lonely planet

India

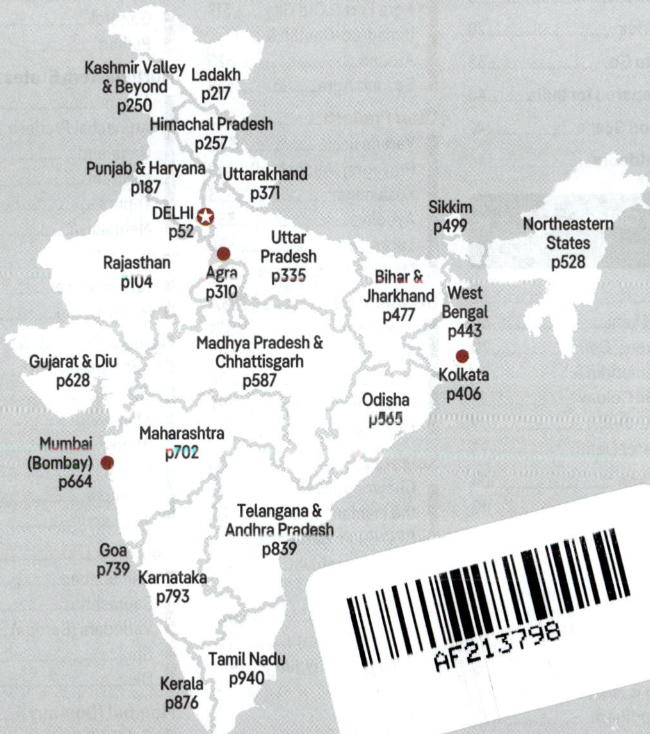

Isabella Noble, Margot Bigg, Joe Bindloss, Mark Eveleigh, Prachi Joshi, Puneetinder Kaur Sidhu, Christabel Lobo, Joanna Lobo, Pooja Naik, Paul Stafford, Meena Thiruvengadam, Shikha Tripathi, Dr Jenny Walker

CONTENTS

Plan Your Trip

The Guide

Theyyam **(p928), Kannur**

Mehrangarh (p162), Jodhpur

Toolkit

Storybook

ABHILASH KV/SHUTTERSTOCK

Valiyaparamba Backwaters (p929), Kerala

INDIA

THE JOURNEY BEGINS HERE

India has been a major character in my life since the late 2000s, when on arrival in Agra – like so many other travellers – I was instantly mesmerised by the ethereal beauty of the Taj Mahal. And yet every India visit still feels like a thrilling new adventure. I've backpacked around Delhi, Rajasthan and Himachal Pradesh with my brother, explored eight different states with my India-loving father, spent blissful solo time in the Andaman Islands and even met my partner at a beachside cafe in Puducherry. India's sultry south has been luring me back for years, after first landing in lushly green Kerala more than a decade ago, and it's been a joy to see the region's inspired arts, culture and food scenes blossom. Whenever I return, I head straight to vibrant Kochi to stroll around galleries, devour lightly spiced *vada* and feast-worthy vegetarian *sadya*, sip steaming *kaapi* in raintree-shaded squares and start days with early-morning yoga bathed in the tropical breeze.

Isabella Noble

@isabellamnoble

Isabella is Spain-based, British-Australian travel journalist who has been spending time in India for over 15 years and has written 50-plus Lonely Planet guidebooks. She wrote the Kerala and Plan Your Trip chapters.

My favourite experience involves lingering over a fiery sunset on northern Kerala's peaceful **Valiyaparamba Backwaters** (p929), where palms nod gently along the shoreline and temple song echoes across the water.

WHO GOES WHERE

Our writers and experts choose the places which, for them, define India.

TSCREATIONZ/SHUTTERSTOCK

While Delhi certainly earns its reputation as a noisy and oftentimes chaotic city, it's also full of nature-filled parks and tucked-away green spaces where it's easy to forget about the big-city bustle. One of my favourite such spots is **Lodhi Garden** (p86), a massive park in the heart of the city. Not only is it filled with plants, parrots and plenty of walking trails, but it also feels a bit like an architecture museum, with beautifully preserved Lodi-era tombs across its grassy lawns.

Margot Bigg

@margotbigg

Margot lived and worked in Delhi for six years and continues to visit regularly. She wrote the Himachal Pradesh chapter and updated the Delhi chapter.

DAVID EVISON/SHUTTERSTOCK

Walking between the ruined temples and step-wells scattered around inside the walls of the **Kumbhalgarh Fort** (p157) north of Udaipur is one of the most relaxing experiences in Rajasthan. You'll leave the crowds behind at the Badal Mahal palace, and share the quiet pathways with songbirds, chipmunks and buffalo, plus the odd waving farmer. Combined with the fabulously ornate Jain temples at Ranakpur, it's one of the state's most rewarding days out.

Joe Bindloss

@joe_on_travel

Joe has been writing about Asia since the 1990s, and he was formerly Lonely Planet's Destination Editor for the Indian Subcontinent. He wrote the Agra and Rajasthan chapters.

JAMES R.D. SCOTT/SHUTTERSTOCK

A nocturnal kayaking experience on Flat Bay, in the **Andaman Islands** (p984), ranks among the world's most spectacular wildlife experiences. Sure, the presence of crocodiles added an undeniable thrill, but it was the bioluminescent plankton – slipping through my wake like shimmering emeralds – that I'll never forget. Add tropical snorkelling and jungle trails and the Andamans provide every temptation necessary for 'going the extra mile'.

Mark Eveleigh

@markeveleigh

The author of a book about his 1225km hike across Spain, Mark rarely turns down an opportunity for a long hike. He wrote about the Andaman Islands, Telangana & Andra Pradesh and Bihar & Jharkhand.

IMAGESOFINDIA/SHUTTERSTOCK

The rock shelters of **Bhimbetka** (p608) are an archaeological wonder, particularly the cave paintings within, some of which are over 30,000 years old. What's fascinating is that same rocky canvas was used from the Mesolithic era to as recently as the Middle Ages, so you can literally see the art evolving in complexity, from stick figures to detailed animal drawings. Even the scenes change from hunter-gatherers to pastoral pursuits – Bhimbetka is truly an anthropological marvel.

Prachi Joshi

@delishdirection

Prachi is a Mumbai-based freelance journalist who writes about travel, food, art and culture. She wrote the Madhya Pradesh & Chhattisgarh chapter.

EZDAN/SHUTTERSTOCK

I can never get enough of **Varanasi's** (p340) lively side-lanes, ancient and historic, and as legend has it, as old as time, where colourful havelis, hidden temples and buzzing bazaars offer an unfiltered experience of local life. A sensory overload of sights, sounds and aromas, the none-too-clean alleys with brimming shops, chanting pilgrims and delicious street staples are both chaotic and endearing at the same time. Especially for the intrepid traveller!

Puneetinder Kaur Sidhu

@cuttinglooseinsta

Puneetinder is a travel and food writer and lives by one motto: Travel. Eat. Write. Repeat. She wrote the Uttar Pradesh and Punjab & Haryana chapters.

SAIKO3P/SHUTTERSTOCK

Hampi (p823) overwhelms in the best possible way. The vast, boulder-strewn landscape and exquisite ruins create a stunning tension between scale and detail that's irresistible to the eye. But this beauty carries weight. These ruins were once the centre of the thriving Vijayanagar empire, which ruled much of southern India until it was undone by ambition and conflict. At sunset, when the stones turn rose-gold, the site feels otherworldly.

Christabel Lobo

@whereschristabel

Christabel is a writer and illustrator based between South India, the UAE and Washington, DC. She wrote the Karnataka chapter.

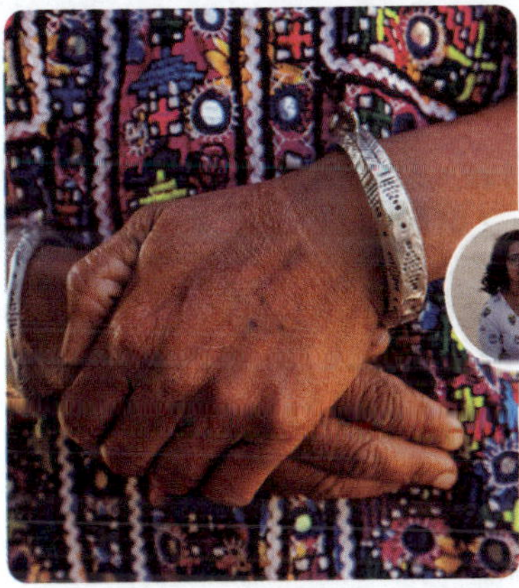

EMILY MARIE WILSON/SHUTTERSTOCK

There is nothing quite like **Kachchh** (p655). India's rich textile history comes alive in the region, especially in the smaller towns and villages around Bhuj. It is a privilege to watch the artisans, craftworkers and masters of ajrakh, rogan art, lacquerware, embroidery, bandhani, pottery, brocade and pit-loom at work. The artisans are warm, friendly and extremely talented, and their works are quite a treasure.

Joanna Lobo

@thatdoggonelady

Joanna Lobo is a freelance journalist, editor and author based in Goa who enjoys writing about food, travel and everything that makes her heart happy. She wrote the Maharashtra, Gujarat & Diu and Goa chapters.

KOBBY DAGAN/SHUTTERSTOCK

I've called Mumbai home for nearly three decades, yet I only truly got under its skin two years ago, when I began leading walking tours in the city. At 5.30am, **Sassoon Docks** (p674) – loud, pulsating and frenzied – comes alive in a different light, or rather the lack of it, with the smell hitting you before the sights and sounds. Learning about the Kolis – the city's indigenous fisherfolk community – and understanding how their lives and livelihoods are woven into Mumbai's very veins was a fascinating revelation.

Pooja Naik

@poojanaik05

Pooja is a travel writer with a penchant for food, art, and culture. She wrote the Mumbai chapter.

There are pleasant surprises throughout West Bengal, but hiking the **Singalila Ridge** (p470) remains the most extraordinary. Delving up the rocky spine; leaving paved roads behind; stopping by prayer-flag-bedecked Buddhist temples in the clouds; being completely disconnected from the outside world for four days; arriving in villages where farming and living are unchanged in millennia, all in the shadow of mounts Everest and Khangchendzonga, is a humbling travel experience.

ABHISHEKDEYPIXELS/SHUTTERSTOCK

Paul Stafford

@paulrstafford

Paul is based in Birmingham, UK; when not entangled in a web of words and pictures he travels for Lonely Planet and plays gigs as half of the alternative rock duo PHWOAR. He wrote the Kolkata, West Bengal and Odisha chapters.

In a country that can overwhelm the senses, **Chettinadu** (p971) feels like an oasis. This collection of towns a few hours' drive from Madurai is known for its grand historic mansions, small-scale artisans and spicy twist on Tamil cuisine. The streets are quiet in the morning. Inside small workshops, artisans churn out everything from tiles and savoury snacks to totes and cotton saris. Time feels like it slows down here, and there's no place I'd rather relax in Tamil Nadu.

DIVYAN/SHUTTERSTOCK

Meena Thiruvengadam

@meenathiru

Meena writes about travel, culture and the arts and is the founder of the travel site travelwithmeena.com. She is an Indian-American of Tamil descent and wrote the Tamil Nadu chapter.

Changthang (p241) may come across as wilderness, but it is the reward for those who go the extra mile, quite literally. The far-flung eastern part of Ladakh merges into the great Tibetan plateau, like its endless plains, nomadic culture, and kiang herds, that also know no boundaries. Years ago when I first crossed over from the Spiti Valley into Changthang and laid my weary eyes on the sapphire oasis of Tso Moriri after walking days across the cold desert, I was born again – I've kept visiting ever since.

DMITRY RUKHLENKO/SHUTTERSTOCK

Shikha Tripathi

@shikha_trip

Shikha is a writer, photographer and outdoor enthusiast whose work and play take her on extensive journeys across the Himalaya. She wrote the Ladakh and Uttarakhand chapters.

RON RAMTANG/SHUTTERSTOCK

Travel the Seven Sister States of the Northeast overland rather than flying and you'll find that all roads lead back to **Assam** (p534). We came to count each return to the plains – with their meticulous tea estates and paddy fields, the gentle Assamese culture of dance, colour and ritual, and the birdsong that floats above the jungle – as a homecoming and grieved when we eventually flew home.

Dr Jenny Walker

@jennywalkertravel

Jenny is a higher education consultant, an author of an academic book on desert travel literature, and co-author of an off-road guide to Oman; she has contributed to over 60 Lonely Planet titles since 2002. She wrote the Northeastern States and Sikkim chapters.

CONTRIBUTING WRITERS

Khursheed Dinshaw

@khursheeddinshaw

Khursheed contributed the Land Before Time essay. She is an Indian freelance travel writer and photographer. She holds two records in the India Book of Records *for the first bloggers meet and the highest bloggers meet in India, at Khardung La.*

Ruby Hembrom

adivaani.org

Ruby contributed the Indigenous Indians essay. She is a Kolkata-based Adivasi (Indigenous Indian) writer and the founder of Adivaani, a non-profit archiving and publishing outfit for and by Adivasis.

Ravikant Kisana

@buffalo.intellectual

Ravikant contributed the meet the Indians essay. He is an India-based professor and researcher who has done ethnographic fieldwork across the country, and is the author of Meet the Savarnas: Indian Millennials Whose Mediocrity Broke Everything, *published by Penguin Random House in 2025. He performs and podcasts under the moniker 'Buffalo Intellectual'.*

Jyoti Nisha

@jyotinisha

Jyoti contributed the Beyond Bollywood essay. She is an academic, writer, filmmaker and producer based in Mumbai, India, who works on gaze, caste, gender and cinema.

Dr Ruchika Sharma

@ruchikasharma23

Ruchika contributed the History in 15 Places essay. She is a Delhi-based historian and lecturer who also makes YouTube videos on history with a side of eyeshadow.

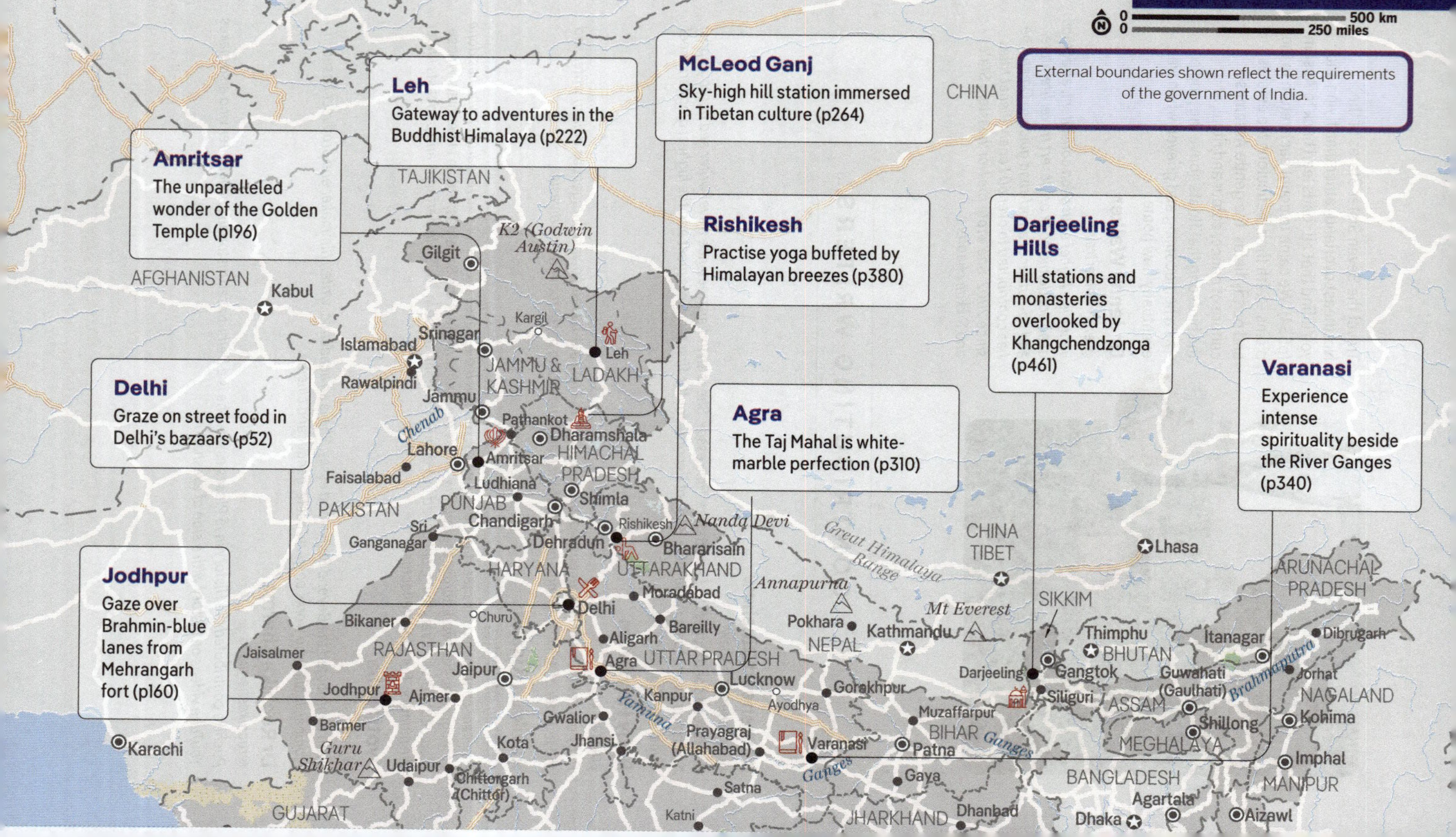
0 500 km
0 250 miles
External boundaries shown reflect the requirements of the government of India.
Amritsar
The unparalleled wonder of the Golden Temple (p196)
Leh
Gateway to adventures in the Buddhist Himalaya (p222)
McLeod Ganj
Sky-high hill station immersed in Tibetan culture (p264)
Rishikesh
Practise yoga buffeted by Himalayan breezes (p380)
Darjeeling Hills
Hill stations and monasteries overlooked by Khangchendzonga (p461)
Varanasi
Experience intense spirituality beside the River Ganges (p340)
Delhi
Graze on street food in Delhi's bazaars (p52)
Agra
The Taj Mahal is white-marble perfection (p310)
Jodhpur
Gaze over Brahmin-blue lanes from Mehrangarh fort (p160)
CHINA
TAJIKISTAN
AFGHANISTAN
Kabul
PAKISTAN
Islamabad
Rawalpindi
Gilgit
K2 (Godwin Austin)
Kargil
Srinagar
Leh
JAMMU & KASHMIR
LADAKH
Jammu
Pathankot
Dharamshala
HIMACHAL PRADESH
Chenab
Lahore
Amritsar
Faisalabad
Ludhiana
PUNJAB
Shimla
Chandigarh
Sri Ganganagar
Rishikesh
Nanda Devi
Dehradun
Bhararisain
HARYANA
UTTARAKHAND
Delhi
Moradabad
Bikaner
Churu
Bareilly
Aligarh
Jaisalmer
RAJASTHAN
Jaipur
Agra
UTTAR PRADESH
Jodhpur
Ajmer
Barmer
Karachi
Guru Shikhar
Udaipur
Chittorgarh (Chittor)
Kota
Gwalior
Jhansi
Yamuna
Kanpur
Prayagraj (Allahabad)
Lucknow
Ayodhya
Varanasi
Ganges
Satna
Katni
GUJARAT
Great Himalaya Range
Annapurna
Pokhara
NEPAL
Kathmandu
Mt Everest
CHINA TIBET
Lhasa
Gorakhpur
Muzaffarpur
BIHAR
Patna
Gaya
JHARKHAND
Dhanbad
SIKKIM
Darjeeling
Gangtok
Siliguri
Thimphu
BHUTAN
Itanagar
ARUNACHAL PRADESH
Dibrugarh
Brahmaputra
Jorhat
NAGALAND
Kohima
Guwahati (Gaulhati)
ASSAM
Shillong
MEGHALAYA
BANGLADESH
Agartala
Dhaka
Imphal
MANIPUR
Aizawl

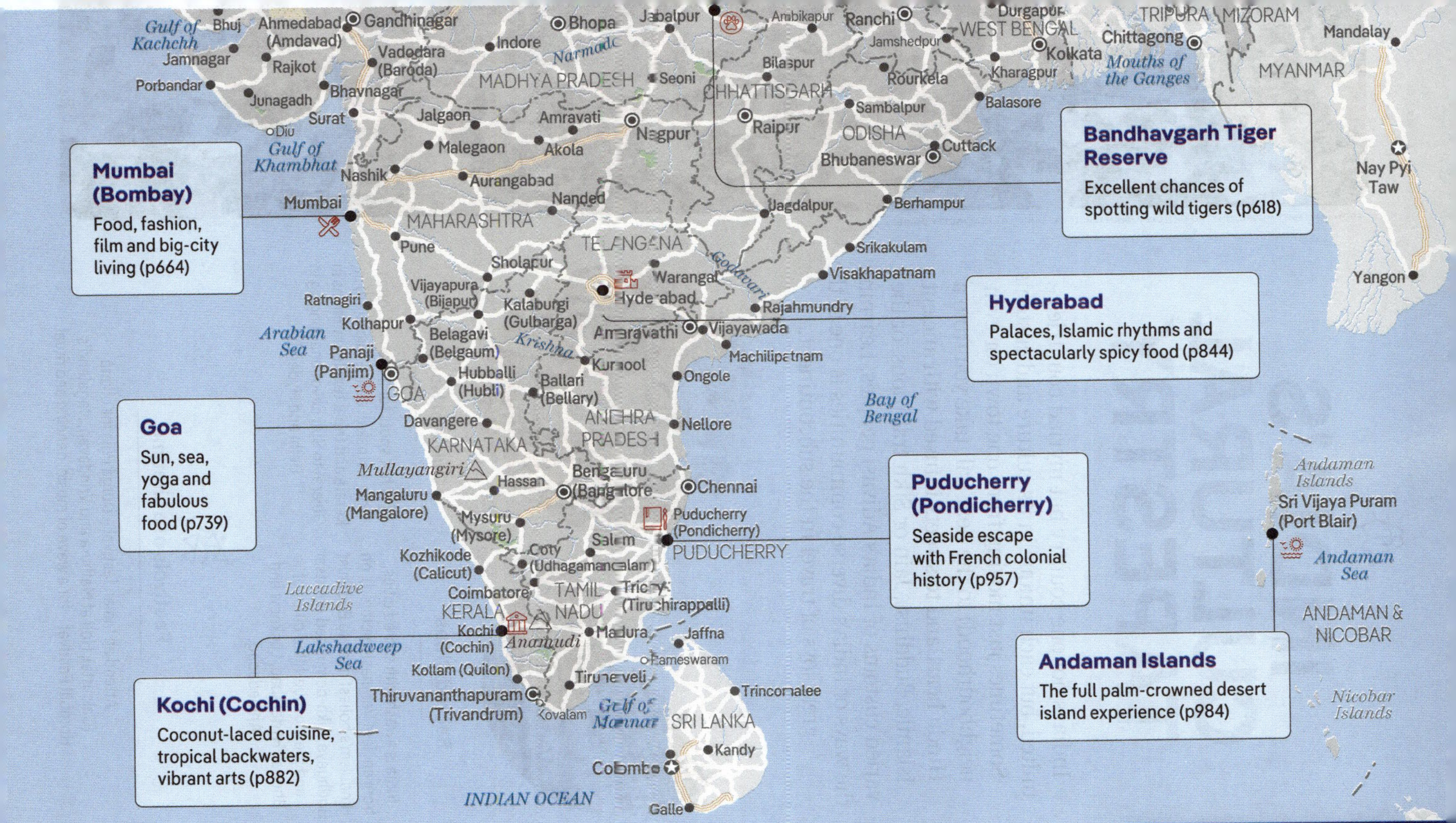
Mumbai (Bombay)
Food, fashion, film and big-city living (p664)
Goa
Sun, sea, yoga and fabulous food (p739)
Kochi (Cochin)
Coconut-laced cuisine, tropical backwaters, vibrant arts (p882)
Bandhavgarh Tiger Reserve
Excellent chances of spotting wild tigers (p618)
Hyderabad
Palaces, Islamic rhythms and spectacularly spicy food (p844)
Puducherry (Pondicherry)
Seaside escape with French colonial history (p957)
Andaman Islands
The full palm-crowned desert island experience (p984)
Gulf of Kachchh
Bhuj
Ahmedabad (Amdavad)
Gandhinagar
Bhopal
Jabalpur
Ambikapur
Ranchi
Durgapur
WEST BENGAL
TRIPURA
MIZORAM
Mandalay
Jamnagar
Rajkot
Vadodara (Baroda)
Indore
Narmada
Jamshedpur
Kolkata
Chittagong
Mouths of the Ganges
MYANMAR
Porbandar
Junagadh
Bhavnagar
MADHYA PRADESH
Seoni
Bilaspur
CHHATTISGARH
Rourkela
Kharagpur
Balasore
Surat
Diu
Jalgaon
Amravati
Nagpur
Raipur
Sambalpur
ODISHA
Cuttack
Bhubaneswar
Gulf of Khambhat
Malegaon
Akola
Nashik
Aurangabad
Nay Pyi Taw
Mumbai
Nanded
Jagdalpur
Berhampur
MAHARASHTRA
TELANGANA
Pune
Sholapur
Srikakulam
Warangal
Godavari
Visakhapatnam
Yangon
Vijayapura (Bijapur)
Kalaburgi (Gulbarga)
Hyderabad
Ratnagiri
Rajahmundry
Kolhapur
Amaravathi
Vijayawada
Arabian Sea
Belagavi (Belgaum)
Krishna
Machilipatnam
Panaji (Panjim)
Kurnool
Hubballi (Hubli)
Ongole
GOA
Ballari (Bellary)
Bay of Bengal
Davangere
ANDHRA PRADESH
Nellore
KARNATAKA
Mullayangiri
Bengaluru (Bangalore)
Andaman Islands
Hassan
Chennai
Mangaluru (Mangalore)
Sri Vijaya Puram (Port Blair)
Mysuru (Mysore)
Puducherry (Pondicherry)
Salem
PUDUCHERRY
Kozhikode (Calicut)
Ooty (Udhagamandalam)
Andaman Sea
Laccadive Islands
Coimbatore
TAMIL NADU
Trichy (Tiruchirappalli)
KERALA
Kochi (Cochin)
Anamudi
Madurai
Jaffna
ANDAMAN & NICOBAR
Lakshadweep Sea
Rameswaram
Kollam (Quilon)
Tirunelveli
Trincomalee
Nicobar Islands
Thiruvananthapuram (Trivandrum)
Kovalam
Gulf of Mannar
SRI LANKA
Kandy
Colombo
INDIAN OCEAN
Galle

INDIA'S CULTURAL TAPESTRY

India is not one country but myriad countries – united, but each unique in its culture and customs. Sometimes just moving from one town (or even neighbourhood) to the next will take you from a Hindu heartland to streets infused with ancient Islamic, Buddhist, Jain or Sikh traditions, or the varied customs of India's Adivasi peoples. Learning the ways of India's diverse communities is one of the great joys of travel in the subcontinent.

FROM LEFT: MATT MUNRO, DMYTRO GILITUKHA/SHUTTERSTOCK, SANDEEP RASAL/GETTY IMAGES

Sacred Cities

India is awash with sacred cities, from ancient Varanasi (pictured), on Hinduism's holiest river, to Buddhist Bodhgaya, Sikh-dominated Amritsar and the mosque-filled cities of Bhopal, Hyderabad, Lucknow and Ahmedabad.

Cultural Hot Spots

Visit hot spots for Indian art forms, from Kathakali dance (pictured) in Kerala and tribal textile traditions in Gujarat to Sufi devotional singing in Delhi and Hyderabad.

Festivals of a Lifetime

Attend an Indian festival – Durga Puja inKolkata (Calcutta), Holi at Mathura and Vrindavan, Nagaland's Hornbill Festival – for a wave of music, dancing and ritual.

Ganesh Chaturthi festival, Mumbai (p664)

BEST CULTURAL EXPERIENCES

Explore the ancient ghats (riverside steps) beside the holy Ganges in ❶ **Varanasi** (p340) and tune into the sacred heart of Hinduism.

Be moved by *qawwali* (devotional singing) at the Sufi dargah (tomb) of Hazrat Nizamuddin in ❷ **Delhi** (p52) – a hauntingly beautiful Islamic tradition.

Experience the vital vibes of magnificent ❸ **Mumbai** (Bombay; p664), where spirituality thrives alongside fashion, food, finance and film.

Use ❹ **Bhuj** (p652) in Gujarat as a gateway to mesmerising encounters with the kaleidoscopic clothing of the Adivasi people of Kachchh (Kutch).

Learn about South India's traditional performing arts in Kerala's ❺ **Kochi region** (p882), home to unique art forms and renowned training academies.

AWE-INSPIRING ARCHITECTURE

With 5000 years of architectural heritage and a whopping 44 UNESCO World Heritage Sites, India is a treat for history fans. Every last corner of the country is dotted with regal palaces, mighty monuments, tremendous tombs and imposing forts combining military might with whimsical flourishes. Many jewels are scattered around the countryside, but even in India's burgeoning megacities, ancient step-wells, Mughal mausoleums and centuries-old temples pop up among the office blocks and shopping malls.

FROM LEFT: ULTIMATE TRAVEL PHOTOS/SHUTTERSTOCK, MANOJ PANDEY (NIKON)/500PX, SYLWIA BARTYZEL/LONELY PLANET

Magnificent Monuments

From royal observatories to the Taj Mahal in Agra and the tomb of Humayun (pictured) in Delhi, India is home to some of the world's most memorable monuments.

Royal Cribs

India's historic royal palaces are a window onto a life of extraordinary opulence. Stay overnight at some of the best, perhaps in Jaipur (p110) or Hyderabad (pictured; p844).

Forts to Spare

Formidable forts lord over the Indian landscape, spinning a tale of combat, conquest and resistance. Rajasthan is fort central, but *garhs* (fortresses) dot every Indian state.

Taj Mahal (p314), Agra

BEST ARCHITECTURE EXPERIENCES

Be awestruck by the magnificent ❶ **Taj Mahal** (p314) in Agra, built by a grieving Mughal emperor for his lost bride.

Marvel at the intricate, ancient rock-cut cave art of UNESCO-listed ❷ **Ajanta and Ellora** (p720) in northern Maharashtra.

Wander the boulder-studded landscapes and evocative temples of ❸ **Hampi** (p823), the ruined one-time capital of the mighty Vijayanagar empire.

Hike through Brahmin-blue laneways to Jodhpur's ❹ **Mehrangarh fort** (p162) – a medieval marvel, rising dramatically from rocky desert cliffs.

Witness the lavish life of a maharaja at ❺ **Mysuru Palace** (p808), one of the world's grandest residences, lit at night by 100,000 bulbs.

WILD INDIA

Tigers roam deep in the jungles of India, but these stripy stars are just the start of the Indian wildlife experience. Skies buzz with birds; myriad species of deer, gazelles and antelopes frolic in the forests; snow leopards haunt the mountains; and the beach-lined coast is visited by everything from sea turtles to dolphins.

BEST WILDLIFE EXPERIENCES

Spot your first tiger in the wild at ❶ **Bandhavgarh Tiger Reserve** (p618) in Madhya Pradesh.

Have a jumbo-sized wildlife encounter at ❷ **Bandipur National Park** (p810) in Karnataka, a top-tier destination for seeing wild elephants.

Go looking for big cats in Rajasthan's beloved ❸ **Ranthambore National Park** (p127), best known for its roaming tigers and leopards.

Scan for snow leopards in the barren mountains of the ❹ **Stok Range** (p229) in Ladakh, favoured territory of the predator locals call the 'grey ghost'.

Trek into the Western Ghats forests of Kerala's ❺ **Periyar Tiger Reserve** (p911), home to tigers, elephants and great hornbills.

Big Cats

Beyond majestic tigers, keep your eyes peeled for leopards, Asiatic lions in Gujarat and elusive snow leopards (pictured) in Ladakh, Himachal Pradesh, Sikkim and Uttarakhand.

Supersized Wildlife

In the forest reserves of Karnataka, Kerala, Tamil Nadu and the Northeast, bears and tigers share cover with elephants (pictured), mighty gaur (Indian bison) and one-horned Indian rhinos.

FROM LEFT: SHIVANG MEHTA/SHUTTERSTOCK, JIMMY KAMBALLUR/SHUTTERSTOCK

Birds, Birds Everywhere

Grasslands, forests and lakes across the country are alive with jewel-like bee-eaters, ballerina-like cranes and sharp-taloned raptors, while parakeets are as common as pigeons.

RAJESH NARAYANAN/SHUTTERSTOCK

Nilgiri Mountain Railway (p978), Tamil Nadu

EPIC TRAIN RIDES

Most of India's steam trains may have rumbled on to the great railway yard in the sky, but this is still one of the most atmospheric places on the planet to ride the rails. Train routes trundle through jungles and deserts, rattle through villages and cities and even climb high into the Himalaya and Western Ghats.

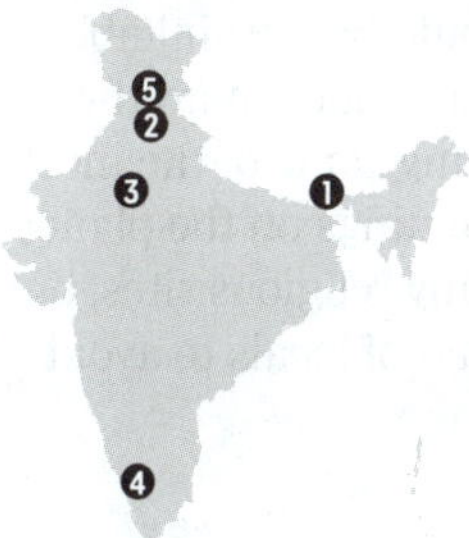

BEST RAIL EXPERIENCES

Rumble into the Himalaya aboard the toy train from New Jalpaiguri, Ghoom or Kurseong to ❶ **Darjeeling** (p161).

Roll into Shimla in style on the ❷ **Toy Train** (p302) from Kalka, following the same rails as British colonial administrators and the Indian officials who later evicted them.

Experience the ❸ **Palace on Wheels** (p127), India's most famous luxury train, connecting Delhi to Rajasthan's landmark cities.

Feel the clickety-clack of one of the world's few cog railways on the UNESCO-recognised ❹ **Nilgiri Mountain Railway** (p978) to Ooty, in Tamil Nadu's Western Ghats.

Spin through Maharashtra and beyond aboard the luxurious, royal-blue ❺ **Deccan Odyssey** (p127).

Toy Trains

The fading days of the Raj are echoed in the century-old 'toy trains' that clatter from the plains to hill stations such as Ooty, Shimla and Darjeeling.

Epic Journeys

India is flush with memorable lowland rail routes, from the Mumbai–Goa *Mandovi Express* known for its food, to services through dramatic desert landscapes.

SACRED SITES

Coming to India without visiting a temple, mosque or monastery would be unthinkable! India's sacred sites are a window onto the nation's soul, as well as being some of the most flamboyantly decorated buildings on the planet. Visitors are welcome at many religious sites, but respectfully follow the lead of locals to avoid intruding.

BEST RELIGIOUS BUILDING EXPERIENCES

Boggle your mind at the panopoly of painted deities, demons and celestial beings adorning Madurai's ❶ **Meenakshi Amman Temple** (p966).

Feel the powerful buzz of belief at Amritsar's captivating ❷ **Golden Temple** (p198), the most important shrine for India's 21 million Sikhs.

Join the Sufi pilgrims thronging the tomb of ❸ **Khwaja Muin-ud-din Chishti** (p134) in historic Ajmer, following in the footsteps of Akbar and Jehangir.

Marvel at the carving-covered ❹ **Sun Temple** (p581) in Konark, then soak up more Odisha spirituality at nearby Puri.

Peek between blushes at the erotic Chandela carvings etched into the Hindu and Jain temples of ❺ **Khajuraho** (p598), in Madhya Pradesh.

Tremendous Temples

Hindu temples in India can be restrained or flamboyant, timeworn or gleaming-new, but they're always beautifully adorned. Find them everywhere from Khajuraho (pictured) to the high Himalaya.

Magnificent Minarets

India's Islamic architecture is majestic. Sky-piercing minarets set the scene in the old Muslim quarters of cities such as Delhi (pictured), Ajmer, Bhopal, Hyderabad, Lucknow and Agra.

FROM LEFT: DMITRY RUKHLENKO/SHUTTERSTOCK, SAIKO3P/SHUTTERSTOCK

A Plurality of Faiths

Don't overlook India's other religions. Tibetan Buddhist monasteries, ancient Buddhist stupas, Sikh gurdwaras, Christian churches, Jain temples and Adivasi shrines all are worthy of exploration.

JOSE HERNANDEZ CAMERA 51/SHUTTERSTOCK

Rue Francois Martin, Puducherry (p957)

BEST COLONIAL HISTORY EXPERIENCES

Wander Edwin Lutyens' planned New Delhi, including ❶ **Connaught Place** (p70), and uncover traces of India's precolonial history amid the British-built architecture.

Drift through the ruined and intact basilicas of ❷ **Old Goa** (p751) near Panaji (Panjim), once one of the biggest cities in Asia.

Discover the memories in stone and marble of Britain's first colonial capital in ❸ **Kolkata** (p412) – swapped for Delhi when Bengali leaders started agitating for autonomy.

Stroll the colourful districts in breezy ❹ **Puducherry** (p957), the most famous leftover from France's empire in the Indian Ocean.

Gaze over to the Himalayan snowline from the Ridge in ❺ **Shimla** (p300) – still a favourite hill escape from the heat.

COLONIAL-ERA REMNANTS

The attempts of former colonial powers to rebuild Europe in Asia have been thoroughly reclaimed by the world's largest democracy, but lingering traces of this often troubling historical period are a key part of understanding modern India's story – and can be both charming and challenging to visit.

Colonial Capitals

Discover convincing facsimiles of European architecture in former colonial cities such as Delhi, Lucknow and Puducherry (Pondicherry) and all along the Goa coast.

Head for the Hills

India's hill stations swim with nostalgia, but historic high-altitude escapes such as Darjeeling, Shimla, Nainital and Ooty were vital hubs for Indian culture even in their heyday.

SAND & SURF

India's tropical beaches sweep from surf-whipped strands of gold to busy urban sands dotted with street-food stalls and coconut carts in cities like Mumbai and Chennai. The loveliest stretches of coastline are all in the south of the country, where a lively surf scene has blossomed in recent years. Whether you fancy catching waves, going paddleboarding offshore or simply relaxing on the sand, you're spoilt for choice.

Safety

Strong currents and riptides are common off southern India's beaches, so always take care when in the water. Some beaches in popular tourist destinations have lifeguards.

Beach Etiquette

While swimwear is usually fine on touristy beaches, it's best to cover up off the sand. Many Indians choose to swim fully clothed.

Surf Scene

South India's surf scene is booming. Look for reputable schools and camps affiliated with Surfing Federation of India (SFI) or International Surfing Association (ISA).

FROM LEFT: SAURAV022/SHUTTERSTOCK, TRAVELVIEW/SHUTTERSTOCK, JAVARMAN/SHUTTERSTOCK

Varkala (p915), Kerala

BEST BEACH & SURF EXPERIENCES

Beach-hop around northern Goa, home to knockout beaches like ❶ **Morjim** (p758) and ❶ **Mandrem** (p759) and a thriving surf scene.

Pick between riding Kerala's tropical waves or relaxing on gold beaches beneath soaring red-laterite cliffs in ❷ **Varkala** (p915).

Go surfing along the undeveloped Karnataka coast, where laid-back ❸ **Udupi** (p820) is India's original wave hub.

Escape to the remote Andamans for the chance to go snorkelling with dugongs off ❹ **Shaheed Island** (Neil; p1000) or relaxing on Swaraj Island's (Havelock's) ❹ **Radhanagar Beach** (p997).

Head to tiny ❺ **Kovalam** (p953), a fishing village turned surf-scene epicentre on Tamil Nadu's Coromandel Coast.

SAURAV022/SHUTTERSTOCK

Kerala's backwaters (p898)

EVERY SEASON

Spanning diverse landscapes, elevations and climatic zones, India is truly a year-round destination. While the October-to-March winter season is the top time for most places, India's varied microclimates mean there's somewhere worth visiting in every season, even at the height of the monsoon. Let the weather and the festival calendar steer you towards the trip of a lifetime.

Wildlife Wonders

January to March/April is generally the best time to spy many wild creatures in India's nature reserves, but check regionally as things vary.

Festival Time

Whenever you're in India, there's bound to be a fabulous festival looming (p39), from Mysuru's (Mysore's) dazzling Dasara (September/October) to Tamil Nadu's Pongal harvest festivities (usually January).

BEST SEASONAL EXPERIENCES

Evade the monsoon with an elevated escape to ❶ **Leh** (p222) in Ladakh – a summertime hub for yoga, meditation, hiking and more.

Explore ❷ **Kerala's backwaters** (p898) by kayak, houseboat or punt-powered canoe from December to March for tip-top tropical weather.

Enjoy the first snows of winter in Himalayan hill stations such as ❸ **Nainital** (p386) in Uttarakhand – pick a hotel with a fireplace!

Hike West Bengal's spectacular ❹ **Singalila Ridge** (p470) in October and November when the skies are clearer and the weather is still warm.

Head to Tamil Nadu's capital ❺ **Chennai** (p946) around mid-December for fabulous dance and Carnatic music programmes.

MIND, BODY & SOUL

Wellness is a reason to travel to India all by itself. Many of the world's favourite wellness traditions evolved in the subcontinent, from yoga and meditation to Ayurvedic medicine. Practising at the source is a profoundly moving experience – some travellers come for a weeklong retreat and end up devoting a lifetime to self-discovery.

FROM LEFT: YURAKRASIL/SHUTTERSTOCK, CHRISTOPHE BOISVIEUX/GETTY IMAGES

An Ancient Practice

More than 150 million Indians practise yoga, and holistic hubs such as Goa (pictured), Kerala and Rishikesh draw droves of yogis, from novices to teachers.

Transformative Meditation

Murmured mantras fill the air at Buddhist hubs such as Bodhgaya, Leh and Dharamshala, with classes for new meditators and silent retreats for serious practitioners.

Ayurvedic Experiences

Ayurvedic clinics and hospitals are found all over India, but Kerala, Goa and Uttarakhand are particularly known for their wide-ranging Ayurvedic resorts and treatment plans.

BEST YOGA, MEDITATION & AYURVEDA EXPERIENCES

Tune into one of India's oldest traditions with a dawn yoga session overlooking the misty waters of the Ganges in ❶ **Rishikesh** (p380).

Take your pick of drop-in yoga classes to start the day with sun salutations before basking on the beach at ❷ **Arambol** (p756) in Goa.

Begin your meditation journey with Tibetan Buddhist guides at the ❸ **Tushita Meditation Centre** (p267) near McLeod Ganj, in the Himalayan foothills.

Join Buddhists from across the globe at a meditation session in ❹ **Bodhgaya** (p480) in Bihar, where the historical Buddha attained enlightenment.

Book in for an in-depth holistic treatment plan at a well-established Ayurvedic resort near ❺ **Kovalam** (p924) in Kerala.

REGIONS & CITIES

Find the places that tick all your boxes.

Ladakh

SURREAL MOUNTAINSCAPES AND DEEP BUDDHIST FAITH

The call of the wild is tangible in the mountains of Ladakh – the Buddhist-majority eastern section of Kashmir, sitting bone-dry in the rain shadow of the high Himalaya. Traveller hangout Leh is just the starting point for a powerful journey through mountains, monasteries and magic.

Himachal Pradesh

MISTY MOUNTAINS AND HIMALAYAN HERITAGE

The front door to the Himalaya rises to the north of Delhi, sliding through green foothills to the world's tallest mountains. Buddhist and Hindu culture mingle in these elevated valleys, home to favourite traveller haunts – such as McLeod Ganj and Manali – and full of outdoorsy adventures.

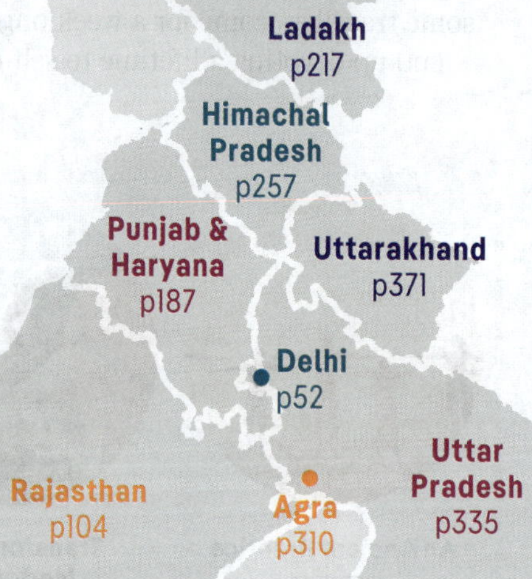

Punjab & Haryana

LUXURIANT FARMS, HALLOWED LAND AND HAPPY-GO-LUCKY PEOPLE

Split in two when India and Pakistan went their separate ways, Punjab is infused with the spirit of the legendary Grand Trunk Road. It's also the heartland of Sikh culture, home to the gleaming Golden Temple at Amritsar, while fringing Haryana offers fascinating history off the beaten track.

Rajasthan

FABULOUS FORTS AND PAINTED CITIES

Rajasthan encapsulates the romance of medieval India. The circuit from Delhi to the colourful cities of Jaipur, Jodhpur, Udaipur and Jaisalmer is a perfect primer for new arrivals. With more time to spare, forts, temples, palaces and tiger reserves – both on and off the tourist trail – await.

Delhi

INDIA'S ACTION-PACKED CAPITAL

The nation's capital is marinaded in history. Eight great cities rose and fell beside the banks of the Yamuna River, each leaving behind a fabulous legacy of mosques and monuments, tombs and temples. Travel here isn't always restful, but it's tirelessly fascinating.

Agra

INDIAN ICONS AND MUGHAL MAJESTY

Gifted celebrity status by India's most famous building – the magnificent Taj Mahal – Agra is the gateway to a world of Mughals, mosques and medieval masonry. Alongside Jaipur and Delhi, it's the third point of the so-called Golden Triangle, and a must-visit for history buffs.

Uttarakhand

MOUNTAINS, MAGIC AND MYSTICISM

The plains slide into the Himalaya in the state of Uttarakhand, famous for its historic hill stations and mountain temples. Here you'll find some of India's most iconic experiences, from yoga in Rishikesh to safaris at Corbett Tiger Reserve, and the mountain trails of Garhwal and Kumaon.

Uttar Pradesh

FAITH, FINE FOOD AND FABULOUS CRAFT

There's more to 'UP' than Agra! India's most populous state is traversed by the River Ganges and home to some of the country's most sacred cities – including marvellous, mesmerising Varanasi, and the meadows where Krishna frolicked around Mathura. Fine food awaits too, particularly in historic Lucknow.

Sikkim

THE LOST MOUNTAIN KINGDOM

The serene doorway to the fascinating Northeast, Sikkim is a place to find inner peace in mountain valleys scented by Himalayan breezes, and lorded over by Khangchendzonga, the world's third-highest peak. Rewarding hikes to mountain viewpoints and Buddhist monasteries await.

Bihar & Jharkhand

HALLOWED LANDS, ESPECIALLY FOR JAINS AND BUDDHISTS

Bodhgaya, where Buddha attained enlightenment, is a magnet for Buddhist pilgrims, while Jains flock to sacred Parasnath Hill. Trace Buddha's life at Bodhgaya, Rajgir, Vaishali and Nalanda, or explore the excellent museums in vibrant Patna, on the banks of the Ganges.

Northeastern States

STRONG TRADITIONS IN A LANDSCAPE OF EXTREMES

Leaning towards Southeast Asia in culture, temperament and topography, the Northeastern States offer an entirely distinct experience from travelling in 'the mainland' – the local term for anywhere southwest of Assam. Strong tribal identities, abundant wildlife and soaring mountain landscapes well reward the effort of reaching the region's Sister States.

Kolkata

INDIA'S ENIGMATIC CITY OF JOY

Kolkata – still Calcutta to many – is India's capital of culture, best embodied by the films of Satyajit Ray and the poetic writing of Rabindranath Tagore. Visiting the city on the Hooghly River can be an intense experience, but it's also a fine place to connect with Bengal's creative spirit.

West Bengal

MOTHBALLED CAPITALS AND HIMALAYAN ADVENTURES

The sinuous state of West Bengal is bookended by natural wonders. To the south lie the tiger-filled mangrove forests of the Sundarbans, while the northern Himalayan foothills serve up thrilling hill stations, such as Darjeeling. In the middle are ruined former capitals of old empires, plus Bengal's cultural nucleus at Shantiniketan.

Southern India on p26-7

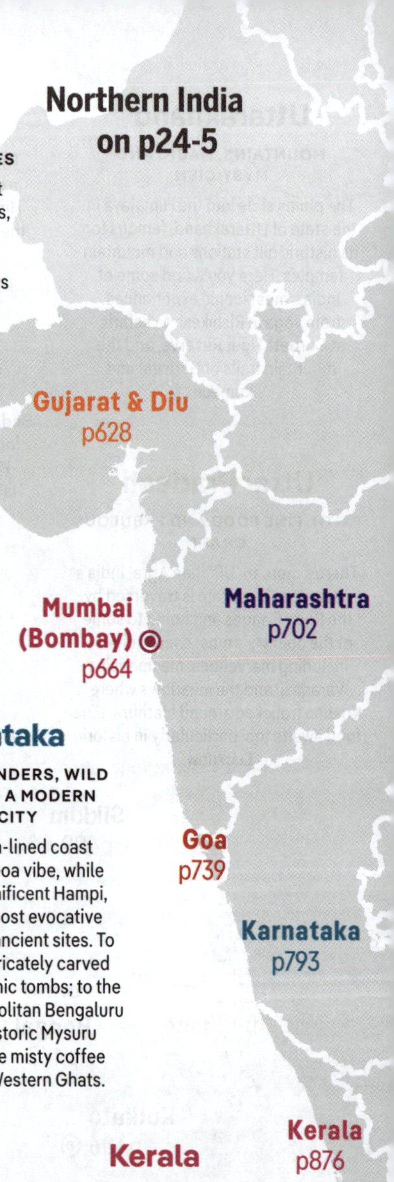

Gujarat & Diu

RICH HERITAGE, TEXTILES AND VARIED LANDSCAPES

Often underrepresented on India's tourist circuit, Gujarat offers a rewarding tapestry of UNESCO-listed monuments, gorgeous havelis (ornately decorated residences) and palaces, ancient Harappan sites, intricate step-wells, dinosaur relics and craft traditions. The topography brings variety too: from the salt flats of the Rann of Kachchh to Gir's dry deciduous forests.

Mumbai (Bombay)

INDIA'S CAPITAL OF COMMERCE AND COOL

Movies, money and glamour make the world go round in Mumbai, India's second city. History – both ancient and modern – spills into the streets of a city celebrated for fine-dining, fashion, finance and the moviemaking machine that is Bollywood. Strap in – it's quite a ride!

Maharashtra

ANCIENT ARCHITECTURE AND NATURAL BEAUTY

Beyond Mumbai, Maharashtra unfolds as a rich, varied symphony – home to UNESCO-protected sites like the Ajanta and Ellora Caves, the youthful urban energy and food culture of Pune, the palm-dappled beaches and deep cultural heritage of Sindhudurg, and the ancient city of Nashik, now the centre of India's flourishing wine region.

Karnataka

HISTORIC WONDERS, WILD NATURE AND A MODERN MEGACITY

A short, beach-lined coast continues the Goa vibe, while inland lies magnificent Hampi, one of India's most evocative (and climbable) ancient sites. To the north are intricately carved temples and Islamic tombs; to the south are cosmopolitan Bengaluru (Bangaore), historic Mysuru (Mysore) and the misty coffee estates of the Western Ghats.

Goa

BEACHES, CULTURE AND PORTUGUESE HERITAGE

India's favourite hub for sun, sea, sand and seafood, Goa is a heady blend of Indian and Portuguese cultures. While scattered hippie resorts remain, the beach scene is going upmarket, particularly at mealtimes, and Old Goa and historic Panaji (Panjim) offer a glimpse back through the centuries.

Kerala

BACKWATERS, BEACHES AND SOUTHERN CULTURE

Kerala's fame precedes it, but this lush southern state still dazzles with powder-soft beaches, thriving arts and crafts scenes, lively historical port cities and evocative cultural experiences, not to mention the beauty of the languid backwaters. Mix time on the coast with wildlife-spotting adventures in the rugged Western Ghats.

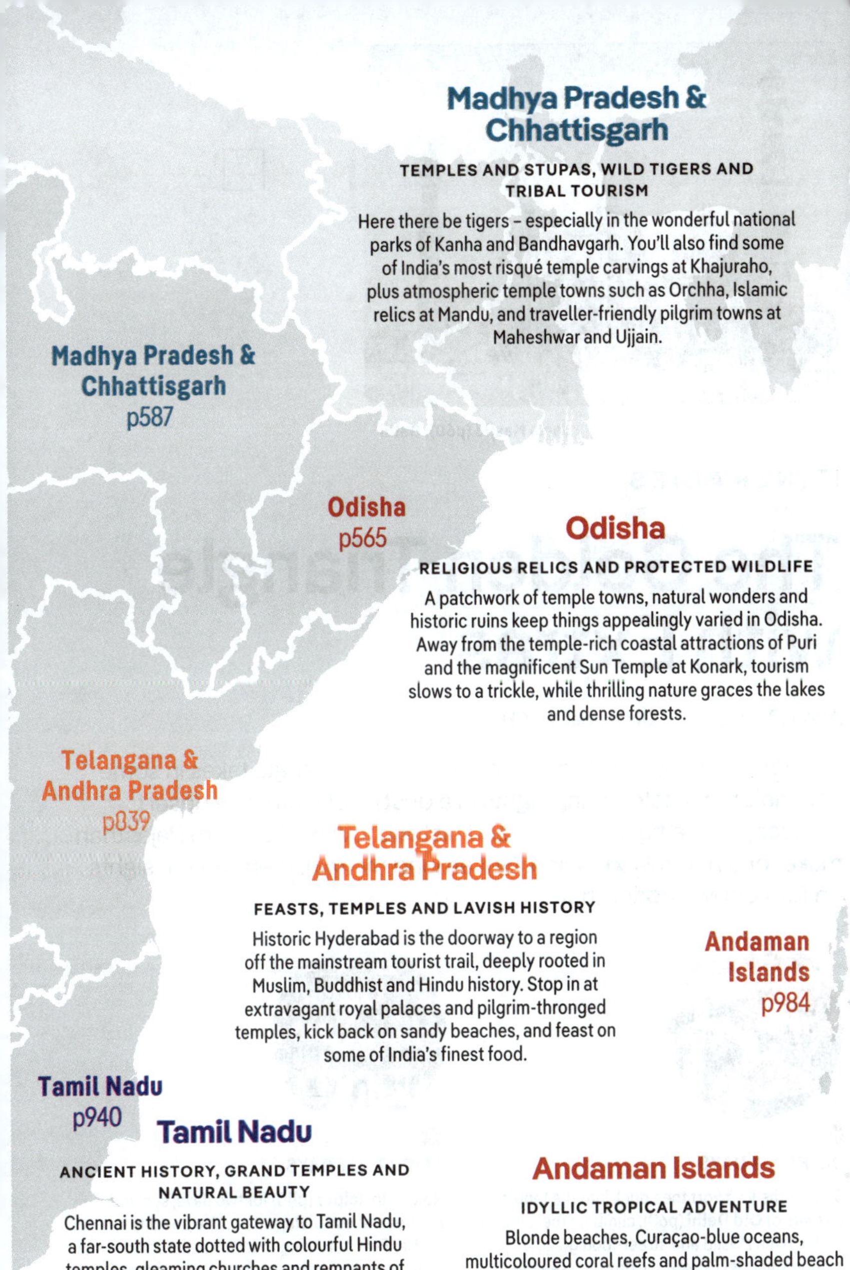

Madhya Pradesh & Chhattisgarh

TEMPLES AND STUPAS, WILD TIGERS AND TRIBAL TOURISM

Here there be tigers – especially in the wonderful national parks of Kanha and Bandhavgarh. You'll also find some of India's most risqué temple carvings at Khajuraho, plus atmospheric temple towns such as Orchha, Islamic relics at Mandu, and traveller-friendly pilgrim towns at Maheshwar and Ujjain.

Odisha

RELIGIOUS RELICS AND PROTECTED WILDLIFE

A patchwork of temple towns, natural wonders and historic ruins keep things appealingly varied in Odisha. Away from the temple-rich coastal attractions of Puri and the magnificent Sun Temple at Konark, tourism slows to a trickle, while thrilling nature graces the lakes and dense forests.

Telangana & Andhra Pradesh

FEASTS, TEMPLES AND LAVISH HISTORY

Historic Hyderabad is the doorway to a region off the mainstream tourist trail, deeply rooted in Muslim, Buddhist and Hindu history. Stop in at extravagant royal palaces and pilgrim-thronged temples, kick back on sandy beaches, and feast on some of India's finest food.

Tamil Nadu

ANCIENT HISTORY, GRAND TEMPLES AND NATURAL BEAUTY

Chennai is the vibrant gateway to Tamil Nadu, a far-south state dotted with colourful Hindu temples, gleaming churches and remnants of India's colonial past. Come here to experience ancient history, Carnatic music, *bharatanatyam* dance, creative visual arts, thrilling mountain treks and more than 1000km of beaches.

Andaman Islands

IDYLLIC TROPICAL ADVENTURE

Blonde beaches, Curaçao-blue oceans, multicoloured coral reefs and palm-shaded beach huts. Is this India or Southeast Asia? Sheltering Adivasi communities and ocean-going elephants, some islands remain tantalisingly undiscovered, while Swaraj Island (Havelock Island) and Shaheed Island (Neil Island) are becoming established fixtures on the Indian travel circuit.

RICHIE CHAN/SHUTTERSTOCK

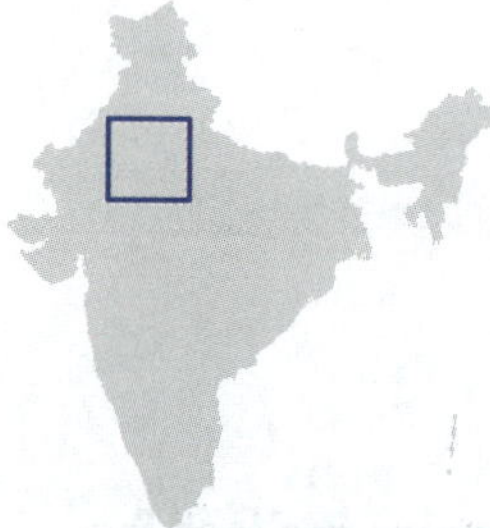

Jama Masjid (p60), Delhi

ITINERARIES

The Golden Triangle with Extras

Allow: 7 days **Distance:** 1000km

Linking Delhi, Agra and Jaipur, India's Golden Triangle takes in some of India's most astounding sights in a dusty but evocative desert landscape. The tiger reserves and historic towns of eastern Rajasthan make for a natural extension. Get around by train, then see the sights on foot or by autorickshaw.

1

DELHI ⏱2 DAYS

Start at the Red Fort then duck into the tangled bazaars of **Old Delhi** (p60), climbing the minaret of the Jama Masjid and street-food grazing around Chandni Chowk. On day two, see the sights of New Delhi, and head to Humayun's Tomb and the Hazrat Nizamuddin Dargah, or the Qutb Minar ruins. Set aside some time for fine dining and souvenir-shopping at the state emporiums on Baba Kharak Singh Marg.

2

JAIPUR ⏱2 DAYS

Roll on to **Jaipur** (p110) for two days, soaking up the richness of Rajasthan. Use one day for Amber Fort, returning to town via the Jaigarh and Nahargarh fortresses and royal cenotaphs. On day two, explore the City Palace, Jantar Mantar and Hawa Mahal, then use the afternoon for Old City shopping or the City Museum, and the evening for a slap-up meal around MI Rd.

FROM LEFT: EMAD ALJUMAH/GETTY IMAGES, SUNIL LODHWAL/SHUTTERSTOCK, RUDIERNST/SHUTTERSTOCK, ONDREJ PROSICKY/SHUTTERSTOCK, ROOP_DEY/SHUTTERSTOCK

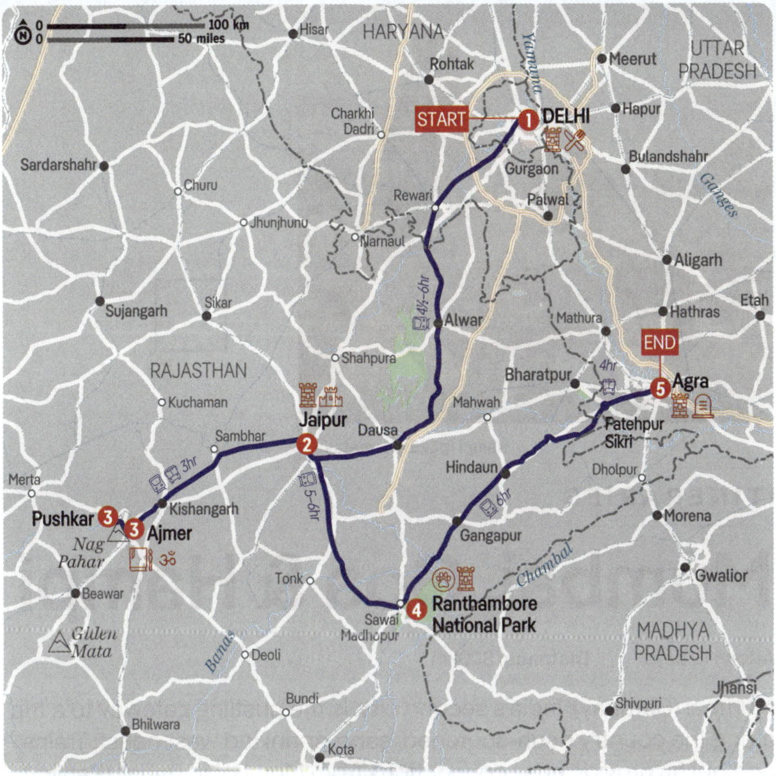

3

PUSHKAR & AJMER 1 DAY

Take a day in **Pushkar** (p130), for a taste of the hippie trail, or **Ajmer** (pictured; p134), to explore the city's rich Islamic history. In Pushkar, tour the city's lakeside ghats and visit one of India's only Brahma temples. In Ajmer, focus on the old city bazaars, the atmospheric tomb of the Sufi saint Khwaja Muin-ud-din Chishti, and the Jain sculptures of the Soniji Ki Nasiyan Temple.

4

RANTHAMBORE NATIONAL PARK 1 DAY

Returning to Jaipur, break the train journey to Agra at this famous **tiger reserve** (p127), just outside the town of Sawai Madhopur. Contact hotels ahead to schedule a tiger safari, then spend the rest of your time exploring the temple-topped battlements of Ranthambore Fort. Mornings offer better chances of tiger sightings, but on any trip, you'll see deer, antelopes and birdlife.

5

AGRA 1 DAY

Agra (p310) is rightly famous as the home of the Taj Mahal, and you'll want to devote half a day to exploring this magnificent tomb and its surrounding gardens. Spend the other half at rambling Agra Fort, perhaps with a souvenir stop to buy a pietra dura–inlaid chess set.

Detour: *Alternatively, see the Taj then zip to nearby* ***Fatehpur Sikri*** *(p331), for a day exploring Akbar's abandoned royal capital.*

D'JULY/SHUTTERSTOCK

Hampi (p823), Karnataka

ITINERARIES

Mumbai, Goa & Hampi

Allow: 10 days **Distance:** 890km

Mumbai (Bombay), India's second city, is the bustling gateway to a trip along the country's sun-scorched, sand-sprinkled west coast. Trains and buses provide easy connections from Mumbai to Panaji (Panjim), the Goan capital, where you can hop across to the beach, then head inland to the wondrous, temple-topped royal ruins of Hampi.

1

MUMBAI ⏱3 DAYS

India's capital of film, finance and fashion, **Mumbai** (p664) is a whole lot of fun. A few days will give you time to find your feet and appreciate the grand architecture of Marine Drive and Chhatrapati Shivaji Maharaj Terminus, tour the museums and maybe take a dawn trip to the Sassoon Docks or the boat to Elephanta Island (pictured). Relish mealtimes – Mumbai has spectacular food for all budgets – before boarding the overnight Goa train.

2

PANAJI ⏱1 DAY

Before you zoom to the beaches, take a day in the Goan capital **Panaji** (p744) to soak up its Portuguese flavours. Eat well – Petisco Kitchen & Bar and Viva Panjim are top picks – then visit the Church of Our Lady of the Immaculate Conception (pictured), and zip over to Old Goa to see the timeworn ruins of a city that was bigger than Lisbon or London in the 18th century.

FROM LEFT: SAIKO3P/GETTY IMAGES, SAIKO3P/SHUTTERSTOCK

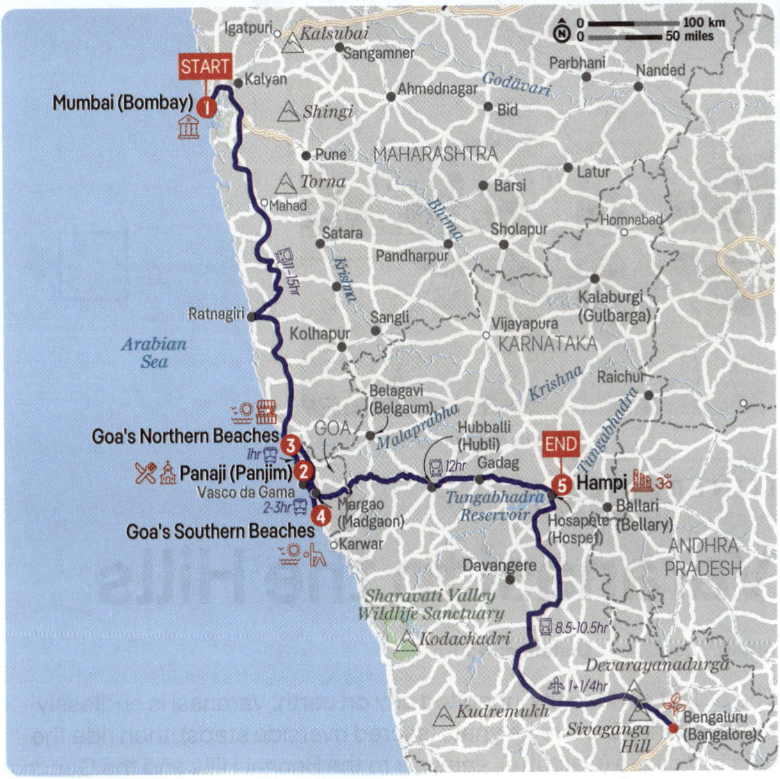

3

GOA'S NORTHERN BEACHES ⏱ 2 DAYS

Devote two days to the beaches that made **Goa** (p739) famous. North of Panaji, you'll find idyllic Anjuna, Mandrem and Arambol and a hint of the hippie Goa of old. Try to visit for Anjuna's famous Wednesday flea market, and after dark, seek out feni, Goa's famous cashew or coconut liquor, or just sip a cold beer in a driftwood beach-bar with your toes in the sand.

4

GOA'S SOUTHERN BEACHES ⏱ 2 DAYS

For more beach action, go south to the less-crowded sands at **Agonda** (pictured; p788) or **Palolem** (p788). A yoga session on the beach is a treat, or you can rent a kayak or surfboard for watery fun. To escape the bustle, hike to **Cola Beach** (p788) from Agonda, or head south to quiet **Galgibaga beach** (p787), a nesting site for olive ridley turtles.

5

HAMPI ⏱ 2 DAYS

Connect through Vasco da Gama to reach Hosapete (Hospet) and the legendary ruins at **Hampi** (p823) – the train gets busy; book well ahead. Over two days, explore the sprawling ruins of the old Vijayanagar capital, scattered among rocky outcrops that lure rock climbers.

Extension: *Travel south from Hampi for a couple of days in* ***Bengaluru*** *(Bangalore; p796), enjoying the perfect climate and booming dining scene.*

FROM LEFT: VIKAS SHRIVASTAV/SHUTTERSTOCK, CAPRICORN STUDIO/SHUTTERSTOCK, DMYTRO GILITUKHA/SHUTTERSTOCK

DANIELRAO/GETTY IMAGES

Victoria Memorial (p416), Kolkata

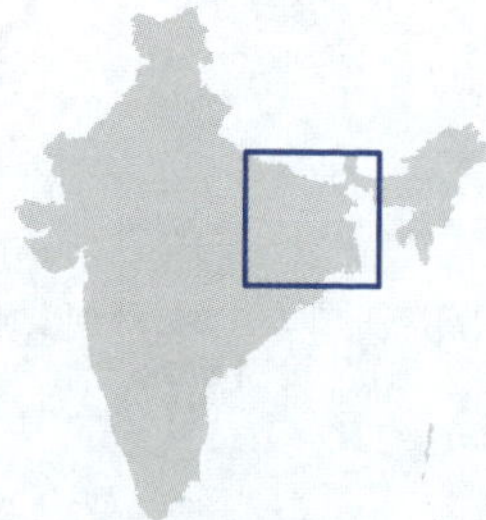

ITINERARIES

Varanasi to the Hills

Allow: 9 days **Distance:** 1430km

The oldest continually inhabited city on earth, Varanasi is endlessly atmospheric. Explore its ghats (sacred riverside steps), then ride the rails to Kolkata (Calcutta), gateway to the Bengal Hills and the Ganges Delta. Start with urban riches, cruise through steamy swamps and finish with soul-lifting Himalayan views in the hills.

1

VARANASI ⏱ 2 DAYS

Varanasi (p340) is a place of powerful religious intensity, rich history and profound encounters with mortality. Explore its riverside ghats, where pilgrims ritually bathe and cremation fires burn, and you'll be moved and perhaps a little shaken by the emotions it inspires. Take a boat trip on the holy River Ganges to find calm before a long overnight train trip to Kolkata.

2

KOLKATA ⏱ 2 DAYS

The capital of West Bengal, **Kolkata** (p406) is one of India's most exciting cities, and quite undeserving of its bad rap. Have a lavish dinner along Park St, or a street-food lunch at Dacres Lane, then tour the grand, colonial-era Victoria Memorial or the Marble Palace (pictured), and you'll see Kolkata in a very different light. Before you leave, zip up to Kumartuli to watch deity-sculptors at work.

FROM LEFT: ROOP_DEY/SHUTTERSTOCK, MILOSK50/SHUTTERSTOCK, SOUMYAJIT NANDY/SHUTTERSTOCK, NEELSKY/SHUTTERSTOCK, ROOP_DEY/SHUTTERSTOCK

3

SUNDARBANS ⏱2 DAYS

Take an overnight trip from Kolkata to **Sundarbans Tiger Reserve** (p450) and (with luck) you *may* spot tigers burning bright in the atmospheric swamps of the world's largest mangrove forest, sprawled across the islands of the Ganges Delta. Safaris travel by boat, with an overnight stop on a mangrove channel or island – bring mosquito repellent and a sense of wonder.

4

SHANTINIKETAN ⏱1 DAY

As you head north from Kolkata, schedule a day in cultured **Shantiniketan** (p458), founded by Bengal's great poet, Rabindranath Tagore. The Visva-Bharati university exists to preserve and promote Bengali culture, and many buildings on the campus are the canvas for its budding artists. If you can, come in late December for the Poush Mela, marked by performances from Bengal's *bauls* (wandering minstrels).

5

DARJEELING ⏱2 DAYS

Connect through Kurseong to pick up the toy train to **Darjeeling** (p461), the queen of India's historic hill stations. The architecture of the Raj sets the scene, but most visitors are drawn by tea tours, the fascinating Himalayan Mountaineering Institute, trips to colourful Tibetan Buddhist gompas (monasteries), walks in the hills and epic views towards 8586m Khangchendzonga, the world's third-tallest peak.

ITINERARIES

Shimla to Ladakh

Allow: 7 days **Distance:** 720km

The high mountains of the Himalaya represent another India altogether. On this trip by bus, motorcycle or 4WD through the highest mountains on earth, rain-starved mountain valleys shelter ancient temples and Buddhist villages that feel untouched by the centuries. This is also India's activity capital – bring walking boots and a sense of adventure!

Hidimba Devi Temple (p276), Manali

1

SHIMLA ⏱ 1 DAY

This mountain odyssey kicks off in **Shimla** (p300), Himachal Pradesh's most famous hill station, where you can sip tea on the terrace of a colonial-era hotel, gazing towards distant views of the mountains you might soon hike through. Fit in a trip to the hilltop Jakhu Hanuman statue and a walk along the Ridge, Shimla's famous pedestrian esplanade, followed by a browse through the craft shops.

2

PARVATI VALLEY ⏱ 1 DAY

Break the journey north to Manali in the **Parvati Valley** (p284), a longtime hub for footloose, tie-dye-oriented travellers. From Bhuntar, buses trundle up the valley to Jari and Kasol, where you can chill amid peaceful mountain scenery. Doing nothing – with or without, ahem, herbal assistance – is a common way to pass the time here, but numerous hiking trails thread through the hills.

FROM LEFT: RAHUL D'SILVA/SHUTTERSTOCK
IMAGESOFINDIA/SHUTTERSTOCK,
JON CHICA/SHUTTERSTOCK

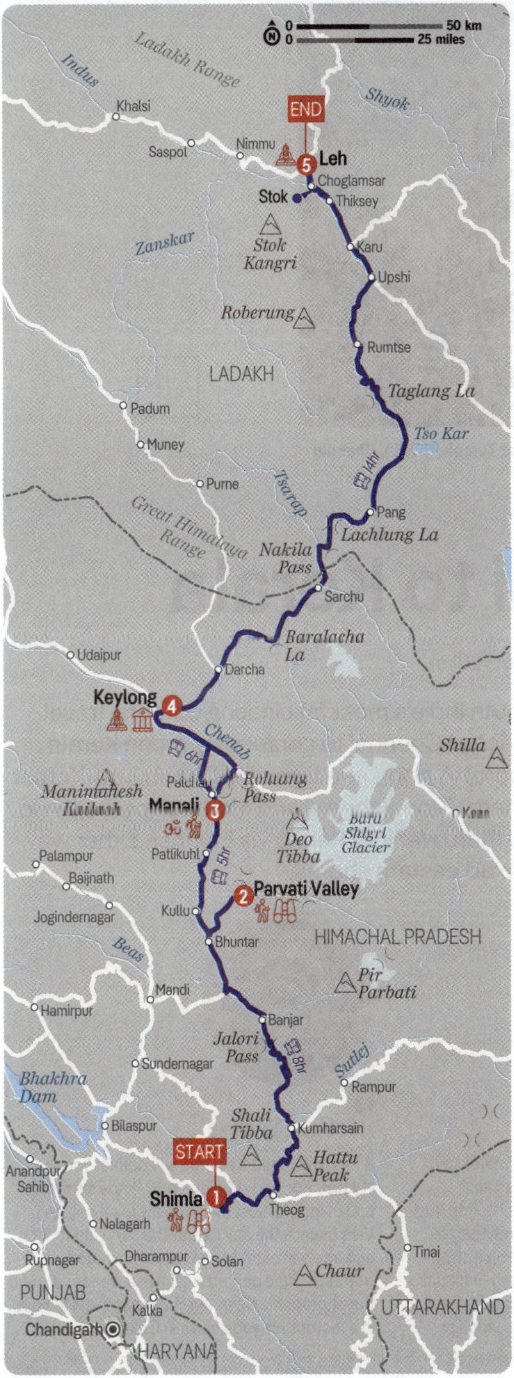

3

MANALI 2 DAYS

It will take half a day to rumble to **Manali** (p276), passing extraordinary scenery on the way. Visit the historic Hindu Hidimba Devi Temple, and devote a day to outdoorsy action – say paragliding, or mountain-biking down vertiginous trails, or a breathless hike into the hills. Before you leave, take a pre-supper stroll around Old Manali and Vashisht for a glimpse of this mountain resort's hippie heyday.

4

KEYLONG 1 DAY

The journey to Leh is a long, bone-shaking two-day trip, and the best place to break the journey is compact **Keylong** (p288), with its Buddhist monasteries and hill-tribe museum (rather than stopping at desolate Sarchu). Get some rest and acclimatise – there's a full-day journey ahead through a high-altitude desert landscape to reach the soothing respite of Leh.

5

LEH 2 DAYS

With the time it takes to get to **Leh** (p222), many travel by air to speed up the journey out of Ladakh, leaving more time to view Leh's Buddhist heritage. With the altitude, go slowly exploring old Leh's historic gompa and palace, perhaps detouring to the monastery at Thiksey (pictured).

Detour: *Consider crossing the valley to* ***Stok*** *(p229) for a day to hike in an arid desert moonscape or for a longer snow-leopard-spotting tour.*

JAYAKUMAR/SHUTTERSTOCK

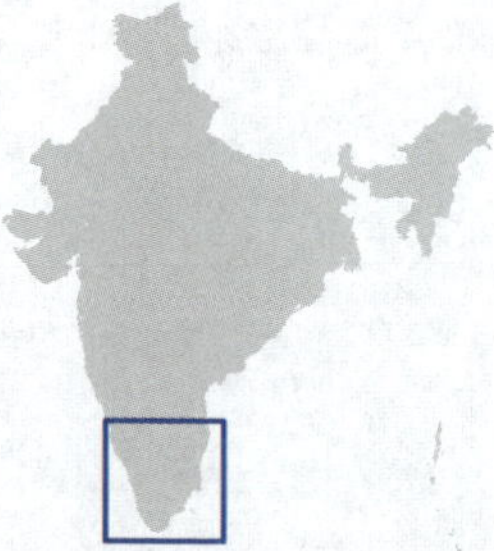

Kapaleeshwarar Temple (p952), Chennai

ITINERARIES

Chennai to Kerala

Allow: 10 days **Distance:** 920km

For a taste of steamy South India's most fascinating corners, travel from historic, well-connected Chennai to gorgeously green Kerala via ancient Mysuru (Mysore). A popular alternative Chennai-to-Kerala route is south to Puducherry (Pondicherry) and Madurai (perhaps via Chettinad or Thanjavur), then over into Kerala via Munnar. Either way, finish up on Kerala's relaxed eastern shores.

1

CHENNAI 2 DAYS

Kick off in spice-scented **Chennai** (p946), and use a couple of days here to sample Tamil Nadu's magnificent vegetarian cuisine. Pop into the colour-crammed Kapaleeshwarar Temple in Mylapore and, if time allows, add on a stroll along Marina Beach. The Government Museum (pictured) is another highlight, but save time also for some of the south's liveliest bars, such as Radio Room.

2

MYSURU 2 DAYS

A long overnight train ride will deliver you to **Mysuru** (formerly Mysore; p804), the setting for one of India's most magnificent royal palaces. Visit once in the day to tour the royal chambers, and again at night to view the illuminated frontage. Time permitting, have a wander around the photogenic Devaraja Market and stretch out in a restorative yoga class in Gokulam.

FROM LEFT: ANDREA CHIOZZI/SHUTTERSTOCK, ISHOWCAM/SHUTTERSTOCK, PAUL HARDING 00/SHUTTERSTOCK, MYLOUPE/UIG VIA GETTY IMAGES, WIRESTOCK CREATORS/SHUTTERSTOCK

3 WAYANAD 2 DAYS

A shorter bus ride will get you to the mesmerising **Wayanad Region** (p932), in Kerala's cool Western Ghats. Explore caves, temples and hiking trails or take a 4WD safari to spot elephants and other jungle creatures in Wayanad Wildlife Sanctuary. Charming homestays will have you considering a longer stay.

Detour: *Break up the southbound journey with a beach stop in untouristed* ***Kannur*** *(p927), which has train/flight links to Kochi.*

4 KOCHI (COCHIN) 2 DAYS

From Wayanad, take a taxi or bus to Kozhikode (Calicut) on the Kerala shoreline, then catch a train, bus or flight to **Kochi** (p882). Ease in at one of Fort Kochi's arty cafes and wander the old quarter, perhaps on an expert-guided tour. Allow time for Mattancherry, Kochi's spice-trading district, home to an ancient palace with Hindu murals (pictured), and for exploring the surrounding backwaters by kayak or boat.

5 VARKALA 2 DAYS

Travel south through Alappuzha (Alleppey) – perhaps with a stop for a canoe or houseboat ride through Kerala's famous backwaters – to reach **Varkala** (p915), the state's loveliest beach retreat and surfing epicentre. Yoga, surf classes, paddleboarding and visits to Varkala's revered Hindu temple are all on the menu. Or just flop on the sand – after travelling the width of India, you've earned it!

WHEN TO GO

The cooler, drier winter draws the crowds, but the rainy lowland summer brings perfect travelling weather in the mountains.

The popular image of India steaming in the tropical sun isn't 100% accurate. In the run-up to the monsoon in April and May, you'll get heat and humidity, but the north can be surprisingly cool during the dry winter months. The roads into high-altitude valleys in areas such as Ladakh are kept open by the courageous Border Roads Organisation, but from November to March many passes close and the only easy way in is by air.

The monsoon season from late May to September drenches the countryside, making many national parks inaccessible and closing down accommodation in coastal destinations. But this is also prime time for fascinating festivals and exploring the high Himalaya, as snow clears from the roads.

The south has its own local climate – typically hot and (often) sticky year-round. Wherever you are, elevation is the key to cooling down – hence all those hill stations. If you come in winter, as many do, be ready for transport delays due to winter fog.

I LIVE HERE

MOUNTAIN SEASONS

Aditya Damani, co-founder of Cat & Cow yoga guesthouse in Dharamshala. *@catcow.in*

The ideal time to visit Himachal Pradesh is from April to June, before the monsoon sets in. Daytime temperatures average around 25°C, with evenings cooling down to 15°C. For me as a yogi, it's an excellent time to practice Buddhism and meditate, and it's also the ideal season for hikes like the beginner-friendly Triund Trek, a stepping stone (pun intended) to many more snowlines. Autumn, from mid-September to mid-November, is also beautiful.

RAVI_SHARMA1030/SHUTTERSTOCK

Monsoon rain, Delhi (p52)

MONSOON

Hitting from May to September – but becoming more erratic with climate change – the monsoon delivers up to 90% of India's rainfall, sometimes triggering landslides in the hills and floods in the plains. Some southern regions experience an additional autumn/winter monsoon.

Weather through the Year – Delhi

JANUARY	FEBRUARY	MARCH	APRIL	MAY	JUNE
Avg. daytime max: 17–27°C	Avg. daytime max: 21–32°C	Avg. daytime max: 27–36°C	Avg. daytime max: 32–37°C	Avg. daytime max: 33–42°C	Avg. daytime max: 27–40°C
Days of rainfall: 2–4	Days of rainfall: 2–4	Days of rainfall: 1–4	Days of rainfall: 3	Days of rainfall: 2–11	Days of rainfall: 6–16

POLLUTION LEVELS

Pollution is a health hazard in much of India, but especially across the north between Diwali and February. Though most glaring in Delhi (often labelled the world's most polluted capital), it's also an issue elsewhere. Stay indoors, keep hydrated and wear an anti-pollution mask.

Biggest Religious Festivals

Holi, the festival of colours, sees everyone doused in vibrant powder, marking the demise of the demon Holika; powder flies particularly enthusiastically in Mathura and Vrindavan (p366). **February/March**

Ramadan (Ramazan), the Muslim month of fasting, finishes with everyone dressing up for a fabulous feast at **Eid al-Fitr**; the eating is particularly good in Delhi, Hyderabad and Lucknow. **February/March (2027/2028)**

Rama's victory over demonic Ravana sees riotous celebrations and the burning of giant effigies during **Dussehra**, especially in Mysuru (p804), Kota (p142) and Kullu (p283). It follows Navratri/Durga Puja, when effigies of Durga are ritually immersed. **September/October**

Diwali, India's festival of light, is a wonder of candles and fireworks, illuminating the streets to mark the return of Rama and Sita from exile. Bring earplugs for the noise. **October/November**

I LIVE HERE

HYDERABAD FESTIVALS

Jonty Rajagopalan is the founder of Detours, an innovative tour company in Hyderabad. *@jonty_detoursindia*

One of my favourite experiences in Hyderabad is the Bonalu festival in July and August. *Bhojanalu* (food) is offered to goddess Mahakali in gratitude for having helped people overcome famine. I love the sight of women carrying pots of food to Kali temples and how Golconda Fort turns into a massive kitchen! On the final weekend, I enjoy the colourful floats that head in procession to the Kali Temple in the old city.

Top Cultural Festivals

Bringing Sankranti kiteflying traditions into the modern age, **Gujarat Kite Festival** (p631) fills the skies over Ahmedabad with colour. Troupes fly giant constructions while children battle with penny-priced paper fighting kites. **January**

Kerala's yearly harvest festival **Onam** (p918) is celebrated by people of all faiths, with processions, dragon-boat races and feasting on *onasadya*, a glorious vegetarian spread on a banana leaf. **August/September**

Livestock trading is just the beginning at Rajasthan's most famous cultural festival. **Pushkar Camel Fair** (p132) is thronged by acrobats, performers, religious pilgrims and vast numbers of camels. **October/November**

The increasingly popular annual **Hornbill Festival** (p553) in Kohima is a must for tribal culture in Nagaland, featuring more than 400 dancers and a magnificent heritage village. **December**

HEATING INDIA

The mercury hit 51°C in Phalodi in Rajasthan in 2016, while Delhi sweltered at a record almost 50°C in 2024. Temperatures of over 45°C are becoming increasingly common. The effect is particularly pronounced in the mountains, where melting glaciers are contributing to lowland flooding.

JULY	AUGUST	SEPTEMBER	OCTOBER	NOVEMBER	DECEMBER
Avg. daytime max: 30–35°C	Avg. daytime max: 28–36°C	Avg. daytime max: 27–35°C	Avg. daytime max: 26–32°C	Avg. daytime max: 20–31°C	Avg. daytime max: 15–28°C
Days of rainfall: 11–24	Days of rainfall: 13–24	Days of rainfall: 7–15	Days of rainfall: 2–11	Days of rainfall: 2–12	Days of rainfall: 1–6

FROM LEFT: OLEH_SLOBODENIUK/GETTY IMAGES, AMAZON

Woman wearing *salwar kameez*

GET PREPARED FOR INDIA

Clothes

Long sleeves and trousers/skirts Prioritise loose-fitting, thin, breathable long trousers or skirts and long-sleeved shirts. In general, it's best to avoid tight-fitting, sheer or revealing clothes, though some Indians now wear less-conservative clothing in beach destinations and certain destinations in big cities.

Local attire Many women in India wear a *salwar kameez* (long shirt and loose trousers); both men and women wear long kurta shirts. Many travellers choose to adopt Indian clothing.

Layers and sun protection For the hills, and the north in general in winter, bring warm fleece layers, a hat and (for higher elevations) proper mountain-wear. A reliable SPF is essential, too.

Something smart Fit in at trendy bars, posh restaurants and high-end hotels with at least one smart outfit.

Practical shoes Bring sturdy shoes for hiking/sightseeing, and slip-on, kick-off sandals for beaches and religious sites.

Swimwear Many Indians prefer to swim clothed. Swimsuits/bikinis are usually fine on touristed beaches (such as Goa or Kerala), but cover up off the sand.

Georestricted Websites

Many Indian websites (from official government pages to local businesses) are georestricted, so you may not be able to access them until you're on the ground. If necessary, try contacting business owners directly (by email/phone) instead.

READ

Midnight's Children (Salman Rushdie; 1981) India feels like a character as well as a setting in this magical realist exploration of Independence.

The God of Small Things (Arundhati Roy; 1997) The first female Booker winner spins a profound and moving tale of Kerala heartbreak.

Heart Lamp (Banu Mushtaq, tr. Deepa Bhasthi; 2025) International Booker Prize–winning story collection about Muslim women in southern India.

Gods, Guns and Missionaries (Manu S Pillai; 2024) Leading contemporary writer and historian delves into the making of India's modern Hindu identity.

Manners

Religious etiquette Remove shoes before entering homes or religious sites, and heed extra rules at shrines. Some temples and mosques are only open to worshippers or to men; mosques may ask women to cover their hair. At some Jain temples, leather items are banned and menstruating women are requested not to enter. Buddhist stupas should be circumnavigated in a clockwise direction.

Taking photos Ask before taking photos of people. Photography is prohibited at many religious sites (you may need to leave your phone/camera with attendants) and often on bridges.

Greetings and meals The default (Hindu) greeting in many regions is to say *namaste*, with a slight bow and hands held together at the chest. Muslims greet each other by saying *salaam alaikum* (peace be with you) – the correct response is *alaikum salaam*. Always shake hands, eat and pass food with your right hand, and wash hands before/after eating.

Touching people Don't touch people unless invited, such as to shake hands. Avoid touching anyone on the head, or with your feet (and don't point the soles of your feet towards people or religious images) – doing so is considered insulting.

Displays of affection Be discreet. Couples holding hands and kissing is generally rare in public, and attitudes towards LGBTIQ+ people remain conservative in many areas. However, Indian men and women often hold hands with members of the same gender group as a sign of friendship.

Language Don't assume people speak English, or even Hindi. These languages are used for government business, but India has more than 100 distinct languages. Try to learn the local words for 'hello', 'excuse me' and 'thank you' in the regions you visit.

WATCH

Pather Panchali (Satyajit Ray; 1955) Ray's masterpiece, one third of the Apu Trilogy, hauntingly evokes Bengali village life.

Mother India (Mehboob Khan; 1957) An outpouring of national pride, exploring motherhood, sacrifice and Indian identity.

Sholay (Ramesh Sippy; 1975) The action smash that thrust Amitabh Bachchan into superstardom; much copied, never bettered.

The Lunchbox (Ritesh Batra; 2013) A misdelivered *dabba* (lunchbox) sparks a romantic Mumbai story of two lives.

Homebound (Neeraj Ghaywan; 2025) An intimate portrait of love and longing set in Northern India.

All We Imagine as Light (Payal Kapadia; 2024) Poignant drama following the lives of three nurses in modern-day Mumbai.

LISTEN

The Sounds of India (Ravi Shankar; 1958) A fine primer for the versatile skills of India's sitar maestro.

Aashiqui (Nadeem Akhtar Saifi & Shravan Kumar Rathod; 1990) Tearjerking love songs from the masters of the 1990s soundtrack.

Aap Kaa Surroor (Himesh Reshammiya; 2006) The bestselling Indian album of all time, full of rousing modern melodies.

Therukural (Arivu; 2019) Politically candid debut album by Tamil rapper Arivu, who garnered international acclaim with *Enjoy Enjaami*.

ONKAR ABHYANKAR/SHUTTERSTOCK

Chaat (snacks) seller, Varanasi (p340)

THE FOOD SCENE

Travelling in India is a daily feast – for the eyes, the ears, and particularly for the taste buds. Prepare to indulge.

Spices from India were once worth more than gold, and priceless would be a good description for the country's cooking culture today. Nowhere else makes such confident and creative use of herbs and spices, or embraces such an elaborate variety of ingredients and techniques, from cooking on superheated charcoal in a clay oven to steaming in pastry-sealed pots.

Countries across the globe owe their spice racks to India's medieval traders, but imported ingredients (such as chillies, potatoes and tomatoes) were seamlessly absorbed into domestic recipes, alongside cumin, cardamom, cinnamon, turmeric, ginger and pepper – once the favoured source of spicy 'heat' in national cooking.

Today, India's cuisine is a fascinating melange of homegrown traditions, myriad regional cooking styles drawn from diverse faiths, cultures and empires, and culinary ideas imported from the Middle East, Central Asia, China, Southeast Asia, the Indian Ocean and Europe. International cuisines are gaining traction too, often thanks to local chefs returning with fresh ideas from stints abroad.

The Culinary Map

Indian food can be broadly divided into North Indian food – rich dishes influenced by the cooking of Central Asia – and South Indian food, usually richly spiced. It's often said that South India is more vegetarian than the North, but rates of vegetarianism are actually higher in northwest states and several of the most meat-eating states are in fact southern. Recent figures suggest

Best Indian Dishes

BIRYANI
Layered rice steamed with meat or vegetables; big in Hyderabad and Lucknow.

PALAK PANEER
Spiced spinach stewed with cubes of unfermented cheese.

BUTTER CHICKEN
Chicken cooked in a buttery tomato, ginger and garlic sauce.

KATI ROLL
A Kolkata special – kebab meat or spicy paneer, wrapped in a rolled *paratha*.

around 30% of the population identify as vegetarian, while 70% now consume at least some type of meat. Vegetarianism is traditionally intertwined with Hinduism, often associated with higher Hindu castes, something still evident in politics today.

Vegetables are not merely a side dish in India – a plate of *sabzi* (vegetables) is a main course, with most dishes named for their ingredients, such as *aloo gobi* (potato and cauliflower curry), or the style of preparation. Kebabs and breads cooked in the tandoor (clay oven) and served with buttery sauces are perhaps the most famous dishes from the north, while dosas (savoury lentil-flour crepes), *idli* (steamed, fermented rice cakes) and *uttapam* (thick savoury rice pancakes with onions, chillies and coriander) are southern signatures.

Many menus feature Chinese-inspired rice and noodle dishes, from gentle-on-the-palate *chow mein* (fried noodles) to the ubiquitous chilli chicken. In the far north, Tibetan-inspired dishes such as *momos* (stuffed dumplings) are popular. Many restaurants make a feature of serving 'Indian, Chinese and Continental' – a mishmash of dishes from India, China and Europe.

Finish any meal by cleansing your palate with handful of fennel seeds and sugar crystals (or colourful sugar-coated fennel known as *mukhwas*).

FROM LEFT: ASMIPHOTOSHOP/SHUTTERSTOCK, ABHINAVS7/SHUTTERSTOCK

Idli **(steamed, fermented rice cakes)**

Rich Regional Cuisines

Mughlai cuisine dominates menus in the north, and the influence of Central Asia is tangible in dishes such as samosas, pilau (spice-flavoured rice) and many of India's favourite kebabs. Saffron, cardamom,

FOOD & DRINK FESTIVALS

Ganesh Chaturthi (p712) This major Hindu festivity is particularly big in Maharashtra, with celebratory sweets (pictured) and vegetarian meals.

Onam (p918) The feast-like vegetarian *onasadya* is a key part of Kerala's harvest festival.

Hornbill Festival (p553) Nagaland's main annual event is the perfect chance to sample regional tribal dishes.

Eid al-Fitr (p39) Muslims mark the end of the fast by seeking out Hyderabad's best *haleem* (wheat and mutton stew).

Grub Fest *(instagram.com/thegrubfest)* A multiday event devoted to all things edible in Delhi's Jawaharlal Nehru Stadium (dates vary).

Explorers Club A celebration of India's burgeoning gin scene, and the largest gin festival in the world (varying locations/dates).

Goa Food & Cultural Festival A big showcase of Goan arts and cuisine; check for upcoming dates.

MASALA DOSA
Thin, crispy fermented lentil- and rice-flour crepe, stuffed with spiced potato mash.

TANDOORI CHICKEN
Tandoor-roasted chicken, marinaded in yoghurt, also available as tikka (chunks).

MEEN MOLEE
Kerala's favourite fish dish, rich with coconut milk, tamarind and pepper.

DHAL
Any of dozens of regional variations of spicy stewed lentils.

black pepper, dried fruits and nuts feature prominently. Parsi cuisine – most commonly associated with Mumbai – blends central-Indian cooking traditions with flavours from Persia. In the east, Bengali food gets its distinctive flavour from mustard oil; mutton and fish – particularly *bhekti* and *hilsa* – are popular, and Bengali sweets are famous India-wide.

In the south, locally grown spices dominate the widely varied cooking. Goan cuisine shows strong Portuguese influences in its use of pork and vinegar, while the menus of Mangaluru and Kerala feature plenty of seafood and coconut (the rich Mappila recipes of northern Kerala are a hyper-regional treat). Carnivores should seek out the meaty cuisines of Hyderabad in Telangana and Chettinadu in Tamil Nadu.

Vegans & Vegetarians

Vegetarians are wonderfully catered for across the country. Indian food is divided into veg and non-veg (meaning 'contains meat, eggs or fish'); 'pure-veg' means made in a meat- and egg-free kitchen. Many vegetable dishes contain ghee (clarified butter), *dahi* (yoghurt), paneer (unfermented cheese) and other dairy products. Vegans should always double-check and list off things like ghee, butter etc to avoid. South Indian dishes like dosas and *idlis* are usually dairy-free.

Bread or Rice?

As a general rule, meals in the south are more likely to come with rice as the main starch, while breads are most common for mopping up sauces in the north. Plain boiled rice is the default, but you'll also find variations, such as *jeera* (cumin) rice, curd rice and lemon rice (in Kerala); pilau with vegetables, served as a standalone meal; and *poha (*flattened rice grains with curry leaves, potato, chilli and lemon).

Thali

India's breads are a remarkably varied feast all of their own, from the simple unleavened chapati (or roti) to puffy tandoor-cooked naan, flaky *parathas*, fluffy stuffed *kulcha* and deep-fried, pillow-like *puris*.

Meet the Thali

In many parts of India, the default meal is the thali – an assortment of sauces with rice and/or chapatis, usually curd and a pappadam (lentil crisp), and often a dessert. It's usually served on a special metal dish, also called a thali, or on a banana leaf in the south (where it may just be called a 'meal').

ALCOHOL IN INDIA

Gujarat, Bihar and Nagaland are India's only dry states at the time of writing, along with the Union Territory of Lakshadweep (with the exception of a couple of tourism spots there). Several other states, including Kerala, have toyed with prohibition, and stringent alcohol laws apply across the country. Most states have regular dry days, when liquor shops, restaurants and bars are banned from selling alcohol. Gandhi Jayanti (2 October) is usually a dry day in most places. In many destinations, alcohol is served only in smart restaurants, bars and/or hotels, or by local liquor shops, and taxes are typically high. Goa still has the country's lowest alcohol tax, despite a slight increase in recent years. In touristy destinations you may come across unlicensed restaurants serving alcohol covertly in mugs or similar. Steer well clear of backstreet distilleries offering bootleg alcohol, as alcohol poisoning incidents (often involving methanol) are common.

TOP: SMDSS/SHUTTERSTOCK ; FROM LEFT: MANASWIPATIL/SHUTTERSTOCK, RAINBOW_DAZZLE/SHUTTERSTOCK, ABHISHEK MANE/SHUTTERSTOCK, SRI WIDYOWATI/SHUTTERSTOCK

Local Specialities

Street-Food Snacks

Samosas Deep-fried, wheat-flour triangles, usually stuffed with spiced peas and potatoes.
Kachori A deep-fried portable pastry, filled with spiced veg, including potato, pulses or sweet pumpkin.
Pakora/pakoda & bhajia Veg fritters, fried in gram (chickpea) flour batter.
Chole bhature Spiced chickpeas with a puffed-up *puri* (fried bread) for dipping.
Vada pav Mumbai's favourite burger – a spicy potato cake, topped with chutney in a white bread bun. Glorious!
Aloo tikki Fried potato cake, topped with yoghurt, sweet chutney and *sev* (crunchy chickpea noodles).
Namkeen A vast assortment of crispy pulse- or potato-based savoury snacks.
Jalebi Super-sweet, super-sticky whorls of fried dough, soaked in syrup.
Petha Candied ash gourd; look for vendors pursued by hungry bees.
Halwa Central Asia–inspired sweetmeats, prepared from semolina or vegetables plus dried fruit and nuts.
Chaat Savoury roadside snacks of varying textures, drenched in chutneys.

Delicious Drinks

Chai Tea, flavoured with sugar and milk. Masala chai adds spices like cardamom, cinnamon and ginger.
Kaapi South India's beloved filter coffee, typically prepared with chicory in a stainless-steel tumbler.
Lassi Cooling yoghurt-based drink – sweet or sour.

Dare to Try

Vindaloo An incendiary Goan staple of pork or another meat flavoured with vinegar.
Mirchi pakoda Plump green chillies, stuffed with potato and fried in gram-flour batter.
'Jumping chicken' Frogs' legs – a speciality in Goa, Mumbai, Sikkim and Northeast India.
Bhang chutney A piquant staple in Uttarakhand food, made from hemp seeds.
Chaprah Red-ant chutney is an Adivasi favourite in Chhattisgarh.
Alternative protein Silkworms, crickets and snails are integral to Nagaland's cuisine.

MEALS OF A LIFETIME

Indian Accent (p84) The best of Indian fine dining: Manish Mehrotra's inspired creations at Delhi's The Lodhi.
Papa's (p691) Mumbai's most-hyped 12-seater, with a bucket-list-worthy, India-forward tasting menu.
Goan feast (p761) The ultimate Goan lunch awaits, courtesy of home chef Shubhra Shankhwalker.
Suvarna Mahal (p118) The full royal-palace experience, fabulous food included, at the Rambagh in Jaipur.
Lucknow family meals (p362) Sunaeyaa Kappoor brings to life forgotten flavours of Awadh on a home terrace.
Mattancherry street-food tour (p889) Savour diverse layers of Kerala's cuisine on a culinary walk.
Cafe Bahar (p645) Join the lunchtime queue for Hyderabad's top biryani, packed with spices.

THE YEAR IN FOOD

SPRING

Freshly harvested fruit and vegetables flood menus – a great time enjoy to *palak* (spinach), carrot-based *gajar ka halwa*, and fresh papaya and strawberries. March to June is delicious Alphonso mango season on the west coast.

SUMMER

Curd is popular in sweltering May, but once the monsoon breaks, it's all about comfort foods – such as sweet *ghewar* in Rajasthan and *pakora* across the plains. Spicy soups, such as *rasam*, also go down well.

AUTUMN

After the rains, festivals cram the calendar, associated with all sorts of special foods. Sweets such as *motichoor laddoo* and *rasgulla* are popular to offer (and eat) for Navratri, Dussehra, Durga Puja and Diwali.

WINTER

Winter warmers include rogan josh (Kashmiri lamb) and peppery, meaty *nihari* stew; and health-promoting dishes, such as Kerala's vegetable-and-coconut *thoran* and Rajasthan's *bajra khichdi* (pearl millet).

FAT JACKEY/SHUTTERSTOCK

Markha Valley (p232), Ladakh

THE OUTDOORS

Rising from deserts and steamy jungles to the highest mountaintops, India was made for outdoor adventures, from hiking and wildlife safaris to beach yoga.

India is big the way continents are big, so you'll find terrain for every kind of adventure. The Himalaya forms a natural obstacle course for hikers, climbers and mountain-bikers, plus skiing in winter and rafting in autumn. Moving from rocky ridges to dusty plains and deserts, central India is all about short hikes and wildlife adventures, including tiger safaris. The land rises up again in the south, with hilly hikes and wildlife encounters in the Western Ghats, and beachside activities await in Goa, Kerala, Karnataka and the Andamans.

Highland Adventures

The Himalayan foothills are a trekking playground, with epic trails through Ladakh, Himachal Pradesh, Uttarakhand, West Bengal, Sikkim and Arunachal Pradesh. Routes for cold-weather avoiders await in the Western Ghats and central hills. Autumn is generally the best trekking window; in Ladakh, summertime rules.

Numerous agencies can get you out on the trails, though a growing number of routes require permits. Ladakh is best for independent trekking. Top routes include the Markha Valley in Ladakh, the Singalila Ridge in West Bengal, the Goecha La Trek in Sikkim and numerous high-altitude trails in Uttarakhand.

Hiking is just the beginning – rafting rivers thunder down from the mountains, while lofty peaks entice mountaineers. For

Supersized Adventures

CAVING
Caverns burrow through the Indian hills; the **Borra Caves** (p869) near Visakhapatnam in Andhra Pradesh are illuminated by psychedelic lights.

SKIING
You can ski and snowboard in the Himalaya! **Solang** (p279) near Manali and **Auli** (p385) in Uttarakhand are top spots.

PARAGLIDING
Launch yourself on a soaring tandem flight over the Himalayan foothills from **Billing** (Bir; p273), conveniently close to Dharamshala.

FAMILY ADVENTURES

Zipline over a desert fortress; high-speed thrills await at Jodhpur's **Mehrangarh** (p162).
Splash down in **Palolem** (p788); swim, rent kayaks and paddleboards, go cycling, or go dolphin-spotting on an outrigger boat for instant family fun!

Take the Toy Train to **Darjeeling** (p461); the full route will test kids' patience, but short joyrides by steam train to Ghoom are a blast.
Drift along the backwaters of **Kerala** (p898) on a kayak or punted canoe – an active(ish) family adventure that can take you away from the crowds.

Spend time on a local family farm, perhaps **Hansali Organic Farm** (p205) near Patiala in Punjab.
Spot tigers the family-friendly way – **Ranthambore National Park** (p127) is an easy stop between Jaipur and Delhi or Agra, with a rambling fort as bonus fun.

warm-weather rock climbing, head to Hampi and Badami in Karnataka.

Motorbiking is another Himalayan hit, particularly around Manali and Leh – two towns linked by India's most dramatic motorcycling route (local operators rent out bikes and offer guided trips). For more low-key pedallers, bikes are available for hire in many tourist hubs.

Wildlife Encounters

Elephants, rhinos, tigers and leopards are just the headline acts on a wildlife roster spanning hundreds of endemic species. Winter and spring are the best seasons for wildlife spotting – many wildlife zones are impassable during the summer monsoon.

India's 106 national parks and tiger reserves cover every kind of terrain, from the jungles of Kerala to the mountains of Ladakh. Visit on jeep safaris or on foot rather than on elephant-back to avoid harming these vulnerable creatures.

Madhya Pradesh, Rajasthan, Kerala, Karnataka, Assam and Uttarakhand have some of the best national parks. Bandipur, Periyar and Mudumalai come top for elephants, while Bandhavgarh, Kanha, Corbett, Ranthambhore and and Tadoba Andhari deliver reliable tiger sightings.

Birdwatching is a treat too, with highlights including Keoladeo National Park in Rajasthan and Neora Valley National Park in West Bengal. Over in the Andamans, there's the unique chance to swim with dugongs.

Beachside Fun & Holistic Pursuits

Beach resorts, particularly around Goa and Kerala in the south, offer rafting, kayaking, paddleboarding, diving, snorkelling, and boat cruises to spot dolphins and other marine life. Many locals bathe fully clothed; while swimwear is often fine in touristy destinations, it's best to cover up away from the sand.

For serious divers, the best reefs are off the Andaman and Lakshadweep islands. Surfers are drawn to the breaks between Puducherry and Chennai in Tamil Nadu; Ashwem and Agonda in Goa; Varkala and Kovalam in Kerala; and Udupi and Mangaluru in Karnataka.

Travellers with an interest in yoga (and wellness) head to Goa, Kerala, Mysuru and Rishikesh for classes, retreats and training. Kerala is India's capital of Ayurveda – herbal and therapy-based traditional medicine.

Meditation tempts seekers of self-knowledge into the mountains – particularly Tibetan Buddhist areas such as Ladakh and Himachal Pradesh – and to lowland sacred sites such as Bodhgaya.

SERIOUS YOGA
Those keen to dig deep into the roots and intricacies of yoga can join professional teacher-training courses, including in **Rishikesh** (p380).

A TASTE OF MOUNTAINEERING
Take on 615m-tall **Kang Yatse II** (p232) from the Markha Valley near Leh; guides are essential, booked through local agencies.

ICE RIVER TREKKING
Use the frozen Zanskar River as a trekking trail on the winter-only Chadar Trek, linking Ladakh and **Zanskar** (p244).

MOUNTAIN SPORTS
Manali (p276) options include summertime zorbing, winter snowtubing, and, reputedly, yak skiing (being hauled up the slopes by a yak).

ACTION AREAS

Where to find India's best outdoor activities.

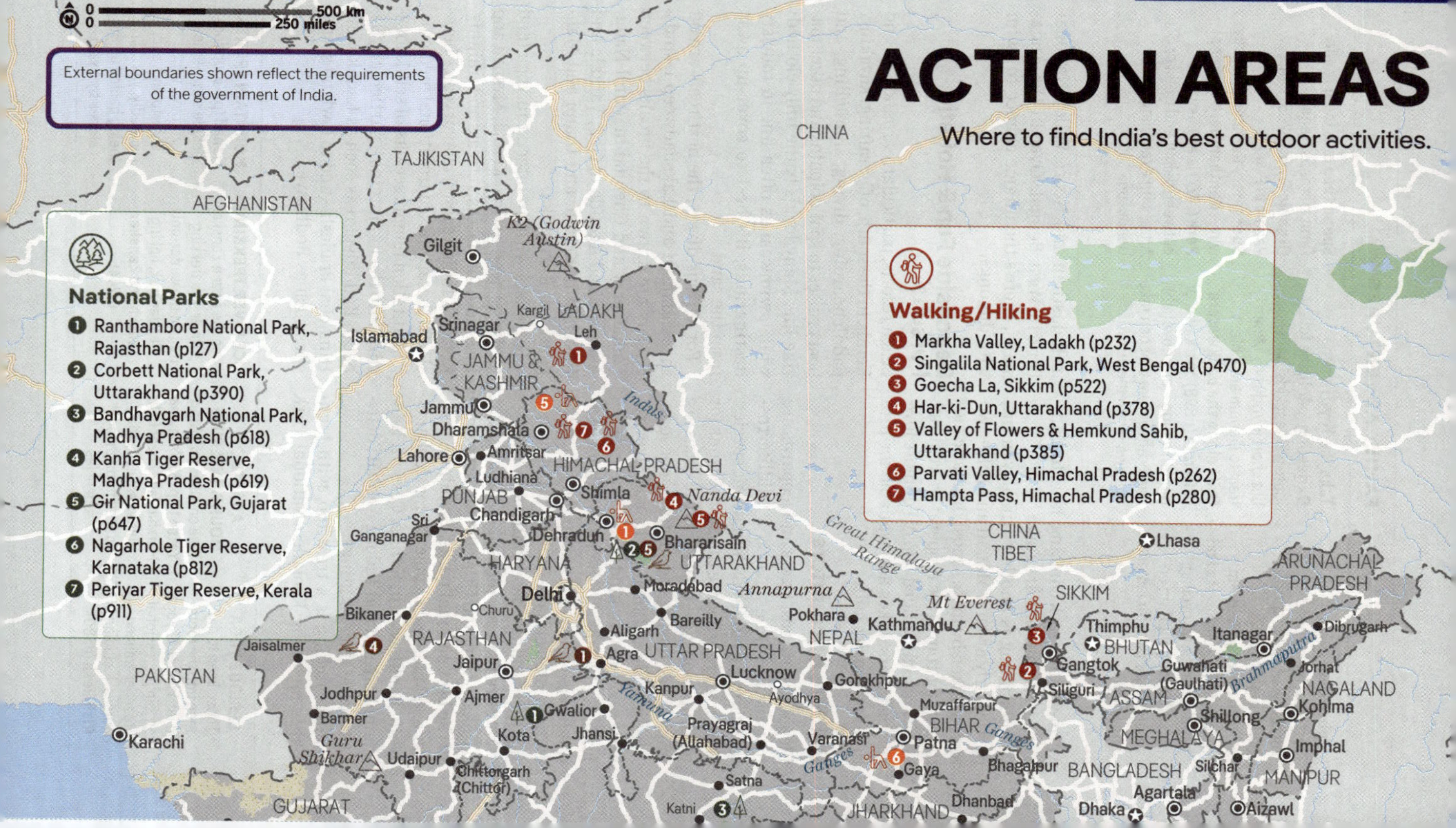

Beaches

1. Canacona Beaches, Goa (p786)
2. Varkala, Kerala (p915)
3. Morjim & Around, Goa (p758)
4. Gokarna, Karnataka (p822)
5. Kovalam, Tamil Nadu (p953)
6. Rushikonda, Andhra Pradesh (p867)
7. Swaraj Island (Havelock), Andaman Islands (p995)

Birdwatching

1. Keoladeo National Park, Rajasthan (p124)
2. Bandipur Tiger Reserve, Karnataka (p813)
3. Thattekad Bird Sanctuary, Kerala (p919)
4. Kichan, Rajasthan (p170)
5. Corbett National Park, Uttarakhand (p390)
6. Sundarbans Tiger Reserve, West Bengal (p450)
7. Mollem National Park, Goa (p781)

Yoga & Meditation

1. Rishikesh, Uttarakhand (p380)
2. Mysuru, Karnataka (p804)
3. Varkala, Kerala (p915)
4. Arambol, Goa (p756)
5. McLeod Ganj, Himachal Pradesh (p264)
6. Bodhgaya, Bihar (p480)

INDIA

THE GUIDE

Chapters in this section are organised by hubs and their surrounding areas. We see the hub as your base in the destination, where you'll find unique experiences, local insights, insider tips and expert recommendations. It's also your gateway to the surrounding area, where you'll see what and how much you can do from there.

Jaigarh fortress (p123), Jaipur

ABIR ROY BARMAN/SHUTTERSTOCK

Researched by
Margot Bigg

Delhi

INDIA'S ACTION-PACKED CAPITAL

Transformed time and again by the rise and fall of empires, India's capital will saturate your senses and defy your expectations.

Delhi's culture, cuisine and charisma draw influences from every corner of the country. Here you can buy artisan crafts from all over India, sample the best in regional food, see the latest developments in contemporary art and explore the city's many layers of a fascinating, blood-soaked past.

Like other great historic cities, Dehi's modern daily life unfurls among the ruins of its past. Street sellers cook up *chhole bhature* (chickpea curry with puffed fried bread) in the walls of crumbling *havelis*,(traditional, ornately decorated residences), AirPod-eared runners speed past gracious Lodhi tombs, and traffic swarms through once-impenetrable fortresses. At least eight significant settlements, with eight different names, have occupied this flat plain by the banks of the Yamuna River, and each has left its mark. From the 12th-century remains of the Hindu kingdom at Lal Kot, to the triumphant Qutb Minar erected by the conquering Afghan invaders, to the breathtaking Mughal architecture of the Red Fort and Humayun's Tomb, to the colonial-style colonnades of Lutyens' Delhi, this city is littered with reminders of the transitory nature of imperial power.

BILL PERRY/SHUTTERSTOCK

For the visitor, there's a choose-your-own-adventure of possibilities. You can head to Old Delhi for a chaotic and sensual feast, winding through mazelike lanes to hunt down street treats and treasures to take home. You can explore the hipster cafe culture in the leafy southern suburbs, with galleries and international street art. You can let your tastebuds plan the itinerary, sampling flavours from across the country, as well as the creations of chefs innovating modern Indian cuisine. You can discover the spiritual life of the city, visiting age-old temples, gurdwaras, mosques and shrines. Or you can sign up for a residential retreat, take a yoga or meditation course, explore Ayurveda or consult an astrologer.

As 21st-century suburbs continue to extend the Delhi metro area beyond its historic core, the National Capital Region is accelerating into its future, without losing connection to the past. Right now is a great time to visit – you'll find a city changing almost before your eyes.

THE MAIN AREAS

OLD DELHI
Monumental history and labyrinthine markets. **p60**

LUTYENS' DELHI
Avenues of the British Raj. **p70**

NIZAMUDDIN & LODHI COLONY
Enchanting tombs and gardens. **p81**

SOUTH DELHI
Indie India: cafes and creativity. **p89**

GREATER DELHI
Archaeological wonders. **p95**

For places to stay in Delhi, see p102

OLEG PODZOROV/SHUTTERSTOCK

Above: Qutb Minar (p98); Left: Ceiling, Sheesh Gumbad tomb (p86), Lodhi Garden

Find Your Way

Delhi's efficient metro will get you close to most places; combine it with taxis and autorickshaws to conquer the megacity's vast sprawl. In Old Delhi, you're best off on foot or cycle rickshaw to immerse yourself in the bustling lanes that are the lifeblood of the city.

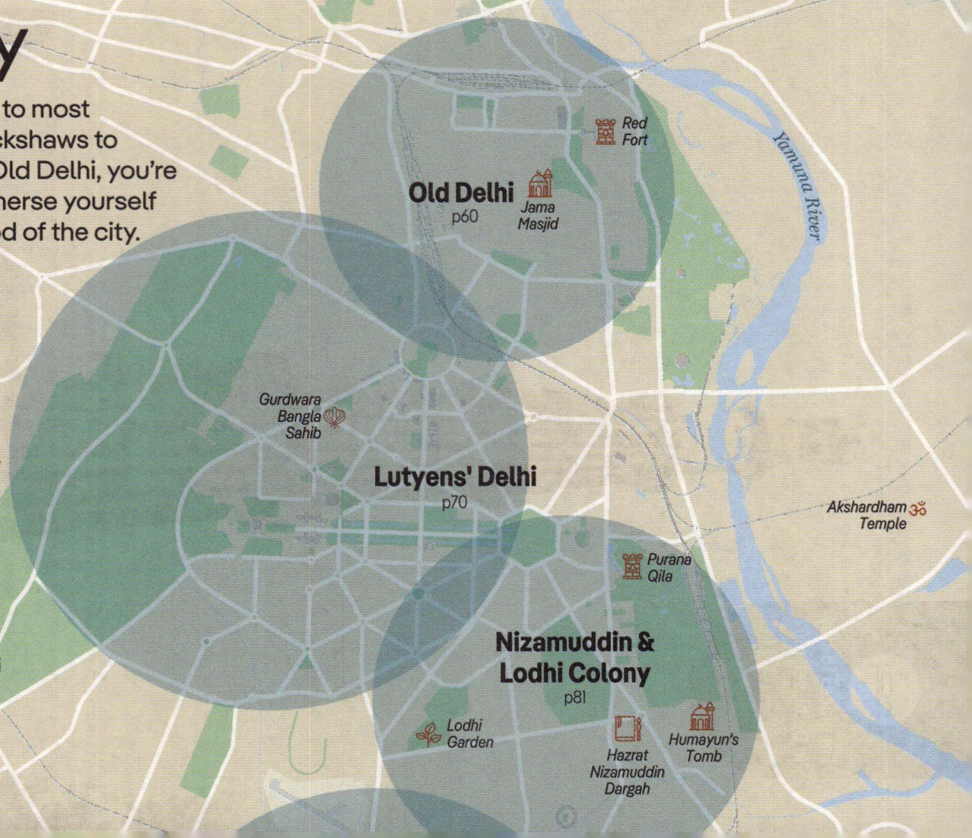

FROM THE AIRPORT

The metro's Airport Express (orange line) is the easiest and quickest way from **Indira Gandhi International Airport** into the city (₹64; 16 minutes to New Delhi Railway Station). Delhi Traffic Police operate prepaid taxi counters just beyond arrivals and outside the terminal. Fares are based on destination, with extra charges for luggage and nighttime rides.

METRO

Delhi's metro is fast and efficient, with information in Hindi and English. The first carriage is for women and children only. Smart Cards are generally better value than Tourist Cards or individual ride tokens. Unlike Tourist Cards, Smart Cards can be used on the Airport Express.

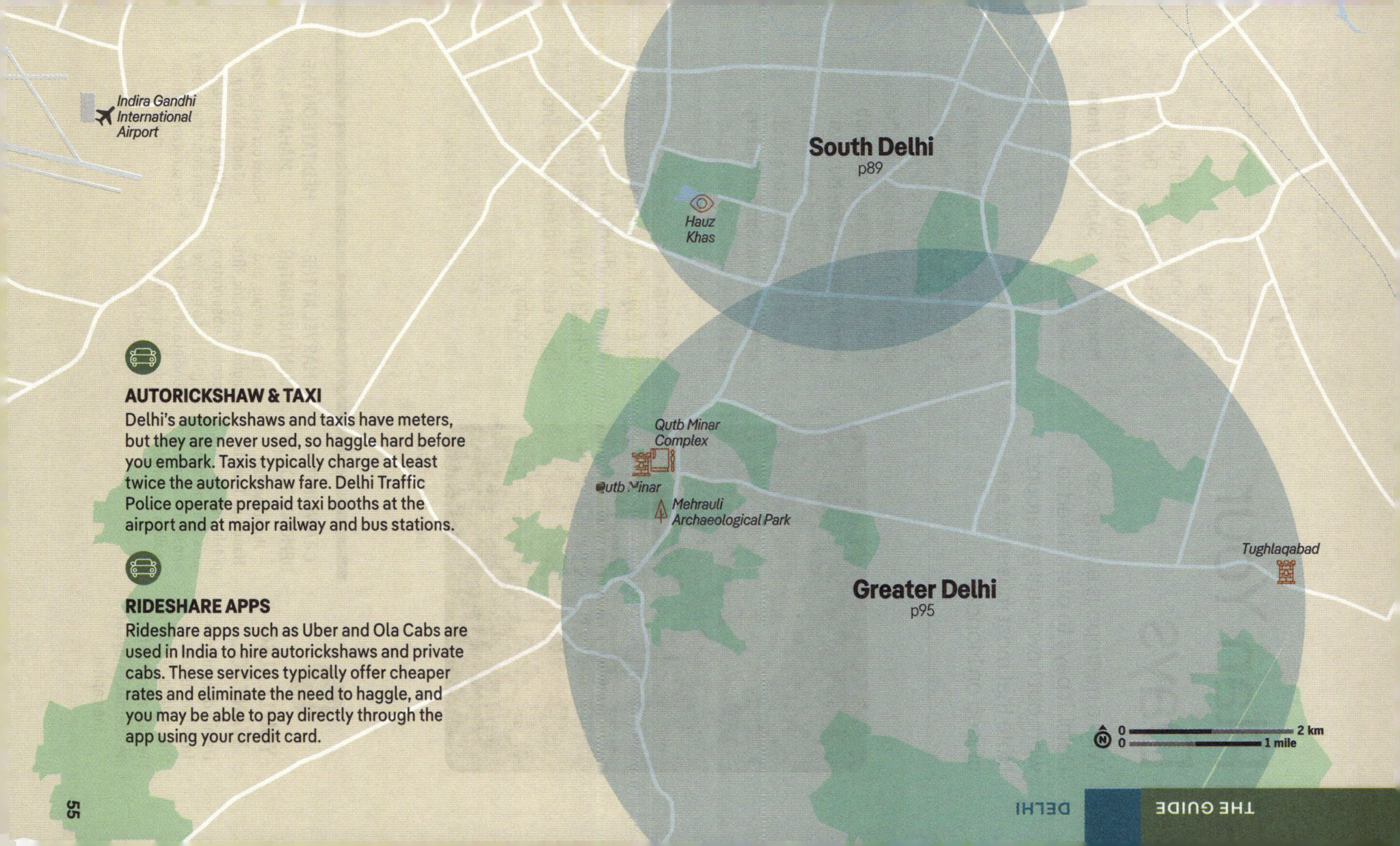

AUTORICKSHAW & TAXI

Delhi's autorickshaws and taxis have meters, but they are never used, so haggle hard before you embark. Taxis typically charge at least twice the autorickshaw fare. Delhi Traffic Police operate prepaid taxi booths at the airport and at major railway and bus stations.

RIDESHARE APPS

Rideshare apps such as Uber and Ola Cabs are used in India to hire autorickshaws and private cabs. These services typically offer cheaper rates and eliminate the need to haggle, and you may be able to pay directly through the app using your credit card.

Plan Your Days

With a metropolis as large as Delhi, it pays to plan ahead to work out how you'll get around. Note that most museums are closed on Monday.

ARNAV PRATAP SINGH/SHUTTERSTOCK

India Gate (p76)

Day 1

Morning

● Start your morning off with a visit to historic Lutyens' Delhi, with stops at the **National Gallery of Modern Art** (p75) and iconic **India Gate** (p76).

Afternoon

● Now head over to **Humayun's Tomb** (p83), where the Mughal magnificence will knock your socks off. Then descend into the subterranean **Humayun's Tomb World Heritage Site Museum** for an artefact-filled educational experience, followed by a stroll at the adjacent **Sunder Nursery** (p84).

Evening

● Enjoy a fine-dining experience at acclaimed **Indian Accent** (p84) or head to **Khan Market** (p87) for fancy eats with a side of high-end shopping.

YOU'LL ALSO WANT TO...

Delhi's delights run from the historic to the esoteric. Get off the tourist trail to find the alternative joys of the capital.

CRAWL INTO A DEMON'S MOUTH

Jhandewalan Hanuman Temple (p74) houses demons, gods and goddesses who spurt blood and swallow you whole.

MARVEL AT THE JANTAR MANTAR

The enormous, and slightly eccentric, 18th-century **observatory** (p70) has a massive sundial and world-time clock shaped like an inverted heart.

MEDITATE ON THE MAHATMA

Follow our self-guided **Gandhi history walking tour** (p69) to learn about the leader's personal and political story.

Day 2

Morning

- By now you've acclimatised enough to tackle the onslaught of Old Delhi. Spend the morning at the **Red Fort** (p64) then take our **Old Delhi Walking Tour** (p66) into the bazaars of **Chandni Chowk** (p61).

Afternoon

- Climb the minaret of the **Jama Masjid** (p60) for sweeping views over the city, and reward yourself with a mocktail on the rooftop of **Gumbad Cafe** (p68) or a kebab at **Karim's** (p60).

Evening

- Take the metro over the river to **Akshardham** (p88) for a temple experience that pulls out all the stops. Arrive just after sunset for a water-and-light fountain show.

Day 3

Morning

- Get an early start for a trip to the 13th-century **Qutb Minar** (p98). Combine it with a ramble through **Mehrauli Archaeological Park** (p97).

Afternoon

- Combine lunch and retail therapy, either at South Delhi's **Hauz Khas Village** (p89), great for vintage decor and trendy restaurants, or nearby **Dilli Haat** (p92), which features craft vendors from across the country and food stalls representing cuisines from almost every state.

Evening

- Head north to **Connaught Place** (p70) for drinks and people watching. Grab a pint at microbrewery **Ministry of Beer** (p78) or a cuppa at tea shop **Cha Bar** (p75).

TAKE A YOGA CLASS

Join locals for **traditional yoga classes** (p94) where deep, meditative asanas take precedence over dynamic, fitness-focused sequences.

HEAD TO THE KITCHEN

Try your hand at making perfectly round chapatis, or at least learn to whip up some dhal, at a **cooking class** (p94).

LAUD THE LOO

Learn about the importance of sanitation, and see some historic latrines, at the whimsical **Sulabh International Museum of Toilets** (p100).

IMMERSE YOURSELF IN THE ARTS

Check out **contemporary art** (p75) or **stand-up comedy** (p92). See **live music** (p91), or **play some yourself** (p91).

HELP ME PICK:

Delhi's Historic Sites

One of the world's oldest continually inhabited cities, Delhi has had many incarnations, some easier to distinguish than others. It's commonly agreed there are eight historical sites below the modern megacity, including the 11th-century Hindu metropolis with its fort at Lal Kot, the cities of the five Delhi sultanates, Shahjahanabad of the Mughals and British Lutyens' Delhi. The bones of these fallen empires show through the skin of the modern capital in stunning reminders of its often gory past.

Where To Go If You Love...

Modern Interpretation

The Victorian-era barracks erected by the British inside the **Mughal Red Fort** (p57; 1648) have been converted into museums and temporary exhibition spaces that provide an excellent introduction to Delhi's heritage and 20th-century Indian history. The subterranean **Humayun's Tomb World Heritage Site Museum** (p84) opened below the site in 2024.

Sheer Wow Factor

Mughal **Humayun's Tomb** (p83; 1570), the model for the Taj Mahal, is hard to beat for its architectural glory, though the **Qutb Minar** (p98; 1199) comes close. Dating from the first sultanate, this sandstone tower is one of Delhi's oldest yet best-preserved monuments.

SAIKO3P/SHUTTERSTOCK

Jantar Mantar (p70)

Historic Curios

Maharaja Jai Singh II's oddball **Jantar Mantar** (p70) was the height of astronomical technology in 1724. **Agrasen ki Baoli** (p71; built in the 14th century) is a large and atmospheric step-well that seems to descend both into the earth and back in time. The spooky F**iroz Shah Kotla** (p78; 1354) of the third sultanate is said to be haunted by djinns.

Picnic-Friendly Parkland

Many of Delhi's historic sites are set in beautifully maintained gardens that provide green escapes from the city. Try **Purana Qila** (p81; 1538; a great picnic spot), **Hauz Khas** (p91; ruins surrounded by arty cafes, greenery and the lake-like tank), **Sunder Nursery** (p84; newly created parklands with a Sunday market) or **Lodhi Garden** (p86; a fabled date destination). There's a great kids' playground (only adults with children allowed in) near **India Gate** (p76).

Place-to-Yourself Rambles

Almost forgotten in the south of the city, 12th-century **Mehrauli Archaeological Park** (p97) is threaded with forested tracks frequented by shepherds and wild pigs and sprinkled with the remains of the first sultanate. The slightly creepy ruins of sultan Ghiyus-ud-din Tughlaq's stern **Tughlaqabad Fort** (p100; 1321) offer great views across Delhi, but see few visitors. This would be a great place to set a murder mystery.

Spiritual Significance

The **Hazrat Nizamuddin Dargah** (p85; 1325) is Delhi's most mystical experience. The busy shrine of the Sufi saint receives hundreds of pilgrims daily from many different faiths. One of the biggest mosques in India, the **Jama Masjid** (p60; 1656) can accommodate 25,000 worshippers.

ORHAN CAM/SHUTTERSTOCK

Humayun's Tomb (p83)

HOW TO

Hire a car and driver Historic sites tend to be further afield and some are a long way from a metro station. Hire a car for the day to maximise your time.

Budget Foreigners pay more at Archaeological Survey of India sites than Indians. Buy tickets online to save ₹50 off major sights and skip the ticket queue.

Get a guide You'll get a lot more out of a visit if you hire a guide or at least bone up on a bit of history before you arrive.

Opening hours Most major attractions are open daily or every day except Monday.

Know Your History

The first recorded city in Delhi, Lal Kot (1052–60), was built under the reign of Anangpal Tomar in what is now Mehrauli. It later came under the rule of Prithviraj Chauhan, who ultimately lost it to Muhammad of Ghor. Ghor's general, Qutb-ud-din Aibak, ended up in charge after Muhammad's death, establishing the Delhi Sultanate. He commissioned Delhi's first mosque, Quwwat-ul-Islam, and the towering Qutb Minar (in 1199), but the latter was ultimately completed by his successor, Iltutmish. The Sultanate's next rulers, the Khilji Dynasty, constructed a new capital around Siri Fort (1303) to defend against the Mongols.

The Khilji were defeated by the Tughlaq sultans, who built Tughlaqabad Fort (1321), though it was abandoned just six years later. Firoz Shah Tughlaq then built Firozabad centred on Firoz Shah Kotla (1354). Timur (Tamerlane) stormed through town in 1398, opening the door for the Sayyid and Lodhi dynasties, the last of the Delhi sultanates, whose tombs are scattered around Lodhi Garden. Babur, a descendant of both Timur and Genghis Khan, was the first Mughal emperor. He seized Delhi in 1526 and his son Humayun began work on what is now called the Purana Qila. A century later, Shah Jahan gained the Peacock Throne at the cultural zenith of the Mughal empire. He built Shahjahanabad around the Red Fort. The Mughals were defeated by the British in 1858 and British rule ended with Independence in 1947.

Old Delhi

MONUMENTAL HISTORY AND MAZELIKE MARKETS

GETTING AROUND

Old Delhi's sights are nicely concentrated and best visited on foot; it's fascinating to walk the bustling lanes in any case. If you get tired, just hail a passing cycle-rickshaw. Taking a guided tour is a great way to get accustomed to Old Delhi's streets.

TOP TIP

Old Delhi has a big personality, but it's also hectic and stressful, with crazy traffic and touts. If you like to chill at the end of the day, don't book your accommodation here. There are more relaxed options further south.

Old Delhi, aka Purani Dilli, is the anarchic, charming and unmissable heart of the city. With tangled lanes wriggling around some of the city's most important attractions, old-style bazaar shopping and fantastic street eats, you haven't really been to Delhi until you've come here. It's well worth delving off the main thoroughfares into the narrow alleys – for one thing, you'll pay less than on the larger streets, but you'll also get the sense that you're going backstage, where Old Delhi's real daily life takes place.

Shah Jahan moved his capital here from Agra in 1648, in the same year that work was completed on his wife's mausoleum, the Taj Mahal (p314). He named the city Shahjahanabad and built the Red Fort and the Jama Masjid, while his daughter Jahanara Begum designed Chandni Chowk. The half-moon-shaped walled city had 14 gates, including Kashmiri Gate and Ajmeri Gate, which are still important city landmarks.

Delhi's Magnificent Mosque

An oasis of calm in the heart of Old Delhi

The **Jama Masjid** *(adult/child ₹400/free)* can hold a mind-blowing 25,000 people. The marble and red-sandstone structure, known also as the 'Friday Mosque', was Shah Jahan's final architectural triumph, built between 1644 and 1658. The four watchtowers were used for security. There are two

EATING IN OLD DELHI: BEST RESTAURANTS

Karim's: While purists say it's changed for tourists, Karim's remains Delhi's most famous Mughlai kebab and mutton restaurant. *9am-1am* ₹₹

Lakhori: Inside the beautifully restored Haveli Dharampura, this is an atmospheric place to dine at courtyard tables on Mughlai and local dishes. *noon-10.30pm* ₹₹₹

Madan Café: Friendly, pint-sized, roadside eatery that's among the cheapest places to get a meal along Paharganj's Main Bazaar. *7am-11pm* ₹

Cafe Delhi Heights: Inside the slick Red Fort Centre, this pure-veg branch of the hip cafe has surprisingly good-value thalis and snacks. *9am-9pm Tue-Sun* ₹

minarets standing 40m high, one of which can be climbed for amazing views.

There are numerous entrance gates; the eastern gate is closest to the metro and was originally for imperial use only, while the northern gate has a car park. Expect to pay for an additional ₹200 ticket if you want to climb the 121 steps up the steep and narrow southern minaret (access from the northern gate). From the top of the minaret, you can see how architect Edwin Lutyens incorporated the mosque into his architectural planning: the Jama Masjid, Connaught Place and Samvidhan Sadan (former parliament house) are in a direct line.

Visitors should dress conservatively and remove their shoes before entering the mosque, though you can carry your shoes with you inside if you wish to leave from a different gate, or are worried about losing them (many locals do this). The mosque is closed noon to 1.30pm; tourists can't enter during prayers.

Market Meanderings

Walking through one of Delhi's oldest markets

Old Delhi's main drag, **Chandni Chowk**, is a mix of shops, restaurants and houses of worship, bookended by the Red Fort (p66) and Fatehpuri Masjid. Tree-lined and elegant in Mughal times, the thoroughfare is now mind-bendingly chaotic, with tiny little ancient bazaars tentacling off it. In the Mughal era, Chandni Chowk centred on a pool that reflected the moon, hence the name 'moonlight place'. Motorised vehicles are not permitted between 9am and 9pm, and while this doesn't keep them all out, it's a far more pleasant experience to walk through here during the day than at night.

The 17th-century **Fatehpuri Masjid**, built by Fatehpuri Begum, one of Shah Jahan's wives, is a haven of tranquillity after the frantic streets outside. The central pool was taken from a noble house, hence the elaborate shape. After the First War of Independence (1857), the British sold the mosque to a Hindu nobleman for ₹19,000. It was returned to Muslim worship 20 years later in exchange for four villages.

Story Time in Old Delhi

A little cultural centre with big ideas

Tucked down a narrow residential lane, in a masterfully restored 19th-century *haveli*, **Kathika** *(kathika.in; ₹1500, after 2pm ₹500)* is a hybrid cultural centre and museum, though it feels more like the home of a collector of whimsical ephemera than anything else. Black-and-white photos line the walls, depicting scenes from early-20th-century Delhi life, while an eclectic mix of statues, antique furniture and even a staircase lined with rotary phones add to the vintage appeal. Cultural experiences, complete with Indian classical music and dance, take place daily in the courtyard, with additional plays, storytelling sessions and other activities at Neem Haveli (p102), Kathika's sister property/guesthouse, across the lane. Following the lead of most Delhi attractions, the property is shut on Mondays.

BEST OF QUEER DELHI

Batool Ali is a trans woman who runs walking tours exploring Delhi's queer history. *@DelhiQueerHeritage Walks; dilliqueerheri tagewalks@gmail .com*

Here are her top recommendations.

Depot 48: Live-music nightspot with queer events on Thursday night, including drag nights.

Jugmug Thela: Queer friendly outdoor cafe.

Kitty Su: Inclusive and elite club near Connaught Place; but they might look twice at your shoes before letting you in!

Pride: Pride *(@delhi queerpride)* is now celebrated for an entire month (November/ December), with events and art exhibitions, especially at the **Goethe Institute**, our longstanding ally. There's also **Rainbow Lit Fest** *(rainbowliterature festival.com)*.

Walking Tours: Our tours visit important sites like Hijron ka Khanqah (p97) and reveal Delhi's queer history, which dates back hundreds of years.

HIGHLIGHTS
1 Jama Masjid
2 Red Fort

SIGHTS
3 Chandni Chowk
4 Chatta Chowk
5 Diwan-i-Am
6 Diwan-i-Khas
7 Fatehpuri Masjid
8 Gandhi Darshan
9 Gandhi Darshan Park
10 Kathika
11 Lahore Gate
12 Moti Masjid
13 Naubat Khana
14 Ramakrishna Mission
15 Rang Mahal
16 Red Fort Centre

SLEEPING
17 Haveli Dharampura
18 Hotel Ajanta
19 Hotel Cottage Yes Please
20 Hotel Godwin Deluxe
21 Major's Den Guesthouse
see 10 Neem Haveli
22 Zostel Delhi

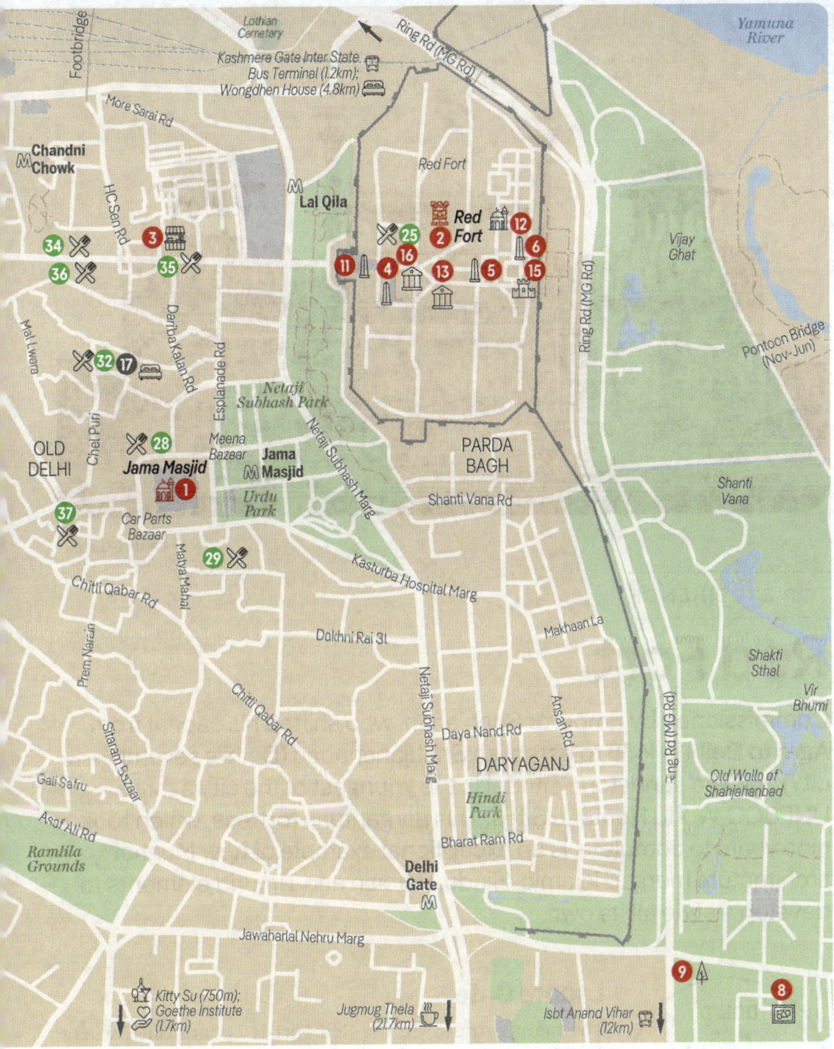

EATING
- **23** Bade Mia Ki Kheer
- **24** Bikaner Sweets Corner
- **25** Cafe Delhi Heights
- **26** Everest Cafe
- **27** Exotic Cafe & Restaurant
- **28** Gumbad Cafe
- **29** Karim's
- **30** Krishna Rooftop Cafe
- **31** Kuremal Mohan Lal
- **32** Lakhori
- **33** Madan Café
- **34** Natraj Dahi Balle Corner
- **35** Old Famous Jalebi Wala
- **36** PT Gaya Prasad Shiv Charan
- **37** Shyam Sweets
- **38** Sita Ram Dewan Chand

SHOPPING
- **39** Main Bazaar
- **40** Paharganj Fruit Market
- **41** Paharganj Vegetable & Spice Market
- **42** Spice Market
- **43** Tooti Chowk

DMITRY RUKHLENKO/SHUTTERSTOCK

Lahore Gate

TOP EXPERIENCE

Red Fort

Commissioned by Emperor Shahjahan, who shifted his capital from Agra to Delhi in 1638 to establish Shahjahanabad (Delhi's seventh city), this red sandstone citadel is the youngest of the city's three UNESCO World Heritage Sites. This gargantuan fortress, which took nine years to complete, is an exceptional example of how Mughal architecture merged Islamic, Hindu, Persian and Timurid elements to develop a style all its own.

DON'T MISS

- Lahore Gate
- Red Fort Centre
- Naubat Khana
- Diwan-i-Am
- Rang Mahal
- Diwan-i-Khas
- Moti Masjid

Lahore Gate

The main entrance to the Red Fort is Lahore Gate, where Jawaharlal Nehru first raised the tricolour flag of a newly independent India back in 1947, a tradition that takes place every year to honour Independence Day. You can still see bullet marks on the gate that date from the First War of Independence (Indian Uprising) in 1857. Just beyond the gate is **Chatta Chowk**, a roofed arcade that's lined with shops selling scarves and other souvenirs.

PRACTICALITIES

- asi.nic.in/pages/WorldHeritageRedFort
- adult/child ₹600/free
- sunrise-9pm Tue-Sun

Red Fort Centre

Just beyond Chatta Chowk, inside repurposed barracks dating to the British era, the Red Fort Centre tells the story of the fort through a series of four interpretive areas, collectively known as Afsana, along with a 360-degree immersive augmented reality experience, Afreeen, that takes visitors back in time to the era of Shahjahan's rule. The centre is ticketed separately from regular Red Fort admission, and tickets with *(₹150)* and without *(₹100)* the Afsana experience are available.

Naubat Khana

Past the Red Fort Centre, the Naubat Khana, or 'drum house,' is a three-storey structure embellished with carved designs that were originally painted with gold. This structure was once used by musicians, who performed here five times a day, and doubled as a parking area for elephants and other mounts.

Diwan-i-Am

Behind the Naubat Khana, the Diwan-i-Am (Hall of Public Audiences) was where the emperor once received the public, who would come here to air their grievances. At the back of the hall, protected by plexiglass, sits a white marble throne inlaid with precious stones. Behind it, a series of pietra dura panels depict images of flowers and birds; there's also one of Orpheus and his lute. The panels are believed to have been created by French jeweller Austin de Bordeaux.

Rang Mahal

So-named because its exterior was once a riot of colour, the Rang Mahal was part of the zenana (secluded women's quarters). A cooling artificial stream, the *nahr-i-bihisht* (river of paradise), once helped regulate temperatures within. Two of its apartments feature *sheesh mahal* (palace of mirror) in which fragments of mirrors are arranged on the walls to create beautiful reflective designs when illuminated by candlelight.

Diwan-i-Khas

The Diwan-i-Khas (Hall of Private Audiences) was where the emperor would meet with courtesans and other officials. It features aisles of decorated arches supported by marble piers ornamented with semi-precious stone inlay. A wooden ceiling over the hall was painted in 1911 and is crowned with *chhatris* (domed canopies). It was here where Bahadur Shah Zafar became the last Mughal emperor in 1857, only to be exiled by the British later the same year.

Moti Masjid

To the west of Diwan-i-Khas, the Moti Masjid was built by Aurangzeb for his personal use back in 1662. The white mosque surmounted by three onion-shaped domes is quite the sight from outside, but the interiors are off-limits to visitors.

JAI HIND SOUND & LIGHT SHOW

After sunset, the fort transforms into the venue for *Jai Hind*, a sound-and-light show that uses projection mapping and narration by veteran Bollywood superstar Amitabh Bachchan to tell the story of the fort over the centuries. The show begins at the Naubat Khana, continuing to the Diwan-i-Am, and culminating at the Diwan-e-Khas (the only seated part of the experience).

TOP TIPS

- You can pre-book Red Fort Centre and sound-and-light show tickets at *in.bookmyshow.com*. Only some sound-and-light shows are in English and timings vary, so check at the time of booking.
- Independence Day (15 August) is celebrated with aplomb at the Red Fort every year, with a 21-gun salute and a flag-raising ceremony at Lahore Gate. Expect massive crowds and arrive early if you plan to attend.
- Snacks from across India are available onsite at Cafe Delhi Heights (p60).
- The Red Fort has ramps and accessible pathways with loaner wheelchairs available on request.

WANDER THE BAZAARS OF OLD DELHI

All your senses will come alive as you venture into the historic heart of the city – especially your taste buds.

START	END	LENGTH
Red Fort	Fatehpuri Masjid	2km; 1½hr

Allow at least half a day to explore the historic buildings and modern museums in the 1 **Red Fort** (p64). When you're starting to get hungry, come out through the 2 **Lahore Gate** (p64) and cross the road (take the underpass) to the red sandstone 3 **Digambara Jain Temple**. Head down 4 **Chandni Chowk** (p61), which is (mostly) motor-free between 9am and 9pm. Turn right just before McDonalds to 5 **Bhagirath Palace Electrical Market** (p80). On the corner of the next major street to the left is the 6 **Jalebi Wala** cooking up amazing *jalebis* (deep-fried syrupy dough swirls). It's on the corner of the 7 **Dariba Kalan** market, where silver jewellery, ornaments and old coins are sold. Continue to the next main street to the right, the 8 **Kinari Bazaar** (p80).

When you reach a fork, head right to a street of *paratha* sellers; 9 **PT Gaya Prasad Shiv Charan** is the most famous. Follow the dog leg back to Chandni Chowk. Directly across the road is 10 **Natraj Dahi Balle Corner**, a tiny place selling *dahi balle* (lentil fritters in yoghurt) on the corner of a narrow *gali* (lane). Keep heading west on Chandni Chowk, exploring specialist lanes like 11 **Nai Sadak**, opposite the town hall, lined with stalls selling saris, shawls, chiffon and *lehenga-cholis* (blouse and skirt combos) or the 12 **Ballimaran** market, specialising in sequined slippers and fancy, curly-toed jootis (slip-on shoes), before taking respite in 13 **Fatehpuri Masjid** (p61).

Sights & Smells of the Spice Market

Grab your camera and your hankie

It feels as if little has changed for centuries in the fabulously atmospheric, labyrinthine **Spice Market** (Khari Baoli), as labourers hustle through the narrow lanes with huge packages of herbs and spices on their heads while sunlight pours down through cracks in the hessian sacks hanging overhead for shade. The colours are wonderful - red chillies, yellow turmeric, green cardamom pods - and there's so much spice in the air, people walk around unable to suppress their sneezes.

There are eye-catching displays of everything from lentils and rice to giant jars of chutneys, pickles, nuts and tea, and you can buy small packets of items, despite it being a wholesale market.

Paharganj Main Bazaar Madness

Everything you didn't know you needed

Backpacker Central, this crazy-busy bazaar that runs through Paharganj sells almost everything you want, and a lot you probably don't. It's a great place to pick up souvenirs and gifts, with shops selling incense, costume jewellery, colourful stickers of deities, and loose-fitting 'backpacker uniform' apparel. Haggle with purpose and beware the street-side henna scam, where *mehndi*-wallahs will quote a price for a beautiful henna tattoo only later to reveal that the price was not per hand but per inch.

There are rooftop cafes (p68) surrounding **Tooti Chowk**, about midway along **Main Bazaar**. Just south of Main Bazaar is a street-side **Fruit Market**, around the corner from which the **Vegetable & Spice Market** is the best place to shop for spices in Paharganj.

STREET FOOD

Old Delhi sizzles with the sound of *Dilli-ki-Chaat* (street-food snacks) being fried, boiled, grilled and flipped.

Dahi bhalle: Fried lentil balls served with yoghurt and chutney.

Aloo tikki: Spiced potato patties.

Shakarkandi: Sweet potato baked on coals, sold in winter.

Aloo chaat: Fried potato with chickpeas and chopped onions, garnished with spices and chutney.

Chhole bhature: Breakfast favourite of spicy chickpeas, accompanied by puffy, fried bread with a light paneer filling.

Chhole kulcha: Less greasy version of *chhole bhature,* made with mushy boiled chickpeas and a soft, fluffy bread.

Nihari: Goat curry eaten with roti; a popular breakfast in Muslim neighbourhoods.

EATING IN OLD DELHI: SWEETS & STREET EATS

Old Famous Jalebi Wala: Century-old place that does Delhi's - if not India's - finest *jalebis* (deep-fried, syrupy dough). *8am-9.30pm* ₹

Kuremal Mohan Lal: The Kuremal family have been making *kulfi* since 1906, with options like pomegranate, fig and watermelon. *11am-11pm* ₹

Bikaner Sweets Corner: Try *kaju barfi* (cashew-and-sugar sweet) or *gajar halwa* (soft, ghee-and-carrot dessert sprinkled with nuts). *8am-11pm* ₹

Shyam Sweets: *Ghiya ki barfi* (bottle gourd sweet) in summer and *gajar pak* (carrot cake) in winter. *8am-9.30pm Mon-Sat, to 6.30pm Sun* ₹

Natraj Dahi Balle Corner: Tiny place famous for *dahi bhalle* and crispy *aloo tikki.* *10.30am-10pm* ₹

PT Gaya Prasad Shiv Charan: The most popular joint in this street of *paratha* sellers, said to date back to Mughal days. *7am-10pm* ₹

Bade Mia Ki Kheer: Established in 1880; super-delicious, creamy, cardamom-scented *kheer* (rice pudding). *10am-11pm* ₹

Sita Ram Dewan Chand: Paharganj hole-in-the-wall serving just one tasty dish - *chhole bhature* - plus lassis. *8am-6pm* ₹

INTERCITY BUS & TRAIN STATIONS

There are three main railway stations in Delhi: **Delhi Junction** (aka Old Delhi Railway Station), **New Delhi Railway Station** across from the Paharganj backpacker enclave, and **Hazrat Nizamuddin Railway Station** near Humayun's Tomb. Make sure you know which station your train is leaving from. All three connect to the Delhi Metro.

Most northbound state-run services leave from the large **Kashmere Gate Inter State Bus Terminal** (ISBT) in Old Delhi, accessible by metro (exit gate 7), while buses headed to Uttar Pradesh and Uttarakhand often depart from the **Anand Vihar ISBT**. Most destinations are served by both local buses and more comfortable, more expensive air-conditioned private buses, some with sleeper berths.

NICOLO' ZANGIROLAMI/SHUTTERSTOCK

Spice Market (Khari Baoli; p67)

Peaceful Retreat in Paharganj

Meditate at Ramakrishna Mission

Amid the chaos of Paharganj, the **Ramakrishna Mission**, the temple that gives the metro station here its name, is a wonderfully calming escape, with a landscaped garden leading to a simple meditation hall with an exhibition space in the basement *(closed noon-4pm)*. The morning and evening *aarti* (auspicious lighting of lamps or candles), at 5am and sunset, are atmospheric times to visit. At other times, people simply meditate in peace.

EATING IN OLD DELHI: ROOFTOP RESTAURANTS

Krishna Rooftop Cafe: Popular Paharganj restaurant overlooking Tooti Chowk serving cold beers and a traveller-friendly menu. *7.30am-midnight* ₹

Exotic Cafe & Restaurant: Currently the most popular of the rooftop joints overlooking Tooti Chowk; it opens late and serves cold beer. *7.30am-midnight* ₹₹

Gumbad Cafe: On the rooftop of the Hotel Aiwan E Shahi, no-alcohol Gumbad has an unbeatable view over the Jama Masjid. *12.30pm-1am* ₹₹₹

Everest Cafe: Up several flights of stairs west of Tooti Chowk, this Tibetan spot serves up *momos*, noodles and North Indian staples. *9am-10.30pm* ₹

A MOVING WALK THROUGH GANDHI HISTORY

Gandhi is revered as the father of the nation and was one of the most influential figures of the 20th century globally.

START	END	LENGTH
Delhi Gate	Raj Ghat	2km; 2½hr

The sights on this tour (all free) celebrate Mahatma Gandhi's saint-like reputation in India; keep in mind you won't find commentary from critics who accuse him of sexual abuse and racism.

Take the metro to ❶ **Delhi Gate** and walk along Jawaharlal Nehru Marg, straight past Gandhi Hindustani Sahitya Sabha (a small NGO), to the ❷ **National Gandhi Museum** (closed Monday). It preserves some of Gandhi's personal belongings, including his spectacles and two of his teeth. Cross busy Mahatma Gandhi Marg to ❸ **Gandhi Darshan Park**. Walk through these peaceful landscaped gardens to the ❹ **Gandhi Darshan** on the eastern side. This pavilion displays photos relating to the Mahatma and the boat he used to cross the Mahi River at Kanapur during the Dandi (salt) march, as well as a replica of the cell at Yervada where he went on hunger strike.

Cross Satyagraha Marg to reach ❺ **Raj Ghat**; you'll have to walk east a little to enter through the security gate. This peaceful, well-maintained park contains a simple black-marble platform marking the spot where Mahatma Gandhi was cremated. It's inscribed with what are said to have been Gandhi's final words, 'Hai Ram' ('Oh, God'). Every Friday (the day he died), commemorative prayers are held here at 5pm. Another poignant Gandhi Museum is at Gandhi Smriti, where the Mahatma was assassinated in 1948.

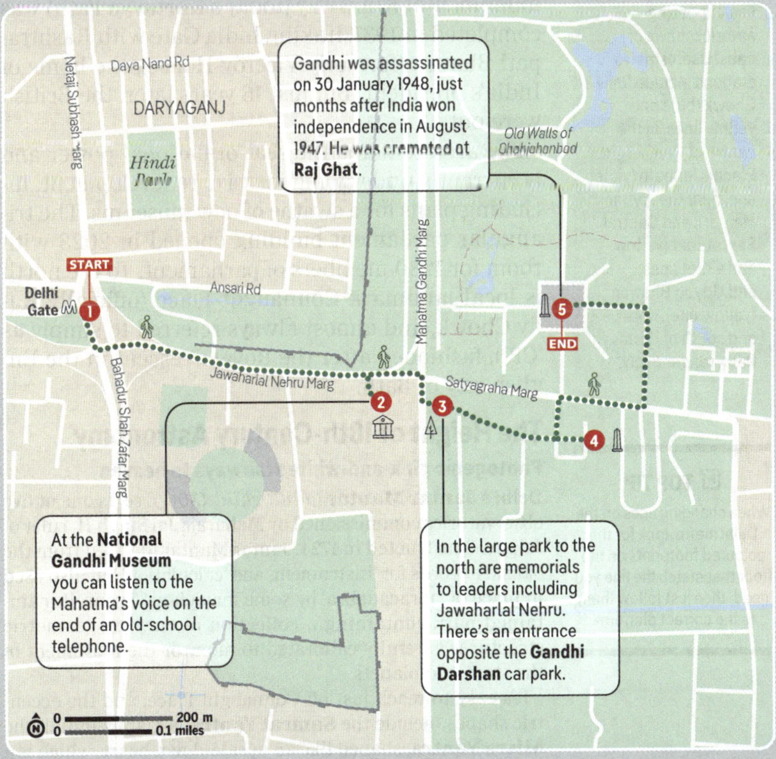

Lutyens' Delhi

AVENUES OF THE BRITISH RAJ

GETTING AROUND

This area's wide, tree-lined avenues are pleasant to walk along, but distances can be vast, so you'll want to make use of passing autorickshaws or cabs. Useful metro stations include Rajiv Chowk (blue and yellow lines, in the centre of Connaught Place), Janpath (violet line, near the Jantar Mantar), and Central Secretariat (yellow and violet lines) and Udyog Bhawan (yellow line), north and south of Kartavya Path, respectively.

Just like Shah Jahan before them, the British moved their capital here from somewhere else. Some say the move from Calcutta (now Kolkata) in 1911 aimed to place the capital in a more central location; others claim anti-colonial sentiment in Calcutta had made it untenable. Whatever the reasons, they clearly planned to stay, and set about building a New Delhi of grand imperial buildings and spacious boulevards. Architect Edwin Lutyens was behind much of the design. His monumental Kingsway (today's Kartavya Path) was completed in 1931, linking India Gate with Rashtrapati Bhavan (formerly Viceroy House), the home of India's president. But just 16 years later, the British were out.

The area remains the seat of national power and is currently undergoing massive redevelopment, including plans for a swathe of new museums. The triangular parliament building opened in 2023 with room for 1280 members of parliament. To the north is local landmark Connaught Place (officially Rajiv Chowk, and almost always referred to simply as 'CP'), fashioned after the Royal Crescent in the English city of Bath.

TOP TIP

When changing lines on the Delhi metro, look for the coloured footprints on the floor that match the line you need, then just follow them to the correct platform.

The Height of 18th-Century Astronomy

Photogenic pink-and-white stairways to heaven

Delhi's **Jantar Mantar** *(adult/child ₹300/free)* is one of five observatories commissioned by Maharaja Jai Singh II, ruler of Jaipur. Constructed in 1724, Jantar Mantar (derived from the Sanskrit words for 'instrument' and 'calculation' but also used in place of 'abracadabra' by some magicians) is a well-maintained park containing a collection of curving geometric structures carefully calibrated to monitor the movement of the stars and planets.

It's easy to reach just off Connaught Place, and the eccentric shapes include the **Samrat Yantra**, a giant sundial; the **Misra Yantra**, shaped like an upside-down heart, which is a world-time clock; and the **Ram Yantra**, with rows of windows to observe the positions of celestial bodies. Unfortunately, the tall buildings in this part of the city render many of the semi-accurate instruments unusable.

Atmospheric Agrasen ki Baoli

Delhi's most popular step-well

The atmospheric 14th-century **Agrasen ki Baoli** is one of Delhi's most beautiful *baolis*. It was once set in the countryside, till the city grew up around it; 103 steps descend to the bottom, flanked by arched niches that are frequented by pigeons. This free attraction is a great place for a break among the office towers southeast of Connaught Place and has garnered more attention since it was used as a shelter by Aamir Khan's alien character in the 2015 movie *PK*. After visiting the *baoli*, turn right and walk for about two minutes to see a small dhobi ghat filled with clothes and bed linens (the best views are from the right of the adjacent Shiva temple).

Shopping at the Government Emporiums

Fill your pack before you head back

Handily lined up in a row along Baba Kharak Singh Marg are half a kilometre of treasure-filled **state emporiums** representing artisans from across India's states. While some have the air of torpor that often afflicts governmental enterprises, shopping here is like travelling around India – top stops include Kashmir, for papier-mâché and carpets; Rajasthan, for miniature paintings and puppets; Uttar Pradesh, for marble inlay work; Karnataka, for sandalwood sculptures; and Odisha, for stone carvings.

In the same complex is the Craft Council of India's **Kamala Crafts Shop** with beautiful crafts, curios, textiles and homewares designed with flair and using traditional techniques but offering some contemporary, out-of-the-ordinary designs.

A couple of blocks east on Janpath, the government-run multilevel **Central Cottage Industries Emporium** is a wonderful treasure trove of fixed-price, India-wide handicrafts. Prices are higher than in the state emporiums, but the well-presented selection of woodcarvings, jewellery, pottery, papier-mâché, stationery, brassware, textiles (including bedspreads and cushion covers), toys, rugs, beauty products and miniature paintings makes it a glorious one-stop shop for beautiful crafts. The **Tibetan Market** is across the road.

BAOLIS

Baolis (step-wells) are beautiful pieces of historic design that solve the problem of the low water levels in Delhi's plains. They typically feature long stone staircases into the ground, giving access to groundwater and storing rain. Some *baolis* were used for drinking and others for bathing. Naturally, they became community meeting places. Many are extremely beautiful, with arches, pavilions, shaded passageways and columns supporting *dalans* (colonnaded verandas) over multiple levels that take advantage of the cool microclimate. Delhi once sported over 100 *baolis*; only around 30 survive today.

EATING IN LUTYENS' DELHI: CHEAP EATS

Naturals: Branch of the Bombay ice-cream sensation with creamy, fresh flavours such as coffee-walnut, jackfruit, mango and chocolate. *10am-1am* ₹

Haldiram's: The CP outlet of this popular chain is busy with families tucking into street-style and fast eats. Pick up *namkeen* and sweets. *8.30am-10.45pm* ₹

Kake da Hotel: No-frills, always-busy hole-in-the-wall dating from 1931 that's hugely popular with local workers for its Mughlai and Punjabi dishes. *noon-12.30am* ₹

Coffee Home: Right next to the government emporiums, this Delhi Tourism–run garden courtyard serves up South Indian snacks like masala dosas. *11am-8pm* ₹

LUTYENS' DELHI

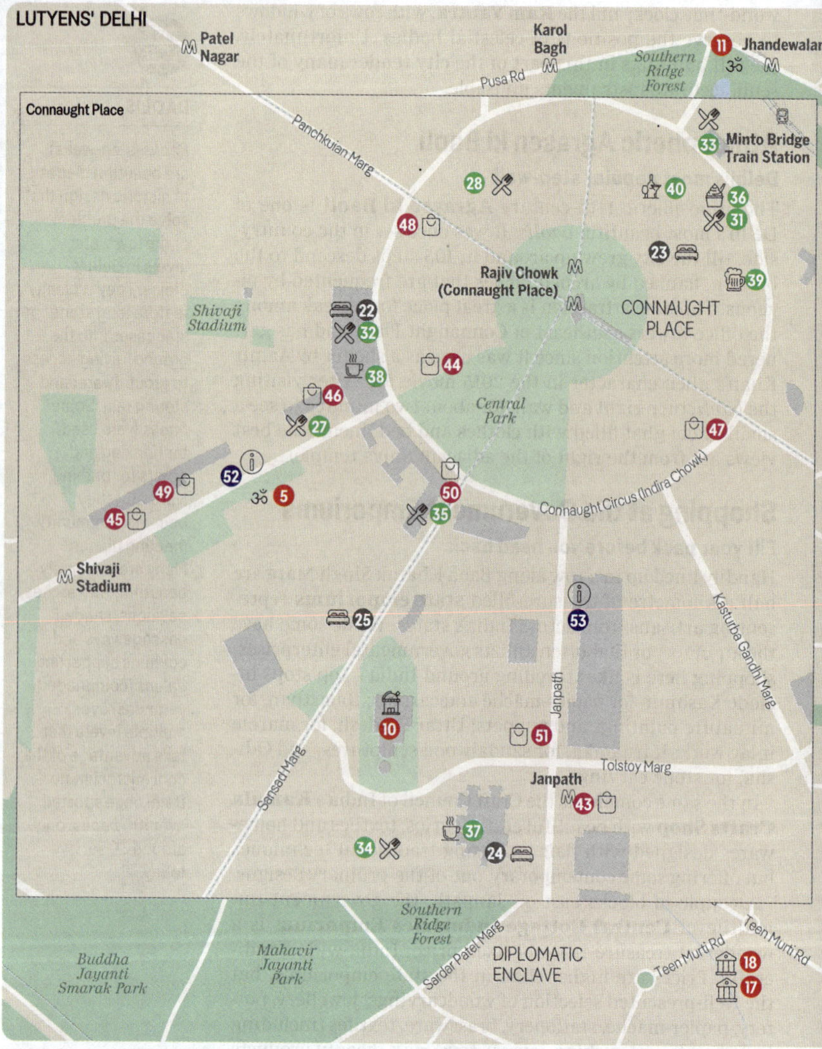

HIGHLIGHTS
1 Gurdwara Bangla Sahib

SIGHTS
2 Agrasen ki Baoli
3 Firoz Shah Kotla
4 Gandhi Smriti
5 Hanuman Temple
6 Hawa Mahal
7 India Gate
8 Indira Gandhi Memorial Museum
9 Jama Masjid
10 Jantar Mantar
11 Jhandewalan Hanuman Temple
12 Kartavya Path
13 National Crafts Museum & Hastkala Academy
14 National Gallery of Modern Art (NGMA)
15 National Museum
16 North Secretariat
17 Pradhanmantri Sangrahalaya
18 Prime Ministers' Museum & Library
19 Shaheedi Park
20 South Secretariat

SLEEPING
21 CP Villa Bed & Breakfast
22 Hotel Alka
23 Hotel Palace Heights
24 Imperial New Delhi
25 The Park, New Delhi

EATING	34 Kerala House Samridhi Canteen	38 Madras Coffee House	44 Fabindia
26 Andhra Pradesh Bhawan Canteen	35 Kwality	39 Ministry of Beer	45 Kamala Crafts Shop
see 13 Cafe Lota	36 Naturals	40 Unplugged Courtyard	46 Khadi Lounge
27 Coffee Home	see 42 Triveni Terrace Cafe	**ENTERTAINMENT**	47 Oxford Bookstore
28 Dasaprakash	**DRINKING & NIGHTLIFE**	see 41 Kamani Auditorium	48 Rikhi Ram
29 Diggin	see 24 1911 Restaurant	41 Little Theatre Group	49 State Emporiums
30 Gulati	see 25 Aqua	42 Triveni Kala Sangam	50 The Shop
31 Haldiram's	37 Atrium	**SHOPPING**	51 Tibetan Market
32 Hotel Saravana Bhavan	see 47 Cha Bar	43 Central Cottage Industries Emporium	**INFORMATION**
33 Kake da Hotel			52 iCentre
			53 India Tourism Delhi

BEST SHOPPING IN LUTYENS' DELHI

Khadi Lounge: Known for its excellent *khadi* (homespun cloth), this shop also sells handmade paper, incense, spices and natural soaps.

Fabindia: Surprisingly well-priced, high-quality clothes in funky Indian fabrics, plus stylish homewares.

The Shop: Gorgeous little boutique selling clothing and homewares.

Rikhi Ram: A tiny old shop dating from 1920 that sells classic and electric sitars, tablas and harmoniums.

Oxford Bookstore: Great selection of books in English. There's a tarot reader here and a stall selling designs by Atulyakala, a network of deaf artists.

MINIMACROSPACE/SHUTTERSTOCK

Jhandewalan Hanuman Temple

Sikh Temple with Devotional Music

Magnificent white-marble gurdwara topped in gold onion domes

The **Gurdwara Bangla Sahib** was constructed at the site where the eighth Sikh guru, six-year-old Harkrishan Dev, stayed before his 1664 death. Despite his tender years, the guru tended to victims of Delhi's cholera and smallpox epidemic, and the waters of the large tank are said to have healing powers. It's full of colour and life, yet tranquil, and live devotional songs waft over the compound.

As at all gurdwaras, free meals are served to pilgrims daily at the onsite *langar* (community kitchen). Remove your shoes and socks and cover your head before entering the temple – headscarves are available to borrow.

Crawl into the Mouths of Demons

Watched over by a giant Hanuman

Jhandewalan Hanuman Temple is not to be missed (it's actually hard to miss) in Karol Bagh. The 34m-tall Hanuman statue that soars above both the roads and the raised metro line presides over a ramshackle collection of rooms

EATING IN LUTYENS' DELHI: SOUTH INDIAN

Andhra Pradesh Bhawan Canteen: The canteen at this state house serves cheap and delicious unlimited South Indian thalis. *8-10am, noon-3pm & 7.30-10pm* ₹

Kerala House Samridhi Canteen: Kerala House offers bargain set meals with authentic Keralan spices. Lunchtimes are wildly popular. *8-10am, 12.30-3pm & 7-9pm* ₹

Hotel Saravana Bhavan: Fabulous dosas, *idlis* and other South Indian delights. A second branch is a couple of blocks away on Janpath (queues at both). *8am-11pm* ₹₹

Dasaprakash: Good-value South Indian breakfast and classic meals with blue booths and tasteful murals. *8am-midnight* ₹₹

for worship. In the lower floor, accessed through a demon's mouth, a fake cave is filled with beautifully dressed deities, some drinking the blood of Kali as it spurts from her beheaded neck. The closest metro station is Jhandewalan, one stop from Paharganj's RK Ashram Marg Station.

There's another **Hanuman Temple** just off CP, that's fittingly overrun with troops of monkeys.

Five Thousand Years of Indian History

Ancient and intricate artisan work

As part of the Central Vista project redevelopment, the collection of ancient treasures in India's National Museum collection was set to move into Yuge Yugeen Bharat in 2026 or 2027. Under construction at the time of writing, the museum is slated to become the world's largest with 950 rooms, housed in the **North** and **South Secretariat** buildings flanking Kartavya Path.

For now, the dusty **National Museum** *(nationalmuseumindia.gov.in; adult/child ₹500/free)* continues to house wonders like the mind-bogglingly ancient, sophisticated figurines from the Harappan civilisation, almost 5000 years old, including the remarkable *Dancing Girl*. There are also some fine ceramics from the even-older Nal civilisation. Other items include Buddha relics, exquisite jewellery, miniature paintings, medieval woodcarvings, textiles and musical instruments. Don't miss the immense, five-tier wooden temple chariot, which was crafted in 19th-century Tamil Nadu from teak, sandalwood and acacia. As with most major museums, it's closed on Mondays.

The Anubhav Tactile Gallery has 22 touchable objects designed for people with a visual impairment.

Contemporary Art & Its Centuries-Old Roots

Indian modernism 101

The **National Gallery of Modern Art** (NGMA; *ngmaindia.gov.in; adult/child ₹500/free*) is a must-visit for anyone interested in Indian art and its cultural impact both internationally and at home. The old wing, housed in the gracious warren of rooms of Jaipur House, holds the **Routes & Roots** exhibition, where modern displays in English explore India's influential languages of representation with symbols such as the lotus, yoga chakras, Buddhist mudras and the written language of Sanskrit.

DANGERS & ANNOYANCES

Crime

Delhi is relatively safe in terms of petty crime, though pickpocketing does happen in crowded areas like Paharganj and Connaught Place. Police have identified Kashmere Gate, Rajiv Chowk (in CP) and New Delhi as the worst metro stations for theft and pickpocketing.

Fake Tourist Offices

Many Delhi travel agencies falsely claim to be government tourist offices. Official government info is available at the **India Tourism** office on Janpath and the **Delhi Tourism iCentre** near the state emporiums.

Roads

Notoriously congested; take extreme care when crossing them, or walking along narrow lanes without footpaths.

See more on touts (p77), pollution (p92) and women travellers (p88).

EATING & DRINKING IN NEW DELHI: CAFES

Cha Bar: Choose from dozens of hot and cold teas at this hugely popular Connaught Place spot, along with decent bites. *9.30am-9.30pm*

Atrium: Enjoy a genteel afternoon tea at the Imperial hotel. Sip tea and nibble dainty sandwiches; served buffet style in the afternoon, Thursday to Sunday. *10am-10pm*

Diggin: This Italian cafe pairs pizzas, pastas and salads with an extensive menu of cocktails, from Bellinis and Rossinis to sangria by the pitcher. *11.30am-10.30pm*

Madras Coffee House: An artists' hangout since 1935, this place serves everything from classic South Indian coffee to blackcurrant shakes. *11am-10pm*

TAKE A STROLL THROUGH LUTYENS' DELHI

The grand thoroughfare orginally designed by Edwin Lutyens is being transformed to reflect a new chapter in Delhi's history.

START	END	LENGTH
Central Secretariat	National Gallery of Modern Art	3.5km; 3½hr

Take the metro to 1 **Central Secretariat**. The new Parliament of India, opened in 2023, is just to the north, but walk south to 2 **Kartavya Path** (also known as Rajpath, and previously, Kingsway). At the time of writing, the area was involved in massive redevelopment works, but Kartavya Path itself was finished, with accessible toilets and underpasses to avoid busy roads.

Until the new Yuge Yugeen Bharat National Museum opens in the former North and South Blocks, the dusty 3 **National Museum** (p75) continues to house the country's historic treasures. Keep going east to 4 **India Gate**, Lutyens's 42m stone triumphal arch, paying tribute to around 90,000 Indian Army soldiers who died in WWI, the Northwest Frontier operations and the 1919 Anglo-Afghan War. Photographer-touts will offer to take your photo with this renowned symbol. Beyond it is the 5 **National War Memorial**. Head south of here, past a huge, excellent children's playground, and cross busy India Gate Circuit to 6 **Bikaner House**, which hosts exhibitions and cultural events for galleries and NGOs, as well as a small craft market. Take a snack break at onsite Diggin or head around the corner to 7 **Gulati** (p80) for the city's best butter chicken. Then continue around India Gate Circuit to the 8 **National Gallery of Modern Art** (p75) for a crash course in Indian modernism and iconography.

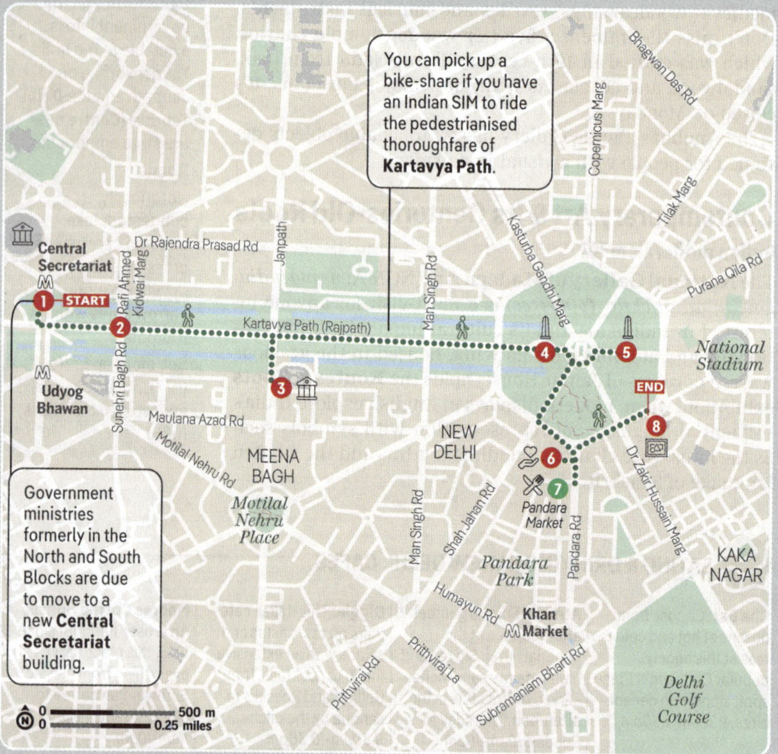

The new wing's **In the Seeds of Time** exhibition charts the development of Indian modernism in chronological order. The first gallery contrasts Mughul miniatures with Orientalist European paintings; then spirals up the floors through the 19th and 20th centuries, as artists responded to both Western expressionism and the freedom movement at home. You'll come out somewhere in the 1980s with strong experimentation and abstraction. The collection includes important works by the Bengal School, the Calcutta Progressive Group, and superstars such as Rabindranath Tagore, Jamini Roy and Amrita Sher-Gil. Free curator-led tours are held at 10.30am, 1.30pm and 3pm; as with most major Delhi museums and some monuments, it's shut on Mondays.

Track India's Remarkable Political Journey

Patriotic museums tell the story of the nation and its leaders

Schoolkids are bussed into the leafy enclave southwest of Kartavya Path to learn the story of modern India and the leaders who overcame the tyranny of British rule in this collection of museums.

The stately Teen Murti Bhavan was built for the British commander-in-chief and became the official residence of Jawaharlal Nehru (India's first prime minister). It now hosts the **Prime Ministers' Museum & Library** *(pmml.nic.in; free)* devoted to Nehru's life and work; the bedroom, study and drawing room are preserved as if he's just popped out. Behind it is the new **Pradhanmantri Sangrahalaya** *(pmsangrahalaya.gov.in; adult/child ₹200/100)* in a building designed to resemble the hands of the Indian people holding aloft the *dharmachakra* (wheel) of the national flag. It's a high-tech space documenting the administration of each of India's prime ministers with English-language sound-and-light shows at 7.15pm.

Around the corner, the **Indira Gandhi Memorial Museum** *(indiragandhi.in/en/memorial; free)*, in the residence of the controversial former prime minister, is devoted to her life and her political-heavyweight family. It displays her personal effects, including the blood-stained sari she was wearing when she was assassinated in 1984 – in the back garden a glass-covered pathway traces her final steps before she was shot and killed by two security guards. Many of the simply furnished rooms in the house are preserved as they were, providing a window into the family's life.

Nearby, **Gandhi Smriti** *(gandhismriti.gov.in; free)* is the poignant memorial to Mahatma Gandhi in Birla House. He was shot dead on the grounds by a Hindu zealot on 30 January 1948, after campaigning against intercommunal violence. The house itself is where Gandhi spent his last 144 days. The exhibits include film

GANDHI'S LEGACY
For more on the Mahatma, see the Gandhi walking tour (p69).

TOUTS

Be aware of touts at the airport, train stations and tourist areas. Taxi and rickshaw drivers frequently act as touts for hotels, and may claim that your accommodation is full, poor value, dangerous, burnt down or closed. Any such story is a ruse to steer you to a hotel where they will get a commission. Men who approach you at Connaught Place run scams to direct you to shops and tourist agents, often offering to help you find your way, secure your belongings or avoid stepping in rubbish.

Touts at New Delhi Railway Station endeavour to steer travellers into private travel agencies where they earn a commission. Touts may tell travellers that their tickets are invalid, there's a problem with the trains, or there's no way onto the platform.

THE FIRST WAR OF INDEPENDENCE (INDIAN UPRISING)

In May 1857, Bengali cavalrymen of the East India Company rose up against their officers in Meerut. While this was said to be sparked by the introduction of a rifle believed to be greased with cow and pig fat – unacceptable to both Hindus and Muslims – the uprising was a reaction to the negative impacts of company rule, not just animal fat.

Participants rallied around Mughal Emperor Bahadur Shah Zafar and quickly captured Delhi and the Red Fort, though they were not united under strong leadership. By September, British forces had reoccupied the city.

Bahadur Shah Zafar was exiled to Burma and the British Government took over the administration of India from the Company, establishing the British Raj.

JIMMONKPHOTOGRAPHY/SHUTTERSTOCK

footage, modern art and spartan rooms preserved just as Gandhi left them. The small clothes shop within the grounds sells garments made from *khadi*, homespun cotton that was championed by Gandhi during the Independence movement.

Visit Haunted Firoz Shah Kotla

Twelfth-century fortress where djinns lurk

Firozabad, the fifth iteration of Delhi, was built by Firoz Shah Tughlaq in 1354, the first city here to be built on the river. Only the fortress, **Firoz Shah Kotla** *(adult/child, ₹300/free)*, remains (most of Firoz Shah's city was plundered to build Shahjahanabad), with crumbling walls protecting the **Jama Masjid** (Friday mosque) and the pyramid-like **Hawa Mahal**, topped by a 13m-high sandstone Ashoka Pillar inscribed with

DRINKING IN NEW DELHI: BARS

Aqua: Enjoy poolside cocktails and sparkling wine spritzers at this casual spot at the Park Hotel. *11am-12.30am*

Unplugged Courtyard: You could forget you were in CP in the big courtyard garden shaded by a lantern-strewn banyan tree. Live music, wood-fired pizza. *12.30pm-1am*

1911 Restaurant: The main restaurant at the Imperial, built in the 1930s, resonates with bygone splendour, and has an extensive cocktail menu. *11.30am-12.30am*

Ministry of Beer: CP's first microbrewery is on point with multiple bars and vibes, including a laid-back leafy courtyard plus an upstairs bar with DJs. *noon-1am*

Gandhi Smriti (p77)

3rd-century-BCE Buddhist edicts, which Firoz Shah had transplanted here.

There are pitch-dark tunnels under these structures that are said to be the abode of djinns (spirits) and people come to light candles and incense to appease them.

Nearby is **Shaheedi Park** *(adult/child ₹50/25, weekends ₹100/50)*, with sculptures and statues about India's freedom struggle constructed using 250 tonnes of upcycled waste.

Open-Air Traditional Crafts Museum

Artisan work from across India

Much of the lovely **National Crafts Museum & Hastkala Academy** *(nationalcraftsmuseum.nic.in; adult/child ₹300/free)*, located near the Purana Qila (p81), is in the open air, including tree-shaded carvings and life-size examples of village huts from various regions of India. Displays celebrate traditional crafts with a 30,000-strong collection, including beautiful textiles on display indoors, such as embroidery from Kashmir and cross-stitch from Punjab. There's a textile academy on the same site where students come to learn traditional skills. Artisans sell their products in the rear courtyard. The museum also includes the excellent Cafe Lota (p80), a semi-open spot with a large menu of inventive dishes, along with an excellent shop with high-end gifts made by artisans from across the country.

DAY TRIPS FROM DELHI

Delhi-based travel operator **Mohd Shafi Billo** *(indiainside travel.com)* shares his recommended day trips from Delhi.

The Taj Mahal, Agra: (p314) Agra is just three hours away from Delhi by cab. Apart from the Taj Mahal, visit Agra Fort and Itimad-ud-Daulah. On the way back, stop in Mathura, considered the birthplace of Lord Krishna.

Jaipur: (p110) Jaipur, also known as the Pink City, is just four to five hours from Delhi. While there, you can visit the Amber Fort, the Hawa Mahal and the City Palace Museum, and shop at local bazaars.

Rishikesh: (p380) Rishikesh is about four to five hours from Delhi. It's a hub for yoga and meditation, and a popular place for river rafting. It's worth staying until sunset to see the *aarti* (lighting of lamps or candles) on the banks of the Ganges River.

TOP DELHI FESTIVALS

Republic Day (Kartavya Path; 26 Jan) A spectacular military parade.

Beating of the Retreat (Vijay Chowk; 29 Jan) More military pageantry.

India Art Fair (NSIC Exhibition Grounds; Feb) Exciting contemporary art from across South Asia.

Eid-al-Fitr (Mar/Apr) Fairs, street food and celebrations, especially around the Jama Masjid.

Independence Day (Red Fort; 15 Aug) India celebrates its independence from Britain.

Ramlila (Ramlila Maidan; Sep/Oct) Dussehra, a Hindu celebration of good over evil, is honoured with a theatrical telling of the Ramayana)

Diwali (Oct/Nov) Expect fairy lights, *diyas* (oil lamps) and (prohibited) fireworks during the annual Festival of Light.

Celebrate Diwali in Delhi

The festival of light

Across India, Diwali (October/November) marks the triumph of light over darkness, good over evil, and knowledge over ignorance. It's a time when homes are lit up with *diyas* (oil lamps), lanterns and candles, while families gather for feasts and celebrations. In the run-up everyone is eager to decorate their homes, buy a new outfit and stock up on *mithai* (sweets).

In Delhi, Diwali melas (fetes and fairs) appear around the city while malls and markets are decorated with Diwali lights. Get into the spirit at places like Dilli Haat (p92) and Khan Market (p87), which are buzzing in the lead-up to Diwali. Head to Chandni Chowk (p61) for *mithai* and dried fruit. Get your palm decorated with henna, stock up on *puja* idols, and especially lights (try Asia's biggest electrical market at **Bhagirath Palace**). **Kinari Bazaar** is the city's favourite place to pick up beads, sequins and bling. Delhi's **Blind School Diwali Mela** is a seasonal institution with upmarket stalls selling shawls, saris and scented beauty products.

Delhi's Sikh community also celebrate Diwali, as it marks **Bandi Chhor Diwas**, the day Guru Hargobind reached Amritsar after being released from a Mughal prison. Gurdwaras are lit up for a few nights leading up to Diwali. Head to Gurdwara Bangla Sahib (p74) to celebrate with a special *langar* (community meal).

Diwali also marks the opening of Delhi's performing and fine arts season; check the websites of venues such as **India Habitat Centre** *(indiahabitat.org)*, **Triveni Kala Sangam** *(trivenikalasangam.org)*, the **Little Theatre Group** *(ltgdelhi.org)* and **Kamani Auditorium** *(kamaniauditorium.org)* for what's on.

EATING IN LUTYENS' DELHI: BEST RESTAURANTS

Triveni Terrace Cafe: In a peaceful garden-courtyard inside Triveni Kala Sangam, this great-value cafe overlooks a dance rehearsal space. *10am-8pm Mon-Sat* ₹₹

Cafe Lota: Bamboo slices the sunlight into flattering stripes at the outdoor restaurant of the Crafts Museum with a modern take on regional dishes. *8am-9.30pm* ₹₹₹

Gulati: Many say this place on restaurant-heavy Pandara Rd makes the best version of Delhi's homegrown dish *murgh makhani* (butter chicken). *noon-midnight* ₹₹

Kwality: A club-like ambience with live songs tinkling from the grand piano in the evening, this place has been going since 1940. *noon-11pm* ₹₹₹

Nizamuddin & Lodhi Colony

ENCHANTING TOMBS AND GARDENS

In the area just south of New Delhi, the city takes a breath, spreading into green space and exclusive enclaves dotted with gardens, golf courses and parkland. This elite neighbourhood is packed with historic sights, including some of Delhi's most atmospheric and affecting. You're sure to be moved by the fervent devotion at 14th-century Hazrat Nizamuddin and the romance of the 15th-century Lodhi tombs. And you can contrast the grandiosity of 16th-century Humayun's Tomb, built as the Mughals were on the rise, with the poignant late-Mughal decline of 18th-century Safdarjung's Tomb.

Today, the neighbourhood is an important centre for arts and culture. In Lodhi Colony, the tall walls of housing estates have been splashed with colour by 50 international street artists, while in the kitchens of exclusive restaurants and the sleek boutiques of fashion designers, India's rich traditions are mixed with Western and Eastern influences to create some of the city's most innovative contemporary offerings.

GETTING AROUND

The yellow and violet lines of the metro pass through the area, and will take you a short walk from Khan Market (p87), but for most other sights you'll need to combine the metro with an autorickshaw or taxi, or walk at least a kilometre to reach your destination. Akshardham, on the other side of the Yamuna River, is walking distance from its eponymous metro station on the blue line.

Peaceful Purana Qila

Chilled alternative to the Red Fort

Shh, whisper it quietly: the **Purana Qila** *(adult/child ₹300/free)* is better than the Red Fort. Delhi's 'Old Fort' isn't quite as magnificent in size and grandeur, but it's far more pleasant to explore, with tree-shaded landscaped gardens to relax in and crumbling ruins to climb over (and even under, in the case of the tunnels by the mosque).

Ringed by a moat, part of which has been refilled with water, and accessed through the majestically imposing **Bada Darwaza** gateway, this 16th-century fort is where Mughal Emperor Humayun met his end in 1556, tumbling down the steps of the **Sher Mandal**, which he used as a library.

The fort had been built by Afghan ruler Sher Shah (1538–45), during his brief ascendancy over Humayun. It's well worth a visit, with its peaceful gardens studded with well-preserved

TOP TIP

Save money with a three-attraction ticket to Humayun's Tomb, the Humayun's Tomb World Heritage Site Museum and Sunder Nursery *(adult/child ₹950/50)*.

HIGHLIGHTS
1 Hazrat Nizamuddin Dargah
2 Humayun's Tomb
3 Lodhi Garden
4 Purana Qila

SIGHTS
5 Athpula
6 Bada Gumbad
7 Humayun's Tomb World Heritage Site Museum
8 Isa Khan's Tomb
9 Khairul Manazil
10 Khan-i-Khanan's Tomb
11 Lodhi Street-Art Precinct
12 Mohammed Shah's Tomb
13 Qila-i-Kuhran Mosque
14 Sabz Burj
15 Safdarjung's Tomb
16 Sheesh Gumbad
17 Sikander Lodi's Tomb
18 Sunder Nursery

SLEEPING
19 Lodhi, The
20 Lutyens Bungalow

EATING
21 Big Chill Cakery
22 Carnatic Café
23 Green Mantis
see 19 Indian Accent
24 Perch

DRINKING & NIGHTLIFE
25 Café Turtle
26 Latitude 28

ENTERTAINMENT
27 Waste to Wonder

SHOPPING
28 Khan Market

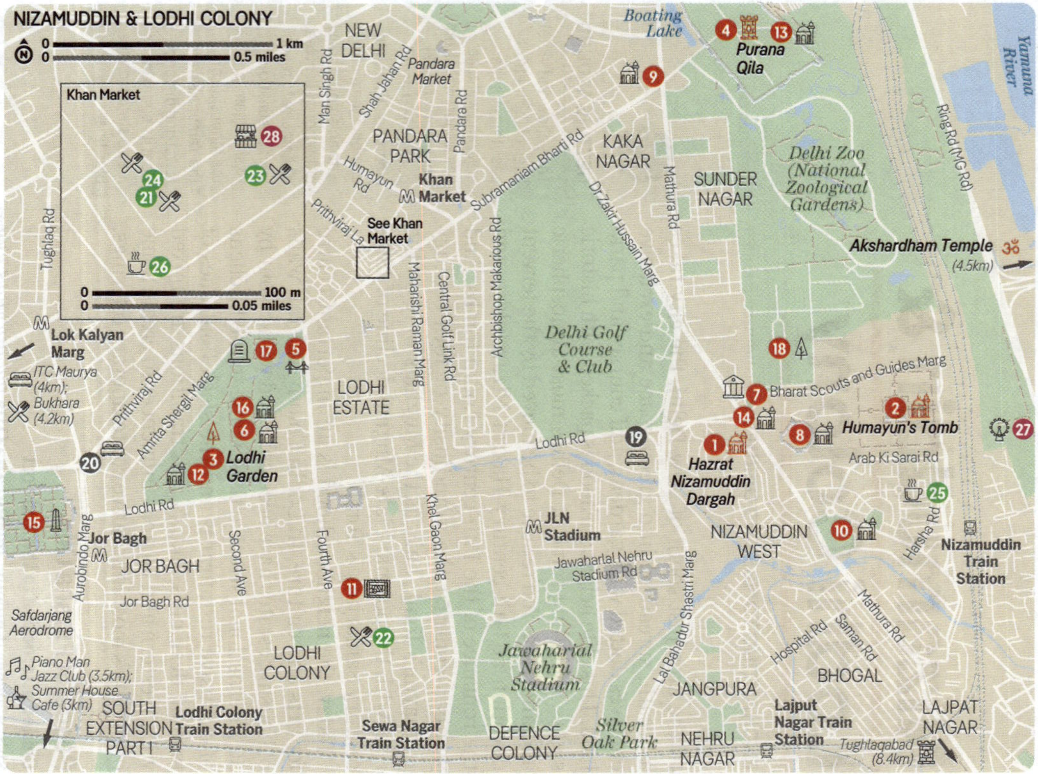

ancient red-stone monuments, including the intricately patterned **Qila-i-Kuhran Mosque** (Mosque of Sher Shah), behind which are tunnels to explore and parts of the outer walls that can be climbed. There's also a small **museum** *(closed Friday)* set within the walls just inside Bada Darwaza gateway.

An elongated lake has been created from the fort's former **moat**, and in late afternoon is well worth wandering along as the sun lights up the towering walls above it, making for fabulous sunset photos.

Across busy Mathura Rd are more relics from the city of Shergarh, including the beautiful **Khairul Manazil** mosque, still used by local Muslims and a favoured haunt of flocks of pigeons.

The Stunning Model for the Taj Mahal

Persian and Mughal architecture merge in Humayun's Tomb

UNESCO-listed **Humayun's Tomb** *(asi.nic.in/pages/WorldHeritageHumayunTomb; adult/child ₹600/free)* is sublimely well-proportioned, seeming to float above its symmetrical gardens. It's thought to have inspired the Taj Mahal, which it predates by 60 years. Constructed for the Mughal emperor in 1570 by Haji Begum, Humayun's Persian-born wife, the tomb marries Persian and Mughal elements. The arched facade is inlaid with bands of white marble and red sandstone, and the building follows strict rules of Islamic geometry, with an emphasis on the number eight. This was where the last Mughal emperor, Bahadur Shah Zafar, took refuge before being captured and exiled by the British in 1857.

The beautiful surrounding **gardens** contain Nai-ka-Gumbad, or 'Barber's Tomb', which features a double dome and two graves inscribed with verses from the Quran. While rumour has it that the emperor's barber is entombed in this elegant shrine, archaeologists are not actually sure who lies within the two graves inside. Nearby stands the **Nila Gumbad**, named as such because of its blue *(nila)* tiled dome. Its lack of a double dome is unusual for the era, and while it's said to have been built in 1625, some speculate that the tomb may predate that of Humayun. On the southwestern corner of Humayun's Tomb, the **Arab Sarai** is a massive structure that may have been used to house mullahs – or simply the craftsmen who built the emperor's tomb.

Sabz Burj, an early-Mughal tomb in the roundabout on Mathura Rd, has been beautifully restored to reveal its blue,

BEST OF DELHI ON THE SCREEN

While nowhere near as celluloid-slick as Mumbai, Delhi has its memorable moments on screen.

Delhi 6: Named for Old Delhi's postcode, this 2009 film delves into communal tensions as a non-resident Indian arrives in town from the US.

Delhi Crime: Netflix drama series released in 2019 following a Delhi Police investigation into a gang rape.

Rang De Basanti: A 2006 box office megahit chronicling a group of Delhi University students fighting corruption against the backdrop of some of Delhi's most scenic spots.

Band Baaja Baarat: A couple from modest West Delhi make it as wedding planners in posh South Delhi in this 2010 rom-com.

Delhi Belly: Three Delhi friends become entangled in international crime in this 2011 film.

EATING & DRINKING IN NIZAMUDDIN & AROUND: CAFES

Latitude 28: On the top floor of Khan Market's Good Earth homewares store, this beautiful cafe pairs global fare with tasty teas, spritzers and wine. *11.30am-11pm* ₹₹₹

Café Turtle: A cosy cafe in Nizamuddin's Full Circle Bookstore serving soups, salads and sandwiches (branches at Khan Market and in Greater Kailash). *10am-8pm* ₹₹

Big Chill Cakery: Cakes and coffee at this bakery side project of Delhi's beloved Big Chill Cafe. *noon-midnight* ₹₹

Carnatic Café: Clean, efficient and delicious Karnataka specialties served in two adjacent restaurants in the Lodhi Art District. *9am-10.30pm* ₹₹

BLENDING PERSIAN & INDIAN STYLES

Haji Begum commissioned Persian architect Mirak Mirza Ghiyas to design her husband's tomb, and features such as the azure tiles recall Persian styles, while elements like the inverted lotus finials and small *chhatris* (domed pavilions) are drawn from Indian tradition. The Persian-style 'double dome' was the first to be built in India, allowing for an impressively bulbous outer dome, with a lower dome enclosing the internal space.

Like the Taj Mahal gardens it inspired, the tomb is surrounded by 25 acres of landscaping laid based on Persian *charbagh* (four garden) design. It's divided into square quarters by water channels, each of which is subdivided into nine smaller squares.

green and gold tilework onion dome. To the right as you enter the complex, **Isa Khan's Tomb** is a fine example of Lodhi-era architecture, constructed before Humayun's Tomb in 1548. Further south is the monumental **Khan-i-Khanan's Tomb** *(adult/child ₹250/free)*, plundered in Mughal times to build Safdarjung's Tomb (p87).

What Lies Beneath

A subterranean museum that scratches below the surface

The newest addition to the neighbourhood, the **Humayun's Tomb World Heritage Site Museum** *(htmuseum.org; adult/child ₹300/25)* launched in 2024 as India's first 'sunken museum'. This subterranean wonderland, developed by the Aga Khan Trust for Culture, shines a light on Delhi's history through rich exhibits complemented by detailed interpretive panels covering topics ranging from Mughal garden design to *qawwali*, a still-thriving form of Sufi devotional music that developed under poet Amir Khusro during the Delhi Sultanate. Restoration geeks will appreciate the extensive displays focused on recent conservation work at the tomb and its surrounding areas. The museum connects to Sunder Nursery on one side and Humayun's Tomb on the other so that you can visit all three on a circuit; consider visiting the museum before the tomb itself if you want a bit of pre-visit context.

Beautiful Reclaimed Gardens

Mughal gardens bloom again at Sunder Nursery

Extending from just beyond Humayun's Tomb and the Humayun's Tomb Heritage Museum, **Sunder Nursery** *(sundernursery.org; ₹200)* was fairly overgrown until recent renovations brought this 36-hectare expanse Mughal gardens back to something approaching their former glory. It's now a vast landscaped heritage park with clipped lawns, delicate waterways and a network of paths dotted with fruit trees, flower beds, tree-shaded benches and numerous **Mughal tombs and pavilions** plus a lotus pond that's itself shaped like a lotus. Some structures in the garden still lie in a state of ruin; others have been lovingly restored. There are loads of events, including an organic farmers market on Sunday morning, bee workshops, heritage and nature walks, and performances for kids.

EATING IN NIZAMUDDIN & AROUND: STYLISH DINING

Green Mantis: Fill your table with beautifully plated sushi, bao, dim sum and soups at this vegetarian spot in Khan Market. *noon-10.30 pm* ₹₹₹

Bukhara: Sit at a low table and eat with your hands (bibs provided) at this spendy spot that celebrates cuisine of the Northwest Frontier region of Pakistan. *12.30-2.45pm & 7-11.45pm* ₹₹₹

Perch: A pared-down aesthetic, waiters in pencil-grey shirts, soothing music, international wines and pleasing international snacks. *8am-8pm* ₹₹₹

Indian Accent: One of the capital's top dining experiences. Chef Manish Mehrotra works magic with seasonal ingredients. Dress smart, book ahead. *noon-2.30pm, 6.45-9pm & 9.45pm-midnight* ₹₹₹

PRADEEPGAURS/SHUTTERSTOCK

Waste to Wonder

Another great kid-friendly attraction east of Humayun's Tomb (take an auto), the **Waste to Wonder** park *(waste towonderpark.com; adult/child ₹50/25)* has large sculptures beautifully constructed out of reclaimed materials like bicycle chains, pipes and scrap metal in a landscaped garden. They depict world wonders like the Eiffel Tower, Taj Mahal and Rio's Christ the Redeemer, plus 40 car-stomping dinosaurs.

Mystical Shrine Hidden in a Tangled Bazaar

Holy Hazrat Nizamuddin Dargah

Visiting the marble shrine of Muslim Sufi saint **Hazrat Nizamuddin** is Delhi's most mystical, magical experience. You'll find the dargah among bazaars selling rose petals, attars (perfumes) and offerings, and on some evenings you can hear the *qawwali* (Sufi devotional singing) amid crowds of devotees. The ascetic Nizamuddin died in 1325 at the ripe old age of 92. His doctrine of tolerance made him popular not only with Muslims, but with adherents of other faiths, too.

Later kings and nobles wanted to be buried close to Nizamuddin, hence the number of nearby Mughal tombs. Other tombs in the compound include the graves of Jahanara (daughter of Shah Jahan) and the renowned sufi poet Amir Khusro. Scattered around the surrounding alleyways are more tombs and a huge *baoli* (step-well). Entry is free, but donations are customary. Both men and women should cover their heads and remove their shoes before entering the shrine. Women may not enter the inner sanctum.

DELHI'S BEST TOURS

It can be hard to get under the surface of such a densely packed city. Luckily, several fantastic tours give you a more personalised view.

Delhi By Cycle: Bike tours around specific neighbourhoods or the banks of the Yamuna; helmets and child seats are available. *(delhibycycle.com)*

Delhi Heritage Walks: Historian-led tours focused on significant areas in the heart of Delhi and beyond. *(delhiherit agewalks.com)*

Delhi Queer Heritage Walks: Explore LGBTIQ+ Old Delhi and beyond and learn about the many influential queer figures in Indian history. *(@delhiqueer heritagewalks)*

Reality Tours & Travel: Offers a range of city tours, including respectful visits to Sanjay Colony, a slum area of Delhi. A bonus: 80% of profits go to charity. *(realitytoursandtravel. com)*

Street Connections: This fascinating walk through Old Delhi is guided by former street children. *(walk. streetconnections. co.uk)*

LEGEND OF THE SULTAN & THE SUFI

Sufi saint Hazrat Nizamuddin is one of India's most famous Sufi mystics. In 1321, Nizamuddin was building a *baoli* (step-well) for his *khanqah* (spiritual centre), while the sultan, Ghiyus-ud-din Tughlaq, was fortifying the city against invasion by the Mongol khans. Tughlaq requisitioned Nizamuddin's labourers to work on the fort, but secretly they returned to work for Nizamuddin at night. When the sultan heard this, he banned the supply of oil to Nizamuddin so lamps could not be lit for the work. In turn, Nizamuddin cursed the fort to desolation.

Today, Nizamuddin's must-see dargah (p85) and *baoli* attract thousands of pilgrims every week, while Tughlaq's fort (p100) has fallen into eerie ruin.

MR.ASHISHSOLANKI/SHUTTERSTOCK

Safdarjung's Tomb

Lovely Lodhi Garden, Delhi's Green Escape

Peaceful parkland with 15th-century tombs

In 1936 Lady Willingdon, wife of the then-Governor-General of India, had two villages demolished to landscape a park containing a collection of Lodhi-era tombs. Today, lush, tree-shaded **Lodhi Garden** – a favoured getaway for Delhi's elite, local joggers and courting couples – helps protect more than 100 species of trees and 50 species of birds and butterflies, as well as half a dozen captivating 15th- and 16th-century tombs from the Sayyid and Lodhi duynasties.

The twin tombs of **Bada Gumbad** and **Sheesh Gumbad**, both built in 1494, the bulbous **Mohammed Shah's Tomb** (1450) and the fortress-like walled complex of **Sikander Lodi's tomb** (1518) are the park's most notable structures, but also look for **Athpula**, an eight-pier bridge spanning a small lake, which dates from Emperor Akbar's reign.

Fifty Global Artists Hit the Wall

India's first street-art precinct

Scattered through the blocky streets of **Lodhi Colony**, a former British-era housing estate, are murals from over 50 Indian and international artists. A project of the St+art India Foundation, many works take inspiration from Indian culture and heritage.

Standouts include the stunning typographic shadow work of *Time Changes Everything* by the late Hanif Kureshi (aka Daku), which changes based on the light, like a sundial. Other must-sees include the rainbow birds of *Colors of Soul* by Mexican artist Senkoe, Holi-inspired *We Love Delhi* by Daku and French duo Lek & Sowat, *Nature's Arch and Visions of Altered Landscapes* by Canada's Li Hill, incorporating a real archway and tree to separate symbols of east and west, the lace-inspired *New Delhi* by Poland's NeSpoon, playful and colourful *Impressions of Lodhi* by Singaporean Yip Yew Chong and *Original Aboriginal* by Australian Kamilaroi artist Reko Rennie, with bold geometric patterns.

Learn more at @startindia.

Fashion Fix

Pick up high-end clothes and homewares at India's most exclusive market

Khan Market is Delhi's most upmarket shopping enclave, and among the most expensive places to rent a shop in India. Its often-packed pedestrian-only lanes are lined with boutiques specialising in fashion, books and homewares, and stalked by Delhi's elites and foreign expats. It's a great place to pick up fusion fashion and lifestyle products, and a good place to eat and drink. For handmade paper, check out **Anand Stationers**, or try **Mehra Bros** for cool papier-mâché ornaments. For elegantly packaged Ayurvedic beauty products, browse **Kama Ayurveda** or **Forrest Essentials**. Literature lovers will have a heyday here. **Faqir Chand** houses piles of books stacked from the floor to ceiling in a way that may appear haphazard, but staff seem to know where everything is. A few shops away, **Bahrisons** feels slightly more organised, and has a dedicated shop for kids' books. Home decor aficionados will find loads of options across the market, with particularly high-quality (and expensive) products at **Good Earth**. Ubiquitous Indian clothing and houseware chain **Fabindia** has separate clothing and home decor shops here. For beautiful block-printed bedsheets, tablecloths, dresses and sleepwear head to the Khan Market branch of celebrated Jaipur company **Anokhi**,

Palm-Lined Gardens at Safdarjung's Tomb

Late-Mughal decorative style

Built by the Nawab of Avadh for his father, the grandiose, highly decorative mid-18th-century **Safdarjung's Tomb** *(adult/child ₹300/free)*, set within palm-lined gardens, is an example of late-Mughal architecture.

Historians often compare the tomb with Humayun's (p83), which was built during the ascendancy of Mughal power in 1570, and on which Safdarjung's was modelled. By the late-Mughal period there were insufficient funds for all-over marble, so materials to cover the dome were taken from the mausoleum of Khan-i-Khanan (p84), and it was finished in red sandstone. You can see the mismatched pieces in the central dome, and close up you may notice unfinished stonework and detailing. However, these are picky complaints – the tomb is still a stunning piece of architecture.

CAPITAL OF MUSIC

Su Real *(@realsureal)* is an award-winning music producer and DJ known for pioneering new genres in India. Here are some of his recommended music venues

Piano Man Jazz Club: The best venue for live western music in the capital. A well-equipped modern stage, low-key classy-casual ambience and great programming of rock, jazz and indie bands from around the country.

Summer House Cafe: When you just need a shameless night out with your mates belting pop hits at the top of your lungs, then spilling your drink on the dancefloor as you attempt the Macarena while the DJ plays the latest Fred Again remix, SHC hits the spot!

Qawwali at Hazrat Nizamuddin Dargah: (p85)The especially adventurous can seek out the legendary *qawwali* performances in the inner courtyard of Hazrat Nizamuddin Dargah.

WOMEN TRAVELLERS

Delhi has, unfortunately, a deserved reputation as being unsafe for women. Precautions include never walking around in lonely, deserted places, even during daylight hours, keeping an eye on your route so you don't get lost (download a map that you can use offline) and taking special care after dark – ensure you have a safe means of transport home with, for example, a reputable cab company or driver.

The first carriage of metro trains are reserved for women and young children only – look for the pink sign on the platform. There are also a number of cab services with women drivers operating in Delhi – try **Sakha Consulting Wings** *(sakhaconsultingwings.com)*.

SEAN HSU/SHUTTERSTOCK

Akshardham Temple

Theme-Park-Style Modern Temple

Delhi's largest temple

The Gujarati Hindu Swaminarayan Group's **Akshardham Temple** *(akshardham.com; entry free, adult/child exhibit pass ₹260/160, water show ₹110/80)*, built in 2005, is breathtakingly lavish. Artisans used ancient techniques to carve the pale red sandstone into elaborate reliefs, including 20,000 deities, saints and mythical creatures. The centrepiece is a 3m-high gold statue of **Bhagwan Shri Swaminarayan** surrounded by more fabulously intricate carvings.

The exhibitions ticket includes a narrated **boat ride** that takes visitors through 10,000 years of Indocentric history, a similar **animatronic experience** and a film about the early life of Swaminarayan. Soon after sunset, a **water fountain show** brings all the spectacle to a climactic finale every day of the week except for Monday, when the temple is closed.

Visiting the temple is more of a theme-park experience than a spiritual one, such are the tourist crowds and the security, but the architecture of the main buildings and the artisanship in their carvings is exceptional. A shame, then, that you cannot take photographs. Electronics (including phones and cameras) are prohibited, but there's a secure cloakroom at the entrance. There are snack and water vendors within the complex and a huge outdoor food court near the exit. The temple is in Delhi's eastern suburbs, but just 200m walk from the Akshardham metro station.

South Delhi

INDIE INDIA: CAFES AND CREATIVITY

Like a fringe festival where the edgiest acts perform, South Delhi skirts the city with its cafe culture, live-music venues and independent designers. There are a handful of must-see attractions here, including the breathtakingly beautiful Lotus Temple, Dilli Haat – Delhi's most chill handicrafts market – and the lovely ruins of Hauz Khas Fort, but South Delhi's real charm is in wandering the village-style enclaves dotted around this large area where the city's creatives break out their stuff. In Hauz Khas Village you'll find retro '90s fashion, crate-diving record stores and open mic stages. Over in Shahpur Jat, independent clothes designers have set up shop beside hipster coworking spaces and stand-up comedy venues.

This is also the best part of town to hunt down a yoga or meditation class, get an Ayurvedic massage, or try your hand at cooking.

GETTING AROUND

Sights in South Delhi are somewhat spread out so they're difficult to visit in one hit – plan accordingly. The yellow and violet metro lines run north–south through the area and the pink line runs east–west; these can get you near your destination, but you'll usually need an autorickshaw or taxi as well (or be prepared for a bit of a trek).

Come with Me to HKV

Delhi's bohemian village

Hauz Khas Village (HKV) is an arty little district of cool cafes, live-music venues, tattoo parlours and offbeat fashion right beside the Hauz Khas ruins (p91) – great for a lazy afternoon bleeding into the evening. Swing off the brash main drag to seek out the cobbled backstreet that twists around to the northwest, crammed with boutiques selling clothing, handicrafts, contemporary ceramics, handmade furniture and old Bollywood posters.

If you're looking for gorgeous furniture pieces (or just want to gawk), head to **Country Collection**, which sells handcrafted cabinets, doors and more, including many vintage pieces (they ship worldwide). Music fans won't want to miss **Pagal Records**, while bookworms should take a peek at **Kunzum**, a cosy bookshop down an alley near the entrance to the ruins.

Also check out contemporary art galleries in HKV such as **Lokayata Art Gallery,** near the entrance to the village (just look for the giant iguana on the roof), and nearby **Creativity**

TOP TIP

Delhi is a land of many acronyms, and many neighbourhoods are routinely referred to in a shortened form. A few handy ones to add to your lexicon include CP (Connaught Place), GK (Greater Kailash), HKV (Hauz Khas Village) and SDA (Safdarjung Development Area).

SIGHTS
1 Creativity Art Gallery
2 Deer Park
3 Firoz Shah's Madrasa
4 Firoz Shah's Tomb
5 Lokayata Art Gallery
6 Siri Fort

ACTIVITIES
7 Kerala Ayurveda Life
8 Saffron Palate
9 Sivananda Yoga Vedanta Nataraja Centre
10 Tushita Mahayana Meditation Centre
11 Yoga Studio

SLEEPING
12 Bed & Chai
13 Colonel's Retreat
14 Haveli Hauz Khas
15 Home@F37
16 Hyatt Regency Delhi
17 Legend Inn
18 Minimalist Poshtel & Suites

EATING
19 Coast Café
20 Dirty Dough Pizza by Moets
21 Evergreen Sweet House
22 Kori's
23 Lakeview Bistro
24 Lama Kitchen
25 Naivedyam

DRINKING & NIGHTLIFE
26 Blue Tokai
27 Gypsy Cafe
28 Hauz Khas Social

ENTERTAINMENT
29 Happy High
30 Piano Man Jazz Club

SHOPPING
31 Arjun Arora
32 Country Collection
33 Dilli Haat
34 Hauz Khas Village
35 Kunzum
36 Midland Books
37 Pagal Records
38 Shahpur Jat Village

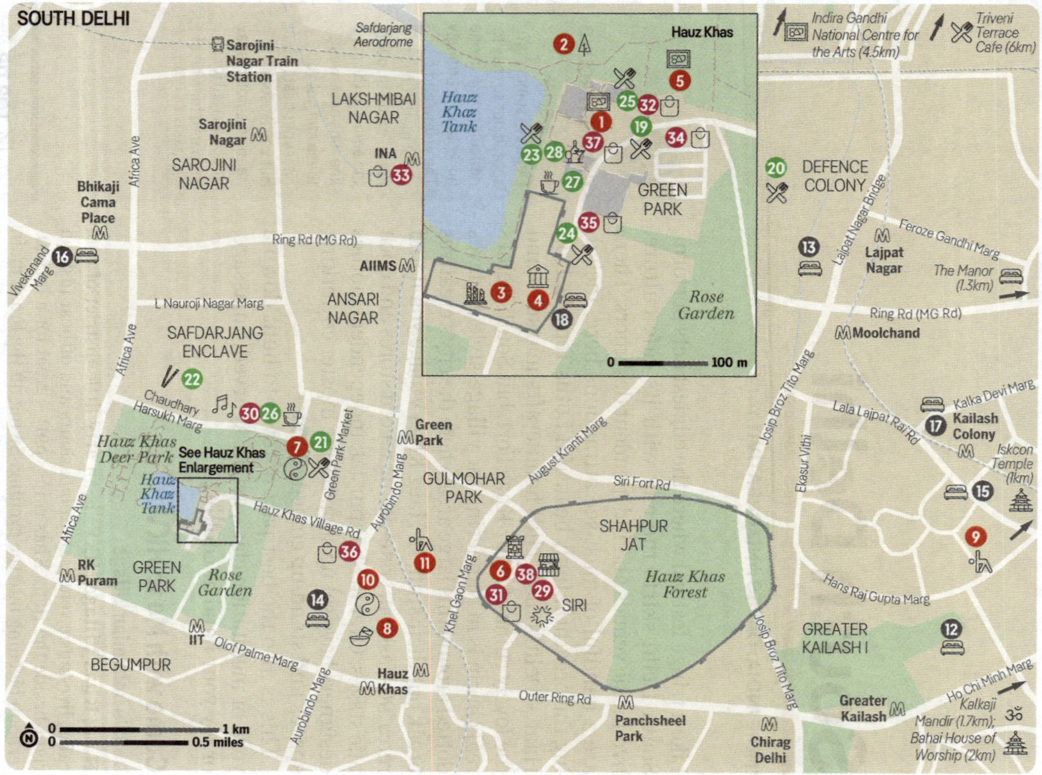

Art Gallery, founded in 1999 and focusing on Indian contemporary art.

There are lots of bars and clubs on the main road, many with nightly live music, but the most atmospheric venues overlook Hauz Khas lake and the lush greenery surrounding it. Check out **Gypsy Cafe**, a shoes-off, cushions-on-the-floor spot where musos gather to jam. You're welcome to pick up an instrument and join them – there's a djembe, guitar, didge and cajon. As the sun sets head to **Lakeview Bistro** for folky live music and a pool table or upmarket restaurant-bar-club **Hauz Khas Social**, with an urban warehouse-style interior of stone walls, high ceilings and amazing views over the ruins, forest and lake.

To reach HKV, take an autorickshaw or taxi to the boom gate – vehicles are restricted in the village. On the way, look for the numerous Lodhi-era tombs scattered along the access road; they're beautifully lit at night. If you come during daylight, you can also take a metro to Green Park and cut through **Deer Park**, behind Green Park Market. Follow concrete paths to a well-stocked deer enclosure near the edge of HKV; you'll need your phone GPS to find the way.

Peaceful Ruins by the Lake

The atmospheric remains of Hauz Khas

Hauz Khas *(adult/child ₹300/free)* means 'noble tank', and Sultan Ala-ud-din Khilji's reservoir once covered 28 hectares. It collected enough water during the monsoon to last Siri Fort, HQ of the second Delhi sultanate, through the dry season. Today it's much smaller but still a beautiful place to be, thronged by birds and surrounded by parkland. Overlooking it are the impressive ruins of Firoz Shah's 14th-century **madrasa** and **tomb**, which he had built before his death in 1388. You can take a 1km walk around the perimeter of the lake, which is particularly lovely at sunset, when the water glows pink and bats depart from their roosts into the sky.

To reach the lake shore, walk to the end of all the HKV shops, and enter the grounds near Firoz Shah's madrasa, from where you can look out over the lake before climbing down to the water's edge.

WHY I LOVE SOUTH DELHI

Margot Bigg, Lonely Planet writer

Many visitors to Delhi, Indian and overseas alike, view the city through the lens of congested areas such as Chandni Chowk, which – as exciting as it can be in short spurts – can feel exhausting to many. South Delhi defies those stereotypes. Here, you find walkable, tree-lined neighbourhoods, many of which feel more like little villages than simple localities. And while much of South Delhi was built up during the years after the Partition, there are still plenty of reminders of the ancient past among the shiny shops and leafy lanes, from the Lodhi-era tombs tucked behind Green Park Market to the medieval madrasa on the verdant edge of Hauz Khas Village. It's this mix of greenery and history that makes South Delhi my favourite part of town.

EATING & DRINKING IN HKV: OUR PICKS

Lama Kitchen: Branch out beyond *momos* at this spot near the entrance to the ruins that specialises in dishes from Nepal and Sikkim. *noon-11.15pm* ₹₹

Naivedyam: Superb South Indian restaurant feels like a temple, with a wood-carved interior and waiters dressed as devotees. *10am-11pm Mon-Fri, from 9am Sat & Sun* ₹₹

Coast Café: Experience the flavours of the Malabar coast, from fish curry to fluffy *appam*, at this chic cafe spread across two sun-drenched floors. *noon-11pm* ₹₹₹

Hauz Khas Social: This massive spot with a rooftop overlooking the Hauz Khas ruins pairs hearty pub food from around the world with a huge drink menu. *11am-1am* ₹₹

DELHI AIR QUALITY

Pollution is a serious health hazard in Delhi, which regularly tops the list of the world's most polluted capitals – it can reach 80 times the World Health Organization's recommended limit. Symptoms include sore eyes, coughing and sore throat. Air pollutants can also cause or worsen cardiovascular and pulmonary diseases and cancer. Winter (November to February) is the worst time.

Various apps track air quality, including UN-affiliated IQAir, the 'Air quality' layer on Google Maps, and 'Shit! I Smoke', which measures how many cigarettes you're passively smoking.

So what can you do when air quality is bad? Stay indoors if possible, close windows and use an air purifier. If outside, wear a properly fitting KN95 mask, avoid heavy exercise and remember to drink lots of water.

DMITRY STRIZHAKOV/SHUTTERSTOCK

Bahai House of Worship

Fortress of Fashion

Eclectic village inside the fort of Delhi's second city

Only some of the walls remain of 14th-century **Siri Fort** built by Ala-ud-din Khilji as the second of the eight historical cities of Delhi. The walls are impressive nonetheless, and kept Siri safe from six Mongol invasions at a time when the Mongol empire was the largest contiguous empire the world has ever seen. It is said that the heads of 8000 Mongols are buried in the foundations.

Within the boundaries of the walls, there's an auditorium, a sports complex and the enclave of **Shahpur Jat**. This urban village contains an artsy collection of high-end clothing boutiques, health-conscious cafes and no-frills eateries, many hidden among graffiti-splattered alleyways. It's one of Delhi's more intriguing places to shop; try **Arjun Arora** for lavish Indian women's clothing suitable for wearing to weddings. **Happy High** *(@happyhighin)* comedy club hosts stand-up, workshops and improv jams in a mix of Hindi and English.

Chill Outdoor Market

Shopping with less hustle

Right beside the Dilli Haat-INA metro station, **Dilli Haat** *(₹100)* is a popular, though somewhat stage-managed, open-air food and crafts market. The market is spacious and wheelchair-accessible, with colourful, photogenic stalls selling regional handicrafts from all over India. It's a great place to shop, but bargain hard.

MORE GREAT SHOPPING?

Head to the **state emporiums** (p71) for handicrafts from across India, **Khan Market** (p87) for high-end design, and of course, **Chandni Chowk** (p61) for bazaar shopping to beat them all.

The market is operated by Delhi Tourism, which also organises regular live music and dance performances, as well as art exhibitions, from various parts of India. At the far end are food stands where you can sample cuisine from every corner of the country.

While this is the original (and best-known) Dilli Haat, there are two additional Delhi Tourism-supported outposts in the Pitampura and Janakpuri neighbourhoods.

Temple Town

A trio of temples

Designed for tranquil worship, Delhi's beautiful Lotus Temple, officially called the **Bahai House of Worship** *(bahaihouseofworship.in)*, offers a rare pocket of calm in the hectic city. This architectural masterpiece was designed by Iranian-Canadian architect Fariborz Sahba in 1986. It is shaped like a lotus flower, with 27 delicate-looking white-marble petals. The temple was created to bring faiths together; visitors are invited to pray or meditate silently according to their own beliefs and there's an almost tangible feeling of serenity inside the space. The attached visitor centre tells the story of the Bahai faith. Photography is prohibited inside the temple and all interior visitors must remove their shoes and maintain silence. The temple is closed on Mondays and admission numbers are limited the rest of the time, so be prepared for queues.

South of the Lotus Temple, **Kalkaji Mandir** *(skmpsc.org)* is among South Delhi's oldest and most famous temples. While the current structure dates to the 18th century, it's possible that a temple has stood here since the third century BCE. Devotees flock here to take *darshan* (an auspicious viewing) of the temple's Kali idol, so expect long waits and bring an offering (available for sale just outside). Interestingly, this temple is run by a number of different priest families who take turns attending to its maintenance and performing rituals.

To the north of the Lotus Temple sits the **Iskcon Temple** *(iskcondelhi.com)*, the Delhi headquarters of the International Society for Krishna Consciousness (sometimes referred to outside of India as 'Hare Krishnas'). This modern temple is an interesting place to learn about Krishna and his consort Radha and to find out more about the organisation and its mission. There's also a bookshop and an excellent veg restaurant, Govinda's.

BEST PERFORMING ARTS

Piano Man Jazz Club: The real thing. Skilled musicians play at this popular, dim-lit, atmospheric place with speakeasy vibes.

Triveni Kala Sangam: Delhi's school of visual arts, music and dance hosts regular performances, and houses a cluster of art galleries and the lovely Triveni Terrace Cafe (p80).

Indira Gandhi National Centre for the Arts: Culture vultures descend for classical and vocal recitals, dance performances, film screenings and literary fests.

India Habitat Centre: An important Delhi cultural address, with art exhibitions performances and concerts, mostly free.

Mandi House: Synonymous with Delhi's theatre scene, this central neighbourhood is home to the Little Theatre Group (p80), Kamani Auditorium (p80) and more.

EATING & DRINKING IN SOUTH DELHI: OUR PICKS

Evergreen Sweet House: Part veg cafe, part sweet shop, this Green Park institution has been around since 1963 with its veg snacks, *chaat*, thalis and dosas. *8am-11pm* ₹

Kori's: Come for the *jimbap*, *teokbokki* and Korean-style thalis *(dosirak)* and stay for the karaoke at this Korean joint. *11am-11pm* ₹₹

Dirty Dough Pizza by Moets: Don't let the unappetising name deter you from snagging a gourmet pie from this Defence Colony pizzeria by culinary institution Moets. *noon-11.30pm* ₹₹

Blue Tokai: The branch of this top-notch espresso chain right next to Piano Man Jazz Club is full of hot-deskers tapping on their laptops. *10am-11pm*

DELHI'S BEST BOOKSTORES

Faqir Chand Bookstore: Compact shop filled with piles of books that has been keeping Khan Market (p87) readers supplied with literature since 1951.

Bahrisons: Another Khan Market favourite with a more organised selection and a dedicated shop for children's literature.

Full Circle Bookstore: Cosy bookshop with branches in Khan Market, GK-1 and Nizamuddin, with a great selection of art books and onsite cafe.

Midland Books: No-frills spot in Aurobindo Market (near Hauz Khas Village) with two floors stacked to the ceiling with books, many by Indian authors.

Yoga, Meditation & Wellness

Nurture body and soul

In the Kailash Colony neighbourhood, the **Sivananda Yoga Vedanta Nataraja Centre Yoga** *(sivananda.org/delhi)* offers multi-session beginner courses and 90-minute drop-in classes for practitioners who are familiar with the Sivananda sequence of asanas. Come on a Sunday morning for a free introductory drop-in class or in the evening for a free community *satsang*. Wear loose-fitting clothes that cover your shoulders and knees.

In the Hauz Khas neighbourhood, the **Yoga Studio** *(theyogastudio.info)* offers a wide range of yoga styles, including Vinyasa, Yin and Ashtanga every day of the week. Drop-in and classes passes are available. A few blocks away, **Tushita Mahayana Meditation Centre** *(tushitadelhi.com)* offers guided Buddhist meditation sessions in a peaceful, temple-like meditation hall in the Padmini Enclave, and also on Zoom. Check the events calendar online for timings. Sessions are free; donations are welcome.

In the nearby Green Park neighbourhood, **Kerala Ayurveda Life** *(keralaayurvedalife.com)* offers a range of treatments, including *abhyangam*, a herbal oil massage offered by two therapists (women for women and men for men), and *shirodhara*, in which oil is slowly streamed onto the top of your forehead through a specially designed vessel. Note that the centre has two outlets, but they're directly across the road from each other.

Curry in a Hurry

Learn the basics of North Indian cooking

Saffron Palate *(saffronpalate.com)* offers award-winning Indian cookery classes run by the charming Neha Gupta on the rooftop of her family home; they last for around three hours. The classes, which start at 11.30am or 5pm, culminate in an Indian meal and can include a trip to a local market.

Travelling Spoon *(travellingspoon.com)* connects locals with travellers wishing to experience home-made meals. You can choose from a clutch of hosts happy to cook, teach and serve traditional cuisine from the comfort of their homes. To find one, search for New Delhi on the website; prices depend on the host and meal served.

Greater Delhi

ARCHAEOLOGICAL WONDERS

Delhi has well and truly burst its britches and spilled over the borders of the National Capital Territory (Delhi NCT). The city of Gurugram (still often called by its former name, Gurgaon) is technically the largest city in Haryana, but is closely tied to Delhi, including by the metro. It has become the capital's de-facto financial and technological hub. Meanwhile, the new international airport set to open in Noida is actually in Uttar Pradesh. Together these areas are known as Delhi National Capital Region (NCR).

As the city continues to sprawl, flash new malls and apartment complexes are sprouting between some of the most historic parts of the capital. It was at Mehrauli that Qutb-ud-din Aibak established the first Delhi Sultanate, and the mosque he built, India's first, can still be visited beside the Qutb Minar. The austere ruins of Tughlaqabad are further east.

GETTING AROUND

Attractions in this area are spread out. The yellow metro line swings through on its way to Gurugram and will take you to DLF Cyber City, but for other attractions, you're best off taking an autorickshaw or cab. The easiest way to get around is to arrange a car and driver for a day through your hotel to visit multiple sites.

SAIKO3P/SHUTTERSTOCK

Quwwat-ul-Islam Masjid (p99)

TOP TIP

You can buy tickets online for a ₹50 discount at Archaeological Survey of India (ASI) sites like Qutb Minar, Tughlaqabad, Hauz Khas, Purana Qila, Jantar Mantar, Humayun's Tomb, Safdarjung's Tomb, Firoz Shah's Tomb and the Red Fort. Go to *asi.payumoney.com*.

HIGHLIGHTS
1 Mehrauli Archaeological Park
2 Qutb Minar
3 Qutb Minar Complex
4 Tughlaqabad

SIGHTS
5 Adham Khan's Mausoleum
6 Hijron ka Khanqah
7 Iltutmish's Tomb
8 Iron Pillar
9 Jahaz Mahal
10 Jamali Khamali Mosque
11 Lal Kot
12 Madrasa
13 Metcalfe Boathouse
14 Quli Khan's Tomb
15 Quwwat-ul-Islam Masjid
16 Rajon ki Baoli
17 Tomb of Balban
18 Tughlaq's Tomb
19 Zafar Mahal

SLEEPING
20 Svelte Delhi

EATING
21 Cafe Stone
22 Canvas V
23 Diva – The Italian Restaurant
24 Olive Bar & Kitchen

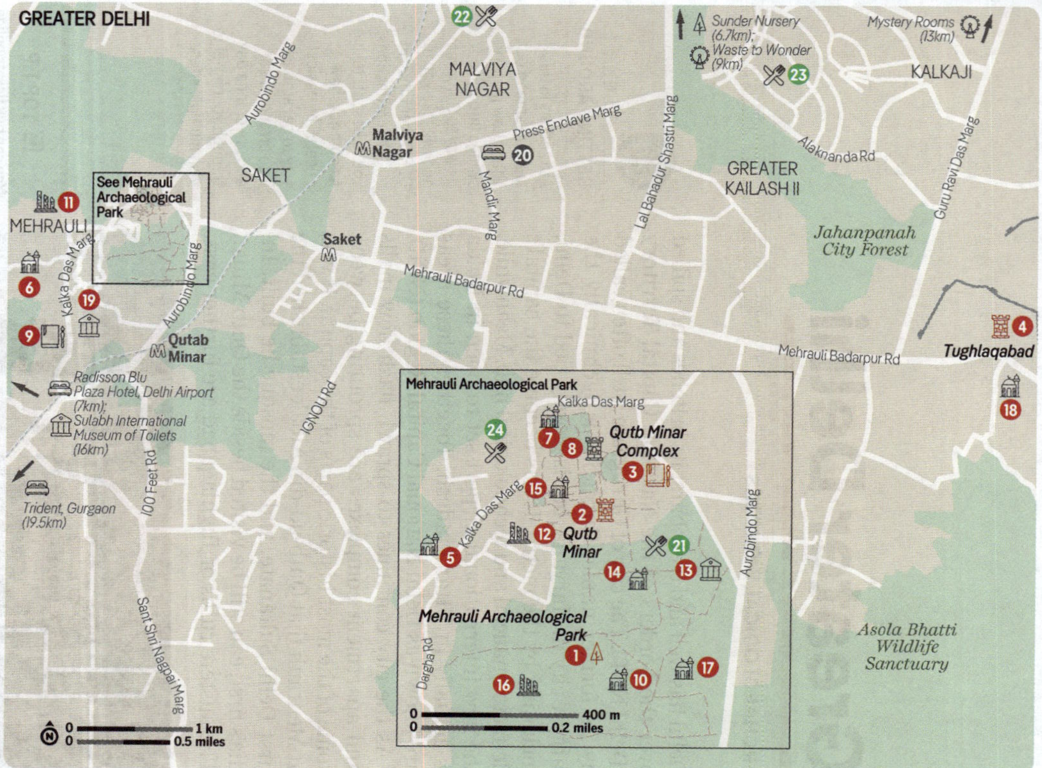

YAMASK/SHUTTERSTOCK

Rajon ki Baoli

Stumble across History in the Forest

Mehrauli Archaeological Park's atmospheric ruins

There are extraordinary riches scattered around Mehrauli, with more than 440 monuments dotting the forested park and the village behind it. In the **Mehrauli Archaeological Park** *(free)*, the most impressive are the 16th-century **Jamali Khamali Mosque**, attached to the **tomb of the Sufi poet Jamali**, and the time-ravaged **tomb of Balban**. To the north is **Quli Khan's Tomb**, a Mughal-era tomb converted into a monsoon-season residence by the East India Company's Thomas Metcalfe in the 19th century. It overlooks lakeside **Metcalfe Boathouse**, once a Lodhi-era tomb. Nearby, the lovely Cafe Stone (p101), with views of the Qutb Minar, is a great place to pause for a bite. To the west is the 16th-century **Rajon ki Baoli**, one of Delhi's finest step-wells, and more ruins are scattered through the forest.

You can walk to the park from Qutb Minar metro station by crossing the pedestrian overpass over busy Anuvrat Marg, then heading north for 500m.

More historic monuments are scattered through the busy streets of Mehrauli village, southwest of the Qutb Minar, but are more difficult to locate. They include **Adham Khan's Mausoleum** (Bhool Bhulaiya), on a busy intersection; just west of here stretch the pre-Islamic walls of **Lal Kot**. To the south is the crumbling **Zafar Mahal**, the last palace built by the Mughals, and **Hijron ka Khanqah**, a Lodhi-era burial ground for *hijras* (the transgender, intersex and eunuch community) that is beautifully maintained by the *hijra* community today. South again is the Lodhi **Jahaz Mahal** ('ship palace').

NOIDA INTERNATIONAL AIRPORT

Nearing completion at the time of writing, Noida International Airport (also known as Jewar Airport) will relieve pressure on Delhi's existing Indira Gandhi International Airport. Technically located in Uttar Pradesh in the new YEIDA City development, it will serve the National Capital Region (NCR).

The first two runways were slated to open in 2026, with a further six to be added in the future. A 31km highway will link the airport with Faridabad on the Delhi–Mumbai Expressway. There are also plans to connect the airport to the Delhi Metro at Faridabad, as well as linking it to the capital via high speed rail.

VIBGYOR STUDIOS/SHUTTERSTOCK

TOP EXPERIENCE

Qutb Minar Complex

The UNESCO-listed Qutb Minar was the first thing Qutb-ud-din Aibak built after overthrowing the Tomar Rajputs at the end of the 12th century. Partly built using stones from destroyed structures of Lal Kot, the minaret emphatically announced a new regime was in town. Muslims would rule Delhi from this time until the coming of the British.

DON'T MISS

- Qutb Minar
- Quwwat-ul-Islam Masjid
- Iron Pillar
- Madrasa
- Iltutmish's Tomb

Qutb Minar

Commissioned in 1199, this stunning red-sandstone tower lends the complex its name. The astonishingly well-preserved minaret is 73m high, tapering from a diameter of 14.32m at the base to an elegant 2.75m at the peak via a series of alternating angular and rounded flutings. It was completed in stages, with the first two stages built by Aibak and the next three by his successor Iltutmish.

PRACTICALITIES

- asi.nic.in/pages/WorldHeritageQutbMinar
- adult/child ₹600/free
- sunrise-8pm Tue-Sun

When the tower was struck by lightning in 1368 it lost its top floor. Firoz Shah Tughlaq, ruler of the third Delhi Sultanate, repaired the damage and added a 5th floor for good measure. This impressive structure introduced India to Islamic architecture and it's still the world's tallest brick minaret.

Quwwat-ul-Islam Masjid

At the foot of the Qutb Minar stands the first mosque to be built in India. An inscription over the east gate states that it was built with materials obtained from demolishing 27 temples; many of the carved pillars here were repurposed from Lal Kot. As well as intricate carvings, the walls of the mosque are studded with sun disks, *shikharas* (rising towers) and other recognisable pieces of Hindu and Jain masonry.

Iron Pillar

In the courtyard of the Quwwat-ul-Islam Masjid is a 6.7m-high iron pillar that is much more ancient than any of the surrounding monuments. It hasn't rusted over the past 1600 years, due to both the dry atmosphere and its incredible purity. A six-line Sanskrit inscription indicates that it was initially erected outside a Vishnu temple, possibly in Bihar, in memory of Chandragupta II, who ruled from 375 to 413 CE. Legend has it that Anangpal, the 8th-century Tomar king credited with founding Delhi, brought it to the site. Scientists are at a loss to explain how the iron was cast using the technology of the time.

Iltutmish's Tomb

Qutb-ud-din Aibak was succeeded by Aram Shah, followed by Iltutmish, who ultimately consolidated the sultanate's hold on India into the Mamluk dynasty.

Iltutmish is entombed in a magnificent sandstone and marble mausoleum, almost completely covered in Islamic calligraphy. Legend has it that he believed his sons were too decadent for the job of ruling the sultanate, so he named his daughter Razia as his heir. However she got there, Iltutmish's daughter Razia Sultana (r 1236–40) became the first female Muslim ruler of India, and the only female Muslim to ever rule Delhi.

Madrasa

Ala-ud-din Khilji, ruler of the second Delhi Sultanate, built a sprawling madrasa (Islamic school) and tomb at the rear of the complex in 1315, 116 years after the Qutb Minar was erected. You can poke around the ruins, which have not survived as well as the towering minaret.

DELHI'S FIRST SULTAN

Born as an enslaved child in Turkestan, Qutb-ud-din Aibak was trafficked to a Persian judge, in whose household he learned horse riding and archery. He was again trafficked to the Ghurid emperor and, starting in the stables, rose up the ranks until he was in charge of northern India and conquered several kingdoms, including parts of what is now Delhi. By 1206, he had officially reclaimed his autonomy as the first sultan of Delhi.

TOP TIPS

- Despite the name, the Qutb Minar metro station is about 2km from the Qutb Minar itself, along busy Anuvrat Marg. If you decide to walk, you'll go straight past the entrance to Mehrauli Archaeological Park (p97), so visit en route.
- From the metro, cross the pedestrian overpass and head north along busy Anuvrat Marg.
- The Qutub Festival showcases classical music and dance forms from across India and takes place here every November/December.
- Save ₹50 by buying a ticket online ahead of your visit.

BEST OF DELHI FOR KIDS

DelhibyCycle: This outfit can kit you up with a child seat to pedal through the Old City and beyond.

Sunder Nursery: Check the website for children's activities from beekeeping to live performances – a great way to meet local kids.

Waste to Wonder: Climb into a car-dinosaur or stumble upon the Statue of Liberty.

Museum of Illusions: Create Insta-friendly optical illusions with mirrors and more.

Escape Rooms: Try one of Delhi's escape rooms – **Mystery Rooms** and **Hidden Hour** have locations across the city.

VIKAS KAUSHIK/500PX

Magnificent 14th-Century Ruined Fort

Explore underground rooms in jungle-clad Tughlaqabad

Half reclaimed by jungle and gradually being encroached on by villages, **Tughlaqabad** *(adult/child ₹300/free)* was Delhi's third incarnation, built by Ghiyus-ud-din Tughlaq in 1321 against Mongol invasions, and abandoned just six years later. In contrast to the decorative flourishes of the Lodhi Sultans and Mughals who came after him, Tughlaq's taste was for stern and functional defensive bastions. There are fantastic emerald-green views from the high points; interlinking underground rooms, which you can explore, were used as storehouses. There's also a creepy *baoli* to explore.

The sultan's well-maintained sandstone tomb (included in the entry ticket) once stood in the middle of a lake, but is now separated from his fallen city by a road. It's almost as well fortified as the fortress.

It does get hot out here, so bring plenty of water and snacks – there's nowhere to buy anything. To reach the fort, take an autorickshaw from the Govind Puri metro station.

Royal Flush

Learn about the wonders of sanitation

Gimmicky as it may sound, the **Sulabh International Museum of Toilets** *(sulabhtoiletmuseum.org; free)* provides an illuminating look at the history of toilets while highlighting

Tughlaqabad

the importance of sanitation access. The museum is part of Sulabh International – a massive social service organisation known for promoting and providing innovative and low-cost lavatories across the country; it's also one of the few major museums in Delhi that's open on Mondays.

Highlights include an outdoor area showcasing different types of easy-to-build latrines that don't require manual waste removal, along with indoor galleries where toilets and urinals from around the world are proudly displayed (along with plenty of cheeky panels that lightheartedly highlight the best in toilet humour). There's also a gallery dedicated to menstrual hygiene designed to dispel misconceptions and taboos around periods, plus a large exhibit centre featuring a virtual reality game for kids and a short narrated film about the organisation and its mission. Docents are onsite to provide tours and information; make sure to ask to see the kitchen, where biogas created from human waste is used to power the stove.

EATING IN GREATER DELHI: OUR PICKS

Canvas V: Chic spot with plant-based versions of North Indian faves such as *dhal makhani* and *soya chaap* plus some funky inventions. *noon-midnight* ₹₹₹

Diva – The Italian Restaurant: Celeb chef Ritu Dalmia flexes her Italian culinary wizardry at this elegant favourite, which opened back in 2000. *12.30-11.30pm* ₹₹₹

Olive Bar & Kitchen: For a stylish lunch, dinner or high tea after visiting Qutb Minar, follow the road around to this haven of a *haveli* courtyard. *12.30pm-midnight* ₹₹₹

Cafe Stone: Garden cafe in Mehrauli Archaeological Park overlooking a lake with burgers, coffee and waffles, plus a weekend pop-up outdoor kitchen. *10am-7pm* ₹

Places We Love to Stay

₹ Budget ₹₹ Midrange ₹₹₹ Top End

Old Delhi

Map p62

Zostel Delhi ₹ Large, clean, colourful hostel with a pool table, cafe and good wi-fi. Beds with lockers, lights and charge points are in six- or eight-bed dorms, one is female only. There's rooftop chill space.

Major's Den Guesthouse ₹ In a relatively quiet spot on a road parallel to the Main Bazaar, this Paharganj classic is an old-school budget favourite, but some rooms lack windows and air-conditioning.

Hotel Cottage Yes Please ₹₹ A longtime favourite among Paharganj regulars, this convenient spot offers spacious, clean rooms, some with colourful decor that appears vaguely inspired by street art.

Hotel Godwin Deluxe ₹₹ Run by the same owners as the similar Grand Godwin next door, Godwin Deluxe offers good service, and comfortable, spacious, clean rooms accessed by a glass lift or marble spiral staircase.

Hotel Ajanta ₹₹ This long-established spot features marble-floored rooms, crisp white sheets and spacious rooms, plus room-service from onsite Cafe Vagabond.

Wongdhen House ₹₹ This solid property in the Majnu-ka-Tilla Tibetan enclave offers simple but sleek rooms and a restaurant serving Tibetan food, sushi, and Thai dishes.

Haveli Dharampura ₹₹₹ Tucked away in Old Delhi, this is a beautifully restored *haveli*, full of Mughal atmosphere. Watch *kabootar bazi* (pigeon flying) and *patang bazi* (kite flying) from the rooftop; weekend *kathak* performances are a real treat, as is the elegant onsite restaurant, Lakhori (p60).

Neem Haveli ₹₹₹ Across from Kathika (p61), and owned by the same people, this lovingly restored 19th-century *haveli* features a few beautifully furnished rooms adorned with antiques. A large neem tree grows out of the central courtyard, where cultural performances regularly take place.

Lutyens' Delhi

Map p72

Hotel Alka ₹₹ An excellent onsite Indian restaurant, fair room rates and a convenient location in the heart of Connaught Place make up for this friendly property's clean if gaudily decorated rooms.

Imperial New Delhi ₹₹₹ Opened 1936, this historic heritage hotel on Janpath features elegant rooms with classical or art-deco touches and a massive private art collection that's liberally displayed across rooms, corridors and restaurants.

CP Villa Bed & Breakfast ₹₹₹ A good deal just 1km from Connaught Place, this place has a lovely garden and spacious rooms with private courtyards. The atmosphere is homey and relaxed, with regular rooms plus a spacious apartment that's great for families.

Hotel Palace Heights ₹₹₹ Small-scale boutique hotel with some of busy Connaught Place's nicest rooms, with gleaming white linen, and caramel and amber tones. The onsite Zaffran Restaurant serves Indian favourites.

The Park, New Delhi ₹₹₹ Conveniently close to the Jantar Mantar, this sleek property with a fab pool trades in historic charm for hip modernism.

Nizamuddin & Around

Map p82

ITC Maurya ₹₹₹ Situated in Chanakyapuri, Delhi's diplomatic enclave, this luxurious property offers plush, contemporary rooms and easy-access to Bukhara (p84), a beloved restaurant serving cuisine from the Northwest Frontiers Province of Pakistan. The spa, Kaya Kalp, is among Delhi's most highly regarded places for pampering.

Lutyens Bungalow ₹₹₹ Rambling bungalow with a colonial-era feel, surrounded by verandas, veggie gardens and hanging lamps. Particularly good for kids because of the rambling space, and the lovely swimming pool. You'll receive a warm welcome like you're visiting family.

The Lodhi ₹₹₹ One of Delhi's finest luxury hotels, with huge, lovely rooms and suites, some with private plunge pools. Amenities include extensive wellness facilities and multiple restaurants, including fine-dining favourite, Indian Accent (p84).

South Delhi

Map p89

Bed & Chai ₹ Among the best value in South Delhi, this French-run backpacker guesthouse offers clean, comfortable rooms with private bathrooms (the cheapest rooms have separate but private facilities).

Minimalist Poshtel & Suites ₹₹ Conveniently situated in the heart of Hauz Khas Village, this spot offers bright rooms and apartments with Scandinavian-style furnishings. The Japanese-style capsule 'rooms' here are essentially curtained-off dorm beds surrounded by walls, a step up from a typical hostel.

Home@F37 ₹₹ Stylish decor, private balconies, HEPA air purifiers and a good breakfast buffet make this 21-room spot in a converted Kailash Colony home a comfortable stay.

Legend Inn ₹₹ Founded by Captain MS Kohli, the leader of the first Indian expedition to summit Mt Everest in 1965, this mountaineering-themed spot has a climbing wall in the foyer and free loaner gear for guests who want to do a bit of top-roping. Rooms are simply furnished and comfortable.

Colonel's Retreat ₹₹₹ Tucked away in the quiet, tree-shaded lanes of Delhi's affluent Defence Colony neighbourhood, this intimate guesthouse features elegantly furnished but homey rooms with plenty of natural light plus a fab terrace restaurant.

Haveli Hauz Khas ₹₹₹ Located in a leafy South Delhi neighbourhood, this family-run B&B is set in a spacious mansion with marble interior, verandahs, terraces and manicured lawns. Six well-appointed rooms have spotless ensuite bathrooms and are full of Indian art, books and collectibles. The Studio room offers the lowest rate, but requires climbing up a spiral staircase.

Hyatt Regency Delhi ₹₹₹ This massive property attracts a mix of business travellers and tourists, and if you come in the winter, there's a good chance you'll see a wedding or two taking place. Lavish buffet breakfasts and a convenient location equidistant between the IGI Airport and Central Delhi seal the deal for many travellers.

The Manor ₹₹₹ In Delhi's posh Friends Colony West neighbourhood, situated handily midway between Humayun's Tomb and the Lotus Temple, this cosy boutique hotel features minimalist contemporary rooms and sprawling lawns flanked with pollution-negating trees and shrubbery.

Greater Delhi

Map p96

Radisson Blu Plaza Hotel, Delhi Airport ₹₹₹ One of a handful of similarly priced, solid options near the Indira Gandhi Airport, this massive property with a gorgeous terraced pool is a convenient place to spend the night before or after a flight. Don't miss the hearty Mughlai fare at the Great Kebab Factory onsite.

Svelte Delhi ₹₹₹ If you've ever wanted to stay at a mall, now you can. In the heart of the Saket District Centre, this business hotel has contemporary rooms, a terrace pool and easy access to a few malls' worth of shops and restaurants.

Trident, Gurgaon ₹₹₹ Southeast of the airport, off the main highway that connects Delhi to the satellite city of Gurgaon, this business hotel offers a luxe ambience with lower rates than what you'll find in Delhi, with contemporary, Mughal-inspired accents and a gorgeous sunken pool surrounded by fountain features.

MRINALPAL/SHUTTERSTOCK

Hyatt Regency Delhi, South Delhi

Researched by
Joe Bindloss

Rajasthan

FABULOUS FORTS AND PAINTED CITIES

Painted palaces, lavish temples, desert dunes and wildly romantic hilltop forts – Rajasthan is India as you've always imagined it.

Enter a world of towering fortresses bursting from rocky crags, looming over tangled medieval lanes. Wander palaces decked from floor to ceiling with mirrored mosaics and intricate paintings of Rajput armies and dancing deities. Rattle across dusty deserts by train and bounce by 4WD through tiger-stalked national parks. This is what Rajasthan is all about.

A one-time playground of Mughal emperors and maharajas, this patchwork of once-independent princely states is where the India depicted on medieval miniature paintings comes vividly to life. Rajasthan is a living monument to India's intense history – indeed, it's hard to travel more than a few kilometres without stumbling across another lavish royal palace or time-scarred fortress.

WHATAFOTO/SHUTTERSTOCK

Some of these regal cribs are still inhabited by the royal families who founded them, while others have been turned into extravagant hotels. Still more live on as fascinating museums to the opulent lifestyle of monarchs who were literally kings and queens of all they surveyed.

Visiting Rajasthan today means hopping between the captivating coloured cities where these rulers held court, stepping on and off the tourist trail. Jaipur, Udaipur, Jaisalmer and Jodhpur rank among the most visited cities in the subcontinent, while other towns lie almost untouched by mass tourism. A little bit of hard sell in Rajasthan's more touristy corners is a small price to pay for sights this dazzling.

THE MAIN AREAS

For places to stay in Rajasthan, see p184

MICHAEL BLANKI/SHUTTERSTOCK

Above: Green Gate (p115), Pritam Niwas Chowk, Jaipur; Left: Jaisalmer Fort (p171)

JODHPUR
A medieval vision in blue.
p160

JAISALMER
Desert fort perfection.
p171

BIKANER
A mesmerising monument to royal life. p179

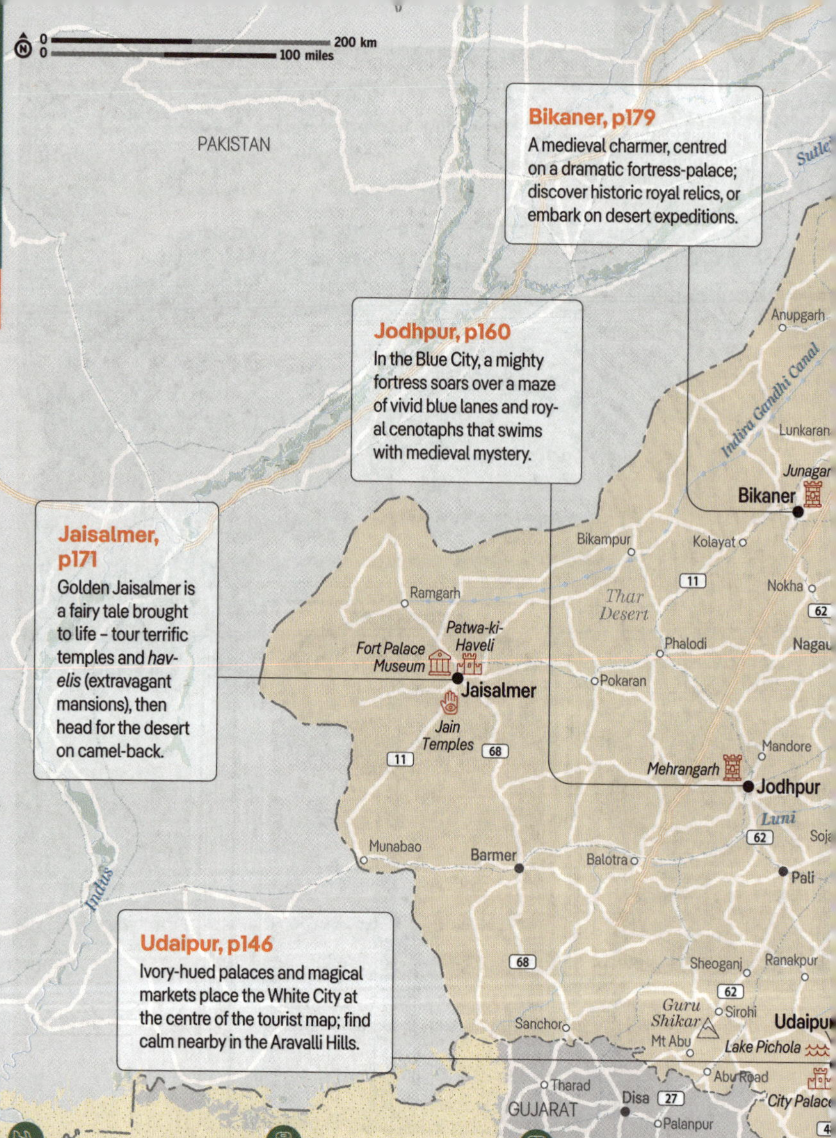

Bikaner, p179

A medieval charmer, centred on a dramatic fortress-palace; discover historic royal relics, or embark on desert expeditions.

Jodhpur, p160

In the Blue City, a mighty fortress soars over a maze of vivid blue lanes and royal cenotaphs that swims with medieval mystery.

Jaisalmer, p171

Golden Jaisalmer is a fairy tale brought to life – tour terrific temples and *havelis* (extravagant mansions), then head for the desert on camel-back.

Udaipur, p146

Ivory-hued palaces and magical markets place the White City at the centre of the tourist map; find calm nearby in the Aravalli Hills.

AIR

In gigantic Rajasthan, flying can save you many uncomfortable hours of travel by road or rail, at a carbon cost. Indigo and other budget carriers zip from Jaipur, Delhi, Mumbai and other major Indian cities to Jaisalmer, Jodhpur, Udaipur, Bikaner and Kota.

BUS

The crammed buses of the Rajasthan State Road Transport Corporation (RSRTC) go almost everywhere, supplemented by more comfortable air-con, '2x2', '2+1' and 'Volvo' buses run by myriad private companies. Always check the departure point – it may not be the main bus stand.

TRAIN

The most comfortable way to reach every corner of Rajasthan. Trains link most towns, including fast and comfortable Vande Bharat services to key cities. There's heavy demand for seats so book ahead, particularly for trips to Jaipur, Jaisalmer, Jodhpur, Udaipur and Ranthambore National Park.

Find Your Way

Rajasthan is India's largest state, so be ready for some long bus and train rides. The odd domestic flight or overnight bus or train ride can save time, but expect cold nights and foggy mornings from November to March.

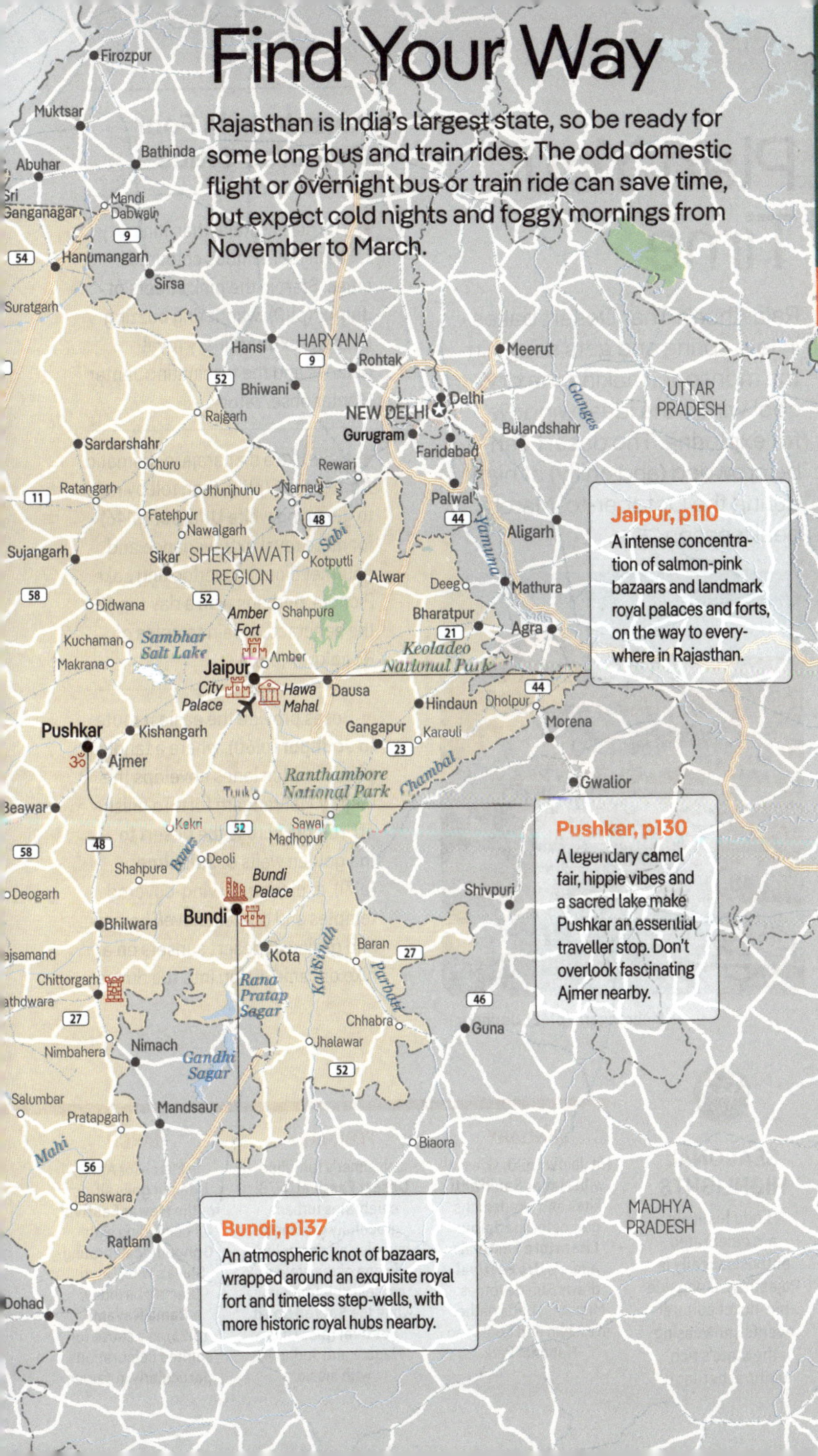

Jaipur, p110

A intense concentration of salmon-pink bazaars and landmark royal palaces and forts, on the way to everywhere in Rajasthan.

Pushkar, p130

A legendary camel fair, hippie vibes and a sacred lake make Pushkar an essential traveller stop. Don't overlook fascinating Ajmer nearby.

Bundi, p137

An atmospheric knot of bazaars, wrapped around an exquisite royal fort and timeless step-wells, with more historic royal hubs nearby.

Plan Your Time

Rajasthan's Thar Desert bakes in late spring and gets soggy in the monsoon, making the dry, cool winter the ideal window for exploring. The desert can be crowded (and chilly) at night during the October-to-March peak season.

NILA NEWSOM/SHUTTERSTOCK

Mehrangarh (p162), Jodhpur

Rajasthan in Four Coloured Cities

- The classic Rajasthan itinerary takes in four famous coloured cities. Start in the pink streets of **Jaipur** (p110), wandering buzzing bazaars, extraordinary royal palaces and the fascinating Jantar Mantar observatory.

- Make like a maharaja in dramatic **Amber Fort** (p112), then roll by rail to gleaming white **Udaipur** (p146) for more royal extravagance and gourmet dinners overlooking Lake Pichola, perhaps with a day trip to the spectacular Jain temples of **Ranakpur** (p157).

- Buses provide the easiest route to **Jodhpur** (p160), where a tangle of bottle-blue lanes envelops the mighty Mehrangarh fort. To finish off, rumble across the desert to the golden walls of **Jaisalmer** (p171), exploring carving-covered temples and opulent *haveli* homes and gazing at desert sunsets on a hike or camel safari into the dunes.

SEASONAL HIGHLIGHTS

Hindu festivals are celebrated enthusiastically in Rajasthan, alongside big-ticket cultural events showcasing the state's rich cultural heritage.

JANUARY

Hit Jaipur (p110; skies fill with **Makar Sankranti** kites and wordsmiths gather for the **Jaipur Literature Festival**. Ajmer's **Urs Festival** draws Sufi devotees. Migrating birds gather in Kichan and Keoladeo National Park.

FEBRUARY

Jaisalmer's fun-filled **Desert Festival** (p178) celebrates turbans, gracefully groomed camels and desert life, in one of the state's biggest celebrations, while the **Sacred Spirit Festival** (p163) fills Nagaur and Jodhpur with music.

MARCH

In March (or April), Udaipur goes all-out for the **Mewar Festival**, coinciding with **Gangaur** (celebrating Shiva's wife, Gauri). Rama's birthday, **Rama Navami** (p123), is a cause for spirited celebrations, particularly in Jaipur.

Two Weeks of Desert Adventures

- Before striking out west for the desert landscapes, see the royal forts and palaces of **Jaipur** (p110) and the seemingly bottomless step-well at **Abhaneri** (p126), then spot tigers burning bright in **Ranthambore National Park** (p127).

- Slingshot through **Kota** (p142) and the Sufi city of **Ajmer** (p134) to experience hippie vibes and sacred rituals in **Pushkar** (p130), then explore the dry hills around **Udaipur** (p146). Admire Jain temples in **Ranakpur** (p157) and fortress ruins in **Kumbhalgarh** (p157) then feel the desert spill into the city streets in atmospheric **Jodhpur** (p160).

- Step off the mainstream tourist map at the desert palace of **Nagaur** (p169), then cross to fortified **Jaisalmer** (p171) to watch sunset over the desert, closing the loop with a camel safari from charming **Bikaner** (p179).

Undiscovered Rajasthan

- To see Rajasthan's underexplored gems, use **Jaipur** (p110) as a stepping stone to **Keoladeo National Park** (p124) – a veritable Garden of Eden for birdlife each winter – and the overlooked royal residences at **Bharatpur** (p124), **Deeg** (p125) and **Alwar** (p126).

- Arrange a car and driver in Jaipur to tour mural-filled *haveli* mansions in **Shekhawati** (p128), then continue to historic **Bikaner** (p179) for camel safaris away from the crowds. Connect to **Jodhpur** (p160) by rail and mingle with Jain pilgrims in scenic, nature-filled **Mt Abu** (p158).

- Trains will take you from Abu Rd to the fascinating Sufi city of **Ajmer** (p134) and on to enormous **Chittorgarh** (p146) fort. Use buses to explore the painted palaces of **Bundi** (p137) and **Kota** (p142), before riding the rails back to Jaipur.

MAY

As temperatures spike ahead of the monsoon, locals head to the green hills of Mt Abu to enjoy the **Summer Festival** (p159), and take long walks in the cool fresh air.

AUGUST

As the monsoon slows, Rajasthan marks **Ganesh Chaturthi**, with statues paraded at Ranthambhore Fort (p128) to celebrate Ganesh's birthday. Rajasthan's lakes are full to capacity and the desert is at its greenest.

OCTOBER/NOVEMBER

The legendary **Camel Fair** (p132) draws camel aficionados and multitudes of pilgrims to Pushkar in October or November. Kota burns huge effigies of the demon king Ravana for **Dussehra** (p143) in October.

DECEMBER

Peak season for Indian weddings, birding in reserves such as Keoladeo, and star-gazing on desert safaris. Local fairs take place in Kumbhalgarh and Ranakpur, while Mt Abu hosts its lively **Winter Festival** (p159).

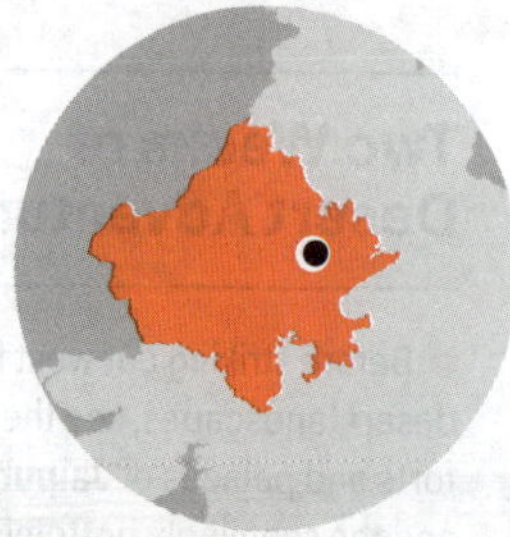

Jaipur

ROYAL HERITAGE | SPECTACULAR ARCHITECTURE | PALACE STAYS

☑ TOP TIP

Jaipur is at its calmest and most atmospheric early in the morning before the shops open, when locals gather at temples and chai stands to ease into the day. As activity builds, be vigilant when crossing the road – Jaipur traffic takes no prisoners.

Exuberant Jaipur is where many travellers get their first taste of Rajasthan. Maharaja Sawai Ram Singh II had the city painted in salmon tones in 1876, reputedly as a gesture of hospitality to the visiting Prince of Wales, and even today, buildings in the Old City must be painted pink, giving the city a remarkable aesthetic coherence.

For travellers, Jaipur is a place to dive headlong into Rajasthan's royal history in dramatic Rajput palaces and time-tumbled forts. Just north of the city, Amber Fort is one of the nation's defining monuments, while the royal Janta Mantar observatory reveals the maharajas at their most playful. Best of all, Jaipur is a living, breathing Indian city, so tourism slots in with lively local life, culture and commerce. Visit the Govind Dev Ji temple north of the City Palace and you'll discover a Jaipur that moves to older, more profound rhythms than the tourist dollar.

See Jaipur Like a Royal

MAP P118

Get a queen's view of the Old City

The city's most-distinctive landmark, the 18th-century **Hawa Mahal** (*obms-tourist.rajasthan.gov.in/place-details/Hawa-mahal; adult/student ₹202/102*) is an extraordinary gingerbread house of a residence, fronted by a delicate honeycomb

GETTING AROUND

The best way to appreciate Jaipur is on foot, but you can also zip around by unmetered taxi or autorickshaw, or summon a ride on Uber or Ola. A single metro line provides easy connections from the train station to the Old City.

A new airport metro line is planned – until then, airport transfers are easiest by taxi or autorickshaw. Make sure you go to the right terminal – the international and domestic terminals are separate and poorly connected.

City buses are handy for reaching Amber Fort and the Jal Mahal (board near the Hawa Mahal). Hotels can arrange a car and driver for wider exploring. For longer journeys, head to the RSTDC bus stand at Sindhi Camp or the busy train station on Station Rd.

SIGHTS
1 Amrapali Museum
2 Central Museum
3 Museum of Meenakari Heritage (MOMH)
4 Nahargarh
5 Sanganeri Gate

ACTIVITIES
6 Cyclin' Jaipur
7 RTDC Transport Unit

SLEEPING
8 Hotel Arya Niwas
9 Hotel Pearl Palace
10 Madhuban
11 Moustache Hostel
12 Narain Niwas Palace Hotel
13 Rambagh Palace

EATING
14 Handi Restaurant
15 Jaipur Modern Kitchen
16 Niro's
17 Old Takeaway the Kebab Shop
see 9 Peacock Rooftop Restaurant
18 Rawat Kachori
see 13 Suvarna Mahal

DRINKING & NIGHTLIFE
see 24 Anokhi Cafe
see 12 Bar Palladio
19 Curious Life
20 Curious Life
21 Forresta Kitchen & Bar
22 Lassiwala
see 9 Native Cocktail Room
see 13 Polo Bar
23 Stepout Cafe

SHOPPING
24 Anokhi
25 Fabindia
26 Rajasthali

of tiny porthole windows and multicoloured glass panels that allowed the ladies of the royal household to secretly peek out at the jostle of the city bazaars. Its five stories are linked by narrow, claustrophobic passageways, and selfie-takers throng the front facade of a monument known locally as the Palace of the Winds or Palace of Breeze. A few rooms display stone carvings, but the most enjoyable experience is sneaking a peek at the streets below through the doll's-house-like windows (great fun for kids). Climb to the upper levels for stunning views over the City Palace (the very top terrace is closed to visitors).

Continues on p117

KANOKRATNOK/SHUTTERSTOCK

TOP EXPERIENCE

Amber Fort

Rising over a rocky valley north of Jaipur, Amber Fort (Amer Fort) is almost a fortified city, enclosed by invader-repelling yellow and pink sandstone walls. Its battlements gaze over Mughal-style gardens, ancient stone temples and a crocodile-haunted lake. Inside the walls, extraordinary audience halls and royal apartments reveal the complex ceremonial and private life of Sawai Jai Singh II, the 18th-century maharaja of Jaipur.

DON'T MISS

- Suraj Pol
- Jaleb Chowk
- Diwan-i-Am
- Ganesh Pol (Ganesh Gate)
- Jai Mandir
- Sukh Niwas
- Zenana apartments

Suraj Pol

From the ticket office on the Jaipur road, a zigzag pathway climbs to the imposing fort gates, or you can save yourself the 10-minute walk and pay for a transfer by 4WD (around ₹600 return) or electric buggy (₹40 one way). At the top, the soaring Suraj Pol (Sun Gate) was built to accommodate royal elephants – it's best to avoid transfers by elephant today as carrying passengers is harmful to these vulnerable animals. Beyond Suraj Pol lies the fort's first courtyard – once the only space open to the maharaja's ordinary subjects (and even then, only for special occasions).

PRACTICALITIES

● obms-tourist.rajasthan.gov.in/place-details/Amber-Fort ● adult/student ₹502/152, composite ticket ₹1102/552 ● 8am-8pm

Jaleb Chowk

Victorious Rajput armies once displayed their captured booty to adoring crowds in Jaleb Chowk, the fort's public courtyard, enclosed by robust walls. You'll enter via Suraj Pol if you come on foot, or **Chand Pol** (Moon Gate) if you come by 4WD. Before you enter the royal part of the fort, glance up to the screened balconies where the women of court viewed proceedings in the square. Steps lead up to the revered **Siladevi Temple**; photography is banned but non-Hindus can step through the silver repoussé-work doors to view the marble interior.

Diwan-i-Am

From Jaleb Chowk, a stairway climbs through the lavishly frescoed **Singh Pol** (Lion Gate) to the fort's second courtyard, where courtiers, military officials and invited dignitaries were granted audiences with the maharaja. The Diwan-i-Am (Hall of Public Audiences) is an airy, open structure, supported by rows of columns crowned by elephant-shaped capitals. Latticed galleries above allowed members of the royal household to view ceremonies in the courtyard without being seen.

Ganesh Pol

Marking the transition to the royals' private quarters, Ganesh Pol is a riot of frescoes and carvings, Fusing elements of Hindu and Islamic architecture, this grand gateway is covered in painted flowers and foliage, surrounding an image of Ganesh seated on a hexagonal throne. An alternative route to the upper levels winds through the maze-like royal *hammam* (Turkish-style baths) in the southeast corner of the courtyard.

Jai Mandir

The maharaja's personal apartments surround the third courtyard, centred on elegant **Aram Bagh**, a Persian-style pleasure garden. On the west side is the Jai Mandir (Hall of Victory), a space for private audiences, adorned with inlaid panels, bas-reliefs of insects and flowers, and intricate mirror mosaics.

Sukh Niwas

On the east side of the third courtyard is the Sukh Niwas (Hall of Pleasure), with a time-worn ivory-inlaid sandalwood door and a surprisingly modern-looking design scheme of floral carvings and vase-shaped niches. A channel once carried cooling water through this space to the gardens.

Zenana Apartments

The secluded women's quarters surround the fourth courtyard – designed so the maharaja could visit his wives and concubines without anyone else knowing. Be sure to explore the warren of passageways inside the walls, which lead to unexpected chambers looking out over Amber village through lace-fine *jalis* (fretwork windows). See if you can find the mechanism in the northeast corner that once hauled water to the upper levels using clay pots attached to a rope.

GUIDE & SHOW

Official guides (*from ₹400*) can be arranged by the fort entrance and they'll help you see more of this labyrinth of a building. Alternatively, pay for an audio tour *(₹200-250)*, though this won't cover less-explored corners.

Every evening, a lively, ticketed sound-and-light show *(₹250)* in English and Hindi illuminates the fort walls at 6.30pm – take in the spectacle from the ticket complex below the main gate.

TOP TIPS

- Visit as soon as the fort opens at 8am to beat the crowds.
- Visit on a two-day composite ticket covering Amber Fort, Nahargarh fort, Hawa Mahal, Jantar Mantar, Central Museum, the Isarlat minaret and Sisodia Rani ka Bagh.
- Follow side passages whenever you see them – they invariably lead somewhere interesting.
- Visitors with mobility issues will need extra help navigating the fort's steps and stairs.
- Grab something light from the Jaleb Chowk food stand, recharge at the Cafe Coffee Day branch northwest of the Zenana, or reserve a table at the swanky, royal-themed **1135AD Restaurant**.
- Arrive and leave by bus to avoid inflated taxi and autorickshaw fares.

DON MAMMOSER/SHUTTERSTOCK

Peacock Gate (Varsha Deori)

TOP EXPERIENCE

City Palace

A grand gateway on Tripolia Bazaar marks the maharajas-only entrance to the City Palace, elegant home of Jaipur's maharajas, founded by Jai Singh II. Visitors can enter via two side gates on the east side of the palace to view opulent interiors and extravagant royal heirlooms. Being mostly on one level, it's one of the most wheelchair-friendly sights in the city.

DON'T MISS

- Mubarak Mahal
- Painting & Photography Gallery
- Armoury
- Sarvato Bhadra
- Pritam Niwas Chowk
- Chandra Mahal

Mubarak Mahal

The main public admission to the City Palace is via the eastern gateway, known as Virendra Pol, on the lane running behind Tripolia Bazaar. You'll enter a vast, open courtyard dominated by the **Mubarak Mahal** (Welcome Palace), built in the late 19th century for Maharaja Madho Singh II to receive visiting dignitaries.

A stylistic stew of Islamic, Rajput and European ideas, it was designed by British architect Sir Swinton Jacob. Today, it forms part of the Maharaja Sawai Mansingh II Museum, displaying a superb collection of royal *choga* and *atamsukh* robes and other ceremonial outfits, including the capricious clothing of Sawai Madho Singh I (it's said he was 2m tall, 1.2m wide and weighed in at 250kg).

PRACTICALITIES

citypalace.org • adult/child or student ₹1010/510; composite ticket including Jaigarh ₹1260/660; guides from ₹400 • 9.30am-6.30pm (night opening 6.30-7.30pm)

Painting & Photography Gallery

Off the courtyard is the Maharaja Sawai Bhawani Singh building, displaying a fascinating collection of historic paintings – many daubed with real gold paint. Alongside deity paintings and cloth maps of medieval cities, old photos depict Jaipur's royal life, including snaps taken by early adopter of technology Sawai Ram Singh II in the 19th century.

The Armoury

In the courtyard's northwestern corner, the Anand Mahal Sileg Khana, formerly the Maharani's Palace, houses the bristling royal armoury. Kids will be gruesomely fascinated by the elaborately decorated guns, knives, talwar swords, clubs, maces and katar punch-daggers – a favoured weapon for Rajasthani royals. Check if the armoury is open; it closed for renovations in 2025.

Savarto Bhadra

A filigree, elephant-guarded white marble gateway leads on to the second courtyard containing the Sarvato Bhadra, a marble-paved pavilion that was used as the Diwan-i-Khas (Hall of Private Audience), where the maharajas consulted their ministers. Decorated with floral motifs in white and sandstone pink, the pavilion contains two enormous silver ewers – reputedly the largest silver objects in the world – full of holy water from the Ganges.

Sabha Niwas

East of the Sarvato Bhadra, a doorway leads to the lavish Sabha Niwas, an extravagant, chandelier-lit state room decked out with thrones, royal treasures and portraits of past maharajas, which served as the maharaja's Hall of Public Audiences. The same courtyard contains the **Rath Khana**, displaying howdahs (elephant saddles), palanquins and elephant armour.

Pritam Niwas Chowk

West of the Sarvato Bhadra, a gateway leads to Pritam Niwas Chowk – an open courtyard flanked by four glorious gates representing the seasons. The Peacock Gate (Varsha Deori) depicts autumn, the Lotus Gate (Grishma Deori) signifies summer, the Green Gate (Vasanta Deori) represents spring, and the Rose Gate (Sharad Deori) embodies winter.

Chandra Mahal

Beyond Pritam Niwas Chowk is the private palace, the Chandra Mahal, the wedding-cake residence of the present royal family. You can take a special 45-minute Royal Tour of selected areas for ₹5000/3000 (adult/child). For a taste of royal living to take home, the **Princess Diya Kumari Foundation** *(princessdiyakumarifoundation.org)* shop sells stylish clothes and homewares, supporting disadvantaged women.

GUIDES & TOURS

Official guides *(from ₹400)* and audioguides *(₹200)* are available to point out the palace's most fascinating features. It's worth taking a guide, if only to discourage the turbaned palace attendants, who can be a little overbearing in their enthusiasm to pose for photos for tips. To access the chambers used by the present generation of the royal family, book onto a pricy Royal Tour.

TOP TIPS

- Come early to avoid crowds. Try try to be first through the doors when the palace opens at 9.30am.
- Buy a composite ticket (valid for two days) for entry to the City Palace, the royal cenotaphs and the Jaigarh fortress at Amber.
- Recharge at the palace's stylish Baradari (p118) restaurant, serving cocktails and globe-trotting menus (including royal Rajasthani cuisine), or the **Gallery Cafe** atop the Savarto Bhadra.
- See the palace in a different light by visiting at night, from 6.30pm to 7.30pm.
- Combine a visit to the City Palace with a turn around the Jantar Manta observatory (p117) across the road.

A JAIPUR OLD CITY WALK

Get the measure of Jaipur on this Old City stroll.

START	END	LENGTH
New Gate	New Gate	5km; 2hr

Enter the Old City at 1 **New Gate**, and follow fabric-filled Bapu Bazaar east past the nostalgic 2 **Golcha Cinema**. At 3 **Sanganeri Gate**, turn north into 4 **Johari Bazaar**, lined with fancy frontages and silversmiths producing fancy *meenakari* (enamelwork). Duck into the vividly colourful 5 **fruit and veg market**, grab a sweet treat at 6 **Laxmi Misthan Bhandar** (p119) or a lassi on 7 **Gopal Ji Ka Rasta**, then pass the minarets of the 8 **Jama Masjid**. Cross temple-ringed 9 **Badi Chaupar** to reach the fantasy frontage of the 10 **Hawa Mahal** (p110).

Just north, a doorway leads to the filigree-fronted 11 **Sri Ram Chandra Ji temple** and, beyond, the 18th-century 12 **Kalki Mandir**, with its statue of the horse mount of the future Vishnu. Cross the road and peek through the 13 **Sireh Deori** gateway at a succession of arches leading to the City Palace.

Return to Badi Chaupar and turn west onto 14 **Tripolia Bazaar**, passing 15 **Tripolia Gate**, the maharajas' private palace entrance. Get an overview from atop the 16 **Isarlat minaret** (p121). Continuing west, peek at the bangle market on 17 **Maniharon ka Rasta**, and sniff along spice-scented 18 **Chandpole Bazaar**. Turn left into 19 **Khajane Walon ka Rasta**, admiring the gleaming white deities in the marble-carving workshops. Wind up by following clothing-centred 20 **Indira Bazaar** back to New Gate.

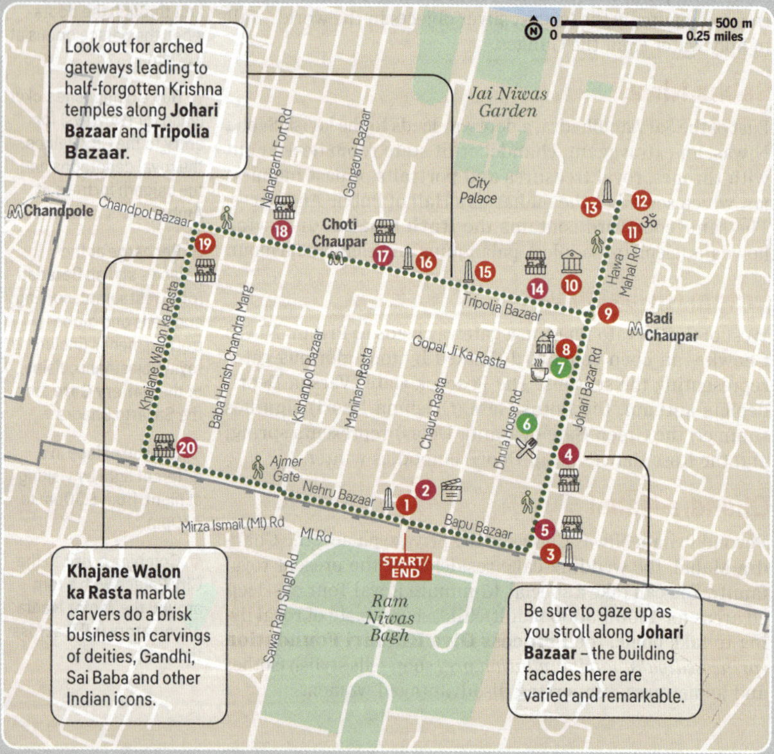

Continued from p111

The entrance is on an alley running north from Tripolia Bazaar, but you can also get here via a passageway just north of the palace on Hawa Mahal Rd, beside the pink, courtyard-style **Sri Goverdhan Nath Temple**. Visit with a two-day composite ticket, which also covers the Amber Fort, Central Museum, Jantar Mantar, Isarlat and Narhargarh.

Unleash Your Inner Astronomer at Jantar Mantar

MAP P118

A royal fantasy, with a purpose

Southeast of the City Palace, the fascinating **Jantar Mantar** *(tourism.rajasthan.gov.in/jantar-mantar.html; adult/student ₹202/102, composite ticket ₹1102/552)* was constructed in 1728 as an astronomical observatory, on the orders of the scientifically curious Jai Singh II. Anyone with a scientific leaning will love investigating this collection of curious objects, used to measure the movements of celestial bodies.

The name comes from Sanskrit *yantra mantrana* ('instrument of calculation'). Stairs to nowhere climb over calibrated crescents, dangling disks and rings form giant astrolabes, and marble-lined basins allow precise calculations of the movements of the spheres. The Laghu Samrat Yantra – a supersized sundial – can measure the time accurately to within 20 seconds (you can test it, if the sun is shining).

Elsewhere, small structures track the constellations of the zodiac, while the enormous Samrat Yantra soars skywards, measuring the movement of the sun. A guide *(from ₹400)* is highly recommended if you want to learn how each fascinating instrument works, or read up on the instruments at *jantarmantar.org*. The site is best explored on a composite two-day ticket.

Soak in Jaipur's Spiritual Side

MAP P118

Understand the city through its temples

The Old City has dozens of courtyard-style temples, all free to visit. However, many stand quiet as the city's religious attention is captured by the huge **Govind Dev Ji temple** *(donations appropriate)* behind the City Palace. Constructed by Maharaja Jai Singh II in the 18th century, it enshrines a particularly sacred Krishna image, drawing pilgrims day and night.

After visiting, grab sweets or a veg snack at **Govindam**, just north of the entrance. South of the palace, the often

BEST MARKETS

The Old City of Jaipur is one big marketplace, but every area has its own specialties.

Hawa Mahal Bazaar: Packed with souvenirs, but a little haggling is required.

Nehru Bazaar and Bapu Bazaar: Full of purveyors of *jooti* slippers and block-printed bedding and clothes.

Johari Bazaar: Lined with silversmiths and goldsmiths selling jewellery, tiny deity statues and *meenakari* enamelwork.

Chandpole Bazaar: Good for wholesale spices and tea, and paraphernalia for home shrines.

Maniharon ka Rasta: An alleyway crammed with vendors of multi-hued *lac* (resin) bangles.

Khajane Walon ka Rasta: Jaipur's marble-workers' bazaar, selling small statuettes and carved stone bowls as well as too-big-to-carry statues.

Kishanpole Bazaar: The city's central hub for bikes, toys and paper kites.

DRINKING IN JAIPUR: REFRESHMENT STOPS

MAPS P111 & P118

Crazy Coffee: Small, cosy and calm, in a handy location near the Hawa Mahal; stop in for a sandwich and latte. *9am-11.30pm*

Stepout Cafe: A low-key locals' hangout with a calm garden and lots of hot and cold-brewed coffee options, south of Statue Circle. *7.30am-10.30pm*

Curious Life: A cool stop for light lunches and hip coffees, served in reusable steel cups; there's a branch nearby, opposite the Deer Park. *9am-10pm*

Anokhi Cafe: The cafe at the swish Anokhi store is a peaceful option for coffees, lunchtime salads and healthy plates. *10am-7.30pm*

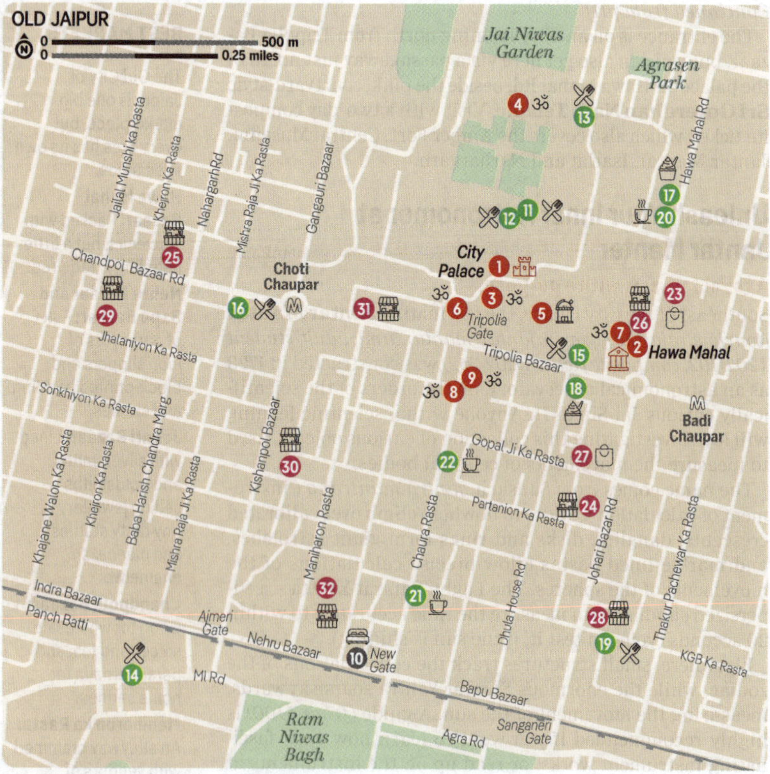

HIGHLIGHTS
1 City Palace
2 Hawa Mahal

SIGHTS
3 Anand Krishna Bihari Ji Temple
4 Govind Dev Ji Temple
5 Jantar Mantar
6 Sri Brij Nidhi Temple
7 Sri Goverdhan Nath Temple
8 Sri Radha Damodar Temple
9 Tarkeshwar Mahadev Temple

SLEEPING
10 Hotel Sweet Dream

EATING
11 Baradari
12 Gallery Cafe
13 Govindam
see 10 Hotel Sweet Dream
14 Indian Coffee House
15 Lala Ji Pakodi Wale
16 Mahaveer Rabri
17 Pandit Kulfi
18 Ramchandra Kulfi Bhandar
19 The Johri

DRINKING & NIGHTLIFE
20 Crazy Coffee
21 Sahu Chai Wala
22 Samrat

SHOPPING
23 Agora
24 Bapu Bazaar
25 Chandpole Bazaar
26 Hawa Mahal Bazaar
27 International Gem Testing Laboratory
28 Johari Bazaar
29 Khajane Walon ka Rasta
30 Kishanpole Bazaar
31 Maniharon ka Rasta
32 Nehru Bazaar

EATING IN JAIPUR: UPMARKET MEALS

MAPS P111 & P118

The Johri: Dine on spectacular vegetarian Rajasthani cooking in a super-classy *haveli* off Johari Bazaar; book ahead. *1-4.30pm & 7.30-11pm* ₹₹₹

Baradari: The courtyard restaurant at the City Palace offers stylish eats in palatial surroundings; book and dress up for dinner. *11am-11pm* ₹₹₹

Suvarna Mahal: The elegant, Renaissance-style dining room at the Rambagh Palace serves an Indian menu fit for royalty. *7-11.45pm* ₹₹₹

Peacock Rooftop Restaurant: Expect heavy demand for tables and fine Indian food atop the Hotel Pearl Palace; evenings bring live music. *7.30am-11pm* ₹₹₹

overlooked **Anand Krishna Bihari Ji Temple** and **Sri Brijnidhi Temple** were constructed by Maharaja Sawai Pratap Singh in the 1840s.

For a morning dose of spirituality, visit the busy **Tarkeshwar Mahadev Temple** – a rare Shaivite temple in Jaipur – where pilgrims offer flowers and pour water over timeworn Shiva lingams (phallic symbols). Across the road is the raised, courtyard-style **Sri Radha Damodar Temple**, devoted to Radha Krishna.

Take a City Tour

MAP P111

See more of Jaipur

To get under the surface of the Pink City, the **Rajasthan Tourism Development Corporation (RTDC) Transport Unit** *(rtdc.tourism.rajasthan.gov.in)* at Hotel Gangaur on Sanjay Marg offers slightly rushed full-day tours of central sights and Amber *(₹600 per person)*, and Pink City by Night tours (*₹1000*), with dinner at Nahargarh fort. However, trips only run if there are enough bookings.

For something more offbeat, various operators run tours of Jaipur in vintage vehicles. Hotel Pearl Palace (p184; *hotelpearlpalace.com; ₹5000 per vehicle)* zooms sightseers around in a WWII jeep; tours run 9am to 5.30pm, with room for four.

Alternatively, propel yourself around on two wheels with the gregarious guides from **Cyclin' Jaipur** *(cyclinjaipur.com; tours from ₹2500)*, based at the Hotel Bissau Palace. Fun-filled cycling and walking tours (there are loads of interesting options) focus on local life, visiting street food stalls, markets and the homes of local families as well as the sights. Cycling trips start early in the morning to beat the traffic.

Eccentric Exhibits in a Local Landmark

MAP P111

Admire the quirky exhibits at the Central Museum

From a distance, Jaipur's **Central Museum** *(Albert Hall; entry ₹302, composite ticket ₹1102)* looks more like a temple or palace, thanks to the whimsy of architect Sir Swinton Jacob, who designed this Indo-Saracenic masterpiece in 1887.

The museum would be worth visiting just for the architecture and the pre-Raphaelite-inspired friezes of world cultures on the walls, but the collection is impressive. Allow an hour to wander the galleries of tribal costumes, Rajasthani instruments, glinting jewellery, medieval weapons, miniature paintings and sculptures.

Don't miss the deity-covered ornamental shields recreating

JAIPUR SOUVENIRS

Jaipur is a shopper's paradise, particularly if you're in the market for jewellery, block-printed textiles (or printing blocks), enamelware, jootis (slippers), marble carvings or handmade puppets. Prepare to bargain for a fair price.

The road in front of the Hawa Mahal has the greatest concentration of souvenir shops, plus **Agora**, an upmarket store and cafe selling gifts with real design flair. More enormous souvenir emporiums line the road to Amber – often paying commissions to autorickshaw drivers who bring in customers.

For fair, fixed prices, try government-owned **Rajasthali** opposite Ajmeri Gate. Upmarket block-printed clothes and homewares are sold at chic **Anokhi** on Prithviraj Marg, and **FabIndia** by the corner of Krishna Marg and Ashok Marg.

EATING IN JAIPUR: TRAVELLER-FRIENDLY STOPS

MAPS P111 & P118

Hotel Sweet Dream: Perched above the Nehru Bazaar hotel of the same name, serving tasty veg curries and cold beers. *7am-11pm* ₹₹

Rawat Kachori: Crispy, well-stuffed kachori (fried pastries) and other savoury snacks to go; conveniently close to the bus stand. *6.30am-10.30pm* ₹

Laxmi Misthan Bhandar: This famous snack vendor's air-con eatery is great for big veg lunches and dinners in peaceful surroundings. *8am-11.30pm* ₹₹

Jaipur Modern Kitchen: Cool, contemporary and popular with the chatty lunch set, serving healthy plates with Mediterranean influences. *8am-11pm* ₹₹₹

GEM SHOPPING 101

Jaipur is famous for precious and semiprecious stones, and many local jewellers offer bargain prices – or a big mark-up for low-grade stones, if you don't know what you're buying. The main gem-dealing area is the Islamic quarter of Pahar Ganj, southeast of the Old City, where you can see stones being cut and polished. Examine gemstones carefully before you buy and be wary of the infamous gem scam, where tourists are fooled into buying overpriced or fake gems with claims they can be sold for a profit at home. Jaipur has several dedicated gem-testing laboratories such as **International Gem Testing Laboratory** *(igtlj.com)* on Gopal Ji Ka Rasta where you can get your stones checked for peace of mind.

ROHINI VACHHER/SHUTTERSTOCK

Jhalana Leopard Reserve

scenes from the Hindu epics and clay figurines of yogis in poses. Visit on the same two-day composite ticket as Amber Palace.

If you're interested in Jaipur's rich jewellery traditions, make an appointment to view the **Museum of Meenakari Heritage** *(MOMH; momhindia.org; free)*, set in a modernist *haveli* and devoted to the city's elegant enamelwork, or the **Amrapali Museum** *(amrapalimuseum.com; ₹600)*, packed with tribal jewellery and art.

Splendid Royal Memorials

Pay your respects to departed royals

Tucked into a green gully below the walls of Nahargarh fort, **Gatore ki Chhatriyan** *(Royal Gaitor; ₹50)* is a regal collection of carved marble *chhatris* – funerary pavilions, topped by handsome domed shelters, built for departed maharajas. The grandest cenotaph commemorates Jai Singh II, but Sawai Pratap Singh and Madho Singh II also have impressive memorials.

Reflecting the gender divisions of the time, Jaipur's maharanis (queens) took their final curtain call in the quieter **Cenotaphs of the Maharanis** *(₹50)*. You'll see more chipmunks and birds than tourists in this peaceful garden of fading *chhatris* on the road to Amber. Both cenotaph complexes are covered by the City Palace composite ticket.

EATING & DRINKING IN JAIPUR: SNACK STOPS

MAPS P111 & P118

Laxmi Misthan Bhandar Sweets: The takeaway snack counter at the LMB Hotel is a treasure trove of sweet and savoury treats. *7am-11.30pm* ₹

Lala Ji Pakodi Wale: A celebrated street-food stand near the alley to the Hawa Mahal, great for kachori, *pakora* (veg fritters) and other fried goodies. *6am-11pm* ₹

Pandit Kulfi: This celebrated *kulfi* (Indian ice cream) stop near the Hawa Mahal doles out a mouthwatering array of flavours. *noon-11.30pm* ₹

Lassiwala: A legendary lassi vendor at 312 MI Rd, much copied but never beaten, serving Jaipur's creamiest lassis in ceramic *kulhad* cups. *6am-4pm* ₹

Epic City Vistas

MAP P111

Get an eagle-eye view over Jaipur

For sweeping views, several elevated viewpoints are accessible using the same two-day composite ticket that covers Amber Fort.

The rocky buttress to the north of the Old City is crowned by the imposing **Nahargarh** *(tourism.rajasthan.gov.in/nahargarh-fort.html; adult/student ₹205/102, composite ticket ₹1102/552)*, Jaipur's third great fortress. Founded in 1734, it was named after prince Nahar Singh, whose restless ghost reputedly demanded the honour in exchange for leaving the fortress in peace.

Inside are several tacky waxworks-style attractions, old wells and the empty but still elegant chambers of the **Sri Madhvendra Bhawan** palace, adorned with floral motifs and murals of royals on elephant-back. Climb to the roof for dizzying views over Jaipur.

Most arrive by taxi or rickshaw (note that the road is too steep for electric rickshaws), but you can also climb to the fort along a 2km path from the end of Nahargarh Rd.

For views downtown, climb to the top of **Isarlat** *(adult/student ₹205/102, composite ticket ₹1102/552)* – the 'Heaven-Piercing Minaret' – accessed from the Aatish hardware market north of Tripolia Bazaar. This ceremonial tower was erected in the 1740s by Sawai Iswari Singh, and it gazes over the Old City bazaars and the City Palace.

Spot a Leopard

Big cats in the suburbs

Jaipur's urban sprawl breaks down into scrubby forest at the city fringes, providing a home for nilgai, monkeys, myriad birds, hyenas and a healthy population of leopards. The Rajasthan Forest Department offers morning and afternoon 4WD safaris in search of these iconic big cats at two sites – **Jhalana Leopard Reserve**, about 11km southeast of central Jaipur, and **Amargarh Leopard Reserve**, about 8km east of the centre off the road to Galta Ji (p122).

The chances of spotting a leopard at either reserve are good, but morning mist can make sightings harder in winter. You can book safaris at both sites online *(obms-tourist.rajasthan.gov.in/place-details/Jhalana-Leopard-Reserve; safari from ₹2000)*, but it's easier to make a booking through your hotel, as they can arrange return transport to the reserves.

GET YOUR MONEY'S WORTH FROM JAIPUR

With so much to see in Jaipur, the cost of entry fees can mount up, but help is at hand. The city offers several excellent 'composite' tickets covering multiple attractions for a discounted price, valid for two days.

The most useful ticket covers Amber Fort, the Jantar Mantar, the Hawa Mahal, the Central Museum, the Isarlat minaret, Nahargarh fort and the Sisodia Rani Ka Bagh garden. A second composite ticket covers the City Palace, Jaigarh fort and the royal cenotaphs.

You'll have to zip around to see everything in two days so make full use of the city's inexpensive autorickshaws, or order rides on Uber or Ola. Take a conventional autorickshaw to reach the Nahargarh and Jaigarh forts (electric rickshaws struggle with the gradient).

EATING IN JAIPUR: MEALS ON MI RD

MAPS P111 & P118

Indian Coffee House: Agreeably institutional, serving tasty South Indian veg breakfasts, lunches and tiffin (snacks) plus strong coffee. *8am-9pm* ₹

Niro's: Established in 1949, licensed, slightly lost-in-time and great for veg and non-veg Indian, Chinese and continental fare. *noon-4pm & 6-11pm* ₹₹₹

Old Takeaway the Kebab Shop: A veteran of the long-established non-veg scene on MI Rd; come for quality tandoori chicken and other meaty treats. *1-11pm* ₹₹

Handi Restaurant: There's a lively buzz at this busy grill-house, known for its sublime lamb and chicken tikka and butter chicken. *noon-11pm* ₹₹₹

OLD CITY TIPS

Raju Meena, guide for Cyclin' Jaipur, shares his tips for exploring the Old City.

Take time in between exploring the sights to see the locals' Jaipur. After wandering around the Hawa Mahal, drop into the **Shri Ram Chandra Ji Temple**, then cross Tripolia Bazaar for tasty *kulfi* at **Ramchandra Kulfi Bhandar**, or try the *rabri* (condensed milk) at **Mahaveer Rabri**, just past Chhoti Chaupar.

If you come to Amber (where I live), explore beyond the palaces. Visit the **Sri Jagat Shiromani Ji Temple** and **Panna Meena step-well**, then climb to the fort-like **Shri Badrinath Ji Temple** for views over the whole of Amber (best at sunset or sunrise). With more time, you can walk on to Sagar lake, below Jaigarh fort.

ALEXANTON/SHUTTERSTOCK

Galta Ji

Take a Sunset Stroll at Jal Mahal

Enjoy sublime palace views

Hemmed in by warehouse-sized souvenir shops on the road to Amber, peaceful Man Sagar lake is thronged by birdlife, including grey and pond herons, shags, egrets and black-winged stilts. It's most famous, however, as the setting for the **Jal Mahal**, a delicate, floating royal pavilion.

Currently closed to visitors, the building was constructed in the 1690s and later restored by Maharaja Jai Singh II. It's particularly appealing at sunset, when the palace is illuminated and the lakeshore is taken over by a family-friendly bazaar. There have long been rumours that the palace will open to visitors – ask locally to see if anything has changed.

Meet the Monkeys of Galta

Simian encounters in a sacred gorge

East of the Old City, a gateway on National Hwy 248 marks the start of the track to the rocky gorge at **Galta Ji** *(donations appropriate)*, where pilgrims ritually bathe in a deep sacred tank, filled by a natural spring that emerges through a cow's mouth spout.

Beyond lie two worn but intricately frescoed courtyard temples, sacred to different incarnations of Vishnu. Galta is known as the Monkey Temple and mobs of macaques and langurs run riot around the complex (keep foodstuffs out of sight).

You can get here from Galta Gate, via a 1km walk (or a ₹300 motorcycle taxi ride), passing the 18th-century, shikhara-style **Surya Mandir**. The gleaming new **Arihant Vatika** Jain temple across from Galta Gate is alive with intricate marble carvings.

Alternatively, take a rickshaw to Galta's rear entrance, stopping into the serene **Sisodia Rani Ka Bagh** *(adult/student ₹205/102, composite ticket ₹1102/552)* – a garden of frangipani trees spilling behind the (closed) palace where Maharaja Sawai Madho Singh was born.

See More of Amber

Bonus forts and backstreet temples

The ridge above Amber Fort (p112) is dominated by the imposing **Jaigarh fortress** *(adult/child ₹500/250, covered by City Palace composite ticket)*, where the royals retreated (via a hidden tunnel) when Amber was in danger. Tall watchtowers guard the walls and a succession of worn palace courtyards lead to a romantic garden fronted by three huge archways overlooking the valley.

Also here is the imposing Jai Vana – the world's largest wheeled canon. Cast and drilled at the fort's foundry, this 50-tonne monster required 100kg of gunpowder to fire, with a range of 30km.

Returning to Amber village, head to the market just beyond the fort ticket complex. Winding alleys lead west past the fort's elephant stables, the ornate, early-17th-century **Sri Jagat Shiromani Ji Temple** and the **Panna Meena** stepwell with fine geometric stairways. All are free to visit.

Nearby is the **Anokhi Museum of Hand Printing** *(anokhi museum.com; entry ₹80; closed Monday)*, an intriguing space in a restored *haveli* where you can learn about the history of Rajasthani block-printing, see printers at work and even print your own scarf, bag or T-shirt.

Festival Time in Jaipur

A packed festival calendar

It's worth planning your trip to coincide with one of Jaipur's big cultural events. In mid-January, the skies fill with kites for **Makar Sankranti**; grab a paper kite and reel from one of the kite shops on Kishanpole Bazaar and join the fun.

Also in January, the **Jaipur Literature Festival** *(jai purliteraturefestival.org)* brings the cream of global literary talent to Jaipur for readings, interviews and talks. In March, this proudly Vaishnavite city pulls out the stops for **Rama Navami**, with processions and temple ceremonies to honour Rama.

JAIPUR'S RULING DYNASTY

The maharajas of Jaipur were the most prominent of the Rajput royal families who ruled vast areas of Rajasthan as independent states, before the Mughals and British curtailed their powers. According to legend, the Kachwaha rulers of Jaipur were descended from Kusha, son of the Hindu god Rama, but the clan's verifiable history is patchy before Dulha Rai in the 11th century. With its royal seat at Amber, the kingdom struggled until Raja Bharmal aligned himself with the Mughals, marrying his daughter to Akbar and helping the emperor dramatically expand his empire. As Mughal power waned, Maharaja Sawai Jai Singh II rebelled and reclaimed his now wealthy kingdom, founding Jaipur as his new capital in 1727.

DRINKING IN JAIPUR: BEST BARS

MAP P111

Native Cocktail Room: The bar at the Hotel Pearl Palace is a great spot to swap travel tales over a cocktail or three. *6pm-midnight*

Forresta Kitchen & Bar: International plates and quality house beers in a tree-dotted garden or rooftop terrace (continue the party next door at Downtown Jaipur). *noon-midnight*

Bar Palladio: The porcelain blue bar at the Narain Niwas Palace oozes elegance and heritage chic; sip indoors or outdoors by candlelight. *4-11pm Mon-Sat, from 1pm Sun*

Polo Bar: Imagine you're shooting pool with maharajas in the swanky, atmospheric bar at Rambagh Palace. *noon-11.45pm*

Beyond Jaipur

The dry country north and east of Jaipur hides historic royal towns, painted mansions and the state's best wildlife reserves.

Places

GETTING AROUND

Alwar and Bharatpur are easily reached from Jaipur by train in three to four hours (the most comfortable option) but crowded local buses run regularly to both towns from Jaipur's RSRTC (Sindhi Camp) bus stand. Ranthambore National Park is awkward to reach by bus, but trains between Jaipur and Delhi or Agra stop at Sawai Madhopur on the edge of the reserve. Get to Sariska from nearby Alwar.

North and east of Jaipur, you'll find some of the state's most and least visited sights. Ranthambore National Park, with its tiger-stalked forests and fortress, is one of India's most popular national parks, while overlooked former royal capitals dot the surrounding plains, alongside some remarkable ruins – including the awesome Chand Baori step-well at Abhaneri.

For nature enthusiasts, Keoladeo National Park and Sariska Tiger Reserve – accessible from Bharatpur and Alwar respectively – offer rewarding encounters with myriad Indian wildlife species, including a kaleidoscope of native and migratory birds.

Getting around this region can be a little convoluted – local buses and branch-line railways connect most towns, but Ranthambore is best visited using long-distance trains between Jaipur and Delhi or Agra.

Bharatpur & Keoladeo National Park

TIME FROM JAIPUR: **3-4HR**

India's best winter birding

South of the dusty town of Bharatpur, a gateway off an anonymous highway marks the entrance to one of Asia's most spectacular birding sites. **Keoladeo National Park** *(05644-222777; entry ₹959, guide from ₹800, bike hire ₹100, autorickshaw tour ₹800)* is a vital breeding and feeding ground for more than 370 bird species, including migrants crossing India from Afghanistan, Turkmenistan, China and Siberia.

During the cooler winter months, a third of the park's 29 sq km can be inundated by floodwaters, luring everything from herons and kingfishers to bar-headed geese, sarus and demoiselle cranes, spoonbills, eagles and flamingos.

Enjoying this richness of birdlife is a highly sustainable activity. Pay the entry fee and walk into the reserve, or explore by rented bicycle or chartered electric autorickshaw, with or without a guide.

Intriguing royal ruins

Dusty but delightful **Bharatpur** was the once-regal capital of the Sinsinwar dynasty, who ruled from the dilapidated, moat-ringed **Lohagarh** *(free)*, or Iron Fort. Enter via the southern

Lohiya Gate to reach the **Sri Bankey Bihari Ji Temple**, thronged by local women at sunset.

Just beyond is the timeworn **Kishori Mahal** palace. You can enter with a ticket for the **Bharatpur Government Museum** *(₹102; closed Mon)*, set inside a second imposing palace 100m further north. The lower levels feature ancient temple carvings and an impressive *hammam* bathhouse, while royal treasures are displayed upstairs in the **Kamra Khaas**, a graceful, jade-green hall with doors adorned with paintings of European ladies and gentlemen.

Maharaja Suraj Mal, who raised the fort in the 18th century, constructed the nearby **Jawahar Burj** tower *(free)* to commemorate his successes against the Mughals.

Follow the bazaars west of the Lohiya Gate to reach the palatial 19th-century **Sri Ganga Maharani Ji Temple**, whose patron goddess is the personification of the River Ganges. Further west are the imposing **Jama Masjid** and **Laxman Mandir**, built during the same period; all are free to visit.

Deeg

TIME FROM JAIPUR: **4-5HR**

Discover a sublimely graceful palace

A 35km bus-ride north of Bharatpur, sleepy Deeg is dominated by the elegant **palace of Suraj Mal** *(Deeg Bhawans; ₹300; closed Fri)*, the 18th-century ruler of Bharatpur, who overran the garrison at Agra and even marched on Delhi in the 1760s.

Bookended by the vast Gopal Sagar and Rup Sagar tanks, this beautifully proportioned palace is surrounded by formal gardens, fountains and trees full of roosting fruit bats. Behind, **Deeg Fort** (show your passport to enter) offers great views from its canon-topped bastions.

Overlooking Gopal Sagar, the 18th-century Gopal Bhavan contains the royal family's lounge – full of faded furniture, wildlife trophies and mechanically operated *punkahs* (fans). Upstairs is a remarkable oval marble dining table, set just 20cm off the ground.

The marble arch in front of the Gopal Bhavan once held the royal swing of Nur Jahan, wife of Jehangir, seized during Suraj Mal's raid on Delhi. To the south are the elegant, black-and-white-marble Suraj Bhavan, and the triple-winged Hardev Bhavan building, once reserved for the royal *zenana* (harem).

Moving anticlockwise around the gardens, you'll reach the Kishan Bhavan, with more faded heirlooms, and the curious Keshav Bhavan (Monsoon Pavilion), with an ingenious

RAJASTHAN'S RULING DYNASTIES

The maharajas of Jaipur were perhaps the most ambitious and successful of the many Rajput royal families who ruled vast areas of Rajasthan as independent states. Claiming lineage from Kusha, son of the Hindu god Rama, the Kachhwaha clan formed a tight strategic alliance with the Mughals when princess Mariam-uz-Zamani married Akbar in 1562, serving as loyal generals under a succession of emperors.

But they had many rivals. The Mewar dynasty of Chittorgarh (and later Udaipur) dominated the Aravalli Hills to the south, while the Marwar dynasty of Jodhpur ruled the western Thar Desert. Closer to Jaipur, tiny Bharatpur state was ruled by the enigmatic Suraj Mal, who maintained capitals at Deeg and Bharatpur, and famously captured Agra in 1761 and Old Delhi in 1763.

EATING IN BHARATPUR & ALWAR: OUR PICKS

Mama Chicken: A branch of the celebrated Agra grill-house, serving kebabs, tandoori chicken (of course) and 'frankies' (kathi rolls). *11am-10.30pm* ₹₹

Hotel Sunbird Restaurant: Nonguests can book in to enjoy the buffet or order from the menu at the restaurant at Bharatpur's Hotel Sunbird. *7am-10pm* ₹₹

Prem Pavitra Bhojnalaya: An Alwar legend serving buttery dhal fry, *palak paneer* and *kheer*. *10.30am-4pm & 6.30-10pm* ₹

Heaven's Shakes: A lively stop for Alwar's hip young things, serving shakes, coffee, cakes and quality dosas and other veg meals. *11am-midnight* ₹₹

ABHANERI'S EPIC STEP-WELL

One of the most enduring features of Indian medieval architecture is the *baori*, or step-well, designed with a cascade of geometric steps and terraces to allow access to water stored from the annual monsoon rains all year round, even when water levels were low. Many *baori* doubled as ceremonial centres, with built-in temples and pavilions for visiting royals and dignitaries. In Rajasthan, one of the most impressive wells is the 8th-century **Chand Baori** *(entry ₹300)*, midway between Jaipur and Alwar, easily reached by chartered car or on a tour. Its sculptural steps drop 20m, and nearby is the ruined 7th-century Harshat Mata Temple, ransacked by Mahmud of Ghazni, who hacked the faces off every deity carving.

mechanism that used jets of water and rolling stone balls to imitate the rain and thunder of the monsoon. On the north side of the compound, the Nand Bhavan features some impressive murals on its supporting columns.

Alwar

TIME FROM JAIPUR: **3-4HR**

Under-explored historic charmer

Inexplicably overlooked by most visitors to Rajasthan, charming Alwar was the capital for a succession of Hindu rulers, including Hemchandra Vikramaditya, who briefly drove the Mughals from Delhi in 1556.

Northwest of the centre, the wonderfully eccentric **Alwar Museum** (*₹105*) is set in the Wedgwood-blue upper levels of the former City Palace, now taken over by government offices and scurrying civil servants. Admire the collection of royal treasures, from ivory ornaments to crocodile-skin shields, then take the stairs just west to reach an astonishingly photogenic tank edged by turreted pavilions and ghats (ceremonial steps).

Above it rises the imposing **Moosi Rani ki Chhatri** *(free)*, the lavish sandstone and marble cenotaph of Maharaja Bakhtawar Singh, renamed for one of his concubines who died on his funeral pyre.

The surrounding lanes are filled with historic temples and royal administrative buildings. Follow Bajaja Bazaar Rd and an arcade of silversmiths east to the colourful **Ram temple** atop the Hope Circus roundabout.

Behind the City Palace, the **Bala Quila fort** (currently closed) hosted Babur, Akbar and the Jehangir, who was exiled here for three years. Unfortunately the access road was destroyed by heavy rain in 2025; check to see if visits are possible.

The fort sits inside a section of Sariska Tiger Reserve & National Park; you can arrange morning and afternoon 4WD trips in search of the park's leopards and tigers.

Sariska Tiger Reserve

TIME FROM JAIPUR: **4HR**

Spot abundant wildlife – and maybe a tiger

Enclosed within the folded Aravalli Hills, **Sariska Tiger Reserve & National Park** (*obms-tourist.rajasthan.gov.in/place-details/Sariska-Tiger-Reserve; safari by 4WD/canter from ₹2100/1700; closed Wed*) is a sweep of craggy canyons sheltering a handful of tigers and leopards and plenty of peacocks, monkeys, boar, birds and deer.

EATING AROUND RANTHAMBORE: OUR PICKS

Shabri Mithaas: The bakery at the Anuraga Palace Hotel serves tasty organic sweets, biscuits and cakes – great for a mid-morning pick-me-up. *8am-8pm* ₹

Ranthambhore Chopati: A cheerful covered food court on the national park approach road, with all sorts of drinks and North and South Indian meals. *10am-11pm* ₹

Fateh's Cafe: A stylish option with an international menu in a vintage bungalow, named for a famous guide and set in a pretty garden. *11am-10pm* ₹₹

Oberoi Vanyavilas Restaurant: This sleek hotel restaurant is the place to come for a five-star feast surrounded by tiger murals. *7am-10.45pm* ₹₹₹

Moosi Rani ki Chhatri, Alwar

Morning and afternoon safaris leave from the park headquarters at the Sariska Gate, but locals also drive in by car to visit the park's revered Hanuman Temple. Book safaris ahead via the official website or through Alwar hotels (you can get here on the Alwar to Jaipur bus).

Ruined forts ring the reserve, including the notorious **Bhangarh** *(entry ₹200)*, founded in 1631 by Madho Singh then mysteriously abandoned. It's said to be the most haunted place in India.

For an interesting overnight stop, **Sariska Lodge** *(sariska lodge.com)* offers secluded cabins dotted around a serene garden near ruined Tehla Fort.

Ranthambore National Park

TIME FROM JAIPUR: **2-3HR**

Spotting tiger stripes

Easily reached by train from Delhi, Agra or Jaipur, **Ranthambore** *(booking.forestrajasthan.com; safari by 4WD/canter from ₹3950/3350)* is one of India's most popular national parks, thanks to famous photos of tigers roaming around its Rajput ruins.

Spilling to the edges of the town of **Sawai Madhopur**, the park is home to huge numbers of chitals, sambar, nilgai and birds, but the resident tigers and leopards can be elusive. Thanks to a slightly haphazard monitoring system, the tiger population is thought to number somewhere between 60 and 88.

Safari operators are granted access to safari zones on a rotating roster. Zone 3, with its hunting lodge ruins and pools that lure tigers and prey, is the most sought-after slot. Zones 1–5 are closed Wednesdays and Zones 6–10 are closed Tuesdays. Safaris by Gypsy (4WD) offer better chances than crowded *canters* (open-topped buses).

INDIA'S MOST LAVISH TRAIN

Ranthambore National Park and Bharatpur are just two of the stops visited by Rajasthan's most famous luxury train. The **Palace on Wheels** *(palaceonwheels.in)* follows a week-long circuit from Delhi around Rajasthan, visiting Jaipur, Ranthambore, Chittorgarh, Udaipur, Jaisalmer, Jodhpur and Bharatpur, then returning via Agra.

Tickets include five-star meals, tours, wildlife safaris and accommodation in lavish private bedrooms in carriages styled after the private trains of Rajasthan's maharajas (when it launched in the 1980s, the train used the maharajas' personal carriages).

Other opulent Indian trains include the **Maharajas' Express** *(the-maharajas.com)* with four routes from Delhi or Mumbai through the central plains, and Maharashtra's **Deccan Odyssey** *(deccanodyssey.com)* with six routes out of Delhi and Mumbai.

SARISKA'S SAD TIGER TALE

In 2005, Sariska Tiger Reserve (p126) took centre stage in one of India's most publicised wildlife dramas, when an Indian journalist broke the news that the sanctuary's tiger population had been completely eliminated by poachers. After public outcry, a government inquiry recommended fundamental changes, including relocating the inhabitants of villages inside the reserve and introducing a support package for affected communities.

Tigers were reintroduced from Ramthambore in 2008, and despite teething problems (including the poisoning of animals by villagers dissatisfied with the level of support) the reserve's tiger population has grown slowly, reaching 50 individuals in 2025, according to forest department reports. Nevertheless, human-animal conflict is an ongoing challenge to the long-term recovery of Sariska's tigers.

While you can book a slot yourself online, many visitors prefer to make arrangements through one of the hotels near the park entrance, who charge a small mark-up for service. Safaris leave at dawn (chilly, but good for tiger sightings) or in the middle of the afternoon.

See more of Ranthambore

Don't let tiger-tunnel-vision blind you to Ranthambore's other attractions. Accessible without paying the national park fee, the 10th-century **Ranthambhore Fort** *(free)* is a wonderfully evocative sprawl of Jain, Hindu and Muslim ruins.

Pilgrims flock to the 13th-century **Trinetra Ganesh Temple** inside the walls, particularly during Ganesh Chaturthi in August or September. Also impressive are the Badal Mahal, with Muslim tombs and a dainty pavilion in a seasonal pond, and the dome-topped Battis Khamba Chhatri. Get here by shared 4WD from Sawai Madhopur station or by taxi.

For a different wildlife experience, consider a boat trip in search of crocodiles in the **National Chambal Sanctuary** *(obms-tourist.rajasthan.gov.in/place-details/National-Chambal-Gharial-Sanctuary-Palighat)* at Palighat, 35km east. Both 'muggers' and gharials can be spotted; Ranthambore hotels can book safaris including transport by car and boat for around ₹4000.

Shekhawati Region

TIME FROM JAIPUR: 4HR

Jhunjhunu's forts, temples and painted houses

North of Jaipur, **Jhunjhunu** is the rail hub for the Shekhawati region. Most of its painted houses have been consumed by urban sprawl, but the grand **Mohanlal Ishwardas Modi Haveli** *(entry by donation)* in the Nehru Bazaar has a train chugging merrily across its facade, and rich murals in its courtyards.

Tucked away in the back lanes running west are the decaying remains of the **Khetri Mahal** *(free)*, a once-opulent palace from 1770. To the north is the small fort of **Badalgarh** *(free)*, backing onto a dramatic landscape of eroded granite outcrops.

Several other memorable buildings are free to visit – swing by the painted **Sri Laxminath Ji Ka Mandir**, the imposing **Dargah of Kamaruddin Shah**, and the eye-catching but controversial **Rani Sati Temple**, fronted by a vast, Mughal-inspired facade. It commemorates Narayani Devi, a Rajasthani noblewoman who died on her husband's funeral pyre.

Meander around magical Mandawa

The most impressive of Shekhawati's painted villages is **Mandawa**, an hour west of Jhunjhunu by local bus. Start at the handsomely painted **Raghunath Temple**, by the ornate Sonthalia Gate, then look for the nearby house adorned with early flying machines. East of the gate, **Hotel Mandawa Haveli** *(hotelmandawahaveli.com)* charges a small fee *(₹100)* to view its murals of deities and airplanes.

West of the bazaar are tower-topped wells and four stunning *havelis* entered on a single ticket *(7734902650; ₹200)*.

Murmuria Haveli is noteworthy for its Venetian landscapes and portrait of Gandhi, while the conjoined **Vishwanath Goenka Haveli & Tarkeshwar Goenka Haveli** feature depictions of village life, wrestlers, elephants and horse riders. Across the road, the **Seth Dayaram Dedraj Goenka Haveli** has an unusual mural that shows either Indra on an elephant or Shiva riding Nandi, depending on how you look at it.

South of the bazaar, **Thalia Haveli** *(8003266001; ₹100)* is filled with vintage household objects and has paintings of smartly dressed Europeans in its *baithak* meeting room. Further south, **Chokhani Double Haveli** *(9829583437; ₹100)* consists of two graceful residences in a single courtyard.

Some grand *havelis* have been converted into stylish hotels; the upmarket **Gulab Haveli** *(seleqtionshotels.com)* features fine paintings of hookah-smoking gentlemen, while the **Hotel Castle Mandawa** *(castlemandawa.com)* is set in the village's sprawling fort.

See more painted villages

From Jhunjhunu, buses buzz out to more painted villages, or you can charter a car and driver to explore (try Yunus Khan in Nawalgarh on 9414491281). An hour south, **Nawalgarh** is home to the spectacular **Dr Ramnath A Podar Haveli Museum** *(podarhavelimuseum.org; ₹300)*, whose lavishly adorned courtyards are alive with murals of steam trains, Hindu festivals, nobles playing the board game *chaupar* and family members peeking out of painted windows.

Just east, facing the dome-topped **Gher ka Mandir**, the **Morarka Haveli Museum** *(7014095073; ₹100)* has graceful murals of noble ancestors and Hindu deities, with an image of Jesus under the eaves on the upper level. West of the centre, the **Vivaana Museum Hotel** *(vivaana.com/vivaana-museum-hotel; ₹150)* is a stylish 19th-century *haveli* that has been filled with eye-catching modern art.

An hour west of Mandawa, **Fatehpur** was hit by severe flooding in 2023, but its elegant *havelis* are slowly being restored. The handsome **Nadine Le Prince Haveli** *(8290760015; ₹200)* features some of the most impressive murals in Shekhawati; check if the French owners have reopened the hotel here.

Nearby, the pretty **Saraf Haveli** *(8309375049; ₹200)* has camels, elephants and palanquins parading across its walls. Just south are several late-19th-century *havelis*, including one with Queen Victoria on its cast-iron railings.

SHEKHAWATI'S PAINTED HOUSES

Shekhawati is renowned for its extraordinary *haveli* homes, built by wealthy 19th- and 20th-century merchants. Set around private courtyards, these lavish residences are painted inside and out with murals of deities, family scenes, and – most strikingly – depictions of the new technology sweeping across India at the time.

Early murals were strongly influenced by Mughal miniature painting and the Hindu epics, while later murals were inspired by the ornamentation of Rajput palaces and European art.

Many *haveli* owners filled their homes with depictions of planes, trains, automobiles, bicycles, telephones, gramophones and other wonders of the modern age that they encountered in big cities such as Kolkata (Calcutta). Most villages have *havelis* that can be visited for a small fee; stroll around and see which are accepting visitors.

EATING IN SHEKHAWATI: OUR PICKS

Khana Khajana: Close to the station, Jhunjhunu's best restaurant serves a stellar menu of Indian veg treats (and great dosas and thalis). *9am-10.30pm* ₹₹

Monika Rooftop Restaurant: This popular, family-run restaurant south of Mandawa bazaar is a great place to pause between *haveli* visits. *8am-10pm* ₹₹

New Bungli Restaurant: Just northeast of the *haveli* action in Nawalgarh, serving delicious Rajasthani curries; call 9414491281 to book. *7am-10pm* ₹₹

Jharokha: The licensed veg and non-veg restaurant at the Grand Haveli & Resort is Nawalgarh's top spot for a romantic dinner. *7am-11pm* ₹₹₹

Pushkar

HIPPIE HERITAGE | SACRED WATERS | CAMEL MAYHEM

TOP TIP
Travel light when you visit Pushkar. You're likely to end up hauling your bags along steep, uneven alleyways, and up multiple flights of stairs. As a holy town, Pushkar is officially 'dry' but beer is served discreetly at traveller restaurants.

The sacred town of Pushkar has a mystique that defies its small size. It's world famous for its hippie heritage and spectacular Camel Fair, but it's also a living pilgrimage centre for Hindu worshippers, who come to pray, meditate and practise yoga by its sacred lake.

The hippies of the 1960s were drawn by the easy availability of marijuana, supplied to fill the chillum pipes of local yogis, but today, the scene is more about hanging out in cafes, getting creative and meditating or saluting the sun on the lakeshore.

Pushkar's holy lake is flanked by ceremonial bathing ghats and milky-blue temples. Non-Hindus are welcome to observe – but not photograph – the colourful *puja* (prayer) rituals that unfold on its shores.

Behind the ghats lie tangled bazaars selling everything from chillums and sacred threads for yogis to tie-dye tees. Many travellers settle in for days, signing up for classes in music, jewellery-making and more.

Ancient Sacred Rituals

Pay your respects at Brahma's holy lake

Sacred **Pushkar Sarover** is surrounded by 52 bathing ghats (all free to enter), thronged by Hindu pilgrims, who come to offer prayers and bathe in the sacred waters. It's fascinating

GETTING AROUND

Buses between Pushkar and Ajmer take an hour to complete the 11km journey, running every hour or so till 7pm. In Pushkar, buses use either the Naya bus stand or the old Marwar (Marwad) bus stand; a few direct daily buses run from Pushkar to Jaipur; for other destinations, connect through Ajmer.

Motorcycles can be rented for local exploring, but Pushkar is small enough to wander on foot. Autorickshaws are of limited use in the winding lanes, but drivers offer transfers to Ajmer for around ₹500. A planned rail line linking Bikaner, Ajmer and Udaipur may make Pushkar's tiny train station more useful.

SIGHTS
1 Brahma Ghat
2 Brahma Temple
3 Gandhi Ghat
4 Old Rangji Temple
5 Old Rangji Temple Museum
6 Pushkar Sarovar
7 Sunset Point
8 Varah Ghat
9 Varaha Temple

ACTIVITIES
10 Cooking Bahar
11 Saraswati Music & Dance School

SLEEPING
12 Hotel Bharatpur Palace
13 Hotel Everest
14 Inn Seventh Heaven

EATING
15 Falafel & laffa stalls
16 Honey & Spice
17 Honey Dew Cafe
18 Narayan Café
19 Om Shiva Garden Restaurant
20 Out of the Blue
21 Shri Venkatesh
22 Sixth Sense

ENTERTAINMENT
23 Pushkar Camel Fair

to settle in and observe, but do so with respect: remove your shoes, and don't smoke, fool around or take photographs.

Some ghats have particular significance. Vishnu appeared at **Varah Ghat** in the form of a boar, Brahma bathed at **Brahma Ghat**, and Gandhi's ashes were sprinkled at **Gandhi Ghat** (Gau Ghat). At sunset, *aarti* ceremonies with devotional songs and sacred flames often take place on the lakeshore, particularly at Brahma Ghat and Varah Ghat; follow your ears to where the singing is loudest.

Be prepared for some pressure to make a donation; there's a long tradition of giving, but also a long tradition of hustling tourists for exaggerated contributions. Only accept a blessing or red thread (the so-called 'Pushkar passport') if you're happy to make a donation, and only give as much as you feel comfortable giving.

As afternoon wears on, half of Pushkar relocates to the ghat beside the Hotel Pushkar Palace – aka **Sunset Point** – to soak in the sunset colours, sip drinks in lakeside cafes and listen to drum circles and swirling religious music (sometimes with trance beats thrown into the mix).

BRAHMA

According to legend, Pushkar's lake was formed by a lotus blossom dropped from the hand of Brahma, the lord of creation. Usually depicted with four bearded faces and four hands holding the Vedas, Brahma sits at the head of the Trimurti – the triad of deities in the roles of creator, preserver and destroyer – alongside Shiva and Vishnu.

Brahma temples were found all over India until around the 5th century CE, when worship of the great creator was eclipsed by veneration of Vishnu, Shiva and Mahadevi. Today, Pushkar has one of world's only active Brahma temples (p132). The town's name – *push* (flower) and *kar* (hand) – comes from the lake's creation myth.

PUSHKAR'S SWEET TREATS

Rajasthan is a state with a sweet tooth, and every town seems to have its own sticky treat based on milk curds, spices, nuts, dried fruit and jaggery (palm sugar). In Pushkar, the treat of choice is *malpua* – small, lightly spiced pancakes made with curd and *khoya* (milk solids), cooked for a second time in a pan full of bubbling syrup. The lane north of Gandhi Ghat is lined with *misthan bhandars* (sweet shops) with big pans full of *malpua* bubbling out front. They're best eaten while hot, with a cup of masala chai on the side. Locals like them for breakfast, but that can be a bit of a heavy sugar hit for foreign palates.

The World's Most Famous Camel Fair

Dive into Pushkar's biggest festival

During the Hindu month of Kartika in October or November, camel drivers from across the Thar Desert groom their favourite camels and begin the long walk to Pushkar for the annual **camel fair** *(tourism.rajasthan.gov.in/pushkar-fair.html)*, held on the town's western fringes since the 19th century.

Already-busy Pushkar becomes an intoxicating swirl of colour, as the streets are mobbed by musicians, mystics, tourists, traders, devotees, camera crews and 50,000 camels, horses and cattle. The mercantile side of the mela (fair) gets going a week before the government-organised festival, when sideshows such as snake charmers and rope-walkers take centre stage.

Highlights for visitors include contests to pick the best moustache and most beautifully decorated camel. Consider joining in the costumed wedding parade or visitors-versus-locals wrestling bout if you're feeling brave.

For visiting Hindu pilgrims, all this hullabaloo is a sideshow to the night of the full moon, when thousands of devotees gather on the ghats beside the lake to wash away their sins and set candles afloat on the sacred waters.

Keep an eye on your valuables, and bring medication and a face-mask if you are affected by dust or animal hair. These inconveniences aside, it's an epic party, and not to be missed if you're anywhere within camel-spitting distance of Pushkar.

One of the World's Only Brahma Temples

Visit a unique Hindu holy place

Topped by a tall *shikhara* tower, the red **Brahma Temple** *(leave cameras in lockers)* to the west of the lake is a fascinating spot. Like many other Pushkar shrines, the original temple was destroyed by Aurangzeb but subsequently reconstructed.

This is one of the only active Brahma temples in the country, and the walls and floor of the surrounding compound are paved with engraved marble dedications to the dead. Note the depiction of Brahma's *vahana* (vehicle) – a goose, or *hamsa* – over the entry gateway.

Another historic temple of note is the 19th-century **Old Rangji Temple** northeast of the lake, blending South Indian *gopurams* (gateway towers) and Mughal-inspired turrets. You can't enter the inner courtyard, but you can visit the small temple **museum** *(₹20)* to view colourful wooden sculptures and a *rath* (chariot) depicting Krishna hiding the clothes of the *gopis* (milkmaids).

EATING IN PUSHKAR: TOP PICKS

Out of the Blue: As blue as its name suggests, blending a street-level coffee bar with a tasteful traveller menu upstairs. *8am-11pm* ₹₹

Sixth Sense: The rooftop restaurant at Inn Seventh Heaven will lift you above the hubbub for Indian veg curries and pizzas with a view. *8am-9.30pm* ₹₹

Om Shiva Garden Restaurant: A traveller stalwart in an expansive courtyard, serving everything from pizzas to quality North Indian curries. *9.30am-11pm* ₹₹

Honey & Spice: A healthy, wholesome air pervades this friendly cafe, serving baked goods, salad bowls and veg stews with brown rice. *8.30am-5.30pm* ₹₹

Few of Pushkar's medieval temples survived Aurangzeb's raids, but you can get a hint of their former grandeur at the partly ruined **Varaha Temple**, east of Varah Ghat, sacred to Vishnu in his boar incarnation.

A Sublime Lake View

Catch Pushkar's sunset or sunrise

To properly appreciate Pushkar, you need to see the town from above, ideally at sunset or sunrise, when the hazy light seems to transport this sacred site back in time.

Southwest of the lake, the **Savitri Mata Temple** is dedicated to Saraswati, but most come here to soak in the dizzying views over Pushkar and its surrounding amphitheatre of rocky hills. An ageing **ropeway** *(return trip ₹180)* climbs from just outside town to the summit, or you can walk up or down (or both) via a winding stairway through a spectral forest of dead trees, joined by hordes of langur monkeys.

Behind the Marwar (Marwad) bus stand, the tiny **Pap Mochani (Gayatri) Temple** is sacred to a goddess who is a personified form of a passage from the Rig-Veda, and it offers soaring views over Pushkar town and the lake. Pick up the steps on the lane immediately west of the bus stand (bring a torch to find your way down if you come for sunset).

Take a Class

Upskill by the lake

Along the main bazaar north of the lake, you'll spot dozens of signs advertising lessons in jewellery-making, Ayurvedic massage, yoga, meditation and all sorts of Indian artforms, from painting and dance to Indian classical music.

One of the most respected schools is the **Saraswati Music & Dance School**, signposted in the lanes running north from Gandhi Ghat. Expert local musician Birju *(9828297784)* teaches a wide range of Indian instruments, from tabla and sitar to the *bansuri* flute, while his brother Hemant *(9829333548)* runs classes in *kathak* (classical Indian dance), Rajasthani folk dances and Bollywood dance. You can sign up for individual lessons, short courses, or long-term training, with the option of group sessions and private tuition; contact the teachers to discuss class options and prices.

Run by another member of the same enterprising family, **Cooking Bahar** *(9829333548; cooking courses from ₹2000)* offers classes in Rajasthani vegetarian cooking, given by the enthusiastic and skilled Deepa.

PUSHKAR'S BAZAARS

The winding bazaar that follows the north shore of Pushkar lake is a nonstop parade of souvenir shops, but the offerings change noticeably as you move from west to east. Near the Brahma temple, stalls target Hindu pilgrims with bangles, religious paraphernalia, jooti slippers, costume jewellery and (incongruously) ornamental swords and air rifles. As you head east, the focus shifts to silver jewellery, hippie clothing, tie-dye skirts, rave T-shirts, chillum pipes and steel cups and bowls painted with floral designs in bold primary colours. Imaginative souvenirs to take home include vintage Indian vinyl records (including the cream of Bollywood), products made from local rose essence and framed posters for Indian household products from the 1950s.

EATING IN PUSHKAR: SNACK STOPS

Narayan Café: A popular breakfast and lunch stop in the bazaar, great for juices and muesli or porridge topped with mounds of fruit. *8.30am-8.30pm* ₹

Falafel & laffa wrap stalls: Backpackers throng this cluster of stalls selling falafel-and-hummus wraps just north of the lake. *9am-10.30pm* ₹

Honey Dew Cafe: A cute and colourful hole-in-the-wall cafe, popular for breakfast bowls and all-day snacks. *7.30am-8.30pm* ₹

Shri Venkatesh: Swing by this family-run, all-veg eatery for quick curries and thalis, with a menu based on the day's market offerings. *noon-10pm* ₹

Beyond Pushkar

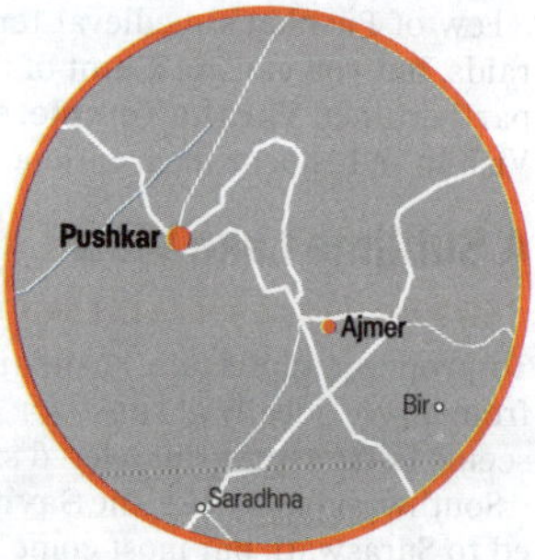

Chill out in Pushkar, then dive into ancient India in Ajmer, one of Rajasthan's most atmospheric cities.

GETTING AROUND

Ajmer is well connected, with buses buzzing day and night across the state from the busy bus stand on Jaipur Rd, and plentiful trains from Ajmer Junction to Jaipur, Jodhpur, Delhi, Agra and other cities. Local buses zip to Pushkar every hour or so until around 6.30pm, or you can take an autorickshaw for around ₹500. Vehicles are banned from the historic heart of Ajmer, so get out and explore on foot.

Pushkar offers an easy introduction to spiritual India thanks to decades of backpacker travel, but in Ajmer, you'll find Indian spirituality as it existed before outside influences changed the subcontinent. This sacred Sufi – and before that, Jain – city is passionate, immediate and unrestrained. Few places in Rajasthan have such an irrepressible energy.

In the backstreets around the dargah (tomb) of Khwaja Muin-ud-din Chishti – one of India's most important Sufi saints – the vibrancy of medieval India pushes through into the present day. Visit Pushkar for the vibes, but devote at least a day to Ajmer to feel India's living spiritual energy, in a city that exists for the benefit of locals rather than the gratification of tourists.

Ajmer

TIME FROM PUSHKAR: **45MIN**

Visit the tomb of India's most important Sufi saint

At the heart of old Ajmer, the **tomb of the Sufi saint Khwaja Muin-ud-din Chishti** *(donations appropriate)* is thronged at all hours by Muslim devotees, who gather here to pray, contemplate, sing devotional *qawwali* hymns, recite from the Quran, and make offerings of flowers, scarves, incense and sandalwood at the saint's gravesite.

Visitors are welcome, but respect is key. Remove your shoes, cover your head, leave your bag and camera in the cloakroom (or back in your hotel), and join the crowds of devotees, who will carry you forward like a living wave. Temple attendants may lead you round and introduce you to some of the Sufi mystics who offer spiritual advice and astrological readings in the courtyard. Leaving a donation is appropriate.

Khwaja Muin-ud-din Chishti came to Ajmer from Persia in 1192 and died here in 1236, after a lifetime preaching a doctrine of tolerance, charity and compassion, earning him great respect from India's Mughal rulers. Keen follower Akbar used to make the pilgrimage to this dargah every year from Agra.

Humayun constructed much of the shrine, and the grand entrance was added by the Nizam

SUFI DELHI

Ajmer is the setting for India's most revered Sufi shrine, but **Delhi** (p52) has a particularly rich collection of dargahs, including the tomb of Nizam-ud-din Auliya, the second-most-important Sufi shrine in the country.

SHAHEDUL SIFAT/SHUTTERSTOCK

Tomb of Khwaja Muin-ud-din Chishti, Ajmer

of Hyderabad in 1915. Other notable features include the 16th-century Akbari Masjid, the Shahjahani Gate (erected by Shah Jahan) and the grand Buland Darwaza gateway, flanked two vast Mughal-era *degs* (iron cauldrons) filled with offerings for the poor.

At the heart of the complex, the saint's dargah is a crowded, atmospheric space, adorned with beaten silver panels and and perfumed with the scent of rose petals. Notes attached to the railings beg for aid or give thanks for wishes granted.

On the anniversary of the saint's death, the **Urs**, in the seventh lunar month, the crowds become an unstoppable mass, and music, singing and the tangible energy of belief fills the compound.

Wander Ajmer's intoxicating bazaars

The **bazaar** running north from the dargah is full of religious stalls, pilgrim restaurants and sweet shops selling the city's famous fudge-like *soham halwa*. Other stalls and shops keep pilgrims stocked up with rose petals, *ittars* (perfumes), incense and topi hats – devotees like to look, and smell, their best when they visit the tomb.

Work your way west along Ander Kote Marg and you'll be hit by mouthwatering smells from the Muslim hotels (canteens) squeezed along the shrine's outer walls, which serve a shifting menu that starts with meaty *nihari* stew in the morning, shifts to biryani at lunchtime, and moves on to tandoori chicken and kebabs in the evening.

Passing through the Mughal-style **Tripolia Gate**, you'll reach the towering arches of **Adhai-din-ka-Jhonpra** *(free)*, an ancient 12th-century mosque adorned with passages of Islamic calligraphy and constructed partly from stones taken

SUFISM IN INDIA

Spend any time in India and you'll notice the tombs draped with green fabric that dot the countryside and backstreets, marking the final resting places of Sufi mystics.

The metaphysical form of Islam, Sufism has its origins in Persia, and its ideas of universality and the personal celebration of spirituality have been part of Islamic philosophy since the time of the Prophet Mohammed.

Roaching India in the 12th century, Sufism was propagated by ascetic teachers such as Khwaja Muin-ud-din Chichti of Ajmer and Nizam-ud-din Auliya of Delhi, who had a profound influence on the emperors of the Mughal dynasty.

Today, Delhi, Ajmer and Hyderabad are the best places to connect with this fascinating and forward-thinking (for its time) belief system, and its uplifting tradition of devotional *qawwali* singing.

RAJASTHAN'S SWEET TOOTH

Rajasthanis love their *mithai* (sweets) and every town has its own specialities that people travel across the state to sample. In Ajmer, it's *sohan halwa* – a tooth-jangling toffee fudge packed with nuts. In Pushkar, it's *malpua*, small, sweet spiced pancakes, soaked in syrup. In Bikaner and Jaipur, the treat to try is *ghewar*, a honeycomb-like ring made from ghee, flour and syrup.

Jaipur is also celebrated for *kunafa* (syrup-drenched bird-nest pastries) and *mawa kachori*, fried parcels, stuffed with milk solids and dried fruit, while Jodhpur is known its *malai roti*, made from creamy milk solids fried in ghee. Local takes on *boondi* (sweetened balls of fried chickpea flour) are popular all over the state – Jaisalmer and Udaipur both have their own versions.

from Jain and Hindu temples destroyed by Mohammed of Ghori in 1198. According to legend, the original building was constructed in just two and half days, and it was one of the first mosques erected in India.

Visit Ajmer's Forts

Beyond the dargah, a track climbs steeply for 3km to the overgrown **Taragarh fortress** *(free)*, constructed in the 8th century by Ajaipal Chauhan, the founder of Ajmer. A golden copy of the shrine of Imam Hussein in Karbala, Iraq, sits inside the walls, and the intact bastions offer wide views over Ajmer's rooftops.

On the far side of the Old City lies **Ajmer Fort** *(adult/student ₹205/105)*, a modest fortified palace constructed by Akbar, which contains a surprisingly well laid out government museum full of old weapons, miniature paintings, rock inscriptions and exquisite Hindu and Jain carvings – a reminder of Ajmer's pre-Delhi-Sultanate history. Interestingly, this was the spot where the British East India company first negotiated trading rights with Jehangir in 1615.

See (Jain) heaven on earth

For all the enlightened attitudes of Sufism, Ajmer's Jains and Hindus suffered terrible persecution under the Islamic Ghurid dynasty, but the **Soniji Ki Nasiyan Temple** *(₹30)* offers a glimpse of the golden age of Jainism in India.

Spilling over three floors are enormous, intricate dioramas created from wood wrapped in gold foil, depicting the Jain concept of the ancient world. On the 2nd level, the holy city of Ayodhya is depicted as a literal city of gold, thronged by people and elephants, with celestial beings floating overhead in bird-headed boats.

More than a metric ton of gold was used to construct these remarkable dioramas between 1870 and 1895, and panels explain how the sculptures recall events from the life of Rishabhadeva (Adinath), the first *tirthankar* (teacher) of Jainism.

EATING IN AJMER: OUR PICKS

Sohan halwa stalls: The bazaar in front of the Ajmer dargah is lined with stalls selling sweet *sohan halwa* – the town's favourite treat. *9am-10pm* ₹

Muslim hotels: The dargah is ringed by eateries serving *nihari* stew for breakfast, biryani for lunch and tandoori skewers for dinner. *6am-2am* ₹₹

Mango Curry/Mango Masala: A hip eatery near the bus stand, divided into veg and non-veg sections, attracting Ajmer's young, cool set. *9am-10.45pm* ₹₹

Ambrosia: Alfresco rooftop dining with a bit of razzmatazz atop the Hotel Ambassador to the east of Anasagar lake. *7am-11pm* ₹₹₹

Bundi

PAINTED PALACES | STUNNING STEP-WELLS | PEACEFUL WANDERING

Southeast of Ajmer, Bundi is a captivating tangle of narrow lanes that coil around one of Rajasthan's most magical palace ruins, whose faded cupolas, filigree balconies and ridge-top battlements dominate the skyline.

This is a place to step off the mainstream tourist circuit, staying in historic *haveli* homes and investigating mural-filled royal palaces, bazaars lined with indigo-blue houses, and deep and mysterious step-wells. Few places in Rajasthan retain so much of the magical atmosphere of centuries past.

Bundi came into its own in the 12th century when a group of Chauhan nobles from Ajmer fled south to escape the ravages of Mohammed of Ghori. They wrested territory from the Mina and Bhil tribes and made Bundi the capital of their kingdom, known as Hadoti. Bundi allied with the Mughals from the late 16th century, but the state retained considerable independence under British rule, before being rolled into the state of Rajasthan in 1948.

TOP TIP

Bundi is a place to wander slowly, soaking up the atmosphere. The ticket for Bundi Palace also covers the Taragarh Fort and Kshar Bagh – easily enough to fill a day – and it's worth devoting a second day to the step-wells and bazaars.

GETTING AROUND

The busy RSRTC bus stand southeast of the Old City has regular buses to Ajmer, Chittorgarh, Jodhpur and Jaipur, and infrequent services to Sawai Madhopur for Ranthambore National Park. For a wider range of destinations, head to nearby Kota (40 minutes) and change to a bus or train.

About 4km from the centre, Bundi's small train station has services to Chittorgarh, Udaipur, Delhi, Agra and Sawai Madhopur; trains to Jaipur, Ajmer or Jodhpur leave from Kota. Autorickshaws buzz around Bundi and drivers offer circuits around the town's step-wells and the sights around Jait Sagar lake. Explore the old town on foot.

HAVE AN AYURVEDIC CONSULTATION

Close to the Nawal Sagar lake and palace, Bundi's charitable **Government District Ayurveda Hospital** *(Dr Vijendra 9950497163; 9am-3pm)* is an interesting place to seek advice on any niggling ailments. Several Ayurvedic consultants run free clinics inside the hospital, prescribing plant-based remedies for all sorts of conditions, from upset tummies to arthritis. Ayurvedic pharmacies line the road in front of the clinic, offering more herbal cures and potions based on natural ingredients sourced from across India, from the Thar Desert to the Western Ghats and Himalaya.

Murals of Bundi Palace

Marvel at timeless, painted perfection

Described by Rudyard Kipling as 'the work of goblins rather than of men', **Bundi Palace** *(bundipalace.com; ₹600)* is an extraordinary, decaying edifice that seems to grow out of the rock of the hillside it stands on. The palace was constructed during the reign of Rao Raja Ratan Singh (r 1607–31) and parts of the compound were occupied by the Bundi royals until 1948, when it was abandoned and taken over by bats and monkeys.

Tickets cover Bundi Palace, the Taragarh fortress and Kshar Bagh, and the palace is worth a few hours of exploring. Entering via the steep causeway climbing to the elephant-topped **Hathi Pol** (Elephant Gate), you'll reach a courtyard garden in front of the **Diwan-i-Am** (Hall of Public Audience; also known as the Ratan Daulat), with its gleaming white marble coronation throne. Steps lead into the **Chattar Mahal**, added by Rao Raja Chhatra Shabji in 1644, with ivory-inlaid doors and some fine but weathered murals set in arched niches.

You'll pass balconies overlooking Nawal Sagar tank en route to the **Phool Mahal**, constructed in 1607, with an ornately decorated ceiling and some tremendous murals, including scenes from an immense royal procession. Beyond lies the late-16th-century **Badal Mahal** (Cloud Palace), with the palace's very best murals, including a wonderful ceiling inspired by the mihrabs (Mecca-facing niches) found in Mughal mosques.

The highest levels offer grand views over the old centre of Bundi through windows screened by metal meshes and stone *jalis* (fretwork screens). As you descend through less decorated chambers towards the exit, look for the original medieval latrine and the giant arch that once supported the royal swing.

Constructed in the 18th century by Rao Ummed Singh, the upper section of the palace is known as the **Chitrasala** *(free)*, and is administered separately by the Archaeological Survey of India.

The chambers behind the palace's pretty garden courtyard contain some of Bundi's best-preserved murals, depicting delightful scenes from the life of Krishna – look out for the playful deity hiding the clothes of the *gopis* (milkmaids).

The rear room to the right is the Sheesh Mahal, and its badly damaged interior still contains some beautiful glass inlay work, while its forechamber contains a fine image of Bundi in its 18th-century heyday. You'll also see plenty of murals of duelling elephants.

EATING IN BUNDI: OUR PICKS

Burg Cafe: A cool newcomer, serving quality coffee, cakes, sandwiches and snacks in a prime location near Nawal Sagar. *8am-10.30pm* ₹

Rainbow Cafe: Up on the roof of Bundi's western gate and family-run, serving – a little slowly – decent Indian and traveller fare. *7.30am-11pm* ₹₹

Morgan's Place: A relaxed rooftop stop, with good coffee, pizzas and other international faves, upstairs at Hotel Kasera Paradise. *9.30am-10.30pm* ₹₹

Bundi Vilas: Feast on Indian treats on the terrace or on the rooftop with fort views at elegant Bundi Vilas; book at 9871632007. *7-10pm* ₹₹₹

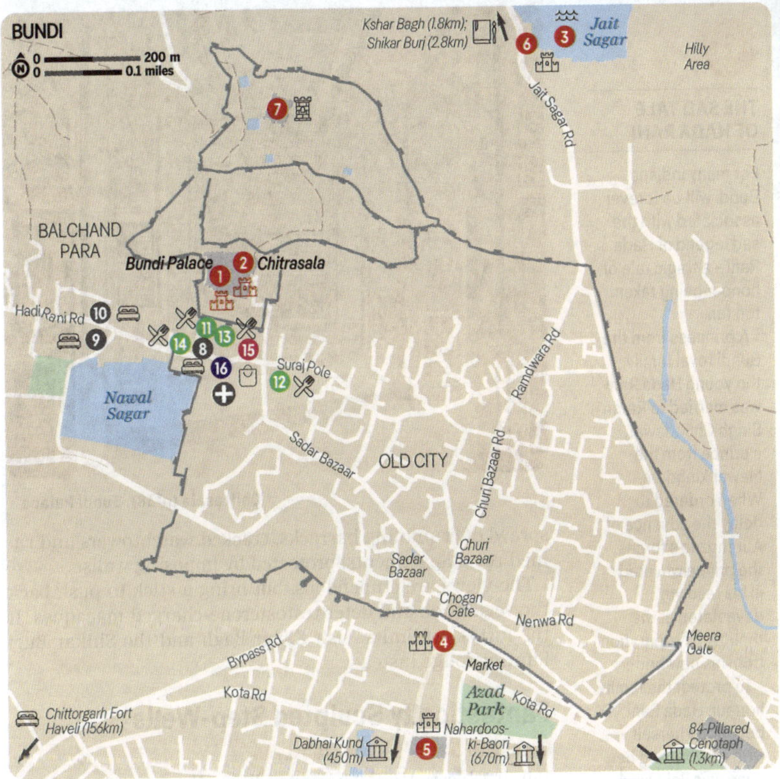

HIGHLIGHTS
1 Bundi Palace
2 Chitrasala

SIGHTS
see 8 Haveli Braj Bhushanjee
3 Jait Sagar
4 Nagar Kund & Sagar Kund
5 Raniji-ki-Baori
6 Sukh Mahal
7 Taragarh

SLEEPING
8 Haveli Braj Bhushanjee
9 Hotel Bundi Haveli
10 Shivam Tourist Guest House

EATING
11 Bundi Vilas
12 Burg Cafe
13 Morgan's Place
14 Rainbow Cafe

SHOPPING
15 Yug Art

INFORMATION
16 Government District Ayurveda Hospital

As the Chitrasala gates are closed at 5pm, monkeys reclaim the palace buildings and chirruping bats flap out from darkened chambers. Give them space – it's their palace now.

Rugged, Ramshackle Ruins

Explore the ruins of Taragarh

Crowning the hilltop above Bundi Palace, the 14th-century **Taragarh** *(entry on Bundi Palace ticket)* is a wonderfully tumbledown fortress, but you'll need to check it's safe to visit at the Bundi Palace ticket desk, as tigers relocated to the new Ramgarh Vishdhari Wildlife Sanctuary have been tracked in the area.

Assuming you get the all clear, you can follow the steep stone pathway uphill above the Chitrasala to reach an overgrown

THE SAD TALE OF HADA RANI

For many Indians, Bundi will be forever associated with the sad legend of Hada Rani – a tragic tale of honour being taken too far.

A princess from the Bundi royal family, the young Hada Rani was married to Ratan Singh Chundawat, a prince from the Mewar kingdom. When ordered to delay the advance of Aurangzeb's forces, the prince wavered in his resolve, devastated at the thought of separation from his new bride.

To protect the family honour, Hada Rani beheaded herself with a sword and her head was delivered to her husband as a message. The prince went on to defeat the advancing Mughal army, before taking his own life to join his bride. Rajasthan's police force has a women's battalion named in her honour.

CHRISTOPHE CAPPELLI/SHUTTERSTOCK

Chitrasala (p138), Bundi Palace

sprawl of crumbling barracks, cracked watchtowers and ruined royal apartments, protected by imposing walls.

The views are stupendous, but bring a stick to push back the vegetation and deter testosterone-charged macaques. If the fort is off-limits, visit Kshar Bagh and the Shikar Burj hunting lodge instead.

Fantastically Sculpted Step-Wells

Dive into Bundi's water features

Bundi is blessed with an outstanding collection of *baori* (step-wells) – vast subterranean water tanks that drop unexpectedly below street level like gateways to a hidden world, designed to collect and store rainwater from the summertime monsoon.

The most impressive and cared-for step-well is the dramatic **Raniji-ki-Baori** *(composite ticket ₹355)*, or Queen's Well, just south of the centre and the Kota road, constructed in 1699 by Rani Nathawati, wife of Rao Raja Anirudh Singh. Plunging 46m, it could have been plucked straight from the Mines of Moria in *The Lord of the Rings*. The composite ticket also covers the Sukh Mahal palace and the 84-pillared Cenotaph.

Other step-wells are free to visit. The matching **Nagar Kund and Sagar Kund** wells face each other in the heart of Bundi's main bazaar, with geometric stairways that plunge to murky depths.

South of Raniji-ki-Baori, **Dabhai Kund** is a much more open-plan construction, flanked by geometric steps on three sides. Further east, the atmospheric **Nahardoos-ki-Baori** is an eerie shaft with galleries on several levels, surrounding a deep central tank. Shrines on the walls appear when the water is low.

History in the Backstreets

See the less-explored Bundi

There's plenty more to see in Bundi. For a rewarding morning stroll, follow the lane curving around the ridge behind the palace to reach **Jait Sagar**, a scenic lake ringed by hills and strewn with pretty lotus flowers in winter.

At the southwest end of the lake, the **Sukh Mahal** *(entry on Raniji-ki-Baori composite ticket)* is a small summer palace surrounded by terraced gardens, where Rudyard Kipling stayed and wrote part of *Kim* in the late 19th century. The attached government museum has temple carvings, paintings and an armoury.

Continue past the lake to reach the **Kshar Bagh** *(entry on Bundi Palace ticket)*, where the elegant cenotaphs of 66 Bundi rulers and queens stand partly reclaimed by greenery. Fork right just after Kshar Bag to reach the ruined **Shikar Burj** *(free)*, a turreted former hunting lodge once used by the Bundi royal family, set beside a step-ringed tank.

If Kshar Bag has piqued your interest in royal funerals, the two-tiered **84-Pillared Cenotaph** *(entry on Raniji-ki-Baori composite ticket)* south of the town was built to honour the son of one of the maharajas' *ayahs* (nurses) about 600 years ago.

Back in town, visit the family-run **museum** *(kiplingsbundi .com; free entry by appointment)* at the charming Haveli Braj Bhushanjee (p184). Run as a hotel by the descendants of the prime minister of Bundi state, this rambling historic home has several rooms devoted to the owner's private collection of craft objects, old paintings, religious paraphernalia, historic weapons and diaries. Drop by to check when they can show you round.

Take a Historical Tour

Discover Bundi's ancient history

It's worth arranging a guide to point out overlooked details and easily missed murals in Bundi Palace; hotels can make arrangements. Speak to the owners of Haveli Braj Bhushanjee (p184) first, as they are particularly well informed.

A more unusual option is to delve into prehistory with Ashwani Sharma *(instagram.com/kukkisworld.bundi)*. The Sharma family are passionate amateur archaeologists, and they have discovered around 70 prehistoric rock-painting sites in the hills around Bundi.

THE BUNDI SCHOOL OF PAINTING

India has many schools of miniature painting, but the Bundi School is perhaps the most refined. Blending ideas from Mughal art and the miniature paintings of the Deccan region, Bundi School paintings are characterised by Krishna themes, the use of pigments made from vegetables, minerals and gold and silver, and an emphasis on vegetation, night skies, moving human and animal figures and stylised representations of water.

With a studio close to Bundi's Nawal Sagar lake, Yug Prasad of **Yug Art** *(instagram.com/ yugartist)* produces paintings in the Bundi style, and can paint you into a miniature painting of a royal scene if you provide a photo, shipping the finished work to you on completion. See the high point of Bundi painting inside the Chitrasala and Bundi Palace's (p138) Badal Mahal.

Beyond Bundi

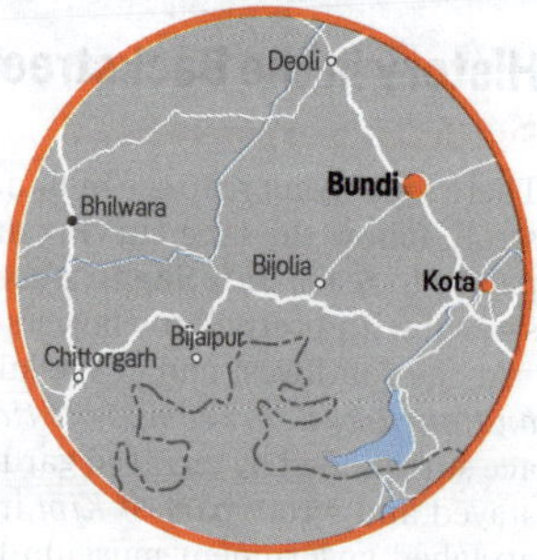

If you enjoyed peaceful Bundi, you'll find a similar off-the-main-path mood in Kota and historic Chittorgarh.

Places

Kota p142
Chittorgarh p144

An easy day trip from Bundi, Kota sprawls beside the Chambal River, Rajasthan's only year-round waterway. Until recently, it was best known for its gigantic coal-fired power station and sprawling palace – home to the Hada rulers of once independent Kota State – but Kota has benefited from a flood of government investment, with a vast revamp of the city's riverside ghats, and a new airport taking shape in the eastern suburbs.

Further west, the sleepy town of Chittorgarh is the setting for largest fort complex in India, nearly 6km long, crowning a high clifftop and studded with temples and ceremonial towers. Kota can be visited from Bundi in a day, but Chittorgarh deserves an overnight trip.

GETTING AROUND

Buses are the easiest way to explore, with regular services from Bundi to Kota, and onward connections from the bus stand near Kota's Swami Vivekanda Circle. Trains also connect Kota Junction station to Chittorgarh, Jaipur, Delhi, Mumbai and other destinations. Local autorickshaw drivers are enthusiastic, but they don't always know where tourists want to be taken – show an address in Hindi or a photo on your phone to make sure you reach the right destination.

Kota

TIME FROM BUNDI: 40MIN

See the seat of Kota's royal rulers

Rising beside the Chambal River, Kota's 17th-century **City Palace Garh** *(kotahgarh.com; ₹500)* was one of the largest royal complexes in Rajasthan in its day. Today, several wings have been taken over by private schools, but the fascinating **Rao Madho Singh Museum** displays everything required for a respectable royal existence, from silver furniture, howdahs and hunting trophies to photos of royal relatives meeting dignitaries from the British Empire. Downstairs is a grand durbar (royal court) decorated with lavish mirrorwork, while upstairs are the elegant royal apartments, adorned with beautifully preserved murals, including the hunting scenes for which the Kota school of painting is renowned.

The throne hall and royal bedchamber in the **Bada Mahal** are extraordinarily lavish spaces, decorated from floor to ceiling with scenes of nature, deities and royal life, and delicate portraits painted on glass mirrors.

In the armoury, look out for the katar dagger mounted with hidden pistols, and a lethal 'scissors katar', with a blade that spreads to widen wounds.

Spare a few minutes to wander the lanes outside the palace gates, dropping by some of Kota's oldest temples.

See the world from Kota's ghats

The ghats lining the banks of the Chambal River have received crores of rupees worth of investment as part of the **Kota**

VISHAL BHATNAGAR/NURPHOTO/SHUTTERSTOCK

East bank, Kota Riverfront

Riverfront *(crfkota.com; entry ₹500, with golf cart transfers ₹600, camera fee ₹500)* development – an Epcot Center-style expanse of gardens, promenades, supersized sculptures and towering, Jaipur-pink reproductions of monuments from across India and the world.

The east bank is dominated by a towering, 70m-tall statue of Chambal Mata, the patron deity of the river, who pours water from an enormous jug as part of the evening laser light fountain show at 8pm and 9pm. Smog from the nearby thermal electricity plant makes for hazy views but evocative sunsets. At the time of writing, only phone and card payments were being accepted for admission.

For more world monuments fun, the **Seven Wonders Park** *(₹10)* by Kishore Sagar lake has a mini Eiffel Tower, Colosseum and Statue of Liberty, and views of the palace-like **Jag Mandir** – constructed as a temple in 1740 – floating in the middle of the lake.

Take a wildlife-spotting boat trip on the Chambal

Upstream from Kota, beyond the barrage, the Chambal River enters the **National Chambal Gharial Sanctuary** *(boat safaris from ₹2600)* section of the Mukundara Hills Tiger Reserve. Despite the proximity of Kota's urban sprawl, dense stands of jungle line both banks of the river, providing shelter for native mammals, birds and reptiles.

Abundant wildlife can be viewed on boat trips along the river, from bird species such as green- and blue-tailed bee-eaters and Bonelli's eagles to otters, crocodiles (both long-snouted gharials and keep-your-arms-in-the-boat marsh muggers). If you're extremely lucky, you might even see leopards, tigers and Indian wolves on the riverbanks.

Morning and afternoon boat trips leave from the Forest Department offices just north of **Chambal Gardens**, about 1.5km south of the fort on the east bank. Contact expert wildlife guide Ravindra Tomar *(9828079769; instagram.com/ravindrasingh.tomar)* to make arrangements in advance.

KOTA'S MAJESTIC MELA

If you're in India for the festival of **Dussehra** (held during the seventh month of the Hindu lunar calendar, in October or November), Kota is a great place to join local people celebrating the triumph of good over evil.

Gigantic papier-mâché effigies of Ravana, the demon king of Lanka, and his brother Kumbhakarna and son Meghnad are constructed and then spectacularly set aflame, symbolising the victory of Rama and the rescue of Sita from the forces of evil.

It's an amazing spectacle – theatrical troupes act out scenes from the Ramayana and there's a huge procession to the mela (fair) ground on the edge of Kota, with plenty of fairground rides, festive food and fireworks to accompany the bonfires.

LANA KRAY/SHUTTERSTOCK

TOP EXPERIENCE

Chittorgarh Fort

The dusty town of Chittorgarh (Chittor) feels like a mere appendage to the gigantic fortress draped along the ridges west of the train station. Rocky cliffs soar above the floodplain of the Berach River, crowned by impenetrable-looking walls and a forest of temples and towers. A looping road encircles the plateau and autorickshaw drivers offer three-hour tours of India's largest fortress for ₹600 to ₹800.

DON'T MISS

- Fort Gates
- Rana Khumba Palace
- Meera & Khumba Shyam Temples
- Tower of Victory & Samidhisvara Temple
- Padmini Palace & Kalika Mata Temple
- Suraj Pol & the Tower of Fame
- Fateh Prakash Palace & Satbis Deori Temple

The Fort Gates

The zigzagging fort access road climbs for over a kilometre from the **Padal Pol** gate at the bottom of the cliffs, passing through six further gateways to reach **Ram Pol**, marked by a small, temple-studded village and the overlooked, bat-filled ruins of the **Rana Ratan Singh Palace**.

Rana Khumba Palace

Following the walls south, the 15th-century Rana Kumbha Palace marks the site of one of three ritual mass suicides that took place in Chittorgarh, as the city fell under siege from Ala-ud-din Khilji in 1303. The time-scarred walls are the setting for a sound-and-light show at dusk *(₹300)*, and nearby are two deity-encrusted temples, absorbed into the fort walls.

PRACTICALITIES

● tourism.rajasthan.gov.in/chittorgarh.html ● 6am–6pm ● ₹600

Meera & Khumba Shyam Temples

Further south are two dramatic 15th-century Indo-Aryan temples, erected by Rana Kumbha. The smaller **Meera Temple** is associated with the mystic poet Meerabai, a 16th-century Mewar princess who was poisoned by her brother-in-law but miraculously saved by Krishna.

Fronted by a statue of Garuda, the enormous **Kumbha Shyam Temple** is dedicated to Vishnu and carved with scenes of medieval life. See more delicate carvings at the **Jateshwar Mahadev Temple** on the edge of the fort walls.

Tower of Victory & Samidhishvara Temple

Passing a ruined step-well, you'll reach the 37m-high Tower of Victory (Vijaya Stambha), erected by Rana Kumbha in the 1440s – most likely to commemorate victory over Mahmud Khilji. Every fabulous millimetre of its nine storeys is covered in carvings but visitors are no longer allowed to climb to the top.

Below the tower is the Mahasati, where many royal widows died on their husbands' funeral pyres, dotted with the ruins of temples ransacked by Ala-ud-din Khilji and Akbar. Some 13,000 women and children perished here during a mass *jauhar* (ritual suicide by immolation) in 1535.

Steps drop to a deep, fish-filled tank known as the **Gaumukh Kund**, fed by a sacred spring emerging through a cow's head spout. Beside the steps is the 6th-century **Samidhisvara Temple**, enshrining a striking three-faced image of Shiva as Trimurti, the Creator, Preserver and Destroyer.

Padmini Palace & Kalika Mata Temple

Pass more wells to reach the monkey-thronged, 8th century **Kalika Mata Temple**, originally consecrated to Surya, the sun god, but rededicated to the goddess Kali in the 14th century. Further south is the graceful 14th-century **Padmini Palace**, with royal apartments flanking a walled garden beside the tower-like **Rani Padmavati Mahal**, floating in a lotus- and lily-filled pool. The original bronze gates to this palace were carried off by Akbar to Agra Fort.

Suraj Pol & the Tower of Fame

On the east side of the fort, the restored **Suraj Pol** was the fort's original entrance, offering epic views towards the misty hills. Just north, attached to the **Sri Digambar Jain temple**, is the ornately carved, 24m-high **Tower of Fame** (Kirti Stambha), dating from 1301 and built to honour Rishabhadeva (Adinath), the first Jain *tirthankar* (teacher).

Fateh Prakash Palace & Satbis Deori Temple

In the centre of the fort, the gleaming white Fateh Prakash Palace contains Chittorgarh's **State Museum** *(adult/student ₹102/52)* with an extensive armoury and informative displays on local history. Nearby is the 11th-century **Satbis Deori Temple** – a collection of fabulously decorated, deity-covered stone shrines, sacred to Adinath.

CHITTORGARH'S TRAGIC SACRIFICE

Rajasthan's medieval rulers were famous – some would say infamous – for choosing death before dishonour. During sieges by solders from the Mughal empire and Delhi sultanate in 1303, 1535 and 1568, the women and children of Chittorgarh opted for mass suicide by immolation while the menfolk of the city marched out to certain death. During the largest of these acts of *jauhar*, an estimated 30,000 residents perished.

TOP TIPS

- Buy fort tickets just south of the Ram Pol gate.
- Visit when the fort opens at dawn to beat the crowds, or come in late afternoon to catch sunset and the 7pm sound-and-light show.
- Vendors sell snacks and drinks, but keep your food hidden from the fort's resident langur and macaque monkeys. For a more substantial meal, try the licensed restaurant at **Hotel Pratap Palace** in town.
- Handy places to stay in Chittorgarh include the Chittorgarh Fort Haveli (p184) in the fort village, and **Hotel Hari Leela Fort View** on the plain below.
- Menstruating women are asked not to enter Chittorgarh's Jain temples.

Udaipur

PALATIAL DIGS | LAKE VIEWS | FINE DINING

TOP TIP
Udaipur is the one place in Rajasthan where the commercialism can be wearing. Try to stay friendly when declining offers from would-be guides, eager souvenir sellers and commission-seeking drivers. Everyone has to make a living, after all, and a polite but firm 'No thank you' usually does the trick.

Entangled by the Aravalli Hills and wrapped around the banks of a shimmering, silvery lake, Rajasthan's 'White City' is swooningly romantic and endlessly atmospheric but sometimes a little overbearing, thanks to its enthusiastic pursuit of the tourist dollar. To get the best from Udaipur, mix up the palace tours with chill-out time in cafes and lavish dinners overlooking the lake, and get out onto the water at sunset to see the city at its most sublime.

With a few days to spare, combine the palaces and temples with walks along the narrow, crooked backstreets. If you don't mind some vigorous sales pitches, this is probably the best place in the state to buy souvenirs, and almost certainly the best spot for a dinner with a view. For a change of pace, hire a car and driver and visit temple towns and historic forts tucked away in the Aravalli Hills.

Cruise Lake Pichola

Float on Udaipur's landmark lake

Glimmering **Lake Pichola** was created in the 16th century by flooding the village of Picholi – one of many vanity projects by the extravagant Maharana Udai Singh II. Gazing out over its silvery waters is one of Udaipur's great pleasures.

GETTING AROUND

Udaipur has daily trains to Agra, Ajmer, Bundi, Chittorgarh, Delhi and Jaipur. For Mt Abu, Chittorgarh or Jodhpur, take a bus from the busy central bus stand, off Sardar Patel Marg. Tickets for private buses are sold by agents around Lal Ghat and Gangaur Ghat; always check where the bus departs. Flights run to Jaipur, Delhi, Mumbai, Bengaluru, Hyderabad and Kolkata from Udaipur's small airport, a 45-minute taxi ride from the centre.

Autorickshaws are the default transport downtown, but squeezing through the narrow lanes can be slower than walking – stroll to the nearest major road and start your ride there. Journeys by taxi start at the parking garage just north of the Chandpole bridge.

Elegant pavilions and palaces stand in the middle of the lake, including the icy white Lake Palace of Maharana Jagat Singh II on **Jagniwas Island**, propelled to international fame by the James Bond film *Octopussy* (today, it's an exclusive Taj hotel).

Further south is **Jagmandir Island**, with its own elegant palace-turned-hotel, built by Maharana Karan Singh II in 1620. The restaurant, bar, spa, gardens and exhibitions inside the Gol Mahal pavilion are open to visitors on boat trips *(₹600–800 return)* run by the City Palace.

Trips leave regularly from the palace's **Rameshwar Ghat** from 10am to around sunset *(₹50 City Palace entry fee applies),* and prices increase mid-afternoon. You can linger as long as you like in the gardens before taking any boat back to shore.

Sunset cruises *(₹500–750)* can also be arranged directly with boat operators at **Lal Ghat** or through hotels and tour agencies, taking a similar circuit around Lake Pichola and its floating palaces.

A Right Royal Dinner Service

Admire the royal crystal

Set inside the Taj Fateh Prakash Palace Hotel in the City Palacecompound, the **Crystal Gallery** *(₹500)* displays an extravagant collection of crystal-handled cutlery and place settings, chandeliers, crystal-framed chairs and even a crystal-framed bed.

Maharana Sajjan Singh placed a massive order with English crystal maker F&C Osler & Co in 1877, but he died before it arrived, so the delivery was packed away, unopened, for 110 years.

The gallery admission fee also includes entry to the downstairs **Durbar Hall**, full of weaponry, royal portraits and dangling chandeliers. You'll need to pay the ₹50 palace compound entry fee to visit; leave cameras and phones with the guard.

A Snapshot of Mewar Life

Visit a prime minister's residence

Beside arch-fronted Gangaur Ghat, the gracious **Bagore-ki-Haveli** *(02942-482322; entry ₹150, camera ₹60)* was built by a Mewar prime minister in the 18th century. Now restored, this maze of a residence is jammed with kitchen implements, traditional board games, puppets, wedding dioramas, weaponry and household paraphernalia.

Continues on p152

ROYAL MEWAR

Claiming descent from Rama's son Lava (Luv), the House of Mewar, Udaipur's ruling clan, is the oldest serving dynasty in the world, founded by the Rajput warrior Bappa Rawal in the 7th century. Its maharanas (princely rulers) were responsible for building most of Udaipur's grand monuments, and were pivotal in holding back – temporarily, at least – the expansion of the Delhi Sultanate and Mughal empire.

Most people associate Mewar with the Sisodia family, who ruled the kingdom from the 14th century onwards. The current head of the House of Mewar, Dr Lakshyaraj Singh Mewar, is the holder of nine Guinness World Records for his charitable, social and environmental work. During **Holi** in February or March, the royal family hosts an extravagant bonfire ceremony inside the City Palace.

EATING IN UDAIPUR: MEMORABLE MEALS

1559 AD: Stylish lakeside dining complete with candles, waistcoated waiters and live Indian classical music. *11am-11pm* ₹₹₹

Sunset Terrace: Spectacular Indian gastronomy with lake views at the Taj Fateh Prakash Palace hotel; book ahead. *7am-10.30pm* ₹₹₹

Khamma Ghani: Dine on top-class Indian dishes amid lawns and lake views at this stylish restaurant with a swimming pool. *11am-11pm* ₹₹₹

Sheesh Mahal: The lavish Leela Palace pulls out all the stops at its lake view restaurant, elevating Rajasthani cooking to haute cuisine. *7-11pm* ₹₹₹

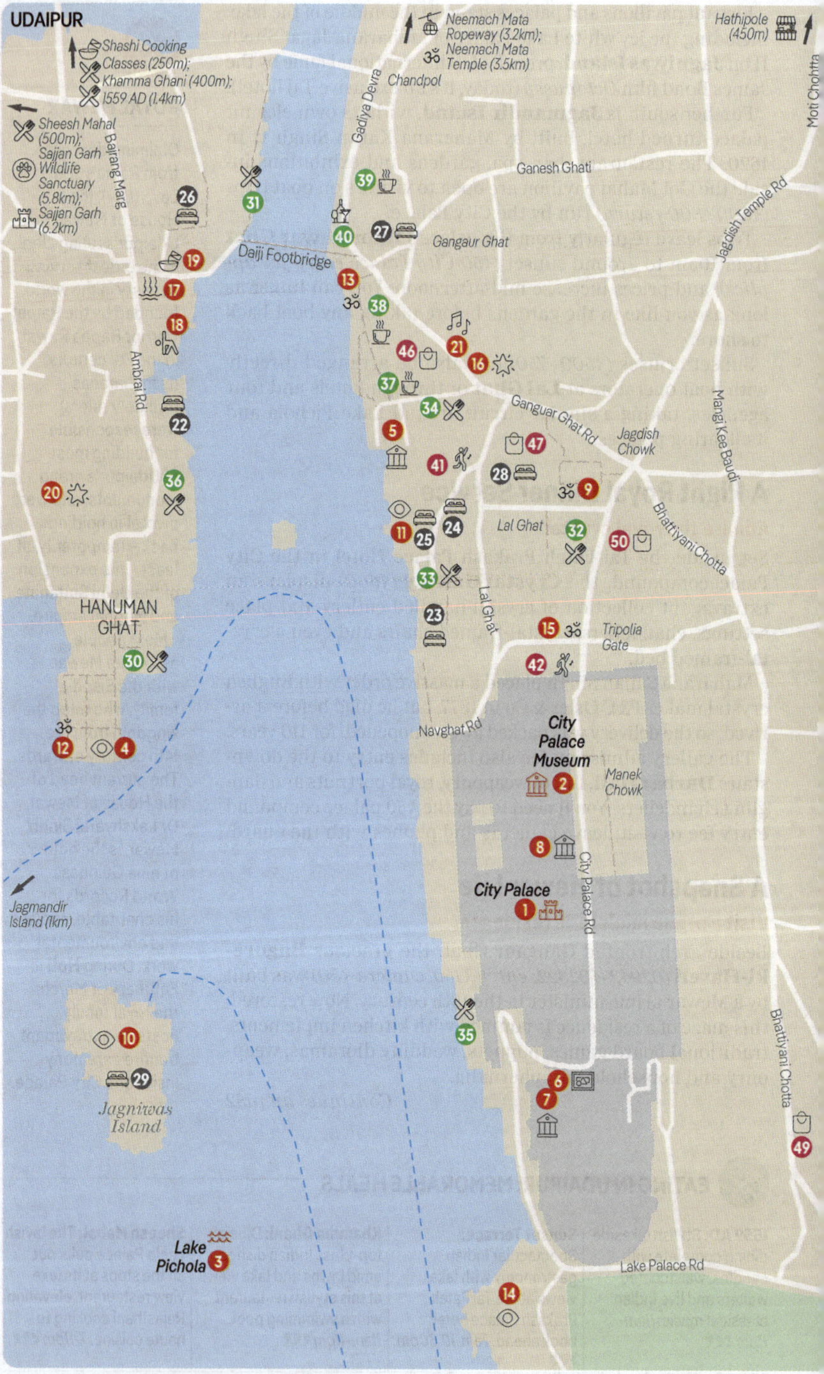
UDAIPUR
Shashi Cooking Classes (250m);
Khamma Ghani (400m);
1559 AD (1.4km)
Sheesh Mahal (500m);
Sajjan Garh Wildlife Sanctuary (5.8km);
Sajjan Garh (6.2km)
Neemach Mata Ropeway (3.2km);
Neemach Mata Temple (3.5km)
Hathipole (450m)
Chandpol
Gadiya Devra
Moti Chohtta
Bajrang Marg
Ganesh Ghati
Jagdish Temple Rd
Gangaur Ghat
Daiji Footbridge
Ambrai Rd
Ganguar Ghat Rd
Jagdish Chowk
Mangi Kee Baudi
Lal Ghat
Bhattiyani Chotta
HANUMAN GHAT
Tripolia Gate
Navghat Rd
City Palace Museum
Manek Chowk
City Palace Rd
City Palace
Jagmandir Island (1km)
Jagniwas Island
Lake Pichola
Lake Palace Rd

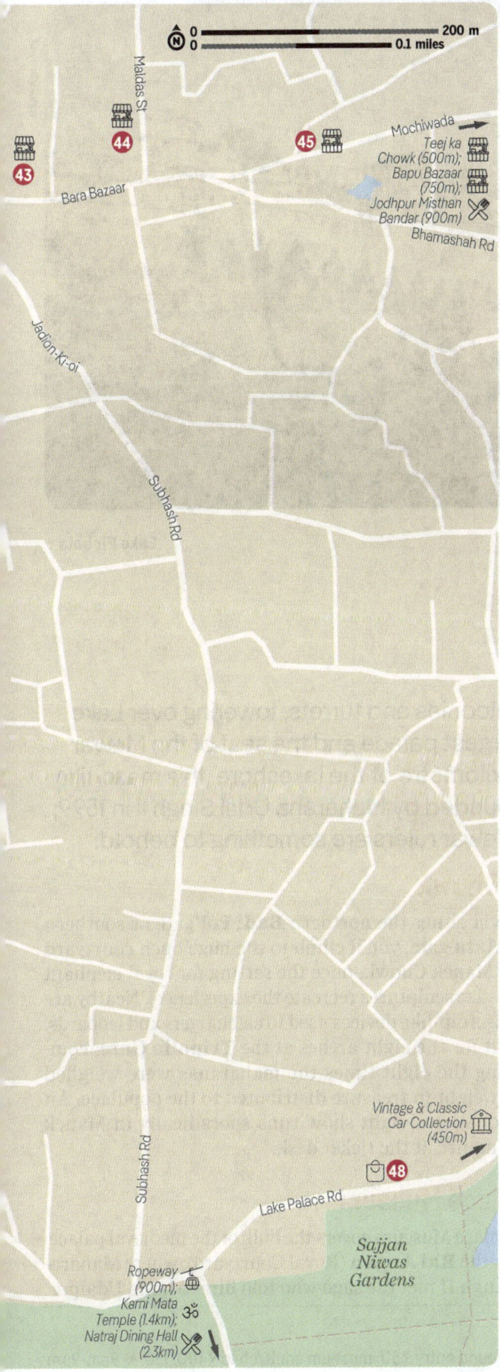

HIGHLIGHTS
1 City Palace
2 City Palace Museum
3 Lake Pichola

SIGHTS
4 Ambrai Ghat
5 Bagore-ki-Haveli
6 Crystal Gallery
7 Durbar Hall
8 Government Museum
9 Jagdish Temple
10 Jagniwas Island
11 Lal Ghat
12 Manji Ka Mandir
13 Ram Ghat
14 Rameshwar Ghat
15 Sri Jagat Shiromani Ji Temple

ACTIVITIES
16 Ashoka Arts
17 Bharti Massage Centre
18 EnteYoga
19 Millets of Mewar
20 Pacific Art
21 Prem Musical Instruments

SLEEPING
22 goStops Udaipur
23 Jagat Niwas Palace Hotel
24 Jaiwana Haveli
25 Kankarwa Haveli
26 Karohi Haveli
27 Nukkad Guest House
28 Pratap Bhawan
29 Taj Lake Palace

EATING
30 Ambrai
see 28 Charcoal
see 23 Jagat Niwas Palace Hotel
31 Little Prince
32 Millets of Mewar
33 Rainbow Restaurant
34 Savage Garden
35 Sunset Terrace
36 Upré

DRINKING & NIGHTLIFE
37 Cafe Edelweiss
38 Jheel's Ginger Coffee Bar & Bakery
39 Nothing Before Coffee
40 Paps Juices

ENTERTAINMENT
41 Dharohar
42 Virasat

SHOPPING
43 Bara Bazaar
44 Maldas St
45 Mochiwada
46 Prem Musical Instruments
47 Rare Arts Exporters
48 Soma
49 Studio Bameer
50 University of Arts

PETE SEAWARD

Lake Pichola

TOP EXPERIENCE

City Palace

A soaring mass of bulging balconies and turrets, towering over Lake Pichola, this is Rajasthan's largest palace and the seat of the Mewar maharanas. Taking up half a kilometre of the lakeshore, this maze-like warren of a residence was founded by Maharana Udai Singh II in 1599; inside, the treasures of the Mewar rulers are something to behold.

DON'T MISS

- Manek Chowk
- City Palace Museum
- The Armoury
- Ganesh Chowk & Government Museum
- The Royal Apartments
- Mor Chowk & Surya Choupad
- Zenana Mahal

Manek Chowk

Entering via either the northern **Badi Pol** gate or southern **Sheetla Mata** gate, you'll climb to the huge open courtyard known as Manek Chowk, once the setting for royal elephant fights (life-size sculptures recreate the experience). Nearby are giant, mousetrap-like devices used to catch tigers and leopards.

Look out for the eight arches at the **Tripolia Gate**, commemorating the eight times the maharanas were weighed and their weight in treasure distributed to the populace. An evening sound-and-light show runs sporadically in Manek Chowk – inquire at the ticket desk.

City Palace Museum

The City Palace Museum covers the bulk of the medieval palace, centred on the **Rai Angan** (Royal Courtyard), where Maharana Udai Singh II met the sage who told him to build Udaipur.

PRACTICALITIES

- citypalacemuseum.org
- palace compound entry ₹50; museum adult/child ₹400/150
- 9am-9pm

Note the sun-topped royal crest of Mewar above the Darikhana ki Pol doorway, then enter via the ornate Toran Pol gate.

The Armoury

Bear right from the first courtyard to reach the astonishing armoury, full of whistle-tooting guards trying to keep the crowds in order. You'll find everything from chain mail trousers to *pattars* (swords with a built-in gauntlet), maces, guns, spears, swords, shields and katar daggers – almost all of them lavishly inlaid and engraved. Look out for the gun-shield, and the backscratcher-like mace shaped like a giant hand.

Ganesh Chowk & Government Museum

You'll pass into open **Ganesh Chowk**, with a gateway leading on to the **Government Museum** *(₹100)*, accessed on a separate ticket. The faded collection includes ivory models, carved temple deities, moth-eaten taxidermy, paintings of maharanas with twirly moustaches, and a collection of turbans, including one worn by Shah Jahan, creator of the Taj Mahal.

Rai Angan

Passing through the mirror-mosaic-covered Ganesh Deodi hall, you'll reach the chequerboard Rai Angan (Royal Courtyard). Rooms along one side commemorate the Battle of Haldighati (1576), where Mewar forces gallantly fought the army of Mughal emperor Akbar to a stalemate. Look out for the bowl of genuine Haldighati battlefield dirt.

The Royal Apartments

Continue through a chain of elegant apartments reserved for the royal household. Of particular note are the **Baadi Mahal** (from 1699), ringed by open pavilions containing fountains and coloured glass, and the **Kishan Vilas**, with miniature paintings from the time of Maharana Bhim Singh (r 1778–1828). Executed in a Mewar-meets-baroque style, the turquoise **Bhim Vilas** is one of the most beautiful spaces in all of Rajasthan.

Mor Chowk & Surya Choupad

Mirrored and painted chambers lead on to the dizzyingly beautiful courtyard known as **Mor Chowk** – with its gasp-inducing mosaics of peacocks, flowers and maharanas. Beyond lies the mural-filled **Surya Choupad**, dominated by a huge metal mask of Surya, patron deity of the Mewar dynasty.

Zenana Mahal

The southern end of the museum is dominated by the 17th-century Zenana Mahal, the royal ladies' quarters. Devote some time to the thoughtful displays on female life in the palace, the collection of musical instruments and the interesting 'Picturing Place' exhibition, exploring Mewar history through old maps.

You'll emerge onto enormous **Laxmi Chowk**, containing a beautiful white pavilion and displays of royal outfits, howdahs (elephant saddles), palanquins and other posh-people-carriers. Exit via Toran Pol to complete the circuit.

MORE ROYAL TREASURES

There's more to the royal estate. South of the museum, the Taj Fateh Prakash Palace – now a luxury hotel – contains the imposing Durbar Hall (p147) and Crystal Gallery (p147). Floating in the middle of the lake are the Lake Palace Hotel (p147) and the Jagmandir Island Palace (p147), accessible on day trips by boat. The collection of royal motors (p154) at the Garden Hotel completes the package.

TOP TIPS

- Tickets are sold at the Badi Pol and Sheetla Mata gates. On top of museum entry fees, there's a ₹50 charge to enter the palace compound.
- The ticket office also sells tickets for the boat trip to Jagmandir Island (p147) and the Crystal Gallery and Durbar Hall (p147).
- Start queuing before 9am to beat the hefty crowds.
- Filling meals of dhal bhatti churma (wheat rolls with stewed lentils) are sold at the museum restaurant on Laxmi Chowk, and at higher prices at the museum restaurant in Manek Chowk.
- A guide (₹500) or audio guide (₹200) is a worthwhile investment; book both at the entrance to the museum.

Continued from p147

Look out for the home temple, the collection of moody *pichwai* paintings and the world's biggest turban, measuring 150m when unravelled. The front courtyard is the setting for performances of Rajasthani folk dances by the **Dharohar** dance group (p155) every evening.

Udaipur's Temples

Explore lavish carvings and spiritual highs

Udaipur is dotted with historic temples that are free to visit, but remove your shoes before you enter and behave respectfully, as these are active places of worship.

The city's grandest Hindu mandir is the towering, multi-level **Jagdish Temple**, poised above the bazaars uphill from Lal Ghat. This carving-crammed Indo-Aryan temple was built by Maharana Jagat Singh in 1651, enshrining a revered image of Vishnu as Jagannath, Lord of the Universe. Its exterior is covered in carvings of elephants, horses, dancing girls, musicians and deities, and a striking statue of Garuda looks on adoringly from an adjacent pavilion. The temple is thronged day and night by devotees, and several tea stands near the base of the steps keep the crowds refreshed.

A short walk uphill towards the palace, **Sri Jagat Shiromani Ji Temple** is another imposing *shikhara*-style temple. Look closely at the carvings and you'll see tigers attacking elephants, elephants fighting elephants, lions pouncing on camels, and the odd erotic scene. More historic temples line the same royal arcade, but are off-limits to sightseers.

Even older are the dozens of neglected stone temples that dot the lake shore between Gangaur Ghat and Hanuman Ghat, many absorbed into neighbouring buildings. At **Ram Ghat**, the view is framed by a statue of the Shiv Dhanush – the bow that Rama broke to prove his divine strength and earn the hand of Sita in marriage.

Head to **Ambrai Ghat** for stunning lake views across to the City Palace and Lake Palace, and drop into the colourful **Manji Ka Mandir** temple – it's sacred to Krishna and draws devotees at sunrise and sunset.

Take In the View

Admire Udaipur's best vistas

Every hotel in Udaipur promises 'the best' view of Lake Pichola but it's easy to take the views to the next level on the **ropeway** *(manshapurnkarnimataropeway.com; return ticket ₹117)* to

BEST SHOPS IN UDAIPUR

University of Arts: Immediately north of the City Palace, this puppeteer-run shop is piled high with vividly colourful Rajasthani puppets.

Prem Musical Instruments: Grab yourself a sitar, tabla, *santoor* or harmonium from this shop run by a trained music teacher on Jagdish Temple Rd.

Rare Arts Exporters: Near Gangaur Ghat; the place to come for heirlooms and medieval militaria, and the paperwork for exporting them.

Soma: On Lake Palace Rd and packed with tasteful block-printed clothes, bed linen and homewares in summery colours.

Studio Bameer: This artist's studio on Bhatiyani Chohatta sells artworks and T-shirts that will invite comments back home.

EATING IN UDAIPUR: ECONOMIC EATS

Little Prince: A traveller favourite on the waterfront at Hanuman Ghat, and always busy thanks to its tasty, pocket-friendly food. *11am-10.30pm* ₹

Savage Garden: Upstairs from Cafe Edelweiss, offering rooftop dining at budget rates; good for soups and pasta. *noon-10pm* ₹

Rainbow Restaurant: Lake Palace views without the razzmatazz (and cost) at a family-friendly waterfront terrace at Lal Ghat. *8am-11pm* ₹₹

Millets of Mewar: Come to this Lal Ghat institution to sample the healthy, hearty millet-based cuisine of rural Rajasthan. *8am-10.30pm* ₹₹

D_ODIN/SHUTTERSTOCK

Jagdish Temple

the ridge-top **Karni Mata Temple** south of the City Palace. While architecturally unremarkable, the temple is dedicated to a goddess whose children are believed to be manifested as rats – there's a more famous Karni Mata Temple (p184) at Deshnok near Bikaner.

North of the old city, a second **ropeway** *(1800-8913898; return ticket ₹200)* climbs to the stone **Neemach Mata Temple**, sacred to Udaipur's protector deity, offering similarly sublime views over Fateh Sagar lake, with its island garden and solar observatory.

The vista is even better from **Sajjan Garh** *(tourism rajasthan.gov.in/monsoon-palace.html; ₹569)*, the monsoon palace of Maharana Sajjan Singh, set at 944m on a soaring hilltop about 5km west of the Old City. The palace was originally planned to be much larger and grander, but the project was abandoned when Maharana Sajjan Singh died unexpectedly in 1884, aged just 25.

The entry fee is steep and the interiors are empty and austere, with just a few marble fountains and wildlife displays, but the views from the open terrace are wonderful, particularly at sunset. Be wary of the langur monkeys at the palace – they're not averse to raiding bags and even climbing into vehicles in search of food.

Autorickshaws can drop you at the zoo-like **Sajjan Garh Wildlife Sanctuary** at the base of the hill, where you can pay the palace entry fee and arrange a taxi transfer *(₹120)* to the palace.

LANDSCAPING UDAIPUR

While frequently embroiled in conflicts with the Delhi, Malwa and Gujarat sultanates, the Mughals, and with rival Rajput dynasties, the maharanas of Mewar devoted considerable efforts to beautifying their kingdom. Lake Pichola was created to supply the village of Pichola with drinking water in 1362 but considerably expanded by Udai Singh II, who moved the Mewar capital to Udaipur from Chittorgarh in 1559. Ceremonial ghats and lavish palaces were constructed both on the banks and out on the water, creating a city that was both a military and trading hub and a super-sized pleasure garden for the royal family. More artificial lakes were created at Fateh Sagar, Swaroop Sagar, Rang Sagar and Doodh Talai, leading early British visitors to describe Udaipur as the 'Venice of the East'.

EATING IN UDAIPUR: DINING WITH A VIEW

Charcoal: Atop Pratap Bhawan hotel, offering grills, curries, Mediterranean platters, TexMex and more with dizzying lake views. *8am-11pm* ₹₹

Ambrai: Views to die for at Ambrai Ghat, with Indian fine dining in a lakeside garden inside the Amet Haveli hotel. *1-3pm & 6.30-10.30pm* ₹₹₹

Upré: Fine dining and fine views from the rooftop at the Lake Pichola Hotel; book *(9116173737)* a slot for dinner from 7pm or 9pm. *1-3.30pm & 7-11pm* ₹₹₹

Jagat Niwas Palace Hotel: Chic dinners in a design-magazine-worthy hotel with sublime Lake Palace vistas. *noon-3pm & 6-10pm* ₹₹₹

UDAIPUR ARTFORMS

The Mewar School is one of the great schools of Indian miniature painting, and it thrived in the 17th and 18th centuries, supported by the Sisodia maharanas. Mewar painters were commissioned to create royal portraits, record momentous battles and political events, and redecorate palaces, *havelis* and homes all over the kingdom, painting on glass or fabric or directly onto the walls.

Today, paper and cloth are the preferred substrates, and a huge industry supplies painstakingly detailed paintings of deities, wildlife and royal scenes for travellers to take home. Look out for moody *pichwai* paintings, featuring stylised depictions of Krishna and related religious themes in strong and often sombre colours – an artform from the Nathdwara region, around 50km northeast of Udaipur.

LLOYD VAS/SHUTTERSTOCK

Bagore-ki-Haveli

See the Royal Motors

Peek into a maharana's garage

Proudly displayed at the Garden Hotel on Lake Palace Rd, the private car collection of the Mewar royal family will make motor-enthusiasts drool. Among the elegant motors in the **Vintage & Classic Car Collection** *(hrhhotels.com/vintage-classic-car-collection.php; ₹330)* are the beautiful 1934 Rolls-Royce Phantom II used in the Bond film *Octopussy*, the Cadillac convertible that whisked Queen Elizabeth II to the airport in 1961, and – more prosaically – a red-and-white 1960s Standard Herald family saloon.

Note the vintage number plates, such as the 1924 Rolls Royce Tourer marked 'Udaipur 2', from the days when the maharanas owned the very first cars in the city. Before you leave, check out the original 1950s petrol pumps in the forecourt.

While you're in the area, it's worth wandering a few more blocks for lunch or dinner at **Natraj Dining Hall**, popular for bottomless Rajasthani thalis and dhal *bhatti* (stewed lentils with wholewheat rolls).

Take a Class

Learn a new skill in Udaipur

Aspiring Indian cooks rave about the sessions offered by **Shashi Cooking Classes** *(shashicookingclassses.com; classes ₹1750)*, which will get you confidently cooking favourite Rajasthani dishes. They're based near the Hotel Satkar Retreat in the Amba Mata Temple area, north of Hanuman Ghat. **Millets of Mewar** *(milletsofmewar.co.in)* periodically offers classes in pulse- and grain-based vegetarian and vegan cooking – drop in and see if courses are running.

For something different, **Ashoka Arts** *(ashokaarts.co.in; classes ₹1000)* at the Hotel Gangaur Palace offers popular introductory classes in Indian miniature painting. Close to the mosque just east of the Leela Palace hotel, the painting classes at **Pacific Art** *(pacificartudaipur.com; classes ₹2600)*, run by gifted brothers Naresh and Jeetu, also get top marks. Contact them in advance to make a booking and avoid the touts who accost travellers in the area.

Musicians can take lessons in sitar, tabla and *bansuri* flute at **Prem Musical Instruments** *(8641073438; classes ₹1500)* north of Gangaur Ghat, run by multi-talented Rajesh Prajapati (Bablu).

Udaipur's Best Night Out

Appreciate traditional Rajasthani dance

Once upon a time, evenings out in Udaipur meant scratchy VHS screenings of the James Bond film *Octopussy* – partly filmed in the Lake Palace (p147) – but now, traditional Rajasthani dance and puppetry shows are the big crowd-pullers, with several companies hosting nightly shows at 7pm.

The most respected show in town is run by **Dharohar** *(dharoharfolkdance.org; tickets ₹250, camera fee ₹125)*, with performances in the courtyard at Bagore-ki-Haveli. It's an entertaining spectacle and traditional Rajasthani dances and puppetry performances are backed by a live band.

Alternatively, try the **Virasat** *(virasatfolkdance.com; tickets ₹250)* show, hosted in a house on the alley just north of the City Palace. Again, the focus is on traditional dance forms and puppetry.

Get a Soothing Massage

Unwind on the lakeshore

Udaipur has some excellent massage and therapy centres. Near the footbridge in Hanuman Ghat, **Bharti Massage Centre** *(bhartimassagecenter.in; massage from ₹1500)* is run by the charming Raju Ansh and family, who have a remarkable skill for identifying where you are holding tension by examining your hands.

For yoga, many budget hotels arrange morning sessions for guests, including the friendly **Nukkad Guest House** near the footbridge to Hanuman Ghat. For more focused yoga, try the spiritually oriented morning and afternoon classes offered by Seethu from **EnteYoga** *(enteyoga@gmail.com; yoga classes ₹750)*, held at Hanuman Ghat at around 8.30am and 5pm.

BEST PALACES IN RAJASTHAN

City Palace, Udaipur: Every section of this bombastic palace has its own unique style of flamboyant interior design.

City Palace, Jaipur: A palace for the maharaja with everything, containing fascinating paintings, photos, weapons and royal treasures.

Bundi Palace, Bundi: An evocative, rambling ruin, with walls like an illustrated manuscript, featuring some of India's finest murals.

Fort Palace, Jaisalmer: The maze-like palace at the heart of Jaisalmer Fort offers epic fort and desert views from its rooftop.

Umaid Bhawan Palace, Jodhpur: An art-deco take on the classic Indian palace, built by a maharaja who liked to move with the times.

DRINKING IN UDAIPUR: REFRESHMENT STOPS

Paps Juices: Inspired juice combinations served with a smile near the footbridge to Hanuman Ghat. *8.30am-8.30pm*

Cafe Edelweiss: A reminder of Udaipur's trippy, hippie days, serving tasty cakes, coffees and juices by Gangaur Ghat. *8am-8pm*

Jheel's Ginger Coffee Bar & Bakery: A hip hangout for young Udaipuris, with seating on several levels overlooking the lake. *8.30am-9.30pm*

Nothing Before Coffee: A popular stop for students staying at nearby hostels, with good coffee and snacks. *8.30am-11pm*

ROYAL MOTOR HEADS

The rulers of Rajasthan's princely states had a deserved reputation for extravagant living, and nowhere was this more apparent than in their parking garages. As India's ruling dynasties embraced influences from across the world during the 19th and 20th centuries, it became a badge of honour for maharajas to drive the latest premium marque automobiles from Europe and America. British-built Rolls Royce tourers and saloons were the prestige cars of choice, with India accounting for a quarter of the company's sales between 1912 and 1947, but sculpted Cadillacs and Buicks came a close second. Udaipur's Maharanas were perhaps Rajasthan's most enthusiastic royal motor heads, but the Maharajas of Jodhpur, Bharatpur, and nearby Patiala in Punjab and Gwalior in Madhya Pradesh, also assembled enviable fleets.

MATTHIAS GRABEN/IMAGEBROKER/SHUTTERSTOCK

Mewar Festival, Gangaur Ghat

Wander the Bazaars

See where locals shop in Udaipur

A maze of bazaars spills beyond the old clock tower on Jagdish Temple Rd. Running east, **Bara Bazaar** is crammed with tiny jewellery and silversmith shops – look out on your left for **Maldas St**, a tiny alleyway jammed with shops selling bangles and fancy saris.

Continue east and you'll hit **Mochiwada**, packed with vendors of jooti slippers and more silversmiths selling bangles and tiny images for home shrines. Further east, beyond the vibrant **Teej ka Chowk** fruit and veg market, lies **Bapu Bazaar**, selling everything needed for local life, from clothes to tools and baby buggies. Pause for excellent kachori topped with chutney and yoghurt at **Jodhpur Misthan Bandar** on Ashoka Cinema Rd.

Heading north from the clock tower, you'll pass shops selling household goods, jewellery, Indian sweets and stainless steel pots before emerging at **Hathipole**, one of the old city gates, where vendors sell fabric and colourful souvenirs aimed at domestic tourists.

Live it up at the Mewar Festival

Udaipur's biggest shindig

Udaipur has a packed festival calendar, from royal-hosted **Holi** celebrations at the City Palace to the folk art traditions of Shilpgram Utsav in December or January, but the biggest event of the year is the **Mewar Festival**, held in March or April.

This enthusiastic celebration of all things Mewar coincides with the Hindu festival of Gangaur, marking the marriage of Shiva to Gauri (Parvati) – a symbol of the perfect union of masculine and feminine energies.

Dancers re-enact traditional Rajput stories, women parade images of Shiva and Gauri through the streets, music fills the lanes around the City Palace and Gangaur Ghat and a royal barge sets sail across Lake Pichola. As well as celebrating Mewar culture, the festival heralds the arrival of spring and the warm weather preceding the monsoon.

Beyond Udaipur

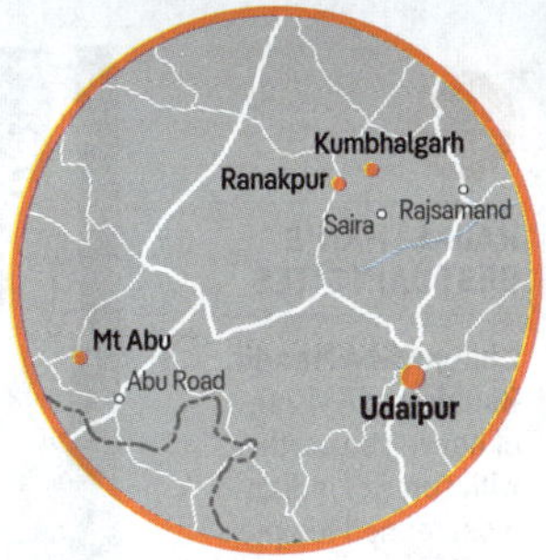

Escape the crush of Udaipur in timeworn ruins and tremendous temples and the relaxing hill station of Mt Abu.

The far south of Rajasthan fringes Gujarat, and many Gujarati tourists are lured here by the area's rich Jain history and temperate highlands. Other draws include an abundance of mock-palace country resorts, and plentiful 'English wine shops' and Punjabi tandoori restaurants, catering to customers from dry, veg-oriented Gujarat.

Once you leave Udaipur, the atmosphere changes noticeably – the region's timeworn forts and ornately carved Jain temples see comparatively few foreign tourists, and the charming hill station of Mt Abu offers a soothing escape from the lowland heat. Mt Abu is an easy stop on the bus journey from Udaipur to Jodhpur; other sites are better reached by chartered car.

Places

GETTING AROUND

Kumbhalgarh and Ranakpur are best reached from Udaipur on a day trip with a chartered car and driver (around ₹4500). If you're travelling to Mt Abu, trains and many bus services operate from Abu Rd, a 28km bus or shared 4WD ride south from the hill station. RSRTC runs a few direct bus services to Mt Abu; more frequent private buses leave from Mt Abu's Koyla Depot bound for Udaipur, Jodhpur, Jaipur and Ahmedabad.

Kumbhalgarh & Ranakpur TIME FROM UDAIPUR: 2½HR

Wander ruined battlements and toppled temples

About 80km north of Udaipur in the tumbling Aravalli Hills, Kumbhalgarh is home to a profusion of palace-shaped country resorts and the 14th-century **Kumbhalgarh Fort** *(tourism .rajasthan.gov.in/kumbhalgarh-fort.html; entry ₹600, sunset sound & light show ₹354)*, only conquered once in its history. It took the combined armies of Amber, Marwar and the Mughal emperor Akbar to breach its strong defences.

Behind its barrel-buttressed walls, the steeply stacked **Badal Mahal** palace features murals of elephants waging war on other wildlife in its empty chambers. Take in the stupendous rooftop views, then escape the crowds on the peaceful pathways that meander between the ancient temples scattered inside the walls.

Loop counterclockwise from the fort gates, passing the multi-level **Vedi Temples**, the column-fronted **Neelkanth Mahadev Temple**, and the ruined but intricately carved **Golerao Jain Temples**, alongside dotted step-wells, dams and farmsteads.

Seek wildlife in the hills

The beautiful, rugged hills of the surrounding **Kumbhalgarh Wildlife Sanctuary** are home to abundant monkeys, birds and deer and rarely seen leopards, wolves and sloth bears. Opposite the Via Lakhela Resort below the fort, the **Forest**

RAJASTHAN'S BEST JAIN SITES

Chaumukha Mandir, Ranakpur: A vision of heaven on earth, with some of India's most refined temple carvings.

Delwara Temples, Mt Abu: The most lavish of Rajasthan's Jain temples, overflowing with deities, scrollwork and wonder.

Jain Temples, Jaisalmer Fort: The five lavishly adorned Jain temples inside Jaisalmer Fort are masterpieces of the stonemasons' art.

Tower of Fame, Chittorgarh: A triumphal tower in Chittorgarh fort celebrating the first Jain *tirthankar* and the Digambara (sky-clad) order.

Soniji ki Nasiyan Temple, Ajmer: Intricate, gilded models tell the life story of the first *tirthankar* at this fascinating, crimson-red temple.

BTWIMAGES/SHUTTERSTOCK

Chaumukha Mandir, Ranakpur

Office *(7014784698)* can arrange morning and afternoon safaris by 4WD for around ₹4300, or you can book through hotels.

You have a better chance of encounters in the Sadri Range near Ranakpur; 4WD safari operators linger by the small **Forest Office** *(8302839196)* near the Jain temple complex.

See Rajasthan's grandest Jain temple

Most people combine a day-trip to Kumbhalgarh with a stop at the spectacular 15th-century **Chaumukha Mandir** *(8696453616; camera ₹100, audioguide ₹200)*, deep in the forest at Ranakpur. Dedicated to Rishabhadeva (Adinath), the first *tirthankar* (teacher) of Jainism, the temple is a riot of filigree spirals, cavorting deities and layered ornamental motifs, like a piece of heaven pushing through onto the earthly plane.

Look out for carvings of five-bodied Akichaka, symbolising the five elements and five negative attachments. Smoking, alcohol, food and drinks are barred, shoes and leather items must be left outside, and menstruating women are not admitted.

Mt Abu

TIME FROM UDAIPUR: 3-5HR

Be blown away by the Delwara Temples

Even by the extravagant standards of Jain architecture, the 11th-century **Delwara Temples**, 3km north of Mt Abu, are something else – a recreation of the heavens in milky marble.

The lavish **Vimal Vasahi Temple** was founded in 1031 by Vimal Shah, a minister from the Chaulukya kingdom in Gujarat. Dedicated to Rishabhadeva (Adinath), it took 1500 masons and 1200 labourers to build and cost ₹185.3 million. Ceilings feature multi-armed deities and mandala-like roof bosses that bring to mind fractal patterns and passionfruit flowers.

The adjacent **Luna Vasahi Temple** is dedicated to Neminath, the 22nd *tirthankar;* it was constructed in 1230, for a more modest ₹125.3 million.

As at other Jain temples, leather articles, cameras and phones must be left with guards at the entrance, and menstruating women are asked not to enter.

Soak in Mt Abu's hill station charm

Rajasthan's only hill station nestles among emerald forests on the state's highest mountain, drawing crowds during Diwali and the **Summer Festival** in June and **Winter Festival** in December.

Reputedly scooped out by Hindu gods using their *nakh* (nails), **Nakki Lake** is the focus for domestic tourists, with boating and chintzy family amusements. Walk around the lakeshore for views of green hills and the cream and red turrets of **Jaipur House** – a summer retreat for the Maharaja of Jaipur.

Duck into the 14th-century **Raghunath Temple**, then climb the hillside to **Toad Rock** for lovely lake views. Stalls south of the lake sell topping-drenched soft ices, theatrically prepared Turkish ice cream, *kulfi* and *rabdi* (sweet condensed milk).

For a taste of 19th-century Mt Abu, order a drink at the **bar** at Jaipur House, wander around the **Polo ground**, then stroll uphill to **St Saviour's Church**, an English-style chapel from 1834.

Explore Mt Abu's green hills

Mt Abu is surrounded by the 289-sq-km **Mt Abu Wildlife Sanctuary** *(9571239361; adult/child ₹550/145)*, an untouched expanse of granite outcrops, lakes, forests and lofty viewpoints, teeming with wildlife, including leopards, crocodiles and bears.

Get a taste on the walk out to Sunset Point; pay the national park fee at the checkpoint south of Nakki Lake, then return to the lake on the Bailey's Walk nature trail via Toad Rock.

To explore these pristine hills responsibly, contact the enthusiastic Mahendra 'Charles' Dan from **Mount Abu Trekking** *(9414154854; mountabutrekking.co.in)* for tailor-made, environmentally sensitive walks.

For even bigger views, sign up for a rock-climbing course with the **Swami Vivekanand Institute of Mountaineering** *(facebook.com/svimadmin; contact the institute for prices and timings)*, or take a taxi to 1722m-high **Guru Shikhar**, Rajasthan's highest point.

MEET THE BRAHMA KUMARIS

Both Mt Abu and nearby Abu Rd are important centres for the **Brahma Kumaris** *(brahmakumaris.org)* – a global Hindu organisation with nearly a million followers, founded in Hyderabad (in present-day Pakistan) in the 1930s. You can identify adherents by their white robes, the Brahma Kumari logo (like an egg made of sun rays) and their use of the greeting 'Om Shanti'. Drop into the free-to-visit **World Renewal Spiritual Museum** in the centre of Mt Abu, or the **Universal Peace Hall** at the Brahma Kumari World Spiritual University north of the centre, or swing by the free laser show at the **Prakashmani Wisdom Park** in Abu Rd. At all these sites, attendants will happily introduce the Brahma Kumari philosophy, with a bit of proselytising along the way.

EATING IN MT ABU

Arbuda: The street in front was named after this ever-popular restaurant, serving quality Gujarati, Punjabi and South Indian veg dishes. *8am-10.30pm* ₹

Chacha Cafe: Offering a bit of everything that's veg, with a licensed bar; eat inside in air-con or outside on the terrace. *11am-11pm* ₹₹

Tandoori Bites: Exceptional tandoori chicken and other meaty treats, served fresh off the charcoal in a simple dining room on the bazaar. *noon-11.30pm* ₹₹

Jaipur House Restaurant: The smartest table in town offers superior Indian, Chinese and European food with sweeping Mt Abu views. *10am-3pm & 7-11pm* ₹₹₹

Jodhpur

PALACE GRANDEUR | EVOCATIVE BACKSTREETS | ROMANTIC DINNERS

> **TOP TIP**
> Jodhpur's hundreds of street dogs can be a menace. Be careful when exploring the backstreets of Navchokiya – dogs here are very territorial, and once one starts barking, others will rush in to join the fray. Carry a bag or umbrella to raise theatrically as a deterrent.

There's more to Rajasthan's famous Blue City than its indigo-coloured alleyways and skyline-dominating fort, but you'll certainly want to devote a couple of days to exploring these iconic sights. The former capital of the princely state of Marwar is perhaps the most atmospheric of the state's medieval cities, hitting the sweet spot between tourist creature comforts and undiluted Rajput culture.

Factor in tangled bazaars, plunging step-wells, royal cenotaphs and rooftop dinners with swoon-inducing views and it's easy to see why this is one of the most visited cities in Rajasthan. Yet the crowds of sightseers seem to melt away in the labyrinthine lanes of the Old City, which never seem to lead where you expect them to.

Sure, there's a bit of hustle in the tourist quarter east of the fort, but it's easy to escape in the bazaars running west and the tightly packed alleys of Navchokiya, tucked behind the fort's less-used Fateh Pol gate.

GETTING AROUND

The maze-like Old City is most easily explored on foot; taxis and autorickshaws will struggle to penetrate much deeper than Sardar Market and the main approach road to the fort, so be ready to walk from the nearest major road to your accommodation along narrow, uneven alleyways. Jodhpur's small airport (a 30-minute taxi trip from the centre) has flights from Jaipur, Delhi, Mumbai, Bengaluru, Ahmedabad and Hyderabad, or there are excellent connections by bus and train to cities all over Rajasthan. Jodhpur train station is 1.5km south of Sardar Market; the bus stand is 2.5km southeast.

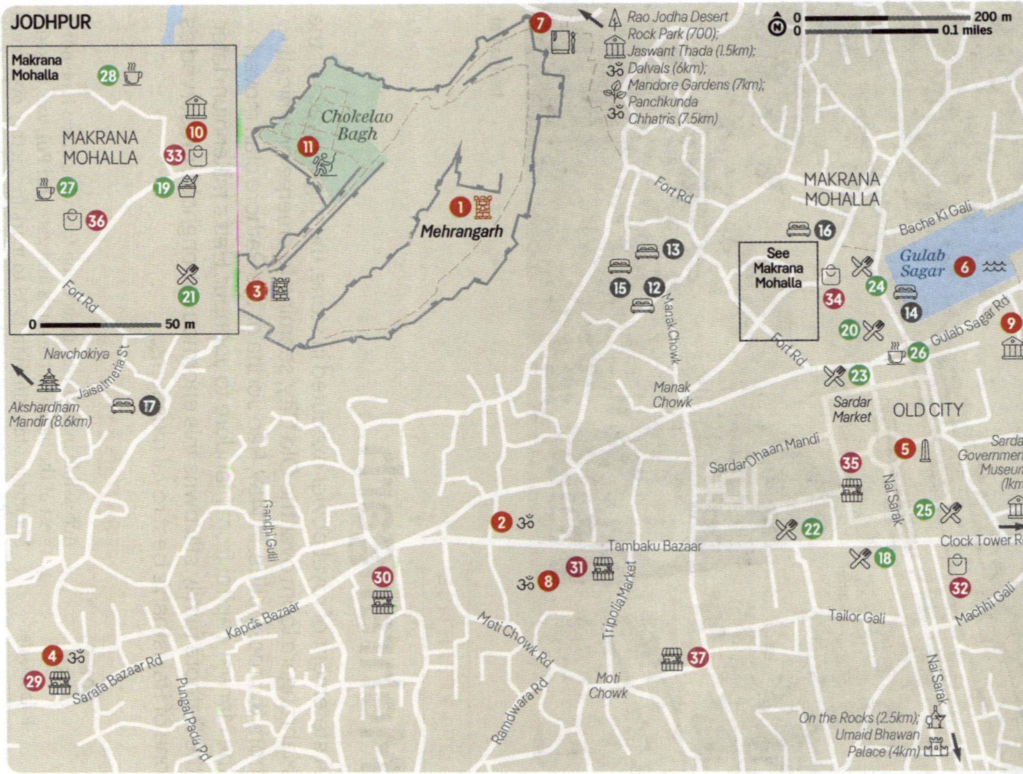

HIGHLIGHTS
1 Mehrangarh

SIGHTS
2 Achal Nath Mandir
3 Fateh Pol
4 Ghanshyam Mandir
5 Ghanta Ghar
6 Gulab Sagar
7 Jai Pol
8 Kunj Bihari Mandir
9 Mayla Bag Ka Jhalra
10 Toorji Ka Jhalra

ACTIVITIES
11 Flying Fox

SLEEPING
12 Kesar Heritage
13 Krishna Prakash Heritage Haveli
14 Pal Haveli
15 Pushp Guest House
16 Raas
17 Singhvi's Haveli

EATING
18 Arora Chaat Bhandar
19 Cold Love
20 Indique
21 Jhankar Choti Haveli Restaurant
22 Nirvana
23 Omelette Shop
24 Panorama 360°
25 Shri Mishrilal Hotel

DRINKING & NIGHTLIFE
26 Cafe Sheesh Mahal
27 Sam's Art Cafe
28 Stepwell Cafe

SHOPPING
29 Daga Bazaar
30 Kapda Bazaar
31 Katla Bazaar
32 Mohanlal Verhomal (MV) Spices
33 Nila
34 Royal Blue
35 Sardar Market
36 Suncity Art Exporters
37 Tripolia Bazaar

ABHISHEKMITTAL/SHUTTERSTOCK

Imritia Pol

TOP EXPERIENCE

Mehrangarh

A statement of royal power executed in stone, the mighty walls of the Mehrangarh loom over the Old City, seeming to emerge organically from the rocky cliffs. In 1459, Rao Jodha of the Rathore clan moved the Marwar capital from Mandore to Jodhpur. Half a millennium later, the Rathore family still owns this enormous stronghold, preserved as one of Rajasthan's best royal museums.

DON'T MISS

- Palace Gates
- Shringar Chowk
- Daulat Khana Chowk
- Sheesh Mahal
- Phool Mahal
- Armoury
- Takhat Vilas
- Palace Ramparts
- Chokelao Bagh

The Palace Gates

Accessible by autorickshaw or on foot via a steep lane northwest of the bazaars, the fort's first gate, **Jai Pol**, was raised by Maharaja Man Singh in 1808 to mark his victory over invading forces from Jaipur. Just beyond, the 16th-century **Dodh Kangra Pol** bears the scars of cannonball hits from the siege.

As you pass through two further gates – **Imritia Pol** and **Loha Pol** with its elephant-deterring spikes – look upwards. Ornate balconies and *jarokha* windows gaze out from the upper levels, while the lower walls are windowless and impenetrable. Note the tragic hand prints marking the *sati* of royal wives on their husband's funeral pyres (the most recent is from 1843).

PRACTICALITIES

- mehrangarh.org
- adult/student ₹800/500; guides from ₹500
- 9am-5pm

Shringar Chowk & Daulat Khana Chowk

Enter the museum via Suraj Pol, looking up at the extraordinary windows topped by long, curved pediments. You'll emerge onto the **Shringar Chowk** (Anointment Courtyard), with an outdoor marble throne and galleries displaying lavishly ornamented royal palanquins and howdahs (elephant saddles).

Beyond, **Daulat Khana Chowk** is flanked by dainty red-and-yellow palaces. One contains a fine collection of miniature paintings from the Marwar school; the other features royal heirlooms, including a gilded palanquin, a solid ivory train set and the sword of the Mughal emperor Akbar.

The 18th-Century Palaces

A teardrop-shaped spiral staircase leads up to the 18th-century **Sheesh Mahal**, with displays of embroidered royal tents and a lavish, deity-dotted mirrored hall (Sheesh Mahal translates to 'Palace of Mirrors').

One level up, the **Phool Mahal** (Palace of Flowers) lives up to its name, with an astonishing gilded ceiling, floral panels dotted with vignette portraits of maharajas, and paintings depicting the 'moods' of the 36 ragas – the melodies and rhythms that form the basis of Indian classical music.

Next you'll reach the royal **armoury**. If it's not open, peek in the windows to see the collection of swords, spears, clubs, maces, knives, guns and other fearsome weapons.

Takhat Vilas

Hung with dangling glass baubles, the ornate Takhat Vilas was the bedchamber of Maharaja Takhat Singh (r 1843–73), whose zenana consisted of 30 maharanis and numerous concubines. From here, you'll enter the **Jhanki Mahal** – the womens' quarters – with lace-like fretwork windows through which the royal ladies could observe events in the palace courtyards. Note the elaborate cradles for infant princes.

Moti Mahal

The most architecturally refined part of the palace, the 17th-century Moti Mahal (Pearl Palace) – a dignified space illuminated by panels set with rainbow-coloured glass – was used for official meetings. The chambers surrounding the adjacent marble courtyards feature some of the finest stone-carving in all of Rajasthan.

Before you leave Mehrangarh, walk south from the Moti Mahal through calm, shady gardens for views over the blue rooftops from the cannon-crammed perimeter wall, topped by the historic **Chamundaji Temple** from 1460.

Chokelao Bagh

For an alternative route back to the Old City, bear left before you reach Jai Pol, and descend to the Chokelao Bagh, a restored 18th-century pleasure garden. The adrenaline-charged **Flying Fox** *(flyingfox.asia; zip lining ₹2000)* offers connected zip lines zigzagging over the walls of Mehrangarh. Exit the fort via the **Fateh Pol** gate into the alleyways of Navchokiya.

MUSEUM SHOP

You could easily do all the souvenir shopping for your whole trip in the Mehrangarh's treasure-trove of a gift shop. Shelves are piled high with everything from block-printed scarves and top-grade miniature paintings to showy jewellery and shimmering outfits inspired by the personal wardrobes of the maharajas and maharanis, plus some excellent books on Rajasthan. Prices are high but this is Jodhpur's best selection of mementos.

TOP TIPS

- Be one of the first through the doors at 9am to view the galleries in relative calm.
- You'll get more from the maze of palaces with an official guide (from ₹500), but the audioguide included in the ticket price is a decent alternative.
- For a ₹50 fee, an elevator lifts visitors with mobility issues from inside Jai Pol to the top of the walls.
- Recharge at the **Cafe Mehran**, just before the museum's main entrance, or the simpler **Palki Cafe**, on the way back to Jai Pol.
- In February, the fort hosts mesmerising Sufi musical performances for the **Sacred Spirit Festival** *(worldsacredspiritfestival.org)*.

EXPLORING MEHRANGARH & THE BLUE CITY

A wander around the magnificent Mehrangarh and Blue City.

START	END	LENGTH
Ghanta Ghar	Sardar Market	3.6km; 2-3hr (incl Mehrangarh)

Start by climbing the 1 **Ghanta Ghar** (p167) clock tower for views over 2 **Sardar Market** (p166), then take the northern exit and turn right past fountain-topped 3 **Gulab Sagar** (p166) and the restored 4 **Mayla Bag Ka Jhalra** (p166) step-well. Cross the causeway over the tank, and go west to Gulab Sagar Rd, then north, turning sharp left to reach the deep 5 **Toorji Ka Jhalra** (p166) step-well. Turn right (uphill) after 6 **Jhankar Choti Haveli**, always following the steepest, busiest lane. When you reach 7 **Hill View Guest House**, go left below the fort walls, looking out for (feathered) black kites soaring overhead, and admiring the street art along Jodhpur's so-called 8 **Blue Corridor.**

At the power lines, turn right and climb past the 9 **Panchmukhi Balaji Temple**, with its five-headed deity image, then a white 10 **Vishnu temple** tucked against the cliffs. Continue west to the 11 **Jwala Mukhidevi Temple**, with its statue of the Pandava king Bhima.

Gaze over the blue rooftops, then descend into the tangled alleyways of Navchokiya near the 12 **Pachetia Sunset Point** cafe. Weave north to the fort's 13 **Fateh Pol** gate, then dive into the maze-like chambers of the 14 **Mehrangarh** (p162). Exit via the fort's 15 **Jai Pol**, and take the footpath downhill to Hill View Guest House, then continue downhill to emerge just northwest of Sardar Market.

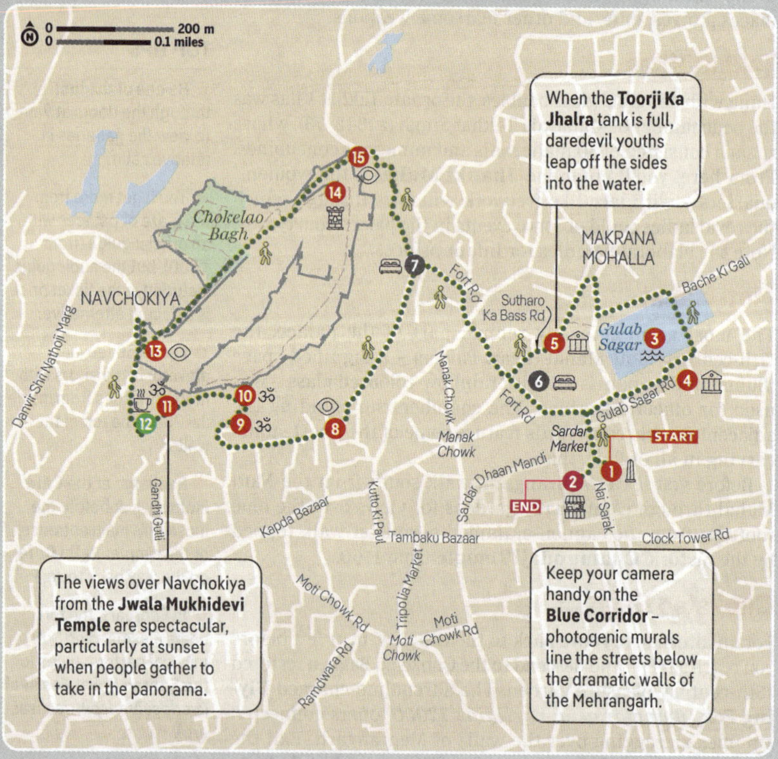

A Magnificent Marble Memorial

Wander around the lake at Jaswant Thada

Across the rocky plateau to the northeast of the Mehrangarh, the marble **Jaswant Thada** *(mehrangarh.org/visit/jaswant-thada; ₹100)* is the funerary memorial for Maharaja Jaswant Singh II, who ruled Jodhpur from 1873 to 1895. Surrounded by smaller *chhatris* (cenotaphs), it's a whimsical collection of spires and marble *jali* screens, hung with portraits of great Rathore rulers.

The adjacent lake forms part of the **Rao Jodha Desert Rock Park** *(mehrangarh.org/visit/rao-jodha-desert-rock-park; entry ₹100, guided walks ₹200)*, protecting an arid landscape of exposed outcrops, drought-tolerant plants, and seasonal pools that attract visiting ducks, egrets, herons, bustards and flycatchers. Arrange guided nature walks at the Jaswant Thada ticket desk.

A Palace for a Modern Maharaja

Visit the palatial home of a modern maharaja

Looking southeast from Mehrangarh, you'll spot the towering domes of the **Umaid Bhawan Palace** *(9414478461; adult/student ₹250/150, guides from ₹250)*, home of the present head of the Rathore clan, Gaj Singh II. Fusing Indo-Saracenic and art-deco features, the palace was designed by British architect Henry Lanchester in 1929, and it reveals a royal family moving with the times.

Several wings are occupied by the lavish, Taj-operated Umaid Bhawan Palace hotel, but you can admire the maharaja's fleet of cars, including a gleaming Rolls-Royce Phantom I and Phantom II and chrome-covered 1940s American saloons, before entering the palace museum.

Inside, rooms display mirror-covered furniture, fancy clocks and other royal heirlooms. Don't miss the elegant Oriental Room, with scenes from the Ramayana, painted in a glorious, part-Indian, part-art-deco style by Polish artist Stefan Norblin.

Jodhpur's Most Extravagant Tombs

Evocative, overlooked royal cenotaphs

About 9km north of the Old City, the sprawling **Mandore Gardens** *(free)* were created around the ruins of Mandore Fort, seat of the Marwar dynasty until 1459, and the towering, rust-red **Devals** *(free)* – an astonishing collection of royal cenotaphs that mirror the architecture of Jain and Hindu temples.

JODHPUR'S JODHPURS

A fashion staple for self-respecting horsey types all over the world, jodhpurs are one of Rajasthan's most famous exports.

It is said that Sir Pratap Singh, a legendary Jodhpur statesman, soldier and horseman, originally designed these pale cream riding breeches – loose above the knee and tapered from knee to ankle – for the Jodhpur Lancers. When he led the Jodhpur polo team on a tour to England in 1897, the novel trousers caught on in London and the fashion spread around the world.

These days, you won't find many jodhpurs for sale in Jodhpur, but you'll see plenty of photos of royals wearing them at the city's palace museums.

EATING IN JOHDPUR: OUR PICKS

Nirvana: Stellar Indian veg cooking, including huge thalis, served on the rooftop above a leafy temple courtyard in the bazaars. *7.30am-10pm* ₹

Jhankar Choti Haveli Restaurant: A courtyard *haveli*, with a broad veg menu, cane chairs, whirring fans and subtle mood lighting. *8am-10pm* ₹₹

Panorama 360°: Reached from the courtyard at Haveli Inn Pal, with spectacular Mehrangarh views and a wide-roaming menu. *7.30am-10.30pm* ₹₹

Indique: On the rooftop at the historic Pal Haveli Hotel, with views and a menu (with tandoori and Rajasthani specials) to die for. *7.30am-10.30pm* ₹₹₹

JODHPUR HIGHLIGHTS

Nikhil Mathur of Pushp Guest House and Bristows Haveli *(bristowsindia.com)* recommends his favourite Jodhpur highlights.

The **Mandore Gardens** (p165) hold some of my most beautiful childhood memories. I still remember going there for picnics with my family and friends, cooking together, and spending entire days surrounded by greenery. Today, Mandore has been beautifully restored, with a stunning museum and an enchanting light-and-sound show, but the memories remain just as strong.

I recommend seeking out the temples of the Old City, home to many ancient temples – the **Achal Nath Mandir**, **Kunj Bihari Mandir**, **Ghanshyam Mandir**, and many more – each marked by centuries of devotion and history. And of course, the newly built **Akshardham Mandir** is a must-visit; its beautifully carved architecture will leave you spellbound.

The *chhatri* of Maharaja Dhiraj Ajit Singh (r 1679–1724) is a magnificent assembly of arches and spires with a tragic backstory – 64 royal wives and consorts were immolated here when the maharaja died.

Also here is a sleepy **Government Museum** *(₹100)* with *pichwai* paintings, temple carvings, royal portraits and musty taxidermy, displayed in the fort's Janana Mahal.

About 1km northeast of Mandore Gardens, the **Panchkunda Chhatris** are the earliest Marwar funerary memorials in Jodhpur, built in the classic Rajasthani style.

Jodhpur's Dramatic Step-Wells

Magical water features

In the lanes north of the Sardar Market, the **Toorji Ka Jhalra** *(free)* step-well was excavated in the 1740s, and it forms the centrepiece of a neighbourhood going through a major renaissance.

The site is most atmospheric when the water level is low, revealing geometric stairways that zigzag down to the water's edge and an ornate arched mock-gateway. Drop into the delightful **Stepwell Cafe** to take in the view over a full-strength espresso.

A short walk south, **Mayla Bag Ka Jhalra** *(free)* is a similarly grand step-well, dropping in stepped tiers just beyond the fountain-topped **Gulab Sagar** tank.

A Snapshot of Marwar History

Visit the surprising Government Museum

Between Mehrangarh and the Umaid Bhawan Palace, the often overlooked **Sardar Government Museum** *(adult/student ₹100/50)* is a little gem. Thoughtfully laid out galleries display Marwar miniature paintings, arms and armour, royal portraits, temple carvings, old photos and maps, taxidermy and crafts. Highlights include stereoscope photos of Indian soldiers in WWI, an ivory train set and a pair of wrestling stuffed tigers.

Hit the Bazaars

Shop the Jodhpur way

Jodhpur's meandering bazaars are a magical place to explore. Start off at **Sardar Market**, constructed in the 19th century by Maharaja Sardar Singh.

DRINKING IN JODHPUR: WHERE TO RECHARGE

Stepwell Cafe: A cool coffee stop with cakes, espresso, snacks, beer and wine, plus views into the Toorji Kna Jhalra step-well. *7.30am-10.30pm*

Sam's Art Cafe: Close to the step-well, with mood lighting and tables dotted around a hoard of art and crafts, plus an extensive menu of drinks and snacks. *8am-10pm*

Cafe Sheesh Mahal: A cute coffeeshop with friendly staff and a great location upstairs near Sardar Market, run by the team from Pal Haveli (p185). *9.30am-9pm*

On the Rocks: A great follow-up to the Umaid Bhawan Palace, with tables set under the trees that are as good for a drink as for a bite. *noon-11pm*

Surrounded by shops selling souvenirs, spices and textiles, you can climb the sandstone **Ghanta Ghar** *(₹100)* clock tower for market views from the upper terrace and a peek at the ancient clock mechanism.

Turn west along Clocktower Rd and you'll hit the main bazaars used by locals for daily shopping, selling everything from garlands for home shrines to *lac* (resin) bangles, glittering saris and steel pots and pans.

Going west from Nai Sarak, you'll reach **Katla Bazaar** then **Kapda Bazaar** – good areas for textiles and brocades – then the silversmiths of the **Daga Bazaar** along Sarafa Bazaar Rd. South of Katla Bazaar, the crowded **Tripolia Bazaar** is known for sequined saris and tie-dye Rajsthani outfits in vivid colours.

As you wander, look out for interesting temples such as the tall-towered **Ghanshyam Mandir** near Navchokiya's Singh Pol gate, and statue-filled **Achal Nath Mandir** and the elephant-fronted **Kunj Bihari Mandir** near Katla Bazaar.

Spice Things Up with a Cooking Class

Make the most of Jodhpur's spices

Sardar Market is dotted with vendors selling packed-for-travel spices, but much-imitated **Mohanlal Verhomal (MV) Spices** *(mvspices.com)* – with conveniently located branches on Nai Sarak and around Sardar Market – is the original and best purveyor.

As well as selling packets of aromatic *jeera* (cumin), cinnamon and other Indian kitchen essentials, the seven daughters of the founder – the self-styled 'Spice Girls of India' – host popular cooking classes *(₹2000)* that will teach you what to do with these fragrant ingredients when you get home.

Learn about desert traditions

Discover Rajasthani life on the city fringes

For a taste of traditional desert life, consider a half-day trip to the **Arna Jharna Desert Museum** *(arnajharna.org.in; ₹150)*, about 23km east of the centre near the village of Moklawas (hotels can arrange taxi transfers).

Spilling over a collection of adobe-style dwellings in a peaceful area of desert near a temple-topped waterfall, displays cover traditional instruments, puppetry, pottery, broom making and local customs – look out for the colourful *kavad* (portable shrine).

BEST SHOPPING IN JODHPUR

Sardar Market: A popular wedding photo shoot spot, and good for spices, saris and scarves.

Royal Blue: A chic gift store well stocked with fashions, trinkets and homewares that will stand out when you get them home.

Nila: Handloom clothes, embroidery, bags and blankets featuring contemporary patterns and subtle blue-and-white colour schemes.

Suncity Art Exporters: A shop for interior designers decking out stylish homes, with upscale furniture and craft objects (and the paperwork to export them).

Mohanlal Verhomal (MV) Spices: The Spice Girls of India sell all manner of spices and curry spice mixes packed to go.

EATING IN JODHPUR: BEST SNACKS

Shri Mishrilal Hotel: Beside the southern gate of Sardar Market, and famed for creamy, saffron-infused *makhania* lassis and other yoghurty treats. *8am-10pm* ₹

Omelette Shop: At the north end of Sardar Market; selling omelettes with spicy fillings to appreciative market shoppers from morning till late. *10am-10pm* ₹

Arora Chaat Bhandar: Top-notch veg snacks (*aloo tikki, channa chaat* and the like) draw huge crowds to this streetside vendor at Nai Sarak. *11am-9.30pm* ₹

Cold Love: Delicious ice creams in natural flavours to slurp while you explore the nearby Toorji Ka Jhalra step-well. *11am-8pm* ₹

Beyond Jodhpur

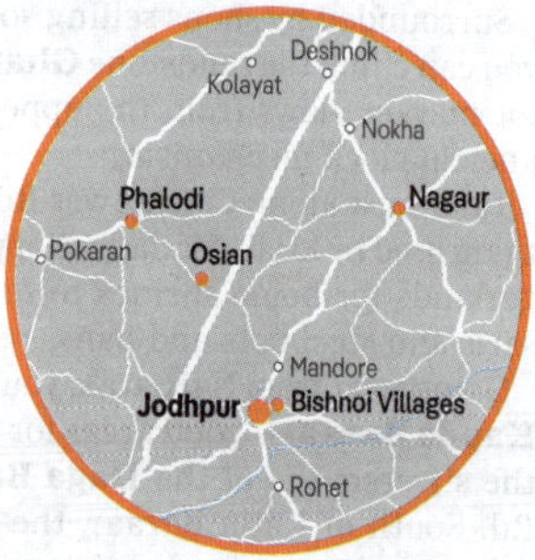

Intriguing desert outposts await in the dry country north of Jodhpur for those willing to step off the tourist trail.

Places

GETTING AROUND

With long distances to cover, and slow backroads to navigate, exploring with a car and driver is the easiest option – hotels and guesthouses in Jodhpur can make arrangements. Visiting Osian and Phalodi together in one day is fine, but Nagaur warrants its own day trip, or you can visit by train from Jodhpur, Bikaner, Jaisalmer or Jaipur. Alternatively, RSRTC buses run from Jodhpur to Osian, Phalodi and Nagaur, with connections on to Bikaner or Jaisalmer.

The arid and underexplored countryside north of Jodhpur is well worth a detour before you head on to Jaisalmer and Bikaner. Here, you'll leave the well-trodden Rajasthan trail and find sleepy towns with stories to tell, dotted with fortress-palaces and ancient Jain and Hindu temples that survived the 800-year jostle for supremacy between Sultanates, Mughals and Rajputs.

The sprawling fortress at Nagaur is perhaps the region's most evocative stop, but it's also worth swinging by Phalodi, a quiet desert bazaar town filled with surprisingly affluent *haveli* homes, and Osian, which pulls in a steady stream of domestic tourists thanks to its finely carved medieval temples and (arguably overhyped) sand dunes and camel treks.

Bishnoi Villages

TIME FROM JODHPUR: 30MIN

Engage with an environmentally friendly community

With time to spare, consider a day trip along the road towards Pali to visit the traditional villages of the Bishnoi sect – followers of the 15th-century Hindu yogi Guru Jambheshwar, revered as an incarnation of Vishnu, whose teachings emphasised protecting the environment.

Wildlife such as blackbuck, nilgai (blue bull), chinkara (Indian gazelle) and desert foxes are easily spotted en route to Bishnoi villages, where residents go out of their way to keep wildlife safe.

At **Khejadali**, a memorial commemorates the 363 Bishnoi villagers who were killed in 1730 protecting a grove of sacred khejri trees from soldiers gathering wood to build a new palace for Abhai Singh, the Maharaja of Marwar. Upon hearing of the massacre, the Maharaja granted special privileges to the Bishnoi as penance.

Many Jodhpur tour agencies offer trips to the Bishnoi villages, but standards vary and some trips can feel a bit exploitative. **Bishnoi Village Safari** *(bishnoivillagesafari.com; tours ₹1250)* is a trusted and reliable operator, with lively trips lasting four hours, run by Deepak and Dhanraj.

Nagaur

TIME FROM JODHPUR: **2-3HR**

A silent, restored wonder

In dusty Nagaur, intoxicating bazaars envelop the enormous and evocatively named **Ahhichatragarh** *(mehrangarh.org; ₹200)* – literally, the 'Fort of the Hooded Cobra'. With Nagaur's off-the-beaten-path location, you might be the only visitor, adding to the magic of wandering its empty palaces.

Part of a two-decade-long restoration project by Jodhpur's Mehrangarh Museum Trust, this 12th-century fort features an elaborate cooling system, with rainwater tanks and ingenious vents on the rooftops feeding cool air and water into the chambers below.

The most impressive of the fort's fountain-ringed palaces is the **Abha Mahal**, containing the bathhouse of Maharaja Amar Singh (r 1634–44). The finest frescoes, depicting female courtly life, are in the **Hadi Rani Mahal**.

Slowly being restored, the murals and mirror mosaics in the **Sheesh Mahal** were painted over by Indian Army soldiers during the 1965 and 1971 India-Pakistan wars. A small exhibition space near the Hadi Rani Mahal tells the story of the fort's impressive restoration. The rear of the fort is given over to Ranvas (p169), a luxury heritage hotel set in the former zenana (women's quarters).

Nagaur also has strong links to Akbar, and to Sufism, thanks to the 14th-century **Tarkin Dargah** *(donations appropriate)*, containing the tomb of the Sufi saint Hamiduddin Nagori. In February, the fort often hosts concerts as part of Jodhpur's **Sacred Spirit Festival** *(worldsacredspiritfestival.org)*.

As you approach Nagaur on the road from Jodhpur, look out for some of India's biggest *gaushalas* – charitable hospitals for stray cows – hosting thousands of rescued cattle.

Phalodi

TIME FROM JODHPUR: **3HR**

Discover a bird-thronged desert outpost

The desert town of Phalodi rose to prominence in the 18th century when Jain salt traders filled its streets with stately *haveli* homes and colourful Jain temples, including Belgian-glass-filled **Sri Godi Parshvanath temple**, northwest of the station.

Built in 1760, the elegant red sandstone Dadha Haveli now houses the Zone Palace by the Park hotel (p169), containing the **Dadha Heritage Museum** *(₹80)*, with a collection of Jain and Hindu manuscripts, sculptures and paintings.

THE FOREST MARTYRS OF KHEJADALI

The bravery of the Bishnoi villagers who gave their lives to protect the khejri trees of **Khejadali** has become a powerful symbol for Indian environmentalists. The Chipko movement (which used direct action to prevent the felling of trees by developers and logging companies in the 1970s and '80s) took direct inspiration from Amrita Devi, the leader of the Khejadali martyrs, who died while shielding trees with her body.

Since 2001, the Indian government has awarded the Amrita Devi Bishnoi Environment Protection Award every year to recognise and support the work of environmental activists and conservation organisations. In 2013, 11 September was declared National Forest Martyrs Day, marked by a fair in Khejadali.

EATING AROUND JODHPUR: OUR PICKS

Bombay Lodge: This sweet shop near Phalodi train station has been dishing out sticky *chum chum* sweets since 1965. *9am-11pm* ₹

Zone Palace by the Park: The restaurant at Phalodi's best hotel serves up tasty vegetarian dishes in the shady interior of an ancient *haveli. 8am-11pm* ₹₹

Swad Restaurant: South of the Sachiya Mata Temple on the main road in Osian, serving tasty veg curries, thalis and dhal *bhatti* plates. *8am-11pm* ₹₹

Ranvas: The elegant dining room at Ranvas in Nagaur Fort offers Rajasthani treats; book ahead on 01582-241271. *7am-10pm* ₹₹₹

RAJASTHAN'S DEMOISELLE CRANES

The Thar Desert may seem parched and lifeless, but the monsoon fills up its seasonal waterholes and every winter, vast flocks of grey and black demoiselle cranes descend on the Thar Desert on their annual migration from Eurasia, Mongolia and China.

Local people in the Jain village of Kichan near Phalodi have been leaving out grain for the cranes for more than 50 years, attracting up to 15,000 every season.

The tradition was started by Rantanlal Maloo, an amateur ornithologist who moved back to Rajasthan from Odisha and started feeding the cranes as an expression of his Jain faith. Today, donors contribute some ₹85 million every year to keep the demoiselles in the manner to which they have become accustomed.

DON MAMMOSER/SHUTTERSTOCK

Demoiselle cranes, Kichan

Tiny **Kichan**, a 5km autorickshaw ride east of Phalodi, bursts into life in the winter months as flocks of migrating demoiselle cranes descend on the village. In the morning and afternoon, you can view the birds on the seasonal lake and the Jain 'feeding home' just off the Kichan–Phalodi road.

Osian

TIME FROM JODHPUR: 1½HR

Temples, dunes and pilgrim markets

The ancient desert town of Osian, 65km north of Jodhpur, was an important trading centre for camel trains on the Silk Road, attracting wealthy merchants who constructed a series of exquisitely sculpted temples, all free to visit *(donations appropriate)*.

Start by exploring the finely carved **Sachiya Mata Temple** (actually a complex of many rust-red shrines) in the centre of the village. Look for depictions of warriors fighting and being devoured by lions on the main *shikhara* and flanking shrines as you wander through the maze of caged passages.

Weave west through the backstreets to reach the handsome stone **Jain Mahavira Temple**, founded in 783 CE. Inside the column-supported main pavilion is an image of Mahavira, the 24th *tirthankar* (Jain teacher), formed from sand and milk coated in gold.

If you don't mind a little company in the desert, 4WD tours trundle over the dunes around Osian, often combined with camel rides and sunset dinners, or overnight stays in desert camps. It's quite touristy, but dune safaris are easy to arrange with operators in town.

DUNE SAFARIS

Osian is one of several popular spots for camel safaris in western Rajasthan – other desert safari hot spots include **Jaisalmer** (p171) and **Bikaner** (p179).

Jaisalmer

DESERT SPLENDOUR | GRAND HAVELIS | CAMEL SAFARIS

Nowhere conjures up the romance of the desert quite like Jaisalmer. Far from everywhere, this handsome outpost glows like gold thanks to the buttery stone used to construct most of its buildings. Watch sunset from the walls of Jaisalmer Fort and you'll feel like you've been transported to a time of camel caravans loaded with opium, silk and spices.

This still-inhabited fort rises from the plain like an extension of the desert itself. Behind its defensive gateways are temples, merchants' mansions and the Fort Palace Museum – alongside craft stalls, embroidery shops, family homes, guesthouses and cafes.

Tourism is modern Jaisalmer's lifeblood, with visitors setting out daily on camel treks across the sands, but staying inside the fort is discouraged because of the impact on water supplies and the fort's fragile structure. Luckily, the surrounding streets are similarly atmospheric, with swirling bazaars wrapped around yet more extravagant *havelis*.

TOP TIP

Book accommodation and transport to and from Jaisalmer well in advance, particularly if you're travelling over popular holidays such as Diwali, when thousands of holidaymakers arrive from Gujarat, filling the streets with traffic.

A Maze of a Palace

Clamber around a maze-like royal palace

Stacked haphazardly above the fourth gate to Jaisalmer Fort, the **Fort Palace Museum** *(02992-252981; entry incl audio guide ₹600)* is the city's most important royal residence, divided

GETTING AROUND

Getting to remote Jaisalmer is relatively easy, thanks to good bus connections and daily trains to its gleaming new railway station from Bikaner, Delhi, Jaipur and Jodhpur. Many trains arrive early in the morning, before hotels are ready to receive check-ins, but staff will serve you tea while you wait for your room. There are also flights from Jaipur, Delhi, Ahmedabad and Mumbai from Jaisalmer's small airport, 13km southwest of the centre.

When leaving Jaisalmer, private buses departing from Hanuman Circle may be more useful than the public buses from the RSRTC bus stand on Shiv Rd. Autorickshaws provide local transfers, but it's easy to explore the main sights on foot.

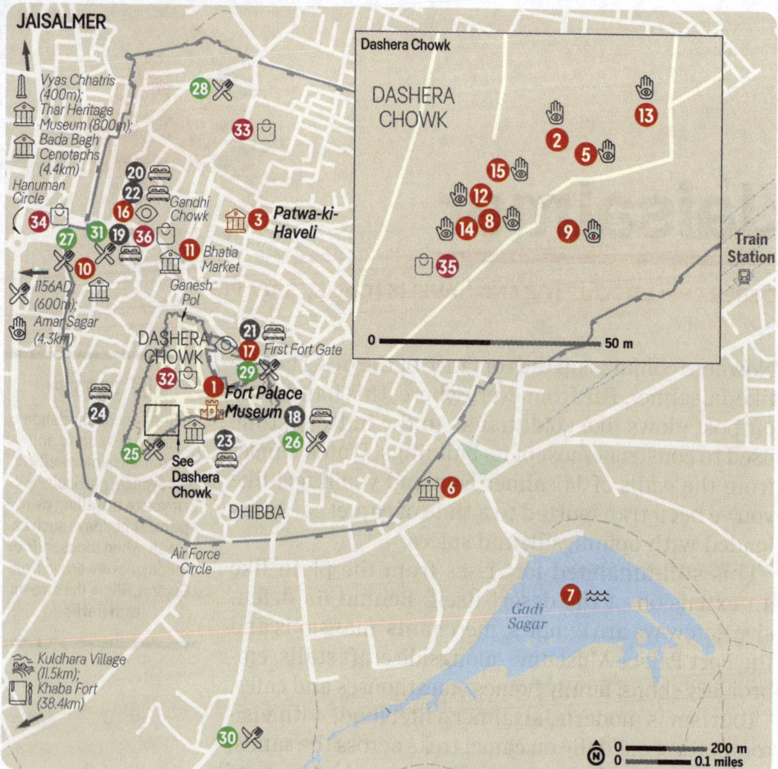

HIGHLIGHTS
1 Fort Palace Museum
2 Jain Temples
3 Patwa-ki-Haveli

SIGHTS
4 Baa Ri Haveli
5 Chandraprabhu Temple
see 3 Department of Archaeology Museum
6 Desert Cultural Centre & Museum
7 Gadi Sagar
8 Gyan Bhandar
see 3 Kothari's Patwa-ki-Haveli Museum
9 Kunthunath & Shantinath Temples
10 Mandir Palace
11 Nathmal-ki-Haveli
see 12 Parshvanath Jain Mandir
12 Parshvanath Temple
13 Rishabhanatha Temple
14 Sambhavanth Temple
15 Shitalnath Temple

ACTIVITIES
see 21 Amrit Travels
see 21 Sahara Travels
16 Thar Desert Tours
17 Trotters

SLEEPING
18 1st Gate Home Fusion
19 Hotel Nachana Haveli
20 Hotel Renuka
21 Hotel Shanti Home
22 Hotel Swastika
23 Moustache Hostel
24 Shahi Palace Hotel

EATING
see 18 1st Gate Home Fusion
25 Big Tree Cafe
26 Cafe +
27 Chandan Shree Restaurant
28 Dosaka
see 21 Flavours
29 Jaisal Italy
30 Jor Bagh
see 3 KB Cafe
see 19 Saffron
31 Trio Restaurant

SHOPPING
32 Bellissima
33 Desert Handicrafts Emporium
34 Gandhi Darshan Emporium
35 Gurus
36 Jaisalmer Handloom

INFORMATION
see 18 Jaisalmer Tourist Guide Welfare Society

into the maharaja's palace, with ornate open balconies, and the lattice-screened queen's palace. The marble throne beside the entrance was used for public ceremonies, while red handprints on the wall mark heart-rending occasions when royal wives died on their husband's funeral pyres.

Inside, narrow stone passageways weave between royal chambers displaying a small collection of medieval weapons, historic photos, thrones and the family tree of the Bhati clan, which boldly claims lineage all the way back to the Hindu god Krishna.

Highlights include the mirrored and painted **Rang Mahal** – which contains the bedroom of 18th-century ruler Mulraj II – and 15th-century sculptures donated by Jaisalmer's medieval temple-builders. There are spectacular 360-degree views from the rooftop over the city and the desert beyond.

The rounded boulders stacked up on the battlements were intended to be rained down onto invading armies, while the low palace doorways were built to force visitors and attendants to adopt a humble pose in case the maharawal (ruler) was in the next room.

An Elegant Royal Crib

See another grand palace

Jaisalmer's other grand palace stands outside the fort and the city walls, topped by a temple-like spire of stacked arches. The finely chiselled **Mandir Palace** *(080-45771900; entry ₹160, camera fee ₹30)*, or Badal Vilas, was built in the early 19th century for Maharawal Mulraj II. It's partly taken up by the Mandir Palace Hotel, but you can view the Zenana Mahal, with displays of kitchenware, weapons and silver furniture, and enter the graceful, finely chiselled Jawahir Vilas, containing the Durbar Hall where the maharawal met officials, hung with giant punkas (fans).

Enter Elegant Haveli Homes

Wander around Jaisalmer's grandest residences

Many *haveli* mansions in Jaisalmer are modern-day facsimiles, but some of the city's original merchants' homes are even grander than the royal palaces. Inside the fort, the charming **Baa Ri Haveli** *(instagram.com/baarihaveli; ₹100)* is decked out with a delightful hoard of family heirlooms – kitchen pots, old cameras and gramophones, antique glass, vintage padlocks and musical instruments. Head to the roof for a wonderful lookout.

East of the fort, the fantastically ornamented but asymmetrical **Nathmal-ki-Haveli** *(free)* was built in the 19th century for Jaisalmer's prime minister by two competitive brothers, whose work was similar, but not identical. One shop inside spills into a mural-filled 1st-floor apartment with an ornate interior balcony; give a donation if you don't make a purchase.

Continues on p176

JAISALMER'S BEST SHOPPING

Bellissima: Tucked inside the fort, and stacked with patchwork, embroidery, bags, cushion covers and more, supporting disadvantaged village women.

Gurus: Imaginative contemporary jewellery from a gifted Jaisalmer artisan; in the fort, close to the Jain temples.

Jaisalmer Handloom: A textiles specialist, with a huge back room filled with wall-hangings, bedding, Rajasthani embroidery and block-print clothing.

Desert Handicrafts Emporium: Near the Jain temple on Patwa Haveli Rd; good for textiles, craft objects, and the odd village heirloom.

Gandhi Darshan Emporium: Fixed-price *khadi* (homespun cloth) and Indian clothing and handicrafts, close to Hanuman Circle.

EATING IN JAISALMER: ROMANTIC DINNERS

Saffron: On the rooftop at Hotel Nachana Haveli, serving superior Indian and international veg and non-veg food (including filling thalis). *8am-11pm* ₹₹

1st Gate Home Fusion: Atop a chic hotel, with dramatic fort views, top-notch Indian and Italian veg dishes, plus beer, wine and cocktails. *11am-10.30pm* ₹₹₹

1156AD: The garden restaurant at Jawahar Niwas Palace is an atmospheric spot for a candlelit dinner. *11am-10.30pm* ₹₹₹

Jor Bagh: Set in a mansion-like building west of Gadi Sagar lake, with superior veg cooking, quality coffee and a pool. *10am-11pm* ₹₹₹

KEVIN STANDAGE/SHUTTERSTOCK

Chandraprabhu Temple

TOP EXPERIENCE

Jaisalmer's Jain Temples

What many visitors remember most from a trip to Jaisalmer is not the palaces or the desert, but the lavishly adorned Jain temples hidden away inside the fort's sandstone walls. Carved from threshold to spire with deities and mystical beasts, and filled with images of the Jain *tirthankars* (teachers), these seven mandirs represent a high point of the Rajasthani mason's art.

DON'T MISS

- Rishabhanatha Temple
- Chandraprabhu Temple
- Parshvanath Temple
- Shitalnath Temple
- Sambhavanth Temple
- Gyan Bhandar
- Kunthunath Temple
- Shantinath Temple

Rishabhanatha Temple

Arriving from the east, the first temple you'll come to is the tranquil Rishabhanatha Temple, with fantastically detailed mandala-like sculptures around its walls, protected by glass panels, and pillars encrusted with *apsaras* (celestial nymphs) and Jain and Hindu deities. On the outer walls of the sanctum are musicians, dancers, deities and warriors battling wild beasts.

Chandraprabhu Temple

Next door is the grand, multi-spired Chandraprabhu Temple, dedicated to the eighth *tirthankar*, whose symbol is the moon. The temple was built in 1509 and its *mandapa* (forechamber)

PRACTICALITIES

● tourism.rajasthan.gov.in/jain-temples-of-jaisalmer.html ● entry with camera ₹250 ● 8am-2pm features a lavish, layered, deity-studded ceiling and intricately sculpted pillars and *toranas* (arched gateways) that conjure up a sense of clouds climbing to heaven. The quality of the stone-carving here rivals the carved marble in the famous Jain temples at Ranakpur and Mt Abu.

Parshvanath Temple

Three more temples are reached via a doorway on the same side of the alley. The grandest is the Parshvanath Temple, accessed through a beautifully carved *torana*, topped by an image of the 23rd *tirthankar*. Inside, the deity-ringed ceiling is painted in bright colours and the sanctum contains a marble statue of Parshvanath. Flanking shrines contain images of the 24 Jain *tirthankars*.

Shitalnath Temple

A doorway to the right leads to the smaller, less ornately decorated Shitalnath Temple, dedicated to the 10th *tirthankar*, represented in the inner sanctum by a striking image made of eight precious metals.

Sambhavanth Temple

Follow the doorway to the left to reach the dimly lit Sambhavanth Temple with eye-catching fretwork windows featuring Jain and Hindu symbols and sandstone and marble statues of the 24 *tirthankars* with disconcertingly staring inlaid eyes. In the temple courtyard, Jain priests grind sandalwood in mortars for devotional rituals.

Gyan Bhandar

Below the temple, steps lead down to the Gyan Bhandar, an underground library of illustrated medieval manuscripts, founded in 1500. Whether it is open to visitors depends on the temple attendants.

Kunthunath & Shantinath Temples

The remaining two temples, Shantinath and Kunthunath, were built in 1536, one on top of the other in a courtyard on the south side of the alley.

The lower **Kunthunath Temple** features sensual carvings of deities, along with a spout shaped like a *makara* (combining features of an elephant and crocodile). Despite the peaceful doctrine of Jainism, many of the figures bristle with weapons, symbolising the struggle against ignorance and ego that is required to reach *moksha* (liberation).

Upstairs, linked to the Parshvanath Temple compound by a walkway, the **Shantinath Temple** features some fine deity-thronged panels on its walls, and a striking gilded statue of the 16th *tirthankar* in its inner sanctum. Look up through the metal grille to view the carvings of wild animals on the temple spire.

JAISALMER STONE

Like the vast majority of houses and hotels in Jaisalmer, the fort's Jain temples are constructed from mustard-yellow 'Jaisalmer stone'. Composed of more than 50% quartz, this versatile, fine-grained material can be chiselled into intricate designs or polished to a buttery sheen. As you'll see from the city's many ornate new-builds, the stone-carving skill used to produce Jaisalmer's historic *havelis* is very much a living art.

TOP TIPS

- Opening hours are subject to change but the mandirs (temples) are usually open to non-Jains in the morning.
- All temples can be visited on a single entry ticket, sold at a ticket window outside, and inspected by the attendants as you go through each gateway.
- Taking photos is permitted with your entry ticket, but avoid taking pictures of idols or the inner sanctums.
- Shoes and all leather items must be removed before entering.
- For refreshments, there are cafes and snack stands in the alley running east to Dashera Chowk.

JAISALMER'S MYRIAD GANESHES

If you spend any time in Jaisalmer, you'll notice the profusion of Ganesh murals adorning almost every house in the city. Painted in brilliant colours on the city's ancient stone walls, these eye-catching panels announce family weddings and other major life events, serving as public invitations to the festivities. As the murals are seen every time anyone leaves or enters the house, the benevolence of the deity shines on the family on an ongoing basis. If the home belongs to the family of the groom, his name will appear first; if it's the bride, she gets top billing. When a new wedding takes place, the mural gets an upgrade from a local artist, which explains why so many panels look freshly painted.

SAIK03P/SHUTTERSTOCK

Patwa-ki-Haveli

Continued from p173
Straddling a narrow lane north of the fort, riotously decorated **Patwa-ki-Haveli** is a cluster of lavish homes adorned from threshold to rooftop with intricate stone carvings resembling honey-coloured lace. They were built between 1800 and 1860 by five jewellery-dealing brothers, and two of these elegant homes are open to the public.

Start at **Kothari's Patwa-ki-Haveli Museum** *(patwahaveli .com; ₹300)* – a maze of gorgeously decorated rooms dripping with regal murals, mirrored mosaics, antique furniture, silk divans and family treasures. Look out for the games room painted with clouds and winged divine beings.

A few doorways down, the **Department of Archaeology Museum** *(adult/student ₹205/55)* is almost eerily empty, but the *haveli*'s bare interiors have a certain spooky charm, with intricately carved stone cupboards and fretwork windows, and a single mirrored chamber.

Crossing the Desert on a Camel Safari

Be a desert dweller for the day

Camels were once Jaisalmer's main form of transport, and agencies and hotels across the city still offer desert camel safaris. However, it's important to have realistic expectations – while there are evocative areas of tumbling dunes, much of the Thar Desert is covered with scrubby vegetation, wind turbines and scattered villages.

EATING IN JAISALMER: LUNCH STOPS

Chandan Shree Restaurant: Inexpensive veg meals, served in a busy dining room, with great *chaat* at its sweet shop around the corner. *8am-4pm & 7-11pm* ₹	**Jaisal Italy:** Set up high beside the fort walls on the way to Dashera Chowk; good for pizzas, pasta and dreamy fort vistas. *7am-11pm* ₹₹	**Trio Restaurant:** Upscale multicuisine meals served at cloth-covered tables on a rooftop by the gates to the Old City. *noon-3.30pm & 6-10.30pm* ₹₹	**Flavours:** Upstairs at Hotel Shanti Home, offering quality Indian and international dishes in front of a grand fort view. *7am-10pm* ₹₹

Better operators skip touristy Sam and Khuri for more remote parts of the desert, starting the trip by 4WD to escape the crowds before transferring to camel.

Most trips include a sunset dinner, singing and dancing around the campfire, then a night on a fold-out bed under a light-pollution-free canopy of stars. Winter brings chilly nights; wrap up warm for overnight trips. Prices for 'non-touristic' safaris to quieter sections of desert start from around ₹2500 for a day trip, and ₹3600 for a two-day overnight trip. Half-day trips tend to focus on touristy areas closer to Jaisalmer.

You'll encounter plenty of desert dwellers, from excited village children to desert foxes and cats, hares, wild asses, black buck, chinkara, sand grouse and bustards, particularly around Desert National Park near Khuri.

Most hotels, and many dedicated camel-trekking agencies, can arrange overnight trips (which leave daily) and longer multiday safaris. Trusted operators include **Trotters** *(trottersjaisalmer.net)* and **Sahara Travels** *(saharatravelsjaisalmer.com)*, with booking offices by the fort walls, **Amrit Travels** *(instagram.com/amrittravelsjaisalmer)* northeast of the fort, and **Thar Desert Tours** *(tharcamelsafarijaisalmer.com)* near the Hotel Nachana Haveli.

Graves with a View

See the cenotaphs of the maharawals

The cenotaphs of Jaisalmer's noble families lie dotted around the city. Start at scenic **Gadi Sagar** lake, excavated by Maharawal Gadsi Singh in 1367. Fronted by the elegant **Tilon-ki-Pol** gateway, the lakeshore is dotted with cenotaphs, shrines and ghats, while the half-flooded pavilions out in the water lure wedding photographers and families in rowboats and pedalos.

About 6km north of the fort, the **Bada Bagh cenotaphs** *(₹300)* – erected for various royal family members between the 18th and early 20th centuries – are grander and more evocative, balanced on the edge of a rocky desert valley. Come at sunrise to enjoy the calm atmosphere before the crowds gather.

Closer to town are the similarly ornate **Vyas Chhatris** *(8875323711; ₹100)*, containing the cenotaphs of members of the Brahmin community. It's a popular spot to watch the sunset. Nearby, you can drop into the cute **Thar Heritage Museum** *(tharmuseum.com; ₹100)*, a personal project for local historian LN Khatri, with an eccentric collection of local folk objects, including an ancient game of snakes and ladders.

SAM & KHURI

The closest sand dunes to Jaisalmer are at **Sam**, 41km west, and **Khuri**, 48km southwest, but don't expect silence and serenity. Along with sunset views and wobbly camel rides, you'll find noisy crowds, rumbling 4WDs and tented desert camps hosting folk music and dance shows.

If you want to commune with the desert, consider a multiday camel safari instead. On the other hand, if you don't mind a bit of carnival atmosphere with your dunes, short camel treks are easy to arrange on arrival. You can reach Khuri by public bus, or either place by taxi. For overnight stays, agreeably informal **Badal House** *(instagram.com/badal_house_khuri)* and swish **Mama's Resort & Camp** *(themamasjaisalmer.com)* in Khuri cover both ends of the market.

EATING IN JAISALMER: CHILLOUT STOPS

Big Tree Cafe: Crowning a bastion at the southwest tip of the fort, serving up thalis, chai and respite from the crowds. *7am-10.30pm* ₹

KB Cafe: A cute rest stop near the Patwa-ki-Haveli, dishing out traveller-friendly fare on a restful rooftop. *8am-9pm* ₹₹

Cafe +: Outside the fort walls near the first gate, with a colourful, shady rooftop where you can escape the hubbub with some dance tunes. *8am-10.30pm* ₹₹

Dosaka: Above-average dosas of all types and sizes, served in a modern, relaxing space north of the fort. *10am-11pm* ₹₹

JAISALMER'S DESERT FESTIVAL

Every January or February, Jaisalmer pulls out the stops for the **Desert Festival** *(desertfestivaljaisalmer.com)*, a fun-filled romp through the colourful culture of the Thar Desert. For three days around the full moon, Jaisalmer throngs with snake-charmers, camels, musicians, sightseers and locals in their best turbans. Visitors can cheer on camel races, camel polo, turban-tying competitions and the contest to find the most unmistakably Rajasthani gentleman in the state. The festivities start at Gadi Sagar lake and end at the Sam dunes. It's an agreeably energetic but busy time to visit, so book transport and accommodation well ahead.

ANIL VARMA/SHUTTERSTOCK

Parshvanath Jain Mandir, Lodhruva

See a Puppet Show

Sample Rajasthan's original live entertainment

On Gadi Sagar Rd, the **Desert Cultural Centre & Museum** *(9799464945; entry ₹100)* was a labour of love for sadly passed local historian NK Sharma, author of the interesting *Jaisalmer – The Golden City* guide. Displays cover everything from the local use of opium to an original kavad (portable folding shrine) and the family stages traditional Rajasthani puppet shows every evening from 6.30pm *(₹200)*.

Take a Tour

See more of Jaisalmer

Guided city tours can be arranged through the **Jaisalmer Tourist Guide Welfare Society** *(9414761175; tours of the fort/havelis/city ₹550/300/1100)* near the fort's first gate, or you can take some interesting village and wildlife trips with independent operators such as Amrit Travels (p177; *amritcamelsafari@gmail.com; tours from ₹1500)*, visiting destinations such as Desert National Park and the architecturally striking Rajkumari Ratnavati Girls School.

Alternatively, throw together your own tour to nearby villages by chartered taxi or autorickshaw. **Lodhruva** is home to the 9th-century **Parshvanath Jain Mandir** *(₹100)*, with intricate fretwork windows and a sculpture of the Kalp-Vraksha (Wish-Fulfilling Tree). Nearby **Amar Sagar** has another finely carved **Jain temple** *(entry with camera ₹150)*, set beside a lake that dries in winter to reveal half a dozen step-wells.

Further from the city are the peaceful oasis at Jaseri Lake and the remains of ancient **Kuldhara** *(₹30)* – a large Brahmin village mysteriously abandoned in the 19th century. More atmospheric is the dusty expanse of ruined homes, temples and *chhatris* behind the heavily restored **Khaba Fort** *(₹30)*, deserted during the same period.

Bikaner

ROYAL MARVELS | HISTORIC BAZAARS | CAMEL TREKS

Bikaner is a vibrant, dust-swirling desert town with a fabulous fort, historic buildings by the dozen, and an energising outpost feel. The capital of a princely state founded in 1465 by Rao Bika, the eldest son of Rao Jodha of Jodhpur, it's less dominated by tourism than other big Rajasthani cities, and life in its maze of bazaars has changed little since Mughal times.

The city also has some of Rajasthan's most delightful places to stay, and famously good food – from elegant restaurant dinners to the delicious, spicy Bikaneri *bhujiya* (crispy fried lentil-flour noodles) sold by every snack shop in town.

This is a place to break the journey between Jaipur and Jaisalmer or Jodhpur, stepping off the tourist conveyor belt for a day or two, and enjoying some fabulous royal architecture, backstreet walks and camel safaris that have a much calmer vibe than in Jaisalmer or Osian.

TOP TIPS

Explore Bikaner early in the day. The bazaars and regal buildings around the fort have a special magic before the traffic gets going and snack shops along KEM (MG) Rd and Station Rd open early serving sweet treats and chai.

Bikaner's Signature Palace

Appreciate the elegance of Junagarh fort

Dominating the centre, Bikaner's enormous fortress – the **Junagarh** *(adult/child ₹600/400)* was raised between 1589 and 1593 by Raja Rai Singh, who served as a general to the Mughal emperor Akbar, and never conquered. Inside its robust walls

GETTING AROUND

Bikaner's tiny airport is served by flights from Delhi with Alliance Air or Indigo, but it's just as easy to get here by road or rail.

Trains run to both Bikaner Junction, just south of the fort, and Lalgarh, about 2km north, with regular sleeper services to Jaisalmer, Jodhpur, Jaipur and Delhi, plus a daytime Vande Bharat train to Delhi. Private bus companies offer more comfortable rides than the public buses from the RSRTC bus stand north of the centre. Get around town on foot or by autorickshaw – you won't have to bargain hard for a fair fare.

HIGHLIGHTS
1 Junagarh

SIGHTS
2 District Collector's Office & District Court
3 Ganga State Museum
4 Ganga Theatre
5 Kote Gate
6 Prachina Cultural Centre & Museum
7 Rampura Haveli
8 Ratan Bihari Temple
9 Sri Rasik Shiromani Temple

SLEEPING
10 Bhairon Niwas
11 Vinayak Guest House

EATING
12 Bikharam Chandmal
13 Café Indra
14 Chottu Motu Joshi
15 Gallops
see 10 Ganesha Coffee Lounge
16 Sattvic
17 U-Turn Cafe

SHOPPING
18 Bikaner Miniature Arts

are two interesting museums, covered by the same ticket, reached through a chain of gateways marked with the hand-prints of tragically immolated royal widows.

As you enter the main courtyard inside the walls, you'll see the **Prachina Cultural Centre & Museum** *(0151-2525609)* to the right, with eclectic displays on the Bikaner dynasty and local folk arts, costumes, jewellery, furniture and ceramics. The main **Junagarh Museum** *(0151-2202297)* is entered through the grand facade to the south. You'll pass through a red courtyard, then the red and white **Karan Mahal Chowk** – used for public audiences – then the graceful, cream-coloured **Anup Mahal Chowk**, flanked by three exquisite palaces built for different members of the royal dynasty.

The **Phool Mahal** to the left features murals of flowers and vases, plus pole-mounted golden royal insignias. Lavishly gilded, the **Anup Mahal** in the centre was the hall of private audiences. To the right is the soothing **Badal Mahal** (Cloud Palace), painted with blue cloud motifs.

Heading upstairs, you'll pass a row of 'nail seats' used by fakirs (Muslim mystics) on the way to the 18th-century **Gaj Mandir** – a symphony of red, white and gold murals and ivory, sandalwood and mirrored glass inlay work.

Descend to reach the royal armoury, bristling with swords and daggers, then the bas-relief covered **Ganga Durbar Hall**. The last royal space is the **Vikram Vilas Durbar Hall**, stuffed with royal heirlooms, including a De Havilland DH-9 biplane bomber donated to Raja Ganga Singh by Great Britain for services rendered in WWI.

Spot More Royal Architecture

Admire the historic buildings around the fort

The streets around the Junagarh are studded with faded administrative buildings, many erected by Maharaja Ratan Singh (r 1828–51) during his 19th-century building spree. Directly east are the **District Collector's Office and the District Court**, housed in stately red sandstone edifices with a noticeable Mughal flavour. Constructed in 1932 by Maharaja Ganga Singhji, the **Ganga Theatre** was the city's first cinema.

Southwest of the fort you'll find the huge, turreted **Ratan Bihari** and **Sri Rasik Shiromani**, built from white marble and red sandstone in a fusion of Hindu and Islamic styles and featuring handsome elevated courtyards. Both are free to visit.

Get Lost in the Old City

Wander a medieval maze

To reach the historic heart of Bikaner, head west on KEM Rd (MG Rd) to the imposing, fortified **Kote Gate**. The surrounding bazaars are dotted with balcony-topped shophouses and rust-coloured *haveli* mansions.

Seek out the **Rampura Haveli** *(basavanarthotels.com/bhanwar-niwas)* near the City Kotwali police station, an elegant home from 1927 hosting the impressive Bhanwar Niwas hotel. Stop to eat at the hotel's Courtyard Restaurant to view the refined interiors. The *haveli* opposite features painted glass portraits on its upper levels.

MEET MASTER MINIATURE PAINTERS

Bikaner is the home of one of India's great schools of miniature painting, drawing on skills handed down by Mughal artists who moved here after Aurangzeb abandoned royal patronage for the arts.

While Hindu legends are popular subjects, the Mughal influence is tangible in court scenes and paintings of desert plants, birds and animals. Head to **Bikaner Miniature Arts** *(bikanerminiaturearts.com)* on Municipal Rd to view the exquisite work produced by the Swami family – some of the finest miniature painting you'll find for sale anywhere in Rajasthan – and observe the artists at work.

Even if you don't make a purchase, you'll get a fascinating introduction to the finer details of the artform, including the grinding of minerals and precious metals to make pigments.

EATING IN BIKANER: OUR PICKS

Gallops: Top-notch continental, Chinese and Indian food (with great tandoori dishes), spilling into a garden near the fort. *10.30am-10.30pm* ₹₹

Café Indra: A cool courtyard hangout on Rangmanch Rd; great for wraps, burgers, veg and non-veg meals and wood-oven pizzas. *11am-10pm* ₹₹

Sattvic: Chic Indian dining southeast of the station in Rani Bazaar; eat in the stylish dining room or out on the rooftop terrace. 7am-11pm ₹₹

Laxmi Niwas Palace: Reserve ahead *(0151-2200088)* for an extremely atmospheric courtyard or dining hall meal at this dreamy palace hotel. *11am-10pm* ₹₹₹

Work your way south (Google maps will keep you on the right track) to reach more interesting free-to-visit sights. The busy **Sri Laxminath Ji Temple** was founded in the 16th century to honour the city's patron deity.

Nearby is the gorgeous, mural-covered **Bhandasar Temple**, reputedly constructed using 40 tonnes of ghee instead of water in its mortar. Just downhill is the modest **Rao Bikaji Tekri**, the city's original fort, dotted with funerary memorials.

Brush Up on Local History

Learn more about Bikaner and the Raj

The neglected but rewarding **Ganga State Museum** *(adult/student ₹100/50)* in the Civil Lines neighbourhood has a collection that spans old photos, dusty taxidermy, medieval weapons, miniature paintings and royal portraits, and an impressive set of lithographs from the time of the 1857 First War of Independence (Indian Uprising), with labels that give a very different take on events to their British-era captions. Also on display is a decree to the Maharaja of Bikaner asking him to rush to Delhi to be present at Akbar's deathbed.

Learn about Camel-ology

An institute devoted to ships of the desert

About 8km southeast of town, Bikaner's **National Research Centre on Camels** *(0151-2230183; entry ₹200, camel rides ₹100)* is devoted to the scientific study of camels, with a camel museum, a stud farm and a camel dairy. You can sample camel-milk treats like chocolate, lassis and *kulfi,* visit the huge herds, take short camel rides and learn about the long history of camel husbandry in Rajasthan.

If you fancy a longer ride, camel safaris lasting anything from one day to a week will take you to isolated desert villages, with good wildlife-spotting opportunities and a quieter mood than safaris from Jaisalmer or Osian. Expect to pay around ₹4000 for a day trip, or ₹6000 for overnight trip. sleeping out under the stars.

To arrange a safari, speak to the wildlife-expert owners of the **Vinayak Guest House** *(vinayakguesthouse@gmail.com)*, or the charming Vijay Singh Rathore, aka the **Camel Man** *(camelman.com)*, who operates from Vijay Guest House (p185). From the same family, Hiteshwar Rathore *(bikanerbycycle@gmail.com; bike tours ₹2500)* runs guided cycle trips around Bikaner city.

BIKANER'S CANNY GENERALS

While some Rajput rulers were legendary conquerors, the maharajas of Bikaner built their status as generals for stronger powers. In the 16th century, Rao Kalyan Mal joined forces with Sher Shah Suri to expel Humayun from Delhi, before about-facing to join Abkar in 1570 as the Mughals regained the upper hand. His daughter married into Akbar's family, and his successor, Raja Rai Singh I, became a trusted general in Akbar's army.

Under the British Raj, the maharajas of Bikaner signed further strategic treaties, allowing the Bikaner state to retain considerable independence. Indeed, relations with the British were so close that Maharaja Sir Ganga Singh, commander of the Bikaner Camel Corps, became the only non-white member of Britain's Imperial War Cabinet during WWI.

MORE CAMEL SAFARI HUBS

As well as Bikaner, other top spots for camel safaris in Rajasthan include **Jaisalmer** (p171) and **Osian** (p170). However, Bikaner safaris are probably the most peaceful.

LUKAKIKINA/SHUTTERSTOCK

Karni Mata Temple

The Rats of Deshnok

A writhing religious experience

About 32km south of Bikaner, the **Karni Mata Temple** *(donations appropriate)* in Deshnok is one of India's most extraordinary places of worship. This vivid pink and white temple is dedicated to the 14th-century female mystic Karni Mata, revered as an embodiment of *shakti* (female spiritual power).

According to legend, when her youngest son drowned, Karni Mata issued a decree that members of her family would no longer die but would be reborn as *kabas* (rats). Accordingly, Karni Mata's shrine is maintained as a sanctuary for untold thousands of rodents, who are fed milk and grain by devotees and have free run of the temple, scurrying across the floor (and over people's feet).

Taxis at Bikaner train station offer return trips to the temple for ₹1000, or you can get here in a hour by local train, or by bus from a stand on National Hwy 89, 3km south of the station (ask locals for directions).

SNACK MASTERS

For many people, Bikaner means one thing: *namkeen.* The city's snack shops do a brisk trade in these crunchy, salty treats, particularly Bikaner's legendary *bhujiya* – thin, crispy, fried dew-bean-flour noodles, laced with chilli and black pepper.

Some 2.5 million people from the Bikaner region are directly employed in the *bhujiya* industry, and in 2010 Bikaneri *bhujiya* was granted protected Geographical Indication status by the government of India.

Station Rd and KEM (MG) Rd in Bikaner are lined with celebrated *misthan bhandar* shops that serve their own brands of *bhujiya* alongside spectacular *kesar fini* (nests of sweet, thread-like noodles) and *ghewar,* a nutty, honeycomb-like ring made from ghee, flour, syrup and saffron.

EATING IN BIKANER: SNACK BREAKS

Bikharam Chandmal: Legendary vendor of Bikaner *bhujia,* sweet snacks and treats, close to Kote Gate. *7am-10.30pm* ₹

Chottu Motu Joshi: This tiny sweet shop is famed for *namkeen, kulfi, ghewar* and *kesar fini* (sweet vermicelli-noodle nests). *6am-11pm* ₹

Ganesha Coffee Lounge: Proper coffee and indulgent cakes in a lounge packed with antiques and personality at the Bhairon Niwas hotel. *11am-11pm* ₹₹

U-Turn Cafe: A hip, calm cafe hangout in the backstreets at Civil Lines; good for coffees and healthy light lunches. *noon-9.30pm* ₹₹

Places We Love to Stay

₹ Budget ₹₹ Midrange ₹₹₹ Top End

Jaipur

Map p111

Moustache Hostel ₹ A hip chain hostel that's almost a hotel; just off MI Rd, with clean dorms and rooms.

Hotel Sweet Dream ₹ A rare cheap hotel in the Old City, with cosy rooms, friendly service and a superior rooftop restaurant and bar.

Hotel Pearl Palace ₹₹ The most popular traveller stop in town, with quality rooms and a great rooftop restaurant. Book well ahead.

Madhuban ₹₹ A courtyard plunge pool, mood-setting murals and smart rooms with antique furnishings – what's not to love?

Hotel Arya Niwas ₹₹ Spotless rooms just off Sansar Chandra Marg, plus a travel desk, classes, yoga sessions and a restful veranda.

Rambagh Palace ₹₹₹ The palatial ex-pad of Maharaja Man Singh II oozes elegance from its five-star restaurant and luxurious suites.

Narain Niwas Palace Hotel ₹₹₹ The *other* swanky palace in town, with grand heritage rooms set in sprawling, leafy grounds, plus an excellent bar.

Bharatpur & Alwar

Birder's Inn ₹₹₹ The sleek choice at Keoladeo, with a pool, a good restaurant and big, bright rooms in neatly tended gardens.

Sparrow Hotels ₹₹ A comfy midranger with bright, spotless rooms and a great location just south of Hope Circle in Alwar.

Ranthambore

Hotel Aditya Resort ₹ A rare cheap Ranthambore stay, with clean, simple rooms and friendly owners.

Hotel Tiger Haveli ₹₹ Quiet, spotless rooms, quality grub and amiable staff, just off the national park road.

Hotel Ranthambore Regency ₹₹₹ Pick of the Ranthambore crop, with a pool, bar, restaurant and lush gardens.

Shekhawati

Hotel Mandawa Haveli (p128) ₹₹ An elegant *haveli* hotel in Mandawa, with painted rooms and oodles of period charm.

Grand Haveli & Resort ₹₹₹ Nawalgarh's top hotel, with a superior restaurant and rooms spread across a painted *haveli* and a modern wing.

Pushkar & Ajmer

Map p131

Hotel Everest ₹ Snug, colourful rooms north of the lake; the charming owners arrange interesting excursions.

Hotel Bharatpur Palace ₹ Right on the ghats, with hospitable owners who charge budget rates for five-star views and fun activities.

Inn Seventh Heaven ₹₹ A tall, rambling courtyard mansion near the lake, decorated with flair and full of calm spaces to relax in.

Hotel Royal Palace ₹₹ A comfy midranger on the bazaar north of Ajmer's dargah bazaar; calmer than most, with a cute restaurant.

Badnor House ₹₹ A homely garden homestay, with a hint of nostalgia and a quiet location away from the clamour in Ajmer.

Bundi & Chittorgarh

Map p139

Shivam Tourist Guest House ₹ Agreeable budget rooms in a brightly painted Bundi house, with cooking classes and activities.

Chittorgarh Fort Haveli ₹ A friendly, comfortable stay in a revamped *haveli* in the village by Chittorgarh Fort's Badi Pol, with great views.

Haveli Braj Bhushanjee ₹₹ A genuinely charming, rambling, 200-year-old *haveli*, run by the descendants of Bundi state's prime minister.

Hotel Bundi Haveli ₹₹ Heritage architecture meets modern comfort in this vintage *haveli* near Nawal Sagar lake in Bundi.

Udaipur

Map p148

goStops Udaipur ₹ A fun hostel with a great Hanuman Ghat setting, a chill-out rooftop and sociable activities.

Nukkad Guest House (p155) ₹ Bright colours set the scene in a guesthouse with the friendliness of Udaipur's hippie days and daily yoga sessions.

Pratap Bhawan ₹₹ Service with a smile and above-average rooms with period trim near Lal Ghat, with good dining upstairs at Charcoal (p153).

Jaiwana Haveli ₹₹ Towering over Lal Ghat, with spotless rooms decorated with tasteful block-print fabrics, and restaurant views.

Karohi Haveli ₹₹₹ Low top-end prices and a wonderful elevated position mark out this venerable *haveli* hotel at Chandpole.

Jagat Niwas Palace Hotel ₹₹₹ A graceful period hotel with design-magazine aesthetics; very stylish indeed, on the water at Lal Ghat.

Kankarwa Haveli ₹₹₹ Heritage-steeped, eclectic and homey, right by the water at Lal Ghat, and set in a genuine vintage *haveli*.

Jodhpur

Map p160

Pushp Guest House ₹ Tucked into the lanes below the fort, run by a delightful family; a home away from home.

Kesar Heritage ₹ Cheery, bright rooms in the Old City, plus friendly owners and a rooftop veg restaurant with a prime fort view.

Krishna Prakash Heritage Haveli ₹₹ KP's has real charm, decked out with Mehrangarh-style murals, plus a pool and quality restaurant.

Singhvi's Haveli ₹₹ The pride of Navchokiya, with eclectic rooms in a *haveli* with a peaceful cafe, minutes from the fort's Fateh Pol.

Pal Haveli ₹₹₹ Handsome heritage in the heart of the Old City, set in the grand mansion built for the Thakur of Pal in 1847.

Raas ₹₹₹ A fabulous modern interpretation of royal living, tucked into exquisite grounds in the Old City, blending heritage and design wow.

Jaisalmer

Map p172

Moustache Hostel ₹ Set in a stone *haveli* by the fort; scores highly for neat dorms and activities.

Hotel Swastika ₹ Pocket-friendly prices, a friendly welcome and clean rooms (and a dorm) northwest of the fort.

Hotel Renuka ₹ Tidy rooms, reasonable prices, and an owner who goes the extra mile arranging tours and safaris.

Shahi Palace Hotel ₹₹ A top-class rooftop restaurant, a genial host and fine rooms with lots of character and Jaisalmer stone trim.

Hotel Shanti Home ₹₹ Appealing rooms and very helpful staff at this charmer near the fort, with an excellent rooftop restaurant.

Hotel Nachana Haveli ₹₹ The posh end of midrange – a courtyard *haveli* with antique-filled rooms and medieval castle vibes.

1st Gate Home Fusion ₹₹₹ Super-stylish digs in a top location, fusing period details with design chic (plus a great restaurant).

Bikaner

Map p180

Vinayak Guest House (p182) ₹ Cosy rooms north of the fort; the naturalist owners run excellent desert trips.

Vijay Guest House ₹₹ A comfortable home in a green garden east of the fort, run by the charming, safari-running Camel Man and family.

Bhairon Niwas ₹₹ A delight by every measure, full of antique heirlooms and run by the charming descendants of Bikaner's prime minister.

ALTRENDO IMAGES/SHUTTERSTOCK

Rambagh Palace, Jaipur

DMITRY RUKHLENKO/SHUTTERSTOCK

For places to stay in Punjab and Haryana, see p215

Above: Golden Temple (p198), Amritsar; Right: Fatehgarh Sahib (p205)

Researched by
Puneetinder Kaur Sidhu

Punjab & Haryana

LUXURIANT FARMS, HALLOWED LAND, AND BIG-HEARTED PEOPLE

Multilayered history, regal flamboyance, age-old syncretism and robust cuisine combine in this luxuriant heritage-dotted region, long dubbed as a cradle of civilisation.

Punjab and Haryana were cleaved from the Indian half of the erstwhile Punjab that witnessed a tumultuous Partition when India and Pakistan split in 1947. Punjab (translating to 'five waters') borrows its name from the five rivers (Beas, Jhelum, Chenab, Ravi and Sutlej) that course through its expanse. Another division in 1966 created Hindi-speaking Haryana on the basis of linguistics; it continues to share Chandigarh as a capital with its Punjabi-speaking neighbour.

AMMY888/SHUTTERSTOCK

Home to the Sikh community, Punjab is generally tourist-friendly on account of its longstanding ties with the UK and Canada. The Golden Temple in Amritsar is without doubt its star attraction. Nonetheless, look beyond and you'll discover a distinct appeal in Patiala's flamboyant past and Kapurthala's structural splendour, especially for history and culture buffs. Kurukshetra, where the epic battle Mahabharata is believed to have been staged, lends credence to Haryana's mythological roots.

Clean, orderly Chandigarh, the Le Corbusier–designed capital, with its wide, treelined roads, public parks and planned neighbourhoods, is in striking contrast to the largely agrarian region that it administers. The City Beautiful, as it is affectionately called, is a cosmopolitan place, housing Nek Chand's fantastical Rock Garden, several amazing cafes and a reasonably lively nightlife. Above all, this region is home to some of the most large-hearted and hospitable folk you are likely to meet in India.

THE MAIN AREAS

CHANDIGARH
Hip and happening capital. p190

AMRITSAR
Home to the Golden Temple. p196

PATIALA
A regal city. p202

KAPURTHALA
Eye-catching architecture. p207

KURUKSHETRA
Mythological roots. p212

Find Your Way

Punjab is a landlocked state in India's northwest and shares an international border with Pakistan. Haryana spreads southeast of Punjab till Delhi, while the mountainous state of Himachal Pradesh lies alongside both to their north.

Amritsar, p196

It's all about faith, history and mouth-watering street food in this atmospheric home of the remarkable Golden Temple.

Chandigarh, p190

The lively capital, shared by both states, is one of India's youngest, most cosmopolitan, well-planned and green urban spaces.

Patiala, p202

Former principality known for its flamboyant rulers, peppered with captivating royal heritage; best experienced at a leisurely pace.

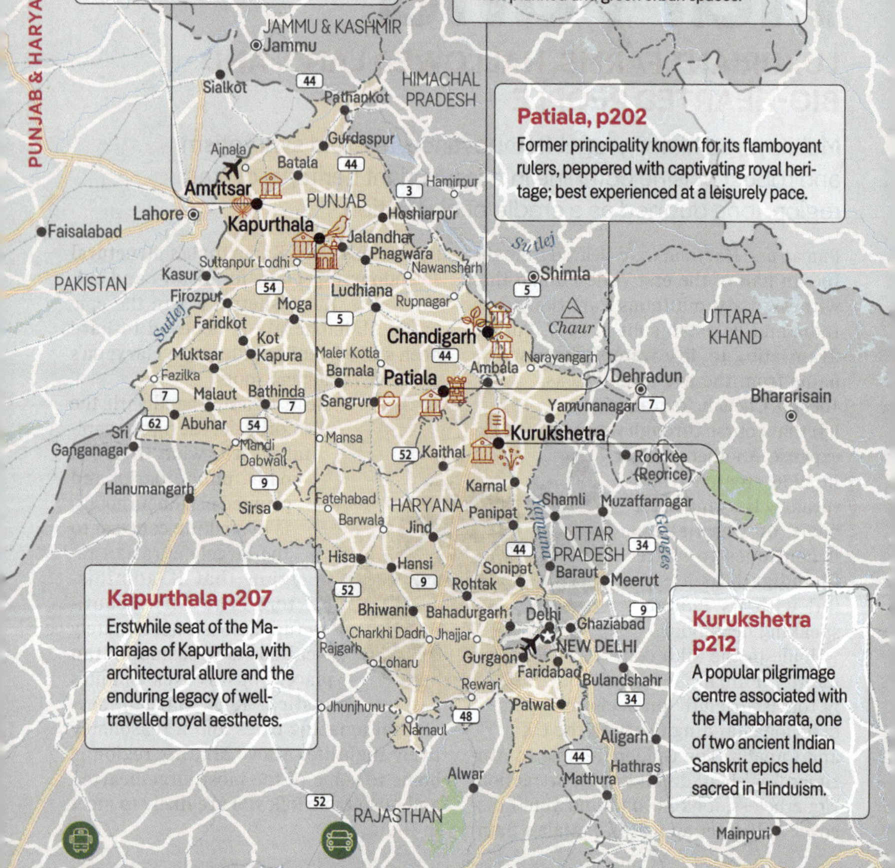

Kapurthala p207

Erstwhile seat of the Maharajas of Kapurthala, with architectural allure and the enduring legacy of well-travelled royal aesthetes.

Kurukshetra p212

A popular pilgrimage centre associated with the Mahabharata, one of two ancient Indian Sanskrit epics held sacred in Hinduism.

BUS

Regular buses run from three Inter State Bus Terminals (ISBT) that serve Chandigarh and Panchkula: ISBT 17 (Sector 17), ISBT 43 (Sector 43) and ISBT Panchkula. They are best used for short intercity hops.

CAR/TAXI

A road trip is one of the best ways to explore the two states. A reasonably well-maintained network of highways places main cities, and the towns spread across their vast flatlands, within an easy drivable reach.

CAMERANEST/SHUTTERSTOCK

Partition Museum (p199), Amritsar

Plan Your Time

Many travellers pass through Punjab to check out Amritsar on their way to Dharamshala, but the region is well worth exploring further to discover its many hidden and understated riches.

In a Rush

- Divide a day in **Chandigarh** (p190) between the **Capitol Complex** (p192) and Nek Chand's incredible **Rock Garden** (p190). Overnight in **Amritsar** (p196), tucking into delicious street food that evening. Early next morning, visit the **Golden Temple** (p198), then drop in at **Jallianwala Bagh** (p199) on your way to the **Partition Museum** (p199) before returning to Chandigarh.

With More Time

- Spend three days in **Chandigarh** (p190) before hopping across to the **Virasat-e-Khalsa** (p195) museum in Anandpur Sahib. Include day trips to princely **Patiala** (p202), and **Kurukshetra** (p212). Head to **Amritsar** (p196 for two days for the **Golden Temple** (p198), **Jallianwala Bagh** (p199), the **Partition Museum** (p199), the **Attari-Wagah Border** (p200), and excellent street food.

SEASONAL HIGHLIGHTS

SPRING
A short spell of great weather between winter and summer. Festivals of Holi, **Hola Mohalla** (p194) and Baisakhi occur March–April.

SUMMER
May andJune are scorchers; best avoided. Most people make a beeline for their preferred Himalayan getaways.

MONSOON
If you love rain and are not fussed about high humidity levels, the plains are the greenest during these months (July–September).

WINTER
The best time (October–February) to be here, although December and January can get very cold and often foggy.

Chandigarh

PLANNED CITY | MODERNIST ARCHITECTURE | HIMALAYAN GATEWAY

TOP TIP

Excellent expert-led walks and half-day/full-day tours offer insight into the important role other architects equally played in the Chandigarh Project alongside Le Corbusier. For details, contact Chandigarh Architecture Lab *(623-9481757)*, Walk Around India *(8283872227)* or Chandigarh and Modernism *(99888 62120)*.

Commissioned in the 1950s by Prime Minister Jawaharlal Nehru, Chandigarh is independent India's first planned city and the joint capital of Punjab and Haryana. Designed as a people-oriented urban space by Le Corbusier, it is divided into orderly, self-sufficient and pedestrian-friendly sectors. Besides, its treelined roads, private gardens, public parks and encircling woodlands make it one of India's greenest cities. Nek Chand's Rock Garden continues to be the city's main attraction, with the Capitol Complex and human-made Sukhna Lake coming in a close second. Shoppers divide their time between the city centre Sector 17 plaza and Nexus Elante Mall, also Chandigarh's main entertainment haunt. Most restaurants and nightclubs crowd Sectors 7, 10, 26 and 35, while pocket-friendly hotels are by and large confined to Sectors 22 and 43. Sandwiched between Mohali (Punjab) and Panchkula (Haryana), it is also a convenient gateway to Shimla in neighbouring Himachal Pradesh.

The Art of Recycling

Explore an alfresco museum

Nek Chand Rock Garden *(₹100; 9am-6pm)*, Chandigarh's top draw, is the result of one man's ingenious imagination. The extraordinary open-air sculpture garden is spread across

GETTING AROUND

Chandigarh's well-marked and orderly sectors, served by broad pavements and cycling tracks, make it a pedestrian- and cycle-friendly city. Download the SmartBike app to hire cycles (30 minutes, from ₹10) from docking stations across the city. Local buses (from ₹10) connect Chandigarh with Mohali and Panchkula, and battery-operated autorickshaws (from ₹50) are readily available. Booking Uber, Ola and Rapido services are only possible with Indian SIM cards. Taxis on hire cost upwards of ₹2000; for reliable service contact Harbans Singh Gill *(981-5208214)* and Harpreet Singh *(981-5587610)*. Consider the Hop-on Hop-off Bus if you're rushed for time.

HIGHLIGHTS
1 Capitol Complex
2 Nek Chand Rock Garden

SIGHTS
3 Capitol Complex Tourist Centre
4 Chandigarh Architecture Museum
5 Garden of Fragrance
6 Government Museum & Art Gallery
7 Le Corbusier Centre
8 Leisure Valley
see 19 Maison Jeanneret
9 Natural History Museum
10 Open Hand Sculpture
11 Secretariat
12 Sukhna Lake
13 Sukhna Lake Nature Trail
14 Zakir Hussain Rose Garden

SLEEPING
15 Anchorage 42
16 Corporate Inn
17 Diamond Plaza
18 Hotel Icon
19 Maison Jeanneret

EATING
20 Au Four
see 16 Back To Source
21 Backpackers Cafe
22 Casa Bella Vista
23 Chhota Banaras
24 Dastaan A Progressive Affair
25 Dochi Pizzeria x Avra
26 Hedgehog Cafe
27 Ikk Panjab
28 Indian Coffee House
29 Koyo Koyo
30 Lykke
31 Pheasant
32 Qisa
33 Sindhi Sweets
34 Sultry Noodle
35 Sundarams

THE CHANDIGARH CHAIR

Pierre Jeanneret was instrumental in making the Chandigarh project possible. Other than executing the plans Le Corbusier created in Paris, he also designed schools, offices, residences and functional furniture. The stodgy Chandigarh Chair is attributed to Jeanneret and his team of Indian architects. The simple teak and cane chair was made by local artisans for public offices, later mass produced, discarded and rediscovered in the 1990s. Bought as scrap by antique dealers, hundreds of them found their way to Europe and North America, and showed up in auction houses, commanding exorbitant prices. In a belated move, a ban was imposed on the sale and export of heritage Chandigarh furniture, making the Chandigarh Chair a coveted design collectible today.

STOCKGALLERY/SHUTTERSTOCK

Nek Chand Rock Garden (p190)

14 hectares, and has been created entirely out of building and home waste. Expect life-size figures of men, women, animals and birds shaped out of broken bangles, cracked china, toilet fixtures, bicycle parts, electrical plugs, rusty coins and bottle caps. Other highlights along an undulating, often constricted passage are an amphitheatre and waterfall. The tiny, easily missed, ticket window is located to the right of the main entrance; anticipate a crowd. Despite leafy surroundings, the stonework gets uncomfortably hot in summer, so carry hats and water.

Corbusier Tour de Force

Visit the Capitol Complex

This UNESCO World Heritage Site features the Legislative Assembly, Secretariat and High Court, as well as the **Open Hand Sculpture**, Chandigarh administration's official emblem. Security is tight and access limited. Visitors are required to join government-run guided walks *(free; 10am, noon & 3pm daily)*. Carry your passports and arrive 15 minutes before the tour commences to register at the **Capitol Complex Tourist Centre**. Entry to buildings is disallowed on weekends and during Assembly sessions, but you can walk up the **Secretariat** ramp for sweeping views of Chandigarh and the Shivalik hills beyond. For more information and advance confirmation, write to *permissioncapitolcomplex@gmail.com*.

EATING IN CHANDIGARH: BEST SNACKS

Indian Coffee House: A venerable institution for affordable snacks served by staff in trademark fantailed hats. Try dosa or mutton cutlets. *9am-10pm* ₹

Sindhi Sweets: A clean, always busy sweet shop known for its tasty *aloo poori* breakfast and Indian fast food, including *channa bhatura*. *9am-10.30pm* ₹

Chhota Banaras: Charming restaurant serving quality Indian snacks and outstanding coffee. Visit for *chaat*, *pav bhaji*, and *tawa bhatura*. *8am-10pm* ₹

Sundarams: Family-run restaurant offering home-style South Indian snacks and set meals. Its *idli sambar*, *upma*, (semolina) and filter coffee are divine. *9am-10pm* ₹

Recreational Waters

Enjoy lakeside walks

The human-made **Sukhna Lake** *(5am-9pm)* is a short stroll east from the Rock Garden. Edged by a promenade and jogging track, it is a popular haunt for families and leisure visitors, as much as for fitness enthusiasts and birdwatchers. Boat rides *(from ₹50)* are available near the small fairground to the left of the lake entrance. Weekends are crowded. You'll want to find a quiet spot further in to relax and watch the sunset. Alternatively, plan an unhurried walk along its forested **Nature Trail** *(6am-6pm)* located down the road between the Rock Garden and Lake Club. For birding guides, contact Chandigarh Bird Club *(987-6151090, 6284541031)*.

The Man in the Shadows

Visit the Jeanneret Museum

Another short walk from the lake will bring you to **Maison Jeanneret**, where Swiss architect Pierre Jeanneret lived during his 11-year stint as Chandigarh's first chief architect. Located in a quiet, leafy sector, it is now a smallish **museum** *(10am-5pm Tue-Sun)*. Jeanneret, Corbusier's cousin, is also synonymous with functional furniture, notably the Chandigarh Chair he fashioned from natural materials. Three good-value guest rooms (p215) are available on the 1st floor; advance booking required.

Building from Scratch

Visit Corbusier's one-time office

Le Corbusier Centre *(₹20, camera ₹50; 10am-5pm Tue-Sat)*, one-time office of the renowned architect, is housed in a low-slung barracks-like building, where sketches, documents, furniture, installations and photograph-filled galleries provide a sense of all that went into urban planning. Reflect over it with a coffee at Buns Bistro, a quiet little cafe behind the museum.

Art, History, Architecture

Explore Chandigarh museums

The **Government Museum & Art Gallery** *(₹30)* houses numerous extraordinary exhibits that include intricate miniatures and contemporary paintings, as well as handwritten manuscripts and a stunning display of Gandhara sculptures. Your ticket includes entry to the adjoining **Natural History**

GARDENS OF CHANDIGARH

Leisure Valley: A beautiful public park, frequented equally by fitness enthusiasts and recreational visitors. *(free, 6am–8pm)*

Zakir Hussain Rose Garden: Best visited in February to March when it is abloom with 1500 varieties and hosts the Rose Festival. *(free, 5am–9pm)*

Terraced Gardens: Verdant home to musical fountains and a popular Chrysanthemum Show held in December. *(free, 6am–8pm)*

Garden of Fragrance: Among the best-maintained gardens of Chandigarh and known for its aromatic botanicals. *(free, 5am–8pm)*

Cactus Garden: An often overlooked, small yet excellent cactus and succulent garden in Panchkula. *(₹10, open 9am–6pm)*

EATING IN CHANDIGARH: OUR PICKS

Jhumroo: Specialises in millet-based delicacies, and reimagined traditional Indian recipes. *10am-10.30pm, from 8.30am Sat-Sun, from 12.30pm Mon* ₹

Hedgehog Cafe: A delightful book-lined cafe and coworking space, frequented for tasty quick bites, coffee and desserts in a busy market. *9.30am-11.30pm* ₹

Au Four: Popular for quality coffees, freshly baked goods, desserts, food on the go (bulging sandwiches and hearty salads) and friendly service. *8.30am-11pm* ₹₹

Back To Source: Organic-food restaurant. Traditional techniques to prepare quality multi-cuisine meals, baked goods and coffee. *9.30am-11pm, from 3pm Mon* ₹₹

HOLA MOHALLA FESTIVAL

This vibrant Sikh festival has taken place since 1701 when it was initiated by Guru Gobind, last of the 10 Sikh gurus. Held annually in March a day after Holi in the historic town of Anandpur Sahib, **Hola Mohalla** is deeply rooted in Sikh traditions. It is a significant event, especially for the Nihangs, a warrior order believed to be the flag bearers of the guru's army, and who stand out – even today – with their eye-catching sartorial style. For three days, Anandpur Sahib comes alive with colourful processions, martial arts displays and music performances. Expect huge crowds, slow-moving vehicles, and traffic jams, so arrive early, and find a seat in the Charan Ganga Stadium, where the procession ends and an indelible spectacle begins.

Museum, of special interest to kids. The **Chandigarh Architecture Museum** *(₹10)* is also part of the same complex, and showcase's the city's planning and development story. The museums are open 10am to 5pm Tuesday to Sunday.

Weavers' Tales

Watch rugs take shape

For an immersive craft experience, head to **Billa Village**, 25km from Chandigarh in Panchkula, to watch artisans weave cotton durries, sometimes with motifs borrowed from Corbusier's artworks. A half-day visit *(₹1500)* includes interactions with generational weavers, trying your hand at a traditional pit-loom, and a meal with artisan families. Contact Lavnish Hans *(7626812118)* to confirm participation.

Verdant Mughal Splendour

Picnic in a cascading garden

Pinjore (Yadavindra) Gardens *(₹25; 7am-10pm)*, a onetime Mughal beauty, was restored to its former glory in the 20th century by Yadavindra Singh, then maharaja of Patiala, and hence bears his name. Located in Pinjore (23km from Chandigarh) in neighbouring Haryana, the garden is laid out in a classic Charbagh pattern with a central water channel, yet unique in its seven descending terraces. Were it not for indifferent upkeep, the gardens – lined with (mostly dry) fountains, mature trees and shrubbery, and featuring great views of the Shivalik hills – would make an excellent picnic spot. It's best to visit during weekdays if you're seeking peace and quiet, as weekends are crowded.

Countryside Capers

Experience conscious living

With a day in hand, plan a visit to Naurangpur village, under 40km from Chandigarh's city centre. Expect to wind through undulating farmlands and patches of forest for about an hour before reaching **Walden Sustainable Living** *(waldenliving.in)*. This family-run, hands-on farm-stay offers an up-close understanding of permaculture and conscious living. Consider a short hike or cycling around the village. We recommend trying the delicious organic lunch *(plus taxes, incl on-farm activities ₹2000)* before or after.

EATING IN CHANDIGARH: OUR PICKS

Backpackers Cafe: Popular travel-themed cafe with quality all-day breakfasts, sandwiches, coffee and desserts. *8.30am-11.45pm* ₹₹

Casa Bella Vista: Charming vegetarian-only European-food cafe fronted by a tiny, well-used garden; popular for wood-fired pizzas. *10.30am-11pm* ₹₹₹

Piccante: The dinner-only Italian restaurant at Hyatt Regency with a fine wine selection; adjoins Shichang, an equally good Asian-food restaurant. *7-11.30pm* ₹₹₹

Koyo Koyo: Excellent Asian-fusion cuisine restaurant. Also has talented mixologists; bao and dim sum are recommended. *12.30-3pm & 7pm-midnight* ₹₹₹

Evolution of a Faith

Visit a Sikh heritage museum

Evoking fort architecture, with its reflecting pools, arcaded walkways, bridges, and upward-curving stainless-steel roofs, the sandstone-clad **Virasat-e-Khalsa** *(10am-4pm)*, spread over 30.4 hectares, is an arresting presence in historical Anandpur Sahib (80km from Chandigarh). The museum recounts the history of Sikhism through a series of beautiful handwoven tapestries, hand-painted murals, dioramas and relief paintings. Take special note of the interpretive mural in the boatlike building depicting daily life in Punjab, across seasons, and set to lilting folk music. Photography is prohibited. Visitors are required to collect their free entry tickets (keep passports handy) from on-site counters located near the car park east of the museum. Expect to spend at least two hours here. Afterwards, visit **Keshgarh Sahib**, which abuts the museum on its west, and is one of Sikhism's five principal *takht* (temporal centres). This gleaming gurdwara is also where the Hola Mohalla procession begins.

Antediluvian Roots

Visit India's first IVC site

If time permits, swing by the **Archaeological Museum** *(₹100; 9am-5pm Sat-Thu)* in Rupnagar on your way to/from Anandpur Sahib. An unsung single-gallery repository near Government College, it is home to a sizable number of Harappan and Iron Age antiquities, all excavated in Rupnagar, the first of independent India's archaeological sites to reveal Indus Valley Civilisation (IVC) remains. Exhibits include painted grey ware (1200–500 BCE), and jewellery, seals and coins from the later Shakya, Kushan and Gupta periods. Expect to also see a glass-encased mock-up of a burial site that was found here. The display is indifferent, but staff are knowledgeable; ask them to show you around.

WHY I LOVE CHANDIGARH

Puneetinder Kaur Sidhu, Lonely Planet writer

It is Chandigarh's newness and orderliness that make it both livable and lovable. Verdurous avenues, open spaces, whimsical roundabouts, well-tended public parks and private gardens add to its charm. It's a cosmopolitan city with a vibrant food and nightlife scene. Driving is a breeze (barring the odd rush hour) and there's little chance of getting lost in its neatly laid-out neighbourhoods. The biggest attraction, though, is its location. You are never more than a couple of hours from a quick dash to the Himalaya. Delhi is a comfortable train ride away, and frequent flights connect it to major Indian metros. Above all, it is home. What's not to love!

EATING & DRINKING IN CHANDIGARH: OUR PICKS

Lykke: Popular haunt for coffee and desserts; caramel custard cake and French toast are top sellers. Other highlights: croissant sandwiches. *9am-11pm* ₹₹

Dastaan A Progressive Affair: Fine-dining restaurant featuring Punjabi/Mod Indian food/drinks; try vodka-laced Gol Gappa shots. *11.30am-11.30pm* ₹₹

Sultry Noodle: Dimly lit and moody Pan-Asian restaurant serving great food and excellent cocktails. Lunch is a quieter option. *1pm-midnight* ₹₹

Qisa: Fine-dining restaurant specialising in reimagined coastal food; try the Sri Lankan pepper fish. *11.30am-11.30pm Mon-Thu, 11.30am-4pm & 7-11.30pm Fri-Sun* ₹₹

Pheasant: A go-to for breakfast and dinner, exuding an old-world charm. Has great food and prompt service by friendly staff. *8-10am & 5-11pm* ₹₹

Ikk Panjab: Fine-dining with hearty Punjabi food and signature cocktails with a twist, in greenery-engulfed cabanas. *12.30-3.30pm & 6.30-11.30pm* ₹₹₹

Dochi Pizzeria x Avra: Frequented by youngsters for quality Neapolitan pizzas and pasta; SFO and Al Funghi pizzas are the superstars. *11.30am-10.30pm* ₹₹

Hops & Grains: The region's first microbrewery – going strong and frequented for quality craft beer and North Indian food. *noon-midnight*

Amritsar

SACRED CITY | SIKH HISTORY | STREET TREATS

TOP TIP
Make it to Amritsar for a green Diwali. See the Golden Temple stunningly illuminated with the help of a hi-tech computerised lighting system. Join thousands of fervent visitors on the candle- and earthen-lamplit walkway and watch the 10-minute ecofriendly fireworks display. It promises to be an unforgettable experience.

Amritsar was founded in 1573 by Guru Ram Das, the fourth of 10 Sikh apostles. It derives its name from Amrit Sarovar (Pool of Nectar), the sacred tank from which rises the striking Harmandir Sahib (Golden Temple). This gilded gurdwara is the most sacred of Sikh shrines and also one of India's most serene sites – this is despite being encircled by a warren of frenetic bazaars: a sensory overload, replete with indelible sights, sounds, aromas and, famously, flavours. In the 18th century, Amritsar was closely associated with Maharaja Ranjit Singh who consolidated warring Sikh confederates, created the formidable Khalsa Raj (Sikh Empire) and kept the British at bay till his death in 1839. Amritsar was also at the forefront of India's freedom struggle, with Jallianwala Bagh being a poignant reminder of colonial brutality. The Partition Museum showcases the aftermath of the bloody severance Punjab experienced in 1947, through stories and artefacts donated by survivors.

Experiencing Spirituality

Visit Sikhism's foremost shrine

Harmandir Sahib, aka Darbar Sahib, is the most prominent gurdwara (place of worship) of the Sikh community. The eye-catching shrine, in the midst of a holy tank, was completed in 1604 under the supervision of Guru Arjan Dev, the

GETTING AROUND

Starting at 4.30am, Amritsar-bound local and deluxe buses (from ₹450) ply frequently from Chandigarh's ISBT-43. Cabs cost upwards of ₹3000 one way. Many of Amritsar's attractions lie within a compact radius, with the remaining not more than 1½ hours away. The old walled-city bazaars can be explored on foot if you enjoy walking. Alternately, e-rickshaws (from ₹100) can ferry you around the crowded and chaotic bylanes. Local cabs (eight hours, from ₹2500) are available for hire, while radio cabs require Indian SIM cards. If you're short on time, the Hop-on Hop-off Bus *(amritsardekho.com; from ₹511)* is an excellent option.

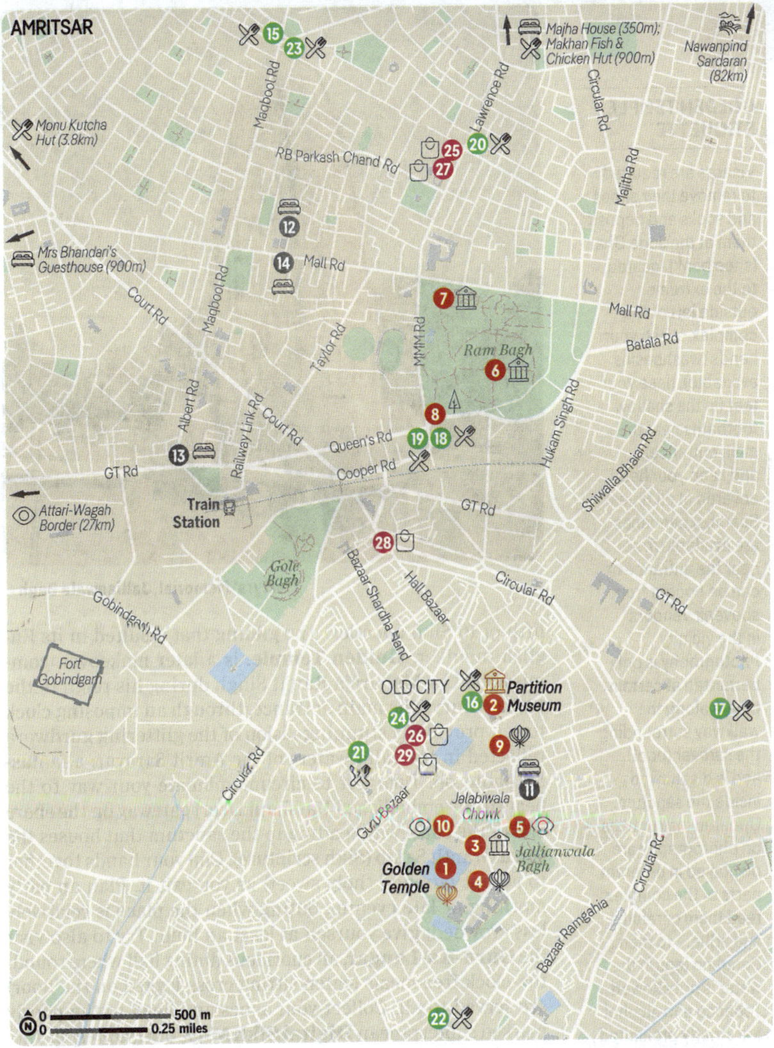

HIGHLIGHTS
1 Golden Temple
2 Partition Museum

SIGHTS
3 Digital Sikh Museum
4 Guru-Ka-Langar
5 Jallianwala Bagh
6 Maharaja Ranjit Singh Museum (Summer Palace)
7 Maharaja Ranjit Singh Panorama
8 Ram Bagh
9 Saragarhi Memorial Gurudwara
10 Udasin Akhara Sangal Wala

SLEEPING
11 Bloom Hotel
12 Bougainvillea
13 KK Continental
14 Ritz Plaza

EATING
15 All India Famous Amritsari Kulcha
16 Bharawan Da Dhaba
17 Bittu Meat Wala
18 Bubby Fish & Chicken Corner
19 Crystal Restaurant
20 Kanha Sweets
21 Kesar Da Dhaba
22 Pehalwan Kulcha
23 Sundar Meat Shop
24 Tara Chand Paneer Bhurji

SHOPPING
25 Harjinder Singh Pappad Wadiya
26 Katra Jaimal Singh
27 Ram Lubhaya Aam Papad
28 Raunaq Punjabi Jutti
29 Shashtri Bazaar

GOLDEN TEMPLE ETIQUETTE

Visitors are required to remove their shoes and socks and deposit them at the Joda Ghar (shoe bank) located to the extreme outside left of the complex. Wash your hands (washbasins available), rinse your feet (in the shallow footbaths near the main entrance), and keep your head covered at all times. Scarves/bandanas are available *(free)* near the entrance or can be bought from souvenir vendors in the vicinity. Photography is only permitted at certain points along the walkway surrounding the *sarovar* (pool). and is disallowed inside the sanctum. Updated instructions on photography are displayed in different parts of the complex; read them carefully and adhere to them. Dangling legs in the water is not allowed. Tobacco and alcohol are strictly prohibited on the premises.

RAMESH R NAIR/SHUTTERSTOCK

Martyrs' Memorial, Jallianwala Bagh

fifth of 10 Sikh apostles. The gilding that resulted in its English moniker, **Golden Temple**, is a later makeover, commissioned by Maharaja Ranjit Singh during his reign in the 19th century. The main entrance, through an imposing clock tower, provides a stunning vision of the glittering gurdwara reflected in the calm waters of the Amrit Sarovar: a fantastic photo op. Turn left to circumambulate your way to the beautifully embellished Darshani Deori gateway on the shore end of the causeway, leading to the sanctum that houses the Guru Granth Sahib (Sikh scripture). Cup your hands together to accept *parshad* (holy sweet) as you exit it. Plan an early morning or late evening outing when the place is relatively less crowded; give yourself at least an hour. Try to also visit the **Guru-Ka-Langar**, an enormous dining hall where round-the-clock free meals (eaten sitting cross-legged on the floor) are served to all. Collect your shoes and head to the poorly marked subterranean **Digital Sikh Museum** *(9am-4pm Tue-Sun)* located up front (entry faces the heritage street).

EATING IN AMRITSAR: VEGETARIAN STREET FOOD

Pehalwan Kulcha: A local favourite since 1953, visited for Amritsar's favourite breakfast – *kulcha-chhole* (stuffed baked flatbread and chickpeas). *8am-2pm* ₹

Monu Kulcha Hut: If you're in the neighbourhood, this is a decent go-to for your *kulcha-chhole* feast; on Loharka Rd. *9am-4pm* ₹

Tara Chand Paneer Bhurji: An old-timer near the Telephone Exchange, frequented for scrambled cottage cheese served with sliced bread. *10am-9.30pm* ₹

All India Famous Amritsari Kulcha: Another popular *kulcha* haunt; visit for its hearty breakfast options. *9am-4pm* ₹

About British Brutality

Visit the Jallianwala Bagh memorial

The horrific massacre at **Jallianwala Bagh**, a walled garden located short of the Golden Temple, was an important milestone in India's fight for freedom. Its bullet-pocked walls, reached through a narrow historical passageway, remain a distressing reminder of the day in April 1919 when British forces killed and wounded 1500 unarmed men, women and children, peacefully protesting a newly introduced draconian act. The large grounds *(free; 7am-7pm)*, host a flame-shaped Martyrs' Memorial – the deep well (now covered) into which many hundreds jumped to shield themselves from unprovoked firing – and four multimedia galleries. Expect crowds, more so on weekends.

Remembering Loss & Resilience

Experience the world's first Partition Museum

This is the first of only two repositories in the world (the other is in Delhi) that showcase the tragic events of the Partition of Punjab at the time of India's Independence in 1947. The multimedia **museum** *(partitionmuseum.org; ₹250; 10am-6pm Tue-Sun)*, housed in a restored wing of the stately 19th-century Town Hall (a short walk from both Jallianwala Bagh and Golden Temple), recounts the horrors of what was the largest migration in human history through newspaper cuttings, hard-hitting photographs, personal effects and moving video interviews of survivors. Schedule at least an hour for a thorough browse of all its stirring galleries.

Leafy Royal Residence

Visit a palace-turned-museum

The **Maharaja Ranjit Singh Museum** *(₹10; 10am-5pm Tue-Sun)* is lodged in a beautifully restored 19th-century double-storey edifice with ruffled arches, once the eponymous ruler's summer palace located at the far end of Ram Bagh Garden (enter from Queen's Rd). Formerly the palace grounds, this garden (which could do with some upkeep) now doubles as a verdurous 34-hectare **public park** (enter from Mall Rd), frequented by outdoorsy Amritsar. Expect to see a fine display of coins, manuscripts, paintings, arms and ammunition. Exhibits include a series of dioramas depicting central figures and pivotal scenes from the maharaja's life. Of particular note is

THE LION OF PUNJAB

A transformative and visionary leader known for his pluralistic ethos and military prowess, Maharaja Ranjit Singh (1780–1839) founded the powerful Sikh Empire in 1799 with Lahore as his capital. By unifying disparate Sikh confederates into the Khalsa Raj, he secured his place in history as Sher-e-Punjab (Lion of Punjab). Under him, Punjab stretched from the Khyber Pass to the Sutlej, and from the Himalaya to Multan. Amritsar became a significant spiritual and political centre after he captured Gobindgarh Fort in 1802, and famously gilded the Harmandir Sahib. He also built the Ram Bagh summer palace, now a museum. Gobindgarh Fort, one-time home to the Koh-i-noor Diamond, is today a Disney-fied tourist attraction *(fortgobindgarh.com)*.

EATING IN AMRITSAR: MEATY STREET TREATS

Makhan Fish & Chicken Hut: Located on Jail Rd, famed for fuss-free Amritsar fish (sole, *singhara*) and chicken preparations. *12.30-11pm* ₹

Bubby Fish & Chicken Corner: Frequented for fried fish, *keema naan*, and smoked kebabs on the busy Cooper Rd curve. *10am-11pm* ₹

Sundar Meat Shop: Clean, no-frills place on Maqbool Rd specialising in brain curry, mutton tikka and *chaamp* (chops). *noon-9.30pm* ₹

Bittu Meat Wala: On the outskirts, amid Jahaj Ghar motor-spare-parts market. Best visited for mutton *burra* and tandoori chicken. *noon-6pm* ₹

BEST SHOPPING EXPERIENCES IN AMRITSAR

Raunaq Punjabi Jutti: There's handcrafted embellished leather traditional footwear at this hugely popular store.

Katra Jaimal Singh: Scout around for colourful embroidered *phulkari* dupatta (scarves) or Punjabi suits in this crammed bazaar.

Shashtri Bazaar: You will find this wholesale market brimming with shawls and stoles; a light, easily packed reminder of your visit.

Harjinder Singh Pappad Wariyan: Swing by for quality *pappad* and *wariyan*, the peppery lentil-based souvenirs synonymous with Amritsar.

Ram Lubhaya Aam Papad: Popular store for tasty treats, particularly candied mango pulp and an array of digestives.

the intricate khatamband work (faceted wood panelling) on the staircase and ceiling of the upper storey. Ram Bagh also hosts the **Maharaja Ranjit Singh Panorama** *(₹10; 9am-7pm Tue-Sun)*, a low-tech museum (Mall Rd end) depicting the Sikh ruler's battles. Expect to remove shoes here.

Jingoistic Jamboree

Witness a patriotic peculiarity

The Beating Retreat ritual is a longstanding military practice signalling the end of the day's activities, marked by a brief flag-lowering ceremony. However, at the **Attari-Wagah Border** (30km from Amritsar) between India and Pakistan, it erupts into a theatrical show of patriotism, cheered on by packed crowds and blaring film songs. Border guards on both sides engage in a 45-minute display of exhibitionism that includes chest-thumping, forceful stomping and high-stepping. Seats fill up quickly, so you should try to arrive early for a ringside view of the spectacle *(free)*, which is held daily at sunset (4.15pm/5.15pm). Remember to carry your passport as ID proof. Only water bottles and phones are permitted inside. Use storage facilities at the tourist reception centre for handbags and other belongings. Shared autorickshaws *(₹150)* are available from the Brothers Dhaba stand near Town Hall; departure 2.30pm.

Agrarian Bliss

Experience life in a Punjab village

Plan a trip to laid-back **Nawanpind Sardaran** (70km from Amritsar) for a spot of relaxation in agrarian surroundings. This compact little village lies along the gently flowing Bari Doab Canal and its charms can be experienced as a day trip from Amritsar. You can stroll around luxuriant fields and citrus orchards, perhaps pop by a goat farm, or drop in at a village home for tea. Consider signing up for a guided tour *(₹1800)* that includes a home-style lunch, refreshments and a chance to try your hand at cooking on a traditional hearth at **Kothi**, a rambling old *haveli* (traditional, ornately decorated residence), which is also a farm-stay. For details, contact Mrs Satwant Sangha *(9417604624)*. Should you enjoy birdwatching, the nearby **Keshopur Wetlands** are a delight in the winter.

EATING IN AMRITSAR: GOLDEN OLDIES

Kanha Sweets: An oldie famous for *puri*, *halwa* and *mithai* (sweets) and savouries; well located on Amritsar's former high street, Lawrence Rd. *8am-9pm* ₹

Kesar Da Dhaba: Legendary family-run *dhaba* (casual restaurant) in Passian Chowk, specialising in Punjabi thali and nostalgia. *12.30-10.45pm* ₹

Bharawan Da Dhaba: Well-known Hall Bazaar spot draws tourists because of its location; food is mostly OK, but *phirni* (rice pudding) is good. *7am-midnight* ₹

Crystal Restaurant: Once Amritsar's top restaurant, serving Anglo-Indian and North Indian dishes. Eat downstairs. *11.30am-11.30pm* ₹₹

AMRITSAR'S ATMOSPHERIC ALLEYWAYS

Walk around the lively, heritage-lined streets of Amritsar's walled city to glimpse its historic past and vibrant present.

START	END	LENGTH
Town Hall	Golden Temple	2km; 2hr

Discover Amritsar's architectural and culinary heritage on this walking tour, starting with the sandstone-clad 1 **Town Hall**. Walk through its chandelier-strung corridor, past Maharaja Ranjit Singh's statue to reach 2 **Saragarhi Memorial Gurudwara**. Turn right into the brass-studded gateway of 3 **Qila Ahluwalia**, once a military fort, now a business-turned-residential complex.

Exit towards 4 **Katra Ahluwalia**, a marketplace with carved windows and elaborate balconies. Turn left towards the Golden Temple for 5 **Gurdass Ram Jalebian Wala**, frequented for his crispy *jalebi*. Try the treacly treat and carry on straight to 6 **Udasin Akhara Sangal Wala**, a subterranean rest house for ascetics.

Turn right into the jeweller-lined 7 **Guru Bazaar** to arrive at gaily painted Chitta Akhara on your left. Up ahead, towards the far end of Bartan Bazaar, is an old banyan tree called 8 **Baba Bohar**. Here, tuck into *puri sabzi* at 9 **Vinod Sweets and Puri**. Take a right for Thakurdwar Darian Mal, a fresco-rich, privately owned Krishna temple, and carry on to Chowrasti Attari.

Up ahead are Katra Hari Singh and the Shahi Taksal, Amritsar's first mint. Opposite it is the Shahni Mandir, its entrance flanked by likenesses of Hanuman and Garuda. Return to the crossing, turn right and walk through Churi Bazaar to end your walk at the 10 **Golden Temple** (p198).

Patiala

PRINCELY PAST | COLOURFUL HANDICRAFTS | PASTORAL ENVIRONS

TOP TIP
The Patiala Heritage Festival is an annual (February–March) crafts fair held in the statue-studded grounds of the striking **Sheesh Mahal** (abutting Old Moti Bagh Palace). This part-European, part-Mughal edifice houses an impressive coin and medals gallery (undergoing renovation at time of research) and a splendid suspension bridge.

This one-time capital of an erstwhile principality of the same name, founded by Baba Ala Singh, is one of Punjab's best-kept secrets. Synonymous with flamboyant polo-playing maharajas, Patiala is home to a striking old fortress, extravagant palaces, once-lavish mansions and leafy gardens. The Mall Rd, its main artery flanked by eye-catching architecture, including art deco cinema halls, runs down the length of the city, loosely separating the old from the new. Qila Mubarak, encircled with animated bylanes, is at the centre of the old city and by far the liveliest part – especially if you enjoy exploring old-world markets selling everything from medicinal herbs to beautiful handicrafts. The newer hot spots are mostly found at 22 (pronounced 'bai') Number, a busy high street curiously named because of the railway crossing it mushroomed around. Amusingly, the city also lends its name to a largish alcohol measure famously dubbed the Patiala Peg.

Genesis of a City

Visit an 18th-century fortress

Qila Mubarak, located in the heart of the old city, was home to Patiala royalty for a near century, since its inception in 1764. Arresting for its blend of Mughal and Rajasthani architecture,

GETTING AROUND

Most of Patiala's main attractions are located within a convenient, easily navigated radius. The city's old bazaars are worth exploring on foot if you enjoy walking, although cycle-rickshaws are readily available to ferry you around the crowded lanes. Local cabs (eight hours, from ₹2000) and battery-operated autorickshaws (from₹250) – contact Dinesh at 7973046842 – are also available. Radio cabs require Indian SIM cards. If short on time, Patiala can be visited as a comfortable 70km day trip from Chandigarh (cabs from ₹3000). Starting at 4.30am, local and deluxe buses (₹90 to ₹300) run regularly and frequently from Chandigarh's ISBT-43.

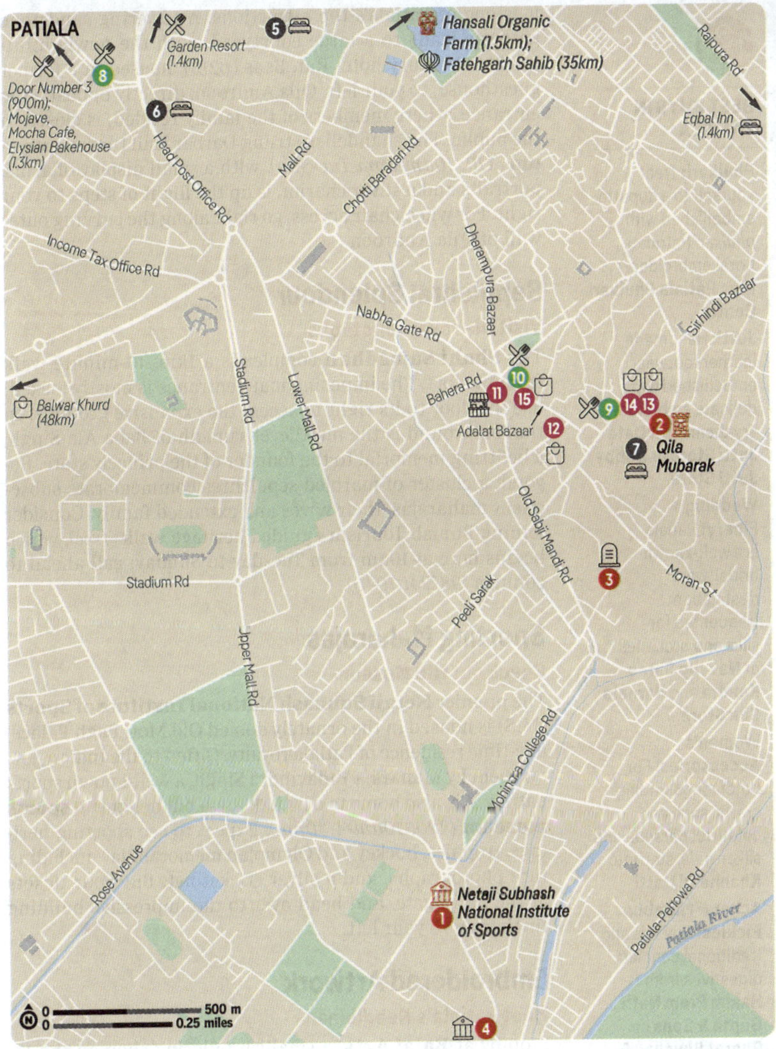

HIGHLIGHTS
1 Netaji Subhash National Institute of Sports
2 Qila Mubarak

SIGHTS
3 Shahi Samadhan
4 Sheesh Mahal

SLEEPING
5 Baradari Palace
6 Mohan Continental
7 Ran Baas

EATING
8 Gopal Sweets
9 Hakim Prem Nath Gupta & Sons
10 Jaggi Sweets
see 5 Royal Glutton

SHOPPING
11 Adalat Bazaar Car Park
see 15 Bajaj Arts
see 15 Barnala Silk Store
12 Dabby Jutti Store
13 Data Jutti Store
14 Khanne Di Hatti
see 15 Navyug Saree Kendra
15 Patiala Phulkari Centre

BEST BUYS IN PATIALA

Phulkari: Treat yourself to a dupatta embellished with *phulkari* (intricate floral embroidery) from **Patiala Phulkari Centre**.

Jutti: Handmade leather footwear embellished with delicate embroidery. Try them on at **Data Jutti Store** or **Dabby Jutti Store**.

Wedding Finery: Patiala is a well-known bridal-wear destination, frequented for silks and brocades at **Navyug Saree Kendra** and **Barnala Silk Store**.

Women's Accessories: For other longstanding crafts, such as colourful *paranda* and silken *nala*, step into **Khanne Di Hatti**.

Achar & Murabba Pickles: Buy this and traditional candied digestives from **Hakim Prem Nath Gupta & Sons** or **Bharat Bhushan & Sons** next door.

it is one of Patiala's top attractions. A towering sandstone gateway leads to a large courtyard, with the newly minted (2025) luxury hotel Ran Baas (p215), housed in a former guesthouse, to your left. Qila Androon, directly opposite the entrance, where members of the family resided, is closed to the public. The chandelier-strung Darbar Hall turned **museum** *(₹10; 10am-5pm Tue-Sun)*, with a small display of arms, portraits and a silver chariot, is up the flight of steps to your right. For wheelchair access, go right along the curving outer wall of Qila Androon.

Sepulchral Splendour

Visit the royal cenotaphs

The **Shahi Samadhan** complex is a 1km, 10-minute walk from the fort. The imposing main entrance is mostly locked; use the door to its right to access the expansive grounds. In the foreground is the multilevel samadh of Baba Ala Singh, a befitting memorial to the founder of the princely state. Beyond, a cluster of marbled sepulchres commemorate subsequent maharajas, their wives and extended family. Consider joining Punjab Tourism's guided heritage walk *(free)*, which begins here at 10am from Tuesday to Sunday; call ahead to confirm *(9872407040)*.

Sporting Maharajas

Check out NIS Museum

The premier **Netaji Subhash National Institute of Sports** (NIS) is housed in the ornately domed Old Moti Bagh Palace, one-time residence of Patiala royalty. Gifted to the Indian government by Maharaja Yadavindra Singh, a well-known sports patron, it is also home to a little-known but delightful **sports museum** *(₹20; 10am-4.30pm)*. Expect to see sporting heritage, trophies, hockey and Olympian memorabilia – including rare photographs, and a silver cricket bat. Buy your tickets at the main gate, and head over to the impressive building further up to your left.

Embroidered Artwork

Meet Patiala's Needleman

Stop by at **Bajaj Arts**, a smallish tailoring shop on the 1st floor of Chatti Darzianwali Gali near Adalat Bazaar car park, to admire the unique artworks of a talented sewing-machine

EATING IN PATIALA: OUR PICKS

Jaggi Sweets: This old Patiala favourite in the lively Adalat Bazaar is best known for *chaat*, *mithai*, samosa and *channa bhatura*. *9am-10pm* ₹

Gopal Sweets: From hole-in-the-wall to most-frequented for fast food, snacks, *mithai* and *namkeen* (savoury nibbles) in Leela Bhawan Market. *8am-10.30pm* ₹

Garden Resort: The city's familiar haunt for a quiet drink and quality Punjabi food. The mutton barra kebabs are noteworthy. *7.30am-11.30pm* ₹₹

Royal Glutton: A range of North Indian, Indian-Chinese, and European meals served in the elegant environs of a heritage hotel. *7.30am-10.30pm* ₹₹

artist. Dubbed the Needleman, he is known for his stunning painting-like embroideries that include detailed, lifelike portraits of Guru Nanak; an exquisite one of Krishna, which took three years to complete; Maharaja Bhupinder Singh of Patiala; Queen Elizabeth II and Steve McCurry's *Afghan Girl*. You may want to call ahead *(9855151496)* to confirm his availability.

A Pastoral Getaway

Experience an agrarian lifestyle

Escape Patiala's chaotic liveliness for some relaxation at the family-run **Hansali Organic Farm** *(hunsalifarm.org.in)* farm-stay (p215). Plan a day trip and the engaging hosts will walk you around their fruit orchards and luxuriant fields. It's a great place to sit back and simply do nothing, but there's also the option to partake in hands-on activities like collecting eggs, milking cows and foraging for your farm-style Punjabi meal *(incl refreshments ₹1500)*. Advance booking required.

Weaving Tradition

Observe traditional rugs take shape

For an immersive textile experience, plan a visit to **Balwar Khurd** village (50km from Patiala), where the highlight is an all-women weaving centre. Led by former advertising professional Kiran Singh, it is focused on reviving dying craft traditions like weaving *panja durrie* (rugs) and *majnu khes* (cotton throws). Once here, you can try your hand at a loom, relish a sumptuous farm lunch and walk it off with a stroll around the village. Your daylong outing *(break-away.in; from ₹3000)* includes all of the above.

Of Faith & Sacrifice

Visit a prominent Sikh shrine

Fatehgarh Sahib (35km) and its twin city Sirhind are also worth a long look-see. The former holds immense significance for the Sikh community, as this is where two of Guru Gobind Singh's four sons (see sidebar) were immured by the Mughals in 1705; **Fatehgarh Sahib** marks the site. Remove shoes and cover your heads before entering. **Sirhind**, located 5km away, was an important provincial capital of the Mughals, who left a sizable footprint in their wake, notably the **Aam Khas Bagh** gardens; and **Rauza Sharif**, a Sufi shrine, and where India's last Afghan ruler is buried.

THE SAHIBZAADE

In Sikh tradition, the sons of Guru Gobind Singh, last of the 10 Sikh Gurus, are referred to as Sahibzaade. His two elder sons, Ajit Singh (aged 18) and Jhujhar Singh (14) died fighting Mughal forces in the Battle of Chamkaur in December 1705. That same month, his two younger sons, Zorawar Singh (9) and Fateh Singh (6) were bricked alive by Wazir Khan, the Mughal Governor of Sirhind, for refusing to change faith. They are widely regarded as the youngest martyrs in Sikh history. Fatehgarh Sahib memorialises the site of their immurement. The week 21–28 December is observed as Shaheedi Hafta (martyrdom week) in Punjab, and is when **Shaheedi Jor Mela**, a three-day religious fair, is held in their memory.

Mojave: Fine-dining place with memorabilia-strung walls. Eclectic menu featuring artisanal burgers, tacos, pasta, soups and salad. *noon-midnight* ₹₹₹

Door Number 3: Contemporary styled restaurant with rooftop seating. Popular world cuisine staples, decent cocktails, attentive staff. *noon-11.30pm* ₹₹

Mocha Cafe: Old hangout with a casual vibe, frequented for coffees, sandwiches, North Indian fare, desserts and live-music gigs. *11am-11pm* ₹

Elysian Bakehouse: Bright, cheery little cafe with coffees and quality bakes, including pastries, cheesecakes and croissants. *11am-10.30pm* ₹₹

EXPLORE PATIALA'S OLD BAZAARS

Get to know Patiala's old-city heritage, animated bylanes, and bustling bazaars often named after the wares they traditionally sell.

START	END	LENGTH
Shahi Samadhan	Adalat Bazaar Car Park	2km; 2 hours

Explore Patiala's atmospheric alleys on this unhurried stroll that begins at 1 **Shahi Samadhan** (p204) in Dal Daliya Chowk. Make your way to the 2 **Bartan Bazaar**, lined with kitchenware shops; stop to observe traditional brass polisher 3 **Gopal Chand** hard at work. Turn left for Qila Chowk, the busy square fronting 4 **Qila Mubarak** (p202). Go past the fort's carved sandstone entrance for 5 **Juttianwali Gali**, replete with traditional footwear and bridal accessories. To your right is Data Jutti Store, and further up is Khanne Di Hatti. Turn left here for Sadar Bazaar; look out for 6 **Hakim Prem Nath Gupta & Sons** (p204), traditional physicians selling pickles and digestives, to your left.

Take the second right onto A-Tank Rd, follow the curve and turn right for 7 **Adalat Bazaar**, Patiala's main market, selling everything from provisions to *phulkari*. Browse for colourful fabric at Tope Khana Mod on the way. Go past Navyug Saree Kendra, one-time clothiers of the royal family, and treat yourself to a plate of *chhole bhature* (deep-fried puris with spicy chickpea curry) at 8 **Jaggi Sweets** (p204) on the right.

Backtrack slightly to enter the lively, art deco 9 **Chhatti Darzian Wali Gali** on the right. Walk up to the 1st floor to admire the embroidered artworks of Needleman Arun Kumar Bajaj (call ahead 98551 51496), then exit towards 10 **Adalat Bazaar** car park.

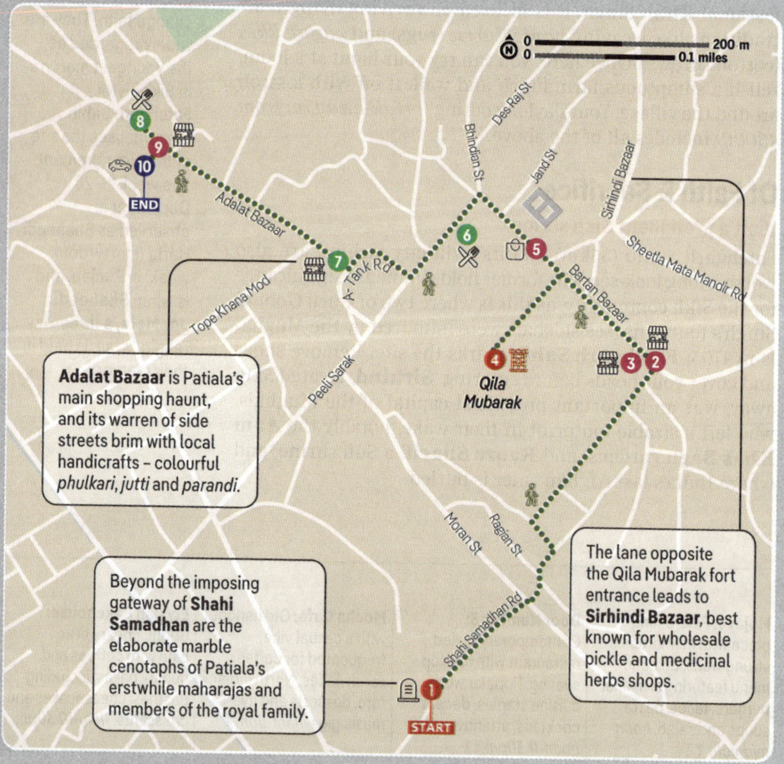

Kapurthala

REGAL PAST | EUROPEAN ARCHITECTURE | PEACEFUL WETLANDS

The erstwhile seat of a wealthy principality founded in the 18th century, Kapurthala is largely known for the architectural legacy of its last ruler, Maharaja Jagatjit Singh. Widely travelled, and an aesthete and a polyglot, he gave shape to modern Kapurthala. An abiding interest in European and Indo-Saracenic architecture is evidenced in the gardens, palaces, villas and places of worship he built. The most striking are the Palace of Versailles-inspired Jagatjit Palace, which houses the Sainik School (closed to the public); and the Moorish Mosque, patterned on the 12th-century Kutubiyya Mosque in Marrakesh, Morocco. Jagatjit Singh's marriage to a young Spanish flamenco dancer, after a whirlwind courtship in Madrid, would become the subject of Javier Moro's bestselling book, *Passion India*. The maharaja's patronage also led to the development of Sultanpur Lodhi, a prominent Sikh centre where Guru Nanak, founder of the faith, spent 14 of his formative years.

GETTING AROUND

Kapurthala is a crowded but neatly laid-out city, with most attractions within a 6km radius of the centre. Other than the Kanjli Wetlands, all of them can be explored on foot if you relish walking. Local cabs (eight hours, from ₹2000) and battery-operated autorickshaws (one hour, ₹100) – contact Sunny at 7009359933 – are readily available. Kapurthala's top attractions can also be explored as a comfortable 68km day trip from Amritsar (cabs from ₹3000). An overnight stay is required if journeying the 172km from Chandigarh (one-way taxi from ₹3000). Alternatively, hop onto a Jalandhar-bound bus (₹350) from ISBT-43 and change for Kapurthala (₹50) there.

Monumental Heritage

Discover the city's European personality

For a self-guided exploration of Kapurthala's striking monuments, start with the Greco-Roman **Jagatjit Club**, once a church, less than 1km from **Jagatjit Palace**. Cross the street, go left by the post office, and through Kamra Bagh to reach **Gol Kothi**, a spherical royal residence from the 1830s. Turn left and carry on straight ahead for **Randhir College** (1856), one of North India's earliest educational institutes. Should they allow access, go by the many-towered **Jubilee Hall** (1916), commemorating 25 years of Jagatjit Singh as maharaja. Exit left for the **State Gurdwara** down the road, and expect it to get congested from here. Go left at the main road; take another left further down the road to get to the Moorish Mosque (1.6km away; p209). Return to the main road and turn right for the **Darbar Hall**, a soon-to-be heritage hotel; across it is the circular-shaped **Baghi Khana** (stables), now a police station.

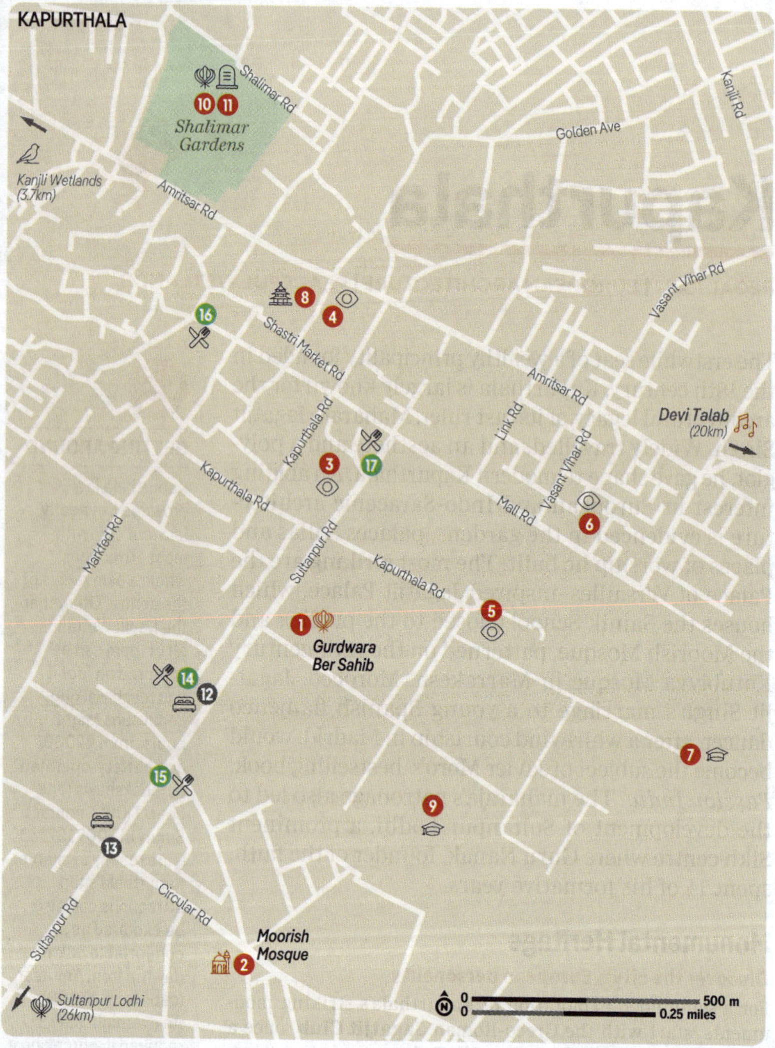

TOP TIP

Many of Kapurthala's architectural attractions are undergoing restoration; others house schools, colleges and government offices. Except for the Moorish Mosque, entry is restricted to most, but they can be viewed from outside. Randhir College and Jagatjit Club sometimes allow a look-around on request, but Jagatjit Palace is out of bounds.

HIGHLIGHTS
1 Gurdwara Ber Sahib
2 Moorish Mosque

SIGHTS
3 Darbar Hall
4 Ghanta Ghar
5 Gol Kothi
6 Jagatjit Club
7 Jagatjit Palace
8 Panch Mandir
9 Randhir College
10 Shahi Samadhan
11 Shalimar Gardens

SLEEPING
12 London Hotel
13 Ramneek Hotel

EATING
14 Dubai Bakers
15 New Ahuja Sweets
16 Pankaj Fast Food
17 Pooja

Moroccan Beauty

Visit the 20th-century Moorish Mosque

The rose-hued **Moorish Mosque** was completed in 1930 and stands out for its distinctive design features: horseshoe arches, a flat, dome-less roof, and a single square minaret topped by a copper spire reminiscent of Almohad architecture. The beautiful sanctum, with richly frescoed walls and an octagonal wood-panelled ceiling, lies opposite the main entrance, across a large colonnaded courtyard. Photography is discouraged. Remove shoes before entering.

In Memoriam of Royalty

Visit rulers' final resting place

The **Shahi Samadhan** (royal sepulchres) are located within a gated enclosure inside **Shalimar Gardens**. The elaborate one to the right of the main entry houses four maharajas, including Jagatjit Singh. The others belong to extended family and wives of the rulers. Pair your visit here with the Panch Mandir.

Patrons of Faith

Visit a stately shrine

The **Panch Mandir** complex, located opposite the colonial-style **Ghanta Ghar** near Shalimar Gardens, was built by Raja Nihal Singh in the 18th century. Its spotless precincts host five shrines dedicated to different deities, including Krishna. The main temple is up a few steps from the entrance and looks stunning on moonlit nights.

Migrating Flock

Swing by for some birdwatching

Kanjli Wetlands lie along the Kali Bien River, 4km from Kapurthala, and attract a number of migratory birds, including mallards, northern shovelers, and ruddy shelducks. For sightings, turn right short of the headwork and follow the wooded bank of the river. Winter arrivals are mostly found along this quiet 2km stretch.

A MUSICAL SOIREE

Harivallabh Sangeet Sammelan *(harivallabhsangeet.com)* is widely acknowledged as the oldest Hindustani classical-music festival in the world. Held annually on the last weekend of December with live performances by a roster of top-billed musicians, it celebrated its 150th edition in 2025. It was first held in 1875 to honour the saint and Dhrupad singer, Baba Harivallabh, at the **Devi Talab** (pond) in Jalandhar, under the aegis of Kunwar Bikrama Singh of Kapurthala. The prince famously rode to Delhi to secure the release of court musician Mir Nasir Ahmed from British incarceration after the dethronement of Mughal emperor Bahadur Shah Zafar in 1857. Mir Nasir Ahmed, a direct descendant of Tansen's daughter, subsequently moved to Jalandhar to instruct his newfound patron.

EATING IN KAPURTHALA: OUR PICKS

New Ahuja Sweets: You'll most likely find *mithai* snacks and hearty North Indian meals at this popular vegetarian restaurant. *7am-11pm* ₹

Dubai Bakers: Kapurthala's go-to for all things bakery (generally eggless) and cafe-style quick bites (sandwiches, burgers). Near the Moorish Mosque. *8am-10pm* ₹

Pooja: Clean, family-run vegetarian restaurant across from Darbar Hall. Its hearty stuffed *paratha* breakfast with lassi goes a long way. *9am-11.30pm* ₹

Pankaj Fast Food: Old favourite frequented for snacks, Indian-Chinese food and fruity shakes; gets the job done when hungry. *10am-10pm* ₹

Beyond Kapurthala

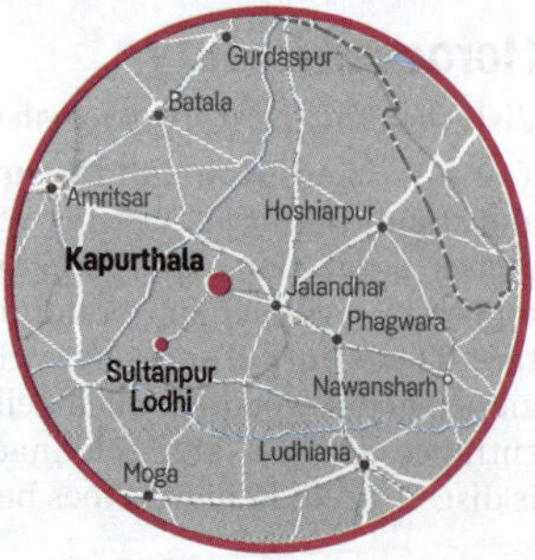

Replace the royal trappings of Kapurthala with spiritual Sultanpur Lodhi, where Guru Nanak first voiced the basis of Sikhism.

GETTING AROUND

The easiest, cheapest way to cover the short distance to Sultanpur Lodhi is by bus. Buses leave Kapurthala bus stand every half hour or so and tickets (from ₹45) can be bought on the spot. Most places of interest in Sultanpur Lodhi are within walking distance of each other; for the odd far-flung ones, hop onto a shared autorickshaw (from ₹20). Alternatively, you can hire a cab for the day (from ₹1500).

Sultanpur Lodhi was founded in the 11th century CE by the Lodis, an Afghan dynasty that preceded the Mughals. It became a major trade hub under the latter, located as it was on the high road between Delhi and Lahore. Today, it draws its fame from the formative years Guru Nanak spent here on the request of his elder sister, Bebe Nanki, a central figure in his life. The young Nanak found employment, married Bibi Sulakhani, and fathered two sons during his stay. This is also where Guru Nanak's divine revelation occurred – elevating Sultanpur Lodhi to the status of a primary Sikh pilgrimage centre, dotted with several historical shrines, including the majestic Gurdwara Ber Sahib.

Sultanpur Lodhi

TIME FROM KAPURTHALA: **40MIN**

Sultanpur Lodhi's most sacred site

Regal-looking **Gurdwara Ber Sahib**, located on the left bank of the Bein rivulet, is without question the town's star attraction. The high-ceilinged three-storey structure features slender pillars, stucco designs and a marble sanctum accessed through silver-clad doors. Completed in 1941 by Maharaja Jagatjit Singh of Kapurthala, the gleaming white shrine stands beside an ancient *ber* (zizyphus), the tree that gives the shrine its name. It is under this tree that Guru Nanak sat in reflection after his daily dip in the Bein. One time he failed to resurface, leading to fears of his drowning. However, three days later he reappeared a few kilometres upstream and voiced a divine revelation that emphasised the oneness of god and humanity. This became the basis for Sikhism. Expect the place to be teeming with followers on Gurpurab (Guru Nanak's birthday); check ahead, as dates change according to the lunar calendar. You are required to remove footwear and cover your head before entering.

In memory of a lifelong confidante

Guru Nanak's elder sister, Bebe Nanki, was the first to recognise his exceptional spiritual quality, and remained an influential figure in his life. The young Nanak relocated to live with his sibling, with whom he shared a deep affectionate bond, and her husband, Jai Ram, facilitated his employment

JIWANJOT/JJSINGH1981/PUBLIC DOMAIN ©

Gurdwara Sant Ghat, Sultanpur Lodhi

as a shopkeeper. The cupola-replete double-storey red-brick building called **Gurdwara Puratan Ghar** (old house) is of recent vintage. It was built in the 1970s under the aegis of a charitable trust to honour the memory of Bebe Nanki, widely acknowledged as the first Sikh because of her unshakeable faith in her brother. Expect to see walls lined with paintings depicting pivotal moments from Guru Nanak's life. The house also enshrines the Guru Granth Sahib; do remember to remove footwear and cover your head before entering.

Life of a householder

Guru Nanak emphasised that spiritual awakening could be attained by living a householder's life, exemplifying this by getting married and raising a family. **Gurdwara Guru Ka Bagh** enshrines a cubical red-brick structure in its basement, said to be the house where Guru Nanak lived after his marriage with Bibi Sulakhni. This is also where their two sons, Sri Chand and Lakhmi Das, were born. In the expansive front yard, a sandstone cupola marks the well the family used for drawing water, and still retains its original brickwork. The facade of this large, elegant, marble-clad shrine features intricate carvings and pietra dura (marble inlay work) panels, punctuated by a finely carved, silver-encased doorway overhung with an equally pretty marble balcony. Once inside, don't miss the sanctum's strikingly painted ceiling with floral mirror-work motifs.

Emergence of a world religion

Gurdwara Sant Ghat commemorates Guru Nanak's reemergence from the Bein rivulet after a three-day disappearance underwater. Located on the western outskirts of the town away from the cluster of main shrines, this is where he is believed to have also composed the Mulmantra (opening stanza of Japji Sahib, the Sikh morning prayer), widely acknowledged as the essence of the Sikh faith.

THE LANGAR TRADITION

The practice of communal meals was enshrined in the tenets of the Sikh faith by its founder, Guru Nanak, who sought to end antiquated ideas of social difference prevalent during his time. By introducing the concept of *sangat* (congregation) and *pangat* (neat rows), and asking his followers to sit together on the floor to eat simple meals *(langar)*, without distinguishing between man or woman, rich or poor, high-born or otherwise, he highlighted the equality of all in the eyes of the creator. The community kitchen at Harmandir Sahib is the world's largest. It serves free vegetarian meals around the clock; averaging 75,000 meals in general, double that on religious occasions and festivals. It's funded by donations and managed by volunteers.

Kurukshetra

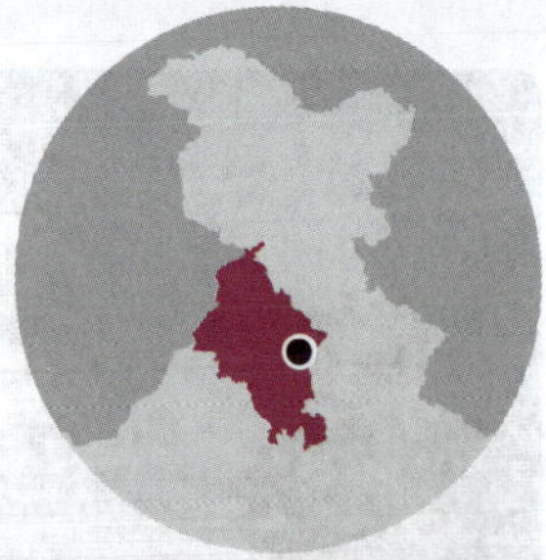

MYTHOLOGICAL MOORINGS | HISTORIC THANESAR | MUGHAL PAST

GETTING AROUND

Kurukshetra is a 90km day trip from Chandigarh. It takes two hours by cab (from ₹3000), which will go into the town as well. Most local buses (₹150) between Chandigarh and Delhi drop you off on the national highway at Pipli, 6km from Kurukshetra. From here, autorickshaws (₹30) ferry passengers to Brahmasarovar. Shared autos (from ₹150) can be hired here to visit the main attractions; solo rides will cost upwards of ₹700. Walking is not a viable option; the main points of interest are widely spread across both Kurukshetra and Thanesar.

Kurukshetra is the setting of the celebrated epic Mahabharata. It recounts an 18-day battle that took place between two sets of cousins, the Pandava and Kaurava; and the town, along with Thanesar (old Kurukshetra), is dotted with sites associated with events that occurred during the war – including the spot where Krishna delivered the Bhagavad Gita discourse to Arjuna. Kurukshetra is also where Brahma, the god of creation, is said to have shaped the universe, adding to its religious and mythological significance for Hindus. Archaeological finds indicate that Kurukshetra's historic footprint dates back to Harshavardhana's rule in the Kushana period (1st–3rd century CE). Excavations at Harsh Ka Tila, a green expanse frequented for outings and walks today, also revealed Thanesar's prominence during the time of the Mughals. The tomb of Sheikh Chilli, the spiritual mentor of Shah Jahan's son Dara Shikoh, is all that remains from the period.

Making of the Universe

Walk around holy waters

The massive **Brahmasarovar** is where Brahma is believed to have created the universe and is one of the town's main attractions. This huge ceremonial tank is divided into two by a central causeway that connects its main entrances. One is across Neelkanthi Yatri Niwas, the other lies beyond Sri Krishna Museum. A walk down the middle brings you to a large metal horse-drawn chariot depicting Krishna's discourse

EATING IN KURUKSHETRA: OUR PICKS

Neelkanthi Yatri Niwas: Reasonably priced, basic North Indian meals and snacks, tea and *paneer pakora* are a must-try. *7-11am, 12.30-4pm & 7.30-10.30pm* ₹

Bikaner Mishthan Bhandar: This is a popular Kurukshetra haunt, clean and fuss-free, frequented for its *mithai*, snacks and baked goods. *6am-10.30pm* ₹

Golden Sweets: Old-time no-frills sweet-shop, best known for its samosa. Newer branch is located near Thanesar train station. *7am-9pm* ₹

Parakeet Resort: Restaurant in government-run tourist complex on Chandigarh–Delhi Hwy. North Indian and fast food. *7-11am, 12.30-4pm & 7.30-10.30pm* ₹₹

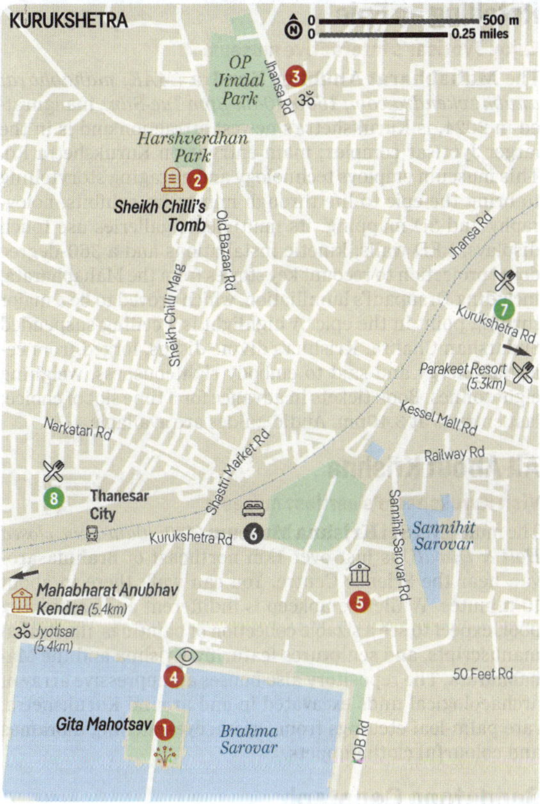

HIGHLIGHTS
1 Gita Mahotsav
2 Sheikh Chilli's Tomb

SIGHTS
3 Bhadrakali Temple
4 Brahmasarovar
5 Sri Krishna Museum

SLEEPING
6 Neelkanthi Yatri Niwas

EATING
7 Bikaner Mishthan Bhandar
8 Golden Sweets
see 6 Neelkanthi Yatri Niwas

MAHABHARATA IN A NUTSHELL

The Mahabharata, one of the two great Indian texts (Ramayana being the other), is, broadly speaking, a mythic tale about feuding cousins that resulted in a fratricidal war at Kurukshetra. Compiled as a poem of 100,000 verses (c 4th century BCE), it centres on the Pandavas and Kauravas. It evolves into an epic of dharma (good) and adharma (evil) following the Pandavas' loss at a deceitful game of dice, and the subsequent humiliation of their wife, Draupadi. Her saviour Krishna's battle-side discourse to Arjuna is called Bhagavad Gita, and is a revered spiritual and philosophical guide for Hindus to achieve self-realisation.

to Arjuna. To experience the place in a different light, consider a visit when the evening prayers at the Sarveshwar Mahadev Temple are underway. Brahmasarovar is also where the **International Gita Mahotsav**, held annually, takes place between November and December. Check for exact dates *(internationalgitamahotsav.in)* before visiting.

A Spot of Spirituality

Where the Bhagavad Gita was voiced

Jyotisar is where Krishna is believed to have imparted the Bhagavad Gita to Arjuna on the eve of the Mahabharata. The holy banyan, under which this discourse on life and duty took place, rises from the edge of a ceremonial water body. Visitors are required to remove their shoes before stepping onto the elevated marble platform that surrounds the tree. One of Jyotisar's two entry points is through a marble archway beside a small parking facility. The other is from the Mahabharat Anubhav Kendra side, with which it shares the premises. Stick around for the half-hour light-and-sound show *(thegitashow.com; ₹30)* about the Gita (in English at 8pm).

THE TALES OF SHEIKH CHILLI

In Indian folklore, Sheikh Chilli is a perpetually broke and lazy but imaginative man known for his elaborate daydreams that often land him in the midst of comical disaster. This lovable, absent-minded character has regaled Indians over many generations with clear moral lessons about hard work triumphing over wishful thinking. Popularly called Sheikh Chilli ke Lateefey, these much-loved tales are available as books and animated versions online. But how did he come to bear the name of a wise saint buried in Thanesar? According to 19th-century traveller David Ross, the Sufi wrote them. In his 1883 travelogue, *The Land of The Five Rivers and Sindh*, he refers to Sheikh Chilli as the 'author of some of the most popular moral tales, allegories, and ballads'.

Retelling an Epic

Enjoy Jyotisar's interactive museum

The **Mahabharat Anubhav Kendra** *(MAK; mahabharat anubhavkendra.com; ₹600; 10am-8pm Tue-Sun)*, inaugurated in 2024, is Kurukshetra's newest attraction and is in the larger Jyotisar complex; main entry is on Kurukshetra Rd. This museum employs technology and engaging storytelling to bring the epic to life through immersive exhibits, holography and 3D mapping. Its multimedia galleries use touch displays, LED walls, kinetic installations and a 360-degree dome projection to recount key stories from the Mahabharata, including Draupadi's humiliation, which proved to be a major turning point in the epic. A highlight is a ceiling-suspended Sudarshan Chakra, Krishna's divine discus, forged from celestial energy and said to embody righteousness, weighing eight tonnes. Book tickets in advance for a time slot of choice; last entry is at 3.40pm. Audio guides are available.

All About Krishna

Visit Kurukshetra's earliest museum

The multilevel **Sri Krishna Museum** *(₹30; 10am-5pm, closed Holi & Diwali)* is just over 1km northeast of Brahmasarovar, near the Science Centre. You can walk there in about 10 minutes. While the upkeep is indifferent and captioning poor, expect to see a sizable collection of paintings, illustrated manuscripts, and sculptures featuring Krishna and the Mahabharata. The repository also houses an impressive array of archaeological finds excavated in and around Kurukshetra, rare palm-leaf etchings from Orissa, eye-catching dioramas and colourful cloth puppets.

Sandstone Cenotaph

Explore a 17th-century Mughal tomb

Sheikh Chilli's Tomb *(sunrise-sunset Sat-Thu)*, said to be that of the spiritual mentor of Dara Shikoh, eldest son of Mughal emperor Shah Jahan, is at Thanesar. The complex is also home to the **Thanesar Archaeological Museum**, housed in an erstwhile madrasa (Islamic college); the remains of a serai (inn); and a spacious car park. The pretty sandstone tomb's terrace provides views of the town, the sprawling Harsh Ka Tila and Pathar Masjid. It's best to buy tickets online *(asi.payumoney.com; ₹250)* beforehand, as internet is patchy and cash transactions are not permitted on-site.

Power of the Feminine

Visit a Shakti peeth

Shakti represents the divine feminine, and **Bhadrakali Temple**, further down the road from the Sheikh Chilli complex, is one of 51 *peeth* (temples) that honour this cosmic energy. Legend has it that Shiva's wife Sati immolated herself to protest her father's disrespect of her husband. When Shiva broke into *tandava* (dance of destruction) holding her lifeless body, this is where her right ankle fell. A silver idol of the deity graces the sanctum. Remove shoes to enter.

Places We Love to Stay

₹ Budget ₹₹ Midrange ₹₹₹ Top End

Chandigarh

Map p191

Maison Jeanneret ₹ Government-run former home of Chandigarh's chief architect, now a museum, with guest rooms on the 1st floor.

Corporate Inn ₹ Centrally located business hotel: very basic, best suited for brief visits; located a short walk from Sector 17 Plaza.

Diamond Plaza ₹ Well suited for short stays, with affordable reasonably clean rooms in a busy market near ISBT-17.

Hotel KLG ₹₹ Close to ISBT-43. You can expect clean rooms, friendly staff and tasty North Indian food.

Hotel Icon ₹₹ Located in the busy Sector 8 market on Madhya Marg, it houses snug rooms and a popular Asian restaurant.

Anchorage 42 ₹₹ Memorabilia-filled home of a married couple (a former naval officer and an artist) promises a comfortable stay and great food.

Dak Bungalow ₹₹ Find eclectic rooms, fine food, and friendly hosts at this farm-stay just off a busy highway outside Chandigarh.

Antler Woods ₹₹₹ Luxurious farm-stay with gracious hosts near Siswan Dam, engulfed by wildlife-rich woodlands and birdsong.

Aura Pottery ₹₹₹ Pottery studio housed in a farm on the outskirts; a minimum two-night stay includes all meals and pottery classes.

Baans Bagh Farm ₹₹₹ Two plush rooms on a massive bamboo-forested farm in Siswan, with superb food and hospitable owners.

Walden Sustainable Living ₹₹₹ Family-run experiential farm-stay an hour's drive from Chandigarh, serving farm-to-table organic food amid tranquil nature.

Amritsar

Map p197

KK Continental ₹ A multistorey hotel with comfortable rooms, friendly staff and limited but tasty food; located close to the train station.

Ritz Plaza ₹ Housed in sprawling grounds on The Mall with an old-world charm; affordable, spacious rooms, and ample parking.

Bloom Hotel ₹ Its convenient location near Golden Temple makes up for smallish but clean rooms and lack of parking.

Mrs Bhandari's Guesthouse ₹₹ A legendary old guesthouse (now looking its age) housed in spacious grounds; also available for pitching tents and camper vans.

Majha House ₹₹ Comfortable, book-lined family home with a well-kept garden and delicious home-style food; also doubles as a cultural space.

Bougainvillea ₹₹ Popular homestay with comfy rooms across two levels and several quirky garden nooks to dine-in; located just off a busy market.

Kothi ₹₹₹ Comfortable rooms on two levels around a central courtyard in a restored *haveli*, welcoming hosts and excellent food.

Patiala

Map p203

Garden Resort ₹ Spacious, simply furnished, comfortable rooms above a popular garden-fronted restaurant serving excellent Punjabi food.

Mohan Continental ₹ Expect basic, affordable rooms, best suited for short stays; located on a busy road across from the main post office.

Eqbal Inn ₹₹ Located away from city centre, the rooms – though adequately sized and equipped with modern amenities – lack character.

Hansali Organic Farm ₹₹ Family-run sustainable farm-stay promises organic meals in Fatehgarh Sahib, a short drive from Patiala.

Baradari Palace ₹₹₹ Heritage hotel with atmospheric rooms on multiple levels, housed in a former royal residence; service could be better.

Ran Baas ₹₹₹ A luxurious heritage hotel housed in an elegant palace inside the historic Qila Mubarak.

Kapurthala

Map p208

London Hotel ₹ This well-located oldie (near Moorish Mosque) offers comfortable short stays in snug rooms; service and maintenance could be better.

Ramneek Hotel ₹ Rooms lack character and need an upgrade, but adequately serve the purpose for a brief stay.

Kurukshetra

Map p213

Neelkanthi Yatri Niwas ₹ Centrally located government-run hotel with spacious rooms, including dorms, and limited but tasty food.

Parakeet Resort ₹₹ A government-run tourist complex in Pipli on the Chandigarh–Delhi Hwy (7km from Kurukshetra) with OK rooms for brief halts.

For places to stay in Ladakh, see p248

DANIEL PRUDEK/SHUTTERSTOCK

Above: Tsemo Gompa (p223), Leh; Right: Alchi Choskhor (p233)

Researched by
Shikha Tripathi

Ladakh

SURREAL MOUNTAINSCAPES AND DEEP BUDDHIST FAITH

In a stark, elemental landscape traversed by four icy, 6000m-plus mountain ranges, Ladakhi culture glows with an inner warmth.

This is a different India. At elevations mostly well above 3000m, sheltered from monsoons by the Great Himalaya Range, Ladakh is effectively a high-altitude desert. It's a place of raw, wild beauty, of scarcely credible mountain scenery and barren rocky wastes, but also speckled with summer oases of greenery along its rivers and around its villages of white-cube houses and flower gardens. The journey to get here, whether you fly in or travel up the spectacular roads from Manali or Srinagar, is a mouthwatering introduction.

FLUID-SHUTTER/SHUTTERSTOCK

All across the landscape, whitewashed stupas, fluttering prayer flags and picturesque gompas (Tibetan Buddhist monasteries) express the profound Buddhist beliefs of the Ladakhi people. The gompas, with their spiritual atmosphere and golden Buddhas, are a highlight of Ladakh travel. So is the landscape itself, which invites you to trek on foot along valleys, through remote villages and over mountains to experience its essence.

The many army camps indicate that not everything is peace and light up here: disputed frontiers with Pakistan and China have brought a large Indian military presence to Ladakh, but also an ever-improving road network that makes it easy to enjoy road trips crossing 5000m-plus passes to outer regions.

At the root of Ladakh's charm remain the Ladakhis themselves, a mountain people of delightfully welcoming traditions and that kind of inner light special to many Himalayan Buddhist cultures.

THE MAIN AREAS

LEH
The atmospheric hub of Ladakhi life. **p222**

NUBRA
Scenic northern valleys. **p237**

CHANGTHANG
Stunning high-altitude eastern lakes. **p241**

ZANSKAR
Remote, traditional southern region. **p244**

Find Your Way

Some 350km from north to south and east to west, Ladakh is a collection of high-altitude valleys and sky-piercing mountain ranges crossed by high passes. The Indus Valley, across central Ladakh, is the most populated part.

Nubra, p237

Northern valleys with forts, monasteries and rivers between soaring mountains, reached by one of the world's highest motorable passes.

Leh, p222

Historic capital overlooked by a Potala-style palace; base for exploring the Indus Valley and organising anything in Ladakh.

Changthang, p241

Barren eastern region with a nomadic population and famously beautiful lakes, notably Pangong Tso and Tso Moriri.

Zanskar, p244

Isolated, still traditional, former independent kingdom reached by smooth roads across awe-inspiring mountain scenery.

TAXI

Bus services are minimal but plentiful taxis have reasonable fixed rates set by local taxi unions, both for short trips and multiday tours (also called 'jeep safaris'). Shared taxis are available on some routes.

MOTORCYCLE

Hugely popular between April and October. Leh travel agencies rent bikes with fixed rates (₹2000 to ₹3500 per day for Royal Enfield models). Main roads are nearly all paved or good-condition unpaved. Petrol stations are fairly plentiful.

MAKKARA/SHUTTERSTOCK

Pangong Tso (p241), Changthang

Plan Your Time

Enjoy Leh as a base for exploring the Indus Valley. Do your best to get out to at least one of the spectacular outlying regions: Nubra, Changthang or Zanskar.

Five to Seven Days

- Two days acclimatising in **Leh** (p222) provides a chance to explore – not too strenuously – its sights and eat some good meals. Then visit some highlights of the Indus Valley, perhaps **Alchi** (p233) and **Thiksey** (p230), before heading out to **Nubra** (p237 or **Changthang** (p241), or both, for exciting road trips across high mountain passes and the spectacular scenery of these remoter regions.

Three Weeks or More

- You'll have time to explore Ladakh's culture and landscapes. As well as Leh, check out **Stok** (p229), **Shey** (p230), **Thiksey** (p230), **Hemis** (p230), **Basgo** (p233), **Alchi** (p233) and **Lamayuru** (p235) in (or just off) the Indus Valley. Take a trek, perhaps a route in the **Markha Valley** (p232) of up to eight days. Tour out to **Nubra** (p237), **Changthang** (p241) and beautiful, old-world **Zanskar** (p244).

SEASONAL HIGHLIGHTS

APRIL & EARLY MAY
Temperatures are more comfortable and nature starts to blossom. Accommodation and restaurants reopen.

MID-MAY TO SEPTEMBER
Tourist numbers peak in June. Delightful September has good weather and few crowds.

OCTOBER TO MID-NOVEMBER
First snows in the valleys normally arrive in November.

WINTER
Yes, it's very cold, but you'll experience Ladakh without the crowds. The roads up to Ladakh can be closed.

HELP ME PICK:

Trekking in Ladakh

There's no better way to enjoy Ladakh's magnificent landscapes and remote villages than on foot, allowing the scenic majesty to unfold gradually as you move along craggy valleys and over prayer-flag-decked mountain passes. Ladakh is criss-crossed by myriad age-old foot and pack-animal trails. New roads have obliterated or dampened the appeal of some longstanding treks, but there are still dozens to walk, and fresh ones are developing.

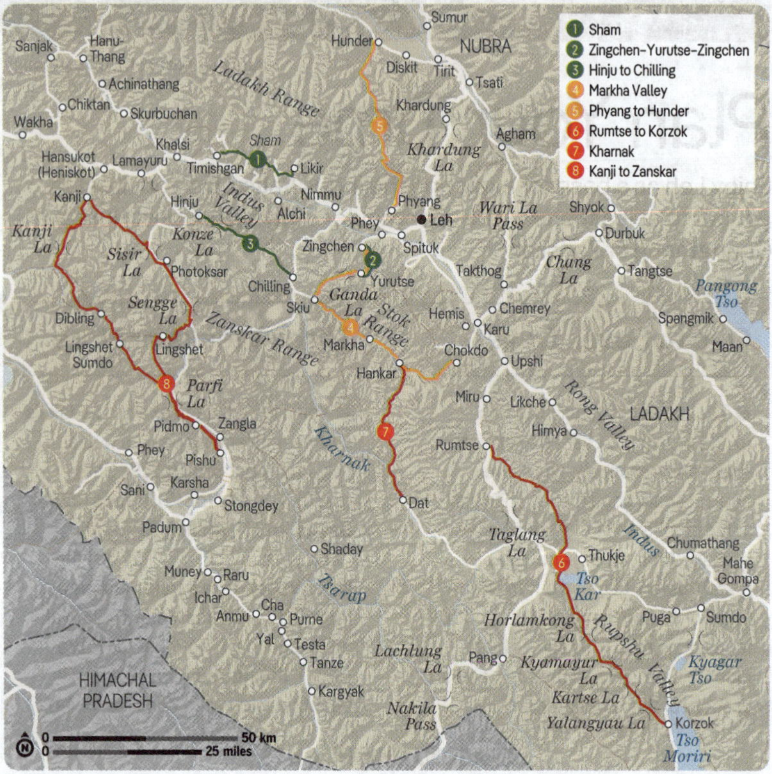

HOW TO

When to go The main trekking season is June to September, but some routes have longer or shorter seasons.

Planning Check sites of recommended Leh agencies such as Hidden North Adventures, Higher Himalaya, Ancient Tracks and Ladakh Traverse.

Before you trek Spend at least two, preferably three, days acclimatising on arrival in Ladakh before embarking on any demanding physical activity.

Don't forget Warm clothes for cold nights, especially if camping; a sleeping bag if camping; water-purification tablets; sturdy sandals for any river crossings.

DIY or Guided?

Markha Valley, Sham, Zingchen-Yurutse, Hinju-Chilling and some routes in Zanskar have village homestays that provide you with a bed, dinner, breakfast and picnic lunch for usually ₹2000 to ₹2500. This enables you to walk with a light pack and, if you wish, without a guide – and experience villager life first-hand. For routes without homestays, Leh's abundant travel agencies can arrange fully equipped camping treks with guides, pack animals, camping equipment, cook, meals and transport. Typical costs are between ₹8000 and ₹10,000 per person per day, varying with group size, distances and other factors. Before signing up, check what is and isn't included.

Carrying all your gear on your own back is a potentially exhausting task at these altitudes that's not recommended for most walkers. An intermediate option if you're self-sufficient and patient is finding your own pack-animal handler with horses, ponies or donkeys to carry your luggage. The minimum cost is ₹800 per animal per day; it can be considerably more in July and August, and in Zanskar. You'll almost always need to engage at least two animals per person and you'll have to pay for extra days required for them to return to the starting point. However you trek, a decent map always helps with planning, navigation and a route overview. A good one readily available in Leh is Milestone's *Ladakh and Zanskar Trekking Map* (1:175,000).

Where to Trek If You Want...

Short Treks

Sham The three- or four-day Likir-to-Timishgan hike in the Sham district has relatively low altitudes (maximum 3880m). Good for acclimatising. The downside: a road now parallels most of the route.

Zingchen–Yurutse–Zingchen A one- or two-day sampler quickly accessed from Leh; ascend from 3370m to 4150m then back down again.

Hinju to Chilling Hard two-day homestay trek: both days are around 20km and nine hours, with the 4890m Konze La on day one and some wild gorge scenery (navigation skills required) and a 4700m pass on day two. It's possible to finish (more easily) at Sumdha Do. If camping, you can take three days.

Medium-Length Treks

Markha Valley Village-to-village along a scenic, though partly road-encroached, valley south of Leh. The most popular route – from Zingchen via the 4960m Ganda La to Skiu, then on to Markha village, the Kongmaru La (5260m) and Chokdo – takes six to eight days. Driving to Skiu village (the road beyond is closed for trekkers), you can do it in five days.

Phyang to Hunder A beautiful, less-frequented, five-day route crossing the Ladakh Range and down into Nubra. Highest pass: Lasirmo La (5440m).

Long Treks

Rumtse to Korzok A tough, exhilarating, seven-day trek in remote Changthang; all above 4000m, with six 5000m-plus passes. Starts on the NH3 highway, passes Tso Khar salt lake and ends at beautiful Tso Moriri.

Kharnak An interesting, challenging variation from the main Markha Valley route heads south after Hankar village, over the 5190m Zalung Karpo La and down to Dat (four days from Markha village) in the relatively green Kharnak district. From Dat you could continue to Tso Khar (three days) or drive to Tso Khar then hike three days to Tso Moriri.

Kanji to Zanskar Challenging alternatives to the Lamayuru-Padum trek across the spectacular Zanskar Range, which has lost much of its charm to road construction, start at Kanji and typically end with a pickup at Pishu, after eight or nine days' walking with several pass crossings. One option goes via the Nigutse La (5100m), Photoksar and Lingshet; another trek crosses the Kanji La (5250m) and continues via Dibling and Lingshet Sumdo.

Leh

HISTORIC HUB| FOOD| MARKETS

GETTING AROUND

Leh is easily walkable, with mostly gentle gradients. Most accommodation is within 15 minutes' walk of Main Market (Main Bazaar), the centre of town. The airport is 4km southwest; a taxi from there to anywhere within 7km costs ₹580. Tempo minibuses and shared taxis from/to Manali, Kargil and Srinagar use the Bombgarh (Bum Ghat/Bomgat/Boom-guard) Taxi Stand, 2.5km south of Main Market. There's also a summer Manali bus by the HPTDC.

TOP TIP

Pre-paid SIM cards from elsewhere in India won't work in Ladakh. You must buy another one here. Jio has good Ladakh coverage; its office is 1.5km south of Main Market. Airtel is good for the Indus Valley, Nubra and around Padum, but not the Markha Valley or Changthang.

Ladakh's historic capital and easily its largest town, overlooking the broad Indus Valley with high mountains in all directions, bustles away beneath its towering 17th-century royal palace. The jumbled buildings of the Old Town on the hillside below the palace give way to central streets of shops, restaurants, travel agencies and markets. To the west and north, many of the winding lanes that once ran between barley fields are now lined with guesthouses and hotels. Newer neighbourhoods to the south lead out towards the airport and large military encampments. In among all this you'll run across dozens of stupas, prayer wheels, *mani* walls (Tibetan stone walls with sacred inscriptions) and temples emphasising Tibetan Buddhism's deep, ancient roots here.

Leh has by far the best range of eating and accommodation options in Ladakh and is a great introduction to the region's scenic grandeur and calm-paced charm. As Ladakh's logistics hub, it's also the place to organise most activities and excursions.

Where Royalty Reigned

Exploring Leh's palace

All over the capital, eyes are magnetised by the sheer-walled **Leh Palace** towering on the hillside. It was Ladakh's 'Lion King' Sengge Namgyal who had the nine-storey palace built, in Tibetan style, when he moved his capital here from Shey in the 17th century. After the Namgyal dynasty was deposed by the 1830s Dogra invasion, the palace fell into ruin. It has been extensively restored since 1982.

An hour is plenty to explore the interior. Two rooms house interesting exhibits: one on the palace's own history and architecture, the other on monuments under the Archaeological Survey of India's protection. But the big highlight for many is the 360-degree panoramas from the 8th-floor roof.

You can reach the palace by working your way on foot up through the Old Town or by driving up circuitous Leh Palace

Rd (a taxi from the town centre costs ₹300/520 one way/return). **Gulzar Hussain** *(8803425501; per person tours under 3hr ₹2000)*, a resident Ladakhi historian, has insightful and engaging walking tours of the Old Town where he grew up.

Victory Peak

Above the palace

From the palace you may well want to continue up to the cluster of buildings on the hilltop above, **Namgyal Tsemo** (Victory Peak). A dusty path climbs from the palace parking area or you can take a circuitous road route from the town below. The first of the three buildings is the highest of Tragspa Bumlde's three Maitreya (future Buddha) temples, the **Tsemo Gompa**, housing a huge, 8m-high, gold-faced Maitreya. Above this stands the red (and very dark inside) **Gonkhang**, a temple home to wrathful protector deities. It was erected by King Tashi Namgyal in the 16th century after defeating an invading army, and it's believed slain enemies are buried below its Mahakala statue.

Crowning the hill are the white-walled remains of Tashi Namgyal's fort-palace, **Tsemo Fort** – it's mostly bare inside, but provides superb panoramas.

A Historic Cultural Centre

Exhibitions and events in the Munshi House

A short walk down into the Old Town from Leh Palace is the 16th-century mansion where the *munshi* (king's secretary) and his household dwelt.

Today it and the adjoining Gyaoo House, both beautifully restored, house the **Ladakh Arts & Media Organisation (LAMO)**, which offers guided tours of the building as well as often-fascinating art and photography exhibits, musical events and film screenings, plus Old Town walking tours.

Discover Leh's Silk Road Heritage

A well-displayed modern museum

Leh was once an important crossroads on the Silk Road trade network, with routes converging from Xinjiang (China), Kashmir, Tibet and India – all four points of the compass. Much of the trade was killed off by the 20th-century closure of borders with Pakistan and China. But you can get a feel

Continues on p226

ACCLIMATISING TO ALTITUDE

The 3500m-plus altitude of Leh and much of the rest of Ladakh causes headaches, fatigue and sometimes dizziness for many new arrivals – especially for those who've flown here. Take things easy initially and drink plenty of fluids, or start on a preventive course of Diamox tablets (available at pharmacies; ensure you are not allergic to sulphates) 48 hours before flying. Several hotels also have portable oxygen concentrators now. If symptoms become severe, you risk potentially fatal acute mountain sickness (AMS). The condition is eminently treatable if you act promptly: call English-speaking specialist **Dr Morup** *(9858060706)* who can attend you at your accommodation. Consultation costs ₹1000 within the town centre, and more as distance increases.

EATING IN LEH: BEST LADAKHI RESTAURANTS

Tsas by Dolkhar: Creative vegetarian food; traditional Ladakhi dishes evolved for contemporary palates. *8-10am & noon-9.30pm* ₹₹₹

Ladakh Organic Food: A calm, five-table upstairs diner at locale D48 in Moti Market with tasty, home-style, vegetarian Ladakhi classics. *8am-7pm* ₹

Namza Dining: Finely crafted Ladakhi cuisine including a highlight Yarkandi pulao (rice cooked in stock and spices). *10am-10pm, closed winter* ₹₹

De Khambir: Convenient central spot for cheap local specialities. Try a *khambir* (Ladakhi bread) pocket sandwich with egg and cheese. *9am-8.30pm Mon-Sat Apr-mid-Oct* ₹

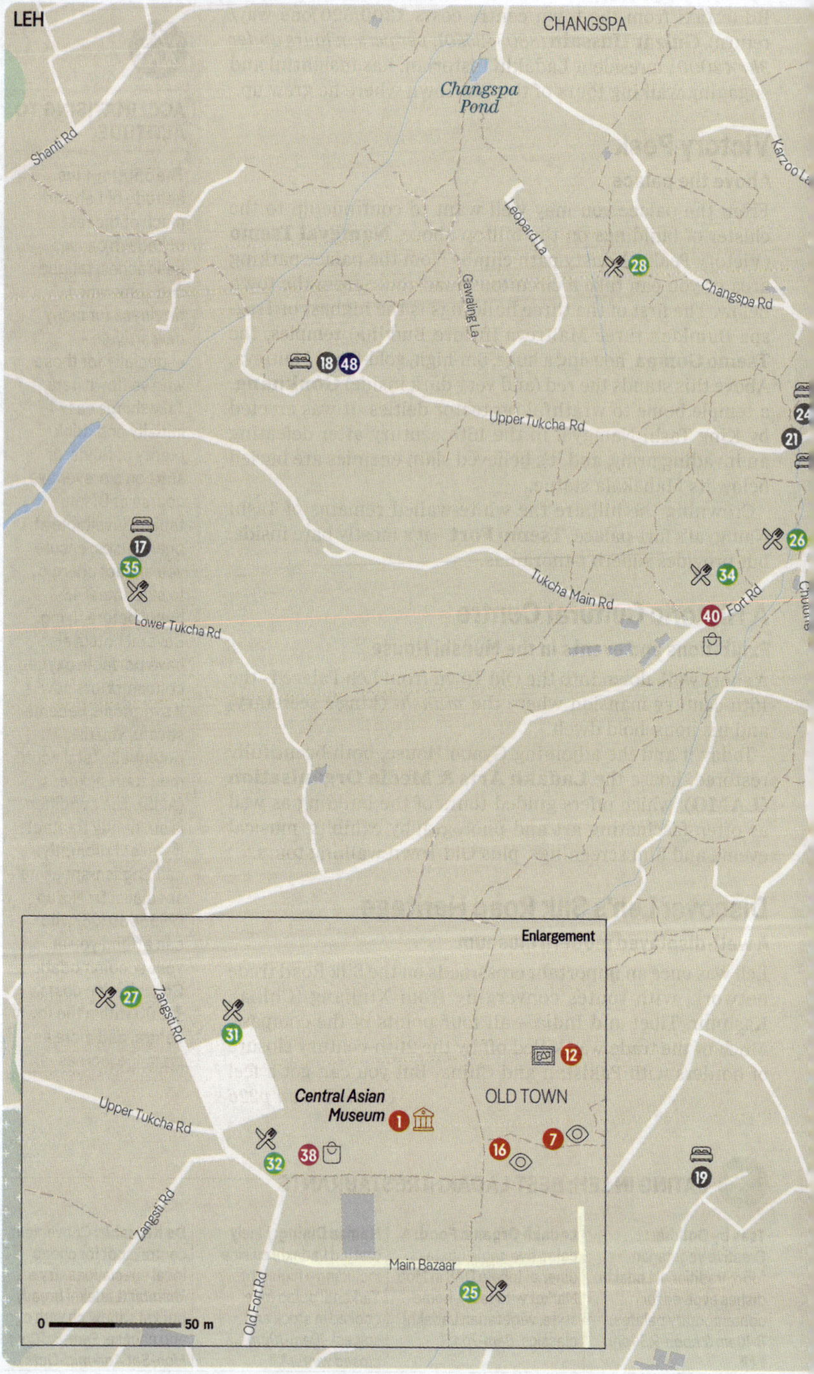
LEH
CHANGSPA
Changspa Pond
Shanti Rd
Karzoo La
Leopard La
Gawaling La
Changspa Rd
Upper Tukcha Rd
Tukcha Main Rd
Lower Tukcha Rd
Fort Rd
Enlargement
Zangsti Rd
Upper Tukcha Rd
Central Asian Museum
OLD TOWN
Zangsti Rd
Old Fort Rd
Main Bazaar
0 50 m
1
7
12
16
17
18
19
21
24
25
26
27
28
31
32
34
35
38
40
48

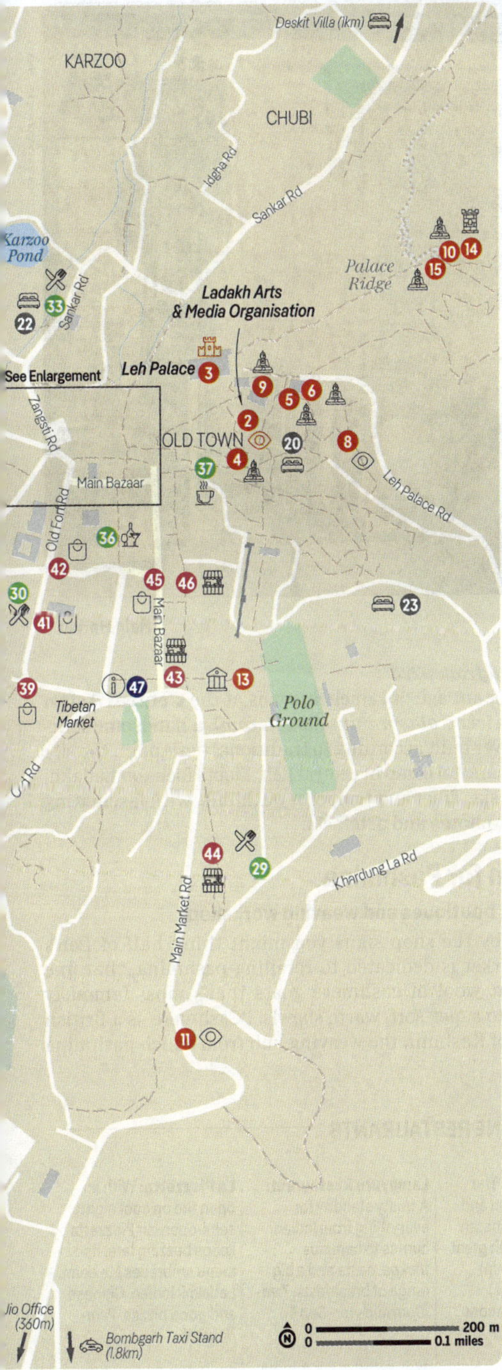

HIGHLIGHTS
1 Central Asian Museum
2 Ladakh Arts & Media Organisation
3 Leh Palace

SIGHTS
4 Chamba Karpo
5 Chamba Marpo
6 Chenresig Gompa
7 Choskor House
8 East Stupa Gate
9 Gompa Soma
10 Gonkhang
11 Leh Main Gate
12 Spindle Art Studio
13 Textile Museum of Ladakh
14 Tsemo Fort
15 Tsemo Gompa
16 West Stupa Gate

SLEEPING
17 Dolkhar
18 Gangs-Shun Homestay
19 Grand Dragon Ladakh
20 Himalayan Bauhaus
21 Hotel Jigmet
22 Kang-Lha-Chen
23 Namgyal Guest House
24 Saiman Guest House

EATING
25 Bodhisattva
26 Chopsticks
27 De Khambir
28 La Piazzetta
29 Ladakh Organic Food
30 Lamayuru Restaurant
31 Leh Cafe
32 Montagne
33 Namza Dining
34 Tibetan Kitchen
35 Tsas by Dolkhar

DRINKING & NIGHTLIFE
36 Ibex Bar & Restaurant
37 Lala's Café

SHOPPING
38 Brand Ladakh
39 Jigmat Couture
40 Leh Vallée
41 Lena Ladakh
42 Looms of Ladakh
43 Main Market
44 Moti Market
45 Nomadic Woollen Mills
46 Nowshera Bazar

INFORMATION
47 Airtel
48 Dr Morup

IN THE SHAN'S FOOTSTEPS

Khenrab Phuntsog is an award-winning wildlife guard and conservationist who brought about awareness of and a tangible increase in the snow leopard population in Ladakh.

A close sighting of the elusive 'ghost' cat or *shan* near Chilling, my home village inside the Hemis National Park, inspired me to pursue this path when I was 12. When I started my career, we had no equipment to rescue these predators; I have used empty gunny sacks, blankets and nets for their rescue! In over two decades, I have led rescues for nearly 50 snow leopards, trained naturalists and trackers, and set up homestay programmes for snow leopard tourism. Rumbak village has leading local trackers and homestays. The Lungmar Remote Camp in Shang Sumdo has great naturalists and superb sightings.

SNEHAL JEEVAN PAILKAR/SHUTTERSTOCK

Main Market

Continued from p223
for the distant age of camel caravans at the **Central Asian Museum** *(centralasianmuseumleh.com),* a handsome four-storey tower built according to traditional designs on the site of an old caravan camp in central Leh. Floors focus on Ladakh, Central Asia, Tibet and temporary exhibits, with fascinating historical photos and artefacts.

Passion for Pashmina

Beautiful boutiques and weaving workshops

Judging by the shop signs you might think half of Leh's Main Market is dedicated to retailing pashmina, that fine undercoat wool of cashmere goats that's most famously woven into super-soft, warm shawls. ('Cashmere' is a British spelling of Kashmir, the weaving hub from which pashmina

EATING IN LEH: MULTICUISINE RESTAURANTS

Chopsticks: This bright, modern pan-Asian restaurant is a good choice for tasty Thai curries, soups and noodle dishes. *11am-9.30pm mid-Mar–early Nov* ₹₹

Tibetan Kitchen: The menu covers Indian and Chinese but the Tibetan is outstanding, with great *thukpa* (noodle soup), *momos* (dumplings) and more. Reservations advised. *1-11pm mid-Apr-mid-Oct* ₹₹

Lamayuru Restaurant: A trusty standby for everything from Indian curries to hummus, *thukpa*, pasta and a big range of breakfasts. *7am-10pm mid-Apr–Sep* ₹

La Piazzetta: With an open fire on cool nights, semi-open-air Piazzetta keeps buzzing late. Its menu embraces Mexican, Ladakhi, Indian, Chinese and good pizzas. *9am-11pm* ₹₹

textiles reached 19th-century Europe.) The finest pashmina wool of all, with fibres just 12µm to 14µm (micrometres) wide, comes from the Changthangi variety of goats, herded by the nomads of Changthang, the high, dry, cold region stretching from eastern Ladakh far to the east across the Tibetan plateau.

Historically Ladakh took little part in processing Changthangi wool, simply selling it on to Kashmiris. But in recent years several initiatives have sprung up, employing local women to process the wool and weave pashmina right here in Ladakh, at the same time providing a shop window for high-quality Ladakhi design. Showrooms where you can browse and buy beautiful, 100% local, high-quality pashmina products, all within a few minutes' walk of each other in central Leh, include high-fashion-leaning **Jigmat Couture**; **Lena Ladakh**, with expensive shawls and more affordable hats and gloves in lovely natural-dye tones; **Nomadic Woollen Mills**, run by a Changthang native; **Leh Vallée**, with relatively inexpensive shawls and cushion covers; and the women's producer cooperative **Looms of Ladakh**. The government-certified **Brand Ladakh** is a cheaper alternative too.

Jigmat, Lena and Leh Vallée also offer the chance to visit their workshops in or near Leh. For a truly hands-on experience, Lena offers a half-day of weaving and dyeing at its workshop in Thiksey (minimum three people; contact them a week ahead). To delve even deeper into the world of Ladakhi textiles, make an appointment (ideally a month in advance) to visit Jigmat Couture's fascinating private **Textile Museum of Ladakh**.

Market Meanders

Discover central Leh

Main Market is lined with three- and four-storey buildings full of restaurants and shops, and has a modern look. For a more old-fashioned atmosphere divert into some of the backstreets, such as narrow **Nowshera (Naushar) Bazar**, strung with barbers, tailors, butchers, astrologers and vendors of everyday clothes. Further south towards **Leh Main Gate** (the principal road entrance to town), **Moti Market** also bustles with townspeople and villagers looking for their everyday needs.

ALCOHOL IN LADAKH

A few, mainly upper-end, restaurants and hotels have alcohol licences, and some other restaurants have beer available off-menu. The nearest thing to a pub in Leh is **Ibex Bar & Restaurant**, open 11.30am to 8.30pm, on Ibex Rd just off Main Market: a bar room with a handful of tables serving bottled beer, wine and various spirits (and some food). Solo women might not feel comfortable there: a better option might be the in-house bar of a premium hotel. The eighth, 15th and last days of each Tibetan month are 'dry' days, when no alcohol – or meat – is sold.

EATING & DRINKING IN LEH: BEST CAFES

Bodhisattva: This cosy, friendly cafe has excellent fresh-ground coffee, cakes, fusion *momos* and more. *9am-9.30pm* ₹₹

Montagne: A menu of global delights is on offer here – fondues, tempura prawns, veg burgers and speciality coffees. *9am-10.30pm Apr-Nov* ₹₹₹

Lala's Café: A former lama's residence, this place serves good coffee, juices and snacks. *9.30am-7.30pm Mon-Sat, 2-8pm Sun Apr-Sep* ₹

Leh Cafe: The perfect spot at the Main Market entrance for people-watching, with cheery staff. Don't miss their fresh apricot cheesecake. *9am-10pm* ₹₹

OLD TOWN DISCOVERY WALK

This rambling tour of Old Leh's hillside labyrinth takes you past dishevelled and restored old houses, colourful temples, dark passageways and eroded stupas.

START	END	LENGTH
Lala's Café	West Stupa Gate	1km; 2hr

From 1 **Lala's Café** (p227), walk east and turn left up a passage beside a *rigsum gonbo* (three small stupas inside a chamber on wooden pillars). A lintel on your right labelled 'Chamba Gonba' marks the 2 **Chamba Karpo**, one of three Maitreya (future Buddha) temples built on the palace hill by the 15th-century Shey-based King Tragspa Bumlde. Past this, turn right then right again (down through a tunnel) onto a wider street. Head left up to the 3 **Himalayan Bauhaus**. From this residence, head right then take the narrow lane on the side, and veer right to the 4 **East Stupa Gate**, one of four stupa-gateways in the Old Town wall. Turning back, head for a large, bare-walled building ahead: 17th-century 5 **Chenresig (Chanrazik) Gompa**, dedicated to Avalokitesvara. Nearby are the red-walled 6 **Chamba Marpo** (Chamspa Lhakhang), another of Tragspa Bumlde's temples, housing a stunning, three-storey-tall Maitreya image, the 1840s 7 **Gompa Soma** and 8 **Leh Palace** (p222). The Maitreya temples (Chamba Karpo, Chamba Marpo and the hilltop Tsemo Gompa) predate everything else on the palace hill by two centuries. Descend from the Gompa Soma to the 9 **LAMO** (p223), and walk straight down to 10 **Spindle Art Studio** in the Onpo (Astrologer's) House, and 11 **Choskor House**, housing an art-conservation studio. Exit the Old Town through the 12 **West Stupa Gate**.

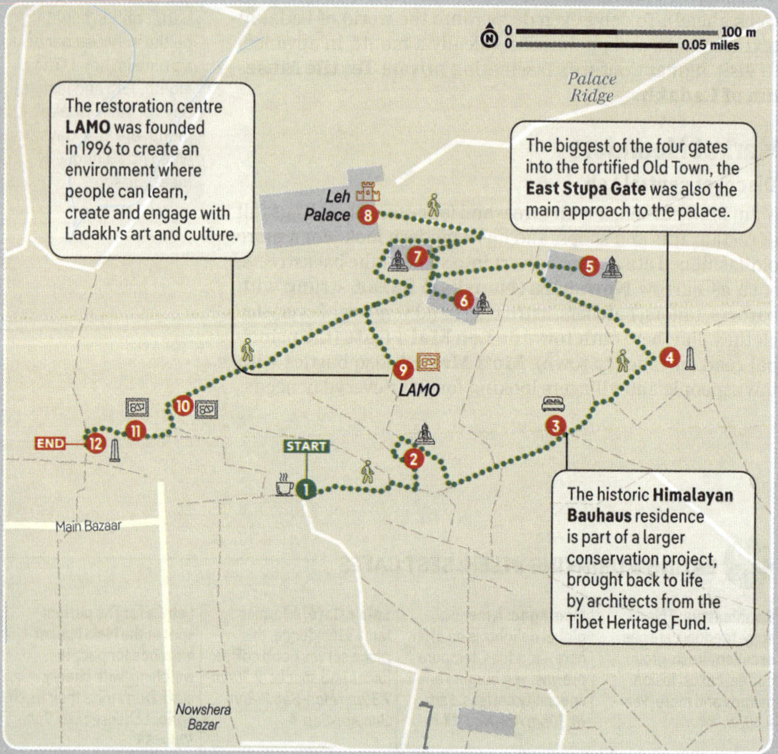

Beyond Leh

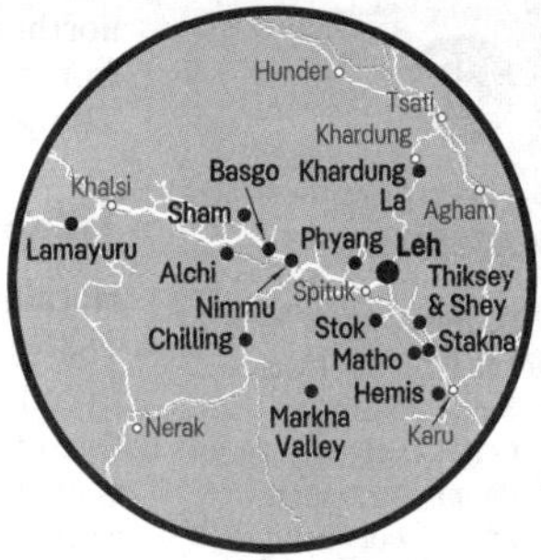

Explore atmospheric monasteries and traditional villages, and trek, cycle or raft your way through stirring mountain and gorge landscapes.

The Indus Valley downstream (west) and upstream (southeast) of Leh is dotted with many of Ladakh's major and most beautiful gompas, whose prayer meetings, festivals and elaborate art give fascinating firsthand experience of the religion's mysteries and beauties. They may be located in villages or isolated in remote valleys; either way, visiting them will also give you a feel for Ladakhi rural life, a cornerstone of its traditional culture, and you'll get to travel through some majestic scenery. The Indus Valley and its tributary valleys and surrounding mountains are, too, an open book for active adventures, with some top treks, mountain biking, river rafting and even snow leopard tracking all easily accessed from Leh.

Places

Khardung La

TIME FROM LEH: **1½HR**

High pass, long downhill bike ride

The 5359m **Khardung La**, on the multi-zigzag road to Nubra, isn't quite the 'world's highest motorable pass' as used to be claimed, but it's still exhilarating to reach its views of the Karakoram range far to the north.

A great way to enjoy it is the Khardung La roll-down *(₹2500-5000 per person; May-Oct)*, where a motor vehicle carries you up to the pass, then you ride a bike 40km downhill back to town!

Many further Ladakh cycling adventures await. Agencies rent mountain bikes *(₹1000-2000 per day)* and also offer guided bike trips.

Stok

TIME FROM LEH: **30MIN**

A royal village

For a 4km stroll exploring this bucolic village, 13km from Leh at the foot of the Stok Range, start at **Stok Palace**, where Ladakh's royal family decamped when ousted from Leh by the 1830s Dogra invasion (it's now an outstanding heritage hotel with an interesting museum). Walk 1km south past a field of white stupas to a huge golden **Buddha statue** just above the modest **Stok (Kurphuk) Gompa**. Continue to the southwest end of the village then follow the road heading

GETTING AROUND

Public transport is limited and slow. Leh's tourist office has bus timetables. Taxis are plentiful. The **Ladakh Taxi Operator Co-operative** *(ladakhtaxiunion.com)*, in central Leh, charges fixed prices (listed on its website) for single- or multi-destination trips. Another option is renting a motorbike (from ₹1500 per day) or scooter (₹1000), available from many Leh agencies.

northeast paralleling the Stok Tokpo stream. About 1.5km from the bridge make a sharp right turn to visit the **Gyap-Thago Heritage Home**.

Thiksey & Shey

TIME FROM LEH TO THIKSEY: **40MIN**

Morning prayers at a major monastery

There's no better way to get a feel for the monastic life central to Ladakh's Buddhist culture than to attend morning prayers. One of the best-attended assemblies (by lamas and visitors) is at the big, beautiful, 15th-century **Thiksey Gompa**, cascading photogenically over a rocky hill 18km from Leh. The daily prayer meeting typically starts at 6am in summer (later in winter), lasting around two hours. The lamas' deep-voiced chanting will alternate with simple reciting of texts, spells of silence, bursts of clapping and thunderous trumpet blasts.

Thiksey Gompa has 10 temples in all. The Maitreya Temple houses an exquisite, 12m-tall golden Maitreya statue, created between 1977 and 1980. Follow signs to the rooftop Lamo-Khang: the temples up here are normally locked, but the views are wonderful.

An old royal palace

Convenient to visit near Thiksey is the old Ladakhi capital Shey. Its recently restored **royal palace** is essentially empty – except for its **temple**, with a colossal 8m-high, golden 17th-century statue of the Sakyamuni (historical) Buddha. You can walk on up the ridge to the 11th-century castle ruins for fine views.

Hemis, Stakna & Matho

TIME FROM LEH TO HEMIS: 1HR

Monasteries with multitudinous festivals

Hemis Gompa, 42km south of Leh, is one of Ladakh's most important, most visited and wealthiest monasteries. Accessed from the main courtyard are an outstanding museum, with Buddhist art and artefacts going right back to a 7th-century Kashmiri gilt-and-copper Buddha statue, and two large, richly bedecked prayer halls. Steps up from the porch of the right-hand 'Main Temple' reach the Guru Lhakhang, containing a giant, wrathful-eyed statue of the Tibetan 'saint' Padmasambhava (Guru Rinpoche). Other temples on the monastery's higher levels are well worth exploring – especially the oldest, the Nyingma Lhakhang.

LEH TRAVEL AGENCIES

Scores of agencies in Leh offer taxi tours, treks, motorbike rental, Protected Area Permits and more. Some recommended outfits and some of their specialities:

Hidden North Adventures: Treks, wildlife trips, motorbike/mountain-bike/taxi tours, motorbike rental.

Ancient Tracks: Treks, snow leopard and other wildlife tours, taxi tours, shared taxis.

Ladakh Traverse: Mountain ascents, climbing (including winter ice-climbing) and trekking.

Ladakh Cycling: Mountain biking.

Himalayan Bikers: Mountain biking.

Wet n Wild: Rafting on the Zanskar and Indus Rivers and multi-adventure trips.

Himalayan Travel Studio: Climbs and mountaineering expeditions.

EATING BEYOND LEH: OUR PICKS

Willow Kitchen: Bistro-like Willow serves well-prepared Mediterranean and Indian fare, and plenty of drinks, in a bright dining room just below Stok Palace. *10am-9pm* ₹₹

Gyap-Thago Heritage Home: Book a day ahead for a full Ladakhi lunch or dinner at this Stok homestay, featuring dishes like *skyu* (barley pasta) and *chutagi* stews. *12.30-9.30pm May-Sep* ₹₹

Café Cloud: Upmarket garden restaurant at Thiksey with soups, salads, burgers, pasta and pizza plus Indian and other Asian dishes. *11am-10pm May-Sep* ₹₹

Alchi Kitchen: Ladakhi cuisine with a deliciously creative modern twist in Alchi. Offers cooking classes too (book ahead). *8.30-10.30am, 11.30am-4pm & 7.30-10pm Apr-Oct* ₹₹

THAISIGN/SHUTTERSTOCK

Thiksey Gompa

Escape the crowds

You can walk south from Hemis' main monastery buildings and through a group of white stupas to follow a footpath that eventually swings north up to the **Gotsang Hermitage** (Rgodtsang Retreat), which predates Hemis Gompa by four centuries. Allow nearly an hour for the trip up, half that back.

A most colourful and popular festival

The liveliest time to visit Hemis Gompa is during **Hemis Tsechu**, one of the busiest of Ladakh's famed monastery festivals. On the 10th and 11th days of the fifth lunar month (in June or July), crowds throng the monastery courtyard to witness superbly dressed and masked lamas performing a series of *chaam* dances enacting the eight miraculous events of Padmasambhava's life, to an accompaniment of drums, cymbals, bells, trumpets and chanting.

On the way back

You can conveniently visit two interesting smaller gompas en route between Hemis and Leh. The 16th-century **Stakna Gompa**, rising photogenically on a rocky crag just west of the Indus River, sports a wonderfully colourful main assembly hall. **Matho Gompa**, at the foot of the Stok Range, is famed for its **Matho Nagrang** (February or March), a festival during which two lamas in trance become oracles, running along the roof blindfolded, performing ritual acts of self-mutilation and predicting events of the coming year.

THE LADAKH FESTIVAL

Held over several days in September (dates vary) at a variety of sites in Leh and elsewhere, the tourism-oriented Ladakh Festival showcases Ladakhi culture. It's a good chance for visitors to see locals in colourful traditional dress and witness Ladakhi dance and music, which otherwise tend to be restricted to private events or cultural shows staged for tourist groups or, in the case of masked *chaam* dances, to annual monastery festivals. Handicrafts, local cuisine and favourite Ladakhi sports like polo and archery get a showing too, with Leh's polo ground reverting briefly to its original raison d'être from its more usual status as a car park.

ECO CRISIS

Ladakh's tourism boom – arrival numbers exploded from around 80,000 in 2010 to over 500,000 in 2023 – is severely straining natural resources. To satisfy tourist demand for showers and flush toilets, many establishments have drilled their own wells, depleting water tables and drying up springs. Waste-management systems struggle to cope with the amount of waste.

Every little thing helps. Limit your water usage: bucket washes use less than showers, and some lodgings have dry toilets available. Carry a refillable water bottle; don't buy plastic-bottled water. Eat locally grown, preferably organic food.

One small enterprise well worth supporting is **Dzomsa**, which sells refills of purified water (₹10 per litre) and offers an ecofriendly laundry service.

Markha Valley

TIME FROM LEH TO ZINGCHEN: **45MIN**

The classic Ladakh trek

The Markha Valley, on the south side of the Stok Range, has long been one of Ladakh's most popular trekking routes thanks to its stupas, gompas, ruined forts and plentiful homestays (which cost mostly ₹2000 for a bed, dinner, breakfast and picnic lunch). Gradients are mostly easy until a high pass on the final day. A recently made road has diminished the remote olde-worlde charm as far as Markha village, but it's lightly trafficked.

The valley starts 5km south of **Chilling**, where the Markha River enters the Zanskar River. It's little loss to skip the initial kilometres as far as the village of **Skiu**. A further 18km (1¼ hours' rough driving or a longish day's walking) reaches a footbridge just before **Markha**, where arguably the valley's most dramatic scenery begins. Three or four days' walking takes you to **Chokdo**, the usual pickup point, via Umlung, Hankar, Nimaling (4850m; with no homestay but a summer tent camp charging ₹1000) and the steep but panoramic 5260m Kongmaru La pass.

The most popular starting point for the well acclimatised, however, is **Zingchen** (Jingchan; 3370m), 23km southwest of Leh. It's three hours' walk from here up to Yurutse (4150m) with its one homestay (backtrack 4km to Rumbak for more options if necessary). The following long day crosses the scenic Ganda La (4960m) and descends to Skiu (there are also homestays at Shingo, before Skiu).

Climb a mountain

The Markha Valley is the springboard for Ladakh's most popular high-peak ascent: **Kang Yatse II** (6185m). It can be summited without technical skills but it's still challenging, requiring a good mountaineering guide and equipment, and the capacity to ascend snowy slopes above 6000m altitude. Expedition packages with local agencies typically last six to nine days and, with acclimatisation time and a buffer day added, cost from about ₹80,000 to ₹100,000 per person. The best season is normally June to September.

Phyang

TIME FROM LEH: **30MIN**

Rural retreat near Leh

For a taste of slow-paced country life, head for Phyang, whose farmsteads are scattered for several kilometres up a valley just a half-hour drive from Leh. The large, old **Phyang Gompa** has a giant modern Buddha inside its Hevajra Temple. The tiny white **Guru Lhakhang** (Padmasambhava temple), with precious old Alchi-style murals, sits up on the rocky east side of the valley about 2km beyond the gompa, with crumbling fortress ruins above it. Trails further up the valley make enjoyable day hikes, and you can even make a five-day camping trek over the mountains to Hunder in Nubra.

SKAMAN306/GETTY IMAGES

Phyang Gompa

The welcoming, comfortable **Hidden North Guesthouse**, belonging to a Ladakhi-Italian family, makes a great base. Owner Tashi Chotak Lonchey runs a gallery of his outstanding wildlife and flora photos, the **Hall of Nature**, down beside the NH1, 1km east of the Phyang turnoff.

Nimmu & Chilling

TIME FROM LEH TO NIMMU: **45MIN**

Rafting adventures

Nimmu, 35km west of Leh, sits just 3km downstream from Sangam, the confluence of the dramatically scenic Indus and Zanskar Rivers and end point of summer rafting trips. Most people book trips through Leh agencies, notably **Wet n Wild** (p230) or **Splash Adventures**. Ideal for families is the relaxed one-hour, 8km Indus float from Tsogsti (₹1200 per person including transport and lunch). The 16km trip from Skorpochey has rapids up to grade II+ or III+ depending on the season (₹2200). Most thrilling is the rapid-strewn 28km (three hours) trip from **Chilling** (III+ or IV+; ₹3000). On the Indus, Phey to Sangam (25km) takes 2½ to three hours but is usually OK for beginners (₹2800). The season runs approximately May to September, with the highest grades usually running in July and August.

Alchi & Basgo

TIME FROM LEH TO ALCHI: **1½HR**

Fascinating expedition into Ladakh culture and history

Alchi sits on the south bank of the Indus, 66km by road from Leh. Tradition attributes the founding of the **Alchi Choskhor** (sacred enclave) to Lotsava (Translator) Ringchen Zangpo, one of 21 young nobles sent to Kashmir in the late 10th century from Guge in western Tibet to study Buddhist scriptures.

LADAKHI FOOD & DRINKS

Ladakhi food is not spicy; sustenance is its primary goal. It shares some dishes with Tibetan cuisine, including noodle-based soup/stews *thukpa* and *thankthuk*, *ngamphe* (*tsampa*, roasted-barley flour) and *mok-mok* (*momos*). But Ladakh has its own specialities. Among them are *chhang* (barley beer) and *gurgur cha* ('butter tea': tea, milk, butter and salt churned together). *Gurgur cha* mixed with *ngamphe* makes *kholak*. *Chutagi* and *skyu* are pasta-and-veg/meat stews. *Khambir* is a wholewheat flatbread; *tingmo* are steamed, unsweetened buns. *Paba*, another staple, is a pea-and-barley meal that's often dunked in *tangtur* (boiled vegetables in curd). *Namthuk* is barley 'soup', like a thin porridge. *Chhurpe* is a hard cheese from the *dimo* (female yak/cow cross); Zanskar produces softer, more palatable *dimo* cheese.

STALKING THE 'GREY GHOST'

Almost 500 snow leopards (out of some 700 in India and a global population estimated between 3500 and 7000) inhabit Ladakh, making this one of the world's more likely regions for spotting these so-called 'grey ghosts'. The best months for sightings are December to March and prime time is the mating season, from around mid-February to mid-March.

Good village bases are Ulley in Sham and Rumbak in the Stok Range foothills. Leh agencies such as Ancient Tracks (p230), Hidden North Adventures (p230), Snow Leopard Quest and Higher Himalaya typically offer packages of around 11 to 12 days (₹100,000-plus per person), of which you'll spend seven or eight based in camps or villages. You'll likely be looking at distant felines through spotting telescopes.

Zangpo translated scriptures from Sanskrit into Tibetan and founded monasteries in Ladakh and Guge, becoming the major protagonist of the 'second diffusion' of Buddhism into Tibet.

Alchi's murals and statuary are artistically unsurpassed in Ladakh and clearly different in style from most Ladakhi monasteries, which were founded centuries later when Tibet itself had supplanted Kashmir as Ladakh's primary source of Buddhist inspiration. It's well worth visiting with a good guide and/or reading up about in advance.

The buildings are outwardly unspectacular: their glories are inside. The first main one you reach is the **Sumtsek Lhakhang**, dominated by three huge (4m-plus) four-armed statues: the white Avalokitesvara, Bodhisattva of compassion; a reddish Maitreya; and orange Manjushri, Bodhisattva of wisdom. Most of the many mandalas on the upper storeys centre on Vairochana, Alchi's primary deity. The second important building is the **Vairochana Lhakhang**, entered through a now-covered courtyard in whose far corners are giant statues of Avalokitesvara and the Maitreya. Its main chamber houses an elaborate four-headed sculpture of Vairochana.

Past the Vairochana Lhakhang are the Lotsawa Lhakhang, where Ringchen Zangpo himself appears in a mural on the back wall, and the Jamyang (or Manjushri) Lhakhang, centred on a highly colourful, fourfold Manjushri sculpture surrounded by strange small animal, human and other figures.

Dramatic remains of an old capital

Basgo, 41km west of Leh, was one of Ladakh's two capitals (with Shey) until the 17th century. Remnants of **Basgo Palace** are scattered picturesquely over pinnacles above the stupa-strewn village. The main building group contains three temples dating from the 15th to 17th centuries, all centred on Maitreya statues (one of them 9m tall) and featuring outstanding medieval murals.

Sham

TIME FROM LEH TO LIKIR: 1¼HR

A relatively easy village-to-village trek

The Sham district comprises a series of north–south valleys descending to the Indus west of Basgo. A three- or four-day hike across Sham from Likir to Timishgan (Temisgam/Tingmosgang) is a relatively easy introduction to Ladakh trekking, with plentiful homestays and low altitudes (highest pass: 3880m). Its remoteness and appeal have been reduced by a road that now links all the villages, but several villages are worth visiting whether you're trekking or not.

Likir has a large and impressive old **gompa**. Timishgan's hilltop palace/castle, **Timishgan Khar**, was a summer residence of the Basgo-based kings. Now semi-ruined, it still has four atmospheric temples, one with an 8m-high Maitreya statue. Ang and Tia (Teya) remain traditional. A possible two-day mini-trek in the generally prettier western half of Sham is to walk from Timishgan up to Ang and Hemis Shukpachan then descend to Rizong Gompa and the NH1 at Uletokpo.

ROBERT HARDING VIDEO/SHUTTERSTOCK

Lamayuru Gompa

Lamayuru

TIME FROM LEH: 2½HR

Slow-paced village with a spectacular monastery

Lamayuru, 113km west of Leh at a 3500m altitude, huddles above a tributary of the Indus around a crag topped by one of Ladakh's largest, most dramatically sited monasteries. The eroded valley landscapes have earned the nickname Moonland.

Lamayuru Gompa has several colourful temples in its main building: look for the tiny cave-niche behind glass in the main prayer hall where the 11th-century mystic Naropa meditated. Missed by many visitors is the Singay Lhakhang, on an outcrop just south of the main building: this Alchi-like shrine, probably from the 11th or 12th century, predates the rest of the complex.

From Lamayuru you can walk up to the summer pastures of Pamz, about 5km west, where locals herd yaks, goats and sheep, or over the Prinkiti La pass (3700m) to Wanla in the Yapola Valley (11km, three or four hours), with its 12th-century ridge-top fort ruins and impressive **Chuchig-zhal Temple**.

Hanle

TIME FROM LEH: 6½HR

High-altitude observatory and night-sky gazing

Hanle first made national news only in recent times, when it was declared India's first Dark Sky Reserve in 2022. Chosen for its clear atmosphere, scant population and absent light pollution, it has an exceptional night sky, with shooting stars popping like effervescent bubbles in a glass of champagne.

On the highest hilltop of Hanle, the **Indian Astronomical Observatory (IAO)** stands at 4500m. The dome-shaped structure is perched on **Mt Saraswati**, opposite the historic 17th-century **Hanle Gompa**. The observatory, a remarkable achievement for Ladakh, is operated remotely from its

SUSTAINABLE TRAVEL IN LADAKH

Rigzin Wangtak Kalon is an engineer turned hospitality professional who ventured into sustainability with a vision to bring meaningful change. @*lchangnagretreat*

My foray into responsible tourism started when I saw that the tourism narrative in Ladakh was going in the wrong direction. I used my engineering knowledge to create a luxurious while fully sustainable retreat made entirely from local material, a model showcase for what was possible. More than a physical place, I focused on experiences like recreating the Silk Road caravan travel, and ideas that will promote and preserve the culture of Ladakh to celebrate its heritage. If we can take that forward while being mindful of our resources, for me, that is the true meaning of sustainability.

SKY GAZING FOR AMATEURS

The IAO (p235) has appointed multiple 'astro ambassadors', trained locals who conduct sessions with their portable telescopes. The Sky Abode Hanle (p248) arranges on-site sessions for its guests. It is also Hanle's first accommodation to offer heated cottages, so stays open the longest, and you can shift indoors in the wee hours to continue the viewing through the glass skylights. Every October, Hanle also observes a week-long 'Star Party', a get-together of night-sky enthusiasts that includes special access to and sessions at the IAO with astronomers.

HARI GOPALAKRISHNEN/SHUTTERSTOCK

Pallas cat

Bengaluru (Bangalore) headquarters using a dedicated satellite link and with the aid of trained local technicians. The IAO crowns the 1074-sq-km **Hanle Dark Sky Reserve** (HDSR), which includes the six hamlets that make up Hanle. While night-sky viewing through these telescopes is reserved for resident scientists, tourists are allowed to enter the observatory for free and explore it from 10am to 5.30pm daily. A digital presentation on the observatory and its night-sky explorations also runs on the 2nd level.

High passes and unique wildlife

Years ago, Ladakh's Khardung La pass (p229) achieved cult status as the highest motorable road in the world, becoming a favourite with motorcyclists. The **Umling La pass** close to Hanle took over the title in 2017 and held it until 2025, when it was surpassed by **Mig La**, now the undisputed king. Barely 64km from Hanle, Mig La may have been opened as the now highest road in the world, but it is still not fully paved like its predecessor, and Umling La remains the more popular driving choice, located around 72km from Hanle. A leisurely drive is rewarded with rare wildlife sightings – part of the Changthang plains, Hanle and its surroundings are home to herds of kiang (a rare Tibetan wild ass) and India's largest population of the Tibetan gazelle. Its wetlands are nesting sights for Ladakh's state bird, the black-necked crane, among other migratory birds like the bar-headed goose. The trophy is a sighting of the elusive Pallas cat that makes Hanle a top choice for photographers and wildlife enthusiasts.

Nubra

STUNNING SCENERY | VARIED CULTURES | MOUNTAIN MONASTERIES

Nubra, the area north of Leh chiefly comprising the valleys of the Shayok and Nubra Rivers, is above all a destination of awe-inspiring scenery: high passes, stark rock mountainsides, snowy peaks, fast-flowing rivers in deep valleys and green oasis villages. The road from Leh makes a memorable introduction as you zigzag almost 2000m upward to the 5359m Khardung La pass (open year-round except after heavy snowfall) where the mighty Karakoram range's eastern end comes into view, before switchbacking more than 2000m down to the Shayok Valley before approaching the broad sandy basin where the Shayok and Nubra meet in a mingling of multiple channels. Most visitors base themselves in the larger villages of Diskit or Hunder and explore from there; Turtuk and Sumur are smaller, less touristed places to hang out.

A militarily sensitive region abutting unresolved borders with Pakistan and China, Nubra still has a remote, somewhat old-fashioned feel, though it's now an extremely popular destination.

TOP TIP

Nubra offers plenty of accommodation options, but only a handful of them stay open in the off-season (typically mid-October to the end of March). Mains electricity in Nubra only operates from 7am to 9am and from 6pm to 11pm. The seasonal accommodation and limited electricity situation is similar in most places outside Leh.

Enter the Hunder Desert Through Diskit

Nubra's main village, with a historic monastery

Diskit sits at the northern foot of the Ladakh Range, about 4km south of the main course of the Shayok River – a pleasant enough base, and on the whole cheaper than nearby Hunder.

GETTING AROUND

The easy way to visit Nubra is by taxi. Leh to Diskit one way costs ₹6000 to ₹10,000 depending on vehicle type, taking 3½ hours including a Khardung La stop. A two-day Leh-Diskit-Hunder-Turtuk-Leh round-trip costs around ₹15,000. Renting a motorbike from Leh is another popular option.

You can also take public transport to Nubra then use local taxis or the few buses to get around. Shared taxis to Diskit and Sumur leave early morning (6am/7am in summer) from the southern entrance to Leh polo ground, and there's a morning bus from Leh bus station to Diskit and Hunder.

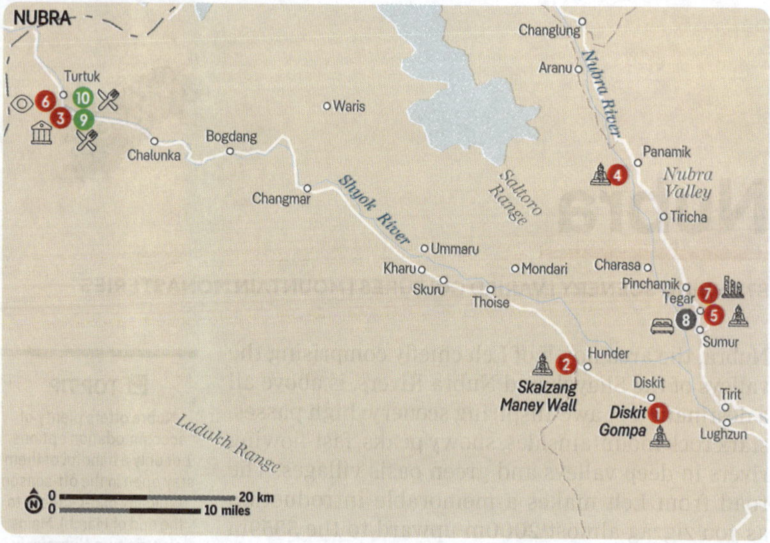

HIGHLIGHTS
1 Diskit Gompa
2 Skalzang Maney Wall

SIGHTS
3 Balti Heritage House
4 Ensa Gompa
5 Samstanling Gompa
6 Yabgo Palace
7 Zamskhang Palace Ruins
see 7 Zimskang Museum

SLEEPING
8 Lchang Nang

EATING
9 Balti Farm
10 Balti Kitchen
see 9 Farmers' House
see 10 Kharmang Guest House

The older area straddling the main street at the village's eastern end makes a pleasant stroll with its stupas, *mani* walls, small shrines and a half-ruined palace.

Diskit Gompa, a cluster of red- and black-fringed white cubes, climbs a ridge high above the village. Picturesque rows of white stupas accompany its 2km zigzag approach road; on the way up you can visit a huge (32m-high), full-colour modern statue of the Maitreya. The monastery itself dates from the 15th century, and its panoramas are superb. Steps within lead up to several colourful temples. The Lachung temple is one of the older ones, dedicated to Tsong Khapa, the founder of the famous 'yellow hat' or Gelug sect to which the 14th Dalai Lama belongs. In the Gonkhang (Protector Deities Temple), a white Mahakala image clutches a withered human arm and blackened skull, supposedly from a hapless Mongol invader.

Walk High-Altitude Sand Dunes in Hunder

Climb to a panoramic fort and see camels

Pretty Hunder, 10km west of Diskit, has Nubra's main accommodation cluster, scattered along its winding leafy lanes. For a spectacular one-hour walk, find the revered **Skalzang Maney wall** (inscribed with the names of 1000 Buddhas) beside Hunder Bridge on the main road. A path leads up the steep hillside to small red and white temples and the very panoramic, scattered remains of a ridge-top fort.

Around Hunder you may spot double-humped Bactrian camels, whose ancestors plied the Silk Road through Nubra until the mid-20th century. Today they give rides to tourists on the dunes east of the village.

Explore Turtuk, the Last Border Village

Journey to a different culture

The trip down the Shayok Valley from Hunder to Turtuk is 80km of scenic magnificence between bare-rock mountainsides above a river often of a vivid turquoise hue, passing just a few small villages and occasional military installations. In Turtuk, the people are culturally and linguistically Muslim Balti, just like their fellow Baltis across the Line of Control (LoC) in Pakistan-administered Baltistan.

Cultivation plots spread all around Turtuk village, and mountains tower above (the LoC runs along the high ridge to the west, just 6km away). Buckwheat is the main crop and the trees yield apricots, walnuts and apples. The lower village along the main road is called **Turtuk Chutang**; on the hillside above (linked to each other by a footbridge) are the densely built western **Turtuk Youl** and the more spread-out, eastern **Turtuk Farol** (which has most of the guesthouses and homestays). It's intriguing to wander the pathways of these slow-paced upper parts.

In Turtuk Youl you'll find the **Yabgo Palace**, a 16th-century summer abode of a dynasty that ruled a slice of Baltistan from Khaplu for many centuries. It's distinctly modest as palaces go but you'll get a short tour, possibly from the current Khan if he's in residence. Over in Turtuk Farol (where signs ask visitors to avoid 'short clothes'), there's the **Balti Heritage House**, a 19th-century home showcasing traditional Balti life. Nearby is the village's long, surprisingly narrow, old polo ground, from where a path leads 500m east to a small Buddhist temple with great views.

Wander Through the Timeless Villages of Sumur & Tegar

Up the Nubra Valley

These neighbouring small villages, a few kilometres up the broad Nubra Valley, provide a relatively rural, off-the-beaten-track base. **Samstanling Gompa**, on an upper road linking the villages (2.5km from Sumur, 1.8km from Tegar), is a popular devotional spot, recently renovated with much colourful paint. Its top-floor prayer room contains several vivid, helpfully labelled deity statues.

LADAKH PERMITS

Non-Indians need a Protected Area Permit (PAP) to visit areas near Ladakh's northern and eastern boundaries, including Nubra, Pangong Tso and Tso Moriri. The permit is available through approved travel agencies, of which there are many in Leh, and will be checked at various points on the roads to the areas in question (carry a few copies). Agencies normally need 24 hours to obtain the permit for you, typically for around ₹1200. A minor hurdle for single travellers is that there must be at least two applicants, but agencies can usually fudge this. Indians and foreigners both have to contribute a ₹400 'environmental fee' to visit Ladakh, payable online at *lahdclehpermit.in* but it's easier to combine it with your permit and get it done via your agent.

EATING IN TURTUK: OUR PICKS

Farmers' House: Global favourites from pasta to sushi to Thai curries in the upmarket Turtuk Holiday Resort. Fresh-picked salads and espresso coffee too. *8am-10pm approx Apr-Oct* ₹₹

Balti Kitchen: Inventive vegan Baltistani dishes such as *kisir* (buckwheat pancake) with *moskot* (walnut puree with chilli), in a charming garden setting. *7am-11pm approx Apr-Oct* ₹₹

Balti Farm: Book a day or more ahead for this live-cooking Balti cuisine tasting menu at the Turtuk Holiday Resort. *8am-11pm approx Apr-Oct* ₹₹₹

Kharmang Guest House: Expect good Balti meals with garden-fresh organic veggies at this popular guesthouse. *meals on request* ₹

NUBRA TO CHANGTHANG

A popular option combining two of Ladakh's most spectacular outer areas in one trip is to continue from Nubra to Pangong Tso via the remote road through Agham and Shayok, meeting the main Leh–Pangong road at Durbuk. Diskit to Spangmik this way is a drive of about 4½ hours plus any stops (Agham, Shayok and Durbuk have drink/food options). Note that the Agham–Shayok stretch has several fords, which may become impassable in July and August, especially in the afternoons. A much longer alternative is via the Wari La pass from Agham.

A four-day Leh-Diskit-Hunder-Turtuk-Shayok-Pangong-Leh taxi trip costs around ₹30,000. From Pangong Tso you can continue to Changthang's other big lake, Tso Moriri, returning to Leh via Tso Kar and the NH3.

GREENSEA/SHUTTERSTOCK

Maitreya statue, Diskit Gompa (p238)

Down in Tegar (Teggar/Tiger/Tigger/Tiggur/Tigur), **Manekhang Gompa** is smaller but older. Above it and a field of stupas on the hillside, the long-abandoned **Zamskhang Palace** will appeal to ruin lovers. The left-hand of two lanes down from the road below the Manekhang leads 300m to the **Zimskang Museum**, an unmarked, 400-year-old house (open on request) full of wooden pillars and beams and with a wonderful, earth-floored, traditional Ladakhi kitchen. For those taken by Nubra's Silk Road history, **Lchang Nang** (p249; *9718204880; prices vary)* in Tegar is a retreat that's launched a three-night programme recreating the magic of the valley's trading past, as you journey on an ancient caravan trail through Panamik, Chamshen and Kyagar villages, with stopovers for meals and stories (it runs from April to October).

To get well off the beaten track, continue north from Tegar and turn west off the main valley road 4km past Panamik to cross to the Nubra's west bank, then hook south 4km to the turnoff for the small, remote, 600-year-old **Ensa Gompa**, high above the road. A lovely *kora* (pilgrim path) takes you past dozens of white stupas to offer fabulous valley views.

Changthang

MAGNIFICENT LAKES | WILDERNESS | BIRDWATCHING

Eastern Ladakh is the western end of Changthang: a high, dry, cold region that stretches far across the Tibetan plateau beyond Ladakh's borders. The Ladakhi part is home to several exceptionally beautiful high-altitude lakes (well above 4000m), and it's the two largest of these, Pangong Tso and Tso Moriri, that draw the great majority of visitors. Getting here is a long road trip, but few who come are disappointed. The scenery en route is spectacular for starters.

This inhospitable terrain supports scattered villages (and army camps, as the region abuts the Chinese frontier). It's also home to the nomadic Changpa people, some of whose camps and herds of yaks, sheep and pashmina goats you will undoubtedly pass as you travel. This is also good trekking and wildlife territory. Many migratory birds breed here in summer, and you may well spot kiang (Tibetan wild asses) roaming the plains. Non-Indians need a Protected Area Permit (p239) to come to Changthang.

Slow Down by Pangong Tso's Brackish Waters

Sublime lake scenery

The journey here from Leh is spectacular – crossing the 5360m Chang La (open year-round except after snowfall) if you come by the most direct route from Leh – and the lake's shimmering beauty, against its backdrop of bare, often snow-capped mountains, exceeds that of any film or photo. **Pangong Tso** is some 150km long (with the eastern two-thirds in Tibet) but rarely more than 5km wide. Its moods and hues change constantly. One moment it may be glistening in the rising sun, in another the skies above may turn it a calm cerulean or translucent turquoise. At other times, overcast skies and winds can turn the lake a forbidding grey, with breaking waves.

The potential downsides are the scrappy nature of the main village, **Spangmik**, and the summer crowds (especially from

GETTING AROUND

You can visit any of the main lakes singly but it's perfectly possible to combine them all in one road trip. The drive from Leh to Pangong Tso takes about four hours; Leh to Tso Moriri is about five hours; and Pangong to Tso Moriri is also about five hours (plus stops in all cases).

Touring (and getting to) Changthang by motorbike is one popular adventure (keep tabs on petrol station locations!). A two-day taxi tour from Leh to Pangong Tso and back costs ₹16,000 to ₹20,000.

TOP TIP

Thinles Dorjay *(9906949183)* organises trips for trekking groups and climbers (book ahead). He's led multiple treks and expeditions across Ladakh for over 20 years, and has won several mountain-biking races in the Himalaya.

LADAKH IN WINTER

We're not joking. Despite temperatures way below zero, you'll probably adapt within a few days, and with far fewer tourists around, local life returns to something like normal at this time of year. Non-touristic restaurants keep going, as do some hotels in Leh (chiefly midrange or top-end), often slashing their rates. In villages you'll often find a homestay to put you up. The main roads within Ladakh stay open most of the time.

Winter is the time of colourful monastery festivals such as **Spituk Gustor** (January) and **Matho Nagrang** (February/March). Ice hockey and skating come into their own on frozen lakes and ponds. There's even the **Frozen Lake Marathon** (February/March) with runners tackling a 21km circuit over ice-covered Pangong Tso!

SIGHTS
1 Kyagar Tso
2 Nyoma
3 Pangong Tso
4 Tsaga La
5 Tso Kar
6 Tso Moriri
see 7 Hidden North Adventures

ACTIVITIES
7 Ancient Tracks

SHOPPING
see 7 Thupstan Shanfan

May to July). Spangmik has loads of accommodation (tent camps, homestays, a few hotels), but **Maan** (Man), 9km beyond, and **Merak**, a further 11km, have similar options and are smaller-scale, more appealing bases.

What to do here other than enjoy the scenery and dip your toes in the chilly water (and take photos)? Boating is for the armed forces only as the Line of Actual Control (LoC) with China crosses the lake about 35km southeast of Spangmik. But you can take a good walk: a track runs along, or close to, the lake shore all the way from Spangmik to Maan and Merak.

Onward to Tso Moriri

Bridging the two lakes

Pangong Tso to Tso Moriri is a great drive through very sparsely inhabited, dramatically barren landscapes. Most people take the easier route via the Tsaga La (4640m) rather than the Chushul–Mahe road crossing the 5400m Kaksang La. After Chushul the scenery becomes increasingly desert-like and the road is often a dusty/sandy unpaved track, running roughly parallel to the LoC, just a few kilometres away in the hills. The **Tsaga La**, 31km past Chushul, is very modest as passes go, just the highest point on a fairly level road.

The road swings from a southeast to a southwest direction and you'll find yourself driving along beside the young Indus River flowing out of Tibet (it rises some 300km away near Mt Kailash). You'll now have a particularly beautiful

50km alongside or near the Indus, with often snow-capped mountains rising ahead. A bridge at Loma marks the turnoff to Hanle and the start of a good paved road surface again. **Nyoma** makes a convenient food stop. At a bridge just after Mahe, turn off south, leaving the Indus. Turn off south again at Puga Sumdo for the final 40km to Tso Moriri, across hills rising to 4830m and passing the lovely **Kyagar Tso**, surrounded by grasslands in a mountain bowl.

Tso Moriri's Grandeur

A lovely and less-visited lake

Tso Moriri, 27km long and up to 8km wide, is not quite as spectacular as Pangong Tso, but by any standards it's a very beautiful lake, flanked by 6000m mountains and with snowy peaks in Himachal Pradesh towering beyond its south end. One of its attractions is that far fewer tourists make it here than to Pangong Tso.

If you're not coming from Pangong, a nice loop is to approach Tso Moriri via the Indus Valley road from Upshi to Mahe, and return via Tso Kar and the 5330m Taglang La on the NH3 Manali–Leh road.

The only village near Tso Moriri's shores, **Korzok** (Karzok), has plentiful varied accommodation but retains a traditional feel, with winding lanes, flat-roofed houses and a gompa and large prayer wheel in the centre. Korzok is the goal of an outstanding week-long trek (see Trekking in Ladakh; p220) over the mountains from Rumtse, and the starting point of another great route, south to Kibber in Himachal Pradesh via the 5578m Parang La (late August and September).

Many visitors stay only one night but lingering longer allows you to take walks into the hills, or along the lake, seeing what birds you might spot, especially at the northern end. A lookout point 2.5km south of Korzok makes an enjoyable stroll, especially at sunset.

Take in Tso Kar's Wild Salt Flats

Birders' delight

The third of Changthang's major lakes is this salt lake beloved of birdwatchers, not far off the Leh–Manali highway. **Tso Kar** is especially famed as a summer breeding ground of the rare black-necked crane, Ladakh's state bird (whose main population is found in Tibet). But it's also a good site for such birds as grebes, bar-headed geese, ruddy shelducks and Tibetan sandgrouse. You may spot argali (wild sheep) and kiang too. The cranes are here from April to October. The lake fluctuates in size but can stretch 7km east–west and 3.5km north–south. The scrappy nearby village of **Thukje** provides a few reasonable accommodation choices.

Birders will also want to visit Tso Moriri, and the Puga Valley between here and Tso Moriri, and possibly Hanle in the far southeast of Changthang. For specialised birding tours contact Leh agencies such as Hidden North Adventures (p230) and Ancient Tracks (p230).

THE TIBETAN CALENDAR

For many important purposes, including setting the dates of festivals and weddings, Ladakhis follow the Tibetan calendar. It's composed of 30-day months, each beginning with a new moon. To dovetail with the moon's actual phases and the 365-day solar year, some days are repeated or skipped, and every couple of years, a month is repeated. Months are numbered, not named. New Year (Losar) is the beginning of the first month, usually falling in February. Ladakhis, however, celebrate Losar two months earlier – apparently a 17th-century king advanced the festivities because he was in a hurry to start a military campaign. At the shop of astrologer **Thupstan Shanfan**, in Leh's Nowshera Bazar, you can pick up a calendar chart giving both Gregorian and Tibetan dates and the main festival dates.

Zanskar

STUNNING SCENERY | REMOTE GOMPAS | HIKING

GETTING AROUND

Sample **Zanskar Taxi Union** *(6006930857)* round-trip rates from Padum are ₹3580 to Zangla and ₹7800 to Phuktal, plus ₹345 per hour waiting time after one hour. One-way out-of-Zanskar rates are ₹18,500 to Leh and ₹22,500 to Manali (both around nine hours). Tempo minibuses and/or shared taxis also run to Leh and Manali (₹2500 per person), leaving early morning from around Padum's central T-junction or the taxi stand 1.5km north. Shared taxis from Leh to Padum leave early morning along Leh main bus station's south side. Taxis from outside Zanskar aren't allowed to make trips within Zanskar. You're required to take local cabs.

This southwest portion of Ladakh, isolated for centuries between the ruggedly beautiful Zanskar Range to its north and Great Himalaya Range to its south, retains a good measure of the traditional, slow-paced Ladakhi lifestyle of yore, with little commercialism and hardly any military installations. That is likely to start changing soon, as new roads bring the outside world a lot closer.

For now, Zanskar remains a charming world of scattered villages, barley fields, hillside monasteries, wide river valleys, deep rocky gorges and awe-inspiring mountainscapes. Approaching it across the Zanskar Range from the north is a journey of hypnotic, ever-changing, savage beauty beneath ice-sculpted rock fangs and between delirious upheavals of geological strata, as you learn to discern subtle tints of yellow, red, green and purple in the grey and brown rock palette.

Padum, Zanskar's only town (a small one at that), is the obvious base for a stay, but there are homestays in many villages.

Cross Over to Zanskar Through Padum

Walks to the local viewpoints

Zanskar's 'capital', Padum (population: around 2000), sits in the middle of the wide, three-armed plain where the Tsarap (Lingti) and Stod Rivers join to form the Zanskar River. An untidy place short on aesthetic charm, its centre is a T-junction where the roads arriving along the three river valleys meet. Most of the better restaurants, among them the Solthap, Changthang and Aley Yato, are within a few steps of here.

Wandering 1km south from the T-junction, look for a red-tile path up beside a line of eight small stupas on Tsarap Rd. This climbs in a few minutes to **Padum Khar**, a boulder-strewn hillock where Padum's fort stood until it was trashed by raiders from Kullu in 1822. Three small, recently built temples

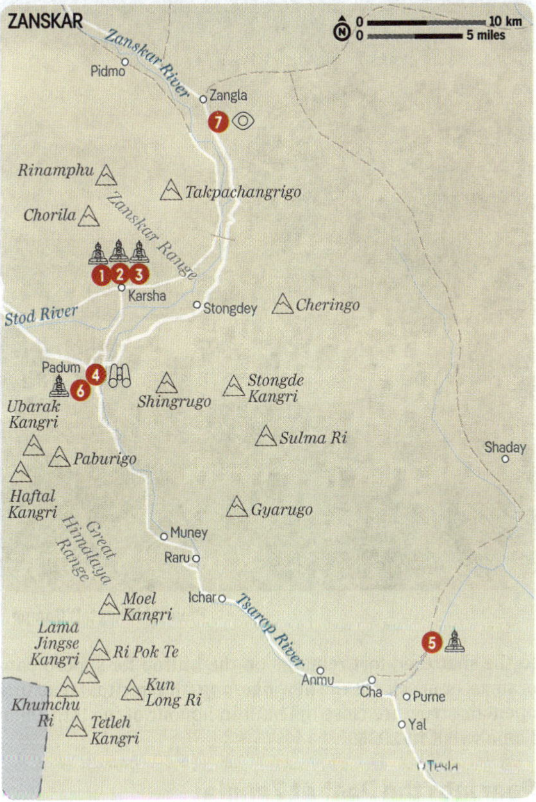

SIGHTS
1 Chukchikjal Temple
2 Dukhang Yokma
3 Karsha Gompa
4 Padum Khar
5 Phuktal Gompa
6 Stakrimo Gompa
7 Zangla Khar

stand here now, and there are good panoramas all around. For even better views walk about 3km west from Padum Khar up to **Stakrimo (Tagrimo) Gompa**.

Dive into Zanskar's Spiritual Heart

Explore a major monastery and nunnery

The whitewashed buildings of Zanskar's largest monastery, **Karsha Gompa**, climb photogenically up a red-rock hillside 10km north of Padum. The gompa contains many shrines: a vehicle road zigzags from the small village below up to its upper parts. Here, off a courtyard, you'll find the two-storey prayer hall **Dukhang Yokma**, brightly painted after a 2009 rebuild, where a small glass-encased stupa enshrines the mummified remains of a revered 14th-century lama, uncovered during the building work.

From the lower part of the gompa a path winds across a cleft in the hillside and on up to the Konchod Drubling nunnery, where the **Chukchikjal Temple**, likely dating from the 11th century, is adorned with early frescoes and a fine statue of an 11-headed Chenresig (Avalokitesvara). You can continue up

TOP TIP

For setting up any activities you might want to do, or for travel bookings, it's best to prearrange everything in Leh. Possibilities include multiday camping treks (through the mountains from Phuktal to Zangla, for example) and rafting on the local rivers.

SACRED LANDSCAPE: VISITING GOMPAS

The Ladakh landscape is an integral, living part of Ladakhis' Buddhist belief, liberally adorned not just with gompas (monasteries) but also with prayer wheels (whose turning is believed to scatter the mantras on scrolls within to the heavens); prayer flags (sending prayers and mantras to the heavens or to purify the surroundings); *mani* walls (long stone rows covered with inscribed stones) and stupas (chortens). Usually white-painted and with a square base, dome-like superstructure, spire and pinnacle, stupas represent the Buddha and are usually constructed to glorify him and gain merit; they may contain sacred relics, holy texts or other precious objects. Buddhists move clockwise around prayer wheels, *mani* walls and stupas; it's respectful for others to do so too.

BALAJISRINIVASAN/SHUTTERSTOCK

Phuktal (Phugtal) Gompa

to the shattered fort remains on the hilltop for superb panoramas, or check out the new *photang* (the spiritual teaching open-air structure close by) built in honour of the 14th Dalai Lama's visit in 2025.

Peer into the Past at Zangla

Ancient royal palaces

Once upon a time (before being annexed by Ladakh in the 17th century), Zanskar was an independent pair of twin kingdoms, with their seats at Padum and at Zangla village, 31km northeast. Zangla makes an excellent half-day outing from Padum. Its crumbling, three-storey old palace, **Zangla Khar**, perches on a high crag about 1km southeast of the village, against an impressive mountain backdrop. It's said to have been founded in the 10th century: several eminent lamas were born here and the scholar Alexander (Sándor) Csoma de Kőrös, known as the 'father of Tibetology' or 'Hungarian Bodhisattva', stayed here in 1823–24 while studying Tibetan language and Buddhism. There's not much inside the palace now, but if you find it closed and you want to look within, try asking for the key at the current home of the former royal family, a large (also old) house overlooking the central plaza-like space down in the village. On request the ex-royals (still respected here) will show you their atmospheric rooftop family shrine. They also run a modest homestay here.

Spirituality Meets Adventure in Phuktal

Canyon walk to a cliffside gompa

Famed **Phuktal (Phugtal) Gompa** lurks secretively in a scenic canyon of the Tsarap River, 54km southeast of Padum. As recently as 2012 you had to trek for at least a day to get here, but access is now a lot easier, by a rough road leading beyond Purne village to within 2.5km of the monastery, leaving you with a walk of about one hour. The beautiful drive from Padum takes about two hours: much of it is unpaved and rough, though it's steadily being improved as it leads ultimately to the Shingo La pass and Manali.

Don't rush the walk, as the altitude is over 3800m. You wend your way upstream above the bright-blue, tumbling river, crossing a sturdy footbridge shortly before reaching the monastery's entrance arch and basic summer guesthouse. Here the gompa finally comes into view, clinging to a cliffside ahead. If you have about 45 minutes to spare, you could approach it by a pilgrim trail that climbs the hillside in front of the guesthouse then runs along the clifftops before dropping down to the monastery's back gate.

The gompa's main temple is built into a large cave; some dark old Alchi-style murals, preserved from a recent rebuild, are pasted on its walls. Up steps to the left, there's another cave prayer hall with a side room housing the monastery's protector deities. Staying in the monastery guesthouse, or in a homestay at the village of **Yogar** across the river, is worth considering if you'd like more time here. There are mountain trails to explore. **Purne** also has a few accommodation options.

An alternative return path leaves the main one just before the sturdy footbridge as you descend, crossing the hillsides high above the west side of the Tsarap to meet the road above Cha village after 5km. However, it's subject to landslides, so ask locally before trying it.

WHY I LOVE ZANSKAR

Shikha Tripathi,
Lonely Planet writer

If Ladakh draws you for its tangible beauty, Zanskar stirs emotion in you. The new road allows easy access to its grand landscapes in an epic drive via Kargil, or a short dash via Chilling. I first reached the place in 2009, traversing the frozen Zanskar River on foot for over a week with a pilgrim's reverence, and now during research, zipped to it by road in five hours; the road may be a lament for some but is a gift for Zanskaris. Zanskar remains a raw, authentic place that holds its own, albeit with a 21st-century sheen. In between the mystique of the Phugtal monastery and the Zangla palace's remains, you'll also now find Padum cafes serving espresso, and I'm not complaining.

TREKKING TO ZANSKAR

The appeal of the classic Lamayuru-to-Padum trek across the Zanskar Range has been hugely diminished by recent road construction. But there are other good routes, principally from Kanji, southwest of Lamayuru. Turn to p220 for tips on these and other great Ladakh hikes.

Places We Love to Stay

₹ Budget ₹₹ Midrange ₹₹₹ Top End

Leh

Map p224

Gangs-Shun Homestay ₹ Very comfortable family home with large rooms and welcoming hosts, in a quiet area 1km west of Main Market.

Saiman Guest House ₹ Bright, spotless, spacious rooms in a great central location; an informative host and free flasks of cardamom and fresh-mint tea.

Namgyal Guest House ₹ Hosting travellers since 1982, friendly Namgyal has varied rooms, all clean, good-sized and very well priced.

Deskit Villa ₹₹ A charming escape in Sankar neighbourhood: bright, sunny rooms, gardens, views and good vegetarian meals.

Hotel Jigmet ₹₹ A short walk from the market and built around a lovely garden, this accommodation has all the offerings of a midrange hotel.

Ayum Ladakh ₹₹ A luxury retreat but at a midrange price, this place sits in an apple orchard away from central Leh.

Dolkhar ₹₹₹ A delightful sustainability-driven boutique stay whose villas marry traditional materials and artisanry with luxurious contemporary design. There's a superb restaurant. Open year-round.

Kang-Lha-Chen ₹₹₹ Long-standing central travellers' favourite with traditional decor, well-maintained rooms and a pleasant garden courtyard.

Grand Dragon Ladakh ₹₹₹ This large, professionally run, top-end hotel has beautiful, luxurious rooms and good dining options. Open year-round.

Riverland Ladakh ₹₹₹ Stanny Wangchuk's high-end homestay offers beautiful Indus views, a thriving kitchen garden and an en suite Jacuzzi for a post-trek soak.

Stok

Gyap-Thago Heritage Home ₹ Superior homestay in a modern but traditional-style family house.

Stok Palace Heritage Hotel ₹₹₹ Your chance to stay in a functioning palace: the balconied suites are comfortably modernised but retain traditional detail. The Chulli Bagh royal garden offers villas.

Shey

Shel Ladakh ₹₹₹ An entire homestay for those who prefer quietude and modern luxury, beautifully set inside a traditional home and five minutes from the iconic Thiksey monastery.

Phyang

Phyang Eco Homestay ₹ Hosted by the sprightly Jigmet Angmo and her warm family, this bright, airy space blends comfort with cultural immersion.

Hidden North Guesthouse (p233) **₹₹** Spacious, panoramic, family-run guesthouse great for a relaxed village stay, providing good meals and rooms at different budgets.

Alchi

Choskor Guest House ₹₹ Friendly guesthouse offering varied en suite rooms, plus a five-person dorm.

Alchi Zimskhang ₹₹₹ Modern hotel near the temple complex, in Ladakhi style with unfussy, comfy, clean and sizeable rooms.

Lamayuru

Dragon Hotel Lamayuru ₹ A clean, affordable stay with good food, spacious rooms and a lovely garden, within walking distance of the monastery.

Hotel Grand Moonland ₹₹ Big pine-panelled rooms with balconies, views and good vegetarian food. Its sister establishment Moonland Hotel is cheaper and also adequate.

Hanle

Padma Homestay ₹ Clean and comfortable with simple, homemade food, and the luxury of attached bathrooms.

Sky Abode Hanle ₹₹₹ Hanle's first accommodation to offer heated cottages, complete with a skylight for night-sky gazing from your room; it also stays open the longest.

Diskit

Zambala Guesthouse ₹ Located close to the main sights and eateries of Diskit, this is a great value-for-money place overlooking the mountains.

Ladakh Ecotel Garden Guesthouse ₹₹ Good-sized, comfy rooms, hot running water, home-cooked local meals and friendly hosts. Open year-round.

Hunder

Galaxy Guest House ₹₹ A welcoming 10-room family-run guesthouse in the heart of Hunder with good en suite rooms, solar hot water and meals from their organic garden.

Nubra Organic Retreat ₹₹₹ Upscale accommodation with premium rooms in a farm. Here you can go cycling and return for a dip in the pool.

Turtuk

Kharmang Guest House ₹₹ Travellers' favourite in Turtuk Farol offering airy, spacious rooms, an organic garden, good Balti meals and a panoramic roof terrace.

Virsa Baltistan ₹₹₹ Surprising luxury in the back country; a celebration of Balti heritage through earthy architecture and traditional cuisine at its fabulous farm-to-table restaurant.

Sumur & Tegar

Nubra Ecolodge ₹₹ Close to the Sumur sand dunes, this family-run retreat has rooms and cottages, with a thriving vegetable garden and Karakoram views.

Lchang Nang ₹₹₹ A luxurious solar-powered retreat in Tegar with elegant garden cottages built of stone, wood and mud, plus fine food and numerous activities and experiences on offer.

Pangong Tso

Thangzing House ₹₹ This guesthouse in the upper part of Maan village has cosy en suite rooms and a huge, bright dining room. Open year-round.

Desert Blue ₹₹₹ Contemporary-styled, upmarket, well-built wooden cabins on the lake shore at Maan.

Korzok

Tsomoriri Guest House ₹₹ Located towards the northern end of the village, with eight sizeable, bright, lake-view rooms.

Hotel Grand Dolphin ₹₹ Congenial guesthouse with well-fitted rooms, comfortable beds and massive windows that frame the beauty of Tso Moriri.

MRIDULABLOG/SHUTTERSTOCK

Grand Dragon Ladakh, Leh

Padum

Zambala Hotel ₹ A good-value option with simple en suite rooms on two floors around a central courtyard.

Heaven Hills Guesthouse ₹ This basic but efficient guesthouse has wooden flooring and electric blankets on request.

Hotel Potala ₹₹ Possibly Padum's best, this 20-room hotel offers comfy, spacious rooms and good bathrooms. Open year-round.

Karsha

Tara Guest House ₹ A basic place like most homes around the monastery that also accommodate travellers, here you'll get a cosy bed, hot water and home-cooked meals.

Zanskar Eco Lodge ₹₹ The best option in the village, with sizeable, bright, en suite rooms, 24-hour solar electricity and a family atmosphere.

Phuktal

Grand Purne Camp & Homestay ₹ This guesthouse with a grand name but modest rooms also has a basic riverside camp, and is walking distance from the Phuktal trailhead.

Tara Mountain Sarai ₹₹₹ An unexpected oasis of luxury in the middle of nowhere, the tented camps here are for remote glamping in a surreal setting.

Kashmir Valley & Beyond

STRIKING PEAKS AND RICH CULTURAL TRADITIONS

Beyond its verdant valleys and snow-capped mountains, the Himalayan region is home to religious and artistic heritage. By Aliya Bashir

Snow-clad mountains, vast green meadows, freshwater rivers and lakes, unexplored valleys and artistic sensibilities that stretch back hundreds of years. These are among a multitude of qualities that the Kashmir Valley and its surroundings are famous for globally.

The Union Territory of Jammu and Kashmir covers an area of 42,241 sq km. The Kashmir Valley covers about two fifths of this, and Jammu the rest.

BHAVEN JANI/SHUTTERSTOCK

Since its conception, Kashmir has been impossibly diverse. Legend has it that Kashmir was a vast lake called Satisar. Kashyapa, an ascetic, struck the mountains at Baramulla with his trident, draining the lake and reclaiming the land. The region was named 'Kashyapamar'. The lore is celebrated in Buddhist, Hindu, Muslim and Jewish cultures in the Indian subcontinent, each catapulting Kashyapa to reverence. Geologic records suggest that earthquakes in the Himalayan ranges surrounding the Kashmir basin lifted it to its current elevation of 1620m, draining the water it once contained. Evidence of this is found in *karewas* – lacustrine deposits believed to have formed during the Pleistocene period when the valley was submerged.

In the third century BCE, the Mauryan emperor Ashoka introduced Buddhism to Kashmir and during the 9th and 12th centuries CE, the kingdom became a centre of Hindu culture, famous in particular for philosopher Abhinavagupta's intellectual contributions to aesthetics, metaphysics and Saiva theology.

Starting with Shah Mir in 1339, Muslim kings ruled over the region for five centuries and introduced rich Persianate art, literature and architecture. Regional scholarship about medieval Kashmir celebrates it as the centre of cultural vivacity reflected in the fusion of Buddhist, Hindu and Islamic traditions.

NASIRAHMEDI2/SHUTTERSTOCK

Above: Dal Lake (p253); Left: Spice market, Srinagar (p253)

Bespeckled Past

In 1819, the Sikh Kingdom of the Punjab under Maharaja Ranjit Singh annexed Kashmir, taking over from the remnants of Mughal rule. After the British defeated the Sikhs in the first Anglo-Sikh War, Kashmir was sold to Gulab Singh, a Dogra chieftain in Ranjit Singh's army, under the Treaty of Amritsar in 1846. Dogras are an ethno-linguistic population in the Indo-Aryan cultural tradition; their native language is Dogri and they mainly live in Jammu. The state of Jammu and Kashmir became a vassal of the British colonial state, safeguarding the porous border, eyed by the expanding Russian empire in the north.

Kashmir remained a fiefdom of ethnic Dogra kings, marked by widespread oppression of the Muslim community. At the juncture of independence from the British and the partition of the subcontinent in 1947 that saw the establishment of two new nation states – Pakistan and India – Kashmir was one of some 550 princely states whose fate was hanging in the balance. These were native territories that were ruled by local princes and indirectly overseen by the British Crown. The ruler of Kashmir, Maharaja Hari Singh, signed an agreement (an 'instrument of accession') with the Union of India, bringing the territory under India's rule. However, parts of the Kashmir kingdom – Muzaffarabad and Gilgit-Baltistan – were integrated with Pakistan. China also claimed (and still claims) ownership of part of the territory, namely the cold, arid deserts of Ladakh, a Union Territory (which was part of the state of Jammu and Kashmir until 2019).

Administration of the bowl-shaped Himalayan territory by India and Pakistan has remained a controversial subject. Many argue that the instrument of accession was a temporary provision and that the Indian state had to hold a plebiscite to allow the local population to choose their political destiny. Sheikh Muhammad Abdullah, a prominent leader in post-princely Jammu and Kashmir, established a special connection with India's first prime minister, Jawaharlal Nehru of the Indian National Congress party, expecting more protection from India. The Indian Constitution (ratified in 1949) offered Kashmir a special autonomous status, granting it a separate constitution, state flag and larger autonomy of internal administration.

Exodus of Kashmiri Pandits

Calls for an independent Kashmir never subsided. In 1987, elections for the state assembly installed the New Delhi–backed Farooq Abdullah as the chief minister. An armed insurgency soon broke out against Indian rule. Pandits, a minority Hindu community, moved to the Hindu-majority Jammu province and other parts of India to escape violence that saw the community being targeted by militant groups. This dealt a severe blow to the region's centuries-old culture of different religions living in harmony. The Indian state responded with a heavy hand, resulting in widespread human rights violations that continue to this day. As many as 66,000 people (by some estimates) have been killed in the political violence, thousands more have disappeared, and an equal number are imprisoned across jails in India, waiting for trials to begin.

Removal of Autonomous Status

In 2019, the Indian government, headed by Prime Minister Narendra Modi of the Bharatiya Janata Party, imposed presidential rule and turned the state into a Union Territory, bringing it under the direct administration of the federal government. In the wake of this political development, Kashmir was put under lockdown with a massive build-up of troops, arms and ammunition on its international borders. An internet shutdown lasted for five months, making it one of the longest such blockades in the world. Since then, Kashmir-based politicians have rallied for elections to be held and statehood restored. At the time of writing, no local government exists and the New Delhi–appointed governor continues to administer the region. In recent years, press freedom has shrunk and journalists are targeted for their work.

HIGHLIGHTS

Dal Lake: The jewel in Kashmir's crown, Dal Lake is home to houseboats, *shikaras* (small boats) and floating gardens, and spans an area of over 18 sq km in Srinagar. It's agateway to the majestic Mughal Gardens, built during Emperor Jehangir's reign. Also in the vicinity is the Tulip Garden.

Gulmarg: Gulmarg is a haven for skiing, and home to the Gulmarg Gondola, the second-highest and -longest cable car in the world, connecting Gulmarg's green meadows to Apharwat in the high snowy peaks.

Gadda Koch: A vibrant market in Srinagar's Zaina Kadal, famous for local spices, Kashmiri copperware and dried fruits.

LAND OF MANY FAITHS

Jamia Masjid, Srinagar: Built in 1400 CE, this mosque stands on 370 wooden pillars, surrounded by a bustling market. It's an important politico-religious centre for Muslims.

Mela Kheerbhawani, Ganderbal: Famous pilgrimage site for Mela Kheerbhawani, an annual congregation of Kashmiri Hindus. The festival also attracts crowds from other religions including Muslims and Sikhs.

Gurudwara Chatti Patshahi, Koh-e-Maran: Named after the Sikh guru, Hargobind Singh, Gurudwara Chatti Patshahi is a pilgrimage site for Sikhs. It is near the shrine of Hamza Makhdoom, a Sufi mystic.

Amarnath Yatra, Anantnag: Amarnath Yatra is an annual Hindu pilgrimage to Amarnath Cave, where thousands of devotees pay respect to Shiva.

EMILY MARIE WILSON/SHUTTERSTOCK

Saffron flowers, Pampore

Kashmir Valley & Beyond Today

On 22 April, 2025, gunmen erupted from the hills into Baisaran Valley, Pahalgam's lush postcard-perfect tourist haven of snow-clad peaks, wildflowers, and grazing ponies. For 20 grim minutes, bullets shattered families, a Mumbai couple, Nepali trekkers and their guide. With 26 people killed, the Pahalgam attack marked one of the deadliest militant attacks in Indian-administered Kashmir since 2019.

Chief Secretary Atal Dulloo has stated that the security in Jammu and Kashmir is 'largely under control' and Chief Minister Omar Abdullah's office said that the government has renewed its focus on peace.

Despite its chequered past, Kashmir remains a visitor's dream. Amīr Khusrau, the 13th-century Indo-Persian Sufi poet and scholar, captures the beauty of Kashmir in his famous verse: 'If there is a paradise on Earth, it is this, it is this, it is this'.

As well as being a hub for heritage arts and crafts, Kashmir is a prime grower of spices and is the world's second-largest saffron producer after Iran. Pampore, on the Jhelum River 16km southeast of Srinagar, is the main saffron-producing area and is popularly known as the 'saffron town'. In India, Kashmiri saffron sells for ₹300,000 per kilo. Every October, the fields surrounding Pampore are covered in purple blossoms, and thousands of saffron growers carefully pluck the stigmas of these flowers at dawn (saffron flowers are very delicate). The stigmas are then dried for a minimum of 12 hours. Kashmiri *kahwa*, a gold-hued drink that derives its flavours from a mix of green tea, cinnamon and cardamom (among other spices) is incomplete without local saffron. Brewed in a traditional copperware kettle, or *samovar,* the drink is served to guests on special occasions, especially at weddings.

Regional handicrafts are renowned for their intricate designs, quality and ingenuity. It's no wonder Kashmir lends its name to the anglicised 'cashmere', after the superbly warm wool from cashmere goats. Skilled artists have a long history of artistic creativity, creating shawls (including cashmere and pashmina), Kashmiri carpets and *namdas* (traditional, felted, woollen rugs), hand-painted papier-mâché articles, wood carvings and silks. The handicrafts are designed, manufactured and finished by craftspeople and serve as a main source of income for a majority of residents in the valley – roughly 250,000 by some estimates. There is a huge demand for their work, which is showcased in both international and national exhibitions and emporiums. Srinagar, Ganderbal and Budgam are some of the main districts involved in handicraft production.

Kashmir's cultural diversity is accentuated by a deep sense of community among locals who find great resonance with each other cutting across ethno-religious identities. Despite growing polarisation globally, Kashmir stands as an example of camaraderie between various ethno-religious and linguistic communities, which is why it was Kashmir was largely peaceful during the genocidal violence of the Partition when dangerous faultlines were exposed elsewhere across colonial South Asia. This dimension of Kashmir possesses a certain degree of circularity and meaning as the region takes its past as a reference point to move forward into the future.

Yet, as days pass, concerns for a secure Kashmir future mount. These concerns range from political and economic to environmental. While glaciers are melting, there is a vast push toward urbanisation that will eat up large tracts of agricultural land. But for visitors, there will be enough to explore once restrictions lift.

SRINAGAR'S ICONIC HOUSEBOATS

Kashmir's signature houseboats first appeared during colonial times, when the Maharaja prohibited the British from buying land in Kashmir. As early as the 1850s, cargo boats were converted into modest houseboats and poled down the Jhelum River (which flows through present-day India and Pakistan). Eventually, navigating the river grew trickier – owing to low bridges and silt buildup – and, as colonial tourism to the valley increased in the summer months, so did demand for more high-end accommodation. The solution? Luxurious, spacious houseboats on Srinagar's Dal and Nigeen lakes – complete with carved walnut and cedar panelling, Kashmiri silk carpets and chandeliers.

Today, due to a systemic dearth of craftspeople to repair them, the future of the houseboats remains uncertain. In the 1970s there were an estimated 3000, but today Dal and Nageen lakes have around 900. Still, the 'super deluxe' ones remain sought after, with plush dining rooms, sitting rooms, bedrooms and private *shikaras* in times of stability.

BITING COLD WINTERS

From the Persian for 'forty grand days', *chillai kalan* is the coldest phase of winter in Kashmir. The phenomenon has historically held cultural and social significance – Kashmiris fire up their clay stoves, fill *kangris* (earthen pots with wicker exteriors) with hot embers and drape themselves in *pherans* (uniquely Kashmiri wool cloaks). Food is always meaty and calorie-dense *harissa*. For decades, this has been a predictable affair: 21 December is 'Pheran Day', the first day of *chillai kalan,* continuing until 31 January, the last day. This is typically followed by two other cold spells – the 20-day *chillai khurd* (small cold) between January 31 and February 19, and the 10-day *chillai bachcha* (baby cold) between February 20 and March 2.

That is, until recently. Shifting snowfall patterns associated with climate change have experts worried about sustained snow cover and groundwater recharge – vital to the farmers of the region, who rely on crops such as apples and saffron.

For places to stay in Himachal Pradesh, see p308

RAGHU KAPUR/SHUTTERSTOCK

Above: Chandratal (p290); Right: Temple bells, Chamba (p274)

Researched by
Margot Bigg

Himachal Pradesh

MISTY MOUNTAINS AND HIMALAYAN HERITAGE

Pack your bags – and your hiking boots – for a land where towering evergreens and grand old palaces give way to gloriously gargantuan Himalayan peaks.

If you're fond of outdoor adventure, you've come to the right place. Himachal Pradesh has long been likened to a natural wonderland, with seemingly never-ending opportunities for trekking, mountaineering and even paragliding. It's in this forested state that you'll find some of India's most famous mountain passes and hiking routes, all amid huge expanses of pine-scented trees and high-desert moonscapes punctuated by the occasional glasslike stillness of an alpine lake.

OBS ZAGREB/SHUTTERSTOCK

Of course, Himachal is not just for the rugged, but even if you're more of a fair-weather outdoors person, the pull of the fragrant pines and crisp mountain air is likely to draw out your inner adventurer. Although Himachal's claim to fame may be its natural beauty, this diverse state is equally enthralling for its cultural offerings. For amidst Himachal's ancient forests and towering peaks, you'll find generations of history preserved in the walls of ancient forts and opulent palaces as well as hundreds of sacred temples, gompas, churches and gurdwaras. You can learn about Tibetan Buddhism at the Dalai Lama's home monastery, hone your chai-tasting skills at a tea estate, and marvel at Victorian palaces and Himachal's own earthquake-resistant *kath-kuni* architecture, all without leaving the state. Just give yourself plenty of time: this place rewards those willing to slow their pace and open their minds and hearts to all of its enchantments.

THE MAIN AREAS

MCLEOD GANJ
Tibetan heritage and home of the Dalai Lama. p264

MANALI
Ancient temples and alpine adventures. p276

KEYLONG
High-altitude hikes and Tibetan Buddhist culture. p288

KALPA
Beautiful timber temples against a Himalayan backdrop. p293

SHIMLA
Architecturally rich Raj-era summer capital. p300

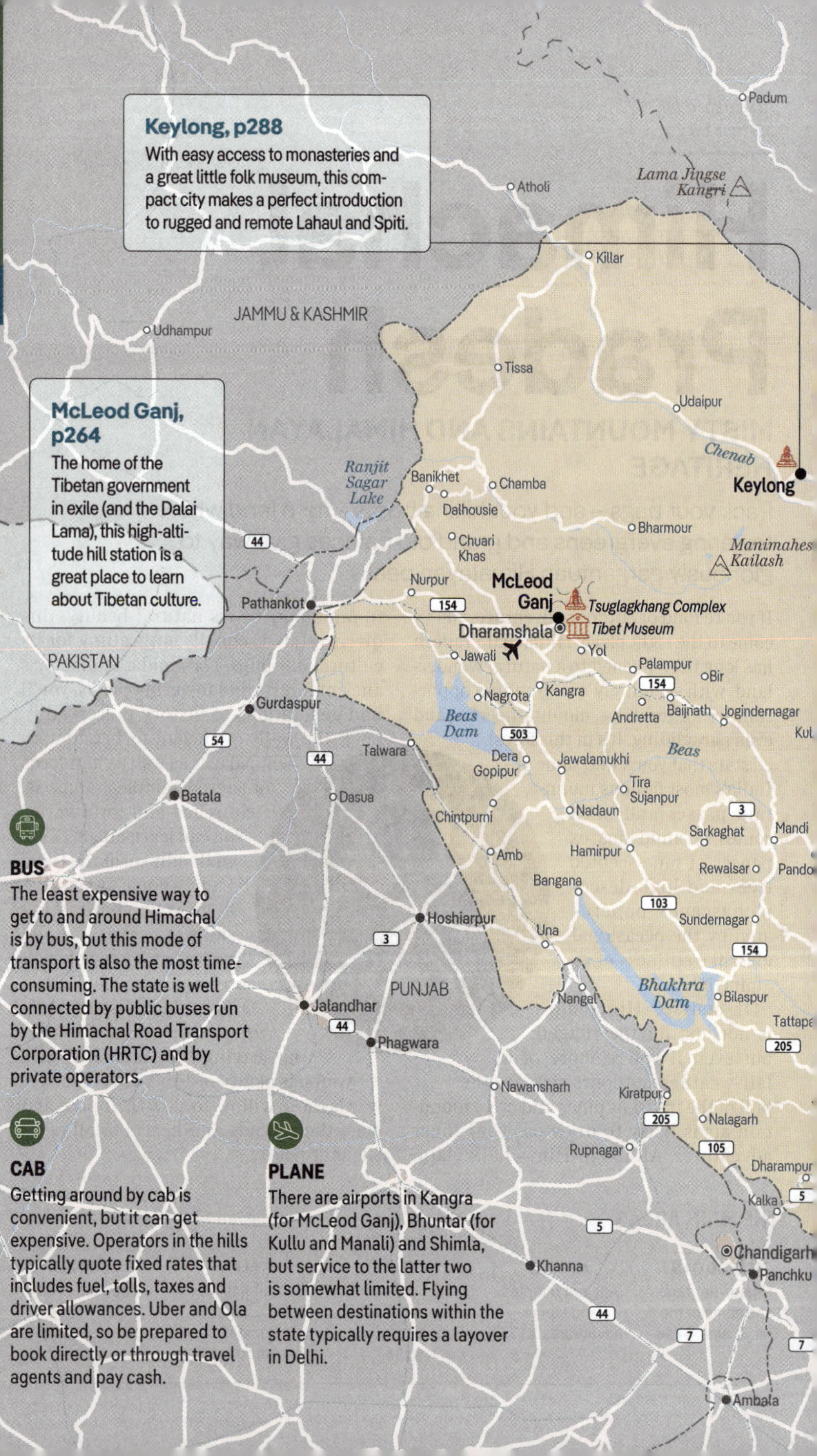

Keylong, p288

With easy access to monasteries and a great little folk museum, this compact city makes a perfect introduction to rugged and remote Lahaul and Spiti.

McLeod Ganj, p264

The home of the Tibetan government in exile (and the Dalai Lama), this high-altitude hill station is a great place to learn about Tibetan culture.

BUS

The least expensive way to get to and around Himachal is by bus, but this mode of transport is also the most time-consuming. The state is well connected by public buses run by the Himachal Road Transport Corporation (HRTC) and by private operators.

CAB

Getting around by cab is convenient, but it can get expensive. Operators in the hills typically quote fixed rates that includes fuel, tolls, taxes and driver allowances. Uber and Ola are limited, so be prepared to book directly or through travel agents and pay cash.

PLANE

There are airports in Kangra (for McLeod Ganj), Bhuntar (for Kullu and Manali) and Shimla, but service to the latter two is somewhat limited. Flying between destinations within the state typically requires a layover in Delhi.

Find Your Way

Himachal Pradesh is enormous, with lots of winding mountain roads, many of which seem to be in a constant state of repair – or disrepair. Travelling even a short distance can take much longer than anticipated.

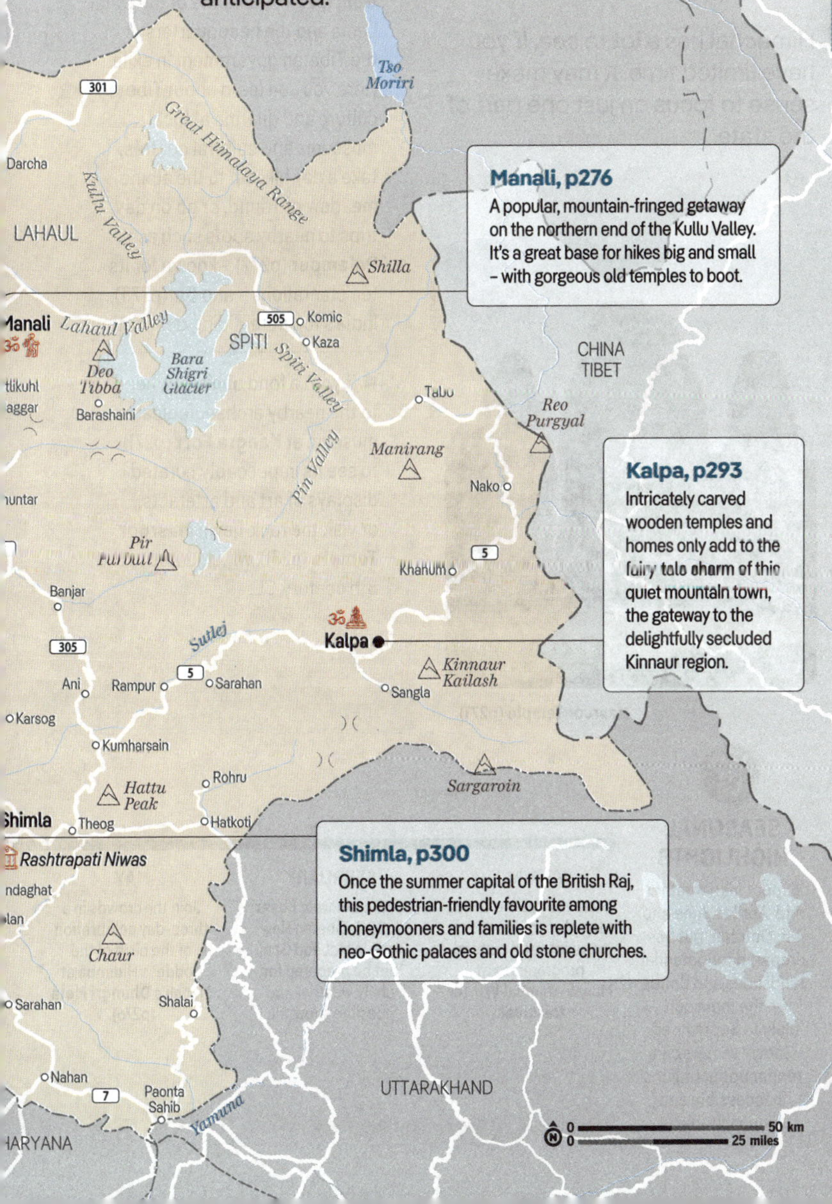

Manali, p276

A popular, mountain-fringed getaway on the northern end of the Kullu Valley. It's a great base for hikes big and small – with gorgeous old temples to boot.

Kalpa, p293

Intricately carved wooden temples and homes only add to the fairy tale charm of this quiet mountain town, the gateway to the delightfully secluded Kinnaur region.

Shimla, p300

Once the summer capital of the British Raj, this pedestrian-friendly favourite among honeymooners and families is replete with neo-Gothic palaces and old stone churches.

Plan Your Time

Himachal has a lot to see. If you have limited time, it may make sense to focus on just one part of the state.

MRINALPAL/SHUTTERSTOCK

Masroor Temple (p271)

Short on Time

- If you only have a few days in Himachal Pradesh, you're best off basing yourself in **McLeod Ganj** (p264), the home of the Dalai Lama and the headquarters of the Tibetan government in exile. Here you can learn about Tibetan culture and dharma at local museums and cultural centres, take a day hike up to the alpine meadow of Triund, or go on day trips to nearby spots such as **Palampur** (p272) – known for its tea plantations – and **Bir** (p273), India's top paragliding destination.

- If you're fond of history, head to the nearby archaeological museum at **Kangra Fort** (p271) to see its impeccably curated displays of art and artefacts, or visit the rock-hewn **Masroor Temple** (p271), which dates to the 8th century CE.

SEASONAL HIGHLIGHTS

Expect mild weather mid-April to June and in October, but be prepared for potential landslides and floods in the monsoon (July to September). Snowy winters can render upper regions inaccessible and inhospitable.

JANUARY

Start your year off with five days of parades, pageants and cultural programmes at Manali's annual **Winter Carnival**.

FEBRUARY

Commemorate **Losar** (p266), Tibetan New Year, in McLeod Ganj, but be prepared for chilly weather and possible snowfall.

MAY

Join the crowds in a three-day celebration of the birth of the goddess Hidimba at Manali's **Dhungri Mela** (p276).

Two Weeks in the Hills

- With two weeks you'll have enough time to visit Shimla, Manali and McLeod Ganj with stops in between. Start with a couple of days in **Shimla** (p300) before making the long drive north to **Manali** (p276), with stops in historic **Kullu** (p283) and **Naggar** (p282) along the way. Make Manali your base for a few days, and consider a side trip to **Barashaini** (p284) for the **Khir Ganga** (p284) hike.

- Then continue to **McLeod Ganj** (p264), breaking your journey up in the lakefront town of **Rewalsar** (p287), before heading to India's paragliding hub, **Bir** (p273), the artist village of **Andretta** (p272) and the tea plantations of **Palampur** (p272). End your trip with a few days learning about Tibetan culture in McLeod Ganj.

Ample Time to Explore

- From **Shimla** (p300), head northeast up the National Hwy 5 (NH5) towards the mountain-view town of **Kalpa** (p293), stopping to see the castle of **Rampur Bushahr** (p297) and temples of **Sarahan** (p296) along the way. From here, make your way to the Spiti region, stopping in **Tabo** (p292) to visit India's oldest monastery.

- Continue up to **Komic** (p291) and **Kaza** (p291) to see more of Spiti's vast landscapes and historic monasteries before dipping down toward **Manali** (p276) via the newly opened **Atal Tunnel** (p289). Consider an overnight trekking adventure with one of the area's many operators before continuing to **McLeod Ganj** (p264), stopping in **Rewalsar** (p287), **Naggar** (p282), **Bir** (p273) and **Palampur** (p272) en route.

JUNE
Check out everything from flower shows to music and dance performances at Shimla's **Summer Festival**.

JULY
Spend a week immersed in mountain traditions at Chamba's **Minjar Mela** (p274), which features folk performances and a massive procession.

SEPTEMBER
Honour the changing seasons among masses of colourful ladra flowers at the quintessentially **Kinnauri Phulaich Fair**.

OCTOBER
Celebrate the victory of good over evil alongside hundreds of *devtas* (deities) and thousands of revellers at **Kullu Dussehra**.

HELP ME PICK:

Himachal Pradesh Hikes & Treks

Himachal Pradesh has long been a favourite among trekkers, offering a wide range of hiking opportunities suited to experienced outdoors enthusiasts and newbies alike. In fact, many people come to the state specifically with the goal of hiking in mind. While some visitors are content with short forest strolls that will have them back to the comfort of their hotel room by nightfall, others get their thrills by braving multinight journeys over glaciated mountain passes.

Treks To Choose If You Love...

Scenic Day Hikes

Chaka Meadows (p293) Follow a stream through forests and meadows until you reach this lovely alpine expanse, which is often blanketed with wildflowers during the warmer season.

Malana (p284) Many people hike to this mountain community in hopes of picking up something to smoke, but you don't have to be a stoner to appreciate the unique culture of this isolated mountain community. Just don't touch anyone or anything, or you'll be faced with a hefty fine.

PRABHKIRAT SINGH/SHUTTERSTOCK

Tosh (p285) Although a newish road means that you can drive to the Parvati Valley town of Tosh, a 3km walk from Barshaini, it's much more fun to take an easy stroll through the woods to get there.

Triund (p267) While many people spend the night at this alpine meadow above the McLeod Ganj suburb of Bhagsu Nag – some en route to Indrahar Pass – Triund makes for a fantastic 10km day hike through flower-filled forests.

Beginner-friendly Overnight Trips

Indrahar Pass (pictured; p268) Although you'll need a guide to help you safely tackle this three-night adventure near McLeod Ganj, you don't need to be an experienced hiker with lots of technical knowledge to carry it out. Just a decent level of fitness and a great sense of adventure will do.

Khir Ganga (p284) An easy 12km hike through the woods leads you to this lovely alpine meadow with hot springs. There are plenty of camps here if you want to spend the night, but many people opt to get up early and visit Khir Ganga on a day hike instead.

Challenging Mountain Adventures

Hampta Pass (p280) Trek from the Kullu Valley near Manali into the moonscapes of Lahaul on this scenic journey, past streams and glaciers and over the 4270m Hampta Pass (.

Pin-Parvati Pass (p285) Expert hikers flock to the Himalaya to attempt this challenging journey, which starts in the Parvati Valley and ends up in Spiti. While crossing the pass will give you real bragging rights, this is not a trek for beginners.

Rupin Pass (p298) Spend a week walking through meadows and up rocky hillsides, making a stop in a cliffside 'hanging village' en route. At the end of your journey, you'll land in Kinnaur.

HIMACHAL PRADESH HIKES & TREKS

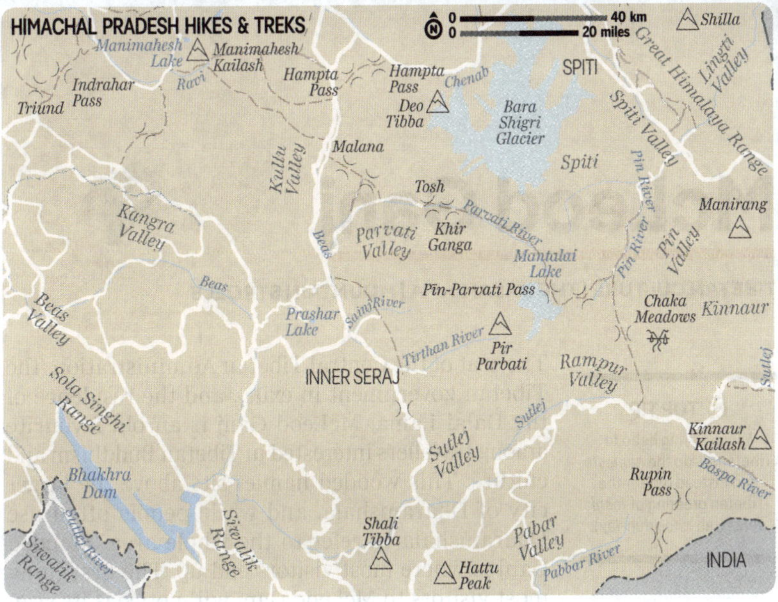

HOW TO

When to go Trekking conditions are generally at their best in May or October, just before or just after monsoon, but this varies by destination.

Book ahead Guided group treks tend to book out well in advance, particularly for popular routes. Reserve your spot as early as you can to avoid disappointment.

What to pack Bring water and snacks if you're on a solo day hike. For guided hikes, ask your trekking operator for a packing list.

Budget Don't just think about the cost of your trek. Factor in all costs, including transportation to the starting point, pre- and post-trek accommodation, insurance and supplies.

Go with a Guide or Go Alone?

The Himalayas and their foothills are no joke, and even if you're an experienced mountaineer or hiker, it's best not to test your luck by attempting any high-altitude or multinight treks on your own. Not only is this the safest way to approach hiking here, but it also makes things much easier. Operators generally take care of arranging trekking/entry permits – required on many routes – and many will help you sort out transport to your departure point. Some operators have their own camps with tents, sleeping bags and support staff who will cook hot meals. Some also offer porterage services, though you'll usually still need to carry some of your own gear, including cutlery, clothing and water bottles.

Reputed operators offering group treks in Himachal Pradesh include **Indiahikes** *(indiahikes.com)*, **Banjara Experiences** *(banjaraexperiences.com)*, **Trekmunk** *(trekmunk.com)* and **Raacho Trekkers** *(raachotrekkers.com)* in Kinnaur and Spiti.

Day hikes or hikes that lead to established villages with good infrastructure, such as Khir Ganga, don't generally require the services of a guide. However, you should still bring a friend along or – at the very least – let someone at your guesthouse know where you're going. You still may find it advantageous to go with a guide, particularly if you want to learn about local flora and fauna or don't have a lot of experience hiking.

McLeod Ganj

TIBETAN CULTURE | THE DALAI LAMA | MOUNTAIN STROLLS

> **☑ TOP TIP**
> When saying hello to Tibetans, skip the *namaste* and instead opt for the Tibetan greeting of *tashi delek* (tah-*shee* duh-*lay*).

The seat of the Central Tibetan Administration (the Tibetan government in exile), and the residence of the Dalai Lama, McLeod Ganj is an old favourite among travellers interested in Tibetan Buddhism and culture. This wooded hamlet sits above the larger city of Dharamshala, and while people often use Dharamshala to refer to the whole area, McLeod Ganj is where most visitors end up. The first thing most visitors to McLeod Ganj will notice is its sizeable Tibetan community. Take a stroll through along Jogiwara Rd, one of the main thoroughfares that runs through town, and you're sure to come across groups of maroon-clad monastics chatting in Tibetan, many of whom live at the Dalai Lama's own Namgyal Monastery. And while the opportunity to learn about Tibetan culture is easily one of this high-elevation hill station's biggest draws, McLeod Ganj also makes an excellent base for exploring the western reaches of Himachal Pradesh.

Monastic Musings

A visit to the Dalai Lama's home

McLeod Ganj's greatest claim to modern fame is the **Tsuglagkhang Complex** *(dalailama.com; free)*, also known as the Thekchen Choeling Complex or – more commonly – as the Dalai

> **GETTING AROUND**
>
> McLeod Ganj is a walkable city, but be prepared to go up and down a few hills. Cabs and autorickshaws are usually available at the Main Square for short trips around town. A couple of minutes' walk north is the town's bus stand, with regular Himachal Road Transport Corporation (HRTC) service to Dharamshala and beyond. You can also get to Dharamshala via the Dharamshala Skyway cable car, which departs from right next to the Tsuglagkhang Complex. The closest airport to McLeod Ganj is the Kangra-Gaggal Airport (DHM), about 20km away, with direct service to Delhi, Chandigarh and Shimla. The nearest major railway station is in Pathankot, 90km west.

HIGHLIGHTS
1 Tibet Museum
2 Tsuglagkhang Complex

SIGHTS
3 Library of Tibetan Works and Archives
4 Men-Tsee-Khang Tibetan Medical & Astro Institute Museum
5 Tsuglagkhang Main Temple Room

ACTIVITIES
6 Kora Circuit

SLEEPING
7 Chonor House
8 Green Hotel
9 Lord Krishna Boutique Stay
10 New Serkong House
11 Ram Yoga House
12 Shree Guest House

EATING
see 8 Green Hotel Restaurant
13 Nick's Italian Kitchen
14 Other Space
15 Snow Lion Restaurant

TRANSPORT
16 Dharamshala Skyway
17 New Bus Stand

LOSAR (TIBETAN NEW YEAR)

Losar is the McLeod Ganj Tibetan community's biggest annual celebration, marking the first day of the year in the Tibetan lunar calendar (which usually falls at some point in February in the Gregorian calendar). Traditions include visiting monasteries, eating *gu-thug* (a type of special nine-ingredient porridge), cleaning one's house, donning new clothes and replacing old prayer flags with fresh, colourful ones. During this time, people also adorn their home altars, known as *chod-shom*, with offerings such as water, incense, Tibetan barley beer and *khapse*, fried biscuits. While there's certainly a strong spiritual side to Losar, it's also a very festive time, with processions and celebrations all around McLeod Ganj.

Lama Temple. This somewhat austere, double-storey complex houses the **Namgyal Monastery**, where the Dalai Lama lives when he's not on the road, along with a couple of small shops selling incense and *thangkas* and a bookshop stocked with tomes penned by His Holiness himself. To access the main part of the complex, you'll need to pass through security (no knives, matches, perfumes or other flammable materials are allowed inside), into a large, spartan covered courtyard. Head up a flight of stairs to the 1st floor to visit the **Tsuglagkhang Main Temple Room**, signposted simply as 'The Tibetan Temple', which houses the Dalai Lama's teaching throne, a giant golden statue of Lord Buddha, and images of Buddhist saint Padmasambhava and deity Avalokiteśvara (aka Chenrezig).

While the Dalai Lama once gave frequent public audiences here, he's slowed down a bit over the years. These days, seeing him in person requires a fair bit of planning – and luck. Up-to-date information about His Holiness's teaching schedule and public appearances is available at his website *(dalailama.com/office/public-audiences)*. To attend a public blessing (typically held on Mondays, Wednesdays and Fridays when he's in town), email *ohhdl@dalailama.com*.

Walking Meditation

Meander along the Kora Circuit

A steep road to the left of the complex's entry gate leads to the **Kora Circuit**, a 1.5km-long circular pathway that traverses a forest adorned with colourful prayer flags and large displays of *mani* stones, carved or painted rocks inscribed with the sacred mantra: *om mani padme hum*. While many people walk the path in a clockwise direction before visiting the Tsuglagkhang Complex, the Kora Circuit is a beautiful spot for a forest stroll. Just be careful if you're carrying snacks, as you'll be sharing the path with large troops of rhesus macaques who are known to get cheeky when the prospect of food is involved.

A Trio of Tibetan Museums

Preserving Tibetan culture and history

About a 1.5km walk from the Tsuglagkhang Complex in the Central Tibetan Administration's Gangchen Kyishong complex, the **Tibet Museum** *(tibetmuseum.org; adult/child ₹20/free)* tells the story of the Tibetan people past and present through a permanent exhibit, aptly named 'I am Tibetan and This is my story'. Through a series of multimedia displays accented with artefacts, visitors are invited to learn about the Chinese occupation of Tibet and the resistance movement that followed while deepening their understanding of Tibetan culture. If you're sensitive, bring tissues along – some of the materials presented can be emotionally distressing.

After visiting the Tibet Museum, head next door to the **Library of Tibetan Works and Archives** *(tibetanlibrary.org; free)*. Founded to store and preserve sacred manuscripts and objects brought over after the Cultural Revolution in Tibet, today it preserves and displays items across three key themes:

Buddhism in Tibet; the teachings of the Buddha; and arts and artefacts from Tibet and the community in exile. Visit the library's museum to see beautifully preserved *thangkas*, mandalas and other sacred objects.

From the library, it's less than a 10-minute walk down Jogiwara Rd to the **Men-Tsee-Khang Tibetan Medical & Astro Institute Museum** *(mentseekhang.org/museum; ₹20)*. Here you can learn about Tibet's scientific traditions through displays of medical instruments, herbs used in medicine and detailed medical *thangkas*. The museum's parent organisation produces the popular Sorig brand of Tibetan creams and medicines, available for purchase on site.

Journey to the Northeast

Bhagsu Nag and beyond

About a 2km walk northeast of McLeod Ganj's Main Square is Bhagsu Nag, a small community that - along with adjacent Dharamkot - has long been a hit among backpackers from abroad, and both areas have plenty of crystal shops and hippie-themed restaurants to show for it. While Bhagsu can feel congested at times, you can easily get out into nature by following a 500m-long path from the town's main **Bhagsu Nag Temple** to the **Bhagsu Nag Waterfall**. The same path eventually leads to **Triund**, a mountain meadow and the first stop on the Indrahar Pass Trek (p268). If you get up early, you can hike to Triund and back on the same day - just give yourself at least four hours each way.

Spiritual Seekers

An Immersive Introduction to Mahayana Buddhist meditation

Spiritual seekers and travellers interested in Tibet's Mahayana Buddhist traditions will find a wide range of courses at **Tushita Meditation Centre** *(tushita.info)*, situated between McLeod Ganj and Dharamkot. Tushita offers a residential 10-day introduction to Buddhism courses along with advanced teachings and retreats for people with some knowledge of Mahayana traditions. If you want to learn the basics of meditation but don't want to commit to a longer course of study, you can sign up for one of its three-day non-residential short courses or drop in for a guided meditation session, held every morning Monday–Saturday. Note that Tushita closes annually from the beginning of December through mid-January.

MUST-TRY TIBETAN TREATS

Momos: Small meat- or veg-stuffed dumplings which are usually steamed but can be fried. Found at nearly every restaurant in McLeod.

Phingsha: A spicy concoction of vermicelli noodles, potatoes, meat and mushrooms.

Tingmo: Tibetan steamed buns made of wheat flour, often served as an accompaniment to main dishes.

Thukpa: A type of noodle soup that's made with thin noodles and prepared with meat and/or vegetables.

Thenthuk: A type of noodle soup similar to standard *thukpa*, but made with pulled flat noodles.

Laphing: A dish of flour noodles, often served cold with a spicy or salty gravy.

EATING IN MCLEOD GANJ: OUR PICKS

Snow Lion Restaurant: Tibetan-run restaurant serving French-press coffee, Tibetan bread baked daily and a solid selection of vegetarian mains. *7am-9pm* ₹

Nick's Italian Kitchen: Combine pizza and pasta with mountain views, and don't forget to check the bulletin board at this backpacker favourite. *7.30am-9pm* ₹

Green Hotel Restaurant: Longstanding traveller favourite offering Tibetan, Indian and Western fare, including tasty homemade fries. *7am-9.30pm* ₹

Other Space: An art gallery meets coworking spot meets cafe with lovely picture windows and views of the Dhauladhar foothills. *9am-9pm* ₹₹

WALKING TOUR

Indrahar Pass Trek (via Triund)

For an intense hiking challenge and spectacular views of the Lower Himalaya, the Indrahar Pass Trek is worth your while. The variation of this route outlined below takes you past Triund (p267), up to the 4342m-high Indrahar Pass and back down again (four days), though some organised treks continue north through the Chamba Valley to Lamu (five days). Trekking conditions are at their most favourable between May and October.

1 Dharamkot

There are two routes to Triund and onwards to Indrahar Pass from McLeod Ganj, and many people go up one way and back down the other. Guided treks often start in the McLeod Ganj suburb of Dharamkot via the Gallu Devi Temple trail, just north of the water tank on Dharamkot Studio Rd, though you can also take a taxi to just beyond the temple and walk from there.

The Hike: The first stretch of the trek normally takes around three to four hours, winding through tree-shaded and rhododendron-lined pathways that give way to an open ridge trail that's rocky in places.

2 Triund

Spend your first night in Triund, an alpine meadow with sweeping views of the Dhauladhar Range of the lower Himalaya. There's a small, state-run **guesthouse**

PRABHKIRAT SINGH/SHUTTERSTOCK

(0189-222-4887) at the top with four simple rooms, though most people on organised hikes stay in tents.

The Hike: Walk for another hour along a mix of rocky ridge trail and rhododendron and oak forest to Snow Line Café. From here, continue for a few more hours to Lahesh Cave.

3 Lahesh Cave

At the snout of the Lahesh Glacier, rocky Lahesh Cave is the closest campsite to Indrahar Pass and a good option if you want to get to the pass early, before it gets too cloudy at the top. Get up early the next day and make your way up toward Indrahar Pass. This particular section is steep and rocky, and is blanketed with snow throughout much of the year.

The Hike: After four or five hours of hiking up a steep incline, you'll reach Indrahar Pass, where you'll have time to take in the views before beginning your descent.

4 Laka Got

Laka Got is a shepherds' camp in a grassy meadow, about an hour or so downhill past Lahesh Cave. Some people opt to forego camping at Lahesh Cave altogether and instead opt to spend two nights at Laka Got instead.

The Hike: Retrace your steps to Triund. From here, you can return the way you came or head south along an alternative trail that will ultimately take you to the Bhagsu Nag Temple (p267).

Beyond McLeod Ganj

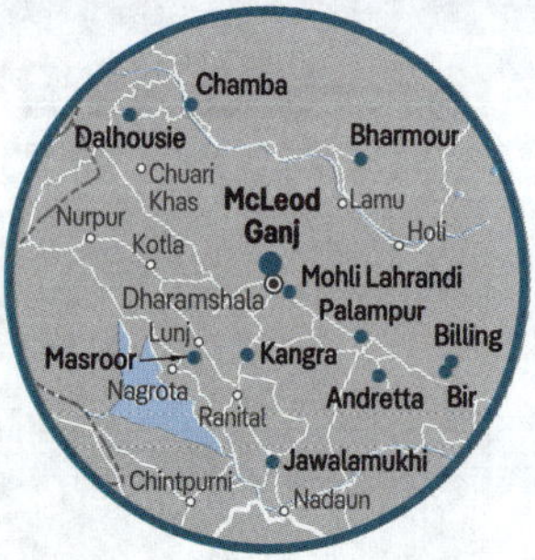

Venture out from McLeod Ganj to ancient forts and temples, cute artist communities and vast expanses of mountains, meadows and tea plantings

Places

No matter what direction you travel from McLeod Ganj, you'll find plenty of surprises. Head south to the ancient ramparts of Kangra Fort or the rock-hewn edifices at the 8th-century Masroor Temple complex, or take the southeastern road to visit the tea plantations of Palampur and the potters' community in neighbouring Andretta. Keep driving and you'll find yourself in the twin towns of Bir and Billing, equally known for magnificent monasteries and paragliding galore.

Or opt for a northern adventure across the Dhauladhar Range to the Chamba Valley. Here you can explore Bharmour's 7th-century Chaurasi Temple Complex or Chamba's 10th-century Laxmi Narayan Temple, before heading to the hill station of Dalhousie to relax among British colonial architecture.

Mohli Lahrandi

TIME FROM MCLEOD GANJ: **40MIN**

Immerse yourself in Tibetan arts and culture

About a half-hour drive southeast of McLeod will take you to Mohli Lahrandi and the **Norbulingka Institute**, named for the Dalai Lama's summer palace in Lhasa. Since its establishment in 1990, Norbulingka has gone above and beyond to promote Tibetan heritage in India, offering educational programmes for artists and craftspeople wishing to immerse themselves in the art of Tibet. Stroll through the centre's gardened grounds, watch artists carve wood and paint *thangkas*, and check out a doll museum featuring dioramas of costumed dolls clad in traditional Tibetan dress. There's also an open-air garden cafe serving tasty vegetarian meals, an on-site guesthouse and – unsurprisingly – a gift shop selling a selection of the high-quality products produced on site.

GETTING AROUND

The area around McLeod Ganj is well-connected by bus, and taxis are widely available from travel agents such as **Buddha Travels** *(9882166383)* for those willing to fork out extra for a more comfortable journey. The Himachal Road Transport Corporation (HRTC) operates regular bus service between McLeod Ganj and destinations across Himachal Pradesh, including Dalhousie, Kullu, Manali and Shimla. Direct service to Delhi is also available.

Kangra

TIME FROM MCLEOD GANJ: **1HR 15MIN**

Historic Himachal at its best

Built more than a millennium ago, **Kangra Fort** *(adult/child ₹250/free)* – the former stronghold of the Katoch Kingdom – is the largest fort in the Himalayan region and among one of the oldest fortifications in all of India. Start your visit at the archaeological museum, a compact but comprehensive collection featuring objects found at and near the fort, including tools dating back to the Palaeolithic era. Other highlights include a gallery full of fine examples of Kangra miniature paintings and a large collection of remarkably intact medieval sculptures and reliefs, most of Hindu and Jain deities. There's also a small garden out front where a few additional pieces are displayed. Note that the museum is wheelchair accessible and has extensive facilities for the visually impaired, including audio guides and signposting in braille, but the fort itself lacks such facilities.

A downhill path to the right of the museum leads to the **Ranjit Singh Gate**, which marks the entrance to Kanga Fort. From here, it's a steep uphill climb up uneven stairs and past carved reliefs to the top of the fort, which offers magnificent views of Kangra and beyond. After taking it all in, head back down and uphill again to the **Maharaja Sansar Chandra Museum** *(kangragroup.com; adult/child ₹100/free)*, a steep 350m away. This compact museum displays a small but ornate smattering of royal paraphernalia, from palanquins to regal costumes, along with a large selection of weaponry. There's also a basic cafe on site serving simple Indian dishes.

Masroor

TIME FROM MCLEOD GANJ. **2HR 20MIN**

Rock-hewn wonders

Perched on a verdant hillock surrounded by woodlands, the 8th-century **Masroor Temple** *(adult/child ₹250/free)* is a spectacular example of Nagara-style rock-cut temple architecture. Often likened to Maharashtra's Ellora Cave Temples (p720) – or even to Angkor Wat – this 14-monument complex is characterised by towering *sikharas* (conical spires), some of which still have their original reliefs of Vedic and Puranic deities intact. In front of the complex stands a tank full of water, which makes for particularly great photos of the temple's reflection when the lighting is right. Make sure to go inside to visit the main sanctum; although it was likely originally a Shiva temple, today it contains idols of Ram, Lakshman and Sita.

Jawalamukhi

TIME FROM MCLEOD GANJ: **2½HR**

An eternal flame

Among the most significant holy sites in the Kangra Valley, the **Jawala Ji Temple** is one of 51 *Shakti peeths*, sacred temples dedicated to the supreme goddess Mahadevi. According to legend, after Lord Shiva's consort – Sati – died, a mourning Shiva carried her corpse around the world. In an attempt to

THANGKA PAINTINGS

You can't go far in McLeod Ganj without coming upon a shop selling *thangkas*, Tibetan Buddhist religious paintings that typically portray religious figures, scenes from the life of the Buddha or mandalas. *Thangkas* are created by skilled artists who first draw the art on a stretched piece of canvas, using a grid to ensure the exact measurements of their subject, before painting it in. The entire process can be long and arduous, and real *thangkas* don't come cheap. The best way to ensure you're getting a genuine article, and that you're contributing to the Tibetan community, is by purchasing your *thangka* from a shop bearing the Tibetan Shopkeepers Welfare Society members' seal.

relieve Shiva of his grief and attachment, Lord Vishnu used his divine disk, the Sudarshana Chakra, to chop Sati's body into 51 pieces. The temple marks the spot where Sati's tongue fell, and the goddess is worshipped here today in the form of Jawalamukhi. To take her blessings, you must descend into a small chamber, which enshrines nine small ever-burning flames, considered her manifestation.

Palampur

TIME FROM MCLEOD GANJ: 2HR

Tea time in the Himalaya

Although most people associate India's tea industry with Darjeeling and Assam, the Himachali town of Palampur has had its own thriving industry since tea was first planted here in the 1840s. In fact, one of the first things you'll notice when you drive into the town is that seemingly every other agricultural plot – and some people's front gardens – are blanketed with bushy tea plants.

You can learn all about how tea is grown and produced at the family-run **Wah Tea Estate** *(wahtea.com; tours with tastings ₹350)*, the largest plantation in the region. Start with a half-hour-long guided tour of the production facilities before heading over to Wah's tea shop for a tasting session. Expect to learn about the art of tea tasting before setting forth to sample 20-odd varieties, from rose-infused black tea to delicately spiced Kashmiri kahwa. If you're feeling hungry, there's a small cafe behind the shop serving dishes such as *kangri dhaam*, a quintessentially Himachali thali feast. The estate also operates an intimate homestay across the road from the main plantation.

Andretta

TIME FROM MCLEOD GANJ: 2½HR

Just south of Palampur, the tiny village of Andretta has been a hub for artists since the first half of the 20th century. A 10-minute drive from Wah Tea Estate will take you to the **Sobha Singh Art Gallery** *(sobhasinghartist.in; adult/child ₹100/free)*. It's housed in the former workshop of Punjabi artist Sobha Singh, who spent much of his life living in Andretta, and features a large selection of his works and ephemera related to his life. From here, it's less than a kilometre to **Chameli Niwas**, the former home of Irish actress Norah Richards, who was instrumental in transforming Andretta into an arts village. Just around the corner sits the **Clayrvoy Studio**, a small shop full of beautiful glazed pottery (the phone number is posted on the door, so if they aren't in, just call). From here, it's just a few more steps to **Andretta Pottery** *(andrettapottery.in)*, an open-air studio offering 15- and 45-minute drop-in pottery classes along with three-month

PICKING THE PERFECT TEA

Surya Jai Prakash, the fourth-generation owner of Wah Tea Estate, offers these tips on how to select tea that's right for you. *@wahtea*

Strength Start with deciding how strong you like your tea. If it's to wake you up in the morning, select an Assam or orthodox black tea. If it's to relax and sip through the day, choose a green, oolong or white tea. Or skip the caffeine and choose a herbal tea.

Flavour Do you enjoy sweeter or stronger tastes? Choose from the fragrance of flowers or notes of spices. Wah has a range of flavours like orange cinnamon, lemongrass, rose or masala, depending on your tastebuds.

Benefits Some teas help with specific ailments, like chamomile for better sleep, or our detox blend.

MINIATURE MARVELS

Head to the **Himachal State Museum** (p303) in Shimla to see a solid collection of Pahari miniature paintings, and compare them with Sikh and Rajasthani versions of the art form.

SUDIP JOTSHI/SHUTTERSTOCK

Paragliding, Bir-Billing

residential intensives for those who want to get serious about clay.

Bir-Billing

TIME FROM MCLEOD GANJ: **3HR**

Tibetan culture in paragliding country

The twin towns of **Bir** and **Billing** are known for two things: paragliding and monasteries. A good chunk of visitors to this part of the state come here for the former, and while many local paragliding operators work primarily with one-and-done tourists wanting to brave a tandem jump, there are plenty of options for more experienced pilots, too. While most guesthouses and visitor-facing facilities are located in Bir's Tibetan Colony of Chowgan, paragliding adventures depart from neighbouring Billing, about 16km north of town.

For those interested in Tibetan culture, there's plenty to see in the area. Notable sights include the palatial **Chokling Monastery** *(chokling-tersar.org/bir-gonpa)*, a huge white structure featuring a grand, chorten-flanked entrance that leads to steep stairs and up into a central courtyard filled with flowers and statuary. It's adorned with row upon row of prayer flags suspended between its stupa and its prayer hall. Chokling's star attraction is an exquisite statue of Padmasambhava, the Indian mystic who founded Tibet's first Buddhist monastery.

About a 20-minute drive out of town, the **Sherabling**

THE OPEN SKIES

Bir-Billing is India's paragliding capital. Here are a few popular operators.

Akash Adventures: Adventure tour operator offering tandem flights plus overnight treks to nearby Rajgundha. *(akashadventures.co.in)*

Golden Eagle Paragliding Club: Tandem paraglides and seven- and 10-day beginner and intermediate courses. *(geparagliding.org)*

Himalayan Sky Safaris: British-run company operating group safaris for all levels and bespoke tandem adventures. *(himalayanskysafaris.com)*

Nayak Paragliding Association: Offers one-day paragliding flights plus camping and trekking adventures. *(82197-61460)*

Skylark School of Paragliding: Runs five- and seven-day programmes for beginner and intermediate skydivers. *(theparagliding.com)*

EATING IN BIR: OUR PICKS

Avva's Café: Pair South Indian favourites with an exceptional variety of coffee drinks at this cosy-sleek spot. *9am-10pm* ₹₹

June16Café: This compact coffee shop serves tasty cakes and espresso drinks plus a solid range of Western breakfast and lunch dishes. *9am-9pm* ₹₹

Musafir Café: Named for a Hindi-Urdu word for 'traveller', this breezy, open-air spot has tasty hot chocolate and friendly vibes. *9am-9pm* ₹

Northern Café: Sample nutritious Tibetan, Indian and continental delights in the open-air covered rooftop of this garden restaurant. *10am-9.30pm* ₹₹

Monastery is a massive complex partially painted in the same rich maroon hue that's worn by Tibetan monks and nuns. It houses over 1000 monastics at any given time. Pop inside to see its magnificent double-storey prayer hall, which houses a gargantuan statue of Maitreya, the not-yet-incarnated Buddha of the future.

Dalhousie

TIME FROM MCLEOD GANJ: **5HR**

Quiet time in the hills

One of the countless hill stations in India bearing the 'little Switzerland' nickname, Dalhousie is a (generally) quiet alternative to more crowded hotspots such as Shimla and Manali, owing largely to its relatively remote location in the northwestern corner of Himachal Pradesh. This cosy spot, founded in the 1850s by then-governor of India Lord Dalhousie, doesn't offer a lot to do beyond wandering, reading and generally slowing down.

The town's British colonial-era architecture is among its biggest appeals, and it's worth paying a visit to the city's oldest Christian house of worship – **St John's Church**, an old stone construction with a few lovely painted glass windows. **St Francis Church** at Subhash Chowk is equally worth seeing and features lovely masonry and stained-glass windows. If you're itching to keep busy, you can take a hike up to **Satdhara Falls**, about a half-hour walk from town, a series of seven waterfalls fed by mineral-rich natural springs. From here, it's only another 15 minutes on foot to **Panchpula**, where you'll find another set of waterfalls and streams surrounded by emerald greenery. Just don't expect a lot of serenity: the area is full of little cafes and souvenir shops, and while it's a scenic place for a meal, it can get crowded.

Chamba

TIME FROM MCLEOD GANJ: **6½HR**

Medieval musings

The district capital of Chamba is one of the oldest cities in the region. It was founded in 920 CE, when Raja Sahil Varman moved his capital here from Bharmour, and many traces of its ancient past remain in the architecture found in and around the city, much of which is centred on the Chamba's central field: the Chaugan. The city's claim to architectural fame is the **Laxmi Narayan Temple Complex**, a collection of six stone temples featuring spire-like *sikharas* and roofs made of slate. The oldest parts were commissioned by Raja Sahil Varman himself, including the temple's Vishnu idol, believed to have been brought from the Vindhya Mountains in west-central India.

Across from the complex, the 11th-century **Hari Rai Temple** is equally remarkable, both for its intricately carved *sikhara* and its mixed-metal idol of Lord Vishnu. It's just down the road from the **Bhuri Singh Museum** *(bhurisinghmuseum chamba.in; adult/child ₹150/30)*, an art and history museum with three floors of art and artefacts. Give yourself plenty of

THE MINJAR MELA

Held annually at the beginning of the month of Shravana (which typically falls in late July), the week-long Minjar Mela is Chamba's liveliest celebration. Taking place primarily in the city's central Chaugan, this mela (fair) features lots of merriment, including folk music and dance performances. Vendors set up shop in booths around the Chaugan and in nearby areas, selling local handicrafts and snacks. Men and women alike dress in their most colourful finery and don *minjars*, silk tassels representing the shoots of corn. The festivities culminate with a grand procession of the local deity, Lord Raghuvir. At the end of the procession, people offer their *minjars* – along with fruits and coins – into the river.

Chaurasi Temple Complex

time, as there's a lot to cover. The ground-floor exhibitions focus on works from the Chamba region, including stone sculptures and *chambarumal* painting (which involves the use of needles to paint on muslin cloth). The 1st floor is full of exquisite examples of Pahari miniature paintings, while the top floor displays anthropological items such as clothes, textiles and musical instruments.

Bharmour

TIME FROM MCLEOD GANJ: 8½HR

Into the ancient kingdom

A 60km drive from Chamba along winding mountain roads will take you to Bharmour, former seat of the Chamba royal family. What remains of the ancient kingdom is the **Chaurasi Temple Complex**, a series of 84 shrines (*chaurasi* means 84 in Hindi), most built between the 7th and 10th centuries CE. The main shrine – the **Manimahesh** – is among the oldest constructions here and features a huge idol of the bull Nandi, Shiva's *vahana* (mount), at its entryway. However, the oldest structure is likely the **Lakshna Devi Temple**, which features the goddess Durga in her Mahishasura-Mardini (destroyer of demon Mahishasura) form.

For a pleasant hike and rewarding views, head up to the **Bharmani Mata Temple**, on a hillock about 4km from the town centre. If you come around the 8th day of the month of Bhadon, which typically falls in late August, you're likely to run into masses of pilgrims. Many come to clean themselves in the temple's holy tank before continuing 26km to **Manimahesh Lake**, an alpine lake below the mountain of Manimahesh Kailash, the final destination of the annual **Manimahesh Yatra**.

PAHARI MINIATURE PAINTING

One of the most celebrated art forms to come out of North India's mountain regions is Pahari miniature painting. Although it was originally inspired by Mughal miniature painting traditions, Pahari painting developed key differences, focusing more on detail and integrating less vivid colours than their counterparts to the south. There are a number of schools within Pahari miniature painting. The Kangra School is perhaps the best known, and often addresses themes of love, poetry, nature and devotion; the Chamba School typically focuses on similar motifs, but artists in this style are known to integrate bolder, deeper colours. Some of the finest remaining examples are on display at the Bhuri Singh Museum in Chamba.

Manali

WOODEN TEMPLES | FOREST STROLLS | MOUNTAIN SCENERY

GETTING AROUND

While much of Manali is walkable, autorickshaws are widely available to get around town or up to Vashisht. For destinations across Himachal Pradesh, Himachal Road Transport Corporation (HRTC) buses depart from the bus station on Mall Rd. There's also frequent direct service to Delhi's Kashmiri Gate bus stand, with upwards of a dozen ordinary and deluxe buses running in a given day, plus seasonal service to Leh. The nearest airport is Kullu-Manali (Bhuntar) Airport, 50km away, with service to Delhi, Dehradun, Amritsar and Jaipur on Alliance Air. Many people rent motorbikes in Manali before heading to Spiti or Ladakh via the Leh–Manali Hwy.

Straddling the River Beas, not far from where the Dhauladhar Range of the lesser Himalaya merges with the Pir Panjal Range, Manali (2050m) has long drawn in a mix of families and honeymooners, adventure-seeking outdoors people and long-term backpackers in search of a cool spot to spend the summer. Although the city is fringed with massive mountain peaks and beautiful forests filled with towering deodar trees, it's not the type of place to go if you're looking for a quiet retreat, especially if you visit during the busy hot season (April to June), when people head up here from the plains in droves, desperate to escape the 40°C-plus weather that stifles lower-elevation cities. And while you should expect plenty of commotion – particularly along the perpetually jam-packed Mall Rd – you're never far from beautiful woodlands and gorgeous old temples, many of which are built in Himachal's quintessential stone-and-wood *kath-kuni* style.

Manali Mandirs

Visiting famous temples

In the wooded outskirts of the village of Dungri, about a 20-minute walk from Mall Rd, sits the **Hidimba Devi Temple**, another *kath-kuni* temple dedicated to the goddess Hidimba Devi, who watches over Manali. Built in 1553 under the order of then ruler Raja Bahadur Singh, this forest temple is topped with a triple roof crowned with a brass cone that gives it the appearance of a pagoda, and is adorned with intricate carvings of deities, animals and decorative designs. Expect crowds, especially if you come during the annual Dhungri Mela, when the goddess' birth is celebrated with three days of music, dance and worship.

Walk northwest for another 25 minutes and you'll reach the **Manu Rishi Temple**, another wood-and-stone temple, this time dedicated to the ancient sage Rishi Manu, who some believe is the originator of the human race. Legend has it

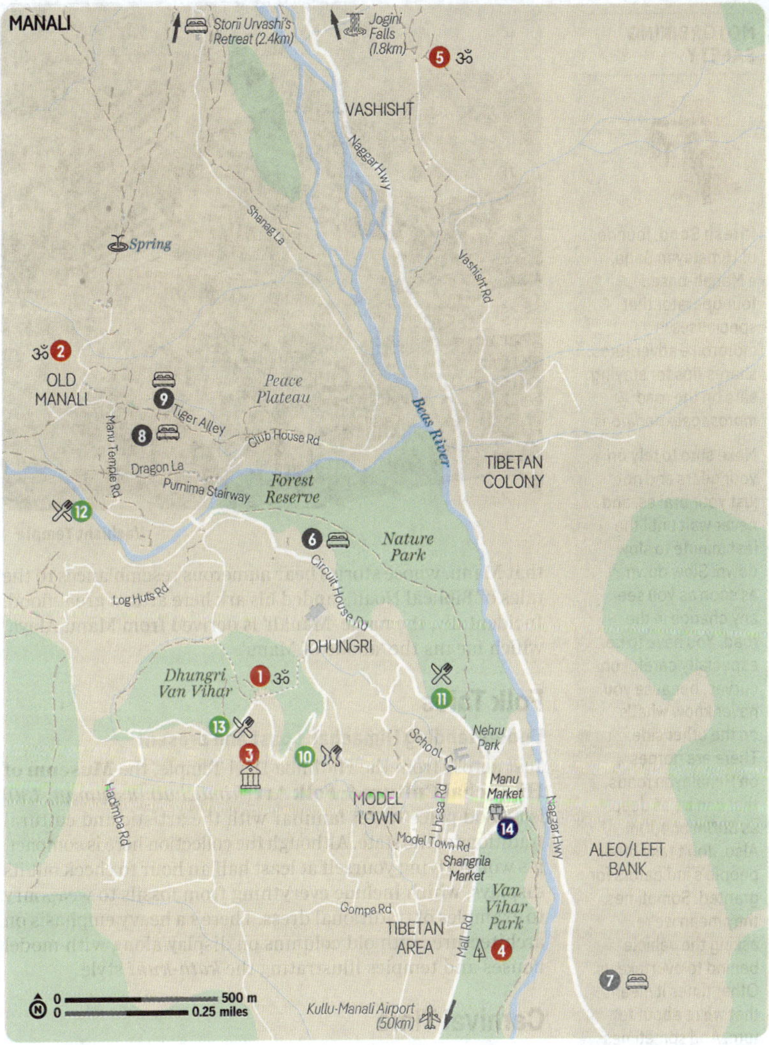

SIGHTS	SLEEPING	EATING
1 Hidimba Devi Temple	6 Baikunth Manali	10 Il Forno
2 Manu Rishi Temple	7 Hill River Resort	11 Johnson's Cafe
3 Museum of Himachal Culture & Folk Art	8 Orchards House - The Hidden Tribe	12 Lazy Dog
4 Van Vihar	9 Zostel Old Manali	13 Southern Souls Café
5 Vashisht Temple		**TRANSPORT**
		14 Bus Station

TOP TIP

Manali's weather can be unpredictable and not just during the cold winter months. The monsoon season can spur devastating flooding and landslides. If you choose to travel during this period of the year, be prepared to be flexible with your itinerary.

MOTORBIKING SAFETY

Ritesh Sood, founder of Himalayan Saga, a Manali-based tour operator that specialises in motorbike adventures, shares tips for staying safe on the road. @ *motosagaexpeditions*

Make sure to rely on your gears and not just your brakes, and never wait until the last minute to slow down. Slow down as soon as you see any change in the road. You have to be especially careful on curves, because you never know what's on the other side. There are gorges on Himalayan roads that can be as deep as 300m or 400m. Also, don't take other people's indicators for granted. Sometimes they mean we're asking the vehicle behind to overtake us. Other times it means that we're about to turn. And sometimes people just forget and leave them on!

OSCAR ESPINOSA/SHUTTERSTOCK

Vashisht Temple

that Manu, whose stories bear numerous resemblances to the tales of Biblical Noah, landed his ark here after a great flood. Incidentally, the name 'Manali' is derived from Manu Alaya, which means the 'abode of Manu'.

Folk Tales

Understanding Himachal's past and present

Just across from the Hidimba Devi Temple, the **Museum of Himachal Culture & Folk Art** *(himachalmuseum.in; ₹30)* is a good place to get familiar with the artistic and cultural traditions of the state. Although the collection here is compact, it's worth giving yourself at least half an hour to check out its displays, which include everything from fossils to weaponry to examples of traditional dress. There's a heavy emphasis on architecture, with old columns on display along with model houses and temples illustrating the *kath-kuni* style.

Carnival Time

Ring in the winter with cultural celebrations

The chilly season is feted with gusto in January during the **Manali Winter Carnival** *(manaliwintercarnival.co.in)*, a five-day celebration of local culture that's been running since 1977. Highlights include traditional music and dance performances, handicraft and food vendors, a carnival parade and even a pageant to crown Manali's 'Winter Queen'. The most spectacular carnival event of them all, however, is a performance of the Maha Nati, a synchronised dance that's performed in unison by upwards of 1500 women from across Himachal.

In the Pines

A walk in the park

Extending west of the Hidimba Devi Temple, **Van Vihar** *(adult/child ₹50/20)* provides an excellent alternative to busy Mall Rd if you're looking for a spot to stroll. Spread out over a few hectares of deodar forest that was planted in the late 19th century, this municipal woodland is a great place for kids who need to burn off some energy, with a massive playground filled with swings and slides flanked in by towering trees, plus a small pond with pedalboats, some shaped like swans to keep the honeymoon set happy. While the playground and pond can get busy during the peak summer season, there's a well-maintained circuit trail that will lead you away from the masses.

Love Your Neighbour

A visit to Vashisht

On the opposite side of the Beas River from Manali, in the neighbouring village of Vashisht, the **Vashisht Temple** has similar architecture to what's found in other area temples, with elaborately carved pillars supporting a two-tiered roof. Peek inside to see its scaled-down shrine, which is designed to resemble local architecture, complete with a slate miniroof and a wood-encased entryway; it houses an idol of the sage Vashisht, to whom the temple is dedicated. The site also has hot springs believed to be both sacred and curative, with separate sections for men and women to bathe. Both are walled in, but the ladies' section has higher walls to keep people from looking in. While you can wear a swimsuit, note that some people strip down to their undergarments or enter with clothes on. Bring a towel.

Head about 2.5km north of the temple and you'll reach the trailhead for **Jogini Waterfalls**, one of the easier and more accessible hikes in the area. A half-hour walk through the forest will take you to the base of the waterfalls, where there's a viewpoint and a small stone dedicated to Yogini Mata. If you're feeling ambitious and don't mind a steep ascent, you can continue to climb for another 20 minutes until you reach the upper falls.

WINTER IN MANALI

Like all major hill stations, Manali attracts big crowds during the summer. Winters here can get busy, too, when travellers from across the country head to the hills with high hopes of glimpsing freshly fallen snow (many for the first time in their lives). Fans of skiing and snowboarding (as well as those who want to hit the slopes for the first time) often take day trips up to nearby Solang Nallah, about 14km north of Manali. **Broza Adventures** *(brozaadventures.com)* offers one-day and week-long skiing courses for beginners. Experienced snow bunnies may want to splurge for a heliskiing adventure with **Himalayan Heliski** *(himalayaheliski.com)*. Note that while Manali's white winters can be enchanting (especially if you witness someone's first glimpse of snow), roads can get treacherous.

EATING IN MANALI: OUR PICKS

Il Forno: Longstanding family-run Italian spot housed in a traditional *kath-kuni* building; famous for its wood-fired pizzas and calzones. *11am-10.30pm* ₹₹

Johnson's Cafe: Cosy lodge-style restaurant inside Johnson's Hotel serving up tasty pizzas and lots of trout-based dishes. *10am-10pm* ₹₹₹

Lazy Dog: Choose from a varied menu of cuisine from around the world, with options ranging from katsu sushi rolls to chicken schnitzel. *noon-11pm* ₹₹₹

Southern Souls Café: Vegetarian spot with indoor and garden seating serving tasty South Indian meals, beyond just dosas and *idlis*. *10am-8pm* ₹₹

WALKING TOUR

Hampta Pass Trek

This popular trek near Manali takes you from the Kullu Valley into Lahaul's Changra Valley via alpine fields where cattle and horses graze, and across the 4270m Hampta Pass. Expect to cross a couple of glaciers and a deep stream along the way. The best time to do this trek is between June and early October, though it's particularly scenic after the monsoon, when rivers rage and meadows fill with blooms.

1 Jobri

The Hampta Pass trek starts in Jobri, about a 90-minute drive from Manali along a zigzagging road. Many trekking outfitters include share-jeep transfers from Manali to the trailhead. This stretch is fairly easy going, with minimal elevation gain, but there are a few rocky, steep areas to cross.

The Hike: Head to Chikka, about a 5km hike from Jobri, passing through a mix of forested trails and mossy meadows.

2 Chikka

Spend your first night acclimatising in Chikka, a sloping meadow surrounded by jagged peaks and stone formations. Fall asleep to the white-noise din of the Rani Stream that flanks the camping area. Plan for at least four hours to make the journey to Balu Ka Ghera, walking through boulder-strewn meadows, alongside rhododendron groves and past a small waterfall.

SUMANKYAL/SHUTTERSTOCK

Hampta Pass

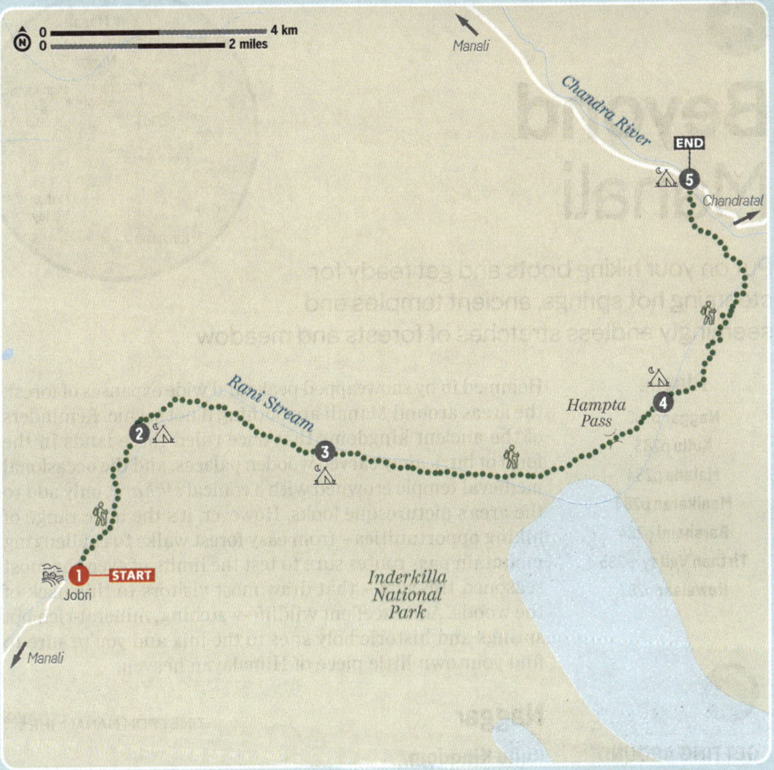

The Hike: The second day of the trek is a bit more strenuous, with around 500m of elevation gain and 9km of hiking. Be prepared to put your boots' waterproofing to the test by crossing a small section of the river.

3 Balu Ka Ghera

Spend your second night at Balu ka Gera camping in a clearing under the shadow of snow-capped peaks. Depending on what time of the year you visit, you may encounter snowfall at your campsite. The third day of the trek will take you over the 4270m Hampta Pass, where you'll want to stop and take in the mountainous magnificence before continuing to your next camp at Shea Goru, 15km from Balu Ka Ghera.

The Hike: Expect a vigorous uphill climb to the pass and a steep, somewhat tricky descent on the other side over boulders and, possibly, snow.

4 Shea Goru

The Shea Goru campsite will likely be a welcome sight after a long and exhausting day of trekking. This flat, riverside meadow is the first campsite in the Lahaul region of Himachal Pradesh and is dotted with tiny flowers throughout much of the hiking season.

The Hike: The final stretch of the trek will take you to Chhatru, about a 10km downhill hike from Shea Goru.

5 Chhatru

On the banks of the Chandra River, surrounded by mountain peaks, Chhatru is where you'll spend your final night, checking out the stars of the night sky on full display. From here, you can return to Manali by road or take a detour to Chandratal (p290), an alpine lake about a two-hour drive away.

Beyond Manali

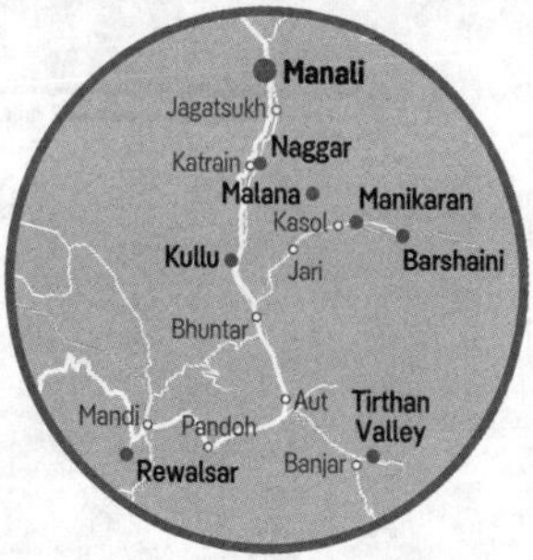

Put on your hiking boots and get ready for steaming hot springs, ancient temples and seemingly endless stretches of forests and meadow

Places

Hemmed in by snowcapped peaks and wide expanses of forest, the areas around Manali are nothing if not scenic. Reminders of the ancient kingdoms that once ruled these lands in the form of intricately carved wooden palaces, and the occasional medieval temple crowned with a conical *sikhara*, only add to the area's picturesque looks. However, it's the huge range of hiking opportunities – from easy forest walks to challenging mountain pass routes sure to test the limits of even the most seasoned trekkers – that draw most visitors to this neck of the woods. Add excellent wildlife-watching, mineral-rich hot springs and historic holy sites to the mix and you're sure to find your own little piece of Himalayan heaven.

GETTING AROUND

While you won't find any trains in the mountainous areas around Manali, the region's towns and cities are typically well-connected by HRTC bus. The National Hwy 3 (NH3) is the region's main thoroughfare, running on a north–south axis from Manali down to Kullu and beyond before turning east toward Rewalsar where the rivers Beas and Tirthan converge. Take the same road north from Manali and you'll soon reach the Atal Tunnel (p289), the gateway to Spiti.

Naggar

TIME FROM MANALI: **1HR**

Kullu Kingdom

Perched above the eastern banks of the Beas River, Naggar – the capital of the Kullu Kingdom until the 17th century – offers beautiful valley views and medieval **Naggar Castle** *(hptdc.in/index.php/the-naggar-castle; closed until early 2027)*. This beautifully preserved property, now a government-run hotel, is a glorious example of *kath-kuni* architecture, characterised by alternating layers of wood and stone, known to keep buildings intact even when rocked by earthquakes, and features intricately carved pillars, arches and balconies with commanding views over the town.

A few steps from the castle sits a *sikhara*-style **Vishnu Temple** dating to the 11th century. Another two-minute walk down the road will take you to the **Tripura Sundari Temple**, a fine example of Kullu architecture, complete with ornately carved pillars and awnings featuring a mix of geometric and realistic patterns (including the profile of two elephant heads touching trunks at the outer entrance of the temple).

From Russia with love

In 1928 celebrated Russian painter Nicholas Roerich and his family moved to India and made Naggar their home. Although Roerich died in 1947, his legacy remains in the form of the **International Roerich Memorial Trust** *(irmtkullu.com/visiting; adult/child ₹200/30)*, a museum that preserves his

MADHUSUDAN SINGH/SHUTTERSTOCK

Kullu Dussehra

former home and the grounds around it. The main house has been transformed into a museum containing works by the artist, most of which are clearly inspired by the landscapes of the Himalaya, before heading up to the 1st-floor balcony, from where you can peep into rooms formerly occupied by the family – and take in Kullu Valley views. Vintage car fans take note: a Dodge convertible dating to 1930 is on display next to the house.

Give yourself plenty of time to explore the gardens and the other property features, which include a souvenir shop, a restaurant and sprawling gardens. Across the road from the Roerich House, the **Urusvati Himalayan Research Institute** features a research library and a small collection of botanical items, plus a folk-art museum displaying crafts from the Himalayan regions.

Kullu

TIME FROM MANALI: 1½HR

Come for Dussehra, stay for the architecture

The capital of the Kullu Valley, Kullu is best known for two things. The first is its beautifully patterned shawls, created throughout the Kullu Valley. The second is its annual week-long celebrations of Dussehra, an annual festival honouring Durga's victory over the demon Mahishasura. During **Kullu Dussehra**, hundreds of colourful *devtas* (deities) are brought in on palanquins from across the region to the city's Dhalpur ground, where a chariot bearing an idol of Raghunath, a form of Ram, awaits to give his blessings. The festivities go on for days, drawing in hundreds of thousands of people from Himachal and beyond.

Even if you can't make it for Dussehra, it's still worth visiting Kullu to see the 17th-century **Raghunath Temple** where the Raghunath is worshipped. The temple is just a two-minute walk from the **Sultanpur Palace**, also known as the Rupi Palace, a curious structure that mixes handsome traditional carved-wood elements with garish, brightly hued trim that gives off circus vibes. The palace houses a large collection of

KULLU SHAWLS

Kullu is famous for its shawls, which are usually woven from sheep's wool and have a twill appearance. Most have muted base colours contrasted by borders and edging featuring brightly hued geometric designs. Kullu shawls tend to run large, measuring 1m by 2m, making them ideal for getting an extra layer of warmth during the region's long chilly season. You'll find shops selling shawls of varying quality across Kullu and around, but if you want to be sure you're getting something of decent quality – and supporting local weavers – head to one of the many showrooms run by **Bhuttico**, a weaver's cooperative founded in 1944. It has numerous showrooms across the state, including in Akhara Bazar in Kullu and off Mall Rd in Manali.

Pahari miniature paintings, but if you don't have any royal connections, you'll have to just view it from the outside – the descendants of the erstwhile family live here to this day.

Malana

TIME FROM MANALI: **3HR 40MIN**

Look, don't touch

About a half-hour-long hike into the hills above Malana Dam will take you to Malana, a self-governing village that some say is the world's oldest democracy. Legend has it that Malana's inhabitants are descendants of Alexander the Great's army, and while there are some doubts to that claim, Malanans do speak a form of the Pahari dialect of Hindi that's distinct from other parts of the region. Then again, so do plenty of people in many less-isolated villages. Malana residents also consider outsiders – foreign and Indian alike – impure, and it's verboten to touch anyone (or anything) in the village. Slip up and you'll be faced with a hefty fine of ₹5000 or more.

Malana's curious backstory is certainly one of its biggest draws, as is its typically Himachali architecture, complete with carved wooden terraces and stacked timber and stone. Among some travellers, however, the village is best known for its high-grade hashish (charas) known as Malana cream. Many people trek up here in hopes of scoring some for themselves, but buyer beware: police checks do happen. No matter your motive, be sure to go with a guide who can help show the way and stop you from committing potentially costly taboos.

Manikaran

TIME FROM MANALI: **3½HR**

Healing waters

Although it's only a few kilometres from the hippie encampment of Kasol, a popular summertime getaway among long-term backpackers and fans of psytrance parties, Manikaran feels worlds apart. This pretty town on the banks of the Parvati River is sacred among Sikhs and Hindus alike, and its **Sri Guru Nanak Ji Gurdwara** is a popular spot for both Sikh pilgrims and for travellers wishing to soak away their aches and pains in the temple's hot spring. A **Shiva temple** sits next to the gurdwara and steam from the hot springs adds a mystical look to both holy structures.

Barshaini

TIME FROM MANALI: **4HR**

Hiking in a trekkers' paradise

On a hill overlooking the Parvati River, Barshaini is more of a base for short guided or independent treks than a destination unto itself. Note that Barshaini does have a smattering of guesthouses for those who don't want to make the drive from Manikaran (40 minutes away), the backpacker enclave of Kasol (an hour away) or the transit hub of Bhuntar (2½ hours away) before heading out on a trek. Plenty of guesthouses are also available in nearby villages such as Pulga and Kalga.

One of the most popular routes takes you to **Khir Ganga**, an alpine meadow at an elevation of just under 3000m. The

GETTING HIGH IN THE MOUNTAINS

For many travellers, the chance to try charas – a type of hashish typically made by rubbing fresh cannabis flowers together to produce a resiny concentrate – is among the Parvati Valley's biggest draws. Charas is typically sold by the *tola* (a historic South Asian measurement that equals just under 12g) and is widely available in spots popular with foreign backpackers. It's frequently smoked out in the open, either in spliff form or in a conical pipe known as a chillum. While many people in Himachal turn a blind eye to charas consumption, keep in mind that it is illegal, and getting caught with even a small amount can land you in serious trouble with the cops.

FAT JACKEY/SHUTTERSTOCK

Khir Ganga

easy-moderate 12km trek itself is part of the fun, taking you through a hilly mix of pine-shaded forests and open meadows. At the end of the trek are two hot spring pools – one for gents and one for ladies (bathing suits required) – plus quite a few camps, restaurants and simple guesthouses. While many people come for the day, or spend just one night, you may run into a few expert backpackers on their first or final leg of the much longer and more challenging **Pin-Parvati Pass** trek.

Among the more difficult treks in the Indian Himalaya, the Pin-Parvati Pass trek takes intrepid hikers from Barshaini to Khir Ganga, onwards to Mantalai Lake, and up over the perpetually snowed-in Parvati Pass before spitting them back out in the tiny village of Mudh in Spiti. The conditions here are harsh throughout the year, so most people attempt the journey in September, after the monsoons. Note that this trek is notoriously challenging and technical, requiring serious mountaineering skills, and should not be attempted without a guide, even if you're an experienced hiker. Organised treks are the way to go and often include the services of porters (as pack animals struggle to make it over the pass).

A shorter day-trek option is to head up to **Tosh**, a popular backpacker haunt surrounded by woods. It wasn't until the early 2010s that the Barshaini road was extended to Tosh, and while many visitors these days go there by road, the trail from Barshaini up to the town offers a great escape into nature, even if just for 3km.

Tirthan Valley

TIME FROM MANALI: 4½HR

Natural magic

A quieter (for now) and more rugged alternative to the Parvati Valley, the Tirthan Valley is a gorgeous spot for trekkers, birdwatchers and anglers in search of one of the last easy-to-access stretches of Himalayan magic. While the town of Jibhi is an increasingly popular spot for quiet mountain getaways, most adventurers start in the town of Banjar, where there

CLIMATE CHANGE & LANDSLIDES

Although occasional landslides are inevitable in mountainous regions, Himachal Pradesh has had a notable increase in landslides, cloudbursts and flash floods in recent years. This is largely attributed to a mix of rapid infrastructural changes, including the widening of mountain roads, and a longer and more intense monsoon season brought on by global climate change. The results have been devastating. In 2025, landslides alone caused over 50 deaths in Himachal Pradesh, and thousands more were impacted. Without passable roads, remote communities lose access to shipments of essential goods such as grains and medicine, while farmers from largely agrarian areas are unable to transport goods for sale. For visitors, growing landslide risks mean taking extra care when arranging travel plans, and possibly reconsidering visiting during the rainy season.

THE HIMACHALI DHAM

Although many restaurants in Himachal Pradesh stick to North Indian mainstays or Tibetan or continental food, it's worth seeking out the state's own take on the thali, known as the *dham*. Often served on special occasions, or to special guests, the feast typically consists of a variety of vegetarian Himachali dishes. It usually includes *madra*, a popular yoghurt-based dish made with *chana* (chickpeas) or *rajma* (red kidney beans), depending on what part of the state you're in. Other typical *dham* dishes include *aloo palda* (another yoghurt gravy dish, this time with potatoes), *sepu vadi* (lentil fritters in a spinach gravy) and *khatta kaddu* (tangy pumpkin), all served with mountainous portions of rice and finished with some sort of dessert.

SAIKO3P/SHUTTERSTOCK

are a few guesthouses and tour operators, before heading deeper into the wild.

A 25-minute drive from Banjar takes you to the **Shringa Rishi Temple**. From here, it's a 45-minute steepish hike through the forest to the village of Chehni. The pinnacle attraction here is **Chehni Kothi**, a 10-storey brick-and-timber tower temple built in the earthquake-resistant *kath-kuni* style dating to the 17th century. A few other shorter towers built in the same style surround it, giving the entire place the appearance of a series of watchtowers. While the interiors are off-limits to visitors, the exterior architecture – and forest views – are the real stars of the show.

Himalayan biodiversity at its finest

A UNESCO World Heritage Site since 2014, the 905.4-sq-km **Great Himalayan National Park** *(greathimalayannationalpark.org; per day adult/child ₹800/500)* protects a swathe of some 25 different types of forest that collectively provide refuge for a wide diversity of wildlife, including some threatened species. A huge range of butterfly species live in the park, as do mongooses, pika, civets, gorals and hundreds of types of bird. Elusive snow leopards are occasionally sighted in the park, particularly during the winter months. The only way to experience the core zone of the park is by obtaining a permit and hiring a guide. You can sort out permits and guide service at the **Range Forest Office** in the village of Sairopa and through operators such as **Sunshine Himalayan Adventures** *(sunshineadventure.com)*, which offers single-day and multinight trekking, birding and wildlife-watching excursions into the park.

Rewalsar

Rewalsar

TIME FROM MANALI: **4HR 40MIN**

A lake for all faiths

At an altitude of around 1360m, **Lake Rewalsar** – also known as Tso Pema (Lotus Lake) – is considered one of the most sacred bodies of water in Himachal Pradesh. Because of its holy status, no fishing is allowed here (though you can buy fish food to throw into the water at the **Fish Feeding Point** on the southeastern edge of the lake). While Sikhs, Hindus and Buddhists alike revere the lake, the Buddhist influence is the most noticeable. It's presided over by a giant golden **statue of Padmasambhava** (aka Guru Rinpoche) and is flanked by numerous houses of prayer. These include the **Gurdwara Rewalsar Sahib**, built in 1930 in honour of Guru Gobind Singh, the 10th Sikh guru, who once stayed nearby. Rewalsar also has three Hindu temples – dedicated to Shiva, Krishna and the sage Lomasha – plus a couple of monasteries. One is the **Tso Pema Monastery**, a beautiful tiered white structure adorned with golden and blue detailing; the other is the **Drigung Kagyud Gompa**, where monks can often be seen meditating. If you do just one thing while you're in town, make it a visit to the **Padmasambhava Caves**, a 10km drive from the lake, where Guru Rinpoche is believed to have spent time meditating. Step inside to see a golden image of the Padmasambhava that's kept continuously illuminated by tiny oil lamps.

MONASTERY ETIQUETTE

While Buddhist monasteries generally have a pretty relaxed atmosphere, and aren't typically hyper strict when it comes to protocols, it's still wise to familiarise yourself with etiquette before you enter. First, like many Hindu temples in India (and even some churches), you'll almost always be required to remove your shoes before entering a temple or meditation hall (shoes are fine on monastery grounds, however). It's also polite to dress modestly. Maintain silence (and keep your phone on silent) while inside. Finally, and perhaps most importantly, do not point your feet at images of the Buddha. If you choose to sit on the floor, you should either sit cross-legged or kneel to avoid accidentally offending someone.

Keylong

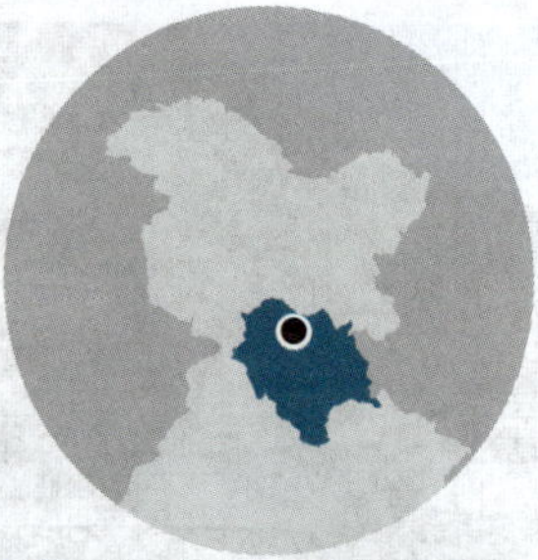

MOUNTAIN VIEWS | ANCIENT ARTEFACTS | FRESCO-FILLED MONASTERIES

Keylong, the district headquarters of Lahaul and Spiti, is where many travellers get their first introduction to the region, particularly if they're coming from Ladakh or Manali. At first glance, this little town doesn't look like much, despite being Lahaul's main commercial and transport hub. While many see Keylong as little more than a good place to stock up on snacks and supplies before venturing across the Kunzum Pass and over into Spiti, it's actually a great place to familiarise yourself with the region – and adjust to life at higher altitudes.

Give yourself a bit of time in and around town and you'll be rewarded with the chance to hike through quiet villages, explore ancient monasteries adorned with Buddhist art and prepare yourself for the cultural traditions you'll encounter as you travel deeper into one of India's remotest regions.

GETTING AROUND

Keylong is compact and its main drag, graciously referred to as 'The Mall', is less than 2km long, and is easy to get around on foot. Seasonal buses to and from Keylong stop at the New Bus Stand on the eastern end of The Mall and connect the town to Manali, Shimla, Leh and Delhi. Private minibuses and shared jeeps are also available to other destinations in Lahaul and Spiti and beyond. **Brokpa Adventure Tours** *(brokpatours.com)* can help arrange tickets.

Museum on the Mall

Learn about local traditions

Right on The Mall in the heart of Keylong, the **Lahaul-Spiti Tribal Museum** *(free)* is a good place to get familiar with some of the cultural traditions of the surrounding region. The extensive collection here includes everything from *chaam* (dance masks) to *thod pa* (ceremonial vessels made from skulls), all labelled in English.

TOP TIP

Keylong sits at an altitude of around 3156m, just high enough to put you at risk of altitude sickness if you don't acclimate carefully. If you've come from a lower elevation, it's a good idea to take things easy for the first day or two while you adjust.

Ghar Valley Gompa

Mountain views and towering thangkas

On a hilltop overlooking Keylong, about 6km by road from the centre of town, the 16th-century **Shashur Gompa** is the head gompa of the Ghar Valley. The views are magnificent, but the real draw is the Tibetan religious art found inside, including intricately painted walls, statues of the Buddha, the goddess Tara and 3rd-century monk Aryadeva, as well as massive *thangkas*, some measuring around 5m in height.

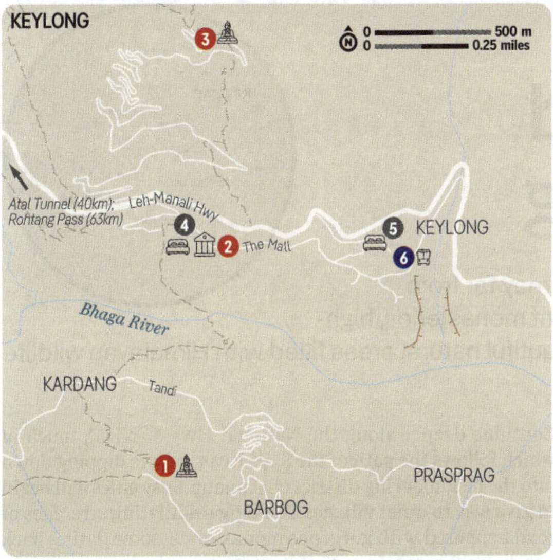

SIGHTS
1 Kardang Gompa
2 Lahaul-Spiti Tribal Museum
3 Shashur Gompa

SLEEPING
4 Kyelang Times Stays & Restaurant
5 Nordaling Guest House

TRANSPORT
6 New Bus Stand

The Journey to Kardang

Walking to Lahaul's former capital

Across the Bhaga River from Keylong, the village of **Kardang** was once the capital of Lahaul. Its key attraction is the **Kardang Gompa**, a Drukpa (Red Hat) monastery that was built in the 12th century, fell into disrepair and was revitalised in the early 20th century by Lama Norbu Rinpoche, who transformed it into a major cultural and educational centre. Inside is a huge prayer wheel, beautiful *thangkas* and frescoes, and a collection of ancient texts, musical instruments and other items.

Although Kardang is just across the valley from Keylong, getting there by car takes about 45 minutes, as you'll need to head west to the Tandi Bridge in order to cross the river, only to head back east once you get to the other side. If you're coming on foot, you can take a stair-path from Vikrant Homestay down to the river, cross the River Bhaga over a small footbridge and then climb uphill for roughly 1km until you reach the main road (Tandi Piukar). From here, you can turn right toward the village or follow the road to the left uphill for another 800m until you reach the gompa.

THE ATAL TUNNEL

Getting from Manali to Keylong used to require driving over the 3978m **Rohtang Pass**, which is usually snowed in from early November until mid-May. In 2020, things got easier thanks to the launch of the **Atal Tunnel**, a 9km tube that zips under the pass, reducing the journey time by upwards of three hours. The tunnel is theoretically open throughout the year, but stretches of the National Hwy 3 (NH3) that leads to the tunnel can shut to tourist traffic when there's significant snow or ice on the road. If you're travelling by car, you can still cross the Rohtang Pass (permits required, available at *rohtangpermits.nic.in*). Motorbikes are no longer allowed on the pass and must use the Atal Tunnel.

Beyond Keylong

You won't have to journey far from Keylong to find ancient monasteries, high-altitude lakes and beautiful natural areas filled with Himalayan wildlife

Places

GETTING AROUND

HRTC buses connect Keylong with other destinations across Lahaul and Spiti and beyond, though service comes to a halt during the winter months. Private shared-jeeps, minibuses and buses are also available when the weather permits. Taxis are an attractive option if you want a bit more comfort and can be relatively affordable if you're travelling in a group or find others to share costs with you. Cabs are available through local providers such as **Keylinga Taxi Service** *(7018778410)*.

Continue deeper along the National Hwy 5 (NH5), much of which follows the path of the Spiti River, before dipping down into the neighbouring district of Kinnaur. Busy cities will begin to give way to quiet villages and long undulating stretches of road peppered with gorgeous monasteries, some dating back nearly 1000 years. In fact, if it weren't for the presence of colourful Indian lorries and road signs in Hindi and English, it would be easy to think you'd crossed into neighbouring Tibet. The cultural and architectural similarities are understandable, of course: both areas were originally introduced to Buddhism by Padmasambhava in the 8th century and their proximity has kept them closely intertwined.

Chandratal

TIME FROM KEYLONG: **4HR**

A visit to the moon lake

At an elevation of 4270m, crystalline Chandratal gets its name – which means 'moon lake' – from its crescent shape. The remarkably clear waters of this mountain lake are enough to merit a visit, but be prepared for a 20-minute high-altitude hike between the car park and the lake's pristine shores. During the springtime, the meadows flanking the water erupt in a flurry of wildflowers. Keep your eyes peeled for kestrels, golden eagles, red foxes, Himalayan ibexes and – if you're very lucky – elusive snow leopards.

Kaza

TIME FROM KEYLONG: **8HR**

The gateway to Spiti

Kaza is many travellers' first introduction to Spiti, but most people use it more as a jumping-off point than a destination unto itself. It's a good place to book bus tickets or taxis, organise trekking experiences or mingle with other travellers at cafes and guesthouses such as Sakya Abode (p309) before heading off to more enticing spots.

Cultural history and wildlife

A half-hour drive north of Kaza, on a 4116m-high hilltop, **Ki Gompa** *(keymonasteryspiti.org)* is not only the largest of Spiti's monasteries, but also among its oldest. Founded by Buddhist sage Dromtön in the 11th century, the monastery provides education for over 200 school-aged monks at any given time. It also welcomes visitors who want to see its superb collection of *thangkas* and other religious paintings along with ancient manuscripts and musical instruments. You can witness a *puja* in the new prayer hall if you come first thing in the morning; come during Losar (which usually falls in February) or during the annual Ki Chaam Festival celebrations to see the gompa's collection of ceremonial masks.

From Ki Gompa, it's only around 8km to **Kibber**, a popular hiking area and the starting point of the 10-night Tso Moriri Lake trek via the Parang Pass. Kibber is also the gateway to the **Kibber Wildlife Sanctuary**, a 1400-sq-km protected habitat for species such as blue sheep, ibex and Himalayan griffon vultures.

Komic

TIME FROM KEYLONG: **9HR**

Visit a monastic museum

Among the highest villages in India with motorable road connections, Komic's main draw is the small **Tangyud Gompa**, a compound featuring a new and active monastery and an older historic building that has housed the **Komick Museum** *(₹50)* since it was inaugurated in 2022. Spread over two floors, the collection showcases a range of permanent exhibits covering everything from cultural history to Spiti's spiritual traditions. Highlights include displays of Spiti clothing and religious items, along with an exhibit on the artisans of Spiti and their creations. Other highlights include 'Nature's Story', which traces the geological history of Spiti, and 'Drink Up', which explores the stories behind Spiti's traditional beverages.

Dhankar

TIME FROM KEYLONG: **9½HR**

A real cliffhanger

Few sights in Spiti are more likely to make you do a double take than that of **Dhankar Gompa**. Straddling a jagged cliff at an altitude of around 3370m, this historic monastery once served a very practical purpose: guarding the surrounding valley from invaders. You can check out the architecture from

PERMITS

Foreign passport holders wishing to visit certain areas of Himachal Pradesh, particularly near the Tibetan border, must obtain a Protected Area Permit (PAP) in advance. These permits are sometimes erroneously referred to as 'Inner Line Permits' (which are actually permits for Indian citizens wishing to visit restricted areas). Permits are currently required for the Pooh area in Kinnaur, as well as Khab, Samdo, Dhankar, Tabo, Gompa, Kaza, Morang and Dubling in Lahaul and Spiti. If you're unsure whether you'll need a permit, check before setting out. Permits are available in Keylong at the **Deputy Commissioner Office** *(01900-202501)* and at the **Assistant Deputy Commissioner's Office** in Kaza *(01906-222202)*. For up-to-date information on requirements and forms, visit *hplahaulspiti.nic.in/foreigner-section*.

EATING IN KAZA: OUR PICKS

Deyzor Hotel Restaurant: Hearty tandoor-cooked Indian dishes or rich Western fare at a bohemian spot. *8am-4.30pm & 6.30-10pm Apr-Nov* ₹₹

Himalayan Café: Traveller fave in Kaza's market with pancakes, falafel and Tibetan *thenkthuk*. Vegan and gluten-free options. *7.30am-10.30pm Apr-Nov* ₹₹

Café Piti: An extensive menu of Tibetan and continental dishes, along with Spiti specialties such as *zara*, a barley dish. *11am-9.30pm Mon-Sat, from noon Sun Apr-Dec* ₹₹

Sól Café: Grab baked goods and refill your water bottle at this travellers' cafe run by social enterprise Ecosphere. *8.30am-9pm May-Oct, 9am-8pm Apr-Nov* ₹₹

HELPING HANDS

Ruchi Dhona, founder of Let's Open a Book - a Manali-based nonprofit free library programme for kids that previously operated in Kaza - shares tips on how to responsibly contribute to improving the lives of local children. *@ruchi_dhona*

Instead of trying to contribute directly, it helps if people can do some research about what NGOs are out there. A lot of people who come to Spiti bring chocolates and stationery with them and then just randomly distribute them to children that they meet, but most children in Spiti have decent access to stationery, even those who go to government schools. Giving away chocolate can complicate existing health issues. Access to dental care is a big issue right now. Instead, donate supplies or cash to an organisation or a school that can use it mindfully.

KIWISOUL/SHUTTERSTOCK

Dhankar Gompa (p291)

below or pop inside to see the collection of ancient paintings and scriptures before making the trek up to **Dhankar Tso**, a small lake with epic views located a tough hour-long hike uphill.

Tabo

TIME FROM KEYLONG: 11HR

Inside India's oldest Buddhist monastery

Founded in 996, **Tabo Gompa** *(tabomonastery.org)* may likely be the oldest continuously operating Buddhist monastery in the country. Although this ancient complex lacks the initial grandeur found at some of Himachal's more picturesque spiritual sights, first impressions can deceive. Step inside the simple mud-hut structures to reveal a fabulous collection of intricate stucco paintings and sculptures. Don't miss the life-sized statues of bodhisattvas in the main assembly hall, one of the oldest parts of the monastery. Tabo also has a number of small caves worth checking out, situated just above the main road. A steep 200m path will take you right to them.

Kalpa

DISTINCT TEMPLES | BUDDHIST GOMPAS | ALPINE HIKES

The hilltop hamlet of Kalpa is as enticing for its traditional timber architecture as for its dizzying views of the snowclad Himalaya. It's a good base from which to begin your explorations of Himachal Pradesh's Kinnaur district, a mountainous region known for its blend of Hindu and Tibetan Buddhist cultural and dharmic practices and for its forests and apple orchards. Kalpa sits on the outskirts of Rekong Peo, Kinnaur's primary commercial and transport hub. While many through-travellers stop in the area just to change buses or get Protected Area Permits to visit Lahaul and Spiti, it's worth sticking around to experience this oft-overlooked stretch of Himachal. With just a few days in Kalpa, you'll see Hindu temples made of carved wood thriving simultaneously alongside Buddhist gompas, hike through mountain meadows or munch on fresh-from-the-orchard apples while gazing out at the grandeur of the Himalaya.

TOP TIP

You can get Protected Area Permits in Rekong Peo with the help of local tour agencies such as **Monk Travels** *(9805530056)*. For a few hundred rupees, agents will sort out your paperwork before marching you over to the nearby Deputy Commissioner's Office to get everything finalised.

Alpine Adventures

On the trail to Chaka Meadows

If you're training for longer treks or just want better views of Chaka Peak to the west of town, it's worth the 2½-hour hike (each way) up to **Chaka Meadows**. A trail leads from Kalpa–Roghi Rd and up along a stream fed by Chaka Peak, through coniferous forests and meadows that fill with wildflowers in summer. Overnight camping is available during the summer

GETTING AROUND

There's a direct overnight bus from Shimla to Kalpa (10½ hours) and another dozen-odd buses that travel between Shimla and the Rekong Peo Bus Stand, about 6km away. Buses between Rekong Peo's Main Bazaar and Kalpa run regularly and taxis are available from the **Kinnaur Taxi Operators Union** *(8091772842)* stand at the bus station if you don't want to make the 90-minute trek to Kalpa on foot. Kalpa itself is small and is easy to get around on foot. As it sits at just below 3000m in elevation and is hilly, pace yourself – particularly if you're coming from somewhere lower in altitude.

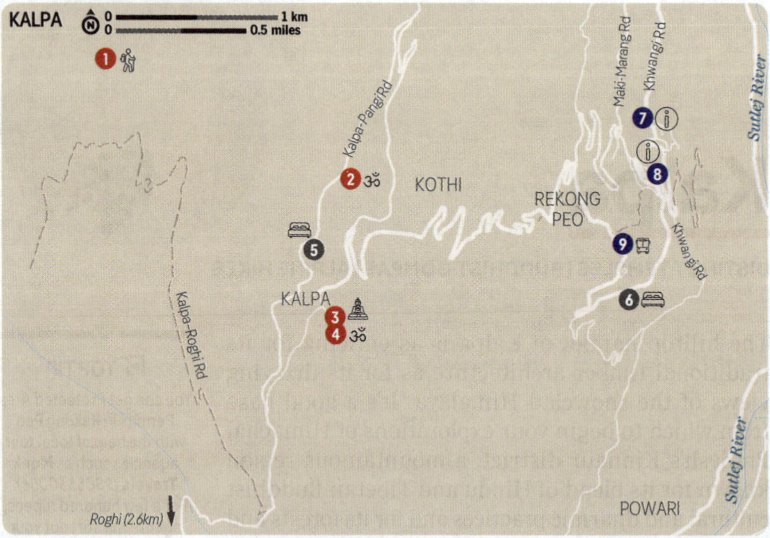

SIGHTS
1 Chaka Meadows
2 Chandika Devi Temple
3 Kalpa Monastery
4 Narayan-Nagini Temple

SLEEPING
5 Grand Shamba-La
6 Wanderers Homestay

INFORMATION
7 Deputy Commisioner's Office
8 Monk Travels

TRANSPORT
9 Bus Stand

season. You can arrange a local guide and book accommodation in advance through **Raacho Trekkers** (*raachotrekkers.com*).

Double Your Prayers

Interfaith explorations

Tibetan Buddhism and Hinduism coexist in Kinnaur, and there are few places this is more apparent than in Kalpa. A five-minute walk from the centre takes you to the **Kalpa Monastery**, a small complex that has been the site of a monastery for three millennia (though the current structure dates to the 20th century). The colourful interiors are often closed to visitors, but you can admire the white chorten at the entrance before circumambulating the main structure clockwise, spinning its brass prayer wheels. Even if you don't see the interior, it's worth coming for the architecture, which includes intricately carved wooden doors and archways crowned by sloping roofs. A two-minute walk from the gompa, the wooden **Narayan-Nagini Temple Complex** has a similar aesthetic, blending Kinnauri carving and pagoda-style roofs more commonly found at Tibetan temples and monasteries.

Village Goddess

Visiting Kothi's Chandika Devi Temple

Between Kalpa and Rekong Peo, Kothi (also known as Koshtampi) is known for its wooden temple complex dedicated to the goddess Chandika, a form of Mahadevi who protects the local area. The **Chandika Devi Temple**'s architecture alone makes a visit worthwhile, with sloping slate roofs and intricately carved wooden trim and pillars set against a backdrop of jagged Himalayan peaks. If you're in town in July, you may get to witness the Dakhraini Festival, when the deity is brought outside and honoured with flowers and a folk dance.

Beyond Kalpa

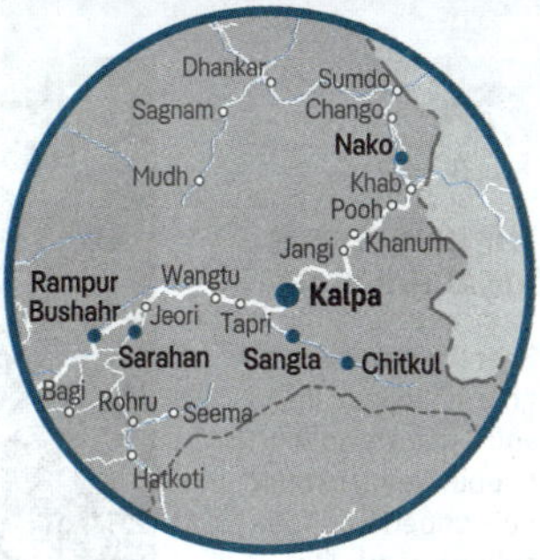

Quiet valley villages dotted with wood-and-slate architecture give way to apple orchards, thick pine forests and towering Himalayan peaks

To get a feel for life in Kinnaur, head beyond the Kalpa–Rekong Peo area, through valleys and along narrow mountain roads, where hairpin turns occasionally give way to villages built on sheer cliffs. Quintessentially Kinnauri temples, characterised by carved wooden edifices crowned with pagoda-style slate roofs, stand testament to the region's historic (and current) Tibetan and Hindu influences, while behemoth mountains beckon intrepid trekkers in search of challenging adventures. Much of the region is split by the National Hwy 5 (NH5), part of which follows the trajectory of the Raj-era Hindustan-Tibet Rd. This connects the region with Shimla to the southwest before turning into the NH505 that continues into the Spiti Valley.

Places

Sangla

TIME FROM KALPA: **1HR 15MIN**

A Sangla Valley stroll

The largest settlement in the Sangla Valley, Sangla is a gorgeous little town where the slate roofs of quintessentially Kinnauri wood-and-stone temples appear to mimic the sloping mountains in the background. It's also the final stop on the Rupin Pass Trek (p298). While many people use the town as a post-adventure transit hub, at most spending the night before catching a bus onwards to Shimla or Delhi, it's worth sticking around to check out Sangla's two main highlights. The first is the **Shree Bering Nag Temple** in the lower part of town, a multi-shrine complex full of beautiful examples of Kinnauri wood carving and a mix of Kinnauri Hindu and Tibetan elements.

From here, it's about a 2km climb up steep trails and stone steps past a centuries-old Badrinath (Lord Vishnu) shrine to the multi-storey **Kamru Fort**. This ancient stone-and-wood complex was once the capital of the Bushahr Kingdom, which ruled the area from the 15th century until the late 19th century, when the British took over administration in the area. Although the kingdom is long gone, the royal family has remained involved in local politics: the titular raja of the erstwhile kingdom is Himachal Pradesh legislative assembly

GETTING AROUND

Public buses depart from Rekong Peo to destinations elsewhere in Himachal and beyond. Taxis are a more expensive, but much more comfortable, option, and make it possible to see a lot in a short amount of time. **Harry Taxi Services** *(9015330063)* in Rekong Peo offers day-trip and overnight services throughout the region. Landslides along sections of the NH5 near the Sutlej River are a frequent occurrence, particularly in areas where hydroelectric projects have loosened the surrounding rock strata.

THE UBIQUITOUS HIMACHALI CAP

Spend any amount of time in Kinnaur and you'll quickly notice people wearing round, flat-topped wool hats adorned with solid-coloured flaps. Known as *thepang*, these caps – worn by men and women alike – serve both as an outward symbol of Kinnauri identity and a protective layer against harsh, and oftentimes frigid, mountain air. More recently, they've come to represent political affiliation (members of the Congress Party often wear caps with green bands while BJP members go for red bands). Similarly shaped hats are found throughout much of Himachal Pradesh and neighbouring Uttarakhand, and each area has its own distinct style. Kullu's caps, for example, typically feature bands with vividly hued geometric patterns.

SAIKO3P/SHUTTERSTOCK

Padam Palace

member Vikramaditya Singh. The fort is home to a temple dedicated to Kamakhya Devi, a form of Kali more commonly associated with tantric Shaktism in Assam – legend has it that the deity housed in the temple was brought to Himachal from Guwahati's famous Kamakya Temple. If you want to go inside, you'll need to wear a cap and a cummerbund, available to borrow out front.

Chitkul

TIME FROM KALPA: 3½ HR

At the edge of India

The final inhabited village before the Tibetan border, Chitkul draws international visitors looking for a relaxed place to take in mountain scenery or a base to do a bit of hiking (just note that you'll need a permit to head east). Smack in the middle of the village is the **Mathi Devi Temple**, a Kinnauri-style structure covered with gorgeous wood carvings.

Sarahan

TIME FROM KALPA: 3HR 40MIN

Kinnauri temple architecture at its finest

Just off the road from Kalpa to Shimla, Sarahan – the erstwhile summer capital of the Bushahr Kingdom – is best known for its **Bhimakali Temple**, an excellent example of Kinnauri temple architecture. It's spread out over three courtyards, with two primary towers dominating the complex, each of which contains a shrine to Bhimakali, a locally revered form of the goddess Durga. The structures here were built by layering stone and timber, a technique designed to help minimise the impact of earthquakes. Note that before entering, you'll need to deposit your camera, phone and any leather goods in lockers. Men will be provided with a small loaner cap to wear while exploring the complex.

Rampur Bushahr

TIME FROM KALPA: **3HR 20MIN**

A castle in the clouds

A good place to break up the journey between Kinnaur and Shimla, Rampur was once the capital of the princely state of Bushahr. Little remains of its regal past save for the city's main attraction: the extravagant **Padam Palace**. This whimsical complex, which features blends of Indo-Saracenic and Kinnauri styles, was commissioned in the early 20th century by then-ruler Raja Padam Singh and includes ornately carved pillars, screens and archways, constructed largely of wood and stone. The gardens are open to visitors free of cost and the exterior architecture alone merits a visit. If you want to spend time inside, you can book a room at the Nau Nabh (p309), a heritage hotel that occupies a renovated adjunct of the palatial complex.

Nako

TIME FROM KALPA: **3HR**

The heart of Buddhist Kinnaur

On the road to Tabo, Nako is a lovely little hamlet set against the Reo Purgyil mountain. Although Nako is part of Kinnaur, in many ways it feels more like Spiti, owing largely to the presence of its star attraction, the **Nako Gompa**, believed to date back to the 11th century. Built in a style similar to that of Spiti's Tabo Gompa (p292), the monastery's biggest draw is its large collection of ancient murals and centuries-old idols made of clay. If you have time, it's also worth taking a gander at **Nako Lake** on the south side of town, where you'll find a small rock shrine said to preserve the footprint of Buddhist saint Padmasambhava (Guru Rinpoche), who many believe meditated here. The lake is also the starting point for the trek to the monastery village of **Tashigang**, about a four-hour walk away. Just be prepared for steep stretches at high altitude and consider hiring a guide to keep you safe. Foreign citizens should bring their passport and Protected Area Permit along with them for the hike.

PHULAICH FAIR

Kinnaur's most spectacular annual event is arguably the Phulaich Fair, also known as Ookhayang, which usually takes place at some point in September during the Hindu month of Bhadra. The festival both honours the shift from summer to winter and pays respects to deceased relatives. During the celebrations, groups of people from towns and villages across the region head up to alpine meadows to collect colourful ladra flowers to bring back to their communities. People also make offerings of floral garlands, rice and wine to their passed-away relatives, which are later redistributed to those in need. While traditions vary a bit across Kinnaur, you can expect to experience plenty of music, dancing and – of course – fragrant blooms.

WALKING TOUR

Rupin Pass Trek

In just under a week, this trek takes you through pine-clad forests and across emerald-green meadows, past a mountain waterfall, over the 4650m Rupin Pass and into Kinnaur. It's considered a moderate-to-difficult journey, with a mix of long days with steep hikes and serious elevation changes and more relaxed stretches that will help you gradually acclimatise. The best time to do this hike is during the May–June summer season or in September or early October, just after the monsoons, road and trail conditions permitting.

1 Bawta

The trek starts in the Bawta area, about a nine-hour drive from Shimla or 12 hours from Kalpa by road. It's wise to arrive in the village the day before to rest up for your expedition, and homestay accommodation is usually included in trekking packages.

The Hike: Expect a short but challenging 5km trek along a steep, tree-lined hillside to the village of Jakha. The journey takes four to five hours.

2 Jakha

Spend the night in Jakha, nicknamed the 'hanging village' because of its cliffside position that makes it appear suspended from the mountain. It's the last village before Rupin Pass. While some guided Rupin Pass treks only go as far as Saruwas Thatch, about six hours from Jakha, many continue for a couple of hours further to Dhanderas Thatch.

AMIT KG/SHUTTERSTOCK

Rupin Pass trail

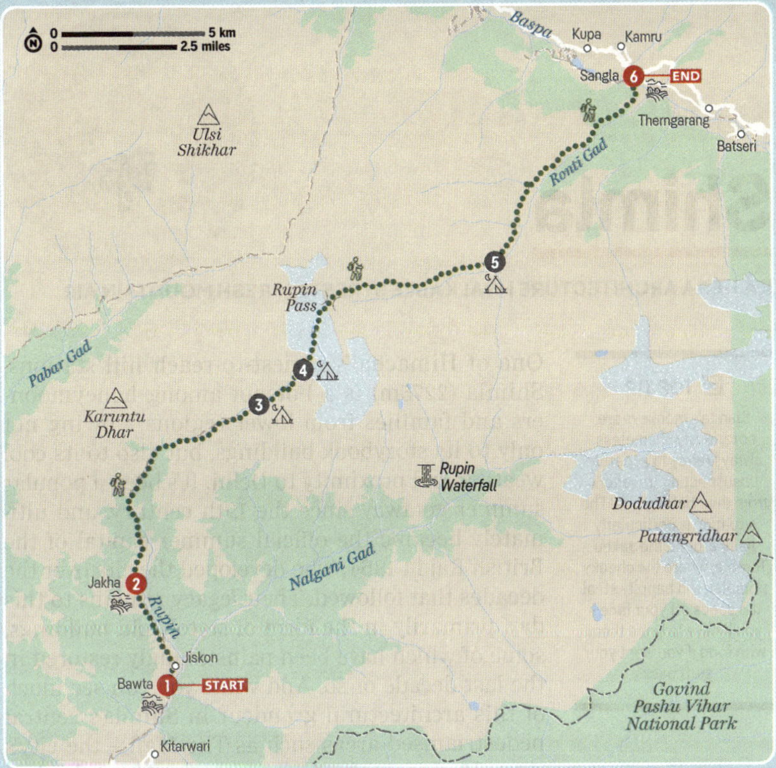

The Hike: Whichever your route, this day of trekking passes through coniferous forests, alongside a river and across a bridge made of snow (weather permitting).

3 Dhanderas Thatch

Arrive at the meadow campsite of Dhanderas Thatch at just over 3500m in altitude and take in glorious views of the Rupin Waterfall, which cascades down a not-so-distant mountain face before transforming into a stream.

The Hike: Get a good night's sleep before continuing your ascent toward the upper part of the waterfall, about a three-hour hike away.

4 Upper Waterfall

Arrive at the Upper Waterfall Camp and take it easy: your job here is to acclimatise so that you'll be in tip-top shape for the challenge of traversing Rupin Pass the next day. A highlight of this stop is the chance to see Rupin Waterfall from the top.

The Hike: Now that you're more acclimated, you'll be ready to make the 12km hike across the 4650m Rupin Pass, climbing up steep snowfields before hiking (or sliding) down to your camp at Ronti Gad.

5 Ronti Gad

It may already be dark by the time you arrive at your final camp, Ronti Gad, on the other side of the Rupin Pass. When you wake up the next morning, you'll be treated to a gorgeous alpine meadow flanked by snowcapped peaks.

The Hike: Make the steep trek through rocky meadows that eventually give way to the small village of Sangla.

6 Sangla

Organised treks end in Sangla. From here, buses reach other destinations in Kinnaur, including Chitkul and Rekong Peo, as well as Shimla and Delhi.

Shimla

RAJ-ERA ARCHITECTURE | WALKABLE STREETS | FRESH MOUNTAIN AIR

TOP TIP

Shimla's monkeys are notoriously shameless, always ready to separate unsuspecting travellers from their belongings. The situation is particularly hairy around the Jakhu Temple, where the cheeky primates will happily steal the specs off your face – you'll have to bribe them with food if you want your stuff back.

One of Himachal's easiest-to-reach hill stations, Shimla (2275m) is a hotspot among honeymooners and families from lower regions – owing not only to its storybook buildings, but also to its cool weather and proximity to Delhi. It's been a popular summer getaway since the 19th century, and ultimately became the official summer capital of the British Raj in 1864, who developed the city over the decades that followed. Their legacy remains to this day, primarily in the form of stately old buildings, some of which have been painstakingly restored in the last decade or so. And while you can see much of this architectural grandeur in Shimla's central pedestrianised areas such as The Mall – the city's shop-lined main thoroughfare – and The Ridge just above it, it's worth venturing out a bit further to get a good feel for what Shimla has to offer.

Curtain Call

A glimpse into Shimla's dramatic past

Ever since it opened back in 1887, the **Gaiety Theatre** *(gaiety.in; ₹25)* has been a hub of cultural life in Shimla. It was designed by Henry Irwin, the architect behind Shimla's Viceregal Lodge and the Mysore Palace in Mysuru (p808). This Gothic Revival structure was originally part of a larger complex,

GETTING AROUND

Shimla is a walker's city, but while most of The Ridge and The Mall are strictly for pedestrians, taxis are easy to come by in non-pedestrian areas. Local buses run on the city's Ring Rd, while long-distance coaches depart from the Inter State Bus Terminal (ISBT) in the Tutikandi neighbourhood, about 6km west of The Mall.

Train service to Shimla is limited to a narrow-rail gauge line that connects the city to Kalka. Alliance Air operates flights between Shimla Airport in Jubbarhatti – 17km away – and Delhi, Amritsar and Kangra (for McLeod Ganj), but service can be unreliable and cancellations frequent, especially when fog levels are high.

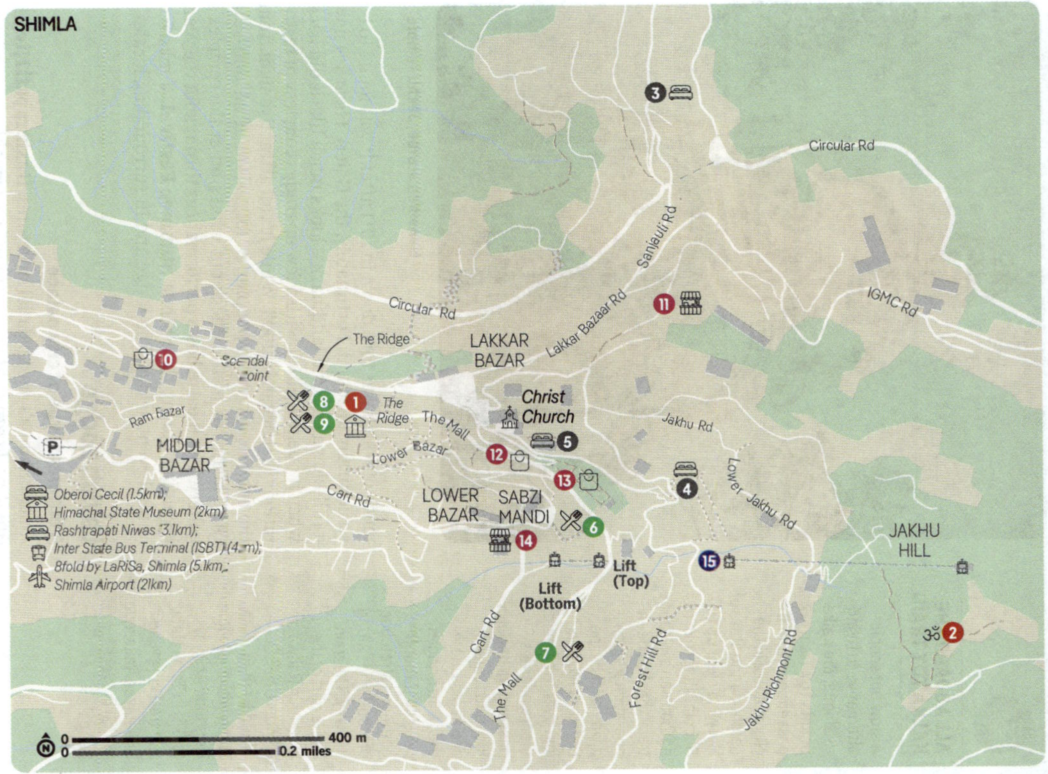

SIGHTS
1 Gaiety Theatre
2 Jakhu Temple

SLEEPING
3 Chapslee
4 Hosteller Shimla
5 YMCA Tourist Hostel

EATING
6 Amaaya
7 Café Simla Times
8 Hide Out Cafe
9 Himachali Rasoi

SHOPPING
10 Himachal Emporium
11 Lakkar Bazar
12 Maria Brothers
13 Simla Shawls by FW
14 Tibetan Market

TRANSPORT
15 Jakhu Ropeway

ALL ABOARD THE KALKA TOY TRAIN

A slow but scenic alternative to flying to Shimla, the Kalka Shimla Toy Train takes passengers from the city of Kalka in the neighbouring state of Haryana clear up to Shimla, all thanks to a 92km narrow-gauge track that has been operational since it was built by the British in 1903. In just over five hours, the train ferries passengers through 100-odd tunnels and across more than 800 bridges, passing through gorgeous stretches of woodlands along the way. The train line is part of the Mountain Railways of India UNESCO World Heritage Site, along with the Nilgiri Mountain Railway (p978) in Tamil Nadu and the Darjeeling Himalayan Railway (p463) in West Bengal.

PAHA1205/SHUTTERSTOCK

Hanuman statue, Jakhu Temple

much of which was torn down in 1911 after it was found to be structurally unsound. Fortunately, the Gaicty Theatre – now a full-blown cultural landmark – looks much like it did back when it opened, albeit with a few upgrades courtesy of restorations that began in 2003. While it's an attractive sight from the outside, it's worth popping in for a show at the 300-seat Old Theatre or just to check out what's on at the complex's gallery. The theatre hosts performances throughout the year, including during the Shimla **Summer Festival**, a massive annual event held at The Ridge and in surrounding locales.

Lavish Lodge

A different type of city palace

Among Shimla's most palatial structures, **Rashtrapati Niwas** (*visit.rashtrapatibhavan.gov.in/visit/rashtrapati-niwas-mashobra-shimla/vm; ₹250*), still referred to locally by its former name, the Viceregal Lodge, is among Henry Irwin's

EATING IN SHIMLA: OUR PICKS

Amaaya: A sophisticated spot that serves hearty Indian and international dishes plus beautifully presented desserts. *12-11pm* ₹₹

Café Simla Times: Dine on Indian, Indo-Chinese and Italian dishes while sitting under a curved frosted-glass roof at this sleek bar and restaurant. *1.30-10.30pm* ₹₹

Himachali Rasoi: Pull up a seat at one of the cedar tables in this cosy cafe, where traditional Himachali cuisine takes centre stage. *12.30-9pm* ₹₹

Hide Out Cafe: Come to this no-frills spot for sandwiches, snacks and delicious espresso drinks. *9am-10pm* ₹₹

finest creations. This Jacobethan-style state house was originally the official summer home of British viceroys under the Raj, and it was here that the Simla Conference, a pivotal event in defining the path for India's eventual independence, took place. It was also the first building in Shimla to have electricity. Today, the palace houses the Indian Institute of Advanced Study (IIAS), and most of the property is off limits to the public. However, you can still wander the fountain-filled gardens or sign up for a tour that will take you into a few key rooms, where you'll be able to admire beautiful teak woodwork and a smattering of period decor.

Art Smart

Himachali history unveiled

A 20-minute walk east of Rashtrapati Niwas will take you to the **Himachal State Museum** *(himachalstatemuseum.in; adult/child ₹150/₹30)*, which occupies an old Victorian mansion that was retrofitted to become a museum. This government-run space, spread out over three floors, houses a massive collection of everything from old coins and stamps to religious sculptures and carvings. There's also a fine selection of miniature paintings, with sections dedicated not only to Himachal's native Pahari art, but also to Sikh and Rajasthani styles. History fans should pay a visit to the Freedom Movement Gallery, which features exhibits recounting the story of the Indian Independence movement with a particular emphasis on the area now known as Himachal Pradesh.

Up & Away

A holy hilltop

Surrounded by trees on the top of Jakhu Hill, the highest point in Shimla, the **Jakhu Temple** is a historic holy place dedicated to Lord Hanuman, the half-human, half-simian servant of Ram and a key figure in the Ramayana. It's also the site of what's allegedly the world's largest Hanuman statue, a 108ft-tall orange depiction of Ram's simian servant that towers over the surrounding tree canopy. Like many Hanuman temples in India, the Jakhu Temple gets lots of monkeys, so avoid carrying food and keep your belongings secure. To get there, you can either take a 45-minute hike up a steep footpath that leads from Christ Church up to the temple (rent a stick to keep monkeys away) or catch a six-minute ride up on the **Jakhu Ropeway** *(jakhuropewayshimla.com; adult/child one way ₹252/200, return ₹467/381)*, which departs from the lower part of The Ridge.

WHERE TO SHOP IN SHIMLA

Himachal Emporium: This state government-run craft emporium sells a wide range of clothing and home decor items from across Himachal Pradesh, all at fixed prices.

Simla Shawls by FW: Choose from a huge selection of high-quality shawls, including the Kullu variety, at this Mall shop across from Rani Jhansi Park.

Maria Brothers: Browse through piles of secondhand books, including rare editions and maps at this beloved Shimla institution, which opened in the 1940s.

Lakkar Bazar: Get ready to bargain at this small market, where you'll find plenty of knickknacks, electronics and home goods alongside shawls and warm jumpers.

Tibetan Market: Pick up colourful prayer flags, chunky beaded jewellery and Western-style apparel from the small vendors at this indoor marketplace.

A WALK BACK IN TIME

Discover Shimla's architectural highlights on this walking tour through the city.

START	END	LENGTH
Gorton Castle	Christ Church	2.8km; 1½hr

Start your walk at 1 **Gorton Castle**, about 600m northeast of the Shimla Railway Station on The Mall. Another three minutes' walk east will take you to the 2 **Railway Board Building**, a fire-engine-red and beige structure made of iron and steel for optimal fire resistance. Continue east, taking your next right onto Gulmarg Rd and walking for another 500m until you get to 3 **St Michael's Catholic Cathedral** (1885), the city's first Catholic church. Stop to admire this large, French Gothic–style stone structure before popping inside to check out its stained-glass windows. Then walk 10 minutes to 4 **Bantony Castle**, the former summer residence of the Maharaja of Sirmaur, its white facade contrasted with dark Tudor accents and sharply slanted red roofs and porticos. Next, head east to the 19th-century 5 **General Post Office**, a red-and-white timber-framed structure that resembles a cross between a Swiss chalet and a candy cane. It's right by 6 **Scandal Point**, among Shimla's most popular viewpoints. About 100m to the east sits Shimla's 7 **Town Hall**, with its mix of grey stone bricks and Tudor Revival detailing. From here, take a leisurely stroll down The Mall before zipping sharply back up to The Ridge to visit neo-Gothic 8 **Christ Church**, among the oldest churches in India.

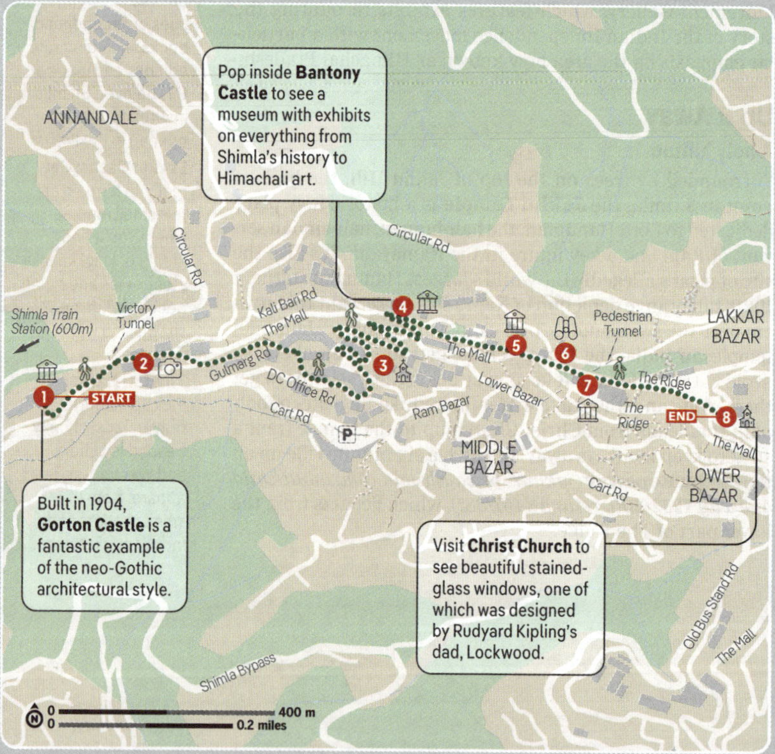

Beyond Shimla

See the quieter side of Himachal Pradesh, where the historic buildings are almost as beautiful as the hilly forests that surround them.

Places

While Shimla is one of the most popular spots in the state, you won't have to journey far to find yourself in more peaceful locations, many with equally gorgeous deodar forests, hilltop views and heritage buildings. Beauty abounds in every direction, but some of the most interesting options - at least for history and architecture fans - are south of the celebrated hill station, often on or near the National Hwy 5 (NH5). Among the deodar forests and towering hills, you'll find laid-back towns built around the historic palaces of royals who once ruled these lands (many of which have since been converted into heritage hotels that exude old-fashioned elegance). Best of all, you'll never be far from natural areas with stellar views.

Chail

TIME FROM SHIMLA: **2HR**

Take that, Shimla!

If you've had enough of Shimla's crowds, a moderately quieter - but not as architecturally rich - alternative is Chail, which was founded by the Maharaja of Patiala after he was ousted from Shimla. He chose this spot, spread across three hills, because it was within view of British-run Shimla, but higher in altitude. Today, the chance to stay in his 1891-built **Chail Palace** *(hptdc.in/index.php/chail-the-palace; adult/child ₹200/free)*, now a Himachal Pradesh tourism board–run hotel (p309), is among the hill station's biggest draws. For a real treat, book the Maharaja Suite, which has an antique fireplace and views all the way to Shimla, at least on clear days. Chail is also home to one of the world's highest cricket pitches, the **Chail Cricket Ground**, about 2.5km from the palace. The area's other big attraction is the **Chail Sanctuary**, 18km north of the palace, which provides a refuge to species ranging from monkeys to Himalayan gorals, bovids that look a bit like a cross between a goat and an antelope.

GETTING AROUND

Destinations along the NH5 are generally well served by bus, but if you plan to go somewhere off this main thoroughfare, you may need to switch buses. Cabs make things easier, and fixed prices are typically set by the **Kalka Shimla Himachal Taxi Union** *(0177-2658225)*. The nearest railway station to the destinations that follow is in Kalka, from where you can catch direct trains to Delhi, the fastest of which (the Kalka Shatabdi Express) only takes around four hours.

WHY I LOVE KASAULI

Margot Bigg, Lonely Planet writer

In the 20-plus years since I first visited Himachal Pradesh, I've seen some of the state's most celebrated hill stations go from relatively chilled-out spots that drew in mostly honeymooners and families in search of respite from the heat of the plains to serious tourism hotspots, complete with chock-a-block traffic and major crowds. I'm grateful that Kasauli retains the relaxed hill-station vibe for which Himachal is known. This is partially because it's spread out, with many of its hotels closer to the famous Lawrence School in neighbouring Sanawar, not exactly walking distance to the town centre. And while Kasauli doesn't have tons of things to see or do, I find that part of its charm, especially when I'm in the mood for quiet time and mountain air.

SUDIP JOTSHI/SHUTTERSTOCK

Kasauli

TIME FROM SHIMLA: 2½HR

History haven

Straddling the Shivalik Hills on the southern edge of the state, Kasauli has long been a popular destination for posh Chandigarhians and Delhiites looking for an easy-to-reach place to escape from the high temperatures to the south. In some ways, it feels like a scaled-down Shimla, with a short shopping drag known as Heritage Market that's flanked by toy stalls and momo hawkers and a smattering of British colonial buildings. The grandest of these is **Christ Church**, a neo-Gothic stone structure which dates to 1853; the gatekeeper usually opens it up for a few hours every afternoon for those who want to take a peek at the stained-glass triptych inside.

Kasauli

NATURAL KINNAURI SNACKS

Kinnaur has long been known across India for its crisp, sweet apples, which flood local markets as soon as the busy October apple-picking season hits. Even if you visit outside of harvest time, you're sure to find dried apples, apple jams and apple juice at shops across Kalpa and beyond. Kinnaur also produces plenty of apricots, and dried versions of the fruit are widely available. If you're more of a savoury-tooth, ask for pine nuts (known locally as *chilgoze* or *neje*), which are harvested from the *Pinus gerardiana* tree that grows throughout Kinnaur as well as in Pakistan and Afghanistan. The buttery flavour and dense nutrient profile make *chilgoze* an excellent trail snack.

While many come to Kasauli simply to take in the mountain air away from the Shimla masses, it's also a great base for visiting the **Dagshai Jail Museum**, roughly 14km away. This free attraction, maintained by a local army unit, preserves the Dagshai Central Jail, a 54-cell prison that was built by the British in 1849. Gandhi himself stayed at the jail for a few nights (as a guest, not a prisoner) while visiting Irish soldiers who were imprisoned following the Connaught Rangers Mutiny of 1920. Ironically, Nathuram Godse, Gandhi's assassin, spent a night here en route to Shimla for trial.

Places We Love to Stay

₹ Budget ₹₹ Midrange ₹₹₹ Top End

McLeod Ganj

Map p265

Shree Guest House ₹ Low-key spot with cosy, compact rooms and deodar tree views.

Green Hotel ₹₹ Well-established favourite among international visitors offering friendly service, great restaurant and a range of simple but spacious rooms, some with lovely views.

Lord Krishna Boutique Stay ₹₹ Comfortable rooms with fantastic valley views, located around midway between the Main Square and the Dalai Lama's temple.

Ram Yoga House ₹₹ Guesthouse with a big focus on yoga and wellness, offering rooms and studio apartments with kitchenettes plus a restaurant serving healthy food.

New Serkong House ₹₹ Peaceful property with spacious rooms and suites adorned with handmade decorative features; just off McLeod Ganj's Main Square.

Chonor House ₹₹₹ Norbulingka Institute–run hotel near the Dalai Lama's Temple featuring bright, mural-adorned rooms, some with lovely views.

Palampur & Andretta

Lodge at Wah ₹₹₹ Small, upscale homestay with a garden restaurant, across the street from Palampur's historic Wah Tea Estate, run by the same family.

Mirage Retreat & Homestay ₹₹₹ Boutique homestay with a welcoming dining area and rustic-chic rooms spread across three houses; across from Andretta Pottery.

Bir

Chokling Art House ₹ Popular hostel opposite the Chokling Monastery with a mix of dorms and private rooms, some with monastery views.

Hideout ₹ Backpacker-friendly guesthouse with simple budget rooms and a small swimming pool in a private garden.

Autumn Home ₹₹₹ Small guesthouse with cosy rooms lovingly decked out with warm hues of red and orange plus a small garden cafe.

Chamba

Proto Hostel ₹ Hostel with modern bunk rooms and colourfully decorated common areas, plus high-speed wi-fi and power backup to entice digital nomads.

Himalayan Orchard Huts ₹₹ Peaceful eco-resort in a quiet natural area just northeast of Chamba with organic garden and easy access to hiking and birdwatching.

Manali

Map p277

Orchards House – The Hidden Tribe ₹ Old Manali budget hotel with large rooms, some with vaulted ceilings, plus beautiful mountain and garden views.

Zostel Old Manali ₹ Reliable chain hostel with plenty of room for socialising, including a garden with a fire pit.

Hill River Resort ₹₹ Contemporary hotel on Naggar Hwy by local chain 'West Western' with big, plush rooms, just across the Beas River from Van Vihar.

Storii Urvashi's Retreat ₹₹₹ Rustic-chic retreat with wood-panelled rooms, some spread across two floors, plus spa and restaurant, among apple orchards on the outskirts of Manali.

Baikunth Manali ₹₹₹ Mid-sized garden hotel with elegant rooms and common areas featuring lots of wood accents, all set among towering conifers.

Naggar

Soham's Chateau De Naggar ₹ Small, multistorey hotel on the south side of town with simple rooms, on-site dining and great valley views.

Naggar Castle ₹₹ Himachal Tourism Department–run heritage hotel housed in a historic castle constructed in the quintessentially Himachali *kath-kuni* architectural style.

NORTH ₹₹₹ Creative campus featuring an architecture studio and rooms housed in contemporary *dhajji* and *kath-kuni* structures.

Kullu

Hotel Sarla Regency ₹ Simple hotel with a restaurant on the banks of the Beas River and budget rooms (some with balconies and/or air-conditioning).

Neeralaya ₹₹₹ Elegant riverfront getaway with beautiful rooms and villas with warm furnishings and exposed *kath-kuni* walls, and a restaurant serving meals crafted from vegetables grown onsite.

Tirthan Valley

Raju's Cottage ₹₹ Set among gardens and orchards on the Tirthan River, this rustic traveller favourite features low-ceilinged timber rooms and tasty meals.

Sunshine Himalayan Cottages ₹₹₹ Spend the night in an elegant pine-clad room or cottage with forest and river views at this small property.

Keylong

Map p289

Kyelang Times Stays & Restaurant ₹ Sleekly furnished inn with a mix of dorm beds and private accommodation plus a restaurant serving Lahauli and Indian fare.

Nordaling Guest House ₹ Popular three-storey guesthouse near the Old Bus Stand with clean, colourful rooms and a popular restaurant.

Kaza

Karze Mud House Homestay ₹₹ Spend the night in a mud house with included homemade breakfast cooked up on a traditional tandoor.

Sakya Abode ₹₹ Double-storey guesthouse set around a garden courtyard with hammocks plus clean rooms and common areas brightened up with Tibetan decor.

Kalpa

Map p294

Wanderers Homestay ₹₹ Family-run guesthouse on the road to Kalpa from Rekong Peo. Big rooms with balconies and fantastic mountain views, plus hearty homecooked food.

Grand Shamba-La ₹₹₹ Comfortable boutique hotel decked out with locally made art and featuring fabulous mountain views.

Rampur Bushahr

Hotel KC Regency ₹₹ Simple but practical oprion with pared-down business-style rooms, some with air-conditioning.

Hotel Nau Nabh ₹₹₹ Sleep like a maharani (or maharajah) in this heritage hotel that occupies part of Rampur's biggest draw: the Padam Palace complex.

Shimla

Map p301

YMCA Tourist Hostel ₹ Centrally located backpacker favourite with hostel-style dorm accommodation plus simple, well-maintained private rooms with shared bathrooms.

Hosteller Shimla ₹ Impeccably maintained chain backpacker hostel with mixed and women-only dorms plus private rooms, some with valley views.

8fold by LaRiSa, Shimla ₹₹ Sleek valley-facing property a short drive from the action with contemporary rooms, a spa and excellent dining options.

Chapslee ₹₹₹ A 19th-century heritage property that puts a major emphasis on recreating the olden days, with opulent rooms and common areas decked out in Raj-era decor.

Oberoi Cecil ₹₹₹ Elegant heritage hotel on the western end of the city, with large, plush rooms and a kids' play area.

Chail

The Palace, Chail ₹₹ The former palace of the Maharaja of Patiala featuring old-fashioned, but elegant, rooms filled with handsome period furniture.

Hotel Grand Sunset ₹₹ Beautifully maintained choice with a restaurant and simple but clean rooms, many of which have sweeping valley views.

Kasauli

Sanawar Heights ₹₹₹ Modern option with plush rooms, many with fantastic views of the surrounding hills, plus a vegetarian restaurant.

Winnies Holiday Resort & Spa ₹₹₹ Popular among honeymooners and families alike, this cosy spot offers a mix of rooms and villas, plus a restaurant, a spa and a compact pool.

Views over Kullu, Naggar Castle (p282)

Researched by
Joe Bindloss

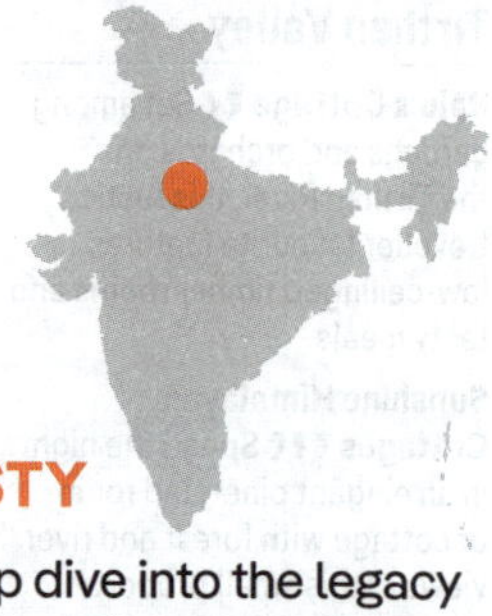

Agra

INDIAN ICONS AND MUGHAL MAJESTY

Come to this atmospheric Mughal city for a deep dive into the legacy of three of India's greatest emperors – Akbar, Jehangir and Shah Jahan.

The home of the Taj Mahal, Agra Fort and a string of other magical Mughal monuments, the city of Agra also has a reputation for hassles that it doesn't really deserve. With sights this iconic, the tourism industry certainly operates at full throttle, but that's a small price to pay for such memorable travel experiences.

Despite its celebrity status, Agra brings India's rich heritage of dynasties and duelling empires vividly to life. Tucked into a bend of the sacred Yamuna River, you'll find towering battlements, regal palaces, beguiling bazaars, the world's most magnificent mausoleum and a string of elegant gardens that follow the Persian *charbagh* pattern in tribute to the Islamic gardens of paradise.

ZORAN KARAPANCEV/SHUTTERSTOCK

Almost everyone starts a visit with a trip to the Taj Mahal – a building of such sublime symmetry that it seems plucked from another plane of existence. Most also add in a trip to Agra Fort, one of India's most spectacular fortresses and the powerhouse of the Mughal empire under Akbar, Jehangir and Shah Jahan.

But there's much more to see. Mosques, mausoleums and monuments – some dating back as far as the Delhi Sultanate – dot the backstreets, and the energetic bazaars spilling north from the fort will remind you that this is a living, breathing city, not just an appendage to its famous mausoleum.

Many visitors see Agra in a rush, ticking off the top sights and moving quickly on to calmer corners of northern India, but it's worth giving the city the time it deserves. There's great eating here, and some charming places to stay, and local-led tours will get you under the surface in a way possible in few other tourist hubs in the area.

Be sure to roam beyond the centre to nearby Sikandra, the last resting place of the Mughal emperor Akbar, and to Fatehpur Sikri, where Akbar's vision for an enlightened capital rose and fell due to poor town planning. With time to spare, visit the wildlife rescue centres on the road to Mathura and support the work charities are doing to help abused bears and elephants.

THE MAIN AREAS

For places to stay in Agra, see p333

MANUEL ROMARIS/GETTY IMAGES

Above: Taj Mahal (p314); Left: Akbar's tomb (p330)

Find Your Way

The Taj Mahal and Agra Fort (and Agra Fort train station) sit 2km apart on the south bank of the Yamuna River. Hotel-crammed Taj Ganj spills south from the Taj, while busy Agra Cantonment train station sits west.

FROM THE AIRPORT

Agra's Kheria Airport is located 7km west of the centre. A prepaid cab to town can cost as much as ₹1000 for the half-hour journey; summon a ride with Ola or Uber for much less.

TAXI OR AUTORICKSHAW

Electric and petrol-powered autorickshaws are the backbone of local transport in Agra, alongside taxis; bargain to get a fair price. Order cheaper rides via Uber and Ola. Agra's expanding metro connects the Fort, Taj and Fatehabad Rd.

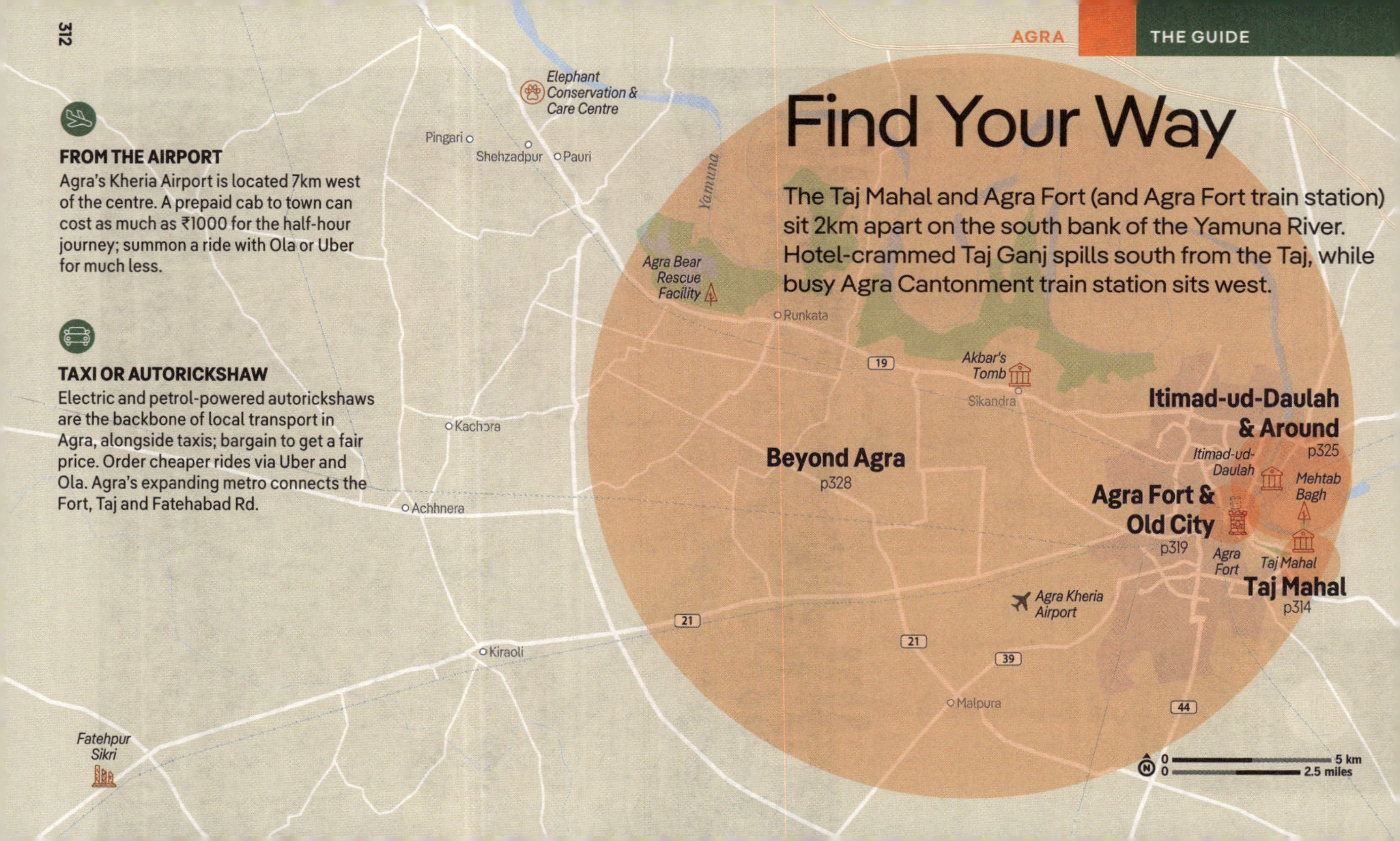

MINH CONG PHAM/SHUTTERSTOCK

Jehangir Palace, Agra Fort (p321)

Plan Your Days

Kick off early to enjoy the city at its calmest. Devote a day to the Taj, Agra Fort and the Old City; use extra days to see the north bank, Fatehpur Sikri and Sikandra.

Pressed for Time

- Set out for sunrise at the **Taj Mahal** (p314), seeing the tomb from all sides, then head over to **Agra Fort** (p321) to observe the evolution of Mughal architecture, and duck into the lanes of the Old City. Spend the afternoon at **Itimad-ud-Daulah** (p325) and the surrounding gardens, catch sunset over the Taj from **Mehtab Bagh** (p326) and then dine in style at **Esphahan** (p327).

A Deeper Dive

- Swing by the **Roman Catholic Cemetery** (p328) to view the Red Taj, a sandstone replica atop a Dutchman's grave, then admire **Akbar's Tomb** (p330) at Sikandra. Continue to **Fatehpur Sikri** (p331) to explore the ruins of Akbar's abandoned royal capital. Bookend your trip with a shopping day in Agra, roaming the bazaars of the **Old City** (p319).

YOU'LL ALSO WANT TO...

SPOT OLD ARCHITECTURE

In the Old City, north and west of the fort, are some of Agra's most striking old mosques, temples and buildings.

FINE DINE

Agra is a place to eat well, so set aside a few lunches and dinners for upmarket Mughlai meals (and other treats) along Fatehabad Rd.

SHOP FOR CRAFTS

Mughal art forms such as carpet-making and marble inlaywork live on in shops dotted around Fatehabad Rd and Sadar Bazaar.

SUPPORT ANIMALS

Make an appointment ahead to visit animal rescue centres along the Mathura road and support their work with bears and elephants.

Taj Mahal

ICONIC PHOTOS | ARCHITECTURAL MAJESTY | POIGNANT HISTORY

GETTING AROUND

Polluting vehicles are banned from a 500m zone surrounding the Taj, but taxis and autorickshaws can drop you at the Shilpgram parking area, 1km from the East Gate, or at Amrood Ka Teela, around 550m from the West Gate. You can walk or take an electric shuttle cart (₹25) to the gates.

The metro has stops fairly close to the West Gate (Taj Mahal station) and East Gate (Taj East Gate) but you'll still need to take an autorickshaw and walk the final stretch. When you exit, you can leave via the East, West or South gates.

TOP TIP

Navigating Taj Ganj can be an exasperating experience thanks to rickshaw drivers and touts trying to coax visitors into using their services. Politely decline if you're not interested and avoid conversations that lead towards a commission-paying shop, hotel or restaurant.

The Taj Mahal is one of those monuments that you imagine long before you visit, and remember long after you depart. Put simply, this vision in white marble – the tomb built by Shah Jahan for his third wife Mumtaz Mahal, who died during childbirth in 1631 – is architectural perfection.

Construction of this dazzling structure, which made 'the sun and the moon shed tears from their eyes' according to the devastated emperor, started in 1632, but it took eight years and 20,000 labourers and craftspeople to complete. The surrounding complex was only finished in 1653.

Shah Jahan's all-consuming grief supposedly turned his hair grey overnight, and he reputedly avoided all contact with the child he blamed for his wife's untimely death. In 1658, the mourning emperor was deposed by his ruthless son Aurangzeb and imprisoned in Agra Fort – gazing out at his matchless masterwork until his death in 1666.

A Mughal Masterpiece in Marble

Be blown away by the Taj Mahal

Before you get to gaze on the wonder that is the **Taj Mahal** *(tajmahal.gov.in; entry ₹1100, centotaph entry ₹200, guides from ₹1500; closed Fri)*, you must first walk or take an electric shuttle from the vehicle drop-off point near the East or West Gates.

Then there are slow security and bag checks (no food, camera tripods, smoking paraphernalia or alcohol) before the magic can begin. There's an X-ray check with separate queues for men and women, and it can take as much as an hour to get through.

But once all that is over, you'll step through the tomb's central gateway to get the view everyone is after, with the Taj's soaring dome and symmetrical minarets lined up at the end of the water channel dividing the tomb's *charbagh*-style gardens.

As you enter, pause to admire the gateway above you, with its splendid calligraphy, tomb-like arches and rows of mini turrets. Inside, the Taj looms dramatically into view for the first time, and it only gets better as you get closer.

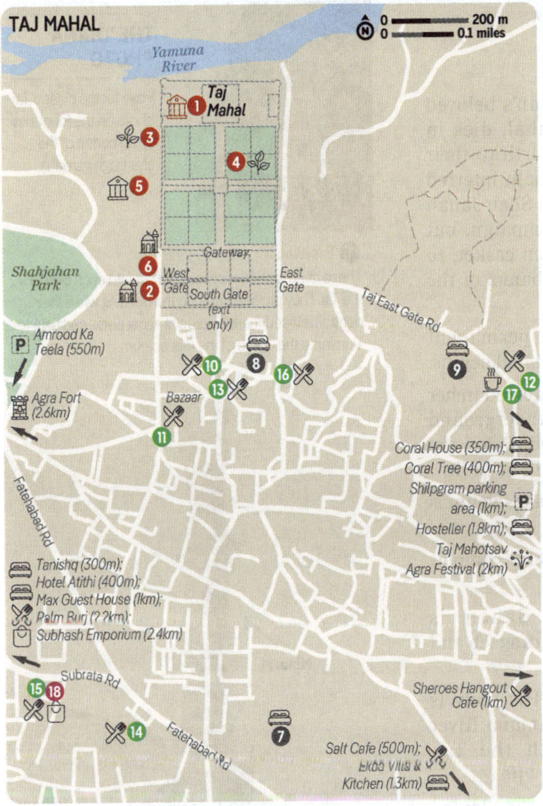

HIGHLIGHTS
1 Taj Mahal

SIGHTS
2 Fatehpuri Masjid
3 Khan-i-Alam Bagh
4 Mughal Garden
5 Taj Museum
6 Tomb of Fatehpuri Begum

SLEEPING
7 ITC Mughal
8 Joey's Hostel
9 Oberoi Amarvilas

EATING
see 9 Esphahan
10 Joney's Place
11 Mukeem Biryani
12 Old England Cafe
see 7 Peshawri
13 Shankara Vegis
14 Sky Deck
15 The Nawaabs
16 Yash Cafe

DRINKING & NIGHTLIFE
17 Blue Tokai Coffee Roasters
see 9 The Bar

SHOPPING
18 Kalra's Cottage Industry

However, you'll likely want to pause to grab the 'Lady Diana' photo (made famous when the British princess visited without her husband) from the fountain at the centre of the gardens.

Don't rush inside the mausoleum; instead, circle the gleaming marble terrace that surrounds the tomb, taking in the surprising perspectives as you gaze up and admire its milky-white perfection.

Pay particular attention to the pietra dura inlays – a tracery of flowers, scrollwork created from 35 types of semi-precious stones, including lapis lazuli, jasper, jade and carnelian. The technique was copied from medieval Italy – and some would say improved.

Created from white marble inlaid with jasper, the Islamic calligraphy surrounding the monumental arches on each side of the tomb gets larger as it rises but appears to be a uniform size when viewed from the ground.

Before you leave, examine the two very similar structures lying east and west of the tomb. The building to the west is a functioning **mosque** used by local Muslims. The building to the east mirrors it, but it faces away from Mecca, and was instead used as a *mehmankhana* (guesthouse). Its name, **Jawab**, means 'answer'.

KEEPING THE TAJ GLEAMING

In the right light, the Taj seems to glow an almost pearlescent white. However, before vehicles and polluting industries were banned from the area, conservators were forced to use everything from careful washing to mud-packs made from Fuller's earth to remove discolouration caused by atmospheric pollution. The battle is far from over – suspended particles from vehicle pollution continue to reach double the recommended limits, contributing to ongoing yellowing of the monument.

Taj Mahal

Timeline

1631 Emperor Shah Jahan's beloved third wife, Mumtaz Mahal, dies in Buhanpur while giving birth to their 14th child. Her body is initially interred in Buhanpur itself, where Shah Jahan is fighting a military campaign, but is later moved, in a golden casket, to a small building on the banks of the Yamuna River in Agra.

1632 Construction of a permanent mausoleum for Mumtaz Mahal begins.

1633 Mumtaz Mahal is interred in her final resting place, an underground tomb beneath a marble plinth, on top of which the Taj Mahal will be built.

1640 The white-marble mausoleum is completed.

1653 The rest of the Taj Mahal complex is completed.

1658 Emperor Shah Jahan is overthrown by his son Aurangzeb and imprisoned in Agra Fort.

1666 Shah Jahan dies. His body is transported along the Yamuna River and buried underneath the Taj, alongside the tomb of his wife.

1908 Repeatedly damaged and looted after the fall of the Mughal empire, the Taj receives some long-overdue attention as part of a major restoration project ordered by British viceroy Lord Curzon.

1983 The Taj is awarded Unesco World Heritage Site status.

2002 Having been discoloured by pollution in more recent years, the Taj is spruced up with an ancient recipe known as multani mitti – a blend of soil, cereal, milk and lime once used by Indian women to beautify their skin.

Today Almost 7 million tourists visit the Taj Mahal each year. That's more than three times the population of Agra.

ARIS ABDULLAH/SHUTTERSTOCK

THE 'DIANA' PHOTO

Pose for the classic Taj photo on the fountains in the centre of the charbagh gardens.

❶ Pishtaqs

These huge arched recesses are set into each side of the Taj. They provide depth to the building while their central, latticed marble screens allow patterned light to illuminate the inside of the mausoleum.

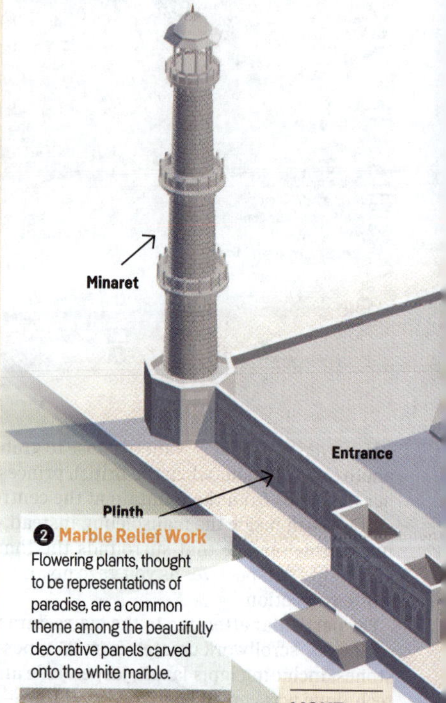

ILLUSTRATION BY JAVIER ZARRACINA

❷ Marble Relief Work

Flowering plants, thought to be representations of paradise, are a common theme among the beautifully decorative panels carved onto the white marble.

FABIOLM/GETTY IMAGES

LIGHT THE WAY

Use the torch on your smartphone to fully appreciate the translucency of the white marble and semi-precious stones.

CHARLES TOMALIN / ALAMY STOCK PHOTO

7 Filigree Screen

This stunning screen was carved out of a single piece of marble. It surrounds both cenotaphs, allowing patterned light to fall onto them through its intricately carved jali (latticework).

ARIS ABDULLAH/SHUTTERSTOCK

6 Central Dome

The Taj's famous central dome, topped by a brass finial, represents the vault of heaven, a stark contrast to the material world, which is represented by the square shape of the main structure.

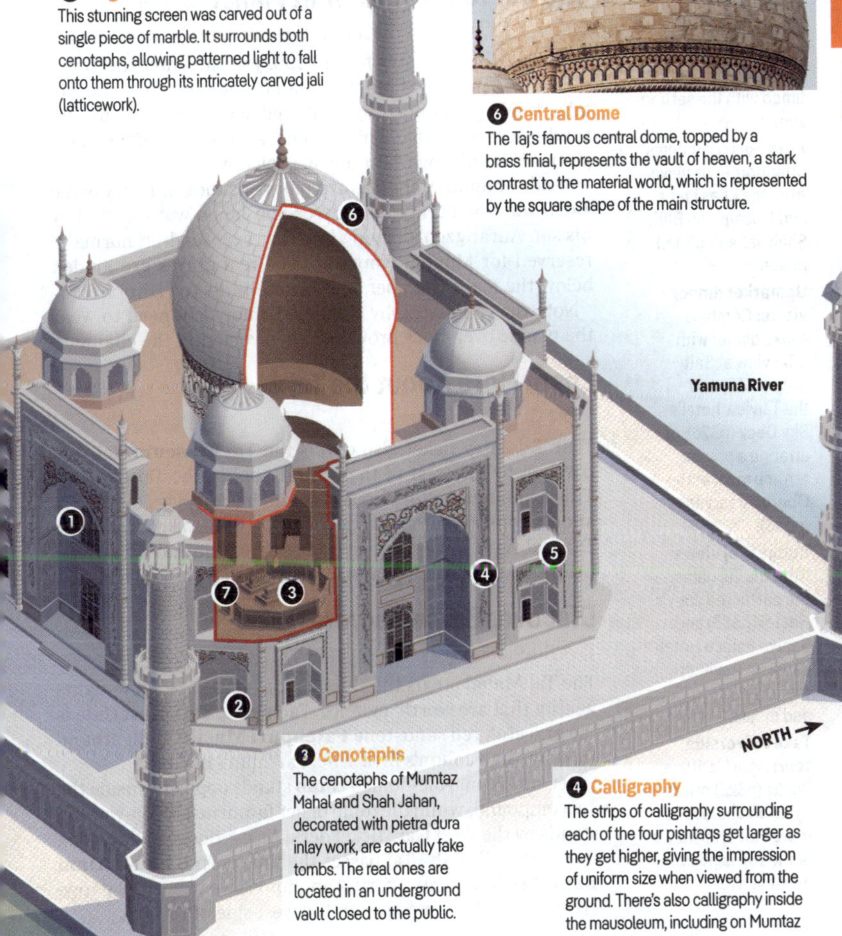

3 Cenotaphs

The cenotaphs of Mumtaz Mahal and Shah Jahan, decorated with pietra dura inlay work, are actually fake tombs. The real ones are located in an underground vault closed to the public.

4 Calligraphy

The strips of calligraphy surrounding each of the four pishtaqs get larger as they get higher, giving the impression of uniform size when viewed from the ground. There's also calligraphy inside the mausoleum, including on Mumtaz Mahal's cenotaph.

FRENTUSHA/GETTY IMAGES

5 Pietra Dura

It's believed that 35 different precious and semiprecious stones were used to create the exquisite pietra dura (marble inlay work) found on the inside and outside of the mausoleum walls. Again, floral designs are common.

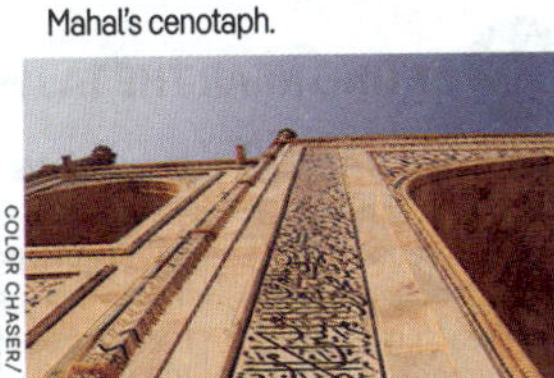
COLOR CHASER/ SHUTTERSTOCK

BEST VIEWS OF TAJ MAHAL

Catch a glimpse of the world's most beautiful building from these top vantage points.

Mehtab Bagh: This north-bank Mughal garden provides close-up views of the rear elevation, best timed with the setting sun.

Agra Fort: Balconies offer gorgeous views from the Khas Mahal and Musamman Burj, Shah Jahan's gilded prison.

Upmarket dinner views: Combine a luxe dinner with a Taj view at Salt Cafe (p327) and the Tajview hotel's Sky Deck (p326), or arrange a private terrace meal at the Oberoi Amarvilas (p333).

Budget Taj views: Near the Taj gates, the partnered Joey's Hostel (p333) and Saniya Palace Hotel serve up traveller-friendly rooftop views and meals.

Take a riverside tour: Agra Heritage Walks (p323) offers cycle and horseback tours that offer views of the Taj rising up over the river.

Many people come for sunrise, hoping to be at the front of the queue when the gates open, but you can still expect a wait. You can exit the compound via the East, West or South Gates. 'Night viewings' from 8pm during each full moon can be booked on the Taj website *(tajmahal.gov.in/night-view.aspx)*.

Every February, the Shilpgram district by the Taj's East Gate is the setting for the **Taj Mahotsav festival** *(tajmahotsav.org)*, celebrating the city's culture and cuisine and the arts.

See the Tomb of Mumtaz Mahal

Meet (well, almost) the makers of the Taj

For an additional entry fee of ₹200, you can enter the Taj to view the Cenotaph of Mumtaz Mahal – actually an elaborate false tomb surrounded by a latticed screen carved out of a single piece of marble. This screen features some of the finest pietra dura inlay work in the mausoleum.

Beside Mumtaz Mahal's grave, offsetting the symmetry of the Taj, is the small cenotaph where Shah Jahan was interred by his son Aurangzeb, denying him the regal send-off normally reserved for Mughal emperors. The real graves are hidden below the main chamber, and are off limits to visitors.

Note that photography is banned, and you'll need to wear the plastic overshoes provided when you enter the chamber.

Learn More About the Taj

Visit the Taj Museum

Your Taj entry ticket also covers the **Taj Museum**, set in a pavilion to the west of the central pool in the Taj gardens. This small but well-laid-out museum has displays on the Taj and its construction. Look out for British-era sketches of the Taj and Agra, an impressive Mughal-era Taj floorplan and portraits of Shah Jahan and Mumtaz Mahal painted on ivory.

Discover Some Secrets

Overlooked extras

The Taj Mahal steals the thunder, but there are a few sights nearby that are worth a glance. Facing the Taj's West Gate is the graceful, red sandstone **Fatehpuri Masjid**, built around 1650 by Shah Jahan's fifth wife, Fatehpuri Begum.

Her simple marble-domed **tomb** stands opposite, inside the Taj compound, while the tomb of her favourite lady-in-waiting stands by the West Gate ticket desk. An overlooked alley along the west wall of the Taj passes the timeworn **Khan-i-Alam Bagh garden** *(free)*, offering an impressive view up the towering walls of the mosque on the west side of the Taj.

EATING NEAR THE TAJ MAHAL: OUR PICKS

Yash Cafe: A Taj Ganj oldie south of the East Gate; good for breakfasts, veg meals and escaping the noise. *7am-10.30pm* ₹

Shankara Vegis: A cosy old-timer near the Taj's South Gate, popular for its veg thalis, rooftop and friendly owners. *8.30am-10.30pm* ₹

Joney's Place: A tiny, no-frills Taj Ganj veteran that's better than the average in the somewhat hectic area right by the Taj. *6am-10.30pm* ₹

Mukeem Biryani: Fragrant lamb biryani (with more meat than bones) at pocket-friendly prices on Taj Ganj's 'biryani corner'. *7am-8.30pm* ₹

Agra Fort & Old City

A HISTORICAL POWERHOUSE

One of the most impressively engineered fortifications in all of India, Agra Fort was the seat of the Mughal court for over a century. Inside its daunting walls stand administrative buildings, barracks, palaces, pleasure gardens, formal courtyards, audience halls and mosques – it was almost a city within a city.

The complex is built over the site of an earlier brick fort known as Badalgarh, which was already a ruin when the forces of the Delhi sultanate arrived. As Akbar shifted his base of operations to Agra, the fort was reconstructed in red sandstone, before being spruced up with white marble by the architecturally flamboyant Shah Jahan.

A short distance away stands the Shahi Jama Masjid from 1648, which served as a key place of worship for the Mughal city. Its striking herringbone-patterned domes rise at the southern end of the old walled city of Agra opposite Agra Fort station.

FIPHOTO/SHUTTERSTOCK

Agra Fort (p321)

GETTING AROUND

The Amar Singh Gate to the south is the sole entry point to Agra Fort, and this is where you buy your entry tickets. A large squatter camp sits opposite, so begging can be an issue here.

The Old City is a short walk or auto ride north from the fort. On arrival, you'll want to explore its tangled lanes on foot, though you can always jump in an autorickshaw if energy levels fall. Get to the fort by autorickshaw, or on the expanding Agra Metro via Agra Fort station.

TOP TIP

Licensed guides *(from ₹500)* will help you get more from the fort's maze of interconnected palaces, chambers and gardens. They'll approach you as you enter and prices are negotiable, so discuss the price before you say yes.

AGRA FORT & OLD CITY

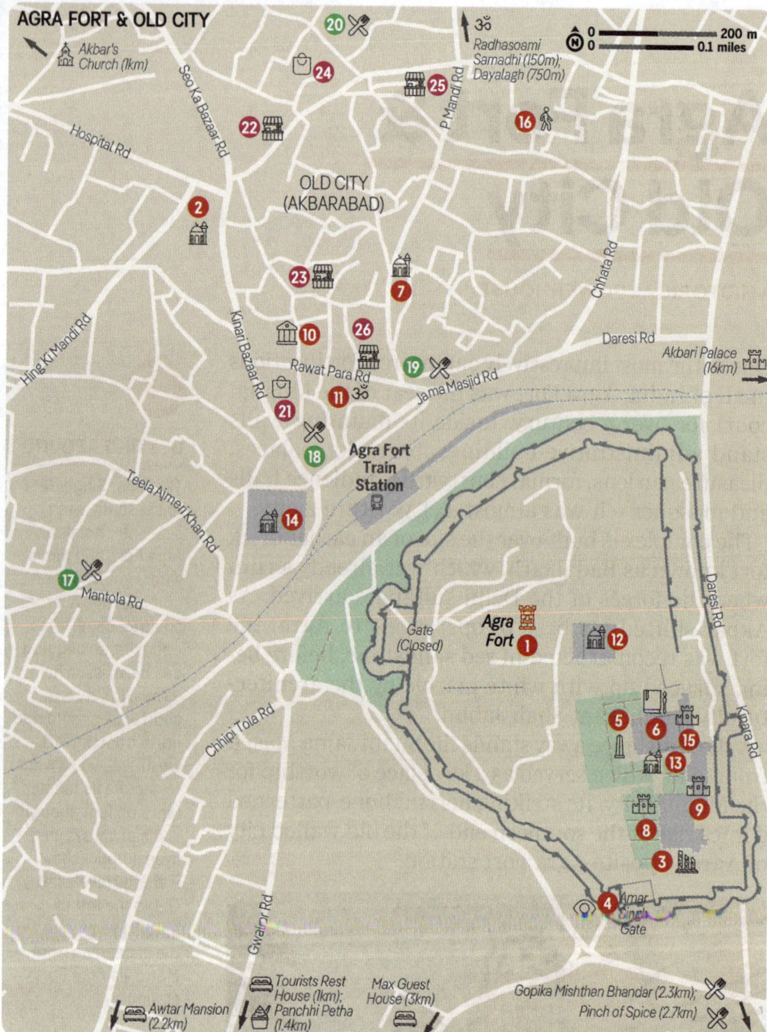

HIGHLIGHTS
1 Agra Fort

SIGHTS
2 Akbari Masjid
3 Akbari Palace
4 Amar Singh Gate
5 Diwan-i-Am
6 Diwan-i-Khas
7 Hazuri Bhawan
8 Jehangir Palace
9 Khas Mahal
10 Kokamal Market building
11 Mankameshwar Mandir
12 Moti Masjid (Pearl Mosque)
13 Musamman Burj
14 Shahi Jama Masjid
15 Shish Mahal

ACTIVITIES
16 Agra Heritage Walks

EATING
17 Abdul Sattar Nashte Wale
18 Chimman Lal Poori Wale
19 Munna Lal Agarwal Pethe Wale
20 Nai Basti Nihari Restaurants

SHOPPING
21 Gopal Das Pethe Wale
22 Kashmiri Bazaar
23 Kinari Bazaar
24 Lala Priya Dass & Sons Perfumers
25 Mal Ka Bazaar
26 Tiwari Gali

Mughal Magnificence

Appreciate the evolution of Mughal creativity at Agra Fort

The city's second must-see sight, **Agra Fort** *(tajmahal.gov.in/agrafort.aspx; adult/under 15yr ₹650/free, Fri ₹600)* was originally constructed as a purely functional fortification, before being glammed up with marble trim, lavish palaces and pleasure gardens.

Known as the Badalgarh, the original brick Hindu fort on the site was seized by Sikander Lodi, sultan of Delhi, after he moved his capital to Agra in 1504, and promptly rebuilt in more solid sandstone. Every subsequent Mughal emperor from Babur to Aurangzeb resided here at one point or another.

It was Akbar who raised the impregnable walls that stand today, and Shah Jahan who gave the place a lavish makeover to create a suitably royal dwelling. It's everything you could ask from a medieval fortress – brutally functional but also elegantly luxurious, befitting a dynasty that blended military ruthlessness with a passion for the arts.

Entering through the ornate **Amar Singh Gate** (note the blue glazed tiles, hinting at Central Asia design ideas), you'll emerge into an open courtyard, with the main palaces lined up to your right. First is the 16th-century **Akbari Palace**, today mainly a ruin, executed in simple red sandstone.

Mughal design had evolved by the time Jehangir created the **Jehangir Palace** in the 17th century, primarily as a residence for the royal wives and concubines. Its sandstone walls are finely inlaid with white marble and covered in a tracery of bas-reliefs that only become apparent as you get closer. Note Jehangir's huge step-in bathtub, displayed in front of the palace.

From the rear courtyard, you'll get your first Taj views as you follow the walls into the ice-white **Khas Mahal**, marking another shift in Mughal aesthetics. At its heart is an elegant marble pavilion, fronted by fountains and gardens and covered in fine carvings and inlays. Head into the corner of the courtyard to peek into the mirrored **Shish Mahal**.

At the far corner of the walls stands the **Musamman Burj**, a graceful, intricately inlaid octagonal tower overlooking the Yamuna, where Shah Jahan spent his final years imprisoned with a view of his wife's tomb in the Taj. This was a gilded prison, but it must have been torment for the grieving emperor after being deposed by his power-hungry son.

Go upstairs past two mosques reserved for personal use by the royals, to reach the marble **Diwan-i-Khas**, where emperors held private audiences with visiting dignitaries. The courtyard in front blends Mughal, Hindu and baroque elements.

Next, enter the vast courtyard housing the enormous **Diwan-i-Am**, whose outsized proportions were intended to project the might of Mughal power to those arriving for public audiences. Note the incongruously placed grave of John Russell Colvin, Lieutenant Governor of the Northwest Provinces, who died here during the First War of Independence in 1857.

CITY OF PEITHA & DALMOTH

You won't be in Agra for long before you notice the astonishing preponderance of shops selling *peitha* (candied ash gourd) and *dalmoth* – the city's most popular savoury *namkeen* snack. Reputedly eaten in Mughal times, *peitha* really took off in Agra in the early 20th century, and it now has protected geographical status. Local shops sell the intensely sweet unflavoured version, as well as novelty varieties flavoured with everything from fruit syrup to chocolate and *paan* (betel nut). Founded in 1926, **Panchhi Petha** *(panchhipetha.com)* has pop-up shops all over the city, or try the appealingly packaged offerings at **Gopal Das Pethe Wale**.

AGRA'S MOST ATMOSPHERIC CORNERS

Tahir Ahmed Qureshi from **Agra Heritage Walks** *(agraheritagewalks.com)* shares his insider tips.

Everyone comes to Agra for the **Taj Mahal**, but this area does not really represent the city. For real cultural flavour, you have to head to **Akbarabad** – the Old City behind the fort. It's easy to get lost, even with Google Maps, so going with a guide is a good idea! Seek out local secrets such as the evening street food scene in **Dayalbagh**, north of Akbarabad. Here, you can also visit the **Radhasoami Samadhi**, the mausoleum of Huzur Swamiji Maharaj, founder of the Radhasoami faith. Looking a bit like the Taj, it's a place to experience what normal city life is like, at a quieter, slower pace.

DON MAMMOSER/SHUTTERSTOCK

Popcorn vendor, Kinari Bazaar

Regrettably, your explorations end here. The gleaming **Moti Masjid (Pearl Mosque)**, whose white domes you can see peeking up beyond the courtyard, is sadly off limits.

Step Into Agra's Storied Bazaars

Walk around the medieval city

Spilling north and west behind the fort, the tangled lanes of **Akbarabad** – Agra's Old City – are best explored on foot or by rickshaw, soaking in the sights, sounds and scents. Allow yourself a few hours to absorb the timeless magic of these atmospheric bazaars.

The road layout here can be confusing, with lanes branching off in all directions, but getting lost is part of the fun. Keep Google Maps open on your phone, and remember you can always ask for directions back to Agra Fort if need be. Plenty of street-food vendors are on hand to stave off hunger while you explore.

Start wandering from the 17th-century **Shahi Jama Masjid** *(free)*, a handsome Mughal mosque with a striking herringbone pattern created using bands of red sandstone

EATING IN AGRA: THE OLD CITY

Chimman Lal Poori Wale: Come for a veg feast of *puris* and assorted sauces at a bargain price near the Shahi Jama Masjid. *8am-9pm* ₹

Abdul Sattar Nashte Wale: A popular Old City breakfast hangout west of the mosque, serving sweet and savoury French toasts. *7am-9pm* ₹

Munna Lal Agarwal Pethe Wale: Old City sweet shop in the bazaars; serving tasty *peitha* and other sweet treats. *8.30am-9pm* ₹

Nai Basti Nihari Restaurants: North of Kashmiri Bazaar, Anar Wali Gali is lined with butchers' cafes serving meaty *nihari* stew for breakfast. *sunrise-10pm* ₹

and white marble. Its elevated courtyard provides a commanding view of Agra Fort and the British-era Agra Fort train station.

From here, you can dive into the bazaars, starting with the market selling extravagant sequinned wedding outfits surrounding the mosque. Running north, the **Kinari Bazaar** starts off selling fancy fashions, but soon gives way to glinting silversmiths and goldsmiths (many residents still keep their wealth in jewellery form, hence the astonishing number of jewellers).

Rawat Para Rd runs east–west, passing the Old City's aromatic, sneeze-inducing wholesale spice market, centred on **Tiwari Gali**, where porters haul sacks full of chillies, cumin and other essential Indian flavourings.

Further north, branching off from Kinari Bazaar Rd, the **Kashmiri Bazaar** caters to Muslim residents with dotted *ittar* (perfume) shops and *nihari* (meat stew) shops. It spills into the **Mal Ka Bazaar**, where wholesalers trade in paper kites.

As you explore, look out for the grand cast-iron balconies of 19th-century trading houses, and ancient mosques such as the **Akbari Masjid** *(free)* on Kinari Bazaar Rd. North of Agra City train station, the baroque-style **Akbar's Church** *(free)* marks the site of a church founded by Jesuit priests with permission from Akbar in 1600.

Take an Old City Tour

See Agra through local eyes

If you don't feel like tackling the bazaars alone, sign up for a local-led walk with **Agra Heritage Walks** *(agraheritagewalks.com)* for an immersive experience in the company of a guide who really knows the area.

The Qureshi family has links to the area dating back to Mughal times, and their excellent tours explore intriguing local angles. Popular options include a handy Agra overview *(₹3675)*, 'A Walk About Mughal Women' tour *(₹3675)* focused on great Agra women, and Old City cycle trips *(₹4000)*.

Longer tours explore the north bank of the Yamuna – you can even explore the riverbank on horseback. All their tours include stops to meet local artisans and sample street food.

Another popular operator is **Agra Beat** *(agrabeat.com)*, with cycle tours, walking tours and themed trips focused on photography, street food and crafts.

ROYAL RESIDENCE RULES

The names of buildings in India's forts and palaces reveal much about the social rules governing court life. While wielding considerable political influence behind the scenes, women of the royal household were restricted to the zenana (women's quarters) and only permitted to gaze on court events through *jali* screens. Rulers received petitions from ordinary citizens under the watchful eye of palace guards in the Diwan-i-Am, a formal hall designed to showcase the might of the monarch. Only approved dignitaries were admitted to the more intimate Diwan-i-Khas to discuss important matters of state. Nevertheless, India's royal families engaged in plenty of 'keeping up with the Joneses' – every palace worth its name has a Shish Mahal (Mirror Palace), Phool Mahal (Flower Palace), Moti Mahal (Pearl Palace) or Badal Mahal (Cloud Palace).

EATING IN AGRA: BEST FAMILY RESTAURANTS

Gopika Mishthan Bhandar: A much-loved local stop for Indian *mithai* (sweets), *namkeen*, and delectable veg snack foods. *8.30am-11pm* ₹

Pinch of Spice: A calm, upscale spot favoured by families, serving quality North Indian staples, backed up by a strong drinks list. *noon-11.30pm* ₹₹

The Nawaabs: A reputable midranger, luring middle-class Agra residents with tasty kebabs, flavoursome sauces and filling biryani plates. *noon-midnight* ₹₹

Old England Cafe: An English-themed cafe that actually looks more like a Tyrolean chalet, serving decent pizzas with proper toppings. *1pm-midnight* ₹₹

STROLL AROUND OLD AGRA

Step into a labyrinth of bazaars on this Old City walking tour.

START	END	LENGTH
Shahi Jama Masjid	Shahi Jama Masjid	2km; 2hr

Start from 1 **Shahi Jama Masjid** (p322) and fuel up for the walk at 2 **Chimman Lal Poori Wale** (p322). Follow Daresi Rd to reach Rawat Para Rd, and stop into 3 **Munna Lal Agarwal Pethe Wale** (p322) for a sweet palate cleanser, then look for the alley on your left leading to the moody 4 **Mankameshwar Mandir**, enshrining a silver Shiva lingam.

Return to Rawat Para Rd and continue west past fragrant 5 **Tiwari Gali** (p323) spice market. As you walk, look up to see the ornate cast-iron balconies of historic mansions – the 19th-century 6 **Kokamal Market building** is particularly impressive. When you reach 7 **Kinari Bazaar** (p323), turn north past a nonstop parade of jewellers, and look out on the left for the easy-to-miss entrance to the 16th-century 8 **Akbari Masjid** (p323). Just north, bear right into 9 **Kashmiri Bazaar** (p323), passing more historic frontages amid the butchers' shops.

Dab on some fragrance at centuries-old 10 **Lala Priya Dass & Sons Perfumers**, then continue into the 11 **Mal Ka Bazaar** (p323), with its colourful kite vendors. When you hit Kala Mahal Rd, where Mughal poet Mirza Ghalib once resided, turn south and look out on the right for the 12 **Hazuri Bhawan**, former home of Huzur Swamiji Maharaj, guru of the mystical Radhasoami faith. Finish by retracing your steps to the Shahi Jama Masjid.

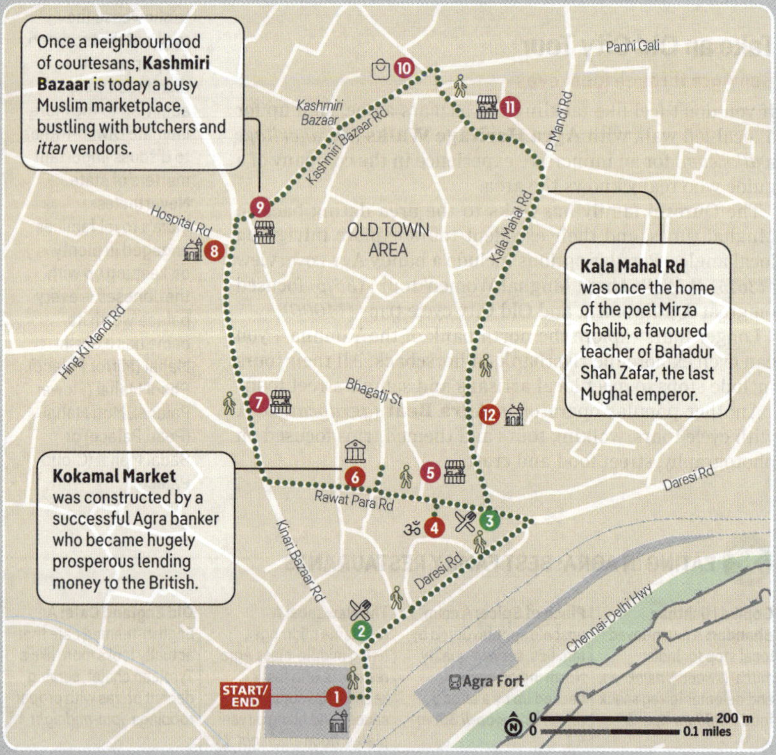

Itimad-ud-Daulah & Around

GREEN GRANDEUR ON THE NORTH BANK OF THE YAMUNA

The banks of the Yamuna were once adorned with more than 40 Mughal gardens, many credited to the botanically inclined Babur. Worn down by the baking Agra summers, the emperor commissioned a series of riverside gardens in the *charbagh* style – divided into four portions in tribute to the legendary gardens of paradise.

The best-preserved gardens are dotted along the north bank of the Yamuna, in an area still studded with flower nurseries. Many of these calm, green spaces became the setting for the tombs of Mughal dignitaries, including the famous Itimad-ud-Daulah, or 'Baby Taj'. The best-known garden is the huge Mehtab Bagh – hailed as much for the views it offers of the Taj across the river as for its planted beds. If it's history you're after, head north to Aram Bagh (Ram Bagh), believed to be the spot where Babur's remains were briefly interred before being relocated to Kabul.

GETTING AROUND

To reach the north bank of the river, take a taxi or autorickshaw or book a ride via Ola or Uber. Itimad-ud-Daulah is about 7km from the west side of the Taj, or 10km from the east side, but the journey can take some time in heavy traffic. Many people charter an autorickshaw to visit multiple gardens, but you can also flag down a ride on the street to hop from garden to garden.

A Rival to the Taj?

Admire Mughal India's first marble monument

The Taj may be hailed as architectural perfection, but it has a challenger. To the north, across the Yamuna, lies the elegant, intricately inlaid **Itimad-ud-Daulah** *(adult/under 15yr ₹310/free)*, the graceful tomb of the Persian noble Mirza Ghiyas Beg.

The name of this jewel-box mausoleum translates to 'pillar of the state' and Beg was indeed a pivotal figure in the Mughal court, serving first as Kabul treasurer, then prime minister, before joining the extended royal family when his daughter, Nur Jahan, married Jehangir in 1611. Set in a *charbagh* garden, the minister's tomb is beautifully proportioned, and less ostentatious than the Taj, while sharing a similar taste for gleaming white marble and intricate floral and geometric motifs.

Blending Mughal and Persian themes, this was the first monument to be built in marble during the Mughal era, and the first to use the distinctive technique of pietra dura, using inlaid semi-precious stones to create ornate patterns of flowers, vases and cypress trees.

TOP TIP

Give yourself half a day and combine a trip to Itimad-ud-Daulah with a visit to Chini Ka Rauza, Aram Bagh and Mehtab Bagh. Aim to be at Mehtab Bagh in the late afternoon to catch the spectacular view as the setting sun sets the Taj aglow (the garden closes promptly at nightfall).

AGRA'S BEST SHOPPING

Beyond the touristy emporiums are some excellent specialist stores to explore.

Subhash Emporium: A Sadar Bazaar purveyor of pietra dura treasures, from boxes to chess sets; in the lobby, see stone-carvers at work.

Kalra's Cottage Industry: Tucked off Fatehabad Rd and showcasing high-quality Mughal carpets – from floral patterns to modern riffs on traditional designs.

Gopal Das Pethe Wale: A ritzy showroom for attractively presented boxes of Agra's famous *peitha* and *dalmoth* (p321).

Tanishq: A jewellery showroom on Fatehabad Rd; come to see how the other half drape themselves with gold and diamonds.

Sheroes Hangout Cafe: This welcoming cafe sells gifts curated to fit into homes overseas, supporting their work to help victims of acid attacks.

The nickname 'Baby Taj' is misleading – the building is squat but refined, with neat corner minarets and a rectangular turret in place of a central dome. However, its delicate pietra dura work was undoubtedly an influence on the Taj, which was constructed a few decades later, while its red sandstone entry gateway shows the influence of earlier Mughal styles.

See Another Side to the Taj

A 16th-century garden with a view

At dawn, you want to the see the Taj from the front; at sunset, it's the view from across the river that dazzles. Agra's largest surviving Mughal garden, **Mehtab Bagh** *(adult/under 15yr*

EATING & DRINKING IN AGRA: BEST CAFES & BARS

Sheroes Hangout Cafe: Inspirational concept cafe run by acid-attack survivors that dishes out fast food and employs recovering victims. *8am-10pm* ₹

Blue Tokai Coffee Roasters: A chain coffee shop serving quality beans that's a welcome haven from the hectic vibe around the Taj. *7am-11pm*

The Bar: Dress up for a drink in the bar at the luxurious Oberoi Amarvilas (p333), known for cool cocktails and enviable Taj views. *10am-midnight*

Sky Deck: Head to the rooftop restaurant at the TajView hotel for drinks and snacks al fresco, perched above Fatehabad Rd. *noon-11pm*

₹300/free) covers 25 acres, facing directly across to the rear elevation of the Taj. Its sprawling planted beds provide a rare calm space in Agra, but most visitors only have eyes for the Taj, rising across the river. If you come for sunset, arrive 30 minutes ahead so you can reach the viewing point in time to catch the show. At other times, the fruit trees, flower beds and ruined fountains make this a pleasant spot to wander and escape the traffic fumes of downtown.

Wander Jehangir's Pleasure Garden

A playground for an emperor

It's said that **Aram Bagh** *(Ram Bagh; adult/under 15yr ₹310/free)*, north of the Itimad-ud-Daulah, was a favourite hangout of Jehangir, who used to come here with members of his harem for pleasurable company. However, the garden is even older, founded by Babur in 1526 but remodelled with elaborate water features and pavilions by Jehangir nearly a century later. This is the most intact of Agra's Mughal gardens, with many fountains and pavilions still standing, and it remains a hangout for young couples to this day.

Legend has it that this was the spot where Babur – a descendant of Timur and Genghis Khan – was interred before his body was relocated to Afghanistan and reburied in the Bagh-e Babur gardens in Kabul, respecting his wish to return to his native Central Asia.

Uncover Agra's Central Asian Influences

A hint of Mughal origins

North of Itimad-ud-Daulah, set in another faded Mughal garden, the **Chini Ka Rauza** *(free)* is the tomb of Afzal Khan, a renowned poet and minister in Shah Jahan's court. The structure shows the clear influence of Islamic tombs in Central Asia, including the use of blue glazed tiles, which were imported from China via the Silk Road.

The tomb's faded inscriptions are said to be the work of Afzal Khan's talented brother, Amanat, who also worked on the calligraphy adorning the Taj. This is the only Mughal structure in Agra aligned with Mecca, and its lavishly decorated interior is styled like a mihrab – the niche indicating the direction of the Kaaba in mosque architecture. While the exterior is heavily worn, the murals inside are still crisp and vibrant.

From the compound, you can see more ruined tombs and garden pavilions dotted along the riverbanks.

GARDENS OF PARADISE

The emperors of the Mughal empire mixed up conquest and battle with time for the finer things in life. Alongside a famous enthusiasm for poetry – best espoused by the work of 19th-century court poet and Agra resident Mirza Ghalib, and the personal writings of Babur, Akbar, Jehangir and Bahadur Shah Zafar – the emperors were captivated by gardens. All of the great Mughal emperors filled their capitals with lavish formal gardens following the Persian *charbagh* plan, with areas of flowers and fruit trees divided into four quadrants by water channels and fountains – mirroring the 'four gardens of paradise' described in the Quran.

EATING IN AGRA: MEALS WITH DAZZLE

Salt Cafe: A glitzy upstairs dining room on Fatehabad Rd that's a glam spot for dinner or a drink with a Taj view. *noon-midnight* ₹₹₹

Esphahan: Book ahead to dine in style at the Oberoi; or go even posher with a private terrace meal (₹17,500 per person). *7-10.30pm* ₹₹₹

Peshawri: You're in the right place for Mughlai food at the top restaurant inside the sleek ITC Mughal; book ahead. *12.30-2.45pm & 7-11.30pm* ₹₹₹

Palm Burj: Cool rooftop dining and drinking for the Insta set in Sadar Bazaar; there are DJs and live music at weekends. *1pm-1.30am* ₹₹₹

Beyond Agra

MORE MAGICAL MUGHAL MARVELS

Heading northwest from Agra towards Rajasthan or Delhi, you can take in a series of magnificent Mughal monuments that will significantly expand your understanding of India's most famous dynasty.

On the outskirts of Agra, Sikandra is dominated by the mausoleums of the Mughal emperor Akbar and his wives and children. Their serene tombs are very different in atmosphere to Agra's grand but crowded monuments. Nearby are two of the region's most important wildlife centres.

Further west, magnificent Fatehpur Sikri was the capital of the Mughal Empire from 1572 to 1585. The site is still an active pilgrimage site for Muslims, who come to pay their respects at the tomb of the Sufi saint Shaikh Salim Chishti.

GETTING AROUND

Mathura buses from Agra's Bijli Ghar bus stand pass Akbar's tomb at Sikandra, or you can arrange a half-day trip by taxi for around ₹2500, dropping by the 'Red Taj'.

To reach Wildlife SOS's animal rescue centres, charter a taxi from Agra (from ₹3000). For Fatehpur Sikri, charter a taxi (from ₹2500) or take one of the regular buses from Agra's Idgah bus stand. On arrival, you can hike to the ruins or take an electric cart for ₹20.

TOP TIP

If you plan to visit the bear and elephant rescue centres, be sure to contact Wildlife SOS in advance so a guide is ready to show you around. Make a day of it by visiting the tombs of Sikandra on the way back to Agra.

Remarkable Memorials

A graveyard with diverse influences

Known as the 'Red Taj', the ornate **grave of Colonel John William Hessing** does indeed resemble a rust-coloured copy of the Taj Mahal. An adventurer by trade, Hessing first served the Dutch East India Company, then the Nizam of Hyderabad, before dying while defending Agra Fort on behalf of the Hindu Maratha kingdom in 1803.

Hessing's grave is one of many striking memorials in Agra's **Roman Catholic Cemetery** *(free)* on MG Rd. Other tombs here are styled like Hindu *chhatris*, Sufi dargahs and Islamic gravestones, commemorating European citizens of Agra who, in the parlance of the time, 'went native', adopting local customs and causes after arriving in the service of foreign empires. The attendant will open Hessing's tomb and other tombs for a tip.

HIGHLIGHTS
1 Akbar's Tomb

SIGHTS
2 Agra Bear Rescue Facility
3 Kanch Mahal
4 Red Taj
5 Roman Catholic Cemetery
6 Sur Sarovar Bird Sanctuary
7 Tomb of Mariam-uz-Zamani

EATING
8 Agra Chaat House
9 Deepee
10 Deviram's Sweets
11 Mama Chicken

TRANSPORT
12 Bijli Ghar Bus Stand
13 Idgah Bus Stand

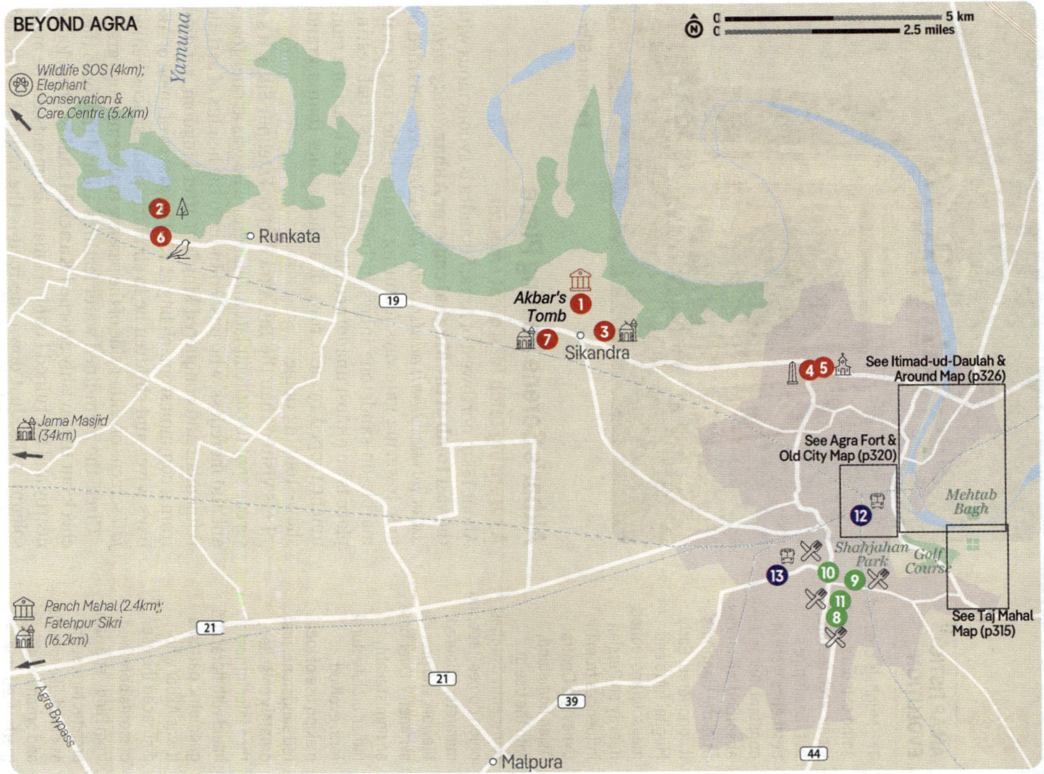

AN ARTISTIC EVOLUTION

The Mughals created some of India's most iconic architecture, but the empire's aesthetics were in constant flux as it absorbed influences from the kingdoms it conquered. Early Mughal forts and mausoleums leaned heavily on Persian influences from the dynasty's Central Asian homeland, with the use of four-centred arches, onion domes, tapering minarets, coloured tilework and precise symmetry. Over time, an unmistakably Indian architectural form evolved, making use of local red sandstone, first ornately chiselled, then later intricately inlaid with floral and geometric patterns. It was Akbar who embraced the use of motifs borrowed from Hindu and Jain architecture, such as cloud-like *toranas* and ornamental *jalis* (perforated stone screens), while Shah Jahan was the pioneer of monuments clad in white marble inlaid with Italian-influenced pietra dura patterns.

ARVIND BALARAMAN/SHUTTERSTOCK

Fatehpur Sikri

Akbar's Serene Resting Place

A surprising tomb for a great emperor

About 15km northwest of Agra, Sikandra is synonymous with the vast **tomb of the Mughal emperor Akbar** *(asiagracircle .in/other-tick.html; adult/under 15yr ₹310/free)*. Guarded by four towering gateways featuring some of the most ornate marble-on-sandstone inlays in India, Akbar's final resting place is an almost unadorned chamber at the heart of a monument topped by neat rows of arches rather than a grand, show-stopping dome.

Less visited than the Taj, Agra Fort or Fatehpur Sikri, it's a serene spot to contemplate an emperor who was at once tolerant and merciless, who pushed India to the heights of artistic refinement and conquered kingdom after kingdom, yet died from a common stomach bug at 63. The graves of some of Akbar's wives and children lie in similarly plain spaces behind *jali* screens on either side of the passage to the emperor's grave.

Circle the palm-lined water features around the tomb then check out the lavishly adorned **Kanch Mahal** hunting lodge nearby and the ruined Lodhi-era mausoleum outside the mausoleum walls. Just down the road is the tasteful brick and sandstone **tomb of Mariam-uz-Zamani** *(adult/under 15yr ₹310/free)*, aka Jodha Bai, Akbar's favourite wife and the mother of Jehangir.

A Wildlife Success Story

See elephants and bears saved from suffering

One of the region's great wildlife success stories, the donation-funded Indian organisation **Wildlife SOS** *(wildlifesos. org)* maintains two important animal rescue centres on the road between Agra and Mathura.

Wildlife SOS was founded in 1995 with the aim of freeing India's 'dancing bears' – captured sloth bears forced to perform cruel tricks using a rope tied through a hole cut into their muzzle. By taking captive bears into protection and providing education and employment opportunities for former bear-trainers from the Kalandar community, the organisation effectively ended bear performances in northern India.

In 2011, the organisation expanded its focus to rescuing elephants injured or traumatised by being forced to carry tourists, lead wedding processions and bless visitors to temples, providing both essential veterinary care and humane living conditions for former working elephants.

With advance notice, visitors can arrange trips to see (and learn about) the 85 sloth bears allowed to roam freely in large enclosures at the **Agra Bear Rescue Facility**, a dedicated section of the **Sur Sarovar Bird Sanctuary** *(₹350)*, about 20km from Agra.

Trips can also be arranged to meet the rescued elephants at the **Elephant Conservation & Care Centre**, about 30km from Agra. For either site, you'll need to pre-book a visiting slot (11am, 1pm or 3pm), pay a donation *(₹1500-2000)*, and arrange transport (Agra taxi drivers offer day trips to both centres for around ₹3000). Volunteer placements can also be arranged.

Wander Akbar's Ghost City

Discover the planned city of an open-minded conquerer

Founded for its proximity to the shrine of the Sufi saint Shaikh Salim Chishti, **Fatehpur Sikri** *(asiagracircle.in/fateh-pur.html; adult/under 15yr ₹610/free, guides from ₹450)* was conceived by the emperor as a model city where citizens of diverse faiths could be accommodated within the Islamic structure of Mughal society.

Unfortunately, the emperor did not give as much thought to the water supply. Akbar's model capital was constructed in 1571, but replaced as capital in 1585 by Lahore, then abandoned to the desert winds due to chronic water shortages. Its ruins lie off the road linking Agra to Bharatpur, accessible by bus or chartered taxi, then a steep uphill walk or low-effort golf cart ride *(₹20)* from the Gulistan Tourist Complex.

Arriving by golf cart, you'll enter by the royal stables, first reaching the **Shabistan-i-Iqbal**, once mistakenly thought to be the palace of Akbar's wife Mariam-uz-Zamani. As you wander through the subsequent courtyards, you'll notice subtle architectural details borrowed from Hindu and Jain temples and Christian churches.

Look out for structures such as the **Haramsara** (women's quarters) – often misidentified as the house of Akbar's loyal

AKBAR & BIRBAL

The much-loved *Birbal Stories* are moral tales of wisdom, friendship and loyalty that have been part of Indian popular culture since at least the 19th century. These fictitious yarns are inspired by the bond between Akbar and his courtier Birbal, the only one of the emperor's most prominent advisers – known as the Navratna (Nine Gems) – to be granted a residence inside the palace complex at Fatehpur Sikri. Most of the stories relate to Birbal finding ingenious solutions to tricky questions, such as being asked to count the number of crows in Akbar's kingdom. Birbal also shows up as a character in Salman Rushdie's novel *The Enchantress of Florence*.

EATING IN AGRA: BEST SNACKS

Agra Chaat House: A gem in Sadar Bazaar's 'chaat gali' specialising in *aloo tikka bhalla* – fried potato cakes, mashed and drenched in chutney. *1pm-10.30pm* ₹

Deviram's Sweets: On MG Road at Pratap Pura, this famous sweet shop is a popular stop for kachoris, samosas and *jalebis*. *8am-10.30pm* ₹

Mama Chicken: An ever-busy fast-food favourite, serving meaty treats from the tandoor and famous 'frankies' (kathi rolls). *noon-midnight* ₹₹

Deepee: A reliable dosa and *idli* stop in the popular Meher Cinema Complex at Sadar Bazaar. *10am-11pm* ₹₹

AKBAR'S NEW RELIGION

While Akbar was as uncompromising as other Mughal emperors in his dealings with rival kingdoms, he was also a man of profound tolerance for his time. Guided by the spiritual teachings of Sufi mystics such as Khwaja Muin-ud-din Chishti of Ajmer and Shaikh Salim Chishti of Fatehpur Sikri, Akbar created a unifying religion known as Din-i-Ilahi, emphasising the shared spirituality inherent in different faiths. While Akbar's new religion found few followers beyond the Mughal court, the emperor abolished the discriminatory *jiyza* tax on non-Muslims, and appointed Hindus, Jains, Christians and Zoroastrians to key positions in his government. In Akbar's royal city at Fatehpur Sikri the Diwan-i-Khas was specifically designed to promote dialogue between faiths.

courtier, Birbal – and the kiosk of the royal astrologer. Your attention will be grabbed by the cascading, open terraces of the **Panch Mahal**, designed to catch nocturnal breezes, and the bridge-traversed **Anup Talao** pool.

Nearby is the huge enclosed courtyard of the **Diwan-i-Am** (Hall of Public Audience), where Akbar held court and reputedly meted out justice by having condemned prisoners trampled by elephants (not always fatally – sometimes a 'light' trampling was enough).

The most unique feature of the ruins is the acoustically brilliant **Diwan-i-Khas** (Hall of Private Audience). At its centre, an ornately carved stone column forms the hub for four stone bridges – Akbar reputedly sat in the middle and debated with scholars and ministers from many different faiths.

Discover Akbar's Spiritual Teacher

A thriving Sufi hub

At the southwest end of the Fatehpur Sikri ruins, the grand, 17th-century **Jama Masjid** *(donations appropriate)* is a working mosque, a historic monument and a place of Sufi pilgrimage.

Dominated by the vast gateway known as the **Buland Darwaza** (note the horseshoes nailed to the gates for good luck), the mosque complex is usually entered from the side, via the Shahi Darwaza. You'll arrive into a vast courtyard dotted with dozens of Muslim graves, many attended by Sufi mystics waiting to offer advice and astrological readings to visiting pilgrims.

The main focus of attention is the white marble dargah (tomb) of **Shaikh Salim Chishti**, Akbar's most cherished spiritual adviser. Non-Muslims can enter the tomb, with its elaborate, lace-like *jali* screens, but leaving a donation is appropriate.

Nearby is the sandstone tomb of the saint's grandson, the Mughal general **Islam Khan**. The west side of the courtyard is dominated by the beautiful **mosque**, featuring lavish marble inlays that bring to mind the patterns on Persian carpets.

Visit respectfully, leaving your shoes outside, and avoid stepping onto graves or getting exasperated with the souvenir vendors and would-be guides who crowd non-pilgrim visitors.

INDIA'S GREAT SUFI SAINTS

Fatehpur Sikri is famous for the tomb of the Sufi saint Shaikh Salim Chishti, and there are several other important saint's dargahs (tombs), including the shrine of **Hazrat Nizamuddin** (p85) in Delhi and the shrine of **Khwaja Muin-ud-din Chishti** (p134) in Ajmer.

Places We Love to Stay

₹ Budget ₹₹ Midrange ₹₹₹ Top End

Taj Ganj & Agra Cantonment

Map p315

Hosteller ₹ A hostel that's almost an upscale hotel, with inviting dorms and rooms, games areas, a rooftop pool and more – all just a 10-minute walk from the Taj Mahal (be sure to pick the branch northeast of the East Gate approach road).

Zostel ₹ Part of the new breed of hotel-style Indian hostels, with inviting, colourful dorms and private bedrooms, a fine rooftop terrace, and a cosmopolitan, sociable clientele.

Joey's Hostel ₹ More like a budget hotel, Joey's is basic but right on the doorstep of the Taj in the slightly hectic Taj Ganj neighbourhood. Taj views from the terrace provide compensation for the noisy location and inconvenience of having to walk from one of the vehicle drop-off points.

Coral House ₹₹ Greenery and flowers define this cheerfully painted homestay just off the pedestrian access road to the Taj's East Gate. Rooms are spotless and spacious, with shady outdoor spaces where you can enjoy being cocooned away from the frenzy.

Coral Tree ₹₹ Beside Coral House, and similarly green and pleasant, Coral Tree is another oasis of calm, placing you close to the Taj but away from the frantic vibe. The pot-plant and flower-filled gardens are a place you can truly relax.

Hotel Atulyaa Taj ₹₹ If you crave a pool close to the Taj, look no further than this gleaming white hotel on the pedestrianised road to the East Gate, with bright rooms and a rooftop terrace and pool.

Hotel Atithi ₹₹ A solid upper-midranger in a great location for the restaurants of Fatehabad Rd; rooms are calm and inviting and there's an outdoor pool.

Ekaa Villa & Kitchen ₹₹ Boutique rooms – clean and comfortable – spread over two floors of Fatehabad Rd and styled with subtle nods to Mughal design. The kitchen dishes out great food, served indoors or out in the garden.

Oberoi Amarvilas ₹₹₹ Agra's most luxurious address offers golf-cart transfers to and from the Taj Mahal. Set in enveloping grounds are a gorgeous pool and elegant rooms with enviable Taj views, plus best-in-class dining and drinking.

ITC Mughal ₹₹₹ Fitting its name, the ITC blends luxury fit for an emperor with modern flourishes like an award-winning spa and a dreamy pool. The Peshawri restaurant (p327) is one of Agra's top tables.

Shaheed Nagar & Beyond

Max Guest House ₹ South of the Taj bustle in the calm Shaheed Nagar district, this simple, low-key guesthouse offers few frills, but the welcome is warm and there's a plant-filled breakfast room (other meals available on request).

Tourists Rest House ₹ Centrally located, with home-style food and an array of well-priced rooms set around a leafy courtyard. It's a 1960s veteran and a favourite with budget travellers. Staff offer free transfers from the train and bus station.

Awtar Mansion ₹₹ Family-run homestay in a nostalgic home set in expansive grounds in the Agra Cantonment area. Expect spacious, tastefully decorated rooms, gracious hosts and activities such as yoga sessions and cooking classes.

Mela Kothi Chambal Safari Lodge ₹₹₹ This family-run rewilded ecolodge, a 60km drive southeast from Agra, is a great place to unwind. Comfortable, attractively furnished cottages share forested grounds with civet cats and a family of nilgai (antelopes).

IZZET KERIBAR/GETTY IMAGES

For places to stay in Uttar Pradesh, see p369

Above: Varanasi (p340); Right: Celebrating Holi, Mathura (p366)

THE MAIN AREAS

VARANASI
Spiritual city on the Ganges.
p340

PRAYAGRAJ (ALLAHABAD)
Confluence of three holy rivers.
p349

KUSHINAGAR
Buddha's blissful resting place.
p353

Researched by
Puneetinder Kaur Sidhu

Uttar Pradesh

FAITH, FINE FOOD AND FABULOUS CRAFT

Welcome to the soul of spiritual India, a heady mix of ancient religions, holy rivers, and antediluvian cities enriched by modern history and syncretic heritage.

Uttar Pradesh (UP) is India's fourth largest and most populous state and its sights are spread out across its massive girth. Iconic Agra (p310), synonymous with the Taj Mahal and Mughal grandeur, is without doubt the star attraction. If you linger to look beyond, you'll find that it is also home to one of the country's holiest cities, Varanasi (variously Kashi, Benaras), famed for its ancient temples and vibrant ceremonies along the banks of the Ganges River. For Hindus, this is the most sacred place to achieve moksha or deliverance from the cycle of death and rebirth. Krishna was born in Mathura; and Ram, the hero of the epic Ramayana, was born in Ayodhya. Prayagraj (Allahabad), where the Ganges and Yamuna Rivers meet the mythological Saraswati, is another important Hindu pilgrimage centre. A dip at the confluence, called Sangam, is believed to cleanse all sins, resulting in the once-in-12-years Kumbh Mela, when millions of salvation-seeking pilgrims converge here.

PRABHJIT S. KALSI/SHUTTERSTOCK

UP is just as closely associated with Buddhism. Buddha gave his first sermon in Sarnath and died in Kushinagar. Both places are now tranquil pilgrimage destinations and draw visitors from around the world. The Muslim Mughals and Nawabs made indelible impressions as well, leaving behind a wealth of architectural and gastronomic masterpieces. As an abiding consequence of the latter, Lucknow, erstwhile seat of the Nawabs, and the modern-day state capital, was designated a UNESCO Creative City of Gastronomy in November 2025.

AYODHYA
Birthplace of Ram. p356

LUCKNOW
Nawabs, kebabs and fragrances. p359

MATHURA & VRINDAVAN
Birthplace of Krishna. p366

Lucknow, p359

Nawabi culture, couture, and cuisine define the lively state capital, and its brush with the British is reflected in its architectural heritage.

Mathura & Vrindavan, p366

Follow in a youthful Krishna's footsteps, temple-hopping your way between the twin spiritual centres. Vrindavan doubles as the international home of the Hare Krishnas.

TRAIN

UP is well connected by train, including high-speed Vande Bharat Express services, which link Varanasi with Delhi via Prayagraj (Allahabad), Delhi with Ayodhya via Lucknow, and Lucknow with Gorakhpur via Ayodhya. Sleeper trains are available, and recommended, to cover longer distances.

AIR

Of the 25 airports in UP, the most useful for travellers are located in Agra, Varanasi, Prayagraj (Allahabad), Gorakhpur, Ayodhya and Lucknow. A low passenger turnout has resulted in airlines reducing operations to Kushinagar's International Airport.

BUS/TAXI

Buses ply regularly across the state and are best used for short hops between cities. For multicity itineraries short on time, hiring taxis is recommended. Reliable cab services are readily available and drivers often double as (passable) guides.

Find Your Way

Uttar Pradesh is a landlocked state in north-central India. Roughly the size of the UK, it's encircled by eight other Indian states and a Union Territory, and shares an international border with Nepal to its northeast.

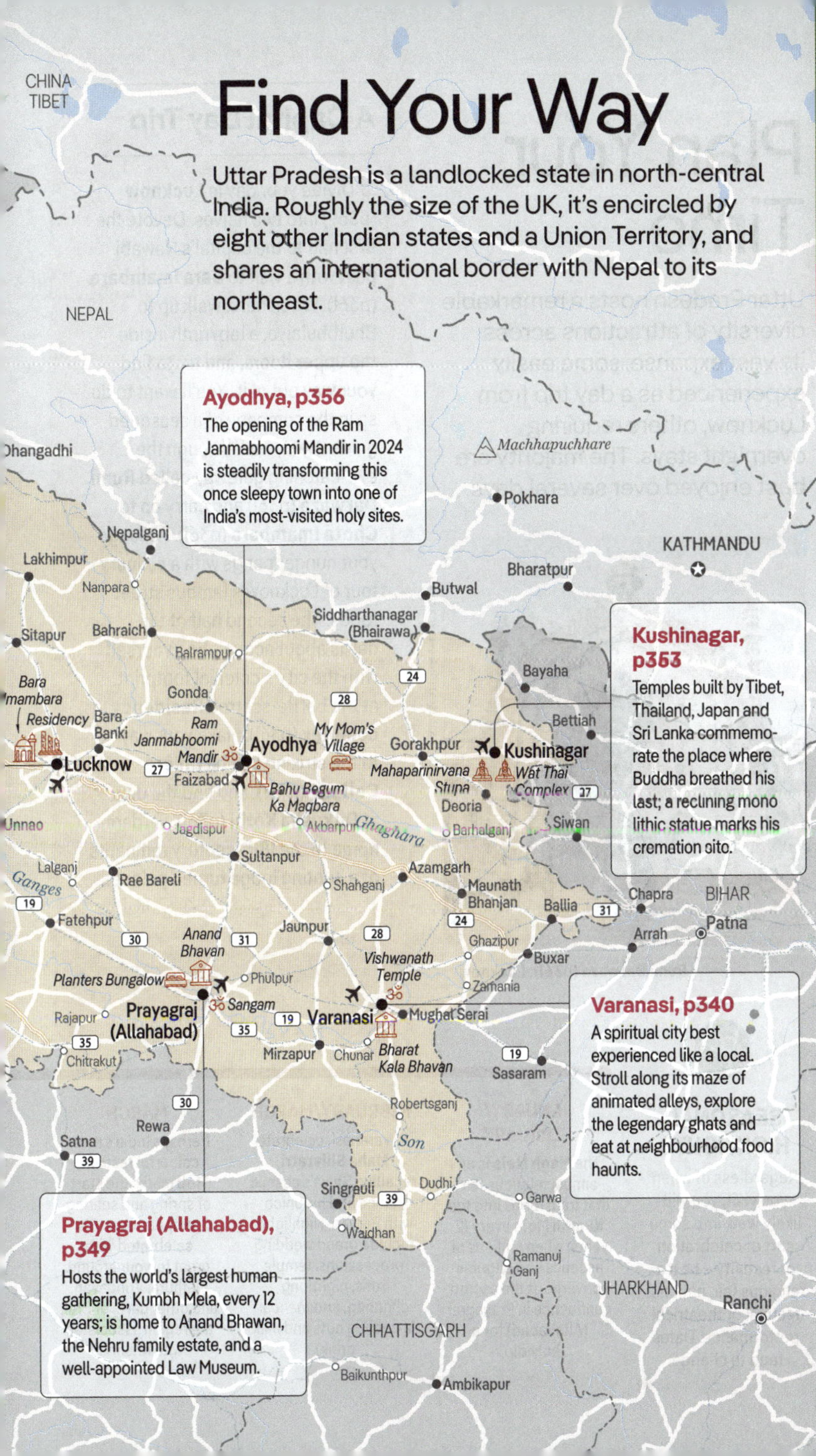

Ayodhya, p356
The opening of the Ram Janmabhoomi Mandir in 2024 is steadily transforming this once sleepy town into one of India's most-visited holy sites.

Kushinagar, p353
Temples built by Tibet, Thailand, Japan and Sri Lanka commemorate the place where Buddha breathed his last; a reclining monolithic statue marks his cremation site.

Varanasi, p340
A spiritual city best experienced like a local. Stroll along its maze of animated alleys, explore the legendary ghats and eat at neighbourhood food haunts.

Prayagraj (Allahabad), p349
Hosts the world's largest human gathering, Kumbh Mela, every 12 years; is home to Anand Bhawan, the Nehru family estate, and a well-appointed Law Museum.

Plan Your Time

Uttar Pradesh hosts a remarkable diversity of attractions across its vast expanse, some easily experienced as a day trip from Lucknow, others requiring overnight stays. The majority are best enjoyed over several days.

VINAYAK JAGTAP/SHUTTERSTOCK

Rumi Darwaza (p361), Lucknow

A Capital Day Trip

● Divide your day in **Lucknow** (p359) into two halves. Devote the first half to the capital's Nawabi past with a visit to **Bara Imambara** (p361). When here, walk up to Bhulbhulaiya, a labyrinth inside the upper floors, and try to find your way out of it. You'll want to do so in the company of a seasoned guide. Next, walk through the eye-catching gateway called **Rumi Darwaza** (p361) and carry on to **Chota Imambara** (p361). Assuage your hunger pangs with a culinary tour of Lucknow's famous street foods. The second half of the day is about acquainting yourself with the city's colonial footprint at the battle-scarred **Residency complex** (p361). Make your way to the striking **La Martinière College** (p361), and end the day at **Dilkusha Kothi** (p361), verdant home to the 18th-century remnants of a hunting lodge turned palace.

SEASONAL HIGHLIGHTS

Regardless of when you visit, you will likely walk into some sort of celebration or festivity – be it a religious fair, national festival or theatrical performance. Dates tend to change.

JANUARY/FEBRUARY

The **Magh Mela** is an annual religious fair that transforms into the **Kumbh Mel**a every 12 years, when millions of ascetics and pilgrims converge at the sacred confluence in Prayagraj (Allahabad) for a holy dip.

FEBRUARY/MARCH

In Varanasi, celebrate **Maha Shivratri**, recalling Shiva's cosmic dance and his union with Parvati. Highlights include grand wedding processions, temple runs, nightlong chanting, and *thandai* (a cooling nuts and milk drink).

MARCH

Perhaps India's most colourful festival, **Holi** marks the start of spring and soaring temperatures. It's celebrated with great fervour around Mathura, Vrindavan, and other parts of Braj, the region associated with Krishna.

Three Varanasi Days

- Give yourself three days to explore **Varanasi** (p340); include a sunrise boat ride and an evening *aarti* (the auspicious lighting of lamps or candles) at one of its ghats. Sign up for an immersive Old City tour, watch skillful weavers and toymakers at work and traditional wrestlers at practice, and tuck into delectable neighbourhood staples. You'll want to spend some time in **Bharat Kala Bhavan** (p344), a 125-year-old repository at Benaras Hindu University; and visit **Sarnath** (p347), where Buddha gave his first sermon. Take a trip to **Prayagraj** (Allahabad; p349) to see the holy confluence, the Nehru family estate and the **Law Museum & Archives** (p351). Look out for the grand architecture of **Allahabad University** (p352) on your way to or from **Khusro Bagh** (p351). Perhaps consider a relaxing stay at **Planters Bungalow** (p352), a British-era heritage home set amid an erstwhile indigo plantation.

A Week in Uttar Pradesh

- After **Varanasi** (p340), head north to **Kushinagar** (p353), the peaceful town where Buddha died, and follow in his final footsteps. You could continue up to Gorakhpur and Nepal, or veer east and stop by at India's latest pilgrimage hot spot, the **Ram Janmabhoomi Mandir** (p356) in Ayodhya. En route, experience UP's bucolic charm at **My Mom's Village** (p358), a heritage farm-stay, an hour's drive from Ayodhya. Continue on to **Lucknow** (p359) and immerse in its gracious hospitality. After your fill of sightseeing and street-side delights, you'll want to wind down over a home-cooked Awadhi meal with a local family. Make a trip to **Kannauj** (p364), the perfume capital of India, and witness the production of attar (alcohol-free perfume oil) through age-old techniques. Also visit a perfume bar to create your signature fragrance.

APRIL/MAY

Buddha Purnima commemorates Buddha's birth, enlightenment and death, as they are believed to have transpired on the same day. It's best observed in Sarnath and Kushinagar, with lighting lamps and prayer ceremonies.

JUNE/JULY

Monthlong Muharram marks the martyrdom of Imam Hussain, the Prophet's grandson. Observed through fasting, large processions and mourning rituals, including self-flagellation, it is historically fervent in Lucknow.

SEPTEMBER/OCTOBER

In the prelude to Dassehra, Ram Lila episodes are performed around the **Ramnagar Fort** (p344) in Varanasi. This retelling of the Ramayana has been performed, sans lighting and sound system, since the 1800s.

OCTOBER/NOVEMBER

Diwali is celebrated pan-India by illuminating homes and lighting oil lamps. It marks the return of Ram to Ayodhya after a 14-year exile and is followed, 15 days later, by the Dev Diwali of Varanasi.

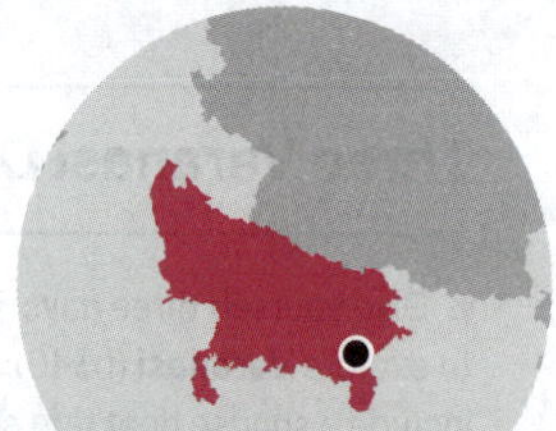

Varanasi

SPIRITUAL CENTRE | RIVER REVERENCE | LIVELY LANES

TOP TIP

Modernised Namo Ghat, just northeast of the Malviya Bridge, is the first fully wheelchair-accessible ghat in Varanasi. Namo, with its striking sculpture of hands in prayer, can be reached by car, and there are ramped pontoons for boarding boats.

Varanasi is everything you imagined about India and then some. Colourful, characterful and unabashedly chaotic, it's the kind of place you go to experience, not merely see. This is where Hindus come to die, hoping for deliverance from rebirth, to cremate their dead, and wash away their sins in the Ganges. Related rituals take place in full public view, and facing the reality of death can be a forceful experience. The intensity of sights, sounds and smells of the Old City, where most places of interest, hotels and restaurants are located, can just as easily overwhelm the uninitiated, or the not-so-intrepid. Stand your ground, nevertheless, because it is this uniqueness that will linger on in the memories long after you leave. As will watching the sunrise from a boat, strolling along the ghats and losing yourself to the crescendo of chants, drums and conch-blowing of a *ganga aarti* (river worship ceremony).

Boat Ride at Daybreak

Magical sunrise on the Ganges

Gliding down the Ganges as day breaks over a slowly stirring Varanasi is unforgettable. Settle into a rowboat, camera at hand, for the hourlong ride south from Dashashwamedh Ghat to Harishchandra Ghat. Observe the riverbank come alive with pilgrims bathing and offering prayers to the rising sun.

GETTING AROUND

The most atmospheric part of town is the Old City, a maze of *galis* (alleys) lining the west bank of the Ganges. However these lanes are too narrow for cars and autorickshaws. If you stay here, you may have to walk in with your luggage. There's road access close to Assi Ghat and Dashashwamedh Ghat, but taxis and autorickshaws can't access the Dashashwamedh area between 9am and 9pm.

The main train station is 5km northwest of Dashashwamedh Ghat; the bus station is across the road. An autorickshaw is around ₹200 to the ghat area. The airport is 24km northwest; a taxi is around ₹1200.

Ghats

Early winter evenings, to coincide with the nightly *ganga aarti*, are also a good time to be on the river. Expect to pay upwards of ₹500 for a rowboat and ₹1500 for a motorboat off the ghat. Customised boat trips with seasoned guides and classical musicians are pricier and require advance bookings *(9415225994; from ₹8000)*. Avoid in the monsoon.

Centred on Shiva

Visit the upgraded Vishwanath Temple

Varanasi's most famous shrine, **Vishwanath Temple** is dedicated to Vishveswara, Shiva as lord of the universe, and paying obeisance here is considered an essential pilgrimage by Hindus. It received a massive makeover with the construction of the **Kashi Vishwanath Corridor**, resulting in a widened approach from the Ganges. High security restricts entry for foreigners to Gate 4 *(shrikashivishwanath.org; ₹700)*. You are required to leave all personal belongings, including phones, in a locker here before joining teeming pilgrims in the huge shrine-lined marble plaza with the sanctum at its heart.

Spectacular Show of Reverence

Delight in an atmospheric aarti

Without doubt one of the most photographed spectacles in Varanasi, the *ganga aarti* is an indelible experience. The 45-minute ceremony at 7pm (earlier in winter) includes a practised routine by priests wielding multitiered fire lamps. It is accompanied by chanting, clapping, drumming, bell-ringing and conch-blowing. Massive speakers belt out bhajans (hymns) at ear-splitting decibels. Generally held at Dashashwamedh Ghat, the riveting ritual is now also conducted at Assi Ghat and **Namo Ghat**. Show up early for a free spot on the steps. Nominal donations may be expected but are not mandatory.

ESSENTIAL TIPS FOR VISITING VARANASI

- Don't take photos at the 'burning' ghats. Resist offers to 'follow me for a better view', where you'll be pressured for money.
- Do not go to any shop with a guide or autorickshaw driver. Be firm and don't do it. Ever. You will pay 40% to 60% more, due to ridiculous commissions.
- When negotiating with boaters, confirm the price and currency before setting out. Many just love to say '100!' and at the end claim they meant dollars or euros.
- Be careful with bhang lassis – they are made with hash and can be very strong (we've heard reports of robberies of intoxicated people).
- Beware of yoga teachers who are mainly interested in hands-on lessons with young women.

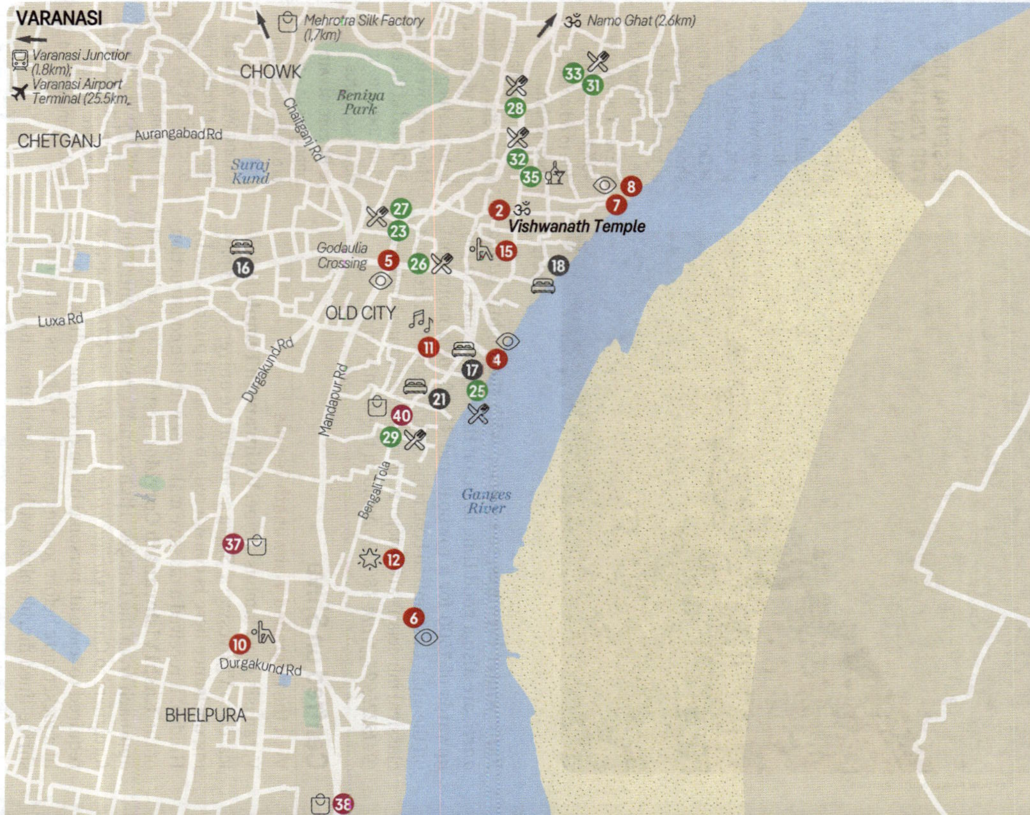

HIGHLIGHTS
1 Bharat Kala Bhavan
2 Vishwanath Temple

SIGHTS
3 Assi Ghat
4 Dashashwamedh Ghat
5 Gowdowlia Chauraha
6 Harishchandra Ghat
7 Kashi Vishwanath Corridor
8 Manikarnika Ghat
9 Ramnagar Fort & Museum

ACTIVITIES
10 Chaitanya Yoga Kendra
11 International Music Centre Ashram
12 Pragati Hindi
13 Varanasi Walks
14 Vasistha Yoga Foundation
15 Yoga Training Centre

SLEEPING
16 Bedzzz Varanasi
17 Brijrama Palace
18 Ganpati Guesthouse
19 Hotel Ganges View
20 Nilay House
21 Wander Station

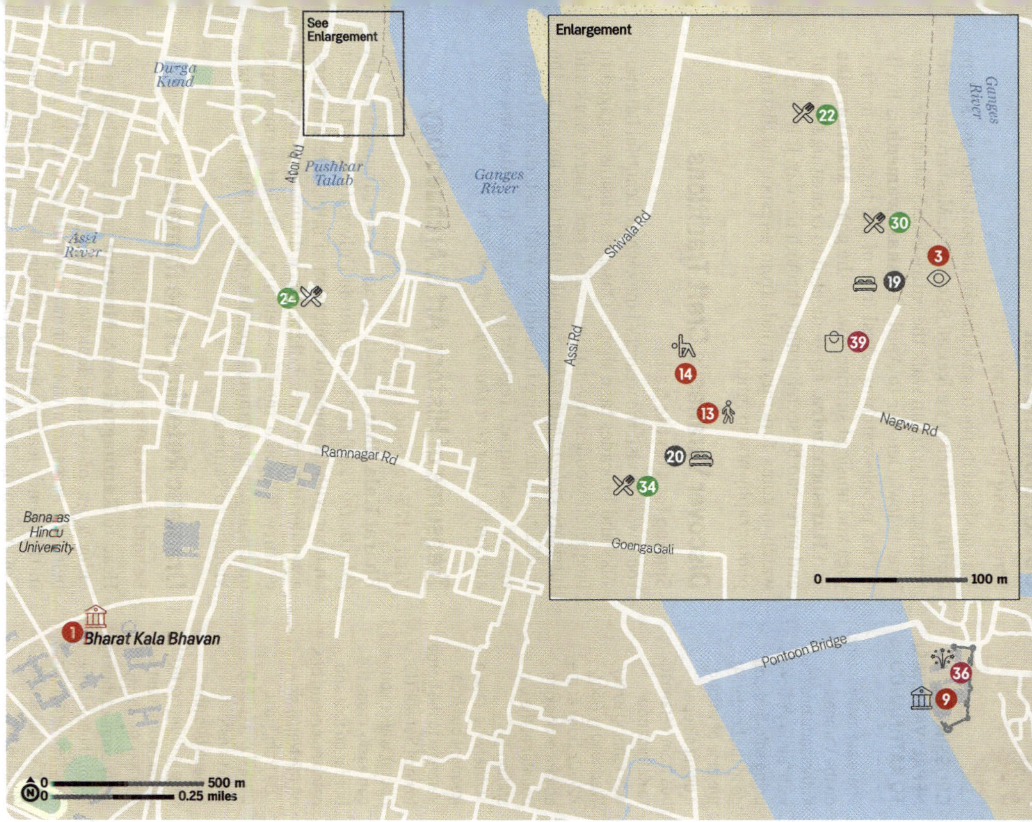

EATING
- **22** Aum Cafe
- **23** Baba Thandai
- **24** Chachi Ki Kachori
- **25** Darbhanga
- **26** Keshari Ruchikar Vyanjan
- **27** Keshav Paan Bhandar
- **28** Lakshmi Chai Wale
- **29** Monalisa Cafe
- **30** Pizzeria Vaatika Cafe
- **31** Ram Bhandar Kachori
- **32** Shree Rajbandhu Sweets
- **33** Shree Satya Narayan Sweets
- **34** Sparrow Cafe

DRINKING & NIGHTLIFE
- **35** Blue Lassi

ENTERTAINMENT
- **36** Ram Lila

SHOPPING
- **37** Baba Blacksheep
- **38** Fabindia
- **39** Harmony Book Shop
- **40** Himalayan Hemp Company

CROSSING TO NEPAL: VARANASI TO KATHMANDU

There are many scams on the Varanasi–Kathmandu bus route, with 'through' tickets being sold that only go to the border. At the time of writing, a direct sleeper bus from Varanasi to Kathmandu was running every Wednesday *(16hr, ₹2150)*; book at the advance-booking counter at the bus station.

Otherwise, take a frequent bus from Varanasi to the border town of Sunauli (10 hours), where you can easily cross the border on foot and catch an onward bus on the Nepal side.

By train, go to Gorakhpur (p353) then transfer to a Sunauli bus (the stop is 100m north of Gorakhpur's main bus station). By air, you'll likely connect through Delhi, though there are often direct flights from Varanasi with Buddha Air.

Get to Know the Ghat

Stroll along the riverbank

Varanasi is at its photogenic best by its boat-lined ghats (steps leading to the river's edge), all 88 of them. Most are meant for bathing, and you can walk the entire length when the water level is low (October to April). **Dashashwamedh** is liveliest for people-watching; **Assi** (one of the biggest), for free yoga and music at sunrise. Two of the ghats, **Manikarnika** and **Harishchandra**, are dedicated to cremating the dead, and pyres can be seen burning through the day. It is okay to watch ongoing funerary rituals from a respectful distance, photography not so much.

Discover Varanasi's Craft Traditions

Sign-up for a textile trail

You'll want to visit the weavers' lanes, where beautiful Banarasi silks and brocades take shape. Observe artisans engaged in lacquered wooden toy-making, soft-stone filigree work and intricate *gulabi meenakari* (pink enamel on metal) in the making. For immersive interactions with custodians of these age-old techniques, register in advance for a daylong craft and textile tour *(breakaway.in; from ₹6000)*.

Treasures of History, Art & Archaeology

Visit a 125-year-old repository

Bharat Kala Bhavan is the spacious on-campus museum *(bhu.ac.in; ₹250)* at Benaras Hindu University. Spend at least an hour with its splendid collection of miniature paintings, a wonderful sculptures gallery (some dating back to the 2nd century BCE) and the 12th-century palm-leaf manuscripts on display at mezzanine level. It's open 10.30am to 4.30pm, Monday to Saturday.

Dramatic Retelling of the Ramayana

Behold Ramnagar's unique Ram Lila

Head to **Ramnagar Fort & Museum** across the Ganges to enjoy a one-of-its-kind depiction of Ramayana's **Ram Lila**, held free across multiple venues around its crumbling fort, in the month leading up to Dassehra (October–November). Come evening, locals throng the town to watch these daily enactments by colourfully attired masked men as they belt out dialogues without microphones or stage lights. Join the audience of old and new patrons, kitted out in their Sunday

EATING & DRINKING IN VARANASI: OLD CITY

Blue Lassi: A tiny, hole-in-the-wall yoghurt shop near Manikarnika Ghat. It churns out the freshest, creamiest and fruitiest lassi – the size of a meal. *9am-10pm* ₹₹

Keshari Ruchikar Vyanjan: This atmospheric, carved-wood spot has been at it for half a century. Indians pack in here for high-quality veg. *9am-11pm* ₹₹

Darbhanga: Some of the best Indian food. The *aloo chaat* is a gourmet-street-food revelation. Inside the BrijRama Palace Hotel; book ahead. *7am-2pm & 3pm-10pm* ₹₹₹

Monalisa Cafe: This relaxed cafe in Bengali Tola is another traveller favourite, with good Wi-Fi, rooftop dining, vegan options and excellent espresso. *7am-10.30pm* ₹₹

best, for a truly memorable outing. Like us, you may want to do it in the company of Ajit Yadav *(9415225994)*, a seasoned and knowledgeable guide.

Realign Your Chakras

Explore yoga and meditation

Try your hand at yoga and meditation at a host of studios across the city. Lessons are held on the hour (6–10am, 4–8pm) at the spartan yet lively **Chaitanya Yoga Kendra** *(chaitanyayogavns.in)*. Likewise, the Sunil Kumar-helmed **Yoga Training Centre** *(+91 991-9857895)* near Meer Ghat, runs daily classes from 6am to 8pm. Courses in ancient knowledge systems are an additional attraction at the **Vasistha Yoga Foundation**. While history enthusiasts do well to sign up for yoga-history walks with **Varanasi Walks** *(varanasiwalks.com)*.

Take Up a Skill

Courses and workshops galore

Discover the beauty of Indian classical music at the family-owned **International Music Centre Ashram** *(inmca.org)*, and learn to play the sitar or tabla *(from ₹1000)*. Should you enjoy cooking, sign up for a three-hour class *(from ₹2500)* at the women-run **Sparrow Cafe** *(790-9007364)*, near Assi Ghat. If craft floats your boat, call **WOV Tours** *(837-6819587; from ₹9000)* to register for a basic *zardozi* (embroidery), *meenakari* (enamel work) or toy-making workshop. Linguists can consider in-person or online classes *(₹500/hr)* with Raju Mukherjee *(933-5376488)* of **Pragati Hindi**.

Enjoy a Spot of Retail Therapy

Procure silk saris and souvenirs

There's no lack of shopping in Varanasi – every street corner beckons with attractive options. However, all that shimmers is not silk. A trustworthy name for educative and restrained sales and affordable buys *(silks from ₹2000, pashmina silk from ₹3000)* is **Baba Blacksheep** *(bababIacksheep.co)*. For fine silks and fabrics at fair, fixed prices, try **Mehrotra Silk Factory** *(mehrotrasilk.in)*, where comfy floor seating allows a leisurely browse. Visit **Fabindia** for contemporary apparel and home accessories; and the **Himalayan Hemp Company** *(himalayanhemp.in)* for sustainable fashion. With its handpicked literary gems, **Harmony Book Shop** *(harmonybooksonline.com)* is a veritable booklover's haven on Assi Ghat.

CROSSING TO NEPAL: SUNAULI TO BELAHIYA

Sunauli offers little more than a bus stop, a couple of simple hotels and a busy border post. The border is open 24 hours (for foot traffic) and the crossing is straightforward, so most travellers carry on into Nepal, pausing just long enough to get their passport stamped.

Moneychangers on the Nepali side change Indian rupees to Nepali rupees at fixed rates *(NRs100:₹60, ₹100:NRs160)*, as the currencies are pegged.

Multiple-entry visas are available on arrival *(15/30/90 days US$30/50/125; children under 10 free)* at the Nepal Immigration Post. You must pay with US cash, and you need two passport photos. Visit nepalimmigration.gov.np for the latest information on Nepali visas.

EATING IN VARANASI: AROUND ASSI GHAT

Aum Cafe: Colourful cafe; good lemon pancakes, astounding lemon or organic green-tea lassis. Lots of veg options. *7am-4.30pm Tue-Sun Jul-Apr* ₹

Sparrow Cafe: Small and cheerful women-run place with checked tablecloths and travel books. Recommended cooking courses run here. *8am-9pm* ₹

Pizzeria Vaatika Cafe: In a prime position overlooking Assi Ghat, this place has a wood-fired pizza oven, a leafy courtyard and homemade cookies. *8am-10pm* ₹₹

Chachi Ki Kachori: Around for over a century, serving only a handful of traditional breakfast dishes, eaten seated on empty oil cannisters. *9-11am* ₹

DELICIOUSNESS AFOOT

Get to know Varanasi's delectable side through its street-side staples, some well-advertised, some unsung, and some little-known.

START	END	LENGTH
Gowdowlia Crossing	Gowdowlia Crossing	3km; 1½hr

Delve into the city's scrumptiousness with a walking tour of its lively alleys. Begin from 1 **Godowalia Chauraha** with an anytime Banarsi staple at 2 **Keshav-Madhav Pan Bhandar**. Carry on along the road for a refreshing glass of *thandai* at 3 **Baba Thandai**. Go past the Foreigner Ticket Office of Vishwanath Temple to arrive at 4 **Lakshmi Chai Wale**, popular for cream-slathered toasts and strong flavourful tea.

Turn right into Thateri Bazar to dig into the breakfast specials at 5 **Shree Satya Narayan Sweets**; try the *gol kachori* (stuffed savoury pastry) with *chana ghugni* (chickpeas), perhaps a crispy *jalebi*. Follow the road to 6 **Ram Bhandar Kachori**, famous for *puri* (deep-fried flatbread), kachori and *jalebi* in the mornings, samosa (stuffed savoury pastry) in the evenings.

Head south towards Kashi Vishwanath Corridor, and turn into Kachori Gali for 7 **Shree Rajbandhu Sweets**; treat your sweet tooth with *malai gillori, kheer kadam* and *rajbhog*. Walk the sugar rush off with a leisurely stroll through the Corridor to 8 **Dashashwamedh Ghat** (p344), and pause here for a spot of people-watching.

Make your way west from here. Stop by at 9 **Keshari Ruchikar Vyanjan** en route to end with *chaat*, Varanasi's most well-known snack. Pop in a few *pani puri*, and tuck into some *tamatar* or *papdi chaat*. Top off with a round of *kulfi* (ice cream) before returning to Godowalia Crossing.

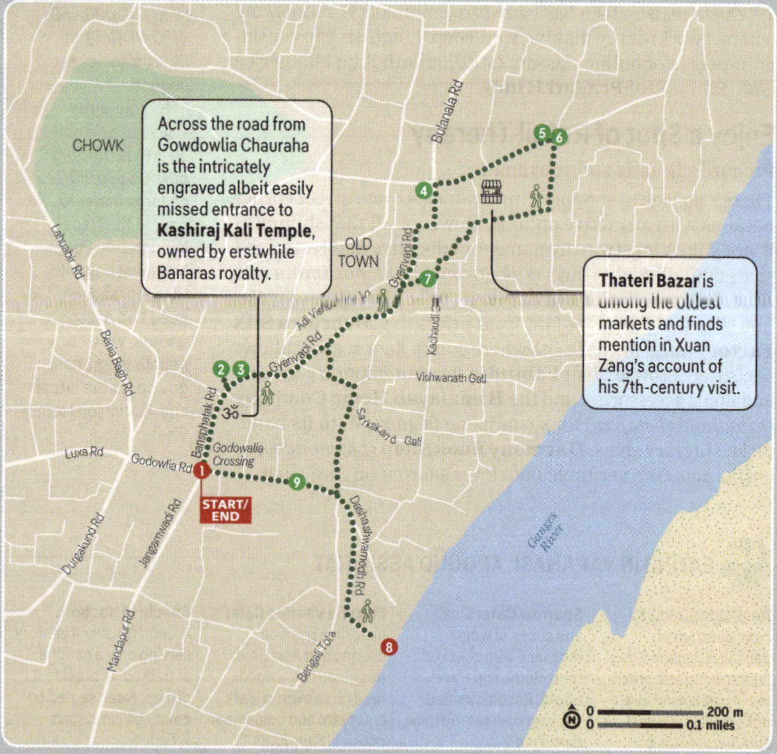

Beyond Varanasi

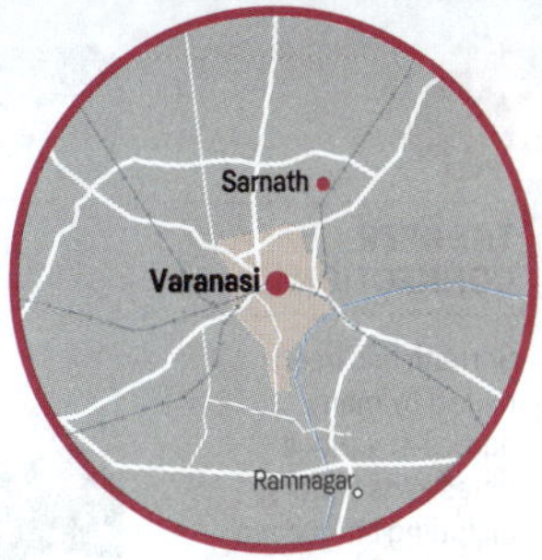

The colour and clamour of Varanasi makes way for Sarnath's quietude, where an enlightened Buddha gave his famous first sermon.

Sarnath is one of four significant sites on the Buddhist circuit, and once featured magnificent stupa and monasteries built by emperor Ashoka in the 3rd century BCE. During his 640 CE visit, Chinese traveller Xuan Zang recorded close to 1500 monks housed in roomy monasteries and a 60m-high stupa. Not long after, Buddhism began its decline, and with the subsequent sacking by Muslim rulers in the 12th century, Sarnath lost its sheen altogether. It wasn't until British archaeologists chanced upon its ruins in 1835 that it regained its importance. Today, followers from around the world flock to its well-preserved remnants, in particular around Purnima (April–May), when Buddha's birth, death and enlightenment are roundly celebrated.

Sarnath

TIME FROM VARANASI: **30MIN**

Sarnath's most sacred site

Enclosed within a large green complex, open from sunrise to sunset, are the vestiges of one of Buddhism's most hallowed places, once believed to be deer-dwelling woodlands. A well-marked path leads to the imposing 34m-high **Dhamek Stupa**, where an enlightened Buddha first shared his wisdom. Its encircling carvings are from the 5th century CE, though some of the brickwork harks back to 200 BCE. The path carries on to the remains of **Mulgandha Kuti Vihar**, the hut Buddha is said to have stayed in for three months. It winds past neatly kept remnants of votive stupa, and to the original location of the 3rd-century edict-engraved **Ashoka Pillar**. Marvel at the undiminished polish of the fragments here. The rest is on display at the site museum, your next stop. Wheelchairs are available with limited access.

Home of India's national emblem

For a better understanding of Sarnath's importance in Buddhist history, the **Archaeological Museum** is best visited after the monastic ruins. A remarkably well-preserved lion capital, which once crowned the Ashoka Pillar and became India's national emblem in 1950, is the most famous exhibit here. It's open 9am to 5pm (closed Fridays); give yourself at

GETTING AROUND

The easiest way to get to Sarnath is by autorickshaw or taxi. An autorickshaw will cost ₹300–400 one way from Varanasi, or figure on around ₹700 for a return day trip, with waiting time. A taxi costs ₹1000 return, with an hour or so of waiting time.

Infrequent local buses *(₹35)* run to Sarnath from outside the Varanasi train station – look for orange buses 107 and 108.

THE DEER CONNECTION

Sarnath has been called by many names at various times in its history, including Mrigadava and Migadaya. Some hotels, shops, and places of business continue to bear these monikers, conjuring up a past replete with *mrigya* (deer) roaming freely. In Buddhism, this gentle herbivore symbolises harmony, happiness and longevity. Buddha's first sermon is commonly believed to have taken place in a deer park. This inspired the twin deer and dharma-wheel emblem, globally recognised as a Buddhist symbol. The future Buddha routinely shows up as a golden deer or deer king in the *Jataka*, a collection of Buddhist fables depicting Buddha's previous lives. Sarnath is itself a derivative of the name Sarangnath, meaning lord of the deer.

HSTUDIO99/SHUTTERSTOCK

Dhamek Stupa (p347)

least half an hour to take in all the single storey museum's beautifully displayed exhibits at leisure. It includes larger-than-life sculptures and an enormous stone umbrella, ornately carved with Buddhist motifs and said to be over 2000 years old. You will also see a rich collection of ancient tools, inscriptions and structural fragments. Weekends can get crowded. It is advisable to buy combined tickets for the museum and ruins in advance *(asi.payumoney.com; adult/child ₹255/free)*. Bags and large items are not allowed; lockers are available for free near the entrance.

Striking frescoed shrine

Not to be confused with its namesake-in-ruins, the eye-catching **Mulgandha Kuti Vihar Temple** is of recent vintage and was completed by the Mahabodhi Society in 1931 to commemorate Buddha's first public discourse. The striking structure with multiple churchlike spires houses Buddha relics and is near the town's main crossing. Step inside the shrine to admire its vibrant frescoes. Painted by Japanese artist Kosetsu Nosu, the intricate mural depicting Buddha's life from birth to death took five years to finish. A bodhi tree (sacred fig) on the premises was transplanted from the one in Sri Lanka that came from the original in Bodhgaya. Entry is free but donations are accepted. It's open 4.30am to 11.30am and 1.30pm to 5.30pm. Visitors are required to leave shoes outside the temple.

Hallowed Jain pilgrimage centre

Sarnath is just as important for adherents of Jainism. The 19th-century **Digambar Jain Temple**, distinct for its golden-coloured *shikhara* (spire) and verdant premises, is located close to Dhamek Stupa. It is dedicated to Shreyansanath, the 11th *tirthankar*, who was born in the nearby village of Singhpuri. His seated likeness, aesthetically fashioned from polished black obsidian stone (used to test purity of gold), graces the sanctum. Painted scenes from the life of Mahavira, founder of the faith, cover the walls here. The peaceful temple complex is open from sunrise to sunset.

Prayagraj (Allahabad)

KUMBH MELA | INDEPENDENCE HISTORY | MUSEUMS GALORE

Prayagraj (Allahabad) is home to the holiest of river confluences. It is on the southeast edge of this city that the Ganges River merges with the Yamuna and a mythical Saraswati. This generally laid-back metropolis, the most celebrated of India's four Kumbh Mela locations, transforms into a sea of humanity every 12 years. Millions of Hindus congregate on the riverbanks for ritual cleansing in holy waters. A foremost administrative centre during the Mughal and British periods, Prayagraj (Allahabad) is equally important in Indian history and modern politics. It was home to the influential Nehru clan, and served as the nerve centre of the Independence movement. For casual visitors, it offers plenty of sights and a host of experiences, from Mughal sepulchres and striking colonial buildings, to literary legacies and enriching repositories. A railway line slices the city into neat halves: a hip and happening Civil Lines and the heaving old-world Chowk.

GETTING AROUND

The stands at the train station and MG Marg are your best bets for autorickshaws and taxis. Consider hiring one for a half-day *(4hr, ₹600)* to take in the town's sights, as they are quite spread out. A taxi will cost around ₹13 per kilometre. Ola rideshares also operate.

Cycle rickshaws are plentiful; pay ₹40 for a short trip of 1km to 2km, but be prepared to haggle for it. *Vikrams* (tempo or a larger version of the standard tempo, ie a large autorickshaw) hang about on the south side of the train station.

A Soul-Cleansing Sacred Confluence

Experience the holy Sangam

A hallowed spot visited all year-round for purifying dips or immersing ashes of the dead, **Sangam** experiences a sizeable increase in footfall around Magh Mela, a six-week-long religious fair held annually in February and March. The arrivals swell to astonishing levels when, every 12th year, it metamorphoses into the mother of all religious festivals, the Kumbh. Hundreds of boat-hands ferry pilgrims and priests, dawn to dusk, from the teeming **Qila Ghat** to the general vicinity of the confluence. Haggle your way into one *(shared boat/solo rides from ₹100/800)* for a closer look at unique ancient customs. Once back on terra firma, make your way to the towering eastern wall of the hard-to-miss 16th-century **Allahabad Fort**, occupied by the Indian army. Here, a small door leads to the only section open to public, the subterranean and shrine-replete **Patalpuri Temple** (open 6am to 5.30pm). Look out for a shrine formed by the roots of the holy Akshaya Vat (banyan

TOP TIP

Many tour operators offer day trips to Prayagraj (Allahabad) from Varanasi. Unless you want to linger to absorb the atmosphere at Sangam during a mela (fair/festival), a day trip is enough to see the main sights.

HIGHLIGHTS
1 Anand Bhavan
2 Sangam

SIGHTS
3 Allahabad Fort
4 Allahabad Museum
5 Allahabad University
6 Khusro Bagh
7 Law Museum & Archives
8 Patalpuri Temple
9 Swaraj Bhavan

SLEEPING
10 Hotel Prayag
11 WelcomHeritage Badi Kothi

EATING
12 El Chico Cafe
13 Indian Coffee House
14 Sardaar Ji Dhaba

DRINKING & NIGHTLIFE
15 Patiyala Peg Bar

tree) in the courtyard above. Keep nominal change handy to leave small offerings at the shrine: ₹5–10 is fair; don't be compelled to give more.

Where India's Fate was Redrawn

Visit historic Nehru family estate

The charming two-storey **Anand Bhavan** *(₹200)*, with its eye-catching wraparound verandas, is the stately home-turned-museum of the Nehrus. They are an influential family that produced five generations of leading political figures, from Moti Lal Nehru to Rahul Gandhi; and two prime ministers in Jawaharlal Nehru and Indira Gandhi, who was also married here in 1942. It was within the elegant, book-lined and high-ceiling rooms of this mansion that Mahatma Gandhi, Jawaharlal Nehru and others effectively planned to bring down the British government. It's filled with personal effects and photos, and you'll require a half hour minimum to take in all the neatly displayed exhibits (open Tuesday to Sunday). Give yourself another 30 minutes to view Indira Gandhi's life-in-pictures in the adjoining **Swaraj Bhavan**.

Repository of Art, History, Literature

Explore delightful galleries

The red-bricked, well-kept **Allahabad Museum** *(₹500)* is home to wide-ranging archaeological and historical artefacts, including the encased pistol of freedom fighter Chandra Shekhar Azad, who lends his name to the expansive park that hosts the museum. Nearly as old as independent India, it showcases rich collections of ancient stone and wood sculptures, miniatures, modern paintings and textiles. You'll find galleries centered on Jawaharlal Nehru and leading literary personalities of Prayagraj (Allahabad). It's open 10am to 5pm, Tuesday to Sunday. Standing within the same complex is the vehicle that carried Mahatma Gandhi's ashes for immersion at Sangam.

Singular Mine of Legal History

Visit India's oldest law museum

A unique, quiet, academic space, the **Law Museum & Archives** *(₹10)* brings alive the history of the Allahabad High Court since its inception in 1866. This repository has a notable collection of old and rare documents pertaining to India's legal history, including Jawaharlal Nehru's application for an assistant law reporter's job. Other exhibits comprise landmark judgments and firman (decrees) issued by Mughal emperors, colonial-period court furniture, judicial robes and portraits of legal luminaries. Open 10am to 5pm, Friday to Wednesday, it's worth an (unexpectedly) enjoyable hour.

Royal Remains

Mughal tombs inside walled garden

Khusro Bagh wears a surprisingly festive air, despite the funerary nature of the monuments it encloses. Open dawn

THE MIGHTY MELA

At the Ardh Kumbh Mela in 2019, 240 million people gathered at the Prayagraj (Allahabad) Sangam (meaning 'river confluence'). It was the single largest gathering of humanity, ever – till the one in 2025, which is said to have attracted a whopping 660 million people.

For each mela, auspicious bathing days are carefully calculated for maximum astrological potency by seers of the 13 *akharas* (religious colleges). These are the most popular times to be in or near the river, and the crowds have turned deadly in the past. In 2013, 42 people were killed in a stampede at the train station; while in 1954, 350 pilgrims died in a stampede to reach the river, an event recreated in Vikram Seth's novel *A Suitable Boy*.

COLONIAL PRAYAGRAJ (ALLAHABAD)

This one-time capital of North-Western Provinces carries a distinct colonial footprint, evidenced in the broad, bungalow-lined roads of Civil Lines, and in its many churches, cathedrals and cemeteries. Allahabad High Court, Muir College and Faculty of Science buildings of **Allahabad University** are imposing examples of British-era architecture. Prayagraj (Allahabad) also features in the writings of celebrated author Rudyard Kipling. For two years he was assistant editor of *The Pioneer*, and lived and worked out of Belvedere House. His earliest works, including *Plain Tales from the Hills*, were published by AH Wheeler & Co of Allahabad. A tour *(holywaters.in; ₹5000)* can uncover the city's little-known historical side.

SHASHANK SHUKLA KOTAHA/SHUTTERSTOCK

Khusro Bagh (p351)

to dusk, the large public garden houses four Mughal tombs. Two belong to Jehangir's first wife Shah Bano and rebel son Khusro, who was blinded and imprisoned after an assassination attempt on the emperor. Between the two stands another attractive sepulchre, constructed by Khusro's sister Nesa Begum, but never used as one. The origins of the smallest structure are unknown. Khusro Bagh's well-laid paths and grounds are popular with fitness enthusiasts, picnickers and cricket-playing youngsters.

A Pastoral Getaway

Experience life in the countryside

For a spot of agrarian life, consider a 45-minute (15km) cab ride to Shavpur village. The highlight here is **Planters Bungalow** *(plantersbungalow.in)*, a 150-year old estate, once the country home of a British indigo planter. A privately held property, lush with guava and mango orchards, fish ponds, ducks and more, it is the city's preferred escape. Spend your time walking or cycling around the acreage, bask in the outdoors and enjoy a hearty meal *(incl on-farm activities, ₹2500)*. Should you desire an extended outing, it also doubles as a heritage stay *(₹10,000)*.

EATING & DRINKING IN PRAYAGRAJ (ALLAHABAD): OUR PICKS

Indian Coffee House: Managed by the Indian Coffee Workers Coop, this super-cheap fuel stop has snacks, drinks, and servers in fancy hats. *8am-9pm* ₹

El Chico Cafe: Cure your hunger in a heartbeat among a forward-thinking Indian crowd. Best coffee in town, plus two hip restaurants above. *11am-10.30pm* ₹₹

Sardaar Ji Dhaba: Karaoke joint with festive decorations and Chinese and Indian dishes. Break out your Punjabi hits. *11am-11pm* ₹₹

Patiyala Peg Bar: This interesting bar for tourists has live *ghazal* (Urdu love songs) performed nightly from 7.30pm. Inside the Grand Continental.

Kushinagar

BUDDHIST CENTRE | SERENE MEMORIALS | INTERNATIONAL SHRINES

Kushinagar is where Buddha died, aged 80 years, making it one of four principal centres of Buddhist pilgrimage in the world (the others are Lumbini in Nepal, Bodhgaya and Sarnath). This sleepy little town, roughly 50km east of Gorakhpur, is home to three major historical attractions, including the site where Buddha is believed to have been cremated. Like Sarnath, Kushinagar too fell by the wayside once Buddhism began to wane, and when Xuan Zang stopped by in 640 CE, he found it in disrepair. In due course, his records led British archaeologists Alexander Cunningham and ACL Carlyle to unearth key Buddhist sites, and bring them back to historical life in 1876. Kushinagar also hosts several temples of recent vintage erected by Buddhist nations. You'll see their elaborate spires and pagoda roofs along the hotel and restaurant-dotted Buddha Marg, which connects Mahaparinirvana Stupa and Matha Kuar Shrine with Ramabhar Stupa.

GETTING AROUND

Despite its flashy international airport, Kushinagar is not easy to reach. At the time of writing, flights were suspended, though there were plans for IndiGo to take over services to/from Delhi, Mumbai and Kolkata.

Kushinagar is also not well connected overland, except with the transport hub of Gorakhpur. Frequent bus services run from Gorakhpur's main bus stand, 400m south of the train station, to Kushinagar *(1½hr, ₹83)*. It's easy to flag down a bus back to Gorakhpur on the main road near the gateway to town. Hiring a return taxi from Gorakhpur will cost around ₹1500, including waiting time.

Where Buddha Departed This Life

Statue portraying his final moments

The sprawling remnant-speckled **Mahaparinirvana Stupa** complex, open sunrise to sunset, is the reason you're likely in Kushinagar. At its centre is a raised platform (inaccessible by wheelchair), with a 2.74m-high stupa marking the place Buddha attained *mahaparinirvana* (freedom from rebirth). Beside it, the Nirvana Temple, a no-frills rectangular hall, enshrines Kushinagar's raison d'être: a 6m-long monolithic statue of Buddha on his deathbed. The 5th-century CE sandstone likeness depicts him lying on his side, eyes closed, with mourning devotees engraved into the base. Visitors are expected to remove their shoes and maintain silence in this stirring, sacred site. Join monks in deep contemplation or circumambulate the stupa where, contrary to instructions, you'll find appeals to Buddha scratched into the protective railing. Take one last picture of the stupa's pretty reflection in the adjoining pool of water before moving on to your next stop.

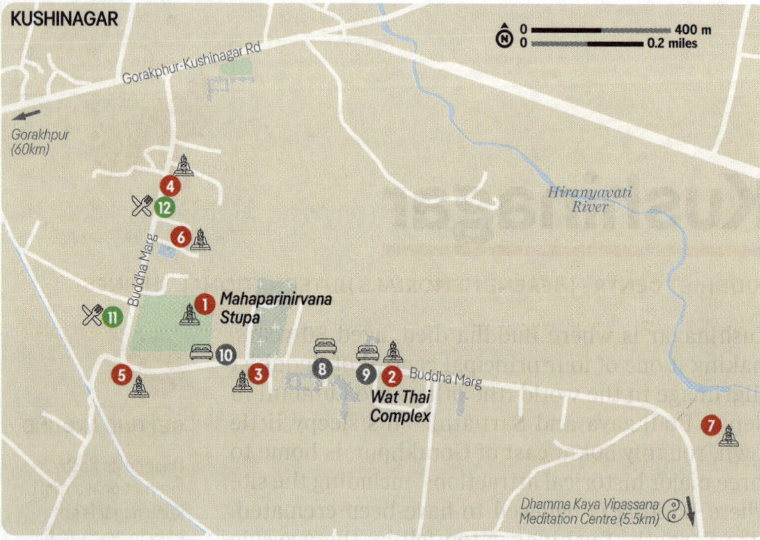

HIGHLIGHTS
1 Mahaparinirvana Stupa
2 Wat Thai Complex

SIGHTS
3 Japan-Sri Lanka Buddhist Centre
4 Linh-Son Vietnam Chinese Buddhist Temple
5 Matha Kuar Shrine
6 Myanmar Stupa and Temple
7 Ramabhar Stupa

SLEEPING
8 Lotus Nikko
9 Royal Residency
10 Tibetan Monastery Guesthouse

EATING
11 Kushinagar Restaurant
see 8 Lotus Nikko
see 9 Royal Residency
12 Yama Cafe

Site of Last Public Discourse

Stop by the smallish memorial

Matha Kuar Shrine is part of a large monastic compound that was unearthed in 1876. It is said to be the place Buddha held his final sermon, and lies diagonally across the road from Mahiparinirvana Stupa's Interpretation Centre. The star attraction here is a 3m-high statue of Buddha seated under the bodhi tree (sacred fig), thought to date back to the 10th or 11th century CE. It is sculpted in black stone, painted golden, and sits on the edge of a little pool in a small room not far from the main gate. It is open from sunrise to sunset, and if you find the memorial door locked, don't turn away. Staff operating the entrance gate hold the key and will give you an unhurried look-see.

> **TOP TIP**
>
> If you find yourself overnighting in Gorakhpur, **10 Park Street B&B** is the coolest choice of hotels. Frequent buses from Gorakhpur to Sunauli on the Nepal border leave from 100m north of the main bus station. Buses to Varanasi depart from the Kachari bus station, about 3km south of the main bus stand.

Stupa in Serene Surrounds

See Buddha's cremation site

Ramabhar Stupa, raised over the site of Buddha's cremation in 483 BCE, is little more than a large dome-shaped mound of red bricks. And yet, the calm, well-tended space has a palpably meditative quality to it, inviting reflection and mindfulness. Find an empty bench along the palm-lined path around the stupa for some quiet contemplation. Or perhaps simply sit and observe pilgrims and monks offering lotus flowers and prayers at its base. Also known as the Muktabandhan Chaitya or Vihar, it is located 1.5km southeast of the Mahaparinirvana Stupaand hemmed in by farmlands. Open from sunrise to sunset, it has spotless facilities.

International Places of Worship

Visit shrines of Buddhist nations

There are numerous modern temples built by Buddhist countries where pilgrims can stay and interact with resident monks. Most are within 2km of the main historical sites, and can be covered by an unhurried stroll along the length of Buddha Marg. The closest to Mahaparinirvana is the extravagantly styled **Myanmar Stupa and Temple** (Maha Sukhamada Chan Thargyi Pagoda), unmistakable thanks to its towering golden stupa and fierce lion statues guarding the entrance. Less than 200m north is the **Linh-Son Vietnam Chinese Buddhist Temple**. Distinguished by its multitiered pagoda-style roofs, it houses a monastery and is easily accessed from the main road. The **Japan-Sri Lanka Buddhist Centre**, a striking brick stupa with a minimalist main shrine reached via a flight of cascading steps, is just under 1km away towards the Ramabhar Stupa. Five hundred metres further up the road is the **Wat Thai Complex**, possibly the most impressive of all international temples. A visual delight in white, gold and grey, it was raised through worldwide donations from the Thai community. Temples are mostly open from 9am to 5pm, with a break between noon and 2pm.

Sign Up For Silence

Consider a vipassana meditation course

If you're in Kushinagar for the long haul, consider signing up for a meditation programme at the **Dhamma Kaya Vipassana Meditation Centre** *(kaya.dhamma.org)*. It conducts 10-day introductory courses in *vipassana*, an ancient Buddhist meditation technique they say was rediscovered by Buddha. The centre is located 6km south of Kushinagar, and has residential facilities with breakfast and lunch (dinner is not eaten). Men and women are separated and silence observed throughout the program. You are required to apply online for a spot in its year-round programmes, starting every 1st and 17th of the month. Courses are free of charge; however, donations are welcome (₹10,000 is considered a fair amount).

BUDDHIST CIRCUIT

Thousands of Buddhists travel to Uttar Pradesh every year to visit Buddhism's most sacred sites – where Buddha threw off his royal privilege, roamed as an ascetic, meditated for seven years, gained enlightenment and set in motion the philosophy of Buddhism and its monastic system.

Lumbini Buddha's birthplace, just over the border in Nepal.

Bodhgaya (p480) Buddha's enlightenment under a Bodhi Tree; and Dungeshwari Cave, where he lived as an ascetic before renouncing his fast at nearby Sujata Stupa.

Sarnath (p347) Buddha's first sermon in the Deer Park.

Kushinagar (p353) Site of Buddha's death.

Significant places in Bihar: Vaishali (p496), Rajgir (p488), Nalanda (p488), Kesariya Stupa (p496).

EATING IN KUSHINAGAR: OUR PICKS

Lotus Nikko: Hotel restaurant that's among the best in town, and nonguests can often get in on the evening Thai buffets. *6am-11pm* ₹₹

Yama Cafe: Run by the welcoming Mr Roy (a wealth of local information), this Kushinagar institution has a simple, traveller-friendly menu. *8am-8pm* ₹

Kushinagar Restaurant: Housed in Rahi Pathik Niwas Hotel. Freshly prepared, multicuisine meals in reasonably clean surroundings. *7am-10pm* ₹

Royal Residency: Great-value, fresh-food buffets are served to guests (and nonguests, with a bit of notice – call 945-5821729). *4-9am, 10am-2pm & 6-10pm* ₹

Ayodhya

RAM'S BIRTHPLACE | PILGRIMAGE CENTRE | FADING FAIZABAD

GETTING AROUND

Private vehicles are not permitted beyond designated parking lots *(₹100)*, which fill up quickly on weekends. Ayodhya's train station is a convenient 10-minute walk from the temple area. Uber and Rapido cabs are readily available if you have an Indian SIM. Battery operated golf carts *(shared, from ₹30)* regularly ply between the town's major points of interest. Alternatively, they can be exclusively hired *(from ₹600)* to visit the main attractions here. It is best to walk, or negotiate your way onto an e-rickshaw *(from ₹20)*, when in Ayodhya's busy old neighbourhoods.

Revered as the birthplace of Ram, and the setting for the epic Ramayana, Ayodhya is one of Hinduism's seven sacred cities, and also the most controversial. Nevertheless, with the opening of the partially completed Ram Janmabhoomi Mandir in 2024, it has gained global traction. Large sections of the town were razed to accommodate the grand structure and revamp Ayodhya for the millions of pilgrims expected to pour in annually. It has a new airport and train station, while a bus terminal is under construction. Large hotels and restaurants are coming up, but options are limited. Ayodhya lies along the right bank of the Saryu River, some 7km from Faizabad, the former capital of the Nawabs of Awadh. However, other than the crumbling old tombs of Nawab Shuja-ud-Doula and his wife Bahu Begum, little is left of its former grandeur, although it has relatively more accommodation to offer.

Ayodhya's Top Sight

Visit Ram Janmabhoomi Temple

The imposing new **Ram Janmabhoomi Mandir**, a striking three-storey sandstone-and-marble structure, is built over 1 hectare in a 28-hectare complex. Ornately carved, inside and out, with gold- and silver-plated doors, it has been constructed in the Nagara style of temple architecture generally prevalent in northern India. There is a towering *sikhara* (spire) over the sanctum, which houses a bejewelled black granite idol of Ram as a five-year-old child, revered as Ram Lalla; and five *mandapa* (congregation halls). The complex will also host several smaller shrines (under construction at time of research) dedicated to other divinities from the Hindu pantheon.

Security is tight; only wallets and passports are allowed inside the main temple. Visitors are required to leave shoes, phones and other personal effects in lockers *(free)* at the large pilgrim facilitation centre operated by friendly staff. Drinking water and restrooms are also available here. Expect serpentine queues on weekends and festivals, and a long walk to the

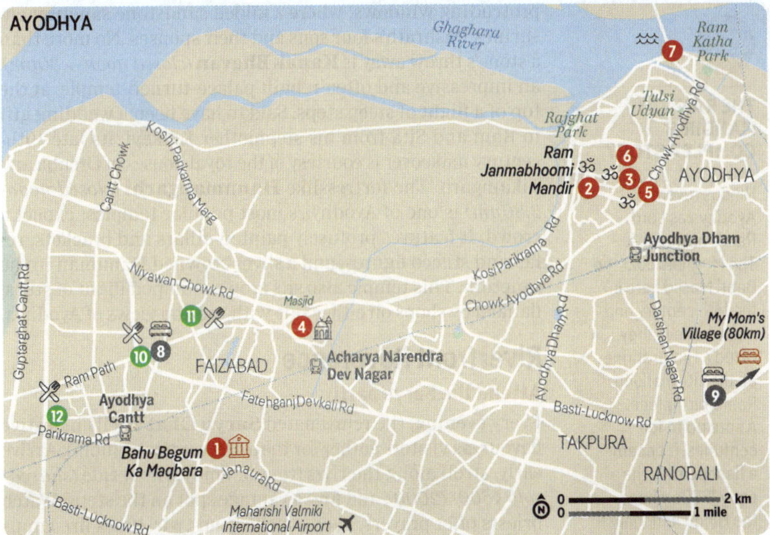

HIGHLIGHTS
1 Bahu Begum Ka Maqbara
2 Ram Janmabhoomi Mandir

SIGHTS
3 Dashrath Mahal
4 Gulab Bari
5 Hanumangarhi
6 Kanak Bhavan
7 Saryu Ghat

SLEEPING
8 Hotel Shane Avadh
9 Ramayana Hotel

EATING
10 Madhur Milan
11 Mahaveer Tikki Chat
see 9 Naivedyam
12 Tipsy Town

main temple from this point on. Wheelchairs with handlers *(from₹150, expected tip ₹50)* are provided on request. You can book ahead *(online.srjbtkshetra.org)* for queue free viewing at special slots, although presenting your passport at time of visit will also get you the same benefit. Like us, you can hire a guide *(Sakshi Upadhaya; 7380536256; ₹2500/day)* to show you around Ram Mandir and other Ayodhya attractions. Ram Janmabhoomi Mandir is open 7am to 11.30am and 1pm to 7pm.

TOP TIP

Entry to the Ram Mandir is free. There are three daily *aarti* lamp ceremonies (but each has only 30 spots). *Darshan* temple visits are possible 7am–11.30am and 2pm–7pm.

The Ramayana Footprint

Explore Ayodha's storied shrines

Dashrath Mahal *(closed noon-4.30pm)*, dedicated to Ram's father, is a 10-minute walk from Ram Mandir. A multistorey arched gateway, in need of repair, ushers you into a large unkempt compound. Further up, another doorway opens onto a courtyard enclosed by brilliantly painted walls with

EATING IN AYODHYA & FAIZABAD: OUR PICKS

Mahaveer Tikki Chat: Famous street *wala* serving only *tikia* (potato patty with *channa*, served on leaf plate). Look for red-and-yellow Hindi sign. *4-9pm* ₹

Tipsy Town: Lovely leafy rooftop restaurant with a view over Faizabad and an international menu. No booze, despite the name. *11am-11pm* ₹₹

Naivedyam: Classy pure-veg restaurant at the Ramayana Hotel in the south of town, with salads, Chinese, curries and pasta. *7-10.30am, 12.30-3.30pm & 7-11pm* ₹₹₹

Madhur Milan: Close to Faizabad's bus station, this place has an international menu and a nice atmosphere, with hanging plants. *10.30am-10.30pm* ₹₹

THE RAM MANDIR'S COMPLEX STORY

Hindus revere Ayodhya as Lord Ram's birthplace. The Mughals built the Babri Masjid here in the 16th century and many believe they razed a Hindu shrine on the site marking Ram's birthplace. A sore point for centuries, it became a flashpoint in the early 1990s when the Hindu nationalist Bharatiya Janata Party (BJP) began campaigning on the issue. In 1992, a Hindu mob demolished the mosque and nearly 2000 people were killed in the ensuing riots.

The problem of what to do with the land went to the Supreme Court. In 2019, it ruled that the Ram temple could be built on the site. Construction began immediately and in January 2024, it was partially opened by BJP Prime Minister Narendra Modi, three months ahead of the national election.

protruding windows, where a gilded sandstone sanctum enshrines Dashrath's four sons and their spouses. No more than a stone's throw away is **Kanak Bhavan** *(closed noon-4.30pm)*, an impressive and often rebuilt palace-turned-temple, at the top of a flight of steep steps. Said to have been a wedding gift to Ram and Sita from his stepmother Kaikeyi, its late-19th-century makeover is courtesy of the royal houses of Orchha and Tikamgarh. The fortresslike **Hanumangarhi** *(closed noon-2.30pm)* is one of Ayodhya's most popular temples; expect a crowd. It features profusely painted pillars and brackets, relief and stucco figures, and a silver crowned Hanuman in the sanctum. This temple also sits atop a cramped flight of steps, flanked by shops on either side with rooftop views of Ayodhya.

Riverfront Reverence

Attend the Saryu aarti

Every evening, the rejuvenated **Saryu Ghat** swells in festive flavour, as visitors gather for the *aarti* ceremony (6pm). Arrive early, stroll along the riverfront or enjoy a boat ride *(shared/solo ₹600/₹2000)*, and find a vantage spot on the steps. Watch priests offer prayers, blow conches and twirl brass fire lamps in a spectacular show of reverence. The Ayodhya Deepotsav, marking Ram's return from exile, is also held here a day before Diwali, when you'll find the riverfront all aflicker in the warm glow of a record-breaking number of *diya* (earthen lamps).

Ruins over Remains

See 19th-century sepulchral heritage

The most dominant feature of Faizabad's skyline is **Bahu Begum Ka Maqbara**, the towering double-domed tomb of Nawab Shuja-ud-Doula's wife. Despite its fall into decrepitude, this beautiful Indo-Persian structure remains an irresistible draw from sunrise to sunset for history and architecture enthusiasts. You'll want to keep clear of the angrily strutting emus that live on the unkempt grounds. The nawab himself is buried a couple of kilometres away, in a visibly less grand tomb surrounded by a neglected rose garden called **Gulab Bari**.

Give Rural Charms a Chance

Experience Ayodhya's lush countryside

My Mom's Village is a women-run sustainable farm-stay *(mymomsvillage.in; ₹9500)* located an hour's drive (on a good day) east of Ayodhya (90km) along the Lucknow–Gorakhpur Hwy. It's a convenient day trip, but an immersive experience mandates an overnight stay. You'll want to take in a village tour, walk around its dense woodlands or go cycling across the 40.5-hectare estate's marked trails. Forage for your food, crunch on local rice-coated vegetables and tuck into delicacies like *phare* (lentil-filled rice-flour shells) and *baingan chokha* (smoked aubergine mash). Perhaps enjoy an outdoor cookout in a mango orchard with the hospitable owners, Puja and Shailendra Singh. Expect peace, quiet and friendly canines in a verdant setting.

Lucknow

INDO-PERSIAN HERITAGE | BRITISH-ERA HISTORY | CULINARY DESTINATION

State capital Lucknow owes much of its refined culture, elaborate architecture, intricate handicrafts and fine cuisine to the Shiite Nawabs of Awadh (1722–1856). A line of provincial rulers of Persian origin, they shaped its unique heritage, and as patrons of art attracted poets, musicians and artists to the court. An equally enthusiastic patronage of culinary artistry lingers on in melt-in-your mouth kebabs, korma (a currylike braised dish) *qaliya* (yoghurt-based meat curry) and fragrant biryani (fragrant spiced steamed rice with meat or vegetables), leading to UNESCO's recognition of Lucknow as a Creative City of Gastronomy in 2025. Its brush with the British is apparent in several telltale ruins that lie along the Gomti River, including the Residency. Today, it straddles two worlds: a wistful past that inhabits its fascinating bazaars and gracious homes, and a frenetically burgeoning metropolis trying to catch up with the times. Glitzy malls notwithstanding, Hazratganj remains Lucknow's preferred go-to for shopping and dining – or *ganjing*, as outings to this vibrant commercial centre are dubbed.

TOP TIP

Check what's on in poetry, stand-up comedy and theatre, as well as what's happening in local news, at *knocksense.com/lucknow*. For LGBTIQ+ events, check *@awadhqueerpride*.

GETTING AROUND

The easiest way to get around is on Lucknow's spotless Metro; however there's currently only one line. It's useful for the bus station, railway station and airport; for other places, combine it with an Uber (if you have an Indian SIM) or autorickshaws – go for one of Lucknow's fleet of white electric autos.

Lucknow is well connected by air, bus and train. Most trains leave from Lucknow NR (usually called Charbagh) rather than Lucknow Junction (150m away) – check your ticket to make sure. Buses and trains link Lucknow with Delhi, Agra, Faizabad, Gorakhpur, Prayagraj (Allahabad) and Varanasi.

HIGHLIGHTS
1 Bara Imambara
2 Residency

SIGHTS
3 Chota Imambara
4 Dilkusha Kothi
5 La Martinière College
6 Rumi Darwaza

SLEEPING
7 Backpacker Den
8 Bilgram House
9 Clarks Avadh
10 Lucknow Homestay
11 Saraca

EATING
12 Cherry Tree
13 Mahmudabad House
see 24 Naimat Khana
14 Oudhyana
see 23 Philtre & Co
15 Royal Cafe
16 Sakhawat
17 Tunday Kababi
18 Tunday Kababi (Chowk)

DRINKING & NIGHTLIFE
19 Penthouse
20 Sharma Ji Ki Chai
21 Sky Bar

SHOPPING
22 Bhairvi
23 Le Press
24 Sanatkada

Nawabi Splendour

Discover the capital's Indo-Persian heritage

The grand, arch-filled **Bara Imambara** (Shiite congregational mourning hall, open 6am to 6pm) is Lucknow's top draw. It was built by Nawab Asaf-ud-Daula over a period of 10 years to provide dignified work for his famine-hit subjects. He and his wife are buried in the huge central hall, one of the world's largest vaulted galleries. Above it, Bhulbulaiya, a curious maze of narrow passages with hundreds of doorways leads to the rooftop, a splendid photo-op with stunning bird's-eye views of Lucknow. The labyrinth entrance is to the outside left of the main hall. If on your own, hire a resident guide *(from ₹100)*, as it is easy to get lost. The impressive three-domed Asafi Mosque (closed to public), and a large *baori* (step-well) flank the *imambara* (tomb dedicated to a Shiite Muslim holy man) on either side.

Beyond this complex is **Rumi Darwaza**, a magnificent gateway said to replicate one in Istanbul. Less than 500m past it is the golden-domed and calligraphy-adorned **Chota Imambara**, open 6am to 5pm. Constructed by Nawab Mohammad Ali Shah on a visibly smaller scale, its chandelier-strung main chamber also serves as his tomb. Both *imambara* require visitors to remove footwear, for women to cover their heads, and a guide to accompany couples. A combined ticket *(on-site ₹500)* provides access to both *imambara*, a 19th-century red-brick clock-tower (open dawn to dusk) and an avoidable portrait gallery (7am to 6pm) overlooking an artificial lake. Half a day is sufficient to visit all at an unhurried pace.

Remnants of an Empire

Explore Victorian-era ruins and buildings

The verdurous grounds of the **Residency** *(₹300)* are speckled with a whole host of well-preserved remains – their walls pockmarked by bullets and cannonballs from the Siege of Lucknow, a major turn of events that preceded the 1857 First War of Independence (Indian Uprising), and sounded the death knell for the British Raj. Every bit of the leafy premises, easily covered in an hour (it's open 9.30am to 5pm), offers a captivating peep into its action-packed history. A well-kept cemetery, where weathered gravestones speak of bloody face-offs, lies to the far end. The main Residency building houses a small museum (closed Fridays) with models of original buildings and sketches of the aftermath.

The understated **Dilkusha Kothi** lies roughly 7km south in the cantonment. A hunting lodge commissioned by Nawab Sa'adat Ali Khan in 1814, the once-turreted grand structure suffered a similar fate to the Residency. You'll find its vestige in a quiet corner of a neatly tended park, dotted with cast-iron benches; the kind of place you bring a book. It's open sunrise to sunset, and tips *(₹50)* are welcome. An attention-grabbing building, Constantia, envisaged as a country residence by French adventurer Claude Martin, stands a couple of kilometres away. It is now **La Martinière College**, a premier

FROM LYON TO LUCKNOW

One of the many prospectors who came to India in the 18th century was Claude Martin, a teenager from Lyon. He joined the French East India Company as a dragoon, presciently switched loyalties, and rose to the rank of Major General in the British East India Company. A man of acute business sense, who famously loaned sizeable sums of money to the nawab, he is also credited with designing some of Lucknow's most notable buildings. Kothi Hayat Baksh (Governor's residence); Kothi Farhat Baksh in the Chattar Mahal complex, a heritage hotel-in-the-making; and Constantia Palace, the grandest of all his residences. He willed a considerable chunk of his wealth towards education, which led to establishing La Martinière colleges in Kolkata, Lucknow and Lyon.

BEST HOME-BASED CULINARY EXPERIENCES

Deeba Ali: Serves delicious everyday Awadhi staples – vegetable curries, kebab and biryani – freshly prepared and generously served in her spotless home. *(8115555529)*

Chetna Srivastava: Offers a curated menu of heirloom dishes like *mangoda* (green lentil fritters) typical of Kayastha cuisine. *(8009222277)*

Naheed Varma: Delectable Awadhi, Rampuri and Kayastha meals served with engaging anecdotes from a storied life. *(98380 03590)*

Sunaeyaa Kappoor: Brings to life forgotten flavours of Awadh, accompanied by soulful Sufi renditions in her Hazratganj homestay. *(9833967411)*

Niharika Bajaj: Runs a quality artisanal cloud patisserie, specialising in desserts, confectionary and savouries; requires 24-hours notice. *(9170258887)*

PRADEEPGAURS/SHUTTERSTOCK

Market, Aminabad

boys' school established in 1845. Visit the sprawling campus, preferably on a Sunday, when you can ask the caretaker for a quick look at the school chapel and Martin's tomb. Pop into the smallish on-campus museum while you're at it. Allocate half a day for all of the above. Alternatively, consider guided tours *(waltzindia.in; from ₹2500)* by engaging storytellers.

Gastronomic Wealth

Eat your way around Lucknow

Famously called the kebab capital, Lucknow is that and more. One way to get acquainted with its street-side deliciousness is to take a culinary tour *(965-1775518; incl food ₹3500)* of Chowk. The city's oldest bazaar, best known for the original **Tunday Kababi**, it also hosts other neighbourhood favourites that dish out a delectable array of *pasanda* (flattened meat kebab), *nihari* (slow-cooked meat stew), biryani (steamed rice with meat/vegetables) and halwa (semolina pudding and the like). There's also an airy *nimish* (a delicate cream dessert) in winter. Refreshing lassi and *thandai* (dairy beverages), appetising *chaat* (Indian snack), and traditional *mithai* (sweets) are available year-round. Or, you can sign up for engaging home-style meals with local families *(deepdiveindia.com; from ₹3000)*. Hazratganj, Lucknow's busy high street, is your go-to for contemporary cafes and restaurants.

EATING IN LUCKNOW: OUR PICKS

Sakhawat: The daily-changing kebabs (*galawat* etc) at this highly recommended locals' haunt are grilled to smoky, crispy perfection. *2-10.30pm* ₹

Royal Cafe: Even if you don't step inside this classy restaurant, don't miss its popular sweet-and-savoury basket *chaat* (snack) stand at the front. *11am-11pm* ₹₹

Cherry Tree: Contemporary cafe running the gamut from peri-peri chicken to penne arrabbiata and Lebanese meze, plus good espresso. *8am-midnight* ₹₹

Oudhyana: Chef Nagendra Singh gives Lucknow's famous Awadh cuisine its royal due at this restaurant inside the Taj Mahal hotel. *12.30-2.45pm & 7.30-11.30pm* ₹₹₹

Custodians of Craft

Go on a textile tour

Chowk is also where Lucknow's finest handicrafts take shape, from intricate embroideries like *chikankari* and *zardozi* to *chattapati* or *tukri* work (a unique silk patchwork). Amble through the lively alleys to observe *chappai* workers block-printing patterns with indigo and glue, and artisans beating metal into utility items, including silver footwear. *Gota-kinari* shops beckon with glittery wares; step into one for a length or two of tinsel lace, then walk through what's left of the flower-sellers' market for floral jewellery. Customised textile tours *(break-away.in; from ₹6000)*, which often include visits to a riverside 'laundromat', are recommended.

Take Home a Coveted Souvenir

New finds in old bazaars

Lucknow's bazaars, a cornucopia of curiosities, are a great place to scout around for bargains. Aminabad is old Lucknow's shopping haunt for household needs; and Chowk is where you go for all things *chikan* (embroidered cloth), including **Bhairvi's** exquisite saris, menswear, and home accessories *(from ₹2000)*. Alternatively, swing by **Sanatkada**, a one-stop-shop for traditional crafts from across the country, and also for delicious Lucknow home staples at its restaurant, **Naimat Khana**. Find hip stores and designer boutiques on Hazratganj and at **Le Press**, Lucknow's most recent retail and food and beverage space, housed in a former printing press.

Savour a Regal Repast

Dine in a 17th century fort

Plan a memorable experience of Awadh's one-time glorious aristocratic past at the rambling old **Mahmudabad Fort**, 60km north of Lucknow. A popular backdrop in Hindi films, this extraordinary edifice, a collection of slowly crumbling rooms, corridors, balconies and courtyards, can be visited as a day trip with advance notice. Sit down to a sumptuous meal of heirloom dishes in once gilded surrounds, before or after a tour of Mahmudabad's shrines, mango orchards and embroidery workshops. If you're rushed for time, consider a curated meal at the owning family's palace – **Mahmudabad House** *(mahmudabad.in; from ₹7000)* – in Lucknow.

LUCKNOW'S KEBABS DECONSTRUCTED

Kakori Kebab: Legend has it that the toothless Nawab of Kakori asked his royal *bawarchi* (chef) to make kebabs that would melt in the mouth. They're made adding papaya (as a tenderiser) and barbecued on a skewer.

Galawat: Served in Lucknow's most famous kebab restaurant, **Tunday Kababi**, where it's referred to as a mutton kebab; in other restaurants it is often called Tunday. Essentially the same as Kakori kebabs, but rather than barbecued they are made into patties and shallow-fried in oil/ghee.

Shami: Raw mincemeat boiled with spices and black gram lentil, then ground on stone and mixed with onions, coriander leaves and green chillies, and shallow-fried.

EATING & DRINKING IN LUCKNOW: OUR PICKS

Philtre & Co: Espresso bar in Le Press shopping complex with indoor/outdoor seating. Decent pick-me-up cuppas and small bites. *11.30am-11pm* ₹₹

Sharma Ji Ki Chai: Much-loved over-50-year-old chai shop. Around the corner, find *chaat* from Jain Chaat Bhandar (small English sign). *7am-8pm, to 2pm Sun*

Sky Bar: Stunning rooftop bar with an infinity pool overlooking the Lucknow skyline. Live music Friday and Saturday. Inside the Renaissance Hotel. *1pm-1am*

Penthouse: Cocktails with an Awadhi twist. Stay on for an exceptional culinary experience featuring Indian, Asian and European staples. *noon-midnight*

Beyond Lucknow

In Kannauj, discover the timeless allure of sensual attar, artisanal perfume oil extracted from botanicals through ancient techniques.

GETTING AROUND

Hiring a taxi *(round-trip from ₹4500)* is the most convenient way to get to Kannauj, well-connected by the Agra–Lucknow Expressway. The cab will also come in handy for exploring the town, as its main points of interest are spread out. Old Kannauj, a warren of lively undulating lanes, on the other hand, is best experienced on foot. Autorickshaws and cycle-rickshaws are plentiful; prices tend to vary. Expect to pay roughly ₹50 for short distance (1–2km) rides.

Approximately 125km west of Lucknow, Kannauj has been an attar-making centre for centuries, by some accounts since the 7th century, when it was ruled by Harshavardhana. With time, particularly the loss of Mughal patronage and subsequent British disinterest, this one-time perfume capital of India all but disappeared from popular imagination, and it would appear an otherwise unremarkable town. Recent efforts towards its revival, and a growing interest in natural and sustainable products, have once again placed the forgotten craft of attar-making in the spotlight. Less than two hours by road, Kannauj is a comfortable day trip from the state capital. Sightseeing options are limited; but you're really here to pleasure the olfactory sense with artisanal flavours and fragrances.

Kannauj

TIME FROM LUCKNOW: 2½HR

The essence of fragrance

At the forefront of reimagining the Kannauj story is Pranav Kapoor, 8th-generation perfumer, chef and founder of Perfume Tourism by **Indian Naturals** *(perfumetourism.com)*. His hands-on perfume-making experiences *(₹18,000 plus tax)* transform a family legacy into an enriching cultural immersion. Expect an activity-filled outing, with visits to an aromatics farm and a traditional distillery, where they use the age-old *deg-bhapa* (copper stills and bamboo pipes) method to extract *ruh* (essence). Join in for seasonal flower harvests, watch rose or jasmine petals disappear into massive stills atop raging wood-fires, perhaps catch pottery shards as they metamorphose into bottled petrichor. Relish a fragrance-paired thali of regional cuisine, and create your signature fragrance at the in-house perfume bar before calling it a day. Take in the lively lanes in the vicinity, where shop owners enthusiastically introduce you to a mind-boggling array of scents and essentials oils. Top-shelf attar can cost upwards of ₹5000.

Stately art deco heritage home

Escape the hurly-burly of Lucknow in the welcome quiet of Tirwa village. Spend a weekend at the distinguished-looking **Anand Bhawan Palace** *(amastaysandtrails.com)*. The six-room mansion, less than 20km from Kannauj, is a convenient

Rose petals at perfume distillery, Kannauj

springboard for acquainting yourself with the craft of attar-making, and to observe wooden *attar-daan* (perfume boxes) and *kuppi* (leather attar containers) take shape in the hands of the last of the artisans engaged in these crafts. You can also dine in the leafy grounds, enjoy a relaxing swim, an unhurried game of billiards or a long sun-soak. Alternatively, observe floral waste being transformed into fragrant incense cones by skilled local women; note this activity requires advance notice. Perhaps spend a fragrant evening with owners Shruti Shandilya and Divyaudit Singh, creating your signature attar at their perfume bar. If short on time, plan a day excursion. It includes a perfume tour, lunch, an optional high tea and visit to Tirwa's Annapurna Devi temple *(from ₹7000)*.

Stepping into the past

Look beyond Kannauj's fragrant personality with a peep into its historical past. The **Government Archaeological Museum** *(₹50)* features a fine display of sculptures, coins, pottery and terracotta figures, including a massive pot from the Kushana period (1st–3rd century CE) on the 1st floor. Keep an eye out for exhibits from the Gupta period (3rd–6th century CE), widely celebrated as the acme of innovation in Indian art and literature. In another gallery, the story of Kannauj's most celebrated ruler, Harshavardhana, unfolds through a series of colourful dioramas. The museum is open 10.30am to 4.30pm, Tuesday to Sunday (except second Sundays).

Training your sense of smell

For an instructive outing, swing by the sprawling campus of the government-run **Fragrance and Flavour Development Centre** *(ffdcindia.org)*, synonymous with quality perfumery research. You can visit its botanical garden, distilling and processing units, and the fragrance development laboratory, an absolute delight for your nose. Expect to take anything between 15 minutes to two hours, depending on who the authorities can spare (when available and reachable) to show you around. It would be best to call ahead and confirm your visit.

KANNAUJ'S TOP FRAGRANCES

Ruh Gulab: This pure rose extract is among the world's most expensive perfumes.

Attar Shamama: Traditional perfumers are said to have their own closely guarded formulations of this warm, spicy blend best worn in the winter.

Ruh Motia: An extract of the jasmine flower, generally harvested during the rainy season, this is a classic monsoon scent with clean and crisp floral notes.

Gul Hina: This sensuous earthy scent comes from the flower of the henna tree, handy in both medicinal and cosmetic purposes, but best known for its staining properties.

Gil Mitti: Bottled petrichor, the unmistakably raw fragrance of moist earth after the first monsoon shower, is made from fresh earthenware.

Mathura & Vrindavan

KRISHNA'S BIRTHPLACE | ARCHAEOLOGY MUSEUM | TEMPLE TRAIL

GETTING AROUND

Shared autorickshaws and buses charge ₹30–40 for the 13km Mathura–Vrindavan run; figure on ₹300 for a private autorickshaw. Uber services are planned for the area. Frequent trains link Mathura with Delhi (two to three hours) and Agra (one hour); buses run from the bus station 1km east.

Sights are quite spread out in the two towns and it's worth hiring a car or an autorickshaw to see them; include time to wander the atmospheric backstreets of Vrindavan. Krishna Balaram Information Centre, on the Krishna Balaram Temple Complex, arranges fixed-priced car services. It's ₹700 for a car to/from Mathura; ₹1500 for a temple tour.

Mathura is famed as Krishna's place of birth and is one of Hinduism's seven holiest cities. Vrindavan is where the venerated Hindu god is believed to have grown up and spent his youth. This makes these twin towns, 13km apart, hallowed pilgrimage centres frequented by devotees from across the country. They are dotted with old and new temples, accessed through constricted streets teeming with visitors, vendors, rickshaws and thieving monkeys. The many ghats along the Yamuna River (Mathura alone has 25) are best experienced at dawn, or post sunset during the evening *aarti* (prayers) ceremony. Vrindavan is also where the International Society for Krishna Consciousness (Iskcon) is headquartered, attracting pilgrims from all over the world. Janmashtami (Krishna's birthday), which falls in August or September, and the colourful festival of Holi in February/March are particularly hectic, when both Mathura and Vrindavan witness fervent celebrations.

A Divinity is Born

Mathura's most significant shrine

The **Kesava Deo Temple**, also known as Krishna Janmabhoomi, shares a wall with the towering white-domed Katra Masjid. Open 5am to noon and 4pm to 8pm, it houses Mathura's most important site: the prison cell in which Krishna was born to his incarcerated parents. A narrow corridor leads to a low-ceilinged and confined space with a silver-encased platform on which Krishna's mother is said to have given birth; his bedecked idol marks the spot. Expect to be jostled around, as the smallish room crowds easily with supplicating devotees.

Of the other two main shrines here, the multistoried eponymous temple, built in 1958, is the first point of interest as you enter the complex. The Bhagvata or Gita Bhavan, located beyond the prison cell, is of more recent vintage (1982), and enshrines likenesses of Krishna and Radha (his consort) at one end of a large hall. The walls are covered in multi-faith imagery, as well as copper plates inscribed with the Bhagavad

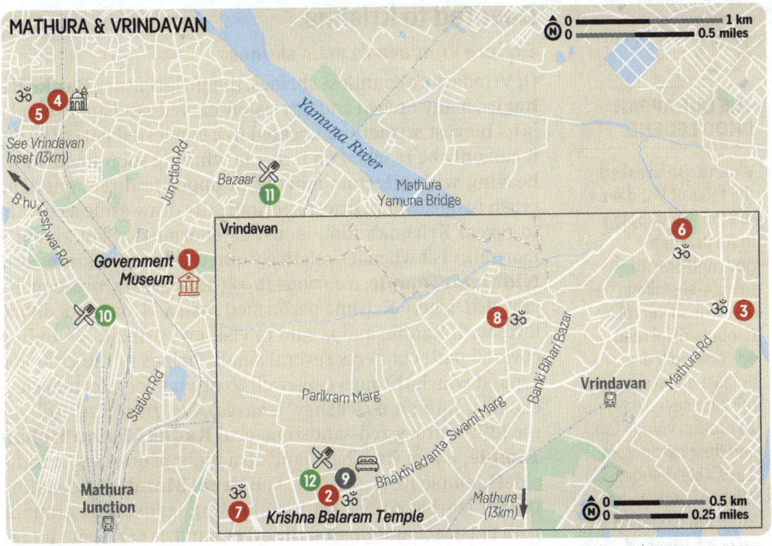

HIGHLIGHTS
1 Government Museum
2 Krishna Balaram Temple

SIGHTS
3 Banke Bihari
4 Katra Masjid
5 Kesava Deo Temple
6 Nidhivan Temple
7 Prem Mandir
8 Radha Madan Mohan Temple

SLEEPING
9 MVT Guesthouse

EATING
10 Agrawal Bhojnalay
11 Brijwasi Holi Gate
12 Govinda's Restaurant
see 9 MVT Restaurant

Gita, the ancient text that lends the temple its name. Security is tight; only passports and wallets are allowed inside. Lockers at nominal cost are available at Gates 1 and 2 to store phones, cameras, electronics and bags. Wheelchair access is limited; anticipate some amount of stair climbing.

A Rich Repository

Visit Mathura's Archaeology Museum

Mathura was one of the most important cities of ancient India, and the **Government Museum** *(admission ₹25, with mobile/camera ₹20)*, located in a relatively quiet end of town near the ghats, is proof of that rich past. It features a splendid collection of sculptures from the Kushana and Gupta periods (1st to 6th century CE). That the town was once a vibrant Buddhist centre is evidenced in the large array of Buddha, *yaksha* (male deity) and bodhisattva likenesses. Among the other larger-than-life figures on display is the striking headless statue of Kanishka, a powerful ruler of the Kushana dynasty. Other galleries showcase equally impressive lots of pottery, coins and prehistoric tools. Despite poorly labelled exhibits and lackadaisical staff, this storied museum is a primary source of information of the time. A must-visit for history and culture buffs, it is rarely crowded, but demands at least 1½ hours to unhurriedly view its remarkable treasures. It's open 10.30am to 4.30pm, Tuesday to Saturday. Note: videoing is not permitted.

KRISHNA'S BIRTHPLACE

A small room in the Kesava Deo Temple commemorates Krishna's birth more than 5000 years ago.

Destroyed and rebuilt a number of times over the past thousand years, the current temple was erected in the 1950s. Towering over it, the **Katra Masjid** was built by the Mughal ruler Aurangzeb in 1670. The question of whether it stands on Krishna's birthplace, as Aurangzeb ordered the destruction of a Hindu temple to build it, is still being decided in the courts.

THE CHHAPPAN BHOG LEGEND

When Krishna asked the folks of Vrindavan to stop worshipping Indra (the rain god) and pray to the life-sustaining Govardhan Parvat (mountain) instead, an enraged Indra unleashed hammering rains for seven days. To protect village folk and their cattle from a possible deluge, Krishna is said to have lifted the mountain on one finger and sheltered everyone, going without his preferred eight meals a daydoing so. In gratitude, the villagers are believed to have prepared *chhappan* (56) dishes to assuage his hunger. This tradition endures today. Come Janmashtami, Krishna's birthday, believers express their reverence by preparing 56 offerings comprising all six tastes, including curd, sweetened butter, *poha* (flattened rice), and *kheer* (rice pudding).

Devoted to Krishna

Explore Vrindavan's main shrines

Of Vrindavan's countless shrines, the 19th-century **Banke Bihari**, a many-arched and intricately carved sandstone temple, is its biggest attraction. Located in a congested part of town, it can only be reached on foot, via winding shop-lined alleys heaving with pilgrims moving in opposite directions. The crush inside, where priests periodically draw aside a curtain to reveal Krishna's idol, is just as enormous. Plan an early morning visit when it's relatively quiet. Less than 1km away is **Nidhivan Temple**, a curious *tulsi* (holy basil) grove, equally crowded, where Krishna performed *ras-leela* (dance of divine love) with Radha, and is said to visit every night. A winding covered path connects several small shrines in the grounds, around which throngs can swell to often uncomfortable levels. Hop into an e-rickshaw *(shared/solo, from ₹20/100)* for the 16th-century, red-sandstone-clad **Radha Madan Mohan Temple**, 1.5km from here, and up a flight of 60 steps. It is the oldest temple in Vrindavan. The **Prem Mandir**, a gleaming Italian marble edifice set in sprawling landscaped grounds with musical fountains, on the other hand, is of recent vintage (2012). Most temples are closed from noon to 4pm.

Hare Krishna Headquarters

Stop by Iskcon temple

The **Krishna Balaram Temple** is the nerve centre of the International Society for Krishna Consciousness, also known as the Hare Krishnas. A large spiritual centre, it houses the samadhi (sepulchre) of the founder Swami Prabhupada (1896–1977), who built this grand marble temple in memory of Krishna and his foster brother Balaram. Also enshrined within the clean, orderly and atmospheric temple are Radha and Krishna with the two *gopis* (milkmaids) Lalita and Vishakha. The campus grounds are a constant whirl of activity, where hundreds of Indian and foreign devotees gather to pray, chant, drum and dance in its chessboard-floored central courtyard. An equal number are here to attend courses and seminars. The temple is closed 12.45pm to 4pm. Comfortable rooms are available in the guesthouse at the back of the temple, and can be booked online *(iskconvrindavan.com; from ₹3500)*.

EATING IN MATHURA & VRINDAVAN: OUR PICKS

MVT Restaurant: Well-run foreigners' restaurant on 2nd floor of the MVT Guesthouse. *8.30am-10am, 12.30-3.15pm & 6.30-9.15pm mid-Aug–mid-Apr* ₹₹

Govinda's Restaurant: On Iskcon campus, this pure-veg place has Indian faves plus some Chinese and Italian dishes. Lots of juices and shakes. *8am-10.30pm* ₹₹

Brijwasi Holi Gate: Popular sweet and snack shop next to Holi Gate. There's a stand-up bench where you can eat. *7am-10.30pm* ₹

Agrawal Bhojnalay: Across the road from the Mathura bus stand, this family restaurant is a clean, calm respite, with booth seats. *9am-midnight* ₹₹

Places We Love to Stay

₹ Budget ₹₹ Midrange ₹₹₹ Top End

Varanasi
Map p342

Wander Station ₹ Clean, bright dorms close to the ghats, with a popular rooftop restaurant where musicians play nightly at 9pm.

Bedzzz Varanasi ₹₹ Modern rooms in yellow and white around a plant-hung atrium with a good restaurant on the roof. Accessible by vehicle, 1km from the ghat area.

Ganpati Guesthouse ₹₹ An old red-brick favourite with a pleasant, shaded courtyard and plenty of balcony space around; fine river views.

Nilay House ₹₹₹ Well-appointed boutique-stay a stone's throw from Assi Ghat, home to the Tea Room cafe, featuring fine teas and home-baked goodies.

Brijrama Palace ₹₹₹ Meticulously renovated riverfront palace, built in 1812 and known as the Darbhanga Mahal, and the most luxurious heritage hotel along the ghats.

Hotel Ganges View ₹₹₹ Beautifully restored colonial-style *haveli* (traditional, ornately decorated residence) overlooking Assi Ghat; crammed with books, antiques and classy furniture. Book ahead.

Prayagraj (Allahabad)
Map p350

Hotel Prayag ₹ Just south of the train station, this sprawling, well-organised, lodging house has wi-fi, a State Bank of India ATM and a cool restaurant.

Planters Bungalow ₹₹ A 150-year-old heritage home amid mango and guava orchards. Spacious rooms, great food and lush outdoors.

WelcomHeritage Badi Kothi ₹₹₹ Not far from Sangam, this famous historic hotel is in a 400-year-old palace that was used by the tax collector during the British Raj.

Kushinagar
Map p354

Tibetan Monastery Guesthouse ₹ By far the nicest of Kushinagar's pilgrim accommodation offerings. En-suite, cold-water bathrooms and fans and relaxing porch-sitting areas.

Lotus Nikko ₹₹ Thai and Japanese groups favour this well-run hotel and for good reason: the rooms are simple but spacious and there's a pleasant garden area.

Royal Residency ₹₹ A great deal, with spick-and-span rooms and nice views over the garden. Bountiful buffets served three times per day at one of its two restaurants.

Ayodhya
Map p357

Hotel Shane Avadh ₹₹ Huge range of rooms in a well-run and busy establishment in Faizabad; one of the better deals in town. Book ahead.

My Mom's Village (p358) ₹₹ A women-led sustainable farm-stay with rooms and independent cottages, home-grown produce and the friendliest of canines.

Ramayana Hotel ₹₹₹ One of the flashiest hotels in Ayodhya, its best rooms have private balconies, the worst have no windows. Helpful staff.

Lucknow
Map p360

Lucknow Homestay ₹ Lucknow's homiest budget option is in the leafy 'Mall Ave' neighbourhood, and is home of Naheed and her family.

Backpacker Den ₹ Neat and clean hostel with good dorms and private rooms, plus a communal kitchen. There's a women-only dorm.

Bilgram House ₹ Well-run homestay with independent units that include a kitchenette and sitting room, and homestyle Awadhi staples.

Clarks Avadh ₹₹ Conveniently located, Lucknow's oldest five-star hotel has comfortable rooms, river views, helpful staff and decent food.

Mahmudabad House (p363) ₹₹ Tastefully decorated suites in a city palace with vintage furniture and incredible food, including curated culinary experiences.

Saraca ₹₹₹ The 1939 Morris car by the entrance sets the tone here; the 41 rooms were once part of a 1936 *haveli* and feature antique furniture. Some have private terraces.

Mathura & Vrindavan
Map p367

MVT Guesthouse ₹₹ Run by the Hare Krishna financial endowment and used mostly by followers, this relaxing, pleasant guesthouse is open to all, and has a great restaurant.

For places to stay in Uttarakhand, see p404

DEEP PAI/GETTY IMAGES

Above: Valley of Flowers National Park (p385); Right: Jageshwar Temple (p396)

Researched by
Shikha Tripathi

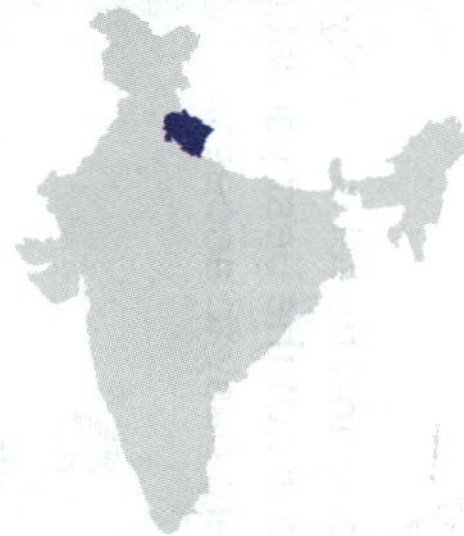

Uttarakhand

MOUNTAINS, MAGIC AND MYSTICISM

This unparalleled mountain state unites faith with adventure. Get your inner and outer bearings streamlined in a giant embrace of spirituality and the great outdoors.

Despite its relatively new identity as a state, Uttarakhand has been India's undisputed 'abode of the gods' since long before it was born in 2000. This is the birthplace of the Ganges, India's longest river, with the country's unofficial yoga capital on its banks, its best whitewater rapids and the most challenging glacier treks upstream. The small state is packed with a surprising number of firsts, be it the country's first national park – set up here even before Independence – or the Beatles' first visit to India to study transcendental meditation. It cradles the highest peak that's entirely in India (only overshadowed by Kangchenjunga, which also spills into Nepal) and has a hardy but delectable cuisine that uses ingredients revered nowhere else. Infuse all of this in an adaptive mountain sensibility typical to this geography, and steep it in colonial-era ambience – visible in its architecture and hill stations – and you have Uttarakhand.

SATISH PARASHAR/SHUTTERSTOCK

Good-natured rivalry divides its two major regions, Garhwal and Kumaon, but the state's most-loved folk song – which celebrates nature and love – unites them. Dialects and traditions differ in just the right doses but the deep spiritual connection, venerable simplicity of many people's lifestyles, and the grandeur of the Himalaya are the glue that holds Uttarakhand together.

THE MAIN AREAS

Find Your Way

Nearly 86% of Uttarakhand is mountainous and travel is mainly by road. Its small size can be deceptive and is not the best yardstick for travel duration, but popular regions are easy to access.

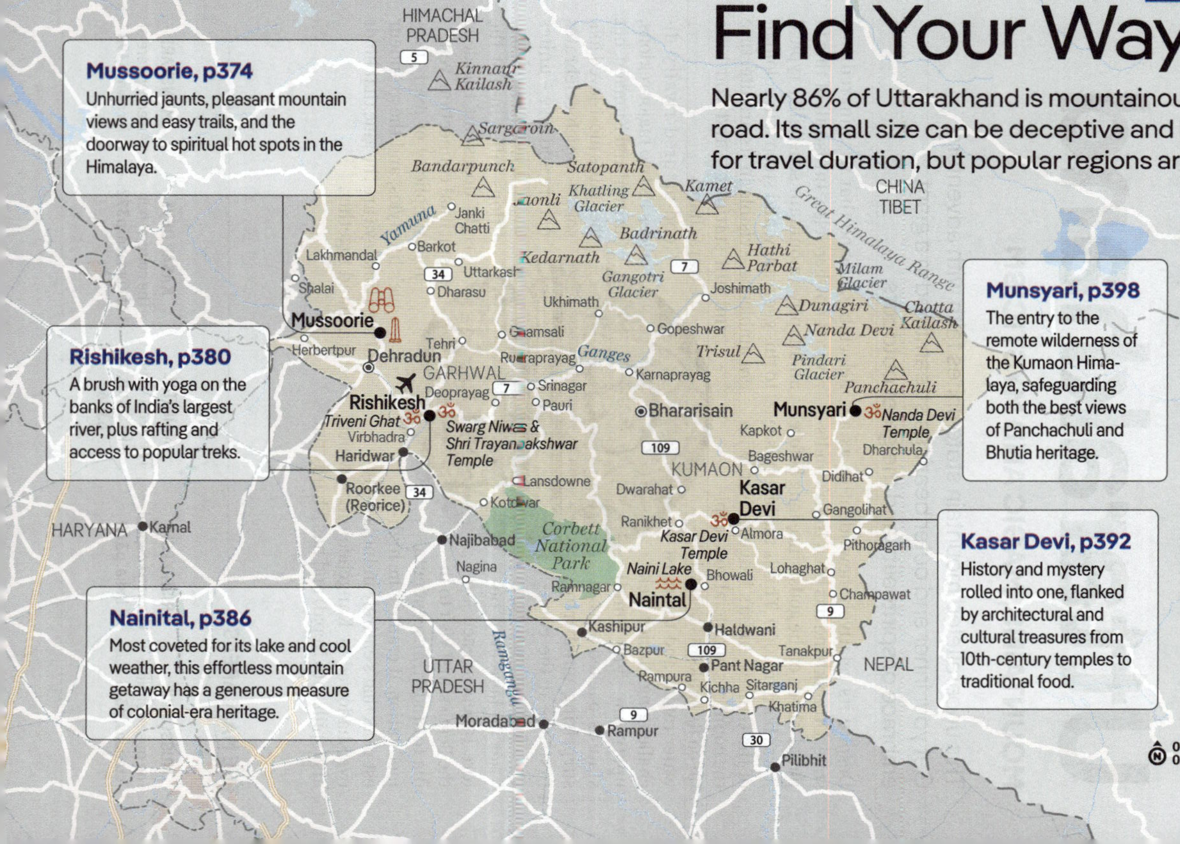

Mussoorie, p374
Unhurried jaunts, pleasant mountain views and easy trails, and the doorway to spiritual hot spots in the Himalaya.

Rishikesh, p380
A brush with yoga on the banks of India's largest river, plus rafting and access to popular treks.

Nainital, p386
Most coveted for its lake and cool weather, this effortless mountain getaway has a generous measure of colonial-era heritage.

Munsyari, p398
The entry to the remote wilderness of the Kumaon Himalaya, safeguarding both the best views of Panchachuli and Bhutia heritage.

Kasar Devi, p392
History and mystery rolled into one, flanked by architectural and cultural treasures from 10th-century temples to traditional food.

AIR

The main flight routes to the state from major airports like New Delhi and Mumbai are to its capital Dehradun. Pant Nagar near Nainital and Bareilly (at the border across in UP) have options too. Chopper services are available for those who want to go up to the Kedarnath temple.

ROAD & RAIL

The popular Delhi–Dehradun–Kathgodam triangle is connected by trains and good government bus services (see *utconline.uk.gov.in*). The shared taxi network is the most convenient way to move around in other locations.

SOLTAN FRÉDÉRIC/GETTY IMAGES

Kumbh Mela, Haridwar (p384)

Plan Your Time

Distances may be misleading on alpine terrain, but concentrated pockets of culture and adventure make it easy to taste a little bit of everything.

3 Days of Highlights

- Head to Landour for mountain views and to walk the **Infinity Loop** (p377). Descend to Rishikesh next for a day of **whitewater rafting** (p382) and an evening of Ganga *aarti* **(river worship ceremony**; p380). Go for a morning safari at the **Rajaji National Park** (p384) on the third day, then head to the **Mindrolling Monastery** (p378) in the capital, Dehradun. Finish off with a meal at **Kalsang Cafe** (p378).

A Week

- With over a week in hand, do the highlights then continue towards Nainital. Stop overnight at **Corbett National Park** (p390), then explore the lake district with short day hikes and birding. End your adventures with **Kasar Devi** (p392), including a day trip to see the **Jageshwar temples** (p396), a walk through **Almora's old bazaar** (p395), and a grand **Kumaoni thali** (p387).

SEASONAL HIGHLIGHTS

SPRING
The state tree, rhododendron, is in bloom around this time. Drive through endless forests of scarlet.

SUMMER
Escape sweltering heat in the mountains. Great for outdoor activities, including treks, rafting and climbing.

AUTUMN
Catch the biggest traditional celebration, the **Nanda Devi Festival** (p397), just before autumn sets in.

WINTER
Go skiing in **Auli** (p385), one of the best winter-sports hot spots not only in the state but in the whole of India.

Mussoorie

MOUNTAIN VIEWS | COLONIAL-ERA ARCHITECTURE | COMFORT FOOD

Still holding on firm to its title of the 'Queen of Hill Stations', Mussoorie sits high on the hills just above Uttarakhand's capital, Dehradun. Concentrated around a 2km ridge with the Garhwal Himalaya on the horizon, it is a hot favourite of domestic travellers – especially in the summer months – thanks to its crisp mountain weather. The town commands impressive views of the vast Doon Valley, which often fills up with clouds, a sight to behold especially during the monsoon. Unique for its winterline phenomenon that mimics a false horizon, this hill station has more than natural beauty. Mussoorie was founded in 1823 by the British, who set up a string of boarding schools here among other colonial-era structures, with their distinct architectural style stamped all over them. Its ever-mushrooming hotels and restaurants spoil you for choice, while its quiet extension, Landour, woos the solace-seeking traveller.

GETTING AROUND

Taxis are available at Library Chowk and Picture Palace. Negotiate ahead. Many distances between places of interest are walkable, but you may need a taxi at day's end. You can also hop on the cable car connecting the Mall Rd to Gun Hill. Horses ply the Camel's Back stretch, though it's best to use them for emergencies rather than joyrides. You can get around by bicycle, available for hire at several places including **Mussoorie Bike Rental** *(9720145638; pickups from Gandhi Chowk; per day ₹500).*

TOP TIP

The popularity of Mussoorie can create frustrating jams on the Dehradun–Mussoorie highway, especially over long weekends; travel on weekdays if possible.

Ghosts of the Past

See heritage and art on a stroll

Mussoorie is dotted with old buildings clamouring for space with the new. There is an occasional glimpse of a bygone era in the worn-out facades of its colonial-era buildings. Start at the **Landour Clock Tower**, beneath which sits the **Mussoorie Heritage Centre**. Local historian Surbhi Agarwal, who was born in this house, walks you through the artefacts on display; some exquisite items are on sale at her father's next-door **store** *(9068804682),* open 10am to 6pm, and a few vintage shops along the same road sell knick-knacks collected from Mussoorie's old homes. Those interested in fine art can check out their nearby contemporary gallery **VR Art Space** *(07454084766),* open 10am to 6pm. Another house of culture off the mall is the **Soham Heritage & Art Centre** *(9897241261; ₹100),* run by painter Kavita and her husband Sameer. The gallery-museum largely exhibits the culture of the Uttarakhand Himalaya and is open 10am to 2pm and 3pm to 5pm

SIGHTS
1 Atal Udhyan
2 Camel's Back Road
3 Gandhi Chowk
4 Gun Hill
5 Kellogg Memorial Church
6 Lal Tibba
7 Landour Christian Cemetery
8 Landour Clock Tower
9 Mussoorie Heritage Centre
10 Parsonage
11 Picture Palace Cinema
12 Soham Heritage & Art Centre
13 St Paul's Church
14 Union Church
15 VR Art Space

SLEEPING
16 Herne Lodge
17 La Villa Bethany
18 Savoy

EATING
19 Café de Tavern
20 Cafe Tea Totaler
21 Char Dukan
22 Landour Bakehouse
23 Little Llama Cafe
24 Lovely Omelette Centre

SHOPPING
25 Cambridge Book Depot
26 Prakash's

TRANSPORT
27 Library Chowk
28 Mussoorie Bike Rental
29 Picture Palace

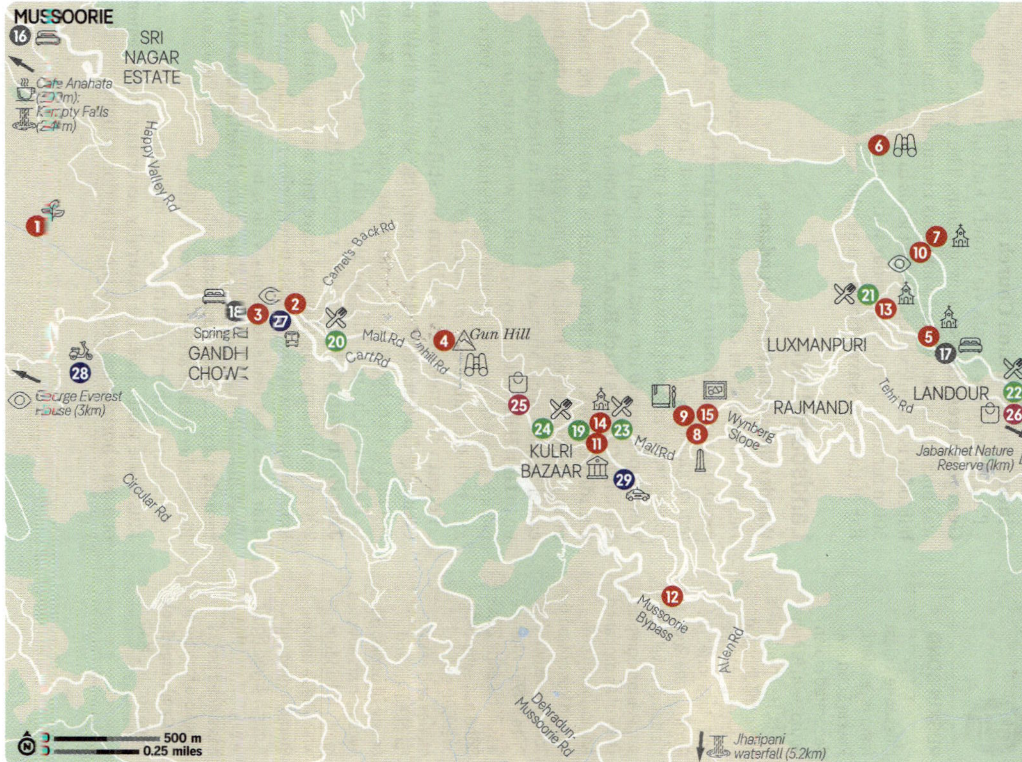

RUSKIN BOND

Mussoorie's most famous resident, Ruskin Bond is a decorated Indian author with British roots. He spent parts of his childhood in Dehradun, Shimla and Mussoorie. *The Room on the Roof*, his debut novel and semi-autobiographical story of an orphaned Anglo-Indian boy named Rusty, won the John Llewellyn Rhys Prize in 1957 when he was in his early 20s. Bond has authored over 500 short stories and essays for children, and nearly 70 books. He lives with his adopted family in Landour, which has a thriving literary community. A much-loved figure in town, the author has signed books available for sale at the **Cambridge Book Depot** on the Mall.

Thursday to Tuesday. On the main mall, the **Picture Palace Cinema** and the **Union Church** are landmarks to tick off.

Prep yourself for a walk via Cloud's End all the way to the **George Everest House**, now in ruins. The iconic building was once the home of the eponymous mountain's namesake, but today is a scenic viewpoint that leads to an even better one 500m further up. Finish your day with a drink at the Writer's Bar of the regal **Savoy hotel**, an aesthetic treat.

Landscape Love

Wander through nature's abundance.

Despite the mayhem of Mussoorie in peak season, you can escape to pockets of nature. The **Jabarkhet Nature Reserve** *(entry/guided walk ₹450/700)* tops the list. Traverse its dense forest trails and wildflower meadows alongside mountain views (open 7am to 1pm and 2pm to 4pm). On a day out on the Mall, hit **Camel's Back Road**, which branches off from near **Gandhi Chowk**. The 3km stretch is an oasis in the middle of the action-packed mall, with pleasant viewpoints and a camel-shaped rock. Midway on the Mall, a steep path spirals up to **Gun Hill**, which shows grand views of the region's main peaks, albeit from amid joyriders and snack sellers. You can also take the **cable car** *(one way ₹75)*.

Recently renamed **Atal Udhyan** but still better known as Company Garden, this botanical paradise set up in 1842 for colonial officers lies at the far end on the road towards **Kempty Falls**, which are wildly popular with Indian tourists; the **Jharipani waterfall** makes for a peaceful alternative. About 200m from Company Garden, leave the tarmac road for a long, leisurely walk on a moss-laden brick road through deodar trees that leads to Happy Valley, home to Mussoorie's Tibetan settlement. The trail ends at the **Tibetan Buddhist temple** next to **Cafe Anahata**, where both the views and Biscoff cheesecake are equally rewarding.

Between October and March, you may witness the famous Mussoorie winterline, the naturally occurring phenomenon of a false horizon caused by the refraction of light.

EATING IN MUSSOORIE: OUR PICKS

Café de Tavern: A centrally located multicuisine eatery on the Mall that panders to your pizza and dessert cravings, and also serves drinks. *11am-11pm* ₹₹

Little Llama Cafe: An Instagram-worthy cafe in Kulri Bazaar that serves great Tibetan food and equally good European dishes. *11am-10pm* ₹₹

Lovely Omelette Centre: This hole-in-the-wall joint has served omelettes since 1918; its bestsellers include cheese and also chocolate (!) options. *7am-2pm & 3-9pm Wed-Mon* ₹

Cafe Tea Totaler: Perfect for a break between mall walks, this place has a lovely sit-out upstairs and several fast-food options. *10.15am-10.30pm* ₹

WALKING THE INFINITY LOOP

A couple of hours' walkabout on Landour's narrow Infinity Loop is the best way to soak in its atmosphere.

START	END	LENGTH
Prakash's	Landour Bakehouse	3km; 2hr

Start from the iconic A Prakash & Co, better known as 1 **Prakash's**, which sells homemade jams (the gooseberry wins hands down) and cheeses in the Sisters' Bazaar area. Go past La Villa Bethany homestay (p404) and turn left at the knot (the figure-of-eight-shaped fork in the road), where steps lead to the 2 **Kellogg Memorial Church**, which also has the famous Landour Language School on its premises.

Keep walking until you cross a stone portico that marks the entry to boutique hotel 3 **Rokeby Manor**, which has a diner best known for its brunches. Past 4 **St Paul's Church** is the language-school-students' haunt 5 **Char Dukan**, a row of tea and pancake stalls.

Follow the loop to reach the viewpoint 6 **Lal Tibba** and catch a breather (and the sunset if it's late). The final stretch is also the highlight: a long path flanked by forests to the right, landmark buildings such as the 7 **Parsonage**, the 8 **Landour Christian Cemetery** with graves of British military men, and old bungalows that cup the hill's contours on one side and overlook stellar views of the Bandarpunch range on the other.

Turn left again and retrace your steps to Sisters' Bazaar, where you can finish your walk with a well-deserved coffee and dessert at the congenial 9 **Landour Bakehouse.**

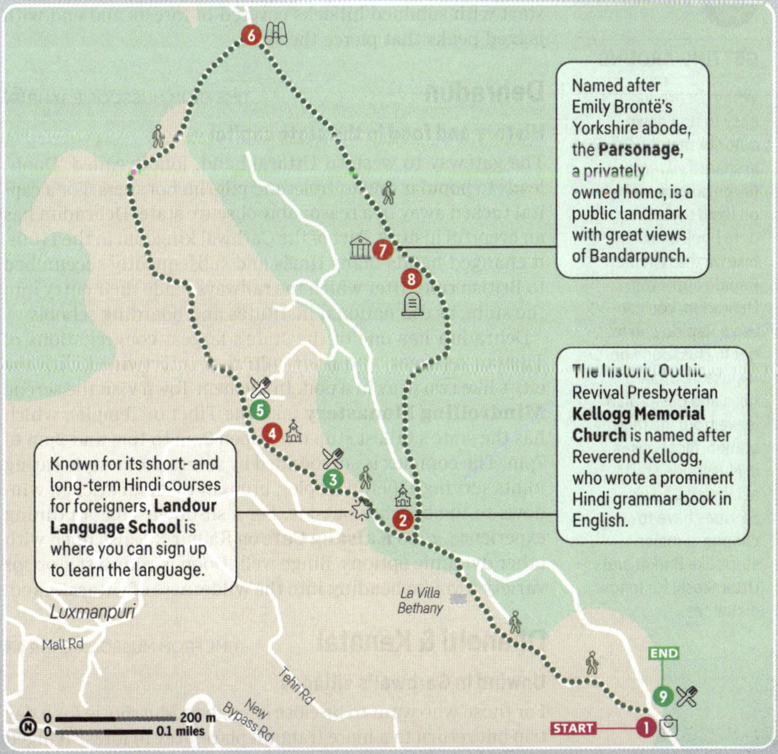

Beyond Mussoorie

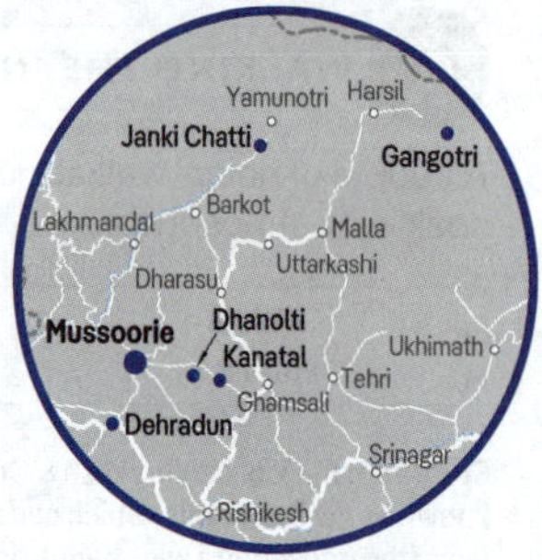

Away from Mussoorie, you will find the less manicured Garhwal: it slowly grows on you, one interesting place at a time.

Places

State capital Dehradun has enough for a day's exploration: slick hotels, institutes of national importance, and dynamic food joints and cafes to satiate you after a trek to Dodital and its high-altitude lake, or the multihued Har-ki-Dun valley. You can pamper yourself here, though it's entirely possible to avoid the capital if you fly into the airport on its outskirts. Deeper in the mountains, the roads beyond Mussoorie introduce you to the slow life, with languorous walks and Himalayan sunsets. They also lead you to the sources of the two largest rivers of India, the Ganges and the Yamuna, as well as landscapes that start with subdued hillocks covered in forests and end with jagged peaks that pierce the skies.

GETTING AROUND

Within Dehradun, it's easy to flag down autorickshaws or hop in shared *vikrams* (large autos running on fixed routes), or to book a taxi or bike on the reliable Rapido app. From Dehradun, you can use a Rapido cab to get to Mussoorie or Rishikesh. Shared taxis and buses also leave from the railway station. Most buses in Mussoorie start at Library Chowk; you may have to change at major stops like Barkot and Uttarakashi for longer distances.

Dehradun

TIME FROM MUSSOORIE: 1¼HR

History and food in the state capital

The gateway to western Uttarakhand, fondly called 'Doon', leads to popular towns, treks and pilgrim hot spots. For a capital tucked away in a reasonably obscure state, Dehradun has an eventful history. Part of the Garhwal kingdom in the 1400s, it changed hands many times and subsequently succumbed to British rule, after which the railways made their entry into the state, as did national institutes and boarding schools.

Dehradun has one of the state's largest congregations of Tibetan refugees, and their culture is intertwined with the city's like two peas in a pod. In Clement Town visit the serene **Mindrolling Monastery** (aka the Tibetan Temple), which has the state's tallest stupa. It's open 9am to 1pm and 2pm to 7pm. The complex is surrounded by several homestyle eating joints serving Tibetan staples, brought through kitchen windows to the benches outside. For a sit-down Tibetan dining experience, go to **Kalsang Cafe** on Rajpur Rd, also lined with other dynamic options. Binge well: Doon is your last stop for variety if you're heading into the wilderness of Uttarakhand.

Dhanolti & Kanatal

TIME FROM MUSSOORIE: 1HR

Unwind in Garhwal's villages

For those who want to be close enough to Mussoorie for a day trip but return to a more tranquil place, stay in forest-fringed

IMAGESOFINDIA/SHUTTERSTOCK

Gangotri

Dhanolti. Continue driving another 40 minutes on tarmac roads through cedar and rhododendron forests and past valley views, and you will get to the grand setting of the Garhwal Himalaya in **Kanatal**, loaded with orchard fruit, crisp air and long periods of repose.

Gangotri

TIME FROM MUSSOORIE: 7HR

Hike to the Ganges' source

A seven-hour drive from Mussoorie via Uttarakashi (notable for India's premier climbing school, the Nehru Institute of Mountaineering), **Gangotri** (3100m; road open May to early November) is a revered *char dham*, one of the four holy sites known as the pillars of Hinduism in Uttarakhand. Being the gateway to the source of the Ganges makes Gangotri special for Hindu pilgrims. The town itself is underwhelming, but the glacial snout Gaumukh, 18km away, makes up for it. The trek is a gradual climb to the glacier where India's largest river flows out from beneath the western face of the Bhagirathi peak. The journey is too long for a day trip from Gangotri but seasoned trekkers can break up the trip with a stunning **Tapovan meadows camping experience** *(9410178414; experiencethehimalayas.in)*.

Janki Chatti

TIME FROM MUSSOORIE: 4½HR

Hot springs and holy glaciers

The quietest of the four *dhams* (spiritual centres), Yamunotri is where the source of the Yamuna River lies. It's a medium-grade 1½-hour trek from Janki Chatti, which has several basic guesthouses to stay in. The **Yamunotri Temple** (3235m) sits in a gorge near the actual source in Kalinda peak. The frozen glacial lake is 1km away and a highly technical climb. You can soak in the hot springs and the vibe of pilgrim bonhomie near the temple instead.

DOON'S HIDDEN TRAILS

Lokesh Ohri, historian and anthropologist, runs citizens' group Been There Doon That, which has immersive walking tours in Dehradun, Mussoorie, Rishikesh and Haridwar. *beentheredoonthat.org*

Our walks focus on the natural, historical and intangible heritage of the region. An example is the unique Pahari-Mughal **monument of Guru Ram Rai Darbar Sahib** in Doon Valley, hidden in plain sight. We also work with mountain communities to equip them with creating curated village experiences. Our group runs **Cafe Laata** in Dehradun, and our book, *Walking with Laata*, gives detailed descriptions of 50 fabulous trails in the region. The Jharipani–Kipling Trail is my favourite walk in Doon, and I also highly recommend the Landour Infinity Loop in Mussoorie.

Rishikesh

GANGES VIEWS | SPIRITUAL PLUNGES | KICKSTARTING ADVENTURE

Many first-time travellers to India may not know Uttarakhand, but it's almost impossible not to have heard of Rishikesh. India's unofficial yoga capital, set on the banks of the country's longest river worshipped by millions of devout Hindus as 'mother Ganges', this is the town that travellers choose for an introductory spiritual deep dive in the Himalaya.

There's never a dull season in Rishikesh. This fairly big town is overflowing with pilgrims year-round, as well as backpackers, yoga practitioners, ascetics and trekking and rafting enthusiasts. Be it Rishikesh's yoga ashrams and its lively evenings on the ghats (stairs leading to the river bank), its food joints and cafes serving simple thalis or gourmet coffee, or the welcome chaos on its crowded bridges and streets, curious visitors love the town's vibe, especially in Tapovan neighbourhood. While most are here on individual pursuits, nearly everyone goes back having tasted a few drops of its divinity.

GETTING AROUND

The most efficient way to move around is by hopping in local shared *vikrams*, eight-seater tuk-tuks that ply fixed routes, or private autorickshaws. You could hire a private taxi for greater distances, but avoid taking one towards Lakshman Jhula or other crammed spots. Instead, get a seat on a shared taxi from Lakshman Jhula or at Swarg Ashram. A great way to get to the eastern bank is by local ferries from Ram Jhula; not only do you get to avoid the pedestrians and bikes on the bridge, you get a more picturesque alternative.

Spiritual Shenanigans

Attend yoga classes and Ganga aarti

Rishikesh is littered with traditional yoga schools, yoga ashrams and private coaching centres. Attend **Anand Prakash Yoga Ashram & Retreat Center** for individual classes and **Rishikesh Yogpeeth** for longer courses. If you just want to dip your toes, many places offer daily drop-in classes.

EATING & DRINKING IN RISHIKESH: OUR PICKS

Little Buddha Cafe: One of the busiest in the Lakshman Jhula area and for good reason; great for European cuisine and Ganges views. *8am-11pm* ₹₹

Beatles Cafe: A tribute to the band that added to Rishikesh's fame, this place in Tapovan has excellent burgers and smoothies, and river views. *11.30am-9.30pm* ₹₹

Govindji Prasadam: Inside the ISKON temple premises at Muni ki reti, this restaurant serves one of the best vegetarian thalis in town. *11.30am-10.30pm* ₹

Bistro Nirvana: In the High Bank traveller enclave; one of Rishikesh's few joints where you can get non-vegetarian options including tandoori items. *8.30am-10.30pm* ₹₹

HIGHLIGHTS
1 Swarg Niwas & Shri Trayanbakshwar Temple
2 Triveni Ghat

SIGHTS
3 Lakshman Jhula
4 Maharishi Mahesh Yogi Ashram
5 Ram Jhula
6 Shatrughan Temple Ghat
7 Swarg Ashram

ACTIVITIES
8 Anand Prakash Yoga Ashram & Retreat Center

SLEEPING
9 Terrakotta
10 Vashishth Guest House

EATING
11 Anna's Mess
12 Arches Cafe
13 Beatles Cafe
14 beMonk Cafe
15 Bistro Nirvana
16 Govindji Prasadam
17 Little Buddha Cafe

INFORMATION
18 Red Chilli Adventure

Complete your cultural induction by attending the famous Ganges *aarti*, a daily evening religious ceremony on the river banks involving devotional music and earthen lamp offerings; go to **Triveni Ghat**, or the quieter **Shatrughan Temple Ghat**.

Sights of Rishikesh

Explore the landmarks around town

The major sights lie upstream, around the two bridges **Ram Jhula** and **Lakshman Jhula**. The latter looks directly at the town's defining point, the **Swarg Niwas and Shri Trayanbakshwar Temple**. Walk 2km on the east bank of the river and south of this hanging bridge to the **Swarg Ashram** spiritual conglomeration of temples and ashrams.

Further south is the **Maharishi Mahesh Yogi Ashram** *(₹600)*, better known as the Beatles' Ashram. The sprawling part-restored, part-dilapidated campus has surreal meditation domes, scattered graffiti art and a permanent photo exhibition by Paul Saltzman set up in 2018 to commemorate the 50th anniversary of the Beatles' visit.

See the stalwarts of the Garhwal Himalaya at sunrise from the **Kunjapuri temple**; note that you have to climb 300 steps. The **Neer waterfall** (or Neergarh waterfall) is a 25m cascade over limestone formations. Less-crowded places include the Himshail waterfall trail and the Pawki Devi temple hike.

Adventure Awaits

Hit the country's best whitewater rapids

Known for some of India's best whitewater rapids, the section of the Ganges close to Rishikesh is synonymous with rafting. Day trips start upstream from Shivpuri and end just a bit short of Rishikesh, with the rafting season running from mid-September to the end of June. **Red Chilli Adventure** *(redchilliadventure.com; per person for 3hr ₹1500)* organises half-day and multiday all-inclusive rafting trips with camping.

Planet Abled *(planetabled.com; message ahead on 99100 19981)* organises disability-friendly tours across India, including in Uttarakhand, and has led rafting trips in Rishikesh for people with physical challenges. For high-end, responsible adventures, pick Delhi-based **Aquaterra** *(aquaterra.in)*.

BUILDING WITH INTENT

In a seismically vulnerable region, the indigenous architecture of Uttarakhand has long demonstrated the art of earthquake-proof building. **Koti Banal**, a village in the Uttarkashi district, birthed the style that has endured earthquakes for nearly 900 years. Structures were built to endure severe temperatures and stand strong on uneven terrain, using local material and construction methods that gave rise to the distinct Koti Banal style of architecture. It was adapted across the state in different forms, especially in Garhwal. The intricate carvings on doors and windows became an art form in their own right known as *likhai*.

TOP TIP

Non-veg food and alcohol is not served in Rishikesh (or Haridwar), specifically in the periphery of the holy river. A few cafes away from the centre serve meat, and you can consume your own alcohol at your hotel.

EATING IN TAPOVAN: OUR PICKS

Tulsi Restaurant: Loved for its savoury crepes, this simple but popular joint has a thoughtful, limited menu. Try the millet cheese pancakes. *9am-9pm* ₹

Arches Cafe: A chic multicuisine restaurant in the midst of a buzzing Tapovan; the outdoor seating here commands a stellar Ganges view. *8am-10.30pm* ₹₹

Anna's Mess: Hidden from plain sight, this elfin garden restaurant is an unabashed celebration of South Indian cuisine. *noon-10pm Wed-Mon* ₹

beMonk Cafe: An unsuspecting doorway opens into a classy world of designer decor and live devotional music while your enjoy your meal. *10am-10pm* ₹₹₹

Beyond Rishikesh

It's time to step up for encounters with the wilderness of Uttarakhand.

Places

Many go to Rishikesh for a journey into the self, yet it's equally a gateway to outdoor adventures, and there's a smorgasbord of activities to pick from. The spiritual essence of Rishikesh spills into Haridwar beyond, but the Ganges also offers wild and spirited voyages in the form of rafting. Where rafting ends, the jungles of Rajaji and its wildlife experiences begin. Upstream, the roads lead to some of the most magnificent places not only in the state but also in the Indian Himalaya. From easy adventures to tricky ones, the region offers something to every seeker: skiing spots, valleys flooded with flowers, rugged mountains and ancient spiritual epicentres where you can feel the pull of Uttarakhand's magnetism at its strongest.

Chopta-Tungnath-Chandrasila

TIME FROM RISHIKESH: 4½HR

On a rhododendron high

One of the state's best day hikes, the **Tungnath Trek** spirals out of the rhododendron bowl that is **Chopta**. Spring is a riot of colours, especially the burst of pink flowers that you see all along on the drive to Chopta, and the even more dense thickets as you climb 3.5km from there to the **Shiva temple** at **Tungnath**. Head a steep 1.5km further to **Chandrashila** peak (4000m) for a rewarding view (five to six hours' return). The rising sun is a sight worth the early morning start. Chopta has little to offer, including options to stay; go to Guptkashi (p404) instead.

Kedarnath

TIME FROM RISHIKESH: 6HR

Seeking blessings in the seat of Shiva

The most revered of the *char dham,* Kedarnath is the seat of Shiva, the cosmic destroyer. From May to mid-November it also has the most dramatic setting, surrounded by peaks towering nearly 7000m. A 14km walk upstream along the Mandakini River and its canyon, the trek to Kedarnath is typically lined with the pilgrim crowd, shops selling *puja* (religious ceremony) items, food stalls and medical stops.

GETTING AROUND

You can get a Rapido cab to get from Dehradun to Rishikesh, but not beyond. Buses take you to main towns like Haridwar and Joshimath, and can drop you off at trailheads if they fall on their route. The most hassle-free option for any remote area is asking your accommodation to book you a taxi. You can also take shared taxis. There are generally multiple travellers heading to the trailheads of popular routes, so car pooling is common.

RHODODENDRON RUSH

Every spring, Uttarakhand's forests roll out the red carpet – made from crimson flowers fallen from its state tree, the rhododendron. Between February and March, trees blossom across the state with predominantly red flowers, though they're sometimes pink and white, and in rare cases, blue. The sight is best relished on treks or long drives on undisturbed routes. The Chopta–Tungnath trail has endless stretches of the pink variety in full bloom against azure skies. For a less-crowded, offbeat option, head to Ranthan Kharak (p403) in eastern Uttarakhand. The flowers' petals are also collected and crushed to make a refreshing drink. During rhododendron season, you're likely to be offered a glass upon arrival at a hotel or a home. Even *pakoras* (fritters) can be made from the petals.

Helicopter rides are a popular alternative to make this a day trip (₹6060 from the Sersi helipad with **Himalayan Heli Services** *(himalayanheli.com)*; or get tickets via your accommodation). Paying extra for an express *darshan* (holy glimpse) of the sacred stone hump can help avoid massive queues. Getting a (free) photometric ID card in Sonprayag centre (open 5am to 6pm), 5km before Gaurikund, is compulsory since the 2013 Kedarnath floods.

Badrinath

TIME FROM RISHIKESH: 8½HR

Dive into the heart of Hinduism

Believed to be the first of the *dhams*, Badrinath (from May to November) is also the only of the four that you can drive up to all the way. Despite its chaotic surroundings, it's popular for its accessibility and its vividly painted structure. A side trip to the timeless Mana village gives a glimpse of what the original Badrinath setting must have been like hundreds of years ago.

Haridwar

TIME FROM RISHIKESH: 40MIN

Religion and rituals

Known for its evening Ganga *aarti*, and of great significance among Hindus for rituals that follow death and mark boys' coming of age, Haridwar is essentially a pilgrim town. Its most famous spot is **Har-ki-Pauri**, the 'Footstep of God', where Vishnu supposedly left an imprint. This is where the action is: from priests and devout Hindus performing prayers and rituals, to the mandatory dip in the freezing waters, or the daily *aarti* on the banks, Har-ki-Pauri is the place.

Every 12 years Haridwar hosts the Kumbh Mela, the largest religious gathering in the world. The monsoon season also sees the Kaanwar Yatra, when thousands of Shiva devotees descend. The crowds are best avoided by non-pilgrim travellers, especially women.

Rajaji National Park

TIME FROM RISHIKESH: 30MIN

Head into the wild

The massive 820-sq-km **Rajaji National Park** *(mid-Nov–mid-Jun)* is most accessible from between Rishikesh and Haridwar (four gates) though it spreads all the way to the foothills of Dehradun (two gates). It was only declared a tiger reserve as recently as 2015, but its deciduous jungles have long been a habitat for deer, elephants and over 400 species of birds. On a **safari** *(₹1100, plus jeep and guide ₹4000)* few will be fortunate enough to spot a tiger, but leopard- and elephant-sighting have good odds. **Veeru Negi** *(rajajijungle safari.com; 9917606031)* is a skilled naturalist who has been around since the park's inception and can organise guided safaris for you.

Leopards, Rajaji National Park

Auli

TIME FROM RISHIKESH: 7HR

Stop and ski

Perched above Joshimath, the epicentre for many of Garhwal's most popular treks, Auli is one of India's few and favourite skiing destinations. The government-run guesthouse **GMVN Auli** (Garhwal Mandal Vikas Nigam) runs skiing courses and has a good bar and the best views. Auli is a great alternative to Joshimath for breaking up your journey en route to higher mountains. In summer, you can still enjoy tremendous views of the mountains, which are an easy 20-minute cable-car ride from Joshimath.

Valley of Flowers National Park & Hemkund Sahib

TIME FROM RISHIKESH: 7½HR

Trekking through a rainbow of colours

This bucket-list trek is loved by hikers for its sheer beauty and short, two-day duration. The **Valley of Flowers National Park** *(₹600; 7am–2pm June–October)*, is part of the Nanda Devi biosphere that transforms into a carpet of flowers between June and September. The monsoon flowering of over 300 species is inimitable, but the valley is equally magical (and drier) outside the main season. Add a third day for **Hemkund Sahib**, a holy place for Sikh pilgrims. The steep 6km ascent can get challenging but is worth it for the reward of the glacial lake at the end. **Eskimo Adventure** *(eskimoadventure.com; 9412413714, 9756835647)* is one of the longest-running adventure outfits in the area for this trek.

UTTARAKHAND'S BEST TREKS

Har Ki Dun: Glacial streams and pristine forests are the hallmark of this undulating trek. *(easy, max height 3510m, three days)*

Dayara Bugyal: Beginner-friendly trek known for its highland meadows and Himalaya views. *(easy, max height 3700m, five days)*

Pindari Glacier: A bowl of mountains and glaciers on the edge of the Nanda Devi sanctuary. *(moderate, max height 3353m, three days)*

Aali Bedni Bugyal: A magical world of high-altitude alpine meadows and unadulterated views. *(moderate, max height 3354m, six days)*

Auden's Col: A legendary trek and rite of passage for seasoned trekkers and climbers. *(difficult, max height 5490m, 15 days)*

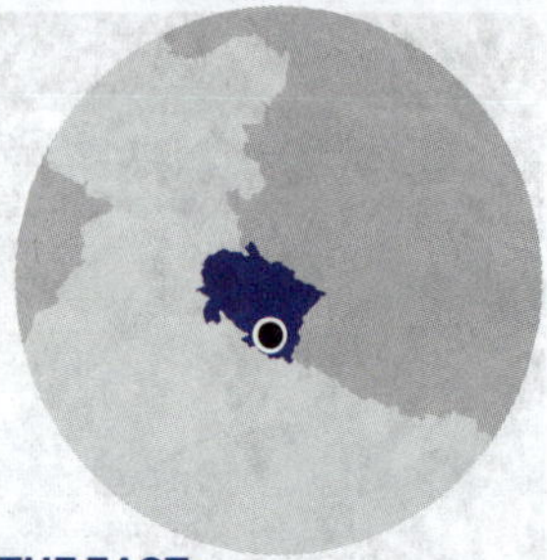

Nainital

LAKE VIEWS | COLONIAL-ERA HISTORY | GATE TO THE EAST

GETTING AROUND

Walking is the best way to get around. For longer stretches, get a cab from its two major points, Tallital and Mallital. If you don't have luggage, hop onto a bike taxi and ride behind the driver; these are a convenient and quick way to navigate through busy areas. Cycle- and e-rickshaws ply the Mall, which is closed to vehicles in the evenings; you have to take the longer college road. Boats are largely recreational but you could hire one to get from one end of the lake to the other.

TOP TIP

Parking can be a nightmare in the high season, so it's best to not do a self-drive trip. There's a ₹300 toll tax each time your vehicle enters the Mall (which is closed from 6pm to 8pm); timings and toll prices may vary with season.

The first non-native claiming to 'discover' Nainital was British sugar merchant Peter Baron, who implored his fellow countrymen to set up a colony here in 1839. Even now the emerald lake, splashed across the valley between seven forested hills, remains Nainital's star draw. From being the summer capital of the United Provinces in a pre-Independence India to becoming a favourite haunt of Bollywood stars and political leaders in the '70s, the town has long been awash in nostalgia: there's the old club with vintage furniture, the library by the lake, its missionary schools and colonial heritage galore. Today, it has reclaimed some of its original image and created a unique identity by infusing its British past with festivals and events that celebrate local culture. Despite heavy domestic tourism, it still has pristine pockets of beautiful woods and impressive viewpoints, far from the madding crowds. Move away from its busy centre and you'll find the Nainital of yore.

Walk the Naini Mall

See the promenade's major landmarks

Take a walk up the Mall (or elbow through it, especially on summer evenings) to find its gratifying spots. Begin at the upper end of the road near the Mallital rickshaw stand, outside the Flats, grounds that were formed by a momentous landslide in 1880. They serve as an all-in-one town stadium today, for everything from cricket matches to annual concerts, flanked by the **Naina Devi temple** and **Tibetan market**. To the right is the historic Boat House Club, a 1910 building where the British socialised over drinks and bridge. India's second-oldest club, it still hosts the annual regatta featuring boats not sailed anywhere else. The club allows non-members to enter for a ₹300 fee (from 10am to 10pm) and enjoy its ideal lakeside location for a pint on a sunny afternoon. Walk further up past restaurants and shops to the historic Grand Hotel, which hosted '70s Bollywood stars, and the recently renovated 1934 lakeside **Durga Shah Municipal Library**

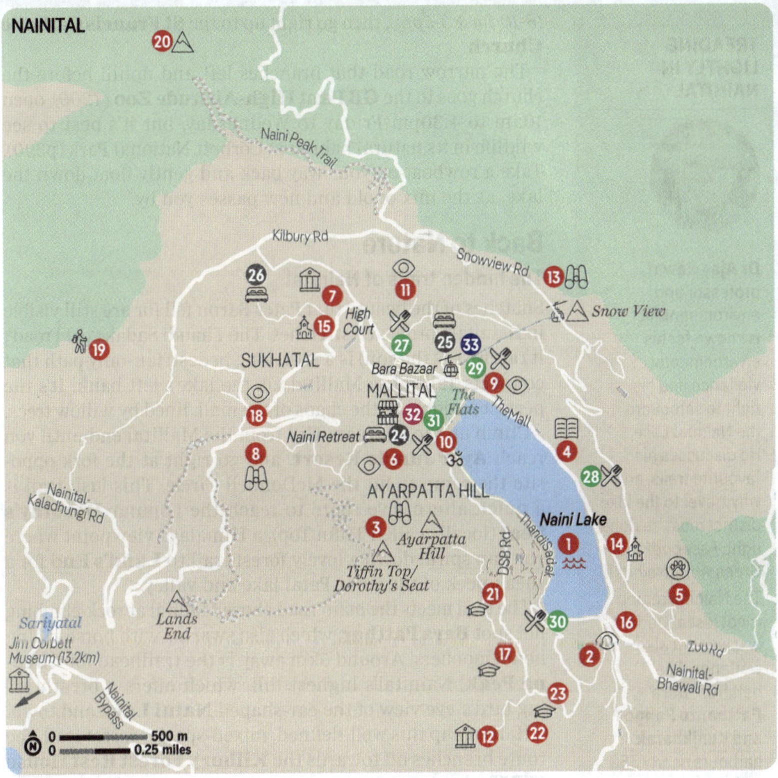

HIGHLIGHTS
1 Naini Lake

SIGHTS
2 District & Sessions Court
3 Dorothy's Seat
4 Durga Shah Municipal Library
5 GB Pant High Altitude Zoo
6 Gurney House
7 High Court
8 Land's End
9 Mallital
10 Naina Devi
11 Pilgrim House
12 Raj Bhavan Governor House
13 Snow View
14 St Francis Catholic Church
15 St John's in the Wilderness
16 Tallital

ACTIVITIES
17 All Saints' College
18 Bara Patthar
19 Camel's Back
20 Cheena Peak
21 Kumaon University
22 St Joseph's College
23 St Mary's Convent

SLEEPING
24 Naini Retreat
25 Palace Belvedere
26 Shervani Hilltop

EATING
27 Anupam
28 Cafe Lakeside
29 Sakley's
30 Simz Cafe
31 Sonam Fast Food

SHOPPING
32 Tibetan Market

TRANSPORT
33 Ropeway Nainital

EATING IN NAINITAL: OUR PICKS

Sakley's: This place evolved from a cubbyhole patisserie to a restaurant serving good Asian food, and still has the town's best desserts. *10am-10pm* ₹₹

Anupam: One of the oldest and best North Indian food joints here. For local flavours, try the traditional Kumaoni thali. *10.30am-10.30pm* ₹

Cafe Lakeside: Ideal for an evening of fancy wine and delectable food overlooking the lake and Mall, or for people-watching. *9am-10.30pm* ₹₹

Sonam Fast Food: A local favourite, 'Sonam's' is a timeless, busy place serving the best Tibetan bites. No tables; takeaway available. *11am-8pm* ₹

TREADING LIGHTLY IN NAINITAL

Dr Ajay Rawat, professor and environmentalist, is known for his environmental vigilance and his fight to safeguard the Nainital Lake. He discusses his favourite trails, and why travel to the lake district must be done right. *Facebook: S3 Green Army Nainital*

The Nainital region is not just abundant in lakes, but also wetlands. The belt from **Bara Patthar to Pangot and Kunjkharak** harbours nearly 350 avifauna species, and birdwatching is a great way to experience the richness of Nainital. This holds true for the the pedestrian-only **Thandi Sadak** too, the offbeat Camel's Back trail, and the towns of Sattal and Bhimtal nearby. I've also had tourists join me with my students in lake-cleaning campaigns, a wonderful way to travel meaningfully.

(8-10am & 3-5pm), then go right up to the **St Francis Catholic Church**.

The narrow road that branches left and uphill before the church goes to the **GB Pant High-Altitude Zoo** *(₹200)*, open 10am to 4.30pm Friday to Wednesday, but it's best to see wildlife in its natural habitat at Corbett National Park (p390). Take a rowboat on your way back and gently float down the lake, as the mix of old and new passes you by.

Back to Nature

The hidden trails of Nainital

Snatches of the beauty that Peter Baron fell for are still visible in Nainital's protected stretches. The Thandi Sadak ('cold road'; it rarely sees the sun) is a mile-long pedestrian-only path that connects Tallital to Mallital via the lake's left bank. It's the perfect antidote to the chaos of the mall, lined by willow trees.

Climb up the Ayarpata Hill from the Mallital end until you reach **Ayar Jungle Resort**, and go right at the fork opposite the camp to hit the McDonnell Circle. This lush trail is a quiet, alternative route to reach the popular **Dorothy's Seat** (locally called Tiffin Top), a Himalaya viewpoint where you can spiral down a lovely forest trail to **Land's End** for a sneak peek of the Khur Patal lake and valley.

The trail meets the main road above Mallital at rock-climbing hot spot **Bara Patthar**, which also swarms with horse-riding honeymooners. Around 5km away is the trailhead for **Cheena Peak**, Nainital's highest hill, which offers a breathtaking bird's-eye view of the ear-shaped **Naini Lake** and town.

Halfway up this well-defined, mixed-species forest trail, the route branches off towards the **Kilbury Forest Rest House (FRH)** through a dreamy oak and cedar forest. This trail was described by hunter-turned-conservationist Jim Corbett as one of his favourites, and remains one of Nainital's best-kept secrets. Adventurers can go up the tricky **Camel's Back** and be assured of near-zero crowds (though it's not advisable to go alone), while you can enjoy heights and lake views on the **Ropeway Nainital** *(return ₹300)* between 10am and 4pm to **Snow View**. You can explore these trails or the lake district with nature and culture guide **Sunil Kumar** *(tranquility treks.in; 9411196837, 8477019549)*, who grew up here.

Jim Corbett Sites

From hunter to conservationist

Edward James 'Jim' Corbett, born in Nainital in 1875, was drawn to the wild at an early age. His remarkable metamorphosis from hunter to conservationist and author (*Man-Eaters of Kumaon* remains one of his best reads) was honoured with India's first national park being named after him. **Gurney House**, where he was born, is now a privately owned home on Ayarpatta Hill. Corbett fans are welcome to pop in; the caretaker gives tours. It's next to the hotel **Naini Retreat**, close to the McDonnell Circle trailhead. The Corbett family spent winters in their Kaladhungi home in the foothills, today the **Jim Corbett Museum** *(9012308933; ₹200)*.

A WALK THROUGH COLONIAL-ERA KUMAON

Nainital nurses a colonial-era hangover stronger than many of its sister hill towns in Kumaon; see the sights on this walking tour.

START	END	LENGTH
Simz Cafe	High Court	4km; 2½hr

Start at 1 **Simz Cafe** and head towards the Thandi Sadak road; go left and ascend the route that kicks off the college road. Cross the 2 **District & Sessions Court**, and stop to see the 1878 3 **St Mary's Convent**. Next is 4 **St Joseph's College**, a school established in 1888, with the town's most recognisable facade. Less than 500m away is the iconic 5 **Raj Bhavan Governor House**, a home for British governors inspired by Buckingham Palace.

Continue down the ridge, below 6 **All Saints' College** and past the campus of 7 **Kumaon University**, until the end of the road above the 8 **Tibetan Market**. You can finish your walk at the 9 **Naina Devi**, a temple dedicated to the goddess that gives the town its name ('Naina' means 'eyes'; in Hindu mythology, this is where goddess Parvati's eyes fell off her burnt body and landed when her enraged husband Shiva did his cosmic dance carrying her).

Otherwise, add a small detour to see remnants of 10 **Pilgrim House**, the house built by Peter Baron. North of here is 11 **St John's in the Wilderness**, an atmospheric church as delightful as its name, and diagonally opposite is the beautiful old secretariat that today serves as the state 12 **High Court**. It stands in the foreground of Cheena (or Naina) Peak, the town's highest hill.

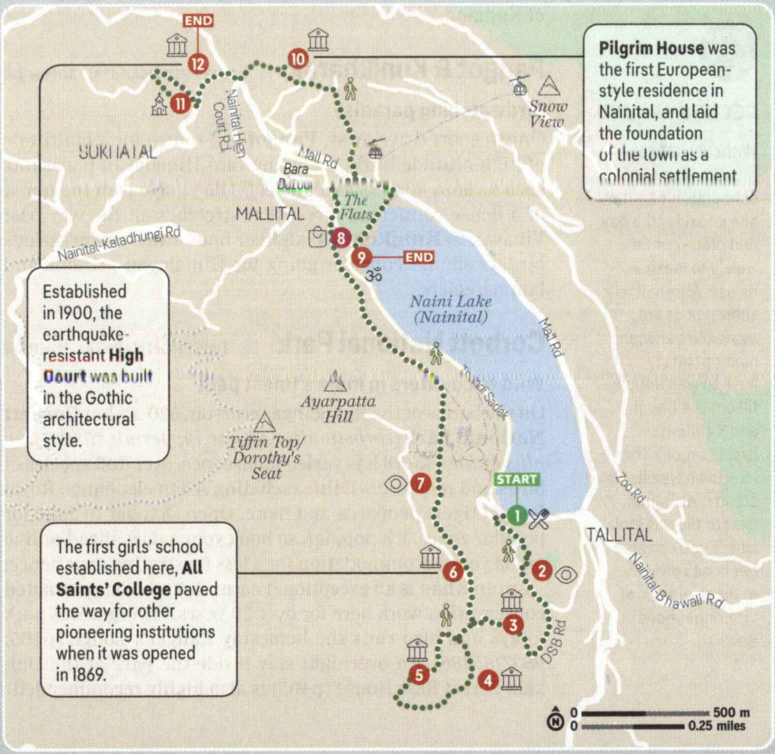

Beyond Nainital

Explore the lake district, with its teeming birdlife, wildlife hot spots, and quiet hamlets.

Places

Nainital has the largest body of water in the entire lake district of Kumaon – no small boast, considering the district also comprises the Bhimtal, Naukuchiatal and Sattal lakes, and a handful of minor ones. It's worth your while to take a day off to explore these beautiful lakes; some travellers stay in quiet Bhimtal and do day excursions from there. Corbett National Park is a must-see destination for wildlife lovers, and with an overnight stop it can also be experienced on your way to Kumaon. Beyond the major towns, small villages and protected forest belts herald your entry to the tranquillity of Kumaon.

GETTING AROUND

Without a reliable public transport schedule, it's best to hire a taxi for the day and plan your time wisely to maximise its use. Alternatively, shared taxis are available between major points (you'll have to wait until they fill up) like Bhimtal and Kathgodam (train station). The intertown Nainital taxi stand is at Tallital, next to the bus stop where you can also get buses directly to these places, or via connections in Bhowali.

Pangot & Kunjkharak

TIME FROM NAINITAL: **30MIN**

Birdwatching paradise

Only a short drive away, **Pangot** is a refuge for a multitude of high-altitude birds, including rare Himalayan pheasants such as chir, koklass and khaleej. The village is in the midst of a dense coniferous forest that stretches all the way past Vinayak to **Kunjkharak**, another hour away, where serious birders should consider going for Himalayan griffons and lammergeiers.

Corbett National Park

TIME FROM NAINITAL: **1¾HR**

Wild encounters in India's finest park

On the banks of the Ramganga reservoir, 520-sq-km **Corbett National Park** *(corbettonline.uk.gov.in; permit ₹6800, jeep plus guide ₹4500)* has varied landscapes, over 600 species of birds and majestic wildlife including Asian elephants, Royal Bengal tigers, leopards and more. Open October to June for popular zones, it's popular, so book your safari ahead online or via your accommodation for a less frustrating experience.

Imran Khan is an exceptional naturalist who has promoted conservation work here for over 20 years. He organises park forays and also runs the homestay Ranger's Lodge (p405; *9837185386)*. An overnight stay inside the park at the Dhikala Forest Rest House (p405) is also highly recommended.

ANURADHA MARWAH/SHUTTERSTOCK

Bengal tiger, Corbett National Park

Ramgarh & Mukteshwar

TIME FROM NAINITAL: 1HR

Draw in Himalaya views

Ramgarh is the detour taken by Indian travellers nostalgic for the 'finer Nainital', and where Nobel laureate Tagore wrote parts of his famous *Gitanjali*. Starting from the sequestered Gagar district in Ramgarh, the area that stretches two hours further up to **Mukteshwar** is also called the fruit belt of Kumaon, and is lined with posh summer homes, boutique hotels and impressive mountain views. It's ideal for being idle, or for long walks with stirring views.

Bhimtal

TIME FROM NAINITAL: 1HR

Dig deep into nature and culture

The idyllic lake town of Bhimtal is great for a day of easy sightseeing and a lazy lunch, or even to base yourself. It has the **Folk Culture Museum** *(Lok Sanskriti; ₹100)*, privately run by decorated historian Dr Mathpal, paddleboats and rowboats to go around the lake, and an intriguing **Butterfly Research Centre** *(₹300)* run by founder and ecologist Peter Smetacek out of his home. You can easily hike down to birding hub Sattal from here, or drive half an hour to see Naukuchiatal lake.

FOR THE LOVE OF BUTTERFLIES

Peter Smetacek runs the Butterfly Research Centre in Bhimtal and has spent six decades documenting butterflies and studying moths. He has authored several books on the subject and is an advocate for conservation of the region. *facebook.com/peter.smetacek.5*

The Raj Bhawan or Government House grounds in Nainital are special because they have been very well protected for over a century. There are many butterflies there from April to June and from September to November. I would also recommend any walks around Kilbury, since the views and the forest are exceptional. Around Bhimtal, the Sattal area is fantastic. And you can always combine it with my favourite – a dip in the lake on a sunny afternoon!

EATING & DRINKING AROUND BHIMTAL: OUR PICKS

iHeart Cafe: A local favourite. Stop for breakfast or brunch, coffee and dessert. Get the signature José or pancake breakfast. *7am-8pm Thu-Tue* ₹₹

Chai Etc.: Juicy mutton *momos* (dumplings) are sold at this stall with a cosy seating area, along with piping hot chai, wraps and bun sandwiches. *9am-8pm Wed-Mon* ₹

Machan: Indulge in a rich North Indian meal complete with tandoori tikka and garlic naan. It's best to not count calories. *9.30am-10.30pm* ₹₹

Pine Crest: If you're after Italian food, this largely word-of-mouth place, just after exiting Bhowali, is the spot for thin-crust pizzas and lasagne. *8am-10pm* ₹₹

Kasar Devi

SPIRITUALITY | MOUNTAIN VIEWS | LAID-BACK LIVING

GETTING AROUND

Kasar Devi is a small village, and within it is an even smaller area that packs in travellers' interests: most guesthouses, shops, cafes and places to see are concentrated on the ridge (a radius of a couple of kilometres) and can easily be reached on foot. For any sightseeing beyond walking range, you'll have to hire a taxi. Every hotel or guesthouse has a set of drivers they work with, best hired for half- or full-day trips. A great way to explore short distances is to rent a motorbike from your guesthouse or **Moksha Bike Rentals** *(7452988522; per day ₹500-1500)*.

Fondly known as the 'Cranks Ridge', an ode to its eclectic residents in the 1960s, Kasar Devi has long drawn poets, mystics, writers and philosophers. Indian spiritual leader Swami Vivekananda, Danish philosopher Sunyata, painter Earl Brewster and Beat poet Allen Ginsberg all stayed here, as did musician Bob Dylan and writer DH Lawrence.

Despite its global appeal, Kasar Devi lingered in obscurity until recent years. Its magnetism is often attributed to the belief that it shares cosmic energy – akin to locations like Machu Picchu and Stonehenge – via openings in the Van Allen belt surrounding the earth. Whatever the merits of the theory, the village continues to be a magnet for creatively inclined travellers, spirituality seekers and, more recently, remote workers in search of an inspiring backdrop and cool cafes. Its newfound popularity has transformed the once-quiet Kasar into a lively community teeming with guesthouses, cafes and art centres.

Rewind to the Past

Walking through the ridge's history

Kasar Devi Temple, the hamlet's first significant building, remains a favourite sunrise-watching spot. About 100 steps lead up to the temple; close by is the Swami Vivekananda rock, where the philosopher is believed to have meditated. After soaking in silence, head to nearby **Drikung Kagyu Meditation Centre**. Painter and poet Ernst Hoffmann has a stupa dedicated to him on these premises – he was better known as Govinda Lama and was one of the first white men to be ordained a monk and establish a Buddhist order.

For an introduction to the history of the ridge, go to **Himadri Handloom**, an outlet 5km away at Dinapani, which has a wall dedicated to the history. You can then head to its patron, the nearby **Panchachuli Women Weavers of Kumaon** (not to be confused with Panchachuli Handloom in Almora), and see

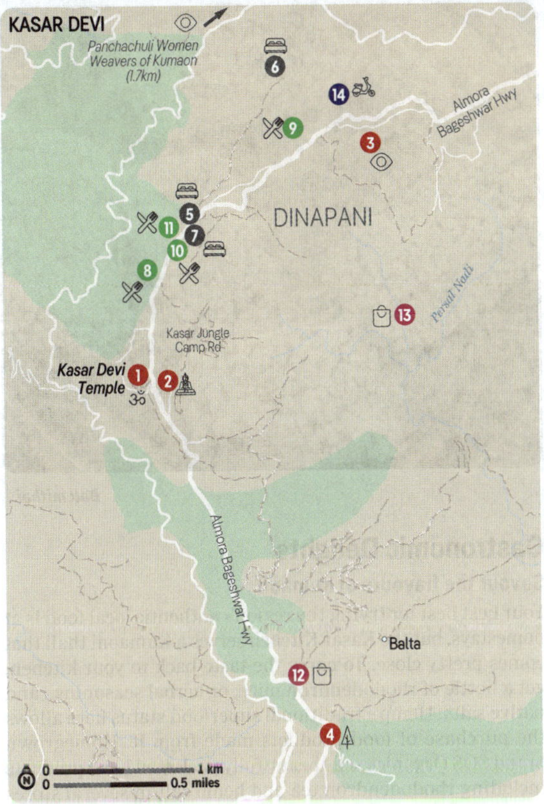

HIGHLIGHTS
1 Kasar Devi Temple

SIGHTS
2 Drikung Kagyu Meditation Centre
3 Himadri Handloom
4 Simtola Eco Park

SLEEPING
5 Freedom Guest House
6 Kumaon
7 Mohan's Mud Houses

EATING
8 Ila Cafe
9 Kasar Kitchen
10 Mohan's Cafe
11 Rainbow Cafe

SHOPPING
12 Lali's Organic Gift Shop
13 Tara's General Store

TRANSPORT
14 Moksha Bike Rentals

the women at work, bringing traditional weaves to life. Their classic products in cashmere and lambswool, married with New Age designs, can be viewed or purchased here. All of these places have free entry, and are open from sunrise to sunset.

Out & About

Experience Kasar Devi's rich outdoors

There are plenty of trails in Kasar Devi, and even a simple jaunt down the ridge reveals elaborate mountain views. On a clear day, you can witness the entire range from Trishul and Nanda Devi in the Kumaon Himalaya to the Panchachuli massif close to the Nepal border. A gentle 2.5km walk down takes you to the Balta waterfall in the quaint village of the same name and, 6km from the ridge, is the **Simtola Eco Park** in Papperseilly, where you can stop for tea and a snack at **Lali's Organic Gift Shop** – a favoured hangout of long-term ridge inhabitants.

TOP TIP

Kasar Devi sits on a ridge facing the Himalaya, and the weather can turn at any time of the year. Come prepared with woollen clothing, rain gear and good hiking shoes for its many trails and varied weather.

HEMP CHUTNEY

The hardy cuisine of Uttarakhand was born out of the need to combat its cold climate and tough conditions. Nutrition was prioritised over taste, but the delectable bhang chutney bridges the gap between the two. Made from bhang (or hemp seeds), used liberally here, this dip inspires curiosity and is an essential part of a local meal. What starts with intrigue usually ends with love for its piquant flavour and gritty texture. The seeds have negligible THC and doesn't cause intoxication (its consumption in this form is legal here). Hemp seeds are considered a superfood with immense nutritional value, and are an integral part of the kitchens of Uttarakhand.

ANILD/SHUTTERSTOCK

Ball mithai

Gastronomic Delights

Savour the flavours of Kumaon

Your best best for trying the region's authentic local food is at homestays, but the Kasar Kitchen serves a Kumaoni thali that comes pretty close. To carry the taste back to your kitchen, get a bottle of rhododendron juice, or herbal seasonings and native salts. Hemp's traditional superfood status here allows the purchase of food products made from it. Homegrown brand SOS Organics sells beautifully packaged local products including rhododendron tea and hemp salt in several stores across Kasar Devi, including **Tara's General Store**, Lali's Organic Gift Shop (p393) and Mohan's Cafe.

On a day trip to Almora, stop at **Lala Joga Sah** and **Heera Singh Jeewan Singh** in the old bazaar if you have a sweet tooth. In the heart of the Lala Bazaar and adjacent to each other, these are generational pioneers of traditional Kumaoni sweets including *singori* (a milk-based sweet wrapped in an indigenous malu tree leaf), *ball mithai* (a chocolate-flavoured sweet covered in tiny sugar balls) and *khechua* (milk and sugar cooked extensively for hours).

EATING IN KASAR DEVI: OUR PICKS

Rainbow Cafe: This place has near-360-degree mountain views, delicious breakfasts spreads and omnipresent dumplings. *9am-9pm ₹₹*

Mohan's Cafe: One of the oldest cafes on the ridge, doubling as a fancy guesthouse. The meals are average but the landscaped setting is spectacular. *9am-8pm ₹₹*

Kasar Kitchen: Run by the cheery Raju Mehta, this is a fantastic place for a value-for-money thali. Basic, neat and efficient, with a grand mountain view. *9am-9.30pm ₹*

Ila Cafe: Enjoy hand-tossed pizzas, baked goodies and surprisingly good coffee for the area. The menu is limited but gratifying. *8.30am-8.30pm Tue-Sun ₹₹*

Beyond Kasar Devi

Rich in nature and Kumaon's cultural history, this is a region of dense forests, ancient temples and traditional architecture.

While most people who visit Kasar barely budge from the ridge, the area's rich cultural and natural history are worth exploring. Ripples of culture emanate from Almora, the old capital of the Kumaon region, where kings built temples that have stood the test of time and residents established a living heritage that travellers can see in *likhai*, enduring artwork on doors and windows of village homes, or in traditional recipes that have not lost their authentic flavours. This cultural legacy stretches all the way to the Jageshwar, Dwarahat and Baijnath temples, a testament to the reign of the Katyuri kings. Up in Binsar, history melts into a wild haven of oak and rhododendron.

Places

Almora

TIME FROM KASAR DEVI: **30MIN**

A walk through the old bazaar

Almora may not show any obvious traces of its cultural heritage, but one gets glimpses down the 1.5km pedestrian-only *pataal* (slate-paved) bazaar. The upper end starts at **Milan Chowk** near the **Nanda Devi Temple**, just before the **Shikhar Hotel**. Interspersed in the maze of general stores, vegetable vendors, jewellers and utensil shops with copperware (the town is known for its ancient copper work) are old homes with intricately carved doors and windows, the hallmark of Kumaoni architecture. Find the biggest concentration at **Khazanchi Mohalla**. Some of these buildings are used for commercial purposes but most remain homes, including the **Lala Badri Shah Memorial House**, outside of which a small plaque commemorates Swami Vivekananda's visit.

A small path branches off to the erstwhile collectorate that now houses the **Almora Fort** (and museum), old British buildings used as offices and a small temple. The market culminates in the **Paltan Bazaar**, where the cantonment begins; this is the most well-preserved part of Almora, with beautiful colonial-era buildings and some trifling ruins.

GETTING AROUND

There are no buses from Kasar Devi, so the best way to do day trips is to prebook a taxi through your accommodation. For short distances, such as to Almora or Chitai, you could also rent a motorbike. For longer trips, catch a bus from Almora to pretty much any major town in the area. Alternatively, get a shared cab from the taxi stand close to the bus stop.

THE FESTIVALS OF ALMORA

Ashok Pande, author and cultural expert, talks about the historic importance of Almora, and how a glimpse of its heritage can still be caught at its festivals. *@AshokPande*

Being Kumaon's ancient capital, Almora was always the hub of culture even before the British arrived. It's still known for its unique tradition of *baithaki* Holi that involves sit-down sessions of classical singing – you can join the audience in any home hosting it. Get a good rooftop spot during the Dussehra procession to see the effigies, the most elaborate you will see in the region. Almora's Nanda Devi Temple hosts one of the most authentic celebrations of the goddess' festival. Over multiple days, witness traditional performances hard to find elsewhere.

Chitai & Lakhudiyar

TIME FROM KASAR DEVI: **40MIN**

One with local experiences

On your way in or out of Kasar, make a quick detour to the temple **Chitai Golu Devta**. Dedicated to Kumaon's beloved god of justice, this place will impress you with its sheer number of bells and disputed,court-case affidavits attached to them. Be prepared to queue up with its throng of local devotees (the monkeys will keep you entertained).

A 15-minute drive further up the same road is **Lakhudiyar**, a rock shelter of historic significance where, in complete contrast to Chitai, you will rarely find anybody – especially travellers. The cave is covered in prehistoric art containing human forms and animal motifs, believed by historians to be among the richest in this part of the country.

Jageshwar Temples

TIME FROM KASAR DEVI: **1½HR**

An amalgam of architecture and religion

The Jageshwar temples are a complex of 125-odd temples built between the 7th and 14th centuries, and are of utmost spiritual significance, especially for Shiva worshippers. The main temple and its sanctum are usually occupied by pilgrims and priests, but the beauty of its carvings and stone edifices can be observed in many of the smaller temples scattered across the premises. Many of these are in the typical Nagara style of architecture built by the Katyuris, one of the last ruling dynasties of Kumaon. Some of the smaller temples were added by different kings from other parts of the country as an ode to their pilgrimage to Mt Kailash, and reflect varied architectural styles from central and Southern India. Don't miss the well-maintained **Jageshwar Archaeological Museum** next door, with idols dating back as far as the 8th century. To appreciate the architecture minus the crowds, slip away to the nearby **Dandeshwar Temple**, where you can seek the same divinity amid a silent cluster of tall deodar trees.

Binsar Wildlife Sanctuary

TIME FROM KASAR DEVI: **30MIN**

A window into Himalayan wildlife

One of the last strongholds of oak in Kumaon, the **Binsar Wildlife Sanctuary** boasts over 200 species of birds, serene mountain sunsets and an interesting history that predates Independence. Starting with pine and rhododendron, the forest dissolves into unadulterated oak – a refuge for barking deer, pine martens, leopards, porcupines and countless high-altitude birds and pheasants. The park was created in 1988 and still retains its five British estates, now run as heritage lodges.

A single road winds up from the ticketed forest checkpost *(open sunrise to sunset; ₹650 & ₹250 per vehicle)* and reaches a clearing 6km up, with an 11th-century Shiva temple on the

MIHIRJOSHI/SHUTTERSTOCK

Crimson sunbird, Binsar Wildlife Sanctuary

right and **Simba Jungle Lodge** on the left. Go for long hikes that branch off from Simba, or hit the popular **Binsar Zero Point trek** starting from the government-run guesthouse at the end of the motorable road. For a deeper tryst with its wilderness, spend a night in the sanctuary. Birding guide **Hem Joshi** *(9410121557)* knows Binsar inside out, and also runs a charming homestay inside the park.

Dwarahat

TIME FROM KASAR DEVI: 2½HR

Kumaon's lesser-known temples and towns

While **Dunagiri** is the best-known temple near Dwarahat, this enchanting village has close to 55 major temples across its surroundings built by the Katyuri kings between the 7th and 11th centuries. **Mahaavtar Baba's Cave** is about 20 minutes away, and devotees of the spiritual leader trek up the small hillside for a glimpse. Stop here for Dwarahat's undulating hills, terraced fields and quiet Kumaoni village life. The temples make for a great day trip from Ranikhet, a quiet cantonment town with Himalaya views, long walks under cedar trees and better accommodation options (p405).

NANDA DEVI

At 7816m, Nanda Devi is the highest mountain completely within India. The peak is also worshipped by Uttarakhand's Hindu population as its patron deity, the Goddess of Bliss. Towards the end of the monsoon period, the **Nanda Devi Festival** celebrates the goddess' return to her maternal abode in the Himalaya foothills The celebration lasts for nearly a week, starting with creating the idol, continuing with temple ceremonies and local fairs, and ending in a fervent procession. Every 12 years, the Raj Jat Yatra commemorates her perilous mountain journey to the abode of her husband Shiva. The grand sendoff is also known as the Kumbh of the Himalaya.

Munsyari

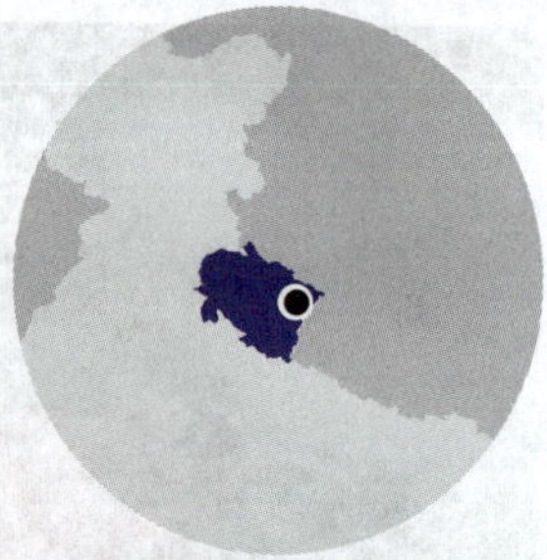

HIMALAYA VIEWS | GLACIER TREKS | HIGH-ALTITUDE WEAVERS

The last defining outpost of Kumaon, Munsyari is where the region ends for most travellers – and begins for serious hikers and mountaineers. As you climb up the Kala Muni ridge and hit the last few kilometres before entering Munsyari, the Panchachuli massif unfurls like a banner hoisted in heaven. While the actual town is essentially a spider's web of shops and houses down in the valley below, the setting couldn't be any grander. Munsyari is also the gateway to Milam Glacier and other Uttarakhand treks.

Part of the Johar Valley, this is where the story of 'Rajula Malushahi', Kumaon's pre-eminent ballad, originates. It's also home to the Bhutia community or 'Joharis', prosperous traders on the Indo-Tibetan border who migrated from higher regions like Milam and created this settlement after the 1962 war with China, and who continue to hold on to remnants of their culture through their traditional weaving, language and food.

GETTING AROUND

Getting here is no mean feat: it takes a solid 11 to 12 hours by road from Nainital or Kathgodam. Once here, walking is pretty much the only option unless you've rented a car. You will find shared taxis near the main market to visit some of the nearby villages but timings aren't fixed. Most shared departures happen in the mornings at around 6am, but local routes to places in the vicinity, such as Sarmoli village or the Nanda Devi Temple, take place often. For a day of sightseeing, hire one of the shared jeeps after fixing a price beforehand.

Above the Clouds

Hikes and high-altitude lakes

From its mythology to its appeal to mountaineers, the **Panchachuli** is Munsyari's star attraction. Sunset on this cluster of five peaks is the town's most famous sight and it can be caught from almost anywhere. The Dana Dhar ridge and the **Nanda Devi Temple** below it are particularly good spots: the circuit also makes for a great evening hike. Follow it by a day of short walks to quaint lakes including **Thamri Kund** (three hours' return) and **Maheshwar Kund** (1½ hours' return), which provide ample birding opportunities. For the best views, do the full-day gruelling but rewarding trek to **Khaliya Top**. A five-hour uphill climb through the Khalia reserve forest takes you straight to the meadows that not only have stunning views of the Indian and Nepal Himalaya, but also give a chance to spot the the rare monal, Uttarakhand's multihued state bird.

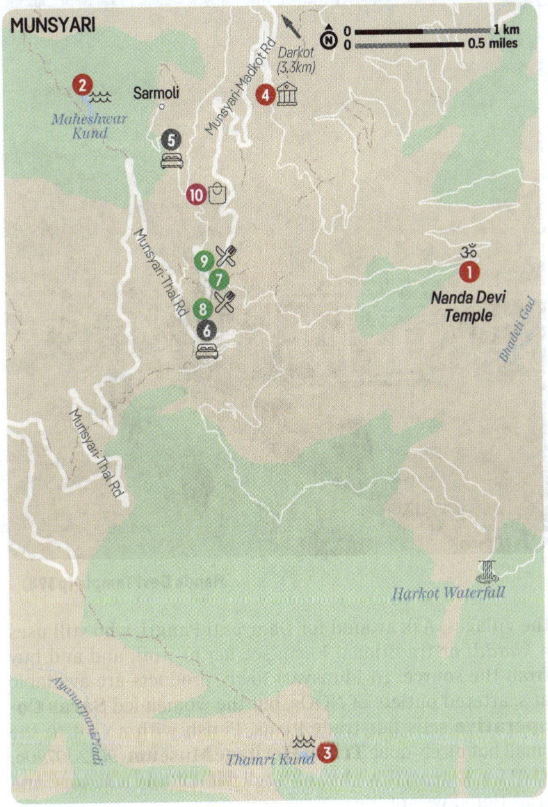

HIGHLIGHTS
1 Nanda Devi Temple

SIGHTS
2 Maheshwar Kund
3 Thamri Kund
4 Tribal Heritage Museum

SLEEPING
5 Himalayan Glamping
6 Snow View Inn

EATING
7 Alpine Glow Cafe
8 Apna Bhojnalaya
see 5 Himalayan Glamping
9 One Soul Cafe

SHOPPING
10 Saras Cooperative

Village Ways

Homestays and traditional living

Just 1km outside of Munsyari town, Sarmoli is a sprightly village that came to life in recent years because of the homestay movement that started here. Stay in one of the homes run by village women to experience the Kumaoni way of life, from sleeping in traditional mud-lined rooms (with cosy beds!) to eating meals prepared from indigenous grains and vegetables, learning about new ingredients and recipes, and most of all, getting to live and interact with a local family. **Himalayan Ark** *(himalayanark.com)*, a community-led tourism initiative, is the oldest running homestay network here. You can also observe the women, known for their high-altitude traditional weaving skills, as they make incredible handwoven pieces such as *thulma* (a coarse bedspread) and *dunn* (a kind of rug), art forms passed down by women to their daughters and daughters-in-law.

If weaving sparks your curiosity, visit Darkot village, 5km away, which has the highest number of weavers out of all

TOP TIP

The drive to Munsyari is spectacular but requires expertise. Navigating tricky roads is tiring, so an overnight midway stop in Chaukori is recommended to fully enjoy the landscape that changes dramatically the following day.

WHY I LOVE MUNSYARI

Shikha Tripathi, Lonely Planet writer

For those who make it as far as Munsyari, the gargantuan mountains are only the first of its rewards. It's the doorway to a high-altitude Narnia that holds wondrous secrets, privy to the few who make it to the other side. The region is integral to Uttarakhand, and yet vastly different in culture and geography; it is home to rare communities and biodiversity, and has a landscape that you may otherwise only discover after days of trekking. My trip there was like falling through the looking glass, and a day hike to Khalia Top (p403) shows you just that. It also hosts a unique version of the state-wide celebration of the Nanda Devi Festival.

HABIB PAPPU/SHUTTERSTOCK

Nanda Devi Temple (p398)

the villages. Ask around for Damyanti Pangti, who still uses a *khaddi* or traditional loom; see her at work and and buy from the source. In Munsyari town, products are available at scattered outlets of NGOs, but the women-led **Saras Co-operative** sells fair-trade items. Finish with a visit to the small but nicely done **Tribal Heritage Museum** *(9012007906; ₹20)* for sharper insights into the community's history and traditional way of life.

EATING IN MUNSYARI: OUR PICKS

Apna Bhojnalaya: A clean efficient kitchen that serves thalis made with fresh produce and local ingredients, and 'Indian Chinese' like Manchurian and noodles. *6.30am-9pm* ₹₹

Alpine Glow Cafe: Beautiful local artwork decorates this tiny spot selling popular fast food like *momos* and greasy but delicious chow mein. *9am-8pm* ₹

One Soul Cafe: An atmospheric community-run option serving as a meeting point for its youth, it offers North Indian and Tibetan snacks. *9am-8pm* ₹

Himalayan Glamping: You're in for a surprise with the upscale local and continental spread here. Prebooked tables only for non-residential guests. *9am-9pm* ₹₹₹

Beyond Munsyari

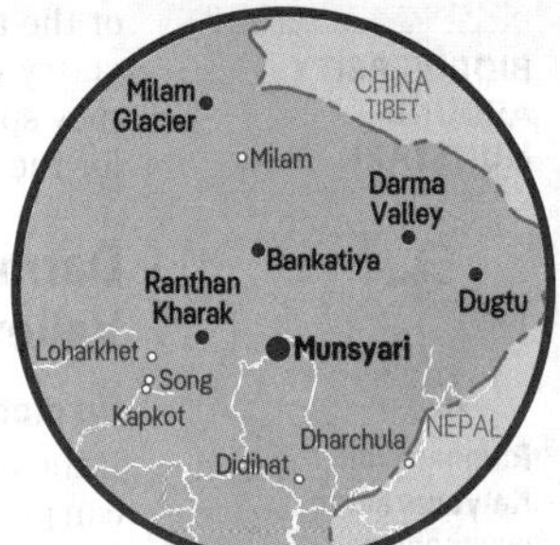

The final frontier this side of the Indian Himalaya: a melange of massive mountains, imposing drives and Kumaon's ultimate wilderness.

For the handful that make it to Munsyari, going beyond it is the litmus test of their love for adventure and unexplored territories. This is a playground for seasoned trekkers, filmmakers and mountaineers who come in search of raw nature, rare wildlife and hidden cultures. A trek to Milam Glacier is an added badge of honour, as is the even more arduous Ralam Glacier trail. From Dharchula, four hours away, the border region splits into three incredible valleys, each with multiple high treks and peaks, elusive nomadic communities and uncommon festivals. Darma is home to the Panchachuli Glacier and the lesser-known but legendary travelling philanthropist Jasuli Devi. Chaundas celebrates the intriguing, duodecennial Kangdali Festival. Meanwhile Vyas is recognised as Shiva's throne with its landmark Om and Adi Kailash peaks.

Places

Milam Glacier p401
Darma Valley p402
Bankatiya p402
Ranthan Kharak p403

Milam Glacier

TIME FROM MUNSYARI: **4½HR TO LASPA ROADHEAD**

Get closer to glaciers and Nanda Devi

Just beyond the last village of the same name on the Indian side of the border, the 3450m-high **Milam Glacier** is accessible via an ancient trade route to Tibet. The week-long iconic trek is now on its way out given the newly built dirt road, so do it before it disappears. It starts with unparalleled views of the Gori Ganga River and rugged peaks as you ascend. You can add a three-day detour to reach the **Nanda Devi East Base Camp** (7816m) and a rather strenuous four-day detour to **Ralam Glacier**.

Since most inhabitants of Milam village (and other hamlets en route) have lived in Munsyari since the 1962 India-China War, it's a good idea to arrange for camping gear and go with a guide who will help you find a homestay or huts wherever available. **Mukesh Laspal** *(7983967725, 8791713529; @laspa_alpine_trail)* organises short and long multiday treks in the area.

October is harvest season in Milam, marking the end of the agricultural cycle for major cash crops such as potato, buckwheat and barley. Together with the penetrating clarity

GETTING AROUND

Get shared taxis from the Munsyari taxi stand to the beautiful Laspa village, the new starting point for the Milam and Ralam treks, and Dharchula, the main town for catching shared taxis for the Darma, Chaundas and Vyas Valleys. Pithoragarh is the district's biggest town and sometimes has heli services *(heritageaviation.in)*. Most taxis leave in the early morning, so prebook (a promise to show up is usually enough). If you don't want to wait, book an entire cab.

BIODIVERSITY AROUND MUNSYARI

Ramnarayan Kalyanaraman, environment researcher, conservation facilitator, rural livelihood specialist and educator, dons many hats. For around 30 years he's worked in Pithoragarh district's remote Greater Himalayan Gori River. *@indiasnature1*

The Khalia region has very rich biodiversity as it spans multiple altitude zones. Together with the Gori Valley and Askot Wildlife Sanctuary, the area factors for about 45% of the birds seen in Uttarakhand. Of trekking trails, the Ralam Valley has to be my favourite. Across the Himalaya, roads are being made at a rapidly destructive rate but the valley along the Ralam River is still untouched. Travellers who respect local and natural resources are welcome to join me on my scientific expeditions.

of the autumn skies, this is a great time to be here for the glassy views and to catch the Bhutia population in action as they spur on their yaks, celebrate their harvest and pack up for the winter.

Darma Valley

TIME FROM MUNSYARI: **8HR TO DUGTU ROADHEAD**

Up close with Panchachuli

If the view of **Panchachuli** from Munsyari isn't enough, you can get super-close to them at the base camp, accessible from Dugtu village in the Darma Valley. Shared 4WD vehicles go all the way up the narrow and sometimes scary road from Dharchula – driven by experienced drivers who might enjoy your misery but will ensure you arrive safely. From Dugtu, an easy rhododendron-laced 1½-hour hike gets you to **Panchachuli Base Camp**. The gargantuan, glacier-ridden massif dwarfs and floors you with its magnitude.

There are plenty of basic homestays in Dugtu and some in Daatu (the quieter village across the Nyuli Yangti rivulet) with a great window into the Rung (Darma community) way of life. A special permit is required to go deeper into the valley beyond the ITBP checkpoint. Festivals like the Kangdali celebration held every 12 years in Chaundas Valley are a rare opportunity to get to know the Rungs and other Himalayan communities better. Jagdish Bhatt at **Alpine Trek** *(8449661443; alpinetrek.in)* is a Pithoragarh-based regional expert and guide who can organise these experiences.

Bankatiya

TIME FROM MUNSYARI: **4½HR TO LASPA ROADHEAD**

The newest trekking jewel in the crown

For everyone who mourns the birth of yet another road and consequently the death of the associated trek, Bankatiya brings hope. Named one of the top three in the 2025 Trek of the Year award by the Uttarakhand Tourism Department in a bid to shift focus to the state's hidden treasures and lesser-known trails, the base camp trek to the peak is a moderately tough one. The journey takes you beyond Munsyari and close to the Laspa village, another detour from the Milam route. The trailhead for this trek, Laspa is also known for its unique celebration of the statewide Nanda Devi Festival. The trail takes you into one of the most raw, unsullied parts of the Himalaya with a thriving biodiversity, all the way to the base of the distinct, hook-like **Bankatiya** (meaning 'sickle' in the local dialect). The glacier of the same name sits here at 4000m, and is better explored as a day trek from Laspa. Hike from Laspa to the Nanda Devi East Base Camp (p401) via Burfu and continue to Milam Glacier, combining two classic treks with the emerging one and in the process bypass the new road.

SHIKHA TRIPATHI

Woman in traditional Rung costume, Kangdali celebration, Chaundas Valley

Ranthan Kharak

TIME FROM MUNSYARI: **30MIN TO KHALIA TOP BASE**

Revisiting the rhododendron

At **Khalia Top**, where the holy grail ends for the typical traveller in Munsyari, the trail begins for the hardy adventurer. From this meadow, a three-day trek takes you to **Ranthan Kharak**, a virginal bastion of rhododendron close to the marked Namik Glacier. Travelling to this part of Kumaon enlists you in a special inner circle of explorers, and is not without its rewards – this lesser-known trek is among the emerging ones, and a massive payoff for those who travel this far in spring in search of the state flower. At the peak of the blooming season, the rhododendron is found here with an abundance and variety unlike other trails in the state. Interspersed with massive *kharaks* (natural clearings) in between dense forests that are a delight to camp in, this trek also has a long ridge section showcasing the iconic Nanda Devi, Maiktoli and Trishul peaks to the west, and the omnipresent Panchachuli to the east. The seclusion of this trail also lends itself to some excellent birdwatching opportunities. The route exits on the other side at the Namik village, which is connected by road.

WEAVING MOUNTAIN CULTURE

Mukti Datta, founder of the award-winning Panchachuli Women Weavers of Kumaon (p392), started her epic journey of women's empowerment from Munsyari and beyond.

In 1995, the Lipu Lekh pass reopened after a gap of 35 years and the historic Trans-Himalayan trade was briefly revived by semi-nomadic Bhutias whose ancestors had been trading for centuries with Tibetans. At the time, I had just begun working with tribal women artisans from Munsyari. I seized the opportunity to apply for a trade permit and crossed into Tibet on a raw journey on foot. My learnings became the seed for this women-led enterprise. This entire region still holds that magic for anyone who wants to go beyond the obvious, while treading lightly and responsibly.

Places We Love to Stay

₹ Budget ₹₹ Midrange ₹₹₹ Top End

Mussoorie

Map p375

Herne Lodge ₹ A guesthouse with pocket-friendly family suites, single rooms and studios spread on a hillside in Happy Valley overlooking pleasant vistas.

La Villa Bethany ₹₹₹ Sunita and Amar Kudle's homestay in Landour is everything a typical Anglo-Indian mountain home should be, from the history to the fusion meals.

Savoy ₹₹₹ Journey back in time through this regal hotel built in 1905, with its architecture, old-school charm, decor and service reminiscent of an era that was.

Dehradun

Mango Tree Courtyard ₹₹ An oasis amid a bustling capital, this thoughtfully crafted boutique homestay (with a branch in Mussoorie) is run by two friends.

LP Residency ₹₹ It's away from the town centre, but makes up for this with its lovely outdoor seating and two in-house, award-winning restaurants.

Dhanolti

Himalayan Splendour Resort ₹₹ In a lush pine-forest setting despite being close to the main road. Spacious rooms and mountain views, but also plenty of stairs.

Barefoot Bungalow ₹₹₹ A wheelchair-accessible, tastefully-done bungalow with fabulous Garhwali food and bedroom windows opening to majestic mountain views. There's also a brand-new branch in Dehradun.

Rishikesh & Around

Map p381

Vashishta Guest House ₹ Unwind in the comforts of this boutique guesthouse while being surrounded by the intensity of the yoga ashrams of Swarg Ashram.

Terrakotta ₹₹ In the midst of busy Tapovan, this hotel holds its own with its slick rooms, appealing breakfast spreads and great access to most attractions.

Atali Ganga ₹₹₹ At this 'active' hotel, you can climb an artificial wall one minute and dine poolside the next. Their newest villas are wheelchair-friendly.

Guptkashi

Village Retreat ₹₹ Return to comfy rooms and a cheery restaurant with grand views after day-trekking to Chopta or taking a chopper trip to Kedarnath.

Buransh Heli Resort ₹₹ Cottages with quality rooms in the midst of a sprawling garden that looks straight at the Chaukhamba mountain massif.

Haridwar

Hotel La Casa ₹₹ In a town brimming with budget hotels, this comfortable stay is worth the extra money for better rooms and good bathrooms.

Pilibhit House ₹₹₹ Aristocratic grandeur meets luxe living at a century-old heritage hotel with alfresco dining and the largest private bathing ghat on the Ganges.

Rajaji National Park

GMVN Chilla ₹₹ Government-run accommodation inside the national park, with beautiful log huts and decent amenities. Location and park access are its biggest wins.

Wild Brook Retreat ₹₹₹ An ecolodge powered entirely by solar energy, with beautiful stone and wood independent cottages.

Auli

GMVN Auli (p385) ₹₹ This preferred government-run accommodation conducts ski courses and has comfortable rooms, excellent views and a licensed bar perfect for apres-ski.

Blue Poppy Resort ₹₹₹ Premium wooden huts with 180-degree views of the most well-known Garhwal peaks, and rare road access through the winter.

Nainital

Map p387

Palace Belvedere ₹₹ Despite needing a facelift this is a perfect midrange hotel, with its history and regal air compensating for what's missing.

Naini Retreat (p388) ₹₹₹ Iconic heritage home that's a melting pot of vintage decor and nostalgia, with an enviable location.

Shervani Hilltop ₹₹₹ An old favourite, this timeless hotel has added revamped, elegant rooms in a plum setting.

Corbett National Park

Dhikala Forest Rest House ₹ A government-run lodge inside the park with basic facilities, but an unrivalled location and experience; book ahead.

Ranger's Lodge ₹₹ The Khans' home, where naturalist host Imran shows rare wildlife documentaries and his wife Kehkashan preps meals and conducts outdoor cooking sessions.

Jim's Jungle Retreat ₹₹₹ While the Ramnagar–Ranikhet road along the reserve is plump with accommodation, this atmospheric place is popular with serious wildlife enthusiasts.

Bhimtal

The Retreat ₹₹ Run by exemplary host Paddy Smetacek (who may share a family recipe if she likes you), this charming forest retreat overlooks Bhimtal Lake.

Fisherman's Lodge ₹₹₹ Boutique retreat on the lakeside with compact but pleasant rooms and an open-air restaurant on the deck.

Naukuchiatal

Moustache Select ₹₹ Close to the boating point, this agreeable place offers a variety of rooms, homely food and lake-view accommodation at an affordable price.

The Lake Resort ₹₹₹ With a prime location that you won't find at other lakesides in the district, this sprawling estate has rooms overlooking a sizeable stretch of Naukuchiatal lake.

Kasar Devi

Map p393

Freedom Guest House ₹ Spacious rooms with decent breakfasts, friendly staff and sweeping mountain panoramas make this value-for-money space a hit with budget travellers.

Mohan's Mud Houses ₹₹ A midrange extension of popular Mohan's Binsar Retreat, these well-furnished cottages have access to its popular cafe.

Kumaon ₹₹₹ The fanciest place on the ridge, with minimalism at its core, this architectural prodigy has heated bathrooms and winsome views.

Binsar

Sakshi Hill Cottage ₹ Experience traditional Kumaoni hospitality and authentic local dishes at birding and trekking guide Hem Joshi's cheerful home inside the sanctuary.

KMVN Tourist Rest House ₹₹ Hands down the best view of Binsar's mountain range. With basic rooms and food, it runs on solar power.

Mary Budden Estate ₹₹₹ A painstakingly restored British bungalow with a cluster of new cottages that match its vibe, the estate takes you back to the colonial-era high life.

Ranikhet

Hotel Chevron Rosemount ₹₹ One of the longest-running hotels in town, with bright rooms, dependable service and a lovely garden.

Holm Farm Heritage ₹₹ A functional bungalow full of history, hidden deep in a forest and commanding fabulous mountain vistas.

Munsyari

Map p399

Snow View Inn ₹ Not unlike the other box-like guesthouses in the main market area, this one has amicable and helpful staff.

Himalayan Glamping ₹₹₹ Luxurious tents and a wooden dining room that serves delicious food in a lush setting looking straight at the Panchachuli range.

EASY ACCOMMODATION ACCESS

Stranded in Uttarakhand with no reliable **accommodation? Go** to the nearest KMVN (Kumaon Mandal Vikas Nigam) or GMVN (Garhwal Mandal Vikas Nigam), modest state-run guesthouses that will meet basic needs and help you plan your forward journey. They almost always have a great location (see *kmvn.in* or *gmvnonline.com*).

THE GUIDE

KOLKATA

Researched by
Paul Stafford

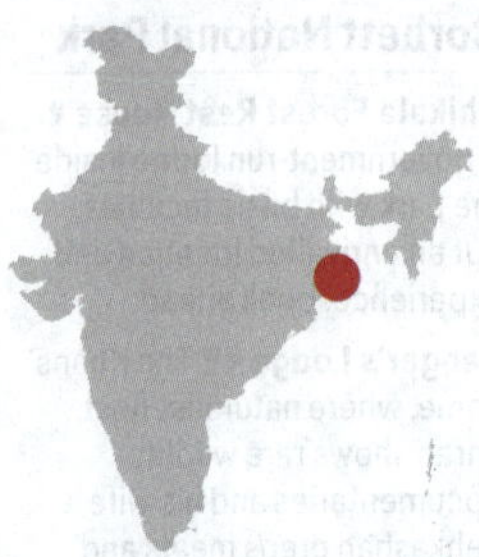

Kolkata

INDIA'S ENIGMATIC CITY OF JOY

Discover the Bengali secret to happiness through Kolkata's creative culture, complex cuisine and heritage-rich neighbourhoods.

Kolkata is known as the City of Joy. But then Kolkata goes by many names. And while they're not all particularly flattering, one thing is certain: India's third-largest city is often misunderstood and unjustly overlooked. Many travellers pass through on their way elsewhere. Those who linger discover it to be a place rich in creativity, education and culture, a hub for the intelligentsia that grows on you.

When Job Charnock selected this rural backwater to serve as an East India Company (EIC) trading outpost in 1690, he was thinking mainly about accessibility and defence. The only settlement of note nearby was Kalikata, surrounding a temple (present-day Kalighat).

RIMA DAS MUKHERJEE/SHUTTERSTOCK

Inequality was inbuilt from the outset. Calcutta, as it was known (and to older generations, still is) , was split into two zones: mansion-dotted White Town (mainly home to EIC employees and British administrators) and the poorer Black Town (Bengalis employed by the EIC). That division would come to define the injustices of colonialism. It's little surprise then that Bengal, and Kolkata in particular, was the fertile ground in which India's Independence movement grew.

In the post-Independence half of the 20th century, colonial-era buildings were allowed to rot, streets and neighbourhoods were renamed after the architects of Independence, and Calcutta became Kolkata. Paradoxically, the Victoria Memorial remains the prize attraction, and more recently, Raj-era relics were revamped alongside a growing Metro network that added or opened extensions to four new lines in 2024–25, suggesting the city is moving into a new, more confident phase of its identity.

Kolkata remains a place where the dichotomies of a burgeoning industrial economy are garishly displayed: the wealth and the poverty, the past and the present, the heart and the hustle, the flair and the filth. Where you choose to place your focus will define your experience of it. Those who lead with their senses soon develop an appreciation of Kolkata's remarkable flavours, enthralling festivals, architectural diversity, intrinsic spirituality and proud history of artistic expression. This place undoubtedly deserves closer attention.

THE MAIN AREAS

CHOWRINGHEE & THE MAIDAN
Historic monuments and city-centre attractions. p412

BBD BAGH, BARABAZAR & OLD CHINATOWN
Religious diversity and heritage architecture. p423

THE HOOGHLY RIVER & HOWRAH
Ghat life and gardens. p429

NORTHERN KOLKATA
Palaces, temples and effigies. p432

ALIPORE & BALLYGUNGE
South Kolkata's historic haunts and dapper districts. p436

For places to stay in Kolkata, see p441

NILADRILOVESPHOTOGRAPHY/SHUTTERSTOCK

Above: Playing cricket, Maidan (p413); Left: Goddess Durga effigy, Durga Puja festival (p434)

Find Your Way

Sprawling Kolkata can seem disorientating at first. The region from Sudder St to Park St has long been the city's main base for travellers. It remains the best choice, particularly for first-time visitors, with its Metro access and proximity to major sights, including the Maidan and Victoria Memorial.

FROM THE AIRPORT

The Metro's Yellow Line opened in 2025, connecting the airport to central Kolkata. Change onto the Blue Line at Noapara for Chowringhee stations. The full journey takes 45 minutes and costs ₹45. Airport buses (V2, VS-1, VS-2) run every 10 to 15 minutes between 8am and 7.30pm.

TAXIS & RIDESHARE APPS

Kolkata's traditional yellow taxis are metered, but are gradually being edged out by safer, more reliable rideshare apps such as Uber and Ola. If you're willing to brave them, moto taxis booked via these apps can beat the traffic snarls. Helmets are always provided.

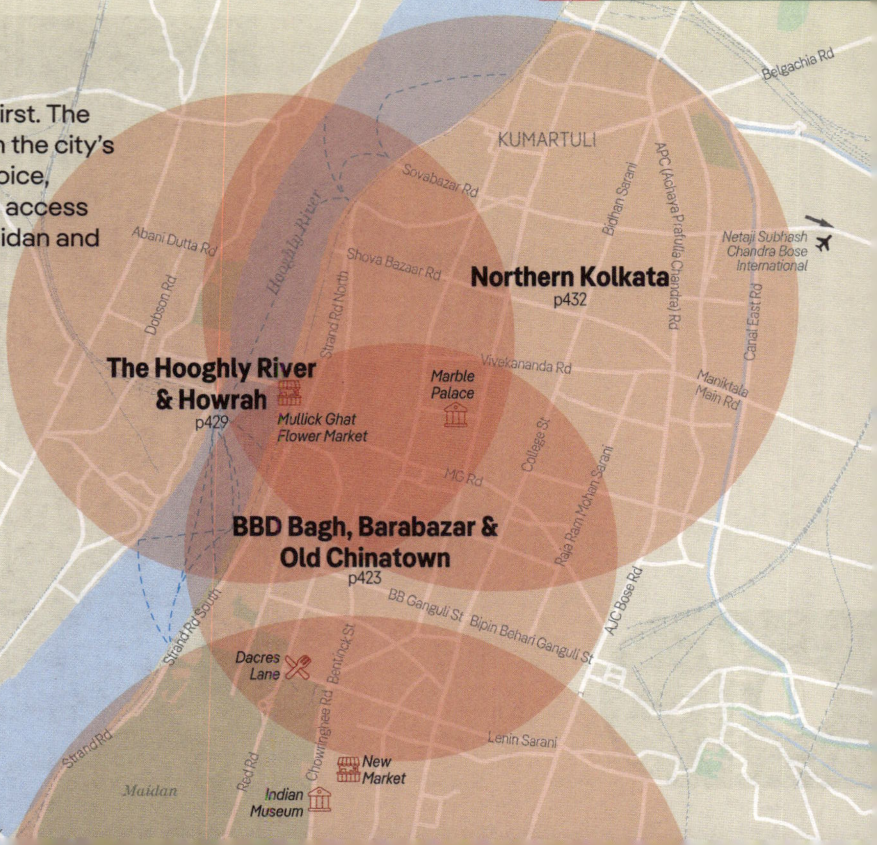

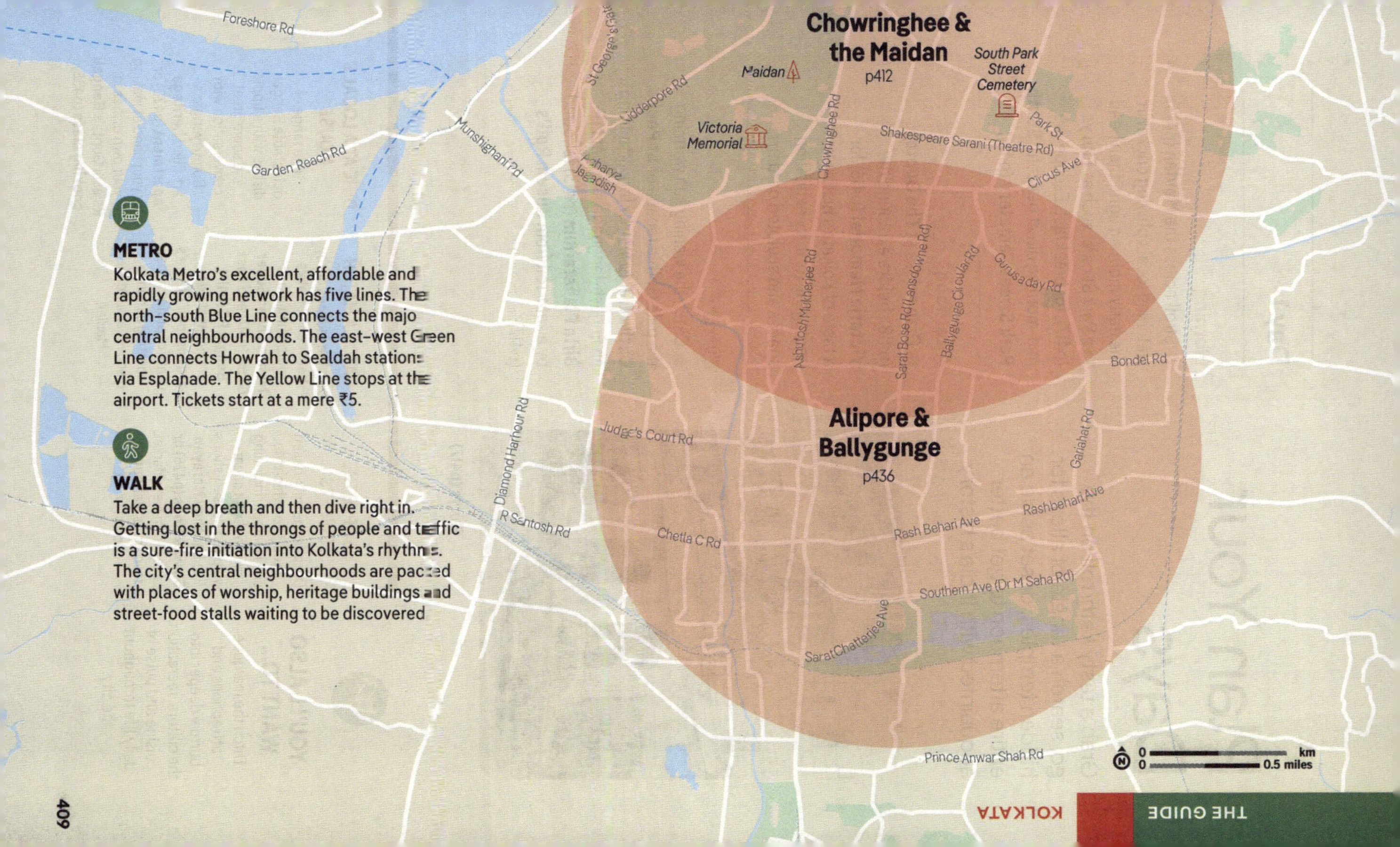

METRO

Kolkata Metro's excellent, affordable and rapidly growing network has five lines. The north–south Blue Line connects the majo central neighbourhoods. The east–west Green Line connects Howrah to Sealdah stations via Esplanade. The Yellow Line stops at the airport. Tickets start at a mere ₹5.

WALK

Take a deep breath and then dive right in. Getting lost in the throngs of people and traffic is a sure-fire initiation into Kolkata's rhythms. The city's central neighbourhoods are packed with places of worship, heritage buildings and street-food stalls waiting to be discovered

Plan Your Days

Grab a tasty *kathi* roll on the go, search a tangle of alleys for hidden temples, or set aside an entire afternoon to get better acquainted with India's history.

PAUL STAFFORD

Flurys (p417)

Day 1

Morning

- Stroll across the **Maidan** (p413), watching locals playing cricket in the early morning light, then head to a Park St cafe, such as **Flurys** (p417), for breakfast. Escape the mid-morning din at peaceful **South Park Street Cemetery** (p421).

Afternoon

- Grab a dosa at **The Guptas** (p418), before exploring the **Victoria Memorial** (p416) for a taste of Kolkata's history and heritage in its lofty exhibition spaces and sculpted gardens.

Evening

- Catch the waning sun warming the pale Gothic facade of **St Paul's Cathedral** (p413), before attending an English-language show at **MP Birla Planetarium** (p413) followed by a *kathi* roll from **Kusum Roll's** (p417).

YOU'LL ALSO WANT TO...

Ditch the marquee attractions and burrow deeper into the culture, recreation, cuisine and pulse of daily life throughout the city.

SAMPLE THE SWEETS

Dig into the milk-based sweets for which the city is famed, including *mishti doi*, at sugar-whipped dessert shops like **Lakshmi Narayan Shaw & Sons** (p425) or cakes from New Market favourites **Nahoum & Sons** (p418).

CATCH A MATCH

Be it the raucous derby between Kolkata's footballing titans **Mohun Bagan Super Giant** (p417) and **East Bengal FC** (p417), or cricket at **Eden Gardens** (p417), there's plenty of professional sporting action to discover around the Maidan.

DINE AT A LOCAL'S HOUSE

Try a range of delectable Bengali dishes with a tipple and some great conversation with Bomti Iyengar's art-filled **heritage apartment** (p420) or try your hand at making your own dishes in Rajashi Gupta's **Bengali cooking class** (p438).

Day 2

Morning

- Get an early start to catch **Mullick Ghat Flower Market** (p430) in full bloom, then wander south into the web of market-lined streets that make up **Barabazar** (p428) to discover churches and temples aplenty.

Afternoon

- Continue to **BBD Bagh** (p423), paying a visit to the **RBI Museum** (p426), perusing an art exhibition at the **Currency Building** (p428) and then visiting the memorials at **St John's Church** (p423).

Evening

- Recover the day's burned calories by indulging in the best local cuisine on a **food tour** (p432), then head to Park St for happy hour at the **Lords & Barons** (p420).

Day 3

Morning

- Wander the streets of **Kumartuli** (p434), observing the idol makers busy at work creating new clay and straw effigies ahead of the next Durga Puja. Next, delve into all things Rabindranath Tagore at his ancestral home, **Jorasanko Thakurbari** (p435).

Afternoon

- Wander through the gleefully eccentric **Marble Palace** (p434), then hop on the Metro south to Jatin Das Park station to get a different take on Kolkata's colonial-era history at **Alipore Museum** (p439).

Evening

- Head back into the centre to seek out the delicate flavours of Bengali cuisine at **6 Ballygunge Place Chowringhee** (p419) or hearty Mughlai dishes at **Zam Zam** (p418).

PERAMBULATE THE PARKS

Kolkata is a verdant city with a long legacy of well-tended gardens, including the **Agri-Horticultural Society** (p437), the **Botanical Gardens** (p437) and leafy public parks such as **Rabindra Sarovar** (p440).

TAKE A HOOGHLY FERRY

Enjoy a **Heritage River Cruise** (p429) at sunset from one of the Hooghly River ghats or use the regular passenger ferries to hop between sights, such as **Belur Math** (p435) to **Kumartuli** (p434) via Bagbazar Ghat.

EXPLORE TRENDY BALLYGUNGE

Visit a contemporary art gallery in chic **Ballygunge** (p439), shop for handmade Bengali textiles at boutique stores such as **Byloom** (p439) and **Weaver's Studio** (p439), then sample the neighbourhood's **coffee culture** (p440).

TACKLE KOLKATAN ART

Explore the galleries of Kolkata, with Independence-themed exhibitions within the complex of the **Alipore Museum** (p439), local works at the **Birla Academy of Art & Culture** (p439) and paintings by the Indian masters at **CIMA** (p439).

Chowringhee & the Maidan

HISTORIC MONUMENTS AND CITY-CENTRE ATTRACTIONS

TOP TIP

Many museums are closed on Mondays, so it might be worth planning this as a rest day. Alternatively, take one of our self-guided walking tours. Some sights that do remain open on Mondays include St Paul's Cathedral, MP Birla Planetarium, and South Park Street Cemetery, among others.

Chowringhee and the Maidan, loosely deemed central Kolkata, host most of the city's major sights alongside excellent restaurants and some of the city's best accommodation. Thanks also to its great Metro links, Chowringhee is where most visitors usually base themselves for the duration of their stay.

Northern Chowringhee is dominated by the sprawling chaos of New Market, south of which lies the capacious Indian Museum and Park St, Kolkata's pulsating nightlife hub. Chowringhee is bordered along its western edge by the Maidan, a great green lung in the urban centre, where some of the finest heritage architecture, including the Gothic St Paul's Cathedral and the Indo-Saracenic Victoria Memorial, is situated.

Elsewhere, the respective homes of Netaji and Mother Teresa elicit important conversations about the perils of idolising individuals and ideologues. You might not come away with any conclusive answers, but you will gain a deeper appreciation of Kolkata's central importance in the history of India.

GETTING AROUND

Walking is still the best way to get around the streets of Chowringhee, where you will learn how to sidestep, slalom and dodge the incessant parade of life's obstacles. When venturing further afield, the Metro is a vital and most welcome conduit, with many stops on the north–south Blue Line between the Esplanade and Netaji Bhawan stations.

Rideshare apps Uber and Ola are also effective tools to navigate this busy area. As with elsewhere in Kolkata, wheelchair access is extremely poor. However, some sights, including South Park Street Cemetery and the Victoria Memorial, offer a semblance of wheelchair accessibility.

Sporting History

Exploring the morning Maidan

Central Kolkata's urban tangle is stayed by the vast green expanse of the **Maidan**. Getting acquainted with it early on will ensure you always have a place of respite. At roughly 4 sq km, the largely unmanicured recreational space originally hosted the neighbourhoods of a nascent Kolkata. In 1756, these were flattened to allow the cannons of Fort William (renamed Vijay Durg in 2025 and still used as a military base) clear lines of sight, following the city's sacking by Siraj-ud-daula, the Nawab of Bengal, and the subsequent Black Hole incident that saw a number of British prisoners die of suffocation.

The Maidan is at its best in the hour after sunrise, when Kolkata is serene and the fields are full of locals playing spirited games of cricket, football and occasionally the slap-happy rough and tumble of kabaddi in the golden-lit smog. A wander through this pancake-flat park is the perfect addition to an itinerary that includes the Victoria Memorial (p416).

PARK LIFE

The Maidan may well be India's largest inner-city park, but there are plenty of green escapes in urban spheres throughout the subcontinent, including Bengaluru's **Cubbon Park** (p797) and Delhi's **Lodhi Garden** (p86).

Stained Glass & Gothic Style

Admiring St Paul's Cathedral's detail

Tucked into the southeastern edge of the Maidan is the gleaming white edifice of **St Paul's Cathedral** *(stpaulscathedralkolkata.org; adult/child ₹10/free)*. With its lofty square bell tower and Gothic Revival architecture exemplified by its finials and tracery, it presents as one of Kolkata's more incongruous buildings. Look for the stained-glass **West Window** by Pre-Raphaelite artist Sir Edward Burne-Jones, depicting various Biblical figures including St Paul. There's a wheelchair ramp into the church around the back.

Family-Friendly Chowringhee Rd

Planetarium shows and dark dioramas

North of St Paul's Cathedral is the squat, broad dome of **MP Birla Planetarium** *(mpbirlaplanetarium.org; ₹140)*. Audiovisual shows within are a tad dramatic as they explore the universe's marvels. English-language shows take place daily at 1pm and 6pm, with tickets available up to 30 minutes beforehand, leaving enough time to visit nearby St Paul's Cathedral while you wait.

Around 350m south of the planetarium is the wonderfully odd **Nehru Children's Museum** *(nehrumuseum.com; adult/child ₹20/10)*. Although time-worn and often overlooked, its two floors of elaborate diorama models, depicting tales from Hindu folklore, are delightfully wild, weird and get pretty dark once the war scenes and she-demons get involved. And yet kids and adults alike absolutely lap it up. Other rooms display dolls wearing traditional dress from around India and the world.

SMASHING CHAI

Street kiosks in Kolkata serve up their chai in little red, unglazed clay cups known as *bhar* (or *kulhar* in Hindi). You may notice some of them in ruins on the street outside. That's because it's customary to throw away or break the cups after one use to keep the *bhar* makers in work. The practice was once common across India but *bhar* is gradually being replaced by plastic. There's an ongoing discussion about reviving *bhar* cups to counter the growing blight of discarded plastic cups. However, many point out that the fuel burned to fire these disposable clay cups doesn't exactly make *bhar* environmentally friendly. One thing is certain: the flavour of masala chai served in *bhar* is far superior to that served in plastic.

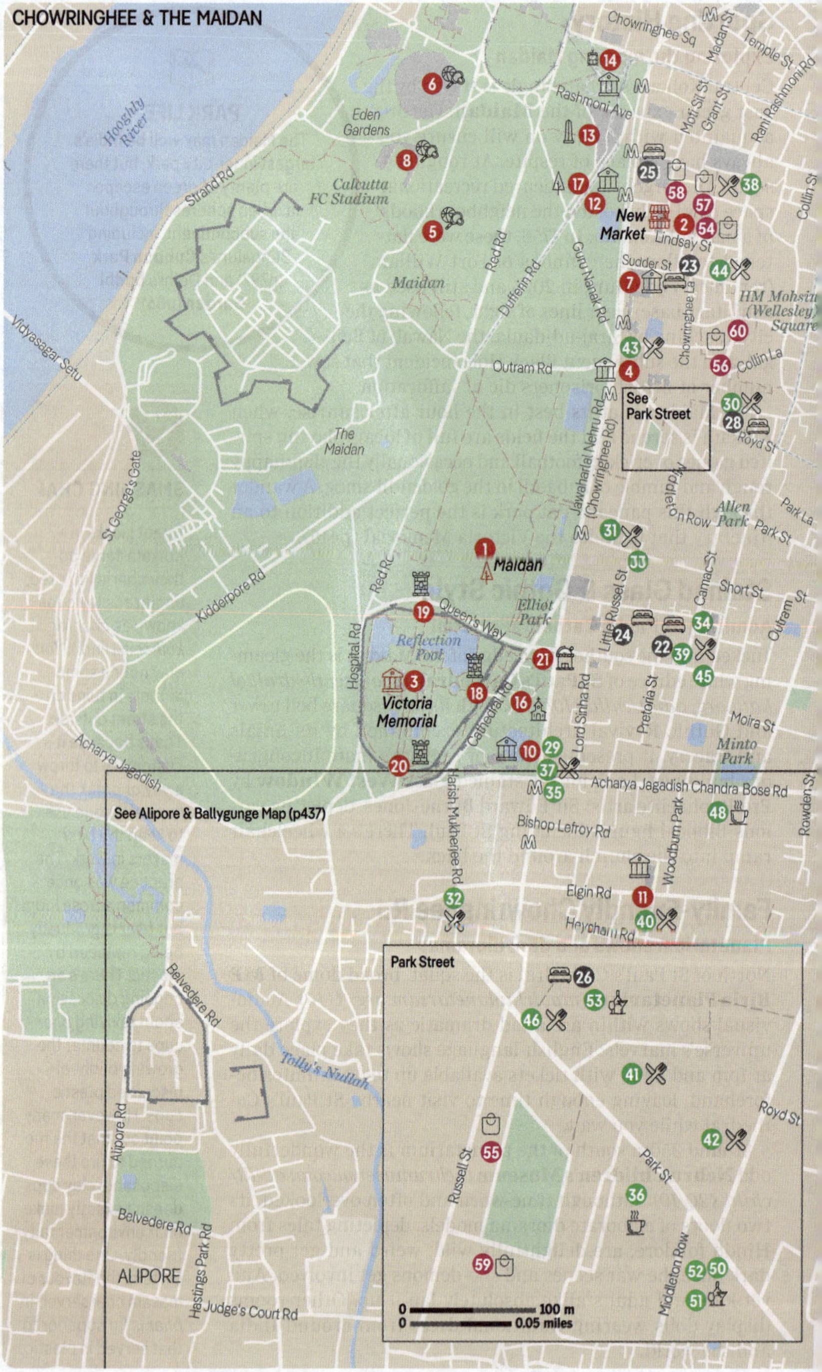
CHOWRINGHEE & THE MAIDAN
Hooghly River
Strand Rd
Eden Gardens
Calcutta FC Stadium
Maidan
The Maidan
Vidyasagar Setu
St George's Gate
Kidderpore Rd
Red Rd
Dufferin Rd
Outram Rd
Guru Nanak Rd
Rashmoni Ave
Chowringhee Sq
Madan St
Temple St
Rani Rashmoni Rd
Moti Sil St
Grant St
Collin St
New Market
Lindsay St
Sudder St
Chowringhee La
HM Mohsin (Wellesley) Square
Collin La
See Park Street
Royd St
Jawaharlal Nehru Rd (Chowringhee Rd)
Middleton Row
Allen Park
Park St
Park La
Short St
Camac St
Little Russel St
Outram St
Maidan
Elliot Park
Queen's Way
Reflection Pool
Hospital Rd
Victoria Memorial
Cathedral Rd
Lord Sinha Rd
Pretoria St
Moira St
Minto Park
Acharya Jagadish
Acharya Jagadish Chandra Bose Rd
Rawdon St
See Alipore & Ballygunge Map (p437)
Harish Mukherjee Rd
Bishop Lefroy Rd
Woodburn Park
Elgin Rd
Heyrcham Rd
Belvedere Rd
Tolly's Nullah
Alipore Rd
Belvedere Rd
ALIPORE
Hastings Park Rd
Judge's Court Rd
Park Street
Russell St
Royd St
Park St
Middleton Row
0 100 m
0 0.05 miles

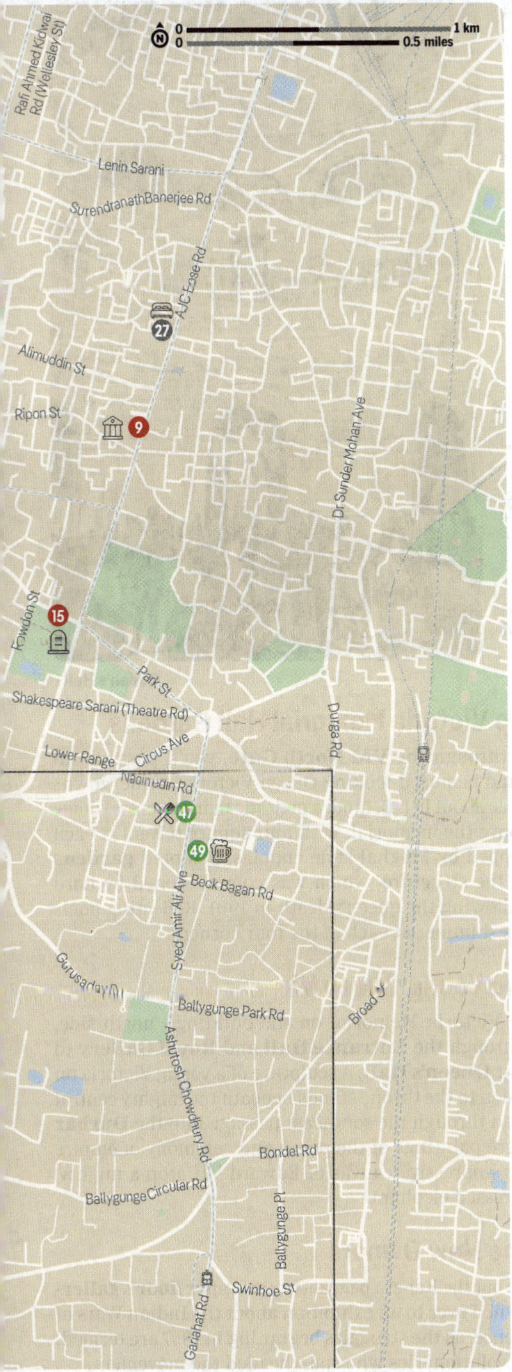

HIGHLIGHTS
1 Maidan
2 New Market
3 Victoria Memorial

SIGHTS
4 Asiatic Society Museum
5 East Bengal FC
6 Eden Gardens
7 Indian Museum
8 Mohun Bagan Super Giant
9 Mother Teresa's Motherhouse
10 Nehru Children's Museum
11 Netaji Bhawan
12 Press Club Kolkata
13 Shaheed Minar
14 Smaranika Tram Museum
15 South Park Street Cemetery
16 St Paul's Cathedral
17 Upper Maidan
18 VM East Gate
19 VM North Gate
20 VM South Gate

ACTIVITIES
21 MP Birla Planetarium

SLEEPING
22 Astor
23 Elgin Fairlawn
24 Kenilworth
25 Oberoi Grand
26 Park Hotel
27 Shaw Guest House
28 Sunflower Guest House

EATING
29 6 Ballygunge Place Chowringhee
30 Arsalan
31 Balaram Mullick & Radharaman Mullick
32 Balwant Singh Dhaba
33 Blue Poppy Thakali
34 Bombay Shiv Sagar
35 Cosy Locus
36 Flurys
37 Haldiram
38 Hotel Sidheshwari Ashram
39 Kaidi Kitchen
40 Kewpie's
41 Kusum Roll's
42 Mocambo
43 Motherland Café
44 Raj's Spanish Café
45 The Guptas
46 Trincas
47 Zam Zam

DRINKING & NIGHTLIFE
48 Artsy
49 Irish House
50 Lords & Barons
51 Myx
52 Peter Cat
53 Tantra
see 26 Tavern

SHOPPING
54 Chamba Lama
55 Good Companions
56 Home of Bengal Hand Embroidery
57 Nahoum & Sons
58 Pumposh
59 Russell Exchange
60 Sasha

TOP EXPERIENCE

Victoria Memorial

Although the march of time is restoring Bengali names to Kolkata's streets and landmarks, changing the name of its most beloved monument remains unthinkable. The white marble Victoria Memorial, with its striking cleanliness amid the palls of Kolkatan smog, set amid landscaped grounds, is a monolithic monument commemorating a monarch whose legacy is nothing if not divisive in these parts.

PAUL STAFFORD

Queen's Hall

TOP TIPS

- For a less-crowded first impression, enter through the VM South Gate. The monument here is fronted by a Victory Arch.
- The VM East Gate, closest to Sudder St, is used as an exit only.
- To encounter the memorial at its most magisterial, visit an hour or two before sunset.

PRACTICALITIES

- victoriamemorial-cal.org
- ₹500
- 10am-6pm Tue-Sun

Visit the Victoria Memorial Hall Gardens

Entering through the **VM North Gate**, you'll pass an enthroned and bemused-looking Queen Victoria statue, gowns draped wide about her. Behind, a majestic marble central dome towers above the memorial, with four square towers at each corner topped by Mughal-style cupolas. Sculpted **gardens** surround the structure, which was commissioned by Lord Curzon following the queen's death in 1901. Reflecting pools and ponds shimmer at each of the four corners.

Meet the Young Queen Vic

Enter the Victoria Memorial on the building's north side, passing through the **Entrance Hall** and **Royal Gallery** to the circular **Queen's Hall**. A sculpture of a young Victoria on her accession to the throne stands beneath the mighty central dome. Head through the southeast passage into the **Durbar Hall**, where paintings of the pomp and ceremony of empire include an impressive canvas of Edward VII atop a mighty, lavishly dressed elephant.

Up to the New Owners

To balance out the Raj-era pageantry, the **upper floor's galleries** are turned over to an exhibition about the Indian Wars of Independence, as the struggles beginning in 1857 are termed, and the revolutionaries who spearheaded the movement.

Martyrs & Museums

History in the Upper Maidan

The **Upper Maidan** is decidedly leafier than the southern section, its trees concealing a series of private sporting and social clubs, including **Press Club Kolkata**, the oldest journalists' club in India. The most notable structure, however, is the creamy, lighthouse-like **Shaheed Minar** *(free)*. It was originally built by the British in 1828 to commemorate the early 19th-century military successes of Sir David Ochterlony. In 1969 it was rededicated to those who died fighting for Indian Independence and named the Martyrs' Monument (Shaheed Minar). Immediately north is Esplanade, where you can catch the historic local trams. A disused tram car now serves as the **Smaranika Tram Museum** *(₹20)*, which explores their first use in 1873 and electrification in 1902, before any other city in Asia. It's closed on Thursdays.

Head to a Ball Game

Professional sports around Eden Gardens

Kolkatans love sport. Every patch of flat grass you come across will likely have been co-opted by footballers and cricketers at all times of day. The floodlights on the Maidan's northwestern fringe belong to hallowed grounds: those of rival football clubs **East Bengal FC** *(eastbengalclub.com)* and **Mohun Bagan Super Giant** *(themohunbaganac.com)*, one of Asia's oldest teams, founded in 1889. The Kolkata derby (known as the Boro Match) is one of India's hotly anticipated contests.

Sporting fervour reaches fever pitch at nearby **Eden Gardens** *(cricketassociationofbengal.com)*, where Indian Premier League (IPL) and international cricket matches draw tens of thousands. Built in 1864, it was Asia's first cricket field. Finding ticketing and scheduling information is not always straightforward. Check trusted websites such as ticombo.com or the District by Zomato app, which is also useful for booking entertainment experiences in many other Indian cities.

Shop Hard, Play Hard

Seeking bargains in New Market

New Market is still officially known as Sir Stuart Hogg Market, with its red-brick, clocktower-fronted facade remaining one of Chowringhee's signature buildings. It has housed a warren of silver-tongued sales people and busy commerce since

SAFER TRAVEL IN KOLKATA

Women travellers: Although safer than cities like Delhi, it is highly recommended to avoid walking in unlit areas at night. The rear carriage on Metro trains is reserved for women only (marked in pink).

Transport overcharging: Drivers of taxis, tuk-tuks and hand-pulled rickshaws occasionally overcharge. Always negotiate use of the meter, or a set fee, in advance.

Touts: New Market and Sudder St attract commission-seeking touts. Don't believe tales of hotels being shut or roads closed. Whenever approached, politely decline any offers and keep walking.

Food safety: The days when eating out in India felt like risking food poisoning are waning. If in doubt, eat at places packed with locals.

Pollution: Keep a mask handy on pollution-heavy days, especially in winter.

EATING IN CHOWRINGHEE: BEST FOR BREAKFAST & LUNCH

Raj's Spanish Café: Tucked away in a cosy courtyard strung with fairy lights off Sudder St; the muesli, fruit and curd bowls offer a health kick. *9am-9pm* ₹₹

Kusum Roll's: On Park St, arguably Kolkata's finest *kathi* rolls, stuffed with fillings and usually eaten right here on the side of the street. *11.30am-midnight* ₹

Flurys: Legendary 1920s Park Street cafe with a sickly pink confection decor; it serves great breakfasts and coffee. Try the rum balls. *6am-11pm* ₹₹₹

Motherland Café: Modern-style option poaching eggs to perfection alongside great 'crepes' (more akin to galettes). Coworking space. *8am-9pm* ₹₹₹

KOLKATA'S PICE HOTELS

In Kolkata *pice* hotels are no-frills dining spots once aimed at migrant workers (*pice* is a derivation of the Hindi word *paisa:* the pence to India's rupees that are no longer in circulation). These workers came to Kolkata from poorer surrounding states such as Bihar and Odisha (Orissa). Nowadays they are used by people from all walks of life. You can generally still get a good three-course meal for about ₹300. Meals, served on banana leaves, may include a fish or prawn dish along with various vegetable sides and a bowl of rice.

JON HICKS/GETTY IMAGES

1874. If you look even remotely like you're not a local, you'll be accosted by a bevy of touts. The best ploy is to smile and say 'I'm not here to buy anything, thanks' and keep walking. Early morning tends to be the calmest time to visit.

Amid the stalls, **Nahoum & Sons** have been selling old fashioned plum and fruit cakes from their wizened store since 1902. The lemon cakes are best. **Chamba Lama** sells Tibetan jewellery and Buddhist sculptures. There are some authentic antiques here but always insist on seeing certification for silver items. **Pumposh** (the Kashmiri name for 'lotus') has sold cashmere shawls here since 1925 and it's now a third-generation family-run store. Bartering is encouraged.

EATING IN CHOWRINGHEE: OUR PICKS

Hotel Sidheshwari Ashram: Traditional *pice* hotel serving authentic Bengali cuisine on banana leaves. Try the *posto bora* (poppy-seed fritters). *10am-3pm & 7-10pm* ₹

The Guptas: Delicious, buttery naans and dosas at this cosy, wood-panelled spot along Shakespeare Sarani. They also do a great *sambar idli. noon-10pm* ₹

Arsalan: Mughlai cuisine, such as biryani, is all the rage in Kolkata and this branch on Muzaffar Ahmed St (aka Ripon St) is among the best. *10am-midnight* ₹₹

Mocambo: Serving up gourmet dishes such as devilled crab and fish Florentine since 1956. The decor harkens back to that era as well. *11.30am-11pm* ₹₹₹

Kaidi Kitchen: There's a weird prison aesthetic (*kaidi* means 'prisoner') here, with tables set behind bars. Try the stuffed *litti chokha* balls. *7am-midnight* ₹₹

Kewpie's: An institution in Kolkata, located right around the corner from Netaji Bhawan. A dab hand at a *daab chingri* (prawn curry). *noon-3pm & 7-11pm* ₹₹

Bombay Shiv Sagar: Classics from South India and Maharashtra (the cheese *pav bhaji* doesn't dishonour the original), plus Bengali Chinese dishes. *11am-10pm* ₹₹

Zam Zam: Inexpensive, cheerful and soaked in ghee, Zam Zam does light, fragrant biryanis. Kolkata's premier budget Mughlai restaurant. *noon-midnight* ₹

New Market (p417)

Travel by Hand

Chowringhee's hand-pulled rickshaws

One form of transport that is virtually synonymous with Kolkata is the hand-pulled rickshaw. They're a curious anachronism in an app-forward world of Uber ridesharing. Their operators, almost exclusively men, often pull the same wood-framed rickshaw their fathers and even grandfathers once pulled. But while this was once seen as a fascinating way to experience city life and a little piece of its heritage at the same time, hand-pulled rickshaws are nowadays a blast from a past that many people would like to forget.

There's an increasing unease about having somebody pull you around a city, veins and sinews bulging under the duress of your, and the cart's weight. After all, this Japanese invention was brought to India by the British. As such, it invokes images of classism, with some branding it simply inhumane.

In the short term, at least, such attitudes do little for the men, and their families, who rely on the income. The rickshaw

TEXTILES IN KOLKATA

Kolkata and the wider West Bengal state have long been important for textile production. Popular techniques and styles include *kantha* embroidery, a style rooted in rural communities, where old materials were upcycled by emblazoning them with stitched depictions of flowers, animals and even stories. A traditional weaving technique is *jamdani*, which imbues fabrics with elaborate patterns.

Boutique stores selling handcrafted Bengali textiles, where sellers work directly with the artisans, are dotted throughout Kolkata, including a handful in Chowringhee, such as **Sasha** (selling *jamdani* fabrics and handmade crafts), the **Home of Bengal Hand Embroidery** (selling leather and embroidered fabrics) and the **Good Companions** (selling embroidery since the 1930s). Ballygunge is another top place to find textile boutiques.

EATING IN CHOWRINGHEE: OUR PICKS NEAR METRO STATIONS

6 Ballygunge Place Chowringhee: Try dishes such as *machher malaikari* or *daab*. Rabindra Sadan Station. *12.30-3.30pm & 7-10.30pm* ₹₹₹

Blue Poppy Thakali: This neat Nepali eatery is accessed via a courtyard south of Middleton St. The *jhol momos* are a highlight. Maidan Station. *noon-9pm* ₹₹₹

Cosy Locus: The dinner buffet offers decent value here with both meat and vegetarian options. À la carte is cheaper. Rabindra Sadan Station. *10am-midnight* ₹₹

Trincas: Opened in 1927, Trincas is a legendary Park St spot serving *kung pao* chicken, lobster thermidor and cocktails. Park Street Station. *11.30am-11.30pm* ₹₹₹

ART & DINNER

Bomti Iyengar, local art dealer, invites guests into his heritage apartment in Chowringhee, where his team prepares exceptional Bengali dinners. He shares his thoughts on Kolkata's best art experiences. Make bookings with Bomti via email. *bomtiyengar@yahoo.com*

People come to my house and they think they're walking into a gallery. The food and art go well together. It's not about food on the table, it's an experience. It's a slice of my life that I'm sharing.

Elsewhere, if you want to see good art in Kolkata, **CIMA** (p439) shows high-end contemporary art. Indian masters, mostly. Then there's the new art space at **Alipore Museum** (p439), which is also very interesting, with some temporary exhibitions besides a small collection.

PAUL STAFFORD

South Park Street Cemetery

pullers often migrate to the city from poorer rural communities, and the reality is that they do their job with great dignity amid the difficult and dangerous streets of this choked megacity, caught in the folds of a caste system that won't be ironed out overnight.

Mammoths, Mummies & Mughal Art

Discovering the Indian Museum's treasures

A deep legacy of Indian architecture and artistry is on display at what is billed as one of the country's premier museums. Opened in 1814 by the Asiatic Society, the broad remit of the collection at the **Indian Museum** *(indianmuseumkolkata.org; ₹500)* includes a woolly mammoth skeleton, artefacts recovered from the Buddhist 1st century BCE site of Bharhut, and an Ancient Egyptian mummy. No wonder it's known locally as Jadu Ghar (The House of Magic).

Ground-floor highlights include artefacts from Bodhgaya, a numismatics room with an impressive silver coin (c 336–23 BCE) featuring Alexander the Great atop his horse Bucephalus, and various Hindu sculptures from around the country. The series of Mughal miniatures in the upper floor's Painting Gallery are the highlight of the museum's art holdings, providing a glimpse at daily palace life behind the royal walls.

DRINKING IN CHOWRINGHEE: BEST BARS

Peter Cat: This charming establishment has liveried staff, low lighting and beer served in brass tankards. Popular food includes *chelo* kebabs. *noon-11pm*

Tavern: One of the better LGBTIQ-friendly bars in Kolkata, Tavern, located behind Trinca's, hosts 'Pink Social Thursdays' and nightly live music. *noon-11.30pm*

Lords & Barons: Rooftop hangout with DJs spinning tunes, happy-hour specials from opening until 6pm and hookah. *noon-midnight*

Irish House: On the 5th floor of INOX (Quest Mall), this smart bar has an early evening happy hour. The locally made Caldera wheat beer is great. *noon-1am*

Although it's a large museum, you're unlikely to need more than a few hours here.

Clubs & Diamonds

Sample the Park St nightlife

Kolkata's nightlife scene lags behind that of other Indian cities. Although the trendy exurbs of Lake Town and New Town have some modern offerings, they remain dislocated and distant from downtown Kolkata. However, things are changing in Chowringhee, with new brewpubs, upscale clubs and bars opening all the time. Nevertheless, nightlife is still primarily centred around Park St, which slices diagonallly through Chowringhee. Start with the scene's diamonds: Peter Cat and Trincas (p419) have both thrived for decades with the liveliest staff and dim lighting. To take the night to another level and sample Kolkata's budding club scene, try **Tantra** or **Myx**, both small but lively spaces.

A Grave Nature

Strolling South Park Street Cemetery

The first burials at **South Park Street Cemetery** *(entry with/without camera ₹50/25)* began in 1768, with its clusters of imposing pagoda-, pyramid- and obelisk-shaped tombs reflecting the same British penchant for the Gothic and neoclassical in death that characterised their buildings in life.

As one of central Kolkata's most peaceful and overlooked spaces, it's a refuge for much flora and fauna, with 65 species of plant, including Buddha trees, jasmine and bottlebrush, their roots gradually inching their way into the brick tombs. Meanwhile mongooses, chipmunks and birds make the most of the cemetery's protection. The grandest monument is that of Sir William Jones, who founded the Asiatic Society, which maintains a small **museum** on Park St.

Home of a Fighter

Visiting Netaji Bhawan

Cheerful green wooden shutters lend character to **Netaji Bhawan** *(netaji.org; adult/child ₹50/20)*, the ancestral home, turned museum, of Subhas Chandra Bose (Netaji). It was from here, in 1941, that Netaji escaped British-imposed house arrest to Germany, before fighting alongside the Japanese against British forces during WWII. Visitors are greeted by his

THE ENDURING INFLUENCE OF SATYAJIT RAY

Mid-20th-century Calcutta was thrust into the global consciousness by one of the all-time greats of Indian cinema, Satyajit Ray. His films, which are much more sophisticated than Bollywood's general output, are humanistic and deeply influenced by Italian Neorealism. They eventually came to define, and then influence, Bengali culture.

Pather Panchali is up there in the pantheon of all-time great directing debuts. It would become the first instalment of the 'Apu Trilogy', named after the film's young hero. However, it's in his Kolkata-based films, a highlight being *The Big City*, that Ray captures the evolution of India's cultural values, and the friction of that shift, so succinctly. Ray continued to paint Kolkata on a silver-screen canvas throughout his career and his films remain incredibly relevant.

EATING & DRINKING IN CHOWRINGHEE: COFFEE & SWEETS

Haldiram: Jaggery, ghee and syrup are the most important ingredients of the sweets made here. The *laddu* is particularly good. *8am-10pm Mon-Sat, from 10am Sun* ₹₹

Artsy: For good coffee, Artsy is reliable, but when it comes to hot chocolate, this is the place to be. Goes great with their Biscoff cheesecake. *9am-10pm* ₹₹₹

Balwant Singh Dhaba: Legendary hole in the wall famed for its *doodh* (milk) cola, which is exactly what it sounds like. *24hr* ₹

Balaram Mullick & Radharaman Mullick: Try the dairy-based desserts here, such as soft, creamy *sandesh* and pots of sweet *mishti doi*. *10am-9pm* ₹₹

NETAJI & MOTHER TERESA: CONTROVERSIAL FIGURES?

Subhas Chandra Bose (1897–1945), aka Netaji, is lauded in Hindutva circles for his militarism in conjunction with Indian Independence. Frequently incarcerated for committing acts of 'civil disobedience' against British colonial laws that were widely considered unjust, Netaji escaped to exile in Germany and allied with the Axis powers, a fact routinely ignored by Netaji's devotees and sidestepped in museums dedicated to him.

Catholic nun Mother Teresa (1910–97), aka St Teresa of Calcutta, established the Missionaries of Charity in Kolkata as a refuge for dying and destitute people. The attention it gained also created a perception that the people it helped were indicative of Kolkata as a whole: poor, desperate, sick. Her legacy once seemed unimpeachable, now some pose the question: white saviour or self-sacrificing saint?

RITESH RANJAN SETT/SHUTTERSTOCK

Getaway car, Netaji Bhawan (p421)

not-inconspicuous Wanderer getaway car, before filing past Netaji's bed and his study, which is now painted in the Indian flag's colours and preserved behind glass with a reverence befitting the importance of his fight for his country's independence.

NETAJI MONUMENTS

Subhas Chandra Bose may have spent many crucial moments in his subversive, anti-colonial career in Kolkata, but he was born and raised in the comparatively provincial Cuttack, in Odisha. His ancestral home is now the **Netaji Birth Place Museum** (p577).

A Revered & Maligned Tomb

Paying respects at the Motherhouse

Kolkata was long defined in the West by images of abject poverty, particularly of children, that became the focus of Mother (now Saint) Teresa's work in the city. While the city has managed to shake that image for something closer aligned to reality, **Mother Teresa's Motherhouse** *(missionariesofcharity.org; free)*, which is closed on Thursdays, is still doing its charitable work, operated by the Missionaries of Charity that Mother Teresa established in 1952. Christian pilgrims in particular visit to pay homage at St Teresa of Calcutta's tomb, museum and the shrine that has been made of her spartan room.

BBD Bagh, Barabazar & Old Chinatown

RELIGIOUS DIVERSITY AND HERITAGE ARCHITECTURE

Once the East India Company's administrative hub, BBD Bagh (Benoy-Badal-Dinesh Bagh; formerly Dalhousie Square) is now named after three key members of the Indian Independence movement who in 1930 assassinated Norman Simpson, Inspector General of Prisons in Calcutta at the time. The area retains spectres of its past: looming edifices, bound by the Hooghly River to the west. Some of these architecturally fascinating buildings are mouldering and crumbling, others are repurposed, co-opted or still serve their original purpose. Further north you run into Barabazar, which once housed the EIC's innumerable clerks and servants. Nowhere illustrates Kolkata's religious diversity like Barabazar, with its profusion of churches, synagogues and mosques. Heading away from the river, some of the city's longest-standing stores, selling everything from guns to musical instruments, can still be found in Old Chinatown. Beyond is Kolkata's main university district around College Square, where booksellers line the streets.

TOP TIP

A day on foot in Kolkata can be a tiring yet rewarding experience. Wear comfortable footwear and light, breathable fabrics. If you plan to be outdoors later in the afternoon or in the early evening, bring insect repellent with you to top up when the blighters really start biting.

Black Holes & Revelations

Dark history at St John's Church

Dating back to 1784, **St John's Church** *(stjohnschurchcni.org; ₹10)* retains a large cache of colonial-era history. The two-storey, hexagonal **Mausoleum of Job Charnock** (founder of

GETTING AROUND

Exploring on foot is the best, and sometimes the only way to get around the highlights of these contiguous neighbourhoods. Expect to get lost, too. Part of the joy is in stumbling upon something unexpected, be it an alleyway lined with the workshops of sitar makers, to the huge Raj-era mansions housing fascinating museums or subversive galleries. A tram links the southern side of Lal Dighi tank in BBD Bagh to Esplanade and the Maidan. To buy advance train tickets for journeying beyond Kolkata, head to the Eastern Railways Foreign Tourist Bureau (bring passport and passport photos), on Fairlie Place Rd.

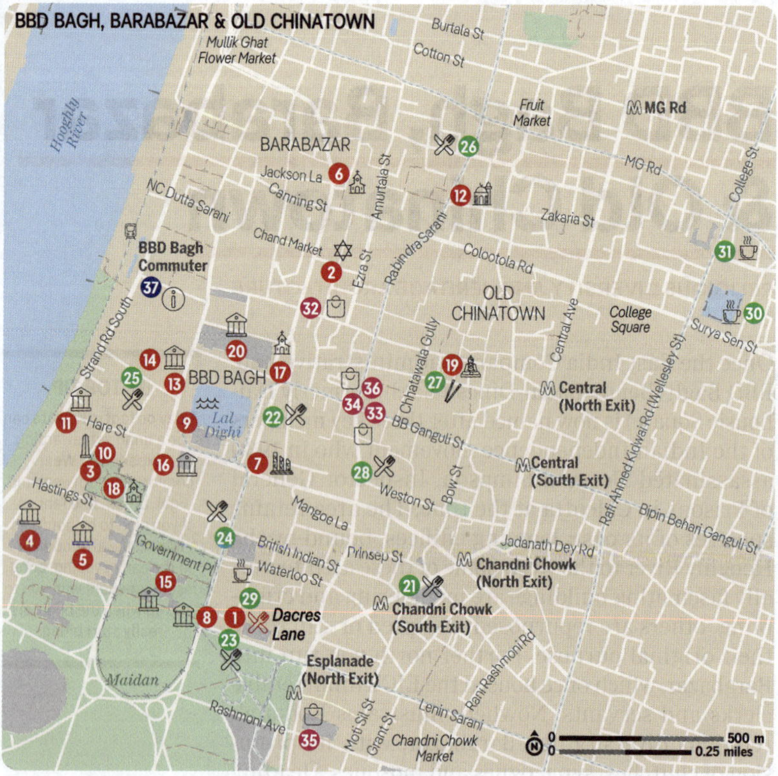

HIGHLIGHTS
1 Dacres Lane

SIGHTS
2 Beth El Synagogue
3 Black Hole Memorial
4 Calcutta High Court
5 Calcutta Town Hall
6 Cathedral of the Most Holy Rosary
7 Currency Building
8 Esplanade Mansion
9 Lal Dighi
10 Mausoleum of Job Charnock
11 Metcalfe Hall
12 Nakhoda Masjid
13 Old GPO Building
14 Postal Museum
15 Raj Bhavan
16 RBI Museum
17 St Andrew's Church
18 St John's Church
19 Toong On Temple
20 Writers' Buildings

EATING
21 Anand
22 Bhoj Company
23 Chitto Babur Dokan
24 Chutney Co
25 Fairlie Place Rd Food Stalls
26 Royal Indian Hotel
27 Tung Nam Eating House
28 Vojon Rosik
30 Food Square
31 Indian Coffee House

DRINKING & NIGHTLIFE
29 Faltu Tea Centre

SHOPPING
32 A Tosh & Sons
33 ML Bhunja & Co
34 Musical Instrument Zone
35 Pen Hospital
36 Saekar

INFORMATION
37 Eastern Railways Foreign Tourist Bureau

EATING AROUND BBD BAGH: OUR PICKS

Vojon Rosik: A good place to try a Bengali-style thali. They also do 'combos', which are set menus branching out from the thali. *11am-10pm* ₹₹₹

Chutney Co: Artful dosas and *idli* are available all day with a fantastic range of delicious dips. There's also a daily rice bowl special. *11am-9pm* ₹

Bhoj Company: Classic Bengali dishes, such as *bhetki paturi* (barramundi fish marinated in a mustard sauce) and *ras malai* for dessert. *noon-10pm* ₹₹

Anand: Adivasi handicrafts on the walls and (despite the bizarre pricing structure) great-value tiffin (snacks) from around India. *11am-9pm Thu-Tue* ₹₹

Calcutta as we know it today) is located in the church grounds, as is the **Black Hole Memorial**, dedicated to those who died in the Black Hole Prison in the original Fort William.

Within the church, the **office of Warren Hastings**, the first British Governor General of India, is on the right after you enter. Also look out for the **Last Supper painting** by 18th-century German artist Johann Zoffany, left of the altar.

Heritage, Culture & Art

Discover Kolkata's culture at Metcalfe Hall

The imposing neo-Greek architecture of **Metcalfe Hall** *(₹20)* was inspired by the Tower of the Winds in Athens. The impressive Corinthian pillars hold up a large entablature with the building's name in gold leaf. A fine restoration, completed in 2019, is indicative of the change in local attitudes towards heritage architecture, and now the building is repurposed to hold a wonderful museum exploring the arts and culture of Kolkata, with sections on dance, literature and the Durga Puja. The building, originally intended as a library, is named after Charles Theophilus Metcalfe who, in his short tenure as Governor General of India (1835–36), established freedom of the press in Kolkata. It is closed on Mondays, like most museums in the city.

Iconic GPO & Museum

Do the rounds of India's postal history

The **Old GPO (General Post Office) Building** towers over the water tank **Lal Dighi** and the surrounding streets. The 37m corner dome is supported by Ionic-Corinthian pillars. Moreover, the building retains its original function. Left of the main post office entrance, on the south side of the building, is the **Philatelic Bureau** *(free)*, exhibiting Indian stamps through the years. They explore some esoteric areas of India and Kolkata's history, including the city's love of football and a series of tiger stamps from 1973 to commemorate Indira Gandhi's Project Tiger initiative. The **Postal Museum** *(free)* is further west. Its exhibits, which trace the pre- and post-Independence history of India's postal service, include a selection of swords issued to security officers tasked with guarding post offices.

Street-Food Alley

Sampling Kolkata's flavours on Dacres Lane

Kolkata boasts one of India's most iconic street-food scenes. Wherever you go, you'll find steam rising from grills and pans, throwing their aromatic scents into the melee of street life. BBD Bagh is the best place in central

REGIONAL EATS

Kolkata may be the capital of Bengali food, but there are plenty of other fantastic culinary idioms to discover throughout the country, including Mumbai's **Parsi cuisine** (p683) and the **Dilli-ki-Chaat** (street-food snacks; p67) of Old Delhi.

KOLKATA'S MUST-TRY STREET FOOD

Two Kolkatan street-food classics are *kathi* rolls (a *paratha* fried with an egg and filled with grilled onions, chilli and paneer or meat of choice) and *phuchka* (known elsewhere as *pani puri*). For a great breakfast dish, try *kochuri* (deep-fried bread stuffed with savoury fillings) with *aloo tarkari* (potato curry) or *chholar dal*. Alternatively, try *aloo dum* with *luchi* bread from Fairlie Place Rd's food stalls, which makes for a great snack on the go. **Lakshmi Narayan Shaw & Sons**, a famous spot near Sovabazar Sutanuti station where Netaji ate in his youth, serves crunchy *piyaji* (onion *bhaji*) and delightful *aam chops* (mango fritters). Mughlai dishes such as biryani, inspired by the culinary influences of Persia and Turkey, are also a popular street food in Kolkata.

QUIRKY SHOPS IN BBD BAGH & CHOWRINGHEE

Kolkata's historic neighbourhoods teem with delightful anachronisms; shops that endure despite the march of modernity.

Saekar: Head down the alley beside Mondal (another instrument shop) to Saekar, which has some excellent handmade *dotara* (two-stringed instruments) and *dhol* drums.

A Tosh & Sons: Selling packages of Darjeeling and Assam tea since 1897; next to the Indian Tea Board building.

ML Bhunja & Co: The place to buy antique guns since 1948, with several historic weapons on show.

Pen Hospital: Selling and healing dip nib fountain pens in Esplanade since the 1940s.

Russell Exchange: Operated by the same Kolkatan family that bought it in 1940, this is said to be India's oldest auction house. Sunday noon auctions are an experience.

BALAJISRINIVASAN/SHUTTERSTOCK

Parathas vendor, Dacres Lane

Kolkata to experience this. The unmissable street-food destination is **Dacres Lane** (aka James Hickey Sarani), best at breakfast and lunch times. Stalls to aim for in this busy narrow alley north of Esplanade are **Chitto Babur Dokan** for their chicken stew, made with carrots and green papaya, followed by a masala chai in a *bhar* cup from **Faltu Tea Centre**. Another option are the **food stalls** on the south side of Fairlie Place Rd.

Economic Experiences

All things money at RBI Museum

Everything you ever wanted to know about money and the banking system of a nation can be discovered at the **RBI Museum** *(therbimuseum.rbi.org.in; free)*. The subject matter could easily be dry and factual, but this is a fantastic, well-considered exhibition that includes a look at how the use of money evolved, plus a chance to test the weight of a (not real) gold bar. Some interactive games keep younger visitors entertained. The collection is housed in a beautifully preserved heritage building.

EATING & DRINKING IN BARABAZAR & COLLEGE SQ: OUR PICKS

Indian Coffee House: Legendary spot near College Square with Indian Independence links and underwhelming coffee. Upper-level seating is best. *noon-8pm* ₹

Food Square: A simple space popular with students. Try their refreshing *paan sharbat* drink made with grated betel leaf, liquorice, fennel and rose. *11am-9pm Mon-Sat* ₹

Tung Nam Eating House: The wonton and heaped noodles plates have long made this a favourite Chinese food spot for Kolkatans. *noon-3pm & 6-10pm Wed-Mon* ₹₹

Royal Indian Hotel: One of Kolkata's historic *pice* hotels, serving Mughlai dishes such as biryani or mutton curry on banana leaves since 1905. *10am-11pm* ₹₹

BBD BAGH HERITAGE & ARCHITECTURE ON FOOT

Wander through a Kolkata that clings to its past while belonging very much to the city's present.

START	END	LENGTH
Dacres Lane	RBI Museum	2.75km; 3hr

Begin on 1 **Dacres Lane** with a good cup of chai, or a fish fry from Chitto Babur Dokan. Fuelled up, head to the delightful 2 **Esplanade Mansion**. Built in 1910, it is one of Kolkata's few art nouveau buildings, with circular balconies and a cupola. From here, walk north, then west, glimpsing the mighty 3 **Raj Bhavan**, the West Bengal governor's residence, on the way to 4 **St John's Church** (p423).

Next, drop south to Esplanade Row to pass 5 **Calcutta Town Hall** with its grand portico and the beautiful neo-Gothic edifice of 6 **Calcutta High Court**, established in 1862. Turn north when you reach Strand Rd. The Hooghly River is now on your left beyond Millennium Park, with its fairground rides of dubious health and safety compliance. In two blocks, you'll reach column-fronted 7 **Metcalfe Hall** (p425).

Continue north, then east onto BTM Sarani (formerly Koilaghat St) to the 8 **Old GPO Building** (p425), with the Postal Museum next door. At Netaji Subhas Rd, head north to the mighty 9 **Writers' Buildings**, the East India Company's former headquarters. Construction started in 1776. Its strawberries and cream exterior and baroque statues crowning the eaves reveal its former grandeur. The block south of this is dominated by peaceful 10 **Lal Dighi** (p425). Finish this tour one block south at the 11 **RBI Museum**.

FAITH & COMMERCE STROLL THROUGH BARABAZAR

Take in a hearty dose of Kolkatan street culture through the markets and religious institutions along this self-guided route.

START	END	LENGTH
Currency Building	Beth El Synagogue	2.8km; 3hr

Bengali for 'Big Market', Barabazar is mercantile chaos at its most fascinating, interspersed with glimpses of its foundational diversity. Start at the ❶ **Currency Building**. Its upper level was demolished to help stabilise the crumbling structure. Walk north from here to ❷ **St Andrew's Church**, a still-active branch of the Scottish Diocese. Curving rows of seats fan out from the pulpit, where the Holy Communion is delivered at 9.30am on Sundays and 1pm on Thursdays.

From here, head east, passing the sign chisellers to the ❸ **musical instrument zone** where sitars and *mridangam* (percussion instruments) are handmade. Continue east, passing ❹ **ML Bhunja & Co**, a gun shop in business since 1948. Cut north, weaving through Old Chinatown, where Kolkata's waste pickers live and work. Taoist ❺ **Toong On Temple**, which marked its centenary in 2024, lies just south of lively Tiretta Bazaar.

At ❻ **Nakhoda Masjid**, a cluster of cream, sienna and gold domes and minarets pose a bulwark against the busy market streets outside. Next, push west along Amratala La (beneath the yellow Khan Zareen sign) to Portuguese Church St where you'll find the two towers and gold-carved doors of the ❼ **Cathedral of the Most Holy Rosary**. Nearby, the interior of ❽ **Beth El Synagogue** (Jewish people only) is a medley of stained glass and wrought iron.

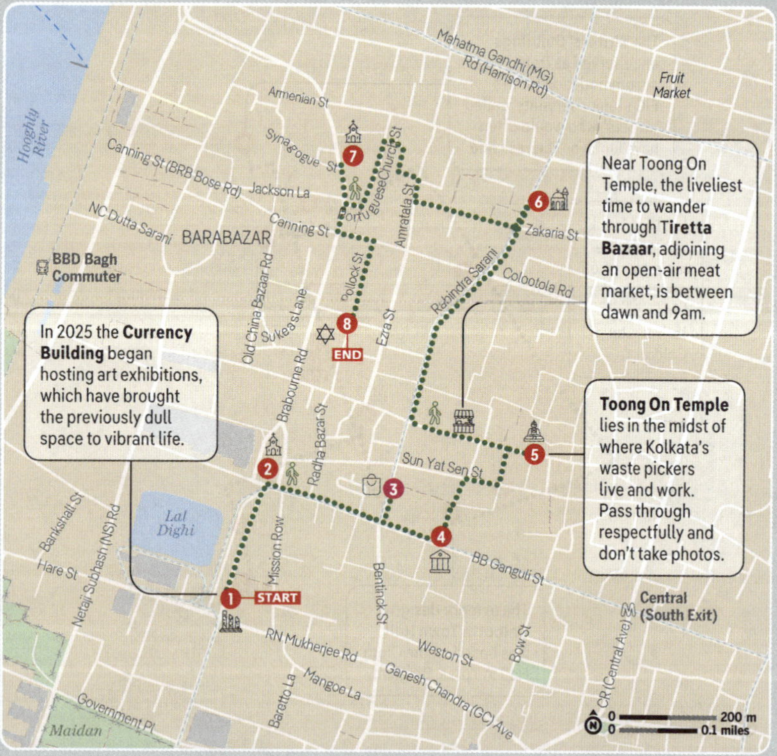

The Hooghly River & Howrah

GHAT LIFE AND GARDENS

Much of Kolkata's best tourism infrastructure lies east of the Maidan and many visitors leave without ever having seen the Hooghly River to the west. Located a couple of kilometres away from Chowringhee, this distributary arm of the Ganges feels completely detached from the city. In fact, the silty river is so vast that it has always served more as an impediment rather than a focal point of urban life. But it is still sacred to many people and the various ghats along the river's eastern bank offer a window onto other facets of Kolkatan life, including Mullick Ghat's flower market and its wrestlers, training in the early morning light. Howrah, on the Hooghly's western bank, is practically a separate city. Most people only venture that way to reach the train stations of Howrah Junction and Shalimar, but Howrah's Botanical Gardens and rail heritage are worthy of visits in their own right.

GETTING AROUND

With only two bridges spanning the Hooghly River in Kolkata, including the cantilever Howrah Bridge, the river remains a big part of the cause of the city's choked roads. Getting to or from Howrah Junction would often require a slow taxi journey or a boat crossing. The extension of Kolkata Metro's Green Line in 2025 went a long way to improving the situation and Howrah has never been more accessible. The eastern bank still feels detached, and while you can get small boats across the river from a number of points, getting to the riverfront from areas like Chowringhee is easiest by rideshare.

The Boats of Shipping Ghat

Take a Hooghly River cruise

All along the Hooghly River, ghats are abuzz with the comings and goings of boats, skiffs and ferries. The ferries shepherd people across the water to places like Howrah Station and Belur Math temple. For a guided trip, take the **Kolkata Heritage River Cruise** *(₹190)* run by the West Bengal Transport Corporation (look for the blue ticket booth) from **Shipping Ghat** in BBD Bagh. Boats depart at 4pm and 6pm daily, with additional trips on weekends at noon and 2pm. Tours pass beneath the Howrah Bridge (p430) during the 90-minute cruise. **Vivada Cruises** *(vivadacruises.com; ₹1850)* runs an evening cruise on newer boats from the same ghat. The three-hour trip includes a stop at Belur Math (p435) for 45 minutes and on-board snacks.

SIGHTS
1 Chotelal Ghat
2 Howrah Bridge
3 Rail Museum
4 Siyaram Akhara Byayam Samity

ACTIVITIES
5 Kolkata Heritage River Cruise
6 Vivada Cruises

SHOPPING
7 Mullick Ghat Flower Market

TRANSPORT
8 Howrah Junction Railway Station
9 Shipping Ghat

TOP TIP

Aim to visit the river at sunrise if you wish to catch the flower market and watch wrestlers in full flow around Mullick Ghat. Visit at sunset if you're looking for the best photos, to take a cruise or simply to stroll the riverbank at its most atmospheric time of day.

Blooms Under the Bridge

Scents and stances at Mullick Ghat Flower Market

The 705m-long **Howrah Bridge**, built by the Brits in 1943, has been an emblem of Kolkata since it was completed. Spanning the coffee-coloured waters of the Hooghly River, the symphony of steel latticework churns with honking traffic around the clock, while many more people cross on foot. Its official name is Rabindra Setu, but you're unlikely to hear anybody calling it that.

Beneath the bridge's eastern span, **Mullick Ghat Flower Market** buzzes in a blaze of orange and yellow, atop a hash of shredded newspaper. The fast-paced hawking of floral wares reaches its zenith in the early morning, when wholesalers auction in bulk to the vendors. Garlands of orange and yellow marigolds and, less commonly, red hibiscus flowers, are presented at Hindu temples during special occasions, but bought year-round to celebrate big life events such as house warmings and weddings.

THE GREAT GHATS

India's riverside ghats are legendary for their importance to Hinduism, not least of all Varanasi's **Manikarnika Ghat** (p344). **Triveni Ghat** (p382) in Rishikesh is a place for religious ceremony, while ghats of a very different kind, Karnataka's **Western Ghats** (p814), are some of the prettiest mountains south of the Himalaya.

BALAJISRINIVASAN/SHUTTERSTOCK

Street vendor, Mullick Ghat Flower Market

Walk up to the lip of Howrah Bridge, which crosses above the market, for the best photos.

Head 150m south then turn towards the river at Chotelal Ghat, passing between the red and white buildings to reach **Siyaram Akhara Byayam Samity**, the last of Kolkata's *kushti* wrestling rings (it's free to observe). Combining spiritual practice with intense physicality, the wrestlers' morning training is a remarkable thing to witness. Arrive between 4am and 7.30am for a chance to see them working out. There's another session in the evenings.

A Junction Between Worlds

Mainlining rail history at Howrah Station

India's busiest railway station is **Howrah Junction**, a public transit behemoth first opened in 1854. The current carmine and beige station building was built in the first decade of the 20th century and subsequently expanded to its current 23 platforms. Its square towers and profusion of arches gives it an air of steady order amid chaos, which is generally upheld by the events within. More on India's rail history can be discovered nearby at Howrah's **Rail Museum** *(₹30)*, with a collection of historic locomotives and a **working toy train** *(₹10 extra)*.

THE WRESTLERS OF MULLICK GHAT

Kushti (aka *pehlwani*) is a form of Indian wrestling that has Mughal origins, which in turn flowed into India from Persia (the Persian word for wrestling is *koshti*). The banks of the Hooghly were often seen as the ideal place to practice, with its mud and cool breezes coming in from the water. Today, **Siyaram Akhara Byayam Samity** is the last of the *kushti* training centres (called *akhara*) in Kolkata. Boys start training here as young as six years old, learning the principles of focus, body strengthening and discipline to become *pahalwans* (wrestlers). You will often see the wrestlers training in the morning, from sunrise until around 7.30am, and practitioners are often very open and welcoming to curious passersby.

Northern Kolkata

PALACES, TEMPLES AND EFFIGIES

GETTING AROUND

In the north, Kolkata remains anchored to the Hooghly River. The Metro's Blue Line runs parallel to the river and everything in between these two conduits is roughly demarcated as the main region containing neighbourhoods of interest to visitors north of the Maidan. Then there's Rabindra Sarani, the main road that runs in between the Metro line and river, where traffic is often at a standstill. Trams are the best way to navigate this bustling street, clustered with businesses of all kinds. Pay the conductor (around ₹10) once you've boarded. Rideshare apps offer the most efficient way to get around this area.

Sprawling out from what the British East India Company originally dubbed 'Black Town', Kolkata's northern neighbourhoods were a swell of life that helped define Bengali cuisine, spirituality, creativity and independence. Some of India's greatest politicians, gurus, mystics and literary icons were shaped in these humble streets, and nourished at the food stalls of Shyambazar.

Perhaps the most compelling reason why Kolkata holds the unofficial title of 'India's literary capital' is down to one man: Rabindranath Tagore. His ancestral home, Jorasanko Thakurbari, lies on the major thoroughfare Rabindra Sarani. Swami Vivekananda was also born here, going on to found Belur Math, which enlivens the Hooghly riverbanks. Those same banks are the source of clay, used in the production of effigies and idols that are integral to the city's Durga Puja celebrations each September or October. Idol makers and artisans of the Kumartuli neighbourhood make these effigies throughout the year.

Mustard Oil & Fish

Sample Bengali cuisine on a food tour

Often using sharp-edged mustard oil as a base, then balancing and accenting it with ingredients such as coconut, nigella seeds, cumin and vegetables, Bengali cuisine produces some of India's most refined dishes. A full spread at dinner might include *luchi* (fluffy bread), *posto bora* (fried poppy-seed cake), *chola dal* (lentil curry), *shukto* (a bittersweet vegetable stew), *mochar ghonto* (banana flour curry) and, perhaps most importantly in Bengal, *macher* (fish) and *chingri* (prawns) prepared in a variety of curry styles such as *kalia* (stronger, with lots of ginger and garlic) and *jhol* (lighter and fragrant). Always leave room for the equally important dairy-based desserts. For a brilliant, off-the-beaten-track Bengali cuisine tour, check out those offered by **A Chef's Tour** (*achefstour.com; ₹3500*), which explore Shyambazar and other northern neighbourhoods.

HIGHLIGHTS

1 Marble Palace

SIGHTS

2 Jorasanko Thakurbari
3 Kumartuli Idol Makers
4 Siddhivinayak Temple

ACTIVITIES

5 A Chef's Tour
6 Calcutta Walks

SLEEPING

7 Broadway Hotel
8 Calcutta Bungalow
9 City Central Hostel
10 LaLiT Great Eastern
11 Polo Floatel

EATING

12 Allen Kitchen
13 Bhojohori Manna
14 Golbari
15 Lakshmi Narayan Shaw & Sons
16 National Economic Restaurant
17 Putiram
18 Sufi Palace

TOP TIP

The best time to visit Kumartuli is right before Durga Puja in autumn. With the monsoon season usually over by this point, there's one final burst of fervent creative energy in order get all the idols ready for the celebrations.

DURGA PUJA

Recognised by UNESCO for its intangible cultural heritage, the **Durga Puja festival** transforms Kolkata (as well as much of West Bengal and Assam) during the month of Ashwin, seventh month of the lunisolar Hindu calendar (usually late September or early October). It is Kolkata's most majestic festival, where effigies (aka sculpture-idols) of the 10-armed goddess Durga, who is often depicted riding a lion, along with other deities are displayed all around the city in *pandals* (temporary temples). These effigies are worshipped, paraded and then ultimately submerged in the Hooghly River. Every community has its own *pandal*, which often blocks entire roads or commandeers a local park. The one in Kumartuli is generally said to be among the city's best each year.

SUN_SHINE/SHUTTERSTOCK

Idol maker, Kumartuli

Straw Gods

Meeting Kumartuli's idol makers

Kumartuli is a neighbourhood in northern Kolkata where deities are born. Well, at least, their likenesses are. Using straw frames, clay from the river and paint, sculptors *(kumars)* craft and paint idols in their street-front workshops, often with a mezzanine above, used as living quarters. Skills are passed down generations and many established families in Kolkata have their go-to *kumar* in the run-up to the **Durga Puja**. Most **Kumartuli idol makers** have their workshops on Potter's Lane, also known as Banamali Sarkar Street. It's easy to explore on your own, but a guided tour from **Calcutta Walks** *(calcuttawalks.com; ₹2500)* can provide better access to the workshops and artisans.

Geese, Gods & General Eccentricity

Embrace the Marble Palace weird

Everybody in Bengal seems to have a story about the **Marble Palace** and the Bengali trading family who built and continue to own it, members of which once travelled around Calcutta in a carriage pulled by zebras. The palace was built in 1835 by Raja Rajendra Mullick. Legend has it that he once bought an entire trading ship's consignment of antiquities when it docked in the city. The palace is packed with sculptures (some in duplicate) of Greek gods in marble and bronze, grand pianos, billiards tables, Belgian glass and Chinese Ming vases. The 19th-century floor of the music room and dance hall is particularly exquisite.

If you're walking to the Marble Palace along Muktaram Babu St from Mahatma Gandhi (MG) Road Metro station, don't mistake the first large columned building you come to as the palace. This is just **Siddhivinayak Temple**, humble by comparison. In theory, you are required to first obtain a permit from the West Bengal Tourism office in BBD Bagh to enter the Marble Palace, but baksheesh still worked at the time of research: pay the gate guard on arrival and also to anybody mandatorily assigned to show you around the interior of the palace. Around ₹100 to ₹200 each should suffice.

On entering the Marble Palace grounds, you'll be directed to follow the path past the extravagant fountain first, then away from the palace's west side to a small **aviary and menagerie**, which only adds to the absurdity. Finally, circle back to the palace for a guided tour of the interior. The palace is closed on Mondays and Thursdays.

India's Nobel Laureate in Literature

Explore Rabindranath Tagore's principal residence

Feeling more like a series of government offices than an ancestral home, **Jorasanko Thakurbari** *(Tagore's House; ₹150)* is where Rabindranath Tagore, India's greatest poet, polymath and only Nobel Laureate in Literature (1913), was born and died. Known popularly as Thakurbari, it plays a central role in Bengali cultural life. Visitors wander from room to room following a circuitous route that emphasises the size of the palace. A series of picture-forward exhibitions details Tagore's life and travels in Thailand, Japan and China. Alas, you won't leave knowing a great deal about the man or his work, but more about the myth of him, a missed opportunity on the part of the curators here. However, the minimalism of the room where Tagore died on 7 August 1941 is very moving.

A Guru's Spiritual Stronghold

The shrines and temples of Belur Math

Belur Math *(belurmath.org; free)* was founded by Swami Vivekananda, a disciple of Ramakrishna, and was completed in 1938, after his death. There's an Orthodox Christianity meets Mughal palace vibe going on with the architecture of this complex's various temples, further adding to the sense of a mixing of religious ideologies that pervades the site's ideology. Of the peach-coloured riverside temples, **Swami Brahmananda Temple** is located on the site where its eponymous Sri Ramakrishna disciple was cremated. **Maa Sarada Devi Temple** is dedicated to the 'spiritual consort' of Ramakrishna, also on the site of her cremation.

QUINTESSENTIAL BENGALI TASTES OF KOLKATA

Avik Mitra, who leads food tours from Chowringhee to the wider Shyambazar area for A Chef's Tour (p432), names his favourite dishes and where to try them. *achefstour.com*

Mutton curry, Golbari: Mutton is red goat meat, which can absorb a lot of spices and flavours. At Golbari, they replace the chilli with cinnamon.

Prawn batter cutlet, Allen Kitchen: Started by a Scotsman, who helped show Bengalis how to use fish to make interesting culinary treats.

Golda chingri malaikari, Bhojohori Manna: A lobster prawn curry cooked in a delectable coconut sauce, which plays second cousin to the rich prawn meat.

Mishti doi, Putiram: The only shop that serves this yoghurt with a crystal white colour. There's no added sugar; they harness the natural sweetness of milk.

EATING IN NORTHERN KOLKATA: OUR PICKS

Allen Kitchen: Historic eatery opened in 1884 known for its prawn batter cutlet. Near Sovabazar Sutanuti station (close to Kumartuli). *1-9.30pm* ₹

Bhojohori Manna: This restaurant forms part of the Hati Bagan Star Screen complex (the first Bengali cinema). Great place to try regional cuisine. *noon-10pm* ₹₹

Sufi Palace: Mughlai biryani restaurant close to MG Road Metro station. The chicken *reshmi kebab* is a classic. *noon-11pm* ₹₹₹

National Economic Restaurant: Dirt-cheap diner opened in 1920 and never updated. It only does tea, eggs and toast. As if nothing else were needed. *7.30am-9pm* ₹

Alipore & Ballygunge

SOUTH KOLKATA'S HISTORIC HAUNTS AND DAPPER DISTRICTS

TOP TIP
In addition to being closed on Mondays, like most sights in Kolkata, many of the art galleries throughout the city often close at the slightest hint of a celebration or religious holiday.

Many of the temples and villages that existed when the East India Company's ships first docked in Kolkata were located to the south. These included Kalighat Temple, although the current iteration was built in 1809. The Alipore area of Kolkata was the site of many colonial-era buildings, including a jail that now serves as the powerful Alipore Museum, which highlights the Indian Independence movement's struggles and sacrifices in chilling detail.

But it's much more than history that makes South Kolkata special. There are green spaces aplenty, including the pleasant grounds of the Agri-Horticultural Society and, further south in Ballygunge, Rabindra Sarovar lake and park. Ballygunge is the city's hipster central, with a buzzing cafe culture, great shopping and dozens of small, subversive art galleries. Stick around long enough to take a deep dive into the world of Bengali cuisine on a personalised cooking class in a family home.

The Green Lungs

A verdant escape from the bustle

One striking thing about southern Kolkata is that it's greener than other parts of the city, Maidan aside. Some of the spaces have been lovingly preserved and tended for centuries,

GETTING AROUND

Distances are much greater between the sights of southern Kolkata than other neighbourhoods in the city. Getting from one place to another may require taking an autorickshaw or using a rideshare app (wait times are rarely longer than five minutes). Ballygunge, however, is Kolkata's most walkable neighbourhood. Its pavements are mostly even, accessible and clean. The Metro's Blue Line runs down the middle of southern Kolkata. To save money on transport, take it to the stop nearest your destination and then get an autorickshaw onwards. Kalighat Metro station connects to the tram network, which serves southern Ballygunge and Golpark.

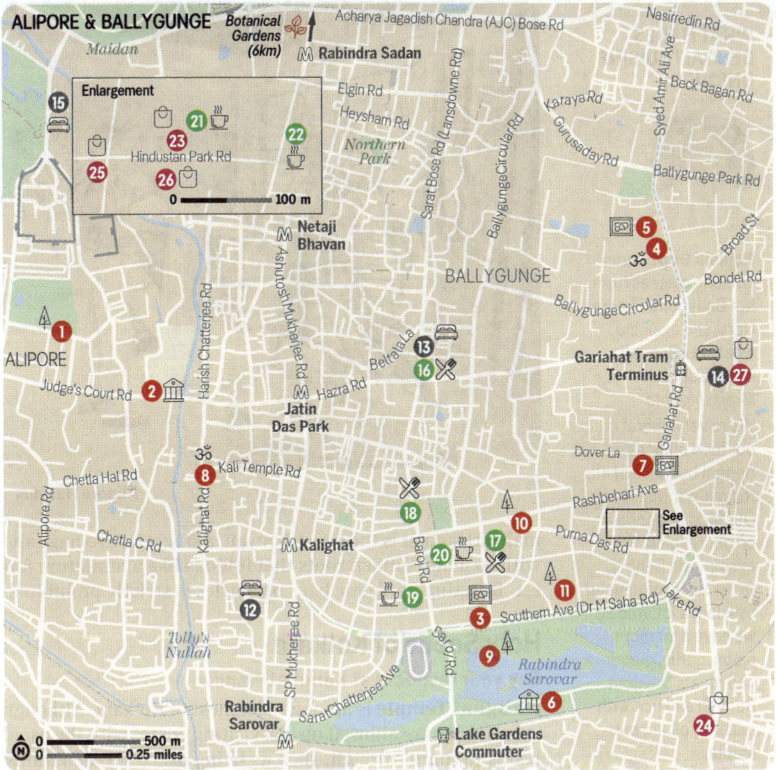

SIGHTS
1 Agri-Horticultural Society
2 Alipore Museum
3 Birla Academy of Art & Culture
4 Birla Mandir
5 CIMA
6 Durga Museum
7 Experimenter
8 Kalighat Temple
9 Rabindra Sarovar
10 Triangular Park
11 Vivekananda Park

SLEEPING
12 Bubble Beds Kolkata
13 Corner Courtyard
14 Ivy House
15 Taj Bengal

EATING
16 Corner Courtyard
17 Kolkata Rajbari
18 Tamarind

DRINKING & NIGHTLIFE
19 Art Café
20 Café by the Lane
21 Cup eBong
22 Marbella's

SHOPPING
23 Byloom
24 Dakshinapan Shopping Centre
25 Made in Bengal
26 Sienna
27 Weaver's Studio

including the gardens of the **Agri-Horticultural Society** *(₹100)*, with entrance on Belvedere Rd only. Founded in 1820, it is set over 30 acres with a miniature lake and a beautiful rose garden at its core, a welcome addition to Kolkata's fragrance palette.

Across the river, 3.5 miles south of Howrah, lie the **Botanical Gardens** *(bsi.gov.in; ₹100)*, officially called Acharya Jagadish Chandra Bose Indian Botanic Garden. The gardens are ideal for birdwatching and walking, with over 12,000 plant species. Highlights include the Cactus House and the ruins of Roxburgh House, built for botanist William Roxburgh. The

WHAT MAKES BENGALI CUISINE UNIQUE?

Rajashi Gupta runs cooking classes from her Ballygunge home. Here, she examines what sets Bengali cuisine apart. *@rajashigupta*

We're very liberal in our food choices in Bengal because of all the many influences. Our food depends on our religion. For example, in Bengal, we've been influenced by Islam a lot. And so we have a lot more onion, garlic, ginger and meats like goat. But fish and rice with mustard oil are our staple.

In Bengal, we have a unique way to serve our thalis, offering one thing at a time, instead of having everything in bowls. It goes: rice, dhal, fry, vegetable, fish or meat and then, after the meal, we give chutney and poppadom last, because we believe it's good for digestion.

SUPRABHAT/SHUTTERSTOCK

Alipore Museum

main attraction is the Great Banyan, a single tree so huge and with so many sunken roots that it looks like a miniature forest. Bringing in plastic bags or bottles is strictly prohibited.

Holy Seeds of Kolkata

Pay your respects at Kalighat Mandir

Kalighat Temple is among the holiest in Kolkata. Although non-Hindus are allowed inside, visiting comes with the usual hoops to jump through, such as being asked for 'donations' and finding a place to safely stash your shoes (the stalls left of the entrance will let you store them in exchange for buying a ₹20 garland of hibiscus flowers to offer inside). Once inside you'll have to join the serpentine queue and wait, along with the devout.

Kitchen Classics

Bengali cooking classes at Triangular Park

There's no better way to learn all about Bengali cuisine than in the kitchen of a private home. Near **Triangular Park** in Ballygunge, **Rajashi Gupta** *(@rajashigupta)* opens her kitchen up to the world to impart her wisdom in the ways of the local flavours. Rajashi runs two types of classes. The

EATING IN SOUTH KOLKATA: BEST RESTAURANTS

Tamarind: Specialising in South Indian dishes, Tamarind does chicken *Chettinad* and *kothu paratha* as well as anywhere down south. *noon-9.30pm* ₹₹₹

Kolkata Rajbari: One of Kolkata's top restaurants for quality Bengali fare such as *chingri malai* (prawn curry) and Bengali-style thalis. *noon-11pm* ₹₹₹

Tollygunge Club: The uber-upscale Tollygunge has a handful of air-conditioned, elegant restaurants and bars. There is a strict dress code here. *5am-11pm* ₹₹₹

Corner Courtyard: If you're in the mood for something less spice-centric, the decent Italian pasta dishes and pizzas here will be most welcome. *noon-10pm* ₹₹₹

'basic' is a two-hour class where you will learn to cook a dhal, a vegetable or meat dish (depending on visitor preference) and either Indian bread or rice. 'Special' classes last around four hours and include instruction on making dhal, two different types of vegetable or meat dishes, chutney, rice and a handmade bread. Classes end with a sit-down meal and are kept to a maximum of three guests, although Rajashi's home kitchen can accommodate groups of up to five people, at a push. Book directly via her Instagram.

Step Behind Bars

Confronting the past at Alipore Museum

A cheerful-looking red building with green wooden window shutters and upbeat music on entry, **Alipore Museum** *(independencemuseum.in; ₹30)* does a good job of disguising the fact that this was a prison until 2019. Established in 1906, it once housed dissidents who didn't fall in line with the British Raj's way of thinking. Today, the prison and its grounds are a vast, open museum. You can visit the cells, including that of Jawaharlal Nehru (India's first PM), Netaji and other exponents of Indian Independence. The gallows are particularly chilling. People deemed enemies of the British state were condemned on the small death row before being hanged. Other prisoners, kept in a building overlooking the yard, were forced to witness this ultimate punitive measure. A gallows scaffold remains in place.

The sprawling complex also contains an art gallery, a Police Museum showcasing weapons used in the armed resistance, and a variety of exhibitions dotted throughout the various prison buildings, including one detailing the history of plots, assassination attempts (including a book bomb that never exploded) and uprisings during the Raj era.

Kolkata's Cutting Edge

Art in southern Kolkata

Arguably the city's best contemporary art gallery is **CIMA** *(cimaartindia.com; free)*, located on the 2nd floor of a building a minute's walk north of **Birla Mandir temple**. The gallery's exhibitions change regularly, usually dividing space between hot names on the Indian art scene with the works of Indian old masters such as Amrita Sher-Gil, Benode Behari Mukherjee and B Prabha.

Ballygunge is dotted with smaller galleries, the primary one being **Birla Academy of Art & Culture** *(birlaart.com; ₹20)*. It showcases annual

ARTISTIC EXPRESSION IN INDIA

One of the finest collections of post-Independence Indian art is held at Delhi's **National Gallery of Modern Art** (p75), plus Mumbai's **Jehangir Art Gallery** (p681). Diverse themes and eras of Indian art are explored in Bengaluru's **Karnataka Chitrakala Parishath** (p802).

SHOPPING IN BALLYGUNGE

If you're looking to buy top-quality Bengali textiles, look no further than the excellent boutique stores of Ballygunge and Golpark.

Weaver's Studio: For handmade textiles. The clothing range is inventive and chic, while always working directly with artisans.

Byloom: Hindustan Park Rd is elevated by its high-quality crafts stores and cafes, most notably Byloom, which has some beautiful saris and kurta.

Made in Bengal: Boutique specialising mainly in women's clothing such as saris, but also selling handcrafted purses, jewellery and artwork.

Dakshinapan Shopping Centre: State-government initiative with official stalls selling handicrafts from states across India.

Sienna: Primarily a cafe, but the well-curated attached boutique sells a wonderful selection of homewares, local food products and clothing.

WHY I LOVE KOLKATA

Paul Stafford, Lonely Planet writer

For a traffic-choked megacity, Kolkata retains a surprising warmth that always astounds me, cropping up at the least expected of moments. You have to work for it though; this is not the kind of place that tells you how it wants to be loved. It's a city for the senses: the rough red clay of the *bhar* chai cups; the sweet and spicy melange of an *aam chop* (mango fritter) from a street-food vendor whose family has made them this way for over a century; the blare of a foghorn as boats swash across the Hooghly in the early morning smog. Each urban scene is filled with optimism and life, where heritage and modernity juxtapose in endlessly endearing ways.

exhibitions of regional works. Look for the giant statue of Krishna down the alley to the left (west) of the building. The biggest buzz continues to be around **Experimenter** *(experimenter.in; prices vary by exhibition)*, which has been breaking the mould with multiple-format contemporary art exhibitions.

Work & Play

Drink in the Ballygunge cafe culture

As one of Kolkata's more affluent neighbourhoods, southern Ballygunge, along with neighbouring Golpark, is the ideal place to stay for visitors familiar with Kolkata who are looking for a quieter, cleaner slice of the city. A proliferation of galleries, parks and boutiques is set around leafy, clean streets that are enhanced with occasional bursts of street art. The best place to experience the energy of the area is at one of the many cafes. By day, they make for stylish places to meet with friends or get some work done, while at night, many transform into bars, with food service and live music. Some, like Café by the Lane, even provide the instruments.

Birds & Durgas

A walk around Rabindra Sarovar

South of Ballygunge, the verdant escape of **Rabindra Sarovar** forms what is arguably Kolkata's best park. It folds around a large central lake, whose islands harbour colonies of squawking cormorants, while colourful kingfishers perch on branches around the edge. The sculpted park's walkways pass rowing clubs and sports fields. On the lake's southern shore, the **Durga Museum** *(free)* displays some of the largest and most artful surviving Durga effigies from the Durga Puja. Immediately to the north is **Vivekananda Park**, where every square inch of grass is given over to cricket pitches and batting cages.

DRINKING IN BALLYGUNGE: BEST CAFES

Marbella's: This cute little LGBTIQ-friendly cafe has an elegant greenhouse serving tasty shakes and a good kombucha. *10.30am-11pm*

Art Café: Creative wicker-ceiling fixtures adorn this stylish hangout. The *momos* and other Tibetan dishes have inspired a dedicated local clientele. *noon-9pm*

Cup eBong: Located behind Byloom, there's a cosy vibe in this cafe. Popular for its pork sausages (difficult to find in Bengal) and fried breakfasts. *9am-10pm*

Café by the Lane: Kitschy indoor decor with an 'icons of rock music' theme. The piano is free to play. *11am-2am Wed-Sat, from 9am Sun-Tue*

Places We Love to Stay

₹ Budget ₹₹ Midrange ₹₹₹ Top End

Chowringhee & Central Kolkata

Map p414

Shaw Guest House ₹ There's a healthy collection of good-value accommodation near the Motherhouse. Shaw remains the best for its spartan yet clean rooms.

Sunflower Guest House ₹ One of the better low-budget choices near Park St, in a historic building.

Siamton Inn ₹₹ Clean, spacious rooms in a modern hotel. Free breakfast and a (very small) gym add value. Ask for a room on an upper floor.

Red Arrow Residency ₹₹ Located in the last building you come to down a side street, Red Arrow is clean and free from most traffic noise.

Hotel Ichamati ₹₹ Tucked into the third storey of a multipurpose building, the rooms are small but surprisingly comfortable for the price.

Oberoi Grand ₹₹₹ Kolkata's best hotel. A classic old-school accommodation with an evening turndown service. It closed in 2024 for renovations; reopening was set for late 2026.

Elgin Fairlawn ₹₹₹ Built in 1783, the Elgin Fairlawn is a delightfully anachronistic slice of Raj-era hospitality. Breakfasts on the veranda are particularly charming.

Kenilworth ₹₹₹ A stunning heritage building overlooking a fairy-light-strewn garden. Some rooms are in a modern annexe.

Park Hotel ₹₹₹ In an unbeatable location on Park St if you're looking for nightlife, with bars, restaurants and clubs in the same building.

Astor ₹₹₹ The black-and-white photos inside the Astor emphasise that this hotel, located in a beautiful heritage property, has a storied history.

Northern Kolkata

Map p433

City Central Hostel ₹ A few blocks from College Square, this is one of the few truly decent hostels in Kolkata if your budget is tight. Dorms are mixed.

Polo Floatel ₹₹ Those keen to get up close with the Hooghly can spend a night on the river in this moored boatel. Tastefully designed, with a great restaurant.

Broadway Hotel ₹₹ With painted wooden shutters and a colonial-era carapace, this decent lower-midrange hotel also has its own restaurant and bar.

Calcutta Bungalow ₹₹₹ An impeccably preserved piece of architectural heritage – from the original brickwork to the pilasters, this is one of Kolkata's most charming properties.

LaLiT Great Eastern ₹₹₹ Luxurious pools, architecture, furnishings and interior design are all reasons why the LaLiT has been among central Kolkata's top hotels since 1840.

Alipore & Ballygunge

Map p437

Bubble Beds Kolkata ₹ A great budget option close to Ballygunge, with shared, female-only and male-only dorms, plus a small rooftop garden.

Corner Courtyard ₹₹ More than a restaurant, the Corner Courtyard is also an excellent hotel with a cheery interior style in a building built in 1904.

Taj Bengal ₹₹₹ One of the few Kolkata properties that feels like it might not be in a megacity. Luxury befitting the brand and fantastic restaurants.

Ivy House ₹₹₹ A beautifully designed boutique hotel on a peaceful Ballygunge street, with four-poster beds and breakfast included.

Outer Kolkata

ITC Royal Bengal ₹₹₹ Kolkata's 'it' hotel opened in 2019 and has gone on to become one of India's premier luxury stays in the ensuing years.

Rajbari Bawali ₹₹₹ To the south of Kolkata, this beautifully restored heritage property was built around 250 years ago by the Zamindars of Bengal.

Raajkutir ₹₹₹ Over towards the New Town area of Kolkata among some of the city's finest modern hotels, Raajkutir blends traditional style with modern amenities.

ARPAN GOLAY/SHUTTERSTOCK

For places to stay in West Bengal, see p475

Above: Darjeeling (p461); Right: Japanese Peace Pagoda (p465), Darjeeling

Researched by
Paul Stafford

West Bengal

MOTHBALLED CAPITALS AND HIMALAYAN ADVENTURES

From southern mangrove swamps to northern mountain forests, West Bengal is a place of immense natural beauty. Dig down and you'll unearth a fascinating cultural heritage.

West Bengal is among India's most geographically diverse states. Dipping its mangrove-covered toes into the warm Indian Ocean in the bulbous south, there are watery wildernesses aplenty. As the state becomes narrower to the north it is almost cleaved in half by the bifurcating Ganges, then squeezed between the borders of Nepal, Bhutan and Bangladesh until it rises thousands of metres into the Himalaya massif, offering glimpses of the world's highest mountains.

RAHUL D'SILVA/SHUTTERSTOCK

Rivers are common features, and major obstacles, throughout West Bengal, historically fragmenting the state so that some regions have a closer kinship linguistically and culturally with neighbouring countries. You'll see beautiful examples of Buddhist monasteries, Islamic mosques, Christian churches and Hindu temples. West Bengal's cuisine is just as diverse, with mustard- and coconut-infused prawn curries in the south and hearty *momo* dumplings and *thukpa* soups in the north.

Despite all that diversity, Bengalis possess a unique sense of identity. Long considered an independent-minded state, it was once the Mughal empire's wealthiest province, its Murshidabad palaces attracting the attention of European trading companies. The rest is history. Discover it for yourself: the creative university town of Shantiniketan, the terracotta-temple-rich streets of Bishnupur, tigers and rhinos in the forests and the charming hill towns of the north all welcome visitors in and send them away awed.

THE MAIN AREAS

THE HOOGHLY
Heritage architecture and religious legacies. **p446**

MURSHIDABAD
Riverside ruins of a former capital. **p453**

DARJEELING
Tea, mountains and monasteries. **p461**

Find Your Way

Most people arrive in West Bengal at Kolkata or Bagdogra Airports. From both, railway lines and roads fan out across the Indian subcontinent, making it easy to get off the beaten path with the minimum of hassle.

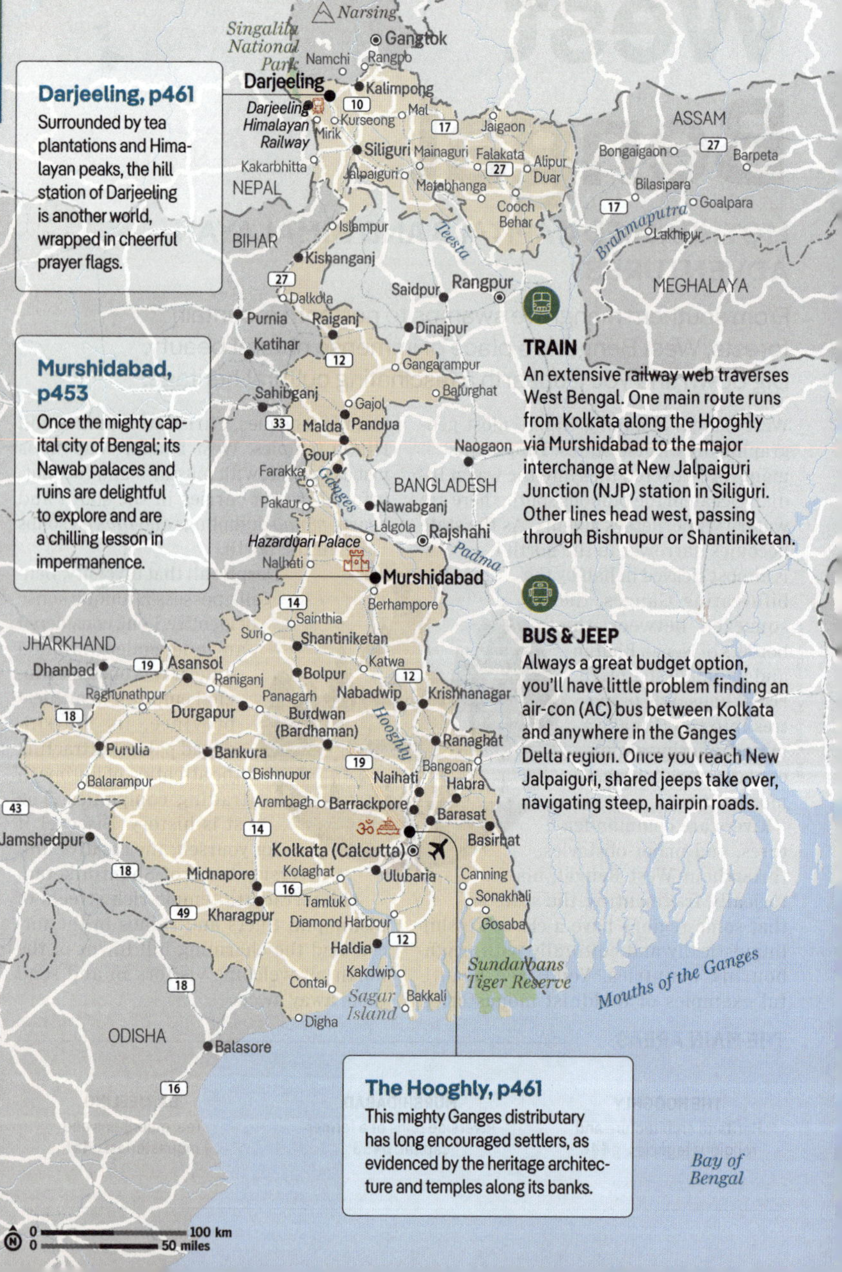

Darjeeling, p461

Surrounded by tea plantations and Himalayan peaks, the hill station of Darjeeling is another world, wrapped in cheerful prayer flags.

Murshidabad, p453

Once the mighty capital city of Bengal; its Nawab palaces and ruins are delightful to explore and are a chilling lesson in impermanence.

TRAIN

An extensive railway web traverses West Bengal. One main route runs from Kolkata along the Hooghly via Murshidabad to the major interchange at New Jalpaiguri Junction (NJP) station in Siliguri. Other lines head west, passing through Bishnupur or Shantiniketan.

BUS & JEEP

Always a great budget option, you'll have little problem finding an air-con (AC) bus between Kolkata and anywhere in the Ganges Delta region. Once you reach New Jalpaiguri, shared jeeps take over, navigating steep, hairpin roads.

The Hooghly, p461

This mighty Ganges distributary has long encouraged settlers, as evidenced by the heritage architecture and temples along its banks.

DEBARUP/SHUTTERSTOCK

Lamahatta Eco Park (p473), Tukdah

Plan Your Time

Some visitors head straight for the mountains; others tour the Sundarbans Tiger Reserve and move on. But spare a thought for the overlooked gems in the middle of the state.

Time for Tigers & Tea

- Using Kolkata as a base, take a tour of **Sundarbans Tiger Reserve** (p450) to look for Bengal tigers, then spend a day exploring heritage sites along the **Hooghly** (p446). Hop on a train to **Murshidabad** (p453) to gawp at the opulence of the **Hazarduari Palace** (p453). Jump in a jeep at Siliguri to reach the cooler climes of **Darjeeling** (p461) and a warming cup of tea.

Two-Week Full Spread

- Take the long way north, visiting the terracotta temples of **Bishnupur** (451), then kick back with the creatives in **Shantiniketan** (p458).Explore the Sultanate of Bengal's ruined capitals at **Gaur** and **Pandua** (p459). Once in the Himalayas, visit the historic **Makaibari Tea Estate** (p464) near Kurseong, then take a five-day trek along the utterly magnificent **Singalila Ridge** (p470).

SEASONAL HIGHLIGHTS

SPRING

The climate in the mountains is warm and dry, perfect for watching the first flush being picked on the tea estates.

SUMMER

Intense heat precedes torrential downpours, which make getting around challenging. Wildlife can be more active.

AUTUMN

Durga Puja takes over in September or October, before the ideal six-month window to visit the Sundarbans begins.

WINTER

The best time to visit lowland West Bengal, when temperatures rarely break above 25°C. The busiest time for domestic tourism.

The Hooghly

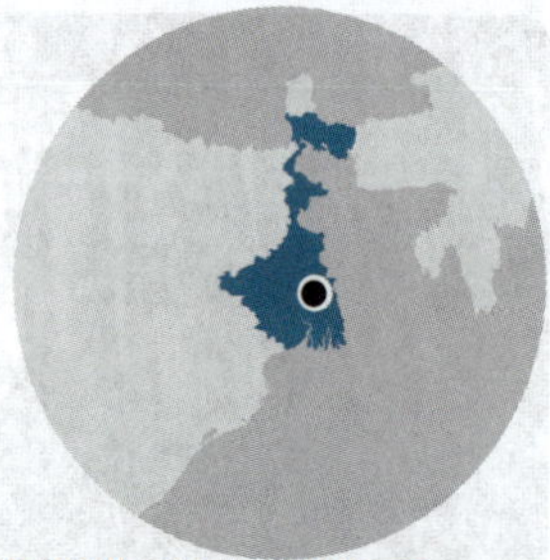

HERITAGE ARCHITECTURE | TERRACOTTA TEMPLES | WILDLIFE CRUISES

GETTING AROUND

Trains are by far the most convenient way to get up and down the Hooghly River. Starting from Howrah Junction Railway Station, one to three trains depart for Bandel Junction (from ₹50; one hour) every hour. This stopping service visits Serampore, Hooghly and Chandan Nagar stations along the way, each of which provides access to one or more of the sights detailed here. From Bandel, you'll need to hire a *toto* or an autorickshaw to get between places (₹600 for around three hours). For Chandannagar and Serampore, shared autorickshaws (₹20) ferry back and forth between the stations and the main sights.

As the Ganges River approaches West Bengal, it begins to fragment into the world's largest river delta. Among this mess of waterways, the Hooghly River proved the most attractive and navigable option to traders. A series of riverfront towns north of Kolkata initially formed when various trading companies and crowns, keen to cut out middlemen in the Middle East, sought permission from the ruling Mughals and, later, the Nawabs of Bengal to build warehouses and trading outposts. This region of India, rich in spices, Bengal silk, indigo and saltpetre (used as a food preservative as well as in gunpowder production), attracted the French to Chandannagar, the Portuguese to Bandel, the Danes to Serampore and (although little remains of their presence) the Dutch to Chinsurah. The ensuing trade also created a wealthy local mercantile class. The medley of historic heritage buildings left behind covers all major religions with plenty of intriguing architecture.

Lotus Domes & Terracotta Temples

Admiring Hanseswari Mandir's singular style

Above the rural town of Bansberia rise the 13 sharp-tipped lotus *sikharas* (spires) of **Hanseswari Mandir** *(free)*, a Hindu temple presided over by the goddess Kali. The spires are weathered so that it looks as though the petals have begun to rot. Around to the left of the main structure is the broad sweep of terracotta panelling that forms Vasudev Temple. Quite distinct from neighbouring Hanseswari, it's built in a historic Bengali style seen most commonly in Bishnupur. Negotiate a rate (around ₹600) with *toto* drivers outside Bandel station for a round-trip journey including Hanseswari, Bandel and Hooghly Imambara, ending back at Hooghly station.

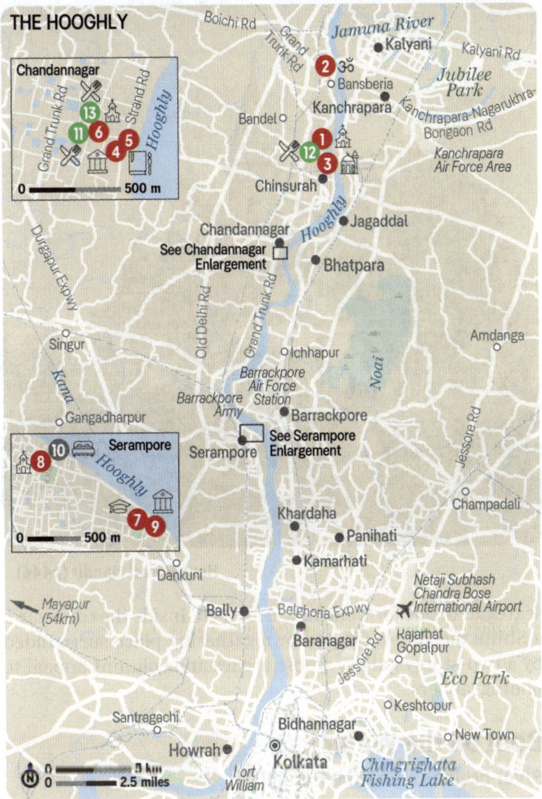

SIGHTS
1 Bandel Basilica
2 Hanseswari Mandir
3 Hooghly Imambara
4 Institut de Chandernagor
5 Jora Ghat
6 Sacred Heart Catholic Church
7 Serampore College
8 St Olav's Church
9 William Carey Museum & Library

SLEEPING
10 Denmark Tavern

EATING
11 Adda
12 Barfi
13 Cafe Destination
see 10 Denmark Tavern

A Christian God Amid the Devas

River views from Bandel Church

The marble cladding on **Bandel Basilica** *(bandelchurch.com)* gives it the air of a modern edifice, but this was in fact the first major church to be built in Bengal. The Portuguese, who were well ahead of their European counterparts in the international trade game, settled here as early as the 1530s. The only clear reminder of this is this church, started in 1599, a full 91 years before the British were to take root in the area further south. There's a nautical theme running throughout the church, particularly in the chapel to Our Lady of the Happy Voyage. Head up the tower rooftop for views of the Hooghly.

TOP TIP

It's possible to visit all sights along the Hooghly on a self-guided day trip from Kolkata. Set out early (7am) from Howrah, heading to Bandel Junction first, then work your way gradually back south to ensure you can make it back to Kolkata before sunset.

An Indo-Saracenic Mosque

Climb the towers of Hooghly Imambara

Roughly 1.5km south of Bandel Basilica is the stately **Hooghly Imambara** *(₹20),* completed in 1861. Its facade is dominated by a handsome twin-towered clock. Climb the *paan*-speckled stairs to the top of a tower for views from the building's courtyard to the boat-dotted Hooghly. The two towers are

THE GANGASAGAR MELA

Follow the Hooghly River (a distributary of the sacred Ganges) south of Kolkata and you will soon come to the Bay of Bengal. At this confluence of great water landmarks, on the south side of Sagar Island, the world's second-largest gathering of Hindus takes place in what is called the **Gangasagar Mela**. However, while you'd have to wait between four and 12 years for the largest holy gathering, the Kumbh Mela, to take place, Gangasagar's event is an annual one, occurring in the middle of January each year around the 14th and 15th. Some 4.5 million pilgrims (with this number said to be rising rapidly every year) descend upon **Kapil Muni Ashram** to bathe in the holy estuarine waters.

PAUL STAFFORD

Hanseswari Mandir (p446)

segregated: one for women, one for men. Inside the courtyard, a Shiite mosque is fronted by a gathering place surrounded by a two-storey gallery whose arches and columns appeal to photographers.

Boat on the Water

River cruises along the Hooghly

If you've got some cash to spare, multiday boat cruises turn a trip up the Hooghly into a decadent excursion. Highly recommended is the seven-night Historic Hooghly cruise with **Assam Bengal Navigation** *(assambengalnavigation.com)*, which heads from Kolkata to Farakka (for visiting Gaur and Pandua), where the Hooghly branches from the Ganges. **Antara Cruises** *(antaracruises.com)* runs an alternative in spring, which heads only as far north as Mayapur, unless you want to bed in for 19 nights, in which case they have a cruise from Kolkata to Varanasi each October. For something shorter (and at around ₹10, much cheaper), there are many passenger ferry crossings all the way up the river. These include the ferries from Serampore to Barrackpore, and from Chandannagar to Jagaddal, which would make for fun picnic excursions to break up your trip.

WATER WORLDS

As a tropical country with a healthy amount of monsoon rainfall, plus the water basin for the world's highest mountain range, India is no stranger to waterways. In particular, there are memorable multiday trips on houseboats in the backwaters of Kerala at **Alappuzha** (p897).

The French Connection

Explore Chandannagar's French-inflected riverfront

Chandannagar's pretty waterfront promenade is overlooked by a series of heritage buildings painted banana yellow and now housing colleges and branches of local civil administration. The focal point is between **Sacred Heart Catholic Church**, built in 1875, and the heritage arch of **Jora Ghat**, which is stared down by a statue of Mahatma Gandhi. Nearby, **Institut de Chandernagor** *(₹20)* fills the former French Governor's superb mansion. The museum portion that is open to visitors gives interesting historic insight into the main European players along the Hooghly, as well as presenting a dusty assemblage of period furniture and trinkets devoid of explanation.

Colleges & Churches

A wander through Serampore

Jute and jaggery are two long-standing industries in Serampore, 25km north of Kolkata. Sat next to a large jute factory, the colonnaded portico of **Serampore College** *(serampore college.ac.in)* rings with the sounds of students playing cricket and football on the adjacent field. To visit the **William Carey Museum & Library** *(free)* here, you must first obtain a permit from the principal's office. Apply online ahead of time via the college website or head up to the 1st floor of the office building by the eastern gate on arrival. The museum explores William Carey's life. The British Baptist came to India in 1793 and worked in an indigo factory before eventually setting up the college in Serampore. Get a shared autorickshaw to cover the dusty 1km north to find the portico-fronted **St Olav's Church** (closed) and the renovated **Denmark Tavern**.

HISTORY ON THE HOOGHLY

It all started with Vasco da Gama's first successful voyage around Africa's Cape of Good Hope, whereby he reached Calicut (now called Kozhikode) on India's Kerala coast on 20 May 1498. His arrival opened the floodgates for a series of European-led expeditions in search of a more lucrative alternative to the spice and silk trade via the Middle East. Bengal's eminence as a producer of both, plus its ease of access to those with ships, kickstarted a wave of colonisation that immeasurably changed the region. The Portuguese were already building their first church at Bandel before the British East India Corporation (EIC) was even officially founded in 1600.

EATING & DRINKING ALONG THE HOOGHLY: OUR PICKS

Cafe Destination: Travel-themed Chandannagar cafe serving tasty pizzas and artfully made coffees and mocktails. *11am-11pm Mon-Sat, to 4pm Sun* ₹₹

Adda: This charming coffeeshop behind Chandannagar's Sacred Heart Catholic Church has good coffee and snacks such as popcorn chicken. *11am-9.30pm* ₹

Denmark Tavern: Famed restaurant with a diverse menu, with Bengali, Chinese, Italian and hot takes on Danish cuisine. *noon-9pm* ₹₹₹

Barfi: Don't be put off by the name, for the Bengali dishes served at this whimsical place near Bandel Basilica are top notch. *noon-10pm* ₹₹

Beyond the Hooghly

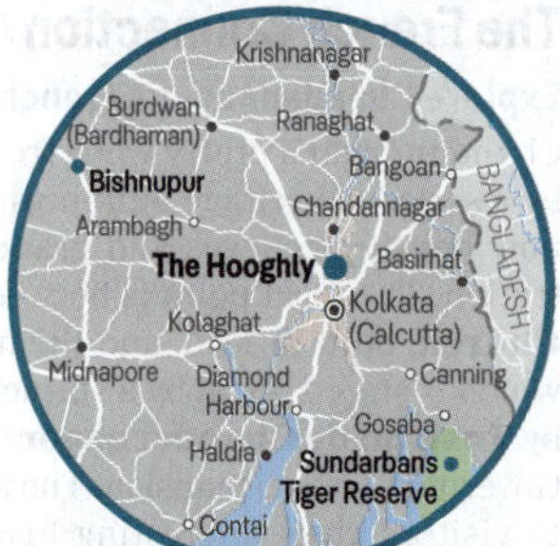

Search for elusive Bengal tigers through dense mangroves and hop between some of India's finest terracotta temples.

Places

Sundarbans Tiger Reserve p450
Bishnupur p451

The southern reaches of West Bengal offer plenty of unique day-trip experiences from the Kolkata region. In the southeast, branches of the Ganges River feed into a delta whose thick Sundarbans mangrove forests have long posed challenges to humans. But they provide a vital lifeline to wildlife, particularly for overhunted prize game mammals such as Bengal tigers. Nowadays, rapid modes of transport and modern engineering have made the once-insurmountable rivers no more challenging to cross than a border between friendly states. But as long ago as the 7th century CE, the Malla rajas in Bishnupur were exhibiting creative and architectural ingenuity of their own while building their intricately carved terracotta temples.

Sundarbans Tiger Reserve

TIME FROM KOLKATA: 4HR

Swamp cats

All the silt washed down from the Himalaya is dumped into an alluvial delta that has given rise to India's largest expanse of mangrove-tangled swampland. It's no surprise that a place so inhospitable for humans harbours the largest surviving tiger population on the planet. A UNESCO World Heritage Site since 1987, **Sundarbans Tiger Reserve** *(Sundarbans National Park; sundarbantigerreserve.org)* protects a 1330-sq-km chunk of India's share of the huge mangrove forest, with the majority lying over the border in Bangladesh.

But if you thought that all that black, white and tan would stand out nicely against the verdant backdrop,

THEY'RE GRRRREAT!

Seeing tigers in the wild is the ultimate bucket-list experience in India. Your best chance of spotting one is in Bandhavgarh and Pench National Parks, and Kanha and Panna Tiger Reserves. All four are in **Madhya Pradesh** (p587).

EATING IN BISHNUPUR: OUR PICKS

Taste Ride: All aboard for this quirky Bengali restaurant, with excellent paneer and chicken curries and friendly service. *11am-10pm* ₹₹

Fire & Ice: The menu takes its cues from Mexico (burritos and quesadillas), Tibet *(momos)* and the USA (burgers and fried chicken). *10am-10pm* ₹₹

Aami Bangali Bishnupur: The Bengali thalis are excellent here, served in a space overlooked by murals about the city's heritage. *noon-10pm* ₹₹₹

Hotel Annapurna Restaurant: Simple restaurant serving tandoori, Indian and continental dishes, such as butter chicken. *2-11pm* ₹₹₹

think again: Bengal tigers are notoriously difficult to spot. The roughly 101 individuals thought to exist in Sundarbans Tiger Reserve (as of a 2025 survey) spend most of their time deep in the wilderness and are spied most commonly taking a drink from, or swimming in, the delta's myriad channels.

Regardless, the voyage out of Kolkata, one of the world's most polluted cities, into the serenity of the mangroves is part of the charm of Sundarbans trips. And saltwater crocodiles, gharials, snakes, kingfishers and Ganges river dolphins are possible sightings on boat safaris, which stick to a limited range of waterways, often shared by dozens of other tour boats. While this hampers the chance of any sightings, it helps to decrease human interference in these fragile habitats.

Within the park, a couple of worthwhile out-of-the-boat experiences include **Sajnekhali**, with its **observation tower** and the **Mangrove Interpretation Centre**. Note the **shrine to Bonbibi** as you enter the walkway. The 'lady of the forest' is a guardian spirit, worshipped by both Hindus and Muslims for protection against the demon Dakkhin Rai, who assumes the form of a tiger to attack human beings. **Dobanki Watch Tower** is located deeper inside the mangroves. A 450m-long elevated walkway through the mangrove canopy offers the best chance to see a wider range of wildlife such as chitals (spotted deer), monitor lizards, horseshoe crabs and wild boar.

October to February is the best time to visit, with tiger sightings anecdotally highest in March and April. But most people leave having never seen one. Sundarbans Tiger Reserve is closed on Tuesdays. Due to the considerable travel time to get to the national park from Kolkata, tours that stay for at least one night are recommended.

Bishnupur

TIME FROM KOLKATA 3HR

Silken verse at a Baluchari workshop

Bishnupur is the home of authentic Baluchari silk, where saris sporting depictions of mythological scenes are still woven by hand. The staff at **ANUVAB** *(free)* openly welcome visitors to look around their production rooms. Head down the passageway and turn right into the garden where the clunk and clack of six working Jacquard looms is joined by the tap-tap-tap of the pattern designer hammering out the next story designs as the artisans create these lustrous garments. Photos are encouraged and you can check out and buy the finished works in the store at the front.

GETTING AROUND

Reach Sundarbans Tiger Reserve on public transport from Kolkata via Canning and Gosaba on buses and local ferries. Budget a whole day. Organised tours will have you there in four hours, while also arranging the national park boat trip. Bishnupur is served by two daily trains from Shalimar and Howrah. Take a tuk-tuk *(₹100)* from the station to Ras Mancha. When ready to tour the other temples, hire a *toto* or an autorickshaw locally *(₹400 for three hours)*.

SUNDARBANS TOURS

Tours include accommodation on a safari boat or at camps on Satjelia Island. Ask in advance about additional fees.

West Bengal Tourism Development Corporation (WBTDCL): State-government tourism agency with four monthly tours from Kolkata. Packages from ₹12,000 per person. *(wbtdcl.wbtourismgov.in)*

Vivada Cruise: Luxury two-night trips once a month October to December. From ₹41,000 per person (twin share). *(vivadacruise.com)*

Tour de Sundarbans: One- and two-night tours, staying in a lovely ecovillage. From ₹6500 per person. *(tourdesundarbans.com)*

Sundarban Eco Trip: Good value tours from Kolkata from ₹5000 per person. *(sundarbanecotrip.com)*

Sunderban Tiger Camp: If you're travelling DIY, this Satjelia Island resort runs boat trips directly from the property. Prices vary. *(waxpolhotels.com/sunderban-tiger-camp-dayapur)*

TOP EXPERIENCE

Historic Bishnupur

From the 7th to 18th centuries, the Malla rajas of Bishnupur ordered the construction of scores of brick temples covered in terracotta panelling. The unique architectural style blends Odishan, Islamic and Bengali sensibilities. The best work, mostly from the 16th and 17th centuries, sees the terracotta panels carved with painstaking detail, depicting pastiches of life alongside stories from Hindu epics and fables.

PRADIP GHOSH/SHUTTERSTOCK

Shyam Rai Temple

The Stout Opener

All trips begin at **Ras Mancha Temple**, where you'll find the main ticket booth. Built in 1587, this temple has a broad pyramidal roof and three concentric square, bubble-domed galleries. At its core is a small shrine where idols may have been placed. Take a break at **Acharya Jogesh Chandra Purakriti Bhaban** *(₹25)*, aka the District Museum. The handsome red and yellow building houses 10th to 12th-century Vaishnavite statuary.

The Temple Cluster

Hire one of the *totos* outside to run the temple loop, beginning at **Shyam Rai Temple**, displaying Bishnupur's most impressive terracotta tile work, notably the Rama battle scenes above the three-door archways on the building's west side. **Jor Bangla Temple** (1655) looks like two ornamented houses glued together topped by a brick *charchala* central tower. Lower panels are rich in animal imagery. **Radhashyam Temple** (1758), with Radha-Krishna carvings on the south side, is nearby. Just north is the mottled, champagne-coloured **Lalji Temple** (1658), presided over by playful chipmunks.

Madan Mohan Temple (1694) has ornamentation exhibiting the finest detail of all, with dancing and party scenes from *Krishnalila* and the lower reaches of the west and east sides dedicated to birds.

TOP TIPS

- Tickets are available at Ras Mancha; they also cover access to Jor Bangla and Shyam Rai. Entry to the rest is free.
- Hire a *toto* from the temple zone (₹400 for three hours) to trundle around all the temples. Trips always follow the same route, starting at Ras Mancha.

PRACTICALITIES

- asikolkata.in
- ₹300
- 7am-5pm

Murshidabad

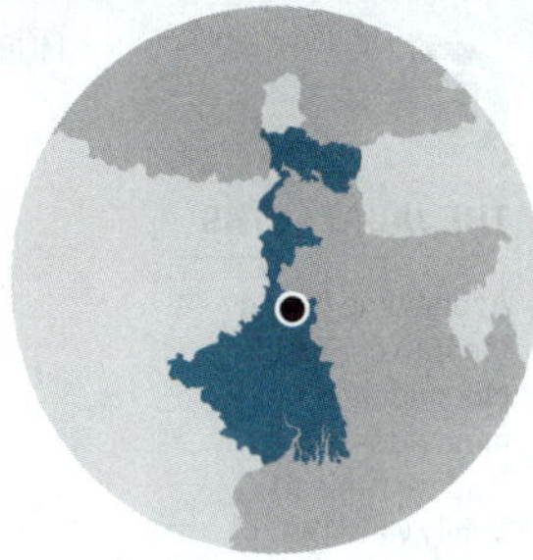

ROYAL PALACE | CITY RUINS | BENGALI HISTORY

Murshidabad was the last capital of an independent Bengal, from 1704 to 1757. The city is named after its first governor Murshid Quli Khan (one of the last truly loyal vassals to the Mughal emperor Muhammad Shah). Bengal's inherent wealth (it was the richest province in the Mughal empire at the time) propped up the ailing empire through its anarchic decline, until the East India Company seized de facto control of the region, thanks to the help of the Jain money-lenders, who effectively played kingmaker. Many of the stately Jain palaces, such as the House of Jagat Seth, are outdone only by the Nawab's opulent Hazarduari Palace. Nevertheless, during the 18th and 19th centuries, roaring trade imbued Murshidabad with the fabulous wealth that built the main sights on show today. Evidence of this former glory litters the streets, with the larger, modern city Berhampore, immediately to the south.

TOP TIP

Aim to visit Monday to Thursday. Hazarduari Palace is closed on Fridays and gets overcrowded on weekends, an issue common to sights throughout West Bengal. If you plan on staying overnight in the area, you'll find most of the better-value hotels south of Murshidabad in the contiguous city of Berhampore.

Fabulous Wealth

Discover Hazarduari Palace's excesses

Built between 1829 and 1837, magnificent **Hazarduari Palace** *(asiraiganj.in; ₹000)* is said to have 1000 doors, but it's the neoclassical synchronicity of this imperious building that strikes the viewer. Designed by the Scottish architect Duncan McLeod for the Nawab of Bengal, Mubarak Ali Khan II, it is

GETTING AROUND

Trains from Kolkata's Sealdah Station run to Murshidabad, where regular shared autorickshaws ply the road north, passing Hazarduari Palace as far as the House of Jagat Seth. It's possible to walk between sights, particularly those further north, although it's around 3km between Kathgola Bagan and Hazarduari Palace. For onward trains north, cross to the western side of the Hooghly River (which is also called Bhagirathi by locals) to Khagraghat Rd (near Berhampore), or to Azimganj Junction stations for trains north to Malda and New Jalpaiguri or south to Kolkata.

THE JAGAT SETHS

At one time during the 18th century, Murshidabad's most powerful (and wealthiest) family were the Marwari Oswal Jain financiers. Nawab of Bengal Alivardi Khan bestowed the title of Jagat Seths ('Bankers of the World') upon them in 1723, when they masterminded a way to safely send money from Bengal to Delhi, even when the Mughal empire was crumbling everywhere else. It was called the Hundi System. Before that, money was sent in physical form, as gold and silver pieces, which were risky to transport, particularly if having to pass through enemy territory. The Hundi System presaged modern banking by allowing deposits in local banks and the transfer of wealth merely by piece of paper, making it far harder to detect and catch couriers.

every inch the combination of British imperial immodesty and Bengali ambition.

Within lies a vast **museum collection** of Bengali and European relics, including a sedan chair that could be affixed to an elephant, cases of weaponry and antique furniture. The architectural pinnacle is **Durbar Hall**, the circular, dome-topped throne room. Another highlight is the **Musnud of the Nawabs**, a black-slate, 16-sided throne on which Robert Clive and Nawab Nazim of Bengal sat together in 1766, after the British wrested control of the region. As the palace itself attests, it was a most unusual power coup.

Facing the palace across a broad lawn that contains a slightly leaning **clock tower** and two arabesque Medina mosques is the 207m-long **Nizamat Imambara** (Bengal's largest). This Shiite ceremonial building was built during the reign of Nawab Mansur Ali Khan in 1847.

A Careful Family

Pry into a Jagat Seth's secret spaces

In the early days of trade with European powers, the rulers, traders and bankers of Bengal became fantastically wealthy. Much of that wealth is still on faded display in Murshidabad. The **House of Jagat Seth** *(₹150)* is the mansion built by Bengal State's wealthy bankers, who devised a system of payments that kept the ailing Mughal empire afloat. Follow the arrows through the main mansion, which has lost much of its sheen, into the warren of underground rooms, with their collections of porcelain, coins, weaponry, carved ivory and statuary. These apt, secretive spaces and their collections are indicative of a family who took great measures to protect their own and the Mughal's wealth.

DOCTORS PHOTOGRAPHY/SHUTTERSTOCKA

Katra Masjid

Grave of a Founding Father

Pink-hued remembrance at Katra Masjid

With two fortified octagonal corner towers and a soft, pink-hued brick frame, topped with multiple iced gem cupolas, **Katra Masjid** *(free)* is a rather beguiling mosque, built in 1723. The small structure on the eastern side of the courtyard is painted white (although white paint usually develops a tropical patina after a monsoon or two) and conceals the **grave of Murshid Quli Khan**, Murshidabad's founder. Guides usually loll about at the entrance (negotiate fees to around ₹50).

EATING IN MURSHIDABAD & BERHAMPORE: OUR PICKS

Hotel Hazarduari: This pleasant hotel restaurant (open to non-guests) does great Mughlai cuisine, with fragrant biryanis. *10am-11pm* ₹₹

Shish Mahal: Kebabs, tandoori dishes and curries are offered at this restaurant attached to Hotel Samrat. Also does decent mocktails. *11am-11pm* ₹₹

Gopal Dar Chop: Fantastic little street-food shack selling *macher* (chicken) and *aam* (mango) chops (fried fritters), among other options. *5-8pm Sun-Fri* ₹

Mummaz Momo: Located 1km south of Murshidabad Junction, this place does *momos* in inventive styles (try the tandoori *momos*). *4-9pm Wed-Mon* ₹

HISTORIC MURSHIDABAD BY TOTO

Trawl through the embers of a former regional capital city and discover the riches still gleaming amid the ruins.

START	END	LENGTH
Kathgola Bagan	Katra Masjid	6.5km; 6hr

Hire a *toto* or a more comfortable autorickshaw for six hours (around ₹700) from Murshidabad train station. First head to ❶ **Kathgola Bagan**. The ticket office is at the end of a long, shaded driveway. Gardens of poppies and lavender surround this imposing colonnaded palace of a Jain family, which overlooks a placid, palm-fringed tank. The ❷ **House of Jagat Seth** (p454), 600m west, belonged to Murshidabad's powerful Marwari Oswal Jain financiers. Visits follow a set route through its mothballed past.

❸ **Nashipur Rajbari**, 250m south, was also a Jagat Seth palace, although this one has the air of a McMansion, partly due to the modern white fountain out front. It was undoubtedly once a grand palace but, except for a lovingly preserved grandfather clock, the antiquities within and the whole north wing of the building are in an advanced state of decay. Another 600m south, passing through sparsely populated farmland, ❹ **Namak Haram Darwaja** is little more than a ruined gateway beside the road, seemingly leading nowhere. Another 500m south is the modest ❺ **Tomb of Azimunnisa Begum**, daughter of Murshidabad's founder, Murshid Quli Khan, set at the centre of a tended garden.

From here it's a 1.5km jump to ❻ **Hazarduari Palace** (p453) and its neighbouring Nizamat Imambara, then another 2.5km to the pink-hued ❼ **Katra Masjid** (p455).

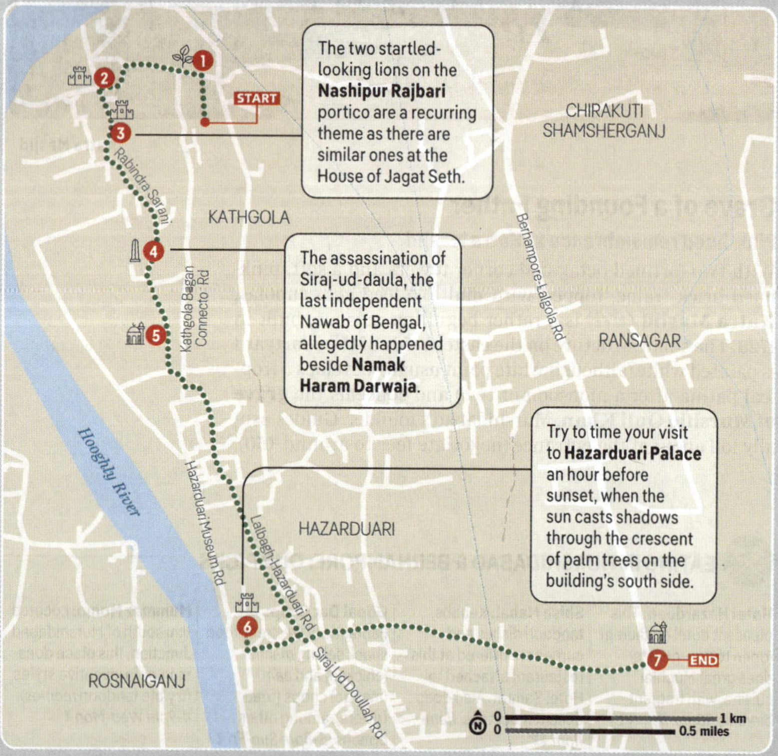

Beyond Murshidabad

A creative university town founded by Rabindranath Tagore, plus the Sultanate of Bengal's ruined former capitals, are among the rich offerings near Murshidabad.

Tombs and temples on the west side of the Hooghly continue a historical conversation started in Murshidabad. Southeast, Shantiniketan is Rabindranath Tagore's enduring gift of creative education to Bengal and the world. Visit his former homes at the Rabindra Bhavana and soak up the creative atmosphere. North of Murshidabad, West Bengal narrows to a tight corridor, crossed laterally by the Ganges and constrained between the borders of Bangladesh (east), and Bihar and Jharkhand (west). It's here that you'll find the busy little city of Malda, a good jumping-off point for trips to Gaur and Pandua, both former capital cities of the Sultanate of Bengal (1352–1576). As with Murshidabad, the intriguing heritage of these crumbling ruins hints at a former grandeur.

Places

Baranagar & Khusbagh

TIME FROM MURSHIDABAD: **30MIN**

Hooghly west bank sights

A handful of lesser-known sights along the west bank of the Hooghly complete the picture of historic Murshidabad. **Khusbagh Tomb Complex** *(free)* houses the modest resting place of Siraj-ud-daula, alongside that of his predecessor and father, Alivardi Khan. Head 12km further north to Baranagar for the riverside temples of **Char Bangla** *(free)*. The four small terracotta Hindu temples, built in a similar architectural style to those found in Bishnupur, face one another across a small green. The northernmost temple exhibits some exquisitely detailed scenes from Hindu mythology.

Tarapith

TIME FROM MURSHIDABAD: **2¼HR**

Tara's third eye?

The crush of visitors at what is essentially a small temple complex in **Tarapith Temple** *(sebaitsouvik.com)* reflects its importance as one of the *Shakti peeth* (places where the body parts of Sati, aka Kali, fell across South Asia). Tara's third eye is said to have fallen in this spot. There is little for non-Hindus to see, beyond taking in the busy fervour and energy of the site,

GETTING AROUND

Buses connect Berhampore (for Murshidabad) to Suri, where you can change for a bus to Bolpur (Jambuni bus stand, then take a *toto* to Shantiniketan) and Bishnupur (change at Durgapur). Trains connect Malda with Kolkata, Khagraghat (for Murshidabad) and New Jalpaiguri (for Darjeeling). Hiring private *totos* or a car and driver (through most hotels) are best for taking control of your itinerary. In Shantiniketan, contact Gaurav at Sarkar Travels on +919434634201. Intercity trips costs upwards of ₹5000 per day.

THE FUTURE OF INDIAN ART

Riti Sarkar, recently graduated Visva-Bharati art student, keeps Tagore's nature-centric approach to creativity alive through her own work. *@poems_and_art_2000*

I present my works through the things which we see daily. It can be a branch; it can be a leaf; those things are my brushes. They are all made from found objects, which are extremely organic. Not plucked from trees, but which I got from the ground.

It's very inspirational to walk around the leafy Visva-Bharati campus every day and see sculptures by the great artists, including a very famous one called Santhal Family, which depicts members of an Adivasi group. This was done by Ramkinkar Baij, who is considered the father of modern sculpture in India.

PAUL STAFFORD

Shonibarer Haat, Shantiniketan

and it's not worth queuing on busy days as it can take many hours to file through the inner sanctum. But a visit makes for a neat detour when travelling between Shantiniketan and either Murshidabad or Malda.

Shantiniketan

TIME FROM MURSHIDABAD: **3HR**

On the art trail

Bengal's revered Nobel Laureate in Literature, the polymath Rabindranath Tagore, first opened a school in Shantiniketan (meaning 'the Abode of Peace') in 1901. By 1921, it had become **Visva-Bharati** *(visvabharati.ac.in)*, a university that today educates around 10,000 Indian and international students. Because its courses generally favour humanities subjects, the northern suburb of Bolpur has long been considered the driving force of Bengali culture.

The university's leafy art school campus, **Kala Bhavan**, is off-limits to visitors without a student chaperone, unless you take the Sunday guided tour (bookable at Rabindra Bhavana Museum). It is peppered with revered sculptures, such as **Santhal Family**, which you can see from the roadside.

More easily accessible art is found at **Prakriti Bhavan** *(prakritibhavan.org; ₹30)*, whose four galleries feature sweet,

EATING IN SHANTINIKETAN: RESTAURANTS & CAFES

Kasahara: Visva-Bharati students tend to hang out at this buzzing budget cafe, which drums up a fantastic masala chai. *9am-10pm* ₹

Rustic Flavours: Owner Sukanya's homemade Bengali meals explore the highlights of local cuisine. Contact for times and reservations. *hours vary* ₹₹₹

Ghore Baire: There's a pleasant profusion of mosaic tables and alfresco dining space at this popular Bolpur-based Bengali eatery. *noon-9pm* ₹₹

Umul the Himalayan Café: Tibetan classics such as *momos* and *thukpa* (noodle soup) are served alongside fried-rice dishes at this budget spot. *7am-11pm Mon-Fri* ₹

nature-themed sculptures in stone, wood and bronze. **Srijani Shilpagram** *(ezcc-india.org; adult/child ₹20/10)* is a folk village containing recreations of traditional homes from India's eastern and northeastern states, each one daubed in folkloric paintings.

Market in the woods

On every day except Wednesday, a woodland floor on the northern edge of Shantiniketan is transformed by a vibrant selection of jewellery and textiles in every imaginable colour. Formerly the sole preserve of Adivasi folk artists, **Shonibarer Haat** (aka Sonajhuri Haat) is sadly losing out to wholesalers, although some authentic pieces can still be found. Come on Saturday afternoons, the main market day, when the wares patchwork more than a square kilometre and *bauls* (wandering minstrels) play local folk music, often accompanied by dancers.

Tagore's seasonal homes

Surrounded by the university campus, the **Rabindra Bhavana** *(visvabharati.ac.in; ₹300)*, aka Uttarayan, features five houses in various modernist styles, set amid exotic gardens. Tagore would move between these homes depending on the season; Punascha was his springtime house, for example. If this seems all a bit excessive, the replica of his Nobel Prize in Literature medal (the stolen original was never recovered) in the site's memorabilia-filled **Rabindra Bhavana Museum** is a reminder that his writing certainly wasn't hindered by the practice. The site is open from Friday to Tuesday.

Gaur & Pandua TIME FROM MURSHIDABAD TO MALDA: 3½HR

Pandua's mosques and mausolea

To the south and north of regional transport hub **Malda** lie two separate ancient cities, Gaur and Pandua, that each served as the Sultanate of Bengal's capital city. Hire a car and driver for the day (for around ₹4500) to visit both.

Pandua (*malda.gov.in*), called Adina by locals, lies to the north and was the sultanate's first capital from 1352 to 1390. Its main relic is the mighty **Adina Masjid** *(Jama Masjid; free)*. Built from 1364 to 1374 by Sultan Sikandar Shah, the ornamental brickwork is reminiscent of architecture seen in Persian and Silk Road cities – the seeds from which the Mughal empire grew. Follow the path along the wall, its lower half of thick granite blocks topped with brickwork uppers, until you reach a doorway on your right with thick lintels decorated in five ornamental bands. Within lies Shah's *qabr* (tomb). The mihrab (prayer niche) is to the right of the door. Left of the door are cloisters, topped with the remaining section of a bubbled roof that once included hundreds of domes and pillars of a gallery running the full way round the site.

ART & MUSIC AT POUSH MELA

For five or six days around Christmas, Shantiniketan holds its annual festival of music, dancing and, above all, art and poetry. **Poush Mela** is a celebration of the creative spirit that continues the ethos established, in part, by Rabindranath Tagore over a century ago. It is attended by artists and other creatives from across the region and the world, and the campus is transformed by creative energy and temporary exhibitions. Most notably, it's the best time to experience the music of Bengal's wandering minstrels, known as *bauls*. And it wouldn't be a Bengali mela without some delectable local sweets, such as creamy *payesh* rice pudding.

TAGORE'S (MANY) OTHER HOMES

Part of Tagore's indelible legacy is that every home he or his wealthy family ever lived in is now some sort of tourist destination. The most celebrated is his birthplace and ancestral home, **Jorasanko Thakurbari** (p435), in Kolkata. There's also one in the Darjeeling Hills at **Mangpoo** (p474).

BEST SMALL RUINS IN GAUR

Ballal Bati: The ruins of a once-huge palace lie untouched in a field. Nearby, the mighty Baisgazi Wall towers over wooded farmland.

Chamkatti Masjid: Small mosque (c 1475) named after a group of Muslim devotees called skin-cutters, who gashed themselves with knives.

Tantipara Masjid: This less-imposing mosque is full brick from the ground up, with four granite pillars down the middle that once held a roof.

Lottan Masjid: The brickwork both within and without this mosque contains hints of the original enamel in blue, green and white.

Kotwali Darwaza: Temporarily hand over your passport at the guarded booth to access this fortified medieval gateway on the India–Bangladesh border.

To the south, **Eklakhi Mausoleum** *(free)*, built 1412 to 1415, is a vast cuboid burial site topped with a bulky onion dome. The space has excellent acoustics within and contains three graves. Walk round to the left, through the gate and along the brick path past rural homes to reach the **Qutub Shahi Masjid** *(free)*, built in 1582 after the fall of the sultanate. Note the lotus carvings and the throne atop the steps. Climb inside the niche below it and look up to see an elaborate hidden rose carving. You might need to find somebody back at Eklakhi to open the gate for you.

Gaur's ghosts on the border

Gaur *(malda.gov.in)*, also known as Gour and Gauda, was the Sultanate of Bengal's most significant city. It served as capital from 1466 to 1565, but its regional importance can be tracked back to at least the 8th century. Today, the city lies in ruins right up to and beyond the Bangladeshi border, a former stronghold reverted to grazing land by the shifting sands of power and time.

The road south from Malda to Gaur is often lined with trucks laden with building materials, getting ready to cross the border into Bangladesh. Just before the crossing, the brunt of the ruined city of Gaur materialises through the trees on both sides of the road. The ruins' faded permanence is a striking juxtaposition with the transience of a border crossing. The largest cluster of relics, surrounded by artificial ponds and farmland, is down country lanes to the west of this road.

Turning off the main road, the lane passes right through the 1655 gateway **Lukochuri Darwaza** to arrive at **Kadam Rasul Masjid** *(free, although donations requested)*, which sports some of Gaur's best ornamental brickwork. The Prophet Mohammed's footprint is said to have been enshrined in stone here. The one on show is a replica; the original was removed decades ago.

Nearby, the impressive dome of the 1450 **Chika Masjid** (*Chamkan; free*) starts practically from the top of the walls, which are uncharacteristically devoid of ornamentation. Facing this mosque in the same precinct is **Gumti Darwaza** (1512), with two semi-columns straddling a doorway below a beehive dome. The original enamelling of the bricks is still visible.

Around 600m to the north, the five-storey 1489 **Firoz Minar** *(free)* stands stately upon a mound. A tight spiral staircase inside is usually out of bounds. Parakeets screech from the eaves.

A further 1km north, hefty **Dakhil Darwaza** *(free)* was built in 1425 and was the main northern entrance to the fortress of Gaur. Nearby, only two of the three arched gateways to the 1526 **Boro Sona Masjid** *(Baradwari; free)* have survived, along with a corridor topped by 11 domes.

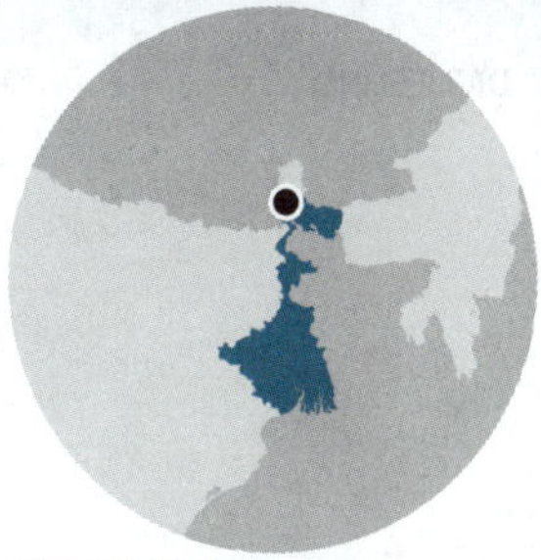

Darjeeling

ORANGE PEKOE | MOUNTAIN VISTAS | BUDDHIST MONASTERIES

The moment you leave the Ganges plain behind, the scenery, climate, dress and principal language all change. Whereas rivers control the geography to the south, the restless Himalaya foothills prevent huge cities from forming in the north. Initially developed as a hill station retreat for East India Company employees and their families, Darjeeling is surrounded by a sea of emerald tea plantations and the occasional vibrant interlude of a Buddhist monastery. Autumn and spring are the best seasons to visit, winter is cold and often cloudy, while monsoon season from June to September is best avoided. All of this is presided over by the perma-frosted Khangchendzonga (the world's third-highest mountain; 8586m). The earnest toot of its steam train, chugging up the mountain since 1881, still rings out three times a day. Of late, Darjeeling is struggling with rapid growing pains, but the city remains a good base for exploring smaller settlements on the surrounding ridges.

TOP TIP

Find accommodation as close as you can to Chowrasta or along the main roads running from it. There's not a great deal to see in the sprawl of suburbs beyond and the hilly walking can be particularly tiring at Darjeeling's 2000m-plus altitude.

Darjeeling Teatime

Tea estate tours and tastings

Many of the first [illegible] were around Darjeeling and Kurseong, using tea plants derived from some smuggled out of China by the British. Darjeeling tea is often served on its own or with a slice of lemon. It is never combined with milk.

Continues on p464

GETTING AROUND

Shared jeeps are the camels of the Himalaya. Once you get north of the Siliguri sprawl, the landscape is navigated by a relentless parade of switchbacks. You'll find Darjeeling's main jeep stand at the Old Market on Hill Cart Rd. Ticket booths are mostly roadside and clearly marked. Tickets to Kalimpong are sold inside the market. Look for destination placards in the jeep windscreens. The Toy Train (aka DHR) runs from Darjeeling to New Jalpaiguri. Steam engines run from Darjeeling to Ghum only. Darjeeling is enjoyable to explore on foot, particularly the pedestrianised zone around Chowrasta. Local taxis are pricey.

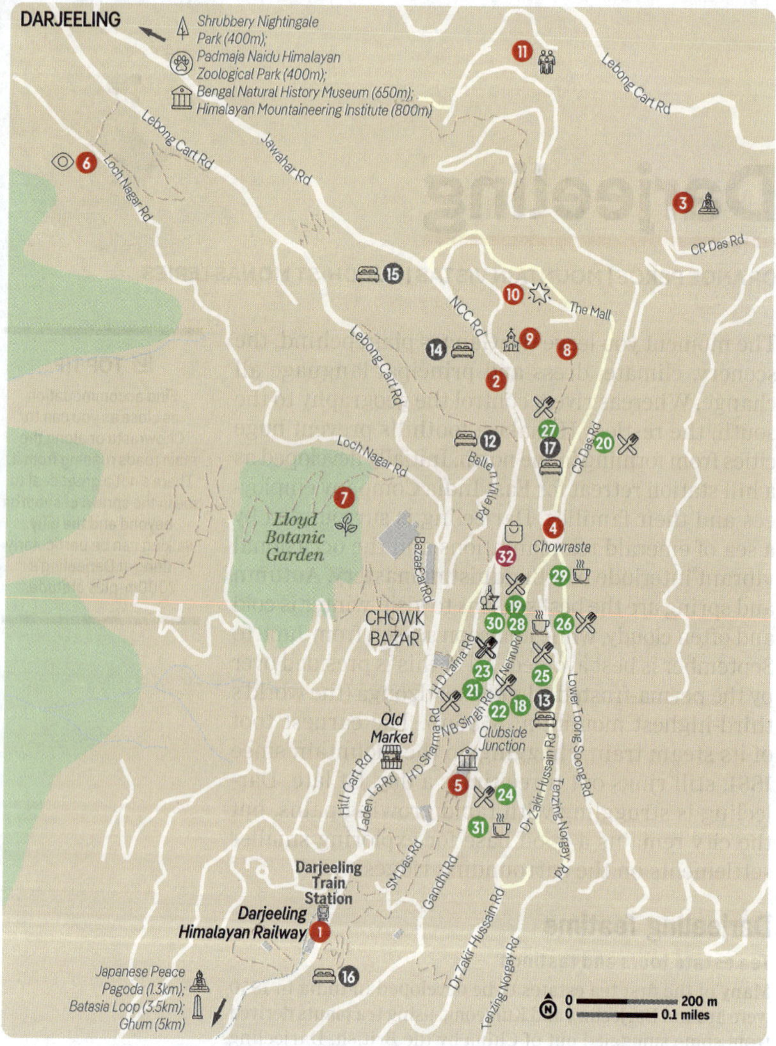

HIGHLIGHTS
1 Darjeeling Himalayan Railway

SIGHTS
2 Bhanu Bhawan
3 Bhutia Busty Gompa
4 Chowrasta
5 Darjeeling Clock Tower
6 Happy Valley Tea Estate
7 Lloyd Botanic Garden
8 Observatory Hill
9 St Andrew's Church

ACTIVITIES
10 Darjeeling Gymkhana Club
11 Tibetan Refugee Self-Help Centre

SLEEPING
12 Elgin Darjeeling
13 Hideout Backpackers Hostel
14 Ivanhoe Hotel
15 Mayfair Hill Resort
16 Summit Swiss Heritage Resort & Spa
17 Windamere Hotel

EATING
18 Dekevas
19 Glenary's
20 Grains Pure Veg
21 Keventer's
22 Kunga
23 Mahakal Restaurant
24 Noryang Tibetan Kitchen
25 Sonam's Kitchen
26 Tom & Jerry Café
27 Wuthering Bites

DRINKING & NIGHTLIFE
28 Glenary's
29 Himalayan Coffee
30 Machhan Tea Bar
31 Sol Café
see 17 Windamere Hotel

SHOPPING
32 Mayukh Tea

TOP EXPERIENCE

Darjeeling Himalayan Railway

The Darjeeling Himalayan Railway, aka the Toy Train or DHR, is still going strong after more than 150 years. The most characterful journeys take place by steam train (known as a 'Steam Joyride'), which run up to four times a day in peak season between Darjeeling and Ghum (taking 1 hour and 40 minutes). This unique trip blends mountain life with heritage.

A Head of Steam

Darjeeling Train Station is the starting point for steam-train journeys between Darjeeling and Ghum, and diesel services all the way to New Jalpaiguri Junction (NJP; [illegible]). Darjeeling's station, where you can buy tickets if you haven't bought them online, is charming in its traditional ramshackle way. The Toy Train's ageing steam locomotives, such as the 804B built in Glasgow in 1925, chug and jolt and jerk their way into the station, often behind schedule, and link to the carriages.

Swing Round the Batasia Loop

Belching steam, trains grind along the narrow-gauge tracks beside, over and sometimes on Hill Cart Rd, with jeeps and cars scrambling to move out of the way. Seating can get a little cramped, but you can get up and hang out the door (with care) to get better photos.

The first stop is **Batasia Loop**, where clever engineering ingenuity was employed to navigate a steep incline. Trains stop here for around 20 minutes. The descent into Ghum is particularly exciting as the carriages whip right past grocery shops, their vegetables arranged only inches away from the train.

TOP TIPS

- Some Ghum trains are diesel. Make sure to book the steam option; it'll say 'steam' somewhere on the service name when booking.
- Services with 'vista' in the title uses carriages with ceiling windows, for better views.
- Diesel trains ply the full route from Darjeeling to New Jalpaiguri, climbing 2100m.

PRACTICALITIES

● irctc.co.in ● one-way steam ₹1500, diesel from ₹1000 ● 6-10 daily (steam & diesel) from Darjeeling to Ghum

ABHISHEK SAH PHOTOGRAPHY/SHUTTERSTOCK

TOP TEA TIPS

Moubani Roy Choudhury, former tea taster, has developed a taste for the best brews. Here, she shares tips on which tea estates to buy from and where to try tea.

If you want to buy tea here, I recommend buying loose tea from the standalone shops, not the packages of tea, where nobody can see what's going into it. From my tasting experience, if you're looking to buy good tea and are looking at which garden it came from, the best gardens are Goomtee and sister garden Jungpana. Then the Goodricke Group that own Margaret's Hope and Castleton.

Happy Valley Tea Estate has tea-tasting sessions and they will take you walking through the tea gardens. This is best for beginners wanting to start learning more about tea.

PAUL STAFFORD

Tea tasting, Happy Valley Tea Estate

Continued from p461

Happy Valley Tea Estate *(tour & tasting ₹100)*, founded in 1854, is one of 87 tea estates in the hills around Darjeeling. From late March until mid-November, the temperature is high enough for the variety of tea known as orange pekoe (which references the tea's colour, not its flavour) to grow. Visit during these months and you'll get the chance to watch tea plucking and processing in action. There's usually no plucking on Sundays, so the factories are quieter on Mondays. The best time to visit is during the production months, but Happy Valley runs factory tours throughout the year. Tours are followed by a short tea tasting of the different 'flushes' (the four main harvesting phases). The **Makaibari Tea Estate** *(makaibari.com; tours ₹100)* near Kurseong is another great spot for a tour of a tea-processing plant and garden. Meanwhile, **Ging Tea House** *(gingteahouse.com)* and **Glenburn Tea Estate** *(glenburnteaestate.com)* are luxury tea properties in the remote hills, where all-inclusive stays are available at a premium.

Mountaineers Both Human & Animal

Climbing up to the Himalayan Mountaineering Institute

The Nepalese sherpa Tenzing Norgay, who became the first man, along with Sir Edmund Hillary, to summit Mt Everest in 1953, is celebrated in Darjeeling like a son. To visit the **Himalayan Mountaineering Institute** *(HMI; hmidarjeeling.com)*,

DRINKING TEA IN DARJEELING: OUR PICKS

Glenary's: With a restaurant, pub, bakery and teahouse, there's always plenty of activity at this long-standing favourite. *6am-10.30pm*

Machhan Tea Bar: Ascend the stairs from the Gandhi Rd entrance of Hotel Peak to Peaks to reach this cool rooftop bar. *11am-7pm*

Windamere Hotel: High tea with scones and sandwiches is available at the historic Windamere. Advance reservations only. *afternoons*

Mayukh Tea: A good place to buy tea to take home. Good-quality flushes in attractive packaging, plus in-store tastings before buying. *9am-9pm*

you must first buy tickets for **Padmaja Naidu Himalayan Zoological Park** *(darjeelingzoo.in; ₹180)*. Walk up through the zoo in order to access the HMI and other museums at the site. This happens to be one of India's better-kept zoos, with leopards, tigers and red pandas. Continue straight ahead after entering, past the Asiatic black bears, to reach the **HMI's Mountaineering Museum**, where a statue of Norgay stands near his *samadhi* (cremation spot) in the courtyard outside.

Within the museum, there's an excellent model of the entire Himalaya range. Upstairs is the **Everest Hall of Fame**, listing the 13 routes used to scale the mountain successfully, with a portrait of Norgay, plus a selection of his climbing gear used in the May 1953 expedition. Also within these grounds, the **Bengal Natural History Museum** *(darjeelingzoo.in)* explores Himalayan flora and fauna.

Buddhist Darjeeling

Monasteries and a refugee centre

Down the eastern slope of the ridge holding Darjeeling is a jumble of neighbourhoods. From Chowrasta, it is possible to hairpin the 1.5km down (ask locals for directions if you're unsure) to the **Tibetan Refugee Self-Help Centre** *(tibetancentredarjeeling.com; free)*. This remarkable space was set up to empower refugees (who fled conflict with China in their home country) to make a living while keeping their heritage alive. The resultant centre includes carpet, woodworking, textiles and painting workshops, an orphanage, a small monastery and a community kitchen. The Tibetan handicrafts shop is an excellent place to pick up local souvenirs.

On a different spur of the eastern slope is the serene **Bhutia Busty Gompa** *(free)*. It was once sited at the top of Observatory Hill until the British Raj forced its relocation. Catch the prayers at 3pm, when you can view the temple's unique murals of Buddha's life.

To take part in a prayer session, head to the **Japanese Peace Pagoda** *(free)* at 4.30am and 4.15pm, when the drumming *puja* (prayer session) starts within the temple on the left after you enter. Visitors are encouraged to take a seat and pick up a hand drum to help keep the beat for as long as they like during the 90-minute session. The 28m-high Peace Pagoda behind the temple is open from the morning until the end of evening prayers.

TIBETAN BUDDHISM IN EXILE

Although Buddhism emerged around **Bodhgaya** (p480), it spread throughout Asia, only to be supplanted by Islam and Hinduism in much of India. Since the 1950s, it has boomeranged back to India via Tibetan refugees, particularly in **Dharamshala** (p264) and at sites across Sikkim, such as **Rumtek Gompa** (p510).

THE DARJEELING HILLS' MUST-TRY DISHES

Momos: Classic snack that leapt from mountains to worldwide culinary fame. Perfect steamed and dipped in spicy *achar* pickle.

Mokthuk: Takes *momos* to the next level by cooking them in a garlic and ginger broth with vegetables such as carrot and cabbage.

Thukpa: Hearty, healthy soup dish that uses plenty of vegetables, including onions and mushrooms, handmade rice noodles and a good amount of chilli.

Thenthuk: Somewhere between a *mokthuk* and *thukpa*, *thenthuk* often includes meat, such as mutton or chicken, veggies and thick handmade noodles.

Tongba: Fermented millet drink that has a low level of alcohol and a somewhat earthy, lightly sour flavour that's much better than it sounds.

Titora (aka titaura): A sour, sweet, chewy fruit snack, often made with mango or tamarind.

WHY I LOVE DARJEELING

Paul Stafford, Lonely Planet writer
There's something humbling about being in the mountains. Perhaps it's their imperceptible gravity, or the sense that nature builds the finest skyscrapers, but I always feel calmer in their presence. Watching the sun rise and set over them somehow stirs the soul. The tranquillity of Buddhist monasteries in the shadow of the world's highest mountains, the delicate teas, the delightful Tibetan food and the gentle charm of its locals make Darjeeling a special place to be. It's starting to get a little too popular for its own good, but it remains the quintessential hill station. If the crowds get too much, I just jump into the back of a shared Jeep and get a little closer to those mountains.

A Planter's History of Old Darjeeling

Wandering the hill station's heritage landmarks

The oldest, Victorian-era part of Darjeeling, crowning a ridge running north to south, can be found around the triangular wedge of plaza known as **Chowrasta**. This pedestrianised area is a good starting point for exploring Darjeeling's heritage-laden core.

Start by heading northeast along the Mall, where you'll find steps on your left heading up to **Observatory Hill** *(free)*. Despite the name, all you'll see are trees, temples and prayer flags. This sacred space is shared by Buddhists and Hindus both worshipping Mahakala, a Buddhist Dharma protector and incarnation of Shiva; it's a neat religious intersection where the only conflict is over who can plaster the greater surface area with their respective flags and bells. Back at the bottom of the steps, if you continue to follow the path north, you'll pass a series of **balcony lookout points** (the true observatories), offering some of Darjeeling's best Khangchendzonga views, especially at sunrise.

Looping back southwards along NCC Rd, you'll pass the rather garish **Bhanu Bhawan**, headquarters of the Gorkhaland Territorial Administration (GTA; p472), the predominant political power in the area. Opposite, an uphill side road leads to a cluster of tea planters' institutions, such as **St Andrew's Church** (open Sunday mornings only), first built in 1843. Just behind the church is **Darjeeling Gymkhana Club** *(darjeelinggymkhanaclub.com; temporary membership ₹177)*. Built in 1909, it has some some great health facilities. All of these sites were frequented by planters in the early days of Darjeeling.

Back on NCC Rd, follow the pedestrianised upper road, past the historic yet worn **Windamere Hotel** *(windamerehotel.com)*, which still does a traditional high tea on request. Following the Mall south as it becomes Nehru Rd brings you to the **Darjeeling Clock Tower**, built in 1850.

EATING IN DARJEELING: BEST RESTAURANTS

Noryang Tibetan Kitchen: The women running this fantastic culinary bolthole make noodles and *momos* by hand. Best restaurant in town. *10am-9pm* ₹

Wuthering Bites: Beautiful conservatory and food terrace with good mains (such as grilled fish) and a 3pm-to-7pm happy hour. *8am-10pm* ₹₹₹

Dekevas: Try the Tibetan *thukpa* at this snug restaurant. The menu also takes inspiration from Vietnam (bao) and South Korea *(kimbap)*. *9am-9pm* ₹₹

Kunga: A good place to try authentic Tibetan dishes such as *thenthuk*, *thukpa* and their really tasty cheese *momos*. *10am-6pm* ₹₹

Mahakal Restaurant: Bengali thalis are served in the afternoon in this simple spot beneath Hotel Mahakal. Free top-ups if you're still hungry. *8am-10pm* ₹

Glenary's: There's an evening restaurant upstairs and an all-day, stodge-centric cafe with mountain-view terrace on the middle floor. *6am-10.30pm* ₹₹₹

Tom & Jerry Café: As you'd expect from the name, there's a big *Tom & Jerry* theme here. They serve good burgers and indulgent milkshakes. *9am-8pm* ₹₹

Grains Pure Veg: In the Udaan resort near Observatory Hill, with top-notch Indian curries and Tibetan dishes. *12.30-3.30pm & 7.30-10.30pm* ₹₹

PAUL STAFFORD

Observatory Hill

Orchids & Wisteria

Exploring Darjeeling's botanic garden

The mountains around Darjeeling are verdant throughout the year and filled with floral blooms for half of it. Despite the rapid growth of the town sequestered on a hillside, there are still plenty of patches of nature to discover, the longest standing of which is **Lloyd Botanic Garden** *(₹20)*, opened in 1878. There's a wisteria, brought here from the Botanic Gardens in Kolkata on opening, that dates back to this time.

As it scales the steep mountainside, this 40-acre site spans three climate zones: upper indigenous, middle coniferous and lower exotic, the last holding conservatories, including 110 species of orchid in the **Orchidarium**. The park is a lovely place for a stroll or to bring a picnic.

CROSSING THE BORDER FROM WEST BENGAL

It's possible to continue your travels beyond India by crossing land borders into Bangladesh, Nepal or Bhutan from the northern half of West Bengal. Borders here are dynamic, so check in advance for the latest restrictions.

Bangladesh Buses from Siliguri run straight to Dhaka via the main crossing at Petrapole–Benapole. South of Malda and Gaur, the Mahadipur border crossing is usually open also.

Bhutan Cross the land border at Jaigaon–Phuentsholing. Most non-Bhutanese or Indian citizens must first obtain clearance from a Bhutanese tour operator and, often, a visa in advance.

Nepal Cross via the land border into Nepal from India at Panitanki–Kakarvitta. As of 2026, this crossing was open to all nationalities, but has been known to close.

EATING & DRINKING IN DARJEELING: BEST BREAKFASTS & CAFES

Sonam's Kitchen: Great-value breakfasts including West Bengal's fluffiest pancakes. Sonam often works alone. It's worth the wait. *8am-2pm* ₹₹

Keventer's: Mountain views and 'English-style' breakfasts that are anything but. Think fried Spam and link sausages instead. *8am-6pm Fri-Wed* ₹

Himalayan Coffee: Spruce spot serving quality coffee, pancakes and all-day breakfasts. Old-school backpacker meets urban coffeehouse. *9am-8pm* ₹₹

Sol Café: Try the Tibetan butter tea here, alongside some good omelettes and pancakes for breakfast. There's Korean food in the afternoon. *9am-9pm* ₹₹

Beyond Darjeeling

More tea, more Buddhist monasteries and more views of the ever-captivating Khangchendzonga. That, and fewer tourists than Darjeeling.

Places

Ever expanding and gradually shedding its montane charm, Darjeeling has still got it, but for how long? It's worth exploring further afield for a more traditional version of the West Bengal Hills. If you want to base yourself somewhere more bucolic, try the comparatively smaller and calmer Ghum, Kurseong (both connected via train to Darjeeling), Kalimpong or Lava, which are ideal for forays into the wilderness or as an easier-going alternative to Darjeeling. Over by the Nepali border, one of India's best multiday treks runs along Singalila Ridge, with mesmerising vistas of four of the world's five highest mountains, days away from the nearest road. Down near Lataguri, rhinos and leopards abound in Gorumara National Park.

GETTING AROUND

Hill Cart Rd is the key artery into the mountains, flanked, crossed and often shared with the Toy Train. Darjeeling is connected to Ghum by this steam train, while diesel engines run from New Jalpaiguri Junction (NJP) via Siliguri and Kurseong. Shared jeeps are ubiquitous, with stands outside Siliguri and NJP stations (and if you find a safe spot on main roads you can flag them down, too). Shared routes within towns are handled by Maruti Suzuki Omnis.

Tiger Hill

TIME FROM DARJEELING: **1HR**

Sunrise with the world's tallest peaks

Every morning, a convoy of jeeps parades out of Darjeeling and up into thinner air, clambering up 2590m Tiger Hill *(shared jeep/private rental ₹400/2500)* to catch the sunrise warming the face of the mighty **Khangchendzonga**. Often piercing above the cloud that commonly shrouds Darjeeling in the early mornings, Tiger Hill offers an impressive view of mountains up to 250km away. If the weather is just right, you'll even be able to see **Mt Everest**, which seems lower than Khangchendzonga due to the curvature of the earth.

If it's winter, a hat, thick socks, scarf and gloves are advisable, as it can drop below freezing, although chai-wallahs bring some respite. To get here, you'll need to book onto a tour. Check in with local operators **Adventures Unlimited India** or **Ashmita Trek & Tours**. Disputes between landowners over ownership of Tiger Hill have forced occasional road closures, so even if you're planning to get here by other means, it's worth checking that Tiger Hill is open before setting out.

Ghum

TIME FROM DARJEELING: **25MIN**

Monasteries in and around town

Most visitors only stop briefly in Ghum (aka Ghoom) on their way back from a Tiger Hill sunrise escapade, to visit **Samten Choeling Gompa** *(free)*, referred to as Ghoom Monastery

ANIRUDDHA RAY/SHUTTERSTOCK

Tiger Hill

by locals. Within resides a huge **Maitreya Buddha** with blue eyes. Elsewhere, chants have reverberated around **Yiga Choeling Gompa** *(Sterling or Old Monastery; yigachoeling.com; free)*, on the western side of Ghum, since 1850. You might need to ask one of the monks for the doors to be unlocked.

From Ghum, a small, winding mountain road leading up the eastern side of the ridge towards Darjeeling brings you to **Mak Dhog Gompa** *(Alubari; often closed)*, fronted by fearsome dragons and lions on the eaves of its four-storey, tiered edifice. Head 2.5km north on Hill Cart Rd, however, and you'll come to **Dali Gompa** *(free)*, set into the hillside. Its museum has a good exhibition of Buddhist ceremonial clothing and masks. There's also a selection of traditional artefacts brought to India from Tibet by monks fleeing Chinese persecution alongside, inexplicably, a Zinedine Zidane France 1998 World Cup shirt and signed football.

Training days

Ghum Railway Museum (*free*) is housed above the train station and explores the history of the DHR. When building the Toy Train railway, the gradients were occasionally too steep even for the narrow gauge trains to run, so innovative loops, where the track passes over itself, were devised. At the core of the loop, the Batasia Loop (p463) is the most prominent, with an eco-garden and a war memorial dedicated to Indian soldiers who have died since Independence in 1947.

TRANSPORT AROUND DARJEELING

When arriving in the Dooars region at the foot of the Himalaya by train, chances are you'll disembark at either Siliguri Junction or, increasingly, New Jalpaiguri Junction (NJP) station. Both have jeep stands nearby. At NJP, exit the station on the north side, then head right until reaching NJP Railway Station Rd. Shared jeeps run from early morning until 4pm. Placards in jeep windscreens announce the destinations of Gangtok, Siliguri, Darjeeling, Kalimpong and Kurseong *(fares generally ₹300-500)*. The closest major airport is Bagdogra. **Wizzride** *(wizzride.com)* runs daily shared trips between Bagdogra Airport and Darjeeling and Kurseong in comfortable Innova cars. Book and pay online in advance. Tour companies also organise private transfers to the airport. Prices are around ₹2800 from Darjeeling to Bagdogra (2½ hours).

EATING IN GHUM & KURSEONG: OUR PICKS

Margaret's Deck: Hovering on stilts over a tea garden, with the cafe at the back. Pots of Darjeeling start at ₹350. *8am-7pm* ₹₹₹

Santa Banta Dhaba: It's the tandoori *momos* that make this place a distinct culinary experience, beside the Batasia Loop in Ghum. *8am-9pm* ₹₹₹

Cafe Kurseong Diaries: There's a replica of the Toy Train here, above Amarjeet Hotel. Try Nepali dishes such as *thukpa* and *momos*. *8am-10pm* ₹₹

33Dream Café: This LGBTIQ-friendly spot is a minute from Kurseong train station, with good cake and rooftop views. *8.30am-8.30pm* ₹₹

WALKING TOUR

Singalila Ridge Trek

Rewarding, enchanting and utterly exhausting, hiking the Singalila Ridge is an extraordinary experience. You will need at least four days (if you're a keen hiker) or six days to complete the full route, which follows the line of the India–Nepal border before dropping into a remote valley. Protected by the Singalila National Park, the trek explores a version of the Darjeeling Hills little changed in centuries. The following is for a five-day itinerary.

1 Mane Bhanjang

Start early. Permits and guides are mandatory for hiking the Singalila Ridge. No matter where you're coming from, foreign nationals must register at the **Office of the District Magistrate** in Mane Bhanjang. This is the first of many checkpoints (bring at least seven passport photocopies). Next, visit the **Highlander Guides & Porters Association** (*highlanderguidesandporters.com*) to organise your mandatory **guide** *(per day ₹1500)* and additionally, if you don't want to carry your own luggage, a **porter** *(per day ₹1200)*.

The Hike: From this point onwards, your planning, routing, accommodation booking and organisation will be taken care of by your guide.

2 Mane Bhanjang to Sandakphu

Since the trail between Mane Bhanjang and Singalila National Park became a paved road, the first, steep stages of the route are best covered by jeep. Luckily, the **Land Rover Owner's Welfare Association** *(₹2500)* has a fleet of beautiful old British Land Rovers from the 1950s. They still do the job. Stop off at **Chitrey Monastery** on the Nepal side, and the **Tonglu Viewpoint**

PAUL STAFFORD

Singalila National Park

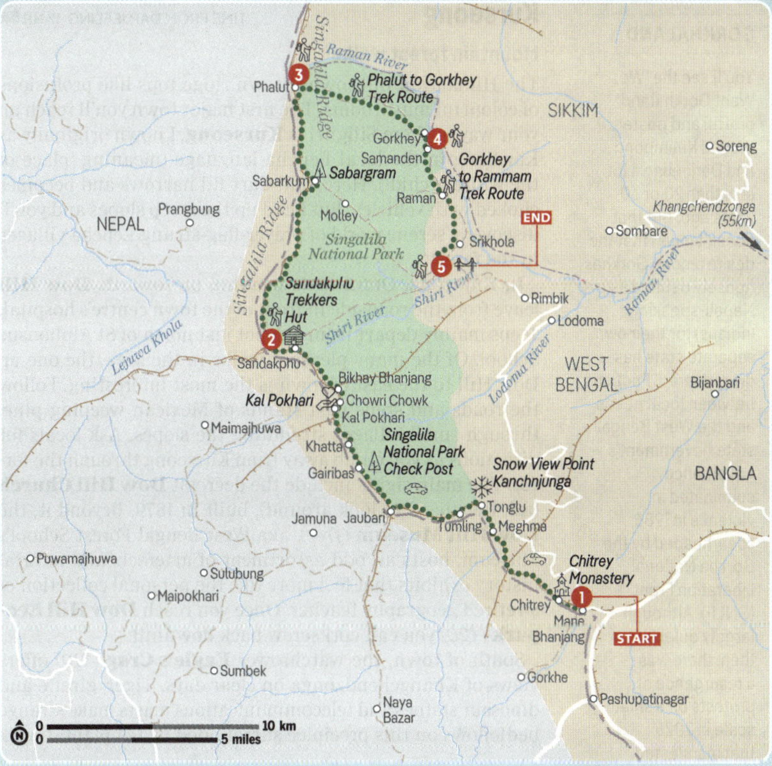

at 3070m for your first glimpse of Khangchendzonga. Soon you'll enter **Singalila National Park** and the paved road ends.

The Hike: Around 13km from Gairibas, but over a vertical kilometre of ascent. Look out for red pandas in this area. Stop for lunch in Kal Pokhari, the last chance before reaching Sandakphu.

3 Sandakphu to Phalut

Get up early to watch the sunrise over **Khangchendzonga**, **Everest**, **Lhotse** and **Makalu**. From this vantage point you can really appreciate why the Nepalis called Khangchendzonga 'Sleeping Buddha', with its head on the left and its feet on the right. You'll likely be feeling the altitude at 3636m, particularly when hiking, but the beautiful grassy slopes of **Sabargram** and yak-filled wilds of **Phalut** are worthwhile.

The Hike: It's 21km, with not much ascent but challenging given the altitude and distance.

4 Phalut to Samanden

Head downhill off the ridge, through a jungle of rhododendron forests and an understorey of thick bamboo and into **Gorkhey**. Keep an eye out for red pandas.

The Hike: The 18km are tough on the knees as you descend, via steep slopes, over a vertical kilometre. The farms of Samanden are a world snatched from a past time.

5 Samanden to Srikhola Bridge

Finally, you'll pass through the jungle on the same old trails used by villagers if they want to get anywhere, before tracking to **Srikhola**.

The Hike: After 18km in and out of valleys, at Srikhola there are regular shared jeeps from Srikhola Bridge back to Darjeeling; or from Rammam, if your guide books ahead.

GORKHALAND

You'll see the 'We Want Gorkhaland' graffiti and posters around Kalimpong and Darjeeling a lot less than 20 or 30 years ago. But that doesn't mean that the desire among Gorkhas (loosely defined as Nepali-speaking Indians) for their own separate state has disappeared. Frictions between local needs and the West Bengal state government's governance culminated in violence in 1986, spearheaded by the Gorkha National Liberation Front (GNLF). Although largely quiet since then, there was a resurgence of protests on a small scale in 2025 that manifested discontent at the destruction of the local area by what many locals consider to be unscrupulous developers in Kolkata and by disrespectful tourists coming from the plains of West Bengal and leaving much more than footprints behind.

Kurseong

TIME FROM DARJEELING: 1¼HR

Mountain forest walks

The Himalayan hill towns crown ridge tops like profusions of colourful mushrooms. The first major town you'll reach on your way up from Siliguri is **Kurseong**, known originally as Kar Sang in the local Lepcha language (meaning 'place of the white orchid'). Here, Hill Cart Rd narrows and becomes choked with vehicles. But head up the steep slopes and you'll discover a serene world of prayer-flag-strung Lepcha villages in the forest.

In Kurseong, Omni taxis heading up towards **Dow Hill** leave from the roadside in front of the town centre's hospital. Jeeps mainly depart from a depot just north of St Alphonsus School. Of the many pleasant walks in the area, the one up Dow Hill to the east of town is the most interesting. Follow the roads and steps past stands of Mexican weeping pine, through small villages straddling the slopes. Ask locals for directions as you climb away from Kurseong through the forest. The main sights include the decrepit **Dow Hill Church** (ask the guard to look around), built in 1879. Beyond it, the **Dow Hill Museum** *(free),* aka West Bengal Forest School's Museum, hosts an odd assortment of artefacts and natural history exhibits that feel more like the personal collection of a retired geography teacher. Once you reach **Dow Hill Eco-park** *(₹20)* you can corkscrew back downhill.

South of town, the watchtower **Eagle's Crag** *(₹10)* offers views of Khangchendzonga on clear days. Tiger, giraffe and dinosaur statues and telecommunications masts make strange bedfellows on this precipice surrounded by tea plantations.

Kalimpong

TIME FROM DARJEELING: 2¾HR

Natural mountain spaces

The Lepcha town of Kalimpong comes from an earlier name 'Kaa-Len-pung', which translates to 'we gather on the ridge'. This feels apt for the majority of towns in the hills. It was this location, however, that made it strategically attractive to the British. The town bustles around the main motor stand near the Mela Ground and the **Macfarlane Memorial Church**, built in 1891, looks out over the town. It was heavily damaged by a 2011 earthquake, with the tower's broken pinnacles still visible in front of the church on the ground. Two services on Sundays cater to the town's 14% Christian population.

EATING IN KALIMPONG: OUR PICKS

Melting Pot Bistro: A top choice: stylish and clean, with a broad array of local, pan-Indian dishes and excellent pizzas. *11am-10pm* ₹₹

Art Café: Follow signs through the shopping centre to this wonderful spot with perfect coffee and great music. *9am-7pm Fri-Wed* ₹₹

Roxberry Pub & Café: The cool place. Enter through a black-light portal for beer and pool tables or the laid-back upstairs cafe. *noon-10pm* ₹₹

Mama Mia: Burgers and pastries are the strong suits of this in-house restaurant at Mayfair Himalayan Spa Resort. *10am-8pm* ₹₹₹

Wander a few blocks beyond the commercial core and you'll discover a calmer slice of mountain life, complete with nurseries growing cacti and orchids for sale around the world. **Shanti Kunj Nursery** *(free)*, with five large greenhouses growing these orchids and cacti, some almost 60 years old, is open to visitors. So, too is **Pine View Nursery** *(₹50)*, which has a few greenhouses and a cactus jungle.

Kalimpong's monasteries

The emerald green of the bamboo- and pine-dressed hillsides is frequently broken by the crimson, mustard, cobalt and white of Buddhist prayer flags. **Geden Tharpa Choling Gompa** *(free, donations welcome)* is Kalimpong's most interesting monastery. A giant golden Buddha, flanked by four gleaming white stupas on either side, holds a commanding view over the colourful rooftops of Kalimpong's buildings. The monastery **museum** contains some interesting artefacts, including *kangling* trumpets made from bone.

Tongsa Gompa *(free)* is a pretty little monastery close to the town centre, set in peaceful grounds. **Durpin Gompa** *(free)*, 4km south of the town centre, is the largest monastery in the region. Its views are somewhat blighted by the presence of telecoms towers and other expansions of the city.

On the other side of town, the ground floor of **Lepcha Gumba** hosts the **Lepcha Heritage Museum** *(free, donations welcome)*. To find it, head through the unassuming yellow gates, then down the path and round the back of the small monastery surrounded by prayer wheels. The museum offers crucial insight into who the Lepchas are and everything they hold dear.

Tukdah

TIME FROM DARJEELING: 1HR

Nature walks at Lamahatta Eco Park

Fronted by pretty, marigold-filled gardens and presided over by a grove of magnificent, yet non-native, Japanese cedar trees, **Lamahatta Eco Park** *(₹20)* offers a series of hiking trails through the forest. The main trail is a stone-paved 2km path up through avenues of bamboo to a 'lake', which is more like a human-made tank (reservoir) strewn with prayer flags.

There's another steep trail that leads up behind the park into the forest proper. Head up to your left, away from the road, before looping around to your right as the path forks. Or keep going to the top of the ridge. Sturdy walking boots are recommended. You are likely to encounter plenty of birdlife, including the pretty kalij pheasant, on these quieter trails.

MULTIDAY MOUNTAIN TREKS

The Himalaya of India offer limitless possibility for challenging and rewarding hikes that get you well away from the trappings of urban India. One highlight is the eight-day trek to **Milam Glacier** (p401) in Uttarakhand.

SUSTAINABLE ACTIVITIES IN KALIMPONG

Yachna Rizal, owner of Art Café in Kalimpong, suggests the best ways to support sustainable businesses around Kalimpong. *@artcafe.kpg*

Walks with locals are a great way to discover Kalimpong's heritage that most visitors miss: Bunty *(@buntysilentnature walks)* runs a great trip. Gangjong Paper Factory, where paper is made from the pulp of the *lokta* plant, is a must-visit: the owner *(8293125989)* gives a personal tour of his factory. Dumthok Lee is reviving the age-old Lepcha handloom tradition with her aunt; you can reach out to her via *@dumthok_lee*. Painter Hemlata Pradhan *(@htnha_kalimpong)* immortalises local orchids and other plants on paper and runs natural-history art classes.

Contact us at Art Café for village food experiences, where you can dine with a local family.

RABINDRANATH TAGORE

As India's sole laureate of the Nobel Prize in Literature, Rabindranath Tagore looms large in Bengali culture. He helped found Visva-Bharati university in Shantiniketan and you find his artworks in galleries all around India. He was much more than a poet and novelist: he is lauded for his philosophy, work in social reform and for his musical composition. The national anthems of both Bangladesh and India were written by Tagore. If his prodigious creative and intellectual life isn't enough, he also lived far and wide throughout Bengal. By the time of his death, aged 80 in 1941, he is believed to have lived in at least 57 homes. Some of them were ancestral, particularly Jorasanko Thakurbari (p435) in Kolkata and his five houses at Rabindra Bhavana (p459) in Shantiniketan.

Mangpoo

TIME FROM DARJEELING: 1¼HR

A Tagore home in the mountains

Rabindranath Tagore moved to the hills in the later part of his life under doctors' orders to rest. **Rabindra Bhavan** *(₹25)* is now preserved as part of the great Indian polymath's legacy. The museum offers some fascinating insight into Tagore's life and work, plus the thinking behind it. As the first Asian and non-European to win the Nobel Prize in Literature, in 1913, Tagore was knighted in 1915. He would later renounce it in 1919.

Mangpoo is an important place for cinchona production, the bark of which produces the quinine used in the treatment of malaria and in other medicines. As such, the house is surrounded by thick jungle.

Lava

TIME FROM DARJEELING: 4¾HR

Seeking red pandas in Neora Valley

Lava gives a sense of how the ridge towns of the Darjeeling Hills once looked before poorly managed overdevelopment engulfed them. From here, thick stands of undisturbed old-growth forest stretch all the way to the Bhutanese border. Roughly 88 sq km of this forest is protected as **Neora Valley National Park**, a vital habitat for endangered red pandas and around 300 species of stunning birds, such as Ward's trogon and the satyr tragopan.

You can hire a jeep and driver-guide for the day, such as **Joseph Lephcha** *(9932095242; day trip ₹4000),* from practically any hotel in Lava. The park entrance is 6km northeast of Lava, towards the pretty village of **Kolakham**, and is accessible by certified guide only.

Lataguri

TIME FROM DARJEELING: 4½HR

One-horned wonders in Gorumara

Around 65 one-horned rhinos are thought to live in the 115-sq-km expanse of preserved forest in **Gorumara National Park**, just north of Lataguri. Two types of safari tour take place in an open-backed jeep known locally as 'gipsies'.

The first visits the watchtowers, such as **Jatraprasad**, placed around the fringes of the forest, overlooking salt licks along the river. The low brush here means mammals are easier to spot. Bookings and departures for these tours are from Lataguri's **Gorumara Ticket Counter** *(jeep, driver & guide ₹1680)* on the road north to Chalsa (closed on Thursdays).

The second safari tour departs from the **Lataguri Forest Range Office** *(jeep, driver & guide ₹2200),* located around 600m south, closer to the centre of Lataguri. This tour (running Thursday to Tuesday) heads through the forest into its depths at dawn. There's a better chance of an up-close wildlife encounter on this option.

It's worth asking to 'share' on either tour, as there will often be a spare spot going with another group.

Places We Love to Stay

₹ Budget ₹₹ Midrange ₹₹₹ Top End

Bishnupur & Serampore

Map p447

Hotel Annapurna ₹₹ Minutes from Ras Mancha, Annapurna scores high on modern comforts such as good mattresses and showers.

Denmark Tavern (p449) ₹₹₹ A lovingly renovated heritage inn with rooms ranged around an open-plan central courtyard overlooking the Hooghly.

Berhampore & Murshidabad

Hotel Samrat ₹₹ Staff at this respectable option are particularly helpful if you need advice on arranging your onward journey.

Bari Kothi Heritage Hotel ₹₹₹ Located in Azimganj, across the river from Murshidabad, this comprehensively restored former Jain palace built in 1774 is an impressive piece of heritage accommodation.

Shantiniketan

Diya Homestay ₹ Shantiniketan's top budget choice, on a quiet backstreet with basic en suite rooms at close to hostel-dorm prices.

Nayana's Homestay ₹₹₹ Namesake owner Nayana is great at helping you arrange trips and onward travel. Meals can be included.

Malda

Golden Park ₹₹ A clean, modern hotel set back from the main highway to Pandua. Ideal if you have an easy means of transport or are willing to take taxis.

Continental Lodge ₹₹ Compact rooms kept to a high standard for the price, right in Malda's city centre, close to the main taxi stand.

Darjeeling

Map p462

Hideout Backpackers Hostel ₹ The terrace views are worth a stay alone, although it's a nightmare to find (ask around). Best-value option near Chowrasta. Dorms only.

Ivanhoe Hotel ₹₹ Get a heritage room without the overinflated price, just a few minutes' walk from Chowrasta.

Summit Swiss Heritage Resort & Spa ₹₹ On the south side of Darjeeling, this spa hotel has tired-looking heritage rooms and modern deluxe accommodation. A 20-minute walk from the Japanese Peace Pagoda.

Mayfair Hill Resort ₹₹₹ While many top-level heritage properties in Darjeeling have let standards slip, Mayfair remains elegant amid a fresh veneer.

Windamere Hotel (p466) ₹₹₹ Entertaining guests since the early 20th century but built in the 19th. Windamere's guest areas feel refreshed after a solid revamp.

Elgin Darjeeling ₹₹₹ A former summer residence for the maharaja of Cooch Behar, the Elgin remains a classy, comfortable hotel. Request an attic room for an extra dose of historic charm.

Kurseong

Dreamhome Stay ₹₹ Take an Omni taxi to this cosy family-run place perched midway up Dow Hill. Rooms with balconies have the best views.

Dew Drop Home Stay ₹₹ At the foot of Eagle's Crag, this cheery little mountain home offers good sunset views.

Kalimpong

Shikher ₹ Set in peaceful, flower-filled grounds, Shikher is located on a ridge with views of Khangchendzonga and the surrounding valleys close to Tharpa Choling. Breakfast included.

Mayfair Himalayan Spa Resort ₹₹₹ This gorgeous Mayfair property is set amid a sprawl of historic buildings. Loads of facilities, including a library, spa, restaurant and bar, plus good wheelchair-accessible rooms and facilities.

PaliGhar ₹₹₹ Luxury farmstay on the lower slopes of peaceful Deolo Hill. All meals are provided and there are opportunities to take nature hikes and learn about traditional farming.

Elgin Silver Oaks ₹₹₹ Exquisite 1920s heritage hotel with plush furnishings and a sense of history [illegible] atmosphere throughout. Ask for a garden-view room.

Siliguri

Loft Hotel ₹₹ Simple, clean and spacious rooms arranged around a central courtyard, 1km from Siliguri Junction station and bus stand.

Mayfair Tea Resort Siliguri ₹₹₹ This luxury property north of Siliguri is a good chance for a final cuppa before catching a flight or train elsewhere.

For places to stay in Bihar and Jharkhand, see p497

VIKASH KR SINGH/SHUTTERSTOCK

Above: Parasnath Temple (p487), Parasnath Hill; Right: Golghar (p495), Patna

Researched by
Mark Eveleigh

Bihar & Jharkhand

HALLOWED LANDS, ESPECIALLY FOR JAINS AND BUDDHISTS

Apart from the Buddhist holy city of Bodhgaya, these two resource-rich but economically challenged states are almost unknown to foreign tourists.

It's said that Bihar took its name from *vihar*, the Sanskrit word for monastery. Buddha reached enlightenment at Bodhgaya, a great Buddhist university once stood at Nalanda and most of the leading lights in the Jain religion attained moksha (enlightenment) on the intensely spiritual Parasnath Hill.

RAH L D'SILVA/SHUTTERSTOCK

In contrast, the sprawling city of Gaya is a religious centre for Hindus, while the even bigger Patna is important for Sikhs as the birthplace of Guru Govind Singh. Indeed, Patna was one of India's most powerful cities for nearly a millennium, though remarkably little remains these days of its celebrated past.

Beyond the cities, Bihar and especially Jharkhand – which was divided from it in 2000 to meet the autonomy demands of the Adivasi (tribal) population – is a starkly contrasting world of rural hamlets and gritty steel and mining towns.

The region's reputation for lawlessness and outbursts of Maoist and Naxalite militancy has significantly improved in the past decade; you'll find few places in lowland India more refreshing and relaxing, for example, than the idyllic mountain paths of Parasnath. The local tourist authority's mantra 'Blissful Bihar' might be a little overstated and the fact that the state is alcohol-free (though Jharkhand isn't) certainly keeps international holidaymakers to a minimum. With a little resilience and a sense of adventure your travels here will reveal a fascinatingly offbeat aspect of India that you're sure to remember with fondness.

THE MAIN AREAS

BODHGAYA
Buddhists and backpackers gather round the Mahabodhi tree. p480

PATNA
History museums and street art on the Ganges. p492

Find Your Way

As well as taking trains and long-distance buses you can arrive by a at Patna and Gaya (close to Bodhgaya). Bihar and Jharkhand extend across an area that is roughly half the size of Germany, or about the size of Florida.

Patna, p492

Beyond Patna's dreary 1970s concrete you'll find a modest artistic side in a metropolis that's surprisingly hassle-free and welcoming.

Bodhgaya, p480

The Mahabodhi Temple complex is the uplifting epicentre of a 'Buddhist circuit', with traveller facilities, study opportunities and a plethora of temples.

TRAIN

There's a well-served network of railways. Gaya and Parasnath are stops for many trains between Kolkata and Varanasi. A ticket between Gaya and Patna costs around ₹500 and can be booked through India Rail's official ConfirmTkt app.

BUS & CAR

Clunky local buses ply the roads while overnight sleepers cover some handy long-distance routes Tour agents in Bodhgaya and Patna offer affordable taxi tours if you want to do the Buddhist circui in more comfort.

PACCEKA/SHUTTERSTOCK

Buddha statue, Dungeshwari Cave (p484)

Plan Your Time

It would take about 14 hours to road-trip from northern Bihar to southern Jharkhand, but most sights of visitor interest are relatively close to Patna or Bodhgaya, the main hubs for foreign travellers.

With Five Days

- After arriving in **Bodhgaya** visit the **Mahabodhi Temple** (p482) and stroll the monastery district. Meet fellow travellers and share a taxi tour to **Dungeshwari Cave** (p484). Head to Gaya for the train to **Parasnath** (p486) and next morning do the Jain pilgrimage hike from **Madhuban** (p486). Take a train from Parasnath to Varanasi or Kolkata or head through rural Bihar to **Patna** (p492).

An Extra Week

- Take the high road from Gaya to historic **Rajgir** (p488). Sidestep the melee of tourists and find some solitude at **Vulture Hill** (p489) before heading for calmer **Nalanda** (p488) and its manicured ruins. Take a train to **Patna** (p492), explore the city's museums and artistic side then loop southwards to spend a few days meditating and soaking up the spirituality of old **Bodhgaya** (p480).

SEASONAL HIGHLIGHTS

SPRING
In March, **Bihar Diwas** (p495) celebrates the state's 1912 reinstatement with concerts on Patna's Gandhi Maidan.

SUMMER
Monsoon rains alleviate the worst of the heat and fill the region's waterfalls.

AUTUMN
Hindu pilgrims head to Gaya (and Bodhgaya) for the 15-day **Pind Daan** festival which usually falls in September.

WINTER
The **Sonepur Mela** (p494), India's biggest cattle fair, takes place in November/December on the north bank of the Ganges near Patna.

Bodhgaya

BUDDHIST MONUMENTS | MEDITATION | INTERNATIONAL FOOD

TOP TIP

It can be hard to differentiate the many genuinely kind, spiritual people from scammers. Be polite but sceptical, and trust your instincts. Disturbingly, it's not unknown for touts to masquerade as monks even within the grounds of the Mahabodhi Temple.

Bodhgaya is to Buddhists almost as Mecca is to Muslims. Around 2600 years ago, this is where Prince Siddhartha attained enlightenment to become Buddha (the 'Awakened One') while sitting beneath a bodhi tree. A 19th-century genetic successor to that 'Maha' (Great) Bodhi Tree is the focus of the Mahabodhi Temple Complex. With thousands of pilgrims from all around the world, Bodhgaya is one of India's most cosmopolitan small cities (although you'll see very few tourists).

Streets surrounding the complex are a cacophony of trinket sellers, food and chai stands, and cows chewing on rubbish piles. It's an architectural beauty pageant too, with countless ornate monasteries, many built in iconic national styles by international Buddhist communities. You'll encounter more Buddhist monks and nuns here than anywhere else in India and will mix with beggars, barefoot pilgrims and a few European soul-searchers. It's all part of a chaotic human and architectural landscape, but there are a few pockets of blissful meditative calm once you know where to look.

GETTING AROUND

Uber is yet to arrive in Bodhgaya but autorickshaws (known simply as 'autos') prowl for custom on every corner. Vedanta Routes *(vedantaroutes.com)* can take the hassle out of bus/train bookings and can arrange tours all over the region. The bus station is 1.5km west of the Mahabodhi Temple, with comfortable double-decker sleeper coaches running far and wide. Allow up to 45 minutes for the 12km auto ride from Bodhgaya to Gaya Junction (the nearest train station) or 30 minutes for the ride to Gaya airport. Scooties (mopeds) are available for rent from ₹400 per day or you'll get a vintage Royal Enfield for about ₹2500 per day.

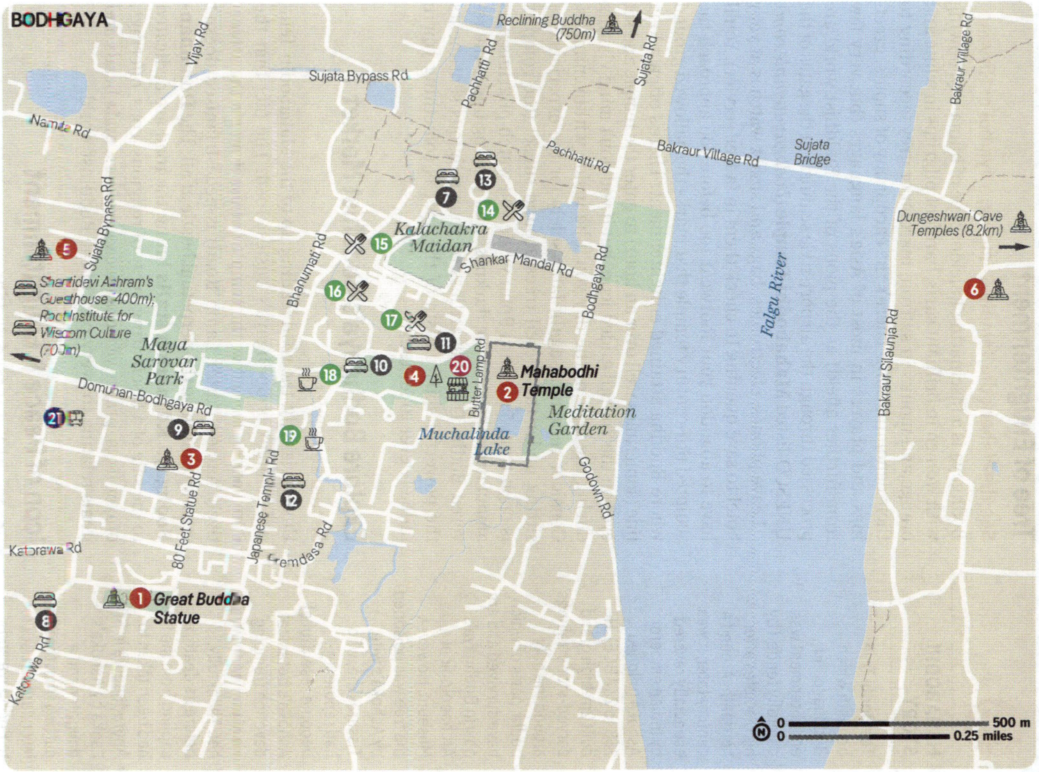

HIGHLIGHTS
1 Great Buddha Statue
2 Mahabodhi Temple

SIGHTS
3 Chalaymanmurti Buddha
4 Jai Prakash Butterfly Release Park
5 Metta Buddharam Temple
6 Sujata Stupa

SLEEPING
7 Beauty Guest House
8 Bodhgaya Hotel School
9 Buddha Heritage Resort
10 Hotel Mahayana
11 Kirti Guesthouse
12 Maya Heritage Hotel
13 Rahul Guesthouse

EATING
14 Hari Om International Cafe
15 Lhasa Restaurant
16 Mohammad Restaurant
17 Ram Sewak

DRINKING & NIGHTLIFE
see 14 Carrot Cake & Coffee
see 17 Espresso Brew
18 Gautam Lassi Corner
19 Puja Tea Store

SHOPPING
20 Domuhan-Bodhgaya Rd market stalls

MAHABODHI STORY

The Bodhi Tree beneath which Buddha found enlightenment was carefully tended by his disciples after his death. Around a century later, it was especially revered by Indian emperor Ashoka (reigned 268 to 232 BCE). He built 2m-high grand carved-stone 'railings' around the holy bodhi, parts of which have survived and are now in Bodhgaya's Archaeological Museum. However, the tree was poisoned by Ashoka's wife, Tissarakkhā, who had reputedly become resentful of Ashoka's botanical devotion trumping his attention towards her. Thankfully, before its death, a sapling from the tree had been taken to Anuradhapura in Sri Lanka by Ashoka's daughter and a cutting from that was later carried back to Bodhgaya and planted where the original once stood.

Tree of Enlightenment

See the Mahabodhi Temple Complex, a symbol of Nirvana

Bodhgaya is a fascinating kaleidoscope of humanity, flowing with women in brilliant saris, barefoot pilgrims in white and orange,and monks in saffron, maroon or grey (according to their denomination). There's the cacophony of shouts, greetings and prayers in most of Asia's languages (but very few from further afield) as the pious of the Buddhist world are processed through the airport-style scanners at the gates of the UNESCO-listed **Mahabodhi Temple** *(bodhgayatemple.com)*.

Leave phones, electronics, bags and smart watches at your hotel to save queuing to check them in (a free service). You'll have to abandon your footwear too before you approach the sculpted 6th-century temple that marks the hallowed ground where Buddha attained enlightenment. There's often a long line (sometimes well over an hour) to enter the temple and set eyes on the 2m-tall gilded icon, but if you don't mind visiting during the heat of the day you'll be inside within minutes. Consider returning again later solely for the experience of sitting under the sacred trees around sunset (the complex is open from 5am until 9pm) while you watch pilgrims perambulating through the darkness and praying under the revered Bodhi Tree. Regardless of your religious sentiments the powerful spiritualism of the spot is something you're unlikely ever to forget.

Explore Bodhgaya's Buddhist Market

Sacred souvenirs

Unsurprisingly, the road leading up to the Mahabodhi Temple Complex is Bodhgaya's busiest road. The fact that the 80m section closest to the temple (where it meets the attractively named Butter Lamp Road) is pedestrianised doesn't seem to minimise the perpetual bustle at all. The **Domuhan-Bodhgaya Rd market stalls** lining the road are dedicated to the sale of a fascinating array of religious icons, offerings, prayer flags, prayer wheels, incense holders, mala beads and items relating to every part of the Buddhist world.

Icon of Peace & Enlightenment

Gaze up at the seated Buddha

Even seated in the *dhyana* mudra meditative pose the **Great Buddha Statue** *(great-buddha-statue.com)* rises to a height of

EATING IN BODHGAYA: CHEAP EATS

Mohammad Restaurant: Worth finding in the alleys of Kalachakra Maidan for hearty breakfasts, delicious juices and great curries. *7am-10.30pm* ₹

Hari Om International Cafe: Features the staples of half a dozen countries, including *khichdi* (ancient recipe of spiced rice and lentils). *7.30am-10pm* ₹

Lhasa Restaurant: A meaty Tibetan menu with vegetarian options in a quirky venue. Manchurian beef and *phing thang* glass noodles are favourites. *7am-10pm* ₹

Ram Sewak: A great place to meet locals as you're seated at shared tables. The vegetarian-only menu is extensive and the food delicious. *6.30am-10.30pm* ₹

ARNAV PRATAP SINGH/SHUTTERSTOCK

Great Buddha Statue

25m. It's become an icon of Bodhgaya since it was consecrated in 1989 by the Dalai Lama. It's said that 12,000 stonemasons worked on the project over seven years and that the hollow statue contains over 16,000 small bronze Buddha figures. Take a stroll towards town from here – between 80 Feet Statue Rd and Japanese Temple Rd – and you'll come across Japanese, Bhutanese, Mongolian, Cambodian and Thai temples.

Flight of Freedom

Release a butterfly to save a bird

Among its roses and tall, straight palms, a key feature of **Jai Prakash Butterfly Release Park** *(adult/child ₹200/₹100)* is a breeding programme and education centre for native butterflies. Butterflies are raised here and there's an interpretation centre (hours vary) where staff will explain the process. The key idea is that Buddhist pilgrims can release a butterfly as an act of merit, but it's an option that's available for the general public too *(₹250)*. It's an environmentally sound alternative to the harmful practice of releasing birds (which has led to poaching of wild birds in many Buddhist countries). The park is an oasis of peace amid the clamour of central Bodhgaya and it's pleasant to wander the flower gardens seeing how many butterfly (and bird) species you can spot. Look out in particular for the lovely Indian jezebel, the blue tiger and the common crow butterfly, which plays a central part in the pollination of sacred bodhi trees *(Ficus religiosa)*.

UNDERSTANDING BODHGAYA'S PILGRIM SEASONS

Rahul Kumar, owner of Vedanta Routes, has a wealth of knowledge from the entire region. *vedantaroutes.com*

Our busy season is from November to March. Outside of these months accommodation prices drop dramatically and some regional restaurants (Tibetan, Thai, etc) close. September is an incredibly vibrant time because the 15-day Pind Daan festival tends to fall in this month (although dates vary because of the Hindu calendar). This festival focuses on Gaya city at revered Vishnupad Temple (closed to non-Hindu visitors), but hotels fill to capacity throughout the area. Once the Hindu pilgrims (sometimes more than a million) have finished making offerings to the ancestors, many come to pay their respects at Mahabodhi Temple here in Bodhgaya.

Spiritual Solitude

Visit Sujata Stupa

Sujata Stupa supposedly commemorates the spot where the milkmaid Sujata lived. It is said that she helped to break Gautama Buddha's fast by feeding him *kheer* (creamy rice pudding). The stupa was built in the 2nd century BCE but, despite its historical interest and spiritual importance, the well-maintained complex surrounding the great red-brick stupa sees very few visitors.

An autorickshaw will cost less than ₹40 to carry you the 2km from the Mahabodhi area, but a stroll across the mighty Falgu River is a memorable part of the Bodhgaya experience that few visitors get to enjoy. At the eastern end of the 500m-long Falgu bridge you'll walk through a vibrant little vegetable market while the western end is most notable for some of the best chai stalls (with recyclable terracotta cups) and delicious local sweets that will fuel your return stroll back to town.

Sujata Stupa is open 24 hours and the hour around daybreak is particularly blissful.

Over the River

Over the river to the Dungeshwari Cave

The tiny **Dungeshwari Cave** *(free)* is where Buddha is said to have starved himself almost to death as an ascetic before discovering the Middle Way. Local guides might tell you he was here seven years, but his entire journey of enlightenment was only six. Regardless, it's a hallowed and popular spot, with porters trying to entice pilgrims into *saliyangs* (single-poled sedan chairs). It's a timeless human-powered form of transportation that might struggle to compete with the new ropeway (cable car) set to open in late 2026.

The 30-minute drive from Bodhgaya will take you on a bumpy road through rural landscapes with ancient banyan trees and traditional Adivasi hamlets with their *jhopari* (adobe dwellings) plastered with drying cow-dung patties used for fuel. The cave itself (accessible on foot via a steep 10-minute climb) is a very scenic spot with views far across the plains to Gaya and Bodhgaya, where during Buddha's time there would have been nothing but jungle haunted by tigers and elephants. Today Dungeshwari Cave is a powerfully evocative location – somehow fittingly humble, despite glittering with gold-leaf – and once you've ducked into the sauna-like cave you'll be blessed by the resident priest.

BEST BUDDHA STATUES

Great Buddha: A Bodhgaya highlight, this statue is surrounded by 10 smaller sculptures of Buddha's disciples.

Reclining Buddha: Completed in December 2023, India's biggest reclining Buddha is gilded and 30m long (although still trumped by versions in Myanmar). It's north near the riverside road to Gaya.

Chalaymanmurti Buddha: A walking, golden figure in Sotuheast Asian style with right handheld in the Abhaya mudra (reassurance gesture).

Metta Buddharam: A gleaming white seated Buddha backed by a sparkling mirror-tiled prayer hall, around 700m north of the bus station.

Tilaya Buddha: A little-known copy of the Great Buddha at the roadside as you drive from Bodhgaya to Nawada.

DRINKING IN BODHGAYA: BEST COFFEE & TEA

Espresso Brew: An appealing coffee shop where Saif (the helpful and friendly owner) dispenses travel advice along with great coffee and brownies. *8am-9pm*

Gautam Lassi Corner: You might come here for the fruit lassis (every flavour imaginable) but stick around for the good curry. *8am-10pm*

Carrot Cake & Coffee: You'll find backpackers and monks hanging out at 'C3', enjoying the reliable wi-fi along with the famous carrot cake. *8am-9pm*

Puja Tea Store: Puja serves unusually delicious chai (in terracotta cups) and enjoys practising her English in her little stall near the Bangladeshi Monastery. *8am-9pm*

BODHGAYA'S MULTICULTURAL MONASTERIES

Take a stroll through the architectural diversity of some of Bodhgaya's most spectacular temples and international monasteries.

START	END	LENGTH
Great Buddha Statue	Namgyal Monastery	3km; 1hr

Although this walk is gorgeous at dawn, you'll want to start out at 8am if you want to find ❶ **Great Buddha Statue** (p482) open to visitors. Loop south through the expansive ❷ **Palyul Namdroling Monastery** *(8am-5pm)*, with its palatial main temple. Next head east to modernist ❸ **Indosan Nipponji Temple**, outwardly an exercise in quiet Japanese understatement, but inside there's a vivid mural depicting a multicultural mass of humanity praising a central Buddha.

One block north, the ornate ❹ **Royal Bhutanese Monastery** has some unusual 3D frescoes as well as images of the kings of Bhutan. Visually stunning, the intricate multi-roofed ❺ **Watthai Temple** provides a colourful flavour of Thailand with ample gilding and manicured gardens.

The strikingly contemporary ❻ **Bangladeshi Monastery** has a 'museum' room of scenes from Buddha's life. Haunting two-voice mantras resonate and you might get a welcome coffee. Meditation is at 6pm.

Beyond the entrance to the richly endowed ❼ **Archaeological Museum** *(9am-5pm; adults/children ₹10/free)* and the iconic ❽ **Mahabodhi Chinese Temple** is the ❾ **Shechen Tennyi Dargyeling Temple**, one of the most spectacularly ornate temples in the city.

Past ❿ **Jai Prakash Butterfly Release Park** (p483), facing the Mahabodhi Temple Complex entrance you'll find ⓫ **Namgyal Monastery** *(9am-5pm)*, housing a Mee-Tse-Khang clinic of Tibetan traditional medicine.

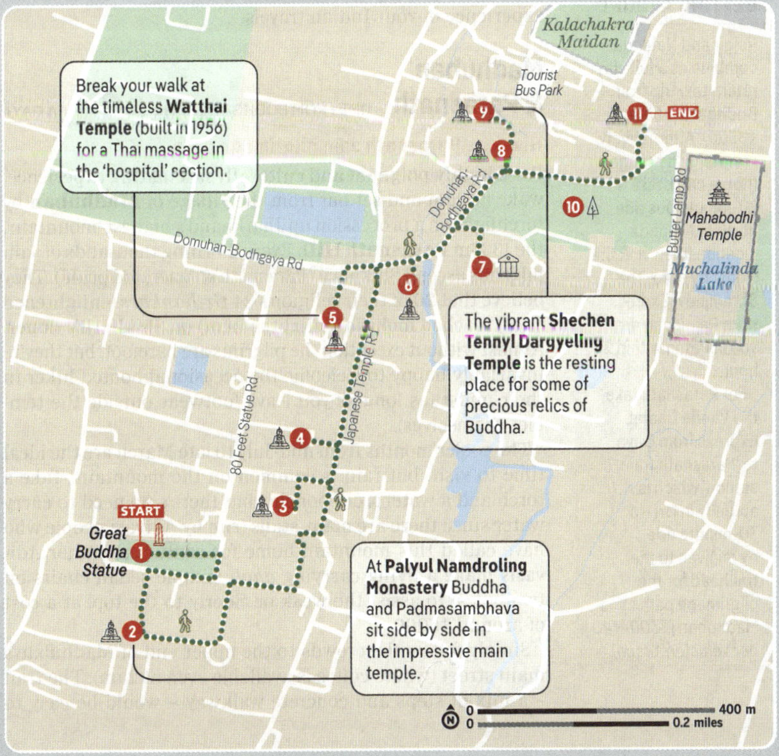

Beyond Bodhgaya

Relatively unknown to international travellers, this area has a wealth of powerfully evocative Buddhist and Jain religious sites.

Places

Gaya, Bodhgaya's big brother, is mostly useful to visitors as a transport gateway since Vishnupad Temple, the main attraction, is off-limits to non-Hindus. Rajgir and Nalanda are key stops on a Bihar 'Buddhist circuit' and, while they're worth an overnight visit, they can be accessed conveniently on a day trip. The road weaves among craggy ridges and some of India's most extensive stretches of rice paddies, with toddy palms serving as lightning conductors.

Nalanda is important to Jains as a possible birthplace of Lord Mahavir, but more significant is Parasnath, the site of a unique mountain pilgrimage that could be the most enduring experience of your Indian travels.

GETTING AROUND

Rajgir and Nalanda combine as a full-day return taxi trip from Bodhgaya *(about ₹3500)*. Alternatively, tour Rajgir by tonga (horse cart), take a 20-minute bus ride north to Nalanda junction, then visit the sights by auto. The Shramjeevi Express from Rajgir can drop you in Patna within 2½ hours.

For Parasnath take the Vande Bharat Express from Gaya to 'Parasnath train station' which is actually in Isri – a 30-minute ride by minivan to the trailhead for the pilgrimage path at Madhuban *(₹300/₹40 per vehicle/person)*.

Madhuban & Parasnath

TIME FROM BODHGAYA: 3½HR VIA GAYA

Hike the Parasnath Jain pilgrimage path

For a highly poignant and culturally fascinating experience, wake at 2am and set out from the village of **Madhuban** by torchlight on a procession up Jharkhand's highest 'mountain', the 1336m **Parasnath Hill**. Every morning thousands of Jain pilgrims ascend Shikharji (Parasnath's 'venerated peak'). They believe that 20 of their religion's 24 *tirthankars* (enlightened ones) reached moksha (enlightenment) on Shikharji's slopes. Almost without exception the pilgrims are barefoot, but they're invariably happy to welcome the occasional booted hiker in their midst (as long as you leave footwear outside the temples themselves).

The cooler months from mid-July to late March are the ideal time to visit, but rain is common on the mountain. Take a torch and a waterproof poncho, but there's no need to carry water since there are many stalls (run by Adivasi people who have called this mountain home for centuries). Other Adivasis make a living carrying *dholi* (simple sedan chairs on two poles) to assist the weak or elderly to the top, at a cost of around ₹6000.

Simply follow the crowds to the upper end of Madhuban's main street (where coffee is available even at 2am). The trail – a mix of steps and concrete walkway – would be easy to

S B STOCK/SHUTTERSTOCK

Parasnath Temple

follow even without the 'candlelit' procession. Expect to reach the peak after about three hours walking to enjoy sunrise (or, more often, swirling clouds).

It would be possible simply to enjoy the views (best from Temple 7) and then head back down, but many Jains stress that, while outsiders are welcome, this is a place of worship and non-Jain visitors (barefoot or booted) should treat it as a pilgrimage rather than a simple hike. It's recommended therefore that you set out with the intention to complete the 9km circumnambulation of the series of 'temples' situated on various *tonk* (outcrops) on the summit.

Most are tiny shrines housing a symbolic footprint, but a few are statuesque temples. Most notable is the dramatic white-stone **Parasnath Temple** on the highest peak, which is the climax of the 27km walk (9km up, 9km around the ridge, and 9km back). Note that there's only one toilet (at Jal Mandir, about halfway around) – this is one of the main reasons why many Jains avoid food and water until after they have completed their pilgrimage.

Steep steps lead to Parasnath Temple, and on a misty day it is indeed reminiscent of, as the Jains say, the 'stairway to heaven'. Leave your shoes at the bottom of the steps and you will be welcome to enter this unique holy place and might even be invited to descend, crouching under the low ceiling, into the basement where a shrine protects the ancient footprints of one of the Jains' greatest *tirthankars*.

Walking back down to Madhuban takes around two hours, initially on a different route. The entire hike can be tough on the knees as the elevation gain across the eight- to nine-hour hike is 1400m. Motorbike taxi-riders tout for passengers *(₹1000)* but, should you be tempted, bear in mind that the trail down is narrow and slippery and there have been fatalities among riders and passengers.

TRAIN VIEWS

When taking a train between Gaya and Parasnath, look through the right-hand windows just east of Gurpa station. On a clear day you'll see the glint of a gilded pagoda sitting high on a gravity-defying crag above the tree line. This fairy-tale scene is **Gurupada Giri** (aka Kukkut Oada Giri, or simply 'Gurpa Hill'), where Buddha's 'last disciple', Mahakasyapa, attained nirvana. According to some versions of the legend, the crag opened up specifically to create a throne for Mahakasyapa. Thereupon he sat and meditated and, some believe, he remains alive to this day awaiting the arrival of Maitreya, the future Buddha. King Ajatashatru of Rajgir reputedly came in search of the holy man and saw him but couldn't quite reach him.

BEING RESPECTFUL ON PARASNATH HILL

Anshul Jain, 21, from Jaipur, has walked the Parasnath Hill pilgrimage nine times.

People have their own beliefs about the pilgrimage and a good Jain doesn't judge. International tourists are welcome to wear shoes, but we prefer to go barefoot. Personally, I choose to fast entirely and I make it my own rule never to sit while on the mountain. If I need to rest, I do so standing. If we're mentally prepared we never get blisters. Foreigners expect our feet to be bleeding after 27km on the concrete, but few Jain people suffer at all. There's a deliciously spicy herb tea called *ukaali* – like a Jain energy drink – that's offered for free at some places on the mountain. It is permissible too for those fasting and you shouldn't miss it.

Explore temple town

Other than the competing throng of *dholi*-carriers at dawn and the minibus drivers *(shared/private taxi to the station ₹40/₹300-400)*, Madhuban, with its 20 or more major temples, is refreshingly hassle-free. It's notable for pilgrims, roaming cows and some spectacular temples (most open to visitors at no charge). Be prepared to encounter naked elderly men – the most spiritually advanced Digambara Jains (Digambara nuns are not so 'sky-clad').

You'll pass the beautiful arches of **Shri Tees Chaubisi Digambar Jain Mandir** near the top edge of town if you head for Parasnath Hill, but return later (around 8pm is ideal) to see it packed with worshippers dancing wildly to devotional music every evening during the pilgrimage season. The more humble but spectacularly carved **Shri Aninda Parshvnath Digambar** has an air of history about it and a friendly caretaker who is happy to show visitors around at no charge.

The **Acharya Shri Shanti Sagar Dham** is worth visiting to see the four-storey statue of the second *tirthankar*, Ajitanath Bhagwan (naked of course). The **Jain Museum** *(₹10)* is slightly underwhelming, with 38 colourful dioramas illustrating the religion's history.

The fabulous new **Shree Digambar Jain Gunayatan** – surely one of the most spectacular temples of modern times – is worth visiting even while building work continues. The **Gunayatan Theme Park**, just across the road, was also expected to be completed in 2026 but is unfortunately an architectural eyesore in such a spiritual town. When opened it will offer high-tech, simulator-seat experiences elucidating religious themes, notably the 14 'soul positions' of Jainism.

Rajgir

TIME FROM BODHGAYA: 1½HR

Ride a cable car to the mountaintop stupa

Vishwa Shanti Stupa is a spired white dome, dedicated to world peace, on a modest yet holy mountaintop overlooking Rajgir. The attraction for most seems to be in getting there on the ropeway *(9am-5pm; adult/child ₹250/free)*. This eight-seater cable car – thankfully having supplanted the single-seater hanging steel chairs – takes four minutes to reach the stupa.

The craving for spiritual peace is not enhanced by the troops of marauding monkeys that swarm like bandits around the stupa. Leave the throngs of sightseers and monkeys behind

EATING NEAR RAJGIR: OUR PICKS

Wat Thai Latthiwan Mahavihara: Between September and March the Thai Buddhist nuns here offer simple free breakfasts (donations welcome). *9am-noon* ₹

Punjabi Rasoi: Excellent Punjabi and local dishes with an outlet in Rajgir centre and a new one at the ropeway station. *11am-9.30pm* ₹₹

Litti Chokha Vendors: Inexpensive but tasty street snacks opposite the tonga stand in Rajgir. Green Hotel next door has seating. *hours vary* ₹

Chulha Bistro/Mitti Farms: This charming place for organic food is about halfway along the Bodhgaya–Rajgir road. *9am-11pm* ₹₹

ASIM VERM/SHUTTERSTOCK

Vishwa Shanti Stupa, Rajgir

by taking the woodland walk back down the mountain. The route is unmarked but take the steps on the left and you can't go wrong. A well-maintained jungle path, complete with myriad butterflies and mosquitoes, leads you back via **Vulture Hill** (Gijjhakuta), where four tiny caves are associated with Buddha's main disciples.

Visit Buddha's bath

Venu Van *(tourism.bihar.gov.in; ₹150)* is best described as an 'oasis' near the heart of perpetually bustling Rajgir. Imaginative landscaping includes floral tunnels, hanging walkways, a herb garden, a Japanese garden, a meditation centre and well-designed play areas for children.

The gardens, which would be worth visiting just for the iconic Indian flora and birdlife, are yet another Buddhist treasure since it's said that they're on the site of a bamboo grove that was given to Buddha by his convert King Bimbisara. Legend has it that Bimbisara's security personnel were so strict that when the king was late returning from his evening bathe in the Saraswati River they refused to readmit him. So he spent the night with his friend Buddha.

It's believed that the only feature that survives from historical times is the **Karanda Water Tank** where Buddha bathed (and which was being equipped with pedalos at the time of research).

KING BIMBISARA OF MAGADHA

Rajgir rose to greatness as Girivraja, 6th-century BCE capital of the Magadha kingdom ruled by semi-legendary King Bimbisara. Both Buddhists and Jains (who call him Shrenika) credit Bimbisara with taking an intimate interest in their founders' spiritual teachings, both Buddha and Mahavir having spent serious time here. The king is credited with building Rajgir's 40km 'cyclopean' (ie encircling) wall, sections of which remain visible on the city's surrounding hills. Later in life he was imprisoned by his son and usurper Ajatashatru, who went on to found his own capital at Pataliputra (now Patna). These days an excavated area is signposted as being the site of Bimbisara's jail though non-archaeologists would be hard pressed to see much pattern to the scattered rocks.

PRADEEPGAURS/SHUTTERSTOCK

Nalanda University Ruins

TOP EXPERIENCE

Nalanda & Rajgir Historical Sites

A wander around the UNESCO-listed Nalanda Ruins takes you back to when this was one of the ancient world's great universities. In a day-trip tour from Bodhgaya you can to combine a visit to this and several other of Nalanda's historic treasures with a cable-car ride to Vishwa Shanti Stupa and a restful wander at nearby Venu Van in Rajgir.

DON'T MISS

- Nalanda University Ruins
- Xuan Zang Memorial Hall
- Kundalpur Digambar Jain Temple
- Son Bhandar
- Nalanda Archaeological Museum

Nalanda University Ruins

The huge expanse of shrines, stupas and monasteries at the UNESCO-listed Nalanda Ruins *(nalanda.nic.in; ₹600)* was once one of the world's greatest universities. The name is said to have derived from the Sanskrit phrase *na alam da* – 'the gift of knowledge knows no bounds'. It was founded about 450 CE and functioned uninterrupted for 800 years. There are six brick temples and 11 monasteries, but so little survived after its abandonment around the 13th century that the site

PRACTICALITIES

● tourism.bihar.gov.in ● Nalanda University 9am-5pm; ₹600 ● Xuan Zang Memorial Hall 8am-5pm; ₹200 ● Kundalpur Digambar Jain Temple 24hr; ₹10 was mere undulations when it was finally excavated in 1916. Today it's a spectacular place to explore and there's good signage throughout in English. The scale of the entire monastery complex is breathtaking, and the intricate sculptures and cramped, windowless cells (home to countless monks) are particularly thought-provoking.

Xuan Zang Memorial Hall

Much of what's known about Nalanda University's heyday comes from reports written by Chinese traveller Xuan Zang (602–664 CE) who spent six years at the complex. One of the world's first guidebook writers, he made an epic 17-year journey around India with a 'backpack' full of scrolls, which resulted in 657 sacred texts. His travels are beautifully illustrated and explained (in English) at the Xuan Zang Memorial Hall *(tourism.bihar.gov.in; ₹200)*, where the highlight is a beautiful wall of metal inlay panels depicting his adventures. The hall is a 2km auto-ride from Nalanda Ruins, but the walk, past a lake surrounded by grazing buffalo, is appealing if it's cool.

Kundalpur Digambar Jain Temple

Though some Jains place it at Vaishali, the Digambara Jains cite Kundalpur village, 1.5km from Nalanda Ruins, as the birthplace of Lord Mahavir, founder of Jainism in its present form. At Kundalpur Digambar Jain Temple, the central temple tower features Mahavir unaffectedly naked and clad only in a rainbow of coloured spotlights. Digambara holy men eschew clothes, but you'll be expected only to eschew your shoes (and perhaps any leather belts or watch-straps) before you enter.

Son Bhandar Caves

Son Bhandar archaeological site *(free)* is a 20-minute drive south of Nalanda – and could conveniently be combined with a visit to Vishwa Shanti Stupa (p488). The two man-made caves were excavated by a Jain sage around the 3rd or 4th century CE. According to legend they were King Bimbisara's treasury, but a small tip for one of the caretakers will reveal even more colourful legends: a secret door is said to lead to a 2km-long tunnel and allegedly even British cannon-fire was insufficient to open it. Script carved into the back wall is in an unknown language, but it's believed that when the words are finally spoken aloud the door will automatically swing open to reveal unimaginable treasures. (So far even Google translate can't crack the code.)

Nalanda Archaeological Museum

Some fine original statuary that had remained buried for centuries at Nalanda Ruins is now displayed across the road in the small but rich Nalanda Archaeological Museum *(tourism.bihar.gov.in; free with ticket to Nalanda Ruins)*. There's also a fine statue of Vishnu removed from Son Bhandar Caves. A historical building in its own right (founded in 1917), the museum was undergoing refurbishment at the time of research but was due to open in 2026.

NALANDA & RAJGIR'S MODERN ATTRACTIONS

The extensive **Rajgir Wildlife Safari** (aka Forest Park) is a crowd-puller for domestic and regional tourists with a safari park, interpretation centre, 3D movie and cycle zip-wire. Locals flock here specifically for the **Sky Bridge**, a glass-floored platform projecting 30m over a deep forested valley. It's unique for Bihar but can feel tame if you've experienced similar elsewhere. Queues, especially at weekends, are often appalling.

TOP TIPS

- The quintessential way to explore the sights from central Rajgir is by tonga (a lofty horse-drawn carriage). The standard tour *(around ₹800)* includes the stones labelled King Bimbisara's Prison.
- If you travel by public transport it's likely to take at least two days to take in the historic riches of this area. If time's short consider shelling out around ₹3500 on a reliable Bodhgaya-based driver who knows the area. Vedanta Routes *(vedantaroutes.com)* can arrange tours.
- If you're well organised, a day touring the archaeological sights of Nalanda and Rajgir can easily be combined with a visit to Vishwa Shanti Stupa.

Patna

GREAT MUSEUMS | STREET ART | HIDDEN HISTORY

If you can look beyond the mouldering 1970s concrete architecture and the deafening din of its traffic, Patna is a remarkably friendly metropolis. Many locals seem disproportionately delighted to find a foreigner taking an interest in Bihar's rich historical roots and are proud of the way that their city has started to blossom over the last decade.

Nothing is more symbolic of the transformation than the sleek, world-class Bihar Museum, which is the main must-see attraction. While lacking the modern sheen, the historic Patna Museum (a leading light dating back to 1917) still retains the romance of past ages.

Little else in Patna even hints that this was once the capital of the mighty pan-Indian Mauryan empire (322–180 BCE), but this is a place that repays those who take time to explore and soak up the urban atmosphere, fuelled perhaps by some great local cuisine and a burgeoning cafe culture.

GETTING AROUND

The 110km/h Vande Bharat Express connects Patna with Gaya in just over 1.5 hours. The Uber app exists in Patna (but not Gaya), but in practice it's usually much faster just to flag down one of the ubiquitous autos on the street. Expect to pay around ₹100 for a half-hour journey. Traffic can become congested (even by Indian standards) during rush hours and you might often find that it's quicker simply to walk.

TOP TIP

While Patna has hundreds of hotels, almost all the budget options, and even some midrange choices, lack the necessary permissions (or will) to host foreigners. Beware that booking websites rarely alert you to this caveat.

Bihar Unveiled

Explore the fabulous Bihar Museum complex

Bihar Tourism describes the province as 'the cradle of Indian civilisation', and for an understanding of its historic influence throughout the region head for the world-class **Bihar Museum** *(biharmuseum.org; adult/child ₹500/₹250)*. You could spend all day wandering its thoughtfully laid-out halls learning about history dating back the Stone Age, the Magadha era and the city's part in the first pan-Indian empire. The depth of information is exhaustive, but the museum is so well planned that a visitor's curiosity is drawn from room to room. The interactive children's section is impressive too, offering fascinating information for adults as well. The Potbelly Restaurant (more a sort of canteen) is on hand, but for a change of scene head 1.5km up Bailey Rd to the Patna Museum where the cafeteria (p495) is infinitely more appealing.

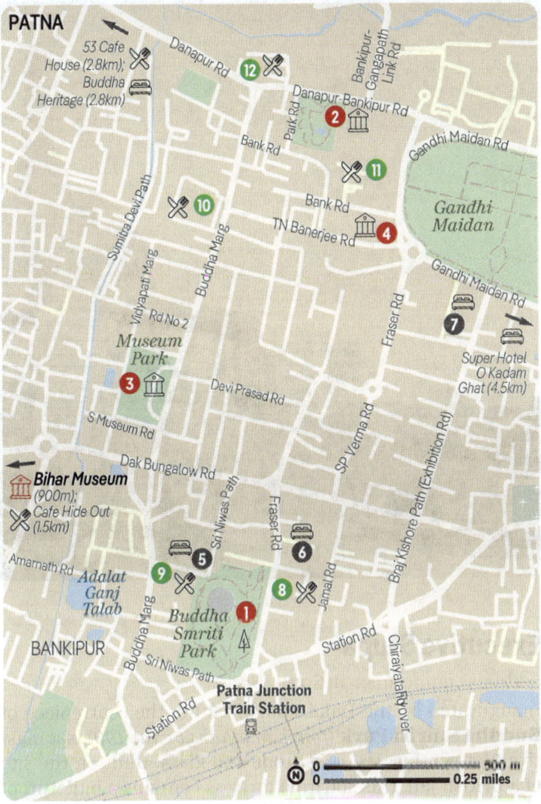

SIGHTS
1 Buddha Smriti Park
2 Golghar
3 Patna Museum
4 Shrikrishna Science Centre

SLEEPING
5 Capital House
6 Hotel Astor
7 Lemon Tree Premier

EATING
8 Blue Moon
9 Bonkers Cafe
see 3 Cafeteria the Park
10 Craft Coffee
11 Lighthouse Cafe
12 Litti Chokha Stall

The two museums (both closed on Mondays) are affiliated and the bulk of the Bihar collection came from the historic **Patna Museum** *(biharmuseum.org; adult/child ₹250/₹125)*, which was founded in 1917. The lovely museum building was mostly built in 1928 and – reminiscent of a particularly spectacular Mughal palace – is known locally simply as 'Jadu Ghar', the Magic House.

Patna Museum's modern wing houses a display that captures the cultural and historical importance of the Ganges as it flows through Bihar. It is interactive enough to keep children entertained too. At the time of writing, the main building was being renovated and the US$20 million makeover was expected to be completed in late 2026. The museum (complete with a new sculpture garden) will then be dedicated to the post-1764 era.

Shrikrishna Science Centre *(sksciencecentre.org; ₹50)* could be India's most entertaining museum. Kids will love the outdoor Jurassic Park–themed model dinosaurs and adults will be enthralled by the fascinating collection of science experiments in the main building. Some are fully explained (with signs in English), but you're left to puzzle others out for yourself.

SONEPUR MELA LIVESTOCK MARKET

Sonepur Mela, one of Asia's biggest livestock markets, takes place during Kartik Purnima (usually in early November). It lasts for two weeks and is held at Sonepur, 8km from Patna on the northern bank of the Ganges. More than just an animal market, it is also a religious event with thousands of pilgrims coming to bathe in holy waters and pray at Sonepur's Harihar Nath Temple. Once famous for its immense elephant market, Sonepur Mela is now focused more on cattle. In his best-selling 1991 book *Travels on my Elephant*, Mark Shand described at first hand the dramatic experience of trying to deliver and sell his elephant Tara at the Sonepur Mela.

ARNAV PRATAP SINGH/SHUTTERSTOCK

Executive Stupa

Buddhist modernism in Smriti Park

Inaugurated by the Dalai Lama in 2010, the centrepiece of **Buddha Smriti Park** *(tourism.bihar.gov.in; ₹90)* is a massive 21st-century stupa in stone and glass. Built on the site of a British jail, this spiritual fortress contains a bulletproof glass chamber containing six stupa-shaped Buddha reliquaries. The once-formidable security has relaxed a lot and, while you should leave bags at the gate, visitors are now permitted to enter with phones and cameras. Apart from the stupa, the highlight of a visit to the park is the excellent museum which opens its doors to a new group at a quarter to each hour. The visit starts with a 10-minute film depicting Buddha's life and then the group is ushered into a series of rooms with fascinating exhibits offering an insight into Buddhism around the world. There's even a blacked-out man-made meditation cave with a sort of mini amphitheatre where you can sit in peace until you have to move on, back to the realm of the bleating autos out on Patna Junction. The memorial park is

EATING IN PATNA: OUR PICKS

Blue Moon: In an alley beside V2 Mall, this is one of several stalls famous for amazing-value hot rolls (made with roti and a variety of fillings). *noon-10.30pm* ₹

Litti Chokha Stall: Bihar's chickpea doughball snacks are served with tangy salsa at street stalls at the northern end of Buddha Marg. *hours vary* ₹

Bonkers Cafe: Central cafe with lasagne, burgers, tandoor dishes and a great selection of enticing juices. *24hr* ₹₹

Lighthouse Cafe: Italian coffee and international cuisine on the 17th floor of Bihar's tallest building. Revolving banquet floor above. *noon-10pm* ₹₹

Stupa, Buddha Smriti Park

closed on Mondays and tickets cover admission for a maximum of two hours.

Gargantuan Granary

Patna's Raj-era icon

The distinctive **Golghar** *(tourism.bihar.gov.in; ₹10)*, a bulbous granary like half a giant onion, rises from the city's edge near Patna's Gandhi Maidan. Just as that dusty park (the setting for the Bihar Diwas festival on 22 March, which celebrates Bihar's 1912 reinstatement) is sometimes optimistically referred to as Patna's green lung, the 29.5m-tall Golghar (literally Round House) granary never quite lived up to expectations. It was built by the British in 1786 to avoid a repeat of the devastating 1770 famine. A plaque on the dome's northern side (marking it as Golghar #1) has a blank space for the date when the granary was filled. The local populace promptly pointed out the difficulty of hefting heavy sacks of grain up 142 spiralling steps to the small hole in the onion's top. Needless to say, Golghar #2 was never built.

MAGADHA LEGACY

Bihar was an epicentre of power, trade and military might from about the 6th century BCE and remained a cultural powerhouse and a centre of learning in northern India for more than 1500 years. With the Ganges River providing sustenance and transport through the region, Magadha's imperial capital was established in Pataliputra (to the east of modern day Patna – and not to be confused with the ritzy neighbourhood of the same name that's been constructed in the city's west). It was in the Magadha region that both Jainism and Buddhism were born and for this reason, although international tourism is still relatively rare, Bihar continues to attract large numbers of pilgrims to this day.

DRINKING IN PATNA: BEST COFFEE SHOPS

Craft Coffee: Striving for perfect coffee, this place (in City Centre Mall) is investigating how artificial intelligence could improve its roasting. *11am-10pm* ₹₹

Cafe Hide Out: This chain of international-style cafes started in Patna. The Boring Rd branch has covered rooftop seating. *11am-11pm* ₹

53 Cafe House: In Patna's coolest garden restaurant the coffee's good and you might also order one the best curries you ever tasted. *3-10pm Sun-Fri, 11am-11pm Sat* ₹₹

Cafeteria the Park: At the cafe in Patna Museum you'll get excellent iced coffee, topped with thick ice cream (ask for a spoon). *10.30am-9pm Tue-Sun* ₹₹

FROM PATNA TOWARDS KATHMANDU

This drive takes you from the Ganges to the foothills of the Indian Himalaya.

START	END	LENGTH
Patna's Ganges Bridge	Satyagraha Park	200km; 5hr

Drive north out of Patna on the 1 **Ganges Bridge** and in two hours you'll reach Vaishali. A relic-casket found here in 1960, believed to contain cremated ashes of the historical Buddha, lies beneath a corrugated metal dome at 2 **Buddha Relic Stupa**. A vast 3 **Buddha Samyak Darshan Museum & Memorial Stupa** opened in 2026 to house the priceless reliquary. Stroll to the large 4 **Peace Pagoda** and 5 **Archaeological Museum**, where the most off-beat exhibit is the 'squat-stone' for a 2000-year-old toilet pit. The 6 **Kolhua Complex**, 5km north, is a calm archaeological park where pilgrim groups meditate around a brick stupa among the foundations of monastic buildings. At 7 **Kesariya Stupa**, 55km further northwest, excavations are showing that a grassy hillock is one of the world's biggest stupa ruins, commemorating the spot where the dying Buddha donated his begging bowl.

Continue north for 45km to 8 **Mahatma Gandhi Smarak** in Motihari, where Gandhi's satyagraha (non-violent civil resistance movement) started in 1917 when he championed oppressed farmers who'd been forced to produce indigo for British dye-makers.

Motihari is also notable as the birthplace of George Orwell. His father's cottage is now the little 9 **Orwell Museum** in Satyagraha Park. If you're heading for the Nepalese border it's a 55km drive from here to the border at Raxaul.

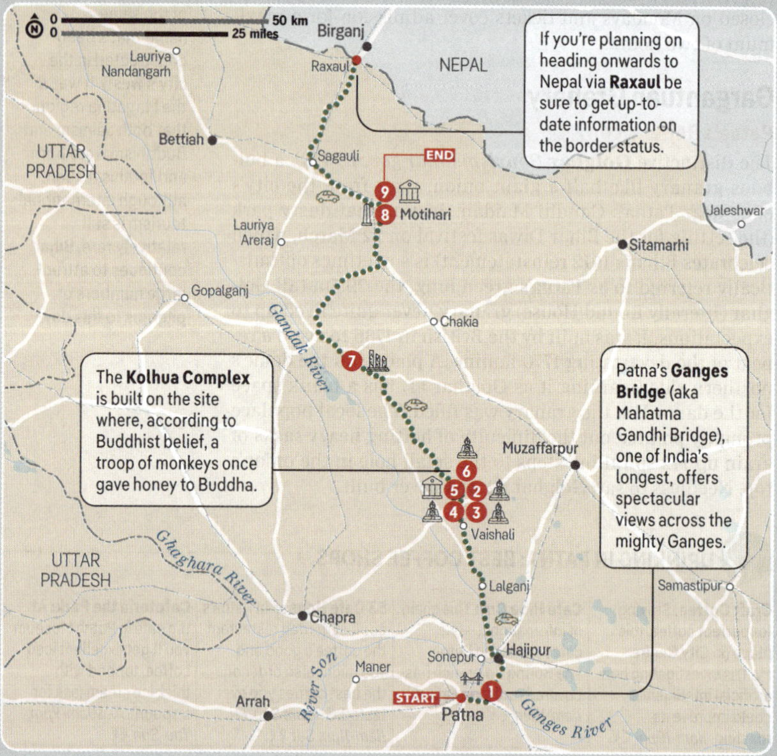

Places We Love to Stay

₹ **Budget** ₹₹ **Midrange** ₹₹₹ **Top End**

Bodhgaya

Map p481

Rahul Guesthouse ₹ An ideal budget bet with an owner and manager who are a wealth of travel advice. The top floor is quietest and its terrace has the best views.

Beauty Guest House ₹ A friendly, family-run cheapy. Simple, clean fan and air-con rooms are standard, but the view from the roof is a real bonus.

Root Institute for Wisdom Culture ₹ There's a range of rooms (and dorms) at this meditation retreat that hosts courses and instruction.

Kirti Guesthouse ₹ Popular with monks on long-stay retreats, this guest house has spacious rooms (air-con and fan) with a view from the back over the Butterfly Park.

Shantidevi Ashram's Guesthouse ₹₹ Stylishly distressed furniture and handicrafts create a boutique feel in this very personable place with mini garden. One of Bodhgaya's few boutique hotels.

Bodhgaya Hotel School ₹₹ Stay in comfortable, well-appointed rooms while supporting a project that provides vocational training for underprivileged youths.

Maya Heritage Hotel ₹₹ Big, airy rooms have lots of homely touches. Staff are welcoming and it's way better than many Bodhgaya hotels that cost twice the price.

Hotel Mahayana ₹₹ Central yet an oasis of calm, right in front of the lovely Butterfly Park. Clean, well-equipped rooms are decorated with Tibetan elements.

Buddha Heritage Resort ₹₹ A step upmarket with the convenient on-site Siddhartha Restaurant and a 25m pool in which to escape the Bihar heat.

Gaya

Hostel Relax Homestay ₹ A simple but welcoming budget choice that's an ideal option if you have an early or late train since it's just 2km from Gaya station.

Sri Vishnu View Hotel ₹₹ A business-style hotel, near Vishnupad Temple zone and just a stone's throw from the ghats.

Madhuban & Parasnath

Gulab Mansion ₹ Huge rooms with massive beds (designed for families). The 8am check-out time is rarely a problem since you'll either be trekking or catching an early train.

Chandra Lok Bhawan ₹ A soulless tower-block hostel of the sort that's typical in Madhuban. It's comfortable, clean and well located for dawn pilgrimages.

Rajgir & Nalanda

Hotel Sagar Inn ₹ A slightly bland convention/events-type hotel but good value if you're determined to stay in central Rajgir.

7 Hills ₹₹ Impressive, super-comfortable contemporary hotel with a small pool, gym and keen staff. On the outskirts of Nalanda town. Fabulous value at walk-in prices.

Patna

Map p493

Super Hotel O Kadam Ghat ₹ A rare cheap option in Patna. About 30 minutes east of the city centre but recommendable for outstanding views over the mighty Ganges.

Capital House ₹₹ A business-style hotel that's excellent value in an ideal location, just around the corner from the 24-hour Bonkers Cafe.

Hotel Astor ₹₹ Rooms are compact but stylish and offer good value by Patna's (relatively expensive) standards. Handy for the station.

Buddha Heritage ₹₹ If you don't mind staying further from the centre, this Patliputra option is more characterful. Events are often held on the rooftop.

Lemon Tree Premier ₹₹₹ Business hotel with spa, gym and (unheated) rooftop swimming pool, plus a Zen-like calm to its spacious foyer.

For places to stay in Sikkim, see p527

DEBARUP/SHUTTERSTOCK

Above: Goecha-La Trek (p522); Right: Red panda, Himalayan Zoological Park (p508), Gangtok

Researched by
Dr Jenny Walker

Sikkim

THE LOST MOUNTAIN KINGDOM

Soaring Himalayan peaks and steep, misty woodland trails, interspersed with Buddhist temples, Nepali-Hindu shrines and a rich diversity of tribal cultures merge in this lofty kingdom.

Bending to receive a silk *khada* – the ceremonial scarf honouring guests – a visitor at a hotel in Gangtok is asked by the host where he's from. 'India,' he says; 'Welcome' is the response. It's a telling exchange because it belies a sense on both sides of the state border that Sikkim is a land apart. An independent kingdom until 1975, Sikkim retains an independent spirit, leaning less towards lowland India than Nepal (the language of which has become Sikkim's lingua franca). Bordering Tibet and Bhutan, Sikkim shares with these two Himalayan neighbours a deep faith in Buddhism and it has become a focus of religious tourism. Following in the footsteps of pilgrims as they journey from gompa to gompa through the deeply incised valleys of the so-called 'Green State' makes for a fascinating introduction to the region as a whole.

ROHIT NAIR.PHOTOS/SHUTTERSTOCK

Around 70% of Sikkim is forested and it's the first state in India to be declared all-organic. This impressive achievement echoes the general Sikkimese concept of living in harmony. No longer quite the crimeless state it once was, Sikkim is still a gentle place to visit, offering warm cultural encounters, delicious meals and a sense of retreat in rural homestays. Most foreign visitors come to trek towards Khangchendzonga (8586m), the world's third-highest mountain, but there's much to be said for going nowhere in particular and letting the reticulated mountain roads dictate a slower pace of travel.

THE MAIN AREAS

GANGTOK
Sikkim's capital and cultural hub. p504

PELLING
Rural town with spectacular Himalayan views. p514

Find Your Way

With Pakyong Airport rarely operational, access to Sikkim is by bus, taxi or shared 4WD from Siliguri (West Bengal) or Bagdogra Airport. Darjeeling and/or Kalimpong make fine stopovers en route. The Siliguri–Rangpo railway is under construction.

SHARED 4WD

Apart from a limited bus service, almost all public transport on Sikkim's labyrinth of narrow hairpin roads is by shared jeep. Ten passengers squeeze aboard, including two beside the driver: booking the two front-seat spaces for one person avoids claustrophobia.

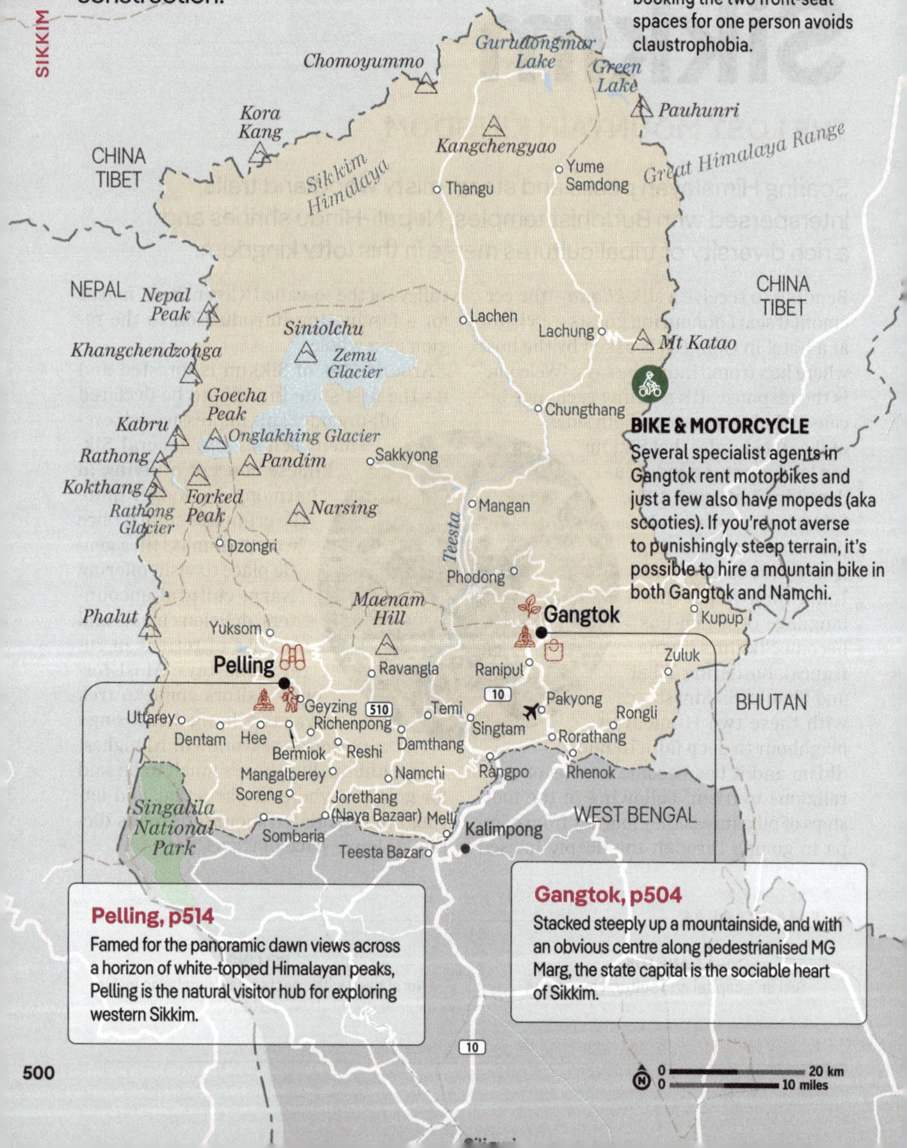

BIKE & MOTORCYCLE

Several specialist agents in Gangtok rent motorbikes and just a few also have mopeds (aka scooties). If you're not averse to punishingly steep terrain, it's possible to hire a mountain bike in both Gangtok and Namchi.

Pelling, p514

Famed for the panoramic dawn views across a horizon of white-topped Himalayan peaks, Pelling is the natural visitor hub for exploring western Sikkim.

Gangtok, p504

Stacked steeply up a mountainside, and with an obvious centre along pedestrianised MG Marg, the state capital is the sociable heart of Sikkim.

NATTEE CHALERMTIRAGOOL/SHUTTERSTOCK

Tsomgo Lake (p503)

Plan Your Time

Be prepared to change itineraries according to current road conditions: landslides and highway works can render route sections miserably difficult or close them altogether, sometimes for months.

With a Few Days

- From Siliguri or Kalimpong head to **Namchi** (p519). Admire the two religious mega-structures, hike along **Tarey Bihr** (p520) or relax in a cafe-bar. Next day drive to **Pelling** (p514), visit the Chenrezig statue and historic **Rabdentse ruins** (p516), but sleep early enough to wake at dawn for spectacular Himalayan views, best at sunrise. Return south via Jorethang to Darjeeling (West Bengal).

More than a Week

- Start in **Gangtok** (p504) with a sunset walk along MG Marg. After dawn at Enchey Gompa get back to town via our **walking tour** (p509). Arrange a ride via **Rumtek** (p510), the **Martam Rice Terraces** (p511) and **Temi tea fields** (p519) to Ravangla with its **Giant Buddha** (p518). Enjoy **Pelling** (p514) then magical **Yuksom** (p520) for a one-day monastery hike or longer mountain trek.

SEASONAL HIGHLIGHTS

SPRING
Clear skies and mild temperatures. Peak blooming times for rhododendrons. April and May bring high-season prices.

SUMMER
Summer can be misty and so wet that roads are washed out, and some hotels close June to September.

AUTUMN
Good trekking months. Much closes down during Tihar, aka Diwali (October/November), and transport is often full.

WINTER
Losoon's end-of-harvest festival at many monastic locations, notably Old Rumtek. Snow in higher mountains from January.

NEED TO KNOW:

Permits & Travel Tips

For non-Indian visitors, visiting Sikkim is slightly complicated by the need to apply for an entry permit. Entry permit applications, however, are easy to organise, either in advance or on arrival, and Sikkim tour agencies can help, if required, with the paperwork. In addition to the entry permit, further stipulations (namely joining a small-group tour) apply if you wish to travel to some designated areas within Sikkim, while some border zones are entirely closed to foreigners. For information about trekking and mountaineering permits, see p522.

Applying to Enter

Before entering Sikkim, foreigners must obtain an entry permit. These are referred to as either ILP (Inner Line Permit) or RAP (Restricted Area Permit). These are free and applications can be made in advance when applying for an Indian visa. They can also be applied for in India at tourist offices in Siliguri and Bagdogra Airport (until 4pm), and in Darjeeling, Delhi or Kolkata (at Sikkim House). Applications can also be made on arrival at a Sikkim state border post (generally 8am to 7.30pm only).

To make an application, you will need photocopies of your passport data page and visa for India, together with one or two passport-sized photos.

Although you can request up to 30 days, most ILPs are initially valid for two weeks. Extending is possible for a second two weeks at the Foreigners Registration Office (FRO) at Tadong (6km from Gangtok) or the Superintendent of Police at Tikjuk (4km from Pelling).

Getting an Entry Stamp at the State Border

If travelling into Sikkim by road, it is imperative that foreigners stop at one of the three currently accessible state border posts (listed below) for their ILP to be stamped. This is rather more of a challenge than it sounds given this procedure is not required for Indian citizens and so drivers of shared 4WDs and buses may not stop at these posts unless specifically asked.

Without your ILP stamped on entry, hotels will not be able to permit you to stay and you will be required to backtrack to the nearest state border post.

To/From Assam

These state border posts between Assam and Sikkim both issue and stamp ILPs for Sikkim.

Rangpo The main crossing point between West Bengal's Siliguri and East Sikkim, this is the main entry point for Gangtok. Note that a new road bridge means that the main Siliguri–Gangtok highway currently bypasses Rangpo checkpoint. To get your ILP stamped you'll need to divert along the old road.

Melli This state border post connects West Bengal's Kalimpong with South Sikkim, giving the most direct access to Namchi.

Jorethang This minor state border post allows a direct route for travellers using small vehicles between West Bengal's Darjeeling and Pelling in West Sikkim.

Pakyong Airport At the time of research flights had been suspended, but if the airport reopens, the permit office is likely to follow suit. If using the Gangtok helicopter, get your ILP at Bagdogra Airport's Tourist Office.

It is not currently possible to cross between Sikkim and any neighbouring country (ie Nepal, China and Bhutan).

DEBARUP/SHUTTERSTOCK

Khangchendzonga massif (p514)

Additional Permits & Closed Areas

To travel in some restricted parts of Sikkim, a further permit is required in addition to the ILP. These internal permits require foreigners to be accompanied by a registered tour guide, or in some instances by a driver who may act as a guide, and are only issued to groups of at least two people.

Note that it is not possible for foreigners to share a 4WD with Indian citizens when travelling in restricted areas. The rules regarding who can travel where, how and when change quite frequently, so it's best to check with a tour agent well in advance if you are keen to reach any of the following.

Nathu La & Tsomgo Lake Despite being a popular day trip for Indian tourists, visiting the Tibetan border post at Nathu La is not permitted for foreigners. It is possible to reach Tsomgo Lake with a guide through a registered tourist operator, but it is usually very crowded and perhaps not the most rewarding experience.

Dzongu Foreigners must obtain a permit for Dzongu (p512) through a registered travel agency and must be accompanied by a guide.

North Sikkim The dramatic scenery in the Far North is a main attraction of Sikkim, with Lachung (p513) the most popular destination with foreign visitors. Permits, guides and transport must be arranged through a registered travel agent. At the time of writing, the north was still being impacted by the Glacial Lake Out Flow (GLOF) of 2023/24 and subsequent landslides due to heavy rain in 2025. This has damaged roads, particularly around Mangan, which is currently mostly being bypassed en route to Lachung until repairs are completed.

Gangtok

LOST ROYALTY | RED PANDAS | WALKABLE CENTRE

GETTING AROUND

MG Marg at the centre of town is flat but to reach anywhere else involves a steep hike. Shared taxis shuttle along the main roads, or the Gangtok Ropeway is a fun way to reach Deorali from the palace area. Shared 4WDs to Ranka start from near West Point Mall; for Mangan from Vajra Taxi Stand; for most other Sikkim destinations from the multistorey Deorali 4WD Stand; and for Siliguri and Darjeeling from the Siliguri Bus Stand a little further down. Try **Throttle Rentals** *(instagram .com/throttlerentals)* on Tibet Rd for reliable motorbikes, or **Hill Bike** *(89187 33644)* rents mountain bikes.

Sikkim's capital and only real city is a cheerful, lively place of brightly painted buildings rendered dramatic by being layered in steep tiers up a precipitous mountain ridge. When clouds clear, the snow-topped tip of Khangchendzonga soars above ridges on the northwestern skyline, visible from windows, rooftops and especially well-positioned viewpoints.

More than specific sights, Gangtok is appealing as a place for meeting fellow travellers: gathering a group saves on 4WD fares and helps get necessary permits if heading north or east. Tucked within the city's confusing spirals of steep lanes and stairways lies its wide socio-commercial heart known as MG (Mahatma Gandhi) Marg. Mostly pedestrianised, this street has all the facilities a visitor needs, including tour agents, money changers, souvenirs, photo printers and countless restaurant-bars. Contrastingly calm and partly wooded areas nearby enfold Buddhist monasteries and the Chogyal Palace, the former royal residence.

The Passeggiata

Stroll along MG Marg

Join the gently buzzing crowd for Gangtok's quintessential visitor experience: a leisurely stroll along the partly pedestrianised main shopping and restaurant strip of MG Marg and its southern extension Namnang Rd (aka Kashira Pradhan Marg). The ambience is best at dusk, especially around New Year when the trees sparkle with festive lights, the giant red panda statue glows orange and the monument to the promenade's namesake is illuminated in bright green.

Look out for a couple of architectural highlights among the pastel-coloured shopfronts, including the facade of the **Dragon Wok** Chinese restaurant, with its pair of ornate dragons, and kiosks selling *paan* (mixture of betel nut and leaves for chewing). The vintage textile emporium **Bansal Trading** is also worth a visit; it's been in business for 80 years or more

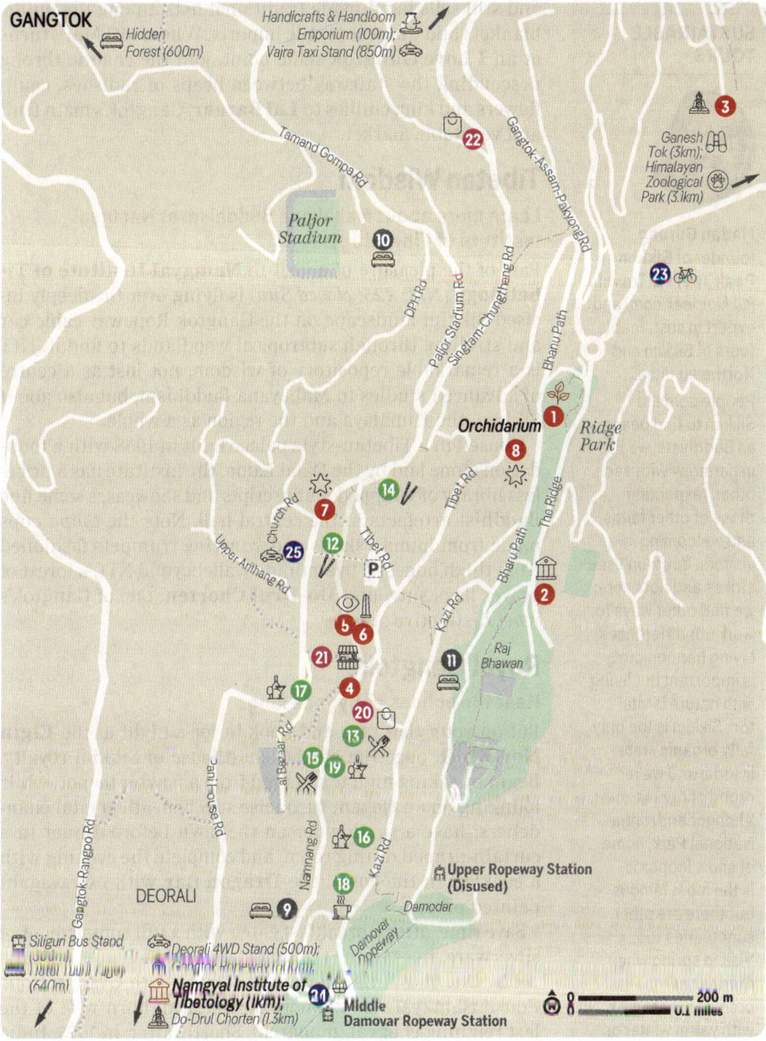

HIGHLIGHTS
1 Orchidarium

SIGHTS
2 12 Chogyals Exhibition
3 Enchey Gompa
4 I Love Gangtok Sign
5 Mahatma Gandi (MG) Marg
6 Red Panda Statue

ACTIVITIES
7 STDC
8 Throttle Rentals

SLEEPING
9 Dzongkar
10 Elgin Nor-Khill
11 Hotel Pandim

EATING
see 22 Cafe Fiction
12 Dragon Wok
13 Nimtho
14 Shuffle Momos
15 Yak Bar

DRINKING & NIGHTLIFE
16 Gangtok Groove
17 Jungle Bar
18 Sikkim Coffee
19 Yak Bar

SHOPPING
20 Bansal Trading
21 Lal Bazaar
22 Rachna Bookshop

TRANSPORT
23 Hill Bike
24 Namnang Ropeway Station
25 Shared 4WDs to Ranka

SUSTAINABLE TOURS

Madan Gurung, founder of **Sikkim Peak Tours & Travels** *(sikkimpeak.com)* and expert in sustainable tours of Sikkim and Northeast India.

People come to Sikkim to find peace: as Buddhists, we live in harmony with each other, respecting those of other faiths and welcoming visitors. You won't see strikes and riots here: we find other ways to work out differences. Living harmoniously is important but living with nature is vital too. Sikkim is the only fully organic state in India and we're proud of our reserves. Khangchendzonga National Park, home of snow leopards, is the most famous but there are other sanctuaries too. Visit in spring when rhododendrons and orchids bloom, trek with yak in winter or book a rural homestay and you'll soon feel the spirit of Sikkim.

and still sells hand-made traditional hats among the quilts, blankets and Chinese textile imports. Where MG Marg turns at an **I Love Gangtok** selfie point, join the chaotic throng descending the stairway between heaps of radishes, cauliflowers and king chillies to **Lal Bazaar**, Gangtok's main fruit and vegetable market.

Tibetan Wisdom

Learn more about Mahayana Buddhism at Namgyal Institute of Tibetology

Part of the pleasure of a visit to **Namgyal Institute of Tibetology** *(NIT; ₹25; closed Sun)* is flying over the deeply incised Sikkim landscape on the Gangtok Ropeway cable car and strolling through subtropical woodlands to find it. NIT is a remarkable repository of wisdom, not just as a centre of advanced studies in Mahayana Buddhism, but also about Sikkim, the Himalaya and the region as a whole.

Housed in a Tibetan-style palace built in 1958 with a foundation stone laid by the Dalai Lama, the institute has a priceless library of wrapped manuscripts and showcases some fine Buddhist artefacts in the central hall. Note the *thöpa* cups made from human skulls and *kangling* trumpets fashioned from thigh bones. A five-minute walk beyond NIT, a forest of prayer flags surround **Do-Drul Chorten**, one of Gangtok's most distinctive stupas.

Royal Gangtok

Hear the echoes of bygone kings

Put on your glad rags and book in for a night at the **Elgin Nor-Khill**, once the official guesthouse of Sikkim royalty. Begin by taking high tea, served from a pewter teapot, while lounging on an elegant turquoise sofa beneath crystal chandeliers; have a sundowner on the lawn before dinner in a curtain-draped dining room, and complete the evening with a cocktail in the cosy little **Dragon Bar** with extravagant painted pillars.

Save time, after a breakfast eaten with a full complement of silverware, to examine the royal family photos adorning the walls. One shows Indira Gandhi talking with Gyalmo Hope Cooke Namgyal, the glamorous American-born wife of the last reigning chogyal (monarch). Shortly after, in 1975, India annexed Sikkim, ostensibly to protect the Nepali community from prejudice. With a covering referendum, Indian troops broke down the palace gates and put the chogyal under house

EATING IN GANGTOK: OUR PICKS

Shuffle Momos: Upper-floor dumpling house with a cult following thanks to the super-succulent *momos*. Fabulous views and great juices. *11.30am-9pm* ₹

Nimtho: Attractively presented thalis (plate meals) of Sikkimese, Nepali and Tibetan food in a beautifully designed restaurant. *11am-9.30pm* ₹₹

Cafe Fiction: Breakfasts, sandwiches, fried rice or ramen in the cosy cafe beneath the excellent Rachna Bookshop. *9am-7pm Mon-Sat* ₹₹

Yak Bar: Range of delicious pan-Asian dishes served on the open-air terrace make this a prime MG Marg dining experience. *11am-10pm* ₹₹₹

Tashi Viewpoint

arrest. The palace, a modest villa, is still private but inside the north gate the small **12 Chogyals Exhibition** *(free)* documents the dynasty.

Mirror, Mirror, On the Wall...

Selfie-taking at the Orchidarium

Sikkim is a paradise for orchids and the Noble Orchid is the state flower. At Gangtok's new **Orchidarium** *(₹350)*, in Ridge Park, 100 of the state's 500 species are on display and the signage does a good job of showcasing these magnificent plants – the largest plant family after daisies. Some species, such as the bee orchid, mimic an insect to attract pollinators – a clever piece of evolution given that despite a record number of seeds per pod (some three million) orchids are hard to propagate. Have a go at the **Great Orchid Chase** – finding specific blooms by their descriptions – and you'll feel something of the orchid mania that seized collectors in the 19th century when the first specimens were sent from Sikkim to Holland.

It may be narcissistic, but don't leave without visiting the **mirror room**. Here you'll find exotic displays of dendrobiums reflected in floor-to-ceiling mirrors that offer garlanded self-portraits stretching into infinity.

ORCHIDS

Once you start looking, you'll see photogenic orchids everywhere, clinging in the wild to branches of gnarled trees, or gracing the balconies of rural homes. If orchid mania takes hold, visit nearby **Arunachal Pradesh** (p544; with 600 species, it's the orchid state of India. And in Assam's **Kaziranga** (p539), there's a priceless collection of rarities.

BEST VIEWS AROUND GANGTOK

Tashi Viewpoint: Fine Khangchendzonga views 7km northwest of the centre. Tour 4WDs heading to North Sikkim pass close by.

Pangthang: Spectacular Himalayan views from the roadside, and from a few middle-of-nowhere hotels. Accessible en route to the Fambhonglo Nature Reserve.

Paragliding: Get airborne with Sikkim Paragliding *(sikkimtourism.gov.in/Public/ThingsToDo/Paragliding)*; the launch point itself has splendid city and valley views.

Ganesh Tok: From the observation platform or nearby road, city views at Ganesh Tok align the royal palace with Enchey Gompa, a 20-minute walk below.

STDC Helicopter Rides: The flight (₹3100) from Gangtok to Bagdogra with STDC *(sikkimstdc.com/HeliService General/HeliGeneral Reservation.aspx)* offers fine views en route.

SIKKIMESE FOOD

Forget what you think you know about 'Indian' food: Sikkimese palates lean towards Tibet with beef and pork, dumplings and dairy dishes among local favourites.

Ubiquitous *momos* (stuffed dumplings) are Sikkim's answer to fast food, while *thukpa* (rich noodle soup) is often fermented and laced with organic veg such as *gundruk* (spinach-like greens), *kinima* (soya beans) or *sinki* (radishes). Also popular are *karela* (bitter gourds) and *sisnoo* (nettles), while spicy gravies might incorporate fried *ningro* (fiddlehead ferns), *bareh* (ground-orchid bud heads) and wickedly hot king chillies.

Dairy derivations such as *churpi* (local cheese) appear in soups but also as hard cubes to suck, or in Bhutanese dishes like *ema datshi* (yellow cheese and chilli).

Non-veg? Try *phaksha paa* (pork and veg), *phalay/phale* (pasties or pies) and *shapta* (beef wok-fried in slices).

Cultural Hubs

Buying books and crafts in Gangtok

Rachna Bookshop *(rachnabooks.com)* is a marvel with English-language publications on Sikkimese history and culture, covering everything from mysticism to gender identity in the Himalaya. There are thought-provoking talks, and the bookshop's **Cafe Fiction** and on-site **Bookmans B&B** offer a chance to meet like-minded travellers.

Similarly inspiring, the **Handicrafts & Handloom Emporium**, next to the PAP Office, supports Indigenous crafts and brings employment to the disadvantaged, and has many fine wood carvings, hats and textiles for sale.

Panda in the Park

Spotting Sikkim's state mascot

If you've strolled along MG Marg and wondered which animal is represented by the prominent giant, orange **statue** in the middle of the promenade, it's a red panda. The real-life version is altogether more gorgeous and if you visit the **Himalayan Zoological Park** *(sikkimstdc.com/GeneralPages/Details/Himalayan-Zoological-Park/199/Details; ₹250; closed Thu)*, one of India's best-maintained animal parks, you'll understand immediately why this beautiful animal has been adopted as the state mascot.

The park's panda research centre is currently home to several breeding pairs and sightings are pretty much assured in the ample red panda enclosure where they spend much of the day lounging in trees. The birth in 2025 of two cubs marks a milestone in the protection of this endangered bamboo-eating species (unrelated to giant pandas) after years of setbacks.

The whole park, surrounded by dense thickets of bamboo and wild hilltop forest, is a treat to explore, though there is no guarantee of sighting many of the other animals (including rare clouded leopards and Himalayan bears) due to the expansive, semi-wild enclosures. From the zoo's ticket booth, opposite Ganesh Tok (p507), it's 1.6km to the main area (near the aviary) and then plenty of walking from one enclosure to another, so hiring a return taxi from Gangtok makes sense.

DRINKING IN GANGTOK: SOCIAL HUBS

Gangtok Groove: Spacious upstairs music bar with fair-priced cocktails; live music currently suspended but likely to return. *1-11pm*

Sikkim Coffee: Perfect lounging to revive after our Downhill Gangtok walking tour. Some profits go to supporting red panda conservation. *9am-8.30pm*

Jungle Bar: Off-beat, top-floor bar with fun decor and two viewpoint outdoor spaces in addition to the main drinking den. *11am-10pm*

Yak Bar: The doorway marked Tashi Delek Hotel leads to this popular open-air bar with fire pit, sunset views and twinkling lights. *noon-8.30pm*

DOWNHILL IN GANGTOK

There are few places in Sikkim where you have the pleasure of a downhill-only walk – this Gangtok classic is one of them.

START	END	LENGTH
Enchey Gompa	MG Marg	2½ km; 2hr

Hop in a taxi to beautiful 1 **Enchey Gompa**. Although one of the oldest and most revered Buddhist monasteries in Sikkim, the present buildings are relatively recent, dating from the early 20th century. People from around Sikkim come to visit two important shrines (Kangsol Lhakhang) here, one believed to be potent in wish-fulfilment.

Return to the entrance gate, walk straight ahead and turn left, passing stands of bamboo and tree ferns. Take the stairway at the first hairpin (before reaching 2 **Hotel Mount Siniolchu**). Descending through conifers, briefly rejoin the lane then at the next corner walk past the 3 **Sentry Post** and descend more steps to the 4 **Tamarind Hotel**. Turn right and continue downhill to the 5 **Nehru bust roundabout** with Indian flag and call in at the 6 **Orchidarium** (p507) to enjoy the magnificent blooms.

Continue along Ridge Park and enter a gateway in front of 7 **12 Chogyals Exhibition** (p507) and skirt the palace to the splendid royal monastery, 8 **Tsuklakhang**. Enjoy expansive views as you leave from the other side of the complex. Turn sharp left, pass the 9 **Secretariat Building** and, at the Mines & Geology Dept sign, descend a long zigzag of red steps. You'll emerge on Kazi Rd outside 10 **Hotel Fair View**. Turn left to find the 11 **Namnang Ropeway Station** and continue downhill to arrive at 12 **MG Marg**.

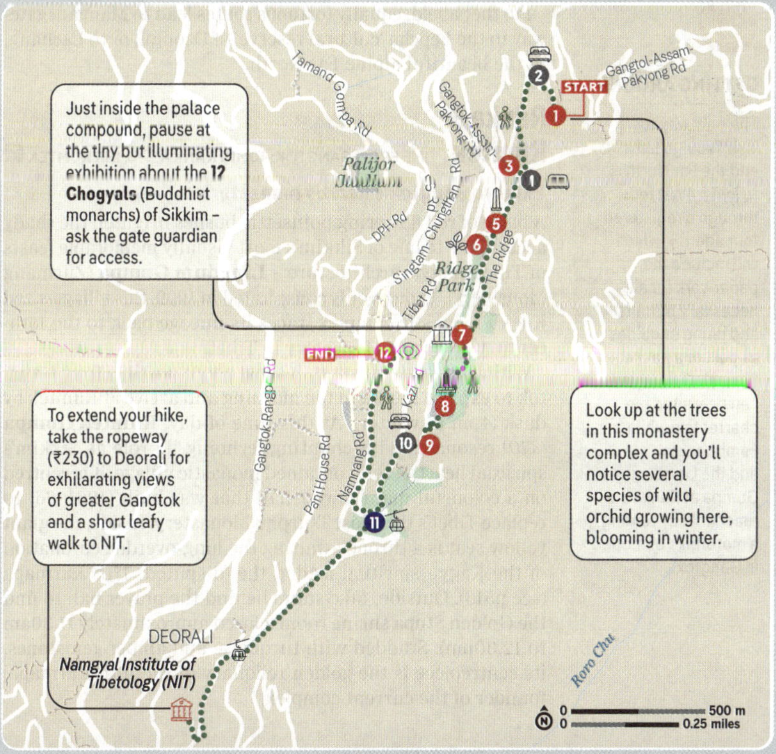

Beyond Gangtok

Monastic villages and terraced valley views around the capital give way to wilder mountain scenes as you head towards the high Himalayan hinterland.

Places

GETTING AROUND

The only way to visit Tsomgo Lake and the Far North is to join a 4WD tour through a registered tour agency, which will include the paperwork for all necessary permits and hiring of guides as part of a package. Rumtek and Martam can be visited by charter taxi while Fambhonglo and the Lingdum Gompa at Ranka are reachable by renting a motorbike or moped in Gangtok.

Significant monasteries at Ranka and Rumtek offer interesting excursions from Gangtok, but just because they sit on opposite sides of the same valley, don't think that this means they can easily be combined in the same visit. As with all roads beyond the capital, no road leads anywhere fast, as they zigzag relentlessly up and down the steep mountainsides. It's something of a miracle that some of the roads were ever made – and the stretch between Gangtok and the pretty village of Martam, known as the 'edge' cost many construction workers their lives.

Further afield, equally tortuous routes lead to Mangan, gateway to the Lepcha 'cultural reserve' of Dzongu, or to Lachang, in the beautiful alpine Far North.

Ranka & Rumtek

TIME FROM GANGTOK: **40MIN RANKA**, **1HR RUMTEK**

Explore Gangtok's nearby monasteries

A blaze of red flowering poinsettia bushes brighten the shady access lane to one of Sikkim's most visually memorable feasts of Tibetan-style architecture – **Lingdum Gompa** (Zurmang Monastery). Though only consecrated in 1999, this village-sized Kagyu monastic complex traces its lineage back to the 15th-century Surmang Monastery in Tibet.

With your own transport, it's just about possible from Gangtok to explore Ranka in the morning and arrive at Rumtek by dusk (4pm in winter). At this time of day, **Rumtek Gompa** *(₹10)* resonates with chanting, echoing its role as Sikkim's spiritual heart. A self-contained monastic village, it is centred on a colourful main prayer hall that was built (1961–66) to replace Tibet's then-lost Tsurphu Monastery. Inside, the giant yellow seat is a throne awaiting the long-overdue coronation of the Kagyu spiritual leader, the (disputed) 17th Karmapa (see p516). Outside, take stairs behind the prayer hall to find the Golden Stupa shrine room (closed approximately 11.30am to 12.30pm). Studded with turquoise and amber gemstones, its centrepiece is the golden reliquary of the 16th Karmapa, founder of the current complex.

IMAGESOFINDIA/SHUTTERSTOCK

Rumtek Gompa

Martam

TIME FROM GANGTOK: 1HR

Enjoy the fruits of local labour

Chance upon Martam's marvel of green terraces in spring and you'll find them cascading down the hill in a vivid sequence of lime and olive green. By September the paddy is beginning to bronze and by November the important business of harvesting begins. Oxen still assist in the process, and in 2025 the ancient Bhutia tribe of Martam inaugurated its first annual festival to mark the occasion – an event opened to visitors in a desire to share and preserve their local traditions.

Festivals such as these, with pop-up communal kitchens set within the terraces, bonfires of juniper, and millet beer handed around in bamboo cups by women wearing traditional handloomed attire, are a wonderful way to engage with local communities and learn about their customs. Martam Village Homestay (p527) offers the chance to make a night of it, while local company **Ease Tours & Treks** *(easetourssikkim.com)* can arrange camping and walking trips on forest and terrace paths. Visitors can also learn how to make *momos* from Bhutia villagers, while nearby **Bamboo Retreat** offers traditional herbal and hot stone *dotto* baths, given a day's notice.

Martam is close to Rumtek, and the less-visited **Old Rumtek Gompa** *(₹10)*, famous for festival Chaam dances (p512). Also in the vicinity are the classically styled **Mila Bhir** cliff carvings. Himalayan bears have been sighted along the road near here, straying perhaps from the Fambonghlo Wildlife Sanctuary that embraces the ridge top.

Hiking in Fambonghlo Wildlife Sanctuary

Having slogged 1km off the main road via a rough, super-steep zigzag track, it's astonishing to find high-spirited weekenders picnicking around an improbably isolated cafeteria. This is the **Fambonghlo Wildlife Sanctuary**, with decorative pond,

LEPCHA LESSONS IN NATURE

Yishey Doma, award-winning writer of *Sikkim: Soul of the Himalayas* and host of Martam Village Homestay.

In Martam we're flanked by forests rich in birdlife and steeped in local lore and walking our village paths amid drifting mists and choruses of crickets is an experience. You may be invited into a local home for tea and snacks – an opportunity to learn about Bhutia tribal ways. Our culture is deeply shaped in faith-healing traditions, rooted in reverence for nature, and our community protects and worships springs, trees and stones. During the farming season, you can forage for edible roots, shoots and leaves, and we can teach you to cook our favourite dishes. At night you'll sip local millet brew and listen to foxes, barking deer and the squeaks of flying squirrels.

labelled trees and a 180-degree viewpoint ('Chuli') overlooking Gangtok. However, it's only by hiking the 5km **Nampung Trail** (around two hours up) that you'll discover the bird-filled woodland, which is the sanctuary's real hallmark.

CHAAM DANCES & FESTIVALS

Sikkim's *chaam* dances feature masked monks acting out parables and stories from the life of Guru Padmasambhava, the saint who brought Tibetan Buddhism to the Himalayan region. Part morality play, part country fair and part exorcism, performances are supported by a crew of clowns, demons and dancing snow lions, entertaining crowds that combine puzzled tourists and spellbound locals dressed in their festive best.

These events are most reliably performed during the Sikkimese end-of-harvest festival **Losoong** (aka Namsoong), when you can see performances at many monastic locations including Lingdum, Phensang (between Gangtok and Mangan), Ralang (north of Ravangla) and most notably at Old Rumtek.

Mangan & Around

TIME FROM GANGTOK: 3HR

Discover Dzongu

The 'protected' Lepcha tribal area of Dzongu is Sikkim at its most unspoilt, best experienced at a family homestay. From butterfly-watching hot spot **Passingdang** village, a 7km hairpin lane with shortcut walking trails leads to Lingthem with its steeply terraced paddy fields and attractive **Lingthem Gompa**, approached via mossy forest steps. Snowy peaks pierce the clouds on the horizon.

Some sub-villages of upper **Tingvong** also have fine Khangchendzonga views. Getting there has the added excitement of crossing the opalescent **Teesta River** on a very long suspension footbridge. Thereafter you'll need to have pre-arranged transport or walk; the multi-hour hike to isolated little **Tholung Gompa** is an option.

Dzongu's gateway is **Mangan**, spreading up a steep wooded slope from the commercial strip. Once an essential stopover on the road north, it's been bypassed since the GLOF in 2023 and subsequent flash floods in 2024. The Toong–Naga road, however, reopened in 2026 and the town may yet regain its former status.

Gangtok–Mangan round trip

Around half of Sikkim is covered in dense subtropical forest and in November the hillsides erupt in shivering pink petals from the flowering wild cherry trees. Engage a 4WD and you can loop through the forest on a long day's outing from Gangtok.

For the outbound route, travel via **Pangthang** for the glorious early-morning views of snow-capped Himalayan mountains, have lunch in **Mangan** and then return via the less-frequented 'Seven Sisters Route'. The road passes the minimal foundation ruins of **Tumlong Palace**, site of Sikkim's third capital, near the colourful 2023 **Zangdopalri (Mindrolling) Gompa** and hefty 1884 **Labrang Monastery**. Back on the main road, continue to Phensang (with another important gompa) and pass the multi-stage **Seven Sisters**, the most impressive of several roadside waterfalls. To see the topmost falls, climb the stairs to the vantage point.

EATING BEYOND GANGTOK: RURAL EATS

Green Tara Food Corner: John Lennon and the Dali Lama look on as you slurp tasty *thukpa* with monks at Lungdum Gompa. *7am-6pm* ₹

Gloria Bae: Nachos, cakes and barista-made coffee in an oasis of urban chic near Rumtek with a terrace panorama of Gangtok. *9am-8pm* ₹₹

Martam Rice Valley Resort: A perfect perch to admire the rice terraces over Indian and Nepali food. Call ahead for Sikkimese food. *10am-7.30pm* ₹

Bamboo Retreat (p511): Phone ahead to have a full Sikkimese thali ready for your arrival at this idyllic hotel near Rumtek. *by arrangement* ₹₹₹

SIHASAKPRACHUM/SHUTTERSTOCK

Seven Sisters waterfall

Around 17km before Gangtok take a few minutes to wander the atmospheric forested glade called **Kabi Lunchok**, where memorial stones commemorate the 13th-century Bhutia-Lepcha friendship, or blood treaty, between clans.

Lachung

TIME FROM GANGTOK: **2-3 DAYS RETURN**

A Far North adventure

Ask any tour agent for their favourite place in Sikkim and they'll tell you to go north. Even city dwellers born in Gangtok describe an irresistible urge, belonging perhaps to a collective sense of being highland people, to track down the state's most rugged places. For foreigners, getting to the Far North is complicated by travel restrictions and the need for permits (p502), making it traditionally a destination largely for keen trekkers (p522).

If you're unphased by booking a tour for the long journey on rough roads, though, then consider going to **Lachung**, visitors stay for either one or two nights before being escorted along the scenically memorable 23km drive to the peak-rimmed **Yumthang Meadow**. It's particularly lovely in spring when alpine flowers are in bloom and grazing *dzo* (yak-cow crossbreeds) are brought to graze. En route, the basic road cuts through the **Shingba Rhododendron Sanctuary** (blooming in May); passes an opal-blue lake formed by landslides; and ducks beneath towering trees bearded with epiphytes.

While lovely, numerous local 4WD tours at the meadow reduce its tranquillity, but it's possible to continue 30km further along to the lesser-visited **Zero Point**, an area of alpine tundra at a breathless 4825m altitude. Although the scenery is less dramatic here, the sense of isolation is poignant, particularly among the shivering snack sellers proffering Maggi and shots of Honey Bee brandy.

FOUNDATION MYTHS

One version of Sikkim's semi-legendary royal narrative tells the story of three Tibetan monks converging on Yuksom from north, west and south and then heading east to find a ruler for what would become Sikkim. They settled on a certain Phuntsok Namgyal of the Bhutia clan, whose distant ancestor Gye Bumsa was the Tibetan prince who had sealed a friendship pact with Sikkim's Lepcha community at Kabi Lunchok. Phuntsok was crowned the first chogyal (literally 'righteous ruler') in 1641 and his lineage would last until 1975, albeit ruling from four different capitals as they struggled in battles with Nepali competitors. Meanwhile, under royal patronage, the foremost lama, Lhatsun Chempo went on to found most of the key monasteries in Western Sikkim; or at least to identify their future sites.

Pelling

KHANGCHENDZONGA VIEWS | RELIGIOUS STATUES | HIKING ROUTES

If you're partial to a morning lie-in, you'll want to make an exception in Pelling: the dawn views of snow-covered Khangchendzonga are spectacular, and watching the light trickling down the icy massif is a key Pelling experience. In fact the view is pretty much the raison d'être of this small ridgetop town, which now comprises a cascade of hotels built to allow visitors to enjoy sunrise from their window. That said, Pelling has a few other attractions, including nearby historic monasteries, 18th-century ruins at the end of a forest stroll and a giant statue above a modern sky walk. Accustomed to visitors, this friendly travellers' town also makes a sociable hub for planning onward journeys towards the high mountains and complements Gangtok's big-city ambience with its altogether more rural context.

Nearby Tikjuk is West Sikkim's bureaucratic township – handy if you need to extend your ILP.

GETTING AROUND

A bus leaves Pelling for Siliguri each morning. **Father Tours** operates a shared 4WD from Pelling to both Gangtok and Siliguri. Many other shared 4WD routes pass through, but to get an assured seat you'll need a local person phone to reserve for you. Or head first to Geyzing using shared taxis departing from the Zero Point junction opposite Hotel Garuda.

Twin hostels **Wake in Himalayas/ Mochilero Ostello** *(mochilerostello.in)* have a couple of mopeds that guests can rent. Hotels (notably the Kabur) and several tour agencies around Zero Point can organise taxis for local rides and sightseeing loops.

Pelling's Sound & Light Show

Catching a Himalayan daybreak

Few spectacles of human ingenuity can match the one that nature performs twice daily across the **Khangchendzonga** massif. The drama begins well before sunrise when the blue whistling thrush plays the opening salvos of the dawn chorus in an extraordinarily complex melody. This is followed by a rhythm section of insistent calls, courtesy of a great barbit, and a percussive wheeze by the chestnut-headed tesia. Soon dogs join the orchestra of sounds just as the first sliver of sun slides along the land of the leopard above the clouds. The sun gains in momentum and the tonal outlines change key: what began as a hint of pink on the distant snow deepens into a deep crimson. Just as you reach for your camera for the critical moment, the sun floods into the valley and splashes against sleepy Pelling: suddenly it's fully day and you missed it!

Thankfully, nature performs the same spectacle every morning and, to a lesser extent, each evening too. Clear views, even

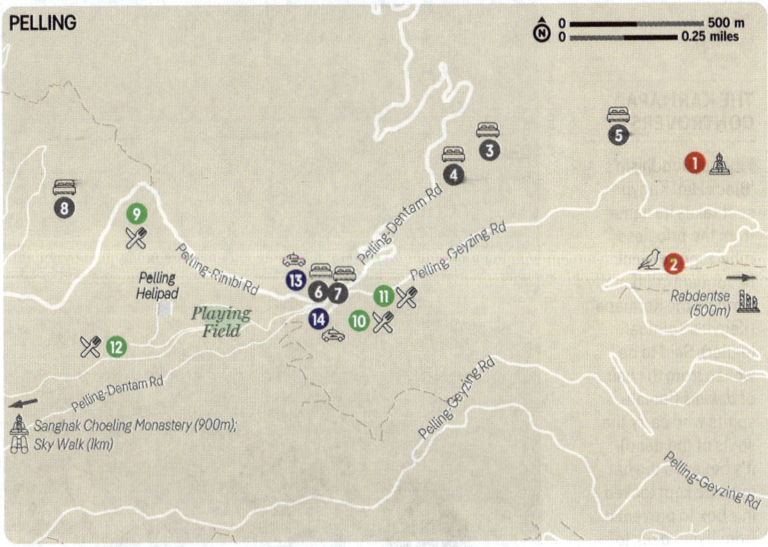

SIGHTS
1 Pemayangtse Gompa
2 Sidkeong Tulku Bird Park

SLEEPING
3 Chestnut Magpie Retreat
4 Chumbi Mountain Retreat
5 Elgin Mount Pandim
6 Hotel Garuda
7 Hotel Kabur
8 Wake in Himalayas/ Mochilero Ostello

EATING
9 Grains by Udaan
10 HavMor
11 Hotel Kabur
12 Purple Cottage

TRANSPORT
13 Father Tours
14 Shared taxis to Geyzing

in the dry season, are far from guaranteed, however, so make the most of every chance to catch the show.

Compassion Personified

Grapple with perception at the feet of Chenrezig

An elderly woman in traditional clothing removes her shoes and steps gingerly onto the glass. She tests it with a bounce and then strides along the walkway with confidence, careless of the three-storey 'drop' exposed below. As she does so selfie-taking lads, old enough to be her grandsons, cling to the side or take cautious steps along the diagonal girders. Of course the **Sky Walk** *(₹100, cash only)*, built in 2018 and the first of its kind in India, is completely safe but it's all about perception.

Other elders, as if bent with the toil of rice planting, pace up the 178 steps towards **Chenrezig**, spinning prayer wheels as they advance towards the giant four-armed bodhisattva of compassion whose most recent modern reincarnation is believed to be the Dalai Lama. Young families follow inside and pay respects at the 'monument within a monument' of Chenrezig's 1000-armed, 11-headed form – reincarnated as such having tried and failed over many lifetimes, according to Tibetan mythology, to pass on his knowledge of enlightenment to humankind.

TOP TIP

If you're keen to watch both sunrise and sunset from Pelling, it pays to check the timing. Factor in about 30 minutes prior to either to [illegible] and dusk. Note that it gets dark much earlier in Sikkim than in more westerly parts of India.

THE KARMAPA CONTROVERSY

Tibetan Buddhism's 'Black Hat' Kagyu sect takes its name from the priceless ruby-topped black headgear traditionally worn by the Karmapa (Kagyu's spiritual leader). Said to be woven from the hair of *dakinis* (female spirits who carry the souls of the dead), it's believed the hat must be kept locked in a box to prevent it from flying back to the heavens. Only the Karmapa should open this box.

But who is the current (17th) Karmapa? In the 1990s, a major controversy divided the Kagyu sect, with two claimants put forward as the 16th Karmapa's reincarnation: **Ogyen Tinley Dorje** *(kagyu office.org)*, recognised by the Dalai Lama, and **Tahye Dorje** *(karmapa.org)*. In 2026, although better relations prevail, the dispute remains unresolved.

SAIKO3P/SHUTTERSTOCK

Even without the spiritual freight of symbolism carried to the ample feet of Chenrezig's seated form, it's worth climbing up the ramp to the monument's plinth. From here there are fine views of **Pemayangtse**, **Dubdi** and, on a clear day, the very distant Great Buddha of Ravangla (p518).

Returning, call in at the small but perfectly formed 18th-century **Sanghak Choeling Monastery** – particularly beautiful when the cosmos daisies and painted window frames glow in the sunset. A new cable car is still under construction, but it's just a 2km walk downhill to Upper Pelling.

Walking Through History

Rabdentse to Pelling via Pemayangtse Gompa

The Pelling area has several royal connections that keep it close to the heart for many Sikkimese today, and walking between these sites makes for a fine day out. From **Sidkeong Tulku Bird Park** (alas, poorly maintained) a 20-minute woodland path leads to **Rabdentse** *(free)*, the site of Sikkim's second royal capital between 1670 and 1840. Although there's not much to see of the erstwhile palace, other than a stone throne and some chortens (stupas), the site is significant for Lepcha people as a place of brave resistance against invading Gurkha armies. The views from here are exceptional.

Back at the bird park, walk uphill for 1km to **Pemayangtse Gompa** *(₹100)*, a three-storey monastery built on the site

Buddha Park (p518), Ravangla (Rabong)

of a 1647 shrine. Considered the 'Mother of Monasteries' in Sikkim, it was a royal monastery, and there's a picture here of His Highness the 12th monarch, whose reign ended with the accession to India in 1975. Head upstairs inside the main prayer hall where a dusty museum, harbouring musical instruments and fur-lined hats, wraps around an elaborate seven-tiered model. Representing **Zangtok Palri** (Padmasambhava's heavenly abode), it was completely handmade by a single dedicated lama in a five-year labour of love.

End a tour of royal connections at suitably regal **Elgin Mount Pandim** (*elginhotels.com*). Dating from Sikkim's last era of royal governance, this elegant hotel has a gorgeous interior of velvet sofas and a grand open verandah terrace with mountain vistas. From here a concrete walkway returns to Pelling through woodlands.

ESCAPE TO RANIDHUNGA

Sweeping views underline the commanding ridgetop location of Rabdentse, Sikkim's second royal capital after Yuksom. Yet it wasn't impregnable, and in 1788 the little citadel was sacked by Gorkha Nepalis. The wife of the chogyal, escaping in the nick of time, was whisked away by her protectors and kept hidden in an inaccessible small cave beneath a smooth rocky outcrop that to this day is known as **Ranidhunga**, the Queen's Boulder. Marked with a large trident, the site is also considered a Hindu holy spot with footprints in the rock seen as a symbol of Sita (consort of Rama). It's possible to visit along a 3½-hour woodland walk west from the Chenrezig Stupa, best in early April when the rhododendrons bloom.

EATING IN PELLING: TRAVELLER FAVOURITES

Hotel Kabur: Twinkling lamps, local and backpacker menu options and a terrace view make for a cosy dining experience. *10am-8.30pm* ₹

Grains by Udaan: Vegetarian cuisine with a creative gourmet twist. Hidden downstairs in the Pine Crest Hotel, it has big views and a great cocktail list. *8am-10pm* ₹₹

HavMor: This bright eatery with hatch servery and souvenir counter is the best place in Pelling for South Indian food, notably masala dosas. *7.30am-8pm* ₹

Purple Cottage: Suhana's cafe offers local cuisine in a charming environment with a mini library. Near the cable-car station. Bargain homestay rooms too. *9am-6pm* ₹

Beyond Pelling

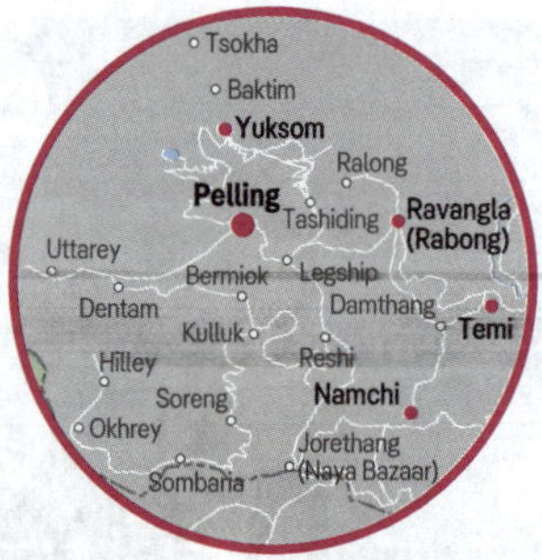

Rustic hamlets, friendly small towns and gigantic religious statues make Western Sikkim a region that anyone can fall in love with.

Places

Perhaps because of the way light falls across the valleys here, or the deeply incised landscape in which only the ridgetops seem connected while the riverbeds are swallowed up by the clouds below, the land beyond Pelling has a certain magic about it that is compelling to the patient traveller. In the past, every hilltop was crowned with a monastery so that messages could travel from crest to crest without the need for time-taking descents. Today the monasteries remain, even if their role has changed, as do the old tracks linking one village to another. Hiking these paths, visiting monasteries en route, is a chief attraction of the area, while higher-altitude treks beckon the adventurous towards Khangchendzonga National Park.

GETTING AROUND

Shared 4WD routes mostly radiate from hubs at Geyzing, Namchi and Jorethang. Towns and bigger villages also have daily services to Gangtok and Siliguri, usually departing fairly early in the morning and returning afternoons. Check the latest state of the roads. At the time of research, for example, long-term roadworks between Kewzing and Legship were adding an hour to Ravangla–Pelling journeys. The Legship–Jorethang road is contrastingly fast.

Ravangla (Rabong)

TIME FROM PELLING: 2¾HR

A pilgrim's park

Whatever one's beliefs, it's hard not to feel a sense of awe on first sight of the 41m-tall golden statue that dominates Ravangla's **Buddha Park** *(Tathagata Tsal; ₹200)*. Set in an attractively landscaped garden, the Buddha is approached via fountains, exhortations to do good cited from sacred teachings, and gentle piped music repeating the *om mane padme hum* mantra. Inside the statue are priceless Buddha relics donated from all around the world, and many pilgrims end their Buddhist Circuit – a multiday pilgrimage that includes 10 days in Sikkim – in meditation here. To learn more about Buddha's life, follow the murals that spiral up around the statue's interior. An 'eco-car' and wheelchairs are available if required.

The main road from Ravangla to Kewzing (and thence Pelling) passes the beautiful old **Yungdrung Kundrakling** temple, dating back to the 8th century and unusual as one of only two monasteries in India practising the pre-Buddhist Bon religion. Look carefully as one of the 20 resident monks here pray and you'll notice the prayer wheels are turned anticlockwise.

At Pathing, across the valley near the Buddha Park, a large gash in the hillside shows the enormous damage caused by landslides – an ever-present threat during summer rains.

Temi

TIME FROM PELLING: 3¼HR

Tea tasting among cherry blossoms

In Sikkim, Temi is synonymous with organic tea, grown in the 178-hectare tumble of terraces that cascade down the hillside. Viewed from above, the terraces are a vision of loveliness, especially in November when the cherry trees that decorate the twisting roads through the tea gardens are perfect in pink. At any time of year, road-side stalls offer tea tasting and snacks and charge a modest fee *(₹50)* for a wander through the terraces.

During 'plucking season' (March, April and October) it's also possible to visit **Temi Organic Tea Factory** *(₹200)*. Visitors gravitate towards a big I Love Temi sign but it's more interesting to take the steps down from the factory's eastern side and stroll over to a new viewing platform. Walks amid the bushes from here are free and the valley views undisturbed. Alternatively, walk down from the **Organic Tea Point** cafe (3.7km by zigzag road) along a tea-bush trail marked initially with prayer flags. Most transport between Gangtok and Ravangla or Namchi travels via Temi.

Namchi

TIME FROM PELLING: 2¼HR

Larger than life

If you've been wondering where Sikkim's trend for giant religious statues started, it was here in Namchi with the building of **Samdruptse** *(₹75)* in 2004. This 45m-tall seated statue of Padmasambhava (Guru Rimpoche), painted in shimmering copper and gilt on a lotus plinth, crowns a 2131m-hilltop behind which the Khangchendzonga massif makes a magnificent backdrop.

Consider a 1km diversion from Samdruptse to **Ngadak Gompa**, whose large 2014 prayer hall contains some of the richest new Buddhist murals in Sikkim. Beside the hall is the reputedly haunted shell of a far older monastery building built over the palace of Pedi Wangmu, the Sikkimese queen who overthrew her half-brother in 1700, had him killed and later fell victim to his followers.

Some 5km southwest of Namchi, Samdruptse's Hindu counterpart is the remarkable assembly of buildings at **Char Dham** *(₹100)*. Here a 33m-tall statue of Lord Shiva is the culminating focus of an impressive architectural park that recreates many of India's greatest pilgrimage sites, including those at

SIKKIM'S BLACK & RED GOLD

Never heard of *Cordyceps sinensis?* You'll not be alone. Referred to locally as **caterpillar fungus**, this eccentricity of the vegetable kingdom grows on the pupae of ghost moths to form a long tube-like fruit. Given its traces of arsenic, opinion is divided as to its health benefits, but it features in traditional Tibetan *sowa rigpa* (herbal medicine) dating back to the 8th century, and the Chinese prize it as an aphrodisiac. Only occurring between elevations of 3000m to 5000m, this rare entopathogenic fungus grows well near Martam and it outstrips black cardamom in value, earning the name 'Himalayan black gold'.

Meanwhile, locally grown *dalle khursani*, crimson, round and one of the hottest chillies in the world, is deserving of the sobriquet 'red gold' – less for its individual value than for the quantity sold and eaten.

EATING & DRINKING IN & AROUND NAMCHI: THE ARTS SCENE

Jimmy's Lagerhouse: The sociable owner is a Hendrix fan and his bar has become the hub of Namchi's dynamic arts scene over beer and a bite. *11am-11pm*

Box 1449: Right on pedestrianised 'Central Park' square, this inviting venue mixes inventive cocktails, has open-mic nights and serves fabulous tandoori food. *8am-7pm*

Teens: Add creamy *kewa datshi* (a Bhutanese potato dish) to the Nepali set meal to create a melange of delicious flavours and textures. In Namchi. *9am-10pm* ₹₹

Kudzu Restaurant: In Solophok near Namchi and set in a rose garden with selfie opportunities among blooms. Stay for mocktails or a meal in the attractive restaurant after. *8am-7pm*

BEST FOR NATURE

Fambonghlo Wildlife Sanctuary: Guides are available for birding and plant identification at this sanctuary on a steep ridge above Martam.

Himalayan Zoological Park: Offering the best chance to see (or better still adopt under the 'My Chield' scheme) a red panda or clouded leopard, this Gangtok research centre is more nature park than zoo.

Shingba Rhododendron Sanctuary: Ablaze with the flowers of this famous shrub in spring, the sanctuary is part of the 'Valley of Flowers' (April to July) near Lachung.

Varsey Rhododendron Sanctuary: The sanctuary borders Nepal in West Sikkim and is home to wild pandas and bears.

Khangchendzonga National Park: Reaching 8586m, and famous for the elusive snow leopard, this UNESCO site is also the home of blue sheep, black bears and blood pheasants. *(national-parks.org/india/khangchendzonga)*

Rameswaram, Dwarka and Jagarnath. A small pavilion at the bottom of the site, beside a statue of a hunter named Kirat (an avatar of Shiva), scopes a very different kind of faith and you may bump into a shaman here whose blessings lean towards an animism as ancient as the surrounding hills.

Walking a knife edge

Examine a photograph of **Tarey Bihr**, Namchi's answer to Aizawl's Reiek in Mizoram (p557), and you'll swear it has been photoshopped. This locally dubbed 'grand canyon of Sikkim' is too neatly divided between cliff and forest, the path too straight, the balding drop off the edge impossibly steep. But it's every bit true. The ample 3km path along this extraordinary cliff face is the project of the local community in Sadam and has become a popular place to enjoy the sunset and engage in nearby adventure sports such as bungee jumping. Don't get too close to the edge – the drop from this 3048m line in the sky is almost a nose dive into the Teesta River, marking the boundary between Sikkim and neighbouring West Bengal.

Yuksom

TIME FROM PELLING: 1¾HR

The patient traveller

Unless you're seasoned in off-roading over potholes in a packed 4WD, there'll be a point during your Sikkim travels where you'll find yourself gripping the seat in white-knuckle fear. With nothing stitching the road to the mountainside but a wing and a prayer, the discomfort of being squeezed into a space with 10 others that's barely big enough for eight pales into insignificance as the driver coaxes his grumbling Sumo up virtually vertical inclines and has several goes at getting it round a corner. It's wholly terrifying when he swerves to miss oncoming traffic on a track barely big enough for a moped. Any satisfaction in reaching the top is dashed, however, by the sight of a tiny Suzuki Alto that must have been lifted there by magic.

To take the fear factor out of overlanding in Sikkim, call in a professional, such as level-headed **Raj Kumar Subba** *(6296955867)*. This expert driver patiently makes a virtue of approaching the road with 'mutual cooperation' and, with your safety assured, your trip teetering along the narrow zigzags high above racing rivers will prove a highlight instead of a horror.

Discovering Yuksom's crowning glory

Tiny but magical, Yuksom is known today mostly as a launching post for high-altitude treks towards **Khangchendzonga** – at 8586m and one of the 'Five Treasuries of Snow', it's the third-highest peak after Everest and K2. Scaling the holy summit is not permitted in Sikkim, but treks in the surrounding national park abound (p522). To get an idea of the park's biodiversity, call in at the 24-hour **information centre** *(free)*, opposite the **park check point** in Yuksom where trekkers are briefed by their guides before setting off for celebrated **Goecha-La Pass** (4950m).

LAKKANA SAVAKSURIYAWONG/SHUTTERSTOCK

Camping on Goecha-La Trek (p522)

Yuksom itself has an illustrious history as the first capital of the Sikkimese nation. The first chogyal was crowned in 1641 in what's now **Norbugang Park** *(₹20)*. A centuries-old cedar tree in this woodland garden of prayer flags shades the open-air **coronation throne**, with the top spot reserved not for the king but for the foremost of three crowning lamas, Lhatsun Chempo. It's believed the lama left his 'footprint' here in stone.

The distinctive **Yangthang Rinpoche Shrine**, just across Norbugang's south wall, features a large, wild-eyed statue commemorating Lhatsun Chempo's 20th-century 'reincarnation'. It's particularly striking seen across the village from **Tashi Tenka**, once the site of a royal complex. Though no historical buildings remain here, it offers one of the best views of Yuksom's wild, forested mountainsides, accessed via a short uphill path.

Continues on p526

BEST BOOZE IN SIKKIM

Thungba: Boiling water poured into a mini churn of fermented millet seeds releasing alcohol. It is drunk through a bamboo straw – not too soon, not too late. Available at Pelling's Restaurant Treat.

Rhododendron Wine: Mild, distilled spirit infused with petals. Himalayan Vines in Dentam makes a good sweet version.

Dansberg Premium: Quality lager beer made by Yuksom Breweries, founded by Sikkimese Bollywood star Danny Denzongpa, who appeared in *Seven Years in Tibet*.

Fireball: Sikkim's signature brandy. Comes in a red globe novelty bottle.

Old Monk: India's classic rum. Though not actually made here, it's sold very cheaply in Sikkim and available in eccentric souvenir bottles shaped like a monk.

EATING BEYOND PELLING: LOCAL FAVOURITES

Mama's Kitchen: Excellent Sikkimese and Bhutanese thalis cooked from scratch; order a couple of hours ahead. Behind Yak Hotel in Yuksom. *8am-7pm* ₹

Traditional Inn: A stalwart of the traveller scene in Yuksom, this is a favourite for *momos* and 'something crispy' *(pakoras)* in the evening. *6.30am-9pm* ₹

Zumthang Restaurant: Near Ravangla, on Kewzing Rd, this all-organic 'fooding and lodging' makes a fine lunchtime thali (and has great rooms here too). *11am-2pm* ₹₹

Third Space: Cheerful new cafe below Dentam Bazaar with a barista who makes a science out of the art of coffee making – best supped with a slice of delicious homebaked cake. *10.30am-7pm* ₹₹

HELP ME PICK:

Hiking & Trekking in Sikkim

Sikkim is a paradise for mountaineers and trekkers. But you don't need to be a Tenzing or a Hillary to enjoy engaging with the mountain wilderness here – there are plenty of shorter treks and day hikes that offer rewarding insights into Sikkim's high-altitude tundra and lower-lying forests. Parts of the Far North of Sikkim are off limits and no-one is permitted to climb to the top of Khangchendzonga (considered sacred by many), but other options abound.

Which Trek If You Like...

Mountain Classics from Yuksom

Goecha-La Trek The classic Sikkim trek, this high-altitude nine-nighter threads through forests, alpine meadows and glacial valleys to Goecha-La pass (4950m) close to Khangchendzonga.

Dzongri Trek This shorter six-night version of the Goecha-La Trek is aimed at those with less time but still keen to reach the iconic views offered by the longer trek.

Kasturi Round-Trek One of the highest in West Sikkim, this 11-night trek circles through Khangchendzonga National Park (p520), ascends Goecha La Pass and ends in Tashiding.

Ridge Treks from Uttarey

Uttarey to Nambu Round-Trek A stunning eight-nighter in the Singalila range, this trek rims the Nepalese border to Goecha La with expansive views of Mt Everest, Khangchendzonga and other peaks.

Uttarey to Yuksom Round-Trek One of Sikkim's longest treks, this 14-nighter combines part of the Uttarey to Nambu Round-Trek (with views of Everest et al) but ends in Yuksom via Goecha La.

Sandakphu Trek An easier, six-night trek along the Singalila Ridge beside the Nepalese border, this route offers views from Sandakphu of Khangchendzonga (resembling a sleeping Buddha).

Dafeybhir Trek A three-nighter along the Nepalese border ridge from near the 3590m-Phokteydara peak descends from Chewa Bhanjyang (3140m) via mossy forests and the Mainebus Waterfalls with a 360-degree view of Everest and Khangchendzonga and the peaks in between en route. The nine-night variant continues north along the ridge from Chewa Bhanjyang.

Flower Routes

Barsey Rhododendron Trek This five-night trek starts from the Tenzing Hillary Park in Uttarey and explores the Varsey (Barsey) Rhododendron Sanctuary (p520) with the chance of red panda sightings.

Sikkim Green Lake Trek A nature-lovers' 12-nighter in North Sikkim, this trek starts from Lachen, passing through meadows and streams with many wildflowers and birds along the route.

Village Hikes

Monastery Hike This perfect day hike (p524) starts in Tashiding (or, for a shorter walk, from Silnon Gompa) and is punctuated by three beautiful monasteries en route to Yuksom.

Pelling-Yuksom Hike A two-day Pelling–Khecheopalri–Yuksom hike starts with a steep descent on village trails to the valley. Thereafter much of the route is on roads, but it's enjoyable nonetheless.

DEBARUP/SHUTTERSTOCK

Goecha-La Trek

TREKKERS BRIEFING

If these rules seem obvious, think of Everest:

Don't litter – put all your rubbish in the provided ₹500 garbage bag, which you have to show on your return.

Don't pick flowers, discard fruit peel or gather seeds, and respect Sikkim's credentials as an organic state.

Stay with your team, behind your guide, and avoid visiting other tents or the kitchen tent at night.

HOW TO

When to go Trekking is possible all year (snow and weather dependent). Arguably the best time is March to May (flowering rhododendrons) and October to November (dry; clear skies).

Book ahead Trips can be booked a couple of days in advance with agents in Gangtok and Yuksom, but it's better to book further ahead: guides, drivers and porters are independent and appointing the best takes time.

Before you go Get fit! On arrival, you need time to acclimatise – even a low-altitude trek starts above 2000m.

Budget Roughly US$350 for a 10-day, all-inclusive Goecha-La trek, including permit, guide, transport, porter, food and accommodation.

Getting Organised

Permits & Tours

A multiday trek at higher mountain altitudes must be booked through a registered tour agency. The agency takes care of all the details, including permits, licensed guide, support staff, accommodation and transport. Trekking locations are subject to continual official review. See p502 for areas currently open to foreigners.

For shorter, low-altitude treks and village walks, permits are not required but hiring a local guide (through a tour agency or homestay) is likely to enhance the experience.

Some recommended trekking agencies:

Khangri Tour Trek & Expeditions *(khangrii.com)* Founder Tshering Dorjee Lachungpa has over 30 years of experience in pioneering treks (ask about his mushroom trail) and is committed to ecotourism.

Sikkim Peak Tours & Travels *(sikkimpeak.com)* Founder Madan Gurung is expert at tailor-making itineraries that include treks in Sikkim and throughout the Northeast of India.

Mountain Tours & Travels *(trekkinginsikkims.com)* Given two days, this Yuksom agency can usually find the necessary guides, permits, pack-yaks and tents for a simple trek.

Sikkim Tourism *(sikkimtourism.gov.in/Public/TravellerEssentials/pap)*. Lists other registered tour agencies.

WALKING TOUR

Monastery Hike from Tashiding

For a highly enjoyable introduction to rural Sikkim, the hike between monasteries from Tashiding to Yuksom is hard to beat. No permits are required for the relatively easy stroll between villages but a guide, such as mountain guide **Shumiran Rai** *(8927794271)*, will enhance your understanding of points of interest and keep you on the right track. The route is comparatively flat, but reserve energy for clambering up steep forest paths to each of the monasteries.

1 Tashiding Gompa

Don't be surprised to see Westerners seated in meditation beside the great dharma bell: Tashiding Gompa, with its forest of chortens, is an important stop for pilgrims. Atop a conical hill 3km from Tashiding, the monastery is one of Sikkim's holiest, the site having been chosen, according to myth, when Guru Rinpoche (Padmasambhava) rode in here on a flying lioness.

The hike: It begins with a long, steep haul. For less of a route march, visit Tashiding Gompa the night before, stay at Silnon Homestay (p527) and start walking from there.

2 Silnon Gompa

The delight of Silnon Gompa is less the building and more the location. On a tiny hilltop, dressed with colourful cosmos and marigolds, its flanking conifers frame a view of snow-capped **Narsing** and **Siniolchu**. Stay the night at the homestay here, and you'll catch the whole Himalayan ridge bathed in ruby red at dawn.

The hike: From Silnon the walk leads downhill to Nessa, beside gardens of precious black cardamom, and terraces of cabbages and pepper vines.

ANANDOART/SHUTTERSTOCK

Tashiding Gompa

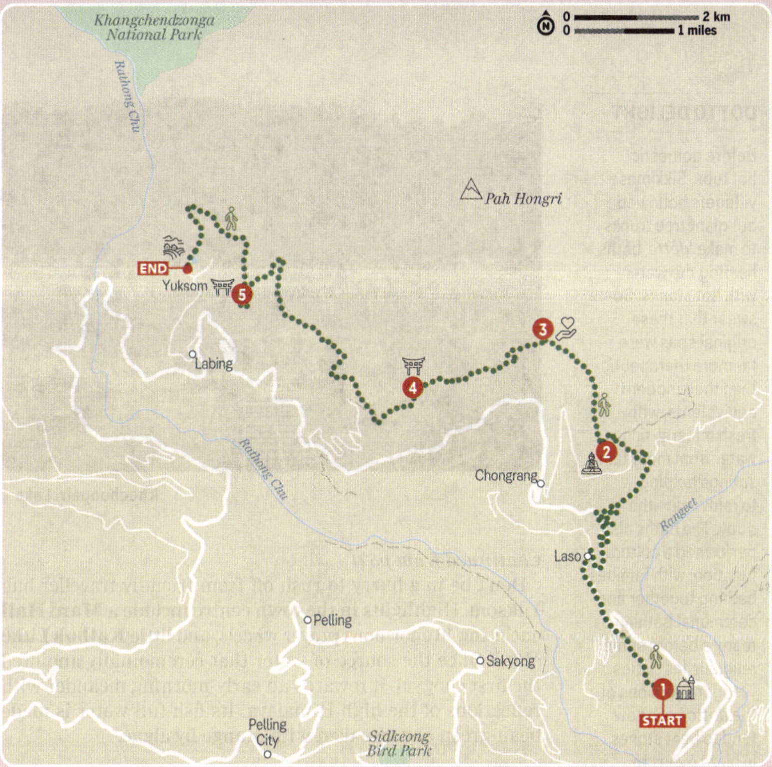

3 Pokhari Dara

At this small hamlet, local Lepcha residents in golden wellies wave you up to a small pea-green lake where prickly gourds and epiphytes dangle from the trees. Each morning a farmer brings cows to be watered outside the homestead here, notable for its traditional bamboo, mud and thatch outbuildings.

The hike: The trail flattens out through the village, where houses are decked with ears of corn and pots of orchids, before climbing steeply up a forest path, slippery after rains.

4 Hongri Gompa

Emerging from the forest to an open hillside fringed with rhododendrons and poinsettia, you'll be rewarded with panoramic views and prayer flags encouraging you to keep defying gravity. On its solitary hilltop, Hongri Gompa is one of the oldest in Sikkim, although recent restoration has breathed new life into aged paintings.

The hike: Head back down into the forest, where wild orchids and monstera cling to the trees and clumps of bamboo rustle in the wind, and emerges onto the road near Tsong.

5 Dubdi Gompa

Pause to enjoy a masala tea beside **Kholatar Elephant Falls** before weaving through subtropical woodland up to Dubdi Gompa (p516; *Yuksom Monastery; ₹20*). The oldest in Sikkim, it was built in 1701 and is prized for its beautiful murals. Catch it at dusk and you'll see sunlight exploding through the trees, refracted in rising smoke from incense burners – a fitting end to an inspiring hike.

The hike: The route down from Dubdi Gompa shortcuts along steep village tracks, emerging in Yuksom with its cheerful gardens of datana and sleeping dogs.

DOTTO DELIGHT

Before domestic hot tubs, Sikkimese villagers hollowed out giant tree trunks to make *'dotto'* baths, heating the water with hot stones. Some swear that these original spas were far more therapeutic than their modern equivalents, with fresh mineral-rich water from mountain springs helping to rejuvenate the body. The baths also performed a cultural function, with families bathing together and communal bathing a feature before some religious festivities.

Modern versions of the *dotto* bath now tend to heat stones in pizza ovens to save on firewood, but they often come with other refinements such as water infused with *tangzi* mountain herbs.

Visitors can try *dotto* at various places around Sikkim, with a day's notice, including at the **Mhenla Spa** in Pelling's **Chumbi Mountain Retreat**.

IMAGESOFINDIA/SHUTTERSTOCK

Khecheopalri Lake

Continued from p521

Don't be in a hurry to rush off from friendly traveller hub Yuksom. Highlights in the town centre include a **Mani Hall** enclosing 18 enormous prayer wheels, and little **Kathok Lake** *(₹20)*. Once the source of water that ceremonially anointed the first chogyal, it rewards an early-morning meander with reflections of the high Himalaya. Its fish-full water is made bean-green and streaked with orange by algae.

Birding above the canopy

Halfway between Pelling and Yuksom lies forest-enclosed **Khecheopalri Lake** *(₹30; 8am-4pm)*, renowned for two things: wish-fulfilment and birdwatching; go during migration and you may get lucky on both counts. Considered holy by some, given its apparent resemblance to Buddha's footprint, the lake is reached along a 10-minute stroll through an avenue of prayer wheels, garlanded with flags. Although several ducks and waders grace the water, the best birding is from a pavilion above the canopy, reached along a steep woodland path from the glass-boxed **Guru Rinpoche statue** at the waterfront. Flycatchers, barbets and the Himalayan monal make attractive sightings here.

Make an overnight trip of it by visiting the **Tashi Choling nunnery** near the car park, have lunch at **Latop's Pizza** and follow signs uphill to **Sonam Homestay** in idyllic **Khecheopalri village**.

Places We Love to Stay

₹ Budget ₹₹ Midrange ₹₹₹ Top End

Gangtok

Map p505

Hotel Pandim ₹ A great budget option with mountain panoramas from the top-floor deluxe rooms and the Tibetan-styled cafe.

Hidden Forest ₹₹ A library, flower nursery and kitchen garden make an idyllic setting for cottage rooms set amid blooming shrubs and orchids 2km out of the centre.

Dzongkar ₹₹ Ideally located and fairly new, with neat, modern rooms and minor design quirks. It's handily situated at the quiet end of the main drag beyond MG Marg.

Elgin Nor-Khill ₹₹₹ Heritage hotel built originally to accommodate royal guests, this 20th-century relic retains old-charm elegance and appealing if slightly dated rooms.

Rumtek & Martam

Martam Village Homestay ₹ Rooms, with grand views of the famous rice terraces, are hotel quality but the experience is delightfully local with delicious Sikkimese food.

Bamboo Retreat ₹₹ Set in an idyllic permaculture garden, this beautiful mansion offers various experiential opportunities for cultural insights and comfortable lodgings.

Pelling

Map p515

Hotel Garuda ₹ The backpacker classic. Adequate rooms, museum-like foyer-lounge, amazing views, shrine room and delicious Sikkimese food (guests only).

Hotel Kabur ₹ This cosy, well-located traveller hub is a midrange hotel yet still at bargain walk-in foreigner prices. The terrace views are wonderful.

Chestnut Magpie Retreat ₹₹ The birds at this rural retreat of fine modern chalets wake you for the unsurpassed views of a Himalayan dawn from each balcony.

Chumbi Mountain Retreat ₹₹₹ Unforgettable marvel using monastic design elements to create a real Sikkimese treasure, set in glorious grounds and with a celebrity guest list.

Yuksom & Around

Limboo Homestay ₹ Choose from compact en suite rooms inside or loveable cottages in the idyllic garden, surrounded by forest. Owners are helpful with trekking ideas.

Lake View Nest ₹ Sweet wooden homestay all alone at the western end of Khecheopalri village, with attractive rooms (shared bathroom), meditation room and vegetarian food.

Silnon Homestay ₹ A friendly, traditional village homestay with simple rooms (shared bathroom) beside Silnon Gompa – perfectly located for the monastery hike to Yuksom.

Tashi Gang Hotel ₹₹ Looming above a beautiful mature garden of datana, local sunflowers and poinsettia, this somewhat vintage hotel (B&B only) has peak views a short stroll from Yuksom.

Namchi

Bliss Makhim Residency ₹ Contemporary decor and superb views from balcony rooms.

Hotel Maenamla ₹₹ Rooms are bright if boxy and better than most Namchi options. The star feature is a small rooftop swimming pool with views.

Ravangla

Lingmoo Residency ₹ Midrange rooms at budget prices at a family-run hotel a short walk south of Ravangla's main market area.

Buddha Retreat ₹₹ Decorated with Sikkimese colour and flare, this comfortable hotel has spring beds, ample sitting space and smart bathrooms.

Mangan

Wongden Cardamom Homestay ₹ Rooms are basic but balcony options have dazzling dawn views of Khangchendzonga. Great home-cooked food and help with permits.

Planter's Home ₹₹ Comfortable rooms in a property with a 1930s Raj-era feel in a peaceful semi-rural setting high above town.

Lachung

Kalden Residency ₹ Simple but loveable homestay in rooms around a local-style house. Affordable rates for walk-ins, but overpriced online.

Yashree Lachung ₹₹ A step above most of Lachung's offerings, somewhat raised above the town beside the monastery entrance.

Researched by
Dr Jenny Walker

Northeastern States

STRONG TRADITIONS IN A LANDSCAPE OF EXTREMES

A culturally diverse, religiously complex and proudly tribal area, the Seven Sister States of Northeast India reach from paddy plains to Himalayan plateaus.

Waving down a ubiquitous Toyota Innova marked 'Northeast India Tourist Permit', a guard at the barely detectable border between Tripura and Mizoram peers at the two passengers in the backseat. Spitting out a large red dollop of *paan* (mixture of betel nut and leaves for chewing), he inserts his head through the window and shouts 'Selfie!' Smiles over, the serious business of inscribing the names and visa details of the travellers in an aged ledger is conducted. There's no space for permit details – a new requirement for travelling in Mizoram – so the party is waved on with a 'Happy Christmas' instead.

SADANANDA SAIKIA/SHUTTERSTOCK

Similar forms of friendly, bureaucratic exchange across the Seven Sister States (so-named in 1972) are repeated across this remote northeast region, hinting at both the challenges and the joys of travel here. If unphased by the need for permits, and the long and often treacherous journeys on roads that don't deserve the name, you'll find the latter easily outstrip the former. Although Manipur is currently off-limits due to inner strife, the other six states – each entirely distinct – richly reward the effort to get there with magnificent landscapes, abundant wildlife and a fascinating mix of traditions that surface above the region's rapid modernisation. Seldom visited by foreigners, the region is a popular destination for home visitors who come from as far as Kerala for an adventure. With hiking, rafting, safaris and distinctive food on offer, it's easy to understand why.

THE MAIN AREAS

ASSAM
Hindu plains hub of the northeast. **p534**

ARUNACHAL PRADESH
Buddhist communities in Himalayan landscapes. **p544**

NAGALAND
Tribal state of Hornbill Festival fame. **p550**

MIZORAM
Highland tribes, proud of Christian traditions. **p555**

For places to stay in the Northeastern States, see p563

AHEH SH/GETTY IMAGES

Above: Nohkalikai waterfall (p562), Cheerapunjee;
Left: Water buffalo, Kaziranga National Park (p540), Assam

TRIPURA
Rural and rich in rice and rubber.
p558

MEGHALAYA
Temperate, modern and edged by escarpment. p560

MANIPUR
Currently off-limits for tourism due to internal tensions and not covered in this chapter.

Find Your Way

Forget what you think you know about time and distance: travelling in Northeast India redefines the terms. Tiny on the map, each state is huge in experiences offered and journeys here are in slow time.

Assam, p534

Famous for tea production and one-horned rhinos, Assam's plains border each of the sister states, making Guwahati the region's main travel hub.

Arunachal Pradesh, p544

With the eastern Himalaya soaring up to the Chinese border, this spectacular state offers high-altitude adventure beyond the capital Itanagar.

Nagaland, p550

Crowds are plentiful at Kohima's annual Hornbill Festival, the roots of which can be traced to remote villages near the Myanmar border.

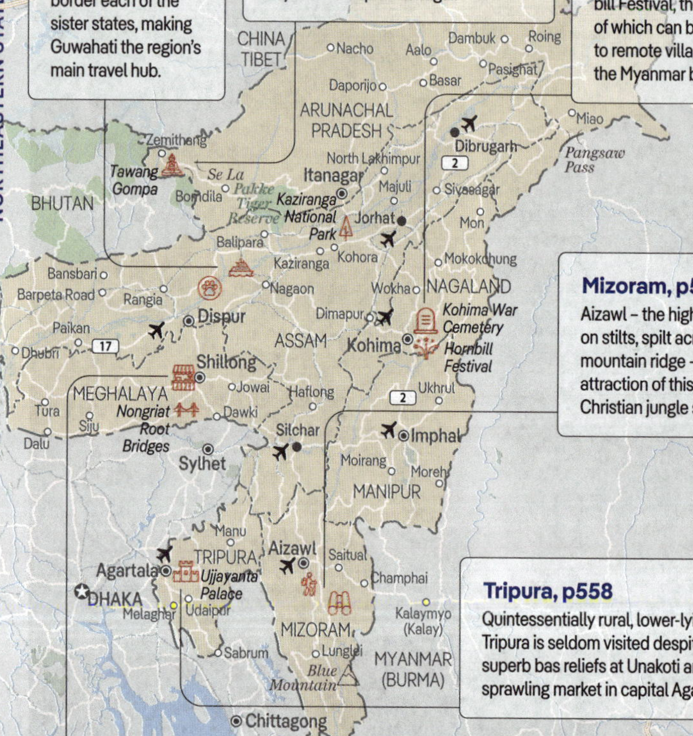

Mizoram, p55

Aizawl – the highland city on stilts, spilt across a mountain ridge – is a chief attraction of this strongly Christian jungle state.

Tripura, p558

Quintessentially rural, lower-lying Tripura is seldom visited despite superb bas reliefs at Unakoti and a sprawling market in capital Agartala.

Meghalaya, p560

Home of forest pines and unique living bridges, Meghalaya boasts cool hill stations at Shillong and Cherrapunjee (wettest place on Earth).

SHARED TAXI & PRIVATE TOUR

Shared jeeps (generally Tata Sumos) reach even the most inaccessible mountain villages, but travelling by public transport is generally overcrowded and often dangerously fast on poor mountain roads, with landslides frequent during the monsoon. Hiring a private car and driver through a tour agency offers a safer option and helps facilitate the paperwork.

TRAIN, BUS & BOAT

Train makes an excellent way of entering Assam, the main travel hub of the Seven Sster States, with regular services between West Bengal's Siliguri and Assam's capital Guwahati. Beyond the capital, though, bus is the main form of intercity transport, while boats across the Brahmaputra help connect with Arunachal Pradesh.

Mask making, Majuli Island (p542)

Plan Your Time

Plan on around six weeks to visit all six currently accessible sister states. Distances are small but a 40km journey takes around an hour, on average, by private car in the dry season, and nightfall comes early.

Plains & Mountains in a Week

- Enjoy a week between Assam and Arunachal Pradesh. Begin in the plains capital of **Guwahati** (p534), watch rhinos in the tropical forests of **Kaziranga National Park** (p540) and cross the Brahmaputra to ancient **Majuli Island** (p542). Meet Arunachal's Apatani people in **Ziro Valley** (p546) or climb up through tropical rainforests to **Tawang** (p546) via high-altitude **Sela Pass** (4170m).

A Fortnight's Cultural Immersion

- Fly into **Shillong** (p560), in the hills of Meghalaya, visit a Khasi homestay and learn about regional customs at the **Don Bosco Museum** (p561). Descend to the plains of Assam to catch nightly dance performances at **Kaziranga** (p540) en route to **Kohima** (p550), site of fierce fighting in WWII. Visit nearby **Naga Heritage Village** (p554) in Kisama for an introduction to the 17 tribes of Nagaland.

SEASONAL HIGHLIGHTS

MONSOON

June to September sees humidity and downpours. Expect landslides and flooding to disrupt travel.

POST-MONSOON

Perfect for safari and safer trips into the mountains, October and November mark the peak season.

WINTER

Christmas and New Year celebrated across much of the region. Snows grace mountains until late March.

SPRING

In April the Assamese celebrate New Year. April and May are also glorious months for flowers.

NEED TO KNOW:

Permits & Travel Tips

The Northeastern States have garnered a reputation over recent decades as somewhat restive politically and a risk for foreign travellers. While the unrest is now mostly in the past, some planning and precaution is required to ensure safe and efficient travel in the region. This includes gaining permits to a few areas and avoiding others, particularly the state of Manipur.

Travelling Safely in the Northeasterm States

Many ethnolinguistic groups in the Northeast continue to feel disadvantaged in the face of illegal immigration from neighbouring countries and are angered at perceived government apathy in managing the situation. Some still harbour aspirations to become independent states, while the border of Arunachal Pradesh is yet to be recognised officially by China. Student unions are powerful across the region, and strikes and other forms of protest can flare up quickly.

Despite these potential concerns, at the time of writing only the state of Manipur was off-limits to tourists due to internal unrest (and is therefore not covered in this chapter), while the other six states presented no threat to travellers. The largest safety issue is likely to be long journeys on often inadequate mountain roads at the mercy of rash jeep drivers. Nonetheless, it pays to be vigilant and to check regional news while travelling.

Tour Agents

To get the most out of a short trip, in the safety of a properly maintained vehicle with a professional driver, book a tour through a reputable tour agency. These agencies take care of all the paperwork and liaise with independent local guides, whose cultural insights greatly enhance a trip.

Xohojatri Travels *(9864625574)* goes above and beyond to deliver the best service for customers. Apurba Kalita, the Assamese owner of this highly competent agency, knows the region well and works with a network of knowledgeable local guides to tailor-make the best itineraries.

Two other reliable agencies are **Purvi Discovery** *(purvidiscovery.com)* and **Alder Tours & Travels** *(aldertoursntravels.com)*.

BORDER CROSSINGS

Despite long international borders, the Northeastern States offer few opportunities for onward travel to other countries beyond India. There are currently no official land crossings with China open to tourists, and travelling to Myanmar (from Mizoram or Nagaland) is currently deemed a security risk. There is a small crossing between Samdrup Jongkhar in Assam and Gelephu in southern Bhutan but this requires the arrangement of all documentation (including payment of a Sustainable Development Fee in Bhutan) for either country in advance. To cross from Bangladesh into India (through Meghalaya or Tripura), you need a paper visa (not an e-visa), obtained in advance, giving express permission to use a particular border. If exiting into Bangladesh, visas on arrival are not guaranteed.

EXPLOREWITHINFO/SHUTTERSTOCK

Chakzam iron bridge (p547), Arunachal Pradesh

TOP TIPS

Bring spare passport-sized photos and take multiple copies of your passport, visa and protected area permits (PAP) to surrender at police checkpoints if required.

Check the latest advice from your Foreign Office before leaving and the following news agencies on arrival:

Northeast Today *(northeasttoday.in)*

Time8 *(time8.in)*

TNT *(thenortheast today.com)*

Permits for the Northeastern States

Rules and regulations regarding travel in the Seven Sister States change frequently but, as of 2026, Arunachal Pradesh and Mizoram were the only two currently accessible states requiring foreign visitors to obtain a permit.

Arunachal Pradesh

You are not permitted to enter Arunachal Pradesh without a Protected Area Permit (PAP). The PAP is valid for 30 days from the specified starting date and costs the rupee equivalent of US$50. A minimum of two travellers must apply together for the PAP, detailing their intended itinerary. Note that foreigners are not permitted north of a 5km zone around Tawang, putting Bom-La out of bounds. The PAP is most easily obtained through a registered tour operator (see *arunachaltourism.com/tour-operators.php*). Some agencies offer this service for a fee without the need to book a tour.

welcomearunachal.com/travel-info/protected-area-permit-pap-for-foreigners

Meghalaya

All visitors must register through the Meghalay Tourism app before arrival, providing passport and itinerary details for an E-Invite. You must also register with the local police within 24 hours of arrival at the Foreigners Registration Office (FRO).

welcomemeghalaya.com/travel-info/ilp-requirement-clarification-not-required-for-meghalaya

Mizoram

Foreigners need a PAP or Restricted Area Permit (RAP) obtained via the e-FRRO (Foreign Regional Registration Office) portal or Ministry of Home Affairs (MHA). You must register at the Foreigners Registration Office (FRO) within 24 hours of arrival.

mizoramtourism.com/about/4

Nagaland

While PAPs are not currently required, you must register at the nearest police station within 24 hours of arrival.

police.nagaland.gov.in/entry-permits

Assam

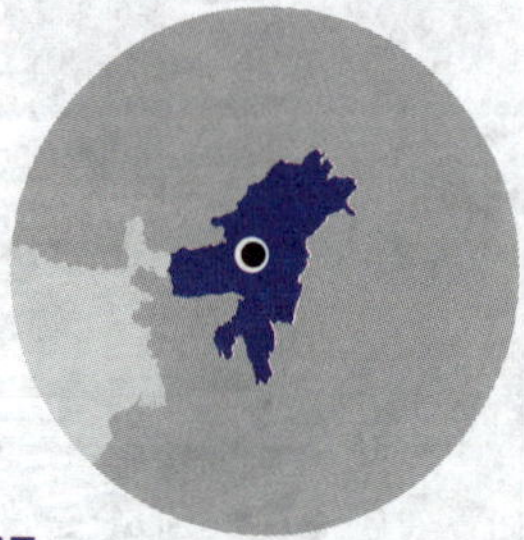

RIVER CRUISES | WILDLIFE SAFARI | ISLAND RETREAT

TOP TIP

It may be a natural travel hub for the whole region but don't be in a hurry to leave Assam! Guwahati, on the banks of the Brahmaputra, is an intriguing capital city with a hallowed Hindu temple, Kaziranga (of rhino-spotting fame) makes a tourist-savvy alternative hub, and Majuli Island is a peaceful retreat.

On the train home to Guwahati, an Assamese family cradle a small plastic basket, packed with a blanket and a new deity, represented in brass. They're returning from Nepal and clearly cherish the new addition to their travelling party, taking it in turns to secure the icon as the train slides through a landscape of paddy fields. They're joined by visitors from Kerala bound for Arunachal Pradesh and keen to see snow.

Although predominantly flat, Assam has long lured travellers from mainland summers as the gateway to cooler climes. Equally, it is not unusual to see 'AS' prefigure car number plates in the other six states, each of which Assam borders. Assam's corridor of plains – part paddy, part tea and part riverine jungle – forms the natural hub of the region, an obvious baseline of cultural and natural wonders from which to mount trips along the Brahmaputra and up, at every state border bar West Bengal, to higher lands.

State Treasures

A visit to Assam State Museum

Ask a local what Assam is famous for and they'll tell you 'tea, one-horned rhinos and Zubeen Garg' – the recently deceased, adored (and now deified) pop singer. Visit **Assam State Museum** *(museums.assam.gov.in; ₹300)*, though, and you'll quickly find a host of other reasons to celebrate the state.

GETTING AROUND

While it's tempting to hop on a flight from Guwahati to the other capitals of the region, travelling by land is a much better way of recognising Assam's unique position as the connective tissue that binds the Seven Sster States together. Almost entirely flat, the state is relatively easy to get around with trains, buses, shared taxis and ferries across the Brahmaputra all readily available. Roads are mostly in good condition but major highways are few and travelling is slowed by other road users, including the occasional wild elephant or hay-bearing buffalo cart.

Begin a tour of the multi-level museum in the basement with its perfectly crafted temple sculptures, some of which predate Assam's enduring Ahom Kingdom (1228–1826). Note too the 14th-century Ganga (river deity) on the ground floor whose ample feet rest on a crocodile and whose elongated earlobes depict wisdom. Good signage in English helps interpret the carvings and gives backstory to the Hindu symbolism.

Save time for the upper floors, whose village and textile galleries tell Assam's story from a less lofty perspective. Although tin roofs have all but replaced the traditional thatch of traditional Assamese housing, the concept of *namghar*, or village hub, endures and village life continues to echo the Ahom *khel*, or clan structure of local life.

Say It with Silk

Shopping for handloomed textiles

Mahatma Gandhi apparently once said that Assamese women weave fairytales into their clothing, and if you've visited the superb examples in the textile gallery in the state museum you'll understand what he meant. Less obvious is the predominant thread. Silk is garnered most famously from the cocoons of mulberry-eating silk moth caterpillars, but it can also be spun from the spent cocoons of a domesticated moth, earning the resultant *'eri'* fabric the term 'nonviolent' or 'peace silk'.

Walk around **Fancy Bazar** in Guwahati and shops such as **Silk House** *(10am to 8.30pm)* dazzle with colourful *eri* silks, many boasting elaborate floral designs favoured in Assamese *mekhela chador* (two-piece sari). **Nirmaan Fabrics** *(facebook.com/nirmaanfabric)* on GNB Rd, opposite state emporium **Jagaran**, sells *eri* scarves designed for a Western market, while Rabha and Khasi communities near Guwahati showcase Indigenous sericulture – contact **7weaves** *(brintha@7weaves.com)* to arrange a visit.

Riding the Brahmaputra

Sunset river cruises from Guwahati

In Guwahati you can walk beside the Brahmaputra along MG Rd in the company of parakeets and woodpeckers or take the **ropeway** *(₹120)* opposite **Nehru Park** to the northern bank. But only boarding a boat will give you a feel for the pulse of the water. One-hour sunset cruises are operated from the **Gateway of Assam** – built to welcome British viceroy Lord Northbrook when he arrived by steamer from Kolkata in 1874 – or book top-deck seats with **Brahmaputra Cruise Private Ltd** *(alfrescogrand.com; ₹150)* to enjoy a sundowner and I-pop. Wear long sleeves and bring mosquito repellent.

LUXURY CRUISES

If the prospect of spending more time riding the Brahmaputra appeals, then consider booking a berth on a cruise operated between October to May by **Assam Bengal Navigation** *(assambengalnavigation.com)*. Four- to 10-night journeys to **Majuli Island** (p542) offer a floating retreat.

BRAHMAPUTRA

Bisected by the mighty Brahmaputra, Assam is almost two states in one. There's the populous southern side, where big cities such as the capital Guwahati, Dibrugarh and Jorhat bring familiar modern bustle to the plains. To the north, in contrast, life continues at a slower pace – suggestive, many Assamese will tell you, of an earlier era under the independent Kingdom of Ahom.

Responsible for this twin character, the Brahmaputra is more than just 'the bit in the middle'. So vast it is still only crossed by six significant bridges in Assam, it encompasses Majuli Island – the largest river island in the world. Amplifying with the monsoon and contracting in the winter, this vital water source, held holy by Hindus, is forever reinventing its course.

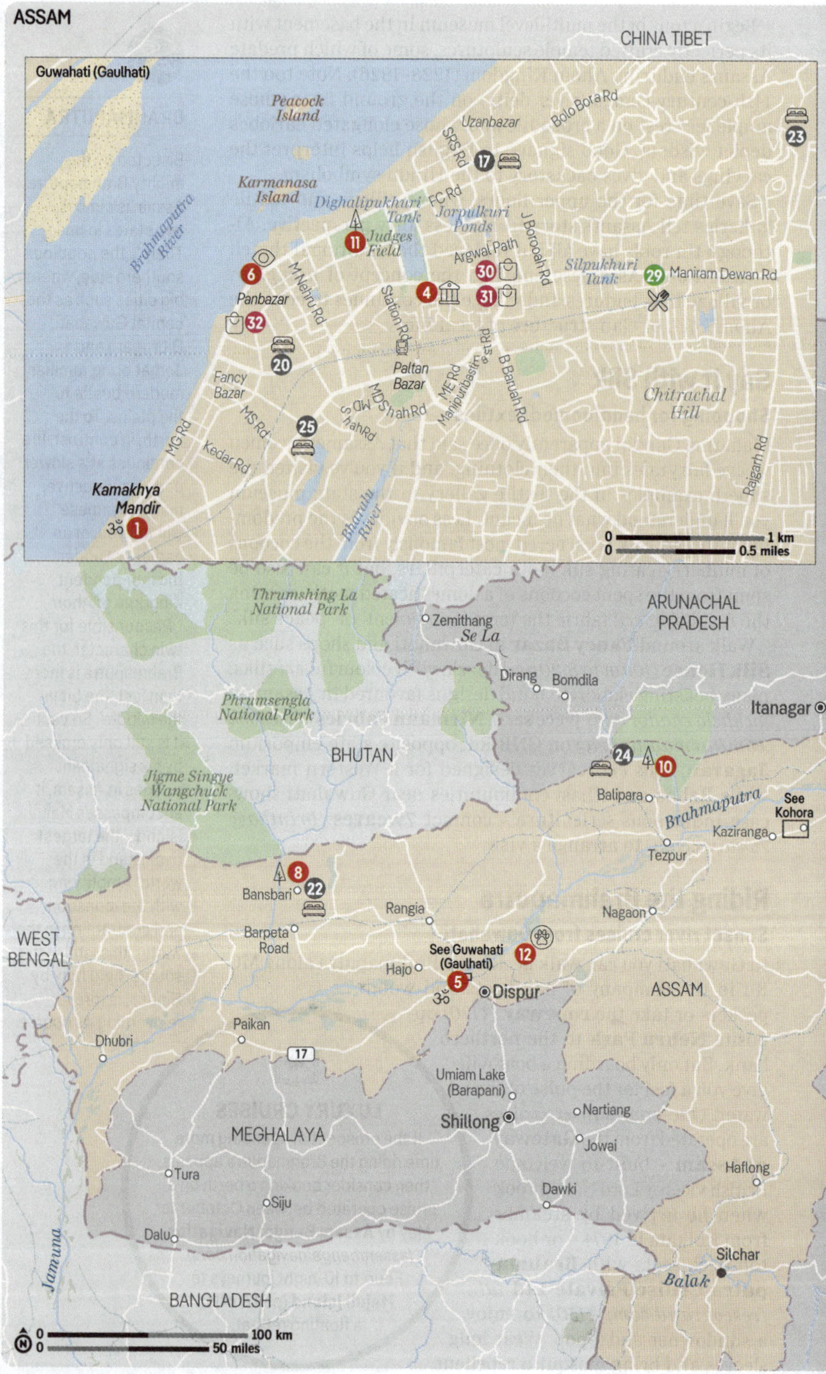
ASSAM
CHINA TIBET
Guwahati (Gaulhati)
Peacock Island
Karmanasa Island
Brahmaputra River
Uzanbazar
Bolo Bora Rd
SPS Rd
17
23
Dighalipukhuri Tank
FC Rd
Jorpulkuri Ponds
J Boroaah Rd
11
Judges Field
Argwal Path
Silpukhuri Tank
29
Maniram Dewan Rd
6
M Nehru Rd
30
4
31
Panbazar
Station Rd
32
20
Paltan Bazar
1st Rd
B Baruah Rd
Chitrachal Hill
Fancy Bazar
MD Shah Rd
ME Rd
Manipuribastin Rd
MS Rd
25
MG Rd
Kedar Rd
Bharalu River
Raigarh Rd
Kamakhya Mandir
1
0
1 km
0.5 miles
Thrumshing La National Park
Zemithang
Se La
ARUNACHAL PRADESH
Dirang
Bomdila
Itanagar
Phrumsengla National Park
BHUTAN
24
10
Jigme Singye Wangchuck National Park
Balipara
Brahmaputra
See Kohora
Kaziranga
Tezpur
8
Bansbari
22
Rangia
Nagaon
WEST BENGAL
Barpeta Road
See Guwahati (Gaulhati)
12
Hajo
5
Dispur
ASSAM
Paikan
Dhubri
17
Umiam Lake (Barapani)
Nartiang
Shillong
MEGHALAYA
Jowai
Haflong
Tura
Siju
Dawki
Dalu
Silchar
Jamuna
Balak
BANGLADESH
100 km
50 miles

HIGHLIGHTS
1 Kamakhya Mandir
2 Kaziranga National Park

SIGHTS
3 Ahom Temples
4 Assam State Museum
5 Bhubaneswari Mandir
6 Gateway of Assam
7 Kaziranga National Orchid & Biodiversity Park
8 Manas National Park
9 Museum
10 Nameri National Park
11 Nehru Park
12 Pobitora Wildlife Sanctuary
13 Salmora Pottery Workshops
14 Samaguri Satra
15 Selek Ghat Bamboo Bridge
16 Treasured Wheels Museum

SLEEPING
17 Baruah Bhavan
18 Chameli Memsaab Bungalow
19 Dekasang Cottage
20 Dynasty
21 Infinity Resort
22 Manas Jungle Retreat
23 Prabhakar Homestay
24 Prasanti Cottages
25 Vishwaratna Hotel

EATING
26 Heritage Jaysagar
27 Maihang
see 19 North East Kitchen
29 Paradise

SHOPPING
30 Jagaran
31 Nirmaan Fabrics
32 Silk House

TRANSPORT
33 Avijatri Travels

TOP EXPERIENCE

Kamakhya Mandir

Packed into a narrow, barred cage, keeping your place in a crush of expectant temple-goers, you'll inevitably question the wisdom of choosing to enter Guwahati's Kamakhya Mandir. It's certainly not an option for the claustrophobic. But then the gate guardian unlocks your queue, and you join the surge into darkness, towards flickering sanctuary lamps. Being among devotees paying their respects in the hushed and garlanded inner sanctum is a privilege not easily forgotten.

SAURAV PURKAYASTHA/GETTY IMAGES

Ambubachi Festival

TOP TIPS

- For inner temple visits, be ready to donate ₹300 to ₹500 at main points of blessing and at several holy shrines on exiting in addition to paying the entrance fee.
- Buy a *genda* (marigold) garland (₹100) before entering.
- Stroll to hilltop temple **Bhubaneswari Mandir**, part of the Kamakhya complex, or walk the 1.5km woodland trail down to the main road.

PRACTICALITIES

● maakamakhya.org
● ₹501 (₹1500 'special ticket' to enter inner temple) ● 7.30am-1.30pm & 3.30-7pm

Pilgrimage Site of Tantric Worship

Revered as the most holy shrine of *shakti* (tantric worship centred on Maa Kamakhya, also known as Kameswari or the goddess of desire), this Hindu temple is visited by millions each year. Around 200,000 pilgrims per day stream into the temple grounds during June alone despite temperatures soaring above 45°C.

It's possible to visit the outer temple complex for free, but it's only by entering the entombed shrines inside the temple's narrow inner confines that the strength of devotion over centuries can be fully felt.

The temple is 8km west of Guwahati, in the Nilachal Hills. The ground itself (elevated above a landscape of plains) is significant in Hindu legend as the site where the yoni (vagina; female fertility symbol) of Sati landed when her distraught husband Shiva scattered the pieces of her dead body.

Annual Festival

Shakti devotees believe that Maa Kamakhya menstruates annually (in June) and that the waters of the Brahmaputra run red at that time accordingly. The temple is closed for the first three days of the four-day **Ambubachi Festival** but celebrations attract thousands of pilgrims on the fourth day.

Bihu Beauties

Kaziranga's cultural showcase

If your only acquaintance with an orchid is of a hybrid variety bought on Mother's Day or rendered in plastic in hotel foyers, then make sure you visit **Kaziranga National Orchid & Biodiversity Park** *(₹500)*. There are 2000 species of orchid and 400 of them grow wild in Assam – that represents 90% of all species found in India. Protected and studied at the orchid park, many of these species are on display, challenging even an aficionado's notion of orchid evolutionary ingenuity. Although April is the best time to see wild orchids bloom, the park showcases orchids all year round, including rare blue *vanda* and other endangered species. Engage a knowledgeable guide from the park staff (the park is run as an NGO for the benefit of the whole village) and you'll find you begin to favour the tiny delicacies of nature over the blousey hybrids of horticulture.

Orchids feature in the **Rongali Bihu** (April) – the state's most famous festival celebrating the Assamese New Year – when women don beautiful handloomed clothing and tuck trusses of foxtail orchids in their hair. The graceful Bihu dance, among other dances such as the unnerving bamboo dance, are performed nightly at 6.30pm in a spectacular **cultural programme** *(₹300)* throughout winter – wear something warm.

Also worth visiting in the park grounds is a pavilion of traditional musical instruments made of frog skin and horse hair, and mango and jackfruit tree wood, used during festivities. Knowledgeable **Dijen Gogoi** *(YouTube: Imu Music)* can demonstrate each handmade instrument.

Treasured Wheels

Vintage car collection

There's a certain irony that in the same year that Kaziranga Park launches its agro-tourism initiative with ox and horse carts championing slow travel, a neighbouring venture focuses on the human fascination with speed. The lifetime project of Piklu Deka, the **Treasured Wheels Museum** *(₹500)* began with a red Renault 4CV, was joined by a Fiat 500 Topolino, and now comprises a priceless collection of heritage vehicles, each meticulously restored in a workshop surrounded by tea gardens. Cyclists will love the folding bike designed for paratroopers.

BEST TOURS

Apurba Kalita: Offers the best advice on touring Assam and the sister states; goes over and above in tailoring excellent itineraries around your interests. *(WhatsApp 9864626574)*

Mrinal Chandra Rag: A highly experienced, professional driver from Assam who rigorously maintains the speed limit – a boon on mountain roads. *(WhatsApp 9101171513)*

Kaziranga Wild Trail: Reliable local jeep company; arranges park paperwork, selects guides and collects guests from their hotel. *(kazirangawildtrail.in)*

Arabinda Borah Kaziranga National Park: An enthusiastic wildlife guide, aware of latest wildlife sightings in the park and keen to help guests spot the Assamese Big Five. *(9859627061)*

Raju Boruah Majuli Island: A member of Majuli Island's Mishing community; offers an insider's perspective on local culture. *(WhatsApp 7896151773)*

EATING AROUND ASSAM: OUR PICKS

Paradise: This Guwahati restaurant on MRD Rd puts together traditional lunch thalis that feature local delicacies such as fish *tenga* wrapped in a banana leaf. *10.30am-10.30pm* ₹₹

Maihang: Generous thalis of Assamese favourites (including locally grown mustard leaves, bamboo shoots and fermented fish dishes) offer a night out from your homestay. *10am-5pm & 7-10pm* ₹₹

Heritage Jaysagar: An attractive tank-side restaurant, the Heritage offers Indian, Chinese and international bites and a bit of boating after. *10am-10.30pm* ₹₹

North East Kitchen: A simple roadside venue offering authentic Assamese favourites, this modest restaurant is is popular with local guides. *10am-5.30pm* ₹

HELP ME PICK:

Assam's National Parks

Assam protects several key areas of low-lying riverine forest. These national parks are richly diverse in habitat and home to many large mammals, including the Assamese 'Big Five', and hundreds of species of birds. While all share similar opportunities for safari, each park is distinct in character and offers a different wildlife experience. Each park takes time and effort to reach, so it pays to understand in advance which park best suits your interests.

Which National Park If You Like...

The Big Five

Home to the Assamese 'Big Five' – Bengal tiger, one-horned rhinoceros, elephant, wild water buffalo and swamp deer – **Kaziranga National Park** *(kaziranga-national-park.com)* is the most visited of Assam's protected areas and famous throughout India for its large rhino population. Stretching along the southern rim of the Brahmaputra, much of the park is densely forested but there are also large open areas of grassland and wetland. It's here that the park's rhinos are often seen, grazing peacefully beside water or clambering out from the tall grass. With over 2600 rhinos (two-thirds of the world's one-horned population) resident here, a sighting is almost guaranteed.

Hiking in Tiger Territory

It's one thing to know tigers are present from the safety of a jeep but it's quite another when you are on foot. At **Nameri National Park** *(assamtourism.gov.in/Nameri-National-Park.php)*, contiguous with Arunachal Pradesh's Pakke Tiger Reserve, guided hikes in the company of an armed ranger take place twice daily and involve crossing into tiger territory on a small wooden boat.

Take the afternoon hike, and as the sunlight fades (as early as 4pm in winter) you'll notice a change in the character of the forest. As you wonder who is watching whom, listen for the wing flap of roosting hornbills and sense the tension among the resident samba as the nocturnal big cats awake.

Rafting Across Borders

One of the best parts of visiting **Manas National Park** *(assamtourism.gov.in/Manas-National-Park1.php)* is the opportunity to raft along the Beki River. This beautiful body of water marks the boundary between Manas and Bhutan's enormous Royal Manas National Park. The border doesn't mean much to the water buffalo who are often spotted crossing the river, despite the swift current. Elephants, rhinos and tigers are all similarly good swimmers if more elusive to spot, especially given the distraction of navigating shimmering – but gentle – rapids. Look out for large herds of gaur (Indian bison) and rare dholes (wild dogs) on the jeep ride to the launching point.

Rafting at Manas or Nameri costs about ₹3600 per person for a 2½-hour trip.

Shorter Travel Times

Just 60km and a two-hour drive from Guwahati, the small **Pobitora Wildlife Sanctuary** *(assamtourism.gov.in/Pobitora-Wildlife-Sanctuary1.php)* makes it feasible to spot a one-horned rhino on a morning safari and be back at your capital homestay for dinner. Take a pair of binoculars with you as the park is a hotspot for birding, with 375 resident species and many migrants.

DHRITIPURNA/SHUTTERSTOCK

Nameri National Park, Assam

HOW TO

When to go By and large, the dry winter season (November to April) is best for wildlife viewing.

What to wear It's cold in an open jeep on an early-morning safari and on returning to base at sundown, particularly in winter – take a coat or blanket.

What to pack Mosquito repellent is a good idea during and after the monsoon. A hat and binoculars are essential.

Budget Entry to each park costs foreigners around ₹650, ₹200 for a still camera permit and ₹2500 for jeep hire. Hiking at Nameria costs about ₹3000, all in.

Arranging a National Park Visit

DIY or Guided Tour While it's feasible, if you have plenty of time, to turn up on public transport to each of Assam's wildlife parks and then book a safari from the main entrance (open 7am to 10am and 1.30pm to 3pm), it's more practical to prebook an activity through **Assam Tourism** *(assamtourism.gov.in/Safari-packages.php)*. Alternatively, most nearby accommodation can arrange a safari; this has the advantage of free pickup and dropoff by jeep and help in obtaining the required permits and guides. A list of tour operators and guides is available from the Assam Tourism website. This option helps ensure you engage appropriate help for your area of interest, particularly if you are looking to spot species other than the in-demand Assamese Big Five.

Elephant or Jeep Each of Assam's wildlife parks offer early-morning safaris seated on an elephant. While this may seem to offer an ecofriendly way of engaging with the jungle, elephant riding is now widely condemned by experts on animal welfare grounds and is likely to be phased out from Assam's national parks within the decade. An elephant's spine is not conducive to supporting heavy weights and the method of training domestic elephants to become docile when young is now considered unethical. Taking a jeep safari instead offers the much better experience of viewing elephants in the wild in their natural habitat.

TOP EXPERIENCE

Majuli Island

The Mishing people of Majuli Island have been welcoming visitors to their rural idyll for centuries. Attracted by the island's many *satras* (Hindu Vaishnavaite monasteries renowned for cultivating the arts), even 17th-century Ahom kings crossed the Brahmaputra to pay their respects here. Today, though, a visit to Majuli is less about sights and more about retreat – into a quieter space running on local time.

ASHWIN KARANTH/SHUTTERSTOCK

Fishing nets, Majuli

TOP TIPS

- Admire the jigsaw precision of vehicles being loaded on tiny, Majuli-bound ferries and spot river dolphins during the one-hour crossing.
- Wake at sunrise to watch Chinese nets being dipped in and out of dawn mists.
- Hire a bike and head for the bamboo bridge at Selek Ghat where birds abound at sunset.

PRACTICALITIES

- majuliisland.in • best visited in dry season
- reached by boat only

Sinking Back into Nature

Hidden among temporary sandbanks that rise and sink with the seasons, **Majuli** is the world's largest river island. Try to put a size on this low-lying landmass, though, and it's like trying to measure a meal that's still being consumed. Bite by bite, the Brahmaputra is snatching the land back. Not that the inhabitants seem unduly troubled by the continuous erosion – the Indigenous Mishing go about their lives in time-honoured rhythms, tending pigs, goats and geese and embracing a continuity of culture informed by belief and expressed through craft industry.

Tradition of Hospitality

'I grew those!' beams a monk who, still wearing his motorbike helmet, snatches a leaf from the lunch his wife has spent hours preparing. 'Very happy!' he says by way of goodbye to his homestay visitors. Being embraced by the warmth of welcome is a highlight of Majuli, no less memorable than the **museum** *(₹100)* of royal gifts in 18th-century **Auniati Satra** or watching young apprentices making masks at **Samaguri Satra**. It's a welcome extended to all, with a lame calf sheltering among yet-to-be-fired pots in the pottery workshops of **Salmora**, and crumbs shared with red-whiskered bulbuls by the riverbank.

Royal Relics

The Ahom Kingdom of Sivasagar

Sivasagar, meaning 'ocean of Shiva', may be overstating the scale of the town's ancient reservoir but the name does at least capture the depth of history associated with the **Ahom Temples** arranged majestically along its southern bank. Founded in 1228, it was from the surrounding royal complex that the Ahom Kingdom ruled much of Assam between the 16th and 19th centuries.

Most imposing of the trio of pyramidal temples is 33m-high **Shivadol**, dedicated to Shiva and built by the Ahom queen, Ambika, in 1734, but there are many other tanks, temples, palaces and *maidams* (funerary mounds) besides, scattered across the local plains and hilly, wooded knolls. These make for a fascinating day trip from nearby Jorhat or a half-day's diversion en route between Kaziranga and Nagaland. The best way of touring Sivasagar's **sites** *(₹500 for 5 monuments)* is by taxi, or **Avijatri Travels** *(7606060737)* offers half-day tours.

Making Time for Tea

Assam's famous tea gardens

If you're a tea drinker, you'll be no stranger to Assam's connection with *Camellia sinensis v assamica*. Some estimate that 440,000 tonnes of Assamese black tea are produced annually, and travelling across the state you'll find a landscape martialled into neat, evergreen rows, shaded with occasional trees draped in pepper vines. Visiting one of Assam's tea gardens is a good way to understand the role of tea in the state economy and to learn how tea is grown and produced. **Kaziranga National Park** *(kaziranga-national-park.com; 9212553107)* can advise on tea gardens that offer guided tours or, better still, you can stay overnight in a plantation cottage, such as Chameli Memsaab Bungalow (p563) in Jorhat, and learn how to make the perfect cuppa.

PRESERVING INDIGENOUS CULTURE

Shiela Bora
University professor and Prabhakar Homestay (p563) host with husband Mahesh, who has devoted his retirement to making beautiful paper from rhino dung. *WhatsApp 94350 33222*

Tourism is picking up in the Northeast region and there is much to see here. My major concern, though, being a historian and having spent my life interacting with tribal communities, is that Indigenous peoples must be allowed to continue to live their own kind of life, speak their own languages (many of which have no written form), and observe their own customs without being overwhelmed by the commoditication of their culture.

Visitors can help ensure that Indigenous communities benefit from the revenue generated from tourism by engaging a local guide to learn about these special cultures, buying local crafts or booking into a village homestay.

Arunachal Pradesh

HIMALAYAN LANDSCAPES | ANIMIST CULTURE | BUDDHIST MONASTERIES

TOP TIPS

Ask your homestay where most visitors come from and they'll tell you 'India'. China has never formally recognised Indian sovereignty here – a point exploited by Arunachal student bodies when negotiating for equal opportunities.

Stop at the various military museums en route to Tawang to learn about the 1962 Sino-Indian conflict and discern a modern Great Game in progress.

Central heating in hotels is uncommon so bring thermals, socks and a hat in winter and be ready to wear them to bed.

Gently holding a small, downy chick between fore-finger and thumb, a Hija village shaman, dressed in collar and tie, rhythmically intones the words of his ancestors, handed down through generations. The rest of the party have been imbibing strong millet beer in the winter sunshine and are contributing to the convivial atmosphere and the discussions about the American president, college education and the rising cost of living. Nothing, though, distracts from the important business of chanting, a precursor to reading the future in nature's signs.

Tradition – be it religious or cultural in nature – is an important part of life in the Himalayan state of Arunachal Pradesh. Communities here are proud of their tribal roots and keen to share their customs with visitors. Visit Ziro or high-altitude Tawang and you'll spot more in common with neighbouring China than the plains of Assam, and it's no coincidence that the Indian army has a strong presence here.

Busy Buying Something & Nothing

Itanagar's busy central market

Nobody visits **Itanagar** for the sights, despite a passable state museum. What attracts the crowds is the **Bazaar**. Many shoppers have had a mammoth trip to get here (12 hours from Tawang) and there's an urgency to the thronging crowds who

GETTING AROUND

A helicopter service connects Guwahati in Assam to Arunachal capital Itanagar. Flights, rail services and a good road also connect Itanagar with Dibrugarh in Eastern Assam. The Trans Arunachal Highway (TAH), replacing single-track roads with two lanes, is nearing completion and is a destination in its own right, with hairpin bends towards Tawang and a newly opened tunnel avoiding 4170m Sela Pass. Modern buses are operated by **Zainab Travels** *(zainabtravels.com)* to Tawang and Ziro while shared jeeps connect smaller towns.

HIGHLIGHTS
1 Tawang Gompa

SIGHTS
2 Ball of Fire Museum
3 Bomdila Pass
4 Chakzam Iron Bridge
5 Clock Tower
6 Dul Dul Tharpa Ling Gompa
7 Jaswantgarh War Memorial
8 Jawaharlal Nehru State Museum
9 Major Bob Museum
10 Museum
11 Naara Aaba
12 Nuranang Falls
13 Pakke Tiger Reserve
14 Pamu Yalang
see 15 Sela Pass
15 Sela Tunnel
16 Sri Nag Temple
17 Thupsung Dhargye Ling Buddhist Monastery
18 Urgelling Gompa

SLEEPING
19 Cygnet Inn Trendz
20 Gonpalok Homestay
21 Hotel Yangzom
22 Lempia Ude Homestay
23 Lungta Homes
24 Yogstel Backpackers Hostel

EATING
see 2 Chindits Cafe
25 Marquee Restobar
26 Taste of Tawang
27 Ziro Degrees

SHOPPING
see 5 Traditional Mix & Match

INFORMATION
28 PAP Checkpoint Bhalukpong

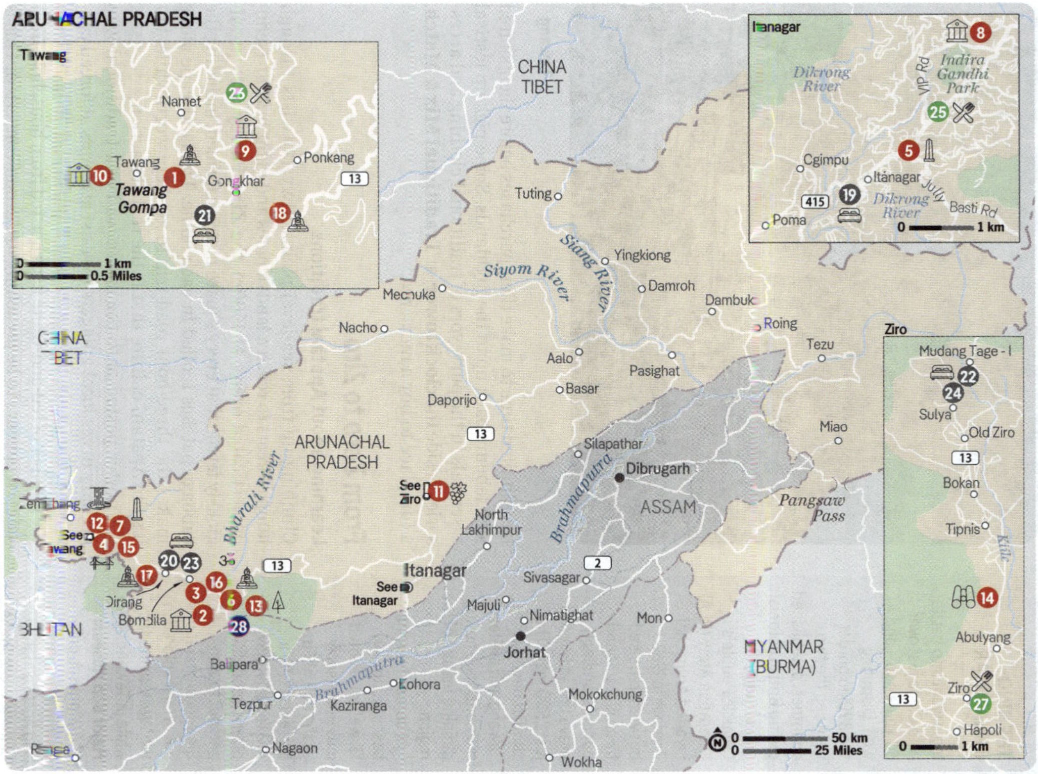

THE SINO-INDIAN WAR

India went into battle with China just over 60 years ago - and won. Disputing the 890km border between the two countries, established during British colonial rule of India, the Chinese People's Liberation Army (PLA) invaded Arunachal Pradesh in 1962 but were repulsed by an ill-equipped but outstandingly brave Indian force of just 2500 men. The conflict began in Tawang and military memorials are now a defining feature of the region.

At some of the many bases along Hwy 13, well-presented museums (such as the **Ball of Fire Museum** *(₹70)* in the Tenga Valley) offer a geopolitical perspective on Sino-Indian relations not often explored in the Western media, while in Tawang, the **Major Bob Museum** *(₹70)* focuses on local engagement and hosts a nightly cultural programme. The bases often open their canteens to passing travellers and sell warm clothing from the mess shop.

MUBARAK_KHAN/SHUTTERSTOCK

Tawang

have limited time to make their purchases before their shared jeep labours back up to the highlands. Some pick up festival essentials in the purveyors of traditional clothing and accessories beside the **clock tower**, at **Traditional Mix & Match**, a fun place to buy a memento.

From Zero to Ziro

Learning about Apatani traditions

Climbing up from sea-level plains, Hwy 13 twists through jungle forests to reach a land of pines and giant *mithun* (semi-domesticated oxen). At 1500m, the **Ziro Valley** is so prodigiously fertile that every square metre is farmed, including the cabbage patches tended in each home. The landscape alone makes the three-hour road trip to get here worthwhile, but it's the Apatani culture that is the real attraction.

A poster pasted onto the rattan wall of a traditional Ziro granary urges local villagers to resist attempts at forced conversion. Curiously, the poster is in English and, judging from the number of red-and-white flags hoisted from household front gates, it appears to be preaching to the non-converted. This is when you'll notice the eggshells carefully lined up on sticks in the tessellated fields of rice and scattered across the bamboo groves. But then you'll see a man on a motorbike wearing a hornbill-beaked hat and sporting a bun of uncut hair in place of a helmet, or the tattooed face of an elderly woman praying in a 'church hall' *(meder nelo)* but of the Donyi-Polo animist religion, and you'll realise that you're witnessing a culture bending but not breaking in the winds of change.

The best way to engage with this culture in transition is to hire an Apatani guide, such as **Nada Nobin** *(8794949199)*, who will help you explore Ziro villages, sip organic kiwi-fruit wine at **Naara Aaba**, and walk up to sacred **Pamu Yalang** for a panorama. To go further afield, contact NGO **NgunuZiro**

(8974954810; facebook.com/NgunuZiro) for treks in the **Tale Valley** and advice on permits to hike from Aalo and Mechuka.

In the Footsteps of the Dalai Lama

Tawang monasteries

With a little town centre of shops selling Chinese teacups, pungent spiky yak hats (still worn locally), handloomed textiles and assorted woollens, the expanding town of Tawang makes for an interesting stroll. But the main reason to visit is **Tawang Gompa**: founded in 1681 and famed for its priceless library of Buddhist manuscripts, it's said to be the second-largest Buddhist monastery after Lhasa's Drepung Monastery. Home to 400 lamas, whose chanting echoes around Tawang at sunrise, the gompa carves a crescent into the hillside visible from afar. Opposite the beautifully decorated prayer hall is a **museum** *(₹20)* with skull utensils and thigh-bone instruments, where black-and-white photos show the current Dalai Lama in plain clothes visiting Dirang during his escape from Tibet.

Nearby **Urgelling Gompa** (mornings only) is famed as the birthplace of the sixth Dalai Lama. Born in 1683, and from the local Monpa tribe, he allegedly struck the ground here and an oak tree grew. The same tree (or its descendant) attracts a chorus of birds at dawn.

Other gompas and sites of interest are scattered around the Tawang Valley, but foreigners are currently only permitted to travel within a 5km radius of the town, putting destinations such as the **Bumla Pass** on the Chinese border out of bounds.

River Diversions

Tawang's Iron bridge and waterfall

Draped in prayer flags and flung across the Tawang Chu, there's a little-visited treasure of early engineering. The **Chakzam iron bridge** was built in 1420 CE by Thangtong Gayalpo, a Tibetan monk, and has withstood flood and fighting to become the cherished symbol of the two local communities that it links. It takes a moment to balance on the honeycomb of woven rattan and bamboo that rests on the bridge's suspended iron chains, but the elasticity is part of its resilience and crossing the water in measured bounces is an exhilarating experience.

While in the neighbourhood, call in at the **Nuranang Falls** *(₹40)*, just off Hwy 13 at Jang. With a 100m drop, the falls are particularly spectacular after noon and during the monsoon.

ARUNACHAL'S TRIBAL DIVERSITY

One of the pleasures of travelling in the wooded hills of Arunachal Pradesh is the opportunity to meet members of various tribal groups – some 26 in all, and including the Adi (Abor), Nyishi, Tagin, Galo, Apatani and Monpa people. Although modernity has brought a certain cultural homogenisation to the region, villages still retain many distinctive tribal traditions, and Indigenous languages are widely spoken at home.

Animist beliefs remain prevalent, formalised into Donyi-Polo (sun and moon worship) in the 1970s in response to the rapid adoption of Christianity – now the state's most prevalent religion. It is not uncommon, though, to see a Christian star next to the Donyi-Polo flag (red sun on a white background) or a string of Buddhist prayer flags adorning a rural Hindu shrine.

EATING IN ARUNACHAL PRADESH: SOCIAL HUBS

Marquee Restobar: (Itanagar) In busy Ganga Market this wood-decked venue serving international food is a popular local hang-out. *11.30am-3.30am* ₹₹

Chindits Cafe: (Tenga Valley) This small mess canteen attracts Tawang travellers and offers South Indian food at the military base opposite the Ball of Fire Museum. *10am-7pm* ₹₹

Taste of Tawang: (Tawang) On the main road, this friendly Tibetan restaurant is a hub of local chat and a good place to meet the Monpa people. *11am-9pm* ₹₹

Ziro Degrees: (Ziro Valley) Reflecting Ziro's reputation as the rock capital of the Northeast, this rock-playing 1st-floor restaurant and bar is one of Ziro's favourite meeting spots. *noon-10.30pm* ₹₹

DRIVING TOUR

A Trip to the Roof of the World

Tawang, high up in the Himalayan foothills, is about as near as you can get to the neighbours without falling over the border. With Bhutan on one side and China on another, the strategic nature of this spectacular steep-sided valley is obvious, and military bases and museums form a fascinating part of the approach route. Although Tawang has several attractions, the two-day road trip to get there is a major part of the experience.

1 Sessa Valley

Beginning your trip at the **PAP checkpoint** in Bhalukpong, you'll quickly sense that you are passing into border territory, not just geopolitically but geographically too. Enjoy the transition from dense jungle to terraced farming as you climb to reach Hwy 13 on the Trans Arunachal Hwy.

The Drive: Skirt Pakke Tiger Reserve and climb instantly from the plains to the slopes of the Sessa Valley, rising in a tumble of bamboo, palms and banana plants, laced with bromeliads and orchids.

2 Tenga Valley

Travelling northwest along Hwy 13, pause at aesthetically perfect **Dul Dul Tharpa Ling Gompa**, gracing a bend in the river, and visit nearby **Sri Nag Temple**, built to appease the mate of an adder killed during road construction. Continue to the **Ball of Fire Museum** (p546) and have tea in **Chindits Cafe** (p547) in the first of many military bases.

The Drive: On reaching Hwy 13, follows the Tenga River and you'll notice a subtle change in

RAHUL D'SILVA/SHUTTERSTOCK

Dirang

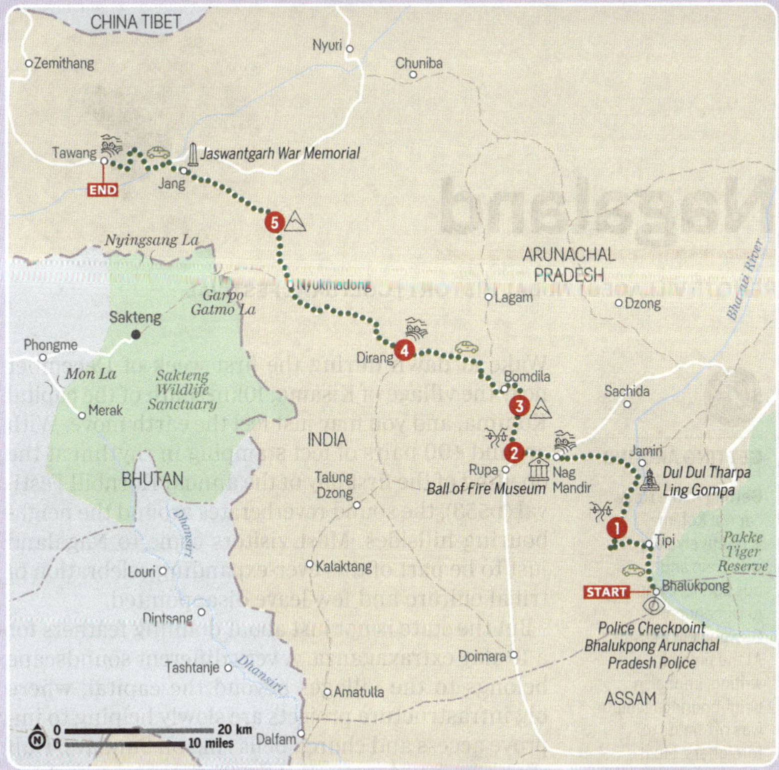

woodland as tropical hardwoods are replaced by more temperate species.

3 Bomdila Pass

At a sudden breach in the mountain ridge, Bomdila Pass gives an expansive view of the snow capped mountains of the Eastern Himalaya. Stalls selling bamboo shoots, kiwi fruit and warm clothing mark the spot.

The Drive: Bypass the town of Bomdila (a possible overnight stop), cross the pass and descend into Dirang via the fortified old town of Dirang Dzong with its many traditional houses.

4 Dirang

Famous for neatly cultivated fields, kiwi-fruit gardens and hot springs, picturesque Dirang makes a good place to overnight. Allow time to walk over the town's suspension bridge and visit Dirang's fine **Buddhist monastery**.

The Drive: From Dirang the drive takes a dramatic turn as it zigzags up a dozen hairpin bends to reach the famous Sela Pass.

5 Sela Pass

At 4170m, Sela Pass is breathtakingly high and affords spectacular views of pine-clad mountains. Just beyond Sela Pass, take a leg stretch (move slowly to avoid altitude sickness) around Sela Lake before the final descent into Tawang Valley. Stop at **Jaswantgarh War Memorial** en route to understand the courage of Indian soldiers repelling the Chinese army in the 1962 conflict.

The Drive: The route towards Tawang is either via Sela Pass or a shortcut through Sela Tunnel. Roads here are maintained by Border Roads Organisation (BRO), whose iterations about road safety make an entertaining read ('Check your nerves on my curves') but make little difference to local driving habits.

Nagaland

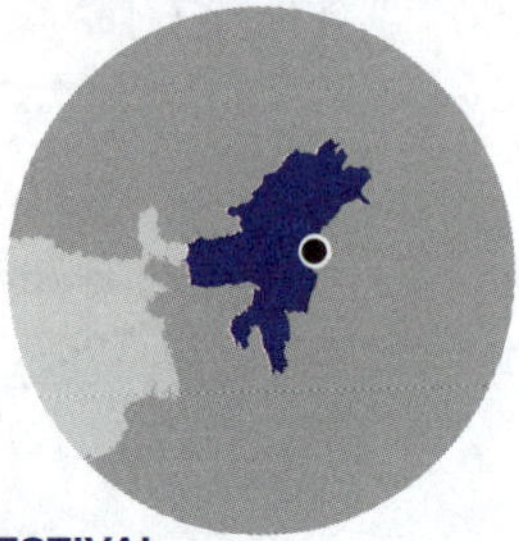

REMOTE VILLAGES | TRIBAL HISTORY | CULTURAL FESTIVAL

GETTING AROUND

Getting to the Naga capital Kohima is relatively easy with train and bus connections to Dimapur and Guwahati in Assam. At the time of writing, Imphal in neighbouring Manipur was off-limits to foreigners. Most roads beyond Kohima are in a poor state of repair, with annual landslides hampering the effort to build new roads. Allow extra time for travelling to further flung villages here – the 300km journey from Kohima to Mon Village, for example, currently takes at least nine hours. Hiring a taxi or a car with a driver is the best way to make efficient use of time.

Wake at dawn during the first week of December near the village of Kisama, 10km south of the capital Kohima, and you may just feel the earth move. With around 400 pairs of feet stamping in rhythm at the opening of the first day of the annual Hornbill Festival (p553), the sound reverberates around the neighbouring hillsides. Most visitors come to Nagaland just to be part of this ever-expanding celebration of tribal culture and few leave disappointed.

But the state is not just about donning feathers for a 10-day extravaganza. A very different soundscape belongs to the villages beyond the capital, where big infrastructure projects are slowly helping to improve access and church bells ring on Sundays. Half the state remains covered in pristine forest, making it an ecological hotspot of the Northeast, and visiting remote villages and hiking in the steeply wooded hills could keep the adventurous traveller occupied for days.

Put to Rest

Paying respects at Kohima's War Cemetery

No-one has played a game of tennis here for a very long time but there's something touching about seeing the white lines of the court still in place. They once graced the lawns of the British Deputy Commissioner's bungalow on the terraced hillside overlooking the modern town of **Kohima**; few could have predicted that on 4 April 1944 they would frame one of the bloodiest battles of WWII.

Today, the lawns crown the **Kohima War Cemetery**, honouring the 1400 British, Indian and Allied soldiers killed in and around Kohima in the resistance against the Japanese invasion of India. Also honoured are the 917 Hindu and Sikh soldiers who were cremated rather than buried.

To learn how the Allied victory here represented a turning point in the campaign to resist Japanese advances, visit the **WWII Museum** *(entry/mobile camera ₹10/50)* in the Naga

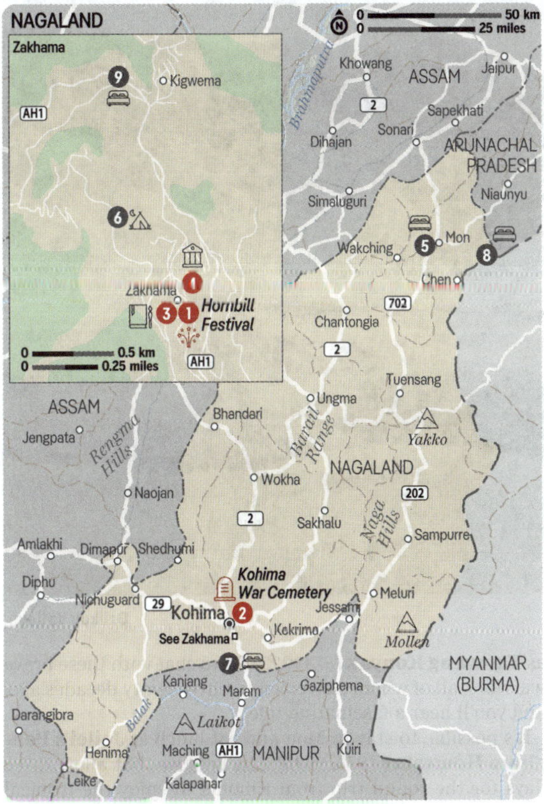

HIGHLIGHTS
1 Hornbill Festival
2 Kohima War Cemetery

SIGHTS
3 Naga Heritage Village
4 WWII Museum

SLEEPING
5 Aihan Homestay
6 Camp Dzukou Trails
7 Dzükou Valley Guesthouse
8 Jellei's Punghom Home Stay
9 Seasons Homestay

Heritage Village (p554). This excellent museum tells a compelling story through the testimony of local witnesses, and captures the period with displays of military uniforms and equipment.

Breakfast in Myanmar

Visiting a Konyak village near Mon

The king and queen of the remote village of Longwa, 40km and around two hours from Mon, have the distinction of sleeping in India and eating their meals in their open range kitchen in Myanmar. If you make it this far into the wooded hinterland of Nagaland, chances are you'll meet them. Their headman's home, with its trophies and spears, literally straddles the border, and it's possible to cross the invisible line at will.

But visitors tend to come to **Mon** less for the architectural curiosity of a cross-border palace and more for the opportunity of meeting the Konyak elders, many of whom are former headhunters. Identified by the tattoos applied to their faces and chests, and adorned with various ornaments representing their past lives in combat, they now make a living from their looks by charging for photographs. Engage a local guide such

TOP TIP

When a market vendor offers a wriggly pupa to try, it's hard to welcome the experience. The people of Nagaland, however, are ahead of the curve in eating more sustainably produced forms of protein so treat the crickets, snails and silkworms as an opportunity to expand your palette, if you're not a connoisseur of alternative foods already.

A BETTER LIFE

Wangnao Wangchung
Grandfather and former headhunter, Longwa Village

I was only 25 years old when they made me a headhunter. There was a dispute over land and we were selected to protect our village and the forest we relied upon, and to revenge those we had lost. The tattoos hurt but we wore them with pride. It was only later we realised it was better to share love and peace. We began hunting wild pig instead. Now I see visitors paying respects in our village and I'm glad but I also have regrets. Life was hard and we did what we did without much choice. Young people now have education and opportunities so be happy, be free and stay blessed...and come back with our photos!

PAPU RAJOWAR/SHUTTERSTOCK

Dzükou Valley

as **Yaowang Konyak** *(8732092289)* to chat with these brave warriors, all of whom converted to Christianity decades ago, and you'll hear a fascinating tale.

It's possible to stay in Mon and eat lunch at **Jeilei's Ponghum Homestay** *(8732093138)* in Longwa, but allow three days for the round trip from Kihoma to enjoy the tropical vistas, bursts of Mexican sunflowers and roadside markets selling pineapples.

Making the Most of the Monsoon

Hiking the Dzükou Valley

It's unremittingly steep, but the hike up to **Dzükou Valley** *(₹200, payable at Dzükou Valley Guesthouse)* rewards with the unusual spectacle of grasslands of miniature bamboo crowning the tropical cloud forest. Beautiful in spring when rhododendrons bloom, it's full of birdsong in summer, and in winter wild cherries add a splash of colour to the woodland. If approached from **Viswema**, the first 8km is covered by jeep, leaving a one-hour climb to the rim of the 'hidden valley'. It's possible to stay at the basic guesthouse and descend to **Zakhama** the next day. Local **Wild Hill Adventure** *(wildhilladventure.com)* offers all-inclusive packages from around ₹6000.

ANITA IN TRAVEL/SHUTTERSTOCK

Nagaland dance troupe, Kohima

TOP EXPERIENCE

Hornbill Festival

Once a year, members of each of the 16 officially recognised tribes of Nagaland send a dance troupe to the capital Kohima for the annual Hornbill Festival. What began as a small cultural celebration has since developed into a major spectacle of traditional clothing and dance attracting thousands of visitors. It makes an exciting focus of a trip to the Seven Sister States.

DON'T MISS

- The lineup of participants before the opening ceremony
- First-night concert
- Eating Indigenous foods
- Shopping for handicrafts (and particularly blankets) on-site

Opening Ceremony

Whatever anyone tells you about the first day, don't miss it! Yes, it probably won't start on time; yes, there will be lots of slightly tedious formal speeches by visiting dignitaries; and yes, the individual tribes perform again on day two with similar pageantry. But it's only on day one that you get to feel the nervous tension of the massed troupes of 400 dancers, each in their feathered and blanketed finery, as they chant and stamp outside, burning off energy as they welcome visitors

PRACTICALITIES

● hornbillfestival.com ● 1-10 Dec at the Naga Heritage Village in Kisama ● ₹150 per day (possible extra per concert)

and prepare to file into the stadium. Being part of the show is an honour that passes to a different clan of each tribe every year, so the opening is a big day for the participants, young and old alike.

Kisama Heritage Village

While the focus of the festival is on the presentations that take place in the stadium on each of the 10 days of the event, part of the fun for the visitor is bumping into the performers around the **Naga Heritage Village**. Each tribe has its own traditional *morung* (young people's dormitory) – magnificent constructions of bamboo, rattan walls and thatched roofs – in this showcase village, and during the festival participants retire here between performances. Sipping rice beer, taking selfies with the dance troupes (usually at their request) and haggling over tribal handicrafts are the highlights of the whole event.

Trying Something Crispy

The cultural programmes and concerts run all day and into the night too, but there's no need to leave the grounds for refreshments. A whole assortment of interesting Indigenous food is cooked up in each of the *morungs,* and pop-up restaurants offer menus of breathtaking variety (dried squirrel, pork innards, grasshoppers, spiders, palm civet and porcupine). More familiar staples are available in the on-site cafes.

Taking Time Out

However mesmerising the dazzle of colour and hypnotic the sound, the festivities become hard to absorb after day two. It's time to take a break and return to real life. Visiting a local village helps give context to the Hornbill's cultural expression while showcasing modern life in its tribal incarnation.

The beautiful Angami village of **Khonoma**, 20km from Kohima, makes for an enjoyable half-day excursion, particularly in the winter when the wild cherry trees are in full bloom and the cascade of terraced fields are bronzed post-harvest. Angami residents act as village guides *(₹150)* and will show visitors the village's three forts, traditional *morungs* (no longer used as dormitories but still functioning as meeting places), *mithun* skulls, and gardens of mustard, peas, beans and cabbage slotted around the village.

For a trip just down the hill from the festival site, call in at **Kikywema** *(₹140)*. The village was requisitioned by the Japanese in WWII and General Sato was headquartered here. Villagers acting as guides will show you his earthquake-proof house, take you past chopped wood piles ready for winter, show you the many uses of bamboo, and steer you into a *morung* cafe for a sumac tea.

KEEPING FAITH WITH THE ANCESTORS

Zayie Sodz, Angami tribe member and Hornbill Festival participant. *Instagram: zayie sodzii-O*

We're proud to be representing our tribe at this festival as it's our chance to showcase our culture to the world, to revive old traditions and translate them into something of meaning for the new generation. Many things of value are being lost through modern life, including our languages. This is our chance to celebrate the connection with our rural roots. Come and visit our villages and we'll make you feel at home!

TOP TIPS

- Book accommodation in and around Kohima at least six months ahead during all 10 days of the Hornbill Festival.
- The stadium is open-air and gets very cold at night – buy a tribal blanket from the craft centre within the grounds.

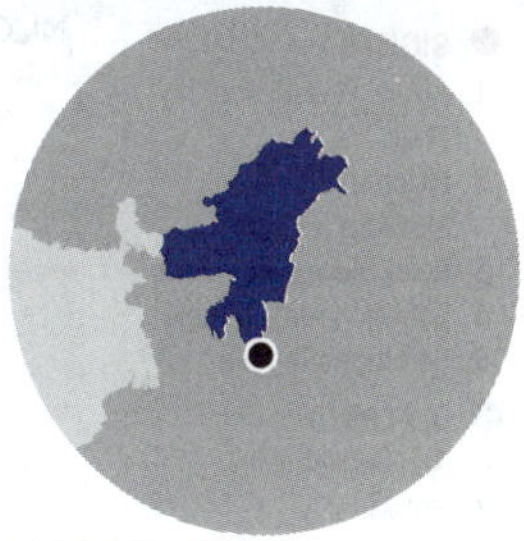

Mizoram

WOODED RIDGES | INTRIGUING CAPITAL | CHRISTIAN IDENTITY

Just when you think you have the Seven Sister States weighed off, you cross the border into Mizoram and realise that yet again this is a state that couldn't be mistaken for anywhere else. Mizoram's most defining feature is the long, steep ridges of hills that run roughly north–south across the state, and they make for a beautiful landscape of temperate wooded valleys and clouded uplands. Renowned throughout the Northeastern States for the cleanliness of its towns, Mizoram is largely litter-free. It is also notable for the absence of 'honking' (beeping of car horns), which locals attribute to the concept of 'being considerate of others', as informed, they avow, by strongly held Christian beliefs.

There's less in the way of identified sights in this seldom-visited and scarcely populated corner of the Northeast, but therein lies part of its attraction: a visit here is as authentic a travel experience as it gets.

GETTING AROUND

Driving from neighbouring Tripura to Mizoram is a lesson in topography as the hills start to rise in a slow long ripple across the state, each ridge higher than the last. As if cresting a wave, roads twist up to each hilltop only to slide back down into a sea of tropical forest on the other side. Inevitably, then, it takes hours to get anywhere.

Aizawl (p556)

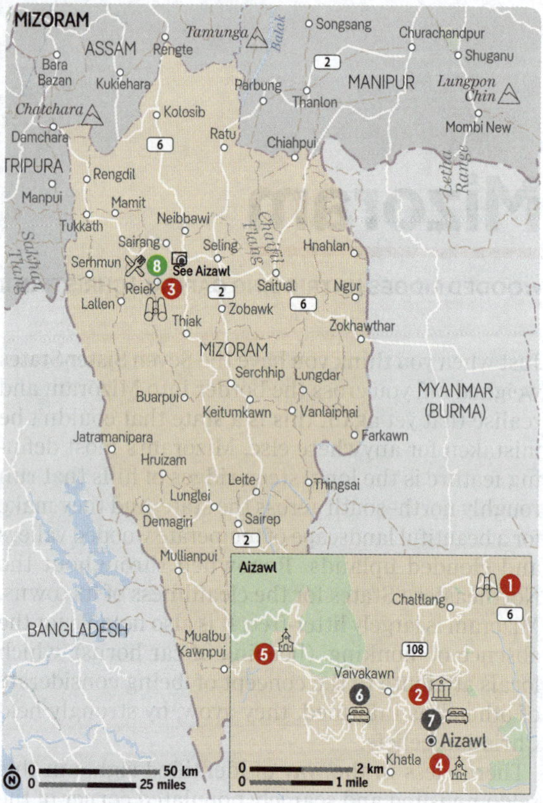

- **SIGHTS**
  1 Aizawl Peak Resort Sky Walk
  2 Mizoram State Museum
  3 Reiek Viewpoint
  4 Salvation Army Temple
  5 Solomon's Temple
- **SLEEPING**
  6 Annexe Homestay
  7 Hotel Floria
- **EATING**
  8 Greenhills Restaurant

City on Stilts

Mizoram's capital Aizawl

Asked why most of Mizoram's villages and indeed the capital **Aizawl** are flung across the hard-to-access hilltops, locals will tell you it's because they are highlanders at heart and can't bear to be bereft of the sunshine by being buried at the bottom of the valley. Unwilling to compromise on this point, the various tribal communities have had to come up with ingenious ways of balancing on a knife edge – most noticeably through the use of wooden stilts, largely replaced these days by reinforced concrete piles. A bungalow from the front is invariably, therefore, a skyscraper at the back. View Aizawl from afar (a magnificent sight at dusk when the painted facades appear to melt into the hillside) and it looks like a fondant icing that has been poured from above.

Various churches vie for being the cherry on top, a prominent contender being the **Salvation Army Temple** on Zodin Sq. The enormous **Solomon's Temple**, on the city outskirts, is another, with space for a 2000-strong congregation.

TOP TIPS

Don't rush the capital. Aizawl is an exciting labyrinth of stairways and twisting roads, churches of every denomination and lanes of woollen-wear shops. It's a particular delight at Christmas when the lights are so numerous they might just be spotted from the moon and the Salvation Army plays carols as people shop for the festivities.

While in town, pay a visit to the **State Museum** *(₹50; Tue-Fri)*. With some interesting Mizo cultural displays and photographs, it shows the development from, as one local guide put it, 'headhunter to the Hallelujah Chorus', and credited in no small part to Welsh missionaries. You may want to avoid the basement of stuffed animals that appears to belong to the former era.

Walking on Air

A skywalk at Aizawl Peak Resort

Following the regional fashion for skywalks – a concept borrowed from China – the new **Aizawl Peak Resort platform** offers quite a challenge to visitors. Dangled over a cliff, many metres above the valley floor, it takes nerve to walk out in socks across the transparent glass floor, particularly when your guide (a licensed paraglider) leads the way by clinging gingerly to the edge and sticking to the metal grid lines. If you can bear to let go, the view across the city and out to the wooded ridges beyond is spectacular. You can recover afterwards over lunch in the on-site restaurant.

Hiking up to the Sunset

Ridge-top Reiek

There are several rewarding overnight excursions into the Mizo countryside from Aizawl, including **Hmuifang**, 52km south of the capital, and the **Blue Mountain** – at 2157m it's Mizoram's highest peak. The easiest trip, though, is the 25km drive to the pretty village of **Reiek**, where you can enjoy a typical Mizo lunch of organic vegetables and boiled pork at **Greenhills Restaurant** before hiking up to the **viewpoint** to catch the sunset. Taxis hang around the government guesthouse at the bottom of the hike if you want a shortcut to the base of the peak. From there it's just a 20-minute hike up through magnificent grasslands to the edge of the escarpment and one of the most expansive views in all the Seven Sister States.

Evergreen Tours & Travels *(8069247161)* can organise camping trips to all three destinations if you're short of time or weary of cramped public transport.

BEST NORTHEAST ADVENTURES

Assam: Hike in tiger territory in Nameri National Park (p540), bump along multiple mini rapids in Manas National Park (p540) or hire a bike from birdwatching guide Jyoti Narayan Sarma *(9435657282)*.

Arunachal Pradesh: Go mountain biking, rock climbing and river island camping in Mechuka with Adventure@Mechuka *(nthadventure.com)* or go rafting with Galaxy Travel & Adventure *(WhatsApp 6009718246)*.

Nagaland: Hike up to a hidden landscape on the Dzükou Valley trek (p552).

Mizoram: Jump off a cliff near Aizawl with professional paragliding pilot Ruatsanga RS *(WhatsApp 9856883556; rs_skyhawk)*

Tripura: Extend a visit to Unakoti (p559) by trekking the well-marked 4km woodland track from the neighbouring Eco Park.

Meghalaya: Swing across the Dympep Valley on two 120m-long ziplines or go bungee jumping with Pioneer Adventure *(pioneeradventuretour.com)*.

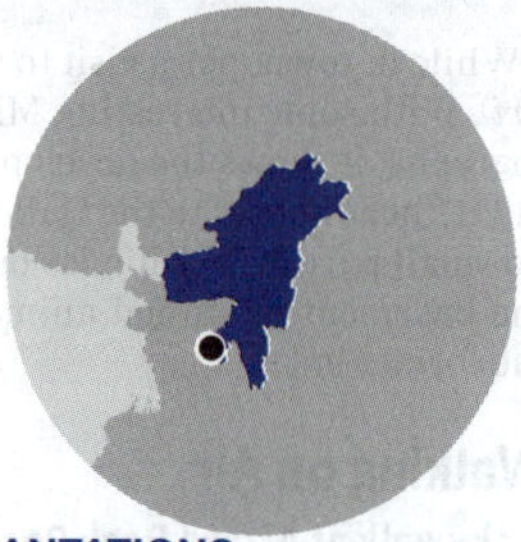

Tripura

TRIBAL DIVERSITY | HINDU HERITAGE | RUBBER PLANTATIONS

Each morning just after dawn an aged elder emerges from the forest above the monuments of Unakoti and takes a crumpled plastic bottle from his basket. Unseen and unsung, he tips some of the water onto a stone lingam and brushes away yesterday's offerings of frangipani flowers, rubbing the stone clean. Ritual complete, he takes a puff from his long-handled pipe and shuffles back through the leaf mould into the jungle, disappearing as completely as the spectacled leaf monkeys in the canopy above him.

The connection with both spirit world and nature in the largely Hindu state of Tripura is almost tangible in the hilly patchwork of paddy and rubber plantations dotted with small shrines. By contrast, modern Agartala leans towards the plains. Home to a diverse cross-section of the state's 19 tribes, joined recently by an influx of Bangladeshis whose country borders Tripura on three sides, Agartala is an intriguing city worthy of a day or two's visit.

GETTING AROUND

Almost an enclave on the eastern fringe of Bangladesh, Tripura is easier to reach from Dhaka than the capitals of the neighbouring states of India. As such, this may be the one capital best reached by internal flight from Guwahati – a 23-hour bus journey away or 17 hours by train. Buses and shared taxis from Agartala reach the main points of interest around Tripura, but reckon on a two-day epic to reach Aizawl across the border in Mizoram. As with the other Northeastern States, hiring a car and driver is easily the best way of combining rural destinations in a limited timeframe.

TOP TIPS

Visit Agartala's Ujjayanta Palace late in the afternoon when the dramatic lighting contributes to its stately grandeur.

Fit for a King

A visit to regal Ujjayanta Palace

Ujjayanta Palace is a grand mixture of classical and Mughal styles, built in 1901 by a British architect for Maharaja Radha Kishore, whose successors ruled here until Tripura's accession to the Indian union after Independence. Prefaced by two prominent Hindu temples, **Sri Laxminarayan Mandir** and colourful **Jagannath Mandir**, it is flanked by two lakes and makes a pleasant place to while away a morning. Within the palace is the extensive **Tripura State Tribal Museum** *(₹500)* with relics from the Maharaja's time, and galleries showcasing Tripura's 19 tribes. Look for the summary of the creation of Bangladesh. The 10 million Bengali refugees that fled here contribute to the cosmopolitan nature of the city today.

Temples & Tanks Tour

Rural excursion to Neermahal from Agartala

On a day trip to **Neermahal Palace** *(₹30, small boat round trip ₹400, ₹50 each on faster big boat)* in Melaghar, near the

HIGHLIGHTS

1 Ujjayanta Palace
2 Unakoti

SIGHTS

3 Jagannath Mandir
4 Neermahal
5 Sri Laxminarayan Mandir
6 Tripura State Tribal Museum
7 Tripura Sundari Mandir

SLEEPING

8 Cozy Nook
9 Ginger

border with Bangladesh, you'll pass through a landscape of terraced fields, wrapped round small hills of rubber trees. It makes for a picturesque landscape – if an unlikely setting for a floating palace. Built in 1930 in a combination of Hindu and Islamic styles, and graciously reflected in the **Rudra Sagar Lake**, single-storey Neermahal stretches across an island and can only be reached by boat. The palace is now empty but it's easy to imagine it once brimming with royal festivities.

Walking among Gods

The bas reliefs of Unakoti

In the middle of a wooded ravine, around a four-hour drive from Agartala, a rock face looms out of the jungle. It takes a while to see the bas reliefs inscribed across the surface, but then your eye settles on a beatific face, the 10m-tall visage of Shiva. The archaeological site of **Unakoti** *(free)* should be ranked a world wonder, but chances are you'll have it to yourself. Almost vertical staircases lead to the cliff top offering a vantage point across the site and down past three Ganesh figures, carved into the waterfall. Follow paths into a forest and stay until noon to catch the sun trickling down the rock face, settling on a headdress here and a Nandi bull there.

TRIPURA'S FESTIVALS

With a rich culture of tribal diversity, Tripura celebrates many different festivals throughout the year. One such festival, the **Kali Puja**, takes place in October or early November at the 16th-century **Tripura Sundari Mandir**. At this time pilgrims flock to this russet-coloured temple in Udaipur to bathe in the temple tank – to the chagrin, one expects, of the resident fish.

At Unakoti, according to Hindu mythology, Lord Shiva stayed for a night en route to Kashi. When his 9,999,999 followers failed to recommence their journey before sunrise, he turned them to stone. The **Ashokastami Festival** takes place here in March or April in a combination of tribal custom and Hindu worship of the rock-cut gods and goddesses.

Meghalaya

ESCARPMENT LANDSCAPE | ROOT BRIDGES | MARKETS

GETTING AROUND

Meghalaya is one state in the Northeast where the roads by and large are good and the journey up from the plains of Assam is facilitated by a major highway. There are also flights connecting Shillong with Kolkata. Getting to other major cities in the region is relatively easy on private buses (bookable from the Police Bazar), while shared taxis are the most common way of reaching sights of interest in Meghalaya. For main tourist destination Cheerapunjee, the **Khasi Hills Tourist Taxi Association** *(WhatsApp 9863023694)* or **Meghalaya Tourism** *(meghalayatourism.in)* offer reliable, if more costly, services from Shillong.

If grandmother is sitting at the head of the table in your homestay at dinner time, it may not be just coincidence. The Khasis of Meghalaya are fond of telling visitors that theirs is a predominantly Christian, matrilineal state – a factor reflected in the opportunities for women in state governance and the fact that 44% of women here are in formal employment. The matrilineal system is one among many cultural details expounded upon in the renowned Don Bosco museum in Shillong.

Known today as the Scotland of the East, on account of the pine-clad hills and copious rains, easygoing Meghalaya has many other attractions beyond the capital, from quiet boating on upland lakes to exploring caves abounding in fossils. Not to be missed is the dramatic escarpment at Cherrapunjee (Sohra), where India falls off the cliff to the vast plains of Bangladesh below. Chances are you'll wish you'd allowed more time for a visit.

Shopping in Shillong

Two of the capital's busiest bazaars

The state capital of Meghalaya since the creation of the Seven Sister States in 1972, **Shillong** is a regional entrepôt with shopping part of the capital experience. Begin a visit at busy **Iew Duh** *(Bara Bazar; dawn-dusk Mon-Sat)*. Dodge potato porters carrying impossible loads, step over bamboo cages of live roosters, duck down alleyways of fish traps and edible frogs, and you'll come to a corner where ironmongers sell arrows – used in the state obsession with archery.

Pause for lunch at **City Hut Dhaba**, where smoked ham and potatoes is a local treat, and then at dusk head to **Police Bazar** (PB) where, at the junction with seven busy roads, shops sell basketry, meticulously made and sold at bargain prices. Escape the crowds for a walk around **Ward's Lake** *(₹25)*, or crank up the evening at **Cloud 9**, where a DJ makes for a fun Friday.

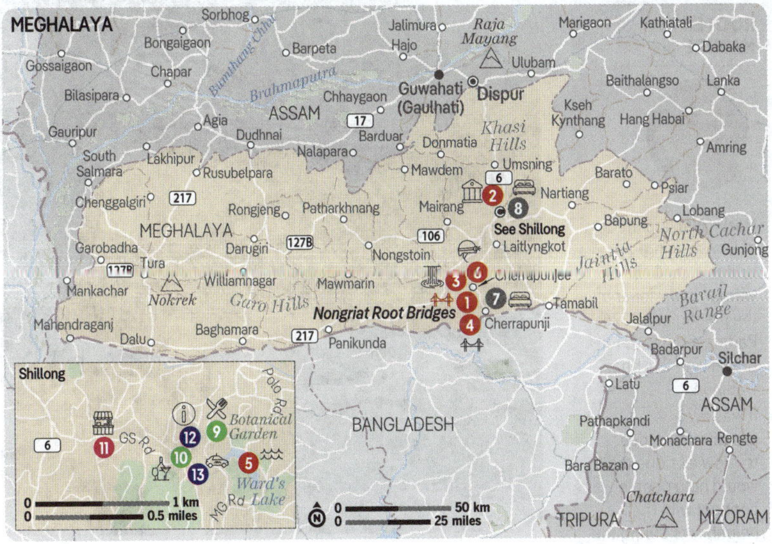

HIGHLIGHTS
1 Nongriat Root Bridges

SIGHTS
2 Don Bosco Museum of Indigenous Cultures
3 Nohkalikai Falls
4 Umkar Root Bridge
5 Ward's Lake

ACTIVITIES
6 Arwah Cave

SLEEPING
7 Polo Orchid
8 Risa Pines Homestay

EATING
9 City Hut Dhaba

DRINKING & NIGHTLIFE
10 Cloud 9

SHOPPING
11 Iew Duh

INFORMATION
12 Meghalaya Tourism

TRANSPORT
13 Khasi Hills Tourist Taxi Association

Rockets, Religions & Indigenous Rights

Visit the Don Bosco Museum

On top of a hill in the Shillong district of Mawlai, the unique **Don Bosco Museum of Indigenous Cultures** *(dbcic.org; ₹100)* does a magnificent job of representing life in the Northeastern States by reflecting on the role of religion, science and nature in the cultural practices of the region's 250 Indigenous cultural communities.

Housed in a whimsical building with a daring skywalk strapped to the roof tiles, the five-storey museum explores India's role in the space race, covers the region's key industries and crops – including the special place of bamboo as 'nature's gift to the Northeast' – and provides a helpful summary of the region's main religions. One floor is reserved for telling the story of Don Bosco, the Christian missionary and saint from Italy whose legacy includes the largest number of technical schools in India.

TOP TIPS

If you have time to pick just one place in Meghalaya to visit, make it Cherrapunjee. Vying with a neighbouring town as wettest place on Earth, it is celebrated for its many waterfalls and is popular with local tourists in search of cooler climes during the monsoon season (May to August).

ROOTED IN NATURE

Harly War, architect of Umkar living bridge, near Seij village, and winner of the prestigious 2026 Padmashri Award for preserving this Khasi tradition.

It was my grandfather's idea to grow a bridge that would help people connect with their neighbours during the monsoon. I was just 10 or 11 years old when I started learning from him how to train the roots of the *Ficus elastica* tree to build the structure. It wasn't easy work as we had to divide our time between tending our garden terraces and livestock, but the villagers were encouraging.

I've come to love this tree and my granddaughter now continues the work. It's important to hand on the skills, to keep growing things for tomorrow. Our bridge keeps expanding, with an upper passage now in the making. Of course, we owe our success to nature – it's a partnership after all.

TALUKDAR DAVID/SHUTTERSTOCK

Living bridge, Nongriat

Bring a Brolly

Cherrapunjee – wettest place on Earth

High up on an escarpment overlooking the plains of Bangladesh and just a two-hour drive from Shillong, **Cheerapunjee** (Sohra) makes for Meghalaya's best excursion. Chief among the region's many attractions are **living bridges**, formed from the roots of wild fig trees, that keep neighbourhoods connected during torrential summer rains. The most famous root bridge is the 500 year-old double-decker at **Nongriat**, accessed via 2600 steps down and 500 steps up, cut into the almost vertical hillside. There are many others, though, including **Umkar Root Bridge** *(₹40)*, whose 'architect' lives in the forest nearby.

Other must-see sights include the **Arwah Cave** *(₹50)*, where marine fossils are scattered across subterranean walls, and 340m-**Nohkalikai** *(₹40)*, said to be the highest single-drop waterfall in India. The viewpoint here makes a fine place to watch the sunset beyond the escarpment.

While locals extol the virtues of a monsoon visit, foreign visitors may beg to differ as the area's potholed roads dissolve into mud and hiking paths crumble under the record volumes of rain (nearly 2.5m back in 1995). Engage excellent Khasi guide **Banshailang 'Babit' Lynnong** *(WhatsApp 9233211585)* to bring local insight to your visit.

Places We Love to Stay

₹ Budget ₹₹ Midrange ₹₹₹ Top End

Assam

Map p536

Prabhakar Homestay (Guwahati) ₹ Professor Sheila and her husband Mahesh enjoy hosting enquiring travellers in their lovely home and are a mine of information.

Chameli Memsaab Bungalow (Jorhat) ₹ A fine example of a planters' home surrounded by mature trees and tea gardens, this guesthouse offers a quiet stopover en route to Sivasagar.

Baruah Bhavan (Guwahati) ₹₹ A period piece of 1950s architecture, this guesthouse on MC Rd has attractive rooms and offers home-cooked meals.

Vishwaratna Hotel (Guwahati) ₹₹ Right in the heart of the city, this business hotel is a favourite for weddings and has an excellent restaurant and a bar.

Dynasty Hotel (Guwahati) ₹₹ Treat yourself to some luxury at this smart airport hotel at the end of your Northeast travels.

Infinity Resort (Kaziranga) ₹₹ Surrounded by woodland alive with birdsong, this old-style lodge is close to the central zone gate.

Dekasang Cottage (Majuli Island) ₹₹ Comprising a cluster of whimsical buildings with a tribal flourish of thatch and bamboo, this friendly guesthouse is perfect for dawn strolls along the river.

Prasanti Cottages (Nameri) ₹₹ Near the border between Arunachal and Assam, this government lodge of simple cottages boasts a pretty garden and easy access to Nameri.

Manas Jungle Retreat (Manas) ₹₹ Delicious meals are delivered to your bungalow porch here while rhinos are sometimes spotted grazing in the bush nearby.

Arunachal Pradesh

Map p545

Lempia Ude Homestay (Ziro) ₹ Nothing beats sitting around the central woodfire in the kitchen of this Apatani homestay – except perhaps having breakfast in the winter sun on the terrace.

Yogstel Backpackers Hostel (Ziro) ₹ This new hostel with dorms and a genuine travellers vibe is destined to become a backpacker favourite and has great terrace views.

Gonpalok Homestay (Dirang) ₹ The friendly host here spoils guests with local feasts served in enormous guest rooms that overlook the kiwi-fruit orchard.

Lungta Homes (Bomdila) ₹ The attentive retirees who open their home to guests here grow kiwi fruit in a beautiful garden with cloud-forest views and the best *puri* breakfasts.

Cygnet Inn Trendz (Itanagar) €€ A half-hour downhill walk from the central bazaar, this modern business hotel offers buffet meals and takeaway breakfasts for an early getaway.

Hotel Yangzom (Tawang) ₹₹ A short walk from ancient Urgelling Gompa, this well-managed woodland retreat is a tad lower (and therefore a tad warmer) than the noisy town centre.

Nagaland

Map p551

Seasons Homestay (Kohima) ₹ Forget the Hornbill Festival (within walking distance): the whole tribal experience of welcome, family customs and local foods is delivered here.

Camp Dzukou Trails (Kisama) ₹ Despite being cold in winter, this camp near the Hornbill Festival site is run by affable Mushie and offers a great way to continue the party.

Aihan Homestay (Mon Village) ₹ More guesthouse than homestay, visitors here enjoy their own suite and have access to the terrace for valley views laced with Mexican sunflowers.

Mizoram

Map p556

Annexe Homestay (Aizawl) ₹ Slightly resting on earlier laurels, the annexe still has the view even if it's lost the energy, and remains good value.

Hotel Floria (Aizawl) ₹₹ If you like being in the thick of it, this excellent, amiable hotel is as central as it gets, has superb city-wide views and takes pride in its fine restaurant.

Tripura

Map p559

Cozy Nook (Dharmanagar) ₹ Not everyone's idea of creature comforts, but this roadside hotel is clean, the food freshly prepared and the location handy for visiting Unakoti.

Ginger (Agartala) ₹₹ A contemporary city hotel with comfortable rooms, a boutique ambience and staff who care.

Meghalaya

Map p561

Risa Pines Homestay (Shillong) ₹₹ Join the family for dinner in this cosy home – one of the best homestays in the Northeast.

Polo Orchid (Near Cherra-punjee) ₹₹₹ Near the Seven Sisters Falls, this eco-chic resort with bar, pool and restaurant offers luxury and grand mountain views.

For places to stay in Odisha, see p585

TIMELESS STUDIO/SHUTTERSTOCK

Above: Rajarani Mandir (p571), Bhubaneswar; Right: Great Chariot (p582) detail, Konark Sun Temple

Researched by
Paul Stafford

Odisha

RELIGIOUS RELICS AND PROTECTED WILDLIFE

Treading the unfrequented paths of Odisha, intrepid travellers are rewarded with archaeological spectacles, story-rich culture, and wildlife-blessed forests and coastlines.

Within India, Odisha is celebrated for its delicate cuisine, natural spaces, creative storytelling through dance and art, and historically significant spiritual places. You'll find Jagannath, the third of the *char dham* – India's four holiest pilgrimage temples – in the state, along with Konark's UNESCO-listed Sun Temple, built in the shape of a mighty chariot pulled by stone horses. Despite Odisha's proximity to Kolkata, few international visitors venture south. Thus, a couple of the holiest temples are off-limits to non-Hindus but, given that state capital Bhubaneswar's nickname is the 'Temple City', you'll never be short of attractions.

PAUL STAFFORD

Historically, the region named Kalinga spawned a capable seafaring empire until its ruling dynasty was felled by King Ashoka in 260 BCE. The new emperor famously adopted Buddhism following the war to atone for the bloodshed he caused. The state's primary Buddhist sites are joined by important Jain temples, which thrived together before Hinduism supplanted both religions from around the 7th century CE.

While quality of life in the cities is undoubtedly improving, Odisha remains one of India's poorest and least urbanised states. One of India's largest regions of Adivasi tribal-group territory is tucked into the state's remote southwest. The beautiful, handcrafted Adivasi art, jewellery and clothing make for wonderful souvenirs. But Odisha is also changing rapidly: in 2024, Chief Minister Naveen Patnaik and his Biju Janata Dal party lost their quarter-century political monopoly to Mohan Charan Majhi of the Bharatiya Janata Party (BJP).

THE MAIN AREAS

BHUBANESWAR
Hand-carved temples and Odishan culture.
p568

PURI & KONARK
Hindu pilgrimage sites and lake excursions.
p578

Find Your Way

Odisha cuts a vast wedge immediately south of West Bengal and Jharkhand. Most major sights are near its 450km Bay of Bengal coastline. Inland, the forests and Eastern Ghats are rarely visited.

Bhubaneswar, p568

The Temple City offers the perfect introduction to the region through engaging museums, local-crafts galleries and dozens of historic temples.

Puri & Konark, p578

Odisha's spiritual hub sees visitors descend on its mighty temples in droves, before decamping to the beaches.

TRAIN

The East Coast Railway, shadowed by highway NH16, is the region's key artery. It passes through Bhubaneswar and branches off to meet Puri. Regular express trains run from both cities to Kolkata, Chennai and Delhi.

BUS & CAR

Buses ply similar routes to the trains, while also connecting smaller towns like Konark. Fares are low, although schedules can be haphazard. The efficient alternative is hiring a car and driver, starting at ₹4000 per day.

Drying saris, Puri (p578)

Plan Your Time

Odisha's top sights converge on a relatively compact region of Odisha around Bhubaneswar and Puri. Venture further afield to discover rare species clinging to remote pockets of wilderness.

Time Poor, Relic Rich

- Visit scores of historic temples in **Bhubaneswar** (p568). Starting with **Rajarani** (p571), take a **self-guided heritage walk** (p570) towards holy **Lingaraj** (p570). Head to **Udayagiri and Khandagiri Caves** (p571) to discover the city's Jain heritage. Stop by **Konark Sun Temple** (p581) and **Archaeological Museum** (p581), then grab a bus to **Puri** (p578) and **Niladri Beach** (p580).

A Week or More

- Investigate Odisha's remote wildlife refuges, such as **Chilika Lake** (p583), where you can seek Irrawaddy dolphins at Satapada, paddle the marshes at Mangalajodi, and marvel at olive ridley marine turtles near Rambha. Head north to croc-infested **Bhitarkanika National Park** (p575). Stop by ancient Buddhist ruins at **Ratnagiri, Udayagiri and Lalitgiri** (p576) along the way.

SEASONAL HIGHLIGHTS

SPRING

The summer heat begins early, starting to rise in March and becoming uncomfortably hot in late April and May.

SUMMER

The monsoon holds the state in its sweaty grip. But this doesn't disrupt the huge **Rath Yatra festival** (p580) in June or July.

AUTUMN

By October, the monsoon rains ebb and the heat subsides, but it doesn't become comfortable until November.

WINTER

November to February are peak visiting months, with pleasant weather. **Konark Dance Festival** takes place in December.

Bhubaneswar

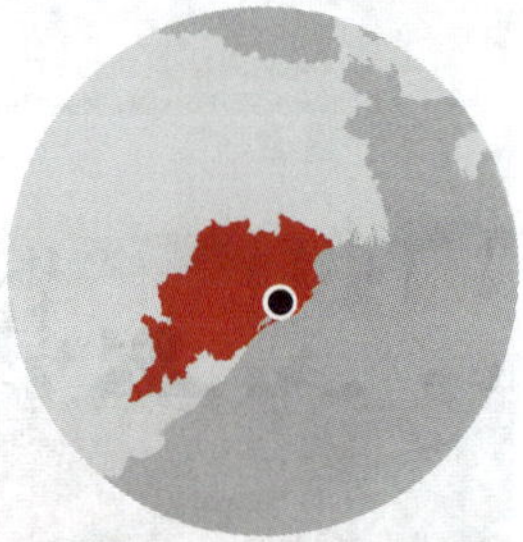

TEMPLE ARCHITECTURE | ODISHAN CULTURE | HISTORIC ARTEFACTS

TOP TIP
The **Odisha Tourism Development Corporation** *(OTDC; bookodisha.com)* runs excellent-value daylong coach tours of Bhubaneswar and the surrounding area. Additional group tours to Konark and Puri, or to Chilika Lake, are also available. The OTDC has offices and good-value hotels at major tourist towns. Also useful is *odishatourism.gov.in.*

It doesn't take long to discover why Bhubaneswar is dubbed the 'Temple City of India'. Among the hundreds of holy shrines, it's the few dozen medieval, sandstone Hindu temples to the south, plus the Jain caves to the west, that elevate the Odishan capital. The stone temples belong to a period of fervid construction from the 7th to 12th centuries BCE, in which several thousand shrines are said to have fanned out from Bindu Sagar tank, before a succession of Muslim invasions reduced many to rubble.

Bhubaneswar, which may first appear like a humdrum city, is Odisha's main transport hub, and the busy religious schedule brings regular bursts of festive energy to the streets. The growing raft of modern hotels (some as good as you'll find anywhere in the country), flavourful Odishan-cuisine-centric restaurants, and informative state history and culture museums make it a place well worth basing yourself for a few days.

Dead Kings & Elephant Heads

Discovering Bhubaneswar Temple City's riches

Medieval sandstone temples flanked by mango trees are dotted throughout the Old Town of Bhubaneswar, which is aptly named **Ekamra Kshetra**, or 'place of the mango trees'. Around a dozen major temples can be visited by people of all

GETTING AROUND

The area around Bindu Sagar is walkable but, as with many Indian cities, beset by hazards and poor air quality. The Ola and Uber apps work best for hiring taxis, particularly transfers to and from Biju Patnaik International Airport. For more freedom, hire a car and driver from Odisha Tourism Development Corporation (OTDC), starting at around ₹2900. For trains, advance tickets can be reserved at window 3 of the reservation office, in the building connected to Bhubaneswar Station's west entrance. Local and regional buses leave from the Master Canteen Bus Stand in front of this entrance.

★ **HIGHLIGHTS**
1 Mukteswar Mandir
2 Odisha State Tribal Museum

● **SIGHTS**
3 Bindu Sagar
4 Kala Bhoomi
5 Kedar Gouri Park
6 Lingaraj Mandir
7 Odisha State Museum
8 Rajarani Mandir
9 Sri Ram Mandir

● **ACTIVITIES**
10 Odisha Tourism Development Corporation
11 Orissa Dance Academy

● **SLEEPING**
12 Adventure Luxury Hotels
13 Cozzet Victoria
14 Crown
15 Hotel Pushpak
16 Mango Hotels
17 Pravuprasad Homestay
18 Trident

● **EATING**
19 Cafe Indistinct Chatter
20 Ekamra Vihar Street Food
see 15 Golden Bird
21 Kanika
22 Narula Sweets
23 Narula's
24 Sri Ram Mandir Tiffin Centre
25 Tangerine
see 15 Truptee

● **ENTERTAINMENT**
26 Mukteswar Dance Festival

● **SHOPPING**
27 Ekamra Haat
28 Market Building
see 28 Utkalika

● **TRANSPORT**
29 Biju Patnaik International Airport
30 Master Canteen Bus Stand

EXPLORING BHUBANESWAR'S HISTORIC CORE

Discover why Bhubaneswar is referred to as the Temple City of India on this self-guided walking tour of Ekamra Kshetra.

START	END	LENGTH
Rajarani Mandir	Ekamravana	2.5km; 3hr

Set amid pretty gardens, 1 **Rajarani Mandir** is a remarkably well-preserved temple, particularly given that it was never officially consecrated. Take some time to appreciate the delicacy of the carvings covering the building.

From here, turn west on Tankapani Rd from 250m. At Lewis Rd, cross over and head south until reaching 2 **Kedar Gouri Park**, hosting a cluster of the city's most beloved temples. The small 10th-century temple on your right is 3 **Mukteswar Mandir**. Next to Mukteswar sits the unfinished 4 **Siddheswar Mandir**, while 5 **Parsurameswar Mandir**, a Shiva temple dating back to 650 CE, lies at the western end of the park.

Continue west on Kedar Gouri La, then turn south onto Bindu Sagar Rd, passing 6 **Bindu Sagar** tank to 7 **Ananta Basudev Mandir**. Aim to arrive around midday when workers hurry back and forth with huge pots of rice and dhal to feed visitors.

South is the mighty 8 **Lingaraj Mandir**, arguably the finest temple in Bhubaneswar, but closed to non-Hindus. However, there's a free-to-access viewing platform on the temple's north side (politely decline the 'donation' scammers who have nothing to do with the site). Finally, wander through the beautifully sculpted 9 **Ekamravana**, a botanical garden that hugs the fringes of Bindu Sagar.

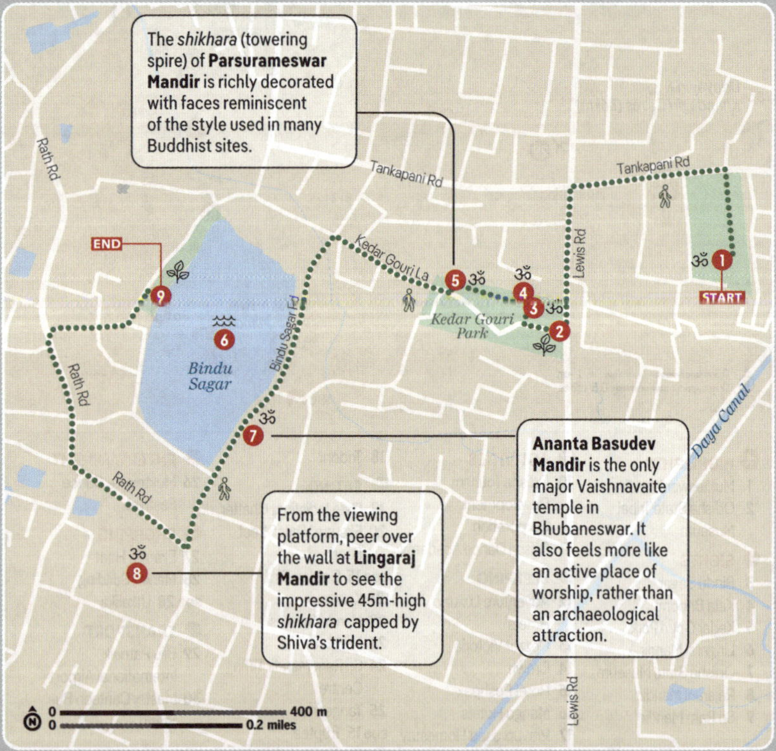

faiths in the southeast of the city. One of the best-preserved is **Rajarani Mandir** *(asi.paygov.org.in; foreigner/Indian national ₹250/20)*. The temple was never consecrated. One theory suggests the death of King Mahasivagupta V in 1110 CE, as the temple was being completed, was considered to be inauspicious. Note the *naginis* (half human, half cobra) carved into the pillars either side of the doorway.

Nearby, a cluster of three temples sits in **Kedar Gouri Park** *(free)*. The most impressive, **Mukteswar Mandir**, fronted by a delicate *torana* (archway), ornamented with elephant heads and reclining female figures. The story of the monkey and the crocodile, taken from the Sanskrit Panchatantra fables, is carved into a lintel frieze on the south side.

Dwellings Fit for Jain Ascetics

Cave life in Udayagiri and Khandagiri

The **Udayagiri and Khandagiri Caves** *(asi.payumoney.com; foreigner/Indian national ₹250/20)* are 33 Jain cave dwelling retreats. Starting in the 1st century BCE, they were excavated from natural fissures in the rock of two neighbouring hills: Udayagiri (18 caves) and Khandagiri (15 caves). Buy tickets from the booth left of the entrance gate at **Udayagiri**, which has the most intriguing caves. Udayagiri's long entrance ramp leads to **Hathi Gumpha** (Elephant Cave; Cave 14). Inside, a 117-line inscription is carved into the ceiling about King Kharavela, the Kalingan ruler under whose direction the caves were created.

To the left, cut into a large, freestanding boulder, is **Sarpa Gumpha** (Snake Cave; Cave 13). Look for the three-headed cobra above the upper chamber. Behind this, rock-cut steps lead to **Bagh Gumpha** (Tiger Cave; Cave 12), carved to look like the gaping mouth of a tiger. The steps continue up past this to the foundations of a former military outpost, offering good views of Khandagiri.

As the path leads down the other side, **Dhanaghara Gumpha** (Cave 15), with a double-pillared entrance guarded by a *dvarapala* warrior, is accessible across some rocks to the right. Note the sloping floors and rock pillow inside the chamber, to allow a relatively more comfortable sleep to the Jain ascetics who lived here.

The main path continues down to **Ganesha Gumpha** (Cave 10), where a *dvarapala* and two stout elephants carrying wreaths with their trunks stand guard. The beautiful friezes within depict the story of King Udayana and Princess Vasavadatta's romantic elopement on elephants, taken from the Sanskrit play *Svapnavasavadattam*.

Rani Gumpha (Queen's Cave; Cave 1) is a two-storey, three-wing monastery complex with the site's most delicate stonework. The upper level's arcade has exquisite relief carvings of elephants amid a celebratory procession, plus a striking battle scene. Other highlights include **Chota Hathi** (Cave 3), with its carved elephants above the door and the two-storey **Jaya Vijaya Gumpha** (Victory Cave; Cave 5), which has a carving of a bodhi tree flanked by worshippers.

DECODING ODISHA'S TEMPLE IMAGERY

Various recurring motifs make an appearance in the carved sandstone tableaux adorning temples around Odisha. One of the most ubiquitous images is of lions standing atop elephants. This is known as the *gajasimha* and represents the triumph of life's higher spiritual goals (the lion) over material earthly desires (the elephant).

The rather phallic shapes everywhere are *lingams*. A mark of Lord Shiva, they symbolise, among other things, creation and destruction. The yoni is a feminine counterpart, representing Shakti, and is often depicted as a lipped disc. A lingam resting atop a yoni, ie the lingam-yoni, represents cosmic unity. You'll see them everywhere, including the temples themselves: the towerlike *shikhara* is the lingam and the smaller, rounder *jagamohana* (assembly hall) is the *yoni*.

ODISHAN CUISINE

Sampling Odishan cuisine – subtly sharp and punchy – is a paramount joy of travelling through the region. A good place to start is with *dalma*, a vegetable dhal made with potato, plantain, pumpkin, aubergine and occasionally gourd and green papaya, in a heavily spiced oil of turmeric, cumin, ginger, asafoetida and mustard seeds. Mustard oil is commonly used, as are ghee, ginger and chilli. Three other top dishes to try are *saaga* dishes that fry leafy greens such as spinach in *pancha phutan*, a commonly used spice-and-oil mix of cumin, mustard, aniseed and fenugreek. *Machha* (fish) and *malai* (prawn) are commonly used in curry dishes. Both are ubiquitous along the coast. *Besar* indicates the main ingredient is cooked in a mustard-paste sauce.

PAUL STAFFORD

Udayagiri and Khandagiri Caves (p571)

You'll find ascetics roaming the paths of 18th-century temple-topped **Khandagiri**. Climb the steps and keep right when the path forks, climbing the steps to **Ananta Gumpha** (Eternity Cave; Cave 3). The damaged friezes, protected by a metal grille, include worshippers at a bodhi tree, elephants, birds and flowers.

Treasures of State

Encounter Odishan art and archaeology

Odisha State Museum (*odishamuseum.nic.in; adult/child ₹20/10*) showcases the rich historic vein of creativity and lore running through the region. The ground floor's three **archaeology halls** hold an impressive array of carved Buddhist, Jain, Vaishnavaite, Shaivite and Shakti (where the supreme holy power is perceived as female) deity statues created between the 3rd century BCE and late medieval period. Among the highlights is a chilling depiction, in the second hall, of Chamunda, one of the seven Brahmanical Tantric goddesses known as *saptamattrikas*, who manifest as divine mothers but also as warrior goddesses. Other highlights include Jain relics from the nearby Udayagiri and Khandagiri Caves.

Upstairs, there's a room of bronze sculptures and galleries exploring **Odishan folk arts**, including delicate *patachitra* (cloth paintings) done by the Chitrakars of Puri, who were once commissioned to paint exclusively for Jagannath Temple.

EATING IN BHUBANESWAR: BEST RESTAURANTS

Narula's: Lots of tasty North Indian dishes in this air-conditioned restaurant above a clothing store. Fantastic butter paneer masala. *8am-11pm* ₹₹

KANIKA: Authentic Odishan cuisine, such as *chingudi chhecha* with river shrimp in garlic, chilli and mustard oil. *noon-3pm & 7-11pm* ₹₹₹

Golden Bird: Hotel Pushpak restaurant (nonguests welcome) with a great *chhatu besar* (mushrooms in mustard-paste sauce). *hours vary* ₹₹₹

Tangerine: Dishes from across India and China on this restaurant's extensive menu, close to the train station. *noon-3pm & 7-11pm* ₹₹₹

You'll also discover silver filigree jewellery, carved horn work, terracotta decorations, and lacquer and cowrie shell art, plus a collection of valuable palm-leaf manuscripts.

In Step with Odisha's Beat

Take a class at Orissa Dance Academy

Odissi dance is regarded as one of the major Indian classical dance styles. This wonderfully expressive art form employs every aspect of the body, including the face, to help tell spiritual tales written by ancient poets. While it usually offers longer courses, you can arrange a private, one-on-one class at **Orissa Dance Academy** *(orissadanceacademy@gmail.com)*. Prices for a one-hour class start at ₹750 per person. If you're visiting in the middle of January, catch Bhubaneswar's **Mukteswar Dance Festival** *(odishatourism.gov.in)*.

Bhubaneswar's Unique Artisan Crafts

Encountering Adivasi creativity

The local customs, clothing and lifestyles of Particularly Vulnerable Tribal Groups (PVTGs, aka Adivasi) are examined at **Odisha State Tribal Museum** *(ostm.in; foreigner/Indian national ₹50/10)*, 5km west of Master Canteen. Highlights include the first room's Adivasi tribal jewellery, including the thick neck bands of the Bonda people, coin necklaces of the Koya, and thick waist chains of the Desia Kandha. On the south side of the airport, **Kala Bhoomi** *(odishatourism.gov.in; foreigner/Indian national ₹50/10)* broadens the creative focus to all forms of traditional artistry from Odisha, such as appliqué and silver filigree.

Check out the unusual straw pictures, known as *sikki* or golden grass. **Utkalika** *(utkalikaodisha.com)* in Bhubaneswar's **Market Building** or the stalls at **Ekamra Haat**, near **Sri Ram Mandir** are great places to pick up handmade souvenirs.

FOLK ARTS AROUND INDIA

Besides Odisha's rich folk-art scene, many of India's future artists train at the university in **Shantiniketan** (p459) in West Bengal. You can find traditional dance masks on **Majuli Island** (p542) in Assam, and fine textile art at **Kachchh** (Kutch; p655) in Gujarat.

THE HIDDEN HISTORY OF ODISSI DANCE

Odissi dance practitioner/teacher **Sayani Chakrabati** reveals how the art form came about (*orissadanceacademy@gmail.com* for dance-class bookings).

Odissi dance started with the *mahari* dance performed by *devadasis* (temple dancers). *Deva* means 'the Lord' and *dasi* means 'the servant'. We also say the 'wife of the gods', the ladies who become *maharis* when they dance for the Lord.

But how could the lady show her love? She knew that the Lord could see everything, but she also knew that she couldn't go and touch him, so it was in the form of dance and music. In the temple, dancers would enter a very small, very secluded room. The *mahari* would offer her prayers, then dance in private for the Lord.

EATING IN BHUBANESWAR: CAFES & BREAKFAST

Ekamra Vihar Street Food: The streets north of Sri Ram Mandir are packed with food trucks. Try Narula Sweets nearby for dessert. *hours vary* ₹

Sri Ram Mandir Tiffin Centre: Budget spot serving *dahi vada* for breakfast and large portions of *dalma* (dhal cooked with potato). *7am-9pm* ₹

Truptee: Breakfast *idli* or pancake-like *uttapam*, both made with fermented rice and lentil batter. The adjoining sweet shop has dessert. *7am-10pm* ₹₹

Cafe Indistinct Chatter: A name that subtly tells you to keep it down while serving decent coffee alongside waffles and cheesecake. *8.30am-10pm* ₹₹

Beyond Bhubaneswar

Discover key episodes from Indian history in the countryside beyond Bhubaneswar, from ancient edicts to national parks.

Places

GETTING AROUND

From Bhubaneswar, regular trains head to Cuttack on their way to cities such as Kolkata further north. Getting elsewhere around the state on public transport involves bus rides at unfixed times. Even visiting Dhauli, 8km south of Bhubaneswar, requires a 2km walk from the nearest bus stop. Hire a car and driver for a day or two to save time and see more. Alternatively, take a tour organised by the OTDC offices at Puri or Bhubaneswar.

The wilderness landscapes of Odisha are filled with endangered wildlife, including crocodiles and olive ridley marine turtles at Bhitarkanika National Park northeast of Bhubaneswar, and wild elephants in Chandaka-Dampara Wildlife Sanctuary. These increasingly constrained patches of protected wilderness are enveloped by the pastoral existence of one of India's least urbanised states, where over 80% of the population still lives. Occasionally, the paddy fields are broken by the ancient ruins of temples and religious universities, such as those of Ratnagiri, Udayagiri and Lalitgiri, which are spread across a swathe of farmland midway between Bhubaneswar and Bhitarkanika. Meanwhile, the historic rock edicts left by King Ashoka in Dhauli after a battle to the south of Bhubaneswar are among the country's oldest political source material.

Dhauli

TIME FROM BHUBANESWAR: **40MIN**

See Ashoka's Rock Edicts

Most people visit Dhauli to trudge up the steps to the **Shanti Stupa** *(free)*. This striking Buddhist peace pagoda, completed in 1972, gleams white atop the forested Dhauli Hill. It's fronted by a large marble plaza, and visitors wander around in a clockwise direction. Views from the northern side overlook a key battlefield where King Ashoka's army took a decisive victory in 260 BCE. Following this, he decided to forsake weaponry and war for the nonviolent ways of Buddhism.

Eleven of his 14 resultant decrees were etched into a boulder at the foot of the hill to become the **Ashoka Rock Edicts**. Among other things, they prohibit the killing of animals, and order provision of healthcare for both humans and animals, self-control and purity of mind. To find them, head down to the

A CHAIN OF PEACE PAGODAS

Nichidatsu Fujii (aka Fuji Guruji) helped build a series of peace pagodas across Asia. Another prominent site in India is the **Japanese Peace Pagoda** (p465) in Darjeeling.

PATRICK HORTON/GETTY IMAGES

Saltwater crocodile, Bhitarkanika National Park

eastern entrance of the site. The inscribed stone itself is to the right of the gate (don't walk uphill).

Chandaka-Dampara Wildlife Sanctuary

TIME FROM BHUBANESWAR: **30MIN**

Where the elephants roam

Much of the landscape around Bhubaneswar is dominated by farmland or broad alluvial plains. Unless you head 20km west. Here, a 175-sq-km tract of land was turned into **Chandaka-Dampara Wildlife Sanctuary** *(foreigner/Indian national ₹400/40)* to help conserve a wilderness vital to the region's wild elephant population. Wild boars, spotted deer and rhesus macaques are also common sightings, while leopards and sloth bears are largely rumours. There are also over 100 species of bird. **Dampara** is the main entry point from the Bhubaneswar side, and you'll need to hire a taxi to get there. Tours are by open-sided safari vehicle, which incur an additional fee of around ₹1600 per vehicle per hour, hired at the entrance.

Bhitarkanika National Park

TIME FROM BHUBANESWAR: **3½HR**

Crocodiles for miles

Cleaved in two by farmland, the 672-sq-km **Bhitarkanika National Park** *(wildlife.odisha.gov.in; ₹40)* comprises a block of riverine jungle around the Baitarani–Brahmani delta and a separate wedge of coastal mangroves. The national park's main centre is **Dangamal**, where you'll find a small museum and the park's main jetty. You'll also likely see live red fiddler crabs, rhesus macaques and chitals (spotted deer) here.

BEST ALTERNATIVE WILDLIFE EXPERIENCES

Satkosia Tiger Sanctuary: Boat tours head through Satkosia Gorge from either Badamul or Tikarpada. Tiger sightings are highly unlikely.

Similipal National Park: Most visitors come for the waterfalls, although you may spot wild elephants. Melanistic black tigers are making a comeback, too.

Debrigarh Wildlife Sanctuary: Ideal stop if travelling from Odisha's coastal region to major Madhya Pradesh nature reserves, such as Kanha.

Karlapat Wildlife Sanctuary: An option when heading into Adivasi tribal territory. Birds and deer are the main observable wildlife.

Bhetanai: Tiny village (five hours south of Bhubaneswar) with a small population of majestic Indian antelope known as blackbuck.

TOP EXPERIENCE

The Diamond Triangle

Deep in the Odishan countryside, surrounded by mud-and-thatch villages with free-range goats and haystacks, are the ruins of three hilltop monastery complexes, Ratnagiri, Udayagiri and Lalitgiri, collectively known as the Diamond Triangle. At one time, this was one of the world's focal points for Buddhist thought and learning. Today it is completely overlooked.

Ratnagiri

TOP TIPS

- Nonexistent public transport links, plus the sites being located 10km from one another, means you will need to hire a car and driver.
- Ratnagiri's museum, located 100m down the road from the main entrance, gives the best introduction to all three Diamond Triangle sites.

PRACTICALITIES

- odishatourism.gov.in
- Ratnagiri: foreigner/Indian national ₹200/15; Lalitgiri: foreigner/Indian national ₹200/15; Udayagiri: free
- All sites 9am-5pm, closed Fri

Hills of Jewels

Ratnagiri ('Hills of Jewels') is the monastery complex located furthest north. It has the best-preserved ruins: two monasteries dating from the 5th to 13th centuries. The first has a beautifully carved pale-green chlorite doorway, leading to a courtyard with a splendid Buddha statue flanked by bodhisattvas.

Sunrise Hill

Udayagiri (not to be confused with Udayagiri in Bhubaneswar) lies 10km west of Ratnagiri. It is split into two sections: **Udayagiri-1** and **Udayagiri-2**. Both are cradled by serene, forest-covered hills. Udayagiri-1 contains a brick, double-storey monastery and shrine complex, with a large inscribed Avalokitesvara image. Udayagiri-2 would have been the grander site, as evidenced by the huge statue toppled on its side.

The Oldest Site & Newest Museum

Lalitgiri is the oldest site, with some terracotta artefacts dating it back to at least the 2nd century BCE. Located 11km south of Udayagiri, it would be the least impressive of the three, but for **Lalitgiri Museum**, which holds the Diamond Triangle's best collection of artefacts, including Gallery 4's fascinating reliquaries made of khondalite, which contained a soapstone, gold and silver casket housing an important monk's bone fragments, wrapped in gold leaf.

NATUREHOLIC_SANGRAM/SHUTTERSTOCK

A conservation effort has seen a resurgence in the numbers of saltwater crocodiles from around 95 in the mid-1970s to 1826 as of a count in 2025. The best time to see the crocodiles is at low tide, when the sun is hottest. If you have a boat to yourself, ask your guide to slow down whenever you wish to get closer. The motors scare the reptiles back into the water. Other common sightings include eight species of kingfisher and wild boar.

You'll likely be hassled into hiring a boat from **Paramanandpur** village's **Khola Jetty**, just outside the park. These are slightly cheaper, costing ₹3500 to charter a full boat for three hours. If you're happy to share, stand firm and ask for a single ticket, which costs ₹350. These boats depart in the early morning and at midday, plying the croc- and birdlife-rich waterways between Khola and **Dangamala**. Full-day boat tours *(₹7500)* are the only way to reach sites within the park such as **Bagagahana heronry** (best in summer and autumn) and **Gahirmatha Marine Sanctuary** (for olive ridley marine turtles). The best time to visit is November to February, although the park is closed in the first week of January for an annual wildlife census.

For independent visits, speak to Bubu at Heritage Tours (p580) in Puri or Ashish at **Alternative Tours** in Bhubaneswar for more information.

Cuttack

TIME FROM BHUBANESWAR: **1HR**

Makings of a revolutionary

Resistance was very much on the mind of a young Cuttack resident named Subhas Chandra Bose in the early 20th century. In a pretty, whitewashed mansion 2km south of the fort, bought by his lawyer father Janakinath Bose in 1885, Subhas Chandra was born in 1897. Known as the **Netaji Birth Place Museum** *(foreigner/Indian national ₹100/20)*, in reference to Bose's honorific title, the prison gallery is designed to recreate a sense of life for Netaji during his many periods of incarceration. He escaped house arrest in 1941, first for Afghanistan and then Berlin in Nazi Germany (a period that is conveniently airbrushed by the museum), before returning to Southeast Asia in 1943 to spearhead the Indian Independence Movement in East Asia. Bose died in Taiwan in 1945.

BEST OTHER SIGHTS BEYOND BHUBANESWAR

Chausath Yogini, Hirapur: Fascinating, squat, circular temple; interior decorated with carved statues of various female deities and their incarnations.

Pipli (aka Pipili): Craft village known for its tiny mirror appliqué decorations, 16km south of Bhubaneswar.

Odisha State Maritime Museum, Cuttack: Odishan maritime history from the days of Kalinga onwards.

Barabati Fort, Cuttack: Remnants of 10th-century fortress and palace built by the Somavamshi dynasty.

Nandankanan Botanical Garden: Tranquil escape from the busy city. Contains a nature reserve located next door to a zoo famed for white tigers.

EATING IN CUTTACK: BEST RESTAURANTS

Golden Spoon: Fish tanks and wooden interiors make dining feel like being inside a ship. Many vegetarian dishes. *noon-3pm & 7-11pm* ₹₹

Blast: Located 2km south of the Maritime Museum, Blast's menu runs long. Try the rooftop terrace in the evening. *noon-11pm* ₹₹

Barabati: Unfussy spot close to Netaji Birth Place Museum with decent chow mein and other Chinese dishes. *11am-3pm & 6-10pm* ₹₹

Dada's Biryani: Longstanding spot with slow-cooked mutton biryani. Biryanis are usually made for two to four people only. *noon-3pm & 6.30-10pm* ₹₹

Puri & Konark

SPIRITUAL CENTRES | RELIGIOUS FESTIVITIES | BEACH TIME

TOP TIP

Puri is a beach city, but you'll feel exposed in a bikini or swimming trunks. Many visitors are here on religious pilgrimage, and taking a dip in the Bay of Bengal is a part of the experience, but everybody does it clothed. Sunbathe and swim in a T-shirt and shorts.

Puri was rooted on the backpacker map during the Hippie Trail days, but its status as a preeminent spiritual centre for Hindus has long been heralded, thanks to the looming presence of Jagannath Mandir, the third of the four *char dham*, considered to be India's holiest temples. Puri's long stretches of coarse sand beach, parts of which are well protected and maintained, make this a decent place to slow things down. These days the banana-pancake vendors and backpacker hostels that survived into the early 21st century are gone, replaced by *pani puriwallahs* and budget hotels catering to the domestic market.

Although the hallowed sanctums of Jagannath are off-limits to non-Hindus, there's a second major national temple open to all to the northeast of Puri. Konark's Sun Temple is the jewel in Odisha's archaeology crown, designed like a mighty stone chariot. Together, Konark and Puri form two corners of a triangle completed in Bhubaneswar, a holy trinity of temples and Odishan cultural life.

A Spiritual Behemoth

Drink in the Jagannath Mandir fervour

Pilgrims come from across the Hindu world to pray, supplicate and participate in various rituals at the mighty **Jagannath Mandir**'s inner sanctum. Built in the 12th century, its

GETTING AROUND

Puri's tourist zone runs from Blue Flag Beach east along Chakra Tirtha Rd. Autorickshaws are the best way to get around the town. Puri is served by regular trains from Bhubaneswar and you can reach Delhi, Kolkata and Madras directly from here. Mo Bus runs an express bus service three times a day between Puri and Bhubaneswar Airport (route AE2; ₹200). Konark is a small town, making everything accessible on foot. Konark Bus Stand is roughly 1km east of the temple entrance, with buses departing when full for Puri (one hour) and Bhubaneswar (2½ hours) between 7am and 4pm.

★ **HIGHLIGHTS**
1 Jagannath Mandir

● **SIGHTS**
2 Blue Flag Beach
3 Golden Beach
4 Lion Gate
5 Niladri Beach
6 Swargdwar Beach
7 Swargdwar Cremation Grounds

● **ACTIVITIES**
8 Heritage Tours

● **SLEEPING**
9 Chanakya BNR Hotel
10 Panthanivas Puri
11 Z Hotel

● **EATING**
12 Bangalir Swade Ahlade
13 Chung Wah
14 Honey Bee Bakery
15 The Grand
16 Wildgrass Restaurant

● **DRINKING & NIGHTLIFE**
17 Neeladri Café

ODISHA'S TOP FESTIVALS

Adivasi Mela (Jan) Folk art and handicrafts made by Odisha's Indigenous peoples are celebrated in Bhubaneswar.

Konark's Dance Festivals (Feb & Dec) Odissi dance performances in front of Konark's Sun Temple. Main event in early December, with smaller February festival.

Pana Sankranti (Apr) Marking the first day of the Odishan Hindu solar year. At Maa Sarala Temple near Tirtol, priests walk on hot coals and host melas (fairs).

Rath Yatra (Jul/Aug) Representations of Lord Jagannath are ceremonially conveyed through Puri between Jagannath Mandir and Gundicha Mandir.

Puri Beach Festival (Nov) Sand-art and music bring the carnival spirit to the sands of Puri's Golden Beach over five days.

presiding deity, Jagannath (Lord of the Universe), is an incarnation of Vishnu. Its main *shikhara* (towering spire) has its stone exposed to better reveal its carvings. It rises to 65m. To deal with recent surges in visitors, a **Heritage Corridor** was constructed around the temple in 2024. This necessitated the demolition of Raghunandan Library and its viewing platform, formerly used by non-Hindus to get a better glimpse of the temple. The best view now is from the upper terrace of **The Grand** restaurant. Wander around the temple exterior, particularly past the **Lion Gate** – aka East Gate – to get a flavour of the fervour at play here.

Life's a Beach

Choose the right spot of sand for you

Practically the entire Odishan coastline is fringed by ochre sand. At **Puri**, there are stark differences between the different qualities of beach. The quietest, cleanest option is **Blue Flag Beach** *(from ₹20)*. The admission fee guarantees a guarded space, free from nuisance vendors, where the beach is regularly cleaned and with access to toilets and cafes. Book local tours operated by the state-run OTDC from nearby Panthanivas Puri (p585) hotel's reception desk.

East of Blue Flag is Puri's best stretch of sand: **Niladri Beach**, which is free to access but remains well cared for by a group of local business tycoons who have planted gardens along its edge and employed local people to keep things clean, rent out deck chairs and offer foot massages. Installations by local artists turn this beach into an open exhibition space. There's also the excellent **Neeladri Café**, run by a local women's self-help group, where you can try what is quite possibly Odisha's best masala chai.

Over on the Jagannath side of Puri (west), **Golden Beach** and **Swargdwar Beach** (*both free*) are raucous with street-food stands, souvenir wallahs and the occasional stage, where live music brings life, light and a lot of people to the sand. The latter is also the site of the hallowed **Swargdwar Cremation Grounds**, where the final earthly act of this lifecycle plays out for dozens of Hindus daily. Naturally, the solemnity of the site demands a degree of respectful behaviour, and complete restraint around camera use. Reach out to Samar at **Heritage Tours** for a respectful, guided visit.

EATING IN PURI & KONARK: OUR PICKS

Wildgrass Restaurant: Lush gardens surround alfresco tables at this top seafood spot in central Puri, with great Odishan fish curries. *11am-11pm* ₹₹

Honey Bee Bakery: If you're keen for a reprieve from spicy food, Honey Bee serves pizzas, pastas and sandwiches. *8.30am-2pm & 6-10pm* ₹₹

Chung Wah: Indo-Chinese rice, noodle and chicken dishes at this LGBTIQ+ friendly spot near Blue Flag Beach. *11.30am-3pm & 6.30-10pm* ₹₹₹

Bangalir Swade Ahlade: Bengali restaurant with an excellent *kochu pata chingri* (prawn curry) served in half a coconut. *noon-4pm & 7-10pm* ₹₹

PAUL STAFFORD

Gajasimha (p582)

TOP EXPERIENCE

Konark Sun Temple

Laced with intricate beauty, Konark's mighty Sun Temple, is a chariotlike juggernaut and a powerful manifestation of Hindu mythological inspiration. Built by Ganga king Narasimhadeva to celebrate a 13th-century military victory, it is the finest example of Kalinga architecture anywhere. It's Odisha's archaeological and cultural highlight, and its only UNESCO World Heritage Site.

DON'T MISS

- Konark Archaeological Museum
- Gajasimha
- Nritya Mandap
- Jagamohana
- Wheel sundials
- Bhadra Deul

Treasures From Another Time

Begin at Konark's **Archaeological Museum** *(additional ticket required; entry ₹10; closed Fri)* to the north of the main site. The museum displays treasures from the temple, including larger-than-life statues of Surya, the sun deity, plus nymphs and handsy couples. There's also a most excellent *leogryph* (half lion, half griffin, obviously). Indian iconography regularly depicts Surya as riding a chariot pulled by seven horses. The Sun Temple recreates this imagery in building form. To get

PRACTICALITIES

- asi.nic.in
- foreigner/Indian national ₹600/40
- sunrise-sunset

KONARK BY NUMBERS

Nothing about the design of this celestial wonder is by chance. Numbers carry great significance at the Sun Temple: the 12 pairs of chariot wheels symbolise the 12 months of the *panchangam* (Hindu calendar). The 24 wheels in total equal the hours of the day. The seven horses mark the days of the week. The eight spokes of the wheel represent the eight intervals of each day.

TOP TIPS

- Stand back from the temple to appreciate the sun chariot in its entirety, with its 24 giant wheels, pulled by seven horses.
- The best time of year to visit for fewer people is on a weekday morning in March or early April. This is the quietest time for domestic tourism outside of the monsoon season and comes right before the heat and humidity become uncomfortable.
- For wheelchair users, the path right around the Sun Temple is step-free. However, it isn't possible to access the upper platforms.
- If you visit later in the day, stick around for the sound-and-light show.

there, follow the main road clockwise to the eastern entrance gate. Nearby, **Konark Interpretation Centre** *(entry ₹50)* contains decent models of the Sun Temple site now, and how it would have looked before the *shikhara* collapsed.

Into the Sun

The Sun Temple is known locally as the 'Living History of Odisha' because the richness of the artwork on its sides vividly displays life in the old Kalinga Kingdom (which incorporated modern-day Odisha). Aside from the usual Hindu iconography, real people and their customs are depicted, bringing this past world out from the mists of time and into the present.

Enter through the Sun Temple's eastern entrance gate. Tickets are sold at the booth to your left. Continue to the **Gajasimha** (main entrance), where the steps are guarded by two huge stone lions standing atop crumpled elephants. Some believe this depicts Hinduism triumphing over Buddhism in the area, but in general it refers to spirituality overcoming earthly desires. The steps lead up the **Nritya Mandap** (dancing platform), which is covered in intricate carvings of dancers and musicians. You can work your way around, or over, it quite freely.

The Great Chariot

On the other side of the Nritya Mandap is the 38m-high **Jagamohana** (assembly hall). The main door is decorated with eight carved jamb styles. It faces east to welcome the dawn's sunlight in one of the temple's many pleasing celestial odes. You can sometimes climb the steps onto the temple's platform, but visitors cannot ordinarily explore inside this structure. Luckily there is plenty to interest you below, such as the remnants of the seven **horses**, leaping ahead of the **24-wheeled chariot**. Two of those wheels, tucked into corners on either side, act as accurate **sundials**, with the left-hand spoke signifying 6am and the right-hand spoke 6pm.

Gardens & Missing Bits

The site's towering structure, the Jagamohana, was merely the lower part of what may once have been one of the world's tallest buildings. The *shikhara,* which once stood around 70m tall, is thought to have collapsed some time before the 19th century. The *shikhara's* base is still intact and sports some impressive chlorite carvings of Surya. As you continue around to the temple's west and north sides, you'll find some of the more risqué erotic carvings and an excellent lower frieze of elephants around the base. Surrounding the main structure are a series of platforms and smaller temples, known as the **Bhadra Deul**, with stone war-stallion statues to the south and elephants to the north.

Beyond Puri & Konark

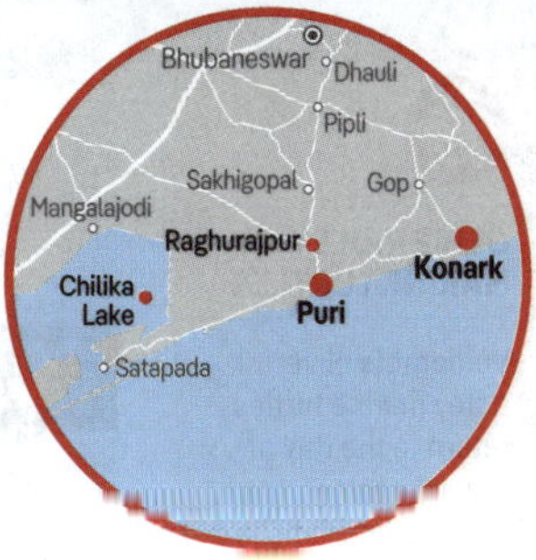

Visits to artist communities and spotting the teeming wildlife of Asia's largest saltwater lagoon make for ideal day trips.

Folk art thrives in the countryside around Puri and Konark. Many of the state's most celebrated art forms, such as palm-leaf etching and *patachitra* (Odishan cloth paintings), are practised in the artists' village of Raghurajpur. Southwest along the coast from Puri and Konark is Chilika Lake, the largest brackish lagoon in Asia. Among the varied settlements dotting the lake's shores, some have become go-to destinations to observe certain endangered species in their natural habitats. These rewarding wildlife encounters include scores of species of waterbird at **Mangalajodi**, Irrawaddy dolphins on boat trips from **Satapada**, and the mass nestings of olive ridley marine turtles on the shores near **Rambha**.

Places

Raghurajpur p583
Chilika Lake p583

GETTING AROUND

Konark is only connected to Puri and Bhubaneswar by bus. Puri has much better connections: Mo Bus runs a service (#80) between Satapada and Bhubaneswar via Puri. OTDC tours run from Puri to Satapada and often make a stop at Raghurajpur. As ever in Odisha, hiring a car and driver, starting at ₹3700 a day, is the best option. A few daily trains pass Mukteswar (for Mangalajodi) and Chilika (for Barkul) stations from Bhubaneswar.

Raghurajpur

TIME FROM PURI: **30MIN**

Drop by the artists' workshops

A small village 10km north of Puri, **Raghurajpur Artists Village** is populated mainly by artists descended from the Chitrakars, families of artists commissioned to paint exclusively for Jagannath Mandir. The Artists Village consists of artists' residences and workshops covered in murals. Watch artists making *patachitra* paintings and palm-leaf inscriptions. Both styles depict stories from Hindu religious texts of deities, particularly Vishnu.

Skip past the stalls on the edge of the village until you reach the 'I Love Raghurajpur' sign. The family at **Maa Bagalamukhi Arts** are particularly lovely. You're expected to haggle, with prices quoted generally 30% to 50% above the work's proper value.

Chilika Lake

TIME FROM PURI: **2–5HR**

Birding in Mangalajodi

Chilika Lake offers one of the most rewarding, eco-conscious experiences in eastern India. It is said to have 334 recorded species of bird, 105 of which are regulars around **Mangalajodi**, a village with a remarkable turnaround story. Villagers used to poach the migratory birds and sell their meat to restaurants. That's until the saving graces of ecotourism gave locals an alternative way of making a living. The exceptional

OLIVE RIDLEY MARINE TURTLES

Vulnerable olive ridley marine turtles return to the Bay of Bengal each winter to mate, and Odisha's coastline provides crucial nesting sites for the vulnerable species. Their timid constitution (read: good sense of self-preservation) means they'll only come ashore to lay their eggs if conditions are just right. Too much noise or light and they return to the sea and reabsorb their eggs. Military bases, harmful fishing practices and lax development rules are putting pressure on traditional laying sites, such as Devi Beach near Konark, and the Rushikulya River's estuary. But responsible travel initiatives are slowly allowing visitors to watch these unique creatures laying eggs, while incentivising local communities in their protection.

PAUL STAFFORD

Chilika Lake (p583)

90-minute **boat tours** weave through the expansive wetlands, gondola-style. The lack of boat motors means you can get extremely close to egrets, pintails, kingfishers, shelducks, godwits, prehistoric-looking purple herons and Oriental white ibis. Request binoculars before you start. Boat and guide hire costs ₹1500 for 90 minutes for one-to-four people.

Spotting dolphins in Satapada

One of the world's few remaining lagoon populations of Irrawaddy dolphins is found in Chilika Lake. **Satapada** is well placed for boat trips to their regular haunts. The village contains the small but informative **Chilika Museum** *(₹10)*, plus kiosks for the most reliable tour organisers, **Dolphin Motor Boat Association**. However, truly ecofriendly organisation is lacking, and boat operators tend to mob the dolphins whenever they're spotted. Solo visitors and groups alike have little choice but to rent their own boat, starting at ₹1300 for an hour for up to six adults and two children, thus increasing the number of boats on the water. Ask your boat driver to back off to a sensible distance. Pay ₹3000 and you'll get a boat for three hours, enough to visit the bird sanctuary on **Nalabana Island** and **Kalijai Temple**, both in the middle of the lake. A cheaper alternative is to take the OTDC daily tour from Bhubaneswar or Puri and ride with other tourists.

Olive ridley marine turtles from Rambha

Rambha is a small village at the southwestern tip of the lake. Boat trips, best booked through OTDC Panthanivas Rambha (p585), seek out birdlife and Kalijai Temple. But the main reason to visit this remoter outpost of Chilika is to witness olive ridley marine turtles coming ashore on the beaches around the mouth of the Rushikulya River. Ask at the OTDC hotel about arranging a local guide. An autorickshaw to the beach costs around ₹750 for half a day.

Places We Love to Stay

₹ Budget ₹₹ Midrange ₹₹₹ Top-End

Bhubaneswar

Map p569

Pravuprasad Homestay ₹ No-frills, clean rooms with thin mattresses at this pleasant family-run homestay in a residential neighbourhood.

Cozzet Victoria ₹₹ This sleek hotel raises the bar in Bhubaneswar for modern style and in-room comfort at its price point. Good on-site restaurant.

Hotel Pushpak ₹₹ The fairy light-speckled facade and lotus-print designs elevate the mood at this charming hotel, located minutes from Odisha State Museum.

Adventure Luxury Hotels ₹₹ Spacious rooms at this hotel with an art deco sensibility, away from the main road but only 10 minutes from the station.

Mango Hotels ₹₹ Clean rooms within easy walking distance of the train station. Café Sundowner is its welcoming rooftop cafe.

Crown ₹₹₹ An outdoor pool and a daily programme of Odishan cultural events mean you can keep exploring the area from your comfortable digs.

Welcomhotel By ITC Hotels ₹₹₹ The rooftop pool and large fitness centre make this yet another world-class hotel in Bhubaneswar.

Trident ₹₹₹ Set in spacious, private grounds, this top hotel's rooms feature carved Odishan stonework. Books up well in advance.

Cuttack & Around

Pramod Convention & Club Resort ₹₹ Tucked away in a leafy suburb of Cuttack, this slightly tired hotel is still among the best in the city.

Kila Dalijoda ₹₹₹ Built in the 1930s, this former hunting lodge is set amid tribal villages of the Munda, Sabar and Santhal Adivasi peoples. The flat, empty roads and forest are perfect for cycling tours run by the friendly owners.

Gajlaxmi Palace ₹₹₹ Located near Dhenkanal, northwest of Cuttack, this former royal palace offers excellent nature-based activities and an upmarket, full-board stay.

Bhitarkanika

Aranyanivas Bhitarkanika ₹₹ The OTDC's property in Dangamala is the best place for independent trips to the national park, also assisting with the organisation of boat trips.

Bhitarkanika Eco Resorts ₹₹ Although Bhitarkanika's accommodation is generally overpriced, this well-maintained and friendly spot is clean and all meals are included.

Killa Aul Palace ₹₹₹ Former royal palace retreat located in Aul village, midway between Bhitarkanika National Park and Ratnagiri, Udayagiri and Lalitgiri monasteries.

Puri

Map p579

Z Hotel ₹ Pronounced 'jed', this lovely heritage property provides the best (and most interesting) budget stay in Odisha. No in-room wi-fi.

Panthanivas Puri ₹₹ OTDC-run property renovated in 2024, a minute's walk from Blue Flag Beach. Nonguests can come here to book coach tours of the locality.

Chanakya BNR Hotel ₹₹₹ Formerly the South Eastern Railway Hotel built during the Raj era, this heritage property, complete with old steam engine in the garden, remains an elegant choice.

Konark & Around

Labanya Guest House ₹ Very basic rooms with no wi-fi, but the lovely pet dog and family-run atmosphere make this one of Konark's best budget options.

Lotus Eco Resort Konark ₹₹ On the road to Puri, this secluded shoreline spot is surrounded by forest at the mouth of the Kushabhadra River. It also has a private beach.

Chilika Lake

OTDC Panthanivas Rambha ₹₹ The go-to property in Rambha for accommodation, Chilika Lake boat tours and trips to see turtles.

Desia Chilika Nest ₹₹₹ A beautiful, end-of-the-road country lodge constructed from wood and bamboo near a small Adivasi community. Direct bookings only via *info@desiachilika.com.*

For places to stay in Madhya Pradesh and Chhattisgarh, see p626

CHETANSONI/SHUTTERSTOCK

Above: Chhatris (cenotaphs; p596), Orchha; Right: Carvings at Vishvanath Temple (p601), Khajuraho

THE MAIN AREAS

GWALIOR
Historic Tomar stronghold with magnificent hilltop fort. p592

KHAJURAHO
World-renowned, UNESCO-listed temples and laid-back village. p598

BHOPAL
Madhya Pradesh capital with beautiful lakes. p604

Researched by
Prachi Joshi

Madhya Pradesh & Chhattisgarh

TEMPLES, TIGERS AND TRIBAL TOURISM

Wildlife, ethnic diversity and spirituality collide in central India: UNESCO-listed religious relics, captivating tribal markets and the world's greatest concentration of wild Royal Bengal tigers await.

Madhya Pradesh and Chhattisgarh sit outside the well-trodden lines of more celebrated neighbouring states, but not for lack of alluring inventory. Spotting a wild Royal Bengal tiger at one of MP's big three tiger reserves (Bandhavgarh, Kanha and Pench) is the principal draw for adventurers, but there is far more to see than big cats. Khajuraho's UNESCO-listed temples showcase some of the finest stone carving in India. These exquisite erotic sculptures are a mere slice of the architectural wonders of a region exceedingly well endowed with palaces, forts, temples and mosques (most gloriously in the villages of Orchha and Mandu). Tranquil Maheshwar and more frenzied Ujjain draw hordes of pilgrims to riverside spiritual havens for which India is renowned, and the UNESCO-listed Buddhist monuments at Sanchi are some of India's oldest.

DR AJAY KUMAR SINGH/SHUTTERSTOCK ©

But MP's somewhat off-the-beaten-path highlights are downright conventional compared to Chhattisgarh, which sits fascinatingly far removed from India's tourist trail. The country's most densely forested state (44%) is blessed with considerable natural beauty, and a foray into the mesmerising tribal zones around Jagdalpur more than justifies a detour. Many of the greater Bastar region's 42 documented tribes engage in some form of tribal art (pointillist paintings, spindly sculptures, painstakingly detailed bell-metal craftwork), which is often on display, along with dizzying inventories of colourful produce and other daily wares, at intriguing daily *haat* (tribal markets) across the region.

INDORE
Cosmopolitan, food-focused metropolis; former Holkar stronghold. p609

JABALPUR
Surrounded by famed tiger reserves. p615

JAGDALPUR
Chhattisgarh hub for Adivasi tribal markets. p621

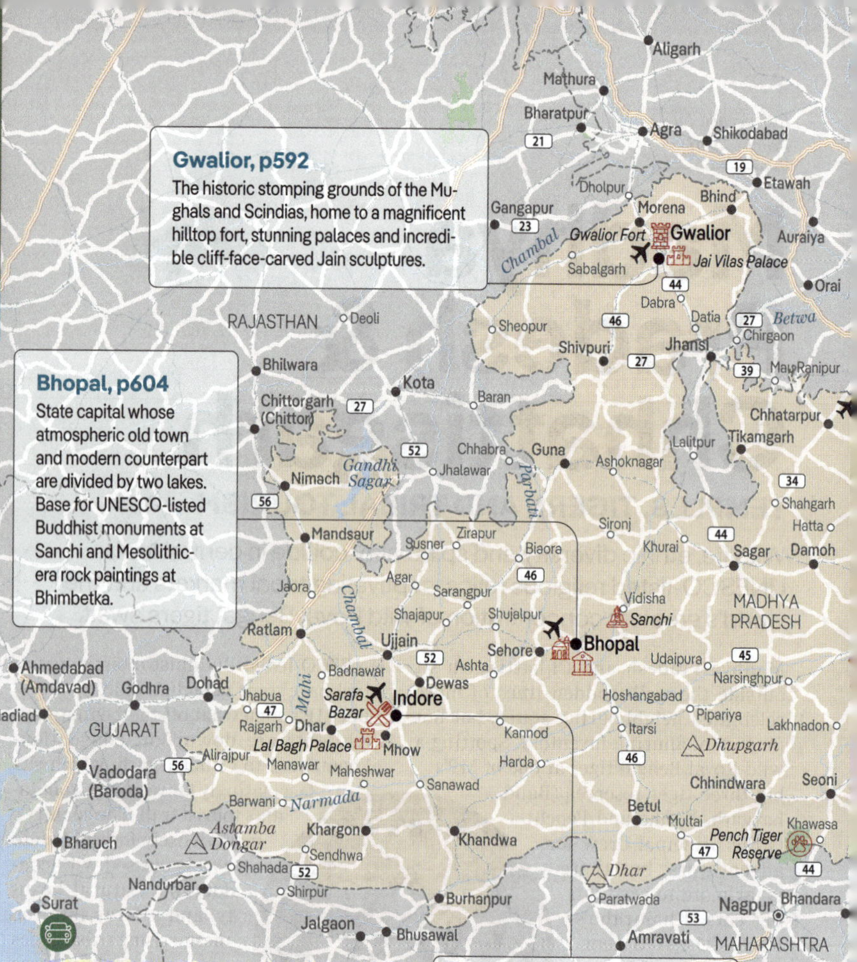

Gwalior, p592

The historic stomping grounds of the Mughals and Scindias, home to a magnificent hilltop fort, stunning palaces and incredible cliff-face-carved Jain sculptures.

Bhopal, p604

State capital whose atmospheric old town and modern counterpart are divided by two lakes. Base for UNESCO-listed Buddhist monuments at Sanchi and Mesolithic-era rock paintings at Bhimbetka.

Indore, p609

Madhya Pradesh's biggest, most cosmopolitan city, with fine Holkar-dynasty palaces, unmissable street food and all the buzz of big-city living.

CAR

Roadways around Madhya Pradesh and Chhattisgarh are generally decent. Several new routes have recently been opened or expanded, including the new four-lane highway between Jabalpur and Nagpur (MH). The eight-lane, 906km Narmada Expressway connecting Gujarat with Chhattisgarh via Madhya Pradesh is in the works. Car hire with a driver is recommended.

TRAIN

With the exception of far-flung destinations, such as the tiger reserves, Madhya Pradesh has an extensive train network *(irctc.co.in)*. It's also home to the ultra-modern Rani Kamalapati (RKMP) station in the suburbs of Bhopal. Opened in 2021, it will completely redefine your idea of an Indian train station.

BUS

Government buses cast a wide net and are supplemented by private companies throughout Madhya Pradesh and Chhattisgarh. As with cars, road improvements have drastically improved bus travel comfort and travel times in the states. **Redbus** *(redbus.in)* is the easiest way of booking buses in advance.

Find Your Way

Good airports, bus stations and rapidly transforming highways means movement in Madhya Pradesh isn't challenging, but distances are certainly considerable (it's India's second-biggest state). Smaller Chhattisgarh is more isolated, but the added effort brings some great rewards.

Khajuraho, p598
Laid-back, traveller-friendly village surrounding the 1000-year-old, blush-worthy, UNESCO World Heritage–listed temples of the Chandela dynasty.

Jabalpur, p615
Eastern Madhya Pradesh industrial and administrative powerhouse serving as the jumping-off point for the state's most famous tiger reserves: Bandhavgarh, Kanha and Pench.

Jagdalpur, p621
Capital of Chhattisgarh's Bastar district and the state's most fascinating destination. Springboard for a head-spinning collection of dazzling tribal markets, art and villages.

Plan Your Time

Madhya Pradesh is a beast, clocking in as India's second-biggest state (308,252 sq km). Distances and travel times are long. Chhattisgarh is more manageable but quite remote, with less tourism infrastructure.

S. THIRU/SHUTTERSTOCK

Stupa, Sanchi (p607)

Madhya Pradesh on the Fly

- If you are only passing through the region on the move to/from more heavily trafficked destinations (such as Rajasthan or Uttar Pradesh), Madhya Pradesh's must-see cultural attraction is the UNESCO-listed **Khajuraho temples** (p600), a mind-blowing testament to 11th-century stone craftsmanship that rates as some of the finest temple art in the world.

- If you are looking for wildlife, look no further than a safari at **Bandhavgarh Tiger Reserve** (p618), where chances of spotting a Royal Bengal tiger in the wild remain high. For the best of both worlds, combine Khajuraho with **Panna Tiger Reserve** (p603), a mere 30 minutes' drive away. Either choice will make for a highly rewarding day or two in the state.

SEASONAL HIGHLIGHTS

Most travellers head for MP in late autumn or winter (October to February) to avoid torrential rain, extreme heat or the dreadfully humid marriage of the two. Tigers, however, are best seen in summer.

JANUARY

Pleasant days (around 25°C), relatively chilly nights (around 11°C). Folk music, dance and tribal handicrafts come together at Bhopal's **Lokrang Festival**.

FEBRUARY

Khajuraho's weeklong **Dance Festival** attracts myriad revellers to India's most titillating town for dance performances, handicrafts and more.

APRIL

Summer temps averaging 40°C barrel down on MP, but thin vegetation and scant water sources make April to June top tiger-spotting time.

A Week to Linger

- Touch down in **Gwalior** (p592) and explore the epic **Gwalior Fort** (p594), one of India's most dramatic and well-preserved hilltop citadels, before moving on to **Orchha** (p596), where excellent village homestays make for a culturally immersive stopover in a tranquil village packed with cultural assets.

- From there, devote two days to wandering the incredible UNESCO-listed temples at **Khajuraho** (p598) and a few more days for tiger-spotting at **Bandhavgarh Tiger Reserve** (p618) or **Kanha Tiger Reserve** (p619), where a bath in the river with a wild elephant is more than acceptable consolation if you don't see a big cat. Finish off in **Sanchi** (p607) for some of India's most remarkably preserved Buddhist architecture.

A Few Weeks to See It All

- Madhya Pradesh rewards slow tourism in spades. The state's major metropolitan destinations – **Gwalior** (p592), **Bhopal** (p604) and **Indore** (p609) – present one to two days each worth of fascinating cultural assets of some of India's most prominent former dynasties (the Holkars, the Tomars, the Scindias), wonderful food and big-city flair. You can while away a week park-hopping between the state's big three tiger reserves: **Bandhavgarh** (p618), **Kanha** (p619) and **Pench** (p620).

- Bliss out for a few days each in **Orchha** (p596), **Khajuraho** (p598) and **Mandu** (p614), taking in ancient temples, stupas, mosques, palaces and the tranquil village atmosphere. And don't miss riverside pilgrimage destinations like **Maheshwar** (p613) and **Ujjain** (p612), or the fascinating tribal markets around off-the-beaten-path **Jagdalpur** (p621).

SEPTEMBER

The last month of the monsoon still drops a daily load of 159mm of rain on the state, but somewhat 'milder' temps averaging 31°C make it a tolerable shoulder season.

OCTOBER

Laying claim to the world's longest festival, **Bastar Dussehra** (p623) keeps Jagdalpur and surrounding tribal villages abuzz for some 75 days in celebration of regional goddess Danteshwari.

NOVEMBER

High season is in full swing, along with nationwide festivals like **Diwali**. Nights and mornings start to be chilly; bring a jacket between now and February.

DECEMBER

Book Bandhavgarh, Pench and Kanha tiger safaris well ahead. Gwailor celebrates 16th-century composer-musician Tansen at the **Tansen Music Festival**.

Gwalior

HILLTOP FORTRESS | ORNATE PALACE | TEMPLES

GETTING AROUND

Madhya Pradesh's fourth-biggest city is a sprawling metropolis, clocking in at 289 sq km. If you are only visiting Gwalior Fort, it is walkable and that is the recommended approach for anyone without mobility or time limitations. Rideshare apps such as Ola and Uber work for getting to and from the fort and around other parts of the city. Otherwise an autorickshaw around the centre is usually no more than ₹100. To Gwalior Airport (GWL) and Gwalior Junction Train Station (GWL), autorickshaws charge around ₹500 and ₹100, respectively.

Gwalior was once the winter capital of the long-gone Indian state of Madhya Bharat (absorbed into the larger state of Madhya Pradesh in 1956), and enjoys a pedigree steeped in longstanding brushes with historic Indian kingdoms that ruled the city and its dramatic hilltop fort for centuries. Legend has it that the city was founded in 8 CE, when a holy man called Gwalipa cured a local chieftain of leprosy with his magic concoction (a temple dedicated to Gwalipa stands at Gwalior Fort today). Over the years, the Kachchhapaghatas (10th century), the Tomars (13th century) and the Mughals (16th century), among others, ruled Gwalior leading up to the Scindia dynasty of the Maratha empire in the 18th century. Today, it's the Tomars (their indomitable 30-year ruler Man Singh Tomar's colourful palace dominates the magical Gwalior Fort) and the Scindias that have left the most evident legacy on modern-day Gwalior.

Royal Pursuits

Explore a 19th-century European-style palace

Get dazzled by the Scindias' lavish lifestyle at **Jai Vilas Palace**, which houses the **Jiwajirao Scindia Museum** *(jaivilas palace.in; ₹850; 10am-6pm, closed Mon)*. The gilded Durbar Hall with two gigantic crystal chandeliers is the centrepiece, but the Banquet Hall will charm you with a model silver train that once ran on the table, distributing wine, food and cigars. Guides by the ticket counter charge ₹300 for an hour-long tour.

EATING IN GWALIOR: OUR PICKS

S.S. Kachori Wala: Iconic breakfast spot for *kachori* (deep-fried stuffed pastry) and *bedai* (crispy flatbread with spicy potato curry). *8am-2pm & 4-8.30pm* ₹

Kwality Restaurant: Locally legendary butter chicken, chicken tikka masala and other rich curries; don't skip the butter naan. *11am-11pm* ₹₹

Panchvati Gaurav: Unfussy restaurant with rustic touches, serving unlimited Rajasthani and Gujarati vegetarian thalis. *1-3.45pm & 7-10.15pm* ₹₹

Silver Saloon: Light-filled multicuisine restaurant at the Taj Usha Kiran Palace with live Indian classical music; preorder the royal Maratha thali. *7am-11pm* ₹₹₹

HIGHLIGHTS
1 Gwalior Fort
2 Jai Vilas Palace & Jiwajirao Scindia Museum

SIGHTS
3 Badalgarh Gate
4 Chaturbhuj Mandir
5 Ganesh Gate
6 Gwalior Gate
7 Hathi Gate
8 Lakshman Gate
9 Man Singh Palace
10 Sasbahu Temples
11 Scindia School
12 State Archaeological Museum
13 Suraj Kund
14 Teli ka Mandir
15 Urvai Gate

SLEEPING
16 Hotel Grace
17 Usha Kiran Palace

EATING
see 17 Silver Saloon

TOP TIP

After sunset, head to the central **Jiwaji Chowk**, flanked by brilliantly lit administrative buildings sporting a mishmash of architectural styles. Then, trawl the warren of streets around it, which is chock-a-block with local markets and street-food stalls.

STEVE ALLEN/SHUTTERSTOCK

TOP EXPERIENCE

Gwalior Fort

Reputedly described as 'the pearl of Indian fortresses' by Mughal emperor Babur, the enormous and majestic Gwalior Fort overlooks the city from the top of an unmissable 3km-long sandstone plateau. Dating to at least the 10th century (and possibly as far back as the 6th), this dramatic fort contains fascinating palaces, temples, museums and other buildings.

DON'T MISS

- Man Singh Palace
- Jain Rock Sculptures
- Hathi Gate
- Sasbahu Temples
- Teli ka Mandir
- State Archaeological Museum
- Suraj Kund
- Badalgarh Gate

Planning & Arriving

Gwalior Fort is an enormous complex that warrants a half-day of exploring. Tackle it on foot from the eastern approach, from which a series of five gates punctuates the worn path up to the fort itself. Taxis and autorickshaws from town will drop you at the lower part of the fort at the **Gwalior Gate** (Kila Gate) near Fort Rd. Many of the major sites – save detours to Teli ka Mandir, Suraj Kund and Sasbahu Temples – can be seen on a leisurely rise-and-fall walk between here and the western **Urvai Gate**, 2km or so from the Gwalior Gate. The fort can be explored independently, but hiring an official guide *(₹2500 for up to four hours)* will greatly enhance your experience.

PRACTICALITIES

- mptourism.com/gwalior-fort-madhya-pradesh-historical-place.html
- ₹300, free for children under 15
- sunrise-sunset

The Gates

Of the fort's original seven gates, five remain, beginning with the Gwalior Gate (Kila Gate), dating to 1660. Shortly thereafter, you'll encounter the **Badalgarh Gate**, named after Badal Singh, uncle of Maharaja Man Singh Tomar, who ruled Gwalior in the 15th century and was the builder of the fort's palaces. Continuing uphill, the 15th-century **Ganesh Gate** precedes a small six-pillared whitewashed Hindu temple to the hermit Gwalipa, after whom both the fort and city are supposedly named. You'll take in a 9th-century rock-cut Vishnu shrine, the **Chaturbhuj Mandir**, before reaching the **Lakshman Gate** (likely dating from the 14th century). Finally, enter the palace area through the magnificent, two-towered **Hathi Gate**, built in 1516.

Man Singh Palace

The imperial-style Man Singh Palace has a colourful exterior, adorned with quirkily ornamented tilework that includes a frieze of yellow ducks and mosaics of elephants, crocodiles and tigers. Otherwise known as the *Chit Mandir* (Painted Palace), this lavishly festooned refuge was built by Man Singh between 1486 and 1516. The four-level structure is considered the only intact pre-Mughal palace in India.

The Temples

The palace ticket also includes admission to the **Sasbahu Temples** (dating to the 9th to 11th centuries; they are behind the sacred **Suraj Kund** pond) and the 9th-century **Teli ka Mandir**, the compound's oldest monument and a perfect fusion of the northern and southern architectural styles of India. It is 1.2km further south beyond the Scindia School from Man Singh Palace.

Jain Rock Sculptures

While sculptures are carved into the rock in various locales around the fort, none are more stunning than the upper set on the western approach between Urvai Gate and the inner fort walls. The nine large (and many smaller) images represent various *tirthankar* (the 24 great Jain teachers) in seated or standing meditating positions, the most impressive of which is the gargantuan, 17m-high standing sculpture of the first *tirthankar*, Adinath.

State Archaeological Museum

The **State Archaeological Museum** *(separately ticketed, ₹400)*, housed in the 15th-century Gujari Mahal palace, is on the right immediately after Badalgarh Gate. The museum's vast collection of sculptures, coins, weaponry and pottery is spread over multiple indoor galleries and an open-air courtyard. The most prized artefact is the 11th-century sculpture *Salabhanjika*, whose enigmatic smile has earned her the moniker 'Indian Mona Lisa'.

SCINDIA SCHOOL

Much of the grounds of Gwalior Fort are occupied by the private boys-only **Scindia School**. Founded as the Sardar School by Maharaja Madho Rao Scindia in 1897 exclusively for the education of Indian royalty and nobility, the prestigious boarding school was renamed the Scindia School in the 1930s. Famous alumni include musician Ananda Shankar (nephew of Ravi Shankar) and actor Salman Khan.

TOP TIPS

- Private vehicles (not taxis or autorickshaws) can drive up the west side through the Urvai Gate; this approach is anticlimactic compared with the formidable view of the fort from the eastern approach.
- Time your visit to sunrise for spectacular views and fewer crowds.
- For a panorama photo up of Man Singh Palace, climb the left-hand-side stairs just before Hathi Gate.
- A nightly sound-and-light show *(₹700)* takes place in English at 8.20pm *(Mar-Oct; 7.20pm Nov-Feb)*.
- Wear comfortable shoes; there's significant walking on uneven cobblestones and copious staircases.
- There's a makeshift snack area on the way to Teli ka Mandir.

Beyond Gwalior

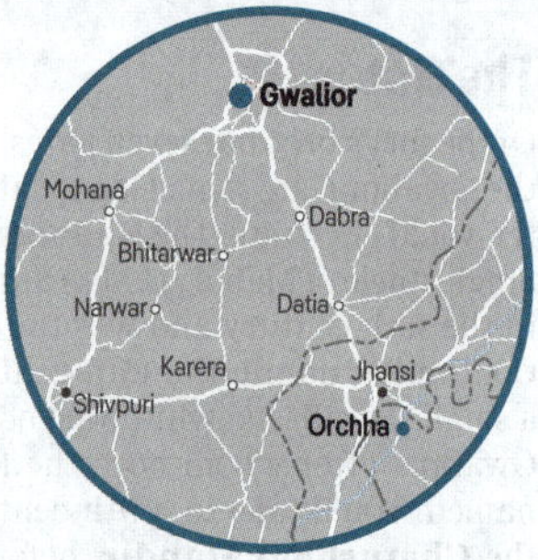

A cavalcade of Mughal-influenced Rajput architecture has turned the once-sleepy agricultural village of Orchha into an unlikely cultural behemoth.

> **GETTING AROUND**
>
> Compact Orchha is easily navigated on foot. The dominating size of Orchha's palaces and temples make for easy navigation from anywhere in town – Jehangir Mahal and Chaturbhuj Temple in particular can be seen from afar. The hamlet of Ganj is about as far away as you're likely to be from the historic fort area and even that's less than a 2km jaunt, at most. Autorickshaws charge around ₹100 to ₹120 between the two.

Tiny Orchha, 120km southeast from Gwalior by car, was little more than a farmland blip on the agricultural radar until the 16th century, when the first King of Orchha, Bundela chief Rudra Pratap Singh, had founded the city and built a fort. Orchha became one of the most important urban areas in this part of India for the following 300 years. It remains a tiny, agricultural village at heart, but a supreme display of Mughal-influenced Rajput architecture in the shape of spectacular palaces, temples and royal *chhatri* (cenotaphs) – along with an intimidatingly large temple dedicated to Rama – have put Orchha firmly on the Madhya Pradesh cultural highlights map. There's rafting in the pastoral countryside, too.

Orchha

TIME FROM GWALIOR: 2¼ HR

Afoot in Orchha Fort

Orchha Fort, built by the Bundela Rajputs, is considerably smaller than Gwalior Fort, but it rises above the village rooftops with no less wow. Begin by crossing the Adawara Bridge to the **Orchha Fort Ticket Office** *(₹750)*, where the admission fees cover seven monuments within the complex and beyond. Head through the main gate to the 16th-century **Raj Mahal**, whose colourful murals depict the likes of Brahma, Vishnu, Buddha, Rama, Krishna, Sita and Ganesh – along with Orchha royalty – dancing, hunting, fighting and wrestling. Up the staircase is **Hotel Sheesh Mahal**, once an 18th-century former royal guesthouse, now a MP Tourism hotel; the gorgeous lobby is perfect for a quick refreshment. Adjacent to the hotel is the entrance to **Jehangir Mahal**, an enormous 17th-century palace with steep staircases and precipitous walkways. Held up as a pinnacle of Indo-Islamic architecture, it's crowned by eight domed turrets and eight slender domed pavilions. On the upper floors, pretty *jali* (stone lattice) windows frame astounding views.

Historic riverfront cenotaphs

Your ticket to the fort includes entrance to the **Chhatris** located 1.2km away on the bank of the Betwa River. Built between the 16th and 18th centuries, these funerary monuments pay

SANGA PARK/SHUTTERSTOCK

Orchha Fort

homage to Orchha's Bundela kings. The 14 richly carved cenotaphs stand on individual elevated platforms and are topped by conical or domed ceilings. Look closely and you might see the vultures that roost atop these monuments. The best view of the cenotaphs is at sunrise from the stepped riverside ghat.

Overnight at a homestay

It can sometimes be hard to crack Indian culture beyond the glitz and gloss of its incredible monuments, palaces, temples and heritage hotels. **Friends of Orchha**, a wonderful homestay programme started by the nonprofit organisation of the same name in 2009, is doing its best to offer a peek behind the curtains in **Ganj**, 1.5km west of central Orchha, connecting travellers with six families in private homes around the village *(rooms from ₹1400)*. You'll be greeted with smiles by wonderful hosts who will serve chai before showing you to your simple but spotlessly clean room, usually with *charpoy* (rope beds) for sleeping and equipped with fans, air coolers, mosquito nets and shared squat toilets. Home-cooked meals are offered *(₹100-300)* and cooking, henna and pottery classes can be arranged. It's more charming than most budget hotels and the interaction with villagers and immersion into village life is nothing short of priceless.

A DIFFERENT SIDE OF ORCHHA

Romi Samele grew up 15km from Orchha but has spent most of his adult life in town. He manages **Friends of Orchha** and OTS Tours & Travel. *@friendsoforchha*

In Orchha, I recommend sitting around the town's famed baobab tree (Kalpvriksh in Hindi) in the evening. It is located just 350m south of the homestay. You should also have a walk around the **Shikaragarh Natural Reserve Forest**. As for eating, the restaurant at Hotel Sheesh Mahal is the best because the food there is always fresh. Nature lovers should also consider river rafting when the flow is up in the river. There is a place near Ganj Mohalla called **Mokam** from where you should try and catch the sunrise.

EATING IN ORCHHA: OUR PICKS

Laxmi Betwa Tarang: The best veg food of Orchha's array of budget options opposite Orchha Fort. Rooftop terrace (few tables). *8am-10.30pm* ₹

Mediterraneo: Standard-casual continental, Chinese and Indian dishes, served on an open terrace on the main road. *9am-11pm* ₹₹

Belpatra: Cheery, light-filled restaurant serving vegetarian thalis, North Indian and Chinese fare. *9.30am-11pm* ₹₹

Hotel Sheesh Mahal: Within Orchha Fort, this historic spot is renowned for its Indian menu and overall freshness. *8.30-10am, 12.30-3pm & 7-10.30pm* ₹₹₹

Khajuraho

UNESCO-LISTED TEMPLES | 10TH-CENTURY EROTICA | PEACEFUL VILLAGE

The Khajuraho Group of Monuments in the northeastern Madhya Pradesh village of Khajuraho postdate the Kamasutra by at least seven centuries, so it wouldn't be inappropriate to speculate that certain Chandela-dynasty artisans were likely avid readers of the erotic arts, in addition to being skilled sandstone carvers. Khajuraho is world-renowned for its three groups of UNESCO World Heritage–listed temples, the most famous of which are blanketed with astonishingly detailed, blush-worthy depictions of the libertine lifestyle of the 10th and 11th centuries CE – sensuous *surasundari* and *apsara* (heavenly nymphs), *nayika* (heroines) and *mithuna* (pairs, threesomes etc of men and women depicted in erotic poses) among them. The temples were constructed between 885 CE and 1100 CE during the zenith of the Chandela dynasty, a Rajput clan who ruled swathes of northern Madhya Pradesh and southern Uttar Pradesh between the 9th and 16th centuries. Today, Khajuraho is an immensely pleasant village that's perfect for walking, cycling and whiling away the time.

GETTING AROUND

Despite sitting firmly on the world's tourism and culture map, Khajuraho is a laid-back village (by Indian standards; population some 30,000) and almost everything of note is in a walkable area along Jain Temple and Main Rds, including the Western Group of temples. Cycling is another great way to get around. Mohammed Bilal at **Bilal Bikes** *(9893240074)*, in the bicycle business since 1982, rents city bicycles and mountain bikes near the intersection of – you guessed it – Jain Temple and Main Rds. A full day costs ₹200 to ₹500 depending on the type of bike.

Read Between the Lines

Museum-hopping in Khajuraho

Your Western Group temple ticket includes admission to the **Archaeological Museum** *(9am-5pm, closed Fri)*, housed in a purpose-built facility north of the Western Group

TEMPLE TOUR?

Khajuraho's UNESCO-listed temples are some of the most astounding Hindu and Jain temples in existence. If you want to continue your Madhya Pradesh temple tour, head to **Sanchi** (p607), 325km southwest of Khajuraho, for its equally impressive, UNESCO-listed Buddhist temples.

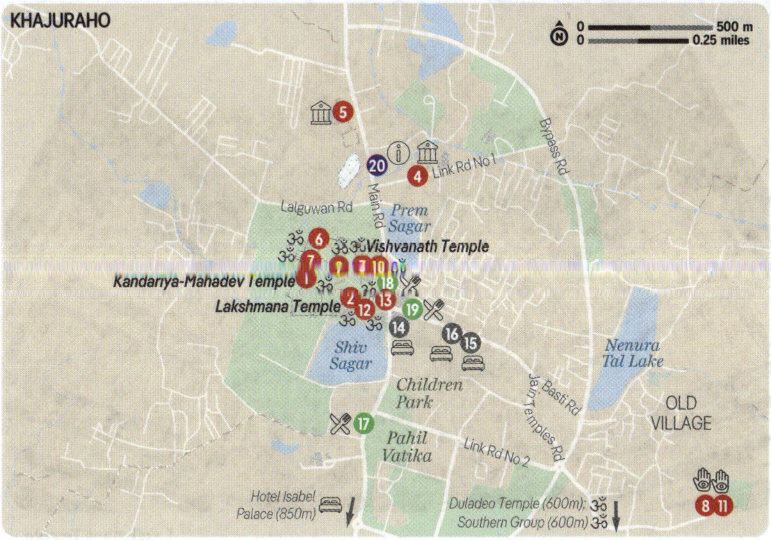

HIGHLIGHTS
1 Kandariya-Mahadev Temple
2 Lakshmana Temple
3 Vishvanath Temple

SIGHTS
4 Aadivart Tribal & Folk Museum
5 Archaeological Museum
6 Chitragupta Temple
7 Devi Jagadamba Temple
8 Eastern Group
9 Khajuraho Temples
10 Nandi Shrine
11 Parsvanath Temple
12 Varaha Shrine
13 Western Group

SLEEPING
14 Dakghar 606
15 Hotel Harmony
16 Hotel Surya

EATING
see 16 Guru Kripa Restaurant
17 Pinch of Salt
18 Raja Cafe
19 Zaheer Paratha & Lassi Corner

INFORMATION
20 Tourist Interpretation & Facilitation Centre

TRANSPORT
see 19 Bilal Bikes

temples. It's worth a visit to add context to your temple experience and features several galleries of Khajuraho sculptures and information panels on Chandela history and art. The nearby **Aadivart Tribal & Folk Museum** *(aadivartmuseum.in; ₹400; noon-9pm, closed Mon)* showcases central India's rich tribal arts through decorative installations.

TOP TIP

MP Tourism's **Tourist Interpretation & Facilitation Centre** on Main Rd between the Aadivart Tribal & Folk Museum and the Archaeological Museum is both friendly and helpful – a welcome change of pace from most city tourism offices.

EATING IN KHAJURAHO: OUR PICKS

Zaheer Paratha & Lassi Corner: This shack draws droves with its lovely chai, refreshing lassi and Zaheer's speciality: stuffed *paratha* (flaky flatbread). *8am-9pm* ₹

Guru Kripa Restaurant: Small, Jain-run restaurant, presenting tasty thalis and a range of North Indian dishes with aplomb. *8.30am-10.30pm* ₹

Raja Cafe: Under a 200-year-old neem tree, this is Khajuraho's top spot for international fare (French toast, fried chicken, pizza) and espresso. *8am-10pm* ₹₹

Pinch of Salt: Khajuraho's nicest independent dining room with bamboo furniture and tribal art on earthen walls. Excellent North Indian dishes. *9.30am-10.30pm* ₹₹

GTW/SHUTTERSTOCK

Lakshmana Temple

TOP EXPERIENCE

Khajuraho Temples

Sex sells and nobody knew that more than the Chandelas, a central Indian ruling dynasty that slathered the temples at Khajuraho with embellished carvings of erotica mostly between 950 and 1100 CE. Khajuraho's eyebrow-raising, UNESCO World Heritage–listed sanctuaries – especially the astounding Western Group – are some of the world's best-preserved temple art.

DON'T MISS

- Lakshmana Temple
- Kandariya-Mahadev Temple
- Vishvanath Temple
- Chitragupta Temple
- Varaha Shrine
- Parsvanath Temple
- Duladeo Temple
- Chaturbhuj Temple

Planning & Orientation

Khajuraho's UNESCO-listed temples fall into three groups: the most famous **Western Group**, which houses the most striking and best-preserved temples, is in the town centre; the **Eastern Group**, is located in the old village, 1.5km or so from the Western Group; and the **Southern Group** is a further 1km south of the Eastern Group. The Eastern and Southern Groups pale in comparison to the Western Group but are worth exploring for those on a deep dive.

PRACTICALITIES

- mptourism.com/destination-khajuraho.php
- ₹600
- sunrise-sunset

Western Group

The fenced-off Western Group of temples are Khajuraho's most striking and most intact, and are arranged in an uncomplicated square pattern that makes for easy navigating. After entering the complex, turn to your right and head over first to the **Varaha Shrine**; inside, an intricately chiselled sandstone carving of Vishnu as his boar avatar (incarnation) stands 1.5m high. Just in front of the shrine, the **Lakshmana Temple** (954 CE) is arguably the best-preserved of all the Khajuraho temples. The orgiastic carvings on the southern side of its base are sure to make the most modest among us blush: a nine-person orgy is followed by man-and-horse bestiality. From here, it's an easy clockwise walk around the complex.

Next up is the 30.5m-long **Kandariya-Mahadev Temple**, the Western Group's largest temple. Built between 1025 and 1050 CE, it is considered the pinnacle of Chandela architecture and is graced with representations of female beauty and sexual acrobatics (some 872 statues in all). Don't miss the gorgeous *sardula* (part-lion, part-human mythical beast) snuggling with a nymph between the Kandariya-Mahadev Temple and **Devi Jagadamba Temple**. At the northwest corner, **Chitragupta Temple** is dedicated to the sun god Surya, a rarity in North Indian temples. Elephant fights and hunting scenes grace its lowest band of reliefs while inside you can spot a tiny sculpture of seven horses pulling Surya's chariot. Lastly, the carvings of **Vishvanath Temple** run the gamut: letter-writing *surasundari*, cuddling babies and miniature camels. The adjacent **Nandi Shrine** houses an impressive 2.2m-long Nandi, Shiva's bull-vehicle.

Eastern & Southern Groups

Temples outside the fenced-in enclosure don't get anywhere near the love that's showered upon the Western Group, but there are worthwhile shrines here. Jain temples dominate the Eastern Group, most notably the largest among them, **Parsvanath Temple**. The exterior walls feature many Hindu deities, suggesting that they were initially built as Hindu temples before being adopted by the Jain community in the 10th century. Some of the best-preserved examples of Khajuraho's most famous images can be seen here, including a woman removing a thorn from her foot and another applying eye makeup (both on the southern side). The Shiva-dedicated **Duladeo Temple**, the highlight of the Southern Group, was among the last of Khajuraho's 85 original temples to be constructed, dating to 1100–50. Of particular note is the lingam (phallic image of Shiva), which features 999 additional linga carved into its base. Another 1.6km away, the **Chaturbhuj Temple** (also part of the Southern Group) is dedicated to Vishnu, whose towering 2.7m four-armed idol has an expressive face and graceful form. The temple dates to 1100 and is the only one in Khajuraho without any erotic sculptures.

TEMPLE PRIMER

Khajuraho's carvings are not just about the erotica (which constitutes barely 5% to 7% of the sculptures). The temples are superb examples of North Indian architecture and Nagara-style symbolism, banded by artistic stonework showing a storyboard of life a millennium ago – deities, warriors, dancers and animals among them – and the majority of carvings focus on more mundane aspects of life.

TOP TIPS

- You must purchase tickets *(₹600)* online.
- Hiring an official licensed guide from near the ticket office *(₹2500/3250 half/full day for up to 5 people)* is highly advisable.
- The three groups of temples are spread out. Hire an autorickshaw or car to get around *(₹750 & ₹1250 respectively for half day sightseeing)*.
- The Western Group of temples are particularly spectacular at sunset.
- Wear shoes that slip on and off easily – you'll be removing them a lot.
- A nightly sound-and-light show *(₹800)* takes place in English at 6.30pm.
- Inclusive tourism agency **Planet Abled** *(planetabled.com)* offers a customised accessible tour at Khajuraho.

Beyond Khajuraho

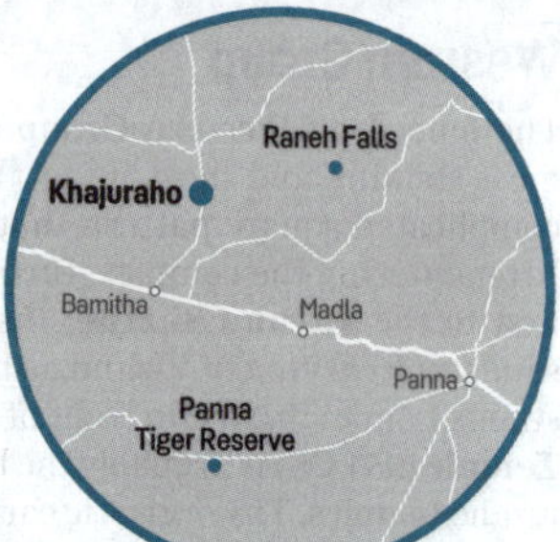

Nature abounds around Khajuraho, where a land of river-cut canyons, plummeting waterfalls and tiger-roamed reserves offers sanctuary for eager outdoorsy types.

Places

Raneh Falls p602
Panna Tiger Reserve p603

GETTING AROUND

You will need to arrange transport both for Raneh Falls, 20km northeast of Khajuraho, and Panna Tiger Reserve, 27km to the southeast. Autorickshaws can transport you to Raneh; for Panna, hire a taxi from your hotel. Within Panna Tiger Reserve, use of a park-registered safari 4WD is mandatory. Safaris can be arranged through the Karnavati Interpretation Centre, 1km from Madla gate, via an agency such as **The Tiger Safari** *(thetigersafari.com)* or your accommodation.

Khajuraho isn't the most notably positioned destination for excursions beyond the village, but a few adventures await should you want a change of scenery from the town's captivating temple art. Raneh Falls, within autorickshaw distance of the village, is the most obvious choice, just a short ride to the northeast. The series of waterfalls in a 30m-deep canyon carved by the Ken River is especially worthwhile after a hard rain. A visit here includes admission to the gharial-protecting Ken Gharial Sanctuary, rounding out a notable day of nature. Panna Tiger Reserve, entered via the village of Madla (a 30-minute drive southeast), is one of eastern Madhya Pradesh's most pleasant tiger parks, not only for big cats but for birding as well.

Raneh Falls

TIME FROM KHAJURAHO: **35MIN**

Waterfalls cascading down a canyon

An easy half-day trip from Khajuraho, **Raneh Falls**, a series of waterfalls in a 30m-deep canyon carved by the Ken River, sit 21km east of town. From Khajuraho, autorickshaws charge between ₹600 and ₹1000 for the round trip, depending on your negotiating skills. The falls' viewpoint is located about 3km from the ticket window from where you can walk, bike or drive; entry fees start from ₹55 (₹330 if you have a car) plus ₹200 for a mandatory guide. The falls are at their mightiest in monsoon season (when you are not likely to be here), but at other times of year the canyon makes for a worthwhile nature excursion at any rate. Look down from the viewpoint and you can see the crater of a millennia-old volcano, while all around it the river-forged canyon is adorned with varying shades of colour, from grey and brown to pink and red. The colours come from granite, dolomite, basalt, quartz and jasper that make up the 5km-long igneous rock canyon.

Spot crocodiles in the river

The Raneh Falls' entry fee includes the nearby **Ken Gharial Sanctuary**, a reserve protecting gharials (critically endangered crocodilians with long, slender snouts that feed exclusively on fish). The viewpoint is 8km from the ticket window.

Along the way, you will probably encounter langurs, spotter deer and sambar deer, not to mention the odd cow. From the viewpoint, the river below shines a bright blue; scan the riverbank and the odd rock in the river to look for the placidly sunbathing gharials. Their muddy brown colour and scaly backs help them blend into their surroundings effortlessly; bring binoculars for a better chance of spotting them as well as muggers (marsh crocodiles) that inhabit the river.

Panna Tiger Reserve

TIME FROM KHAJURAHO: **30MIN**

Track tigers on an uncrowded safari

Southeast of Khajuraho, the **Panna Tiger Reserve** *(weekday/weekend ₹8630/9950)* draws nowhere near the crowds of the trio of tiger reserves around Jabalpur (p615); as a result, safari seats are (relatively) easier to come by. However, that's changing rapidly as the tiger population increases and sightings improve, drawing more visitors. The reserve's core zone is within Panna National Park, 543 sq km of beautiful forests and grasslands, with the crocodile-inhabited Ken (Karnavati) River flowing through it. Poachers had decimated the tiger population here in the late 20th century, but a 2009 reintroduction has gone well, with an estimated 80 tigers now calling the reserve home. The park is also home to leopards and sloth bears, but its birdlife is the biggest draw outside of the striped kitties. Over 200 species are recorded here, including many waterbirds not easily seen in other parks, as well as vultures that nest on the vertical craggy cliffs lining Ken River.

You can also head out in a small boat on the river *(15min boat ride ₹600)*. Time your boat ride to the last hour of your safari; by then the sun will be high up and the crocs will be out sunbathing on the riverbed rocks. Keep an eye out for birds (we spotted a pair of beautiful pied kingfishers), and if you'revery lucky, you may even see a tiger.

WANT TO TRACK MORE TIGERS?

Madhya Pradesh is home to India's highest concentration of tigers. If you're looking to see more, head straight to Jabalpur, 229km south of Panna, the jumping-off point for the big three reserves: **Bandhavgarh** (p618), **Kanha** (p619) and **Pench** (p620).

A FEW DAYS AROUND KHAJURAHO

Yashaswani Bhayal, owner of the Dakghar 606 (p626; *dakghar606.com)* boutique hotel, has lived in Khajuraho for 30 years. These are her greatest hits. *@yashaswanibhayal*

Your culinary journey centres around Raja Cafe's (p599) delectable pizzas and a fusion of continental and Indian dishes. A 25-minute drive will take you to **Bundeli Bakhri** in Madla, ideal for savouring authentic local cuisine. Explore ancient cave paintings at **Brihaspati Kund**, witnessing the majestic waterfall; and discover the wonders of **Bhimkund** (natural water tank), both around Khajuraho. Mandatory visits to the Panna Tiger Reserve and a boat ride along the Ken River paint a vibrant portrait of Khajuraho and the Bundelkhand region.

Bhopal

MUSEUMS | MOSQUES | LAKES

You may have heard of Bhopal as the site of the worst industrial disaster the world has ever known. In 1984, a methyl isocyanate (MIC) gas leak from the Union Carbide plant 3km north of the old city killed some 25,000 people (and counting). Madhya Pradesh's bustling capital isn't immediately lovable – it's mainly used by travellers as a transport hub for the UNESCO-listed Buddhist monuments at Sanchi – but Bhopal still has plenty to offer. Founded by Raja Bhoj, a king of Malwa (western Madhya Pradesh and southeast Rajasthan) in the 11th century, Bhopal has seen its share of conquests, plunder and rebirth throughout the centuries. Today, it's home to fascinating museums and a rich, Indo-Islamic tapestry woven throughout the city. Two attractive lakes, the massive Upper Lake and the more modest Lower Lake, cut the city in two and lend an air of distinction to Bhopal that's palpably different from more typical, river-focused Indian cities.

GETTING AROUND

About 4km separates Bhopal's old city, a labyrinthine area of mosques and bazaars, and its more modern counterpart, known as New Market, with a pair of lakes splitting the difference. Buses and autorickshaws shuffle between the two day and night but rideshare app drivers from Uber and Ola are plentiful and cheap. Bhopal's forthcoming Bhoj metro is under construction, and its inaugural Orange Line is slated to be operational by the end of 2026.

TOP TIP

Head to Bhopal's biggest mosque, Taj-ul-Masjid, in the early morning and you are likely to have the place to yourself – even on Fridays. The empty courtyard lends itself beautifully to photos of the mosque reflected in the central ablution tank.

Queen Bee

Begums who'd built a city

From 1819 to 1926, four formidable begums (queens) – Qudsiya Begum, Sikander Jahan Begum, Shah Jahan Begum and Sultan Jahan Begum – ruled over Bhopal, building not just opulent palaces and grand mosques but also schools, hospitals and the city's first railways and waterworks. In 1877, Shah Jahan Begum broke ground on **Taj-ul-Masjid** *(darululoomtajul masajid.in; free)*, which took a century to complete. Today, India's biggest mosque sits pretty in pink, with a 99-sq-metre courtyard and a prayer hall with 27 scalloped ceiling domes and three gleaming eggshell-like domes on top, all overlooked by two towering minarets. Starting off here, it's an easy 1.1km walk southeast; stop for chai and *jalebi* (orange-coloured coils of deep-fried batter dunked in sugar syrup) at the **Raju Tea Stall** en route to the far smaller **Moti Masjid** *(free)*. Built by Sikander Jahan in 1860, this replica of Delhi's Jama Masjid

★ **HIGHLIGHTS**
1 Madhya Pradesh Tribal Museum
2 State Museum
3 Taj-ul-Masjid

SIGHTS
4 Jama Masjid
5 Kamla Park
6 Moti Masjid
7 Raja Bhoj Statue

ACTIVITIES
8 MP Tourism Boat Club

SLEEPING
9 Jehan Numa Palace Hotel
10 Sonali Regency
11 Ten Suites

EATING
12 Bapu Ki Kutia
13 Manohar
see 9 Under the Mango Tree
14 Wind & Waves
15 Zam Zam

DRINKING & NIGHTLIFE
16 Raju Tea Stall

SHOPPING
17 Chowk

A PERFECT DAY IN BHOPAL

Sonia Rashid is a ceramicist at Koozagari Pottery Studio and the organiser of the Bhopal Potters Market *(@bhopalpottersmarket)*. *@koozagaripottery*

Start with an early-morning walk in **Van Vihar National Park**, Bhopal's small game sanctuary. The road winds between the lake and the forested hills. Follow this up with breakfast at the **Jehan Numa Retreat**. Spend the rest of the day visiting the **Madhya Pradesh Tribal Museum** and the **Chowk**, the old city market around Bhopal's oldest mosque, **Jama Masjid**. Watch the sunset over the Bhopal lake from **Wind & Waves** cafe and enjoy the hustle and bustle of the **Boat Club**. Your finale? **Under the Mango Tree** for excellent Indian cuisine.

is a stunning white marble and red sandstone edifice. Both mosques are open to visitors daily from sunrise to sunset; dress modestly and bring a scarf to cover your head.

History Lessons

Explore the State Museum

Step back in time at Bhopal's **State Museum** *(mptourism.com; ₹400/free adult/child under 15; 10.30am-5.30pm, closed Mon),* a first-class archaeological museum housing multiple galleries ranging from weaponry to ancient Sanskrit manuscripts to postage stamps. Don't miss the 87 10th- and 11th-century Jain bronzes unearthed by a surprised farmer in western Madhya Pradesh, or the 19th-century Rajput, Maratha and Mughal miniature paintings. A new VR Experience Centre offers an immersive journey *(from ₹99)* through the state's heritage sites.

Lore of the Land

Dive into MP's tribal culture

Right next to the State Museum stands the fantastic **Madhya Pradesh Tribal Museum** *(mptribalmuseum.com; ₹400/free adult/child under 10; camera ₹100; noon-8pm, to 7pm Nov-Jan, closed Mon)* dedicated to the tribal people who make up over 20% of the state's population. Inside, to-scale models of Gond and Bhil houses, a decorative wedding pillar, a larger-than-life ceremonial bangle and terracotta funerary votives place you directly into the lives of the communities they evoke.

Still Waters

Scenic lake views

An evening stroll by the Upper Lake is a must-do; there are plenty of small parks and viewpoints along the periphery, including one near a massive **Raja Bhoj Statue**. Nearby, **Kamla Park** *(6am-8pm)* overlooks the Lower Lake.

EATING IN BHOPAL: OUR PICKS

Manohar: Upper-scale cafeteria serving top South Indian breakfasts; order the Mysore masala dosa if you are craving heat. *8am-11pm* ₹

Zam Zam: Fast-food icon. Bhopal's best biryani and even better spicy chicken tikka, grilled over hot coals. *10am-midnight* ₹

Bapu Ki Kutia: Wildly popular lunch icon (thalis from ₹220 to ₹320). No English sign (spy the beach hut and palm tree). *10am-11pm* ₹₹

Under the Mango Tree: Bhopal's best does succulent North Indian barbecue in a mango-tree-flanked garden. *7-11pm* ₹₹₹

Beyond Bhopal

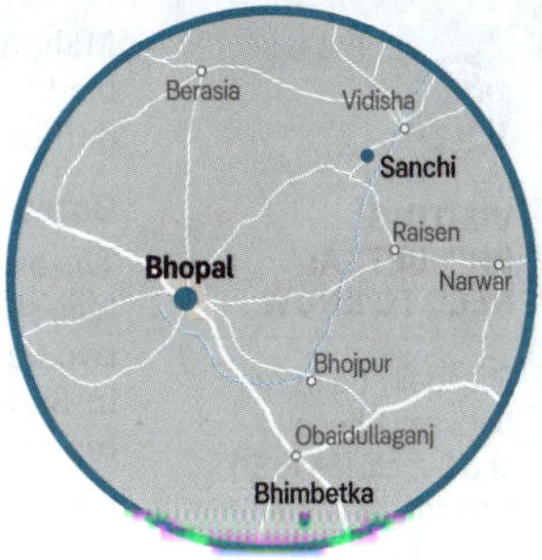

Two UNESCO World Heritage Sites sit within striking distance of Bhopal – Sanchi's 3rd-century BCE Buddhist monuments and Bhimbetka's Mesolithic-era rock paintings.

Ashoka the Great embraced Buddhism after the horrors he had inflicted on Kalinga (Odisha) during the Kalinga War (261 BCE). As penance, he built the Great Stupa at Sanchi, 49km northeast of Bhopal. Sanchi was all but abandoned after the 13th century, but systematic excavations in the early 1900s by archaeologist Sir John Marshall brought it back to life. The rock shelters of Bhimbetka, 45km southeast of Bhopal, were discovered by accident in the 1950s by archaeologist VS Wakankar. Since then, 750 rock shelters – embedded in sandstone and spread over seven hills – have been identified, many with primitive cave paintings. The earliest paintings date to 10,000 BCE, making it the oldest-known rock art in India.

Places

Sanchi p607
Bhimbetka p608

GETTING AROUND

Sanchi is a tiny village that can easily be seen on two feet unless you can't be bothered to climb the 768m (exactly that, according to the sign) uphill to the Buddhist monuments. Autorickshaws ply the route between the train station and the monuments looking for fares. Bhimbetka's roughly 1.5km-long trail winding through the rock shelters can only be accessed on foot, but it is largely paved, with some rock-cut steps to navigate.

Sanchi

TIME FROM BHOPAL: 1½HR

Historic hilltop monuments

The UNESCO World Heritage-listed **Buddhist monuments** *(mptourism.com; ₹600/free adult/child under 15)* at Sanchi sit perched on a hill 900m up the main road; take an autorickshaw (₹50) if you don't want to walk. The compact site takes about an hour to cover; licensed guides *(1-5 people ₹2200)* wait by the entrance.

The showstopper

Take a closer look on the reverse side of a ₹200 banknote – the perfectly proportioned rotundity of the **Great Stupa**, flanked by four incredibly intricate *torana* (gateways), features prominently on it. The stupa was originally constructed by Ashoka in the 3rd century BCE, before being enlarged a century later; the original brick stupa was enclosed within a stone one. Today it measures 16m high and 37m in diameter. A sweeping staircase takes you up the stupa for an up-close view of the dome and gateways.

Beyond the centrepiece

Other worthwhile stupas include the 2nd-century BCE **Stupa 3**, on your left as you approach the Great Stupa; it resembles the Great Stupa in design (albeit smaller). It once contained relics of two important disciples of Buddha: Sariputtra and

VISITING BHIMBETKA: NEED TO KNOW

Four daily trains run between Bhopal and Sanchi (35 to 50 minutes, from ₹150). Alternatively, you can catch a bus (1½ to two hours) from the **Nadra Bus Stand** (Old Bus Stand; half-hourly 1.30am to 9.30pm; ₹70) or hire an Uber (₹1200 or so).

If you're going up to the stupa for sunrise, buy a ticket the day before.

Hoshangabad-bound buses (₹70) from the Nadra Bus Stand will drop you on the highway about 4km from Bhimbetka. From here you can walk (not recommended) or hitch a ride at your own risk; there are no taxis or autorickshaws that ply the route.

It's best to hire a private taxi from Bhopal to Bhimbetka (about ₹2000 for the round trip).

Mahamoglayan. **Stupa 2**, a 240m walk downhill along a cobbled staircase from Monastery 51, showcases chiselled medallions, with flowers, animals and people ringing the stupa.

Gateway grandeur

The breathtaking *torana* flanking the Great Stupa are Sanchi's true shining moment. Consisting of three horizontal bars and two vertical pillars on the top, each depicts various events in Buddha's life. The best-preserved **Northern Gateway** is topped by a broken wheel of law. The **Southern Gateway** narrates Ashoka's life as a Buddhist.

Museum matters

Don't miss visiting the **Sanchi Archaeological Museum** *(₹5; closed Fri)*, which displays archaeological finds from the site, including a 3rd-century-BCE lions-on-lotus capital from the Ashoka Pillar.

Bhimbetka

TIME FROM BHOPAL: 1HR

Back to the Stone Age

Located inside Ratapani Wildlife Sanctuary, the **Bhimbetka Rock Shelters** *(mptourism.com; free; ₹165 per vehicle)* exhibit the earliest traces of human life in India, and provide clear evidence of Stone Age activity at the site. While the rock shelters are distributed over 10km, only a few are open to visitors, organised around a well-marked trail that takes about an hour to complete. Stone plaques give adequate information, but licensed guides *(1-5 people ₹2200)* at the entrance provide additional context.

A sandstone labyrinth

Shaped by wind and rain, the sandstone towers present a surreal picture. When you step inside the so-called **Auditorium Cave**, with its soaring, seemingly Gothic arches, the cavernous chamber feels like an ancient cathedral. Further along the trail, more rock-cut shelters appear, leaving you to imagine how people lived in these caves 30,000 years ago.

Prehistoric art trail

Within these rock shelters, walls have been turned into canvas, depicting scenes of hunting, festivities and war, and even a child's handprint in the Auditorium Cave. The aptly named **Zoo Rock** (rock shelter 4) has some 250 naturalistic animal drawings like deer, elephant, leopard, buffalo, bear and boar. A rudimentary flowerpot in rock shelter 9 could very well be a precursor to van Gogh's *Sunflowers*!

Indore

HOLKAR HISTORY | STREET FOOD | BIG-CITY BUZZ

Vibrant Indore is Madhya Pradesh's biggest city, a fun and fast-paced commercial juggernaut that feels downright cosmopolitan in comparison with the state's other large cities. Founded on the banks of the Kanh and Saraswati Rivers as a 16th-century trading hub between the Deccan plateau and Delhi, Indore rose to prominence with the Holkars, one of India's most powerful Maratha dynasties, beginning in the 18th century. Unfortunately, the Holkars left behind but a smattering of fine Indo-Saracenic palaces and other palatial run-down remnants, peppered about the old city, so most folks don't linger too long here on the way to more inviting environs, such as Mandu or Maheshwar. But Indore has topped India-wide surveys as India's cleanest city (the bar isn't high, honestly, but it does feel notably tidier) and its trendy shops and restaurants, excellent hotels and wonderful food scene warrant more than a passing glance.

Fried snacks, Sarafa Bazar (p611)

GETTING AROUND

Indore isn't the most pedestrian-friendly of cities. Rideshare apps like Uber and Ola remain the best mode of transport. However, for those who feel like hoofing it, Lal Bagh Palace to Rajwada palace is a healthy 2.5km walk. The best hotels and restaurants are considerably northeast of the centre and probably warrant four wheels. The inaugural Yellow Line of the Indore metro operates a limited route from the airport, and is expected to be fully operational by the end of 2026.

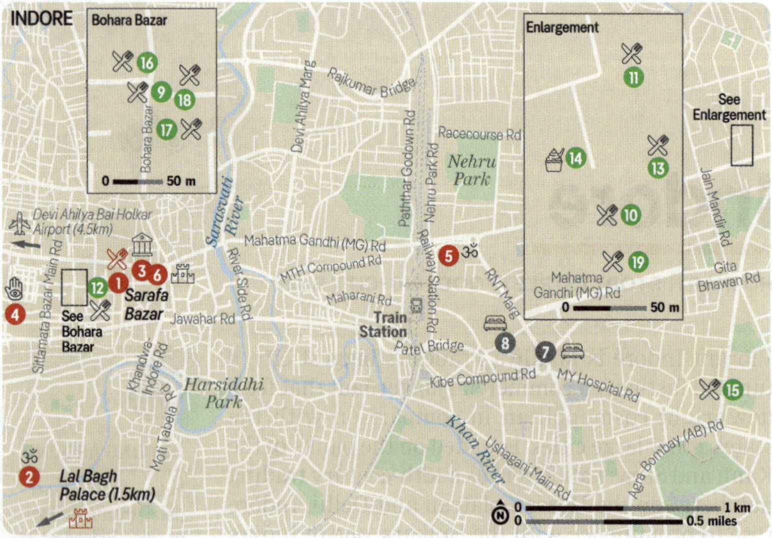

HIGHLIGHTS
1 Sarafa Bazar

SIGHTS
2 Chhatri Bagh
3 Holkar Gallery
4 Kaanch Mandir
5 Krishna Pura Chhatri
6 Rajwada

SLEEPING
7 Hotel Shreemaya
8 The Eden

EATING
9 Bhairavnath Mishthan Bhandar
10 Chappan Dukan
11 Johny Hot Dog
12 Joshi Dahi Bada House
13 Madhuram
14 Nema
15 Prashant Nashta Corner
16 Sawariya Seth
17 Sharmaji Chaatwaale
18 Suresh Chaat Centre
19 Vijay Chaat House

TOP TIP

Indore's Devi Ahilya Bai Holkar Airport is located 9km west of the city centre, but Indore's best hotels are located on the opposite side of town. With traffic snarls a constant in the old town, it can be a time-consuming cross-town jaunt. Plan airport trips accordingly.

Palatial Pursuits

Explore Indore's regal past

The Holkar dynasty ruled Indore from 1732 to 1947. They didn't leave much behind, but what did survive makes for a wonderful half-day of sightseeing. Two lions stand sentinel at the Lal Bagh Fair Grounds gates, past which you'll navigate a tree-lined promenade to reach **Lal Bagh Palace** *(mptourism.com; ₹400)*, the finest building left by the Holkars. The Italian Renaissance Revival–evoking structure, completed in 1926, is considered one of India's most exquisite neoclassical buildings (partially closed for restoration). Visitors may access a few of of the pastel-walled ornate rooms, some with elaborate ceiling frescoes.

The Holkars' original Indore palace, the seven-storey **Rajwada**, was completed in 1766 and features an epic Indo-Saracenic facade. You can enter the palace *(₹400)* to see the courtyard and the austere rooms, but the original exhibits have been moved to Indore's **Central Museum** *(₹400)*. Instead, make your way to the small temple on Rajwada's north side, which houses the **Holkar Gallery** *(₹100)*. It features biographies of Holkar rulers alongside artefacts including armour, religious figurines and utensils. Both palaces and the gallery are open 10am to 6pm (closed Monday).

A Night in the Bazar

Indore's street-food bonanza

A jewellery market just off Rajwada by day, **Sarafa Bazar** turns into a 300m-long nocturnal food-stall strip around 9pm (7pm on Sundays). Seek out local specialities like *bhutte ka kees* (grated maize sauteed with spices and herbs) at **Suresh Chaat Centre** and *sabudana khichdi* (soaked sago with spices, herbs and crushed peanuts) at **Sawariya Seth**. Watch **Joshi Dahi Bada House** toss their *dahi vada* (fried lentil balls soaked in yoghurt with spices) at heights that rival the best Neapolitan pizzaioli. Don't miss the *chhole tikiya* (ghee-fried potato topped with chickpeas, onions, crunchies and spices) at **Sharmaji Chaatwaale**. Dessert? Look no further than nearly world-famous **Bhairavnath Mishthan Bhandar**, aka Rabri Guru, for *rabri* (slow-cooked condensed milk with jaggery and spices).

If Sarafa doesn't satiate your street-food cravings, head to **Chappan Dukan** on MG Rd. This 200m-long open-air food court has 56 shops hawking delights such as *khopra patties* (crispy spiced potato stuffed with coconut and dried fruit) at **Vijay Chaat House**, *garadu* (deep-fried cubes of yam tossed with *chaat masala*, a winter speciality) at **Madhuram** and egg *benjo* (spicy omelette in a thick, soft bun) at **Johny Hot Dog**. End on a sweet note with **Nema**'s *kulfi* (frozen condensed milk dessert).

A PERFECT INDORE DAY

Akash Nagar is a wildlife photographer from Indore who spends eight months of the year in the jungle. *@akash_nagar_photography*

Start your day with breakfast at **Chappan Dukan**, Indore's fantastic street-food promenade. Visit historic sites like the **Rajwada**, **Krishna Pura Chhatri**, **Chhatri Bagh** and **Kaanch Mandir**, the Jain temple famed for its intricate glasswork. Head to the **Lal Bagh Palace** to admire its stunning architecture and lush gardens. Follow with a delicious lunch at **Nafees**, situated in Palasia. Next, visit the holy **Khajrana Ganesh Mandir**. In the evening, enjoy drinks at **Dhuaan**, the rooftop bar at **WOW Crest**, followed by an Indori dinner at **Sarafa Bazar** to complete your memorable day.

EATING IN INDORE: OUR PICKS

Prashant Nashta Corner: Iconic spot for Indori *poha*, a breakfast staple of steamed flattened rice topped with *sev* (crispy chickpea flour noodles). *7am-8.30pm Thu-Tue* ₹

Nafees: Legendary mutton (goat) kebabs, chicken Afghani and other rich curries, some with a Central Asian twist. *noon-11.30pm* ₹₹

Mr Beans: Sophisticated European-style cafe doing good espresso and excellent continental fare (sandwiches, pastas, salads). *10.30am-10.30pm* ₹₹₹

Mediterra: Mood-lit rooftop restaurant at Hotel Sayaji serving upscale global cuisine. Sit on the quieter southwest side for starry-eyed ambience. *7-11pm* ₹₹₹

Beyond Indore

Spiritual pilgrimages to holy riverside towns and a treasure trove of Indo-Islamic monuments lure tranquillity seekers out of bustling Indore.

Places

GETTING AROUND

Mandu is a lovely, slow-paced village that is easy to get around by autorickshaw. All the action in Maheshwar takes place along the Narmada River and is walkable – its sites of interest to travellers are clustered in a very compact area. Ujjain is Madhya Pradesh's fifth-largest city – autorickshaws are the way to go if you don't feel like walking (2km separates Ram Ghat from Mahakaleshwar Mandir, for example).

Indore is a wonderful place to refresh your batteries, but it is the trio of surrounding destinations that is the reason you have ventured here. Mandu (officially Mandav), perched on a pleasantly green 25-sq-km plateau 97km southwest of Indore, is a laid-back village spilling over with UNESCO-listed architectural treasures, many of Afghan origin. The relaxed rural setting is a wonderful place to hole up for a few days to ponder the mutation of the capital of a once-powerful kingdom into just another Indian village. Around 40km southeast of Mandu is Maheshwar, which, along with Ujjain (56km north of Indore), is a captivating pilgrimage destination centred on a holy river, *puja* (offerings) and all the enthralling ghat action that comes with both.

Ujjain

TIME FROM INDORE: 1½HR

On a temple trail

Ujjain is one of Hinduism's seven sacred cities. An electric energy pulses through its vivid melange of famed temples, old city alleyways and *puja* pilgrimages. The **Mahakal Lok Corridor** -adorned with stunning sculptures and mythological depictions – is a grand 900m pathway leading to the revered **Mahakaleshwar Mandir**. Drop behind the conga line through the underground chambers to pay your respects at one of India's 12 *jyoti linga* – naturally occurring, especially sacred shrines to Shiva. A ₹250 VIP ticket lets you enter through a separate gate and avoid the snaking queues, which can be quite long, particularly at *aarti* (auspicious lighting of lamps) times. Later, visit the ancient **Harsiddhi Mata Mandir** (1km away) and **Kal Bhairav Mandir** (6km away and dedicated to Ujjain's guardian deity) to complete the holy circuit.

Join devout pilgrims riverside

On the eastern bank of the Shipra River, **Ram Ghat**, Ujjain's central river ghat, sees steady streams of bathers and pilgrims offering gifts of milk or flowers to the river. Ujjain is one of the four cities that hosts the gigantic Kumbh Mela pilgrimage festival every 12 years. Next stop: 2028.

VINAYAK JAGTAP/SHUTTERSTOCK

Maheshwar Fort and Palace

Maheshwar

TIME FROM INDORE: **2HR**

Go on a spiritual quest

Think of the spiritual riverside town of Maheshwar, 97km southwest of Indore, as a smaller, less chaotic Varanasi, drawing sadhus (ascetics) and pilgrims to its ancient ghats and temples on the holy Narmada River. The best way to head down to the river is through the dominating **Maheshwar Fort and Palace**, dating to Emperor Akbar's days and later expanded upon by Queen Ahilyabai in the 18th century.

The area is divided into the posh Ahilya Fort (p626) hotel, public courtyards and the **Rajwada**, which has a small **gallery** *(₹300)* dedicated to the life of the queen, whose legacy looms large over the town. As you walk down to the river, you will pass **Ahilyeshwar Temple**, which has a shrine dedicated to Lord Rama and a *chhatri*, or memorial, to Ahilyabai. At the river, wander along the atmospheric ghats and consider a **boat ride** *(per person/boat ₹50/500)*. It all makes for an easy half day, but overnighting affords the chance to take in the magical river atmosphere at dawn and dusk; every evening at 8pm, locals and pilgrims perform *aarti* at **Narmada Ghat**.

A WEEKEND IN MAHESHWAR

Rashi Tulshyan is the co-owner of gourmet store and cafe Earthbox *(@byearthbox)*. When she needs a break from Indore, she heads for Maheshwar. *@barefoot_r*

Maheshwar is an ideal weekend getaway. Walk along the banks of the Narmada River, where you can easily find boats and reach **Baneshwar Temple** in the middle of the river. Then, explore the magnificent **Ahilya Fort** (p626), where you should also stay to enjoy the best river views and delicious meals in the hotel. Maheshwar is also a Maheshwari handloom hub. Don't forget to buy Maheshwari saris, suits and dupattas (long scarves) at **[illegible] Handloom**. Have a quick stop at **MPT Narmada Resort** for lunch and for evening snacks at **Labboo'z Cafe**.

EATING IN MAHESHWAR: OUR PICKS

Labboo'z Cafe: Top spot in Maheshwar; a tree-shaded courtyard cafe with snacks, light meals and simple thalis. *8am-8pm* ₹

Banke Bihari Bhojanalay: Steps from Narmada Ghat, this canteen offers wholesome thalis; relish them while seated on the floor. *noon-10pm* ₹

Raaj Bhog: Set 1.5km back from Maheshwar's river. Well-presented veg dishes in a welcoming bamboo structure. Friendly service. *10am-11pm* ₹₹

MPT Narmada Resort: Indian and Chinese staples shine at this river-facing restaurant with indoor and outdoor seating. *noon-3pm & 8-10pm* ₹₹₹

LOVE, INTERRUPTED

Mandu's most enduring legend is the tragic love story of Baz Bahadur, the last ruler of the Malwa Sultanate who reigned from 1555 to 1562, and his consort Roopmati, a beautiful shepherdess who agreed to accompany him to Mandu on the condition that her palace would be within sight of the Narmada River. Baz Bahadur built a hilltop pavilion in Mandu to fulfil her wish. Their idyllic life together was shattered when Emperor Akbar sent his forces to conquer Malwa. Baz Bahadur's small contingent was no match for the imperial army led by Adham Kham, and he fled in a desperate attempt to gather reinforcements. Left behind, Roopmati refused to be captured by the invaders, choosing instead to consume poison.

Weaving magic

Queen Ahilyabai encouraged the development of Maheshwar as a weaving hub, and under her patronage the lightweight cotton-silk Maheswari saris flourished. On your way to Ahilyeshwar Temple, pop into the handloom cooperative **Rehwa Society** to watch the weavers at work *(guided tour ₹250; closed Tue.*

Mandu

TIME FROM INDORE: **2HR**

Historic pre-Mughal monuments

A barrage of UNESCO World Heritage–listed palaces, tombs, monuments and mosques pepper picturesque Mandu, all of which are conveniently divided into three independently ticketed groups of monuments *(₹300 per group)* that are open from sunrise to sunset. Begin with the **Rewa Kund Group** where the 16th-century **Baz Bahadur Palace** stands in pale pink sandstone, curiously mixing Rajasthani and Mughal architectural styles. The gorgeous **Roopmati Pavilion** (a further 400m uphill) is set on a 366m escarpment and affords stunning countryside views.

About 4.5km north of Rewa Kund is the **Village Group**, highlighted by the massive 15th-century **Jami Masjid**, which is one of the finest and largest examples of Afghan architecture in India. Nearby, **Hoshang Shah's Tomb** stands as the oldest marble tomb in India, and was one of the inspirations for the Taj Mahal. Across the street, **Ashrafi Mahal** was a madrasa (Islamic college) constructed by Hoshang Shah; it also holds the tomb of Mahmud Khilji.

Continue 1.7km north to the **Royal Enclave**, which holds numerous 15th- and 16th-century Ghuri- and Khilji-dynasty masterpieces, none more striking than the **Jahaz Mahal**, built on a narrow strip of land between two water tanks. The compound also teems with other photogenic structures such as the **Hindola Mahal** with its sloping walls, **Jal Mahal** or Water Palace, **Champa Baodi** (step-well) and a three-room **Turkish Bath** with stars cut into the ceiling.

EATING IN MANDU: OUR PICKS

Restaurant Gurukripa: The service is not overly friendly, but this simple Mandu veg restaurant is dependable for tasty thalis. *9am-11.30pm* ₹

Hotel Phulwari: Just outside the Royal Enclave, this *dhaba* (casual eatery) specialises in *dal-paniya* (dung-fire-roasted maize bread, eaten with spicy lentil curry). *10am-9pm* ₹

Shivani Restaurant: Canteen-style diner with a vegetarian menu that includes solid thalis plus local specialities. *8am-10pm* ₹

Malwa Resort: Fantastic North Indian dishes, quality service and a cosy ambience. Mandu's best. *8-10am, noon-3pm & 7-10pm* ₹₹₹

Jabalpur

TIGER TRANSIT HUB | WATERFALLS | RIVERSIDE BOATING

Jabalpur is eastern Madhya Pradesh's biggest city and a formidable industrial and administrative hub. Though it's regularly referred to as Sanskardhani (Cultural City), most travellers linger here but a moment on their quest to see a tiger in the famed reserves nearby. However, the city is pleasant enough, albeit devoid of any sights that are going to get your heart racing like a Royal Bengal tiger sighting in the wild. But during British rule, 'Jubbulpore' was an important holiday destination, and the city gave birth to the game of snooker when officers stationed in town decided to shake things up a bit by adding coloured balls to black pool. These days, domestic tourists have long-flocked to this industrial city of *chowks* (market areas) and working-men's taverns for Marble Rocks, an attractive river gorge nearby, and Dhuandhar Falls. There's no reason why foreigners shouldn't visit them either – both are worthwhile stops to/from the tiger reserves.

TOP TIP

The tiger reserves can be visited independently, but there are head-spinning logistics and bureaucracy involved. Save yourself the time and hassle by contacting an agency such as highly recommended Jabalpur-based **The Tiger Safari** *(thetigersafari.com)*.

GETTING AROUND

Most sites of interest to travellers (budget and lower midrange hotels, good restaurants) cluster around the Russel Chowk and Napier Town areas about 1km or so southeast of the town centre. Within this area, most things are walkable. Negotiating skills can get you an autorickshaw from Jabalpur train station or ISBT (bus stand) to Russel Chowk for around ₹50 and ₹120, respectively. Marble Rocks, Dhuandhar Falls and sites around town and further afield are easily reachable using public transport or a private taxi.

SIGHTS
1 Kamaniya Gate

ACTIVITIES
2 Tiger Safari

SLEEPING
3 Kalchuri Residency
4 Rishi Regency

EATING
5 Hytte By Samrat
6 Indian Coffee House
7 Indore Sweets
8 Saheb's Food Junction
9 The Mutton King

TRANSPORT
10 Jabalpur Train Station

Thundering Cascade

Behold the majestic Dhuandhar Falls

Jabalpur itself offers few heavy-hitting sights, but step outside its boundaries and you'll find the city is surrounded by some interesting natural attractions. Just outside the city limits, about 18km west of the centre, **Dhuandhar Falls** *(mptourism.com; free entry on foot, ₹60 for car entry ; 6am-8pm)* is an absolute don't-miss for anyone traversing through Jabalpur. The name comes from two Hindi words – *dhuan* (smoke) and *dhar* meaning flow of water. True to its name, the waterfall creates a smoky mist, coupled with a loud roaring sound as it plunges down 30m. You can get up close and personal with the falls by walking down to the east bank of the Narmada River, past a 1.2km maze of trinket and street-food stalls. Get ready to be drenched by the spray; bring a poncho or a change of clothes. A separate VIP entrance lets you drive right up to the viewing point for ₹250.

A Bird's-Eye View

Take a cable-car ride

The best view of the Dhuandhar Falls comes courtesy of the **Narmada Ropeway** *(round trip ₹145, children under 3yr free; ticket counter 10.30am-6pm, closed 1.30-2pm)*, a cable car system that will transport you in less than five minutes over the falls to the west bank of the river. Sit on the left of the cable car for a spectacular view. Hop off on the west bank where a viewpoint affords a different perspective of the falls. The ropeway may be suspended during peak monsoon season.

INDIA_TRAVELGRAM/SHUTTERSTOCK

Marble Rocks

Rock of Ages

Cruising the River Narmada

About 1km downstream from the falls, India's oldest river chisels through a beautiful gorge known as **Marble Rocks**, where a set of magnesium-limestone cliffs change colours in different light, from white to pink to black. Admire their rugged beauty on a 30-minute boat ride; services run sunrise to sunset from mid-October to mid-June (dates vary). The **Panchvati Ghat** boating site is accessible by 100-odd steps descending from the main road; a lift from **Marble Cafe** offers a return ride at ₹50 but is often out of service. The boat operators are quite pushy and will swarm around you offering their services; purchase a ticket *(from ₹100)* at the designated counter to avoid getting fleeced.

JABALPUR CONNOISSEUR

Saptarishi Saigal, co-owner of The Tiger Safari *(thetigersafari.com)*, is a born-and-raised Jabalpuriya. *@rishisaigal*

Start your morning with a South Indian breakfast at **Indian Coffee House** or try the *jalebi* at **Indore Sweets**, both in Sadar Bazaar. Visit **Dhuandhar Falls** and enjoy boating along the Narmada River flowing through the **Marble Rocks**. In the evening, visit **Gwarighat** and witness theNarmada *aarti* (ritual chanting and worship with oil lamps) at 7pm to take in the city's spiritual side. Pay a visit to **Kamaniya Gate** after 10pm for a street-food dinner. Try *gatpat, dahi papdi* and *aloo tikki,* and finish up with a sweet *malai* roll and hot *kesar* milk. That's a perfect day in Jabalpur.

EATING IN JABALPUR: OUR PICKS

The Mutton King: It is impossible to saunter by the red chicken *shawarma* (₹125) at this elevated food stall and not bite. Rightfully so. *6-11pm* ₹

Indian Coffee House: The nicest and freshest of Jabalpur's many ICHs (Sadar location); great South Indian breakfast, filter coffee and more. *7am-11pm* ₹

Saheb's Food Junction: Looks-wise it doesn't inspire confidence, but Saheb satisfies with its Mughlai curries – fiery if you ask! *11am-11pm* ₹₹

Hytte By Samrat: Buzzing rooftop spot with cocktails and an encyclopaedic multicuisine menu; North Indian is your best bet. *1-11pm* ₹₹₹

Beyond Jabalpur

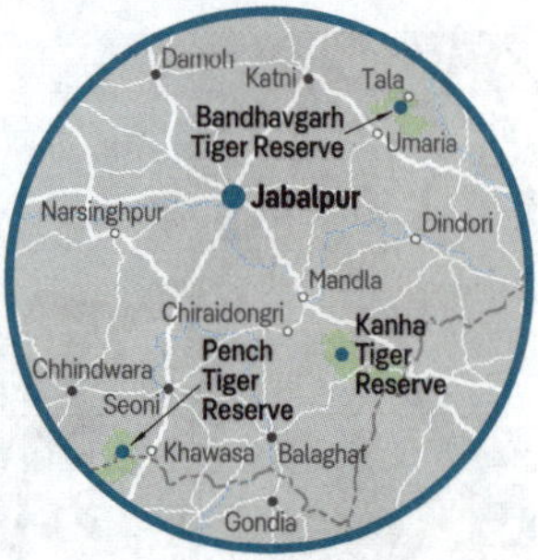

The highest concentration of tigers in the world roar in the three famed Madhya Pradesh tiger parks outside Jabalpur.

Places

Bandhavgarh Tiger Reserve p618
Kanha Tiger Reserve p619
Pench Tiger Reserve p620

Jabalpur is uniquely positioned within striking distance of a an incredible trifecta of India's principal tiger reserves: Kanha, Bandhavgarh and Pench, all sit three to four hours' drive from the city. The first is the most famous (thanks to a setting familiar the world over via Rudyard Kipling's *The Jungle Book* duology), but it's Bandhavgarh that draws the crowds for one simple reason: it's quite easy to spot a tiger. India is home to 70% of the world's tiger population and Jabalpur's surrounds hoard the lion's share (pun intended). If a tiger never materialises, fret not – all three parks are lush, protected forest habitats that yield a rewarding arsenal of mammalian and avian wildlife-spotting opportunities.

GETTING AROUND

It is possible to visit the tiger reserves via public transport, but you are far better off hiring a car and driver, especially if you want to see multiple parks. Within the boundaries of the parks themselves, you cannot stroll around on your own – a park-registered 4WD is required for obvious safety reasons. You will have to choose between a shared canter (18-seat open minibus) or shared/private six-passenger 4WDs (known as Gypsies).

Royal Bengal Tiger Safaris

Easy, tiger!

Madhya Pradesh is home to India's highest concentration of tigers (785 per the 2023 census), most of which roam in the state's three famed tiger reserves around Jabalpur: Bandhavgarh Tiger Reserve, Kanha Tiger Reserve and Pench Tiger Reserve (p620). The best months for tiger sightings are February to June (although temperatures often climb above 40°C between April and June). It is possible to visit all the parks independently, but you are better off hiring a car and driver for travel logistics and getting an agency or your accommodation to handle safari bureaucracy and ticketing. Upmarket hotels pre-secure safari slots to guarantee space for their guests, dramatically reducing the number of tickets available to independent travellers. When you do go, one of the world's great wildlife experiences awaits, so be sure to settle in for two to three days at one park (or one to two days each at multiple parks). And even if you don't see a tiger, you might see leopards, wild boar, gaur (Indian bison), spotted deer and langurs – we even saw the elusive sloth bear in Kanha!

Bandhavgarh Tiger Reserve

TIME FROM JABALPUR: 4½HR

Spot the tiger

The king of MP tiger habitats, the Bandhavgarh Tiger Reserve, 170km northeast of Jabalpur, is the place to come if

SOURABH BHARTI/SHUTTERSTOCK

Bandhavgarh Tiger Reserve

your sole reason for visiting an Indian tiger reserve is to see a tiger, fast. Tiny Tala, 32km northeast of the nearest train station at Umaria, is the main base for visiting the park and from where all safaris begin.

The park is divided into three core zones: **Tala** (entered from the village itself), **Khitauli** and **Maghdi** (or Magadhi), about 5.5km and 6km southwest of Tala along the Umaria road, respectively. Tiger hotspots such as the grassy lawn at Chakradhara (Tala) or watering holes like Sukhi Patiha (Maghdi) and Nigah Nala (Khiltauli) are excellent for producing that mesmerising tiger sighting you're after. Bandhavgarh is justifiably very popular – tiger sightings are frequent. While tigers are not tracked electronically with chips or collars in Madhya Pradesh (scientists instead employ DNA analysis of tiger droppings as well as stripe pattern comparison from camera traps), word travels fast when a tiger is spotted. You may get a brief respite alone with a tiger, but the scene will soon be besieged with Gypsies full of tourists falling over each other for that perfect social media post. That's not to say it doesn't happen at the other parks, but at Bandhavgarh it's especially noticeable.

Kanha Tiger Reserve

TIME FROM JABALPUR: **3HR**

Home of *The Jungle Book*

British author Rudyard Kipling called on the famed forests of the Kanha Tiger Reserve, 135km southeast of Jabalpur, as the setting for his celebrated children's story *The Jungle Book* (1894), and, as such, Kanha is the most internationally recognised of Madhya Pradesh's notable tiger parks. Kanha's sal forests and expansive meadows are far easier on the eye than Bandhavgarh. In addition to tigers, leopards and huge

TIGER SAFARI PLANNING: PART I

Make arrangements as far ahead as possible, as safaris can sell out months in advance.

There are no core zone safaris on Wednesday afternoons.

A finite number of six-passenger safari 4WDs (Gypsies) are allowed in the parks per day, but most can only be booked online *(forest.mponline.gov.in; up to 120 days in advance)* and the website does not accept foreign cards for payment. Paying a hotel or agency to book your safari (typically an additional ₹1000) is the way to go.

A few safari spots can be purchased in person at the gates and/or ticket counters the evening before, but queues can be long and monopolised by locals being paid to hold someone's place.

TIGER SAFARI PLANNING: PART II

Madhya Pradesh foreigner safari prices: ₹5330 entry ticket (an extra ₹1320 on weekends), plus ₹3500 for the Gypsy and ₹1000 for a mandatory guide.

Morning safaris generally start around 6.15am (varies by season), run longer than afternoon safaris (starting at 3pm) and tend to yield more tiger sightings.

Single-seat Gypsy tickets can be purchased (₹900, ₹1110 on weekends), but it's messy; not recommended!

If traditional 4WD safaris are sold out, lumbering, 18-seat open minibuses known as canters are a last-resort option.

Resorts offer the so-called 'American Plan' (includes accommodation and all meals) while the 'Jungle Plan' includes accommodation and meals plus safaris (often two per day). There are very few independent restaurants.

populations of deer and antelopes, including several *barasingha* (swamp deer), which exist nowhere else in the world, call Kanha home. You'll see plenty of langurs, the odd gaur, wild boar and a jackal or two. Safaris venture into four zones within the core zone; **Kanha** and **Mukki** zones have had the most tiger sightings in recent years, followed by **Kisli** zone then **Sarhi** zone. Kisli and Kanha zones are best accessed from the Khatia gate in Khatia village on the western edge of the core zone. To reach the Mukki zone, enter via the Mukki gate on the south side, a 50km, 90-minute drive from Khatia.

A bath with Tara

While tigers are more elusive in the Kanha Tiger Reserve, the scenery, particularly when shrouded in morning mist, makes for wonderful landscape photo opportunities as you clamber about in your Gypsy. But the most thrilling thing to do at Kanha doesn't even involve tigers at all. Check yourself into India's first-ever wildlife lodge, **Kipling Camp** *(kiplingcamp.com)*, where the camp's septuagenarian elephant, a rescue named Tara, allows you to accompany her on her daily 2.5km walk to the Banjar River. Upon arrival, Tara wades in enthusiastically and twists and tumbles about the water for a good 30 minutes or so before allowing you the honour and privilege of bathing her in the river. All of this is illuminated by breathtaking sunsets over one of central India's most stunning river settings.

Pench Tiger Reserve

TIME FROM JABALPUR: **4HR**

Tigers and other wildlife

The Pench Tiger Reserve lies 211km south of Jabalpur and shares real estate with Maharashtra to the west. Consisting of mostly teak-tree forest as opposed to sal, Pench harbours an atmosphere distinctive from the other parks. It can sometimes feel like you have the whole forest to yourself here. The most accessible of the park's three entry points is the **Turia** gate, 12km west of Khawasa on the newly expanded four-lane Jabalpur–Nagpur NH 44. Pench's tiger population has increased in recent years (as have the transport options), which has led to a 30% to 40% increase in visitors. Besides the coveted tigers and leopards, commonly seen wildlife includes chital and sambar deer, jackals, sloth bears and wild dogs.

WANT TO SPOT MORE TIGERS?

If you are on a quest to see more Indian tigers, **Panna Tiger Reserve** (p603), 229km north of Jabalpur, is a less-visited (read: less crowded) option with a tiger population that lends itself to good chances of sightings.

Jagdalpur

TRIBAL MARKETS | WATERFALLS | REMOTE SIGHTS

Although bigger and brasher Raipur is Chhattisgarh's capital, it is Jagdalpur, the capital of the state's culturally rich Bastar district, that makes travelling out of bounds into this deep pocket of central India worthwhile. Located 303km south of Raipur, Jagdalpur was once the capital of the princely state of Bastar, founded in the 14th century and only conceding to the Indian state in 1948. Remnants of the Bastar dynasty are scattered about (the gaily painted Rajmahal or Bastar Palace is the town's main landmark), but Jagdalpur is mostly used as a travel hub to reach the fascinating Adivasi districts in its immediate surroundings. Tribal Chhattisgarh's weekly markets, known as *haat,* afford an incredible opportunity to observe and interact with Adivasi (tribal people) buying, selling and bartering their wares, including gorgeous Ghadwa bell-metal craftwork. According to India's Ministry of Tourism, Chhattisgarh only receives about .04% of India's foreign tourists, which alone is reason enough to venture here.

TOP TIP

Bastar's Adivasi markets serve up a cornucopia of photo opportunities, but do not ever take a picture of a Bastar Adivasi without seeking consent first. Most say yes, so it's not a problem getting pictures, but failure to do so can (understandably) cause offence land you in trouble.

Jagdalpur Jaunt

Get introduced to the Bastar region

Jagdalpur feels firmly off the beaten path, and the vibrant Adivasi culture of the Bastar region – home to eight main tribes spread among more than 3500 villages – offers one of central India's most enlightening cultural adventures. Pay a

GETTING AROUND

Rideshare apps such as Uber and Ola are not yet present in Jagdalpur, so getting around is a throwback to an era when tourists had to negotiate (read: haggle to the death) with autorickshaws over inflated prices. The train station and bus stand sit about 1.2km apart from each other south of the centre. A 4.5km autorickshaw ride across the entire city costs around ₹300 (₹100 if shared), so you can negotiate down for shorter rides.

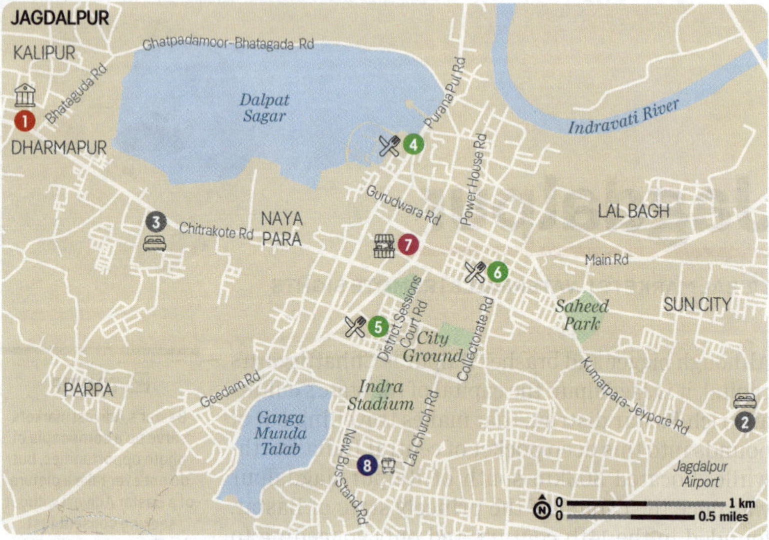

SIGHTS
1 Anthropological Museum

SLEEPING
2 Champa Baag Resort
3 Hotel Avinash International

EATING
4 Bastar Heritage Cafe
5 Hari Om Cafe
6 New Kerala
see 3 Sky Dhaba

SHOPPING
7 Sanjay Market

TRANSPORT
8 Jagdalpur Bus Stand

visit to Jagdalpur's **Anthropological Museum**, 3km west of the centre, which has illuminating exhibits on tribal customs and culture across a range of themes (weaponry, bell-metal and terracotta crafts, recreations of village houses and so on). While the museum is currently shut for renovation (reopening late 2027), a small selection of its exhibits is on display at the premises.

Sanjay Market in the city centre is a hive of activity through the week but goes into overdrive on Sundays, when the Adivasi come in the morning with forest produce like *mahua* (flowers that are used in various food products and are also fermented to produce a clear distilled liquor) and *chaprah* (red weaver ant nests used to make chutney).

Tribal Tales

Enjoy colourful markets and Adivasi culture

Get in touch with Ashit Dubey, aka Babbu *(9425246025; per day from ₹4000)*, Bastar's foremost English-speaking guide on tribal culture. Dubey has spent three decades cultivating relationships with the Adivasi and his unrivalled experience and knowledge are invaluable on a tribal tour. Depending on the day of the week, he will guide you to the vibrant Madia market at **Mardum**, take you on a scenic tour of the Dhurwa village at **Tiriya** or introduce you to the former chieftain of

HARI MAHIDHAR/SHUTTERSTOCK

Bastar Dussehra

the Bison-Horn Madia tribe in **Nainnar** (who might let you don his bison-horn headgear if you request politely). Market locations vary by day, but there's a captivating event daily. Favourites include the mixed market at **Tokopal** (Monday; for Ghadwa bell-metal craftwork, pottery, cane baskets) and the Bison-Horn Madia market at **Bastanar** (Saturday; forest products, terracotta items). Most markets swing into action in the afternoons. The best time of year to visit the tribal villages is between February and May when many hyper-local festivals and village fairs take place, but the weather tends to be hot.

Dinner Date

Relish a tribal meal

In the Bhatra village of **Kurandi** (10km southeast of Jagdalpur), Gurwari will welcome you into her home for a home-cooked meal *(₹2000 for 2 people)* of rice, chicken curry, dried bamboo stir-fry and local gourd stew. Ask to see firsthand how the piquant *chaprah* chutney is made from red weaver ant nests and eggs using a mortar-pestle, and, of course, sample it with your meal.

BASTAR DUSSEHRA

Jagdalpur's **Bastar Dussehra**, usually held in early October, is just the last of 75 days of rituals and preparations that give Bastar Dussehra claim to be one of the world's longest festivals. Dussehra in Bastar celebrates the regional goddess Danteshwari rather than Rama's victory over the demon-king Ravana, a divergence from elsewhere in India. During the final 10 days of the festival, some 84 different villages descend on Jagdalpur with their deities in tow. It all culminates on the last two days with a gigantic *rath* (wooden chariot) being tugged around Jagdalpur by teams of rope-pullers.

EATING IN JAGDALPUR: OUR PICKS

Bastar Heritage Cafe: Artsy cafe serving local Darbha coffee and light bites. Lovely patio views of the 17th-century, royal-built Dalpat Sagar lake. *11am-9.30pm* ₹

Hari Om Cafe: Dependable veg in clean, trendy-adjacent environment (by Jagdalpur's standards). Loads of paneer, noodles, sandwiches and rice bowls. *11.30am-11pm* ₹

New Kerala: South Indian Muslims at it since 1956. Twelve types of biryani (including fish), good rogan josh, plenty of sweets. *11.30am-11pm* ₹₹

Sky Dhaba: North Indian tandoor-grilled kebabs and fragrant curries in a semi-open-air rooftop setting at Hotel Avinash International. *7-11pm* ₹₹

Beyond Jagdalpur

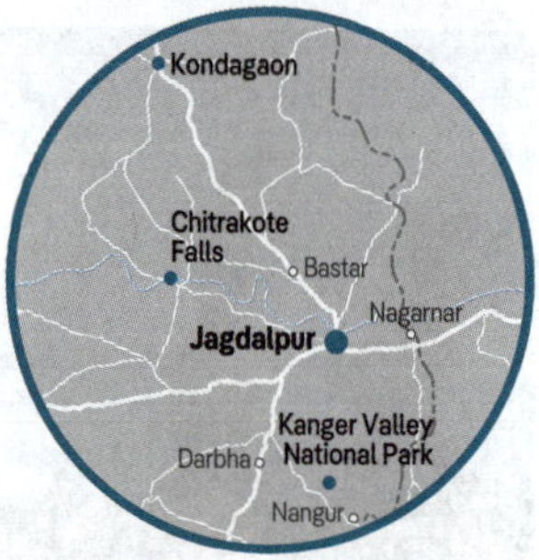

Several waterfalls, including India's widest, and their accompanying natural surroundings are the calling for those looking for non-tribal-related adventures from Jagdalpur.

Places
Chitrakote Falls p624
Kanger Valley National Park p625
Kondagaon p625

GETTING AROUND

Chhattisgarh is isolated and not exactly held up throughout India as a model of public transport. To reach Chitrakote Falls, Kanger Valley National Park and Kondagaon, a taxi is the most convenient, although there are buses to all locations departing from Sanjay Market in Jagdalpur several times throughout the day. Chitrakote buses travel very near the falls; buses to Tirathgarh village can drop you within 1km of the access track to the Tirathgarh Falls.

The greater Bastar region beyond Jagdalpur offers a cornucopia of Adivasi-related cultural experiences, but there's also a wealth of natural attractions in the vicinity of the city, namely a few waterfalls well worth seeking out. Chitrakote Falls, 38km northwest of Jagdalpur, is the widest waterfall in India, often drawing comparisons to Niagara Falls due to its horseshoe-shaped cliff across a series of showers. Kanger Valley National Park, 40km southeast of Jagdalpur, serves up the multi-tiered Tirathgarh Falls and the underground Kotumsar Cave systems with their impressive stalactites and stalagmites. 7Kondagaon, 75km north of Jagdalpur, is a hub for tribal crafts such as bell-metal artefacts, wrought-iron objects, and *tumba* art (decorative carving on dried gourds).

Chitrakote Falls

TIME FROM JAGDALPUR: **55MIN**

Gawk at India's widest waterfall

The impressive **Chitrakote Falls** is often touted as the 'Indian Niagara'. Specifically, it's the horseshoe shape of the falls that draws comparisons with Horseshoe Falls, one of the three waterfalls that make up Niagara Falls. While the numbers aren't quite there (Horseshoe out-drops Chitrakote by 25m and is 490m wider), the high praise isn't entirely off the mark. The spectacular plummet of the Indravati River here spills over from a height of 32m across a 300m-wide span. Depending on the season, the waterfall colour shifts due to climatic conditions. Soak in the entire panorama from the viewing platform or head down the steep steps to the riverside where you can hop in a **boat** *(₹70; 9am-sunset; closed during monsoon season)* and feel the mist of the

WONDERFALL WATERFALLS

Chitrakote Falls is one of India's most impressive waterfalls. If your whistle is wet so to speak, don't miss **Dhuandhar Falls** (p616) in the state of Madhya Pradesh, located 672km northwest of Jagdalpur outside the city of Jabalpur.

falls up close. Buses *(₹100)* leave from **Anupama Chowk** on Chitrakote Rd 500m from Sanjay Market; the last one back to Jagdalpur is at 4pm. A taxi round trip costs around ₹1500.

Kanger Valley National Park

TIME FROM JAGDALPUR: 1HR

Visit waterfallsand caves outside Jagdalpur

An enjoyable outing from Jagdalpur, Kanger Valley National Park covers 200 sq km in a thickly forested valley south of the city, with a number of waterfalls and caves. Visitors head to two main sites. One is **Tirathgarh Falls**, tumbling 35m in several sections down a canyon formed by the Mugabahar River, a Kanger River tributary. Descend some 220 steps to experience the waterfalls at close quarters. Don't miss walking across the rocks to a cluster of Shiva shrines in the middle of the falls.

The other attraction here is **Kotumsar Cave**, where guides lead you through up to 300m of narrow passages, concrete steps and large chambers with many stalactites and stalagmites. Follow Hwy 30 southwest from Jagdalpur to an intersection 27km from the city centre, where the road to the falls (6km) heads off to the right and the ticket office for Kotumsar Cave (10km away along a dirt road) is on the left. Buses to Tirathgarh village (₹45, one hour), leaving Sanjay Market in Jagdalpur several times a day, will drop you at this intersection or at the start of the 1km access track to the falls. A taxi round trip from Jagdalpur is ₹1400 to either the falls or the caves, or ₹1800 for both. The caves can be visited only with a 4WD safari vehicle *(from ₹2300; ticket office 8am-3pm)* with mandatory national park driver and guide. Entrance to the caves is closed from May to October.

Kondagaon

TIME FROM JAGDALPUR: 1½HR

Shop for handcrafted souvenirs

In the heart of Bastar, Kondagaon and its surrounding villages are known for their varied tribal handicrafts. Drop in at **Bastar Aadi Shilp** *(9424278484)*, where Suresh will show you how bell-metal objects are made; visit the village of **Kadaichenda** where almost every family makes beautiful wrought ironworks; and drop in at **Dipak Dewangan**'s workshop in Palari to see how *tumba* art is carved on dried gourds to make decorative objects. Finally, stop by at the government-run **Shabri Emporium** on Bastar Rd to choose from a wide range of traditional handmade items.

CHAPRAH CHUTNEY

Around all the tribal markets in Jagdalpur's vicinity, you'll see small sal-leaf bowls containing a light-brownish and airy substance peppered with tiny white nodules of mysterious origins. What is it? It is the nests of red weaver ants, which are found in abundance around the sal-wood forests in the area. The nests are used to make *chaprah*, a regional tribal chutney that's been held in high praise from world-renowned chefs such as Gordon Ramsay. Ginger, garlic, coriander, chilli powder and salt are ground with the nests (eggs and all) after they are mashed and dried. *Chaprah* is considered to be a superfood and is being proposed for a Geographical Identification (GI) tag.

Places We Love to Stay

₹ Budget ₹₹ Midrange ₹₹₹ Top End

Gwalior

Map p593

Hotel Grace ₹ A good-value hotel near Gwalior Junction, but not without faults, with better rooms and bedding than street-view indications. English spoken.

The Central Park ₹₹ Recently refurbished city-centre hotel with spacious, well-appointed rooms, two restaurants and an outdoor pool. Friendly and helpful front desk.

Usha Kiran Palace ₹₹₹ Central India's most beautiful bar highlights this heritage hotel, originally built in 1880 as a guesthouse for the Prince of Wales (later King George V).

Orchha

King Rama Hotel ₹ Cleaner and quieter than most of Orchha's budget fare but some rooms lack windows; limited breakfast on offer. English spoken.

Hotel Sheesh Mahal (p596) ₹₹ Sleep on the doorstep of the 17th-century Jehangir Mahal; in fact, its eight heritage rooms once made up the 18th-century former royal guesthouse.

Khajuraho

Map p599

Hotel Surya ₹ The lovely courtyard and garden steals the thunder from the rooms, which are standard issue but decently kept; most have garden views.

Dakghar 606 ₹₹ Women-run boutique hotel in the city's former post office; astute stamp art on walls, lovely lounge and rooftop with lake views, and a discerning owner.

Hotel Harmony ₹₹ A striking marble interior courtyard flanks some of Khajuraho's most tastefully decorated midrange rooms; charming rooftop garden restaurant.

Hotel Isabel Palace ₹₹ Family-run hotel away from the main drag; well-worn but clean rooms with garden-facing balconies. Massive, candle-lit rooftop terrace.

Panna Tiger Reserve

Tendu Leaf Jungle Resort ₹₹ Sprawling resort with nature-themed wooden cottages, a convivial riverside deck, herbal spa and a large pool. Multi-cuisine buffet on offer.

Sarai at Toria ₹₹₹ Eco-friendly lodge with tastefully done up mud-houses (minus air-conditioning), run by conservationists and wildlife photographers; open from October to March.

Ken River Lodge ₹₹₹ Luxe riverside resort with a choice of rustic huts, two-bedroom cottages or a double-storey villa; meals served on a *machan* (raised platform).

Bhopal

Map p605

Sonali Regency ₹ Good-value English-speaking cheapie with brightly decorated, smallish rooms overlooking a tiny temple; basic breakfast on offer.

Ten Suites ₹₹ Small boutique hotel in leafy neighbourhood with spacious rooms and foliage-filled bathrooms; myriad open-air rooftops and a welcoming cafe-bakery.

Jehan Numa Palace Hotel ₹₹₹ A 19th-century former royal mansion with pillared walkways and immaculate lawns, home to one of Bhopal's best restaurants and bars.

Indore

Map p610

The Eden ₹ Centrally located hotel with clean and comfortable rooms and English-speaking staff; good breakfast on offer.

Hotel Shreemaya ₹₹ Sparkling rooms and friendly and helpful service that far outweighs the price; very professionally run. Great restaurant and bakery attached.

Hotel Sayaji ₹₹₹ Polished rooms aside, this swanky celebration hotel has six restaurants (three of which rate tops in town). Noisy during wedding season.

Mandu

Shivani Resort ₹ Good-value hotel on Mandu's main road with bright and spacious rooms, some newly added. Well-regarded restaurant.

Malwa Resort (p614) ₹₹ Rooms come with four-poster beds, marble bathrooms and lake views at this MP Tourism hotel. Fantastic multicuisine restaurant.

Maheshwar

Labboo'z Cafe & Lodge (p613) ₹₹ Seven air-conditioned rooms spread among former soldiers' quarters inside the 250-year-old fort gate (lower rooms can be noisy). Best-in-town restaurant.

Ahilya Fort ₹₹₹ Wildly atmospheric heritage hotel with palatial rooms, river views and private verandahs. Top-level service and shifting meal environments, including high tea on a boat.

Jabalpur

Map p616

Kalchuri Residency ₹₹ Steps from the train station, this MP Tourism effort offers spacious, air-conditioned rooms, a rooftop pool and serviceable bar.

Rishi Regency ₹₹ Centrally located hotel with bright, recently refurbished rooms and a well-regarded restaurant serving Indian and international fare.

Bandhavgarh Tiger Reserve

Tala Camp ₹ A simple, family-run jungle homestay just outside Tala Village with comfortable rooms and home-cooked meals; profits often feed park conservation.

Nature Heritage Resort ₹₹ Reliable veteran flush with character (spacious adobe-toned rooms, lush surrounds) for the price. Nice pool, great showers and open-air dining.

Aranyak Resort ₹₹ Good-value property with modern rooms and cottages (some with outdoor showers) as well as ecofriendly mud-houses decked out with rustic flair.

Treehouse Hideaway ₹₹₹ Tigers have been known to appear on the property – luckily, you'll be in a sophisticated sal-wood treehouse. Bush dinners/fabulous tree bar are bonuses.

Pench Tiger Reserve

Kipling's Court ₹₹ Rooms have been upgraded at MP Tourism's Pench property, modernish bathrooms included. Decent playground and multi-cuisine restaurant.

Baghvan ₹₹₹ This luxury Taj Hotel property features bi-level bamboo, sal wood and concrete cottages with wonderful *machans* for sleeping outdoors.

Pench Jungle Camp ₹₹₹ Choose between compact cottages with tribal art and spacious tents (two with lake views). Generous multicuisine buffet offered, plus a small pool and herbal spa.

Saj in the Forest ₹₹₹ Beautiful boutique with Gond art throughout its somewhat-minimalist, comfortable rooms, a mosaic-tiled pool and gorgeous dining room ceramics.

Kanha Tiger Reserve

Motel Chandan ₹ Steps from Khatia gate. There is a recommended restaurant (open to nonguests) and various good-value categories, including rarely seen dorm beds.

Pugmark Resort ₹₹ Twelve high-value primrose-coloured cottages set around a somewhat wild garden. Owner-manager Rahul is the resident artist and naturalist. Small pool.

Salban ₹₹₹ Award-winning luxury homestay near Mukki gate in the spacious home of wildlife experts. Sip *mahua* (Indigenous liqueur) tonics while bird-spotting from the verandah.

Jagdalpur

Map p622

Champa Baag Resort ₹ Marwari-run 'resort' located right by the airport offering simple rooms inside tribal-evoking cottages flanking a colourful courtyard with hammocks and swing chairs.

Hotel Avinash International ₹₹ Jagdalpur's classiest business/boutique hotel with modern rooms, three very good restaurants (including a vegan one) and a surprising rooftop infinity pool.

Ahilya Fort, Maheshwar (p613)

Researched by
Joanna Lobo

Gujarat & Diu

RICH HERITAGE, TEXTILES AND VARIED LANDSCAPES

Gujarat's treasures run deep for a state traditionally more commercial than touristy: vibrant Kachchh (Kutch) textiles, unique wildlife, holy pilgrimage sites and meals fit for royalty.

An unfairly overlooked region in the shadow of Mumbai and Rajasthan, Gujarat as a travel destination has been gaining in popularity in recent years, shining a spotlight on the major attractions of a place better known as a commercial and agricultural powerhouse (and Mahatma Gandhi's homeland). Discovering the deep sense of culture, remarkable architecture and relative religious harmony of its major city, Ahmedabad, inspires a sense of wonder in visitors, its outstanding museums, ancient religious and civic structures and wonderful gastronomic endeavours being unveiled like unsung cultural heroes. Throughout Gujarat, similar moments of revelation await, especially in towns like Vadodara(Baroda) and Sihor. In the tribal villages around Bhuj, world-renowned artisans weave, embroider, dye and print some of India's finest textiles. Fascinating wildlife – including migratory birds, wild asses and growling prides of Asiatic lions – await in the state's excellent nature reserves. Sacred Jain and Hindu pilgrimage sites sit atop mountains that rise dramatically from vast flatlands. In Kachchh, white desert Rann saltscapes stretch to the horizon and play with your visual perspective. Finally, at Gujarat's southern tip, lovers of sand and sea chill out in the former Portuguese island enclave of Diu, a tranquil, independently governed remnant of Portugal's once dominant presence in the region.

ANAND PUROHIT/GETTY IMAGES

THE MAIN AREAS

AHMEDABAD
Architecturally rich, UNESCO-listed Gujarati metropolis. p632

SAURASHTRA
Asiatic lions, architecture and pilgrimage sites. p641

VADODARA (BARODA)
Royal heritage, atmospheric ruins and art. p648

BHUJ
World-renowned textiles and salt desert. p652

DIU
Independently governed island getaway. p659

For places to stay in Gujarat and Diu, see p662

MIHIR SUTARIA/SHUTTERSTOCK

Above: Road through the White Desert (p655); Left: Kachchh (Kutch) embroidery

Find Your Way

Gujarat is India's fourth-largest state by area (191,791 sq km) but travelling between its many culturally rich and historic destinations is relatively straightforward. The 38-sq-km Diu Island is compact and easy to explore.

Bhuj, p652

Kachchh capital featuring world-renowned textile workshops; wild asses, salt desert and artisan villages await beyond.

Saurashtra, p641

Prominent district that is a haven for birding and marine life; a springboard for visiting the world's sole wild Asiatic lion habitat.

Diu, p659

Small island with laid-back beaches and the dilapidated remnants of its life as a former Portuguese colony.

Ahmedabad, p632

A booming metropolis (Mahatma Gandhi's former home) with modern and ancient architecture, museums and atmospheric old city mosques.

CAR & BUS

Gujarat's roads are generally in good condition and distances are manageable, making travel by car with driver (around ₹16 per kilometre) or by bus excellent options. The comprehensive bus network connects all major cities to smaller destination.

TRAIN

Gujarat is covered by an extensive train network, connecting the hub of Ahmedabad, plus Vadodara, Surat, Jamnagar and Rajkot to smaller towns within the state and to major destinations in other parts of India. Check routes and timetables and book tickets via IRCTC *(irctc.co.in)*.

Vadodara (Baroda), p648

A former prominent British princely state, rich in Indo-Saracenic architecture and the legacy of the royal Gaekwad family.

Rani-ki-Vav (p638), Patan

Plan Your Time

Ahmedabad makes for a fairly central base for many attractions, including the Little Rann of Kachchh, but you'll want to consider Bhuj and Junagadh for points further west and south.

An Extended Layover

- Hit the ground running in **Ahmedabad** (p632). Top attractions like **Calico Museum of Textiles** (p632), **Siddi Sayid's Mosque** (p633) and modern architectural highlights in between can be seen in 48 hours. Also take the opportunity to try some Gujarati thalis. Keep a day to visit the marvels near the city, such as the **Adalaj Vav** (p639), **Patan** (p638) and **Lothal** (p640).

Week-Long Deep Dive

- Take in the museums and architectural wonders of **Ahmedabad** (p632), then head west to the **Little Rann of Kachchh** (p655), where wild donkeys are a highlight at the **Wild Ass Sanctuary** (p657). Do a textile tour of the tribal villages surrounding **Bhuj** (p652) before seeking out wild Asiatic lions at **Gir National Park & Wildlife Sanctuary** (p647) in **Saurashtra** (p641).

SEASONAL HIGHLIGHTS

SPRING
March is the sweet spot; average temps barely crest 30°C, tourists dissipate and it is a great time for nature and wildlife viewing.

SUMMER
Many tourists avoid the summer months (beginning of the monsoon), but Gujarat is still cooler than many states.

AUTUMN
Monsoon is in full swing. **Navratri** in September–October is the biggest festival, involving dance, music and food.

WINTER
High-season temps are pleasant. Don't miss the **Rann Utsav** (p656) in Kachchh, or the **International Kite Festival** in Ahmedabad in January.

Ahmedabad

HISTORICAL HERITAGE | GREAT MUSEUMS | TEMPLES & MOSQUES

GETTING AROUND

While rideshare apps like Uber and Ola remain the most convenient option for visitors, Ahmedabad's public transport is extensive. The **Ahmedabad Metro** *(gujaratmetrorail.com)* connects the Old Town to the main train station, Ahmedabad Junction, from where there are departures to Vadodara, Bhuj, Bhavnagar, Mumbai, Jaipur and Jamnagar. The Old City is very walkable. The Sardar Vallabhbhai Patel International Airport is connected to all major cities in India. AC and non-AC buses run from the Gita Mandir Bus Stand to all main destinations within Gujarat (Surat, Vadodara), plus cities in nearby states (Mumbai, Udaipur).

Founded by Sultan Ahmad Shah in the 15th century, Ahmedabad (aka Amdavad, Ahmadabad or Ahemdavad) became India's first UNESCO World Heritage city in 2017 for reasons that are immediately obvious upon arrival. From centuries-old mosques and mausoleums to modernist marvels by Le Corbusier, the city's fascinating feats of architecture draw enthusiasts and specialists alike. CEPT, one of India's top architecture and design universities, is located here as well. Ahmedabad's once-walled Old City, on the east side of the Sabarmati River, is a tapestry of dilapidated *havelis* (traditional, ornately decorated residences), tucked-away temples, mosques, bustling markets, street-food stalls and snaking alleyways. Some 200 *chabutros* (elaborate towering bird feeders made from wood or sandstone) pepper its *pols* (see p636). Today only 20% of the wall remains along with 12 historic gates. Fine restaurants, excellent museums and several major universities characterise the newer parts of Ahmedabad west of the Sabarmati River.

Museum Moments

Ancient textiles and modern art

The collection of antique and modern textiles at Ahmedabad's **Calico Museum of Textiles** *(calicomuseum.org; entry by free guided tour; book ahead; closed Mon)* is said to be second only to London's Victoria & Albert Museum in breadth, scope and importance. You'll stand in awe at the beautiful handmade tapestries, royal garments, exquisite saris, tribal dress, Patola and Mashru weaves and Bandhani tie-dyes.

Kasturbhai Lalbhai Museum *(kasturbhailalbhaimuseum.com; entry by 2hr free guided tour; book ahead)* is housed in the former 1905 bungalow of industrialist Kasturbhai Lalbhai, who founded Arvind Mills, India's largest denim company, in 1897. The collection showcases everything from paintings to hand-painted postcards from pre-Independence India.

SAIKO3P/SHUTTERSTOCK

Sabarmati Ashram

Next door, the **Arvind-Indigo Museum** *(indigoartmuseum.org; free)* is dedicated to various artistic manifestations of the colour indigo. Nearby, the **Kutch Sanskruti Museum** *(instagram.com/kutchsanskrutimuseum; free)* showcases the different tribes, landscapes, textiles and other crafts of the Kachchh region. Look out also for fossils from the Jurassic Mesozoic era.

Gandhi's Ahmedabad Legacy

Visit Gandhi's ashram

Mohandas Karamchand Gandhi (better known as Mahatma Gandhi; 1869–1948) was a lawyer and social activist known for his nonviolent civil disobedience movements during India's struggle for independence. He lived in Ahmedabad from 1917 to 1930 as he fought for India's independence from Great Britain. At Gandhi's former headquarters, the **Sabarmati Ashram** *(gandhiashramsabarmati.org; free)*, you can explore a semi-open-air museum dedicated to his life and work and his spartan living quarters, and see how *khadi* (homespun cloth) is made. Walk along a little further to the **Dandi Bridge**, where Gandhi began his historic Dandi March in 1930, a 24-day march protesting the British salt tax. The entire complex is accessible, and there are toilets and drinking water fountains.

Down by the River

Cross a pedestrianised bridge

Join throngs of locals to watch the sun set over the **Atal Bridge** *(₹50)*, a pedestrianised truss bridge whose design was inspired by Ahmedabad's Kite Festival. The bridge is a hub of activity: here you'll find a flower garden, rest areas, a food court and priceless people-watching opportunities. Go

AHMEDABAD'S HERITAGE

Bhadra Fort: Constructed in 1411, this fort comprises a Mughal palace, a Maratha Kali temple and a British East India Company clock tower.

Hutheesingh Temple: Dating to 1848, this Jain temple is adorned with delicate marble carvings of deities, flowers and celestial damsels.

Siddi Sayid's Mosque: The stunning mosque from 1573 showcases intricate *jali* (carved lattice) windows, two of which depict sacred Hindu and Islamic symbols (a banyan and palm tree).

Bai Harir Vav: Beautiful step-well built in 1499, with five levels of carved and intricate stone columns; there's a mosque alongside.

Kankaria Lake: Artificial lake dating to 1451, with a garden, children's play area and theme park.

TOP TIP

Gujarat is a predominantly vegetarian state, and the repertoire of vegan and vegetarian dishes is varied. In Ahmedabad you'll also find some excellent restaurants specialising in meat dishes; outside these meat-forward restaurants, it is best to stick to vegetarian offerings.

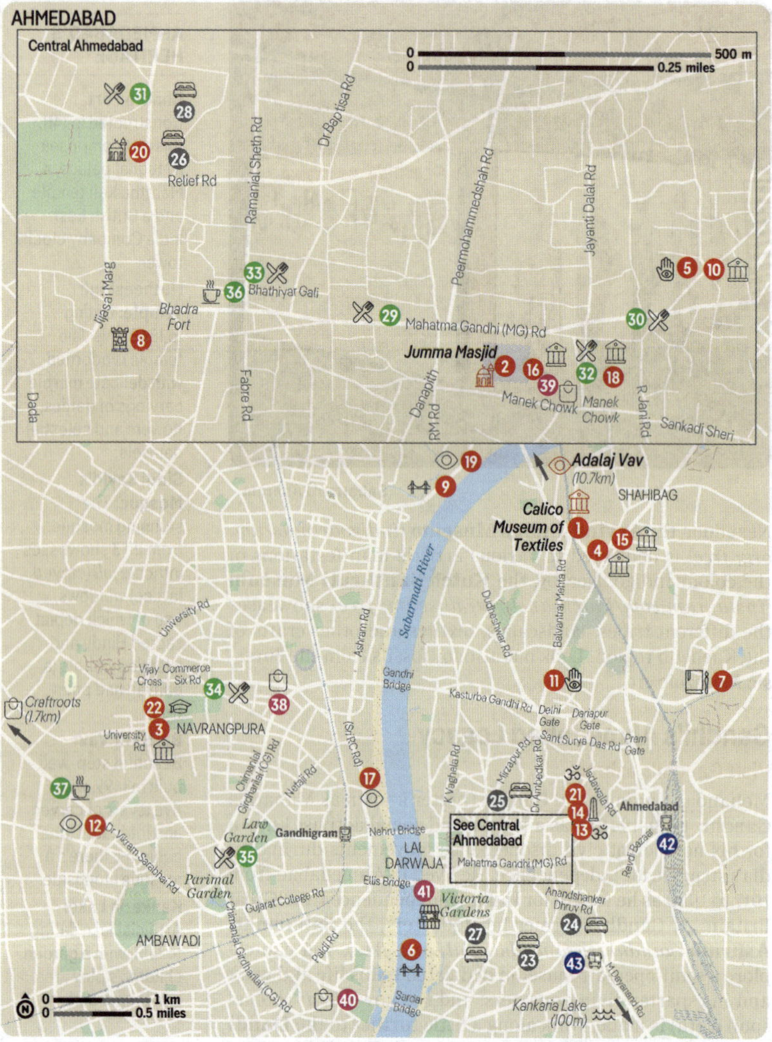

just before sunset to enjoy the weather and watch the night fall over the city. It tends to get crowded on holidays and on weekends, so time your visit wisely.

Experiments & Exhibits

Explore Science City

A government-run space spread over 41 hectares and meant to inspire the scientifically inclined, **Science City** *(sciencecity.gujarat.gov.in; from ₹50)* is fun for the whole family. A combined ticket grants entry to different galleries, giving you the chance to see robots fight each other, explore hands-on

HIGHLIGHTS
1 Calico Museum of Textiles
2 Jumma Masjid

SIGHTS
3 Amdavad ni Gufa
4 Arvind-Indigo Museum
5 Ashtapad Derasar
6 Atal Bridge
7 Bai Harir Vav
8 Bhadra Fort
9 Dandi Bridge
10 Harkunwar Sethani ni Haveli
11 Hutheesingh Temple
12 Indian Institute of Management
13 Kala Ramji Mandir
see 4 Kasturbhai Lalbhai Museum
14 Kavi Dalpatram Memorial
15 Kutch Sanskruti Museum
16 Mausoleum of Ahmed Shah
17 Mill Owners' Association Building
18 Rani-no-Hajiro
19 Sabarmati Ashram
20 Siddi Sayid's Mosque
21 Swaminarayan Temple

ACTIVITIES
22 Centre of Environmental & Planning Technology

SLEEPING
23 Ahmedabad Homestay
24 French Haveli
25 Hotel Elite Inn
26 Hotel Good Night
27 jüSTa Diwans Bungalow
28 The House of MG

EATING
29 Bera Samosa Corner
30 Chandravillas
see 28 Green House
31 Lucky Restaurant
32 Manek Chowk
33 New Irani Restaurant
34 Project Otenga
35 Swati Snacks

DRINKING & NIGHTLIFE
36 Gandhi Cold-Drink House
37 Kaffa Coffee Roasters
see 3 Zen Cafe

SHOPPING
38 Hansiba
39 Manek Chowk
40 NIDUS
41 Ravivari Sunday Flea Market

TRANSPORT
42 Ahmedabad Junction
43 Gita Mandir Bus Stand

scientific exhibits, try immersive virtual reality experiences, learn what astronauts eat, and see fish from all over the world. The experiences extend outside too, with a nature park teeming with birds and butterflies. Each gallery has its own cafe (including one with robot servers) or restaurant. The space is accessible and has drinking water facilities and toilets.

Modern Marvels

Ahmedabad's striking architecture

Ahmedabad's modern architecture delivers one of Gujarat's best surprises. Arresting edifices include the campus of **Indian Institute of Management** *(iima.ac.in)*, designed by renowned American architect Louis Kahn, it is a blend of contemporary brick architecture and Indian elements, with a porous geometric facade. Sign in at the gate and exchange your passport for a visitor's pass. The striking **Mill Owners' Association Building** *(atma.secgen@gmail.com)*, one of four buildings in Ahmedabad designed by legendary Swiss-French architect Le Corbusier, requires a 15-day advance notice for a

BEST SHOPS IN AHMEDABAD

Ravivari/Gujari Market: Every Sunday, the Sabarmati Riverfront comes alive with a market dedicated to antiques.

NIDUS: The NID's (National Institute of Design) on-campus shop stocks independent designs by the institute's alumni and students.

Hansiba: Colourful wall hangings, embroidered shawls, saris and tunics from the Self-Employed Women's Association.

Manek Chowk: The commercial heart of the Old City turns into a food market by night. Buy oxidised silver jewellery from stores near Rani No Hajiro and blouses and Indian traditional wear near Ratanpole.

Craftroots: Showroom for artisanal and sustainable Gujarati apparel, home furnishings and jewellery.

DRINKING IN AHMEDABAD: OUR PICKS

Gandhi Cold-Drink House: Going strong for 100-plus years; try the signature *falooda* (saffron syrup, vermicelli, basil seeds, milk and ice cream). *10am-11pm*

Zen Cafe: A serene, tree-fringed garden cafe next to the Amdavad ni Gufa underground art gallery. *noon-8pm*

Kaffa Coffee Roasters: An oasis aesthetic pervades at this high-end coffeehouse with alfresco seating. *11am-midnight Mon-Fri, from 9am Sat & Sun*

Roastery Culture Coffee Bar: This is worth a detour for the fantastic espresso made mostly from Chikmaglur coffee. *11am-midnight Mon-Sat, to 1am Sun*

CITY OF POLS

The walled city of Ahmedabad is made up of many *pols* – original gated complexes. These are traditional neighbourhoods, dense clusters of houses that share walls and were once designed to foster a sense of community and offer security. Most *pols*, such as **Dhal ni Pol**, **Joshiwada ni Pol** and **Mandvi ni Pol** have a common entry gate with a security alcove above it, an elaborate *chabutro* (bird bath), a well, a small temple, a meeting place, and even hidden escape routes. Ahmedabad has over 300 *pols*, and each comprises hundreds of houses. The highlights of these *pols* include ornate wooden architecture, carvings and elaborate balconies; each house also has bird nest niches.

visit. The brutalist edifice of India's inaugural Pritzker Prize winner, Balkrishna Vithaldas Doshi, can be seen on the campus of the **Centre of Environmental & Planning Technology** (CEPT). Also on the premises is **Amdavad ni Gufa**, an underground art gallery showcasing some of artist MF Husain's original artwork and sculpture, whereas the building's style is officially classed as 'Modern Blobitecture'.

Empty Vessels Tell a Story

India's history told through containers

It may seem a little dull at first glance: a series of pots lining shelves that span a long room and outdoor courtyards. Yet the **Vechaar Museum** *(vechaar.com; ₹50; 3-10pm, closed Mon)* deserves an hour or two of your time. The Vishalla Environmental Centre for Heritage of Art, Architecture and Research (VECHAAR) museum showcases utensils, children's toys, temple items, dowry boxes and nutcrackers. A guided tour will introduce you to some standout pieces like a *surma* (kohl powder used as eye makeup) holder, a foldable cup, 800-year-old paper weights, and a wooden water bottle.

Combine a visit with dining at the in-house restaurant, **Vishalla**. It is a cosy space with swings, little treetop spaces and art on display. The food here is traditional Gujarati and includes an unlimited thali, which is a little more expensive than other places (₹850 as compared to the usual ₹500 to ₹600 range).

EATING IN AHMEDABAD: OUR PICKS

New Irani Restaurant: Former haunt of freedom fighters, renowned for its *bun maska* (buns with creamy unsalted butter) and mutton (goat) dishes. *6.30am-11pm* ₹

Bera Samosa Corner: Four generations have perfected spiced mutton (goat) samosas, sold in 100g increments. Also try their beef samosas. *11am-10pm* ₹

Manek Chowk: Nightly food market. The *dahi puri* (yoghurt and spice-filled deep-fried spheres) washed down with a *jamun* (Malabar plum) shot stand out. *7pm-1am* ₹

Swati Snacks: Canteen-style place serving traditional Gujarati snacks. Try the *patra* (*colocasia* leaf snack) and *undhiyu* (seasonal mixed vegetable dish). *noon-10.45pm* ₹₹

Chandravillas: Praised since 1900 for its breakfast and *jalebis* (deep-fried batter in sugar syrup), this place has starred in Gujarati movies. *8am-7.30pm Mon-Sat, to 4pm Sun* ₹

Lucky Restaurant: Known for their *bun maska*, which are available in different flavours. You dine among tombs of saints. *7am-11pm* ₹₹

Green House: The House of MG's casual semi-open-air restaurant. Gujarati vegetarian dishes, wonderful juices and sweets. *7am-11pm* ₹₹₹

Project Otenga: Culinary haven behind Ahmedabad University Admissions serving Assam delicacies. Try the white sesame chicken. *10.30am-10.30pm Tue-Sun* ₹₹₹

A TEMPLE-TO-MOSQUE WALK

This historic walking tour of the city covers top religious sites, *pols* and architecturally stunning monuments.

START	END	LENGTH
Swaminarayan Temple, Kalupur	Jumma Masjid	2km; 3hr

Uncover the treasures of Ahmedabad's walled city on this morning walk, beginning at the 1 **Swaminarayan Temple**, Kalupur. This multicoloured, wood-carved temple was built in 1822 and is the oldest temple of the Swaminarayan Hindu sect. Exit the temple and head to the 2 **Kavi Dalpatram Memorial**. This small *chowk* (square) features a statue of the Gujarati poet, Dalpatram, plus the facade of his former house.

Cross Relief Rd and head to 3 **Kala Ramji Mandir**, a private Hindu temple (entry granted upon request) with a statue of Lord Ram in black stone. Keep walking until you hit Tankshal Rd and the 4 **Harkunwar Sethani ni Haveli**, with its impressive wooden brackets. Cross the road to visit 5 **Ashtapad Derasar**, a Jain temple that is part of Joshiwada ni Pol, with a wealth of marble and black stone statues.

On the same road, head under Fernandez Bridge, past Madan Gopal Haveli Marg, and further on to Manek Chowk. The raised tomb with cloistered trellises is 6 **Rani-no-Hajiro**, the final resting place of Ahmed Shah's wives. It lies near Ahmed Shah's burial place, 7 **Badshah-no-Hajiro**. Around the corner from here is the 8 **Jumma Masjid**. Built by Ahmed Shah, the sandstone mosque is a stunning example of Indo-Islamic architecture.

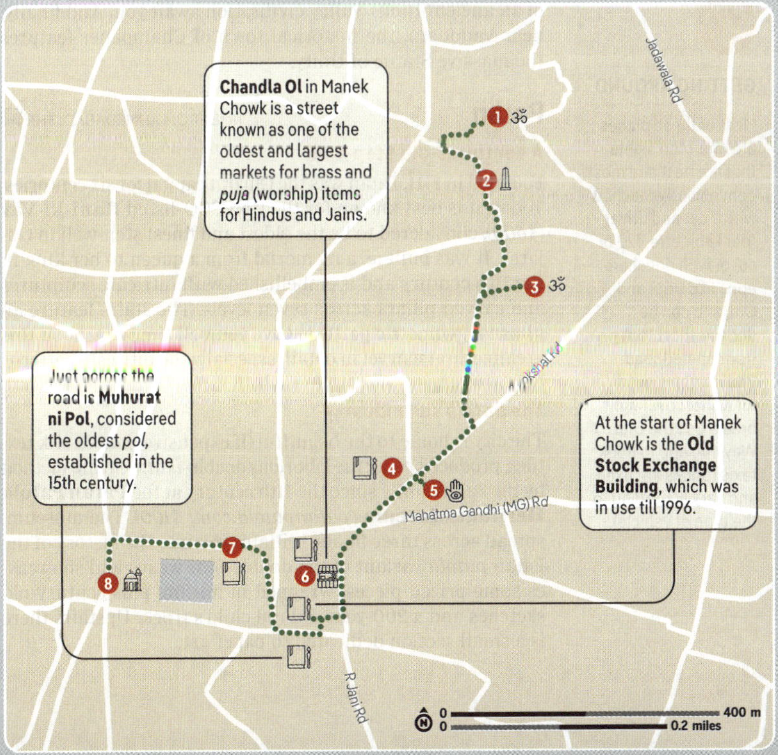

Beyond Ahmedabad

UNESCO-listed archaeological sites, ruins, ornately decorated temples and step-wells encircle Ahmedabad's sprawling cityscape.

Places

GETTING AROUND

Most of these places are one-stop sights that are best and most conveniently reached with a car and driver (per kilometre ₹20 or so) or with rideshare apps like Uber and Ola, and can be done in short trips from Ahmedabad. Bhavnagar is good for a short overnight break. Use the One Way cab app to book taxis (prices are fixed and vary according to the type of vehicle).

Ahmedabad's fairly central location makes it a convenient place from which to visit some of the state's UNSECO World Heritage Sites and historic marvels. There is plenty to see. There is the capital city, Gandhinagar, with its dinosaur fossils and the UNESCO-listed step-well, Adalaj Vav. In Patan, the former Gujarati capital, you will find Patola silk textiles produced using the laborious double-*ikat* weaving method, and the gorgeous Rani-ki-Vav step-well. Modhera's Sun Temple dates to 1027 and is decorated with extraordinarily detailed carvings. At Lothal, southwest of Ahmedabad, the remnants of an ancient Indus Valley civilisation await you. And finally, near Vadodara, the historical town of Champaner features the massive Statue of Unity.

Patan

TIME FROM AHMEDABAD: **3HR**

A centuries-old step-well

Founded in 1411, Patan was the Gujarat capital for six centuries. Today, it is best known for the UNESCO-listed **Rani-ki-Vav** *(₹600),* considered to be the oldest and finest step-well in Gujarat. It was built as a memorial from a queen to her king in the 11th century and is embellished with intricate sculptures and carved pillars across seven levels. The stairs feature an unusual geometric pattern. Give yourself time to take in this architectural marvel in detail, especially the intricate patterns that also appear on *patola* saris.

The *patola* silk industry

The city is home to the beautiful (if expensive) *patola* silk textiles, produced using the laborious double-*ikat* weaving method by the Salvi family since the 11th century at the **Patan Patola Heritage Museum** *(patanpatola.com; ₹100).* The museum, spread across three floors, initiates you into the history of the Patan *patola* variant of the double-*ikat* weave and showcases some prized pieces, wrapped in muslin, plus century-old sketches and a 200-year-old red child's frock. Upstairs there is a small section dedicated to paper art.

HARSHIT TRIVEDI/SHUTTERSTOCK

Rani-ki-Vav, Patan

Gandhinagar District

TIME FROM AHMEDABAD: **40MIN**

Adalaj Vav step-well

The **Adalaj Vav** *(₹300)* is one of Gujarat's finest step-wells, built by Queen Rudabai in 1498. The five-storeys-deep octagonal well is adorned with exquisite Indo-Islamic stone carvings; subjects range from erotic scenes to the production of buttermilk. It has three entrances and the temperature within is always a few degrees cooler than outside. Rudabai's husband, Rana Veer Singh, started building the step-well but died fighting Sultan Mahmud Begada. The sultan fell for the widowed queen, who promised to marry him if he completed the step-well. Once it was completed, in an act of defiance, she threw herself to her death into the well. The sultan killed all the architects in anger and their tombs now lie outside the step-well.

Dinosaurs and fossils

The **Indroda Dinosaur and Fossil Park** *(geerfoundation.gujarat.gov.in; ₹200)* is a special place in Gandhinagar, with fossilised remains and petrified dinosaur eggs. It's easy to spend a few hours here, exploring the zoo and the botanical garden, admiring the blue whale and other massive skeletons at the museum; be prepared to walk. The family friendly space is run by the Gujarat Ecological Education and Research Foundation (GEER). Kids will love the life-sized dinosaur

GUJARAT'S GANDHI CIRCUIT

Dandi Kutir: The museum in Gandhinagar uses technology to offer a dramatic narrative of Gandhi's life.

Dandi Beach: This beach near Navsari is where Gandhi ended his Dandi March – a nonviolent protest against the British tax on salt. It features a memorial and a small museum.

Kaba Gandhi no Delo: Formerly the Gandhi family residence, this *haveli* in Rajkot is now a small museum with an attached weaving school.

Kirti Mandir: This museum in Porbandar is attached to Gandhi's ancestral home and birthplace.

Sabarmati Ashram: This ashram (p633) on the banks for the Sabarmati River served as Gandhi's long term residence; many of his nonviolent protest movements began there.

EATING IN GANDHINAGAR: OUR PICKS

TMS Global Kitchen: Modern restaurant with delicious vegetarian global fusion food, presented with flair. *11.30am–3pm & 7-10.45pm* ₹₹

Cilantro's Global Cuisine: Veg/vegan global fare, such as *khow suey* (Burmese coconut milk noodle soup), on a rooftop terrace. *noon-3pm & 7-11pm* ₹₹

Kansar Garden Restaurant: Multicuisine restaurant doing Tex-Mex nachos, Thai curries and pastas in a cute garden space. *11am–3pm & 7-11pm* ₹₹₹

Greenz: A popular restaurant known for its ambience, its lovely garden area and a globe-spanning menu. Try the sizzler dishes. *11am–3pm & 7-11pm* ₹₹₹

STATUE OF UNITY?

The tallest monument in the world, the 182m-tall **Statue of Unity** *(soutickets.in)* looks out onto the Narmada River, against the backdrop of the Satpura and Vindhyachal hills. The statue is of Sardar Vallabhbhai Patel, India's first Deputy Prime Minister and Home Minister, often referred to as India's 'Iron Man'. He played an instrumental role in uniting India's states after the country had gained independence in 1947. An in-house museum shares details about his importance, and the construction of the museum. The statue came under a lot of controversy, namely because of the expense, which many deemed unnecessary given India's rising poverty, and for displacing many tribal communities from their land.

models and the small zoo. While drinking water is available, food is not allowed and there are no outlets within the park.

Champaner & Pavgadh

DISTANCE FROM AHMEDABAD: **3HR**

An archaeological park

Champaner enjoyed a brief period of 15th-century glory as Sultan Mahmud Begada's one-time capital. Monumental, UNESCO-listed mosques fill the **Champaner-Pavgadh Archaeological Park** *(₹600)*, which is like an open-air museum – it has mosques, water installations, military structures and a palace. It remains the only unchanged Islamic pre-Mughal city in India. Start a tour of the historic city at the Citadel and look out for the carved entrance porch of the striking Jami Masjid, the stone carvings in the prayer hall, the rare brick tomb, and the step-wells that are testimony to the sophisticated water system that existed at the time. The **Kalikamata Temple** on the scenic hilltop at **Pavagadh** is a pilgrimage site and can be reached via a two- to three-hour walk or via a cable-car ride *(₹150)*.

Modhera

DISTANCE FROM AHMEDABAD: **2HR**

A sun temple

Built in 1027 CE by Bhimdev I, the **Sun Temple** *(₹300)* at Modhera is considered the finest work of the sun-worshipping Solanki dynasty. It is dedicated to the sun god, Surya – there are 12 carvings dedicated to him around the inner sanctum hall. The rectangular step-well inside the complex contains 108 shrines. Intricately carved demons, deities and erotic scenes similar to those at Khajuraho (p600) cover the exterior, with 52 sculpted pillars inside the temple depicting scenes from the Ramayana and the Mahabharata. The Hindu god of architecture, Vishwa Karma, is immortalised on the back wall of the temple. The park is vast with many seating areas, and toilet and drinking water facilities. Guides are available *(₹500 per group of up to 10)*.

Lothal

DISTANCE FROM AHMEDABAD: **1¼HR**

Ancient Indus site

You'll need a vivid imagination to reconstruct the once thriving Harappa-era port town at Lothal *(₹100)*, believed to date to 2200 BCE. The site of the once-prominent Indus Valley civilisation lacks dramatic structures, but what is arguably the world's oldest dockyard remains intact, along with washroom drainage systems. There are also the remnants of a warehouse, a bead-making factory, and a citadel that once housed the city's elite. An on-site museum displays artefacts found during excavation.

Saurashtra

BIRDING & WILDLIFE | MUSEUMS & PALACES | ARCHITECTURAL WONDERS

Also known as the Kathiawar Peninsula, Saurashtra was made up of over 200 princely states before Independence, and the villages outside the industrial cities retain a timeless feel. Ancient trading ports like Diu whisper stories of Portuguese conquests and naval battles. There is an abundance of religious sites and pilgrimage spots, such as the seaside temple of Somnath and the dramatic Jain shrines at Palitana. Jamnagar is situated on the Gulf of Kachchh, which provides a haven for waterfowl and marine life within easy reach of the city. Junagadh is unusually rich with Indo-Islamic architecture and is the jumping-off point for seeing the lions at Gir National Park & Wildlife Sanctuary. The seaside city of Bhavnagar has a rich history and ancient frescoes worth lingering over. Near Bhavnagar is Sihor with coppersmiths plying their ancient trade in its narrow streets.

TOP TIP

If you are heading towards South Gujarat destinations like Jamnagar, Junagadh or Gir National Park & Wildlife Sanctuary, you will likely pass through the industrial city of Rajkot. Once the capital of Saurashtra, it has a worth-a-wander old city.

A Lakeside Ramble

Explore the environs of Ranmal Lake

The mid-19th-century artificial **Ranmal Lake** *(₹10)* lies at the heart of Jamnagar. The [illegible] shaded promenade, numerous banyan trees that attract various bird species, and ornate pavilions with enclosed stone balconies. The lake was constructed between 1820 and 1852 by Jam Ranmalji II, the 16th Jam Sahib of the former Nawanagar state, whose gorgeously situated **Lakhota Palace** *(₹50)*

GETTING AROUND

With the exception of Rajkot and Bhavnagar, most of the places in Saurashtra do not use rideshare apps and rely on public transport. Buses go to most destinations but tend to be slow and crowded. Having your own vehicle and driver is the easiest way to get around and see multiple sights in one day. Most of the villages mentioned can be seen within 24 hours. Taxis/cars with drivers can be organised through your accommodation and cost around ₹10 to ₹30 per kilometre (depending on the vehicle).

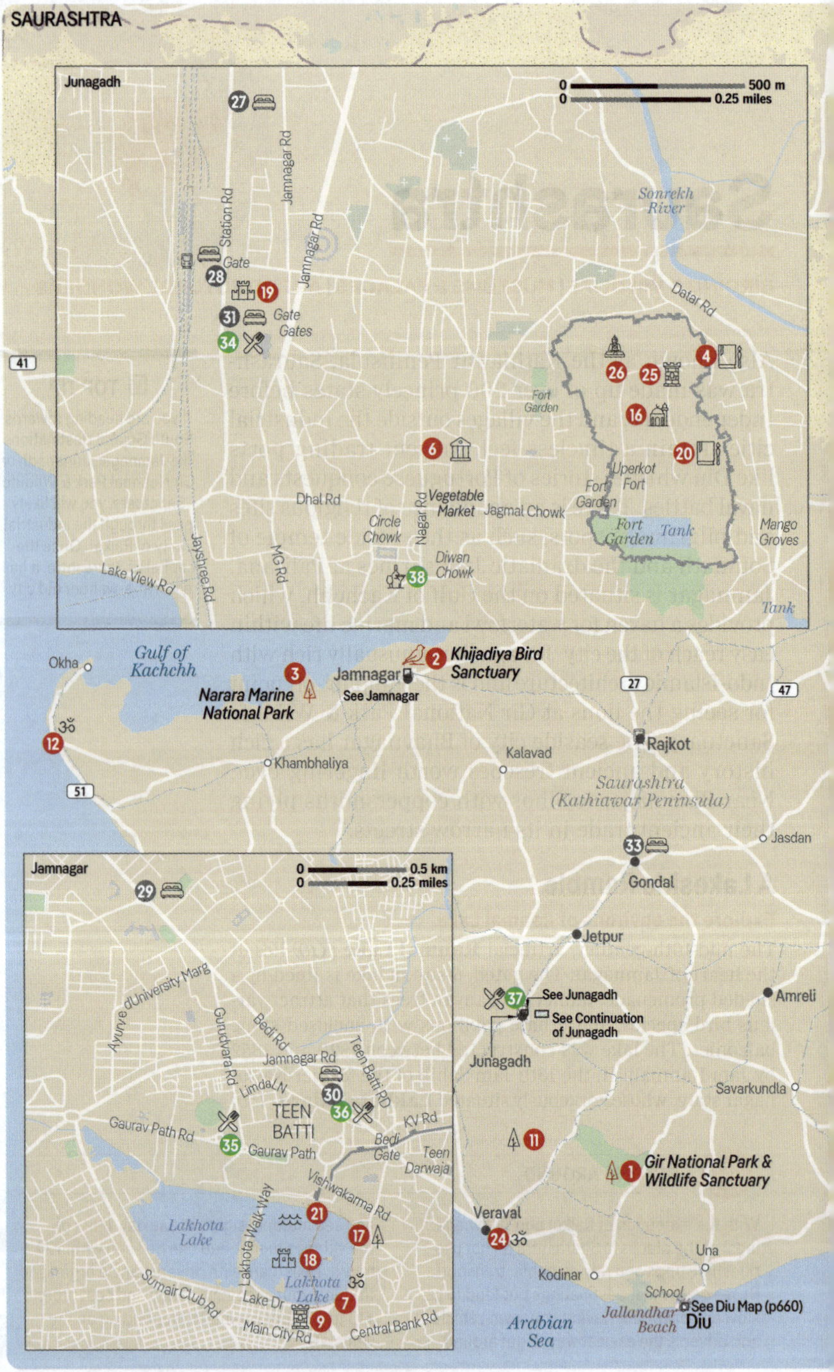
SAURASHTRA
Junagadh
0 500 m
0 0.25 miles
27
Jamnagar Rd
Station Rd
Jamnagar Rd
Sonrekh River
Gate
28
19
31
Gate
Gates
34
Datar Rd
4
26
25
Fort Garden
16
6
20
Uperkot Fort
Fort Garden
Dhal Rd
Circle Chowk
Nagar Rd
Vegetable Market
Jagmal Chowk
Fort Garden
Tank
Mango Groves
Diwan Chowk
38
Jayshree Rd
MG Rd
Lake View Rd
Tank
41
Okha
Gulf of Kachchh
3
Narara Marine National Park
Jamnagar
See Jamnagar
2
Khijadiya Bird Sanctuary
27
47
12
Khambhaliya
Kalavad
Rajkot
Saurashtra (Kathiawar Peninsula)
51
33
Jasdan
Gondal
Jamnagar
0 0.5 km
0 0.25 miles
29
Ayurved University Marg
Gurudvara Rd
Bedi Rd
Jamnagar Rd
Teen Batti RD
Limda LN
30
TEEN BATTI
36
KV Rd
Gaurav Path Rd
35
Gaurav Path
Bedi Gate
Teen Darwaja
Vishwakarma Rd
Lakhota Walk Way
Lakhota Lake
21
17
18
Lakhota Lake
Sumair Club Rd
Lake Dr
7
9
Main City Rd
Central Bank Rd
Jetpur
37
See Junagadh
See Continuation of Junagadh
Amreli
Junagadh
Savarkundla
11
1
Gir National Park & Wildlife Sanctuary
Veraval
24
Una
Kodinar
School
Jallandhar Beach
See Diu Map (p660)
Diu
Arabian Sea

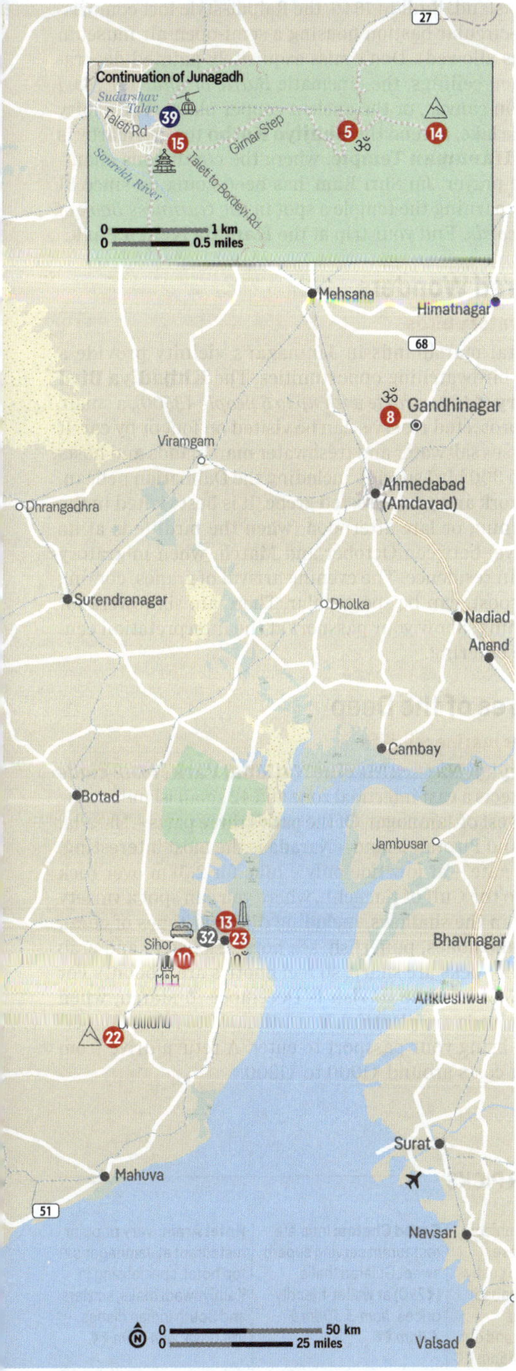

HIGHLIGHTS
1 Gir National Park & Wildlife Sanctuary
2 Khijadiya Bird Sanctuary
3 Narara Marine National Park

SIGHTS
4 Adi Kadi Vav
5 Ambaji Mandir
6 Ashokan Edicts
7 Bala Hanuman Temple
8 Bhavnath Mahadev Temple
9 Bhujiyo Kotho
10 Darbargadh Sihor
11 Devalia Safari Park
12 Dwarkadhish Temple
13 Ganga Deri
14 Girnar Hill
15 Girnar Taleti
16 Jama Masjid
17 Kamala Nehru Park
18 Lakhota Palace & Museum
19 Mahabat Maqbara
20 Navghan Kuvo
see 13 Raj Samadhi
21 Ranmal Lake
22 Shatrunjaya
23 Takhteshwar Temple
24 Temple of Somnath
25 Uparkot Fort

ACTIVITIES
26 Buddhist Caves

SLEEPING
27 Bollevue Sarovar Premiere
28 Click Hotel
29 Hotel Aram
30 Hotel Kalatit International
31 Lotus Hotel
32 Nilambag Palace Hotel
33 Orchard Palace

EATING
34 Geeta Lodge
see 27 Girnar Sky Lounge
35 Grand Chetna
36 Hotel Kalpana
see 30 Le Petit Boulangerie
37 Patel Restaurant

DRINKING & NIGHTLIFE
38 Jay Ambe Juice Centre

SHOPPING
see 10 Kansara Bazaar Road

TRANSPORT
39 Girnar Ropeway

SAURASHTRA'S SACRED SPOTS

The region of Saurashtra is important for its constellation of pilgrimage spots, which sit at the intersection of history, religion and mythology. Dwarka is believed to be Krishna's kingdom. It is home to **Dwarkadhish Temple**, one of the four sacred Hindu sites called *char dham*, and Bet Dwarka, the original residence of Krishna according to legend. The honey-coloured **Somnath Temple**, on the banks of the Arabian Sea, is home to a large black Shiva lingam or *jyotirling* (sacred shrine), one of 12 sacred Shiva shrines in India. The holiest Jain pilgrimage site is Palitana, which is home to the **Shatrunjaya Hill** complex and its over 900 carved marble temples.

sits on an island. Built in 1846, the Rajput-style fort comprises a semi-circular bastion housing a semi-open-air museum (no photos allowed). Don't miss exquisitely painted decorative wooden ceilings, the cinematic *Battle of Bhuchar Mori* painting on canvas, or the ancient copper plates. For a lofty view of the lake, ascend the **Bhujiyo Kotho** tower. Nearby is the **Bala Hanuman Temple**, where the continuous chanting of the prayer 'Jai Shri Ram' has been going on since 31 July 1964, earning the temple a spot in the *Guinness Book of World Records*. End your trip at the **Kamala Nehru Park**.

Feathered Wonders

Spot migratory birds

The coastal marshlands in Jamnagar's vicinity provide a wealth of birdwatching opportunities. The **Khijadiya Bird Sanctuary** *(₹400, vehicle with up to 6 people ₹3500)*, a small, 6-sq-km protected reserve, can be visited on foot or by car. It encompasses saltwater and freshwater marshlands and hosts more than 300 bird species, including the Dalmatian pelican, painted stork and great crested grebe. It is best visited in the early morning or late afternoon (when the birdlife is at its most active) between October and March, when migratory birds are in residence. The evening arrival of cranes, coming home to roost, can be spectacular. There are six towers for birdwatching. Show your passport at the interpretation centre before entering.

Creatures of the Deep

Search for marine wildlife

The 120-sq-km **Narara Marine National Park** *(₹650; guide ₹500)* protects a vast intertidal zone and 42 small islands to the east and west of Jamnagar. Of the park's three parts – Narada, Poshitra and Pirotan Island – Narada is the most interesting. From the gate – at low tide only – hike for 2.3km over rock and reef to the Gulf of Kachchh, where you can spot a variety of sea life in the shallows, including different types of coral, octopus, anemones, pufferfish, sea horses, lobsters and crab plovers (the rocks are sharp, so reef booties are a boon!). For birders, the best time to visit is December to March, when wintering birds are plentiful. You will need to fill out paperwork and bring your passport to enter. A return drive from Jamnagar costs around ₹1000 to ₹1200.

EATING IN JAMNAGAR: OUR PICKS

La-Petit Boulangerie: Excellent bakery at Hotel Kalatit International that feels wildly out of place in Jamnagar – but we are not complaining. *9am-midnight* ₹

Hotel Kalpana: Punjabi, Gujarati and Chinese food, consumed in cushy booths. The Hyderabadi biryani and paneer (cheese) dishes stand out. *10am-4pm & 7-10.45pm* ₹₹

Grand Chetna: Intimate restaurant serving superb sweet Gujarati thalis (₹290) at wallet-friendly prices. *11am-3.30pm & 7-11pm* ₹₹

Hotel Aram: Very popular restaurant at Jamnagar's top hotel, specialising in Kathiyawadi thalis, sizzlers and South Indian dishes like dosa. *7am-11pm* ₹₹

ADIL AHMAD INDIA/SHUTTERSTOCK

Mahabat Maqbara

A Glimpse of Ancient History

Mosques, mausoleums and a venerable fort

The city of Junagadh is packed with fascinating historic sites. The **Mahabat Maqbara** *(₹100)* mausoleum is straight out of an Euro-Indo-Islamic fantasy novel. **Uparkot Fort** *(₹500)* is believed to have been built in 319 BCE by the Mauryan emperor Chandragupta. The fort's 20m-high ramparts enclose a number of painstakingly restored sites and monuments: the controversial **Jama Masjid** (Ranakdevi Mahal), believed to have been built on top of temple remains; a palace converted from a mosque in the 15th century; two step-wells cut from solid rock: **Adi Kadi Vav** and **Navghan Kuvo**; and **Buddhist caves** *(₹300)* – monastic quarters carved out of rock in the 2nd century CE. The fort affords panoramic views of both Junagadh and Girnar Hill.

A Spiritual Quest

Complete a mountaintop pilgrimage

Pilgrims flood Junagadh to scale one of India's most sacred mountains, **Girnar Hill**, home to an astonishing 866 Hindu and Jain temples. Doing so requires a dawn departure and

GIRNAR MAHASHIVRATRI MELA

One of Gujarat's most raucous and entertaining festivals, the Girnar Mahashivratri Mela (otherwise known as the **Bhavnath Mela**), celebrating the deity Shiva's cosmic dance of destruction, is held over five days in the month of Magha (February/March) at the **Bhavnath Mahadev Temple** at Girnar Taleti in Junagadh. Dedicated to Shiva, it's a lively affair of folk music and dancing. Throngs of *nagas* (naked sadhus or spiritual men), arrive seated on elephants, holding flags and blowing conch shells on their way to collective bathing in the Bhavnath temple's tank. In addition to the spiritual aspect, there is free food, handicraft stalls and [illegible]

EATING IN JUNAGADH: OUR PICKS

Jay Ambe Juice Centre: Serving fantastic juices and shakes since 1953. Try the wonderful custard apple shake. *9.30am-11.30pm* ₹

Geeta Lodge: Local families clamber into this tightly spaced favourite for well-priced thalis. Prepare to share your table. *10.30am-3pm & 7-10.30pm* ₹₹

Patel Restaurant: Recommended by locals, ostentatious Patel specialises in superb thalis. Follow the loudspeaker to the 1st floor. *11am-10.30pm* ₹₹

Girnar Sky Lounge: Elevated street snacks, Indian/Chinese combos and continental food on Sarovar Premiere's open-air rooftop. *7.30-11pm* ₹₹₹

BHAVNAGAR HERITAGE

Bhavnagar Heritage *(bhavnagarheritage.com)* is a community-led initiative (working with historians, architects and local citizens) that is dedicated to celebrating and preserving the rich cultural legacy of Bhavnagar and the wider Saurashtra region. It is currently being helmed by Brijeshwari Kumari Gohil from the royal family of Bhavnagar. They have been actively working on revitalising abandoned historic structures in the city through community outreach, responsible restoration such as cleaning drives, public awareness, and even heritage walks. They run a comprehensive website, plus an Instagram account *(instagram.com/bhavnagarheritage)*, showcasing the rich heritage of the city, detailing sites of interest and why they are worth conserving.

considerable effort – there are 9999 steps between you and the summit. The trail begins 5.5km east of the city at **Girnar Taleti**. Luckily, **Girnar Ropeway** *(udankhatola.com; one-way/return ₹400/630)*, Asia's longest, also whisks people over the course of 10 minutes to **Ambaji Mandir**, skipping half of the steps. En route to the trail/ropeway, stop at the **Ashokan Edicts**, where Buddhist emperor Ashoka had 14 edicts inscribed on a large boulder in Brahmi script around 250 BCE.

A Historic Port City

Delve into Bhavnagar's history

A laid-back coastal town in eastern Saurashtra, Bhanvagar was once the capital of a princely state and still preserves some of that history. There are no tours or signboards here so you have to find the places yourself. The city's standout sight is the **Nilambag Palace Hotel**, former home to the Gohil dynasty and now a heritage hotel. Tours are conducted on request *(nilambagpalace.com; ₹500 per person)*, and there's a gift shop on-site. In the city there is also the **Raj Samadhi** site with its sandstone *chhatris* (memorials) to former Gohil rulers. Further south, overlooking the Ganga lake, is **Ganga Deri**. This marble monument was built by Maharaja Takhtsinhji in memory of his wife, Maharani Rajba, who died during childbirth in 1875. Another landmark is the **Takhteshwar Temple**, perched on a hill with sweeping views of the sea and town.

Ancient Ruins & Modern Metalwork

Saunter around Sihor

The erstwhile capital of the Gohil Rajputs (before Bhavnagar took over the role), **Sihor** has been a prominent trading centre since the 5th century BCE. There's a palace on the hill that all the snaking lanes in the city lead up to, and it possesses a rich architectural and cultural heritage. A self-guided tour of the place – it is a 40-minute drive from Bhavnagar – should start at the crumbling **Darbargadh** *(bhavnagarheritage.com)*. The palace complex is in ruins but has some gorgeous, intricate frescoes scattered about on its walls and ceilings. There is a caretaker who can show you around; get permission before entering.

Once you descend from the castle, wander through the dusty lanes admiring the architecture; you may even spot some art deco buildings. In one lane, the sound of rhythmic tapping will tell you that you've arrived at an integral part of Sihor's history and present. On **Kansara Bazaar Road**, you will find brass and copper being welded into pots, bottles, glasses and more. Many smithies have shops attached.

TOP EXPERIENCE

Gir National Park

Gir National Park & Wildlife Sanctuary is the only place in the world where you can see Asiatic lions – majestic creatures that once roamed as far west as Syria and as far east as Bihar. Asiatic lions are smaller than African lions, and they are identified by their prominent belly fold and moderate mane growth in males.

Asiatic lion

Animal Kingdom

Taking a safari through the dry teak woodlands interspersed with grasslands of the national park is a joy – even without the added excitement of searching for big cats like leopards, sloth bears, sambar deer, *chowsingha* (four-horned antelope), gaurs and hyenas. There is an abundance of birdlife, including the crested serpent eagle, the vulnerable greater spotted eagle and the endangered Pallas's fish eagle.

Tranquil Heart

The safari route takes you to what the guides call 'Heaven of Gir' a vast, beautiful body of water surrounded by hills, near Kamleshwar Dam on the Hiran River.

Devalia Safari Park

If you miss out on a permit, your other option for lion encounters is at Devalia Safari Park *(closed Wed)*, a fenced-off part of the park where sightings are guaranteed but stage-managed and overpriced (entry costs the same as a Gir National Park safari).

Rise & Fall of a Species

Widespread hunting decimated the Asiatic lion population with only a dozen left in Gujarat by the 1870s. The Nawab of Junagadh set up a protection zone and, by the beginning of the 20th century, lion numbers began to recover. Today, Gir is too small for the growing lion population, forcing lions beyond the park, leading to higher potential for human–lion interactions.

TOP TIPS

- Carry your passport with you as proof of identification.
- Only 50 slots are available per safari (three daily). Permits must be booked online, at least a month in advance. Tickets cannot be bought at the park and single seat purchases (for the vehicle) are not available.

PRACTICALITIES

- girlion.gujarat.gov.in
- ₹6400, guide ₹400-700, vehicle ₹2000-4500 (up to 6 people)
- 6am-7pm (summer), 6.45am-6pm (winter)

Vadodara (Baroda)

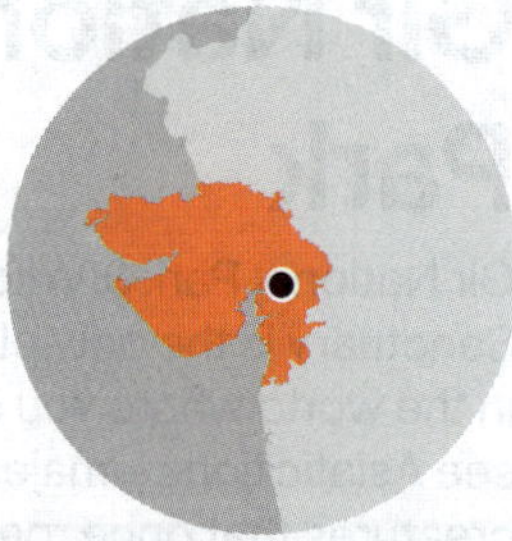

CULTURAL ATTRACTIONS | ART | ROYAL HERITAGE

GETTING AROUND

Vadodara is an hour's train ride from Ahmedabad (multiple trains daily) and is well-connected by train and bus to other major cities, including Bhavnagar and Mumbai. There are flights to major cities like Mumbai and Delhi. It is a 2½-hour drive from Ahmedabad. Within the city, autorickshaws are the easiest and quickest way to travel; agree on a price beforehand. Ola and Uber work here but are scarce – use them to get an idea of the price for certain distances. The One Way Cab app is ideal for trips beyond the city, to the likes of Champaner or Ahmedabad.

Vadodara was the former royal capital of the Gaekwad dynasty from 1732 till 1948. Once the richest princely state in British India, yet smaller than Ahmedabad, Vadodara is sometimes overlooked, yet it offers much value for travellers. It is home to the magnificent Lukshmi Vilas Palace, with its Indo-Saracenic Revival architecture, plus numerous museums. As elsewhere in Gujarat, there are step-wells here too – one on the palace grounds, as well as the 500-year-old Vidyadhar Vav. There are also gardens, such as the tranquil Sayaji Baug. The city's history can be explored in the stunning Baroda Museum and Picture Gallery and the Maharaja Fatehsingh Museum with its collection of paintings by the renowned artist Raja Ravi Varma. Vadodara's food is some of the best that Gujarat has to offer, particularly when it comes to *farsan* (savoury nibbles).

The Gaekwads' Legacy

Learn about royalty

The Maratha Gaekwad family ruled Vadodara for nearly two centuries, from the early 18th century till 1948, leaving an indelible impression on the city. Maharaja Sayajirao III's rule saw Baroda transformed into a wealthy, modern state. Today, the family still lives at the **Lukshmi Vilas Palace** *(instagram.com/lukshmivilaspalace; ₹525),* part of which is open to the public. The 170-room monument is done up in the Indo-Saracenic style. It is the world's largest private residence, and has on its grounds a golf course, the Navlakhi step-well, a dining area and cricket grounds. Within the palace you will find an impressive collection of arms, paintings and statues. The Durbar Hall is particularly impressive with its stained glass and mosaic floors. One kilometre away, on the grounds, is the **Maharaja Fatehsinh Museum** *(₹300),* which features an impressive collection of paintings from Raja Ravi Varma,

HIGHLIGHTS
1 Baroda Museum & Picture Gallery
2 Lukshmi Vilas Palace
3 Tambekar Wada

SIGHTS
4 Aurobindo Ashram
5 Champaner Gate
6 Gendi Gate
7 Kirti Mandir
8 Lehripura Gate
9 Mandvi Gate
10 Narsinhji Mandir
11 Sayaji Baug

ACTIVITIES
12 Central Library Mandvi

SLEEPING
13 Regenta Inn Vadodara
14 Sayaji Hotel Vadodara

EATING
15 Canara Coffee House
16 Gazra Cafe

SHOPPING
17 Khanderao Market

TRANSPORT
18 ST Bus Stand
19 Vadodara Station

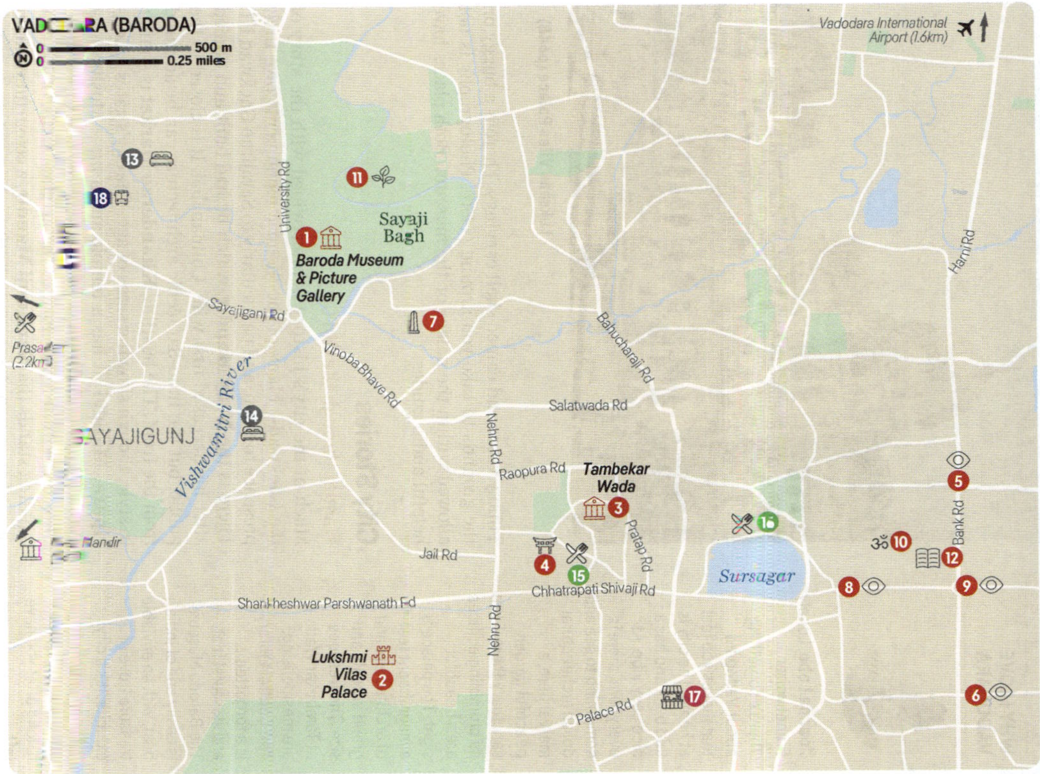

WHY I LOVE VADODARA

Joanna Lobo, Lonely Planet writer

There's something about Vadodara that makes you feel at home. The city is laid back and has a nice easy vibe. At every turn, there is something to see and do: an architectural marvel here, a peaceful garden sanctuary there. Even its crumbling edifices are a beautiful sight. The palace is a magnificent feat of architecture and grand in scale and size. The frescoes at Tambekar Wada are mesmerising. The Central Library is a forgotten architectural feat. The Baroda Museum is easily one of India's best, with an enviable treasure trove of exhibits. It's a city that captures your attention and holds it, long after you have left.

DYNAMOLAND/SHUTTERSTOCK

Lukshmi Vilas Palace (p648)

Tiffany vases and cameo shell carvings. There is a buggy on the grounds to take you around *(₹150)*. Photography is not allowed within the palace or the museum. Both places have helpful audio guides.

City Stories

Wander through the Old City

Much of the city's history is intertwined with the story of the Gaekwads. Many of the historic monuments owe their presence to them, and particularly to Sayajirao Gaekwad III. There is the **Nyay Mandir**, which he had built and named after his deceased first wife, Chimanabai. It is closed to the public, but the Indo-Saracenic architecture can be admired from the front. The bustling **Khanderao Market** is similar in style, though showing signs of age. The city's gates – **Lehripura**, **Mandvi** (it has a temple and a *pir* – Muslim holy man), **Gendi** and **Champaner** – are in the Old City and lie close by. Within a *pol* close to the original Bank of Baroda building stands the **Narsinhji Mandir**, a colourful wooden temple some 280 years old, built like a *haveli*. It is the city's main temple, once patronised by the royal family. Chirag Munjani of **Rural Pleasure Journeys** *(instagram.com/chirag.munjani; group of 5 people ₹2500)* conducts heritage walks in the city. He is a treasure trove of local knowledge.

Faith & Architecture

Explore the city's religious sites

Vadodara has many religious monuments that also offer a glimpse of the city's history. In the city centre is the **Kirti Mandir** monument, which Sayajirao Maharaja had built in the memory of deceased members of his family. It has a high central *shikhara* (rising tower in Hindu architecture) with a bronze finial representing the sun, moon and earth. The bungalow that was once home to yogi and spiritual leader Aurobindo Ghosh, during his 13-year stay in Vadodara, is now **Aurobindo Ashram**. It is a tranquil escape from the city noise, making it ideal for meditation. There is also a small library and some relics of his on site. The on-site shop sells incense, soaps and bath salts made in Auroville, Pondicherry.

A little away from the city centre sits the **Qutubuddin Hajiro**, a mausoleum dedicated to Qutubuddin Muhammad Khan (who had taught Emperor Jehangir Khan). Built in 1586, the double-domed structure resembles Humayun's tomb in Delhi and displays carved Islamic calligraphy.

Fresco Treasures

Admire fresco art

A dilapidated building on the outside, **Tambekar Wada** has a treasure trove of frescoes decorating its interior – the building's main surviving feature of note. Here you can admire the Maratha-style *wada* (mansion) architecture, with its wooden balconies and a central courtyard. The front portion of the house is adorned with tempera paintings, dating from the mid- to late 19th century, that cover the walls and ceilings, depicting stories from Hindu mythology and even some European figures and settings.

A Walk in the Park

Spend time in a green space

An expansive green space, the **Sayaji Baug** gardens are where families go to spend an evening. There is a lot to see – a bonsai park, bandstand and many statues. The highlight here is the **Baroda Museum & Picture Gallery** *(instagram.com/thebarodamuseum; ₹250)*, easily the best museum in the city. It was built in 1894, modelled on the Victoria & Albert Museum in London by Maharaja Sayajirao Gaekwad III. Highlights include *patola* silk saris, leather vases, Persian tiles, bronze figurines, stuffed animals and birds, fossilised dinosaur eggs, [illegible] in a sarcophagus and the skeleton of a blue whale.

VADODARA'S CENTRAL LIBRARY

The **Central Library Mandvi** owes its existence to Maharaja Sayajirao Gaekwad III. It was initially a part of his personal library at the Lukshmi Vilas Palace (p648), before it was moved to its present location. Built in 1910, it was the city's first 'green' building because it was originally designed to not use electricity (though electricity is used today). The three-tier stack area is its most prominent feature, whereas the floors are made of Belgian glass, allowing natural light to illuminate the whole place. The library runs mobile libraries and cinema shows in villages to teach the illiterate. The oldest book here is 1800 years old, and the library fee for the year is just ₹2.

EATING IN VADODARA: OUR PICKS

Canara Coffee House: Small, sweet space doing South Indian classics and and cafe-style food. Look for the cute murals on the wall. *8am-10.30pm* ₹

Gazra Cafe: Overlooking Sursagar Lake, this cafe employs people from the LGBTQIA+ community. Excellent vegetarian food. *11am-9.30pm* ₹₹

Mandap: Situated within a hotel, this is one of the better places to eat an unlimited Gujarati thali. It's a little fancy. *11.45am-2.45pm & 7.45-10.30pm* ₹₹

Prasadam: Another popular thali place serving Gujarati food, including delicious sweets and beverages and side dishes. *11am-3pm & 7-10.30pm* ₹₹

Bhuj

TEXTILES | PALACES | MUSEUMS

GETTING AROUND

Bhuj is well connected by flights from Pune, Mumbai, Delhi and Goa, and by frequent trains to the likes of Ahmedabad, Mumbai, Delhi, Jaipur and Kolkata. Some Bhuj attractions are walkable: the main sights within the Darbargadh palace complex practically sit on top of one another. A 1.8km walk connects them to the Sharad Baug Palace. For attractions further out, negotiate rates with autorickshaws (rideshare apps do not yet work in Bhuj) or hire a car and driver via your accommodation.

The Jadeja Rajputs took control of Kachchh in 1510 and made Bhuj their capital 29 years later. It has remained the most important town in India's largest district ever since. Arguably Gujarat's most entrancing city, it is an ideal springboard for the natural attractions and wildlife around the Great Rann and some of the most famous textile-producing workshops in the world. The city comprises a splendid clutch of somewhat dilapidated, grand palaces full of treasures, sumptuous dining rooms and family heirlooms. The erstwhile Kutch Royal Family still owns most of Bhuj's grand edifices, including Aina Palace (where they worship their ancestors, and the king and his sons perform *dhoop* rituals) and Sharad Baug Palace (their current home). Much of the city was levelled after a devastating 2001 earthquake, the scars of which are still visible in what is left of the city's historic architecture.

Palaces Galore!

Explore royal residences

Begin your exploration of this fascinating city with a look at two historic palaces: **Aina Mahal** *(₹30)*, built in 1752. Its lower floor feels like a cluttered antique market of royal assets. The elaborately mirrored interior is European in style, with blue-and-white Delft-style tiling, and a candelabra with Venetian glass shades. Next door, the 19th-century **Prag Mahal** *(₹70)* is home to the ghostly yet exuberant Durbar Hall with its vast chandeliers; there are are lofty views of 17th-century **Rani Mahal** from the tower's foundations.

The 1867-built Italianate **Sharad Baug Palace** *(instagram.com/kutchroyalfamily; ₹30)* near Hamirsar Lake was the home of the last official ruler of the Kingdom of Kachchh, Maharao Madansinhji. The museum displays his personal assembly of artefacts and heirlooms, such as picture frames made from wild boar tusks and the kingdom's currency collection. The royal family still live on the property; they run

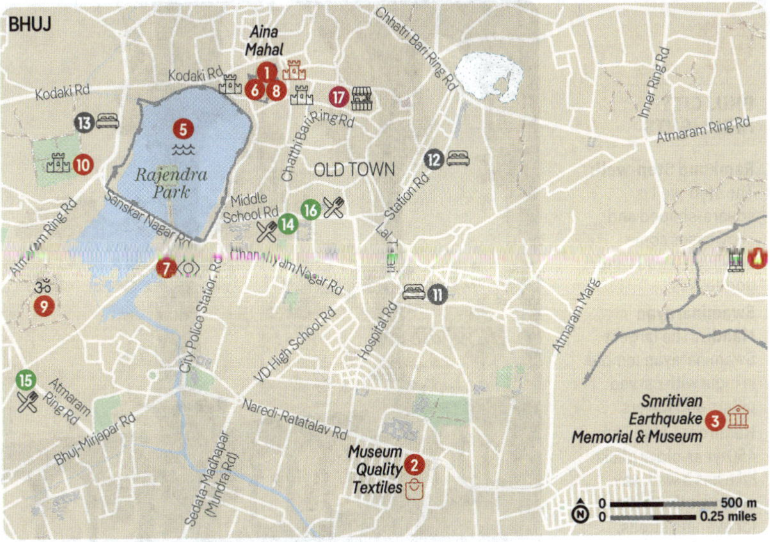

HIGHLIGHTS
1 Aina Mahal
2 Museum Quality Textiles
3 Smritivan Earthquake Memorial & Museum

SIGHTS
4 Bhujia Fort
5 Hamirsar Lake
6 Prag Mahal
7 Ramkund Step-Well
8 Rani Mahal
9 Royal Chhatardis
10 Sharad Baug Palace

SLEEPING
11 Bhuj House
12 Hotel Prince
13 Sharad Baug Homestay

EATING
14 Green Rock
see 12 Jesal
15 Saffron
16 Shankar Vadapav

SHOPPING
17 Saraf Bazar

a homestay and serve delicious local dishes at the **Sharadbaug Dine In** *(instagram.com/sharadbaug_dine_in)*. Call in advance to dine in *(7600384951)*.

Remembering Earthquake Victims

Visit the Earthquake Museum

Bhuj was the epicentre of Gujarat's disastrous 2001 earthquake, which measured 7.0 on the Richter scale and killed 13,000 people in Bhuj alone. The **Smritivan Earthquake Memorial & Museum** *(₹300)*, the largest memorial and museum ever built in modern India, commemorates the tragedy outside town at Bhujia Hill (Bhujiyo Dungar). The museum is divided into seven blocks (Rebirth, Rediscover, Restore, Rebuild, Rethink,

TOP TIP

Parsi families settled in Bhuj after British occupation in the 1800s. They lived in Camp, beyond the walled city of Bhuj. The Bhujwala family's home is now **The Bhuj House** *(thebhujhouse.com)*, a beautiful homestay with great Parsi food.

EATING IN BHUJ: OUR PICKS

Shalimar Hotel & Restaurant: Multi-cuisine restaurant known for its meaty offerings, such as tandoori chicken and *keema* (minced meat dish). *11am-11pm* ₹₹

Green Rock: A fine spot for Gujarati thalis (₹260-300), Punjabi and South Indian favourites. *11am-3pm & 7-10.30pm Sat-Thu, 9am-5pm & 7-10.30pm Fri* ₹₹

Saffron: All-veg Mughlai cuisine in spic-and-span dining room at Hotel Mangalam. Free *khakhra* (thin cracker) is a nice touch. *10am-10pm* ₹₹

Jesal: Rich Punjabi curries, South Indian seafood and Chinese dishes shine at this excellent multicuisine at the Comfort Inn Prince. *7am-10.45pm* ₹₹₹

BHUJ CITY HIGHLIGHTS

Ramkund Step-well: The step-well is square-shaped and showcases some carvings of gods and goddesses.

Swaminarayan Mandir: The largest Swaminarayan temple in India with carved pillars and towers.

Hamirsar Lake: The 450-year-old artificial lake has a walkway around it that's ideal for evening strolls.

Saraf Bazaar: A market offering local goods such as textiles, gold and silver jewellery, handicrafts, antiques, domestic utensils and more.

Bhujia Fort: The fort is a fantastic spot for sunrise and sunset, offering sweeping views of Bhuj city.

Kachchh Museum: Gujarat's oldest museum displays artefacts, crafts and inscriptions dating to the 1st century CE.

PVINCE73/SHUTTERSTOCK

View of Aina Mahal from Prag Mahal (p652)

Relive and Renew). Parts of the museum are dedicated to science and nature, whereas Restore tackles the earthquake itself, with harrowing exhibits of rubble piles with trapped victims, and disorienting emergency telephone control room chaos. Free guided tours point out the museum highlights.

Textile Tales

Marvel at remarkable embroidery

Salim Wazir's late father, AA Wazir, had amassed an incredible collection over 50 years, comprising over 3000 pieces – some as old as 450 years – at the home museum and shop **Museum Quality Textiles**. Many are for sale and the stories behind the pieces are extraordinary. Salim is a wonderful storyteller, and knows the details and history behind every piece, collected from around Kachchh, Saurashtra and Sind. Look out for some stunning dowry bags, *bandhani* (tie-dyed) work, *toplos* (children's caps), *torans* (shield-shaped devices that are part of the local wedding tradition), quilts and camel-leather belts. Give yourself ample time to admire each piece.

Beyond Bhuj

Outside Bhuj lie seasonal salt deserts, wild asses roam the Great Rann of Kachchh, and villages showcase Gujarat's rich textile tradition and other crafts.

Kachchh's beautiful, colourful embroidery work, weaving, tie-dying and block printing are coveted the world over. Bhuj's surroundings, forming part of the great district of Kachchh, include numerous small villages and towns – Ajrakh, Nirona, Sumrasar, Bhujodi – that still practise these different crafts and textile arts. Venturing beyond these villages makes for an abrupt set change. A great arid expanse – the White Desert – emerges 90km or so north of Bhuj. And on the far eastern side of Kachchh, the Little Rann's Wild Ass Sanctuary is a haven for Indian wild asses and other wildlife. Little Rann is part of the Great Rann of Kachchh, a stark landscape that is one of the world's largest salt deserts.

Places

White Desert

TIME FROM BHUJ: 1½HR

Kachchh's saltier side

October to March is the best time to head to the giant salt desert 90km north of Bhuj. The suitably named White Desert is an unsullied sheet of salted earth – part of the greater Thar Desert, which stretches across northwestern India and into Pakistan. A permit *(adult/child/car ₹100/50/50)* is needed to visit, and can be paid for and processed at the carnivalesque **Tent City** (you'll need a photocopy of your passport and visa). The Tent City's food stalls are a great option for lunch. From the parking area, it is a 1.5km walk or camel cart ride (₹50 per person) to a viewing tower overlooking the great salt expanse (and Pakistan beyond). You can get out onto the salt flat to take your perspective-bending photos. Time your day to reach **Kalo Dungar** (Black Hill), Kachchh's highest point

GETTING AROUND

Bhuj is a great base for exploring the surrounding villages. To visit the 7500-sq-km Great Rann of Kachchh with its spread-out sights, including the Little Rann, hire a car and driver in Bhuj (around ₹4000 per day), or better yet, join a tour. Sohail Wazir *(9099689553)*, whose family runs Museum Quality Textiles (p654), conducts excellent tours (₹5000 per day). Delhi-based **Breakaway** *(break-away.in; from ₹25,000)* also offers customised tours of the area.

RANN UTSAV: A CONTROVERSIAL FESTIVAL

Every year, the government stages a festival called **Rann Utsav** *(rannutsav.net)*. Originally lasting a few days, it has now become a three-month affair (October to February), and some say it has lost much of its charm. The original aim was to celebrate Kachchh's rich artistic and cultural heritage and the beauty of the White Desert. Accordingly, there are camel safaris (particularly on moonlit nights), craft stalls and workshops, paintball and ATV rides, and luxury accommodation. All of this unfolds in a temporary tent city. Though the original intentions were good, these days the festival is very commercial, with little to do with Gujarat and its heritage, though the setting is remarkable.

MRIDULABLOG/SHUTTERSTOCK

Tent City (p655), White Desert

(462m), located some 50km from the desert, for sunset views over the salt flat (or inland sea if you visit during the monsoon season). From Bhuj, a car and driver costs about ₹5000 a day.

Dholavira

TIME FROM BHUJ: 2½HR

Ancient Harappan civilisation

A UNESCO World Heritage Site, Dholavira is one of the two largest Harappa-era (3300 BCE to 1300 BCE) sites in India, located on **Khadir Island**. The Bronze Age historic proto-settlement is spread across 49 hectares, giving you glimpses of a well-planned city with an excellent water conservation system. There are reservoirs, wells and water filtration systems, besides the remnants of fortifications, citadel walls and an amphitheatre. Look out for a unique inscription with large pictographic symbols (yet to be decoded), plus the remains of a bead-making workshop, servants' quarters and *bhungas* (traditional mud houses made by the nomadic tribes in the region). There is a museum on-site, detailing Gujarat's other Harappan sites and showcasing some fossils uncovered nearby.

'Road to Heaven'

The unofficial name given to the road across the water, connecting Khavda to Dholavira, is the **Road to Heaven**. This 30km stretch is certainly scenic – depending on the season, you will see either vast stretches of water or glistening white salt on both sides of the road. It is possible to stop the car to take some photos and enjoy the salty air. At the other end of the island, on Khadir Bet Rd, you are likely to spot flocks of flamingos and other waders. Go early in the day to enjoy the birdlife at its most active.

Wild Ass Sanctuary

TIME FROM BHUJ: 4½HR

Where the wild things are

A portion of parched land within the Little Rann is home to the 4953-sq-km **Wild Ass Sanctuary** *(₹1200-1500)*, where wildlife-spotting opportunities include some 3000 or so Indian wild khurs (asses), wolves, caracals, blackbuck and chinkaras (gazelles). From October to March, a bird population of up to 350 species swarms the sanctuary as well – it is one of the few areas in India where flamingos breed in the wild. You can get visitors' permits at the gates (or ask your resort to organise it). 4WD safaris with up to six passengers (including vehicle permit and guide) depart from 6am and cost between ₹3500 and ₹4200, depending on the day of the week. The sanctuary is best reached by private vehicle en route to/from Bhuj; it is a 193km drive east of the city (four hours).

Ajrakhpur

TIME FROM BHUJ: 30MIN

The history of Kachchh embroidery

The excellent **Living & Learning Design Centre Crafts Museum** in Ajrakhpur, run by the Shrujan Trust *(shrujan-lldc.org; ₹100)*, chronicles the many known embroidery styles of the communities in Kachchh, including those of the Ahir, Mochi, Maru/Meghwal and Rabari peoples, among many others. Spread across three galleries, the museum showcases the history of each community's embroidery, the different techniques, and Shrujan's work with 'modernising' the designs. There is a library, and a small crafts studio doing mini-workshops (on request) and an excellent gift shop. The in-house restaurant serves delicious vegetarian food (book a meal in advance).

A centuries-old craft

Ajrakhpur is known for being the hub of block-printing (*ajrakh* means 'block print'), which uses indigo, madder and printed mordants. Sufiyan Ismail Khatri has his own studio, **Ajrakh Indigo House**, and is the 10th generation of the Khatri family to be practising the art. If he is around, he will walk you through around the space, do a demo of the process and show you all his natural colours, especially his indigo vats. He even conducts **workshops** *(instagram.com/sufiyankhatri; ₹3500 per person per day)*. Upon request he can also show you hundreds of blocks, which are imprinted with his designs that ultimately go on the cloth. His studio has an excellent gift shop, too.

Mandvi

TIME FROM BHUJ: 1½HR

Observe traditional shipbuilding

It's worth taking a half-day trip to the laid-back beach town of **Mandvi**, 60km south of Bhuj, to watch skilled craftspeople constructing giant wooden dhows – that would not have looked out of place centuries ago – by hand. Watch the fascinating

A WEAVING VILLAGE

A popular handicraft village near Bhuj, **Bhujodi** is a small town but a major handicraft centre. The Rabari and Vankar communities reside here and, historically, they bartered what they produced – the Rabaris gave them wool from their sheep, and the Vankars crafted them into blankets and garments. Over time, the trade fizzled out and today the Vankars make woven cloth, still using desi wool and cotton (called kala cotton) but for a new audience. One of the prominent community leaders here is **Vankar Vishram Valji** *(instagram.com/vankar_vishram_valji)*, an 11th-generation master weaver and natural indigo dyer, and a recipient of the prestigious UNESCO Seal of Excellence; his designs are internationally renowned.

process at the **Traditional Shipbuilding Yard**, with its attendant rhythmic sawing, sanding and cutting.

Nirona

TIME FROM BHUJ: **40MIN**

An ancient Persian art

Abdul Gafur Khatri and family have revived 400-year-old Persian **Traditional Rogan Art** *(9825753955)* in Nirona. Khatri is a Padmashri Award (Indian's most prestigious civilian achievement award) winner and his whole family is involved in the craft. They are the only family doing *rogan* art in the world and their works are so highly prized that Narendra Modi presented Barack Obama with a *rogan* painting in 2014.

The process is mesmerising: castor oil is boiled and thickened into a jelly and then mixed with pigments to form colour; the paintings are hand drawn using a *kalam* (writing instrument) on cotton or silk. Every piece is unique and unplanned beforehand. Prepare your wallet.

Lacquer art

In a dusty corner of Nirona live the semi-nomadic community, the **Wadas**. They belong to the poorer sector of society, and earn their living largely through lacquer work. They use lac (resin) from trees and have a small makeshift table that they use to add colour to wooden spoons, tops, toys, containers, and rolling pins. The colours are all homemade and they use oil for the shine. While one person does a demonstration, the womenfolk and children get busy propping up a makeshift 'market,' showcasing their handmade beaded bangles, bags, stuffed animals and jewellery. You will need a guide here, as the community only speak Gujarati.

Sumrasar

TIME FROM BHUJ: **40MIN**

A remarkable craft centre

Part-museum, part-international-research-institute, part-shop, **Kala Raksha** *(instagram.com/kalaraksha)* represents work from six communities (Jat, Rabari, Mutwa, Maru/Meghwal, Samaja and Marwada) and is fantastic for picking up applique creations. There's a small museum that gives a brief history of the community, and some embroidery on display. Ask to see the heirloom hall, which contains vintage pieces, some from Sind and Balochistan, too. Call in advance for a short tour of the space and the chance to see the women do *soof* embroidery (it is done from behind, without any pre-traced designs). There's a small store on-site selling bags, garments and tableware.

THE BEAUTY OF KACHCHH

Sohail Wazir, tour guide. *@sohail_wazir_*
Katchchh is one of the most unique regions in the world, where stark landscapes and deep-rooted traditions coexist in remarkable harmony. From the vast white expanse of the Rann to grasslands, wetlands, and desert villages, its natural diversity is striking. Equally rich is Katchchh's living heritage of crafts and textiles. *Ajrakh* printing, *batik*, *bandhani* (tie-dye art), weaving, various embroidery styles, *rogan* painting and bell-making are not museum traditions but everyday practices passed down through generations. Each village holds a distinct craft identity, shaped by history, community and environment. In Katchchh, culture is not displayed; it is lived.

Diu

BEACHES | PORTUGUESE CHURCHES | DELICIOUS SEAFOOD

Still infused with Portuguese history and architecture, the compact island of Diu (one of India's eight specially administered federal regions) is linked by a bridge spanning tidal marshland and salt pans to Gujarat's southern coast. Formerly governed by Portugal as part of the country's Estado da Índia from 1537 till 1961, Diu had served as a major Portuguese port and trading post. Today, the island's Portuguese roots are mostly limited to its churches, crumbling villas and the occasional historic inscription. The streets of the main town are clean (if overly dusty), colourful and quiet once you get off the tourist-packed waterfront strip, and are a joy to stroll. Recent road and jetty constructions have resulted in the destruction of some of the heritage buildings, so today, Diu warrants only a day or two of your time on a Gujarat tour.

A Place in the Sun

Beach-hop around Diu Island

The Arabian-Sea-facing southern coast of **Diu Island** has some decent strands of sand for those craving a low key beach day. Some offer beach bars, restaurants and water sports while others are nearly deserted and pleasant for a stroll. **Gomptimata Beach**, 13km west of Diu Fort (p660), is a long, often empty 2.5km sweep of sand with a small temple. It livens up at weekends. Further east is the crescent-moon-shaped **Nagoa Beach**, backed by numerous resorts, restaurants and bars. Another 7km east brings you to the small, gentle curve of **Chakratirth Beach** near Sunset Point, a small headland at the southern end of the beach. Continuing east, you hit **Chandika Mata Beach**, one of the prettiest and cleanest in Diu (it gets our pick for a beach walk), bookended by large rocks. Our second-favourite is **Ghoghla Beach**, 4.7km north of Diu. It's a long, wide stretch of sand with calm waters, and is one of only two Blue Flag beaches in Gujarat and Diu combined.

GETTING AROUND

Diu is small by India standards – just 38 sq km – and most of the town's main sights are walkable. Rideshare apps – Uber and Ola – do not operate here. There are autorickshaws; agree on the price beforehand. You can catch crowded local buses to Nagoa and Vanakbara from **Jothibai Bus Stand**. It is more convenient to hire a scooter; the going rate is ₹500 per day and a driving licence is required. Try Sai **Bike On Hire** along the waterfront. From Diu's small airport there are flights to Mumbai, Pune, Delhi, Ahmedabad and Goa.

TOP TIP

Diu's far-flung beaches are too close for taxis and too far for autorickshaws. Since there is little traffic, a scooter is the perfect vehicle for exploring the island.

HIGHLIGHTS
1 Chandika Mata Beach
2 Diu Fort
3 St Paul's Church

SIGHTS
4 Chakratirth Beach
5 Church of St Francis of Assisi
6 Diu Museum
7 INS Khukri Museum
8 Lighthouse Diu Fort
9 Zampa Gateway

ACTIVITIES
10 Sai Bike On Hire

SLEEPING
11 Dream Vision Guesthouse
12 Gateway Diu

EATING
13 Apana Foodland
see 6 O Coqueiro
14 Ram Vijay

TRANSPORT
15 Jethibai Bus Stand

A Portuguese Redoubt

Saunter around Diu Fort

Built in 1535, with additions made in 1541, this well-preserved **fort** with its double moat was one of the most important Portuguese forts in Asia. It is a pleasure to wander its ramparts – some of which are walkable – and admire the superb array of cannons, learn about its many bastions, see its empty chapels and enjoy sweeping views of the ocean. Give yourself an hour, ideally in the early evening, for a scenic, leisurely walk. Finish at the more recent **lighthouse**, which is Diu's highest point. If you're after a deep dive into the fort's history, **Make it Happen** *(makeithappen.co.in)* conducts comprehensive tours *(₹499 per person).*

BALAJISRINIVASAN/SHUTTERSTOCK

Diu Fort

The Portuguese Legacy

Discover Diu's historic heart

Vestiges of the island's Portuguese history are still very much in evidence in Diu. Strolling the lanes of the walled town reveals colourful but modest *havelis*. On entering Diu, you face **Zampa Gateway**, part of the city wall, crowded with shops and structures but still showing some carvings of lions, angels and a priest. There are three churches in Diu: the deserted **Church of St Francis of Assisi**, founded in 1593 and built on a platform at the top of some steps; the yellow St Thomas Church, which houses the **Diu Museum** (it has been under renovation for years); and **St Paul's Church**. The latter is the only functioning church of the three – a baroque beauty with a neoclassical facade, founded in 1600 and rebuilt in 1807. Inside, the intricately carved woodwork is the finest among India's Portuguese churches; look for the delicate *volutes* (spiral scroll-like ornaments).

A SUNKEN NAVAL SHIP

The INS *Khukri* was an Indian Navy vessel that was retired after 32 years of service and is now a museum. It was named after an earlier naval ship, also (confusingly) called the INS *Khukri*. During the India–Pakistan War in 1971, the older of the two fell prey to torpedoes fired by a Pakistan submarine near Diu's coast, and sank, taking down 18 officers and 176 sailors with her. Their story is on display at the **INS Khukri Museum**, down the road from Diu Fort. On the other side of the island, on Chakratirth Beach there is a scaled-down replica of the naval ship, plus a **memorial** to the fallen sailors.

EATING IN DIU: OUR PICKS

Ram Vijay: Fourth-generation-run, old-fashioned ice-cream parlour going strong since 1933. Delicious handmade ice cream. *9am-2pm & 4-9.30pm* ₹₹

O Coqueiro: A quiet garden cafe serving seafood and some meat dishes. The food is delicious, especially their Portuguese gravy. *8am-9pm* ₹₹

Apana Foodland: The pick of Ghogla-Beach-facing restaurants. South Indian, Gujarati, Punjabi and Chinese dishes. *7am-3.30pm & 6-10.30pm* ₹₹

Krishna Beach Resort: Fresh fish and seafood for Krishna's excellent fish curries come from their own fishing boats. At Nagoa Beach. *11-3pm & 7-11pm* ₹₹₹

Places We Love to Stay

₹ Budget ₹₹ Midrange ₹₹₹ Top End

Ahmedabad

Map p634

Hotel Elite Inn ₹ Located in the heart of Mirzapur, this hotel offers clean, basic rooms with limited breakfast. The staff are helpful, and you can walk to the old city from here.

Ahmedabad Homestay ₹₹ Two sets of steep stairs lead to this spacious, two-room Old City gem (₹2500) with bath, kitchenette and patio. Breakfast served by basket pulley system!

Hotel Good Night ₹₹ The most inexpensive standard rooms at this dependable cheapie are spartan but spotless. Save here and splurge on food next door at House of MG.

House of MG ₹₹₹ Palatial ex-home of textile magnate Sheth Mangaldas Girdhardas; destination restaurants (Agashiye) and shops (AHMD Trunk), impeccable service and a pool almost too beautiful to swim in. Gujarat's best.

jüSTa Diwans Bungalow ₹₹₹ Gorgeous restored 150-year-old bungalow turned into a boutique heritage hotel bedecked with Gujarati textiles and vintage decor. Spring for the suite for a luxe experience.

French Haveli ₹₹₹ A beautifully restored, steep-staired Gujarati heritage home with five individually decorated, characterful rooms. Some bathrooms are shared. Good breakfast.

Champaner & Pavagadh

Champaner Heritage Resort ₹₹₹ Sitting among mango orchards and eucalyptus forest, this 150-year-old princely estate 12km south of Champaner offers a variety of accommodation (rooms, tents, treehouses).

Jambughoda Palace ₹₹₹ Dine on organic meals slow-cooked over a wood fire with the royal descendants of the Parmar dynasty at this 250-year-old heritage property 25km southeast of Champaner.

Saurashtra

Map p642

Hotel Kalatit International ₹₹ Lower midrange hotel in Jamnagar; the friendly service, good restaurant, Italian espresso and boulangerie win folks over.

Click Hotel ₹₹ Practically in the train station in Junagadh. Spotless rooms, reliable wi-fi and a popular veg restaurant. Staff eager to please.

Lotus Hotel ₹₹ A renovated former pilgrim rest house in Junagadh. Super deluxe rooms (doubles from ₹2700) feature separate toilet and shower areas. Good value.

Nilambag Palace Hotel (p646) ₹₹ Old royal palace in Bhavnagar turned into a hotel with basic rooms within the palace and in cottages outside. Food could be better, but heritage walks are worthwhile.

Orchard Palace ₹₹₹ The erstwhile royal family's former palace guesthouse is now a heritage hotel with art deco furniture, antiques and handicrafts.

Hotel Aram (p644) ₹₹₹ Formal royal property in Jamnagar with various room configurations. Popular all-day restaurant with garden seating.

Bellevue Sarovar Premiere ₹₹₹ Swanky business hotel in Junagadh; international-standard rooms feature all the mod-cons and comforts (plush bedding, hardwood flooring, marble bathrooms).

Gir National Park & Wildlife Sanctuary

Gir Lion Safari Camp ₹₹ Luxury tents and cottages in a serene riverside location. Good food, too.

Araiya Gir ₹₹₹ Well-appointed rooms, some with plunge pools, others looking out onto the artificial lake. Expect a lot of birdsong.

Gir Birding Lodge ₹₹₹ This lodge offers great-value rooms (singles/doubles from ₹7500/8500). Go for a cottage (for the same price you get wooden beds and extra lodge bathrooms).

Fern Gir Forest Resort ₹₹₹ Top-end lodge set within lush grounds features suites with private plunge pools. Brilliant birding in the resort's gardens and daily nature walks.

Asiatic Lion Lodge ₹₹₹ Peaceful lodge 6km west of Sasan Gir set within large grounds. Bungalow-style rooms are simple and spotless; open-air Gir lion documentary screenings nightly.

Vadodara (Baroda)

Map p649

Regenta Inn Vadodara ₹₹ Modern-style hotel with 91 rooms and all-day dining buffet. Close to the main attractions.

Madhav Bagh Royal Heritage Stay ₹₹₹ This guesthouse within a palace has just four rooms, with a serene garden and charming decor.

Royal Orchid Central ₹₹₹ Centrally located hotel with well-appointed rooms, decent breakfast spread and easy public transport access.

Gayaji Hotel Vadodara ₹₹₹ This five-star business hotel is located close to the city sights, and features a rooftop lounge offering good city views.

Bhuj

Map p653

Sharad Baug Homestay (p653) ₹₹ Bed down with the erstwhile Kutch Royal Family at Sharad Baug Palace's former non-veg kitchen and staff quarters.

Hotel Prince ₹₹ Mediocre midrange at best, but quality photography adorns the walls, while comfortable beds and a good restaurant ensure its popularity.

Bhuj House ₹₹₹ Restored 19th-century Parsi heritage house with four rooms looking out over an idyllic courtyard garden; Kachchh embroidery and antique furnishings abound. The food is excellent.

Little Rann of Kachchh

Desert Coursers Eco Lodge ₹₹ Ecotourism pioneer and enthusiastic naturalist Dhanraj Malik oversees the 17 air-conditioned *koobas* (thatch-roofed huts) at this rustic property.

Rann Riders ₹₹₹ Little Raan's top choice, the 28 mirror-pattern-studded *bhungas* (circular huts) or *koobas* have custom-built *tokar* wood furniture. Great food and strong emphasis on sustainability.

Ajrakhpur

The Kutchh Courtyard ₹₹₹ Cosy, peaceful homestay adorned with local art and textiles (it has its own store), offering good vegetarian food and warm service.

Mandvi

Kinara Homestay ₹₹₹ Amicable Kachchh guide Jeetendra Solanki's colourful homestay, featuring vibrant Kachchh textiles and vintage furniture. Wonderful meals.

Diu

Map p660

Dream Vision Guesthouse ₹ Lisbon-born Milesh and partner preside over this classic backpacker crash pad. Leafy garden, good food and helpful staff.

Praveg Beach Resort ₹₹₹ Ghoghla Beach hotel with 35 tin and hardwood barrel cottages. Rain showers, beach-facing patios and nice beach-view bar-restaurant.

Radhika Beach Resort ₹₹₹ Immaculately maintained, condo-like villas set around a figure-eight pool opposite Nagoa Beach.

Gateway Diu ₹₹₹ Sparkling property on Jallandar Beach, with well-equipped rooms offering sea views. Its restaurant, Earth, offers multi-cuisine and non-veg options.

French Haveli, Ahmedabad (p632)

Researched by
Pooja Naik

Mumbai (Bombay)

INDIA'S CAPITAL OF COMMERCE AND COOL

Skyscrapers, festive fervour and a food scene as diverse as its communities – the maximum city enthralls in epic proportions.

Mumbai is maddening and magnetic in equal measure. It dazzles and exhausts, seduces and shocks. The air hums with car horns, chatter and sea breezes, carrying the scents of jasmine, diesel, frying snacks and luxury perfume. Twenty-two million people call this city home – many still fondly calling it by its former name, Bombay – and millions more arrive each year chasing work, opportunity and the silver-screen dream. For all its contradictions – the glamour and the grit, the chaos and the charm – Mumbai remains India's ultimate city of possibility.

As India's financial and creative capital, Mumbai drives the country's economy from its heaving heart. The city contributes more than 6% of India's GDP, and in spirit it is as restless and relentless as New York or London – but with more colour.

Once a cluster of fishing villages inhabited by the Indigenous Koli community, Mumbai evolved through centuries of trade, conquest and colonial ambition. Ancient merchants bartered with Persia and Egypt, and dynasties such as the Chalukyas and Shilaharas left their mark in temples and forts. The Portuguese arrived in the 16th century, followed by the British, who received the seven islands in 1661 as part of a royal dowry. The East India Company transformed the port into a global trading hub, expanding it on reclaimed land and setting the stage for today's metropolis.

AVINASH DEO/SHUTTERSTOCK

Sweat and stardust coexist here. From Marine Drive's arc of art deco facades to Bandra's creative cafes and Bollywood glamour; from the opulence of the Bandra Kurla Complex to the *koliwadas* set against Worli's skyscrapers; and from ruinous mills standing cheek by jowl with fine-dining spots in Lower Parel to the city's green lung in Borivali's Sanjay Gandhi National Park, Mumbai thrives on contrast. Construction cranes dot the skyline as new metro lines and coastal roads reshape the city, but Mumbai's pulse never falters, beating to the rhythm of reinvention. It's a city that demands energy, rewards curiosity and never stands still. For travellers, there's a Mumbai for every mood, every budget, every appetite – and one visit is never enough.

THE MAIN AREAS

COLABA & CHURCHGATE
Architectural gems on Mumbai's southern tip. p672

FORT
Marvellous monuments meet foodie haven. p679

WORLI
Forts, fishing villages, and the rise of the modern skyline. p684

For places to stay in Mumbai, see p701

DLYTRIPPIN/SHUTTERSTOCK

Above: Marine Drive (p677); Left: Painted pots, Dharavi (p689)

LOWER PAREL & THE OLD MILL BELT
Fine-dining splendour and remnants of bygone industries.
p687

BANDRA & AROUND
Bollywood, East Indian communities and urban cool.
p691

BORIVALI
Where northern suburbia meets the national park. p698

Find Your Way

Mumbai is an organised chaos. The traffic can test a monk's patience and the transport system is still catching up, but with a bit of planning, the vast city somehow feels within reach.

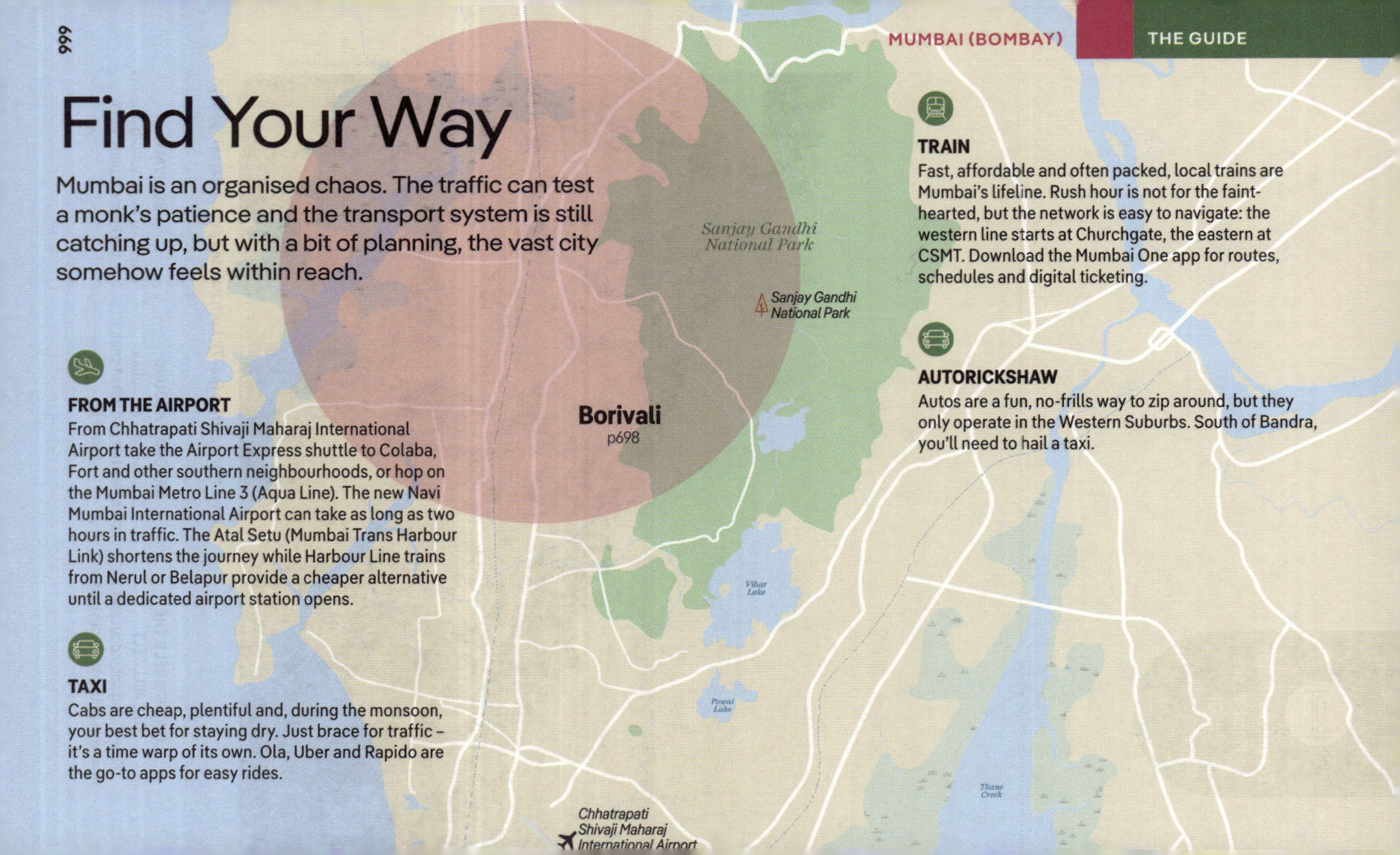

FROM THE AIRPORT

From Chhatrapati Shivaji Maharaj International Airport take the Airport Express shuttle to Colaba, Fort and other southern neighbourhoods, or hop on the Mumbai Metro Line 3 (Aqua Line). The new Navi Mumbai International Airport can take as long as two hours in traffic. The Atal Setu (Mumbai Trans Harbour Link) shortens the journey while Harbour Line trains from Nerul or Belapur provide a cheaper alternative until a dedicated airport station opens.

TAXI

Cabs are cheap, plentiful and, during the monsoon, your best bet for staying dry. Just brace for traffic – it's a time warp of its own. Ola, Uber and Rapido are the go-to apps for easy rides.

TRAIN

Fast, affordable and often packed, local trains are Mumbai's lifeline. Rush hour is not for the faint-hearted, but the network is easy to navigate: the western line starts at Churchgate, the eastern at CSMT. Download the Mumbai One app for routes, schedules and digital ticketing.

AUTORICKSHAW

Autos are a fun, no-frills way to zip around, but they only operate in the Western Suburbs. South of Bandra, you'll need to hail a taxi.

ARABIAN SEA
Nehru Planetarium
Worli
p684
Haji Ali Dargah
p637
Elephanta Island
Fort
Back Bay
Chhatrapati Shivaji Maharaj Vastu Sangrahalaya
Taj Mahal Palace Hotel
Colaba & Churchgate
p672
5 km
2.5 mile

Plan Your Days

Mumbai is one of those cities that will always leave you wanting to return – you can't possibly fit it all in on one visit and it's usually quite hot, so less is more.

SAIKO3P/SHUTTERSTOCK

Chhatrapati Shivaji Maharaj Terminus (p682)

Day One

Morning

- Start early at the **Gateway of India** (p678) to see Mumbai's iconic landmark before crowds and heat set in. Take in the grand **Taj Mahal Palace Hotel** (p672), then head to **Malido Café & Apéro** (p681) for a Parsi-style breakfast.

Afternoon

- Spend the afternoon gallery- and museum-hopping in Fort, visiting **Chhatrapati Shivaji Maharaj Vastu Sangrahalaya** (p681), the **National Gallery of Modern Art Mumbai** (p681) and **Jehangir Art Gallery** (p681). Lunch at **Pancham Puriwala** (p683), the city's oldest restaurant. Stroll **Marine Drive** (p677), the sea-facing, art deco–lined promenade.

Evening

- Head to **G5A** (p687) in Mahalaxmi for a live performance, then end the night with the celebrated 10-course tasting menu at **Masque** (p688).

YOU'LL ALSO WANT TO...

If you've have a longer stay in the city try these quintessentially Mumbaikar experiences.

EXPLORE KHOTACHIWADI

Wander the colourful lanes of this heritage village tucked into the city centre – a pocket of calm amid the metropolis.

HOP ABOARD A FERRY TO ELEPHANTA ISLAND

Start early and sail from Apollo Bandar in Colaba to UNESCO-listed **Elephanta Island** (p674), home to ancient rock-cut cave temples.

TAKE IN DHOBI GHAT'S COLOURS

Mumbai's largest laundry is a staggering open-air complex, with rows of linens in every hue flapping in the breeze.

Day Two

Morning

- Start at **Ram Ashraya** (p690), the legendary Matunga Udupi restaurant (1939), then head to Dadar's **Lalbaug Market** (p689) to pick up freshly ground masalas and spice mixes.

Afternoon

- Drive to Bandra to pose with **Bollywood murals** (p694) on Chapel Rd, wander through Ranwar's Portuguese-era homes and East Indian charm, then stroll **Bandstand Promenade** (p697) and **Bandra Fort** (p697), or browse **Trilogy Curated Bookshop and Library** (p695) for indie authors.

Evening

- If you score a seat at **Papa's** (p691), settle in for chef Hussain Shahzad's 12-seat, 13-course culinary theatre; if not, dive into Bandra's buzzing bar scene at old favourites like **Toto's Garage** (p694) or **The Den** (p694).

Day Three

Morning

- Head to Borivali, where a morning stroll in **Sanjay Gandhi National Park** (p700), the city's green lung, reveals chance encounters with native flora and fauna species, and the ancient rock-cut Kanheri Caves.

Afternoon

- Hop aboard a local train to **Churchgate Railway Station** (p675) in time for a hearty Cantonese lunch and cold beers at **Ling's Pavilion** (p676) in Colaba. Take the rest of the afternoon easy with a light stroll along **Colaba Causeway** (p675), soaking in Victorian architecture and indulging in some streetside shopping.

Evening

- Watch the sunset while enjoying street-food snacks at **Girgaon Chowpatty** (p677). Unwind at **Dome** (p675), a sleek rooftop bar atop the **InterContinental** (p701).

CATCH A CRICKET MATCH

India's premier sport finds its most majestic stage at **Wankhede Stadium** (p676) in Churchgate – there's nowhere better to watch a game.

WATCH A BOLLYWOOD MOVIE

In the home of Hindi cinema, catch a film at an art deco icon like **Eros** or **Regal**: it's a rite of passage.

DISCOVER HIDDEN TIDAL TREASURES

Head to **Juhu Beach**, where low tide reveals a surprisingly rich marine world, from sponges and corals to nudibranchs, moray eels and starfish.

CYCLE ALONG THE COASTAL ROAD

The newly opened 5.25km **Coastal Road** features a dedicated cycling track from Marine Drive to Worli, perfect for an easy ride with sea views.

HELP ME PICK:

Mumbai's Museums & Art Galleries

Mumbai may skip the grand monuments, but it more than compensates with imagination. Its art galleries and museums offer some of the city's most rewarding detours – into national history, Mumbai's layered past, cutting-edge contemporary art, heritage hotels, iconic railway architecture and even the cosmos. Whether you're wandering with family, entertaining curious kids or planning a cultured solo date, this is where Mumbai reveals its thinking, creative side.

Where to Go If You Love...

The Artful Address

Taj Mahal Palace Hotel (p672) The grand dame revived its Taj Art Gallery in 2016, and is now also home to DAG's elegant heritage-wing twin spaces showcasing rotating 20th-century Indian modern masters, from MF Husain to Jehangir Sabavala.

The Culturally Curious

Piramal Art Gallery, NCPA Light-filled, modular space devoted to photography and contemporary visual art, with ever-changing Indian and international exhibitions.

NMACC Art House (p696) A four-storey, ever-evolving exhibition space where bold architecture, immersive installations and global names meet workshops, tech-driven programmes and emerging Indian and acclaimed international talents.

Unmissable Classics

Jehangir Art Gallery (p681) Mumbai's most democratic art space since 1952, where students, stalwarts and first-timers exhibit side by side under one historic roof.

National Gallery of Modern Art (p681) A 1911 landmark where you spiral from Bombay Progressives like Gaitonde and Raza to bold contemporary works – plus the chance of film screenings or pop-up shows.

Dr Bhau Daji Lad Museum (p689) A jewel-box of a museum inside Jijamata Udyan, packing Mumbai's past into dioramas, old maps, mill machinery and decorative arts.

Mani Bhavan Gandhi Sangrahalaya (p677) This creaky, intimate Gujarati townhouse is where Gandhi lived, spun *khadi* and sharpened ideas that would change India: now preserved through his letters, photographs, books and spinning wheel.

Chhatrapati Shivaji Maharaj Vastu Sangrahalaya (p681) Time-travel to 1853 through UNESCO-listed CSMT, decoding FW Stevens' Gothic grandeur and the railway's role in shaping modern India.

Nehru Planetarium (p685) Shrink the universe to bite-size with starry shows, telescope peeks and cosmic galleries at Mumbai's most stellar address.

Bombay Art Society (p695) Founded in 1888, this venerable institution has shaped generations of Indian artists through juried exhibitions and awards – drop in to see history and emerging talent share the same walls.

Modern Musings

Fulcrum (p682) In Kala Ghoda's historic Great Western Buildings, Fulcrum sparks playful debates on art, culture, politics and history.

Art and Charlie (p695) This Bandra bungalow hosts exhibitions, performances, workshops and lively neighbourhood gatherings.

Tao Art Gallery (p686) Vibrant colours, striking sculptures and bold installations define Mumbai's contemporary art scene.

NEKOMURA/SHUTTERSTOCK

Jehangir Art Gallery (p681), Fort

HOW TO

Transport Mumbai's galleries and museums are scattered, often far from trains or the metro, so hiring a car and driver is the easiest way to hop between them without losing time.

Opening hours Always check visiting times and days in advance as many galleries and museums close on specific weekdays or for special events. A quick look online saves disappointment.

Buy tickets online Many places offer free entry, but wherever possible, book tickets online in advance. Some places charge higher fees for foreign visitors at the counter; reserving ahead saves money and avoids queues.

When to go Schedule gallery and museum visits in the afternoon. Mumbai's air-conditioned indoor spaces provide a welcome break from the city's sweltering heat.

Plan a Smart Art Crawl

Mumbai's art scene is sprawling, diverse and wonderfully eclectic, but it's also scattered across neighbourhoods like Kala Ghoda, Fort, Colaba, and Bandra. Start by mapping your must-see stops and grouping them by area to avoid zigzagging across the city. Check opening hours, ticketing policies, and what's currently on show before you head out – rotating exhibitions can make or break a visit.

First-timers or those craving context should consider guided experiences such as **Raconteur Tours** *(mumbaiwalkingtours.com)*, which offer excellent walks through places like Chhatrapati Shivaji Maharaj Vastu Sangrahalaya (p681) or the CSMT heritage precinct. A good guide brings layers – architectural detail, political backstory and insider anecdotes – that transform static displays into living narratives.

Going DIY? Pace yourself. Mix museums with smaller galleries, plan cafe stops between neighbourhoods and leave room for discovery: artist talks, screenings or a gallery you stumble upon by chance. Whether guided or self-led, treat Mumbai's art trail as a slow wander, not a checklist.

Colaba & Churchgate

ARCHITECTURAL GEMS ON MUMBAI'S SOUTHERN TIP

TOP TIP

Start early. Colaba and Churchgate wake up gently. Mornings are cooler, the streets are quieter, and you'll have landmarks like the Gateway of India or Oval Maidan almost to yourself. Plus, it's the best time to catch a breezy walk and a strong Irani chai at a local cafe.

Once a marshy island where Koli fishers cast their nets, Colaba has transformed into one of Mumbai's most southern and iconic neighbourhoods. Linked to the mainland by the Colaba Causeway in 1838, the area evolved from East India Company outpost to a fashionable residential and commercial hub. By the late 19th century, its shoreline was lined with cafes, shops and colonial-era buildings, setting the stage for landmarks like the Taj Mahal Palace Hotel and the Gateway of India – enduring symbols of the city's grandeur and grit.

A little to the north, Churchgate wears its colonial past on its sleeve. Grand Victorian facades still flank the Oval Maidan, relics of an era when the Arabian Sea once lapped their foundations. Named after the old gate that once led to St Thomas Cathedral, Churchgate remains a bustling gateway of another kind today – it's home to one of Mumbai's busiest train stations.

Taj Chronicles

Check into the city's most storied stay

Built in 1903, the **Taj Mahal Palace Hotel** is Mumbai's ultimate symbol of ambition and resilience. A blend of Moorish domes, Florentine arches, Rajput jharokas (projecting windows) and Indo-Portuguese balconies, it reflects the city's

GETTING AROUND

The wide roads make these neighbourhoods perfect for wandering on foot – just bring a hat, good shoes and a sense of adventure. If the humidity gets the better of you, flag one of the pint-sized black-and-yellow taxis that buzz through south Mumbai (autorickshaws don't venture this far), or let apps like Ola, Uber or Rapido do the haggling for you. Just beyond the Gateway of India's northern edge, small docks launch ferries and speedboats bound for Elephanta Island and the coastal town of Alibaug.

HIGHLIGHTS
1 Churchgate Train Station
2 Gateway of India
3 Oval Maidan
4 Taj Mahal Palace Hotel, Mumbai

SIGHTS
5 Wankhede Stadium

SLEEPING
6 Abode Bombay
7 Ascot Hotel
8 Hotel Diplomat
9 InterContinental
10 The Oberoi, Mumbai

EATING
11 Araku
12 Cafe Marina
13 Geoffrey's
14 K Rustom & Co.
15 Koyla Ethnic Cuisine
16 Ling's Pavilion
17 Loya
18 Nksha
19 Pizza by the Bay
20 Sea Lounge
21 Souk
22 Table

DRINKING & NIGHTLIFE
23 Cafe Mondegar
24 Dome
see 4 Harbour Bar
25 Leopold's

ENTERTAINMENT
26 Eros Cinema
27 National Centre for the Performing Arts
28 Regal Cinema

SHOPPING
29 Colaba Causeway

ROCK STARS

The Portuguese named Elephanta Island in the early 16th century, after a large rock-chiselled elephant statue found on the island. The statue was later moved to Victoria Gardens (now called Jijamata Udyan). Beyond the caves on Elephanta Island, Mumbai (and Maharashtra more broadly) is home to several Buddhist and Hindu cave complexes. The region's rich geology – which is largely comprised of swathes of basalt – provides a perfect base for carving. According to the Archaeological Survey of India, there are nearly 1200 caves of varying sizes in the entire state of Maharashtra, out of which roughly 900 belong to Buddhism alone.

OSCAR ESPINOSA/SHUTTERSTOCK

Sassoon Docks

cosmopolitan spirit. Legend says Parsi industrialist Jamsetji N Tata built it after being denied entry to a British-owned hotel nearby, though this remains unproven. When it opened, at ₹6 a night, it was among the few places where a British Viceroy and an Indian Maharaja could share the same lobby.

Pre-dating the Gateway of India (p678), the Taj has long greeted the world at Mumbai's shores. Restored after the 2008 terrorist attacked, its interiors mix Parisian pillars, Turkish baths, German lifts and the city's first licensed bar, the Harbour Bar. Step inside for afternoon tea at the **Sea Lounge** or polish off North Indian noshes at **Loya**.

Sassoon Docks: the City's Salty Soul

Catch the action at Mumbai's oldest dock

Start early to visit the city's oldest and largest working **dockyard**, where Mumbai's fishing life plays out in full colour. Murals and a weathered clock tower mark the entrance to this 1875 Sassoon-built site on reclaimed land, still a vital hub for the Koli community – Mumbai's original fisherfolk.

Arrive before 6am to watch trawlers unload jawla, kolambi and Bombay duck as buyers jostle and workers haul ice-slick baskets through narrow lanes. The dock is split between a local wholesale market and an export zone, both buzzing.

You can take a guided tour of the dock as part of the Mumbai by Dawn experience from **No Footprints** (p685; *nfpexplore.com; 2 people ₹17,000*).

The Island of Stone Gods

Sail to the Ancient Elephanta Caves

Catch a **ferry** (*pnpinfra.com, ₹250 one-way; maldarcatamaran.com, from ₹200 one-way*) from the Gateway of India and sail across the harbour to Gharapuri, or **Elephanta Island** *(elephanta.co.in; ₹550)* – a quiet, green world far removed from Mumbai's bustle. Here, seven ancient rock-cut caves dedicated to Lord Shiva were carved directly into solid basalt between the 6th and 7th centuries. Inside the main cave, a 6m-tall, three-faced Shiva rises from the basalt. Explore pillared halls and shrines, then climb to the hilltop viewpoint for sea panoramas. A small museum near the entrance unravels the site's layered past.

Wander Colaba Causeway

Shop, stroll and soak in colonial charm

Once a causeway linking Colaba to the rest of Mumbai in 1838, this lively boulevard is now one of the city's most popular haunts. Flanked by colonial buildings with arched verandahs and colourful shopfronts, **Colaba Causeway** hums from morning till late at night. Pavement stalls overflow with silver trinkets, embroidered bags, vintage posters and other irresistible souvenirs, while chic boutiques and designer stores sit tucked between them. Stop for a cold beer at **Leopold's** or a coffee at **Cafe Mondegar** and watch the world go by.

Churchgate Railway Station

Trains, history and daily hustle

Opened in 1870, **Churchgate Railway Station** is one of south Mumbai's busiest termini – historically the original end point of the Western Line, and a major suburban terminus from 1930 (after Colaba Terminus closed). The site once formed part of the fortified city wall leading to St Thomas Cathedral, hence the name. The current station is a functional 1950s concrete building, but step outside and you're instantly within Victorian theatre: Gothic spires, stone lions, colonnaded facades and sweeping maidans (open, grassed areas).

Green Grounds

Catch a game of cricket at Oval Maidan

Stretching like a green lung between Gothic spires and art deco towers, **Oval Maidan** is more than a cricket ground – it's a living slice of south Mumbai's past. Once scrubland, it was restored in the mid-1990s and reopened in 1999 as a Grade I heritage site, its 9 hectares now ringed by some of the city's most dramatic architecture. On any given day, office workers cut through towards Churchgate, children practise catches,

BOMBAY TIME

India hasn't always ticked to one clock. During the colonial era, different cities kept their own time. Bombay ran on UTC+4:51:20, Calcutta (Kolkata) on UTC+5:53:28 and Madras (Chennai) followed a standard set in 1802 by British astronomer John Goldingham. The result was a country out of sync by more than an hour, depending on where you stood.

To simplify matters, a central meridian near Mirzapur (82°33′E) was chosen in 1905, laying the groundwork for a single national time. India Standard Time (IST), set at UTC+5.30, was formally adopted after Independence in 1947, with Mumbai and Kolkata finally falling in line by the mid-1950s.

India follows IST year-round: no daylight saving, no clock changes.

EATING & DRINKING IN CHURCHGATE & COLABA: BEST ROOFTOP VIEWS

Souk: A Middle Eastern feast at the Taj, with Syrian-led plates and sweeping harbour views. *12.30-2.45pm & 7-11.45pm* ₹₹₹

Cafe Marina: Relaxed Sea Palace rooftop where breezy harbour views, sunset cocktails, and kebabs and grills set the mood. *4pm-midnight* ₹₹

Dome: Sleek rooftop spot atop the InterContinental where you sip sundowners over sushi with the skyline and Queen's Necklace glittering below. *5pm-1am* ₹₹

Koyla Ethnic Cuisine: Mughal-style shamianas, kebabs, biryanis and hookahs, wrapped into a romantic, old-world-meets-contemporary evening. *7pm-1.30am* ₹₹

TIFFIN TALES

Churchgate is one of Mumbai's busiest stations and the heartbeat of the city's legendary *dabba-wallah* (literally 'food container person') network. Around 125 years ago, a Parsi banker asked for his home-cooked lunch to be delivered to his office. Others loved the idea, demand grew, and visionary Mahadeo Havaji Bachche formalised the system with 100 delivery men – giving birth to today's astounding network. Now less than 5000 *dabba-wallahs* deliver nearly 200,000 tiffin daily, using hand-painted alphanumeric codes to route each metal lunchbox across trains, handcarts and bicycles. Studied by business schools, including Harvard Business School, and admired globally, this human-powered logistics chain is one-of-a-kind. Catch them in action between 11am and noon outside the station.

ARUN SAMBHU MISHRA/SHUTTERSTOCK

Ganesh Chaturthi festival, Girgaon Chowpatty

and clusters of amateur teams run drills as if Ranji Trophy selectors might stroll by (they sometimes do). On weekends, youth coaches bark instructions while balls arc against cinematic backdrops. Nearby, **Wankhede Stadium** – Mumbai's international cricket ground – is also worth a visit.

NCPA, Centre Stage

Mumbai's biggest ideas and best artists under one roof

Tucked beside the Arabian Sea at Nariman Point, the **National Centre for the Performing Arts** (NCPA; *ncpamumbai.com*) is Mumbai's cultural powerhouse. Founded in 1969 by JRD Tata and Dr Jamshed Bhabha, this pioneering multi-venue complex houses five theatres, plus galleries, libraries and cafes.

Expect a rolling calendar of Indian classical music, jazz, contemporary dance, experimental theatre and exhibitions, featuring legends and international touring acts alike. With world-class acoustics and a prime seafront setting, the NCPA continues to shape the city's cultural DNA.

EATING IN COLABA: OUR PICKS

The Table: An upscale Italian spot known for its elegant small plates, chic ambience and sunlit interiors framed by sweeping floor-to-ceiling windows. *noon-4pm & 7pm-12.30am* ₹₹₹

Araku: From earthy millets to aromatic green peppercorns and smooth microlot coffee, it showcases the bold, homegrown flavours of Andhra Pradesh's Araku Valley. *8am-9.45pm* ₹₹

Ling's Pavilion: This Cantonese stalwart has dished out comforting classics from Nanking fried prawns to chop suey for over seven decades. *11.30am-11pm* ₹₹

Harbour Bar: Set within the Taj's opulent 1930s interiors, this timeless bar is the place to unwind with *keema* (curried mince meat) tostadas and a perfectly mixed cocktail in hand. *noon-1am* ₹₹₹

Take a Stroll along Marine Drive

The city's seaside, glittering curve

A sweeping C-shaped boulevard carved out of the Arabian Sea in the 1920s, this reclaimed stretch (officially Netaji Subhash Chandra Bose Rd, though no one calls it that) is one of the city's newest neighbourhoods, and one of its most storied. Art deco apartment blocks curve along the water like a living catwalk of modernist design, forming a UNESCO-listed ensemble. At golden hour, this 3km promenade comes alive with runners, families, ice-cream sellers, dog walkers, camera-toting tourists and young couples. As the sun sinks and the streetlamps twinkle on, the arc of lights becomes the city's most famous silhouette: the Queen's Necklace. At the northern end of **Marine Drive**, the sweep opens out towards **Girgaon Chowpatty**, the city's beloved beach, carnival and public living room in one, although swimming is not advisable owing to the sullied waters.

Gandhi's Nerve Centre

The thinking room of a Freedom Movement

Mani Bhavan Gandhi Sangrahalaya *(gandhi-manibhavan.org; ₹20)* is the creaking, charming Gujarati townhouse where Mahatma Gandhi lived, worked, spun cloth and planned some of his most powerful political actions between 1917 and 1934. Here, Gandhi chose Bombay – not Delhi – as the nerve centre of his activism because of its mix of mill workers, traders, migrants and opinion makers. Today, the museum preserves that electricity in tiny, deeply personal ways: you'll see his spinning wheel, letters, books, photographs, a packed research library and dioramas of key moments. Visiting feels like stepping into the quiet before a storm – the exact rooms where ideas that shaped the nation were first tested, debated, tightened, sharpened and ultimately turned into action.

ART DECO GUIDE

Smiti Kanodia, Founder of **Art Deco Alive!** *(artdecoalive.org)*, pens her thoughts on art deco in the city.

Art deco marks a defining chapter in Mumbai's architectural and cultural story. Emerging in the 1930s and '40s, it introduced streamlined forms, geometric patterns, curves and nautical cues that mirrored Bombay's global outlook. The style coincided with a rising middle class and a subtle assertion of nationalism, visible in Indian names, Indigenous motifs and locally inspired lettering.

Spread across Marine Drive, Shivaji Park, Vile Parle and Matunga, art deco remains one of the city's most distinctive legacies. Landmarks such as Eros and Regal cinemas anchor the narrative, while Dhanraj Mahal near the Gateway blends deco elegance with climate-smart design.

EATING IN CHURCHGATE: OUR PICKS

K Rustom & Co.: Try seasonal favourites or classics such as toffee crunch, roasted almond crunch or *kesar pista* at this Irani ice-cream sandwich shop. *10am-11pm* ₹

Pizza by the Bay: An art deco SoBo classic plating freshly rolled pizzas with sea views and enduring Mumbai swagger. *7am-12.30am* ₹₹

Nksha: A vintage-SoBo glamour setting, where fine-dining North Indian flavours meet art deco design. *12.30-11.30pm* ₹₹₹

Geoffrey's: This English-style pub has wood-panels, dry wit and old-world charm – a cosy spot for a pint and a pizza. *5-11.30pm* ₹₹

TOP EXPERIENCE

Gateway of India

A vast basalt arch commanding Mumbai's harbourfront, the Gateway of India is the city's most recognisable landmark – and the atmospheric front door to Colaba. Completed in 1924 to mark a royal British visit, it began as an imperial showpiece, but was later reclaimed as a symbol of arrival and independence. Come early morning or at sunset for crowds, selfie sticks, balloon sellers, boats chugging off to Elephanta Island and that cinematic sense of standing where India meets the sea.

SNEHAL JEEVAN PAILKAR/SHUTTERSTOCK

Admire the Architecture

Designed by British architect George Wittet, the Gateway of India is a deliberate Indo-Saracenic blend – onion domes, scalloped arches and *chhattris* layered onto neoclassical form. Laid in 1913 and funded by Indian taxpayers, it rose into a 15m dome flanked by bastions and ceremonial chambers. The symbolism is clear: cultural fusion, firmly on colonial terms.

Hire a Guide to Learn about the History

Standing beneath the sweeping basalt arch is impressive enough, but a guide can transform it from postcard to portal. The Gateway of India brims with stories – of royal arrivals, architectural ambition and colonial assertion – that often go untold. With a licensed guide, you'll trace carvings high above eye level, read between the Indo-Saracenic lines and picture the pomp of 1911 when King George V first docked here. They'll peel back layers of power and politics, revealing how this ornate archway became both symbol and stage for the city's evolving identity. Suddenly, you're not just looking at history – you're standing in the middle of it. Guide fees vary but start at ₹500.

TOP TIPS

- Visit at sunrise for soft light and fewer crowds; late nights after 10pm are quieter too.
- Take a short ferry ride into the harbour – the Gateway was meant to be seen from the water.
- Book a sailing lesson with Mumbai Sailing Club *(mumbaisailingclub.com)* or group sail in advance for a rare, refreshing view of Mumbai from the sea.

PRACTICALITIES

- mumbaicity.gov.in
- free to enter and guarded round the clock
- 24hr

Fort

MARVELLOUS MONUMENTS MEET FOODIE HAVEN

South Mumbai's old commercial core, Fort, is where Mumbai's layered history feels closest to the skin. This is where the East India Company literally fortified its power – setting up a walled citadel in the 1700s, conducting ruthless trade and building out the infrastructure that would become the city's financial engine. The walls are long gone, but walk these streets and you still feel the echo: in the colossal neoclassical columns, neogothic spires and Indo-Saracenic facades – all the visual propaganda of an empire determined to stay.

Today, Fort is anything but frozen in its past. The area hums with bookshops, Irani cafes, stockbrokers, lawyers rushing between court hearings, gallery-goers spilling out onto pavements in Kala Ghoda, and office workers queuing for excellent *sandwichwallas* at lunchtime. It's a neighbourhood for purposeful wandering, best taken slowly, on foot, head tilted up.

TOP TIP

Plan your stops around AC breaks. The sun bounces off all that stone – step into a gallery, museum, bookstore or boutique every 20 minutes to browse, buy and cool down. It's the smartest way to explore this neighbourhood.

Shop Till You Drop

Swing by Fort's eclectic stores for your ultimate retail fix

Fort is a magnet for design lovers – a heritage precinct where contemporary India's coolest boutiques sit inside British-era buildings. Start with a pilgrimage to **Sabyasachi**: whether you're buying or just gawking at bridal ensembles, this rose-oil-scented museum of chandeliers, carpets and maximalist detail is unmatched. For a sharper, modern fashion edit, **Ogaan**, **Yam**

GETTING AROUND

Mumbai's first true underground metro – Mumbai Metro-3 (Aqua Line) – threads right under Fort, with a station at Hutatma Chowk and a fast, clean run straight up to Bandra. It finally makes north–south travel feel frictionless. Use the Mumbai One app for seamless digital tickets (no more queueing) before you enter the station. On the streets above, South Mumbai's classic black-and-yellow taxis still zip around and can now be booked via Ola/Uber.

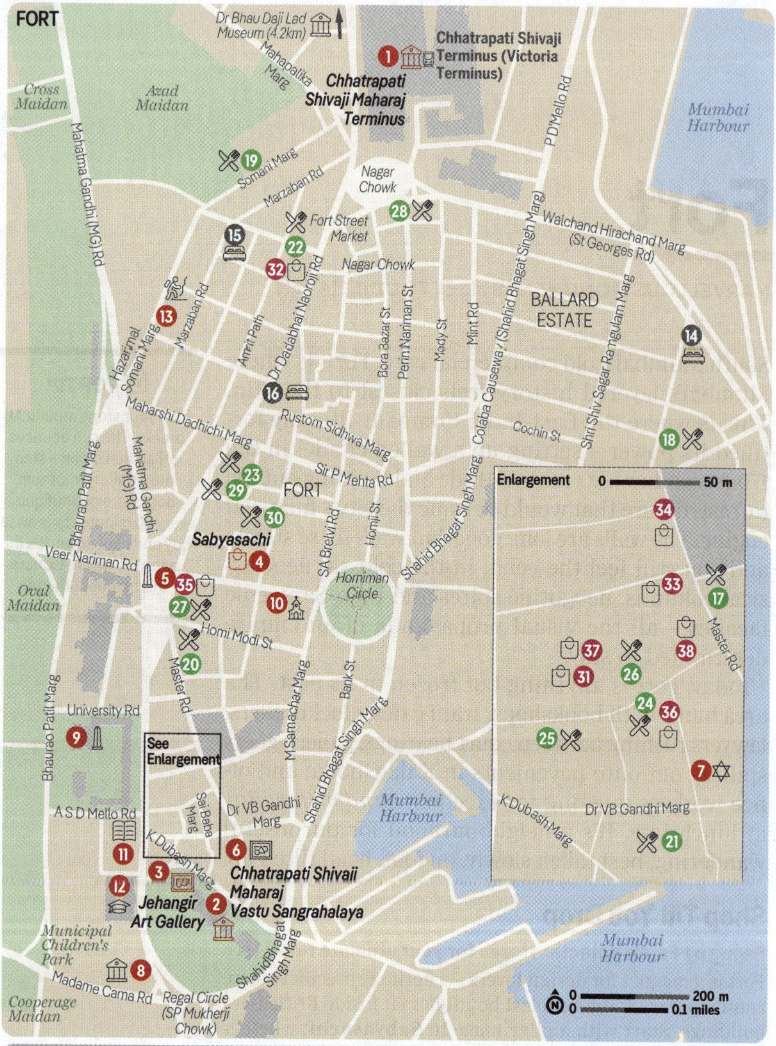

HIGHLIGHTS
1 Chhatrapati Shivaji Maharaj Terminus
2 Chhatrapati Shivaji Maharaj Vastu Sangrahalaya
3 Jehangir Art Gallery
4 Sabyasachi

SIGHTS
5 Flora Fountain
6 Fulcrum
7 Keneseth Eliyahoo Synagogue
8 National Gallery of Modern Art
9 Rajabai Clock Tower
10 St Thomas' Cathedral

ACTIVITIES
11 David Sassoon Library
12 Elphinstone College
13 The Indian Bouldering Company

SLEEPING
14 Grand Hotel
15 Hebbar's Heritage Home
16 Residency Hotel Fort

EATING
17 Americano
18 Britannia & Co
19 Burma Burma
20 Cafe Military
21 Chetana Veg. Restaurant & Bar
22 Ekaa
23 Hotel Deluxe
24 Kala Ghoda Café
25 Khyber
26 Malido Café & Apéro
27 Nandan Coffee
28 Pancham Puriwala
29 Pratap Lunch Home
30 Yazdani Bakery

SHOPPING
31 Bombay Shirt Company
32 Chimanlals
33 Chorus
34 Jodi
35 Kitab Khana
36 Nicobar
37 Ogaan
38 Yam

and **Chorus** offer sculptural, contemporary Indian clothing, while **Jodi** splashes joy across its hand-block prints.

Bombay Shirt Company will measure, design and customise your shirt to the last button. **Chimanlals** is where you buy the kind of paper that makes you want to write letters again. For things to bring home – not just buy – **Nicobar** is your tropical-leaning answer to homeware, tableware and travel accessories. Finally, pause at **Kitab Khana**, a much-loved independent bookshop housed in a century-old heritage building. Linger among its soaring Corinthian columns and browse thoughtfully curated shelves of Indian literature and history.

Museum Musings

Immerse yourself in history and culture

Built in the early 20th century to commemorate Prince George V's 1905 visit, **Chhatrapati Shivaji Maharaj Vastu Sangrahalaya** *(csmvs.in; ₹700 with an audio guide)*, also by Scottish architect George Wittet, is best experienced by browsing its long chronological range. Start with the 2nd-century AD sculptures, then move through Indian, European, Himalayan and East Asian art, textiles, tableware and natural history. Note the dome inspired by Bijapur's Gol Gumbaz with a Taj Mahal–style finial. Once a military hospital (1914–22), it is now wheelchair and lift accessible. Continue 10 minutes on foot to **National Gallery of Modern Art, Mumbai** *(ngmaindia.gov.in; ₹150; closed Mon)* inside the former Sir Cowasji Jehangir Public Hall (1911). Take a few minutes to admire its heritage facade, then follow the spiral stairway down through semi-circular galleries. Prioritise the Bombay Progressives on display – Gaitonde, Raza, Souza, Padamsee – then move on to contemporary names like Nalini Malani. Time your visit for a special exhibition if possible. The museum also runs film screenings, tours and workshops; enquire at reception to see what's on that day.

Art Attack

Wander the halls of Jehangir Art Gallery

Just steps from the precinct, **Jehangir Art Gallery** *(jehangirartgallery.com; free; 11am-7pm)* has anchored Mumbai's art scene since 1952. Founded by Sir Cowasji Jehangir, its light-filled Kala Ghoda galleries have hosted everyone from MF Husain and SH Raza to emerging contemporary voices.

FORT IN FRAMES

Mayank Soni leads Fort Photo Walks, guiding photographers through Mumbai's oldest precincts to frame heritage landmarks on camera. @mayanksoni

Rajabai Clock Tower: The 147-year-old monument dominates the Fort skyline. Viewed from the west and north, it makes for striking frames alongside statues of everyday Indians in traditional attire.

Flora Fountain: The sculpture of the Roman goddess of spring stands out against azure morning skies. The surrounding mythological figures at the four corners are best framed with nearby heritage buildings.

St Thomas' Cathedral: More than three centuries old, this church marks the point from which all of Mumbai's distances are measured. Its facade photographs beautifully from the base, while the stained-glass windows inside are worth documenting.

EATING IN FORT: BEST BREAKFAST SPOTS

Kala Ghoda Café: Pair a strong espresso with a sandwich or burger at this beloved Fort institution, known for its cosy, artsy vibe. *8am-midnight* ₹₹

Malido Café & Apéro: A contemporary spin on Parsi classics, where fluffy herb-and-cheddar omelette *akuri* and *pora* meet excellent coffee and cocktails. *8am-11pm* ₹₹

Cafe Military: This old-school Irani cafe has been dishing out pillowy *brun maska* and hearty home-style *keema* since 1933. Cash only. *10.30am-9.30pm Mon-Sat* ₹

Nandan Coffee: Sample single-origin brews from Kodaikanal alongside South Indian vegetarian fare in a bright, minimalist setting. *8am-10pm* ₹₹₹

STREET EATS

Mumbai's street food culture grew from early waves of migration, when traders, dock and mill workers poured into the city in the mid-19th century seeking work – and quick, affordable, portable meals. Carb-heavy snacks became staples: *vada pav* (a spicy potato fritter in a soft bun), *pav bhaji* (a buttery vegetable mash with bread rolls) and *bhurji pav* (spiced scrambled eggs). Over time, these dishes embedded themselves in the city's collective memory. Around Horniman Circle and Kala Ghoda, generations-old vendors still serve beloved *bhel puri*, *pani puri* and the iconic Bombay sandwich (layered with chutney, potato and beetroot). Each bite tells a story of resilience, migration and ingenuity – how working-class necessity evolved into a culinary identity that fuels the city. Ensure it's hot and freshly made to avoid catching a bug.

ANILD/SHUTTERSTOCK

Yazdani Restaurant & Bakery

With hundreds of exhibitions each year and free entry, it's a place to dip in, linger, and catch the city's creative rhythm mid-flow.

A short walk away, **Fulcrum** *(fulcrum.art; free; 10.30am-7pm Tue-Sat)* extends the conversation. Part gallery, part think space, it hosts exhibitions, screenings and talks that sit at the crossroads of art, politics, history and film – ideal if you want context, debate and ideas alongside the visuals.

Gothic Sights

Admire the architectural details in the periphery

Outside Jehangir the **David Sassoon Library** and **Elphinstone College** flank you like Victorian stage sets. The Kala Ghoda statue – the black horse that lends the precinct its name – still anchors the junction; the original bronze statue now sits inside Byculla's Rani Baug near Dr Bhau Daji Lad Museum (p689). Each February, the **Kala Ghoda Arts Festival** transforms the area into an open-air gallery. Wander past the ice-blue **Keneseth Eliyahoo Synagogue**, ending at St Thomas' Cathedral (p681). A longer walk (20 minutes) or a quick cab north brings you to **Chhatrapati Shivaji Maharaj Terminus** – the neogothic climax. Step back to 1853 on Raconteur Tours' 1½-hour guided walk *(mumbaiwalkingtours.com; ₹500 per person)* through the in-house heritage museum to learn about the birthplace of India's first passenger train. Don't skip it. This railway palace is the exclamation mark on the sentence you've just walked.

Vertical Views

Boulder indoors with a cityscape companion

In a city starved of open rock and outdoor adventure, **The Indian Bouldering Company** *(tibc.co.in)* offers a welcome vertical escape. Set inside a heritage building in Fort, this indoor bouldering gym lets you test strength, balance and nerve on colour-coded routes suited to first-timers and regular climbers alike. No ropes, no mountains – just pure movement, city views and the quiet thrill of climbing upwards when Mumbai usually only sprawls sideways.

Dig into Micro Cuisines

Ethnic food in Mumbai

Mumbai's oldest quarter has long been a melting pot of India's many micro-cuisines – a legacy shaped by centuries of migration. As traders, workers and communities from across the subcontinent poured into this colonial business district, they brought their culinary traditions, leaving behind a trail of small eateries and canteens that continue to feed the city's soul. **Pancham Puriwala** (1848) serves piping hot *puris* (flat dough that puffs up when deep-fried) with tangy *sabzi* (vegetables), the staple in the founder's hometown in Uttar Pradesh. Kerala's fragrant gravies and *appams* (South Indian rice pancakes) find their home at **Hotel Deluxe**, while Mangalorean fish preparations pull crowds to **Pratap Lunch Home**. Maharashtrian thali (plates) and homely Gujarati and Marwari vegetarian fare thrive in humble joints like **Chetana Veg. Restaurant**.

The area's diverse flavours mirror its shifting fortunes – from mercantile hub to modern business district – catering now to hurried professionals as much as nostalgic regulars. Adding another chapter to this story are the Irani cafes, founded by Zoroastrian immigrants from Iran in the late 19th and early 20th centuries, distinct from the Parsis who arrived much earlier in the sixth century from erstwhile Persia. While Parsis established themselves in trade and industry, Iranians opened cafes like **Yazdani Restaurant & Bakery** and **Britannia & Co** serving *brun maska* and chai.

JAIN MENUS

One of Jainism's most fascinating aspects is how this ancient religion's philosophy of nonviolence shapes what's on the plate. Rooted in ahimsa (non-harm), Jain dietary rules favour mindful eating: no root vegetables like potatoes, onions or garlic (pulling them out disturbs soil organisms), no fermented foods (teeming with microorganisms), and restricted leafy greens on certain days (they may shelter tiny life forms). Meals are eaten before sunset to minimise harm and aid digestion. Every bite is *sattvic* (pure), clean and kind.

In Mumbai, where culinary diversity reigns supreme, Jainism's influence runs deep. Nearly every restaurant will cheerfully serve a 'Jain' version – think pizza without onion or garlic, Jain sushi rolls, even Jain tacos.

EATING IN FORT: BEST FINE DINING

Americano: Chef Alex Sanchez' California-inspired spot serves comforting pizzas, pastas and sharing plates. *7pm-1am Wed-Mon, noon-4pm & 7pm-1am Sat-Sun.* ₹₹₹

Burma Burma: Vegetarian and vegan-friendly ode to Burmese cuisine, with signature samosa soup *(samuza hincho). noon-3.30pm & 6.30-10.30pm* ₹₹₹

Ekaa: Chef Niyati Rao redefines Indian dining with globally inspired, ingredient-driven dishes that celebrate local produce and creativity. *12.30-3.30pm & 7.30pm-1.30am* ₹₹₹

Khyber: Northwest Frontier meets *haveli*-style arches and walls adorned with Indian art. Tender *reshmi* kebabs and smoky tandoori dishes. *12.30-4pm & 7.30-11.30pm* ₹₹₹

Worli

FORTS, FISHING VILLAGES, AND THE RISE OF THE MODERN SKYLINE

GETTING AROUND

If you're coming from Bandra or the western suburbs, the quickest route is the Bandra–Worli Sea Link (toll applies; no two-wheelers). By public transport, hop on the Western Railway to Lower Parel or Mahalaxmi and take a short cab ride onwards, or use the Mumbai Metro – Line 3's new stations promise even smoother access. Buses also run frequently along Worli's main arteries.

One of Mumbai's oldest islands, Worli is a place where myth, sea and city-building have long intertwined. Local lore tells of a time when three Hindu goddesses – Mahalakshmi, Mahakali and Mahasaraswati – lay beneath the Worli Creek, their blessings believed to help early builders tame the tides and connect the island to Bombay. What followed is history: a patchwork of fishing villages, rice fields and banyan-lined *pakhadis* (hamlets) gradually transformed by ambitious 18th-century colonial embankments that reshaped the shoreline.

Over the centuries, Worli evolved from a quiet archipelago into a mill district, and later into the glossy, high-rise-heavy neighbourhood that marks Mumbai's modern skyline. Today, it's a study in contrasts – fishers' boats bobbing beside luxury towers, Haji Ali floating serenely offshore, Worli Fort still guarding the creek, and the Bandra–Worli Sea Link sweeping dramatically across the bay. It remains a place where the old city's soul meets its future.

Old Worli Charms

Discover Worli's sights, sounds and scents

Begin by weaving through **Worli Village**'s tiny lanes, flanked by old, colourful houses with *tulsi* (basil plant) shrines at their thresholds and shops selling pav, *khari* and flowers – an evocative warm-up before you reach **Worli Fort**. Climb the steep stone steps into this 17th-century British watchpost, its laterite walls opening into a modest courtyard, a temple and the quirky remains of a once-busy neighbourhood gym. Wander the ramparts for views of fishing boats bobbing in Mahim Bay and the **Bandra–Worli Sea Link** arching across the water. It's an atmospheric spot, especially if you sign up for a street-photography walk with award-winning Mumbai photographer Mayank Soni *(@mayanksonii; ₹950 per person)*, who captures the village's texture and the fort's moody, sea-washed charm.

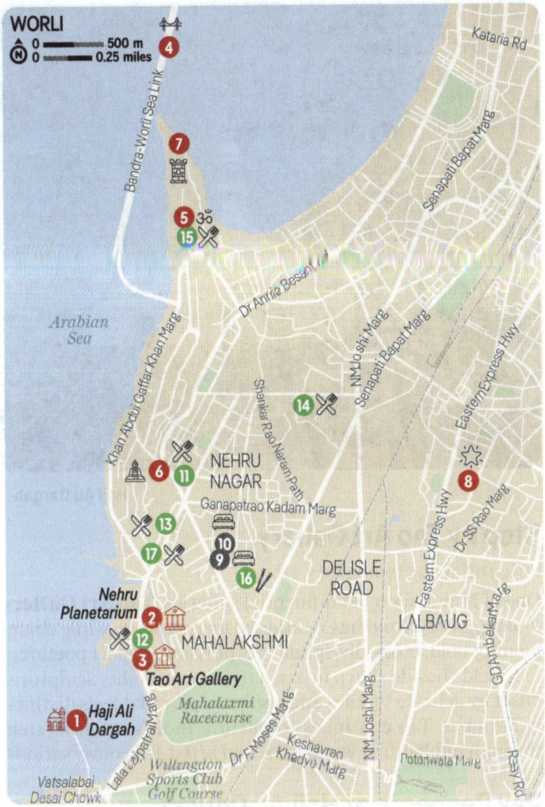

HIGHLIGHTS
1 Haji Ali Dargah
2 Nehru Planetarium
3 Tao Art Gallery

SIGHTS
4 Bandra-Worli Sea Link Bridge
5 Golfa Devi Temple
6 Nippozan Myohoji Buddhist Temple
7 Worli Fort

ACTIVITIES
8 No Footprints

SLEEPING
9 Bloom Hotel – Worli
10 Four Seasons Hotel

EATING
11 City Bakery
12 Copper Chimney
13 Maasli
14 Plum by Bent Chair
15 Slink & Bardot
16 Sun and Moon Korean Restaurant
17 Worli Rane Vadapav

Geek Out on Stargazing

Night shows at Nehru Planetarium

The **Nehru Planetarium** *(nehrucentremumbai.in; ₹150 entry for ages 5+; closed Mon)*, an engaging place to explore the universe. Begin with the 90-minute Stars & Wonders of the Universe show, offered in Hindi, English and Marathi. Visit during an eclipse for telescopes and live demonstrations, or come on a clear evening to try stargazing outdoors. Afterwards, browse the Nehru Centre's galleries or its 30,000-book library. Set aside around three hours if you want the full experience.

AN INSIDER'S WORLI

Harshvardhan Tanwar, co-founder of tour company **No Footprints** *(@nofootprintsmumbai)*

I grew up in Worli when it still felt like a small, self-contained world, long before towers, the Sea Link and the coastal road reshaped its edges. Few realise it was once one of Mumbai's original seven islands, its name possibly drawn from Var – 'upper'.

Guiding people through Worli has sharpened my view. In Koliwada, visitors linger over women bargaining for the morning's catch, children weaving between painted homes, and *bombil* (fish) drying in the sun. At **Golfa Devi temple**, faith distils into a simple nod. A short climb to 17th-century **Worli Fort** opens onto fishing boats, the Sea Link and skyline.

My walks often start with jeera biscuits at **City Bakery**, a pause at the **Nippozan Myohoji Buddhist temple**, then moves through fish thalis at **Maasli** or *vada pav* at **Rane**, ending along Worli Seaface.

TOP TIP

Explore Worli by embracing its striking contrasts – wander through Worli Koliwada's vibrant fishing homes and shrines tucked beneath soaring high-rises – then walk the seafront, best at sunrise or sunset, when waves crash against the promenade and the Bandra–Worli Sea Link glows against the skyline.

SAIKO3P/SHUTTERSTOCK

Haji Ali Dargah

Stop by Tao Art Gallery

Influential contemporary art

One of Mumbai's most influential galleries, **Tao Art Gallery** *(taoartgallery.com)* has weathered market shifts while championing bold, cross-disciplinary expression. Expect poetic colour fields beside sharp urban narratives, weighty sculptures offset by delicate textiles and a spirit of play that feels distinctly Mumbai. Tao continues to nurture India's art ecosystem through publishing, workshops and artist-led conversations.

Pay Respects at Haji Ali Dargah

Pilgrimage to one of Mumbai's most sacred sites

Haji Ali Dargah *(free; 6am-9.45pm, closed during high tide)* is among Mumbai's most atmospheric shrines, best visited at low tide, when the 640m causeway surfaces and the white domes shimmer like a mirage. Built in 1431 as the tomb of Sufi saint Sayyed Pir Haji Ali Shah Bukhari, it showcases Mughal-era Indo-Islamic architecture, from scalloped arches to marble courtyards; inside, the saint's silver-encased tomb lies beneath an embroidered *chuddar* (shawl; keep your head covered and avoid photography). Linger for the mirrored hall or an evening *qawwali* (Islamic devotional singing).

EATING IN WORLI: OUR PICKS

Sun and Moon Korean Restaurant: Authentic favourites from bibimbap and cold spicy noodles to barbecues, *mandu* and a refreshing *patbingsu.* *11am-11.30pm* ₹₹

Slink & Bardot: Indulgent Sunday brunches and a food and drink menu inspired by the Koliwada fishing community. *6.30pm-1.30am Tue-Sun* ₹₹₹

Plum by Bent Chair: This Asian restaurant pairs Insta-worthy interiors with a wide menu of sushi, dim sum and hearty bowl meals. *noon-1.30am* ₹₹

Copper Chimney: Inspired by founder JK Kapur's post-Partition journey, this iconic flagship serves bold North West Frontier classics. *noon-3pm & 7-11.30pm* ₹₹

Lower Parel & the Old Mill Belt

FINE-DINING SPLENDOUR AND REMNANTS OF BYGONE INDUSTRIES

It's hard to imagine this fast-changing belt – Lower Parel and Mahalaxmi – was once the gritty core of Mumbai's cotton industry. In the early 1800s, the area housed British residents, but after cholera swept through they moved out and the mills moved in. With abundant lakes ideal for coal-powered machinery, textile factories drew thousands of migrant men who lived in shared chawls (worker housing) while their families stayed back in their villages. Cotton dust, clattering looms and shift sirens shaped the rhythm of daily life.

Byculla, just south, kept its working-class heart, its markets, workshops and houses of worship offering a raw contrast to polished South Bombay. Dadar, to the north, became a major transit hub – dense, frenetic and deeply lived-in. Nearby Matunga grew into a cultural pocket, famed for its South Indian canteens and coffee culture.

Today, the mills are almost gone. Many stand dilapidated; others have been reborn as grungy, upscale spaces like Masque, while shiny towers, malls and financial headquarters rise around them, reshaping the neighbourhood's skyline.

GETTING AROUND

Both the eastern and western suburban rail corridors slice through the district, offering a quick, congestion-proof way to move around. From Byculla, the eastern line begins at CSMT and rattles north through Parel Loco Workshop and Dadar. The western line from Churchgate glides past Marine Lines and Grant Rd before pulling into Lower Parel and Dadar, then continuing towards Bandra and Khar. Metro Line 3 (the Aqua Line) is steadily [illegible] midtown.

App-based taxis – Ola, Rapido and Uber – remain convenient and reasonably priced, but at peak hours they're often trapped in the city's notorious traffic snarls. When speed, ease and predictability matter, stick to the trains and the metro.

Boundary-Pushing Art in G5A

Cultural hub carved out of a former textile mill

Head to **G5A** *(g5afoundation.org; ₹250-700; noon-10pm Tue-Sun)*, a cultural centre tucked inside a once-forgotten mill compound. As you enter, look for banyan trees muscling through the cracked stone walls of a neighbouring mill – a quiet reminder of how much of Mumbai's textile district has faded into history. On the other side, glassy new towers rise almost by the minute.

Step into G5A's black-box theatre for an experimental performance, a film screening or a conversation with visiting artists. Head up to the terrace, where the moon often hangs

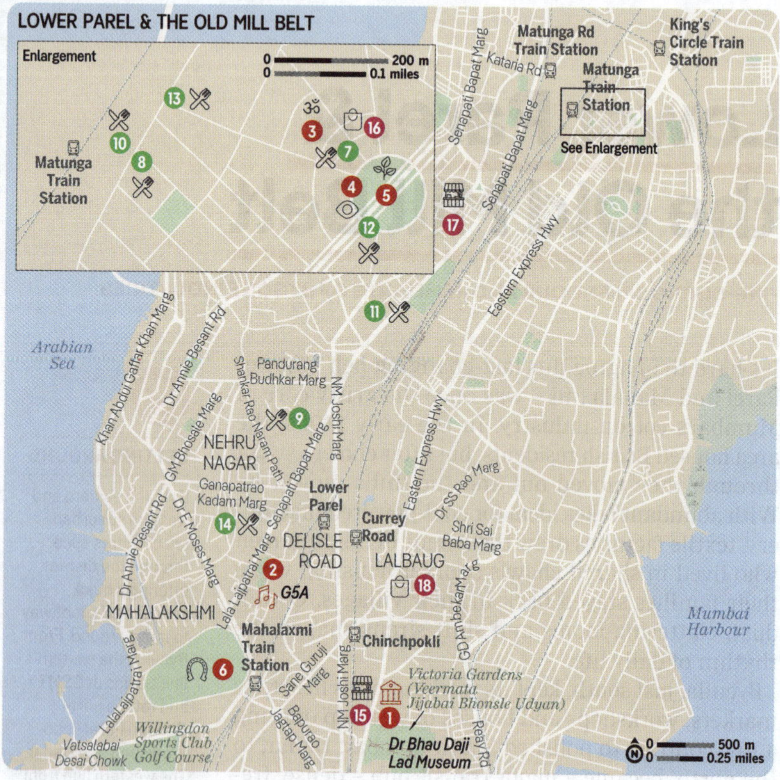

HIGHLIGHTS
1 Dr Bhau Daji Lad Museum
2 G5A

SIGHTS
3 Asthika Samaj Sree Ram Mandir
4 Kings Circle
5 Maheshwari Udyan

ACTIVITIES
6 Mahalaxmi Racecourse

EATING
7 Amba Bhavan Coffee Club
8 Arya Bhavan
9 Bombay Canteen
see 16 Cafe Madras
10 Gupta Chat Centre
11 Jai Hind Lunch Home
12 Koolar & Co.
see 2 Masque
13 Ram Ashraya
14 The Silver Train

SHOPPING
15 Byculla Vegetable Market
16 Cornucopia
17 Dadar Flower Market
18 Lalbaug Market

TOP TIP

Take an early-morning stroll around the **Mahalaxmi Racecourse**. The oval opens to the public at dawn, and you'll find joggers weaving past trainers exercising sleek racehorses – a rare pocket of calm in the city.

EATING IN LOWER PAREL: OUR PICKS

Bombay Canteen: Trendiest restaurant in town; the modern, crisp twist on South Asian fusion will leave your taste buds entertained. *noon-1.30am Mon-Fri, 11am-1.30am Sat-Sun* ₹₹₹

Jai Hind Lunch Home: Seafood stalwart since 1978 for Malvani and Mangalorean classics like fried bombil and stuffed pomfret. *11.30am-3.30pm & 7.30-11.30pm Tue-Sun* ₹₹

Masque: Among Mumbai's finest dining, the tasting menu plates are worth every penny. Book ahead. *7-11.30pm Tue-Sat, 12.30-3.30pm & 7pm-midnight Sun* ₹₹₹

The Silver Train: Palace recipes reworked with flair: think garlic-kissed kheer (rice pussing) and liver-rich raita (yoghurt). *noon-midnight* ₹₹₹

low in the Mumbai haze. In the past, the space has hosted poetry readings by Pulitzer Prize winner Forrest Gander and Indian poet Arvind Krishna Mehrotra, film screenings by filmmaker-writer Varun Grover and sets by touring Norwegian jazz bands.

Go on a Market Crawl

Spices and flowers at Mumbai's busiest bazaars

Start at 5am in **Byculla Vegetable Market**, the city's oldest wholesale veggie market, where BR Ambedkar (architect of Constitution of India) married in 1906. Maharashtra's green belt feeds this place – look for mango ginger, moringa, amla, bitter gourd and tamarind, reminders of India's global, ever-evolving food story.

As you drive towards Dadar's flower frenzy, watch the streetscape shift: glass towers melt into dense, timeworn chawls. These narrow, shared corridors once housed thousands of migrant mill workers drawn here in the 1860s, when the American Civil War pushed Mumbai to the forefront of the world cotton trade. At its peak, 76 mills operated here, men lived 10 to a room and a single bathroom served an entire floor. The 1896 plague emptied the city; a 1981 strike ended most mills, leaving only a few chimneys as reminders until the 1991 economic boom reshaped midtown.

Reach **Dadar Flower Market** by 6am to see Mumbai bloom before sunrise. Under the flyover, marigold mountains, jasmine coils and vendors with towering baskets spill into the lanes of what was once Phool Gully.

Roll onward into **Lalbaug Market**, where petals give way to pepper. In Mirchi Galli, Kashmiri chillies (about ₹260 a kilo) glow ruby red as spice masters roast and grind custom masalas right in front of you.

Visit Mumbai's Oldest Museum

City history under one roof

Dr Bhau Daji Lad Museum *(bdlmuseum.org, ₹20, closed Wed)* sits within Byculla's leafy Jijamata Udyan. Its restored Palladian hall offering an elegant glimpse into the city's social, cultural and industrial past. Inside, you'll find exquisitely crafted clay dioramas depicting 19th-century life in Bombay, alongside rare maps that chart the city's shifting shoreline, ornate silverware from local guilds, mill machinery, wooden models of architectural landmarks and decorative arts from across India. Outside, the original **Kala Ghoda** statue and a towering Elephanta elephant anchor the museum's historic setting.

In October 2025, the museum marked a major cultural milestone when *Mary Magdalene in Ecstasy,* Italian stalwart Caravaggio's radiant 16th-century masterpiece, went on view for a month as part of *L'invenzione della luce* (The Invention of Light) exhibition.

INSIDE DHARAVI

Pooja Ashokkumar, public historian and local guide.

Often dismissed as 'Asia's largest slum', Dharavi is one of Mumbai's most complex working-class neighbourhoods. Once a Koli fishing village, it grew into a migrant-built industrial ecosystem shaped by Tamil leather workers, Gujarati potters and North Indian artisans. Its small-scale industries generate over a billion dollars annually.

My archival project **Bombay Tamil History** *(@bombaytamilhistory)* led me into Dharavi's everyday rhythms. Along 90 Feet Rd, **Hotel Theresa**'s biryani, *parotta* and chicken *saalna* draw queues; **Senthil anna** serves the lesser-known Tamil tradition of cottonseed milk at 5pm. In Kumbhar Wada, potters still fire clay in open kilns; nearby Bombay Tanneries reveals leather transformed from hide to finished goods. Unconventional, industrious and humane – Dharavi is best understood on foot.

MATUNGA FOOD TRAIL

Sample morsels of flavours and history in one of the city's earliest planned suburbs on this walking tour with Vipul Yadav *(@foodie_baba)*.

START	END	LENGTH
Gupta Chat Centre	Koolar & Co	650m; 2hr

Start at 1 **Gupta Chat Centre**, just outside Matunga Central station, and try its cult *sev puri* toast sandwich – a playful, carb-on-carb street snack loved by generations of college students. Cross the road to 2 **Arya Bhavan** (est 2009) for classic Tamil-style *idlis* and *paniyarams* served with sambar and chutney.

Two minutes away is cult favourite 3 **Ram Ashraya** (1939), a quick-service Udupi institution where queues form by 5.30am. Order Mangalore buns, *goli bajje* fritters, seasonal *sheera* and crisp dosas. Walk towards 4 **Amba Bhavan Coffee Club** for a strong cup of filter coffee, pausing en route to notice three-storey art deco residential buildings, South Indian spiritual stores such as Giri at Samrat Nivas, and the colourful, century-old 5 **Asthika Samaj Sree Ram Mandir**, which anchors the neighbourhood's cultural life.

Circle 6 **Kings Circle**, long considered the heart of Matunga, where old-world eateries sit alongside busy colleges and leafy avenues. Tucked into a V-shaped corner is 7 **Koolar & Co**, one of Mumbai's last Irani cafés, with kitschy interiors and vintage posters. Order the wrestler's omelette, caramel custard and Irani chai to close the loop.

Bandra & Around

BOLLYWOOD, EAST INDIAN COMMUNITIES AND URBAN COOL

Once a cluster of fishing and farming hamlets on the edge of the Arabian Sea, Bandra's story stretches far beyond its current cool-kid reputation. Part of the larger 23-island archipelago that became Bombay, it was a thriving settlement long before the city took shape. The Portuguese arrived in 1548, gifting Bandra to nobleman António Pessoa before Jesuit missionaries built a church and college overlooking Mahim Creek. By 1775, after the Marathas and then the British took control, Bandra had grown into a patchwork of 24 *pakhadis* (hamlets), home to communities whose rhythms still echo through its lanes.

In 1950, Bandra was formally folded into Mumbai – and never looked back. Today, it's a heady mix of old and new: Portuguese-era chapels brushing up against boutique cafes, art deco homes jostling with glassy towers, and seaside promenades leading to some of the city's most coveted addresses. From bohemian Bandra West to buzzy BKC and leafy Khar West, this is a suburb that rarely sleeps – or needs to leave its own orbit.

GETTING AROUND

Once you step off at Bandra or Khar Rd station – or the Aqua Line 3 in BKC – autos take over. They're banned south of Bandra but rule the Western Suburbs, zipping through traffic with impressive agility. Hail one on the street or book via Ola or Uber, and always ask the driver to switch on the meter before you climb in.

EATING IN BANDRA: OUR PICKS

Imbiss Meating Joint: A no-frills institution serving serious meat: pork belly burnt ends, house-smoked pork and excellent baby back ribs. *11.30am-2.45pm & 6-10.45pm Tue-Sun* ₹₹

Kaspers: Parisian bistro meets Bandra chic at Will Aghajanian's chef-led space – mud crab gratin with lamb brain, doodled tables and cherubs everywhere. *7pm-1.30am Tue-Sun* ₹₹₹

Papa's: Intimate 12-seater where chef Hussain Shahzad serves a playful, deeply Indian tasting menu. Expect bold flavours and beautiful plates. *from 7.30pm Wed-Sat* ₹₹₹

The Tanjore Tiffin Room: Comforting, home-style Tamil food done right. Start with the tasting thali – bite-sized portions of house specials. *noon-11.30pm* ₹₹

TOP TIP

Bandra comes alive at Christmas. The Catholic community decks out homes and streets with glowing stars, nativity scenes and fairy lights, while carols, pop-up bazaars and community arts fill the air. Check *@thestepsbandra* for festive happenings, or hop on a #BandraBling jeep tour with *@khaki.tours* to cruise past the most twinkling corners of the suburb.

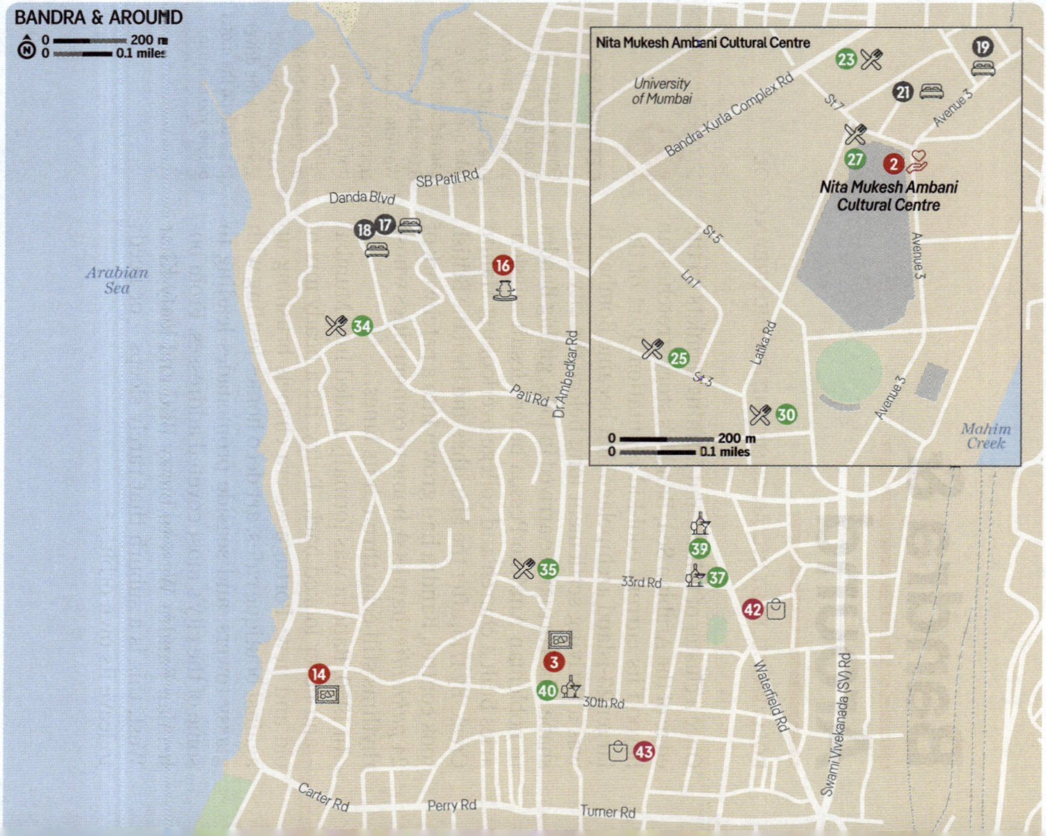

HIGHLIGHTS
1 Father Agnel Ashram
2 Nita Mukesh Ambani Cultural Centre

SIGHTS
3 Art and Charlie
4 Bandra Fort
5 Bandstand Promenade
6 Bomanjee Jeejeebhoy Steps
7 Bombay Art Society
8 Fluxus Chapel
9 Kekee Manzil
10 Mount Mary Basilica
11 St Andrew's Church
12 Steps Bandra
13 Street Art by Bollywood Art Project
14 The Serigraph Studio

ACTIVITIES
15 Adagio
16 Mitti Space

- **SLEEPING**
- 17 GoSolo Stays
- 18 Hammock Hostels
- 19 Sofitel Mumbai BKC
- 20 Taj Lands End
- 21 Trident Hotel, Bandra Kurla

- **EATING**
- 22 Al Bakery
- 23 Bawri
- 24 Café Andora
- 25 CinCin
- 26 IMBISS Meating Joint
- 27 Indian Accent
- 28 J Hearsch & Co
- 29 Kaspers
- 30 Kyma
- 31 Mary Lodge by Subko
- 32 Papa's
- 33 Steps Café
- 34 The Tanjore Tiffin Room
- 35 TwentySeven Bakehouse
- 36 Veronica's

- **DRINKING & NIGHTLIFE**
- 37 Bonobo
- 38 Old Street Café & Bar
- 39 The Den
- 40 Toto's Garage

- **ENTERTAINMENT**
- 41 Mehboob Studios

- **SHOPPING**
- 42 The Comic Book Store
- 43 Title Waves
- 44 Topaz Bookshop
- 45 Trilogy Curated Bookshop and Library

BOMBAY IN BOLLYWOOD

Gully Boy (Zoya Akhtar, 2019) A raw, electrifying portrait of a Mumbai slum kid who finds his voice through street rap, and uses it to punch through class, silence and circumstance.

The Lunchbox (Ritesh Batra, 2013) A misdelivered *dabba* (lunchbox) in Mumbai sparks an intimate correspondence between a lonely widower and a neglected homemaker, quietly reshaping two lives.

Dhobi Ghat (Kiran Rao, 2010) Four drifting lives move between the open-air dhobi ghat of Mahalaxmi and Worli's glassy high-rises, capturing the city's intimacy, distance and quiet collisions.

Jaane Tu... Ya Jaane Na (Abbas Tyrewala, 2008) The metropolis becomes a soft-focus playground for young love — from Bandra Fort sunsets to Xavier's College corridors – turning the city into a warm, lived-in home rather than a spectacle.

RANJIT DAHIYA ARTIST AND FOUNDER BOLLYWOOD ART PROJECT (BAP)

Bollywood Art Project

Cinematic Street Art

Step into the spotlight

The laid-back lanes of Bandra blend Indo-Portuguese cottages, Bollywood lore and star power – sometimes literally splashed across the walls. Spot larger-than-life murals of screen legends, from artsy splatters near **Subko** on Chapel Rd to the glamorous trio of Helen, Waheeda Rehman and Asha Parekh nearby. Wander past a striking portrait of the iconic Raj Kapoor in Ranwar before refuelling at **Veronica's**, a colourful all-day cafe loved by the neighbourhood's creative crowd. Want more than a photo op? Artist Ranjit Dahiya, founder of the Bollywood Art Project (p669), offers immersive **workshops** *(bollywoodartproject.com; ₹3200 per person 6hr session)* where you can paint your own cinematic icon – no experience required.

Stop by Father Agnel Ashram

A quietly powerful space where faiths converge

Pause at **Father Agnel Ashram** *(agnelashram.org)* on Bandstand and look closely. Founded in 1957 by Father Conceicao Rodrigues after he left Portuguese-era Goa, this isn't just a Christian shrine – it's a lesson in syncretism. Spot the bust of

DRINKING IN BANDRA: OUR PICKS

The Den: Neighbourhood favourite for live sports, Tuesday karaoke and nights fuelled by solid drinks and comfort food. *4pm-1am Mon-Thu, noon-1am Fri-Sun*

Bonobo: A buzzy, eclectic bar where DJs spin drum and bass, electronica and funky house for a young, energetic crowd. *6pm-1.30am*

Toto's Garage: A kitschy, high-energy watering hole where the music's loud, the pours are generous and weekends are wild. *5pm-12.45am*

Old Street Café & Bar: Old-school charm with high ceilings, retro decor and Indian and Indo-Chinese fare. *5pm-1.30am Mon-Fri, 2pm-1.30am Sat, noon-1.30am Sun*

Father Agnel at the gate, then look up: an Om above it. Crosses appear alongside elephants, lotuses and the Dhammachakra. Ahead of its time, the Ashram sought to present Christianity not as an imported faith, but as one rooted in and resonant with India's cultural landscape. Today, devotees of all religions visit, and the Ashram also anchors major educational institutions across Mumbai, Goa and beyond.

Creative Corridors

Artists, studios and slow craft

The suburb's creative pulse thrives off Chapel Rd and beyond, where art isn't just exhibited, it's lived. Wander the narrow lanes painted with expressive murals, then drop into **Fluxus Chapel**, a vibrant hub for workshops, screenings and zine culture. Nearby **Art and Charlie** turns a heritage bungalow into an intimate gallery and performance space, while **Adagio** offers analogue culture with guitar lessons and vinyl sessions. For hands-on creativity, **Mitti Space** is a shared pottery studio in Khar West where beginners and seasoned makers alike can learn wheel-throwing and sculpt clay in a welcoming setting. Peek into **The Serigraph Studio**, where signed limited-edition prints bring fine art within reach, then drop by the historic **Bombay Art Society**, a longstanding institution championing Indian artists through rotating exhibitions and open calls.

Paper Trails

Pages, paperbacks and personality-packed bookshops

Bandra's bookstores double as treasure troves and time machines, making them perfect souvenirs to carry home. Browse **Title Waves**, a neighbourhood favourite that hosts author talks and workshops alongside a thoughtfully curated selection. Pop into **Trilogy Curated Bookshop and Library**, a cosy independent bookstore run by passionate bibliophile couple who champion local writers and always have spot-on recommendations. For vintage finds, head to **Topaz Bookshop & Old Mart**, where discounted second-hand books sit beside Agatha Christie paperbacks, P.G. Wodehouse classics, gramophones and vinyl. And for pure nostalgia, visit **The Comic Book Store**, India's first licensed comic shop, stacked with Marvel heroes, Tintin adventures and graphic novels galore.

CATHOLIC COMMUNITIES

Bandra's Catholic identity is rooted in village life and layered migrations. Once made up of around 24 *pakhadis* (hamlets), it was home to Koli fishers, Kunbis (cultivators), Agris (salt-pan workers) and Bhandaris (toddy tappers), forming a largely self-sufficient ecosystem. With fertile land and orchards, Bandra was once a green buffer that also drew British strategic interest.

The Portuguese arrival in the 16th century reshaped the area. Conversion to Christianity altered dress, education and language, with many locals adopting English and clerical work under colonial rule. Later, Goan migrants arrived, prompting older residents to assert the 'East Indian' identity, formalised in an 1888 petition to Queen Victoria.

Walk through Ranwar or Chuim today and this layered past reveals itself in surnames, churches and homes.

EATING IN BANDRA: BEST BAKERIES

Café Andora: Bandra old-timer loved by schoolkids and locals for chicken sausage puffs, roast lamb sandwiches and lemon tart. *8.30am-8.30pm Mon-Sat* ₹

J. Hearsch & Co: This charming place serves old-school bakes and cult Indo-Chinese hits from mawa muffins to lollipops and Schezwan fried rice. *9am-9pm Wed-Mon* ₹

TwentySeven Bakehouse: Here, playful, inventive bakes – from *vada pav* danishes to bright citrus loaves – keep comfort food deliciously off-script. *7.30am-9pm* ₹₹

A1 Bakery: A stalwart since the 1950s, mixing Irani bakery classics with cult quirks – mutton pattices, mawa cake and garlic bread everyone swears by. *7am-10pm* ₹

WHY I LOVE BANDRA WEST

Pooja Naik, Lonely Planet writer

Everyone swoons over South Mumbai – and rightly so – but Bandra has always had my heart. It's the city's original cool kid: effortlessly stylish, a little scrappy and endlessly alive. Here, seaside promenades meet late-night bars, fine dining rubs shoulders with hole-in-the-wall cafes, and art spills out of galleries into the streets. There's history in the churches and bungalows, energy in the music venues and studios, and a sense of community that still lingers despite the gloss. It's where suburbans and townies collide, where I can wander, eat, listen, pause and always feel at home.

SUMIT_YADAV/SHUTTERSTOCK

Nita Mukesh Ambani Cultural Centre

From Boardrooms to Broadway

BKC swaps spreadsheets for stages at the NMACC

Head to BKC, Mumbai's glass-and-steel financial district, and step into the **Nita Mukesh Ambani Cultural Centre** *(nmacc.com)*, a sprawling arts complex that anchors the neighbourhood beyond boardrooms. Catch Broadway-style productions like *The Sound of Music,* large-scale Indian epics such as *The Great Indian Musical,* international ballets, classical concerts, exhibitions and design showcases, all housed across three theatres and gallery spaces that bring global culture into the city's corporate core.

EATING IN BKC: OUR PICKS

CinCin: Savour hand-rolled pasta, wood-fired pizza and a frozen tiramisu in this vibrant, colourful space. *noon-1am* ₹₹

Indian Accent: Chef Manish Mehrotra's celebrated contemporary Indian restaurant nails it in the stylish NMACC. *noon-2.30pm & 6.45pm-midnight* ₹₹₹

Kyma: An airy, alfresco Asian-Mediterranean restaurant blending sushi, mezze and crafted cocktails. *noon-1.30am* ₹₹

Bawri: Delicious Goan fare in a tropically elegant spot in the BKC. Book ahead, and don't miss the tiger prawns. *noon-3.30pm & 7pm-1.30am* ₹₹₹

BANDRA'S GREATEST HITS ON FOOT

Tick off must-see landmarks and historic icons that define the neighbourhood's character.

START	END	LENGTH
Bandra Fort	St Andrew's Church	1.6km; 3hr

Begin at ❶ **Bandra Fort**, a 17th-century Portuguese watchtower perched above the Arabian Sea. Built in 1640 to guard the harbour, its weathered ramparts frame sweeping sea views and sunsets laced with the Bandra–Worli Sea Link (p684). Wander through the newly refurbished terraced garden below, where locals linger, stretch and watch the city exhale.

Exit onto ❷ **Bandstand Promenade** at Lands End, a storied seaside stretch edged with volcanic rock, celebrity homes and colonial bungalows like ❸ **Kekee Manzil**. Climb up to ❹ **Mount Mary Basilica** for neogothic spires, sea breezes and centuries of devotion centred around a 16th-century statue of the Virgin Mary – best decked in September during the Bandra Fair.

Pause at ❺ **Steps Bandra**, also called St Stephen's Steps, a lively community plaza, and then descend via the ❻ **Bomanjee Jeejeebhoy Steps**, tiled in *Starry Night*-inspired mosaics. Pass ❼ **Mehboob Studios** – Bollywood royalty territory – before ending at ❽ **St Andrew's Church**, Bandra's oldest, where restored stone and nine doors hold centuries of faith.

Sign up for a guided group walk with **Khaki Tours** *(@khaki.tours; ₹999 per person).*

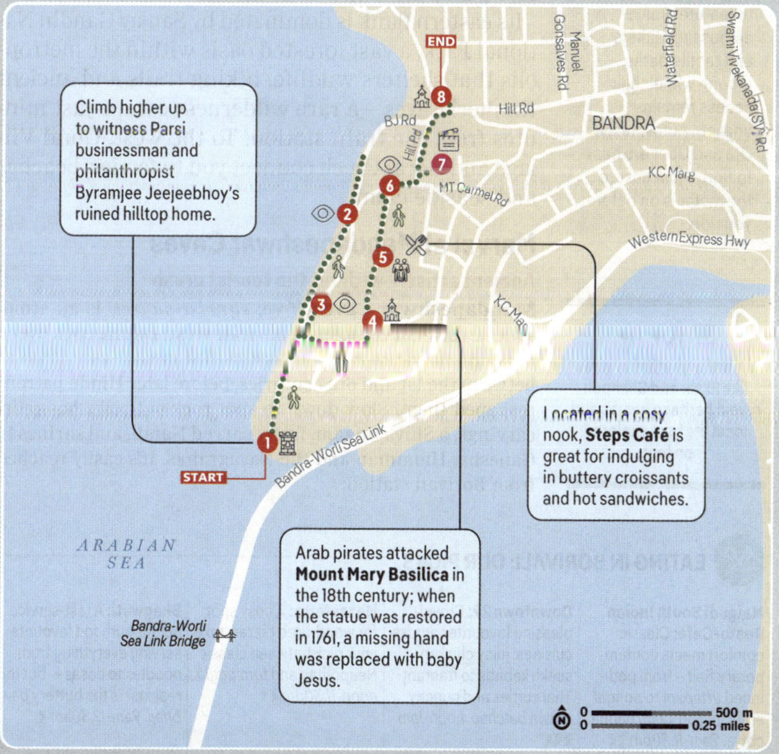

Borivali

WHERE NORTHERN SUBURBIA MEETS THE NATIONAL PARK

GETTING AROUND

Borivali is well connected by the Western Line, Western Express Highway and Metro Line 2A, making travel across Mumbai easy. Its train station was Maharashtra's first to feature braille-embossed railings and tactile paths, though wheelchair access remains uneven. Autos, taxis, Ola and Uber are easy to find – just ensure the meter is on before you ride.

At the northern edge of Mumbai's western suburbs, Borivali is a place many visitors overlook. Once a cluster of small villages like Eksar, Poisar, Shimpoli and Mandpeshwar, it lay scattered on and around Mount Poinsur, between the Dahisar and Poisar Rivers. Its name likely comes from the *bor* bushes of sweet jujube that once grew here. The original inhabitants – tribal groups and East Indians – lived off agriculture and fishing long before the area was urbanised under British rule. Today, Borivali is a bustling residential hub where old *gaothans* (villages) still perch amid gardens and family-run markets.

Its eastern flank is dominated by Sanjay Gandhi National Park, a vast forested oasis within the metropolis that shelters wildlife, hiking trails and ancient Kanheri Caves – a rare wilderness escape just minutes from the train station. To the west, Gorai Village and Gorai Creek connect you to ferries, beaches and seaside calm.

TOP TIP

Walk the *gaothans*: areas like Eksar and Shimpoli reveal heritage homes and local life best explored on foot.

Marvel at Mandapeshwar Caves

Ancient artistry without the tourist crush

Mandapeshwar Caves *(free; sunrise-sunset)* is an atmospheric rock-cut complex in Borivali West. Dating back over a millennium, the caves began as Buddhist meditation chambers between the 1st and 6th centuries, before later Hindu patrons reshaped them. Slow down to spot rock-cut cells, bas-relief carvings, a Shiva lingam, finely carved Nandi, and shrines to Ganesha, Hanuman and the Navagrahas. It's easily reached from Borivali station.

EATING IN BORIVALI: OUR PICKS

Malgudi South Indian Resto-Café: Classic comfort meets contemporary flair – from podi-laced *uttapam* to *pongal* arancini and *kaapi* panna cotta. *9am-11.30pm* ₹₹

Downtown 29: Crowd-pleasing favourites across cuisines: juicy chicken seekh kebabs to fragrant Thai curries and punchy prawn *balchao. noon-1am* ₹₹₹

Mezzaterra: A cosy spot for wood-fired pizzas: take your pick between classic Neapolitan and *formaggio. noon-11.30pm* ₹₹

Bhagwati: A fast-service neighbourhood favourite serving everything from noodles to dosas – but the real star is the buttery *pav bhaji. 9am-12.30am* ₹

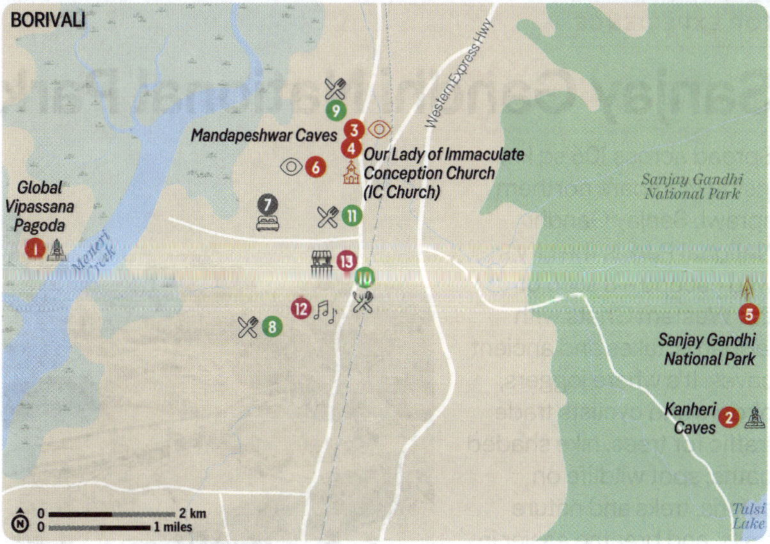

Step into Stillness

Experience meditation at the Global Vipassana Pagoda

Scale and stillness impress at the **Global Vipassana Pagoda** *(globalpagoda.org; free; 10am-6.30pm)* in Gorai. Built in 2009 on a peninsula between Gorai Creek and the Arabian Sea, this vast stone dome shelters an 8000-seat meditation hall. Inspired by Myanmar's Shwedagon Pagoda, it honours the Buddha and the *vipassana* tradition. Try Anapana meditation or a 10-day *vipassana* course (both free). Dress modestly and carry ID. Reach by ferry or road from Borivali or Gorai.

Echoes of Early Bombay

One of the city's oldest churches, still anchoring local life

Our Lady of Immaculate Conception Church *(icchurchborivali.org)* in IC Colony is among Mumbai's oldest Roman Catholic parishes. Founded in 1547 by Franciscans, the Portuguese-style church was later rebuilt by parishioners after falling into ruins in the 18th century. Visit for its calm interiors or on 8 December, Feast of the Immaculate Conception, when pilgrims gather citywide.

Explore Eksar Gaothan

Trace naval history etched in Viragal stones

Eksar Gaothan is one of Mumbai's oldest villages, traditionally home to the Agri community of rice farmers and fisherfolk. Its standout relics are rare Viragals (hero stones) from the Shilahara era (9th–13th century), carved with naval battle scenes and now displayed within the **Club Aquaria** compound. Walk the narrow lanes, pass old homes and glimpse generations still living here, a quiet pocket of history beneath the suburb's modern veneer.

HIGHLIGHTS
1 Global Vipassana Pagoda
2 Kanheri Caves
3 Mandapeshwar Caves
4 Our Lady of Immaculate Conception Church (IC Church)
5 Sanjay Gandhi National Park

SIGHTS
6 Club Aquaria

SLEEPING
7 The Grandeur Boutique Hotel

EATING
8 Bhagwati
9 Downtown 29
10 Malgudi South Indian Resto-Café
11 Mezzaterra

ENTERTAINMENT
12 Kora Kendra Grounds

SHOPPING
13 Jambli Galli

TOP EXPERIENCE

Sanjay Gandhi National Park

Spread across 106 sq km inside Mumbai's northern sprawl, Sanjay Gandhi National Park is the city's wild escape – a slice of the Western Ghats with leopards, lakes and ancient caves. It's where joggers, birders and cyclists trade traffic for trees, hike shaded paths, spot wildlife on safaris, treks and nature trails, and breathe easier in a metropolis otherwise thick with noise and fumes.

Kanheri Caves

FILEDIMAGE/SHUTTERSTOCK

Rock-Cut Cave Complex

The **Kanheri Caves** are a striking complex of over 100 rock-cut chambers carved between the 1st century BCE and 10th century CE. Hewn from basalt, they reveal Buddhist prayer halls, sculptures of the Buddha and bodhisattvas, and an ingenious ancient water-harvesting system. Walk, cycle or drive up to explore this serene hillside sanctuary.

Into the Wild

Take a mini jungle **safari** *(adult/child ₹124/50; Tue-Sun)* through designated lion and tiger enclosures for a chance to see these iconic big cats up close in settings that mimic their natural habitats. The tiger safari spans about 20 hectares and has been redesigned to give visitors a more authentic experience, while the planned lion safari is expanding with more lions arriving from Gujarat. Safaris typically last 30 minutes and run in the morning and afternoon. Beyond big cats, the park shelters 254 bird species, 40 mammals, 78 reptiles and amphibians, and nearly 150 butterflies.

Go Slow with the Locals

Sign up for a **Go Hallu Hallu** *(@gohalluhallu; ₹2100 per person)* slow-walking guided tour for a rare chance to engage with the Indigenous Warli community along the Dahisar River and nearby *padas*. Led by local guides, the experience explores forest-based livelihoods, seasonal food traditions and Indigenous knowledge. Expect village walks, Warli art sessions, (seasonal) tribal fishing and home-cooked meals.

TOP TIPS

- Visit during the monsoon when the forest turns lush, waterfalls appear and wildlife sightings improve.
- Hit the hiking trails early – Kanheri Caves and Shilonda routes are best tackled before midday heat.
- Cycle inside the park on car-free mornings for a peaceful, traffic-free ride through green corridors.

PRACTICALITIES

- entry ₹85/45 adult/child, activities extra
- 7.30am-6.30pm Tue-Sun

Places We Love to Stay

₹ Budget ₹₹ Midrange ₹₹₹ Top End

Colaba & Churchgate

Map p673

Ascot Hotel ₹₹ A classic 3-star stay in Colaba just steps from the Gateway of India and the city's historic sights, offering comfortable rooms and an on-site restaurant.

Abode ₹₹ A stylish Colaba boutique pairing vintage Bombay character with contemporary comforts; art-lined corridors, patterned tiles, bespoke furniture and warm, heritage-inspired interiors.

Hotel Diplomat ₹₹ Tucked beside the Taj Mahal Palace is this well-placed boutique stay with round-the-clock dining and smart spaces for meetings and private events.

InterContinental ₹₹₹ Anchoring Mumbai's art deco seafront, this Marine Drive outpost combines sea-facing rooms with a rooftop pool, skyline views and polished dining.

Taj Mahal Palace Hotel (p672) ₹₹₹ India's most storied hotel, where grand architecture, legendary hospitality and iconic views define a stay.

The Oberoi, Mumbai ₹₹₹ Marine Drive luxury at its finest, with serene, design-led rooms, deep soaking tubs and sweeping sea views.

Fort

Map p680

Hebbar's Heritage Home ₹ A century-old, budget-friendly stay marked by Victorian and Portuguese detailing, vintage furniture and old-world charm.

Residency Hotel Fort ₹₹ A fuss-free, friendly midrange base where comfy rooms, helpful staff and a prime Fort address make exploring old Mumbai refreshingly easy.

Grand Hotel ₹₹ Check into this Ballard Estate charmer designed by Gateway-of-India architect George Wittet, where retro rooms and old-world details keep Mumbai's colonial past very much alive.

Worli

Map p685

Bloom Hotel – Worli ₹₹ Crash at this bright, buzzy Bloom outpost in Worli, where slick yellow interiors, sharp service and a handy location keep things easy and upbeat.

Four Seasons Hotel ₹₹₹ Check in for the views: the rooftop bar, sky-high pool and San:Qi's polished plates steal the spotlight here.

Lower Parel & the Mill Belt

Map p688

The Kin ₹₹ A 15-room boutique hideaway in Dadar where artful travel finds meet marble floors, porthole views, vinyl listening, and buzzy days-to-night dining at Terttulia downstairs.

ITC Grand Central ₹₹₹ Luxury accommodation that blends Victorian-era grandeur with dome-topped drama, throwing in butler service, rooftop sundowners at Point of View and a globe-trotting dining lineup from Dakshin to Dublin.

The St Regis Mumbai ₹₹₹ Shop till you drop at Palladium, then return for butler service, headline-worthy dining (Nikkei at Koishii or rooftop Asian flavours at Mekong), an infinity pool and an evening of Champagne sabering.

Bandra & Around

Map p692

GoSolo Stays ₹ Stay at mixed or female dorms at this boutique Khar hostel in a quaint century-old bungalow steps from local bars, cafes, restaurants and entertainment spots; perfect for solo backpackers to mingle, explore and unwind.

Hammock Hostels ₹ Free breakfast, no curfew and the option to sign up for guided city and food tours – this Bandra hostel is as wholesome as it is laid-back.

Taj Lands End ₹₹₹ All the Taj polish and pampering, minus the Colaba price tag – with Bandra's sea views thrown in for good measure.

Sofitel Mumbai BKC ₹₹₹ Timber floors, marble bathrooms and bold colours, with poolside cocktails at L'OH, six dining options, a luxe spa and grand venues made for power meetings or polished weddings.

Trident Hotel, Bandra Kurla ₹₹₹ A cosier counterpoint to its Nariman Point sibling, this Trident charms with light-filled rooms, oakwood warmth, Botticino's Italian comforts, Maya's Indian classics and a final sugar rush from the in-house patisserie.

Borivali

Map p699

The Grandeur Boutique Hotel ₹₹ Roomy bedrooms, 24/7 room service and free breakfast; perfectly placed for trains, the Global Vipassana Pagoda and Mandapeshwar Caves.

Researched by
Joanna Lobo

Maharashtra

ANCIENT ARCHITECTURE AND NATURAL BEAUTY

With its 2000-year-old cave temples and vast modern cities, the thriving wine region of Maharashtra is full of diverse wonders.

The home state of Mumbai (Bombay) stretches far beyond its capital, with much to offer travellers, from the palm-tree-lined shores of the historically rich Konkan Coast to the ancient architecture, modern cities, medieval hill forts and sprawling countryside inland to the east. The biggest draws for many are the Ajanta and Ellora cave temples in northern Maharashtra, where extremely rare 2000-year-old murals and the world's largest monolithic sculpture will blow your mind. Both are an easy drive from Chhatrapati Sambhajinagar (Aurangabad), a city with a rich culture of artisan crafts and some monumental architecture. Also in the north of the state is the ancient city of Nashik, which sits on the confluence of two holy rivers and serves as a religious epicentre for Hindus. Beyond its old town centre, Nashik is also home to India's up-and-coming wine industry, with vineyards surrounding the city and a handful of wineries open for tasting sessions and excellent dining.

MD NIAZUDDIN NAWAZ/SHUTTERSTOCK

Further south, the mighty tech hub of Pune is a seat of academia with vibrant student nightlife and a music scene to match. And in Maharashtra's deep south lies the Sindhudurg district, with its beautiful coastline, seafood-heavy meals and vanishing artistic traditions. In the eastern part of the state, Vidarbha is Maharashtra's tiger county where Royal Bengal tigers roam forests that are an integral part of their conservation story.

THE MAIN AREAS

PUNE
Tech hub with vibrant student life. **p708**

CHHATRAPATI SAMBHAJINAGAR (AURANGABAD)
Artisanal crafts and monumental architecture. **p718**

SINDHUDURG
Pristine beaches and culturally rich villages. **p723**

NASHIK
India's wine capital and pilgrimage spot. **p727**

VIDARBHA
Haven for wildlife and nature lovers. **p732**

For places to stay in Maharashtra, see p736

ABHISHEK HULLATHI/SHUTTERSTOCK

Above: Tadoba Andhari Tiger Reserve (p734), Vidarbha;
Left: Nandi sculpture, Trimbakeshwar (p731), Nashik

Nashik, p727

India's wine region is home to numerous vineyards that are open to visitors, and is also a popular pilgrimage spot.

Chhatrapati Sambhajinagar (Aurangabad), p718

A handy base for visiting the Ellora and Ajanta Caves, with a rich history of textiles and some striking architecture.

Sindhudurg, p723

The southern coast is lined with palm-tree dotted beaches and culturally rich villages, and features a cluster of fascinating historical sites.

Pune, p708

Students and spiritual seekers flock to this metropolitan tech hub and seat of learning, also home to the controversial Osho's ashram.

Vidarbha, p732

Known for its tiger reserves and wildlife sanctuaries, this district features particularly scenic countryside.

TRAIN

With the line to Aurangabad stopping at Nashik, and another line running southeast through Lonavala to Pune, trains are the cheapest and quickest way to travel between main cities and beyond. Book tickets online in advance using the IRCTC website *(irctc.co.in)*.

CAR & BUS

Hiring a car with driver (₹2500 to ₹6000, depending on the vehicle) is the priciest yet easiest way to get around outside of the cities. Government-run MSRTC *(msrtc.maharashtra.gov.in)* runs a comprehensive luxury and semi-luxury AC bus network spanning all major destinations; book tickets online.

BOAT

Along the Konkan Coast, Ro-Ro ferries and speedboats connect Mumbai to Mandwa (near Alibaug), and to the Konkan Region (Ratnagiri, Sindhudurg). Services between these regions run throughout the day (₹100 to ₹400 per person; from ₹2000 per vehicle). Tickets can be purchased online at *m2mferries.com*.

Find Your Way

India's third-largest state spreads for 720km from north to south and for 800km east to west, bisected by ancient trade routes, modern highways and multiple train routes traversing its expansive interior and lengthy coast.

Plan Your Time

Maharashtra is bigger than it looks on the map, so don't try to pack too much in. Allow ample travel time between destinations and expect the unexpected, particularly when using local transport.

SAIKO3P/SHUTTERSTOCK

Chaitya **(worship hall), Ajanta (p720)**

The Weekend Break

- If you only have a weekend, focus on **Aurangabad** (p718): explore the city's history, eat some delicious street food, and acquaint yourself with the textile traditions that involve weaving **himroo** (p719) and Paithani cloth.

- Aurangabad is a great base for visiting ancient marvels – the Ajanta and Ellora Caves. On Saturday, hit the road early to get to **Ajanta** (p720) as it opens at 9am. Spend the day there, admiring 2000-year-old murals and stone caves. On Sunday, rise early to get to **Ellora** (p720) at 8am to make the most of the mind-boggling monolithic **Kailasa Temple** (p721) before the crowds arrive. On the way back, stop at Khuldabad and, if you have the energy, trek up to the **Daulatabad Fort** (p722).

SEASONAL HIGHLIGHTS

The 'winter' months of November to January mean manageable heat but air pollution is rife. Monsoon (June to August) can be a great season if you don't mind a downpour.

MARCH

Holi parties in Pune are huge and, as the city is nightlife central, expect DJs to feature in the lineup.

JULY

Monsoon season is a great time to visit hill station Lonavala, with the waterfalls at their most impressive and hills rife with greenery.

AUGUST

Naag Panchami Snake festival is celebrated with gusto in Pune, whereas the **Kumbh Mela** festival – the world's largest Hindu pilgrimage – will be at its peak in Nashik in August 2027.

A Week to Spare

● **Pune** (p708) is a great place to start off your Maharashtrian adventure, with its rich Maratha history, deep cultural ties, good food and excellent shopping. Give yourself a day to explore its quirky museums, such as the **RK Laxman Museum** (p710). One evening, trek up **Parvati Hill** (p711) to enjoy sunset views of the city. Keep aside a half-day to embark on a food tour of **Camp** (p712), then take a break in Pune's **Empress Botanical Gardens** (p711).

● After spending a few days here, take the train to **Nashik** (p727), explore the ghats of **Ramkund** (p731) and head out to the holy **Trimbakeshwar Temple** (p731) before acquainting yourself with the thriving wine region around the city by touring different **wineries** (p728).

Slow Travel Time

● Spend a month easing into Maharashtra's zen. Spend a week to 10 days at the 100-year-old **Kaivalyadhama Yoga Institute** (p715) in **Lonavala** (p715). Near Lonavala, spend some time at the **Dharana at Shillim** (p716) spa hotel, soaking in the mountainous surroundings. Then head to the **Osho International Meditation Resort** (p708) in **Pune** (p708) for a week of meditation.

● If you would rather embark on outdoor adventures, go to **Lonavala** (p715) and spend a day visiting the nearby caves and forts. Then proceed to **Vidarbha** (p732), Maharashtra's tiger county, to embark on safaris that will give you the chance to see Royal Bengal tigers, gaurs, nilgai antelope and other animals.

SEPTEMBER

The **Ganesh Chaturthi** festival (p712) is huge across Maharashtra; celebrations are particularly lively in Pune. **Kumbh Mela** will reach its conclusion in Nashik in 2027.

OCTOBER

The Hindu festival of **Dussehra** is celebrated for 10 days in early October (or late September depending on the lunar cycle).

NOVEMBER

Diwali, the Hindu festival of lights, is celebrated with great aplomb across the state, but at the ghats (riverside steps) of Nashik particularly.

DECEMBER

Most attractions are open over Christmas, and New Year's Eve is not an official national public holiday. You will likely find low-key celebrations on 25 and 31 December.

Pune

MUSEUMS | EXCELLENT DINING | MEDITATION CENTRE

TOP TIP
Join the WATC Pune Weekly Events Whatsapp group. WATC stands for We Are The Chompions, a food group *(instagram.com/wearechompions)* with a weekly curation of interesting in-person events that focus on travel, food, heritage & history.

Thanks to the density of universities in the city, Pune buzzes with ingenuity, from its academic prowess to its more recent role of innovative start-up hub. Fuelled by its young professionals and students, the city promises fun nights out, with a vibrant music and cocktail scene. The city is also a hub for good food, catering to every budget. There is a rich history woven into its fabric. Pune was both a domestic and military base of the great medieval Maratha ruler Shivaji, who grew up in the city and later made it his capital; a number of his palaces and temples survive today. There are also remnants of Peshwa architecture visible in the different *wadas* (large mansions). Pune has fun neighbourhoods, quirky museums, buzzing markets and pockets of green. The infamous guru Rajneesh founded his Osho ashram here in 1974 and it remains a popular sight.

A Controversial Guru's Sanctum

Visit Osho international meditation retreat

Many years after his death in 1990, Bhagwan Shree Rajneesh, known widely as Osho, continues to be one of India's most internationally famous and controversial gurus. His sex-positive philosophies made him famous, but murder attempts at his village in Oregon made him infamous. Whether you love or loathe him, his teachings and spiritual practices live on at the **Osho International Meditation Resort** *(osho.com;*

GETTING AROUND

Parts of Pune are walkable but attractions are spread out. Metered autorickshaws are the quickest way to get around; flag one down or use the Ola or Uber rideshare apps. Pune metro is useful for getting to the train station. Pune's airport is connected to most major cities. The Pune Junction train station has inter-city and inter-state trains to Mumbai, Goa, Hyderabad and Chennai, among others. The Pune Station bus stand has buses to Mumbai and Goa; luxury AC buses to Aurangabad and Nashik run from the Shivaji Nagar Bus Stand.

KARAN KHURANA/SHUTTERSTOCK

Pataleshwar Cave Temple (p711)

day pass from ₹1050), which was designed to be 'a spiritual Club Med, as in Meditation'. Here you can put on a maroon robe and join the *sannyasins* (followers) in meditation, use the pool and sauna of the Basho Spa, or sign up for additional therapies (sound healing, hypnosis) at the Multiversity.

Beyond the centre, the verdant **Osho Teerth Park** *(6-9am & 3-6pm)* offers many spots for reflection and meditation, with a gushing stream and birdsong for company. Photography isn't allowed here.

Quirky Museums

Get your culture fix

Let Pune's museums charm you with their historic and unusual collections. Start with **Raja Dinkar Kelkar Museum** *(rajakelkarmuseum.org; ₹400)*, which houses religious icons, musical instruments, utensils and textiles, spread across three floors. **Joshi's Museum of Miniature Railways** *(minirailways.com; ₹120)* has a mini city full of trains and tracks; half hourly shows showcase different kinds of trains and their engines. The **Mahatma Phule Museum** *(₹10)* focuses on anthropological artefacts, engineering models and weapons through the ages. A tour of the **Gandhi National Memorial** in the **Aga Khan Palace** *(₹300)* shows you the rooms where Gandhi was imprisoned (from August 1942 to May 1944) along with his wife, Kasturba, and his secretary, Mahadeobhai

INDIA'S ACADEMIC HUB

Since it comprises 23 universities and over 90 colleges, running undergraduate and postgraduate programmes, it is clear to see why Pune has been dubbed the 'Oxford of the East' and why there is a friendly rivalry between its student populations. Seats of learning include nationally high-ranking institutions such as Dr DY Patil Vidyapeeth, Symbiosis International and Bharati Vidyapeeth and longstanding and revered campuses such as Fergusson College, MIT and Savitribai Phule Pune University. The city can thank the huge population of students for its thriving nightlife, which can be filed next to Mumbai's in terms of liveliness and musical variety, but at a more affordable price.

EATING IN PUNE: OUR PICKS

Surve's Pure Non Veg Restaurant: The place to go for your meat or fish fix. Order the thalis or the *rassas* (spicy curries). *noon-4pm & 7-11pm* ₹₹

We Idliwale Barroom: A chain of restaurants serving South India's *idlis* (spongy fermented rice cakes). Leave space for dessert. *noon-1.30am* ₹₹

Aragma: Fine dining changing menus highlight local ingredients, Indian stories and international cooking techniques. *noon-10pm* ₹₹₹

Paashh: This swanky cafe north of the river uses organic seasonal produce to craft Asian fusion dishes that look like edible art. *8am-10.30pm* ₹₹₹

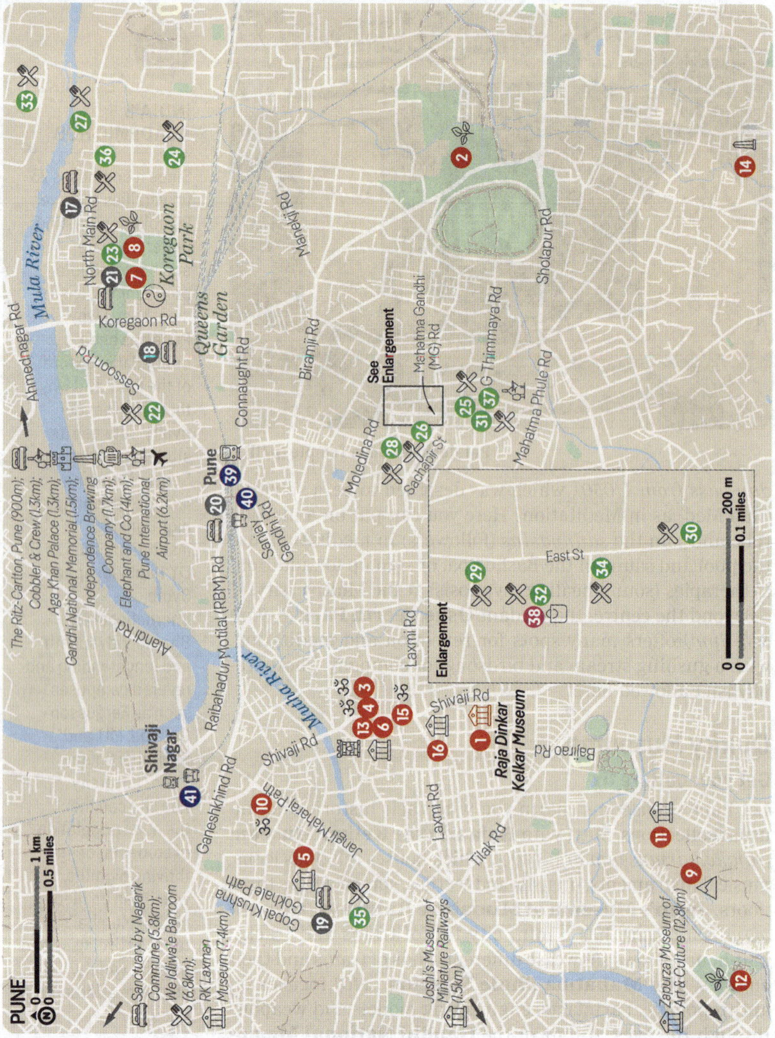

Desai, and details his activities at the time. The latter two died during incarceration – their shrines are in the garden.

Learn about the RK Laxman's iconic satirical cartoon character, the Common Man – representing the average Indian citizen – through the artist's sketches and artwork at the eponymous **RK Laxman Museum** *(rklaxmanmuseum.com; ₹50)*.

If you have the time, take an hour-long journey south of the main city to **Zapurza Museum of Art & Culture** *(zapurza.org; ₹250)*, located on the banks of Khadakwasla Dam. It's a one-stop cultural centre that organises performances and workshops, with an attached art museum displaying lithographs, textiles and jewellery.

★ **HIGHLIGHTS**
1 Raja Dinkar Kelkar Museum

● **SIGHTS**
2 Empress Botanical Gardens
3 Kasba Ganpati Mandir
4 Laal Mahal
5 Mahatma Phule Museum
6 Nana Wada
7 Osho International Meditation Resort
8 Osho Teerth Gardens
9 Parvati Hill
10 Pataleshvara Cave Temple
11 Peshwe Museum
12 Pune Okayama Friendship Garden
13 Shaniwar Wada
14 Shinde Chhatri
15 Shrimant Dagdusheth Halwai Ganpati Mandir
16 Vishrambag Wada

● **SLEEPING**
17 Bloom Hotel – Koregaon Park
18 Conrad Pune
19 Hotel Ketan
20 Sheraton Grand Pune Bund Garden Hotel
21 Sunderban Resort & Spa

● **EATING**
22 Aragma
23 Bai Mu Dan
24 Chafa Cafe and Studio
25 City Bakery
26 Dorabjee & Sons
27 Emmer Bakery
28 Garden Vadapav Centre
29 George Restaurant
30 Kayani Bakery
31 Kohinoor
32 Marz-o-rin
33 Paashh
34 Puna Zarthosti Seva Mandal
35 Surve's Pure Non Veg Restaurant
36 The French Window Patisserie

● **DRINKING & NIGHTLIFE**
37 1000 Oaks

● **SHOPPING**
38 Budhani Bros Waferwala

● **TRANSPORT**
39 Pune Junction Train Station
40 Pune Station Bus Stand
41 Shivaji Nagar Bus Stand

WHY I LOVE PUNE

Joanna Lobo, Lonely Planet writer

This city has the buzz of a city like Mumbai, but with the calm and quiet of Goa. There's always something to do in Pune, abundant as it is in history, interesting museums, cultural spaces and gardens. Each area has something exciting to offer: the abundance of quiet spaces and coffee shops in Koregaon Park, a plethora of eating options and affordable shopping in Camp, a taste of history in the *peths*, and street shopping and educational institutes in Deccan. Traffic is chaotic, but the people are friendly and the food is excellent.

City Stories

Explore gardens and historic monuments

Pune abounds in distinct neighbourhoods, beautiful historic monuments and gardens. On JM Rd, the **Pataleshwar Cave Temple** is possibly the oldest structure in the city – a temple built from a single rock around 750 CE. Over in Wanowrie is the **Shinde Chhatri**, a memorial complex dedicated to the 18th-century Maratha ruler, which contains a temple on site. If you are after a spot of quiet, Pune's gardens offer green therapy. **Empress Botanical Gardens** *(₹20)* is an old favourite, popular for its nursery, children's park, and annual fruit, flower and vegetable show. **Pune Okayama Friendship Garden** or Pu La Deshpande Udyan *(₹50)* is a well manicured garden. There are winding paths, small streams and waterfalls, and little bridges that make for good photo spots. Nearby is **Parvati Hill**: climb the 108 steps to the top to be rewarded with views of five temples, access to the **Peshwe Museum** *(₹20)* that showcases 300-year-old weapons, and sweeping city vistas.

EATING IN KOREGAON PARK: BEST CAFES

The French Window Patisserie: Pet-friendly cafe with open-air seating, freshly baked goods and a selection of vegan treats. *9am-11pm* ₹₹

Chafa Cafe: Local cafe chain, serving global fare and healthy meals in a laid-back space with lots of greenery. Service can be slow. *8am-11pm* ₹₹

Emmer Bakery: Tranquil cafe and bakery with vegan and vegetarian options, and offering wallet-friendly goodies. *9am-6pm Fri-Wed* ₹₹

Bai Mu Dan: This cute cafe does coffee, smoothies, smoothie bowls, salads and gluten-free cakes. Expect crowds in the evenings. *8am-9.30pm* ₹₹

THE IMPORTANCE OF GANESHA CELEBRATIONS

Honouring the birthday of the elephant-headed deity, Ganesh Chaturthi in Pune isn't just a festival. It is a tradition that transcends religion and brings the city together. In 1893, freedom fighter Lokmanya Bal Gangadhar Tilak initiated the tradition of *sarvajanik* (for the people) that epitomises Ganesh Utsav, meant to foster a sense of national pride during British rule. Over the years, the festival has grown, with Ganpati *pandals* (marquees) on every corner, and festivities lasting for days. Some famous idols include Dagdusheth Halwai Ganpati, Kasba Ganpati and Tulshibaug Ganpati. The *visarjan* (immersion of the clay idol in water, symbolising Lord Ganesh returning to Mount Kailash) is a sight to behold.

To learn more about Pune's history, reach out to **Sandeep Godbole** *(9823188898)*, who conducts personalised guided tours. **Ayan Heritage Walks** *(ayanheritagewalks.com)* and **Deccan Drifts** *(instagram.com/deccandrifts)* also conduct walking tours. **Pune Samvad-Chalo PMC** *(instagram.com/punesamvad)* is a citizens' group that organises heritage tree walks. Tour prices start from ₹500, depending on the number of paricipants and the duration.

Chomping in Camp

Visit legendary food spots

Pune Cantonment, or Camp, is well-known for its shopping on MG Rd and East St, the Pune Race Course, its old houses and its legendary food joints.

Start your self-guided food tour at the Aurora Towers end of MG Rd. Off Bootee St is **George Restaurant**, known for its biryani and Persian dishes like *chelo* (barbecued kebab) and *jojeh* kebab (grilled chicken). The bright lights and yellow facade will welcome you to the fast-food joint and cafe **Marz-o-rin** *(marzorin.com)* with its famous sandwiches and macaroni bakes. Nearby is the **Puna Zarthosti Seva Mandal** kiosk that sells fast food like cutlets and burgers. Across the road, enter an alley to find **Budhani Bros Waferwala** *(budhanibros.com)*, started by three brothers and Pune's best place to get potato wafers to date. Take a detour to **Dorabjee & Sons** *(instagram.com/dorabjeeandsonspune)* for some hearty Parsi grub like mutton *keema* (minced mutton dish) and *dhansak* (meat with curried lentils and rice), and keep walking until you reach **Garden Vadapav Centre** for some tasty *vada pav* (deep-fried potato patty served in bread with chutney). Back on MG Road, walk into the **City Bakery** *(instagram.com/citybakeryonline)* and pick up its legendary hazelnut biscuits. Across the road is **Kohinoor** restaurant, the only place that opens at 3am daily, making for an early breakfast spot. Over on East St, pop into **Kayani Bakery** *(kayanibakerypune.com)*, well known for its Shrewbury biscuits, ginger biscuits and *mawa* (buttery sponge) cake. Expect queues.

If seeking an organised food tour, check out Western Routes *(thewesternroutes.com; from ₹1000 per person).*

DRINKING IN PUNE: BEST BARS

Independence Brewing Company: Going strong since 2011, Pune's best brewery has IPAs, lagers and hefeweizen on tap, to name a few. *noon-1.30am*

Cobbler & Crew: Hip cocktail bar doing exciting drinks, accompanied by tasty plates of food. Visit on its jazz nights. Weekends get crowded. *12.30pm-1am*

Elephant and Co (ECO): Fun neighbourhood bar serving craft cocktails, beers on tap and comfort food. *noon-12.30am*

1000 Oaks: Legendary outlet (one of the first pubs in Pune) on East St that specialises in cocktails and North Indian food. *noon-11.30pm*

A WALK THROUGH HISTORY

The area around Shaniwar Wada in Pune is considered its oldest part, and is home to historic monuments, *wadas* (mansions) and markets.

START	END	LENGTH
Shaniwar Wada	Vishrambaug Wada	1.5km; 3hr

Start your tour at the imposing stone ❶ **Shaniwar Wada**, built by Maratha leader Peshwa Baji Rao I in 1732. Only the stone foundations of his seven-storey teak fortress remain, but it's worth seeing the ruins and garden inside.

Turn right onto Ganesh Rd and take a left into Shimpi Ali Path to reach ❷ **Kasba Ganpati Mandir**. The oldest temple in Pune was built by Shivaji's mother in 1630, devoting it to Ganesh. In 1893, freedom fighter Bal Gangadhar Tilak relaunched Ganesh Chaturthi from this temple.

Take Ganesh Rd back towards ❸ **Laal Mahal**, a beautiful villa – all that remains of the vast palace where Shivaji spent his childhood with his mother, Jijabai. Carry on up Ganesh Rd and turn left onto CSM Rd to admire ❹ **Nana Wada**, a huge mansion built in 1780 as the residence of Nana Phadnavis, a minister and statesman of the Maratha Empire.

Follow CSM Rd to ❺ **Shrimant Dagdusheth Halwai Ganpati Mandir**, one of the wealthiest temples in Maharashtra, with a large gold Ganesh idol inside.

Walk along Laxmi Rd, taking a right and then a left to admire ❻ **Vishrambaug Wada**, an ornate mansion that was once the residence of Peshwa Baji Rao II, the last *peshwa* (chief minister) of Maratha confederacy.

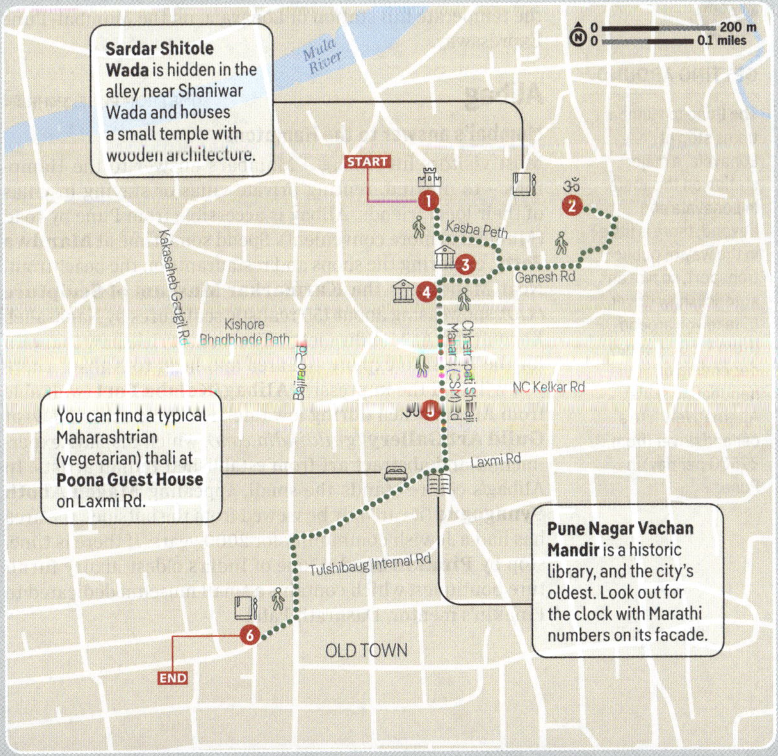

Beyond Pune

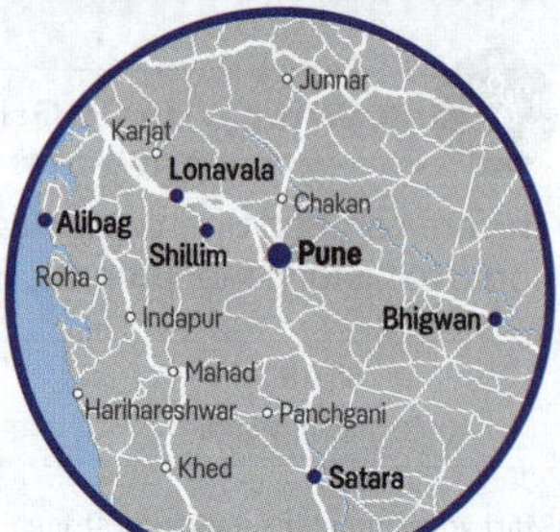

Away from Pune, Maharashtra is rich in hills, lakes, ancient caves, yoga retreats and bird sanctuaries.

Places

There are picturesque landscapes galore to the west of Pune, with the mighty Western Ghats – aka the Sahyadri Mountain Range – rising between the city and the coast. In ancient times, the hills of the range provided shelter to Buddhists, who carved temples into the caves and cliff faces, while the medieval Maratha Empire used the peaks as military lookouts, building (or conquering and repurposing) hundreds of forts in the region. Whether you are an avid trekker, architecture buff or in search of some serenity, it is a great area to explore, either day-tripping from Pune or opting to stay in the temperate hill station of Lonavala, on the Mumbai–Pune Expressway.

GETTING AROUND

The Pune to Mumbai trains stop at Lonavala, a major station on this route. In Lonavala and beyond, there is little in the way of public transport, so hire an autorickshaw driver to take you around (from ₹1500 per day, depending on your negotiating skills). Alternatively hire a car and driver (from ₹2500 per day) in Pune.

Alibag

TIME FROM PUNE: 3¾HR

Mumbai's answer to the Hamptons

Most visitors hit Alibag – Mumbai's answer to the Hamptons – to unwind, renting private villas or staying in villas of their local friends. Alibag is accessible from Pune by road (Mumbai is more convenient). Spend some time at **Mandwa Jetty**, exploring the shops and restaurants on the beachfront. Near Mandwa is the **Karmarkar Museum of Sculpture** *(₹10)*, showcasing about 150 realistic sculptures by Nanasaheb Karmarkar. At Mandwa jetty, hire an autorickshaw (bargain for the rates) to explore the area and head to Alibag. There you will find the impressive **Alibag/Kolaba Fort** (walkable from Alibag beach during low tide). For some art relief, visit **Guild Art Gallery** *(guildindia.com)*, which displays experimental and abstract art from established Indian artists. In Alibag's centre stands the small, appealing **Magen Aboth Synagogue** (it can only be viewed from the outside); the area has had a Jewish community for 2000 years. If there is time, stop by **Pinakin Studio**, one of India's oldest luxury furniture boutiques, which contains a small museum dedicated to Pinakin's mentor, Dashrath Patel.

TUKARAM.KARVE/SHUTTERSTOCK

Khandala

Lonavala

TIME FROM PUNE: **50MIN**

Zen out at a yoga retreat

Treat yourself to a stay at the **Kaivalyadhama Yoga Institute** *(kdham.com; packages from ₹1500)*. It is the oldest yoga institute in the world, where doctors and teachers have been studying the tangible benefits of this yogic practice since 1924. As you walk onto the leafy, tranquil campus, it feels like you're entering a different world. There is a wide range of programmes, from postgraduate degrees in yoga to week-long retreats. Opt for a health reset tailored to your individual needs or enjoy soothing treatments that rebalance your *doshas* (fire, earth and air; the energy sources that govern our well-being) and let your nervous system relax.

A sweet speciality and more

If you have a sweet tooth, a visit to Lonavala is incomplete without carrying back boxes of gooey fudge from **Cooper's Fudge & Chikkis**. Plain chocolate is considered the original and best, but Cooper's now has flavoured versions like coconut, mango and walnut. The original Cooper's Fudge shop at Lonavala market still sees queues, though the fudge is available through the day. Pro tip: one box of fudge (from ₹1400 per kilo) is not enough to sate subsequent cravings! If Cooper's Fudge inspires you to delve deeper into Lonavala's food culture or culture in general, Manasvi Bhatia or **Lonavlaa**

BEST HILL STATIONS NEAR PUNE

Khandala: Misty and lush, this popular weekend getaway is known for its scenic viewpoints and a popular trekking spot, Duke's Nose.

Matheran: The vehicle-free hill station is known for its heritage homes and old-world charm, best experienced in its toy train.

Panchgani: Nestled in the middle of five hills, Panchgani has a pleasant climate, table-top plateau and strawberry fields.

Mahabaleshwar: Iconic hill station famous for its lakes, forts like Pratapgad, temples, colonial-era architecture and strawberry farms.

Bhandardara: A serene place best known for being the base to trek to Maharashtra's highest peak, Kalsubai.

EATING IN LONAVALA: OUR PICKS

Franki's Pizzeria: At this family-run pizzeria, Franki and her father serve wood-fired pizzas to a hungry clientele. Call ahead to dine in. *noon-2pm & 6-9pm* ₹₹

Markaiz: An upscale cafe upstairs from Cooper's Fudge, with a Parsi menu as well as European dishes and sandwiches. *10.30am-11pm* ₹₹

Anglo Indian Cafe: This bright bijou space serves fabulous soups and salads alongside delicious cakes. *11am-midnight* ₹₹

Lola Cafe and Bar: This popular cafe in the heart of Lonavala market sells baked goods and multi-cuisine fare. *11am-midnight* ₹₹

VIPASSANA MEDITATION

Vipassana, a strict form of meditation, was first taught by Gautama Buddha in the 6th century BCE and was popularised again by teacher Satya Narayana Goenka in the 1960s. He opened the **Dhamma Giri Vipassana International Academy** *(giri.dhamma.org)* in Igatpuri, 44km south of Nashik, in 1976. While *vipassana* retreats are found across the world now, the centre is home to the world's oldest and largest *vipassana* institution. Goenka believed that the path to *dhamma* (liberation) was not faith-specific and opened accessible *vipassana* meditation centres globally – all are free to attend – that host incredibly disciplined 10-day programmes for beginners.

Local *(instagram.com/lonavalalocal; tours ₹1000)* organises food crawls, adventure activities and history walks that showcase the region.

Satara

DISTANCE FROM PUNE: 2¾HR

Blooming wonders

Behold a wondrous spectacle of flowers at the **Kaas Plateau**. This UNESCO World Heritage Site comes alive during the late monsoon (from late August to October), when the basaltic soil blooms with over 800 species of wildflowers. Look for the simple orchid, the insectivorous Indian sundew and the highlight: the purple *karvy* flower, which blooms once every seven years. To maintain the fragile ecosystem, only a limited number of visitors are allowed. Tickets sell out fast *(kas.ind.in; ₹150)*. You can walk around and explore on your own on designated trails or hire a guide *(₹200)*.

Shillim

DISTANCE FROM PUNE: 2HR

Wellness check at Dharana

What better place to achieve mental and physical wellness than a sanctuary deep in the hills? **Dharana at Shillim** *(dharanaretreat.com; doubles from ₹45,000)* is a luxury wellness retreat that prioritises healing through wellbeing experiences. You consult with a wellness specialist and undergo bio energetic testing, a body composition analysis and a physical evaluation. Based on subsequent recommendations, you will be handed a strict treatment plan for your stay. Beyond the treatments (we should note these are alternative medical practices), there are complimentary activities like yoga, aqua aerobics, meditation and forest walks. Dharana at Shillim recommends a stay of five days or longer, but can customise your treatment according to your health requirements.

Bhigwan

TIME FROM PUNE: 2HR

Flamingo-spotting

While certainly not the only winged wonders at the **Bhigwan Bird Sanctuary**, the massive flocks of migrating pink flamingos are the main attraction. Visit in winter for reliable flamingo sightings. Also keep your eyes peeled for Eurasian spoonbills, ospreys and the fastest bird of the animal kingdom, the peregrine falcon. The surrounding grasslands are home to mammals such as the Indian striped hyena and Indian grey wolf. Keep aside a whole day for guided tours *(from ₹2000 per person)*, either with Pune-based naturalist organisation and birding specialists **Nemophilist** *(thenemophilist.in)* or with local photographer and birder **Sandip Nagare** *(instagram.com/sandipbhigwanwildlife)*.

EXPLORE CAVES AND FORTS

Discover the peaks, caves and other attractions of the Sahyadri Mountain Range.

START	END	LENGTH
Karla Caves	Pawna Lake	20km; 7hr

Explore the beauty of the Sahyadri Mountain Range, close to Lonavala. Drive northwest from Pune for 55km to the ancient 1 **Karla Caves**. Climb up the winding steps to the rock-cut complex dating to 200 BCE. The Great Chaitya hall (Cave 8) is particularly impressive, with its whale-ribcage-like wooden ceiling and a stupa at the apex.

Drive south for 20 minutes to the 2 **Bhaje Waterfall**, which is just a few minutes' walk from the road. It is at its most impressive during the monsoon (June to October).

A few minutes' drive further are the 3 **Bhaje Buddhist Caves**. They're a 30-minute steep walk uphill and less well-preserved than Karla but still grand, with many of the ornate carvings intact.

A five-minute drive southeast is the base for 4 **Visapur Fort**, with a rocky, forested trail leading to the top, which affords an expansive view of Pawana Lake and Tikona Fort.

About 10 minutes further south lies the well-maintained 5 **Lohgad Fort**, last used by the Maharathi ruler Shivaji as his treasury. It is worth conquering the 300 or so steps to marvel at the bastions, huge gates and panoramic views.

End by driving further south to 6 **Lal Spot Pawna Lake** and take a breather while enjoying the calm waters.

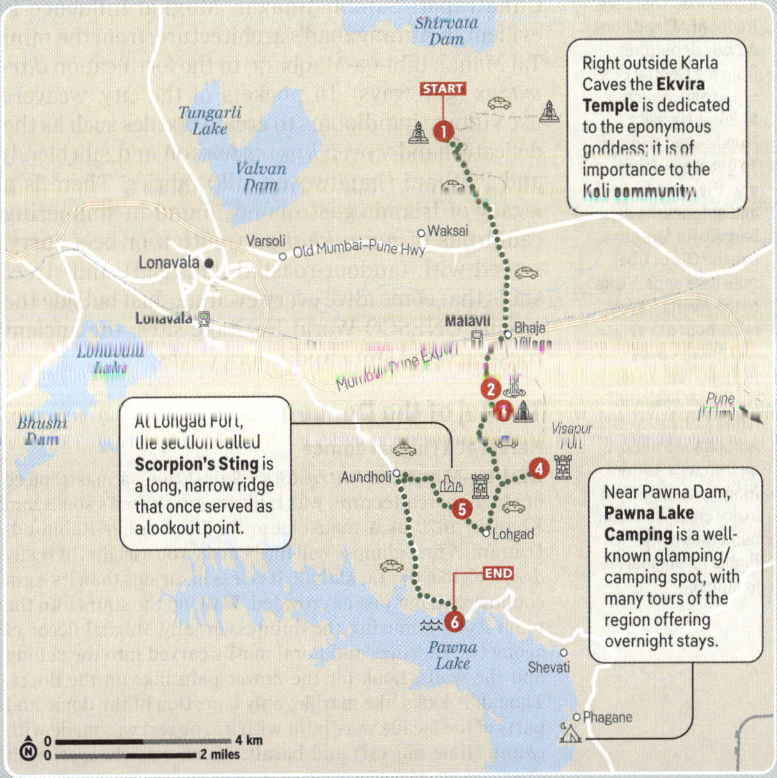

Chhatrapati Sambhajinagar (Aurangabad)

TRADITIONAL TEXTILES | MUGHAL HISTORY | CULINARY CULTURE

GETTING AROUND

From Aurangabad train station there are several daily trains to Mumbai. There are frequent AC and non-AC bus departures from the Central Bus Stand and around to Pune, Nashik, Mumbai and Nagpur. To get around the city, there are taxis and autorickshaws; bargain for fares or use the Ola or Uber rideshare apps. Visits to the Ajanta Caves (a 2½-hour drive) and Ellora Caves (a 45-minute drive) would necessitate hiring a driver. Aurangabad Airport, on the city's eastern fringes, has flights to major cities, including numerous daily flights to Mumbai (45 minutes).

Aurangabad is a sprawling, low-rise industrial hub and education centre in the north of Maharashtra. The city was founded by Malik Ambar, the Ethiopian-born, formerly enslaved African and military leader, who called it Kharki. The last Mughal emperor, Aurangzeb, made this city his capital from 1653 to 1707 and renamed the city. In 2022, it was renamed Chhatrapati Sambhajinagar. Mughal influence is evident in Aurangabad's architecture, from the mini Taj Mahal, Bibi-qa-Maqbara, to the fortification *darwazas* (gateways). In pockets of the city, weavers use vintage handlooms to create textiles such as the delicate, hand-woven *himroo* (cotton-and-silk blend) and Paithani (handwoven silk) fabrics. There is a legacy of Islamic gastronomy, found in simmering cauldrons of *naan khaliya* (mutton or beef curry, served with tandoor-roasted flatbread), and street stalls that come alive every evening. Just outside the city lie UNESCO World Heritage sites: the ancient rock-carved Ajanta and Ellora Caves.

The Taj of the Deccan

Marvel at a Mughal edifice

Bibi-qa-Maqbara *(entry ₹300; 8am-10pm),* a masterpiece of Mughal architecture, was built by Aurangzeb's son Azam Khan in 1679 as a mausoleum for his mother Rabia-ud-Daurani. A first glimpse will likely make you exclaim, 'it really *does* look like the Taj Mahal!' It is less luxurious than its Agra counterpart, but just as crowded. Walk up the stairs into the tomb itself, admiring the quintessentially Mughal decor of geometric carvings and floral motifs carved into the ceiling and the walls. Look for the flower paintings on the doors. Though it looks like marble, only a portion of the dome and parts of the facade were built with it. The rest was made with *chuna* (lime mortar) and basalt, which was cheaper. Visit

HIGHLIGHTS
1 Himroo Factory

SIGHTS
2 Bhadkal Gate
3 Makai Gate
4 Paithan Gate

SLEEPING
5 Zostel Aurangabad

EATING
6 Abdul Jabbar Khaliya House
7 Bismillah Kebab Centre
8 Shama Hotel
9 Zaitoon

TRANSPORT
10 Central Bus Stand

early in the morning or else in the evening; after sunset, the lights come on, illuminating the edifices in a striking way. When leaving, check out the **Armenian tombs** in the front of the monument.

TOP TIP

Buddi Lane and Roshan Gate are popular haunts for a taste of the city's culinary diversity. Many eateries here go back decades and have a loyal local clientele.

The Last of the Looms

Visit a unique *himroo* factory

To witness a truly rare craft, track down Aurangabad's *himroo* textiles. *Himroo* is made of silk and cotton, adorned with specific motifs. The last of the city's handlooms can be seen in action at the **Himroo Factory** *(himroofabrics.in)* on Old Mondha Rd. The Quraishi family have been making *himroo*, Paithani and *bidri* (cloth inlayed with gold and silver) textiles since 1891. The factory is currently helmed by Faisal Quraishi, who will take you around the factory to see the looms and designs, which are so intricate they take months to complete. On request, he will also show off some of their collection of old textiles, some 100 years old. *Himroo* and Paithani saris, shawls and cloth make for great souvenirs. Prices differ between handmade and machine-made cloth. Handmade silk saris cost ₹12,000, whereas those made using an electric power loom will set you back less than ₹5000.

EATING IN AURANGABAD: STREET PICKS

Abdul Jabbar Khaliya House: Legendary takeaway spot serving slow-cooked, cauldron-simmered *naan khaliya*. *noon-10pm* ₹

Shama Hotel: Revamped restaurant, popular at breakfast time for its *paya* (goat trotter curry) and *nalli shorba* (soupy bone marrow dish). *6.30am-9pm* ₹

Bismillah Kebab Centre: Favourite evening spot for the locals who come to eat their beef kebabs fresh off the grill with mint-tamarind chutney. *6-11pm* ₹

Zaitoon: A family restaurant with meat dishes. The Friday, post-*namaaz* (prayers) favourite: mutton *dalcha* (lentil-based stew) stands out. *noon-midnight* ₹₹

MAZZZUR/GETTY IMAGES

Kailasa Temple

TOP EXPERIENCE

Ajanta & Ellora Caves

Dating back two millennia, the UNESCO World Heritage Sites of Ajanta and Ellora epitomise Indian culture, faith and fashion. The Ellora Caves, including the Kailasa Temple, India's ancient engineering marvel, lie 30km northwest of Aurangabad, while the Ajanta Caves, housing ancient Buddhist *viharas* (monasteries) and *chaityas* (temples), built between 200 BCE and 500 CE, are 103km north.

DON'T MISS

Ajanta

- The Reclining Buddha in Cave 26
- Monks' cells in Cave 12
- John Smith's signature on a pillar in Cave 10

Ellora

- Kailasa Temple in Cave 16
- The Buddhist Caves
- The Jain Caves

A Buddhist Treasure

The 29 caves that are part of **Ajanta** are a feat of human ingenuity. In the unfinished caves, you can see the volcanic rock that the monks had to work with – a great example of this is the largest cave, **Cave 4**. The caves are built on different levels in the cliff face, depending on the rock quality. **Cave 9** has a mighty stupa from 200 BCE, with an apse and columns similar in layout to a cathedral. The last accessible space, **Cave 26**, has an extraordinary **reclining Buddha**, the concluding tale in the sequence of caves – his death scene.

PRACTICALITIES

● **Ajanta Caves** ₹600; bus ₹25 one way; 9am-5pm, last bus 4.30pm; closed Mon ● **Ellora Caves** ₹600; 6am-6pm; closed Tue

A Captain's Signature

In 1819, British captain John Smith spotted Ajanta, untouched for 1200 years, from a viewpoint while hunting for tigers. He found **Cave 10**, filled with mud and bats, and carved his signature on one of the front right-hand-side pillars.

Unmissable Frescoes

The incredibly rare, ancient murals in **Caves 1**, **2**, **16** and **17** at Ajanta are usually referred to as frescoes but are technically temperas (painted using a mix of pigment and emulsion). They depict portraits, patterns, mythological stories of Buddha's previous lives, animals, flora, fauna and celestial beings. Don't miss the famous bodhisattva painting in Cave 1. Look up at the ceiling to see the Ajanta lotus, fruits, flowers, cubic and geometric designs and human figures.

The Wonder of Kailasa

At **Ellora**, the biggest attraction is the **Kailasa Temple**. Once you pass through the rock doorway of the low *gopuram* (gateway tower) – with Shaivite carvings lining the left wall and Vaishnavaite carvings on the right – the enormity of this feat of ancient architecture really hits you. Step into the courtyard and gaze up at the *mandapa* (pillared hall) and the pyramid-like *shikhara* (tower) behind it. Don't miss the monolithic elephant sculpture or the Mahabharata frieze on the left side of the *mandapa*. The main shrine features a lingam (phallic image of Shiva). Step to the right side of the courtyard to see the Ramayana frieze on the right-hand wall.

The Buddhist Caves

Just a few minutes' walk from Kailasa Temple there is a cluster of Buddhist cave temples (600–800 CE). **Cave 1** is a *vihara* (Buddhist monastery). **Cave 2** stands out, with its ornate Egyptian-influenced pillars and an imposing seated Buddha that faces the sunset. **Cave 5** is the largest *vihara* in Ellora at 18m wide and 36m long; the rows of stone benches suggest it may have been an assembly hall. **Cave 10** is the only *chaitya* (worship hall) in the Buddhist group and one of India's finest; its ceiling features ribs (meant to mimic wooden rafters) carved into the stonework. The impressive three-storey **Cave 12** is accessed through the courtyard. The shrine on the top floor contains a large Buddha statue, flanked by his seven previous incarnations.

The Jain Caves

The five monolithic Jain caves in Ellora, the youngest here, are home to some exceptionally detailed paintings and carvings of gods, goddesses and other celestial beings. **Cave 30** or Chota Kailash (little Kailash) has similar but less successful stone carving attempts – and **Cave 32**, whose columns are adorned with intricately carved foliage, suggesting Roman influence on the trade routes in the area.

CARRIED AWAY

Ajanta has a fleet of *dholi* (portable 'chair') carriers to carry mobility-impaired visitors up the flights of stairs along the path to the caves. The servsice costs ₹2000 return per visitor; confirm prices before setting off.

At Ellora, there are a few slow e-vehicles for getting around – they cost ₹30 to take you to Caves 29–32, which are 2km from the entrance.

TOP TIPS

- There are hawkers everywhere selling food, trinkets, books and religious figures. They tend to go for the hard sell.
- You may find Indian langur monkeys at the sites – they may seem docile, but don't flaunt food in front of them.
- Hire a guide: government guides at the entrance work on fixed rates (₹2050) and speak English.
- Carry a torch – there is minimal lighting within the caves.
- While photography is permitted, videography is banned.
- You have to remove shoes before entering the caves.
- Visiting during the monsoon means fewer people but slippery paths.

SUFI SHRINES & TOMBS

Mudassir Nadeem, local tour guide, talks about two historic and must-visit places near Aurangabad. *@aurangabadimusafir*

Some 17km northwest of Aurangabad, Daulatabad is a fascinating city. Sufi singer and poet Amir Khusrau came to Daulatabad and loved it so much, he even wrote a *shayari* (a form of poetry) about it. Renowned traveller Ibn Battuta visited Daulatabad in the 14th century. **Daulatabad Fort** is a mix of different architectural styles and monuments from different eras – it includes the Chand Minar (medieval tower), China Palace and Saraswati Bawdi (step-well).

Another fascinating place is Khuldabad. It was once popular with Sufi saints. Here, you will find Aurangzeb's tomb and the tomb of Malik Ambar.

ROSWEL DSOUZA/SHUTTERSTOCK

Fort gate, Aurangabad

Mughal Portals

Admire Aurangabad's gates

When the Mughal Emperor Aurangzeb conquered the city in 1636, he began a grand fortification project, constructing a wall and 52 gates to protect his new regional capital from the growing Maratha Empire to the south. Only 10 gates remain; all are two storeys high, with arched openings and battlement walls.

The oldest and largest, the **Bhadkal Gate**, pre-dates Aurangzeb. It was built in 1612 as a victory gate by Ethiopian military leader Malik Ambar. You'll likely pass through the **Makai (Mecca) Gate** on the way to Bibi-qa-Maqbara (p718), which still has a stretch of city fortification on the side. It faces Mecca in the west. Facing north is **Delhi Darwaza**, the largest gate built by Aurangzeb, there are the ruins of the Jalna Gate to the east, whereas the **Paithan Gate**, facing the holy city of Paithan, lies to the south.

Some roads pass under the gates, others sidestep them. They are best viewed in the daytime.

Sindhudurg

BEACHES | HISTORIC MONUMENTS | ANCIENT ARTS

A vibrant district in the south of Maharashtra, Sindhudurg is where history echoes in quiet corners and villages and the food packs a punch. It's a place that encourages slow travel, but also offers outdoor adventures. Most people visit for its beaches, which are picturesque and uncluttered with shacks or people. The cuisine is predominantly seafood-centred and heavy on the spice. Each village or town within the district has its own charm. The Malvan region is known for its food and the historic Sindhudurg fort. Devgad is the home of the uncrowned king of mangoes, the Alphonso. Sawantwadi specialises in wooden handicrafts and *ganjifa* (traditional handpainted playing cards). The Amboli Ghat is a popular trekking and picnic spot. Vengurla has spiritual significance and beautiful ruins. For many travellers, the region offers a less crowded alternative to Goa, yet Sindhudurg is interesting enough to stand on its own.

GETTING AROUND

Sindhudurg is vast, and the most comfortable (yet pricey) way to travel is by car with driver. Slow, crowded ST (state-run) buses *(stbustimetable.in)* connect Pune and Mumbai with most villages and towns within the region. Autorickshaws can be found at main junctions in villages; bargain for rates. Many hotels in the region will arrange chauffeured cars on request. There are trains connecting Sawantwadi, Ratnagiri and Malvan to Mumbai, Pune and Goa, but most of the stations run far from the coast. Sindhudurg's Chipi Airport has links to major cities around India.

Toy Story

Hub of wooden handicrafts

The town of **Sawantwadi** has a rich history of making wooden handicrafts, namely toys. The toymakers here are best known for their realistic-looking, painted wooden fruit and vegetables. The wood used is from the Indian coral tree, and it is painted in bright reds, greens and yellows, made mostly from natural dyes. All the toys are lacquered, giving them a nice shine. Today, six families carry on this centuries-old craft. The flag-bearers of this heritage, **PD Kanekar** and **Arti Wooden Toys**, can be found in one corner of the Sindhudurg market. There, on dusty shelves, you will find cradles, kitchen sets, religious and mythological figurines, figures from everyday life and animals. The toys are cute, colourful and, in many cases, educational. Think: number games, mechanical toys and more. Mention the child's age, and you will be guided to the right section and shown age-appropriate toys. Purchasing directly from the craftspeople helps to keep this craft alive.

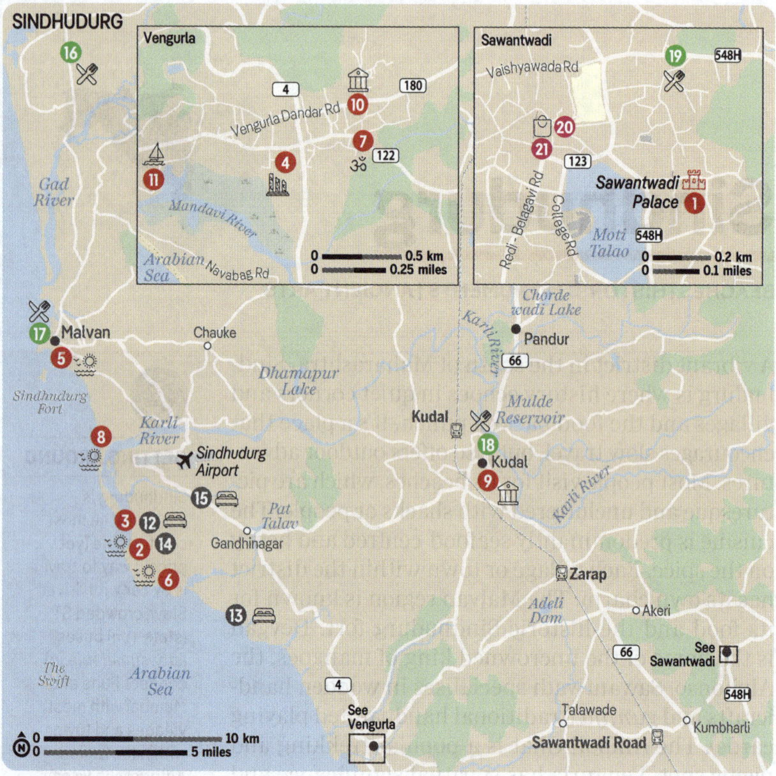

HIGHLIGHTS
1 Sawantwadi Palace

SIGHTS
2 Bhogwe Beach
3 Devbag Beach
4 Dutch Factory
5 Malvan Beach
6 Nivati Beach
7 Rameshwar Temple
8 Tarkali Beach
9 Thakar Adivasi Kala Angan
10 Vengurla Kaladalan

ACTIVITIES
11 Swamini Mangrove Safari

SLEEPING
12 Aryavarta Beach Resort
13 Belantara Beach Front
14 Coco Shambhala Villa Hotel
15 Maachli Farmstay

EATING
16 Hotel Annapurna
17 Hotel Atithi Bamboo
18 Hotel Sanman
19 Shri Mahalaxmi Bhojanalaya Bhalekar Khanaval

SHOPPING
20 Arti Wooden Toys
21 PD Kanekar
see 10 Vengurla Crawford Market

TOP TIP

The region is best explored during the monsoon season (June to October) when waterfalls are at their most magnificent, the land is verdant and the temperatures are pleasant and conducive to trekking.

Dealing a Good Hand

Unique playing cards

Ganjifa are hand-painted playing cards believed to have originated in Persia; they were brought to India during the Mughal reign (1526–1857). They were rectangular and often made from ivory or tortoise shell. Indians made them their own, making the cards round and swapping Persian kings and courtiers for stories and characters from Hindu mythology. *Ganjifa* cards, which have a Geographical Indication (GI) tag, are now found only in select pockets of India.

The **Sawantwadi Palace** (entry ₹30), belonging to the erstwhile rulers of the region, the Bhonsle Sawants, has been on a mission to revive interest in the cards and the related card game since 1971. You can watch artisans paint cards in the palace's **Durbar Hall**, which also features a throne and weapons through the ages. The palace shop has *ganjifa* cards with different themes on sale *(from ₹10,000)*, and its small **museum** also showcases *ganjifa* cards from across India. A more immersive way to learn about the cards is to book either a card-making workshop *(sawantwadipalace .com/home; from ₹500)* or a lesson in playing them *(₹500)*. Hand-painting the cards feels quite therapeutic and they make wonderful keepsakes.

A Reliquary of Forgotten Arts

Shadow puppetry and more

In a quiet part of Pinguli sits a museum dedicated to preserving dying arts like *kalsutri* (string puppetry), *dayati* (shadow puppetry) and *chitrakathi* (storytelling through paintings). The **Thakar Adivasi Kala Angan** *(pingulichitrakathiart. com; ₹50)* highlights 11 local arts belonging to the region's Thakar tribal community. The museum is run by the Gangavne family. Call in advance for a visit to the museum to see old *chitrakathi* paintings, wooden string puppets, and goat-skin shadow puppets. The exhibits don't have much information, but your guide will answer any questions and may even put on a small show for you. Shows require at least 10 people *(₹6000)*. Those seeking to learn more about these art forms may book workshops *(₹2000 for a full day, incl meals)* in advance.

Secrets of the Mangroves

Women-led mangrove tours

In 2017, Shweta Hule launched the **Swamini Mangrove Safari** to give the women in the region a chance to earn a better living. The tours are run by local women, who act as guides and are thereby caretakers of the local mangroves. As part of the Swamini group, eight women organise mangrove safaris in Mandavi Creek, Vengurla. It is a short ride, with about 1.5km covered in an hour. There are four guides to a boat, one of whom talks about the mangroves, their ecological significance and their flora and fauna. Tours *(8806465286; ₹300 per person)* take place throughout the year except during the August to October monsoon season.

WOMEN OF SAWANTWADI

Shraddha Lakham Sawant Bhonsle, chef and hotelier, Sawantwadi Palace @*thesawantwadipalace*

You will hear a lot about the kings, but the queens of the 17th-century Marathwada dynasty were also strong, important characters. The women of Sawantwadi Palace were instrumental in shaping the history of our city and its culture. Rani Jankibai Raje Bhonsle Jankibai was responsible for the creation of the human-made lake, Moti Talao, around which the city of Sawantwadi grew. Rajmata Satvashiladevi Bhonsle revived the Sawantwadi *ganjifa* art form. Rani Saheb Parvati Devi believed that education was important for all, and was the first patron of Rani Parvati Devi College.

EATING IN SINDHUDURG: OUR PICKS

Hotel Sanman: This hotel in Kudal is known for its fiery, coconut-rich Malvani seafood curries and *sol kadhi* (*kokum* drink). *12.30-3.30pm & 7.30-11pm* ₹

Hotel Atithi Bamboo: Five minutes from Chiwla Beach, this simple place serves thalis, fresh fish and rice *bhakri* (flatbread). *11.30am-4pm & 7.30-10.30pm* ₹

Shri Mahalaxmi Bhojanalaya Bhalekar Khanaval: This popular Sawantwadi restaurant dishes up sizeable thalis. *12.30-3.30pm & 7-11pm* ₹

Hotel Annapurna: Malvani dishes like spicy fish curries and *bhakri* really shine at this original minichain outlet in Malvan. *11am-10.30pm* ₹

BEST BEACHES IN SINDHUDURG

Tarkali: A popular destination for its clear waters and water sports like paragliding and snorkelling.

Devbag: A quiet, uncrowded beach that sits at the confluence of the river and the sea. It also offers water sports.

Malvan: This fishers' beach has restaurants, great sunset-watching points and is best known for being the access point to the UNESCO Heritage Site, Sindhudurg Fort.

Bhogwe: One of the quietest and cleanest beaches on this stretch, Bhogwe has white sands and is fringed by palm trees. It is an ideal place to watch the sunset.

Nivati: A peaceful and secluded cove near Nivati Fort, this clean white-sand beach is backed by big black rocks.

JOANNA LOBO

***Ganifa* cards, Sawantwadi Palace (p724)**

Coastal Colour

Explore a coastal region

Once a thriving region under many Indian dynasties, **Vengurla** still retains much of that history in its architecture and culture. Vengurla was a strategic fishing port set up by the Dutch. Here you will encounter the remnants of a **Dutch factory**, built in 1638 by the East India Company. The **Rameshwar Temple** was the hub of the village social life, and remains a popular temple with a small pond. There's a **Crawford market** here too, built by the British; shop here for local produce. The market is home to the **Vengurla Kaladalan** museum that showcases miniature architectural models of famous spots and houses in the region. **Konkan Travel Club** *(konkantravelclub.com)* organises regular tours and trips (and monsoon waterfall trails) in the Sindhudurg region. Its two-hour heritage walk in Vengurla *(₹950 per person)* touches upon history and the place's impressive zero-waste initiatives.

Nashik

GREEN TRAILS | WINE COUNTRY | SPIRITUAL HEARTLAND

A few hours' east of Mumbai, the district of Nashik is replete with ancient traditions, religious ceremonies and ornate wooden architecture. In Nashik town, the old town centre was built on the banks of the Godavari River and hosts the holiest of India's religious gatherings, the Kumbh Mela, every 12 years; the next one will take place from October 2026 to July 2028. Beyond urban Nashik, the wider region is home to rural resorts and eco-stays, surrounded by lakes and reservoirs. More famously, Nashik district (including the towns of Dindori, Igatpuri and Niphad) is home to India's growing wine region with award-winning winemakers. The wine scene has expanded exponentially in the last 20 years, earning Nashik the title of 'India's Wine Capital'. The clean city makes for an excellent getaway, whether you are here for wine, nature, meditation or to soak in the spiritual vibes.

TOP TIP

Nashik will host the Kumbh Mela (the planet's largest religious pilgrimage) from October 2026 to July 2028, with thousands of ascetics and sadhus congregating every day to bathe in the river. The main event, the Shahi Snan (Royal Dip), will be held in August 2027.

Wine-O'Clock

Explore India's budding wine scene

When people speak about wine in India, Nashik is the first place that comes to mind. Nashik's wine production began in 1987 when Madhavrao More established a winery in Pimpalgaon, near Nashik. The Pimpane Co-operative Ltd, as it was known, produced chardonnay and pinot noir but shut down in 2003.

Continues on p730

GETTING AROUND

Public transport is scarce in Nashik, so hiring an autorickshaw with driver is the easiest way to get around. Rideshare apps (GoGreen, Ola and Uber) work within the city but not in the wine region; hire a car with driver to get out to the vineyards. Multiple daily trains connect Nashik to Mumbai; there are also several daily services to Aurangabad. There are flights from Nashik Airport (30 minutes' drive from the centre) to Mumbai, Bengaluru, Delhi and Goa. Regular AC and non-AC buses run to Pune, Aurangabad, Mumbai and other destinations.

HELP ME PICK:

Nashik Wine Region

Grapes have been grown in the rural surroundings of Nashik since ancient times but were only sold as raisins until the wine industry took off. In the late 1990s, two local entrepreneurs realised that the region, with its fertile soils and temperate climate, provided ideal conditions for winemaking. Industry pioneer Sula Vineyards invested in a crop of sauvignon blanc, and the first batch of domestic wine hit the shelves in 2000. Oenophiles rejoice; Nashik hasn't looked back since.

Where to Go If You Like...

Wonderful Views

Vallonné Vineyards Vallonné's picture-perfect vineyards, 30km south of Nashik, sprawl down into the valley along the banks of Mukhne Dam. The fine winery, producing award-winning cabernet sauvignon, merlot, syrah and other tipples, comes with stunning views of the lake and Sahyadri mountains. Vallonné is the only regional producer to make a rosé from cabernet sauvignon grapes. On-site there is a four-room hotel; multicuisine fare is available at the Yelloh restaurant.

Hidden Gems

Grover Zampa Vineyards South of Nashik, on a dusty road to Igatpuri, India's oldest wine producers have a low-key operation, resulting in fantastic, multi-award-winning wines. Here, a vineyard-covered hillside overlooks an appealing farmhouse.

ROHAN_PHOTOGRAPHY/SHUTTERSTOCK

Industry Leaders

Sula Vineyards This large-scale producer is responsible for bringing wine (pictured left) to the masses, and their site is built to accommodate visits from sizeable groups. Facilities include a tasting room, lush gardens, two restaurants, a gift shop and an amphitheatre that hosts SulaFest (India's top vineyard music festival, held in February). They have three luxe hotels on-site: The Source, Beyond, and Haven.

A Boutique Experience

York Winery Recently bought out by Sula, York wines are well-established and well-respected, with a small selection of tipples. They're particularly famous for their Arros blend of shiraz and cabernet sauvignon. It is a quieter tasting and dining experience, with extremely enthusiastic and knowledgeable staff explaining the winemaking process. Their popular restaurant, Cellar Door, serves a broad range of Indian dishes.

Experimental Fruit Flavours

Soma Vine Village Formerly part of Sula's vineyards, Soma broke away to go it alone in 2010 with a host of new innovations. They were the first winery in India to bottle a pinot noir and their Reserve wines are aged in oak barrels. Yet the bestsellers at this winery remain the fruit wines – mango, pomegranate, *litchi* honey and *jamun* honey.

ANIKET GAIKWAD/SHUTTERSTOCK

DHANANJAY BHAGAT/SHUTTERSTOCK

Sula Vineyards

HOW TO

When to go Grape harvest starts in January and continues until March so you're more likely to see the fermentation process in action then.

Booking ahead You can visit the wineries without prebooking but check opening times. Visits to Grover Zampa require prior confirmation.

Budget Most tours range from ₹600 to ₹1250. Eating at these spots can be expensive, as is hiring a car. Budget approximately ₹3000 a day.

Staying there Some of the wineries, like Vallonné, Soma and Sula, have overnight stay options by the Gangapur Lake.

DIY Visits vs Guided Tours

Renting a car with a driver to get around Nashik's wineries (and to be able to sample their wares) undoubtedly gives the most freedom. The wineries are spread out (Vallonné is almost an hour south of Nashik's city centre), so it makes sense to visit the Gangapur wineries (Sula, Soma and York) together, and to do the same with the Igatpuri wineries (Grover Zampa and Vallonné). Some have fantastic restaurants that may tempt you to linger longer (Sula, Vallonné, Chandon), so having your own wheels gives you greater freedom. If you are coming from Mumbai, it is worth arranging a driver for a few days at a daily rate, as taxis in and around Nashik are comparatively costly.

Alternatively, you can arrange your visit via a travel agency such as India Someday (*indiasomeday.com*), whose Mumbai-based team arrange tailor-made tours; Nashik Wine Tours (*nashikwinetours.com*), run by Manoj Jagtap, or Indranil Chowdhuri at Travel with Neel (*travelwithneel.co.in*), who does customised day and overnight tours from Mumbai. Prices start from ₹1000 (a day tour covering three wineries and transport). This means that you will be on their schedule and will have slightly less flexibility, but they also know the pros and cons of each tasting room to make an informed itinerary for your party.

HIGHLIGHTS
1 Sula Vineyards
2 Trimbakeshwar Temple

SIGHTS
3 Anjaneri Fort
4 Dadasaheb Phalke Memorial
5 Deolali Artillery Museum:
6 Grover Zampa Vineyards
7 Harihar Fort
8 Kapurthala Monument
9 Ramkund
10 Soma Vine Village
11 York Winery

ACTIVITIES
see 8 Pandav Leni

SLEEPING
12 Banzai Hotel
13 Beyond by Sula
14 Palm Springs
15 The Parekh Farm
16 Utopia Farmstay
17 Vallonné Vineyards

EATING
18 Budha Halwai
see 14 Hotel Vastu Wada
see 17 Malaka Spice
19 Tales & Spirits Bistro

TRANSPORT
20 Nashik Rd Train Station
21 New Central Bus Stand

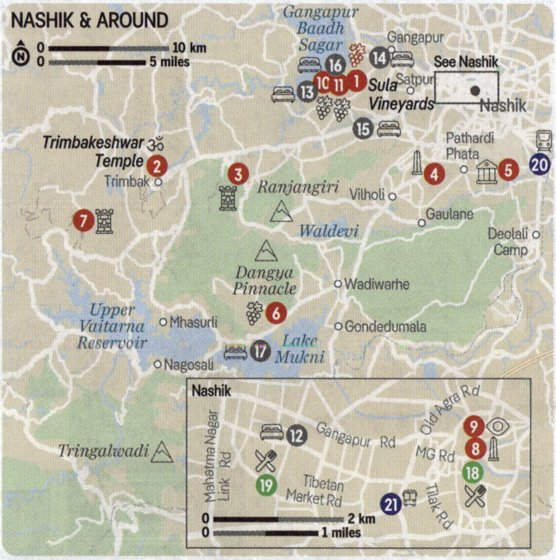

Continued from p727

In 1999, India's wine movement truly kicked off with the founding of the **Sula Vineyards** *(sulavineyards.com)*; Sula remains the most popular wine brand here. In the last two decades, Nashik's wine region has blossomed with over 50 small- and large-scale wineries, such as the **York Winery** *(yorkwinery.com)*, **Reveilo Wines** *(reveilo.com)*, **Grover Zampa Vineyards** *(groverzampa.in)*, **Vallonné Vineyards** *(vallonnevineyards.com)* and **Soma Vine Village** *(somavinevillage.com)*. Many of these wineries offer tours showcasing the distilling process in the factories, plus wine tastings. Tours *(from ₹600 per person)* last about an hour and run throughout the day. Booking ahead is not necessary; the last tours of the day tend to finish by 6.30pm. Vallonné, Sula and Soma have restaurants and accommodation options.

If you are seeking a more intimate, family-run boutique experience, consider **Grape Berry** *(grapeberryvineyard.com)* and **Nipha Winery** *(instagram.com/nipha_winery)*. To shop for a large selection of local wines, visit the **Wine Information Centre** *(instagram.com/wine.information.center)* in Vinchur (1¾ hours' drive from Nashik). Most grape varieties are imported; look out for tipples made from local sharad seedless, sonaka and thompson seedless grapes.

Historic Nashik

Discover the old city

Nashik's spiritual significance runs deep – so deep, in fact, that it is embedded in the city's name. It was taken from a gnarly scene of the sacred Ramayana text, in which Rama's sister has her *nasika* (nose) chopped off. You cannot miss the scenes of devotion in the old town centre: hundreds of Hindus

OSCARESPINOSA/GETTY IMAGES

Hanuman statue on the ghats near Ramkund

visiting daily to perform last rites for the remains of their loved ones, knee-deep in the water, sending their ashes down the Godavari River from the ghats of **Ramkund**. Along the embankments, you will notice the **Kapurthala monument** (the tomb of Maharaja of Kapurthala), plus several temples. There is a plethora of ancient temples to see in the old town centre, as well as old *wadas* (mansions) and *akhadas* (training spaces for wrestlers).

It is also well-worth doing a half-day trip to **Trimbakeshwar**, one of India's most sacred temples to Shiva, containing a highly venerated *jyoti linga* ('pillar of light' and one of India's 12 holiest shrines to Shiva). The temple was built in 1756 on the remains of a much older temple in Trimbak, 28km from the city of Nashik.

Journalist and author **Ramesh Padwal** *(8380098107; ₹1000 per person)* conducts old city tours in the morning and evening, focusing on the history, architecture and even historic snack spots. You can book private tours with Amrita Gangatirkar of **Nashik Heritage Trails** *(@nashikheritagetrails; ₹1100 per person)*, or with Ulka Pawar of **Urbanum Design Studios** *(9619179955; ₹3000 for a group of 5)*. Pratiksha Kothule of **Conservation Tales** *(instagram.com/conservationtales; from ₹1500 per person)* conducts nature hikes and birdwatching excursions in the region.

NASHIK'S HERITAGE HIGHLIGHTS

Pandav Leni Caves: Pandav Leni is a series of 24 rock-cut caves, dating back to the 2nd century BCE.

Harihar Fort: The climb to the top of this imposing fort is rewarded with the sweeping views to take in the Western Ghats (Sahyadri Mountain Range).

Anjaneri Fort: The birthplace of the monkey-god Hanuman according to legend, this fort is an important religious site and comprises Jain temples and a lake.

Dadasaheb Phalke Memorial: The memorial to a legendary face of Indian cinema displays his works and has a meditation centre, gardens and an exhibition hall.

Artillery Museum: Asia's biggest artillery museum houses ancient and modern weapons, an aircraft, cannons and tanks.

EATING IN NASHIK: OUR PICKS

Budha Halwai: This snack bar has been making *jalebi* (deep-fried batter in sugar syrup) and *fafda* (deep-fried gram flour) for a hundred years. *8.30am-9pm* ₹

Hotel Vastu Wada: Homey restaurant specialising in spicy mutton (goat) dishes. Also try the *gul kala* (flatbread with jaggery and ghee). *11am-10.30pm* ₹

Malaka Spice Nashik: Savour the flavours of the Southeast Asian fusion cuisine at this excellent restaurant at the Vallonné Vineyards. *11am-10.30pm* ₹₹

Tales & Spirits Bistro: Freshly rolled sushi plus Mughlai and North Indian fare, devoured in a picturesque garden setting. *noon-12.30am* ₹₹

Vidarbha

TIGER COUNTRY | RICH BIODIVERSITY | LOCAL FEASTS

TOP TIP

About two hours from Nagpur, the Satpura Range is home to Chikhaldhara, the state's only coffee-producing region. To try this coffee, grown by local farmers, look out for the local brand, Korku *(korkucoffee.com)*.

The Vidarbha district occupies the eastern part of Maharashtra, split into two main administrative divisions, Nagpur and Amravati. Home to almost 75% of the state's forest cover, the region is a premier ecotourism spot. Yet it attracts few tourists, losing out to the popular cities on the west coast and the forests of neighbouring Madhya Pradesh. Vidarbha is where you go to encounter wildlife, birdwatch and enjoy the quiet of the forest. If you are looking for Royal Bengal tigers, head to one of the many wildlife sanctuaries, including Tadoba-Andhari, Umred Pauni Karhandla and Tipeshwar. The summer months of March, April and May are the best time to visit the tiger reserves and sanctuaries – the stifling heat means the animals frequent waterholes, offering a better chance at sightings. Vidarbha is also known for its fiery Saoji cuisine, with its meat-heavy, spicy curries. You can find these in roadside *dhabas* (eateries) and at most hotels.

Feast in a Forest

Exceptional dining at Tipai

Quite literally forest-to-table, **Tipai** is a luxury resort that sits on the edge of the buffer zone of the **Tipeshwar Wildlife Sanctuary**. The resort's biggest focus is food, which is

GETTING AROUND

Nagpur is the main city, easily traversed by autorickshaw (either agree on a price beforehand or use Uber). The airport (30 minutes' drive from the city) connects Nagpur to the likes of Delhi, Mumbai, Bengaluru. Regular bus services link Nagpur to all the main cities in Maharashtra (Pune, Mumbai, Nashik, Aurangabad), as well as Delhi, Pune and Goa. Train services link Nagpur to Mumbai, Kolkata, Delhi and Jalgaon (for the Ajanta Caves). It is best to hire a taxi or a car with driver to visit the wildlife sanctuaries from Nagpur.

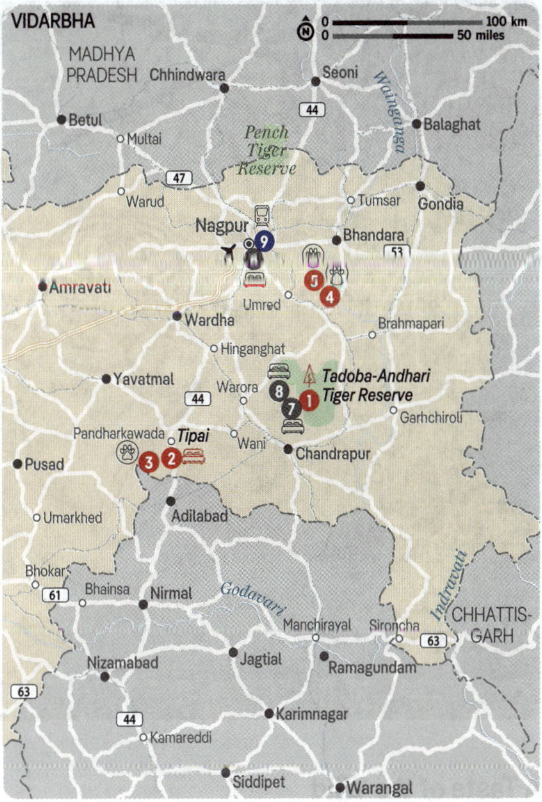

HIGHLIGHTS
1 Tadoba-Andhari Tiger Reserve
2 Tipai

SIGHTS
3 Tipeshwar Wildlife Sanctuary
4 Umred Pauni Karhandla Wildlife Sanctuary

ACTIVITIES
5 Bamboo Forest Nature Conservancy

SLEEPING
6 Pride Hotel Nagpur
7 Tadoba Tiger Valley Resort
see 7 The Spotted Owlet Farm House
8 Waghoba Eco Lodge-Tadoba

TRANSPORT
9 Nagpur Junction Train Station
see 9 ST Bus Stand

prepared in distinctive ways in its on-site restaurants. **Talaabwali** specialises in North Indian dishes, such as succulent kebabs, meaty biryanis and condiments made from seasonal produce. At **Perch**, the lunch menu changes daily to reflect a different Indian region. **Wadi**, near the kitchen garden, features global fare made with homegrown produce from the kitchen garden.

Chef Amninder Sandhu curates all the menus, and has trained local women as her sous chefs; they run the kitchen in her absence. The crowning glory is Palaash, a seven-course degustation menu cooked in *chulhas* (earthen cooking stoves) and on *sigrees* (open fire grills) that celebrates the best of local produce and Indian cooking. Each dish is crafted from local ingredients, presented in a more elevated form: a wild orange sorbet, fried roselle leaf *chaat* (snack), *raan* (leg of lamb, slow-cooked in an underground barbecue pit) served as a taco using *bhakri* (flatbread) and *mahua kala jamun* (caramelised milk-solid dumpling flavoured with the *mahua* flower).

SECRETS OF THE FOREST

Shiv Shankar Gedekar, forest guide, shares wisdom from the woodlands.

Besides tigers, some of the more interesting forest dwellers are the blue tiger butterflies and the loggerhead shrike, also called butcherbird, as it hangs its prey on thorns until it dies. The *gudmar (Gymnema sylvestre)* plant is useful for diabetics and controlling blood sugar as its active compounds (gymnemic acids) interfere with the sweet taste receptors on the tongue and also block receptors in the intestines, reducing sugar absorption. The bitter leaves of the *kalmeg* plant (green *chiretta*) help to bring down fever. The bark of the ghost tree is used to make capsules.

My village of Gothangaon holds a tiger *pola* (tiger-worshipping festival) every year.

MATRISHVA VYAS/SHUTTERSTOCK

A Taste of the Wild

Adventures in a forest lodge

Imagine being woken to a shout of 'There's a tiger on the property!' **Bamboo Forest Nature Conservancy** *(doubles from ₹40,000),* a 10-villa resort, is located within the Umred Pauni Karhandala Wildlife Sanctuary, close to the Gothangaon gate. The space is part of the sanctuary, so animals such as spotted deer, wild hogs and even tigers can be seen there on a frequent basis. The reigning tiger queen of the Gothangaon area is affectionately called Campwaali because she is often seen on the grounds. The rooms are on stilts, and you need security to walk you everywhere due to the risk of animal encounters. The resort raises important questions about whether ecotourism is a lifeline for conservation, and whether one should profit from protecting nature.

Beauty of the Beast

Spot India's national animal

If you are coming in search of tigers, the **Tadoba-Andhari Tiger Reserve** *(mytadoba.mahaforest.gov.in; ₹1800)* should be your first stop. The 'Jewel of Vidarbha' is Maharashtra's oldest and largest national park, and home to a

Tadoba-Andhari Tiger Reserve

thriving population of Royal Bengal tigers (approximately 400), as well as rare four-horned antelopes and leopards. While there, be sure to ask about the legendary tiger, Chota Matka. Tipeshwar Wildlife Sanctuary (p732; *tipeshwarsafaribooking.in; ₹5900*) is one of the newer and lesser-known national parks. The dry deciduous forest is home to around 20 tigers, besides leopards, sloth bears and spotted deer. At **Umred Pauni Karhandla Wildlife Sanctuary** *(₹1500)*, the forest is denser and more mature, thick with meadows, lakes and and a host of migratory birds.

All safari bookings in Maharashtra should be done online; permit slots open 120 days earlier. You have to book and pay for entry, plus a guide and Gypsy safari vehicle *(safaribooking.mahaforest.gov.in; from ₹3000)*. Mobile phones are not allowed on safaris. Carry the ID used to make the online booking.

For a personalised tour with a wildlife expert, reach out to Joydeep Mondal of **Wildchasers India** *(instagram.com/wildchasersindia)*; he organises educational, off-the-beaten-track safaris through all the parks in Maharashtra *(from ₹40,000 per head for a 3-night/4-day tour with 4-5 safaris)*.

Places We Love to Stay

₹ Budget ₹₹ Midrange ₹₹₹ Top End

Pune

Map p710

Sanctuary by Nagarik Commune ₹ Contemporary homestay that feels like a hostel but still offers privacy, with cosy rooms, cafe and a coworking space.

Bloom Hotel – Koregaon Park ₹₹ This branch of funky yellow Bloom is a solid midranger, both well-located and well-stocked with free snacks and any amenities you need.

Hotel Ketan ₹₹ Expect excellent, old-school hospitality at this slightly retro but well-presented property with huge rooms in the heart of the university zone. Don't skip the South Indian breakfast.

Sunderban Resort & Spa ₹₹ This renovated art deco bungalow near the Osho resort effortlessly combines old-world class with boutique appeal, offering deluxe, beautifully presented, spacious rooms laden with antiques.

Conrad Pune ₹₹₹ Five-star hotel close to Pune airport with 351 spacious rooms, luxury spa, temperature-controlled pool, salon and a rooftop restaurant.

Sheraton Grand Pune Bund Garden Hotel ₹₹₹ Located near Pune train station, this 5-star hotel offers multiple dining options, free parking, childcare and a squash court.

The Ritz-Carlton, Pune ₹₹₹ Luxe hotel situated near the airport with plush rooms and suites, multiple dining options, a rooftop bar, a tearoom, a spa and an outdoor pool.

Lonavala

Triose Boutique Hotel ₹₹ A chic little property on a quiet road with extremely comfy beds, elegant rooms and, most importantly, the friendliest management you've ever met.

Manasi Bungalow ₹₹ Cosy boutique homestay in the hills, with good food, curated experiences and handpicked recommendations by Manasvi Bhatia.

Bohemyan Blue ₹₹ Gorgeous eco-tents – lovingly made from layer upon layer of gorgeous textiles – line the serene garden. Unwind in the sun by the pool while birdwatching.

The Machan ₹₹₹ A secluded treehouse hotel with stand-alone baths and dreamy boho rooms. Guided forest bathing and stargazing on offer.

Villas by Chandralok ₹₹₹ Have the quintessential Lonavala experience by renting a villa, like locals do – there are none finer than this boutique stay, with antique-bedecked properties and a great little pool.

Satara

The Fern Residency ₹₹ A 60-room laid-back hotel with a coffee shop, rooftop restaurant and spacious rooms with modern amenities.

Brownstone Resort ₹₹₹ Resort hotel with lake-facing villas offering a peaceful stay. Finding the place may be a challenge.

Chhatrapati Sambhajinagar (Aurangabad)

Map p719

Zostel Aurangabad ₹ This lovely, homey outpost of a trusted hostel chain is a large converted house with an airy atrium dining room, chic dorms and private rooms.

Hotel Kailas ₹ Just a few minutes' walk from the Ellora Caves' entrance, this spot has well-presented cottages around a nice garden, and a great restaurant.

Fern Residency Hotel ₹₹ A smart stay with switched-on staff and ultra-comfy beds, this solid midranger is well-located for visiting the Ajanta Caves.

Lemon Tree Hotel ₹₹ Large rooms with snazzy artwork beckon at this modern 4-star property with a great swimming pool and gym.

Hyatt Place Aurangabad Airport ₹₹₹ Contemporary hotel with well-appointed rooms, on-site pool and restaurant doing buffet meals.

Matheran

Dune Barr House-Verandah In The Forest ₹₹ A 170-year-old British-built mansion turned into a hotel, with rooms furnished with antiques and complimentary breakfast.

Panchgani

Avabodha ₹₹₹ This river-facing three-bedroom villa is a peaceful escape, offering vegetarian food and many offline activities.

Sindhudurg
Map p724

Belantara Beach Front ₹₹ A private beachfront estate with ocean-facing, beautifully decorated rooms, cottages, suites and villas.

Aryavarta Beach Resort ₹₹ Private beach resort with sea-facing rooms, offering Malvani food and organising water sports.

Sawantwadi Palace Art Hotel (p724) ₹₹₹ Sensitively restored palace with six rooms that showcase *ganjifa* art and woodwork. The current owners are chefs so the food is excellent; try the tasting menu.

Coco Shambhala Villa Hotel ₹₹₹ Luxury villa resort close to Bhogwe Beach, with delicious local food, (optional) cultural performances and a great spa.

Maachli Farmstay ₹₹₹ Ecofriendly forest homestay offering a peaceful holiday complete with nature walks, farming and pottery experiences.

Highland Sarovar Portico ₹₹₹ This 50-room retreat near Nivati Beach is a tranquil escape with an outdoor pool and nature or birding walks on request.

Nashik
Map p730

Banzai Hotel ₹ Compact, clean rooms in the heart of the city. This boutique hotel offers flexible check-in and check-out times. Great for solo travellers.

The Parekh Farm ₹₹ Quiet farmhouse and six-bedroom homestay with handwoven textiles, fruit trees and a garden ideal for birdwatching.

WelcomHotel Rama International ₹₹₹ Business and leisure hotel, conveniently located close to major sites and offering well-appointed rooms.

Beyond by Sula ₹₹₹ Sula's second high-end property is ultra-luxurious, with modernist-inspired villas that pull out all the stops to ensure privacy and tranquillity.

Palm Springs ₹₹₹ The finest of the large hotel resorts that surround Nashik, Palm Springs boasts contemporary design and excellent hospitality.

Utopia Farmstay ₹₹₹ Overlooking the Gangapur reservoir, family-run Utopia lives up to its name, with beautiful eco-conscious rooms adorned in salvaged ornate woodwork.

Vidarbha
Map p733

Tadoba Tiger Valley Resort ₹ Simple, spacious rooms and dormitories, with a variety of hot food options.

Pride Hotel Nagpur ₹₹ Clean, well-maintained hotel with spacious rooms, good food and warm and welcoming staff.

The Spotted Owlet Farm House ₹₹₹ Situated in the buffer zone at Tadoba, this retreat has three cottages and a villa with a dipping pool. It organises tours and safaris, too.

Waghoba Eco Lodge-Tadoba ₹₹₹ This luxury safari lodge near Tadoba National Park has spacious rooms, a birdwatching room and great food. Its naturalists are well trained.

Tipai-Wildlife Luxuries (p732) ₹₹₹ Housed in the buffer zone of Tipeshwar Sanctuary, this luxury hotel offers a wilderness holiday, with a natural pool, bespoke dining experiences and knowledgeable naturalists.

Lemon Tree Hotel, Aurangabad

For places to stay in Goa, see p790

CHRISHEPBURN/GETTY IMAGES

Above: Morjim Beach (p758), Pernem; Right: Carnival (p747) installation

Researched by
Joanna Lobo

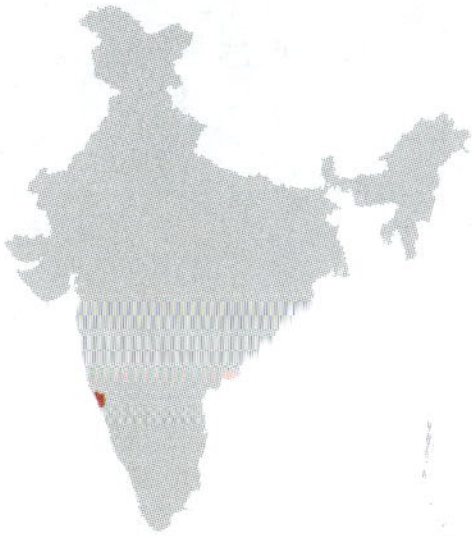

Goa

BEACHES, CULTURE AND PORTUGUESE HERITAGE

Permeated with Susegaad (a sense of contentment), India's favourite holiday destination has it all: a long coastline, beautiful beaches, Portuguese heritage spots and excellent cuisine.

One of India's smaller states, Goa is proof that good things come in small packages. There is something for everyone: history and Portuguese heritage in Old Goa; adventure and water sports along beaches like Calangute, Baga, Palolem and Agonda; music and culture in the form of unique festivals and *fado* and *mando* concerts; exciting food and cheap drinks; and a relaxed vibe almost everywhere you go. Little wonder then that Goa remains India's preferred destination for honeymoons and family holidays, and welcomes numerous foreign tourists.

ASHISH_VASSUP6730/SHUTTERSTOCK

Goa lies on the Konkan Coast in Western India. It has three distinct regions: North Goa, South Goa and Kushavati. North Goa is the trailer, while South Goa is the award-winning movie, with a supporting role by Kushavati.

Historically, Goa was ruled by many kingdoms, but particularly lasting impact came from 451 years of Portuguese rule. The architecture, language, music and food bear European influences, but with a strong Goan touch. The state prides itself on being secular, and most Goans prefer living in harmony.

Goa continues to struggle with overtourism. In recent years, the state and its dining, cultural and ecological landscape has changed irrevocably. Yet, Goa remains a land of plenty, packaging the best of what India has to offer in one beautiful, exciting, adventurous bundle.

THE MAIN AREAS

PANAJI (PANJIM)
Historic capital, buzzy waterfront and festivals. p744

PERNEM
Hippie lifestyle and secluded beaches. p756

BARDEZ
Gentrified villages, green spaces and parties. p760

SALCETE
History, architecture and fun museums. p773

CANACONA
Wildlife sanctuaries, waterfalls and rich history. p786

0 10 km
0 5 miles
Pernem, p756
A large coastal district encouraging alternative lifestyles and activities, with buzzing beaches and diverse and healthy dining options.
Panaji (Panjim), p744
The state's capital is a microcosm of Goa's attractions. People come here for the rich history, lively waterfront, ever-evolving food scene and festivals.
Bardez, p760
A happening, vibrant place with popular beaches, quiet (if gentrified) villages, party destinations and outdoor activities (kayaking, foraging, birdwatching).
KARNATAKA
Terekhol River
Querim
Pernem
Paliem Sweet Lake
Arambol
PERNEM
66
Chapora River
Colvale
Morjim Beach
Morjim
Siolim
Chapora Harbour
Vagator
Anjuna
Mapusa
Mapusa Market
Aldona
Mapusa River
Bicholim
Arpora
Baga
BARDEZ
Saligao
Calangute
Candolim
Porvorim
Chorao Island
Divar Island
Naroa
BICHOLIM
Sanquelim
Onda
SATARI
Valpoi
Mandovi River
Agua da Port & Jail Complex
Panaji (Panjim)
Ribandar
Old Goa
Aguada Bay
Church of Our Lady of the Immaculate Conception
Miramar
TISWADI
Dona Paula
Bambolim
Goa Velha
Mormugao Bay
Mormugao
Sao Jacinto Islet
Agassaim
Zuari River
Cortalim
Usgao
Khandepar
Usgao Tisk
Ponda
Vasco da Gama
Sancoale
MORMUGAO
PONDA
DHARBANDORA
Pequeno Island
Bogmalo
Sao Jorge Island
Grande Island
Verna
The Goan Kitchen
Loutolim
Utorda
66
Western Ghats
Bhagwan Mahavir Wildlife Sanctuary
Colem

BUS

There are state-run buses (Kadamba) and private buses connecting the cities to all the villages. Some buses between major cities are direct and have air-con. Buses are cheap, but often do not run according to schedule and can be slow. No departures after 9pm.

MOTORCYCLE TAXI

Goa's motorcycle taxis are affectionately called 'pilots'. They can be found at most bus stands in the cities and at major junctions in popular villages and towns (minimum fare ₹150).

CAR

The most convenient way to explore the hinterland's lesser-known villages and wildlife sanctuaries is by car. Either rent your own (from ₹1200 per day) or use the GoaMiles app for cheaper taxi fares during peak season.

Find Your Way

To reach many of Goa's sights you need your own wheels. Renting a bicycle, car or motorcycle is straightforward. Public transport is cheap and slow. Goa's two international airports are in Dabolim and Mopa.

Salcete, p773
Portuguese heritage is evident in this region's food, architecture, music and art. Museums offer fascinating glimpses of the past.

Canacona, p786
Sometimes overlooked due to its location in the far south, this taluka (district) is rich in wildlife and natural beauty, including uncrowded beaches.

Plan Your Time

Goa is best explored at leisure. The north is buzzing with parties, markets, concerts, dance socials and other activities. Things are quieter in the south, which is rich in flora and fauna, old architecture and museums.

LLOYD VAS/SHUTTERSTOCK

Panaji (p744)

Pressed for Time

- A few days to spare? Base yourself in **Bardez** (p760), ideally near the popular Baga-Calangute-Vagator-Candolim beach belt. Spend time soaking in the sun at **Vagator Beach** (p766), a typical Goan beach with shacks, water sports, sunbeds and shops.

- Take a quick trip to the new **Fort Aguada Jail** (p764) in Candolim then head over to **Houses of Goa Museum** (p767) for an introduction to Goan architecture. Stop at the **Mario Gallery** (p767) nearby for local crafts.

- One evening, climb up to the **Chapora Fort** (p765) for a sunset view then pub-hop along Chapora's main street. To complete the Goan experience, eat a thali (plate meal) or Goan seafood at **Sudan's Bar** (p765) while sipping on some feni (cashew liquour) or a locally brewed beer.

SEASONAL HIGHLIGHTS

Summer sees sunny weather. Monsoon (June to September) showcases Goa's greener side. Winter is ideal for travel, with temperatures between 20°C and 26°C.

JANUARY

The period between New Year's Day and mid-January offers the spirit of Christmas without the high rates. Stay on to participate in the **Three Kings Feast** (p778).

FEBRUARY

It is a month of arts and literature events, including the popular **Carnival** celebrations across the state, which involves floats, parades and music.

MARCH

The summer season means cashew harvest for the distilled spirits, *urrak* and feni, plus the first mangoes. Look out for the parades of the Hindu festival of **Shigmo** (p747) across Goa.

Seven Days to Travel Around

● In North Goa, set up base at **Arambol** (p756). Explore nearby beaches like **Morjim** (p758), go surfing, and shop at **Mapusa Market** (p760).

● You will need a day to travel to South Goa. On the way, make a pit stop at **Old Goa** (p751) to see the **Basilica de Bom Jesus** (p752) and get a glimpse of St Francis Xavier's preserved body. Stop in **Margao** (p777) with its vintage buildings, churches and good Goan food.

● Spend the rest of your time at the **Agonda** (p788) and **Palolem** (p788) beach stretch in **Canacona** (p786). Trek to the beautiful **Cola** (p788) and **Butterfly** (p788) beaches, seek out the waterfalls and bubbling lake at the **Netravali Wildlife Sanctuary** (p785) and eat some oysters at **Galgibaga** (p786).

If You Have More Time

● Stay in the capital, **Panaji** (p744). You can explore its streets, visit its religious institutions and do a walking tour of its Old Quarters. From Panaji, you can easily reach the islands of **Divar** (p753) and **Chorão** (p751) and explore old Goan village life. **Salcete** (p773) is a short drive away; here you can tour the heritage homes in **Loutolim** (p776) and **Chandor** (p773).

● In the hinterlands lies **Mollem National Park**, part of the Bhagwan Mahavir Wildlife Sanctuary, and home to the state animal, the gaur (Indian bison). Nearby you will find the **Salaulim Dam** (p784), Buddhist **Rivona Caves** (p785), **Usgalimal petroglyphs** (p784) and **Cotigao Wildlife Sanctuary** (p789), which is home to treetop watchtowers – spot the Indian pied hornbill.

JUNE

Monsoon season means fewer tourists. You can go fishing/angling in smaller streams and **manos**, or jump in a well as part of São João celebrations (p772).

AUGUST

The peak of the monsoon season means lush waterfalls, blooming plateaus, plus foraging for seasonal vegetables or glimpsing them on the *matoli*, part of the **Ganesh Chaturthi** (p789) festival.

NOVEMBER

Attend the **International Film Festival of India** screenings in Panaji and take part in **Heritage Walks Festival**, across Goa. During **Diwali**, look for the *narkasur* effigies, burned to symbolise the victory of good over evil.

DECEMBER

Christmas and New Year season is peak time for parties and festivals, such as the **Serendipity Arts Festival**. See the state's community cribs (p779), and Old Man effigies burned on New Year's Eve.

Panaji (Panjim)

GOAN HISTORY | CULTURAL MONUMENTS | EXCITING EVENTS

TOP TIP
The changing decorations at the main traffic junctions, such as at Divja Circle and Miramar Circle, should clue you in about whichever festival or event is being celebrated in the city during your visit, be it Christmas, Serendipity or Shigmo.

Goa's capital city, Panaji (Panjim), deservedly features on most tourists' radar. The city offers a concise, well-packaged introduction to Goa and its culture, history, architecture, food and even its current socio-economic issues. Panjim was a tiny village by the Mandovi River before Portuguese colonisers made it their capital in 1843 and gave it city status. Post-liberation, it was renamed Panaji.

The architecturally rich heritage here is visible in the religious institutions and the old houses and buildings. Historic wards of **Fontainhas** and **São Tomé** offer a glimpse of the European influence on Goan architecture. Panaji's churches, temples and gardens are oases of calm amid city bustle, and there are museums, art galleries and bookstores to keep you occupied, especially in inclement weather.

Today, this constantly evolving city is becoming a hotspot for food, and is the base for numerous festivals and events.

Arty Azulejos

Admire hand-painted tiles

Azulejos, or hand-painted ceramic tiles, are a distinctive feature adorning Goan architecture. The blue-and-white glazed tiles are a stunning sight. You can view them on nameplates outside homes in Fontainhas and in the lobby of the **Institute**

GETTING AROUND

Panaji's attractions are quite spread out and walking is not recommended owing to the lack of proper footpaths and the constant construction. Departures from the bus stand serve Margao, Ponda, Mapusa and other destinations. Find autorickshaws and 'pilots' at the taxi stand (part of the bus stand). Hiring a scooter (*₹450 per day*) or bicycle (most homestays lend them to guests for free) gives you the greatest flexibility; mind the one-way streets in the city centre. The closest train station to Panaji is Karmali (Old Goa), 12km to the east near Old Goa, with services to Mumbai (Bombay).

HIGHLIGHTS
1 Church of Our Lady of the Immaculate Conception

SIGHTS
2 Abbé Faria Statue
3 Centre for Indo-Portuguese Arts
4 Dayanand Bandodkar Statue
5 Goa State Museum & Secretariat Building
6 Indian Customs & Central Excise Museum
7 Institute Menezes Braganza
8 Mahalaxmi Temple
9 Sunaparanta Goa Centre for the Arts

ACTIVITIES
10 Bookworm
11 Goa State Central Library

SLEEPING
12 Hospedaria Abrigo de Botelho
13 Hotel Fidalgo
14 Mateus
15 O Abrigo
16 Old Quarter Hostel
17 WelcomHeritage PanjimInn

EATING
18 Cafe Aram
19 Cafe Bhonsle
20 Cafe Bodega
21 Cafe Real
22 Cafe Tato
23 Kokum Curry
24 Larder & Folk
25 Miguel's-Cocktails & Petiscos
26 Mo's Cafe & Bistro
27 Pakiza
28 Petisco
29 Praça Prazeres

DRINKING & NIGHTLIFE
30 Bebde
31 Miski
32 MTW-Bar & Toasties
33 Tea Trunk

ENTERTAINMENT
see 3 Azulejos de Goa

SHOPPING
34 Velha Goa Galeria

TRANSPORT
35 Divja Circle
36 Panaji Bus Stand

GOA'S BEST LITERARY SPACES

Goa State Central Library: India's oldest public library in Panaji houses two lakh (200,000) books and a laboratory for book conservation.

Bookworm: A children's library and a registered nonprofit in Panaji, hosting activities and events. Also runs a travelling library.

Dogears Bookshop: An independent bookshop in Margao known for its book fairs, festivals and workshops.

The Booktique Goa: An online lending library *(thebooktiquegoa.com)* in Anjuna, where the owner delivers books to customers in North Goa via bicycle.

Literati Bookshop & Cafe: This old Goan home in Calangute houses a bookshop and an attached cafe where you can browse, read and discuss books.

BORNTOGETBUSY/SHUTTERSTOCK

Our Lady of Immaculate Conception

Menezes Braganza. In the latter, there are five floor-to-ceiling panels that depict scenes from the Portuguese poem *Os Lusíadas,* written by Luís Vaz de Camões, and they tell the story of Vasco da Gama's departure from Portugal and his journey to India. At **Azulejos de Goa**, Orlando de Noronha teaches you how to paint these tiles and create a unique memento for yourself *(azulejosdegoa; ₹1500 per person)*. The two-hour class includes an introduction to the history of tile-making and the chance to paint two tiles of your own. De Noronha even fires them for you. You can also browse *azulejos* and *azulejo*-inspired ornaments for sale. Nearby is the **Velha Goa Galeria** *(velhagoa.net)* where you can buy ceramics and *azulejos* (customisable options available).

Step into History

Explore historic monuments

Befitting for a state capital, Panaji is where you go to get your dose of Goan history, through its religious institutions, monuments and museums. One of the most beloved and prettiest sights in Panaji is the majestic church of **Our Lady of Immaculate Conception** *(icchurchpanjim.com)*. Dating back to 1541, this white Portuguese baroque-style church stands tall at the top of the hill overlooking the main square. Its defining feature is a series of zigzag stairs and it houses the second-largest bell in Goa. Nearby, at the Altinho foothill, stands the **Mahalaxmi Temple** *(mahalaxmipanaji.in)*, built

EATING IN PANAJI: OUR PICKS

Oya's Umami: Naga-inspired Asian street fare like soba noodles and smoked pork. Leave space for the mango sticky rice dessert. *noon-11pm* ₹₹

Petisco Kitchen & Bar: A locally beloved restaurant serving chimichurri salad, prawn tacos and breadfruit fritters. Live music some nights. *noon-12.30am Tue-Sun* ₹₹₹

Praca Prazeres: European comfort food like Scotch eggs and roast chicken. Upstairs, the bar hosts music nights. *noon-3pm & 7-11pm Tue-Sun* ₹₹₹

Isabella's Tapas Bar: Modern tapas bar featuring small plates like *patatas bravas*, tempura prawns and garlic clams, plus homemade vermouth. *noon-midnight* ₹₹₹

in 1819. It was one of the first Hindu temples built in the city after the Portuguese arrived, and is dedicated to the goddess of wealth, who is considered to be the main deity of Panaji.

Beyond these religious monuments, Panaji's history can be found in the **Adil Shah Palace**, the city's oldest surviving building. The two-storey structure has a tiled roof and open balcony and now houses the **Goa State Museum** *(free; closed Sat & Sun)*, featuring various artefacts from Goan history, including manuscripts and household items.

The building is flanked by two notable statues: Goa's first chief minister **Dayanand Bandodkar** and **Abbé Faria**, Goa's famous son, known for his pioneering work in hypnotism. A little distance away is the bright-blue **Dharohar Indian Customs & Central Excise Museum** *(₹50)*, whose displays showcase the history and role of Customs in India, as well as smuggled goods like animal skins, tusks and rare idols.

The Art of Fado & Mando

Attend an intimate concert

Imagine a tiny room that morphs into an intimate concert venue. **MadraGoa** *(instagram.com/madragoa.goa; tickets from ₹1500, available via Instagram)* is located inside a 250-year-old heritage home by the Mandovi riverfront and doubles as the **Centre for Indo-Portuguese Arts** *(cipagoa.com)*. Every few weeks, in front of a wall painted to resemble a street in Lisbon, *fadista* (*fado* singer) Sonia Shirsat takes to the stage, regaling an audience with *fado* (a Portuguese musical genre) and *mando* (a Konkani musical genre) songs. Accompanying her are two musicians, and they sometimes include other *fado* singers too. During the break, you can try Portuguese snacks like *pastéis de nata* (custard tart).

Even when there isn't a concert, you can eat Indo-Portuguese snacks at the balcony cafe, **Cháfé Braz**, and buy books in Portuguese, Konkani and English.

Festivals Ahoy!

Seek some entertainment

Through the year, Panaji's gardens, heritage structures, galleries and open spaces welcome exhibitions and festivals. Early in the year, just before the start of Lent, decorated floats and musical nights mark **Carnival**. Similar festivities accompany the spring festival of **Shigmo**. The **Goa Arts & Literature Festival** *(goaartlitfest.com)*, held in February at the

WHY I LOVE PANAJI

Joanna Lobo, Lonely Planet writer

There is never a dull moment in this city. When not making your way through traffic and dodging crater-sized potholes, there are events to attend and restaurants doing old Goan food to visit. The city is the epicentre for everything fun, from festivals like Serendipity to concerts featuring Indian singers and international stand-up acts. There are restaurants, libraries, fascinating museums, concerts in tiny halls, lesser-known Goan dishes, buzzing bars and local chefs doing fun things with food. Every corner has something interesting. It is a city that embraces the old while welcoming the new with the same enthusiasm.

Pakiza: Konkani-Muslim-run place in a tiny lane, serving excellent biryanis and meat dishes, plus stellar fish thalis. *noon-4.30pm Mon-Sat* ₹

Bombil: Sample Goan food, especially fish thalis, in a cute space decorated with murals and miniature 3D landscapes. *noon-4.30pm & 7.30-10pm* ₹₹

Kokum Curry: Comfort Goan Hindu food that is heavy on fish. There is another outlet in Candolim. *noon-4pm & 7-11pm* ₹₹

Miguel's Cocktails & Petiscos: Konkan-Portuguese fusion like *cavalinha* (pickled mackerel with gin gel). *5-11pm Wed-Mon* ₹₹₹

PANAJI'S FLOATING CASINOS

Upon entering Panaji, it is hard to miss the bright lights and noise from Goa's floating casinos. They have always been controversial. For tourists from other parts of India who come in search of gambling, the casinos are an ideal destination – free-flowing liquor, live entertainment and the chance to win some money. For Goans, they are a scourge, polluting the waters, and adding to light and sound pollution. The streets near the jetty are packed with tourists and taxis, causing traffic jams. Many casinos function without adequate CRZ (Coastal Regulation Zone) clearance. Despite this, there is unlikely to be a ban on casinos as they contribute significantly to the state government's coffers.

LLOYD VAS/SHUTTERSTOCK

Carnival (p747) celebrations

International Centre Goa (ICG), showcases contemporary writers from Goa and India, plus cultural performances. Also in February, the **Goa Open Arts Festival** *(goaopenarts.com)* at the **Old GMC** complex features art exhibits, music performance and film screenings. In summer, celebrate the bounty of the treasured cashew apple through cashew drinks, cashew-infused recipes and even cashew stomping at the **Cashew Fest** *(instagram.com/goacashewfest)* at the **DB Grounds**. The new **Purple Festival** *(instagram.com/purplefestgoa)* celebrates people with disabilities through concerts, exhibits, sports and other events. If you are into movies, look out for the **International Film Festival of India** *(iffigoa.org)* in November. Look out for the multidisciplinary **Serendipity Arts Festival** *(serendipityartsfestival.com)* in December, which features workshops, food talks, art installations and musical performances, spread over 10 days across the city.

Breakfast Like a Goan

Get acquainted with Goa's cafe culture

Goa has a unique cafe culture, which has little to do with coffee and much to do with food. These cafes are dining institutions, offering a quick and affordable breakfast (or teatime snacks). Orders are simple: *bhaji* with *pao* (bread) or *puri* (deep-fried dough). *Bhaji* is made in several different ways: with *patal* (thin potato curry), *tamat* (tomato), *batat* (potato), *alsande* (beans), *biya* (cashew nuts), *olmi* (mushrooms) and *salad* (onion tomato mixture). You can also order hot samosas,

EATING IN PANAJI: BEST CAFES

Mo's Cafe & Bistro: A sweet space where dishes are a fusion of Goan and Japanese flavours. Definitely try the drinks. *9am-9pm* ₹₹

Tea Trunk: Beautiful tea room inside a heritage home, specialising in Indian teas and elaborate high tea preparations. *9am-6.30pm* ₹₹

Larder & Folk: Cafe and restaurant serving decadent sandwiches, *bombolinis* (Italian filled doughnuts), good coffee and hot honey doughnuts. *9am-7pm Tue-Sun* ₹₹₹

Padaria Prazeres: Charming cafe-bakery, locally renowned for its *pastéis de nata* (egg custard tart). Popular with tourists and locals. *9am-6.30pm Tue-Sun* ₹₹₹

mirchi bhajiya (fried chilli fritters), deep-fried sweet bread made with bananas, and *chau* (tea) or coffee.

There are many breakfast spots scattered in the capital, serving customers hearty breakfasts in the morning, and filling snacks throughout the day and at teatime. These are no-frills spots, with tables packed close together and the constant buzz of conversation. The system is quick: come, order, eat and leave. They do not encourage lingering over your meal – tables need to be vacated for those next in line. Panaji's two iconic, century-old *bhaji* places are **Cafe Tato**, usually called just Tato's (with outlets in Panaji, Margao and Vasco), and **Cafe Bhonsle** (with outlets in Ponda and Porvorim). Other popular spots include **Cafe Aram** and **Cafe Real**.

Culture Check

Visit Sunaparanta Goa Centre for the Arts

At the top of Altinho Hill sits a beautiful white and blue old house with a grand double staircase and a little courtyard in the centre. **Sunaparanta Goa Centre for the Arts** *(sgcfa.org)* is an arts foundation hosting exhibits on subjects like the ongoing ecological crisis, miniature art, and climate change and its effect on gender roles, among others. It also hosts events including book releases and talks. It is a visual treat too, beyond the art work, offering a glimpse of Goa's unique architecture. The area around its central courtyard is taken up by **Cafe Bodega**, with a menu offering small eats and baked goods along with beverages. It is a great space to get your daily dose of art, while enjoying some quiet from the chaos of the city.

Shredding & Grinds

Practise tricks on a skateboard

Every evening, a small patch of land on the Mandovi waterfront comes alive with the sounds of laughter and the clattering of wheels against a hard surface. This area is the home of **Skate Life Goa**, a community of skateboarding enthusiasts who gather in the evenings to skate. The space is open to all. They host events and workshops once a month at the **Miramar Skatepark** *(instagram.com/skatelifegoa; ₹100)* for people of all age groups. If you are seeking a deeper immersion, **Skate Shala** *(instagram.com/skateshala)* conducts six-day skating camps teaching you the fundamentals of skating *(₹2999; bring your own skateboard).*

GOA'S TOP CULTURAL SPACES

Kala Academy: This space is known for art exhibitions, cultural programmes and concerts. Architecture buffs will appreciate architect Charles Correa's beautiful design.

The Cube Gallery: Moira space that features contemporary art and design shows; its lawn is sometimes transformed into an outdoor sculpture gallery.

Saraya: Beautifully restored home in Sangolda with a cafe and an art gallery that hosts contemporary Indian art shows, workshops and talks.

Alt Food Co: This community space and kitchen for budding chefs in Campal organises community fairs, cooking classes, food parties and workshops.

Art Chamber: This modern art space in Calangute also hosts literary events, workshops and musical performances.

DRINKING IN PANAJI: BEST BARS

Bebde: Locally owned bar and music venue, doing live music, karaoke, jams and music launches, with a side of good food. *6pm-1am*

Miski: Old taverna that is a cosy drinking spot and popular community bar. Service is friendly, the food is Goan and the vibe is retro. *12.30-11pm*

MTW Bar & Toasties: Office by day, bar by night. Laid-back, snug place, offering creative cocktails and filling toasties. *7pm-1am Mon-Sat*

For the Record-Vinyl Bar: A restaurant, bar and music room with exciting cocktails; the innovative menu is heavy on ferments. *12.30-3pm & 7-11pm Thu-Tue*

EXPLORING PANAJI'S LATIN QUARTER

Explore Goa's Portuguese heritage and architecture, and narrow lanes hiding art galleries and bakeries, in Panaji's compact wards of São Tomé and Fontainhas.

START	END	LENGTH
Fundação Oriente	Casa De Moeda	900m; 1hr

Start at the 1 **Fundação Oriente**, which houses an art museum. Next, head northeast until you see the patterned tiles of the 2 **Old Quarter Hostel**, a good coffee stop. Continue northeast along Rua 31 de Janeiro until you reach 3 **Gitanjali Gallery**, showcasing the works of contemporary Indian and Goan artists.

Continue north to the junction and head left to the 4 **St Sebastian Chapel**, built in 1818, home to an unusual crucifixion image of Jesus with eyes open. Further west along St Sebastian Rd, look for an 5 **old well** with mosaic tiling and colourful 'rainbow' steps.

Take Rua de Natal north to the 6 **Confeitaria 31 De Janeiro**, a good pit stop for Goan snacks.

Cut northeast, passing by colourful houses and shopfronts with oyster shell windows, before reaching the 7 **Joseph Bar**, a characterful old-school taverna.

At the north end of Rua São Tomé, the 1849-built 8 **São Tomé Chapel** has a beautiful tiered facade and is dedicated to St Thomas, believed to have brought Christianity to India. Cross the road to the statue of 9 **Dr Miguel Caetano Dias**. He was known for adopting modern European medical standards and revolutionising Goan healthcare. Behind it is the 10 **Casa De Moeda**, the former Mint of Goa (1834 till 1841).

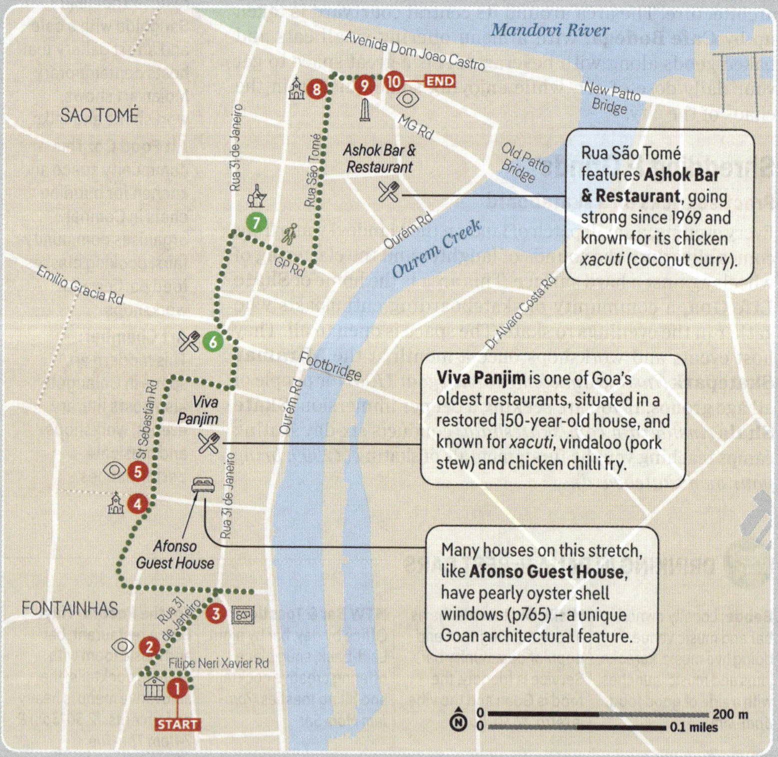

Beyond Panaji

Get to know the city's surrounds, hop between islands, visit churches and temples, and go birdwatching.

If the big city of Panaji gets too much for you, explore the city's suburbs of Taleigao, Caranzalem, Campal, Siridao, Altinho, Santa Cruz and Dona Paula. East of Panaji, across the Ponte de Linhares Causeway, lies the quiet village of Ribandar – the jumping-off point for the islands of Divar and Chorão, picturesque pockets of Goan village life. The most prominent place outside Panaji is Old Goa. The former Portuguese capital of the region, it harbours churches, chapels and other protected monuments, some of which are UNESCO World Heritage Sites. Further west lies the taluka of Ponda, considered to be the Hindu heart of the state and known for its many spice plantations.

Places

GETTING AROUND

From Panaji bus stand, buses to Old Goa stop at the Divar and Chorão ferry points in Ribandar. Regular ferries run to the islands from early morning till 9pm; these are free for pedestrians and two-wheelers (vehicles from ₹20). To explore the islands, hire your own vehicle as the main sights are spread out. Ponda is accessible by infrequent bus. Hire taxis or autorickshaws (from ₹150/km) at the Panaji bus stand.

Old Goa

TIME FROM PANAJI: **30MIN**

Delve into religious art

In the Holy Hill section of Old Goa (Velha Goa), a short walk away from the **Ruins of the Church of St Augustine**, stands a stunning convent and church. The 17th-century **Convent of Santa Monica** houses the **Museum of Christian Art** *(museumofchristianart.com; ₹100)*, a repository of five centuries of Indo-Portuguese art gathered from Goan churches and private collections. It's a small museum, with two floors, and contains the renovated Church of the Weeping Cross.

Things to look out for include a model of St Francis Xavier's tomb, 17th-century altar cards, intricately embroidered vestments, a 1.2m-tall pelican tabernacle monstrance, an Indian rosewood Calvary cross with semi-precious stones, an ivory sculpture of St Anne and the Virgin Mary and a wooden bas-relief carving of St Ursula and her virgins. The museum is accessible, has a gift shop and regularly hosts events and themed walks. You can book a guided tour (*₹300)*, which highlights special pieces and shares additional details of their history, or wander around on your own. Additionally, it conducts themed tours: Retracing Monte Santo and the Holy Hill Tour *(₹1350 per person, book in advance via website)*.

UNESCO World Heritage Site churches

Pilgrim or not, a visit to Old Goa is a must for every visitor to Goa. This is one of the most beautiful parts of the state, with a wealth of historical and religious monuments, as well

MONTE MUSIC FESTIVAL

Every winter (end of January or early February), the **Church of Our Lady of the Mount** hosts a music festival. Started in 2002 and curated by the Fundação Oriente *(foriente.pt)*, the three-day **Monte Music Festival** takes place inside (the acoustics are excellent) or on front lawns of the chapel, and also at Santa Monica Convent. Performances are a mix of Indian and Western classical music, featuring Indian and international artists and some Goan performers too. Entry is free and attendance is on a first come, first served basis. In 2024, the festival branched out to Delhi too.

as ample green spaces. The churches and convents of Old Goa are a UNESCO Heritage Site.

Start your tour at the majestic baroque church, **Basilica de Bom Jesus**, which contains the remains of Goencho Saib (St Francis Xavier), Goa's patron saint. An exposition of these sacred relics takes place every 10 years and is free and open to everyone; the next exposition will take place in 2034. Across the road is the **Sé Cathedral**, home to a miraculous cross to mark the spot where a vision of Jesus is said to have appeared in 1919. A walk through the compound takes you to the **Chapel of St Catherine**, built in 1510 in baroque style and not open to visitors. Nearby is the **Church of St Francis of Assisi** with its wooden pulpit, floral frescoes and a statue of Our Lady of Miracles brought from Jaffna, Sri Lanka. Nearby is the **Church of St Cajetan**, modelled on the Basilica of St Peter in Rome and built in the corinthian style. Walk through the Ruins of the Church of St Augustine (p751), admiring the only surviving part – a laterite bell tower – of what was the largest church complex of the time. End your visit by hiking up a hill to the **Church of Our Lady of the Mount**, which overlooks the Mandovi River and nearby islands and offers the best view of Old Goa.

Ribandar

TIME FROM PANAJI: 10MIN

Goa's glistening salt pans

As you head east from Panaji, you will see mountains of white glistening in the sun just south of the Ponte de Linhares causeway. This is Ribandar, and these are among the few surviving **salt pans** in the state. It is best to explore them under the guidance of architect **Talullah D'Silva** *(instagram.com/tallulahdsilva; ₹500 per person)*, who conducts regular salt pan walks. You will start by learning about the *khazan* land system and how it benefits both local people and nature, then walk through the pans to understand their architecture and how the salt is farmed and collected. At the end, you can taste (and purchase) some of the salt.

Carambolim

TIME FROM PANAJI: 25MIN

Twitchers, rejoice!

One of the most popular birding sites in Goa, Carambolim (Karmali) is a small village close to Panaji. The best bird-watching opportunities are around the **Carambolim Lake**,

EATING BEYOND PANAJI: BEST GOAN-RUN RESTAURANTS

Star Bar: Popular lunch joint by the Mandovi River in Ribandar, known for its thalis, fish and seasonal mussels. *12.30-3.30pm & 7.30-10pm Tue-Sun* ₹

Segundo Bairro: Goan-run space in Dona Paula serving the Goan fish thali, plus decadent desserts. *11am-3.30pm & 7-11pm* ₹₹

Peep Kitchen: This Taleigao institution specialises in traditional Goan food like vindaloo and *xacuti*. *noon-3pm & 7-11pm Tue-Sun* ₹₹

Low & Slow: BBQ joint in Old Goa known for its slow-cooked meats and hearty sides. *7-10.30pm Tue-Sat, 1-3pm & 7-10.30pm Sun* ₹₹

a massive artificial lake that attracts a variety of migratory (between November and March) and endemic species. This wetland and the surrounding fields are home to Indian pond herons, little egrets, common kingfishers, purple swamphens and great cormorants. Go early in the morning, park by the lake, and then station yourself at one of two watchtowers. There are boards describing the species found at the lake and the exotic plants around.

Merces

TIME FROM PANAJI: **15MIN**

A taste of local culture

Deep in the heart of the village of Merces is a family-run cultural space, **Sadhana Dell 'Arte** *(sadhanadellarte.com)* in a beautiful yellow and white renovated home. The house belonged to João Francisco Viegas, the first Goan Catholic licensed money lender in Goa, whose family wanted to honour his memory. Besides promoting local artists, Sadhana houses a co-working space, the **Wineyard Goa** *(instagram.com/wineyard.goa)* bar and **Unbox Labs** *(instagram.com/unboxlabsgoa)*. Unbox Labs is a cultural and event space that hosts film festivals, coding, pottery and dance workshops, community boardgame nights and artist residencies.

St Estevam Island

TIME FROM PANAJI: **40MIN**

An island sojourn

St Estevam Island (Juvem) is an 8-sq-km estuarine islet, offering a glimpse of old Goa in a rapidly changing state. It is a tiny place, ideally suited to a half-day trip. At the heart of the island is **St Stephen's Church**, built in 1575 atop a hillock. Its design mixes corinthian, rococo and baroque influences, and it gives the island its name. The other sight of note is the **Fort Santo Estevão** – originally a watchtower – built on the highest point of the island in 1550. The ***Local Beat*** *(thelocalbeatgoa.com; ₹4284 per person)* provides an exciting way of exploring the island. Its half-day lunch or dinner excursions include a trip to the fort, a riverside picnic, catching crabs and line-fishing, tour prices include traditional drinks and Goan food.

Divar

TIME FROM PANAJI: **50MIN**

Experience island life

A typical Goan island, Divar is one of the state's most picturesque spots. Give yourself a day to tour this island – you can cycle (bring your bicycle with you) or drive around – and immerse yourself in village life. Start by climbing the hill to the **Church of Our Lady of Compassion**, which affords great views of the surroundings. As you pass by the villages, stop to admire the old houses and eat some snacks at a bakery. Take a break at the **Koti Tirth Thali** (or Porne Tirth) ruins dating back to the Kadamba dynasty (10th–14th century CE). The only thing that remains of the original Saptakoteshwar

THE KHAZAN LAND SYSTEM

The *khazan* land system is a unique aqua-agro system that regulates water salinity and ensures equitable distribution of water. *Khazans* are coastal wetlands reclaimed from mangrove forests, which contain a system of dykes, *manos* (sluice gates) and canals that help people farm, fish and pan for salt. In the monsoons, the mud *bundhs* (outer embankments) prevent sea water from overflowing into the *khazan*. The *manos* would control the flow; at high tide, limited water amounts pass through into the fields growing saltwater-tolerant varieties of rice. The water is then collected in a reservoir where fish spawn. At low tide, water is drained out and the adult fish are caught at the *manos*. Some *khazans* are still in use in Goa.

PONDA'S TOP RELIGIOUS STRUCTURES

Shri Manguesh Temple: The defining feature of this popular Hindu temple is the distinctive seven-storey octagonal lamp tower at its entrance.

Shri Shantadurga Temple: This 18th-century Hindu temple was built on a hill and features pyramidal *shikharas* (rising towers), arched windows and stained glass.

Shri Nageshi Temple: One of the oldest in Goa, this 18th-century historic temple features stone idols of gods and goddesses and an old water reservoir.

Shri Mahalasa Narayani Temple: This 16th-century Hindu temple is dedicated to the rare female depiction of the Lord Vishnu.

Safa Masjid: The 16th-century mosque is built in Indo-Islamic style and has a rectangular tank with 44 hammams (individual baths).

EPHOTOCORP/GETTY IMAGES

temple is a pond surrounded by intricately carved niches meant to hold idols.

Divar is known for its festivals. Just before Lent is the three-day **Potekar Festival**, when locals dress up and go from house to house, demanding food and drink. Held in the last week of August, **Bonderam** is a flag festival marking the protests of the villagers and the face-off with the Portuguese over property disputes on the island in the 17th century.

Dona Paula

TIME FROM PANAJI: **15MIN**

The secrets of the Cabo Raj Bhavan fort

Cabo Raj Bhavan is the official residence of Goa's governor, located at the end of a cape in Dona Paula, at the confluence of the Mandovi and Zuari Rivers. Once an important fortress for the Portuguese, it is now open to two-hour-long tours (*rajbhavan.goa.gov.in; ₹500).* There is much to observe and admire on this 36-hectare property, much of it under forest cover. The laterite stone chapel, **Our Lady of Cape**, was once a landmark for seafarers and looks out over the river confluence. Nearby is a shrine holding the reclining statue of St Paulina/Paula. The tour takes in an abandoned jetty, a museum containing old stone carvings, and a garden of medicinal plants.

DevkiKrishna Temple

Ponda

TIME FROM PANAJI: **30MIN**

A mud bath to remember

Every monsoon (June to September), the **DevkiKrishna Temple** in Marcel plays host to an exciting festival called **Chikal Kalo**. It is dedicated to the Lord Krishna and involves recreating many of his childhood games, as well as a *dahi handi* (whereby participants form a pyramid to break a hanging pot of curd to celebrate the Lord Krishna's childhood act of stealing curd). The festivities begin with prayers and rituals at the temple, after which the men and boys of the village oil their bare-chested bodies and head to the grounds in front to play games in the mud. They play musical instruments, sing songs and chant prayers. The festivities end with the breaking of the *dahi handi*, followed by a simple meal.

A SWEET CUSTOM

Rohan Barbosa, Goa-themed content creator, shares a sweet custom that takes place every August. *@finding_feni*

As the monsoon deepens and August arrives, a quiet Goan ritual unfolds. On the first morning of August, many homes begin the day with eating *madachem godd* (palm jaggery) and freshly grated coconut. This tradition, passed down through generations, is meant to protect us during the rainy season, when coughs and colds are common. Rich, nourishing and comforting, it is both food and blessing. My mother never forgets this day and this ritual. The plate is always ready. And with a smile we say, *'Augusto di amka gusto'* ('May August be sweet to us').

EATING BEYOND PANAJI: OUR PICKS

Laxmi Bar: Local restobar known for its affordable seafood, as well as generously portioned thalis. *12.30-3pm & 7.30-10.30pm* ₹

Bappa's Cafe Siddhi: Goan breakfasts like *bhaji pao* (vegetable dish with bread) and *mirchi bhajiya* (fried chilli fritters). *11.30am-3.30pm & 7-11.30pm* ₹

Kuttikar Bar And Restaurant: Lunch place cooking up good thalis and fresh fish. The approach road is bumpy. *noon-3.30pm & 7-10.30pm* ₹

Ana Bar & Restaurant by Vasquito: Bar with an emphasis on Goan and Portuguese dishes like BBQ pork ribs and crab fritters. *11.30am-3.30pm & 7-11.30pm* ₹₹

Pernem

BOHEMIAN LIFESTYLE | SWEET-WATER LAKE | RELAXED VIBE

GETTING AROUND

Arambol and Morjim are connected by relatively infrequent buses to Mapusa, Panaji and the rest of Pernem. The simplest way to explore the village and soak up its atmosphere is on two wheels – most homestays and hotels can help with renting cycles *(₹300 per day)* and motorbikes *(₹450 per day)*. It is easier to park a two-wheeler than a car, especially close to the beach. Some inner roads are narrow and crowded, with stalls spilling onto the street, but for the most part, it is a pretty drive through streets canopied with trees and quiet neighbourhoods.

Goa's northernmost taluka is perhaps best known for being a quiet escape from the tourist-loving crowd to its south. Once a small sleepy fishing village, Arambol, its namesake beach, is today the heart of hippie, alternative living in Goa. Arambol and the neighbouring areas have quiet, beautiful beaches – Morjim is the nesting site for the endangered olive ridley turtles; Ashwem is home to surf schools; and in Mandrem, yoga is popular. Arambol and Morjim became known in the 1960s as a mellow paradise for long-stayers escaping the scene at Calangute. Today, these areas remain a popular haunt of 'free spirits'. Away from the coast, the hinterlands of Pernem Taluka are pockets of calm, where idyllic villages reward those who venture inland. Go further north and you will hit Fort Tiracol, now a heritage hotel. Nearby is secluded Querim Beach, ideal for picnics.

The Bohemian Life

Embrace the hippie lifestyle

The hippie movement of the 1960s and 1970s has made Arambol a favourite destination for those embracing alternative lifestyles. Today you can find associated daily activities and events; look for flyers and posters at shacks and cafes.

Start your day with drop-in yoga classes at **Himalayan Iyengar Yoga Centre** *(hiyogacentre.com; from ₹600; Nov-Mar)*, **Yoga Village** *(yogavillage.in; ₹500)*, which does hatha and yin yoga, or the **Raj Yoga School** *(rajyogaschool.com; ₹500)*, which offers hatha, aerial and vinyasa ashtanga yoga.

Jungle Dance Double Dutch *(instagram.com/jungledance doubledutch)* is a performance venue and cafe deep in a jungle, locally known for its movement arts; you can attend yoga and dance classes *(from ₹500)*, or flow to the rhythm of ecstatic dance. Nearby is **Shunya Wellness** *(instagram.com/shunyawellness; from ₹500)*, which has a cafe, accommodation and an outdoor event space under a banyan tree. Go here for ecstatic dance nights, weekly markets, vocal classes and nunchaku workshops. At the beach, **Goa Drum Circle** *(instagram*

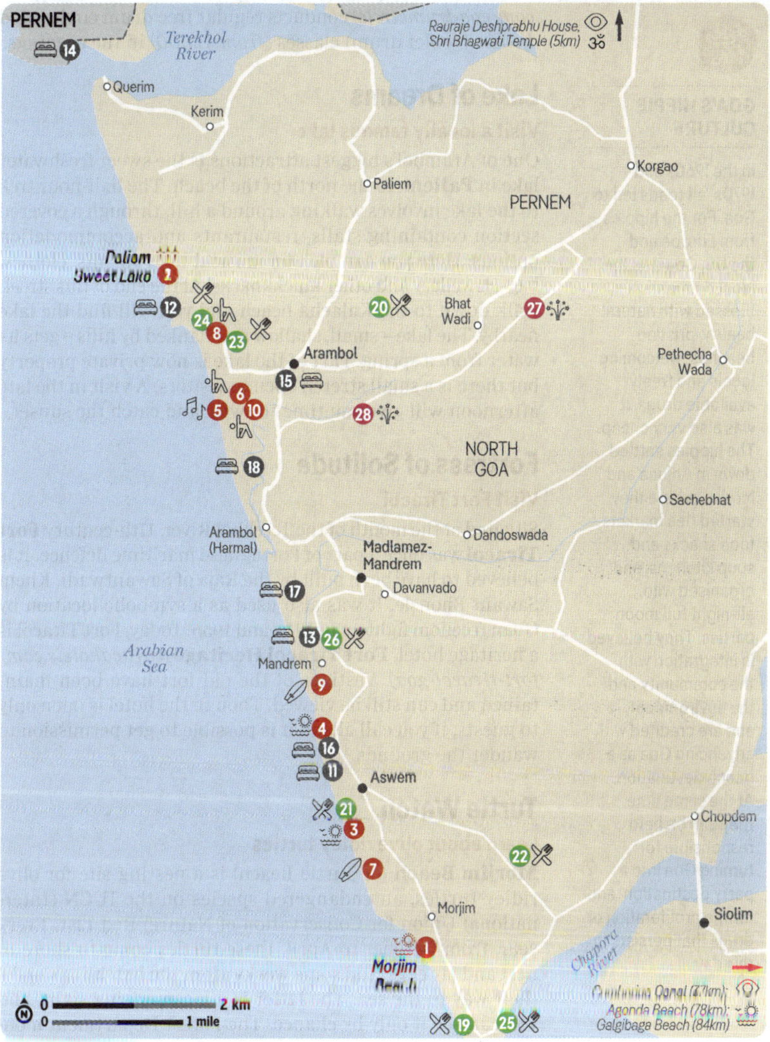

HIGHLIGHTS
1 Morjim Beach
2 Paliem Sweet Lake

SIGHTS
3 Ashwem Beach
4 Mandrem Beach

ACTIVITIES
see 3 Banana Surf School
5 Goa Drum Circle
6 Himalayan Iyengar Yoga Centre
see 11 Jack's Surf School
7 Octopus Surf School
8 Raj Yoga School
see 4 Samudra Surf School
9 Swell Cats Surf Club
10 Yoga Village

SLEEPING
11 Anahata Retreat
12 ATS All Terrain Stay
13 Elsewhere
14 Fort Tiracol Heritage Hotel
15 Happy Panda
16 Palm Grove Beach Resort
17 Vaayu Kula
18 Veda5 Wellness Retreat & Spa

EATING
19 Burger Factory
20 Garden of Dreams
21 La Plage
22 Rice Mill
23 Shantaram
24 Shimon Falafel
25 The Bodhi Tree Cafe and Bar
26 Verandah Goa

ENTERTAINMENT
27 Jungle Dance Double Dutch
28 Shunya Wellness

GOA'S HIPPIE CULTURE

In the 1960s and 1970s, all roads led to Goa. For the hippies from Europe and the US, Goa was the ideal destination – blessed with natural beauty, pristine beaches, welcoming locals and freely available drugs. It was also very cheap. The hippies settled down in Anjuna and Morjim, where they started flea markets, food shacks and soup kitchens, and organised wild, all-night full moon parties. They believed in integration with the community and the environment, and are credited with advancing Goa as a beach destination. At the same time, they can be held responsible for turning Goa into a party destination, and for the proliferation of drugs that persists to this day.

.com/goadrumcircle) conducts regular free drum circles, and *djembe* (goblet drum) classes *(from ₹2000)* in the evenings.

Lake of Dreams

Visit a locally famous lake

One of Arambol's biggest attractions is the sweet freshwater lake in **Paliem**, to the north of the beach. The half-hour trek to the lake involves walking around a hill, through a covered section containing stalls, restaurants and accommodation options. Here you can pick up musical instruments, clothes, bags, jewellery and other knickknacks. At the end of this street, walk down to the Kalacha beach and you will find the lake nearby. The lake – small, shallow and flanked by hills – gets its water from a spring. Part of the lake is now private property but there is a small stretch open to visitors. A visit in the late afternoon will give you time to swim and catch the sunset.

Fortress of Solitude

Visit Fort Tiracol

Situated at the mouth of the Terekhol River, 17th-century **Fort Tiracol** was once a part of Portuguese maritime defence. It is believed to have been built by the Raja of Sawantwadi, Khem Sawant Bhonsle. It was also used as a symbolic location by Goan freedom fighters in 1954 and 1955. Today, Fort Tiracol is a heritage hotel, **Fort Tiracol Heritage** *(saracahotels.com/fort-tiracol-goa)*. Vestiges of the old fort have been maintained and can still be viewed. Though the hotel is open only to guests, if you call ahead it is possible to get permission to wander the grounds.

Turtle Watch

Learn about olive ridley turtles

Morjim Beach (or Turtle Beach) is a nesting site for olive ridley turtles, an endangered species on the IUCN (International Union for Conservation of Nature) Red List. Every year, from October to April, these turtles come to shore to nest and lay eggs, and some weeks after, the hatchlings make their way to the sea. The latter is a mesmerising sight, and you can see it only by chance. The Forest Department monitors the whole process. You can watch the turtles from afar but should not get too close or disturb them. Morjim Beach has a turtle nesting site where you can see the nesting pits

EATING IN PERNEM: OUR PICKS

Shimon Falafel: Popular Lebanese spot known for its falafel and generous servings of vegan dishes, including shakshuka (egg dish). *9am-1am* ₹₹

Shantaram: A raw vegan cafe and shop with an open rooftop space. Try the smoothie bowls and plant-based burgers. *9am-8pm Wed-Mon* ₹₹

Garden of Dreams: Vegetarian garden cafe with a swimming pool. Porridge, smoothie bowls, fruit salads, coffee and raw vegan desserts on offer. *9.30am-6pm* ₹₹

The Bodhi Tree Cafe and Bar: Beachside cafe serving Goan food, juices, sandwiches and some international dishes. *9am-midnight* ₹₹

VLADIMIR SALMAN/SHUTTERSTOCK

Surf lesson, Mandrem

and read more about the species and the guidelines to follow in case you spot a turtle.

Hang Ten!

Hit the waves in Morjim

Surfing is an increasingly popular sport in Goa, aided by a thriving surfing community and surf schools, with ample beginner-friendly spots. Morjim – as well as the nearby **Mandrem** and **Ashwem** beaches – are replete with surf schools offering beginner classes and immersive courses for all ages; they also rent out surfboards. Reach out to **Octopus Surf School** *(octopus.surf)* in Morjim, or **Banana Surf School** *(instagram.com/bananasurfschool)*, **Jack's Surf School** *(instagram.com/jack.surfschool)*, **Samudra Surf School** *(instagram.com/alwaysonemorewave)* and **Swell Cats Surf Club** *(swellcatssurfclub.com)* in Ashwem, among others. Classes take place throughout the year (except the June to September monsoon season). Groups sessions cost around ₹2500/session and include surfboards, board rentals cost ₹500.

GOA'S VILLAGE FESTIVALS

Pednyechi Punav: A festival that centres on the Shri Bhagwati Temple, and supposedly casts out evil and demons from 'possessed' people.

Chorutsav: Villagers of Zarme (Mauxi) and Caranzol in the Sattari taluka recreate a legend of the killing of four innocents. As part of this festival of repentance, four people are buried up to their necks.

Dinya Jatra: A bachelorhood festival in Gaondongorim village, Canacona, where young men perform a dance with decorated sticks in front of a shrine.

Sangodutsav: A procession of canoes along Cumbarjua Canal, depicting mythological scenes, Goan traditions and social issues.

Karvalyo: In Sattari and Bicholim talukas, boys dress up as women and are taken from house to house, as it is believed that their presence brings prosperity.

EATING IN PERNEM: GLOBAL FARE

Burger Factory: Popular chain known for its delicious beef, pork, chicken and veggie burgers. Right on the beach in Morjim. *1-10pm Tue-Sun* ₹₹

La Plage: Hip beach shack in Ashwem with attentive staff, chill vibes and excellent French food. *10.30am-10pm Thu-Tue* ₹₹

Rice Mill: Old rice mill turned into a cosy cafe and jazz bar in Morjim, offering international bites and some Goan food. *9.30am-11pm* ₹₹

Verandah Goa: Hillside restaurant and gin speakeasy in Mandrem, doing pizza, pasta, grilled seafood and meat. *noon-3pm & 6.30pm-midnight Tue-Sun* ₹₹₹

Bardez

BEACHES | PARTY SPOTS | GREEN SPACES

TOP TIP

To keep abreast of local cultural events, follow **Offbeat Goa** *(@offbeatgoa)* on Instagram. It runs a thrift shop, cafe and a Sunday vegan community market, New Earth Gathering.

Bardez is the most vibrant of Goa's 12 talukas, offering a microcosm of the state as a tourist destination. People come here for the sun, sand, surf, water sports, all-night parties, hipster cafes and co-working spaces, exciting and innovative food, local and flea markets, and every kind of entertainment. Yet while Bardez embraces the comforts of modernity, it takes measures to preserve its rich history, and in recent years Goa's culinary buzz has been centred here.

Mapusa is the main city here, known for its vibrant Friday market and for offering easy access to Morjim and Arambol in the north and Panaji to the south. The coast has a long stretch of popular beaches like Vagator, Anjuna, Chapora, Calangute and Baga. Away from beachside action, there are historic forts and churches, quiet backwaters for kayaking or fishing, birdwatching sites, and non-gentrified villages for those seeking some Susegaad.

Scoring a Bargain

Visit Mapusa's Friday market

Mapusa Market (*9am-7pm daily*) is Goa's oldest public market. It is busiest on Fridays, when people from across the state come to sell their wares. Look for women in saris, with flowers in their hair, selling strings of *choris* (Goan sausages), bottles of vinegar, dried fish, and fruit and vegetables from

GETTING AROUND

Mapusa is the main city and is well-connected by bus *(goakadamba.com)* to destinations such as Anjuna, Arambol, Calangute, Candolim, Panaji and Thivim, plus the northern beaches and both of Goa's airports. There are autorickshaws, taxis and 'pilots' available at the Mapusa's Kadamba bus stand, at the main beaches and at village junctions; agree on a price beforehand. Alternatively, rent scooters or cars via your accommodation. Thivim, about 12km northeast of town, is the nearest train station on the Konkan Railway that connects Goa to Mumbai and destinations in Karnataka.

LESHIY985/SHUTTERSTOCK

Mapusa Market

their gardens. The market has different sections catering to earthenware, flowers, woven products, plants and clothes, besides the fish and vegetable sections. Be prepared to haggle. You can pick up food souvenirs here, from the ubiquitous cashew nuts to readymade masalas. There are also food stalls to sate the hungry, doing a brisk trade in thalis, fried fish and snacks like *puri bhaji* (vegetable dish with deep-fried bread). During festivals, the market becomes livelier and more crowded – at Christmas, you will find a crib (p779) here, and during Chaturthi, a Ganesh *pandal* (marquee). Go early for the best selection of the freshest wares.

A Village Feast

Enjoy a home-cooked meal

In the picturesque village of **Camurlim**, a few kilometres from Mapusa, chef Shubhra Shankhwalker cooks from home and offers an elaborate lunch experience in a small farmhouse close to the river *(instagram.com/goafromhome; ₹4500 per person)*. Expect a feast made from ingredients produced by the Gaud Saraswat Brahmin (GSB) community. Shubhra sources the produce, preps, cooks and serves the food herself, all the while talking about the cuisine and sharing recipes. Skip your breakfast because Shubhra's lunches are long and leisurely, with at least 10 courses, including curries, fish prepared several different ways, seasonal vegetables, punchy pickles and chutneys, and other dishes abundant in coconut, *kokum* (purple dried fruit rind), local chillies and spices.

Out & About in the Highlands

Tour the Socorro Plateau

A few minutes' drive away from Porvorim, the laterite **Socorro Plateau** is a biodiverse habitat rich in plants, flowers, insects and birds. It is best to visit the grassland, preferably in the early morning or evening, when the wildlife is at its most active. Carry your binoculars as you will spot many of

GOA'S GREEN WARRIORS

Goa Foundation: Environmental action group *(goafoundation.org)* active in conservation efforts and protection of Goa's natural environment.

Act for Goa: A community platform *(actforgoa.org)*, providing people with the information, tools, connections and opportunities they need to create a better future for Goa.

Goa Worth A Fight: Environmental conservation organisation *(goaworthafight.org)*, advocating for sustainable development and livelihoods.

#MakaNakaPlastic: This movement *(sensible.earth/makanakaplastic)* provides a sustainable alternative to single-use plastics by collecting old clothes and turning them into bags.

Responsible Tourism Collective: A group of businesses *(rtcgoa.org)* committed to promoting sustainable tourism by involving local communities, minimising disturbance to natural habitats and respecting local traditions.

HIGHLIGHTS
1 Aguada Port & Jail Complex

SIGHTS
2 All About Alcohol Museum
3 Anjuna Beach
4 Baga Beach
5 Calangute Beach
6 Candolim Beach
7 Chapora Fort
8 Church of Madre de Deus
9 Ozran Beach
10 Saligao Institute
11 Sinquerim Beach
12 St Alex Church, Calangute
13 St Lawrence Church
14 Vagator Beach

ACTIVITIES
15 Clube de Floresta
16 Coco Padel
17 Dolphin Point

SLEEPING
18 Cavala Seaside Resort
19 Funky Monkey
20 The Beachside Hostel
21 The Park Calangute

EATING
22 Anand Bar Seafood Restaurant
23 Anar
24 Artjuna Cafe
25 Baba Au Rhum
26 Barefoot Goa
27 Bean Me Up
28 Bhatti Village
29 Bomras
30 Caravela Cafe & Bistro
31 Infantaria
32 Kefi
33 Meiphung-North Eastern Kitchen
34 Pousada by the Beach
35 Saltamontes-Garden Cafe & Bar
36 Smoke
37 Sri
38 The Foundry Nagoa
39 The Hungry Hornbill
40 Vinayak Family Restaurant

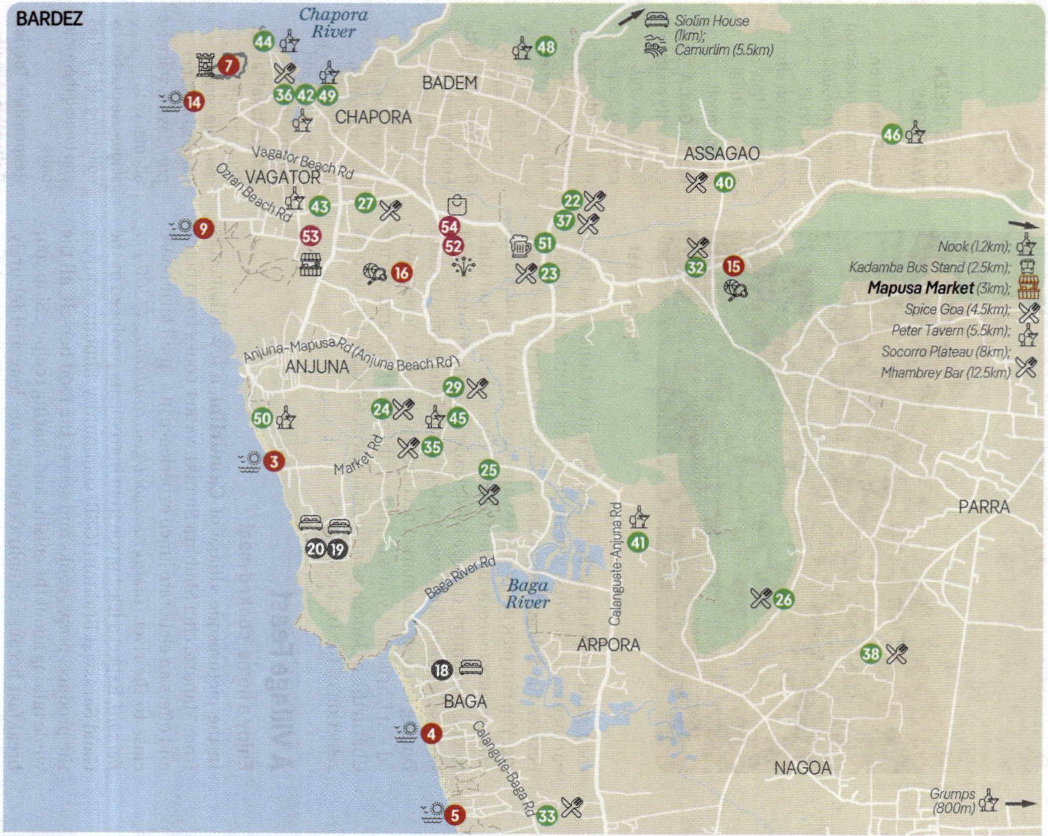

DRINKING & NIGHTLIFE
41 Cajy Bar
42 Darling's Bar
43 Hideaway Cafe & Bar
44 House of Chapora
45 Juna
46 LouLou Cocktail Bar
47 Misfit
48 Pablo's
49 Paulo's Antique Bar
50 Slow Tide
51 Soro
see 42 Sudan's Bar

ENTERTAINMENT
52 Offbeat Goa

SHOPPING
53 Goa Collective Bazaar
54 Good Karma Treasure Shop
55 Ninoskha

INSIDER GUIDES TO GOA

Terra Conscious: An ocean biodiversity experience *(terraconscious.com)* where you will learn about the Indo-Pacific humpback dolphin while respecting marine wildlife-watching guidelines.

Adventure Breaks: Outdoor sports company *(adventurebreaks.in)* offering land- and ocean-based activities, including treks near the ocean, rock climbing, sea cave exploration and coasteering.

Avocet & Peregrine: Birding company *(birding.avocet-peregrine.com)* organising guided day trips, tours and birding stays at twitcher hot spots around Goa.

Khoj-aao! Adventures: Tour company *(khojaao.com)* curating offbeat experiences linked to nature and adventure, like overnight camping, educational and nature trails.

The Goan Friend: Samuel Almeida *(thegoanfriend.com)* runs private excursions in Goa, many of which focus on fishing (deep-sea, spin, line and angling).

MONDADORI PORTFOLIO/GETTY IMAGES

Fort Aguada Jail

the 238 recorded bird species here, including bulbuls, barbets, purple sun birds and starlings. You may even spot a wild boar or jackal; keep a safe distance if you do. Maryanne Lobo of **Plant Walks Goa** *(instagram.com/plantswalksgoa.official; from ₹1000 per person)* conducts walks across Goa, including in Socorro, focusing on medicinal plants.

Queer-Friendly Goa

Inclusive spaces

Goa is relatively queer-friendly, especially North Goa, and there are a number of organisations at the heart of LGBTIQ+ action. **Qrave** *(instagram.com/qrave_official)*, run by multidisciplinary artist Avril Stormy Unger (her drag alter ego is Chutney Mary), arranges queer parties, which take place at different venues and centre on queer and women DJs. Community-specific groups include **Queen Kinara** *(instagram.com/queer_kinara_goa)*, which also throws various events and parties. A **Rainbow Collective** *(instagram.com/arainbowcollective)* puts on drag shows and gender-safe events. The **Audacity Collective** *(instagram.com/the_audacity_collective)* specialises in events such as reading and listening circles. There is also the collective **Queerly Goa** *(instagram.com/queerly_goa)* that helps people keep abreast of all events. Events happen throughout the year, and there is usually something every week.

Arrested Development

Walk around a decommissioned prison

Goa's fight for independence from Portuguese colonial rule is on view at the **Fort Aguada Jail** *(₹600)*. The Aguad fort was constructed in 1612 to guard against the Dutch and contained the Aguada Central Jail. Many Indian (during the national independence struggle in the 1930s and 1940s) and

Goan freedom fighters (in the 1950s, up till Goa's liberation in 1961) were imprisoned here. It was a prison till 2015. The decommissioned 17th-century prison complex looks out onto the Mandovi River and houses interactive museums that touch on Goa's rich biodiversity, its freedom struggle, festivals and prehistoric findings. There are some restaurants and bars on site, and the complex also hosts flea markets and concerts. Look out for the memorial dedicated to Goan freedom fighters. You can tour the space on your own, scanning helpfully placed QR codes for information. **Make It Happen** *(makeithappen.co.in; ₹700 per person)* conducts hour-long engaging tours of Aguada Fort.

Out at Sea

Go dolphin-spotting

The waters off Sinquerim and Candolim Beaches are where you are most likely to spot dolphins. Numerous tour operators offer boat tours between 9am and 5pm; look for the **Dolphin Point** jetty in Sinquerim, on the road heading to Aguada Fort. Most tours head out on a large boat for an hour *(₹400 per person)*. While spotting Indo-Pacific humpback dolphins is the main attraction, you will also get to enjoy views of the palm-fringed coast, fishers at work, the imposing hilltop **St Lawrence Church** and the Fort Aguada Jail.

Charmed by Chapora

Explore a seaside town

Standing guard over the mouth of the Chapora River, the 17th-century **Chapora Fort** was once a strategic military outpost for the Portuguese. Today, it consists of picturesque ruins, with few remnants of its military past, but the 10-minute climb up to the fort is worth it for the bird's-eye view of the nearby beaches, including the neighbouring Vagator (p766), especially at sunset. The route from the parking area to the bottom of the fort is dotted with stalls selling snacks, drinks and trinkets.

Once the sun has set, explore Chapora's lively main street, which is lined with quirky bars and places to eat, with tables right on the street. Start your pub-hop at **Paulo's Antique Bar**, which plays vintage rock and is papered with old posters of musicians. Nearby, **Darling's Bar** has a pool table and is known for its pizzas, while **Sudan's Bar** serves *urrak* (distilled cashew spirit) in season, plus fresh seafood. For more

OYSTER SHELL WINDOWS

Goa's architecture is a unique blend of Indian and European architectural styles. Some of the striking features found in Goa include oyster shell windows, thought to have originated in the 17th century. The window panes are made from mother-of-pearl (nacre) shells and are locally called *capiz*. They were used instead of glass to filter out the harsh rays of the sun, while allowing sufficient light to enter. They also offered homeowners a sense of privacy. The harvesting of certain oyster species has been banned since 2005 due to the declining numbers of said oysters. Look out for their shells in the windows of old Goan Catholic homes across the state.

EATING AROUND MAPUSA: BEST THALI JOINTS

Vinayak Family Restaurant: A popular spot in Assagao known for its seafood thalis and generous portions. Slow service. *noon-4pm & 7-11pm Fri-Wed* ₹

Anand Bar Seafood Restaurant: A tourist favourite, this busy Anjuna joint executes superlative thalis and delicious curries. *12.30-4.30pm & 7-11pm Tue-Sun* ₹

Mhambrey Bar: Tiny laid-back family-run space by the river in Aldona serving no-frills, wallet-friendly thalis. *11am-3pm & 7-11pm Tue-Sun* ₹₹

Spice Goa: Family restaurant whose thalis, fresh fish and fusion seafood dishes have a loyal local following. *11.30am-4pm & 7-11pm* ₹₹

GOA'S ALCOHOL INDUSTRY

In recent years, Goa's homegrown spirit industry has boomed. The state's excise duties are lower than in most other Indian states, so alcohol has always been cheaper here – a big factor drawing in domestic tourists. There is now a growing interest in homegrown drinks, starting with gin (the gin revolution in India started in Goa in 2017), and including vodka, rums, beer, whiskies and also liqueurs. They tick the major boxes: local, homegrown, craft and farm-to-bottle. Goa offers a booming bar and cocktail scene, ease of doing business, an audience open to experimenting and a great vibe.

PEPPY GRAPHICS/SHUTTERSTOCK

Vagator Beach

dining options, consider **Smoke** with its stellar smoked meats, and stalls selling *momos* (Tibetan dumplings) and *shawarma* (spit-roasted kebabs). Finish your night by dancing to techno and trance at the **House of Chapora** *(instagram.com/houseofchapora; 8pm-7am)*, down by the beach.

Superlative Strands

Go beach-hopping

The beaches in Goa's northern belt are among the liveliest and most popular in the state. The northernmost beach is **Ozran Beach**, or Little Vagator, beloved by locals and known for its rock carving of the deity Shiva. **Vagator Beach** is a great sunset spot.

About a 15-minute drive away is the vast sandy sweep of **Anjuna Beach**, which was once a hippie haven and today is home to many beach shacks. South of Anjuna, another 15-minute drive away, you will find the two most popular (and crowded) beaches: **Baga** and **Calangute**.

DRINKING IN BARDEZ: BEST TIPPLE SPOTS

Hideaway: Hip cocktail bar and performance space in Vagator with innovative cocktails. Come for live gigs and feni-based drinks. *7pm-1am Wed-Mon*

Boilermaker: Buzzing bar in Siolim, known for its half-sized cocktails (so that you can try more drinks) and a disco in the bathroom. *6pm-12.30am Tue-Sun*

Slow Tide: Beach-facing shack that serves exciting craft cocktails inspired by Anjuna's hippie past, plus coastal fare. *11am-11pm*

Juna: Anjuna space that identifies as a bar, serves delicious food and has a rotating list of local music acts. *7pm-1am Wed-Mon*

Nook: Small outdoor bar inside Caju Grove Villa, hosting karaoke nights, game nights and parties, and serving local tipples. *6.30-11pm Tue-Sun*

Grumps: Restobar specialising in cocktails highlighting Asian ingredients like yuzu, gochujang and pandan. *7pm-midnight Thu-Mon, 12.30-4pm Sat & Sun*

Pousada by the Beach: Family-run beach restaurant serving excellent seafood, Goan food and classic cocktails. *11am-9pm*

LouLou Cocktail Bar: Attic converted into an intimate bar with a grand piano and interesting cocktails. Go here for the special jazz nights. *7pm-3am*

Further south along the coast, a 15-minute drive takes you to **Candolim**, then to the relatively quieter and cleaner **Sinquerim**. Every beach has shacks and sunbeds and offers water-sport activities; nearby, shops rent out bicycles. Expect crowds, especially during public holidays.

On the Taverna Trail

Imbibe at Goa's old-school watering holes

Goa's tavernas are venerable watering holes, where locals gathered (from the 19th century onwards) to imbibe feni and *urrak* (firewater distilled from cashew apples), gossip and gamble. The number of tavernas are dwindling, but you can still find them in villages and on city corners, and they are still frequented by locals (though not as many as before). Some (including those mentioned below) have undergone a makeover, and are now hip, modern bars with cocktails and good food. Many remain family-run spaces that, much like before, serve the function of the neighbourhood bar. In Arpora you will find **Cajy Bar**, which serves meaty Goan snacks and straight drinks. At **Peter Tavern** in Ucassaim, you can dine on Indian-Chinese fare, and participate in quizzes and parties. **Pablo's** is a popular neighbourhood bar in Anjuna, with a special focus on cocktails and good food.

A Family's Artistic Legacy

Peruse the Museum of Goa

Head deep into Pilerne Industrial Estate to find the **Museum of Goa** *(museumofgoa.com; ₹300)*. A contemporary art space created by artist Subodh Kerkar, it features art spread across three floors, a terrace and a sculpture garden. Much of it is Kerkar's own work – acrylic paintings, and sculptures made using cowrie shells, driftwood, fibreglass and plaster of Paris. One section features artwork by his father, Chandrakant Kerkar, whose paintings are a visual record of old Goan life.

The gallery also hosts temporary exhibitions, and organises workshops, art courses, musical performances and artist residencies. Its weekly informative lecture series, MOG Sundays, are gratis.

Architecture, Goan-Style

Discover the secrets of Goan construction

On a traffic island at the bottom of a steep slope near Torda Creek sits the boat-shaped **Houses of Goa Museum** (*museumhousesofgoa.com; ₹300*). Designed by local architect Gerard da Cunha, it boasts a sloping roof, a plant-covered facade and three floors with a spiral staircase. Inside, there are displays on Goa's architectural history, 3D models of still-standing historic houses, photos, paintings, info boards and elements from centuries-old houses, such as balustrades. Look for sketches showing Goa's history, done by the late Goan cartoonist, Mario Miranda. Across the road is the **Mario Gallery** *(mariodemiranda.com)*, one of many such shops where you can buy products featuring the popular artist.

THE LIFE OF A CARTOONIST

Mario Miranda (1926–2011) was an artist and painter highly regarded for his vibrant, detailed and witty caricatures, especially of Goan life and culture. He was a beloved social cartoonist and his work is still widely displayed around Goa. Born in Daman, he worked as a cartoonist with newspapers in Mumbai, and shuttled between the city and Goa. His colourful characters and cartoons showcased Goa by making fun of everyday life. Mario also did illustrations and fine art, won many awards for his work, and wrote and illustrated several books. After his death, his family established six branches of the Mario Gallery *(mariodemiranda.com)* across Goa to display and sell his work.

THE GENTRIFICATION OF ASSAGAO

The trendiest destination in Goa in recent years, **Assagao** was once a quiet village. It attracted attention because of its proximity to Mapusa and the popular Calangute–Baga–Chapora–Candolim tourist trail. Today, Assagao is a prime example of the rapid gentrification of Goan villages. Some jokingly refer to it as Assa-Gurgaon – a reference to Delhi and Gurgaon folks buying property here. While Assagao is a 'happening' food destination, with new restaurants, bars and coffee shops popping up, this has come at a cost of pricing out locals and the destruction of green spaces. What has happened to Assagao is now spreading to the villages of Siolim, Aldona (p771), Moira and Bastore in North Goa.

MOR TUUL & BRUNO MORANDI/GETTY IMAGES

Church of Nossa Senhora de Penha de França

Play Ball

Join in the padel and pickleball craze

Padel and pickleball are the newest sports finding popularity in the state in the last few years. Padel is a fast-paced, doubles racquet sport played on an enclosed tennis court with walls for rebounds; while pickleball is a mix of tennis, badminton and ping-pong. The state has a slew of new courts, and competitions attract locals and tourists alike.

Assagao has **Clube de Floresta** *(instagram.com/clubedeflouresta)*, which also offers coaching; and **CoPlay at Assagao House** *(instagram.com/coplayofficial; ₹1200 per hr for pickleball, ₹2400 for padel per person)*. **Jolt Method** in Siolim has pickleball and padel courts *(instagram.com/jolt.method; from ₹500)*.

There are half-hour padel slots available at **Padel People** *(instagram.com/padelpeoplegoa; ₹800)* in Socorro and at **Coco Padel** *(instagram.com/cocopadel_goa; ₹1000)* in Anjuna. Many venues offer coaching and equipment rental.

An Intoxicating Experience

Visit an alcohol museum

On a bustling road in Candolim sits a private museum dedicated to alcohol. Businessman Nandan Kudchadkar's **All About Alcohol Museum** *(instagram.com/alcoholmuseum;*

EATING IN BARDEZ: GOAN FAVOURITES

Mafia Cocktail: A brother-sister duo run this place out of their home in Pilerne. No menu; you get what has been cooked that day. *12.30-4pm & 8-11pm* ₹₹

Bhatti Village: Family-run restaurant in Nerul serving typical Goan seafood. A rare place with ox tongue on the menu. *noon-3pm & 7-11pm* ₹₹

Infantaria: Calangute landmark known for its breakfasts, brunches and baked goods like croissants and pancakes. *7.30am-11pm* ₹₹

7 Short 1 Long: Goan dishes served alongside Bel-gin-da (grapefruit, pink peppercorns and gin) cocktails. *12.30-2.30pm & 7-11pm Tue-Sun* ₹₹

₹500) features his collection of artefacts linked to alcohol. You can explore on your own or join a guided tour (included in the ticket price). Guided tours last an hour and focus on some standout displays such as the world's tallest shot glass, bottled showpieces, and vintage cashew distillation equipment. The museum's main focus is feni; you can learn about its distillation, view a rustic still and participate in a tasting at a makeshift taverna.

A Remarkable Place of Worship

Explore Penha de França's church

Penha de França is a small town by the Mandovi River, which gets its name from the imposing riverfront **Church of Nossa Senhora de Penha de França**. This 16th-century church overlooks the confluence of the Mapusa and Mandovi Rivers. Sit on the garden wall to get the best views, including those of the islands of Chorão and Divar, and Ribandar. Visit the church during services (it is shut otherwise), which are held in the mornings *(7-9am)*, to see the restored interior with the gilded gold plating on the altar, wood carvings and paintings. The acoustics here are marvellous.

Unique Flavours

Sample Northeastern Indian cuisine

One of the newer cuisines to have become popular in Goa is that of India's Northeastern states. It is a cuisine that is heavy on pork, meat and fermented foods like *axone* (soybean) and *tungtap* (fish). Over in Siolim is **Alag**, serving *shokupan* (Japanese milk bread) sandwiches, cookies and coffee. While its food isn't from the region, it sources its coffee from the Northeast, its staff is from the region and it has books and an in-house magazine highlighting the region. **Pots and Grillz** in Sangolda does Mizo food and is known for spicy salads, smoked pork and eggplant stew. Livingstone Shazia from Manipur prepares dishes from his home region at the **Meiphung-North Eastern Kitchen** in Calangute – expect *singju* (spicy salad with fermented fish), smoked beef salad and stir-fried pork. There is also **Hungry Hornbill (by Fat Panda)** in Candolim, which does smoked beef with yam, smoked pork, snails and fish curry. Panaji's **Soul Chef** specialises in Northeastern and pan-Asian dishes like steamed fish with local greens, fish cakes and fiery Naga wings.

Get Jiggy With It

Attend a dance social

Goans love to dance, as is evident at any wedding, party or festival. If you want to brush up on your dancing skills, learn a new move or two, and meet new friends while doing so, attend one of the many dance socials (a free opportunity to practise dance with other enthusiasts). Architect Fedora Cotta has created a community of Lindyhoppers via her platform **Lindy Zai** *(instagram.com/lindyzai)*. She conducts classes

BARDEZ' BEST CHURCHES

Church of Madre de Deus: Saligao's neogothic church dates to 1873 and houses a supposedly miraculous statue of the Mother of God.

St Anthony's Church: This 1630-built Siolim church (p772) is dedciated to St Anthony of Padua for saving Portuguese merchants caught in a storm.

St Alex Church: This Calangute church was founded in 1590 and has a dome similar to St Peter's Basilica in Rome.

Church of Our Lady of Miracles: This Mapusa church, founded in 1594 by Franciscans, is known for both Catholics and Hindus attending its services.

Reis Magos Church: The first church built in Bardez (in 1555) features a wooden relief of the Three Wise Men.

GOA'S HERITAGE

Heritage First Goa *(heritagefirstgoa.com)* is a not-for-profit organisation preserving and promoting Goa's rich natural and cultural heritage. It was created by Heta Pandit, Snigdha Manchanda and Jack Ajit Sukija in 2024. They organise events like walks and workshops, including the Walking/Workshops with Icons series, centred on Goan legends, and a Heritage for Sustainability Film Festival. They run an annual **Heritage First Festival** in November – with over 30 walks and workshops across the state. Themes have included Wild Edibles, Kaavi Art and rice-farming workshops, alongside walks focused on *khazans* (coastal wetlands), marine life, sketching, architecture and caves.

NOVONIL/SHUTTERSTOCK

Market spices, Goa

and workshops, and also organises swing socials every few weeks. Siddhaarth Sharma and Naadia Khan run jive and salsa socials at different restaurants. Places like **Saltamontes-Garden Cafe & Bar**, **Misfit**, **Soro** and **Kefi** also host dance socials; they all begin with a short, free dance class. A good way to keep track of the socials in Goa is by checking the OneBoard app *(oneboard.app)*.

Battle of the Brains

Take part in a quiz night

Spend an evening in Goa testing your knowledge against other brainiacs at a quiz night. The **Inquizitiors** *(instagram.com/theinquizitors)* is run by Alroy Fernandes. His general knowledge quizzes include themed nights that focus on subjects as diverse as Harry Potter, sports or Bollywood. Sullivan Noronha of the **Sully One Project** *(instagram.com/the_sully*

EATING IN BARDEZ: BEST CAFES

Caravela Cafe & Bistro: Family-run coffee shop in Candolim dishing up all-day breakfasts, snacks, Goan dishes and its own single-estate coffee. *9am-8pm* ₹₹

Moira Coffee House: Quiet space with good coffee, library and sweet treats worth returning for (try the miso brownie). *10.30am-7.30pm Tue-Sun* ₹₹

Barefoot Goa: This coworking space in Parra doubles as a cafe serving open sandwiches, smoothies and teas. It hosts regular events. *9am-9pm Mon-Sat* ₹₹₹

Bean Me Up: An outdoor vegan restaurant in Vagator whose food menu includes tempeh and seitan dishes, poke and Buddha bowls. *9am-11pm* ₹₹₹

Artjuna@Mojigao: Trendy Anjuna spot with sandwiches, salads and Mediterranean dishes, plus post-lunch cocktails. *7.30am-10.30pm* ₹₹₹

Cafe Lento: All-day breafast spot inviting you to savour chicken soup, crab omelette, ham sandwiches and French toast. *9am-6pm Thu-Tue* ₹₹₹

Baba Au Rhum: Popular French cafe and pizzeria in Anjuna serving quiches, bagels, crostinis and filling sandwiches. *9am-9pm Thu-Tue* ₹₹₹

Kefi: Outdoor Assagao bistro with Mediterranean food like hummus, *shawarma* and kebabs on the menu, ideal for the midnight munchies. *24hr* ₹₹₹

.one_project) conducts quizzes and game nights that tend to get extremely competitive.

Their quizzes happen a couple of times a month at bars and restaurants across the state, including Peter Tavern (p767), **Miri**, **Misfit**, and **Bab's Hideout**. Solo participants are welcome; book in advance as tables run out quickly. Prizes typically include alcohol or vouchers.

One for serious quizz heads, the **Sunday Evening Quiz Club** *(instagram.com/seqcgoa)* conducts quizzes (including themed ones) at auditoriums and halls in Margao and Panaji.

Life at Low Tide

Learn about marine ecology

Blessed with a long coastline, Goa's shallows are home to a wealth of marine life, from seaweed such as sargassum, sea snails and barnacles to anemones and sea urchins. To learn more, join a guided walk with **Marine Life of Goa** *(instagram.com/marinelifeofgoa)* or **Canopy by the Coast** *(instagram.com/canopyby.thecoast; tours from ₹850 per person)*. These walks are conducted by marine biologists and usually take place in the early morning or at low tide. Canopy by the Coast also organises mangrove boat rides and wetlands biodiversity walks. Gabriella D'cruz of **The Good Ocean** *(instagram.com/thegoodocean)* has been working hard to promote local seaweed and its culinary applications; she sells seaweed, too.

To Market, to Market!

Visit a village market

Aside from the bustling village markets, Goa has smaller markets featuring local brands and home chefs. The **Goa Collective Bazaar** *(instagram.com/thegoacollectivebazaar; ₹200)* in Vagator takes place every Friday from 4pm between November and April. This is an open-air night market with stalls showcasing local products, along with a global food court and bar. On most Thursdays (except during the June to September monsoon season), the space in front of the St John de Baptist Church hosts the **Pilerne Heritage Market** *(instagram.com/pilerneheritagemarket)*, centred on Goan food and local homemade items – many of them coconut-, Christmas- or even rice-themed. The Saligao Institute holds a **Made in Saligao market** *(instagram.com/made_in_saligao)* on Tuesdays, also focusing on locally made products and food.

Ambling Around Aldona

Explore a picturesque village

It appears that Goa's villages are taking their turn in the spotlight. Following Assagao (p768) and Siolim, the newest hot spot (as of 2025) is **Aldona**. Away from the beaches but home to tranquil backwaters, Aldona still retains much of its charm. You can explore it on your own, ideally by bicycle. Highlights include the **Corjuem Fort**, across the river, which offers scenic views of the surroundings. Constructed in 1550,

SHOP LOCAL, SHOP SUSTAINABLE

Ninoshka: Fashion designer Ninoshka Alvares-Delaney's brand focuses on sustainable fashion; she works with local artisans and employs a zero-waste philosophy.

Zero Posro: A zero-waste, no-plastic local food movement that connects consumers with small-scale farmers specialising in indigenous grains and fresh produce.

Good Karma Treasure Shop: A thrift shop that does pop-ups, closet cleanses, barter events and more. Donates 25% of its profits to various NGOs.

Art by BU: Artist Vaibhav Salgaonkar *(instagram.com/artbybu)* does vibrant sketches, illustrations and caricatures capturing Goan life, on calendars, coasters, magnets and more.

Goan Parampara: An online store aiming to popularise the traditional Goan *kunbi* weave through saris and other items.

THE FEAST OF SÃO JOÃO

Every 24 June, Goans gather to celebrate the **Feast of St John the Baptist**. One part of the celebration involves jumping into village wells – to symbolise how St John leapt into his mother's womb upon hearing about the birth of Jesus. People make *kopel* (flower wreaths) for their hair and there are Carnival-like processions and float parades, with much singing and dancing. A special celebration happens in Siolim, by the Chapora River and in front of the **Church of St Anthony**. There is a boat parade followed by a musical evening. Places like Colva in the south do smaller, quieter and more traditional celebrations.

ALEX EROFEENKOV/SHUTTERSTOCK

Corjuem Fort (p771)

it was the property of the Bhonsle rulers of Sawantwadi, and rebuilt by the Portuguese colonists in 1705 to boost their defences of Panaji. Check out **St Thomas Church**, built by the Franciscans in 1596, and overlooking the Mapusa River. It has twin bell towers and elaborate biblical-themed frescoes. Close by is the Aldona Market and the **Martinho Lobo Supermarket**, a shop that sells niche food products like imported sweets, cheeses and packaged food. Nearby is **Project Cafe Goa** – an old house that comprises a gallery, cafe and stay option; it regularly hosts art exhibitions. **Prose Patisserie and Cafe** *(prose.co.in)* near Nachinola football ground is a cafe, patisserie and space for pop-up markets. Prose is part of **Arthshila Goa** *(arthshila.org)*, a multipurpose space that features art galleries, readings and an amphitheatre for events. One of the cutest spaces here is **The Owl House** *(theowlhousegoa.org)*, a community centre that educates and then employs neurodiverse adults in the on-site cafe.

EATING IN BARDEZ: BEST BAKERIES

Joseph Bakery: Popular bakery in Mapusa, known for its Goan snacks, sweets and delicious biscuits. *7.30am-8pm* ₹

Bakers Street: Sangolda's famous bakery is frequented for its delicious cakes (especially the chocolate cake) and other sweet treats. *9am-10pm* ₹

CocoaMoga Bake House: Small outdoor cafe and bakery in Parra doing great pastries, some stellar sandwiches and dips. *9am-6pm Tue-Sun* ₹₹

Saint Cloud: The patisserie, bakehouse and cafe in Sangolda is a local favourite for its baked goods, sandwiches and Christmas cake. *9am-9pm Tue-Sun* ₹₹

Salcete

NATURAL BEAUTY | PRESERVED HERITAGE | FASCINATING MUSEUMS

A taluka in South Goa, Salcete is rich in natural beauty and Portuguese heritage. Villages like Loutolim and Chandor are home to some of Goa's oldest, most beautiful and well-preserved homes such as the Figueiredo Mansion and Menezes Braganza House. Salcete has beaches that cater to every kind of traveller, from buzzing ones offering water sports, like Benaulim and Colva, to secluded sandy stretches, ideal for picnics, such as Betul.

Margao is Salcete's main hub and the focus of many cultural and food experiences; it is considered to be Goa's commercial capital. Salcete is home to majestic churches, temple ruins, and art galleries like Carpe Diem. The people here are proud of their history and culture; this is reflected in museums like Big Foot, which are based on personal collections and Salcete's food traditions. You will find unique dining experiences in people's homes and hidden away in picturesque corners and farms.

TOP TIP

Ravindra Natya Bhavan *(ravindrabhavanmargao.com)* in Margao is where you can catch a *tiatr*, a kind of musical theatre unique to Goa. Check the local newspapers, such as *O Heraldo* and *The Navhind Times*, for shows and ticket details.

House Rules

Explore historic Goan homes

Goa's heritage mansions offer an insight into the area's colonial past and Portuguese architectural influences. Some of these houses date back centuries; they have been lovingly restored and are open to the public. Many can be found in Chandor.

Continues on p776

GETTING AROUND

Margao is Salcete's main city, and its centre is easily navigated on foot. The city bus stand has services to all the villages in the taluka. Local transport is available between major cities like Margao, Panaji and Vasco, and to the more popular tourist points and beaches. You will find motorcycle 'pilots' and taxis at the bus stands. Margao's train station, about 2km south of town, serves both the Konkan Railway and local South Central Railways routes, and is the main hub for trains from Mumbai to Goa and south to Kochi (Cochin).

HIGHLIGHTS

1 Carpe Diem Art Cafe
2 Goan Kitchen

SIGHTS

3 Ana Fonte Garden
4 Benaulim Beach
5 Betul Beach
6 Big Foot
7 Casa Araujo Alvares
8 Colva Beach
9 Figueiredo Mansion
10 Holy Spirit Church
11 Largo de Igreja
12 Majorda Beach
13 Margao Municipal Garden
14 Mobor Beach
15 Our Lady of Grace Church
16 Patriarchal Seminary of Rachol
17 Saat Burzam Ghor
18 San Thome Museum
19 Three Kings Chapel

SLEEPING

20 Beleza by the Beach
21 Caravela Beach Resort
22 Heritage Village Resort & Spa Goa
23 Longuinhos Beach Resort
24 Novotel Goa Dona Sylvia Resort
25 Vivenda dos Palhacos

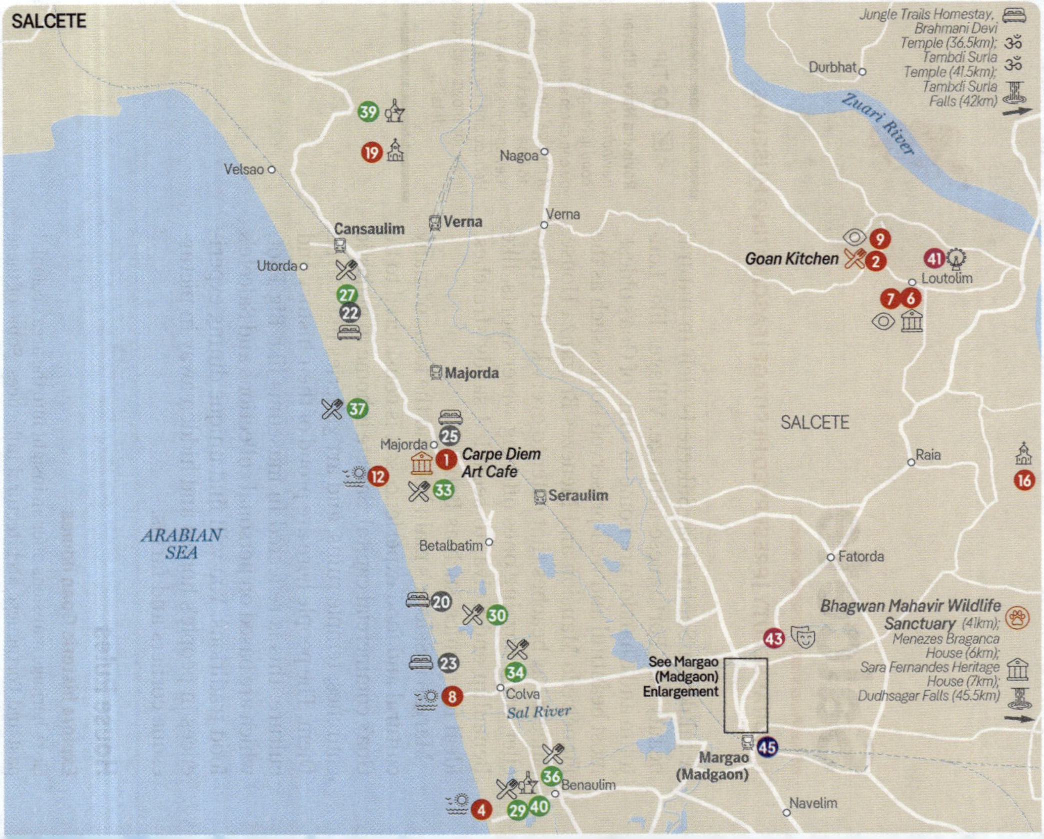

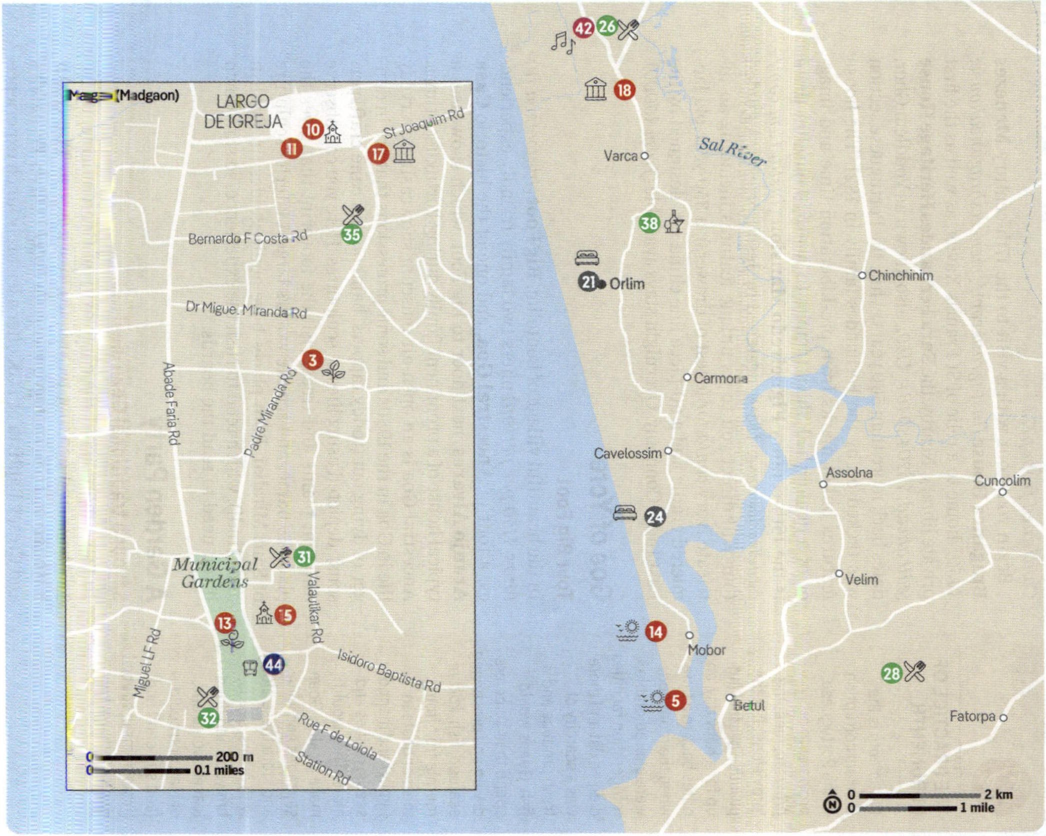

EATING
26 Beno
27 Bonita
28 C'est La Vie
29 Goodfellas
30 Juju
31 Konkani Coastal Food Delicacy
32 Longuinhos Bar, Restaurant & Confectioners
33 Martin's Corner
34 Mon Petit Frère
35 The Goan Kitchen Restaurant
36 Unndo
37 Zeebop by the Sea

DRINKING & NIGHTLIFE
38 Bar SoGo
39 Cazulo Premium Feni
40 Feli

ENTERTAINMENT
41 Ancestral Goa
42 Heritage Home Concert
43 Ravindra Natya Bhavan

TRANSPORT
44 City Bus Stand
45 Margao Train Station

THE PRACTICE OF PURUMENTH

Purumenth is the Konkani corruption of the Portuguese *provimento* or *provisão,* meaning 'provisions'. It is the practice of stocking up for a rainy day, and dates back to a time when the monsoons were unpredictable, refrigeration facilities didn't exist and there was a scarcity of fresh produce and fish. Goans would spend their summers drying and preserving seafood, fish, *kokum* (purple fruit from the mangosteen family) and mango seeds, chillies and more. They would make pickles, Goan sausages and wine, and store these along with grains, seeds, firewood and dried leaves. Come end of May, you could (and still can!) find these items in special *purumenth* markets.

Continued from p773

Begin your tour with a visit to the 17th-century **Menezes Braganca House** *(instagram.com/_menezesbragancahouse; ₹450),* home to a relic of St Francis Xavier, as well as the first private library. Nearby, the **Sara Fernandes Heritage House** *(call ahead: 7620480464; ₹150),* also known as Voddlem Ghor, dates back more than 500 years, while the Portuguese section was tacked on by the Fernandes family in 1821. The house features bullet marks from pre-Liberation time and images of a demolished Shiva temple. In nearby Loutolim there is the 16th-century **Figueiredo Mansion** *(instagram.com/figueiredohouse; ₹350),* designed by Jesuit priests. A guided tour will direct you to its unique features including an intricate ivory *contador* (chest of drawers), a 350-year-old lacquered cradle and a 60-piece fine china set, designed by the East India Company. Overnight stays available *(from ₹5000).*

Goa of Yore

Tour Big Foot

In the beautiful village of Loutolim, **Big Foot** *(bigfootgoa.in; tours ₹150 per person)* offers two family-friendly experiences: a tour of **Ancestral Goa**, and one of the historic **Casa Araujo Alvares**, next door to Big Foot, which showcases a typical house of a prominent family during Portuguese times. Ancestral Goa is an open-air museum showcasing everyday life in Goa in the 1980s and some professions that are in danger of dying out (toddy tappers, bamboo and cane craftspersons), depicted using lifesize sculptures. Here you can observe different plants and trees, visit the footprint that gives the place its name, and see the world's largest laterite sculpture of Sant Mirabai. Both places have audio guides (in English and Hindi), which tend to rush the experience, so slow down if you need to read the boards.

A Garden Party

Savour a traditional Goan meal

To learn more about the complexity of Goan cuisine, its ingredients and cooking techniques, reach out to **The Goan Kitchen** or TGK *(instagram.com/hellotgk).* Oliver Fernandes and Crescy Baptista of TGK offer a leisurely lunch experience *(₹3675 per person; 15 people maximum)* in a shaded patch of Baptista's garden in Loutolim. There's a welcome drink at the start, either feni or *urrak* and some Goan snacks.

Between courses, you can wander around the garden, looking at the well and the kitchen set up in a former storeroom, observe and learn about the ingredients left out to dry, and explore the rustic kitchen set up outside. Here, Baptista conducts a sausage-making demonstration, shows the old baking system *(tizel)* used to make *bebinca* (a 16-layer coconut cake), and talks about spices and souring agents as well as the system of *purumenth* (a local preservation technique). The meal is brought out by local village cooks, and is a feast of Goan dishes, such as *caldeirada* (fish stew), *xacuti*, *sorpotel* (a spicy

CAMERANEST/SHUTTERSTOCK

Ancestral Goa at Big Foot, Loutolim

pork stew) and fish curries. TGK also has a **restaurant** space in Margao with a daily changing menu.

Margao Mayhem

Explore Goa's commercial capital

The second-largest city in Goa, Margao is considered to be Goa's commercial capital. An important settlement during pre-Portuguese times, the municipality catered to all the villages in the Salcete taluka during 300 years of Portuguese colonial rule. Today it's a bustling, chaotic yet culturally rich city. Walk around to take in its main sights. Start at **Our Lady of Grace Church**, built as a chapel in 1812, and now an important site for Catholics. If it is open, drop by the **Margao Municipal Garden** for a breather. To treat the munchies, head to any of the small stalls nearby and snack on *ros* omelette.

THE ROS OMELETTE

One of Goa's most popular street snacks, the *ros* omelette is a fluffy masala omelette smothered with *ros* (typically a chicken curry made with coconut), and served with Goan *poee* (flatbread), or *pao* (bread). Goans find it a cheap and filling meal, and it works as a quick breakfast, an evening snack or a post binge-drinking treat. It is typically sold out of *gaddos* (street stalls) in the evenings, and in small tea shops. You can now find the *ros* omelette in fancier restaurants, too. The origins are contentious but most people believe that the late Ashok Naik created the dish, serving it out of his stall in Margao.

EATING IN SALCETE: OUR PICKS

Feli: Beers on tap, cocktails and small plates, including popular Goan dishes such as *cafreal* (meat cooked in spicy sauce). *5pm-midnight* ₹₹

Bar SoGo: A bar overlooking paddy fields, serving plates of salads, burgers and pastas. Frequent music events and bar takeovers. *noon-1am Wed-Mon* ₹₹₹

Bonita: Arossim restaurant dishing up pizzas, pastas, grilled meats and tacos, with an emphasis on fresh produce. *noon-11pm* ₹₹₹

Juju: Colva restaurant specialising in bold flavours and modern twists on popular Indian dishes and desserts. *12.30-3.30pm & 7-11.30pm* ₹₹₹

Mon Petit Frère: All-day Colva breakfast spot, with stellar egg dishes and pancakes, plus burgers, bar bites and salads after 1pm. *9am-8pm Tue-Sun* ₹₹₹

Beno: Breakfast-to-bar spot in Benaulim known for its gin collection. The food menu comprises breakfast dishes, salads, pastas and burgers. *8am-midnight* ₹₹₹

Zeebop by the Sea: All-day dining spot on Utorda Beach with an extensive seafood menu, plus Goan and Indian food. *11am-11pm* ₹₹₹

Goodfellas: Italian restaurant in Benaulim serving homemade pastas and traditional wood-fired oven pizzas. *1-3.30pm Thu-Tue, 7-11.30pm* ₹₹₹

FINDING FENI

Feni is Goa's state drink. It is made either from coconut sap, and called coconut feni or *maad*, or else from the juice of the cashew apple, and referred to as cashew feni. Coconut feni is often infused with botanicals and herbs, the most popular of which is *dukshiri* (Indian sarsaparilla root) to create different flavours. Feni is a pre-industrial spirit, still completely handmade and all-natural, made without any preservatives or additives. It is distilled in a pot still and uses natural yeast for fermentation. The liquid produced after the first distillation is called *urrak* and is a popular summer refresher. In the past, feni was used to treat ailments, was added to food, and was a part of many religious and cultural practices.

Next head north towards the imposing, Indian baroque-style **Holy Spirit Church** (1675) with its heavily ornamented altars. It was the first church built in the city. This is the fifth incarnation of the building, which was destroyed repeatedly by Muslim raiders. In **Largo de Igreja**, the area around the church, look for the grand **Saat Burzam Ghor** ('Seven-Gabled House'). Of its seven distinctive high-peaked gables, only three remain, though it is still an impressive edifice that can be admired from the outside. If you choose to stick around in the evening, take a walk in the beautiful **Ana Fonte Garden** and admire its musical fountain.

Vintage Technology Treasure Trove

Visit the San Thome Museum

If vintage technology is your passion, then visit the **San Thome (Back in Time) Museum** *(goamuseum.com; ₹200)* in Benaulim. This private museum features curator Thomas Antonio da Costa's extensive collection of calculators, phones, typewriters, cameras, watches, radios and assorted curios spread across three floors. Some outstanding items include a 1940 dictograph, a grandfather clock with an alarm, an artillery shell fired by Iraq on Kuwait from 1991, a bush radiogram from 1948 and frames made with whale bones. It's a self-guided tour, and few of the items have notes or information. Opening hours can be erratic so it is best to call *(9822363917)* before heading over.

On a Cashew High

A feni immersion

At a cashew farm in the hills of Cuelim, you'll find **Cazulo Premium Feni**. Here you can sit in a small natural spring-fed pool, under the shade of trees, while owner Hansel Vaz teaches you to appreciate Goa's beloved cashew liquor during the three-hour Floating Feni tour *(instagram.com/fazendacazulo; ₹2500 per person)*. As tiny fish nibble at your feet, Hansel will talk you through the history of feni. You then tour the farm and the feni distillery, and wander around a cellar containing *garrafões* (large glass containers). Afterwards, you get to taste of Cazulo's different feni offerings – cashew, coconut and *dukshiri* (made with Indian sarsaparilla root) and learn to pair these with food.

Chapel on a Hill

Visit the Three Kings Chapel

Allegedly haunted by the ghosts of three Portuguese kings, one of whom plotted to poison the others but died himself in the process, the **Three Kings Chapel** sits on a hill in Cansaulim. It plays a particularly important role in January during the **Three Kings' Feast**. Three young boys from nearby villages are chosen to enact the story of the three wise men who brought gifts for the baby Jesus. As part of the celebratory procession, they ride up to the chapel on horseback from

BHATAKTA MANAV/SHUTTERSTOCK

Three Kings Chapel, Cansaulim

different parts of the village. You can go up to the chapel, though the interior is not open to visitors the rest of the year; you can still walk around the courtyard and enjoy the views of palm groves, paddy fields, beaches and the Arabian Sea.

Seize the Day

View contemporary art

An art gallery that hosts events, **Carpe Diem** *(carpediemgoa.com; free)* does it all. It utilises the rooms of a venerable Goan home – the main rooms are used for exhibitions, the on-site cafe is in the kitchen and backyard, the storeroom hosts pottery workshops, and the garden is the spot for book launches. Most exhibitions centre on one artist (either Goan or Indian); these change every few weeks. You can wander around the house (no photography allowed in the exhibition space), shop for ceramic magnets and knickknacks, or grab a bite at the attached cafe. Check the notice board for regular workshops (pottery, tie dye, painting).

COMMUNITY CRIBS

Every Christmas, youth groups and groups of villagers get together to create life-size cribs. These are a way of showcasing creativity as well as emphasising Goa's secular nature – it is not just Catholics who participate in this activity. These cribs are huge creations and include replicas of the nativity scene, along with recreations of villages, Goan professions and important religious structures. Many cribs use lights, music and other technology to stand out. Each crib is unique, either in its creation, the materials used (some go all-natural or else recycle waste products) or the theme (often a social message). These cribs are typically placed in open fields and near churches, and are open till late. Entry is by donation.

EATING IN SALCETE: BEST GOAN FARE

Konkani Coastal Food Delicacy: A favourite lunch spot serving delicious thalis and seafood. *noon-3pm & 7.30pm-12.30am* ₹

Unndo: Small, family-run Goan restaurant in Benaulim dishing up simple thalis in a vibrant yellow-hued space; try the prawn *bhaji. 7am-10pm Tue-Sun* ₹

Martin's Corner: Local favourite in Betalbatim offering home-style Goan food, Indian and Chinese dishes; they do live entertainment, too. *11.30am-4pm & 6.30-11.30pm* ₹₹

Longuinhos Bar, Restaurant & Confectioners: Margao institution serving Goan favourites: stuffed crab, *kismur* (shrimp salad) and *xacuti. 9am-10.45pm* ₹₹

BEST BEACHES IN SALCETE

Benaulim Beach: A peaceful beach with a long expanse of white sand, shacks serving good seafood, and some water-sport activity.

Colva Beach: A lively and popular beach, with many food shacks, sunbeds and a variety of water-sport options.

Majorda Beach: A relatively clean beach with few people and dotted with some shacks and sunbeds.

Mobor Beach: A compact, clean beach with calm waters, golden sand and a few tourists, located between the Sal River and Arabian Sea.

Betul Beach: A secluded beach located right on the delta of Sal River, fringed by coconut palms and known for its mussels.

Rachol's Riches

Explore a 17th-century seminary

Built in 1580 atop an old Muslim fort, the oldest and largest seminary in Goa was once an orphanage, a hospital, a catechetical school and home to Asia's third printing press before becoming the **Patriarchal Seminary of Rachol**. Asia's largest Catholic seminary makes for an impressive structure. Upon entering, you will walk past a flowering garden to reach the **church** *(9am-4pm)*, the only section of the 17th-century structure open to visitors. A tour of the church, built in Portuguese baroque style, reveals an antique pipe organ, paintings of saints and copies of the works of Goan artist Angelo da Fonseca. At Christmas, they usually put up an elaborate crib (p779) in the garden.

A Home Concert

Enjoy an intimate musical evening

To attend an unusual concert, step into a 150-year-old house in Benaulim. **Heritage Home Experience** *(instagram.com/soundsfromgoa; tickets from ₹3000)* offers an initiation into the music, dance and cuisine of Goa during the course of an evening. You begin by wandering around the house, admiring its architecture and the garden. To the side, a table is laden with little-known Goan snacks and drinks like *donnem* (rice cones steamed in jackfruit leaves), mango pies and *dedos de dama* (cashew nut and caramel sweets). As the sun sets, make your way to the grand *saala* (hall) where the band Entre Nos occupies a makeshift stage and performs for an intimate audience. The hour-long concert visits different Goan musical stylings like *mandos, dulpods, dekhni* and *fado*. Sometimes there is even a short dance performance. Concerts happen once every few months or by prior arrangement; you can choose between a high tea or a dinner experience.

The Chef's Table

Dine at a cashew farm

Avinash Martins is a popular Goan chef known for his reimaginings of traditional Goan dishes, which he serves at his restaurant **Cavatina Cucina** in Benaulim. A more personal dining experience, however, takes place at **C'est La Vie** *(8805258277; ₹6000 per person, minimum of 6, book 48 hours in advance)*, a chef's table at Avinash's family cashew farm in Velim. Here, Avinash serves a seven-course menu that is Goan but with a twist. There are paired cocktails too, some with feni. The afternoon starts with the making of *poee* (local wheat-dusted flatbread), which is a hands-on experience. The food comes out in courses, with Avinash explaining the ingredients, cooking styles, stories that inspired the dishes and people involved in bringing it to life (fishers, toddy tappers, farmers). Expect dishes like coconut carpaccio, red amaranth spanakopita and hay-smoked mackerel.

SAIKO3P/SHUTTERSTOCK

Dudhsagar Falls (p782)

TOP EXPERIENCE

Mollem

Bhagwan Mahavir Wildlife Sanctuary is the largest wildlife sanctuary in Goa, occupying 240 sq km along the eastern state border and the forested slopes of the Western Ghats. Mollem National Park is the core part of the sanctuary. The forest is home to a variety of flora and fauna, many endemic to the region.

DON'T MISS

- Dudhsagar Falls
- Tambdi Surla Temple
- Endemic birds
- Tambdi Surla Falls
- Temple with erotic art
- Jungle Trails Homestay

Biodiversity Hot Spot

This protected land contains within it plants, butterflies, fish, birds, odonata species, mammals, ants, reptiles, fungi, fish, orchids and lichen. Here, you can find Goa's state symbols – the state tree (crocodile bark tree), the state bird (flame-throated bulbul) and the state animal (gaur). There are bird, dragonfly and butterfly species endemic to the Western Ghats, and Asian small-clawed otters, which are the smallest in the world. A hike or a walk, on marked paths, offers glimpses of the sanctuary's

PRACTICALITIES

● ₹100 ● 7am-5.30 pm

A VILLAGE EXPERIENCE IN THE JUNGLE

Jungle Trails Homestay *(jungle trailsgoa.org; from ₹2000)* is an ecotourism venture in a forest hamlet, run by the women of Talade. They cook an elaborate spread of vegetarian food, and even perform folk dances (on request). It's a simple house, with cow-dung floors, high-roofed ceilings and murals on the walls. Book ahead online as there is no phone service here.

TOP TIPS

- Opting for a guided tour rather than venturing here solo enhances your bird-spotting opportunities. Many homestays conduct birdwatching tours.
- The monsoons are the best time to visit the waterfalls but the trek can be treacherous and the path slippery.
- Vehicles are allowed within the sanctuary (at extra cost), so if you wish to cover a lot of area, take your own car.
- A 4WD tour allows you to cover the park (like a safari) and visit a waterfall on one day – ideal for those short on time.
- Night visits are only permitted with guides and require special permission.

biodiversity. Herpetologist and wildlife photographer, **Nirmal Kulkarni** *(instagram.com/nirmal_kulkarni_; ₹6000-35,000)* conducts wildlife expeditions, including in Mollem, of four to five nights during the monsoons.

Dudhsagar Falls

Dudhsagar Falls rank as one of Goa's top sights. Dudhsagar (meaning 'river of milk') is a four-tiered waterfall, cascading down over 305m and disappearing into the thick forest. There is a trekking route to reach the falls from Kulem village, which takes about three hours. A quicker option is hiring a 4WD at Kulem's Dudhsagar Taxi stand *(dudhsagarjeeps.com; ₹950)* – you will be taken to the foot of the waterfalls and given an hour and a half to swim in the falls. It is best visited in the monsoon, or just after, though the trek is tougher during wet conditions.

Tambdi Surla Temple

Goa's oldest Hindu temple survived both the Inquisition and Muslim rulers because of its remote location in the heart of the forest. The 13th-century **Mahadev Temple** (locally called Tambdi Surla) is dedicated to Lord Shiva. Carved out of grey-black basalt stone and dating back to the Kadamba Dynasty (it bears the coat of arms), inside are bas relief idols, a lotus carved on the ceiling and the intricate carvings on the pillars. To reach the temple, enter from the Bolkornem gate and drive straight. The trek to the **Tambdi Surla Falls** begins just before the entry to the temple.

Birdwatching

The ruby-throated yellow bulbul, Goa's state bird, is just one of the 120 avian species that can be spotted in the sanctuary. Increase your chances by joining a birdwatching tour with **Mrugaya Expeditions** *(mrugayaxpeditions.com; start at ₹3500 half day for 2 people)*. You'll start the day early, at 7am, with naturalist Omkar Dharwadkar, who comes armed with a telescope and binoculars. The first stop is at a small plateau, for a view of fruiting trees and the birds feasting on them. Over the next few hours, you can spot Malabar pied hornbills, black naped orioles, ashy drongos and brown-headed barbets, and endemic birds such as tiny Nilgiri flowerpeckers, Sri Lankan frogmouths, grey-fronted green pigeons and Malabar parakeets.

Erotic Carvings

One of the smaller temples in the sanctuary is the **Brahmani Devi temple**. It stands on the ruins of the old one, which was built with similar basalt rock used for Tambdi Surla. The temple has folk-style reliefs, which now lie on plinths at the base – there are human-animal hybrid figures, women with lamps, peacocks, fighting scenes and, interestingly, a few erotic scenes.

Beyond Salcete

Delve into history with a meal on the side, drink some award-winning whisky and visit a disappearing village.

The talukas of Quepem and Sanguem in the new Kushavati district are often ignored in favour of the more accessible and popular Salcete in South Goa. This is a cleaner, greener and more picturesque part of Goa, with a long history. Quepem town was established by a Portuguese nobleman, Deão Jose Paulo, who not only built an impressive house, but also a church, marketplace and hospital. The taluka itself has a dam dating to colonial times, a temple on a hill and beautiful beaches. In nearby Sanguem, which lies to the east, is the dam that feeds most of South Goa, a village that resurfaces only in summer, and an impressive wildlife sanctuary.

Places

GETTING AROUND

Bus connections in South Goa are quite limited and irregular, especially deep in the hinterlands. Consider renting your own vehicle in Margao, and mapping out routes beforehand as phone connectivity in certain areas may be limited.

Quepem Taluka

TIME FROM SALCETE: **30MIN**

Dine at an 18th-century palace

A half hour drive from Margao leads you to the banks of the Kushavati River and the 18th-century **Palácio do Deão** *(palaciododeao.com; tour incl lunch ₹1500 per person)*. Lovingly restored by Ruben and Celia Vasco da Gama, the house is open for visits and meals *(book in advance: 9823175639)*. The house was originally built by Deão Jose Paulo, a dean of the church and a nobleman credited with founding Quepem.

Ruben conducts a short tour of the space, talking about the restoration work and pointing out some unique features – the chapel where the dean would conduct prayers, a library with rare books and the full-length oyster shell windows (p765) overlooking the verdant garden. After the tour, you can wander about the house and the garden yourself, taking in the many architectural details. Then, head to the verandah for a feast of Indo-Portuguese dishes, eaten against the backdrop of the gushing river. Celia does the cooking – there is no fixed menu, and she uses produce from the garden but expect some stellar Indo-Portuguese dishes like stuffed crabs, pork empanadas, prawn *rissois* (savoury pastry), pumpkin pie and *bebinca* (a layered dessert). Drinks cost extra.

Visit a whisky distillery

Set up in 2008 on the Cuncolim Industrial Estate, **John Distilleries** *(pauljohnwhisky.com; tastings ₹450-1500)* started selling its whiskies in 2015, winning awards and attracting

GOA'S BEST SPICE PLANTATIONS

Tanshikar Spice Farm: This farm (and homestay with cottages) in Neturlim grows a lot of nutmeg, follows organic practices and makes ecofriendly products.

Savoi Plantation: One of Goa's oldest, this betel nut plantation in Ponda also highlights spices and tropical fruits.

Sahakari Spice Farm: Under dense forest cover in Curti, this farm tour includes a look at different spices, coffee and cacao, plus a vegetarian lunch.

Pascoal Spice Village: This spice farm on a riverbank in Ponda has a attached nature retreat and swimming pools, and organises boating activities.

Nandanvan Spice Farm: Besides seeing spices grow at this spice farm, partake in picnics, zip lining and other outdoor activities, and sample local food.

much recognition along the way. The expansive distillery has a visitor centre, which offers two-hour guided tours.

Tours begin with a brief video about the company, and an introduction to the grains and peat. In the distillery, replete with shiny tanks and pot stills, you will learn about the processes involved in whisky production and the importance of the spirit safe. Back in the warehouse, you get to see the cellars, stocked with different casks used to age the whisky. The tour ends at a little makeshift bar, with a whisky tasting. Regular tastings comprise their three flagship whiskies, but you can also opt for the special and limited edition tastings (three more apiece). The reception houses a gift shop where you can purchase whiskies and gin.

Sanguem Taluka

TIME FROM SALCETE: 45MIN

Visit Salaulim Dam

One of the state's most important dams, **Salaulim Dam** *(₹20)*, supplies most of South Goa with water. This artificially constructed earthen reservoir, built in the 1970s, is surrounded by dense forests, and makes for a particularly impressive sight (though photography is not allowed) during the monsoon (June to September), because of its duckbill spillway: when the reservoir fills up, water flows into a semi-circular opening and down a vertical shaft, giving the impression of a sinkhole.

Outside monsoon season, the dam is still worth a visit; you can spot birds like kingfishers and drongos, and spend time picnicking at the botanical garden nearby. You can enter the dam from the bottom, through the gardens and walk up to it, or drive to the entrance from above.

A submerged village

Every monsoon (June to September), the village of **Curdi** gets submerged by the Salaulim Dam. Before the dam was built, the government relocated the people to the surrounding areas. The village resurfaces once a year, usually for a few weeks at the height of summer (April and May). This is when its former residents return to celebrate their old home, with prayers and flowers.

Curdi is a picturesquely desolate place, with a backdrop of water and mountains of greenery. It is accessible by a dirt road and touring the place involves some amount of trekking. You may see the remnants of the Sacred Heart of Jesus Chapel, the Someshwar Temple and its *deepstambha* (lamp pillar), stubs of coconut trees, ruins of houses, and some laterite *tulsi chauras* (podiums containing the tulsi plant). **Soul Travelling** *(soultravelling.in; ₹2599 per person)* offers half-day tours of Curdi that include lunch – you will learn about the rituals performed by the villagers and get to see the atmospheric remains of the village.

Prehistoric petroglyphs

A small hamlet on the banks of the Kushavati River is home to some stunning rock carvings dating back to the Stone Age (around 8000 BCE). The carvings are in **Usgalimal** or

Pansaimol village. Look for the Archaeological Survey of India (ASI) board on the main road, near the **Dandolem Cricket Ground**. Park your vehicle and then follow the well-worn dirt path for about 20 minutes to the site. The carvings are alongside a tranquil river, with the tall trees of a spice farm beyond.

There are over 100 petroglyphs, some extremely well-defined, including a hunting scene, a dancing figure, a bull, a woman giving birth, an animal trap, a peacock and an intricate labyrinth. There is a guard on-site, who, if asked, will point out specific carvings using water squirted from a bottle. There's little shade here, so go either early in the morning or late in the afternoon. The carvings are submerged during the June to September monsoon.

Netravali

TIME FROM SALCETE: **1HR**

Voyage into Netravali Wildlife Sanctuary

Spread over a 211-sq-km area and bordered by Cotigao Wildlife Sanctuary (p789) to the south, **Netravali Wildlife Sanctuary**, comprising decidious forest and grasslands, is the state's largest, with a wealth of reptilian, amphibian and avian life. You can purchase tickets from the Matoni and Dhargini gates *(8.30am-4.30pm, entry ₹100, four-wheelers ₹100)*, which are a 10-minute drive from each other. Established in 1999, the sanctuary is also home to mammals like gaurs, leopards and wild boars, plus the Malabar rose butterfly, which is endemic to the region. There are many (marked) walking paths through the forest too, ranging from 2km to over 12km.

The monsoon season (June to September) is the best time to visit, when the forest is lush and there are mini waterfalls everywhere; trekking may be difficult, so wear appropriate shoes. There are two all-season waterfalls her, **Savri** and **Mainapi**, and both are trekkable; enter from the Matoni gate. Savri is closer and easier to access (half-hour trek from the gate), while the smaller and secluded Mainapi requires a longer trek over steep, uneven terrain (over an hour). There are signboards marking the walking/trekking paths. Also within the sanctuary is the fascinating **Budbudyanchi Tali**, or bubbling lake. There is limited phone connectivity; bring plenty of food and water.

Go strawberry-picking

The hilly areas of Tudav and Verlem, a 12km drive from Netravali, are home to **strawberry farms** *(₹20)*. To get here, you have to enter the Netravali Wildlife Sanctuary (and pay the entrance fee there too). The farms are run by a self-help group, mentored by a farmer from Mahabaleshwar (known for its strawberries). At the farm, there are helpers who will guide you, explaining the process of cultivation and how to pick strawberries. You can buy the berries that you pick. Visit the farms from December to March, when the berries are in season. The farms open at 8am. Go in the morning, before the actual harvest of the strawberries is done. The roads leading to the farms are rough, unpaved and narrow, so drive carefully.

TOP ROCK-CUT CAVES IN GOA

Rivona Caves: Rock-cut laterite caves, believed to have been used by Buddhist monks in the 7th century CE. Around 3km south of Zambaulim village.

Arvalem Caves: Linga (phallic images of Shiva) were discovered in the caves in Bicholim, thought to have been carved in the 6th century CE.

Narve Caves: Two 6th-century CE caves in Bicholim, one of which contains a basalt tiger sculpture, worshipped locally as a *vaghrodev* (tiger god).

Khandepar Caves: Four caves in Ponda, dating to the 9th century CE, with tiered roofs, lamp niches and a lotus medallion carved into the ceiling.

Aquem Cave: This 11th-century CE Pandava cave (cave of Pandavas) is rectangular with simple windows. It is found behind the St Sebastian Church in Margao.

Canacona

WILDLIFE SANCTUARIES | WATERFALLS | BEACHES

The Canacona taluka is the southernmost part of Goa, and doesn't feature on many travel itineraries. But those who do make the trip down there will find scenic, lightly peopled beaches, such as Agonda and Palolem. One of the southernmost beaches is the picturesque Galgibaga – a nesting site for olive ridley turtles and a great place to eat oysters and fresh fish. Canacona has a wealth of flora and fauna, mostly found in Goa's second-largest wildlife reserve: the Cotigao Wildlife Sanctuary. It has well-marked trails for hiking and treetop viewpoints overlooking watering holes. Portuguese history is to be found in the medieval Cabo de Rama fort, which has witnessed many battles. In the hinterlands, you may find yourself charmed by villages that seem timeless. Tourism has arrived relatively recently in this region, and as a result, Canacona still retains much of its natural beauty and tranquillity.

☑ TOP TIP

At the northern end of Palolem Beach there is a small island, **Kankon** (Canacona or Monkey Island), accessible during low tide (be mindful of timings to avoid getting stuck on Kankon). It is ideal for a short trek with great views.

Seaside Aphrodisiac

Eat oysters at Galgibaga Beach

Galgibaga Beach is a beautiful, quiet beach that runs parallel to the Galgibaga River that meets the ocean at the beach's southern edge. It is free of shacks and other structures, and is one of the nesting sites for olive ridley turtles. Another great reason to visit this beach is to eat fresh oysters. Raw oysters

GETTING AROUND

Public transport infrastructure is quite sparse. There are buses to the main towns and villages from the bus stand in Chauri (the main city). It is easiest to use the GoaMiles app to book a taxi to your lodgings and rent a vehicle with their help. Scooters (from ₹450 per day) are ideal for visiting the area's beaches, if you are comfortable taking dirt roads; otherwise, consider renting a car (from ₹1200 per day). The roads are largely empty and make for scenic drives. Connectivity may be limited, so map your route beforehand.

HIGHLIGHTS
1 Palolem Beach

SIGHTS
2 Galgibaga Beach
3 Patnem Beach
4 Sadolxem Bridge
5 Talpona

SLEEPING
6 Bhakti Kutir
7 Casa Galgibaga
8 Casa Jaali
9 Jungle by sturmfrei
10 Kala Bahia
11 Mud Dauber

EATING
12 Cantine Indienne
13 Casa Jaali
14 Santosh Beach Restaurant
15 Surya Beach Cafe
16 The Mill
17 Vidushi's Cow Corner

TRANSPORT
18 Chauri bus stand

BEST FORTS IN GOA

Cabo de Rama Fort: This ruined 17th-century fort in Cola village comprises a chapel of St Anthony, abandoned cannons and great views of the sea.

Reis Magos Fort: Overlooking the Mandovi River, this restored 16th-century fort has some jail cells, a few cannons and a watchtower.

Corjuem Fort: A small 16th-century fort (p771) located in inland Bardez, offering sweeping views of the village.

Mormugao Fort: A simple 17th-century fort with a small cross; it affords views of the harbour in front.

Tiracol Fort: The site of historic Satyagraha marches, this 17th-century fort is now a heritage hotel but is open to visitors interested in seeing its chapel.

GUZEL GASHIGULLINA/SHUTTERSTOCK

Cola Beach

are not commonly eaten in Goa, and do not often feature on restaurant menus. Galgibaga, however, has two popular places known for their raw oysters – **Surya Beach Cafe** and **Santosh Beach Restaurant** *(around ₹450 per plate; both open Nov-Apr)*. The two neighbouring shacks have similar menus: oysters, plus seafood and fish, and some international and Chinese fare. The molluscs are gathered every day from the river nearby, and served in the half-shell with lime juice and Tabasco sauce. Both places can also help organise kayaking and boat trips.

Life's a Beach in Canacona

Seek out the perfect strand of sand

Agonda and **Palolem**, which sit in the middle of Canacona's beach stretch, are also its most popular beaches, known for their calm waters, beach shacks, dining options and nightlife. Many tourists make these beaches their bases when in Canacona. White-sand Agonda is also a turtle-nesting site. Palolem is where you will find the most shacks and water-sport activities. Other popular beaches include **Patnem**, a small beach just south of Palolem, ideal for swimming, and the uncrowded **Talpona**, south of Patnem.

Check out two of this region's most underrated beaches: Cola Beach and Butterfly Beach, just north of Agonda. The access to **Cola Beach** is rough and involves some off-roading – there are 4WDs to take you to the beach and back *(₹500 per person)* from the **parking lot**, or else you can self-drive. Cola Beach is worth the trek because where the river joins the sea you will find a freshwater lagoon; the emerald shade of its waters matches the surrounding greenery.

Butterfly Beach, located in a secluded bay surrounded by large rocks and dense vegetation, boasts clear, shallow waters ideal for swimming. You can get here by boat from Palolem or Agonda *(₹3500-5000 per boat)*. Boat operators will take you on a return trip, allowing around 1½ hours at the beach. Alternatively, park near **Butterfly Cafe** and walk the dirt path down or take a jeep *(₹500 per person)*. Carry food and water if you intend to spend a few hours there.

A River Vantage Point

Stroll a narrow bridge

Just a short ride by car or bike from Palolem Beach, the bright-blue **Sadolxem Bridge** over the Talpona River connects Canacona and Poinguinim. What makes this bridge worth seeing are its surroundings. The river is flanked on both sides by mangrove forests and coconut groves, with boats bobbing on the placid waters. From the bridge, you can see the Talpona River winding its way down from greenery-clad hills.

Where the Wild Things Are

Spot wildlife at the Cotigao Wildlife Sanctuary

Cotigao Wildlife Sanctuary *(₹100)* is a stretch of dense woodland by the Goa–Karnataka border. The second-largest wildlife sanctuary in Goa was set up in 1968 and this 86-sq-km stretch of woodland is home to a number of species of animals and birdlife, as well as some rare old trees. It is worth spending a day or two exploring the place and looking for sloth bears, hump-nosed pit vipers, white-bellied woodpeckers, black leopards, painted bats and Indian pangolins. There are eight hiking trails (ranging in length from 500m to 5km), and cars are allowed to certain points – the reception at the entrance will provide a map and point out the hiking trails and the treetop viewpoint, which look out over the watering holes frequented by the animals. The sanctuary is about a 40-minute drive from the coastal area in Canacona.

MATOLI

Goa's celebrations of the Hindu festival of **Ganesh Chaturthi** have a unique feature, the *matoli*. *Matoli* is a showcase of the bounty of Goan produce, from fruit to medicinal herbs and plants, which are strung up on a wooden frame above the idol of Ganesh. The practice dates back to the time when Goans would forage for plants, herbs and roots, especially during the monsoon season. This foraged produce was incorporated into the festival celebrations too. People used the *matoli* as a way to teach younger generations about ecology and plants (eg which plants were medicinal or poisonous). Every August, *matoli* bazaars pop up across the state – in Margao, Mapusa and Chaudi.

EATING IN CANACONA: OUR PICKS

Cantine Indienne: Canteen-style Palolem spot, serving Tanjore and French food and thalis. Hosts mushroom-related special events. *9.30am-9.30pm Tue-Sun* ₹₹

Vidushi's Cow Corner: A cute Patnem space with a garden, specialising in slow-cooked Indian and Australian food. *9.30am-10pm Tue-Sun* ₹₹

Kala Bahia: A restaurant in Colomb Bay serving global food like paninis, pizzas and schnitzel. Great spot for sunset-watching. *11am-midnight* ₹₹₹

Zest Cafe: Vegetarian and vegan garden cafe by the beach in Agonda, cooking up beautiful plates of ravioli, pancakes and pad thai. *8am-9pm* ₹₹₹

The Mill: Cosy cafe in a restored rice mill, whose vegetarian and vegan menu includes smoothie bowls, wraps and fresh juices. *9am-6pm* ₹₹₹

Kopi Desa: Gastro restaurant on Agonda Beach known for its slow-roasted meats, pastas, fresh bread and herb-infused cocktails. *8am-11pm* ₹₹₹

Casa Jaali: Seaside cafe in Patnem serving cakes, croquettes, rolls, juices and other drinks. Live music some nights. *7am-midnight* ₹₹₹

La Dolce Vita: Agonda Beach restaurant dishing up homemade pastas, wood-fired pizzas and desserts. *noon-4pm & 6-11pm* ₹₹₹

Places We Love to Stay

₹ Budget ₹₹ Midrange ₹₹₹ Top End

Panaji (Panjim) Map p745

Old Quarter Hostel (p750) ₹ Hostel in the heart of Fontainhas with dorms, a private room and an attached coffee space.

Mateus ₹₹ Boutique hotel in a heritage home in Fontainhas with cosy rooms and a shared kitchen.

O Abrigo ₹₹ The compact rooms at this cosy homestay come with attached balconies and garden views. There is an on-site coffee shop.

Hospedaria Abrigo de Botelho ₹₹ Boutique guesthouse in Fontainhas with air-conditioned rooms furnished with antiques. Great breakfast.

WelcomHeritage PanjimInn ₹₹ Three heritage hotels in the Latin Quarter with a rooftop pool, art gallery and luxurious rooms.

Hotel Fidalgo ₹₹ Fancy hotel with mood lighting, deep soaking tubs, massage chairs and a stone fireplace. Other perks include a pool and a 24-hour cafe.

Goa Marriott Resort and Spa ₹₹₹ Luxury beach resort situated on Miramar Beach. Amenities include five restaurants and bars, and a 24-hour fitness centre.

Old Goa

Amrapali House of Grace ₹₹ A pet-friendly hotel in a 100-year-old restored home by the river, with spacious rooms, a private garden and bespoke dining. Close to Old Goa.

Chorão & Divar

The Island Sanctuary ₹₹ Beautifully designed homestay in Chorão. Its two villas and three rooms come with wooden beams, stone flooring and balconies.

Island Pool Villa ₹₹₹ A restored 120-year-old Goan house with a private pool, complimentary breakfast and rooms with four-poster beds and wooden floors.

Dona Paula

Cidade de Goa ₹₹₹ This pet-friendly resort on Vainguinim Beach resembles a Portuguese hamlet. Serves good Goan food, too.

O Pescador by Indy ₹₹₹ Large waterfront resort with outdoor pool, terrace and restaurant specialising in local dishes.

Pernem Map p757

ATS All Terrain Stay ₹ A 30-room hostel with sea-facing rooms, an in-house restaurant and tour desk.

Happy Panda ₹ This traveller-focused hostel by the beach has a cheap bar.

Anahata Retreat ₹₹ Beachfront resort in Ashwem with cottages and villas; also hosts yoga retreats.

Elsewhere ₹₹₹ Four houses and luxury tents overlooking a creek on a private beach in Ashwem.

Veda5 Wellness Retreat & Spa ₹₹₹ Lake-facing cottages close to the beach. Ayurvedic therapies, nutritious food, yoga and meditation are on offer.

Vaayu Kula ₹₹₹ Luxurious, pet-friendly space in Mandrem with beach-facing rooms and an in-house surf school.

Palm Grove Beach Resort ₹₹₹ Luxe bungalows on Ashwem Beach, with in-house restaurant and bar. There is an on-site boutique extension, Little Palm Grove.

Bardez Map p762

The Beachside Hostel ₹ This hostel on Anjuna Beach has dormitory-style accommodation and private rooms.

Funky Monkey ₹ Backpacker hostel close to Anjuna Beach, with a garden, library and yoga space.

Cavala Seaside Resort ₹₹ A resort near Baga Beach with clean rooms, central swimming pool and a bar-restaurant with live music.

Resort Martins Siesta ₹₹ Intimate, boutique resort with 29 rooms, a vegetarian breakfast and an in-house bar.

Siolim House ₹₹₹ Set in a 350-year-old house, this heritage hotel has four-poster beds, antique furniture and private patios.

Ahilya by the Sea ₹₹₹ Gorgeous riverside property in Nerul with two pools, alfresco dining and a martini bar.

Wildflower Villas ₹₹₹ Seven Portuguese-style villas located on a 3-hectare forest estate on a hill in Candolim.

The Park Calangute ₹₹₹ An all-white boutique resort with 30 rooms, two terraces, an outdoor pool and direct access to the beach.

Salcete

Map p774

Longuinhos Beach Resort ₹₹ Popular family beach resort with a pool and rooms to suit a range of budgets.

Heritage Village Resort & Spa Goa ₹₹₹ Beautiful property near Arossim Beach, with three dining options, a central pool and many in-house activities.

Caravela Beach Resort ₹₹₹ Beachside luxury property in Varca with an outdoor pool, spa and golf course.

Beleza by the Beach ₹₹₹ Luxury beach resort nestled between Betalbatim Beach and paddy fields, with three restaurants, a curio shop and concierge services.

Vivenda dos Palhacos ₹₹₹ A century-old renovated house in Majorda, with three distinctive stay areas, garden and pool.

Novotel Goa Dona Sylvia Resort ₹₹₹ Beach resort in Cavelossim with sea-facing rooms and villas, two pools and a poolside bar.

Mollem

Nature's Nest ₹₹ A nature resort located near the sanctuary, comprising mud-lined cottages and a pool fed by a natural spring. Guided tours on offer.

Dudhsagar Plantation ₹₹₹ A farmstay on a 20-hectare organic plantation that has a spice garden and a natural swimming pool. Delicious food available.

Backwoods Camp ₹₹₹ Located by a stream in the heart of the sanctuary, this stone house offers homecooked meals and is run by birders for birders.

Canacona

Map p787

Bhakti Kutir ₹ A health resort near Colomb Beach, organising yoga and meditation classes. The on-site restaurant serves organic food.

Mud Dauber ₹ A homestay and creative space in Sadolxem on the banks of the river, offering a mud bungalow and tent options.

Jungle by sturmfrei ₹ Beachfront hostel in Palolem with dorms and private rooms, a terrace and lounge, bar and workstation.

The Earthen Nest ₹₹ Farmstay in a jungle with mud houses, tents and cottages, a pool and homecooked meals on request.

Casa Galgibaga ₹₹₹ A luxurious lovingly restored Goan villa by the beach, with appealing common spaces and a beautiful garden. Meals cost extra.

Cabo Serai ₹₹₹ A luxury eco-resort consisting of thatched cottages and tents, spread over 5.5 hectares and overlooking the Cabo De Rama Beach.

Casa Jaali ₹₹₹ Tranquil space with Patnem Bay views. Choose between rooms, luxury huts or a beach house with a private garden. Cafe-style food on offer.

Ahilya by the Sea, Bardez

For places to stay in Karnataka, see p836

SAIKO3P/SHUTTERSTOCK

Above: Virupaksha Temple (p826), Hampi Ruins; Right: Stone carving, Ibrahim Rouza mausoleum (p835), Vijayapura

THE MAIN AREAS

BENGALURU (BANGALORE)
Huge city, and a lot of fun. **p796**

MYSURU (MYSORE)
Royal palaces and yoga. **p804**

WESTERN GHATS
Green, coffee-growing hill country. **p814**

KARNATAKA COAST
Golden Sands, great seafood. **p819**

Researched by
Christabel Lobo

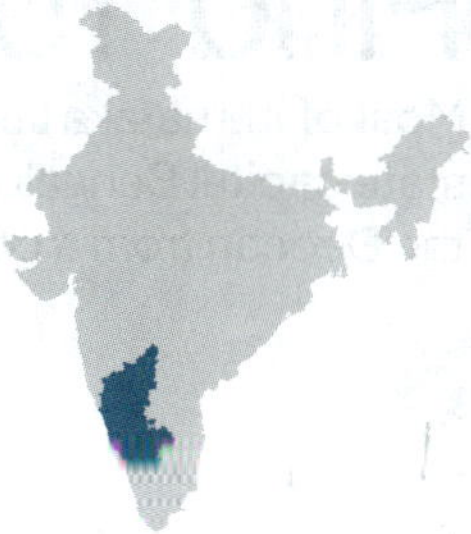

Karnataka

HISTORIC WONDERS, WILD NATURE AND A MODERN MEGACITY

A state of huge variety, from metropolitan buzz to long-ruined cities, dreamy beaches to luxuriant hill country – much of it undeservedly little-known to outsiders.

The IT boom town Bengaluru (Bangalore, the yoga and former royal capital Mysuru (Mysore), the backpacker havens of hauntingly ruined Hampi and beach-bliss Gokarna – these Karnataka highlights are justly celebrated and well-visited destinations. But there's a lot more to this large state that too many visitors hurry through en route between Goa and Kerala or Mumbai (Bombay) and Hyderabad. Much of Karnataka lies on the Deccan, India's central plateau, where successive historic kingdoms shaped the land through exceptional architectural and artistic legacies, including the Chalukyas, the Hoysalas, the Hampi-based Vijayanagar empire and its Bijapur sultanate rivals, and the Mysore Kingdom. Between the Deccan and Karnataka's steamy, beach-fringed coastal strip on the Arabian Sea lie the Western Ghats, verdant hills rising to 1500m or 2000m that catch a lot of monsoon rainfall and grow most of India's best coffee. Drier forests on the ghats' inland side are home to parks and reserves with some of India's richest concentrations of wildlife: tigers, leopards, elephants and sloth bears among them. Culturally, Karnataka reflects the multiple historical influences of its crossroads location: a large majority of the population is Hindu but there are also significant Muslim, Christian and Jain communities. The cuisine is just as varied: while South Indian vegetarian cuisine is popular in the south, the north leans more towards meat, and the coast is deservedly famed for its seafood.

BALAJISRINIVASAN/SHUTTERSTOCK ©

HAMPI
Epic ruined city, psychedelic sunsets. **p823**

BADAMI & BEYOND
Stunningly sculpted cave temples. **p830**

VIJAYAPURA (BIJAPUR)
Magnificent Islamic monuments. **p833**

Find Your Way

Most of Karnataka lies on India's central plateau, the Deccan, with the state capital Bengaluru in the southeast. The Western Ghats separate the Deccan from a coastal strip along the Arabian Sea.

BUS & CAR

The KSRTC state-government bus company runs a comprehensive service. Private bus companies also serve some routes: check *redbus.in*. Renting a car with driver is the most convenient transport; expect to pay around ₹4000 per day.

TRAIN

Trains may be quicker or slower than buses, though often less frequent. See *indianrail.gov.in* for timetables. Online booking is often problematic for foreigners. Travel agencies can help or you can make advance reservations in person at stations.

Badami & Beyond, p830
Wonders of early Hindu temple architecture and sculpture, some built, some carved out of cliffside caves.

Hampi, p823
Legendary ruined city in a surreal boulder-strewn landscape with a big budget traveller scene.

Vijayapura (Bijapur), p833
The magnificent mosques, mausoleums and palaces of the Adil Shahi dynasty.

Mysuru (Mysore), p804
Former royal capital, a well-planned city of palaces and world centre for ashtanga vinyasa yoga.

Bengaluru (Bangalore), p796
IT hub, India's fourth-biggest city: huge beer bars, cool cafes, green parks, terrible traffic, diverse neighbourhoods and great restaurants.

FABIO LAMANNA/SHUTTERSTOCK

Ibrahim Rouza mausoleum (p835), Vijayapura

Plan Your Time

Sojourns at Hampi and/or Gokarna and yoga in Mysuru are the main draws for many. Then there are wildlife safaris, hill-country delights, monumental heritage and big-city life.

Just a Few Days

- Karnataka is a big state; with just a few days you can't really cover more than two places. Depending on your interests, pick any pair from **Bengaluru** (p796; metropolitan buzz), **Mysuru** (p804; palaces and yoga), **Nagarhole Tiger Reserve** (p812; wildlife), **Gokarna** (p822; beaches) and **Hampi** (p823; surreal ruins and traveller scene).

Three Weeks or More

- Experience the progressive capital **Bengaluru** (p796) before heading to Mysuru's magnificent **palace** (p808) then **Kodagu** (p814) and **Chikkamagaluru** (p817) for a taste of hill country. Follow **Gokarna** (p822) beach time with the diverse heritage of **Badami** (p830) and **Hampi** (p823). If you have time, add **Vijayapura** (p833) for monumental Islamic architecture.

SEASONAL HIGHLIGHTS

OCTOBER–JANUARY

Dry and moderate temperatures. Mysuru's mega-festival **Dasara** (Dussehra) is in October.

FEBRUARY–APRIL

Still dry but getting hot. These are the best months for wildlife sightings in parks and reserves.

APRIL & MAY

Head to the hills – regions like Kodagu stay cooler, with misty mornings, forest walks and the first signs of the coming rains.

JUNE–OCTOBER

From late May or June into October. Deluges on the coast and in the Western Ghats; less rainfall on the Deccan.

Bengaluru (Bangalore)

CITY LIFE | EATING & DRINKING | PARKS & LAKES

GETTING AROUND

An efficient modern metro system *(english.bmrc.co.in)* serves two of the three major train stations (KSR Bengaluru and Yesvantpur Junction), the main Kempegowda (Majestic) Bus Station, MG Road, Cubbon Park and Indiranagar. Bengaluru has thousands of Uber and Ola vehicles, autorickshaws and cars. From the airport (Kempegowda International Airport), an Uber to the city centre costs around ₹1200. The cheaper VayuVajra airport bus service *(mybmtc.karnataka.gov.in)* also runs frequently to many parts of the city.

Bengaluru is bright lights, festive beer bars, shiny shopping centres and lots of well-salaried young professionals, as well as green parks, old-fashioned markets and simple vegetarian eateries. Its rapid growth has engendered water supply problems and terrible traffic, but it's a lot of fun and its climate is delightful.

Bengaluru began life in 1537 as a trading settlement. The British established their HQ for the Mysore Kingdom here in the 19th century. The Indian Institute of Science was founded here in 1909 and pioneering educational, research and industrial ventures followed in succeeding decades. Texas Instruments (1985) was the first multinational to arrive, and by the turn of the 21st century the city was already 'India's Silicon Valley'.

Bengaluru has around 15 million people in its agglomeration of neighbourhoods, and competes with Mumbai for India's highest per-capita income. Many people still use its anglicised name Bangalore.

EATING IN BENGALURU: CITY CENTRE & INDIRANAGAR

Burma Burma: Vegetarian Burmese fare in Indiranagar. Go for the mango salad, a curry or rice dish, and *tagu pyian* dessert. *noon-3pm & 6.30-10.30pm* ₹₹₹

Lupa: Small plates, fresh gelato and an extensive wine list at this hotspot offering garden seating and an Italian-inspired dining room. *noon-3.30pm & 7pm-1am* ₹₹₹

Brik Oven: Bengaluru pizzeria chain specialising in thin-crust, wood-fired pizzas with classic and Indian toppings, plus calzones and garlic bread. *8am-11pm* ₹₹

Phobidden Fruit Vietnamese Kitchen: Draws regulars for its hearty pho and fresh spring rolls. *noon-3.30pm & 7-11pm Mon-Thu, noon-11.30pm Fri-Sun* ₹₹

DEBAJIT89/SHUTTERSTOCK

Flower display, Lalbagh

A Walk in the Park

Stroll Cubbon Park and Lalbagh

Bengaluru is called the Garden City with good reason: a wander in some of its beautiful green spaces is not to be missed. In **Cubbon Park**, walking paths are strung between grassy lawns, ponds and flowering trees. The colonial-era **State Central Library** and **Attara Kacheri** (Karnataka High Court), and a trio of museums, are within the park along with the massive 1950s neo-Dravidian-style **Vidhana Soudha**, Karnataka's state parliament.

A couple of kilometres south is delightful **Lalbagh** (*adult/child ₹50/20*), a 1-sq-km botanical park laid out by Hyder Ali in the 18th century. Stroll among beautiful and impressive trees (don't miss the giant silk-cotton tree), a big lake and a century-old glasshouse, and enjoy the views from a 16th-century watchtower. Near the summit, an exposed outcrop of one of the oldest rocks on Earth, the Peninsular Gneiss is where locals come to watch the sunset.

GARDEN CITY

Poornima, author, storyteller, historian and founder of Un-hurried (*unhurried.in*)

You'll be surprised at the range of trees lining Bengaluru's streets or leaning out of compounds. They can range from a simple Indian sampige *(Magnolia champaca)* to the pink South American Tabebuias that Bengaluru is famous for. Visit Lalbagh, Cubbon Park or **Bugle Rock Park** to discover the city's trees.

Birdwatching around the many lakes is another great pastime. Visit **Hebbal** or **Lalbagh** Lakes or lesser-known **Puttenahalli** or **Jakkur Lakes** and spot birds like heron, barbet, pelican and many more. (Check out *bngbirds.com* for a weekend walk.) Trek up the Nandi or Savandurga Hills for a fantastic window to nature and a welcome break from city traffic!

EATING IN BENGALURU: BEST FOR SOUTH INDIAN

Food Street: Popular vegetarian food stalls in Basavanagudi, doling out dosas, *parathas*, *kathi* rolls, pulao, *chhole bhature* and taco-waffle-ice-cream! *5-11pm* ₹

Mavalli Tiffin Rooms (MTR): Legendary name in South Indian comfort food, offering a fantastic vegetarian lunch (₹340). *6.30-11am, 12.30-2.45pm & 3.30-8.30pm Tue-Sun* ₹

Rameshwaram Cafe: Line up with the Indiranagar evening crowds for dosas, *idlis* or rice-like *puliogare*, then eat standing on the pavement. *6.30am-1am* ₹

Bengaluru Oota Company: Thoughtful introduction to Karnataka cuisine; thalis and regional dishes. Reservations required. *12.30-3pm & 7-10.30pm* ₹₹₹

BENGALURU (BANGALORE)
Yesvantpur Junction Train Station (4.4km)
Benji's Coffee (700m)
Blue Tokai (800m); Hebbal Lake (5.4km); Jakkur Lake (11km); Kempegowda International Airport (30km)
0 1 km
0 0.5 miles
Rameshwaram Cafe (3km)
Palace Rd
MV Jayaram Rd
Thimmaiah Rd
Subedar Chatram (SC) Rd
Sampige Rd
NEHRU NAGAR
Sankey Rd
Palace Rd
VASANTH NAGAR
Millers Rd
Bengaluru Golf Course
National Gallery of Modern Art
Kumarakrupa Rd
Cunningham Rd
Ali Asker Rd
Raj Bhavan Rd
Queen's Rd
Racecourse Rd
Infantry Rd
Racecourse
Loop Rd
Sampige Rd
Seshadri Rd
GANDHI NAGAR (MAJESTIC)
Palace Rd
Cubbon Rd
Dr Ambedkar Rd
Cubbon Park
Children's Park
Vidhana Soudha
Seshadri Rd
Dhanavanthri Rd
City Train Station
Museum of Art & Photography
Kempegowda
Kempegowda Circle
Kempegowda (KG) Rd
Sir M Visveshwarya
Post Office Rd
Cubbon Park
District Office Rd
PETE
Pete
Chickpet Rd
Chickpet
Cubbon Park
See Enlargement
Vittal Mallya Rd (Grant Rd)
Kanteerava Stadium
Kasturba Rd
Cottonpet Main Rd
CHICKPET
Avenue Rd
TCM Royan Rd
Nagarthpet Rd
Fort Rd (RajaramMohanroy Rd)
Kasturba Rd
Lavelle Rd
City Market
Mysore Rd
Silver Jubilee (SJ) Park Rd
Sri Narasimharaja Rd
Mission Rd
KR Market
Tippu Sultan Palace Rd
Arumugam Madaliar Rd
Jayachamaraja Wodeyar Rd
Lalbagh Rd
1st Cross Rd
4th Cross Rd
SHANTI NAGAR
Tipu Sultan's Summer Palace
5th Main Rd
Lalbagh Fort Rd
Siddaiah Rd
Kengal Hanumanthiah Rd
Bull Temple Rd
Shankarmutt Rd
1st Cross Rd
Krishnarajendra Rd
Rashtreeya Vidyalaya Rd
Hosur Main Rd
Diagonal Rd
Lalbagh Botanical Gardens
Mari Gowda Rd
WILSON GARDEN
Katte Kulture (3.2km); Perch (6.5km)
Bugle Rock Park (600m)
Vani Vilas Rd
Puttenahalli Lake (7km)
Lalbagh Tank
1
2
3
4
5
6
7
8
9
10
11
13
14
15
16
17
18
21
23
24
25
30
35
40
43
49
54
55

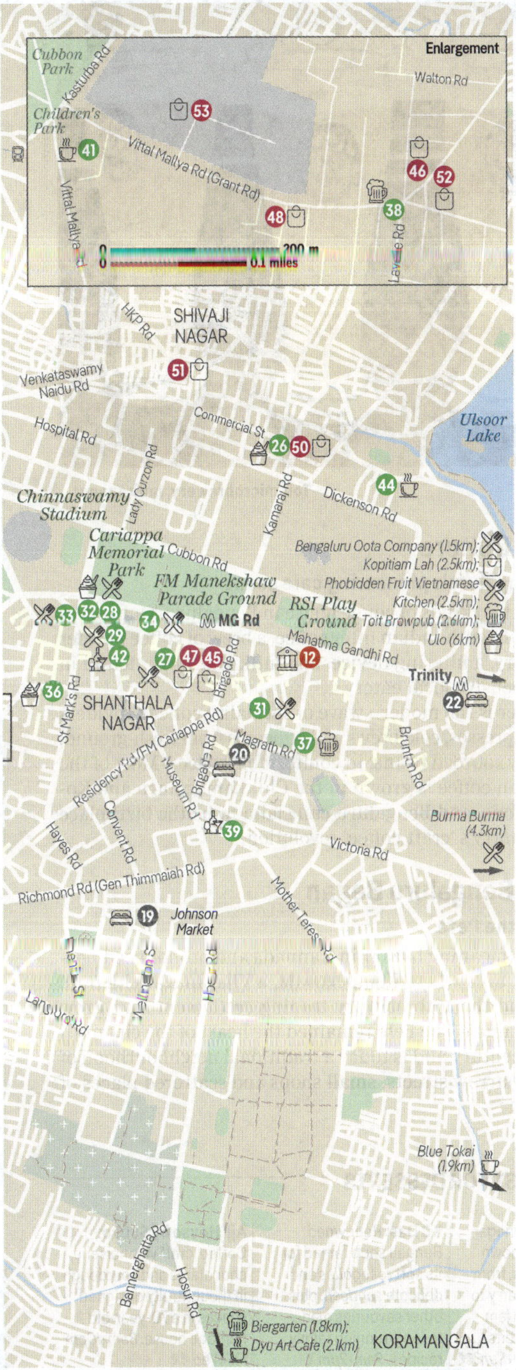

HIGHLIGHTS

1 Cubbon Park
2 Lalbagh Botanical Gardens
3 Museum of Art & Photography
4 National Gallery of Modern Art
5 Pete
6 Tipu Sultan's Summer Palace

SIGHTS

7 Attara Kacheri
8 Bangalore Fort
9 Bangalore Palace
10 Government Museum
11 Karnataka Chitrakala Parishath
12 Kempegowda Museum
13 Mythic Society
14 Sri Anjaneya Swami Temple
15 Sri Ranganathaswamy Temple
16 State Central Library
17 Venkatappa Art Gallery
18 Vidhana Soudha

SLEEPING

19 Casa Cottage
20 Grand Magrath
21 Locul Uptown
22 Taj MG Road
23 Taj West End
24 The Fern Residency

EATING

25 Ajji House by Subko
26 Anand Sweets
27 Brik Oven
28 Church Street Social
29 Empire
30 Food Street
31 Karavalli
32 KC Das
33 Koshy's Bar & Restaurant
34 Lupa
35 Mavalli Tiffin Rooms
36 Smoor Signature Lounge

DRINKING & NIGHTLIFE

37 Arbor Brewing Company
38 Biere Club
39 Bob's Bar
40 Brahmin's Coffee Bar
41 Café Coffee Day
42 Dali & Gala
43 Karnataka Coffee Board Coffee Shop
44 Maverick & Farmer Coffee
see 25 Midle Room
see 25 Wine in Progress:

SHOPPING

45 Blossom Book House
46 Forest Essentials
47 Gangarams Book Bureau
48 Ganjam Jewellers
49 Krishnarajendra Market
50 Mysore Saree Udyog
51 Russell Market
52 San-Cha Tea Boutique
53 UB City

TRANSPORT

54 Kempegowda Bus Stand
55 KSR Bengaluru Train Station

BABA BUDAN

The story goes that Baba Budan, a Sufi from the Chikkamagaluru area, took a liking to coffee in the Yemeni port of Mocha on his way home from a pilgrimage to Mecca in 1670. Since exports of unroasted beans from Mocha were banned, he smuggled seven of them out in his beard, and planted them in his courtyard back home. They thrived and thus India discovered coffee. Baba Budan's revered dargah (burial place; p818) lies in a cave in the hills north of Chikkamagaluru, where the nearby peak Bababudangiri (p818) and its entire range (Bababudangiri Hills) are named after him.

TOP TIP

One-, three- and five-day passes for the metro system, sold at station ticket offices, are convenient. They may or may not save you a few rupees but they do save you having to queue up for a ticket.

MUDACOM/SHUTTERSTOCK

Toit microbrewery, Indiranagar

Coffee Culture

Enjoy Bengaluru's pioneering cafe scene

There are two kinds of coffee house in Bengaluru. One serves traditional South Indian filter coffee, a brew of coffee powder and chicory, a filtering device, and milk and sugar, found in any inexpensive local eatery.

The other is the modern wave of speciality coffee providers serving espressos, cold brews and affogatos from fresh-ground, selectively sourced beans, in comfortable spaces. Most of the best Indian coffee is grown in the Chikkamagaluru and Kodagu regions, and Bengaluru can claim to be the birthplace of the country's 'craft coffee' revolution.

Where Bengaluru Began

A tour of the Pete

The **Pete** (meaning bazaar in Kannada and pronounced *peh-teh*) is the area where Kempegowda, a Vijayanagar chieftan, established the 16th-century trading settlement that grew into Bengaluru. The Pete remained the heart of the city until the 20th century and is today a traditional neighbourhood of crowded narrow streets, small shops and scattered places of

EATING IN BENGALURU: BEST FOR DESSERTS

Anand Sweets: Reliable institution for Indian sweets – especially Mysore *pak*, *badam halwa* and *kaju katli*. Multiple locations. *8.30am-10.30pm* ₹

Ulo: Playful Indiranagar ice-cream shop known for quirky flavours, from sweet corn-blueberry to Edam cheese with jam swirls and praline bits. *11am-midnight Tue-Sun* ₹₹

KC Das: Renowned Bengali shop famed for its soft *rosogollas* and delicate *sandesh*, plus other savouries made to long-running family recipes. *9am-9pm* ₹

Ajji House by Subko: Coffee, craft viennoiserie, chocolates and sourdough in thoughtfully designed spaces in a 70-year-old heritage house. *8am-10pm Fri-Wed* ₹₹

worship. The ideal way to experience it is on a walking tour such as those offered by **Unhurried** (*unhurried.in; from ₹4500*).

The Pete's two main streets, meeting at a focal crossroads, are Avenue Road (formerly Doddapete, Big Pete) and Old Taluk Cutchery (OTC) Rd (formerly Chikpete, Small Pete).

Wandering south down Avenue Rd from the colourful **Sri Anjaneya Swami Temple**, join locals for South Indian filter coffee at the **Karnataka Coffee Board Coffee Shop** (a converted bus). The next stretch of Avenue Rd is strung with shops specialising in stationery, press and textbooks. The fourth street on the right leads to the atmospheric, 16th-century **Sri Ranganathaswamy Temple**, dedicated to a form of Vishnu.

Back on Avenue Rd, silk and other clothing shops start to take over with 250m of OTC Rd dedicated almost entirely to saris. **Krishnarajendra Market**, off the south end of Avenue Rd, is awash with bright piles of fruit, vegetables, spices and flowers. Inaugurated in 1927, the market now also contains a four-storey 1990s building in the middle. Head upstairs to look down on a yard full of yellow, orange and white garlands wound into rings, which make a famous Bengaluru photo op.

Beer City

Sink a pint in a macro microbrewery

Bengaluru's love of beer goes back to colonial times. United Breweries, producer of India's most popular beer brand Kingfisher, was founded here in 1915.

But today it's all about microbreweries. Bengaluru's large middle class has taken to fresh-brewed craft beer so avidly that there are now approaching 100 brewpubs. Some are vast multi-level cathedrals of beer, seating several hundred drinkers. Others are smaller and more intimate, with a focus on experimental brewing and conversation.

Wheat beers are among the most popular brews, but there are plenty of IPAs, pilsners and, lately, stouts on offer too. Try the flights (samplers of six or eight beers) and the many seasonal and novelty beers – flavours of fruits, herbs, spices, caramel – dreamed up by innovative brewers.

Microbreweries also serve all kinds of other drinks and often have great food offerings. Some, like **Toit** in Indiranagar, even open for breakfast.

BENGALURU NEIGHBOURHOODS

The main downtown axis is **Mahatma Gandhi (MG) Road**. The city's original heart, the **Pete**, lies 2km to 5km southwest of here. South, north and east of MG Rd are areas that comprised the **Cantonment** (British garrison) in colonial times, including **Ashok Nagar** (south), **Shivaji Nagar** (north) and the restaurant and nightlife hub **Indiranagar** (east). **Koramangala**, around 4km southwest of Indiranagar, is another nocturnal hotspot. **Basavanagudi**, 3km south of the Pete, and **Malleswaram** (3km north) are neighbourhoods of wide, straight streets, laid out with improved sanitation after a plague epidemic in 1898. The major IT hubs are mostly 15km to 20km from the centre in areas like **Electronic City** (south) and **Whitefield** (east).

DRINKING IN BENGALURU: BEST FOR BEER

Biere Club: Bengaluru's original microbrewery, still one of the best with three human-scale floors and several in-house craft beers. *11am-11pm, to 1am Fri-Sat*

Arbor Brewing Company: Busy beer hall with gleaming tanks brewing a range of on-tap beers; good food and non-boom-boom music. *noon-1am*

Koshy's: Roll back the years with pints of Kingfisher and 'short eats' of baked beans on toast at this venerable establishment. *9am-10.30pm*

Toit: Offering a great pub atmosphere, this microbrewery has been going strong since 2010. Its hoppy-but-not-overly-so India Pale Ale is beer perfection! *8.30am-1am*

KARNATAKA FOOD

Vidya, avid cook, food blogger and Bengaluru food walk leader. *vidyascooking.blogspot.com*
Karnataka is a cultural melting pot, with great regional food variety. Across the state, rice, legumes and millets such as sorghum and ragi remain central to everyday cooking. North Karnataka is known for hearty millet-based dishes paired with spicy vegetable curries and chutneys, while South Karnataka is famous for flavoured rice preparations like *bisibelebath* and *vangi bath*, alongside soft *idlis* and dosas. The coast has varied fish curries. Fusion cuisines from Bengaluru's British and Muslim history gave us *paya* soup (with lamb trotters) and *botti saaru* (mutton soup).

Pre-British Power Centre

Fort remains and a sultan's palace

The Wadiyar kings of Mysore built a mud fort immediately south of the Pete in the 17th century, and the 18th-century rulers Hyder Ali and Tipu Sultan strengthened this into a stout stone-walled fort. All that remains of the fortifications is part of the northern **Delhi Gate**. A plaque on the southeast gate's corner marks the spot where British forces breached the walls in 1791. More aesthetic is Tipu Sultan's **Summer Palace** *(₹250)*, an elegant two-storey structure in teak and stone, with floral murals and fluted columns supporting handsome shell-form arches and a small museum.

Artistic Touch

Bengaluru's top-notch galleries

Don't miss the central **Museum of Art & Photography** (MAP; *map-india.org; adult/child ₹100/30*), a five-floor contemporary space with classic, folk and modern Indian art exhibitions. Across the road, the **Venkatappa Art Gallery** *(₹50)* showcases the work of Mysore royal court painter K Venkatappa, a key figure whose career bridged traditional Indian aesthetics and early modernism. The gallery is also home to works by KK Hebbar and CP Rajaram, whose wood sculptures draw on natural forms.

The large **National Gallery of Modern Art** *(ngmaindia.gov.in; ₹500)* has a top-rank collection of Indian art from early miniatures through colonial-era landscapes to the 20th-century Bengal School. Guided walks *(4pm Wed & Sat)* are a great way to discover the highlights. The **Karnataka Chitrakala Parishath** *(chitrakalaparishath.org; free)* features striking Mysore traditional art, Adivasi art and Himalayan mountainscapes by Nikolai Roerich.

Most of Bengaluru's major galleries and museums are closed on Mondays.

EATING & DRINKING IN BENGALURU: BEST COFFEE SHOPS

Katte Kulture: Indian-grown beans, manual brews and excellent espresso, along with an inventive selection of coffee-infused mocktails. *8am-10pm* ₹₹

Perch: Popular Delhi import pairing specialty coffee and wine with seasonal European plates in a relaxed all-day cafe-bar setting. *10.30am-10pm* ₹₹

Benji's Coffee: Serious coffee spot offering manual brews from carefully sourced beans, attracting regulars here for the house blend. *8am-8pm* ₹

Maverick & Farmer: Roaster-cafe focused on Kodagu-grown coffee beans, serving espresso and filter brews with light bites in a relaxed alfresco setting. *8.30am-11pm* ₹₹

Kopitiam Lah: Inspired by Malaysia's *kopitiams* (coffee houses) serving classic *kopi* made from caramelised Robusta beans with condensed milk. *8.30am-10.30pm* ₹₹

Blue Tokai: This chain's 20th Main Rd branch has a friendly buzz along with fresh-roasted brews, salads, sandwiches and breakfasts. *8am-11pm* ₹₹

Dyu Art Cafe: The coffee aroma will draw you into this Koramangala cafe-gallery with cakes and other eats in a peaceful courtyard. *10am-10.30pm* ₹

Brahmin's Coffee Bar: Renowned Basavanagudi cafe, busy with people stopping for coffee and South Indian snacks. *6am-noon & 3-7pm Mon-Sat* ₹

Museum of Art & Photography

Eating Like a Local

Decoding Bengaluru's everyday eateries

In Bengaluru, restaurants are often called hotels, a quirk of local language that quickly becomes one of the city's great food shortcuts. These are organised less by decor than by cuisine, and learning to read the name on the signboard is often the key to getting well fed.

Cheap South Indian breakfast spots are known as *darshinis* (short for *upahara darshini*). Here you pay first, eat standing at small tables, and move on. Expect *idlis*, dosas, *vadas* (doughnut-shaped deep-fried lentil savouries) and strong filter coffee, served from early morning through evening tiffin time.

Kamat hotels specialise in North Karnataka vegetarian cooking, where dishes tend to be heartier and less coconut-forward than in the south. Look out for classics such as *obbattu*, a sweet chickpea-filled flatbread, or screw-pine *idlis*, whose distinctive aroma comes from being steamed in fragrant pandanus leaves. *Karavali* hotels focus on coastal cuisine, pairing neer dosas with curries such as coconut-rich chicken *kori gassi*, tangy mango fish curry or crisp banana-leaf fish fry. At *Military hotels* meat takes centre stage, in rice-based dishes and slow-cooked soups like mutton biryani and lamb trotter *paya*, often eaten with dosa for breakfast.

BENGALURU'S TOP SHOPPING

Vittal Mallya & Lavelle Roads: Bengaluru's glitziest mall UB City, plus Ganjam Jewellers, Forest Essentials (high-end natural cosmetics) and San-Cha Tea Boutique.

Commercial Street: Devoted chiefly to saris and other textiles: Mysore Saree Udyog is one of Bengaluru's busiest shops.

Sampige Road: Malleswaram's main shopping street, packed with sari stores and sweet shops, plus lively street shopping for bangles and essentials.

Church Street: Bookshop central: Gangarams and the westernmost of three Blossoms have the biggest selections.

Krishnarajendra Market (City Market): A colourful morning scene of flowers, fruit, vegies and spices.

DRINKING IN BENGALURU: OUR PICKS

Middle Room: Intimate bar inspired by Japanese jazz *kissas*, where cocktails shine, and small plates are designed to pair with drinks. *6-11.30pm*

Dali & Gala: Stylish cocktail bar inspired by surrealism; creative drinks with theatrical presentation, plush interiors and a sociable crowd. *5pm-1am*

Wine in Progress: Convivial wine bar pouring wines by the glass, with friendly staff, small bites and welcome conversation. *5-11pm Tue-Sun*

Bob's Bar: Unpretentious Koramangala kerbside pub with Kingfisher, Budweiser and Hoegaarden on tap and people just enjoying a social drink. *11.30am-1am*

Mysuru (Mysore)

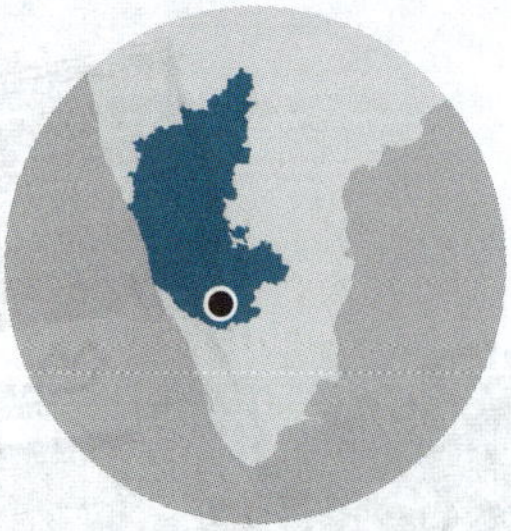

ROYAL PALACES | YOGA | TEMPLES

GETTING AROUND

It's easy and cheap to get around by Uber and Ola autorickshaws. Inter-city buses arrive and depart from the Central (KSRTC) Bus Stand, 1.5km north of Mysuru Palace. The train station, Mysuru Junction, is 2km northwest of the palace. Mysuru Airport, 10km south, has flights to/from Chennai and Hyderabad only. State-run Flybus travels direct between Bengaluru Airport and Mysuru's Central (KSRTC) Bus Stand (3½ hours) almost hourly round the clock.

TOP TIP

Pools at several Mysuru hotels are open to non-guests for a few hundred rupees. Particularly inviting is the 18m oval pool in the Southern Star's (p836) tropical garden.

Former capital of one of colonial India's most important princely states, Mysuru is famed for the exceptionally splendid palace of its erstwhile ruling dynasty, the Wadiyars. It is a city of palaces: seven in all, at least five of them visitable, and a good deal more monumental architecture. One of the outer neighbourhoods, Gokulam, is the home of ashtanga vinyasa yoga, which draws thousands of students from around the world annually. Something of a cultural capital, Mysuru stages one of India's grandest traditional festivals in its 10-day Dasara (Dussehra) celebrations in September/October. Tourism and IT are backbones of its economy and it's famed for silk (Mysore saris are especially fine and expensive because of the gold-and-silver *zari* thread embroidered in them) and sandalwood-oil products (chiefly soap). Officially renamed in 2014, but still widely known by its old name, it has a population of around one million.

Beyond the Palace

Markets, museums and more palaces

The central area around the palace is a planned zone of wide straight streets, large roundabouts around Wadiyar statues, and monumental architecture. At **Devaraja Market**, traders sell colourful traditional items such as garlands, piles of *kumkum* (coloured powder used for bindi dots), bangles and spices – and plenty of fruit, veg and herbs. Bustling bazaar streets extend to the west, south and east. A few minutes' walk south, the large and impressive **Jaganmohan Palace** *(₹100; closed Mon)* was built for the Wadiyars in 1861 and now houses a huge collection of Indian art, including a room devoted to the beloved 19th-century Keralan artist Raja Ravi Varma. Other main colonial-era landmarks are **Government House**, the former British Residency, in large grounds open to the public; and, 5km east of the centre, the enormous 1920s **Lalitha Mahal Palace**, built as a local pied-à-terre for the British governors-general – now a hotel with restaurant and bar open to the public.

HIGHLIGHTS
1 Devaraja Market
2 Jaganmohan Palace
3 Mysuru Palace

SIGHTS
4 Doddakere Maidana
5 Government House
6 Heritage House
7 Kukkarahalli Lake

ACTIVITIES
8 Ashtanga Saadhana
9 K Pattabhi Jois Ashtanga Yoga Shala
10 Mysore Mandala
11 Yoga Bharata

SLEEPING
12 Anokhi Garden
13 Laika Heritage Stay
14 Ranee Bi Roambay
15 Royal Orchid Metropole
16 Southern Star

EATING
see 12 Anokhi Garden Cafe
17 Durrah
18 Depth 'n' Green
19 Dosa Palace
20 Organic Cafe & Bakehouse
21 Sahib's Brick Oven Pizza
22 Santosha Cafe
23 Tegu Mess
24 Vinayaka Mylari

DRINKING & NIGHTLIFE
25 Leaven
26 Minimal Coffee Roasters
27 Ritual Coffee House
28 Sapa
29 SIHI, Patisserie and Boulangerie
30 West End Coffee Company
31 White Teak Coffee Roasters

TRANSPORT
32 Central (KSRTC) Bus Stand
33 Mysuru Junction Station

EATING IN MYSURU: BEST FOR SOUTH INDIAN

Dosa Palace: Busy neighbourhood spot serving crisp dosas, *idlis* and strong filter coffee. The *benne dosa* with ghee or butter is a local favourite. *7am-10pm* ₹

Depth 'n' Green: Popular vegetarian cafe pairing South Indian staples with bowls, sourdough and smoothies. Cosy setting with vegan options. *9am-9pm* ₹

Santosha Cafe: Vegetarian plates, millet dishes and pancakes served in a calm Gokulam space. The lunch thali is especially popular. *8am-8.30pm* ₹

Vinayaka Mylari: Legendary since 1938, famed for soft, buttery Mylari dosas flipped to order. Quick turnover. *6.30am-10pm* ₹

EATING WELL IN MYSURU

Dina Weber, chef and founder of SAPA, on what food visitors often miss when in town. *sapabakery.com*

Many visitors assume Mysuru is entirely vegetarian, but that's a misconception. Meat has always been part of the city's food culture. Dishes like liver fry, brain masala or Kodava-style pork are often served in small non-vegetarian messes like **Tegu** or neighbourhood places like **Bopy's**, so you have to know they exist.

If you want to eat well in Mysuru, don't overthink it. Start with simple tiffin rooms in the mandis (markets), share dishes and follow what locals are ordering. The most meaningful food here, like *patholi*, steamed rice dumplings wrapped in turmeric leaves, is actually cooked at home during festival season.

PRIYA DARSHAN/SHUTTERSTOCK

International Yoga Day, Mysuru Palace (p808)

For greenery and fresh air, join the Mysoreans on the popular 3.5km circuit round tree-girt **Kukkarahalli Lake**, 3km west of Mysuru Palace. Just five minutes away is **Heritage House** *(instagram.com/heritage_house_mysuru)*, a restored centuries-old building that now serves as a vital community space for talks, art exhibits, music nights and workshops. The **Jagannatha Centre for Art and Culture** (JCAC; *jcacmysuru.com*), opened in 2025, hosts exhibitions, performances and hands-on workshops ranging from visual arts and craft practices to music and theatre throughout the year.

Yoga Epicentre

The home of ashtanga vinyasa

Mysuru is a world-famous yoga centre, primarily for ashtanga vinyasa yoga, which was developed here in the mid-20th century, and later popularised in the West by K Pattabhi Jois. Ashtanga vinyasa is a demanding form of postural yoga involving a sequence of *asanas* (postures) linked by smooth transitions with synchronised breathing. Learning and practising it requires very strong commitment: courses here are often for a minimum of one month or longer. You will normally attend group sessions for 1½ or two hours six mornings a week. Class sizes depend on the school and normally range from around

EATING & DRINKING IN MYSURU: OUR PICKS

Anokhi Garden: Gokulam cafe preparing omelettes, sandwiches, smoothie bowls and pancakes. Also a store with upcycled clothing. *8am-2pm* ₹

Organic Cafe & Bakehouse: Casual vegetarian-only cafe and bakery offering excellent bread, soups and filling South Indian lunch thalis. *8.30am-9.30pm* ₹₹

Burrah: Contemporary Indian grill serving smoky kebabs, Kolkata-inspired *kathi* rolls and tandoor dishes. The stylish dining room fills up quickly on weekends. *5-10.30pm* ₹

Sahib's Brick Oven Pizza: Neapolitan-style pizzeria serving excellent wood-fired pizzas with crisp bases, generous toppings and playful flavours. *1-10.30pm Thu-Wed* ₹₹₹

15 to 30 students, though the more established ones can have as many as 70 students in each session. Courses are offered for yoga teacher training as well as practice; for the most popular you should register online months ahead. Hatha yoga and various specialised disciplines are also on offer at several schools, and in recent years a growing number of short-term courses and drop-in classes have become available.

Many schools cluster in the residential Gokulam neighbourhood, about 5km northwest of the city centre. You can get tips about accommodation and much more through social media such as the **Ashtanga Community in Mysore** *(facebook.com/groups/166848013363212)* and **Mysore Ashtanga and Hatha Yoga Community** *(facebook.com/groups/326896780836283)* groups.

Mysuru is also a centre for Aayurveda and other healing arts. The **Indus Valley Ayurvedic Centre**, in a rural setting beneath Chamundi Hill, is an outstanding residential centre with specialist doctors, offering all manner of detox, rejuvenation, beauty, weight and other treatments in packages ranging from one night to one month.

Hill of the Mother Goddess

The temple of Chamundeshwari

Mysuru's protector deity Chamundeshwari, a lion-riding manifestation of Durga, resides on **Chamundi Hill**, where she's believed to have slain the havoc-causing, shape-shifting buffalo demon Mahishasura. A visit to her hilltop **temple** provides (if the air is clear) big views as well as a close-up experience of Hindu devotion. The temple is a winding 12km by road from the city centre; Uber autorickshaws should cost around ₹200 each way (though drivers may ask extra for going uphill!). You can also walk up (and/or down) the 1000-plus **Chamundi Hill Steps** used by pilgrims, which start opposite the **Sri Ayyappa Swamy Temple** in Chamundipuram, passing en route a beautiful, old, rock-carved sculpture of Nandi, Shiva's bull vehicle. Temple queues can be long on weekends.

YOGA SCHOOLS

Sharath Yoga Centre: One of Mysuru's foremost ashtanga schools, shaped by the legacy of Sharath Jois.

Mysore Mandala: Home to BNS Iyengar, the yoga master knowledgeable in ashtanga vinyasa and pranayama teachings.

Anokhi Garden: Welcoming Gokulam studio with drop-in classes, including meditation and restorative sessions.

Samyak Yoga: Well-regarded school offering structured ashtanga vinyasa teacher trainings.

K Pattabhi Jois Ashtanga Yoga Shala: Ashtanga practice courses with Pattabhi Jois' daughter and granddaughter.

Yoga Bharata: Mostly four-week courses in hatha and ashtanga vinyasa.

Ashtanga Saadhana: Ashtanga vinyasa courses with popular Vijay Kumar.

DRINKING IN MYSURU: CUTE COFFEE SPOTS

Leaven: Stylish artisanal bakery for pastries, sourdough and croissants, plus sandwiches and good espresso. *11am-9pm Wed-Mon* ₹₹

White Teak Coffee Roasters: All-day cafe and patisserie offering pour-overs, espresso and beans roasted in-house. Strong wi-fi. *7am-11pm* ₹₹

SAPA: Mysuru staple led by chef Dina Weber known for European-style breads and viennoiserie. Reserve on weekends. *9am-8.30pm Tue-Sun* ₹₹

Minimal: Design-forward cafe focused on single-origin brews, cold brew and espresso; favourite with serious coffee drinkers. *8am-8pm* ₹

Vui Coffee Roasters: Simple breakfast plates, sandwiches, smoothies and organic coffee beans. *8.30am-8pm* ₹

SIHI: Leafy courtyard cafe on a quiet street; hearty sandwiches from buttermilk fried chicken to Moroccan tempeh, plus strong coffee. *10am-9.30pm Thu-Tue* ₹₹

West End Coffee Company: Specialty roaster serving dependable espresso, pour-overs and cold brews, plus sandwiches. *8am-10pm* ₹

Ritual Coffee House: Modern, minimalist coffee bar highlighting local beans through pour-overs and espresso drinks. *10am-7pm* ₹

Public Durbar Hall

TOP EXPERIENCE

Mysuru Palace

Mysuru Palace, the former seat of the Wadiyar maharajas, is one of India's very grandest royal buildings and most visited monuments. Its ceremonial rooms are a glittering sequence of gorgeously decorated halls and fascinating art and artefacts, giving a great sense of the pomp, circumstance and beauty surrounding the royal life.

LIGHTING-UP TIME

The palace is illuminated by 97,000 light bulbs – a glorious sight to behold – for an hour from 7pm on Sundays and national holidays and during Dasara, and for 15 minutes after its **sound-and-light show** *(usually 8pm Mon-Sat)*.

Dolls' Pavilion

The first hall you reach was designed for traditional worship of dolls during Dasara. Today its southern half (where you enter) displays sculptures from the maharaja's collection. Straight ahead is a model of the pre-1897 wooden palace. Further along, look for the mini-pavilion structure with Rajasthani mirror-work, housing a figure of Ganesh playing the lute-like *veena*.

Look down to the right to seven ceremonial cannons and four ammunition carriages. The cannons are still fired during Dasara.

Elephant Gate

Halfway along the Dolls' Pavilion, the visitor route turns left through the ornate Elephant Gate, traditional starting point

PRACTICALITIES

- mysorepalace.karnataka.gov.in (in India only)
- entry ₹1000
- 10am-5.30pm

of ceremonial processions, flanked by two wall-mounted elephant heads. The gate's superb brasswork includes large repoussé elephants below, and, in the centre, a double-headed eagle flanked by hybrid lion-elephants – the state emblem of both modern Karnataka and the old Mysore Kingdom.

Marriage Pavilion

You next pass into the Marriage Pavilion, still the setting for royal weddings and other ceremonies. Maharaja Yaduveer Krishnadatta Chamaraja Wadiyar was crowned here in 2015 and married here in 2016. Take time to absorb the beauty of the octagonal central ensemble with its delicate turquoise-and-gold fluted pillars, colourful stained-glass ceiling, intricate floor mosaics and low-hanging chandelier. The fascinatingly detailed murals of a 1930s Dasara procession were based on photographs and show real people.

Golden Howdah

After passing through rooms of royal portraits, caskets and 'chairs' (thrones), and around the Wrestling Courtyard, you re-emerge in the Dolls' Pavilion, whose northern half displays dolls and, at the end, the remarkable wooden Golden Howdah, decorated with 80kg of intricately worked gold, which carries Mysuru's guardian deity, Chamundeshwari, during the Dasara procession. Take a close look at the fly whisks on either side: their bristles are made from fine ivory.

Public Durbar Hall

Head upstairs to the most magnificent section of all: the hall where the maharaja presided over public gatherings, with mesmerising turquoise-and-gold-painted colonnades. The front of the hall, with terraced seating for guests, looks over the palace grounds. The back-wall paintings, beneath arches inlaid with semiprecious stones, show forms of the goddess Devi, four Wadiyar kings (in the centre) and, to the right, *Sita's Swayamvara*, a Ramayana scene by famed Keralan artist Ravi Varma. The front-ceiling paintings illustrate the 10 incarnations of Vishnu and, in the central panel, the Hindu Trimurti (trinity) gods Brahma, Vishnu and Shiva, plus Chamundeshwari, with the 12 zodiac signs in the sky around them.

Private Durbar Hall

This final main room, entered through rosewood doors with intricate ivory-inlay motifs depicting Krishna, is where the rulers held private audiences and meetings. Richly decorated with green-and-gold columns and arches, chandeliers and stained-glass ceiling panels, this is also where the historic Golden Throne (complete with its own golden staircase and sunshade) is placed during Dasara, the only time it's on public show.

OUT OF THE ASHES

Mysuru Palace was built between 1897 and 1912 after its early-19th-century wooden predecessor burned down in a fire that broke out at the end of Princess Jayalakshmmanni's wedding. It owes its Indo-Saracenic style to British architect Henry Irwin (who also designed the Viceregal Lodge in Shimla), while BP Raghavulu Naidu, a Mysore government engineer, was in charge of the construction works.

TOP TIPS

- To avoid the thickest crowds, visit early in the day (from 10am) on weekdays.
- Touring the palace at a moderate pace takes one to 1½ hours.
- A guide can be invaluable. Official guides are available inside the grounds (*₹300-400 1hr tour*).
- It's well worth walking around the palace grounds and gardens, which contain several centuries-old temples and some grandiose gateways.

Beyond Mysuru

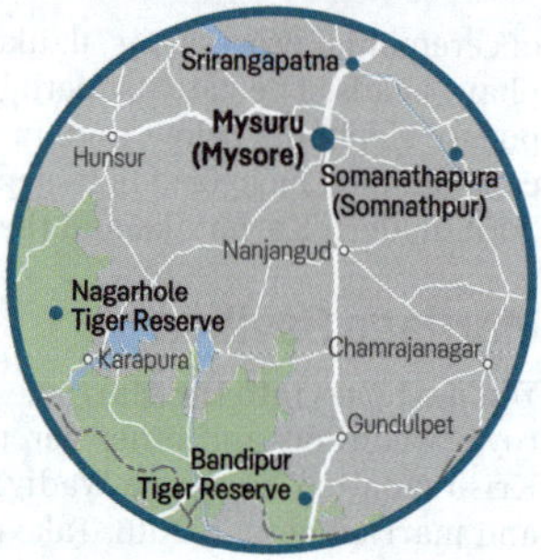

Explore two of India's top wildlife-spotting parks, a fascinating trip into Mysore kingdom history at Srirangapatna and fabulous sculpted architecture at Somanathapura.

Places

GETTING AROUND

Renting a car and driver is a convenient option. A typical rate from Mysuru is ₹3500 to ₹4000 per day. One reliable driver in Mysuru and Bengaluru is Nasir (9845594423). Buses from Mysuru's Central (KSRTC) Bus Stand (p804) will also get you to, or close to, all these places. Accommodation for Nagarhole and Bandipur Tiger Reserves is spread around rural areas, so you may need an autorickshaw or taxi for the final few kilometres.

It's just 1½ hours' drive from Mysuru to two of India's outstanding tiger reserves, Nagarhole and Bandipur, with some of the best wildlife-spotting in the country: tigers, leopards and elephants if you're lucky, and plenty of deer, monkeys and birdlife. You can visit either or both of these reserves in a return trip from Mysuru, or en route to Kerala or other parts of Karnataka. In late 2025 safari operations in both parks were temporarily suspended following three tiger-related fatalities involving local villagers.

Closer to Mysuru you can make close acquaintance with the life and death of the legendary ruler Tipu Sultan at his capital Srirangapatna, and gaze at the sculptural genius of the Hoysala culture from almost a millennium ago at Somanathapura.

Srirangapatna

TIME FROM MYSURU: **20 MINS**

Tipu Sultan's island capital

Srirangapatna, on an island in the Cauvery River 15km north of Mysuru, was once capital of the Mysore kingdom under the 18th-century rulers Hyder Ali and his son Tipu Sultan. It went into decline after falling to the British following a month-long siege in 1799.

Mysore-based **MyCycle Tours** *(instagram.com/meandmycycle; 9886705179; from ₹1450)* does excellent guided bike rides or the town. Buses to Srirangapatna depart every few minutes from Mysuru's Central (KSRTC) Bus Stand (p804). Srirangapatna's Fort area in the west of the island, with several city gates and much of its mighty walls still standing, is walkable but hire an autorickshaw (₹300 to ₹400) or taxi to reach wheelchair-friendly **Daria Daulat Bagh** *(₹250)*, Tipu Sultan's elegant summer palace, with fascinating murals and an excellent museum, and the **Gumbaz**, the monumental domed mausoleum of Tipu, Hyder and Tipu's mother Fakr-Un-Nisa.

SRIRANGAPATNA'S FORT ON FOOT

Explore the historic sites where Tipu Sultan, the 'Tiger of Mysore', lived and met his end.

START	END	LENGTH
Srirangapatna Bus Station	Srirangapatna Bus Station	5.5km; 4hr

From 1 **Srirangapatna bus station**, pass through the narrow 2 **Bengaluru Gate** to the 3 **Jamia Masjid**, with two elegant minarets built by Tipu Sultan. Head north then west to the small 4 **monument** marking the spot where a British officer found Tipu's body after the day's battle on 4 May 1799 (see p812). Walk down to the riverbank at the 5 **Srirangapatna Ghat**, then inland to the sad remains of 6 **Tipu Sultan's Palace**, demolished by the British. Move on to the very large and old 7 **Sri Ranganathaswamy Temple**, dedicated to a form of Vishnu, who reclines on the coils of serpent god Adishesha in the temple's main image.

Along the north side of the island is 8 **Colonel Bailey's Dungeon**, where British prisoners were chained to the wall, reputedly naked with water up to their necks. Pass under the railway and on to the island's western point where an 9 **obelisk** commemorates the British taking of Srirangapatna on 4 May 1799.

Returning, you can cut across the train station footbridge and then climb up the 10 **Flagstaff Bastion** for views before finishing back at the bus station.

HYDER ALI & TIPU SULTAN

Hyder Ali was a commander in the Mysore army who deposed the Wadiyar king in 1761, naming himself Sultan. He expanded Mysore into one of South India's biggest powers, leaving his son Tipu Sultan a kingdom that stretched from the Eastern Ghats to the Arabian Sea. It had a navy and successfully used early rockets in warfare. Mysore came up against regional rivals, including the British, with whom it fought the four Anglo-Mysore Wars. Tipu was a brave and clever general and mostly popular ruler, but was demonised by the British. He lost considerable chunks of territory and was finally defeated and killed when they took his capital Srirangapatna in 1799.

TATHAART/SHUTTERSTOCK

Stone carvings, Keshava Temple

Somanathapura (Somnathpur)

TIME FROM MYSURU: 1HR

Masterpiece of Hindu art

The **Keshava Temple** *(₹250)* at Somanathapura, 35km east of Mysuru, is an outstanding example of sculpture and architecture of the Hoysala kingdom, which ruled most of Karnataka from the 11th to 14th centuries. The soapstone temple's entire exterior is encrusted with detailed carvings of gods, horses, elephants, warriors, musicians, dancers, birds, cattle, sexual positions and more. The more sober interior features lathe-turned columns, and three shrines with images of Venugopala, Keshava and Janardhana, all forms of Vishnu.

A further 25km east lies **Talakadu**, a Kaveri riverside temple site with a cluster of mainly Chola-era shrines from around the 10th century. Public transport from Mysuru is by bus to Bannur then 8km by autorickshaw. A taxi round-trip costs around ₹2500.

Nagarhole Tiger Reserve

TIME FROM MYSURU: 1½ HR

Wildlife-watching on land and water

The 643-sq-km **Nagarhole (Nagarahole) Tiger Reserve** *(nagaraholetigerreserve.com)*, in the forested hills of southwest Karnataka, is home to some of India's largest populations of tigers (141 according to the official census in 2022), leopards (around 200) and elephants (roughly 2500). A special attraction here, in addition to land safaris, is boat safaris on the Kabini River, which for much of the year expands into a reservoir about 2km wide. As the Kabini shrinks in the late dry season (February to April), its grassy banks become a magnet for wildlife.

HOYSALA ARCHITECTURE

There's further superb Hoysala architecture and sculpture at **Halebidu** and **Belur** (p817) which, along with Somnathapura, were added to the UNESCO World Heritage List in 2023.

Sightings on land safaris are always a matter of luck. Elephants are a reasonably good bet, and you're sure to see deer, monkeys and colourful birds. Gaur (large wild cattle), mongoose, giant squirrels and dholes (wild dogs) are all on the cards. Safari drivers keep in touch with each other so if there's an exciting sighting they will head towards it.

The Kabini **water safaris**, in comfortable, open-sided boats, give you the chance to see not just any wildlife visiting the riverbanks but also resident otters and birds from kingfishers to cranes to eagles. These trips start from the Kabini River Lodge and are available only to people staying there or at some other resorts.

Land safaris visit the waterside too, and tend to give better tiger-sighting chances because they also visit forest waterholes. If you're staying at one of the resorts, you will probably get to do both.

For in-person land safari bookings, go to the reserve's **Kakanakote Safari Center ticket office** *(6-9am & 2-6pm)*.

Most Kabini area accommodation is near Karapura village, 80km southwest of Mysuru on SH33. Buses from Mysuru bound for Mananthawadi (Mananthavady) in Kerala will stop there. Roads through the tiger reserve are closed from 6pm to 6am.

Bandipur Tiger Reserve

TIME FROM MYSURU: 1½HR

Safaris with abundant wildlife

This 872-sq-km national park and **tiger reserve** *(bandipur tr.in)* has hilly, dry deciduous forests similar to Nagarhole's Kabini area, and a similar range of wildlife including 150 tigers (according to the 2022 census) and large numbers of elephants and leopards.

Safaris are restricted to a limited area in the park's southeast, straddling the Mysuru–Ooty (Udhagamandalam) road about 80km south of Mysuru. Ideal months for wildlife sightings are February to April, when the dry season is peaking and animals are increasingly likely to visit waterholes.

In-person safari bookings can be made at the **Bandipur Safari Point** *(6-8am & 2-5pm)* beside NH181 about 12km south of Gundlupet.

Accommodation clusters just outside the tiger reserve limits, along the NH181 and near Mangala village, 5km east off the NH181. By public transport from Mysuru, take an Ooty-bound bus and get off at the tiger reserve entrance, or at Gundlupet and take an autorickshaw or taxi from there. Roads through the reserve are closed from 9pm to 6am.

BOOKING SAFARIS

Safaris in Nagarhole *(nagaraholetiger reserve.com)* and Bandipur *(bandipur tigerreserve.org)* Tiger Reserves can be booked online, but systems are clunky, the best seats (in jeeps or canters rather than buses) get booked up far ahead, and sites don't accept foreign bank cards. The easy option, though it may cost more, is staying at a resort or hotel offering a safari booking service, or packages with safaris included. Another possibility for foreigners is to get someone with access to Indian payment systems to reserve for you. You can also book in person at the reserves' safari centres: get there before opening time, though the best (or all) options may be booked out. Book as far ahead as you can, including for resort stays.

Western Ghats

COFFEE COUNTRY | COOL CLIMBS | SCULPTED TEMPLES

Places

TOP TIP

November to January are the ideal months to visit, with low rainfall and moderate temperatures. City dwellers flock here for a rural escape on weekends (especially Sundays) and holidays. Get out and about in the mornings before temperatures start to rise.

Almost one-third of the 1500km length of the Western Ghats – the range of hills paralleling India's west coast – falls within Karnataka. Separating the coastal plain from the Deccan plateau, and soaking up a great deal of monsoon rain, this is a zone where villages and cultivation on the valley floors give way to luxuriant forests on the lower slopes and then treeless grassy slopes rising to ridges scattered with rock outcrops. The Kodagu (Coorg) and Chikkamagaluru (Chikmagalur) districts here grow India's best coffee and entice visitors with their greenery, moderate climate, scenic charm, good walks and abundant countryside accommodation – including many coffee estate homestays (often with superb home cooking). En route between Kodagu and Chikkamagaluru you can enjoy a visit to the Hoysala temples at Belur and Halebidu, superlative works of 12th-century Hindu architecture and sculpture that were added to the World Heritage List in 2023.

Kodagu (Coorg)

Hike Kodagu's highest peak

The walk up **Thadiyandamol** (Tadiandamol; 1748m) in southern Kodagu is exhilarating and practicable for any reasonably fit person. The partly shaded ascent of 500m takes about two hours, the downhill return trip about 1½ hours. The path starts from the end of a paved road 6km south of Kakkabe village and 2km past Nalknad Palace. After a checkpoint *(entry ₹1000)* the views get better and the summit panoramas, up and down the Western Ghats and down into Kerala, are marvellous. Afterwards, check out **Nalknad Palace**, a handsome two-storey residence of the Haleri kings who ruled Kodagu from the 17th to 19th centuries.

GETTING AROUND

Frequent buses run to Madikeri and Chikkamagaluru from Bengaluru, Mysuru and Mangaluru (Mangalore). You then usually need a taxi or autorickshaw to get out to rural accommodation (some places can arrange pickups). For the Yevakapadi/Thadiyandamol area of southern Kodagu, there are frequent buses from Mysuru to Virajpet, from where private buses run to Kakkinakadu and Kakkabe, where you can get an autorickshaw or pickup. Belur and Halebidu are served by buses from Chikkamagaluru, Hassan and each other. A taxi for a full day of local sightseeing costs approximately ₹4500.

HIGHLIGHTS
1 Chennakeshava Temple
2 Hoysaleswara Temple
3 Namdroling Monastery

SIGHTS
4 Bababudangiri Peak
see 3 Golden Temple
5 Madikeri Fort
6 Manikyadhara Waterfall
7 Mercara Gold Estate
8 Mullayanagiri
9 Museum
10 Nalknad Palace
11 Rajas' Tombs
12 Rajaseat Park
13 Sitalayyana Temple
14 Sri Guru Daththreya Baba Budan Swamy Darga

ACTIVITIES
15 Malcode Estate
16 Riverside Estate
17 Victorian Verandaz

EATING
18 Arabica
19 Belli's
20 Coffee Barn Cafe
21 Coorg Cuisine
22 Papera
23 Tavisa
24 The Blue Door
25 Town Canteen

DRINKING & NIGHTLIFE
26 Agastya Coffee
27 Ainmane Cafe
28 Big Cup Cafe
29 The Wheel Cafe

ENTERTAINMENT
see 3 Saga Dawa

For travellers looking to go deeper into the region's rich ecology, Kodagu-based naturalist **Abhishek Uthappa** *(instagram .com/abhi_uthappa)* leads small-group hikes on select routes, including more demanding grassland and forest trails. All treks operate with official forest permissions and ranger accompaniment.

Coffee estate excursions

Coffee cultivation shapes daily life in Kodagu, which produces a significant share of India's coffee. One of the most rewarding ways to experience the region is through short estate visits led by local planters, many of whom now welcome travellers onto their working farms for a few hours.

Mercara Gold Estate, 8km southwest of Madikeri (Mercara), offers guided plantation walks, a small coffee museum, a look at roasting and a cup of estate coffee for ₹300. Others are best experienced through homestays. At **Victorian Verandaz**, 9km east of Madikeri, amiable fifth-generation owner Thimaiah drives you round the large estate in his ancient jeep to observe seasonal farm activity.

A newer generation of Kodagu coffee growers now focus on direct-to-consumer specialty coffee. Visits to **Riverside Estate** and **Malcode Estate** *(from ₹1500)* typically include shaded walks through the estate, introductions to coffee varieties, explanations of harvesting processes and lunch. Most tours finish, fittingly, with freshly brewed estate coffee.

Madikeri

Explore the Kodagu capital

Madikeri is a busy market town spread over several hills, with lots of shops selling local spices, fruit wines, chocolate and coffee. **Rajaseat Park** *(₹20),* full of colourful flowers and kitsch decorative features, enjoys superb views. In the town centre you can walk round most of the walls of **Madikeri Fort**, founded in 1681. Within the fort, the two-storey rajas' palace has been undergoing restoration, but an 1855 church houses the **Government Museum** *(₹10),* with artefacts from centuries of Kodagu history. On the northern edge of town there are more vistas from the **Rajas' Tombs** *(₹10),* domed mausolea where late Haleri kings and queens are interred.

COFFEE HARVEST

Of India's approximately 350,000 tonnes of annual coffee production, Kodagu grows roughly one-third and the Chikkamagaluru district around a quarter. The higher-caffeine robusta variety is more common here than more labour-intensive arabica.

Harvesting happens from November to February, with arabica coming first. It's still done by hand and heavily dependent on seasonal labour. During the picking months, estates employ migrant day labourers – many of them women from neighbouring states and districts – whose skills lie in selectively plucking only ripe red cherries. Growers have two main methods of extracting the beans. One is to spread the fruit out in the sun to dry and the other is 'pulping' by machine to remove the outer fruit, before being dried into green beans ready for roasting.

EATING IN KODAGU: OUR PICKS

Coorg Cuisine: Popular for Kodava dishes such as *pandi* (pork curry) or *baimbale* (bamboo shoots and coconut). *noon-4.30pm & 7-9.30pm* ₹₹

The Blue Door: Estate cafe highlighting local produce, and leafy, relaxed settings ideal for unhurried lunches or quiet evening meals. *1-10pm* ₹₹

Belli's: Casual restaurant near Madikeri's KSRTC bus stand serving Kodagu, Indian and Chinese dishes. Convenient for quick meals before or after bus journeys. *noon-10pm* ₹

Papera: Gonikoppa hotspot prized for pork dishes, including the region's best pork *chudal* – a dry Kodava pork classic with bird's eye chillies. *11.30am-10.30pm* ₹₹

Belur & Halebidu

Highpoints of Hindu art

The Hoysala kingdom, ruling most of Karnataka from the 11th to 14th centuries, produced some of India's outstanding sculpted architecture in the form of temples encrusted with an astounding profusion of deities, animals, nymphs, musicians, dancers and mythological scenes. The World Heritage–listed 12th-century temples at the successive Hoysala capitals, Belur and Halebidu, can both be visited on an easy day trip from Chikkamagaluru or a long day trip from Kodagu or Mysuru. Excellent information panels explain the architecture and sculpture in detail.

Belur's **Chennakeshava Temple**, still a busy place of worship dedicated to Chennakeshava (a form of Vishnu), stands in a walled compound with four other temples. A frieze of elephants runs right round the base of its walls, with up to nine diffferent levels above that. The sculpted scene to the left of the main (east) doorway, with a man holding a large dagger flanked by crowds of people, is thought to show King Vishnuvardhana, who commissioned the temple, and his court. The brackets at the tops of the walls feature superbly carved *madakinas* (demigod nymphs) including (above Vishnuvardhana) one holding a parrot and another holding a mirror.

Halebidu's **Hoysaleswara Temple**, in attractive gardens, is in fact a pair of adjoined Shiva temples. Fine large Nandi bull sculptures sit in their own pavilions just east of the main structures, with Surya the sun god in a further small shrine past the southerly Nandi. The temple's exterior friezes have even more extravagant detail than at Belur, with 11 bands of small-scale carving showing (from the bottom up) elephants, lions, a scroll, horses and riders, another scroll, scenes from the Hindu epics, *makaras* (mythical aquatic creatures), swans, two levels of nymphs, musicians, warriors, goblins, lions and monsters, and finally secular scenes including some amorous couples.

Chikkamagaluru (Chikmagalur)

Tour the Bababudangiri Hills

The Bababudangiri (or Chandradrona) Hills form a crescent-like eastern spur of the Western Ghats rising north of Chikkamagaluru town. With several scenic viewpoints they make a good day's road trip. Head first for Karnataka's highest peak,

THE KODAVAS

The Kodava people comprise about one-fifth of the approximately 600,000 population of Kodagu today. Their origins are uncertain but their roots here go back a very long way. Traditionally hunters and rice growers, their society is formed of several hundred patrilineal, exogamous clans, each with an ancestral *aine mane* (clan house) where they meet for regular ceremonies. Hinduism and Christianity have had some influence in recent centuries but Kodava ceremonies are still led by family elders rather than Brahmin priests. They revere their ancestors as their guiding spirits and their elders as their living guides. Principal deities are the Cauvery River, which rises at Talakaveri, 45km west of Madikeri, and Igguthappa, a god of crops, especially rice.

DRINKING IN KODAGU: CUTE COFFEE SHOPS

Agastya Coffee: Single-origin coffee, sandwiches and light bites, plus a small shop selling packaged Kodagu staples like honey and spices. *9.30am-9pm* ₹₹

Big Cup Cafe: Roastery cafe showcasing estate-grown Chikmagalur coffee, plus pizzas, baked goods and plenty of relaxed outdoor seating. *9am-10.30pm* ₹₹

The Wheel Cafe: In a traditional Kodagu house, this popular cafe serves espresso and coffee-based drinks, sandwiches and light snacks. *10am-8pm* ₹₹

Ainmane Cafe: Simple cafe and retail space for estate coffee, chocolates and regional products. Good for picking up local treats for souvenirs. *9am-9pm* ₹₹

COORG CUISINE

Anjali Ganapathy, chef and founder of PigOut: A Coorg Kitchen Story names her favorite dishes. (*instagram.com/pigout_coorgkitchen*

Coorg cuisine is shaped by the region's forests, rivers and paddy fields. Meals are often paired with steamed rice cakes *(paaputt)*, balls *(kadambutt)* or string hoppers *(noolputt)*. A good place to start is *akki otti*, a soft flatbread made from leftover cooked rice and rice flour. The ever-popular *pandi* curry, known for its signature dark colour and smoky tang, combines pork, black pepper and *kachampuli*, a souring extract made from forest fruit native to the Western Ghats. During the monsoon, look for curries with mud crab, *colocasia* and *baimbale*, a tender bamboo shoot fermented 48 hours before cooking and foraged from riverbanks.

Mullayanagiri (1930m), a steepish 15-minute walk from a car park at the end of a ghat road. There's a small Shiva temple and, at weekends, a *lot* of people. For more of a leg-stretch, start walking 1.5km earlier at the **Sitalayyana Temple**.

A further 23km drive north is **Sri Guru Daththreya Baba Budan Swamy Darga**, a cave shrine sacred to Muslims and Hindus for its associations with two Sufi saints, Dada Hayath and Baba Budan, and the Hindu deity Daththreya, who are all to some extent identified with each other. By some accounts Baba Budan, the legendary bringer of the first coffee beans to India, is buried here. Entry to the shrine is via a caged gangway about 90m long. An unpaved road leads on 3km to **Manikyadhara Waterfall**, believed to have healing properties. After 500m you can detour on foot for a short walk along the crest of the range, dramatically steep on its eastern side. Another side track leads up to **Bababudangiri Peak** (1895m).

Bylakuppe

A day among monks, prayer flags and Tibetan kitchens

Bylakuppe is one of India's largest Tibetan settlements, established in the 1960s for refugees fleeing Tibet, and today it feels quietly distinct from the rest of Kodagu. Most visits centre on **Namdroling Monastery** and the **Golden Temple**, whose vast prayer hall glows with gold statues of the Buddha, Guru Padmasambhava and Amitayus. Arrive early in the morning to watch monks chant during their daily prayer sessions.

If you're visiting in late May or early June, try to time your stop with **Saga Dawa**, one of Tibetan Buddhism's most important months, marking the Buddha's birth, enlightenment and death. At Namdroling this brings extra prayers, circumambulations and a steady stream of pilgrims to the area.

Wander beyond the monastery gates to eat. You'll find simple Tibetan cafes serving steamed *momos* (dumplings), *thukpa* (noodle soup), *tingmo* bread and butter tea, alongside classic Indo-Chinese staples. Foreign visitors do not need a special permit for a daytime visit to Bylakuppe or the monastery; paperwork is only required if you plan to stay overnight in Kushalnagar.

EATING IN CHIKKAMAGALURU: OUR PICKS

Town Canteen: Long-running favourite since the 1960s known for its crisp *benne dosa*, *idli* and strong filter coffee. Busy, affordable and reliably good. *6.30am-8.30pm* ₹

Coffee Barn Cafe: Sweet country-cottage-style cafe north of Chikkamagaluru. Comfort food from omelettes to cake, juices and coffee. *8.30am-6.30pm* ₹₹

Tavisa: Stylish restaurant with a varied Indian and international menu, good cocktails and attentive service. Relaxed lunches and lively evening dining. *noon-11.30pm* ₹₹

Arabica: Highlights regional cuisine – try the rave-worthy Malnad fish fry and stuffed eggplant. Outdoor seating overlooks the lush mountains. *1-3pm & 8-10.30pm* ₹₹₹

Karnataka Coast

SURFING | COASTAL FLAVOURS | SACRED ARCHITECTURE

Karnataka's 340km coast is a humid, palm-fringed stretch of small fishing towns, indie surf spots and alluring backwaters. Beaches are plentiful, but strong currents make many open-ocean stretches better for walking, surfing or simply watching the day end.

Mangaluru is the coast's southern anchor. Fish docks buzz at sunrise and ancient places of worship line narrow, centuries-old trading lanes. Inland, the 15th-century Jain *basadis* of Moodbidri feature intricately carved pillars decorated with dragons and giraffes – rare motifs linked to the Indian Ocean trade networks that once connected this region with Africa, China and the Arab world.

Udupi blends temple devotion with a large student community from nearby Manipal University, creating an unexpectedly lively dining scene. Further up the coast, Murudeshwar and Gokarna shape the pilgrim circuit. Gokarna doubles as an easy coastal base to wander between sandy coves, join yoga sessions and watch the light fade over the Arabian Sea.

Places

TOP TIP

There's no need to fret about haggling over autorickshaw fares in Mangaluru: drivers there (and most in Udupi too) turn on their meters without even being asked.Not in Gokarna though.

Mangaluru (Mangalore)

Fish, flowers and fruit

Dive into Mangaluru's morning markets to feel the commerce that drives this coastal city. The dockside fish markets are at their most frenetic at sunrise, but even by 10am you'll still catch plenty of action as crews unload the night's catch from red fishing boats moored three deep along the quay. Expect wet floors, hundreds of men and women working in a quick, expertly choreographed bustle of unloading, cutting, sorting and packing. Wear closed shoes and allow around an hour to

GETTING AROUND

NH66 runs the length of Karnataka's coast and is generally reliable, but expect stretches of ongoing roadwork and bumpy patches between Mangaluru, Udupi and Gokarna. Buses and trains connect all major towns. Gokarna's nearest train station is Gokarna Rd (9km east) with a handful of express trains daily. Ankola, 22km north of Gokarna, has further options, and also more frequent bus services than Gokarna.

Mangaluru has an airport with domestic and international flights, making it an entry point for northern Kerala as well as Karnataka.

MANGALURU & UDUPI CUISINES

Mangaluru is justly famed for its spicy seafood curries, which come in several varieties: *panna upkari* uses just onions, chilli and tamarind, *hinga udda* includes coconut and the pungent spice *hing* (asafoetida), and *puli-munchi* means tamarind-chilli and that's what it is, plus other spices. Other favourite preparations are ghee roast – seafood or chicken roasted with spices in ghee (clarified butter) – and masala fry (slow-fried or roasted in a spicy masala sauce).

Udupi, 55km north of Mangaluru, gives its name to a cuisine of vegetarian dishes including the dosa, which some claim (and others deny) was invented there, *idlis*, *sambar* (coconut-based sauce often accompanying *idlis*) and *kosambari* (seasoned salad of lentils or other pulses).

wander between the open-air **Mangalore Fish Market** and the larger, covered **Dhakke Fish Market** just 150m away.

From the docks, head to Car St to see the **Flower Market** in its 1940s-era hall, where vendors thread jasmine, marigold and rose garlands for temple offerings from 6am. Around the corner, the **Hampankatta Market** stirs to life with wholesale fruit, vegetables and spice stalls. The surrounding lanes brim with small shops selling everything from souvenirs to electronics and household wares.

Centres of faith

Mangaluru's religious landmarks sit surprisingly close to each other, and seeing a few in one go gives you a real sense of how the city grew around trade, migration and shifting communities. Start at **Kadri Manjunatha Temple**, where the courtyards fill early with devotees making offerings and the smell of incense hangs over the bronze shrines.

Nearly 4km away is **Gokarnanatha Temple**, offering a different mood entirely – shiny *gopurams*, polished floors and a steady flow of visitors moving between shrines. From here, continue to **Milagres Church**, one of the area's oldest Catholic churches, founded in 1680. A 15-minute walk north brings you to **St Aloysius College Chapel**, where vivid late-19th-century frescoes painted by Italian artist Antonio Moscheni cover nearly every surface.

End at **Zeenath Baksh Juma Masjid**, considered to be India's third-oldest mosque, founded in 646 CE. Its wooden prayer hall and carved pillars feel strikingly different from the stone and stucco elsewhere.

Beach and surfing

Tannirbhavi Beach, 12km north of central Mangaluru, is the city's easiest stretch of sand to reach. It can get busy – especially on weekends – and it's not the cleanest beach these days, but it remains a reliable place to watch the sunset. With sometimes strong waves and ocean currents, these seas are for paddling rather than swimming. **Mangalore Surf Club** offers beginner lessons and board rentals.

For more time on the water, head 25km north to **Mulki**, where modern Indian surfing first took root. **Aquatic Indica Surf School** runs sessions on both the calm backwaters and the open ocean, with options ranging from beginner surfing to SUP and kayaking. Waves along this section of coast are rarely more than a metre, making it an accessible place to

EATING IN MANGALURU & UDUPI: OUR PICKS

Girimanja's: Authentic Mangalorean food in simple surrounds. Try any prawn dish and/or a spicy, shallow-fried fish *tawa*. Be prepared to queue. *11.30am-3pm* ₹

Woodlands: Excellent vegetarian fare in Udipi including filling, multi-flavour South and North Indian thalis, with attentive service. *8.30am-3.15pm & 5.30-10.30pm* ₹

Machali: Super-popular, efficient Mangalore-cuisine restaurant. The prawn *panna upkari* curry is great, but try a fried or ghee-roast fish. *11.30am-3.30pm & 7-10pm* ₹₹

Gajalee: Top seafood restaurant in a panoramic bungalow. Go for prawns or pomfret in butter, pepper and garlic. Alcohol available. *11am-3.30pm & 6.30-11pm* ₹₹₹

EWY MEDIA/SHUTTERSTOCK

Gokarnanatha Temple, Mangaluru

learn. Further along, **Kadal Surf School** offers multiday courses and board rentals for more confident surfers.

Keep driving north to the quiet coastal village of **Kodi Bengare**, a narrow stretch of land with the river on one side and the sea on the other. This is home to the **Shaka Surf Club**, co-founded by Ishita Malaviya, India's first professional woman surfer. Lessons, rentals and river sessions run from here, and the calm waters make SUP especially rewarding.

The medieval Africa–China connection

About 35km northeast of Mangaluru, **Moodbidri** offers one of coastal Karnataka's most distinctive Jain experiences. The town's standout is **Saavira Kambada Basadi** *(adult ₹10, camera ₹100)*, a 15th-century shrine supported by hundreds of lathe-turned stone pillars. The symmetry and repetition create a calming rhythm as you walk through and the details require close inspection. Along the plinths and brackets are carvings of animals, mythic figures and unusually, dragons and giraffes – motifs linked to the Indian Ocean trade networks that once connected this region with East Africa and China.

A seven-minute walk away, **Chowta Palace** showcases carved wooden pillars and a traditional courtyard plan – a contrast to the temple's stone precision.

Travellers interested in extending the circuit often continue to **Karkala**, home to a 12m monolithic statue of Bahubali, before returning to Mangaluru.

TEMPLES OF THE COAST

Kadri Manjunatha Temple (Mangaluru): Dedicated to Shiva, with an atmosphere of hushed reverence.

Gokarnanatha Temple (Mangaluru): Joyfully colourful Shiva temple with many glittering shrines.

Krishna Temple (Udupi): In an atmosphere of deep reverence and awe, Krishna is worshipped in his child form Balakrishna.

Shri Murudeshwar Temple (Murudeshwar): The world's third-tallest Shiva statue and second-tallest *gopuram*.

Mahabaleshwara Temple (Gokarna): Home to a powerful Shiva lingam; non-Indians may not enter the inner shrine.

Mahaganapati Temple (Gokarna): Houses a rare standing Ganesh statue.

Saavira Kambada Basadi (Moodbidri): A 15th-century Jain temple known for rare carvings linked to historic Indian Ocean trade routes.

DRINKING & EATING IN MANGALURU & UDUPI: BEST COFFEE SHOPS

TLC Art Cafe: Good breakfasts and locally sourced single-origin coffee in Mangaluru. The wood-oven pizzas are a big draw. *8.30am-9pm Wed-Mon* ₹₹

Roy's Cafe: In Manipal, alfresco dining, strong pours, fresh bakes, pasta, salads and burgers. Fills up fast on weekends. *noon-9.30pm* ₹₹

BuCo: Renowned chef Shriya Shetty's hotspot offering craft coffee and inventive pastries in Mangaluru. *noon-9pm Tue-Fri, noon-10.30pm Sat & Sun* ₹₹

Cafe Flourista: Consistent coffee and a calm atmosphere make this Mangaluru cafe a great pick for afternoon breaks. *10am-9pm Tue-Sun* ₹₹

Gokarna

The pilgrimage and beach town of Gokarna has a clear travel season. From April to October, many beach cafes, cliffside huts and boat services close for the monsoon, and some trails become muddy or unsafe. The narrow lanes, steep headlands and lack of street lights can make driving a challenge here, and several beaches sit far from the centre. If you're here longer than a day or two, renting a scooter is by far the easiest way to get around. Autorickshaws are available, but short trips start at around ₹200 for a 6km ride.

Beach bliss

There are two Gokarnas. One is the small, atmospheric town anchored by ancient temples that draw many Hindu pilgrims. The other stretches south, where a string of sandy coves draws travellers who come for slow days, cliff walks and quiet sunsets. The many beachfront cafes and restaurants mostly have inexpensive rooms in the back.

Closest to Gokarna town (1.5km), **Kudle Beach** is a 700m, broad, west-facing curve framed by low wooded hills. It's one of the easiest beaches to reach and remains popular for its simple cafes and relaxed feel. A short walk or drive south brings you to **Om Beach**, its 800m twin crescents forming the (vague) shape that gave it its name. Signs ban swimming but plenty of people do swim when the sea is not choppy.

From Om, the cliff path narrows and splits into several trails. About 20 minutes (700m) on foot leads to **Half Moon Beach**, a small, calm cove with basic seasonal huts. Another 700m walk brings you to **Paradise Beach**, often quiet in the early morning when the light is soft and the sand still cool. The trails can be confusing, with both steep and easy options, so carry water and avoid walking alone on isolated stretches. Boats from the west end of Om Beach will ferry people out to Half Moon and Paradise *(₹4000 for up to 10 people)*. Sadly, noisy boatloads can disturb the calm of the outlying beaches.

North of town, **Gokarna Beach** runs for several kilometres. The stretch closest to town is busy, but it becomes cleaner and more peaceful as you walk north – with lots of good-value beachside restaurants and inexpensive guesthouses. Strong currents make it unsafe for swimming, but it's a reliable spot for beginner surfers; **Cocopelli Surf School**, run by internationally certified instructor Sandeep Samuel, operates from this beach.

YOGA & AYURVEDA IN GOKARNA

Shree Hari Yoga: Well-regarded school behind Kudle Beach with varied drop-in yoga classes as well as yin yoga and multi-style teacher-training courses.

Namaste Yoga Farm: Twice-daily yoga sessions for beginners upwards are included with stays at this friendly German-owned retreat above Kudle Beach (November to March).

SwaSwara: Deluxe Ayurveda retreat above Om Beach with accommodation in delightful villas with private mini-gardens and yoga decks.

Gokarna Yoga School: Iyengar yoga classes with certified Italian teachers above Kudle Beach, December to March.

Arya Ayurvedic Panchakarma Centre: Courses of Ayurvedic treatment by professional staff, tailored to individual needs, on Kudle Beach.

EATING IN GOKARNA: OUR PICKS

Sunset Cafe: Popular cafe with friendly service on Gokarna main beach. Reliable for simple Indian dishes and snacks; try the peri-peri fries. *9.30am-3.30pm & 6.30-10.30pm* ₹₹

Bhagvan Cafe: Laid-back spot on Middle Beach. Known for good-value plates and tasty starters. The hummus platter is a favourite. *7.30am-10pm* ₹₹

Mantra Cafe: Rooftop cafe at Zostel with views over Kudle Beach. Favourites include the chicken ghee roast and *paneer* ghee roast. *8.30am-10.30pm Thu-Tue* ₹₹

Chez Christophe: Quality, relaxed French place on Gokarna main beach. Head here for fresh organic salads and chicken Normande. *10.30am-10.30pm Thu-Tue, 6-10.30pm Wed* ₹₹

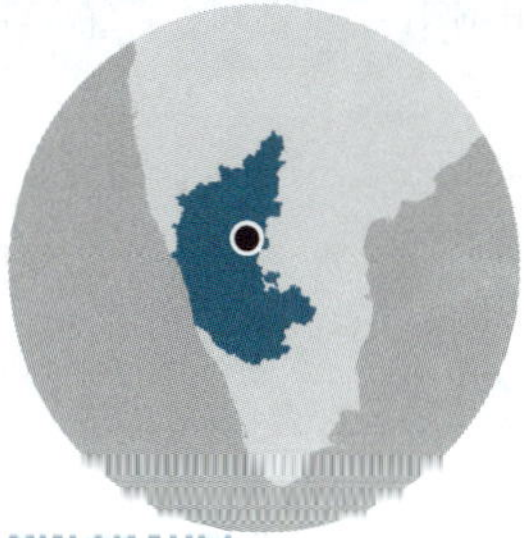

Hampi

ABANDONED CAPITAL | SURREAL LANDSCAPE | SLOW TRAVEL

Once an imperial capital of half a million people, Hampi is today one of the world's most atmospheric ruined cities, with superbly sculpted structures spread across a vast, open landscape of banana groves, rice fields and rust-coloured boulders, where scale is measured as much by walking time as by history.

Hampi was the heart of Vijayanagar, a powerful empire that ruled much of South India under King Krishnadevaraya. Its abrupt collapse came after the Battle of Talikota in 1565, when an alliance of Deccan sultanates defeated the Vijayanagar army, ransacking and abandoning the city. What remains nearly 450 years later is remarkable, offering clear glimpses of its former wealth and ambition.

Hampi isn't just the ruins, though. With its boulder-strewn terrain and unhurried pace – not to mention a certain herb – it's a place a lot of climbers, backpackers, artists and slow travellers choose for an extended stay.

TOP TIP

Most monuments open from sunrise to sunset. Visiting early makes a huge difference as the temperatures are not only cooler, but crowds are thinner and the light is at its best. Vitthala Temple is especially atmospheric at dawn, when the stone chariot catches the first light and the complex is still quiet. An early start there also means you can walk the scenic 1km approach from the car park, avoiding the electric buggies that shuttle visitors later in the day.

Exploring over the River

Villages, swims and hills to climb

North of the Tungabhadra River is a quieter, more rural side of Hampi where villages sit among rice fields, palm groves and rock-strewn hills, best explored by bicycle or scooter.

GETTING AROUND

Hosapete (Hospet), 12km southwest, is the main gateway to Hampi, with long-distance rail and bus services and half-hourly daytime buses to Hampi. Vidyanagar (Jindal Vijaynagar) airport, 37km southeast, has daily flights to/from Bengaluru. One overnight KSRTC bus runs from Hampi Bazaar to Panaji (Panjim; Goa).

Hampi is best explored on foot, bike or scooter. Gearless bikes rent for ₹150 to ₹200 per day; scooters cost ₹300 to ₹500 and can be arranged through most guesthouses. There's a scooter rental point 150m up from the north side of the Hampi Bazaar ferry. Autorickshaws, useful for longer hops, cost roughly ₹1000 to ₹1200 for a full day.

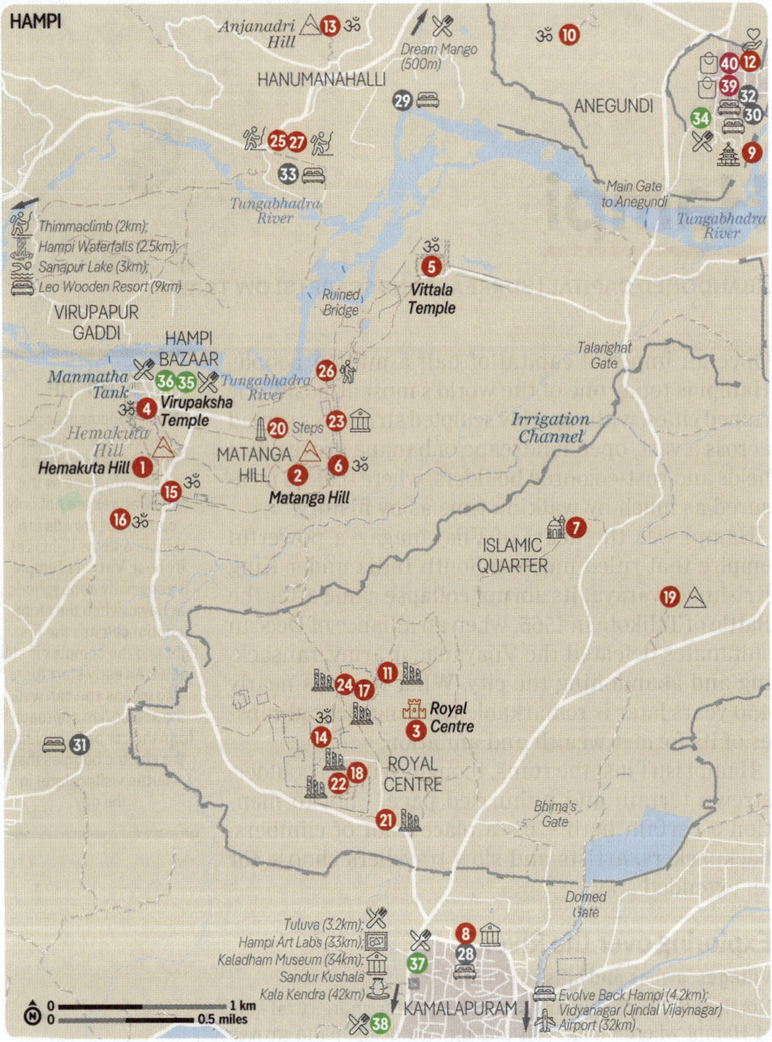

EATING IN HAMPI: OUR PICKS

Mango Tree: Favourite all-vegetarian ('special lunch and dinner' thalis are great) in a peaceful, open-sided Kamalapuram space. *8am-9.30pm* ₹

Cultural Industries Center: Seasonal North Karnataka meals served on banana leaves. Advance booking required at 8088040806. *hours vary.* ₹₹

Hampi Paradise: Long-running restaurant serving filling South Indian thalis, plus chicken and mutton dishes, unusual in this temple town. Cash or UPI only. *7.30am-9.30pm* ₹

Tuluva: Refined spot overlooking a serene infinity pool, spotlighting Karnataka and the Deccan flavours through lunch thalis and à la carte dishes. *12.30-3pm* ₹₹₹

HIGHLIGHTS

1 Hemakuta Hill
2 Matanga Hill
3 Royal Centre
4 Virupaksha Temple
5 Vittala Temple

SIGHTS

6 Achyutaraya Temple
7 Ahmed Khan's Mosque & Tomb
8 Archaeological Museum
9 Chintamani Temple Complex
10 Durga Temple
11 Elephant Stables
12 Gagan Mahal
13 Hanuman Temple
14 Hazararama Temple
15 Krishna Temple
16 Lakshmi Narasimha
17 Lotus Mahal
18 Mahanavami Dibba
19 Malyavanta Hill
20 Nandi Statue
21 Queen's Bath
22 Royal Enclosure
23 Sule Bazaar
24 Zenana Enclosure

ACTIVITIES

25 Golden Boulders
26 Kampabhupa Path
27 Tom's Hampi Adventures

SLEEPING

28 Clarks Inn
29 Epic Island Hampi
30 Peshegaar Guest House
31 Shankar Homestay
32 Srilatha Mane
33 Wanderlust

EATING

34 Cultural Industries Center
35 Dream Catcher
36 Ganesh Old Chillout
37 Hampi Paradise
38 Mango Tree
see 33 Wanderlust

SHOPPING

39 Banana Fibre Workshop
40 Uramma Crafts

Three small passenger ferries cross the river (7am to 5pm), and will carry bicycles.

At **Hampi Waterfalls**, 400m down a road from Sanapur village, the Tungabhadra tumbles down some rocks and people like to jump into river pools when the water's deep enough. **Sanapur Lake** has a swimming spot from some flattish rocks.

East of Hanumanahalli, 570 steps climb panoramic **Anjanadri Hill**, believed by many to be Kishkinda, the homeland of the monkey god Hanuman. A small **Hanuman temple** sits near the summit. Anegundi village lies a further 3km east, its lanes dotted with historic homes, the **Chintamani Temple Complex** and the ruins of Anegundi Fort, which includes an ancient **Durga temple**.

Climb a Rock

Boulders for all

Liberally scattered with rocks of all shapes and sizes, Hampi is a climbers' adventure playground and the undisputed bouldering capital of India. Even if you've never tried the sport before, several experienced, friendly local outfits such as Hanumanahalli-based **Tom's Hampi Adventures**, **Golden Boulders Climbing Shop** and Sanapur-based **Thimmaclimb** will take you for a 2½- or three-hour session *(from ₹1500 per person)* with the necessary equipment and help you get up – and down! – some of those tricky-looking rocks. They also rent gear and lead hikes around the amazing countryside.

LIVING TRADITIONS

Long after the empire fell, Hampi's traditions continue in its villages and workshops. In Anegundi, the **Banana Fibre Workshop** turns banana bark into baskets, mats and various home goods woven by local women, while **Uramma Crafts** offers a close look at local weaving and textile traditions. The restored **Gagan Mahal**, once a 16th-century Vijayanagara royal pavilion, now hosts cultural events and folk festivals throughout the year.

Sandur Kushala Kala Kendra, 42km south of Hampi, sustains craft lineages ranging from Lambani embroidery and *khadi* (homespun cloth) weaving to bamboo work, stone carving and natural dyeing. Back in Hampi, **Hampi Art Labs** brings contemporary artists into dialogue with the landscape through its exhibits and artist residencies, while **Kaladham Museum** offers an immersive way to understand Hampi's layered past.

EATING IN HAMPI: CHILL CAFES

Dream Catcher: Friendly vegetarian Hampi Bazaar rooftop restaurant. Pancakes, *paneer tikka*, Greek salad, pizza and views across the river. *8.30am-10.30pm* ₹

Dream Mango: Laid-back cafe in Hanumanahalli doing everything from burgers to curries, with alcohol also available. 'Chill out' on low cushion seating. *8am-10pm* ₹₹

Ganesh Old Chillout: Long-running Hampi Bazaar fave; everything from continental breakfast to veg pasta and thalis, in cushion-seated surrounds. *8am-10pm* ₹₹

Wanderlust (p837): The airy restaurant at this countryside accommodation near Hanumanahalli is relaxed, with a multicuisine menu. *8am-11pm* ₹₹

FABIO LAMANNA/SHUTTERSTOCK

Virupaksha Temple

TOP EXPERIENCE

Hampi Ruins

The remains of the great city of Vijayanagara are scattered over a vast area in a landscape that only enhances their beauty and mystique. It's possible to tour the most outstanding monuments in one day, but far more rewarding to give yourself several days to explore some of the 3000-odd other structures and soak up Hampi's atmosphere at your own pace.

DON'T MISS

- Virupaksha Temple
- Vitthala Temple
- Zenana Enclosure
- Hemakuta Hill
- Achyutaraya Temple
- Lakshmi Narasimha Statue
- Archaeological Museum

Hampi Bazaar

Hampi village (or Hampi Bazaar as it's often called), at the monumental area's northwest corner, is dominated by the 7th-century **Virupaksha Temple** – the only one of the old city's major temples that's still an active place of worship. You enter through its magnificent 50m-high, 11-tier *gopuram* (where you'll be lent a sarong if you're showing too much leg). A second *gopuram* leads into the inner compound, centred on a pillared *mandapa* (pavilion) dating from 1510 with

PRACTICALITIES

● asi.nic.in/pages/WorldHeritageHampi ● sunrise-sunset ● adult/child under 15 ₹550/free

CLAUDINE VAN MASSENHOVE/SHUTTERSTOCK ©

superb sculptures of multiple motifs – a typical feature of Vijayanagar architecture. *Yalis* (mythical beasts combining features of different animals) adorn the outer pillars. Behind the *mandapa* is the inner sanctum, dedicated to Virupaksha, an incarnation of Shiva.

Stretching 750m east from the temple is a long straight street lined with stone pavilions. This was the original Hampi Bazaar (market) 600 years ago. All Vijayanagara's major temples had markets stretched out in front of them and this one gives some idea of the city's size and importance. Even commoners and bazaar artisans wore pearls and jewels on their ears, necks, arms and fingers, according to 15th-century Persian traveller Abd al-Razzag Samarqandi. Some of the pavilions here still contained small shops or food stalls until a few years ago when the Hampi World Heritage authorities decided to remove such businesses. At the far end of the avenue a pavilion signposted 'Monolithic Bull' houses a large **statue of the bull Nandi**, Shiva's vehicle, facing back towards the Virupaksha Temple.

Hemakuta Hill

Rising to the south of the Virupaksha Temple, the smooth granite slopes of Hemakuta Hill are scattered not just with huge boulders but also more than 30 shrines and temples, including two towering Ganesha statues. It's a popular place at sunset, but don't let the crowds put you off as the views are wonderful. Many of the structures predate the Vijayanagar empire (founded in 1336).

Krishna Temple & Lakshmi Narasimha

The large **Krishna Temple**, built around 1513, has another long market avenue stretching out in front. Not far south you'll find the **Lakshmi Narasimha statue**, an extraordinary

GETTING ORIENTED

The ruins of the old city of Vijayanagara are scattered over a vast area, but the main monuments are mostly concentrated in two main zones. One, known as the Sacred Centre, is the area around and east of Hampi village, on the south side of the Tungabhadra River. The other, the Royal Centre, is 1km to 2km further south, towards Kamalapuram village.

TOP TIPS

- Visit between October to January, when the weather is dry and not too hot.
- The only sites with an entry fee are the Vitthala Temple, Zenana Enclosure and Archaeological Museum. One ticket covers them all for same-day entry.
- Spend dawn at the Sacred Centre and Vitthala Temple, while hills like Hemakuta and Matanga are most rewarding at sunset.
- The Vitthala Temple and Zenana Enclosure are wheelchair-friendly. The Royal Enclosure has a ramp that avoids all except the last three of the steps up to the Mahanavami Dibba.

ROYAL EXHIBITS

It's well worth making the journey to the **Archaeological Museum** (included with Hampi monuments entry) in Kamalapuram village, 4.5km southeast of Hampi village. Its very fine (and well-explained) sculptures, large models of the whole Hampi valley and the Royal Enclosure, and excellent info panels will enlighten on Vijayanagara's history, geography, art and lifestyle.

goggle-eyed representation of Vishnu's man-lion incarnation Narasimha. His four arms and his consort Lakshmi have gone, but her name remains.

Royal Centre

The Royal Centre contains remains of numerous buildings presumed to have been used by Vijayanagara's ruling class. It seems to have suffered the worst at the hands of the post-Talikota plunderers, and a lot of what's here has only been laid bare by archaeologists since the 1970s.

Enter the Royal Centre from the Hampi–Kamalapuram road. On the right is the so-called **Queen's Bath**, a tank surrounded by pretty arcades and balconies (deceptively plain on the outside). Some 350m further, on your left, is the entrance to the **Royal Enclosure**, a walled precinct roughly 300m square. In its northeast corner stands the **Mahanavami Dibba**, a platform from which royalty are thought to have celebrated Dussehra and other festivities. It's faced with wonderful carvings of horses (with riders and handlers), elephants, monkeys, camels, dancers, musicians, warriors, swans, deer and more. The space it overlooks includes several water tanks (notably the beautiful Black Stone Pushkarani) and the King's Audience Hall, a platform reckoned to have supported a 100-pillared hall.

The **Hazararama Temple**, 100m further north, is more intact than other nearby structures and has superb carvings: the entire Ramayana round the outer walls of its inner sanctum, and festival processions on its external walls.

IMAGESOFINDIA/SHUTTERSTOCK

Vitthala Temple

Continue to the **Zenana Enclosure**, a compound named as if it was the royal women's quarters (though there's no actual evidence for this). It has three watchtowers, a treasury building, a palace basement and the **Lotus Mahal**, a building of uncertain purpose but exquisite beauty in its rippling lines of foliated arches. A doorway in the back of the Zenana Enclosure leads out to a handsome row of 11 domed **Elephant Stables**, in Indo-Islamic style.

Vitthala Temple

The **Vitthala Temple** is, along with the Virupaksha Temple, Hampi's most celebrated building – chiefly because of the fabulously carved stone chariot standing in its courtyard (and appearing on the ₹50 banknote). The chariot's wheels used to rotate and it was previously topped by a tower. It's a shrine to the man-eagle Garuda, the vehicle of the temple's presiding deity Vishnu.

The pavilion beyond the chariot (the entrance hall to the inner sanctum) was built in 1554, only a decade before Vijayanagara's fall, and contains some of the most exquisite Vijayanagar sculpture. Its front section features central colonettes producing different musical notes when tapped, as well as reliefs of lovers, human and elephant dancers and what appear to be clowns and wrestlers. On the low frieze round the pavilion's exterior look for Portuguese horse trainers, recognisable by their curved caps.

You can reach the Vitthala either by walking 2km along the **Kampabhupa Path** on the south bank of the Tungabhadra from Hampi Bazaar, or along the 1.2km straight Vitthala Bazaar road from the temple's car park on the Kamalapuram–Anegundi road. Motor vehicles are not allowed on the Hampi Bazaar road, but electric buggies shuttle people back and forth. Wheelchairs are available at the temple.

Achyutaraya Temple & Matanga Hill

You can reach the **Achyutaraya Temple** by walking 500m over a pass from the east end of Hampi Bazaar, or along the Achyutaraya's own 350m **bazaar street** leading south from the Khampabhupa Path. The Achyutaraya sits in a bowl between hills, slightly off the main trails, and receives correspondingly less visitors. Its main entrance is from the north through two partly ruined *gopurams*. The pillared hall to the right inside the first *gopuram* has some superb relief carving – animals, plants, deities including Krishna dancing with a snake – and there's more on the central hall, which housed the temple's main idol (a form of Vishnu).

From the compound's west side a small path leads round behind the south end where a large rock-cut image of the goddess Kali is still a brightly painted object of devotion for local people. Another path winds up **Matanga Hill**, from whose summit you can survey the landscape for kilometres around: another superb sunset (or sunrise) spot, it's slightly harder work to get up to than Hemakuta Hill.

OFF THE BEATEN TRACK

Malyavanta Hill is a great viewpoint, with Malyavanta Raghunatha Temple near its summit, and **Ahmed Khan's Mosque & Tomb** which was built in 1439 in Vijayanagara's Islamic quarter by an officer in its army.

You can reach this area from the Hampi Bazaar side of Vijayanagara along a 4km cycleable track that heads east 350m south of the Krishna Temple and comes out 650m north of the Ahmed Khan turnoff. It runs beside an irrigation channel through classic Hampi landscape. You won't meet very many other visitors around these sites, so it's probably best not to do it alone.

Badami & Beyond

CAVE TEMPLES | HINDU SCULPTURE | ARCHITECTURAL LABORATORY

GETTING AROUND

A day trip of about six hours to Pattadakal and Aihole costs around ₹1200 by autorickshaw or ₹2200 by taxi. Buses run half-hourly or hourly from Badami to Pattadakal and to Aihole, but only a couple connect the two villages.

Badami has a few daily bus and rail services to/from Hosapete (Hospet; for Hampi), Vijayapura, Hubballi and more distant destinations. Badami's bus station is on Station Rd near the town centre; the train station is 4km further north.

TOP TIP

The riches of Badami, Pattadakal and Aihole lie in their Hindu temple architecture and sculpture. Reading up beforehand on what you're going to see, or hiring an authorised guide at the sites, rewards with greater understanding and enjoyment.

It's all about the Chalukyas at Badami. This Hindu dynasty rose to prominence here in the 6th century CE and within 100 years had taken control of a large chunk of southern and central India, encompassing most of what are now the states of Karnataka, Maharashtra, Telangana and Andhra Pradesh. They produced some of India's most remarkable sculptural art, and built a huge number of temples at Badami and nearby Pattadakal and Aihole, amounting to a living textbook of early Hindu temple styles. A couple of days exploring these monuments enables you to enjoy remarkable hilly Deccan scenery, especially the high sandstone bluffs around Badami, and get a feel for small-town Deccan life. The Badami Chalukyas succumbed to the Rashtrakutas in the 750s, though Chalukya successor states soldiered on for a few more centuries elsewhere (and one of them, the Western Chalukyas, built a few late temples at Badami).

Caverns of the Gods

Exploring the Badami cave temples

Badami's famous **caves** *(₹250)* line up along the foot of a cliff above the southwest corner of the picturesque 5th-century **Agastha Theertha tank**. All four have the same basic layout. A two-part porch stretches across the cave mouths, the inner part being larger and often containing superhuman-sized deity figures up to 3m high. Behind this is a hall of sculpted pillars and then, hollowed out in the caves' back wall, the shrine. Caves 1 to 3 were carved out in the 6th century.

Cave 1 is dedicated to Shiva, who appears on the wall to the right outside the porch as Nataraja (the cosmic dancer) striking 18 dance moves in one captivating pose. The main porch has a huge figure of Ardhanarishvara, a combination of Shiva and his consort Parvati, on the right, and Harihara, half Shiva and half Vishnu, on the left.

Cave 2 is dedicated to Vishnu, who appears on the right wall of the porch as his incarnation Trivikrama, and on the left wall as the boar Varaha (emblem of the Chalukya kingdom).

HIGHLIGHTS
1 Badami Cave Temples

SIGHTS
2 Agastha Theertha
3 Archaeological Museum
4 Bhutanatha Temple
5 Malagitti Shivalaya
6 North Fort

SLEEPING
7 Heritage Resort

EATING
see 7 Heritage Restaurant
8 The Bridge

TRANSPORT
9 Bus Station

The largest and most impressive cave is Cave 3. The outer porch has an eight-armed Vishnu and Vishnu as Trivikrama, with a pot-bellied Garuda, Vishnu's man-eagle vehicle, on the ceiling. In the inner porch, Vishnu sitting on the snake Ananta and Vishnu as Varaha appear on the left; Vishnu's lion avatar Narasimha, plus Harihara, are on the right.

Carved in the early 7th century, Cave 4 is a Jain temple. On the left of the main porch stands Bahubali, son of the first *tirthankar* (great Jain teacher) Adinath, with plants growing up his body during his 12-year meditation. The 24th *tirthankar* Mahavir sits in the lotus position in the inner shrine.

Explore Beyond the Caves

Badami's lake and fort

After the caves there's an enjoyable two or three hours to be spent at other sites. Start with Badami's **Archaeological Museum** *(₹5)*, near the Agastha Theertha's northwest corner, then head to the **Bhutanatha (Bhootnath) Temple** and the carved rocks beyond it. Back at the museum, climb the path to the **North Fort**, with two Chalukyan Shiva temples. Finally, there's Badami's best-preserved early Chalukyan building, the **Malagitti Shivalaya** temple, accessed from the town.

DRAVIDIAN VIMANAS & NAGARA SIKHARAS

The early Chalukyan temples at Pattadakal, Aihole and Badami date from a time when distinctly different South and North Indian styles of temple architecture were emerging. The most obvious difference is in the shape of the tower above the temple's inner sanctum. In the southern (Dravidian) style this is a pyramidal set of stepped tiers called a *vimana*. In the northern Nagara style it's a curvilinear tower called a *sikhara*. Slightly confusingly, *sikharas* also crop up on South Indian temples, but in these cases the word refers to a dome-shaped cap atop a *vimana*. *Vesara* and Kadamba refer to towers that are a mix of northern and southern styles.

VISHNU'S AVATARS

Vishnu, the preserver and protector in the Hindu Trimurti (trinity), is commonly said to have 10 avatars (incarnations), which saved the world from different perils. **Krishna** and **Rama** are the two best-known. You're likely to encounter several others in your Karnataka travels. **Varaha** the boar raised the world from the bottom of the sea with his tusks. **Narasimha** the man-lion killed the havoc-dealing demon Hiranyakashipu. **Trivikrama**, aka Vamana the dwarf, turned into a giant to rid the universe of the demon king Bali. **Keshava**, or Chennakeshava, is a form of Vishnu as Krishna: he slew the horse-demon Keshi. **Ranganatha** or Ranganathaswamy is the name given to Vishnu resting on the coils of the snake Adishesha.

North Meets South

The royal temples of Pattadakal

Pattadakal village, 21km east of Badami by road, is home to a World Heritage–listed cluster of 8th-century Chalukyan temples that may have been created as a religious and coronation centre for the Badami royalty. Dedicated to Shiva, they contain superb stone sculpture, and are considered mature forms of the more experimental styles at Badami and Aihole.

Most of the temples are in one grassy **compound** *(₹550)* with informative signboards. Four of the first five temples – Kadasiddeshwara, Jambulinga, Galaganatha and Kasivishveshvara – are clear examples of the curvilinear-towered northern Nagara style. The other three (Sangamesvara, Mallikarjuna, Virupaksha) have southern (Dravidian) stepped pyramidal *vimanas*. The **Virupaksha Temple** is the largest and considered a perfect example of the Dravidian style.

Origins of Temple Architecture

The architectural gems of Aihole

Little **Aihole** has around 100 temples scattered among its houses. Some of its earliest temples, without significant towers, seem to be stone versions of rural wood-roofed temples. The latest of these, the Jain **Meguti Temple** (634 CE), stands on a small hill ascended by 118 steps with views over the village roofs.

Don't miss the 6th-century **Ravanaphadi cave temple**, with marvellous large-scale sculptures, on the village's eastern side. On the left of its entrance hall a 2m-high Shiva, between Parvati and Ganesh, dances with a snake in two of his hands while the seven *saptamatrikas* (a group of mother goddesses) groove along with him. In the inner hall are Vishnu as Varaha and Mahishamardini (Durga killing the demon buffalo Mahisha).

Aihole's central Durga group of temples displays all the stylistic variety that has earned Aihole the 'architectural laboratory' tag. Here there are, among others, early towerless temples such as the Gaudara Gudi and (debatably) the Ladkhan; the Suryanarayana Gudi with a *sikhara* tower; and the **Durga Temple** *(₹250)* itself, whose semicircular west end resembles some Buddhist temples. It has some of the site's best sculpture around its ambulatory (clockwise from the porch: Shiva with Nandi, Narasimha, Vishnu with Garuda, Varaha, Mahishamardini, Vishnu).

EATING IN BADAMI: OUR PICKS

The Bridge: Air-conditioned midrange restaurant in Clarks Inn hotel, reliable for veg and non-veg Indian and some Western dishes. *12.30-11pm* ₹₹

Heritage Restaurant: Even if you're not staying at the resort, worth a trip for Indian vegetarian meals in peaceful surrounds. *7-10am, 12.30-3pm & 7.30-10.30pm* ₹

Hotel Mayura Chalukya: The restaurant at this state-government-run hotel does dependable Indian meals. *7am-10pm* ₹

Sarvaras: Worth seeking out in Aihole for traditional North Karnataka dishes inside a quaint boutique property, plus alfresco dining in the lush garden. *9am-6pm* ₹₹

Vijayapura (Bijapur)

IMPOSING MAUSOLEUMS | ENDURING HISTORY | MONUMENTAL MOSQUES

A historic city epitomising the Deccan's era of Islamic dominance, Vijayapura (historically known as Bijapur) was capital of arguably the most powerful of the five Deccan sultanates formed when the Bidar-based Bahmani Sultanate broke up between 1490 and 1528. Bijapur's ruling Adil Shahi dynasty devoted a lot of energy and money to beautifying their city with mosques, palaces, gardens and tombs, and it's this legacy that draws travellers today. At its peak the Bijapur Sultanate controlled a large chunk of central India, including Goa, and it was a leader of the alliance of Deccan sultanates that destroyed the Vijayanagar empire and its capital at Hampi in 1565. For visitors, Vijayapura feels less like a single sight than a massive city-sized field of over 50 protected monuments – many of them vast tombs, towering minarets and sprawling mosques that rank among the finest surviving examples of Deccan Islamic architecture in Karnataka today.

GETTING AROUND

Vijayapura is well connected to other cities by bus and train, including frequent buses from the centrally located bus stand to Hosapete (for Hampi) and several a day to Panaji (Goa), plus buses and trains to Badami. While you can certainly walk between some of the city's main sights, they're too spread out for most people to comfortably cover all of them in a day on foot. Autorickshaws are plentiful and you could hire one for a day for ₹1000 to ₹1200.

VINAYAK JAGTAP/SHUTTERSTOCK

Gol Gumbaz (p834)

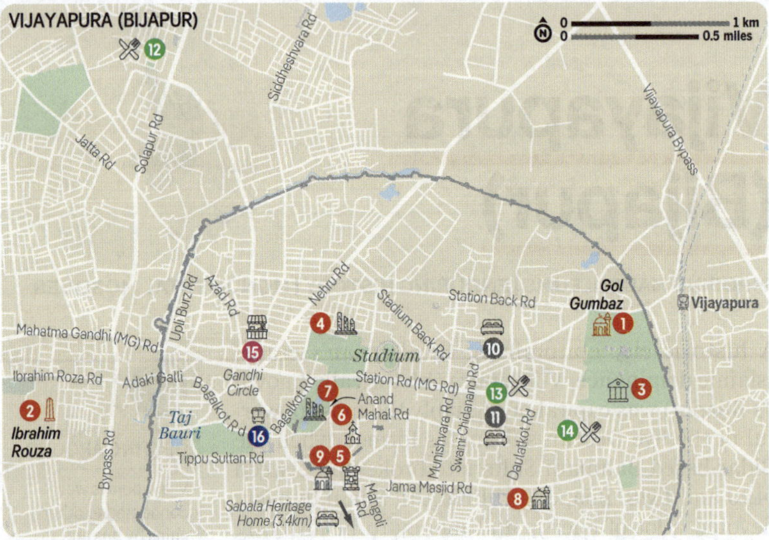

HIGHLIGHTS
1 Gol Gumbaz
2 Ibrahim Rouza

SIGHTS
3 Archaeological Museum
4 Bara Kaman
5 Citadel
6 CSI All Saints Church
7 Gagan Mahal
8 Jama Masjid
9 Karimuddin Masjid

SLEEPING
10 Hotel Madhuvan International
11 Kyriad Hotel

EATING
12 Artha Coffee & Co
13 Niyaaz Restaurant
14 Qaswa Hills

SHOPPING
15 Central Market

TRANSPORT
16 Bus Stand

TOP TIP

In the heart of the Deccan, Vijayapura gets pretty hot by early afternoon, so it pays to set out on your explorations early.

Vijayapura's Finest Tomb

Experience the acoustics of Gol Gumbaz

The **Gol Gumbaz** *(₹250)* awes with its sheer size: a grand dome (the name means Round Dome) on a 47-sq-metre building with seven-tier corner towers sporting their own mini-domes. It's the mausoleum of the seventh Bijapur sultan, Mohammed Adil Shah (r 1627–56), his two wives, his mistress (Rambha), a daughter and a grandson. From the cavernous interior, climb 120 steps inside the southeast tower to the 'whispering gallery' round the base of the dome, with incredible acoustics. A building in front of the Gol Gumbaz houses Vijayapura's worthwhile **Archaeological Museum** *(₹5)*.

EATING & DRINKING IN VIJAYAPURA: OUR PICKS

Qaswa Hills: Buzzing restaurant in Hotel Pearl, renowned for its meat dishes; try a chicken or mutton biryani or kebab. AC and non-AC sections. *7am-11pm* ₹₹

Artha Coffee & Co: Probably the best coffee in northern Karnataka (cappuccino, affogato, frappés, the lot) plus global eats, in a bright, airy space. *11am-11pm* ₹

Niyaaz Restaurant: Longstanding Indian biryani house, founded in 1989, known for its Mughlai dishes and smoky yoghurt-marinated chicken. *11am-11pm* ₹₹

90s Nest Cafe: Casual cafe focused on popular Indian snacks. Its relaxed setting draws a steady crowd of students and young locals. *noon-10pm* ₹

Discovering the Adil Shahis' City

The great monuments of Vijayapura

From Gol Gumbaz it's 1.4km to the **Jama Masjid**, the city's largest mosque, commissioned in 1576 by Ali Adil Shah I and at least partly financed with plunder from Vijayanagara (Hampi). Inside are a large courtyard and a domed prayer hall with beautiful gold-paint inscriptions and decoration on its mihrab.

A kilometre west of the Jama Masjid, the old **Citadel** was once the heart of the city with palaces, gardens and mosques surrounded by walls and a 1.5km moat. Only the moat's northwest quarter has water now. The most impressive remaining structure is the colossal archway of the **Gagan Mahal** royal palace. It's said that this is where the last sultan, Sikandar Adil Shah, surrendered in chains to the Mughal emperor Aurangzeb in 1686. The lawns and benches in front are a popular local relaxation spot.

Just behind the Gagan Mahal stands the austere facade of **All Saints Church**, originally built as a ceremonial gateway into the palace's private complex – it was later converted to a church by the British. Open for a few hours on Sunday mornings, its real surprise lies inside, where colourful stucco work and painted details contrast sharply with the plain exterior.

North across busy Station Rd (MG Rd) stands the **Bara Kaman**, the unfinished tomb of Ali Adil Shah II (r 1656–72), the second last of the dynasty. Originally intended to surpass Ali's father's tomb, the Gol Gumbaz, in grandeur, its arches and columns remain roofless on their high platform. Vijayapura's main **market area** is just west of here.

Vijayapura's aesthetic high point, the **Ibrahim Rouza** *(₹250)*, stands 800m outside the western walls. This mausoleum and its accompanying mosque (similar but not identical) are set in beautiful formal gardens, their upper levels a symphony of varisized domes and spindly minarets. Below, the mausoleum's walls are adorned with wonderful carved calligraphy and geometric designs. Inside are the tombs of the sixth sultan, Ibrahim Adil Shah II (r 1580–1627), his queen Taj Sultana and other family members.

Early Islamic Architecture

A 14th-century mosque built from temple stone

Less visited but historically important is **Karim-ud-Din's Mosque**, southwest of Anand Mahal. Dating to around 1320, it is the city's earliest surviving Islamic structure, built largely from the reused stonework of earlier Hindu buildings. Its low granite roof rests directly on massive stone columns without mortar, while its post-and-lintel construction reflect an early phase of architectural transition in the Deccan. To get a deeper sense of how these monuments fit together, **Walk Bijapur** *(instagram.com/walk_bijapur)* runs free heritage walks every Sunday morning, led by knowledgeable local volunteers who trace the city's layered history on foot.

KARNATAKA TOURS

Travel Next Tours & Travels: Mysuru-based agency arranging transport and guides across Karnataka, including wildlife stays and longer personalised itineraries. *(travel next.org)*

Unhurried: Knowledgeable guides lead food, market, nature and heritage walks in Bengaluru, trips to Hampi and Mysuru, and more. *(unhurried.in)*

Gully Tours: Experienced company offering a range of walks in Bengaluru (including some at night) and Mysuru. *(gully.tours)*

Breakaway: Organises bespoke trips around experiences and themes such as crafts, rural retreats, coffee plantations and wildlife. *(break -away.in)*

Bangalore Walks: Themed tours of the city. *(bangalore walks.com)*

Places We Love to Stay

₹ Budget ₹₹ Midrange ₹₹₹ Top End

Bengaluru (Bangalore)

Map p798

Locul Uptown ₹ Well-run hostel on a quiet lane 3km northwest of MG Rd. Organises interesting walks.

Casa Cottage ₹₹ A hospitable, tastefully renovated, century-old house, with a charming, tranquil garden.

The Fern Residency ₹₹ Modern hotel close to Majestic bus stand and Bengaluru's main train station.

Grand Magrath ₹₹ Long-running hotel near Brigade Rd; spacious rooms, consistent service and a rare rooftop pool in the city centre.

Taj West End ₹₹₹ Began life in 1887 as lodging for British officers, and still oozes colonial-era style, with impeccable modern comforts.

Taj MG Road ₹₹₹ Polished city-centre hotel near MG Rd, with contemporary rooms, an on-site brewery and a standout Chinese restaurant.

Mysuru (Mysore)

Map p805

Rahee Bi Roambay ₹ Well-run, intelligently designed hostel in two characterful adjoining houses.

Anokhi Garden ₹₹ Great option for staying a few days: en suite rooms in Gokulam with kitchen and washing machine; breakfast and yoga available.

Mysore Bed and Breakfast ₹₹ Family home full of personality and artefacts. Affable British host Stephen leads excellent cycling tours. Book ahead.

Laika Heritage Stay ₹₹ Thoughtfully restored heritage home with non-AC rooms, attentive hosts and a quiet residential setting away from Mysuru's busier areas.

Southern Star ₹₹₹ Good-value, well-located hotel: sizeable, well-equipped rooms, two restaurants, and a fine pool in leafy gardens.

Royal Orchid Metropole ₹₹₹ This former royal guest abode provides large, balconied rooms, excellent dining, heritage atmosphere and a classy bar.

Gitanjali Homestay ₹₹₹ Spacious, spotless rooms and generous breakfast, at an eco-minded garden property 6km from the centre.

Nagarhole Tiger Reserve

Evolve Back Kabini ₹₹₹ Luxury riverside lodge on the Kabini backwaters, offering refined villas, plus a strong wildlife focus and guided safaris to Nagarhole National Park.

Kabini River Lodge ₹₹₹ Well-organised former royal hunting lodge with comfortable cottages and a dorm. All packages include boat and land safaris.

KAAV Safari Lodge ₹₹₹ Deluxe rooms, glamping tents and villa right on the edge of the tiger reserve, with a viewing tower and enticing pool.

Bandipur Tiger Reserve

MC Resort ₹₹ Slightly-past-its-best small resort with relatively moderate prices, conveniently located.

The Serai Bandipur ₹₹₹ Elegant, Mediterranean-inspired villas at a luxury resort in the Mangala area.

Dhole's Den ₹₹₹ Contemporary design in pastoral surrounds near Mangala village: spacious rooms with terraces, solar power, organic farm.

Kodagu (Coorg)

Honey Valley ₹ Simple, decently kept rooms on a friendly family's coffee plantation in the luxuriant south Kodagu hills. Sister property Chingaara nearby has larger, more comfortable rooms.

Midland Inn ₹ Low-key guesthouse on a coffee estate near Madikeri, offering plantation walks and homestyle food made with produce from the on-site garden.

Gateway Coorg ₹₹ Hilltop resort near Madikeri with valley views, spacious grounds, plus on-site nature walks and coffee tastings.

Palace Estate ₹₹ Delightful ambience on a characterful coffee and spice farm with welcoming host, excellent home cooking and its own waterfall, at the foot of Thadiyandamol hill.

The Bungalow 1934 ₹₹₹ Comfort, space, attentive service and excellent meals in a revamped family bungalow on a south Kodagu hillside.

Chikkamagaluru (Chikmagalur)

Clover Leaf Home Stay ₹₹ Straightforward cottage rooms, home-cooked meals and evening bonfires on a forest coffee plantation, 9km from Chikkamagaluru town.

Gateway Chikmagalur ₹₹ Intimate 29-room resort near Chikkamagaluru valued for its Ayurveda spa, outdoor pool and tranquil gardens.

Halli Berri Cottages ₹₹₹ A marvellous, relaxed coffee-plantation getaway 25km north of Chikkamagaluru town: stylishly uncluttered rooms, superb meals and an estate tour included.

Trivik Resort ₹₹₹ Standout hilltop retreat with sweeping Mullayanagiri views from its infinity pool, Malnad-focused dining, plus plantation walks, bonfires and coffee cupping sessions.

Mangaluru (Mangalore)

Hotel Manorama ₹ Clean, bare rooms are fair value, and the owner's statuary collection in the lobby makes a memorable impression.

Country Inn & Suites by Radisson ₹₹ One of the more reliable hotels in Manipal, offering a practical base for exploring Udupi, nearby beaches and the coast.

Vivanta Mangalore Oldport Road ₹₹₹ Excellent value with classy service, well-equipped, spacious rooms, a garden pool, bar and terrific buffet breakfast.

Gokarna

Nirvana Café ₹ Fan-cooled rooms along a leafy back garden, all with verandah or balcony and bathroom. East end of Om Beach.

Ananda Cafe ₹ Friendly, family-run budget place 1.2km up Gokarna main beach from the town. Rear rooms in two-storey buildings are best.

Strawberry Farmhouse ₹₹ Plain but decent small cottages, most with views along Kudle Beach.

Namaste Yoga Farm ₹₹₹ Cottages and rooms scattered around a wooded Kudle hillside plot, owned by an amiable German yoga teacher. Tranquil and friendly vibes.

Hampi

Map p824

Wanderlust ₹ Popular spot in the Hanumanahalli countryside with basic cabins, tents and a sociable restaurant.

Epic Island Hampi ₹ Simple bamboo-weave bungalows looking through palms to the river and boulder hills beyond, outside Hanumanahalli.

Peshegaar Guesthouse ₹ Five simple yet stylish rooms decorated with tribal textiles around a pleasant common area with a courtyard garden. Bathrooms are shared, but there are four.

Srilatha Mane ₹ Quaint guesthouse in Anegundi offering three rooms, a courtyard and kitchen access, valued for its characterful setting and well-informed host.

Shankar Homestay ₹₹ Spacious, comfortable rooms and attentive hosts on a tree-covered property near Kadirampur.

Leo Wooden Resort ₹₹ Bijou cottages and excellent restaurant deep in the countryside 5km southwest of Sanapur. Crocodiles in the river, so swim in the pool!

Clarks Inn ₹₹ Professionally run hotel in Kamalapuram with spick-and-span rooms in colourful contemporary style.

Evolve Back Hampi ₹₹₹ The kind of place Vijayanagar royalty would have built if they were around today, out in the sticks beyond Kamalapuram.

Badami

Map p831

Heritage Resort ₹₹ Spacious, airy, inviting AC lodgings in leafy grounds 2km from the centre.

Wada 1 ₹₹ Boutique hotel within the Aihole temple complex, set in a restored 1000-year-old Chalukyan *wada* (courtyard mansion).

Vijayapura (Bijapur)

Map p834

Kyriad Hotel ₹₹ Well-maintained modern rooms and helpful staff, between the centre and the Gol Gumbaz.

Hotel Madhuvan International ₹₹ On a quiet side street, the Madhuvan has plain, clean rooms with optional AC. Cheerful staff and good dining.

Sabala Heritage Home ₹₹ NGO-linked Sabala provides rooms and all-veg meals; runs a craft shop and centre supporting Adivasi women. Semi-rural setting 6km southeast of the centre.

Pravasa Hotel ₹₹₹ Contemporary hotel offering notably spacious rooms and bathrooms, conveniently located about 2.5km from Ibrahim Rouza.

For places to stay in Telangana and Andhra Pradesh, see p875

Above: Charminar (p853), Hyderabad; Right: Sri Venkateshwara Temple (p873), Tirumala

Researched by
Mark Eveleigh

Telangana & Andhra Pradesh

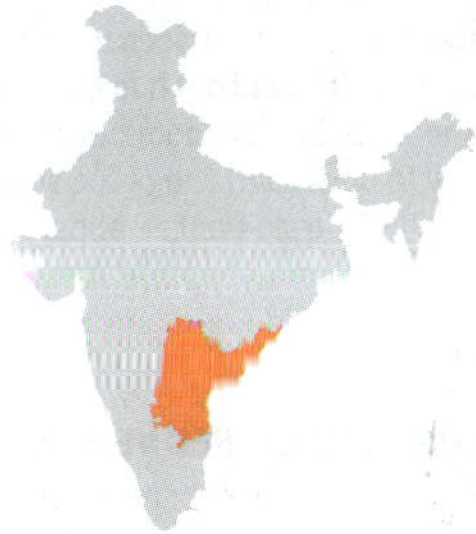

FEASTS, TEMPLES AND LAVISH HISTORY

The buzzing foodie city of Hyderabad is the atmospheric leaping-off point for a hinterland studded with fascinating history and humbling sacred sites.

The ancestral home of India's richest royal family, handsome, historic Hyderabad is the gateway to a region that is underexplored but invariably appreciated by those who make the effort to uncover its charms. Indeed, with direct international flights arriving into Hyderabad's well-organised airport from the UK, Europe, Middle East and Asia, this might well be our favourite first stop in India. Many travellers tour Hyderabad's museums, palaces and mausoleums, then zoom on to Chennai (Madras) or Bengaluru (Bangalore), missing out on the rich history and atmospheric religious sites of rural Telangana and highland and coastal Andhra Pradesh.

VJVENKI/SHUTTERSTOCK ©

The holy hill of Tirumala in the south of Andhra Pradesh is one of India's most important places of pilgrimage, but everywhere you travel in this region the countryside is dotted with the ruins of Buddhist monasteries, ornately decorated Hindu and Jain temples and near-mythical forts.

The two states were one until 2014, and the business of setting up separate state institutions is still ongoing – with a new Andhra Pradesh capital being currently established at little Amaravathi, near Vijayawada.

To get the most from the region, use Hyderabad and Warangal (in Telangana) and Vijayawada and Visakhapatnam (in Andhra Pradesh) as your main hubs for exploring, travelling around by bus, train, chartered taxi and autorickshaw. Take your time, prioritising mealtimes to enjoy to the full the region's lavishly spiced meat and veg cuisine.

THE MAIN AREAS

HYDERABAD
Palaces, pearls and biryani.
p844

VIJAYAWADA
An easy hub for sacred sites.
p860

VISAKHAPATNAM
Museums, beaches and up-country detours. p864

TRAIN

Trains serve all corners of these two states, but services to and from Hyderabad get busy, so book ahead. Delays are common, so it will pay to download one of the several available 'train tracker' apps.

BUS & CHARTERED VEHICLE

Buses are the backbone of rural travel here, and more expensive (and more comfortable) private companies supplement the regular but crowded buses provided by the two state bus companies.

AIR

Bear in mind that a one-hour flight might often be more convenient than a 10-hour overland journey (often at very little extra cost). IndiGo flights from Hyderabad, Vijayawada, Visakhapatnam and Tirupati are a very tempting alternative to long overland trips.

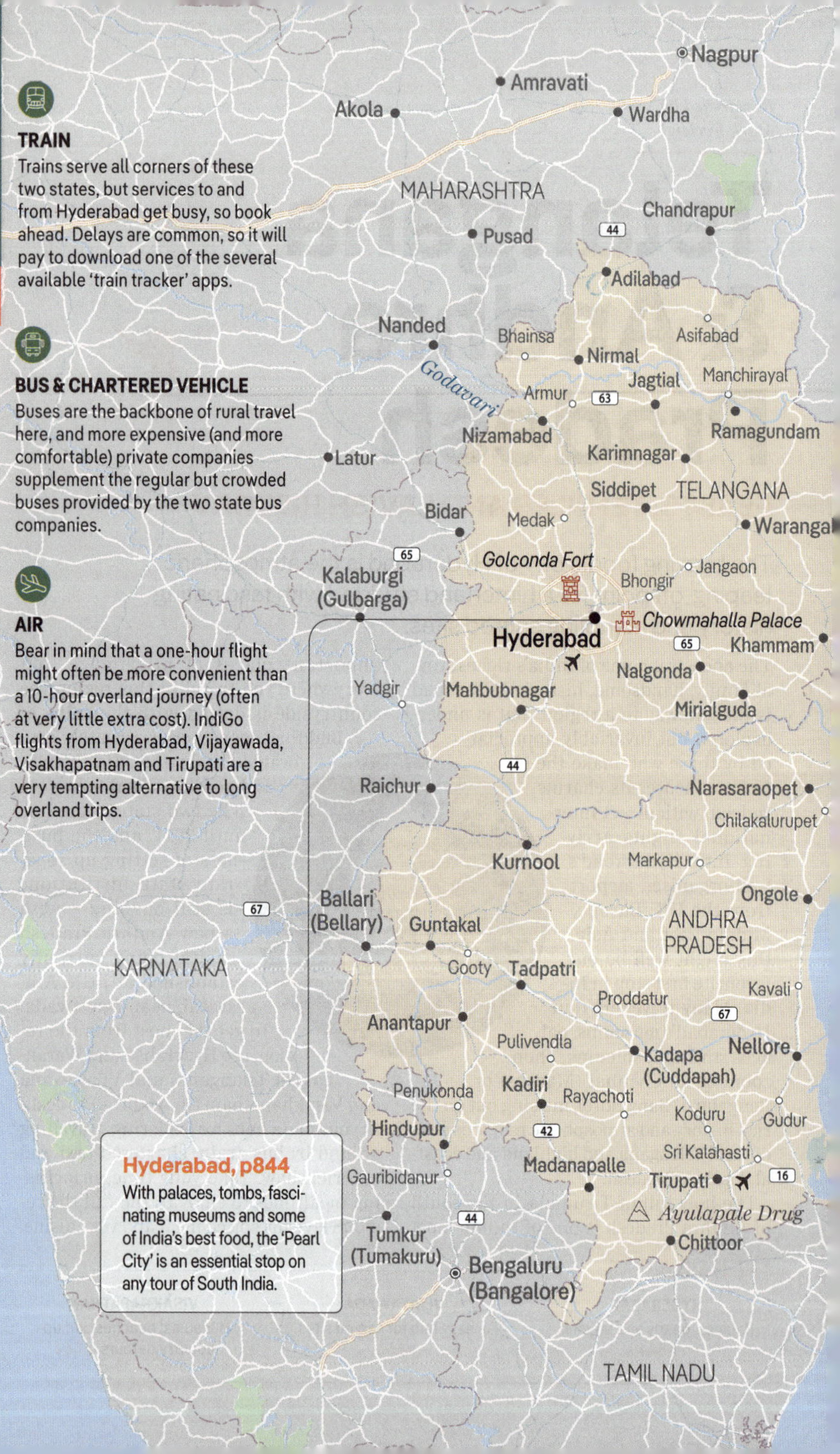

Hyderabad, p844
With palaces, tombs, fascinating museums and some of India's best food, the 'Pearl City' is an essential stop on any tour of South India.

Find Your Way

Hyderabad is the dynamic hub for two states that used to be one. From here, buses and trains fan out across Telangana and Andhra Pradesh. The sacred hill of Tirumala is best reached via Tirupati International Airport.

Visakhapatnam, p864
Hone your surfing skills in Andhra Pradesh's seaside city, or take coastal and highland road trips to historic sites that rarely see a foreign visitor.

Vijayawada, p860
This appealing city is a convenient hub for trips to off-the-beaten-track temples, forts, Buddhist sites and the friendly town of Amaravathi.

Plan Your Time

Must-see Hyderabad is worth several days of your time before setting off to explore the rest of Telangana and Andhra Pradesh. Remote Tirumala is connected with Hyderabad via a one-hour flight or a 10-hour bus.

UNIQUELY INDIA/GETTY IMAGES

Chowmahalla Palace (p845), Hyderabad

Five Days for Hyderabad & Highlights

- Focus your first day on **Hyderabad** (p844), exploring palaces and museums. Fuel your excursions with ample biryani and find time for a leisurely spell in one of the city's cool cafes. Take the train northwest across Telangana to temple-filled **Warangal** (p857) and hire a driver for a half-day excursion to **Ramappa Temple** (p859), one of India's unsung architectural highlights.

- From here head down to **Vijayawada** (p860) to spend a few days exploring **Kondapalli Fort** (p862) and the ancient Buddhist sites in **Amaravathi** (p863), Andhra Pradesh's new capital. Loop back to Hyderabad to shop for souvenirs in the bazaars (or pearls in a trendy mall) and wander among the tropical vegetation and peacocks in **Kasu Brahmananda Reddy National Park** (p855).

SEASONAL HIGHLIGHTS

There's no bad time to visit Telangana and Andra Pradesh. Spring is particularly lovely and, if you don't mind crowds, the festival season (August and September) can be unforgettably vibrant.

JANUARY

With a maximum temperature of around 25°C (13°C at night), the coldest month of the year is ideal for exploring and walking. Many communities celebrate the beginning of the harvest season at this time.

MARCH

An important time for Muslims with **Ramadan** ending in March and for Hindus with **Deccan**, **Mahashivratri** and **Ugadi** festivals being celebrated in this month (although dates vary according to the Hindu calendar).

MAY

A lovely time to travel with the jacarandas in a riot of purple haze. The heat is increasing prior to the monsoon (which begins in mid-June) but spring is a great season to head to Visakhapatnam's beaches or Araku Valley.

Ten Days for History, Coast & Highlands

Begin with a couple of days to soak up **Hyderabad** (p844) history around Chowmahalla Palace, Galconda Fort and the British Residency. Next take a flight for a two-night stay in Tirupati and spend a day joining the barefoot pilgrimage to the incredible temple at **Tirumala** (p873). The direct morning flight is the best way to reach **Visakhapatnam** (p864). Spend a day experiencing the four naval/aviation museums, but be sure to schedule a morning surf session (or just beach wander) at **Rushikonda Beach** (p867). Take the scenic train up to **Araku Valley** (p870) for some highland relaxation and unforgettable slow-cooked bamboo chicken. Hire a driver for the drive back to the coast so that you can detour to visit **Borra Caves** (p869). Fly out from Visakhapatnam International Airport.

Three Weeks to See It All

Allow at least four days to experience the best of **Hyderabad** (p844) – historical sights, temples, parks and bazaars. Move on to **Warangal** (p857) but base yourself in Hanamkonda from where you can explore the iconic temples on foot. Take a morning drive to **Ramappa Temple** (p859) before catching an afternoon train to **Vijayawada** (p860) to spend three days seeing the sights. Visit the Buddhist stupa at **Amaravathi** (p863), then catch the train to **Visakhapatnam** (p864) to see the Varahalakshmi Narasimha Temple and the Buddhist sites along the coast. **Araku Valley** (p870) is a crucial detour before you catch a flight to Tirupati. End your tour in fine style with a barefoot pilgrimage up to the sacred hill at **Tirumala** (p873) before looping back to Hyderabad.

AUGUST

Bonalu Festival, one of Telangana's most colourful Hindu ceremonies, tends to fall in August and is a vibrant celebration of the goddess Mahakali. With the monsoon in full swing you'll see few international visitors and lower prices.

SEPTEMBER

Another month for celebrations, with **Ganeshotsav** (in honour of the iconic elephant-headed god) celebrated throughout Telangana and Andhra Pradesh and **Brahmotsavam** focused especially at Tirumala.

OCTOBER

Dussehra (p39) brings an end to nine days of fasting for many Hindus, a particularly fascinating time to visit Vijayawada's Kanaka Durga temple. The festival of flowers and beauty that is **Bathukamma** also runs into October.

DECEMBER

Winter is the busiest time, with domestic tourists taking city breaks to Hyderabad and the temple towns. Despite the crowds, this can be an ideal time to visit and to make lasting friendships among domestic visitors.

Hyderabad

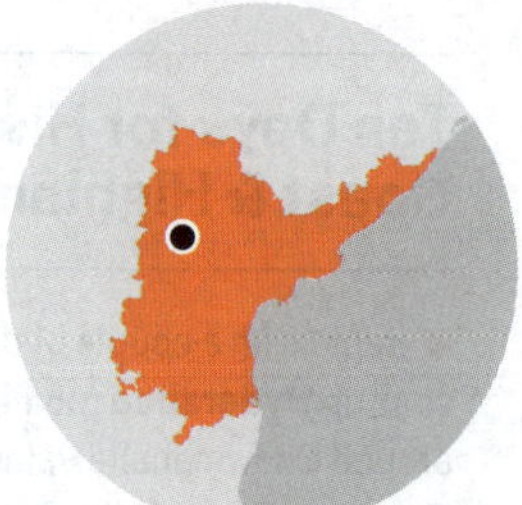

PALACES | TOMBS | FAMED BIRYANI

GETTING AROUND

The metro takes the stress out of exploring Hyderabad and tickets (available via various apps or directly at stations) range from ₹11 to ₹69 for a journey in the city. Autorickshaws (best booked through the Uber or Rapido apps) are also very affordable and simultaneously offer an opportunity to take in the ever-frantic street scenes. Taxis have the benefit of air-con but are more expensive and usually slower. The city is hard to navigate on foot and crossing any major road is a test of courage. Hyderabad's most convenient train stations are Secunderabad, Nampally and Kacheguda.

It can take a little tenacity to hunt down atmospheric corners of the timeless medieval city in what is now a fast-flowing modern metropolis. Take time to get to know Hyderabad, however, and you'll discover an enchanting city where diners invite you to join their table in crammed-to-the-rafters biryani restaurants and museum security guards will zip you round the highlights if you arrive close to closing time.

In the crowded bazaars around minaret-topped Charminar quarter, pearls, precious stones and perfumes have been traded for centuries. Trendy modern neighbourhoods such as Banjara Hills and Jubilee Hills are also great places to shop and dine – flush with money from the city's IT revolution. What is harder to love is Hyderabad's traffic. The efficient metro takes away some of the pain, but there will still be moments when you take an autorickshaw just to avoid the death-defying act of crossing a main road.

A Sprawling Regal Ruin

Climb the ramparts of Golconda Fort

Golconda Fort *(hyderabad.telangana.gov.in; ₹300)*, Hyderabad's most iconic sight, was constructed in the 16th century by the Qutb Shahi dynasty. Inside monumental battlements that run for 4.8km, its grand royal palaces, though shattered and roofless, remain a poignant reminder of the fort's former grandeur.

Start exploring at the base of the hill, where formal gardens, an enormous arsenal and the royal funerary hammam lead to a magnificent sprawl of royal apartments. Some of the chambers retain traces of their original carved stucco, and the vaulted ceilings provide a home for vast colonies of bats. The graceful **Taramati Mosque** is the most impressively ornamented structure here, but you can also see traces of dainty pools in the former **zenana** (women's quarters).

Due to clever acoustic effects, the sound of a hand-clap from a sentry at Fateh Darwaza (the outer so-called Victory Gate)

DMITRY STRIZHAKOV/SHUTTERSTOCK

Golconda Fort

could be heard almost a kilometre away at the Baradari (Reception Hall) on the hilltop. If the thousands of bats squeaking in the darkness of the crypts freak you out, continue onwards to the **Darbar Hall** on the peak, which is dominated by emerald green parrots and skulking lizards. Carry water because 277 shadeless stone steps lead from the southern access to the still-functioning **Jagadamba Mahakali Temple** and the heart of the fortress. The more taxing northern stairway is best used as an exit.

You can get to Golconda Fort by auto or taxi, but it's worth taking a guide who can point out hidden features and recount little-known local and historical anecdotes. **Breakaway** *(break-away.in)* has a team of experienced and highly knowledgeable English-speaking guides and can provide a day-trip tour combining Golconda Fort with many of the city's other main sights *(from ₹6000 for up to 4 people)*.

The Nizams' Palatial Pad

Admire Hyderabad's grandest palace

The opulent **Chowmahalla Palace** *(chowmahalla.in; adult/child ₹400/40)* was constructed in the 18th and 19th centuries as a home for a succession of Nizams (rulers of Hyderabad), starting in 1769 with Nizam Ali Khan Asaf Jah II. The front

HYDERABADI CUISINE

Hyderabadi cuisine, famous across India, is a lavish fusion of southern spices with the rich, meaty flavours of Mughal tradition. The landmark dish is biryani – basmati rice, spices and vegetables, egg, mutton or chicken. Layered in a single pot, it is covered and slowly cooked in its own steam. Huge portions are served at countless biryani restaurants, accompanied by *mirchi ka salan* (a spiced gravy) and yoghurt-based raita. Order slow-*simmered dum biryani* rather than the less refined fried version for authentic, melt-in-the-mouth flavours. The other dish to seek out is *haleem*, a Ramadan delicacy of pounded spiced wheat with lentils and goat, chicken or beef. If spiciness is not to your taste a glass of yoghurt-based lassi (sweet or salted) is the ideal remedy.

EATING IN HYDERABAD: BEST BIRYANI

Cafe Bahar: Air-con upstairs and non-air-con downstairs, but expect queues at both at this favourite spot for lunchtime biryani. *11am-1am* ₹₹

Hotel Shadab: A legendary old-city venue near Madina Circle for biryani – rich, fragrant and alive with the flavours of cinnamon and cloves. *noon-11.30pm* ₹₹

Paradise: A local biryani legend. Branches include a grand flagship eatery near Paradise Flyover Rd in Secunderabad. *11.30am-11pm* ₹₹

Biryaniwalla & Co: A taste of proper homegrown biryani in Banjara Hills, popular with workers on the homebound commute. *noon-10.30pm* ₹₹

HYDERABAD
Krishnakanth Park
SR NAGAR
Balkampet Rd
Yousufguda Main Rd
Yellareddyguda Rd
Ameerpet Rd
AMEERPET
Rd No 36
Rd No 10
42
39
JUBILEE HILLS
Rd No 1
Srinagar Colony Rd
40
45
Rd No 45 Jubilee Hills
46
24
Rd No 3
37
28
Hindu Cemetery
Rd No 3
Panjagutta Rd
Rd No 2
19
Rd No 5
44
43
11
Rd No 14
Jalagam Vengala Rao Park
KBR (Kasu Brahmananda Reddy) National Park
BANJARA HILLS
Rd No 4
Rd No 7
47
Mathur Rd
KBR Lake
21
Road No 8
49
Rd No 10
30
27
DEEN DAYAL NAGAR
Lotus Pond
Rd No 82
Rd No 11
56
Rd No 1
52
Rd No 13
Banjara Lake
Rd No 1 3A
Church Rd
Hakimpet Kunta
Farook Rd
Rd No 12
MASAB TANK
ADITYA NAGAR COLONY
MEHDIPATNAM
Chacha Nehru Park
Masab Tank Rd
TOLI CHOWKI
Mehdipatnam Rd
HUMAYUN NAGAR
Shah Hatim Talab
Asif Nagar Rd
HYDERABAD
Mohammadia Ln
Khader Bagh Rd
PV Narasimha Rao Expy
Gudimalkapur Rd
Tappa Chabutra Rd
Golconda Fort
2
Gudimalkapur Vegetable Market
LANGAR HOUSE
Ford Rd
Langar Houz Talab
GOLCONDA FORT
GUDIMALKAPUR
Golconda Rd
Langar House Rd
Musi River
Musi River
Rd No 82
PLEASANT PARK
Musi River
Upparpally Rd
TEJASWI NAGAR
PV Narasimha Rao Elevated Expressway
UPPERPALLY
Kishan Bagh Rd
Musi River
Puranapul Rd
0 1 km
0 0.5 miles
Nehru Zoological Park

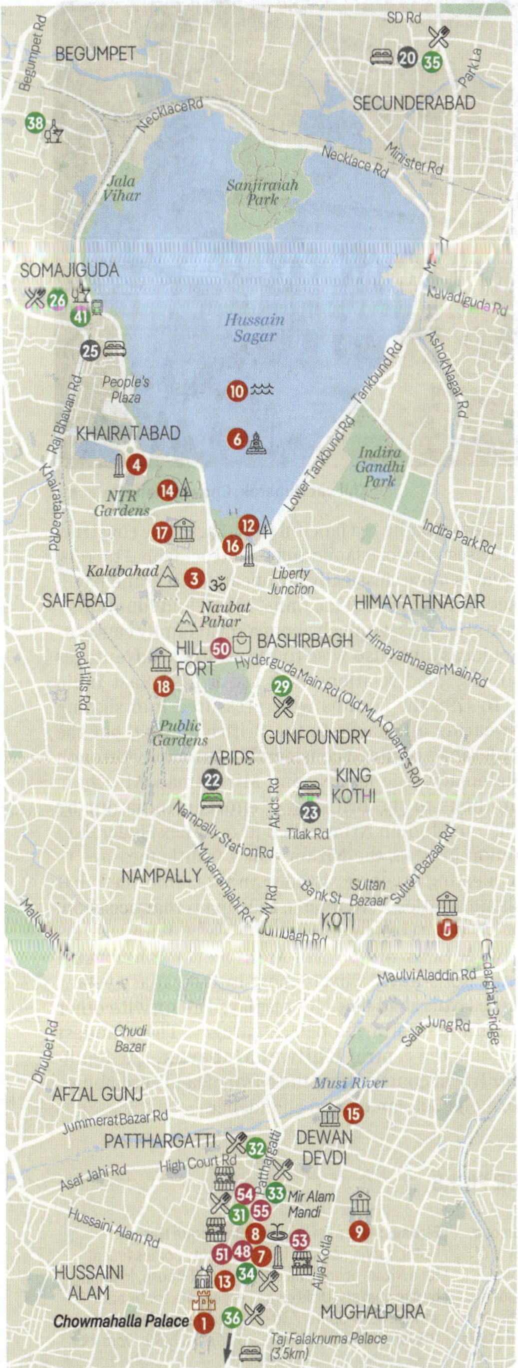

HIGHLIGHTS
1 Chowmahalla Palace
2 Golconda Fort

SIGHTS
3 Birla Mandir
4 BR Ambedkar Statue
5 British Residency
6 Buddha Statue
7 Charminar
8 Gulzar Houz
9 HEH The Nizam's Museum
10 Hussain Sagar
11 Kasu Brahmananda Reddy National Park
12 Lumbini Park
13 Mecca Masjid
14 NTR Gardens
15 Salar Jung Museum
16 Telangana Amarula Smarakam
17 Telangana Secretariat
18 Telangana State Archaeology Museum

SLEEPING
19 Golden Glory Guesthouse
20 Hotel Raj Inn
21 Hotel Urban Eminonoo
22 Royalton Hotel
23 Taj Mahal Hotel
24 The Leela Hyderabad
25 The Park

EATING
26 Aish
27 Barbeque Nation
28 Biryaniwalla & Co
29 Cafe Bahar
see 23 Dakshina Mandapa
30 Firdaus
31 [illegible]
32 Hotel Shadab
33 Meerut Hotel
34 Nimrah Cafe
35 Paradise
36 Pista House
37 Royal Tiffin Centre

DRINKING & NIGHTLIFE
38 10 Downing Street
39 Black Fuel Roastery
40 Broadway
41 Kismet
42 Prost Brewpub
43 Roast CCX
44 Roastery Coffee House
45 True Black

SHOPPING
46 Evolution Contemporary Arts
47 Fabindia
48 Gulzar Houz Market
49 Ikat India
50 Kalanjali
51 Laad Bazaar
52 Malkha
53 Mir Alam Mandi
54 Patel Market
55 Patthargatti Rd
56 Suvasa

TOP TIP

On arrival at Hyderabad's international airport beware of taxi touts in fake uniforms masquerading as rideshare drivers. They operate right in front of the taxi desks (and in full view of airport security). Go directly to speak to staff behind the desks.

DIAMOND GEEZERS

The Qutb Shahis and later the Nizams built their vast fortunes on solid foundations and you won't be in the city long before you realise that jewels – in the form of gold, pearls and especially diamonds – are still what puts the sparkle in Hyderabadi eyes.

The Krishna Valley to the east of Hyderabad was the world's main source of diamonds until the discovery of deposits in southern Africa in the 19th century. The Kollur mine near Vijayawada was reputedly the source of the Koh-i-Noor (p858) as well as the gigantic 340-carat Nizam Diamond, which the last Nizam, Mir Osman Ali Khan, is said to have used as a paperweight. This legendary stone vanished mysteriously during the 1948 annexation of Hyderabad, and its present whereabouts is unknown.

AKELLA SRINIVAS RAMALINGASWAMI/SHUTTERSTOCK

Khilwat Mubarak, Chowmahalla Palace

half of the Chowmahalla is a fanciful Indo-Saracenic construction, with incised stucco, Islamic arches and octagonal turrets, while the rear is more classically European, with grand pavilions flanked by neoclassical columns, lawns and fountains.

The palace's design says much about a royal family captivated by novel ideas, and also wise to the strategic advantages of maintaining good relations with the British East India Company. In 1798 the Nizams were pressured into signing a treaty swearing allegiance to the British empire, but the state of Hyderabad retained considerable autonomy through careful diplomacy. The last Nizam, Mir Osman Ali Khan, donated millions to the British war effort in India during WWII. When the Indian Army rolled in to annex Hyderabad into the union in 1948, the Nizam sent a frantic message to London requesting urgent assistance and was informed that the British authorities were unable to help on that occasion.

Showing off their cosmopolitan tastes came with the territory for the Nizams. Mir Osman Ali Khan commissioned a custom-built Rolls-Royce Silver Ghost in the canary-yellow colours of the Hyderabad flag – it's displayed along with other heirloom automobiles in the palace garages. The grandest building here is the central **Khilwat Mubarak**, a magnificent *durbar* (royal court) where the Nizams held ceremonies under enormous Belgian crystal chandeliers.

EATING IN HYDERABAD: OUR PICKS

Govind Dosa: A cult food stall west of Patthargatti Rd, with *idli* (rice cakes), *vada* (fritters) and spectacular dosas. *7am-midnight* ₹

Pista House: A famous Shalibanda purveyor of *haleem* (meaty, spicy stew) during Ramadan, and other meaty dishes year-round. *11am-11.30pm* ₹₹

Firdaus: At the Taj Krishna Hotel, serving cuisine fit for a Nizam accompanied by live *ghazals* (Urdu love songs). *12.30-3pm & 7.30-11.30pm* ₹₹₹

Barbeque Nation: Quantity comes first at this grill-house, featuring excellent kebabs and fantastic curries. *noon-3.30pm & 6.30-10pm* ₹₹₹

At the rear of the compound, the European-influenced **Afzal Mahal** contains elegant colonial-era furniture and royal heirlooms. Flanking the palace gardens are the **Aftab Mahal**, displaying lavish royal wedding outfits, and the **Mehtab Mahal**, now occupied by palace offices. Palm-fringed fountains and lawns complete the picture of an exclusive private getaway for entire generations of extremely pampered royals.

The Lavish Lives of the Nizams

Explore ostentatious royal homes

Northeast of Chowmahalla Palace, the **Purani Haveli** was the residence of the sixth Nizam, Mahbub Ali Khan (r 1869–1911). The palace has been taken over by the Mukkaram Jah High School, but one wing remains open as **HEH The Nizam's Museum** *(thenizamsmuseum.com; adult/child ₹125/free)*, displaying a king's ransom in royal possessions, including Mahbub Ali Khan's silver cradle and gold-burnished throne. Whole rooms are filled with racks of silver ornaments and models of Hyderabad buildings, donated by grateful royal subjects (and, no doubt, hopeful petitioners). Since it's said that the sixth Nizam never wore the same clothes twice, you have to wonder what he kept in the 54m-long, two-storey Burmese teak walk-in wardrobe.

Another royal residence, the opulent **Falaknuma Palace** (p875; *tajhotels.com*) is an astonishing circa-1884 Indo-Saracenic fantasy. Today it houses Hyderabad's most luxurious hotel. Adorned with stained-glass paintings of European scenes, the palace is built in the shape of a scorpion, surrounded by elegant, peacock-filled grounds on a hilltop south of the Charminar. If you can't stretch to the US$600+ room rates, book in for an exceptional dinner or arrange an afternoon tour with high tea. The Nizam Palaces tour run by **Telangana Tourism** *(tourism.telangana.gov.in)* also swings by the Falaknuma and offers an opportunity to check out the world's longest dining table, seating 101 guests.

Marvellous Mercantile Madness

Untangle the bazaars

Hyderabadis flock to the teeming bazaars around the Charminar monument (p853) to browse, bargain and buy. Approaching from the north you'll first reach **Patthargatti Road**, home to some of the city's most extravagant wedding outfitters, creating astonishing bead-work patterns on lehenga wedding dresses. Mir Chowk Rd runs east to the **Mir Alam Mandi**, the ramshackle wholesale fruit and veg market.

In the **Gulzar Houz** quarter, stores are piled with strands of Hyderabadi pearls, gemstone garlands and glass bottles of *ittar* (Islamic perfume). If you're in the market for pearls, examine the strands carefully, checking the pearls for lustre and smoothness – agreeably wonky 'rice pearls' are less costly than perfect spheres.

You'll know you've reached Charminar proper when you emerge into a manic market selling everything from household

HYDERABAD'S MOST STYLISH STORES

Evolution Contemporary Arts: The best place to shop for sustainably sourced craft and textile souvenirs from all over the region.

Fabindia: Branches in Banjara Hills and Jubilee Hills stock stylish but pricey Indian clothing and homeware.

Kalanjali: Close to the Assembly metro stop and stacked with crafts, knick-knacks, accessories and chic women's designer wear.

Malkha: South of Banjara Hills, environmentally aware Malkha specialises in hand-dyed, hand-printed and handwoven clothing.

Ikat India: This sleek Jubilee Hills store specialises in traditional *ikat* scarves, *dupattas* (long scarves), shawls and clothing, with patterns dyed into the fibres.

Suvasa: High-quality clothing and homeware in Banjara Hills; great for high-end designer *salwar* kameez (traditional dresslike tunic and trouser combination for women), dupattas and kurta (long shirts).

goods to chintzy costume jewellery and tourist trinkets. Look out for dealers in old Indian coins: many from the Raj era (1858–1947) and, occasionally, crude copper coins dating back to the 16th century. The bazaars around the Charminar have done a brisk trade in perfumes since the 16th century, when they supplied fragrances for the court of the Qutb Shahis. You'll see inexpensive prepackaged natural flower scents and extravagant blended fragrances costing upwards of ₹7000 a bottle.

Laad Bazaar, running west from the Charminar, is famed for its bangle shops, specialising in sparkling lac bangles made from insect resin. To the west of Patthargatti Rd, the lively **Patel Market** selling cloth and textiles of every imaginable hue and design cranks into action from around 11am.

Grand Civic Moments by the Lake

Spot statues by Hussain Sagar

Hussain Sagar, Hyderabad's city-centre lake, was created by the Qutb Shahis in the 16th century and today its southern shoreline is crowded with the city's most ostentatious civic monuments.

The southern shore is dominated by a gargantuan 38m-high statue of **BR Ambedkar**, the reformist government minister who inspired 500,000 Dalits to convert to Buddhism to escape the restrictions of the Hindu caste system. Behind him you'll see the Mughal-inspired **Telangana Secretariat** and **Telangana Amarula Smarakam**, a spectacular mirrored sculpture commemorating the 369 students killed while campaigning for a separate Telangana state in 1969.

On the nearby hilltop, the ethereal **Birla Mandir** was constructed in 1976 from gleaming white Rajasthani marble. Fusing northern and southern architectural styles and dedicated to Sri Venkateshwara, a popular incarnation of Vishnu, the temple draws pilgrims throughout the day, and offers magnificent views over the lake and the city skyline. Bags, phones and cameras must be left with the guards at the entrance.

The two lakeshore parks, **NTR Gardens** and **Lumbini Park** *(both adult/child ₹20/10)*, have seen better days. NTR is nevertheless popular with families for its oversized sculptures and (slightly dilapidated) children's rides, while Lumbini is primarily known for the motorboats that shuttle passengers out to see the 18m-high granite statue of **Buddha**, consecrated by the Dalai Lama in 2006.

Hyderabad's History Museums

Dive into Hyderabad history

The royal families of Hyderabad were obsessive hoarders, and their vast collections of treasures have spilled over into the city's museums. **Salar Jung Museum** *(salarjungmuseum.in; ₹500)* exhibits a mind-boggling collection amassed by Mir Yousuf Ali Khan (Salar Jung III), grand vizier to the seventh Nizam. He accumulated enough heirlooms to fill 39 galleries, covering everything from jade mouthpieces for hookah pipes

ANCIENT WATER RESERVOIRS

Akila Chungi – a ceramic artist, spatial designer and co-founder of Black Fuel Roastery – appreciates her city's historic buildings. *@one.pot.dish*

Step-wells hold much more than just water; an incredible insight into subterranean architecture, they're repositories of history, culture, tradition and countless stories.

Bansilalpet Step-well *(₹50)* Restored in 2022, this beautiful step-well has spectacular acoustics and light quality, so check *@gandipet_welfare_society* for details of musical events.

Bapughat Baoli Step-well *(₹20)* Said to have once been a 'pleasure garden', this step-well now serves as a venue for small-group musical performances.

Badi Baoli Step-well *(adult/child ₹10/5)* This is architecturally the most spectacular, and perhaps the best-known - it's the biggest of the six historic step-wells in Qutub Shahi Tombs.

JOSEPH FIDELIS/SHUTTERSTOCK

Buddha statue, Hussain Sagar

and engraved swords to European sculptures and exquisite paintings from all the Indian miniature schools.

Founded in 1951, the museum is all the more evocative for its web of corridors, and the slightly musty smell that brings to mind the bric-a-brac–filled home of some eccentric relative. It's easy to miss whole sections of the collection, so take your time and hunt down quirky pieces like the elegantly carved *Veiled Rebecca* by 19th-century Italian sculptor Benzoni, spectacular (if ecologically disturbing) ivory carvings, extravagant Persian carpets and unusual toys and household items.

Smaller but equally evocative in its own way, the rambling **Telangana State Archaeology Museum** *(adult/child ₹50/25, plus ₹50 to take photos)* is located in a fanciful Indo-Saracenic building constructed by the seventh Nizam as a playhouse for his daughter. Interlinked wings display archaeological treasures, cannons, stone carvings, inlaid metal *bidriware* and hand-painted *kalamkari* fabrics. Unexpected highlights are a 2000-year-old Egyptian mummy (with wonderfully descriptive information – in English and Hindi) plus, incredibly, a clay bowl containing what is believed to be some of the ashes of Buddha (which were unearthed in 1993 at Bavikonda, near Visakhapatnam).

HITS OF TOLLYWOOD

The Telangana film industry – known locally as 'Tollywood' – is massive, accounting for 20% of films made in India. Centred in Hyderabad, the industry is fast gaining on Bollywood, producing up to 200 full-length feature films every year, alongside thousands of hours of television shows for India's 96 million Telugu speakers.

The biggest Tollywood smash of all time was the 2017 historical blockbuster, *Baahubali 2*, the first Telugu film to take more than ₹10 billion at the box office. This action romp almost doubled the take of the previous record-holder, the original *Baahubali* – at the time, the most expensive Indian movie ever produced. A big hit was 2023's controversial *RRR*, an all-guns-blazing, Raj-era retribution tale casting the British Army as vanquished villains.

EATING IN HYDERABAD: OUR CROSS-CITY PICKS

Royal Tiffin Centre: A favourite local hangout with locations around the city including Banjara Hills for tasty dosa snacks and friendly service. *4am-1am* ₹

Meerut Hotel: A hole-in-the-wall near the Mir Alam Mandi covered market, serving inexpensive meat and veg curries with roti. *8am-10pm* ₹

Dakshina Mandapa: The Taj Mahal Hotel's vegetarian restaurant serves fabulously filling thalis. *7am-10.30pm* ₹₹

Aish: This swish eatery at The Park hotel serves regal Hyderabadi set menus, with sorbets between the courses. *12.30-2.30pm & 7-11pm* ₹₹₹

WALKING TOUR

Hyderabad's Royal Heart

Even in a country overflowing with history, Hyderabad's medieval heart stands out for its energy and welcoming vibe. Discover the pulsing heartbeat of the city on this 3.5km walk around markets, palaces, ancient landmarks and sacred sights. It's a walk that takes in some of the city's most vibrant quarters, but keep your wits about you because, even at its quietest, the traffic can be riotous.

1 Salar Jung Museum

If time allows, spend an hour or so admiring the treasures hoarded by the Nizams at the Salar Jung Museum (p850). Be sure to check out all the rooms in this maze-like complex because surprising things pop up in hidden corners.

The Walk: Head 350m west along the riverbank and at the first bridge turn left into the market-area maelstrom of Patthargatti Rd (p849). Walk 500m then turn left into Mir Chowk Rd.

2 Mir Alam Mandi

The old fruit and vegetable market of Mir Alam Mandi (p849) is a lively place to detour into. Perhaps stop for a cup of chai or a refreshing glass of sugarcane juice.

The Walk: Return to Patthargatti Rd and continue southwards through the pearl vendors' section of the market. Just beyond the iconic Khader Yar Khan Mosque you'll pass the first of several enormous medieval arches.

3 Gulzar Houz Fountain

From the Gulzar Houz Fountain you can turn to see the 16th-century arches that guard the approaches to the Charminar. Perfumes are a major stock in trade around here, with scores of dealers waiting to

DAKSHESH TAILOR/SHUTTERSTOCK

Charminar monument

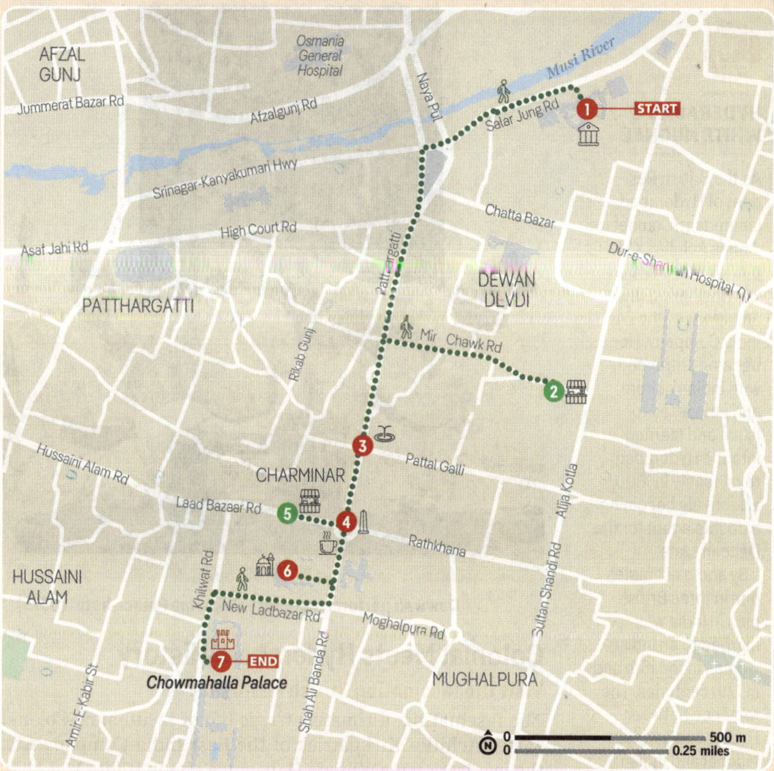

freshen up your personal bouquet with a dab of scent.

The Walk: Shortly before you pass through a second archway to the south you'll be grateful to enter the pedestrianised zone that radiates out from the Charminar.

4 Charminar

The towering Charminar monument was constructed in 1591 to commemorate the founding of Hyderabad. Sky-piercing minarets crown each corner (hence the name, meaning 'four minarets'). Spiral stairways of 50 steps *(₹300)* lead up for unforgettable views.

The Walk: Pause for a cup of Irani tea at Nimrah Cafe to observe the bustle around the Charminar. Turn west into Laad Bazaar.

5 Laad Bazaar

At Laad Bazaar (p850) you'll enter a whole street dedicated to the sale of colourful lac bangles. The best are made from the resin secreted by scale insects, inlaid with beads and semi-precious stones.

The Walk: Back at Charminar turn south again, keeping the majestic facade of the Nizamia General Hospital (built in 1926) on your left.

6 Mecca Masjid

On your right you'll see the city's most important mosque, Mecca Masjid, with room for 10,000 devotees. The imposing facade was reputedly carved from a single block of granite.

The Walk: Turn right under a modern archway into New Ladbazar Rd, where shopfronts are adorned with lehenga wedding dresses, lavishly embellished with beads and sequins.

7 Chowmahalla Palace

End your walk at the grandest downtown residence of the Hyderabad Nizams, Chowmahalla Palace (p845), which will be doubly appreciated by now as a calm haven from the noisy, crowded streets outside.

HYDERABAD'S WHITE MUGHAL

As the British Resident of Hyderabad, Lieutenant-Colonel James Achilles Kirkpatrick was charged with furthering the ambitions of the East India Company. He became entranced with Indian culture, and converted to Islam and married into the Hyderabadi royal family in 1800, effectively becoming a double agent for the Deccan state.

By some estimates one in three British men in India was married to an Indian woman in the 18th and in 19th centuries. The romance between Hyderabad's white Mughal and Indian noblewoman Khair-un-Nissa Begum was cut tragically short – Fitzpatrick died from fever in 1805, and his children were sent to England, leaving Khair-un-Nissa childless and bereaved.

AALOK SONI/GETTY IMAGES

***Qawwali* performance, Taj Falaknuma Palace hotel (p875)**

Colonial Meets Hyderabadi History

Visit the fascinating British Residency

The fascinating, ultimately tragic life of Lieutenant-Colonel James Achilles Kirkpatrick of the East India Company was the inspiration for William Dalrymple's book *White Mughals*, and you can visit the grand house where it all happened. The former **British Residency** *(₹300, plus ₹100 to take photos)* was completed in 1807 for the Lieutenant-Colonel and his bride Khair-un-Nissa Begum, a Hyderabadi noblewoman descended from the Mughal emperor Bahadur Shah I.

Outwardly, the house follows a neoclassical pattern, with a grand Greco-Roman pediment supported by Corinthian columns, but rooms were arranged to allow Khair-un-Nissa to live according to Islamic custom, away from the sight of male visitors. It is said that she never saw the front of the house, and a scale model was built in the gardens to allow her to view the Residency from all sides. The building is hidden away in the grounds of Koti Women's College. There's no

DRINKING IN HYDERABAD: BEST CAFES

True Black: A sleek, modern cafe bar, drawing a hip, well-heeled Jubilee Hills crowd. The coffee selection includes cold coffee on draught. *8am-11pm*

Black Fuel Roastery: Hyderabad's coolest cafe is a great place to chill and chat. Thoughtfully designed by the architect-owner with space for art/music events. *8am-9pm*

Roast CCX: Billed as a 'Coffee & Culinary Xperience' this is Banjara Hills most popular eatery and a great place for coffee, breakfast or dinner. *7am-1am*

Roastery Coffee House: Banjara Hills citizens meet for breakfast in the courtyard garden at Roastery, with a 'Spanish cinnamon mocha' chaser. *8am-11.30pm*

signage on the road since the founders of this relatively new museum (opened in 2022) understandably wish to protect the students from large numbers of visitors.

Tickets allow admission to the main rooms, with an excellent exhibition upstairs on the building's history and its restoration with the help of the World Monuments Fund. Downstairs, the grand **Durbar Hall** is an ostentatious space, with an original teak floor and a lavishly painted and lovingly restored ceiling. Ask in particular to see the basement, where there's a formidably barricaded jail (with a clever security system necessitating four locks). This jail, brought into use after the First War of Independence (Indian Uprising), was originally constructed to store currency that had been produced in the building's subterranean mint. Both the mint and the room opposite it (once a wine cellar) are now used as overflow classrooms for the college.

The Green Lung of the City

Escape the city in an urban forest

'Not all classrooms have four walls' reads a sign in **Kasu Brahmananda Reddy National Park** *(hyderabadtourism.travel; adult/child ₹50/30)*. Known to locals simply as KBR Park, this 1.6-sq-km area of forest and wetlands serves - once as an outdoor exercise area and an education centre promoting environmental awareness.

Less than half the park is open to visitors; the other section, with a huge lake, is left entirely wild as a conservation zone. It's a great place for birdlife and also home to mongoose, snakes and, some say, otters. The last verified census of peafowl in the park in 2014 came up with an estimated population of 418 but the figure is now believed to be closer to 500. The park is particularly colourful in spring when pink trumpet, yellow tabebuia and purple jacaranda trees are in bloom.

KBR opens from 5am to 7pm each day, but is closed between 10am and 4pm to give the habitat a rest from humanity. It's most popular in the hour after sunrise when locals gather to walk, jog and practise aerobics. There is also a 5km **KBR Walkway** *(4.30-9am & 4.30-9pm)* that loops picturesquely around most of the outer edge of the park and features a herbal and medicinal garden, a creeper garden, a birdwatching tower and even a well-maintained (free) yoga *shala* (space). All this without even entering the park!

THE SOUND OF HYDERABAD

Emerging in the subcontinent in the 13th century, *qawwali* singing is closely linked with Sufism – the mystical, esoteric form of Islam – and Hyderabad is one of the best places to hear its haunting, passionate refrains. An acoustic framework for powerfully moving vocal improvisation is provided by the harmonium, tabla and clapped hands or clicked wooden blocks. The Dargah Yousufain Sharifain Sufi temple or the nearby Dargah Hazrat Shah Khamosh are the best places to hear singers in full flow. Worshippers used to sing there on Thursday and Friday evenings but these events have been less consistent in recent years. More reliable are the *qawwali* performances at the Taj Falaknuma Palace hotel (p875), which are usually timed to coincide with lavish dinners or high tea tours.

DRINKING IN HYDERABAD: BEST FOR BEERS

Broadway: Jubilee Hills' biggest, best and busiest bar with gleaming brewing tanks, quality craft beers on tap and a great food menu. *noon-11.30pm*

10 Downing Street: Hidden at the back of Tycoon Mall with a wood-lined interior, like an old English pub (complete with photos of British royalty). *noon-midnight*

Prost Brewpub: Perhaps most famous among the brewpubs in Jubilee Hills; huge, hip and well stocked with house ales. *noon-midnight*

Kismet: Centred around the swimming pool on the 8th floor at The Park hotel, this is perhaps the most scenic sundown cocktail spot in the city. *6am-midnight*

Beyond Hyderabad

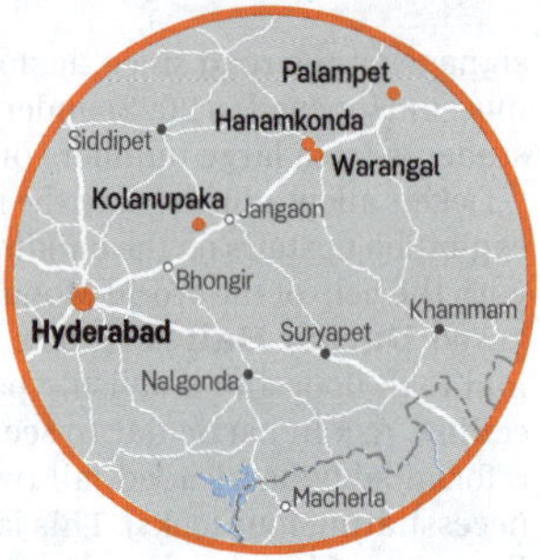

Escape Hyderabad's magnetic pull and you'll find quieter, culturally interesting towns steeped in history, and ancient temples that make for irresistible road-trip destinations.

Places

GETTING AROUND

A chartered car and driver is the easiest way to explore the area around Hyderabad. Devilalnayak Gugulothu *(WhatsApp 9493184944)* is a highly recommended English-speaking driver. However, it can take a long time to get back into the city during rush hour. Warangal is easily accessed by train from Hyderabad or Vijayawada. Travelling by bus you'll need to head instead for the adjacent town of Hanamkonda, about 5km northwest, then take an autorickshaw to Warangal.

It may be hard to drag yourself away from Hyderabad's fabulous food and wonderful historical sites and museums, but more treasures await in the surrounding countryside. Trains and buses can whisk you to Warangal and the dramatic fort that was the capital of the 12th-century Kakatiya dynasty. Hanamkonda, Warangal's twin-town, has a wealth of fascinating and ancient temples.

Kolanupaka Swetamber Jain Temple can easily be reached as a road trip from Hyderabad, but Ramappa Temple is much more conveniently accessed from Warangal or Hanamkonda. While it's possible to reach Ramappa by public transport (just a 1km walk from the village of Palampet), in practice it's likely to be more convenient to visit with a private vehicle.

Kolanupaka

TIME FROM HYDERABAD: 1½HR

Visit a peaceful Jain temple

Kolanupaka Swetamber Jain Mandir *(yadadri.telangana.gov.in)* is a place of unexpected serenity in a region where the most venerated temples tend to attract tens of thousands of visitors. Said to date back 2000 years, it is the resting place of eight valuable idols including a priceless 1.3m-tall statue of Lord Mahavir that's said to be made of a single piece of jade.

No photos (or shoes) are allowed inside, and the main shrine is so wonderfully colourful and abundantly decorated – with beautifully executed inlaid marble and glass chandeliers – that you might find yourself wondering afterwards if you imagined it all. The outside of the temple is almost as spectacular, sculpted out of beautiful peach-coloured sandstone (left appropriately uncovered, with the typical Jain whitewash).

The temple is most easily reached by private car – or by a 15-minute auto ride from Aler train station – and is a convenient stop on the journey between Hyderabad and Warangal.

Warangal

TIME FROM HYDERABAD: **3HR**

Dive into impressive ruins at Warangal Fort

The town of Warangal reached its pinnacle of greatness as the capital of the Hindu Kakatiya dynasty then, subsequently, as the setting for terrible battles during the Islamic conquest of central India. On the southern edge of town, **Warangal Fort** was the scene of three sieges by the forces of Alauddin Khilji and his successors, including the battle where the Koh-i-Noor diamond was wrested from the Kakatiyas, before being whirled away in turn by the Mughals, finally to be seized by the British.

Set inside successive rings of towering bastions, the fort was founded in the 12th century, but it was ransacked and repurposed by a string of Muslim rulers. Large sections of the great wall still survive and, with care, you can even climb the sentry towers to gaze over flooded moats that were once stocked with crocodiles.

There are several appealing sights within the fortress and an ideal first stop is **Ekashila Gutta** *(adult/child ₹20/10)*, a great granite monolith where you'll see a Kakatiya-era temple and an octagonal watchtower. There are dark, narrow steps leading up to the roof, which offers views across Ekashila Lake (which provided water during the successive sieges) and into the great compound of Svayambhu Temple.

It's the ransacked **Svayambhu Temple** *(adult/child ₹300/free)*, partially restored and guarded by four spectacular *torana* gateways, that's the main drawcard within the fortress compound. The toppled stones have been rather scrappily reassembled, but there are some stunning carvings, alongside deities and bas-reliefs. If you've visited the more pristine Ramappa Temple (p859) with its (mostly) immaculately preserved sculptures, you'll notice the contrast here in Warangal's historic fort, where the defaced and beheaded figures tell the tale of violent reprisals after the city finally fell to the marauding armies of the Delhi sultanate. Inexplicably, a particularly well-crafted Nandi statue seems to have escaped the war-clubs and axes.

It's worth making time to stroll through the alleyways of **Mathwada** (the hamlet within the fort that still retains a thriving mixed community of Hindus and Muslims), between the pastel-coloured homes, or even to stop for a cold bottle of Thums Up (Indian cola) and a chat at one of the little village stores.

Even if time is tight, do your best to make a quick detour to the **Kush Mahal** *(entry same ticket as Svayambhu Temple)*, just 100m west of the temple's main gate. This 14th-century Islamic building was supposedly an audience hall, but with its monumentally thick sloping walls (ideal for repelling cannon-fire), it's reminiscent of a particularly austere monastic fortress of the Spanish Reconquista. It's hard not to imagine that it was also designed as a final redoubt in case the fortress was overrun (again). You are free to wander the main chamber and might notice that one of the storage rooms still contains a huge heap of stone cannon balls.

WHAT'S SPECIAL ABOUT WARANGAL?

Devilalnayak Gugulothu, born and raised in Warangal, has travelled all over India as a hired driver and guide. *WhatsApp 9493184944*

I love taking road trips out to Ramappa Temple. Although it's just over an hour from Warangal, the landscape seems to change so much. The series of rains and droughts mean that ancient canals (some engineered by the Kakatiya civilisation 800 years ago) are constantly filling and draining the seemingly endless tangle of lakes that surround (and all too frequently enter) the villages that depend on a mix of farming and fishing. Ramappa Temple is one of the most spectacular pieces of architecture you'll see anywhere and I find it surprising that more people don't head out here to escape the big-city frenzy of Hyderabad.

Hanamkonda

TIME FROM HYDERABAD: **3HR**

Pay your respects at Thousand Pillar Temple

Known officially as Sri Rudreshwara Swamy Temple, Hanamkonda's most important historical site has always been known to locals as Veyisthambhalagudi, **Thousand Pillar Temple** *(hanumakonda.telangana.gov.in)*. You're unlikely to feel cheated by false advertising when you realise that there were only ever 300 pillars here – this ornate, black-granite treasure is pure magic both as a historical site and a fully functioning temple.

Immense and atmospheric, it's a popular stop for Hindu devotees. Unless your visit coincides with a specific festival you're unlikely to find overwhelming crowds here, making it an ideal temple introduction for anyone who might feel intimidated by more famous temples where crowds frequently number into the tens of thousands.

Leave your shoes in the small gardens just inside the security gate and proceed through the gateway to the inner courtyard. Built in 1163, the temple is dedicated to the Trikutalayam – the Hindu holy trinity of Shiva, Vishnu and the sun god Surya. Inside the main shrine you'll see spectacular carvings in shiny dolerite, and many of the granite sculptures have been polished smooth by adoring hands over the centuries.

Between the main temple and the *mandapa* (pillared hall) to the south, raised high on stone plinths you'll see a beautifully sculpted larger-than-life statue of Nandi (the sacred bull that serves as the divine mount of Lord Shiva).

On the eastern side of the compound you'll see an old bathing ghat – no longer used and now the habitat of a large number of big turtles. Behind the temple rises Hanamkonda Hill, site of the original Kakatiya capital. Dotted around the hill and adjacent outcrops are more historic temples, most embellished with contemporary paint jobs and gaudy statues.

Take a trip around Hanamkonda's other temples

Padmakshi Temple lies just over a kilometre southwest of the Thousand Pillar Temple. It's a hybrid Hindu and Jain temple set among balanced boulders and covered in painted 12th-century bas-reliefs. Just stroll 800m across the valley to reach the ornate and vibrant **Sri Siddeshwar Devalayan Temple**, fronted by a fearsome figure of Vatuka Bhairava (a wrathful incarnation of Shiva) adorned in human skulls and wrapped in live cobras. Inside the compound to the right

THE MISADVENTURES OF THE KOH-I-NOOR

Few gemstones have such a storied history as the Koh-i-Noor. Originally mined from the Kollur mine in Andhra Pradesh, legend has it that this gigantic 105.6-carat diamond was once the left eye of the fearsome idol of the goddess Kali (which can still be seen today in Warangal's 7th-century Bhadrakali Temple). After being seized as a trophy by the Delhi sultanate it was relinquished to the Mughals, who forfeited it to the Persian conquerors. It was moved on through the Afghan Durrani dynasty to the Sikh Empire, and was finally ceded to the British as part of the Treaty of Lahore. Today this much-coveted gem resides in the Tower of London, forming the centrepiece for the Crown of the late Queen Elizabeth the Queen Mother.

EATING IN WARANGAL & HANAMKONDA: OUR PICKS

Paradise Biryani: One of Telangana and Andhra Pradesh's most reliable midrange restaurants. Serving excellent biryani since 1953. *11am-11pm* ₹₹

Bharathi Mess: A family-run Warangal establishment that's been going for decades, serving great-value South Indian vegetarian meals. *10am-3.30pm & 7-10.30pm* ₹

Sampradaya Multicuisine Family Restaurant: A Hanamkonda favourite, with attractive design and even more attractive Indian/Chinese menu. *11am-11pm* ₹₹

Cafe Downtown: A vibey touch of cafe culture in Warangal, with cool space for chatting (or working) and great coffee, milkshakes and light meals. *noon-11pm* ₹₹

there's a fascinating five-headed statue of Hanuman (with faces resembling human, horse, wild pig, tiger and, of course, monkey). You might be fortunate enough to be invited into the 3rd-century *mandapa* for a blessing at the sacred lingam (phallic image of Shiva) in the main shrine. Men should remove shirts before entering.

Just a little further up the hill is the mysterious **Kaala Bhairava Temple**. There are no signs and many locals don't even know this temple, which is accessible via 150 or so rough-hewn steps. Be aware that some free-range street dogs den among the rocks – they might bark but they're less intimidating than the monkeys in many other temples.

Hanamkonda's busiest temple is the imposing **Bhadrakali Temple** on the shore of Bhadrakali Lake. Constructed by the Chalukya dynasty in the 7th century, it enshrines a fearsome idol of Kali with a weapon in each of her eight hands. Legend has it that her left eye socket was where the Kakatiya kings originally installed the Koh-i-Noor diamond.

Palampet

TIME FROM HYDERABAD: **4HR**

Visit Telangana's most ornate temple

Telangana's most impressive temple lies around 70km northeast of Warangal near Palampet (best accessed with a chartered car and driver). Built in the early 13th century, the **Ramappa Temple**, the high point of Kakatiya architecture, is one of India's most jaw-droppingly spectacular works of architecture. Every panel is covered in beautifully stylised carvings of wild animals, lovers, wrestlers, musicians, dancers, deities and mythical creatures. Highlights include the frieze of more than 500 elephants (each one unique, some in the process of trampling humans) that encircle the exterior of the building. Life-size dancing girls in polished dolerite (serving as brackets for roof beams) could almost be described as the world's first examples of 'art deco' artwork.

Sometimes known as Kakatiya Rudreshwara Temple, the site was inscribed on UNESCO's World Heritage List in 2021, as much for its artistic integrity as for advanced architectural techniques featuring the use of carved granite, polished dolerite and lightweight, porous 'floating bricks' which reduce the weight of the roof.

There are more 13th-century temples waiting to be explored – some in the process of being overrun by jungle – on the shores of **Ramappa Cheruvu** lake, 1km south of the ruins. At weekends, speedboats leave for excursions across the lake *(₹350 for up to 4 people)*.

DIVIDING TELANGANA & ANDHRA PRADESH

Until 2014, Telangana and Andhra Pradesh were united as a single state – created in 1956 along linguistic lines. The state was always contentious; it brought Telugu speakers from the coast under Hyderabadi control, and it reduced the number of government jobs available for people from formerly independent Hyderabad State. After 60 years of dissatisfaction, the region was formally divided, with two state governments and two pools of reserved government jobs. The practicalities, however, are taking time to resolve. Hyderabad continued to administer both states until 2024 when, in the wake of its electoral victory, the Telugu Desam Party confirmed plans to transfer Andhra Pradesh's capital to the little town of Amaravathi (population 140,000). Watch this space.

Vijayawada

TEMPLES | FORTIFICATIONS | BUDDHIST HISTORY

TOP TIP

Private sleeper buses arrive and depart from ticket stands and designated stops around the bus stand on Vijayawada Rd, and competition keeps prices reasonable for overnight trips to Hyderabad, Visakhapatnam and Tirupati. Most services leave late in the evening; take advantage of the train station cloakroom to store your bags.

A busy commercial and industrial city, Vijayawada is not the sort of place that leaps immediately to mind when planning a journey through India. You won't find many tourists here, but if you're looking for authentic, unhurried backstreet life then you could do a lot worse than base yourself in the tangle of streets south of Vijayawada Junction. The city has some unique attractions (specifically the Kanaka Durga Temple), but what makes a stay here so pleasant is the irresistible opportunity to make road trips to explore sleepy rural towns, ancient Buddhist relics and majestic hilltop battlements.

Vijayawada has excellent transport links by air, rail and road, and some decent places to stay and eat. The Krishna River no longer delivers India's diamonds onto Vijayawada doorsteps, but – at the risk of employing a travel writer's cliché – this city still has a hidden gem or two.

GETTING AROUND

Autorickshaws can take you to the revered Kanaka Durga Temple and the Undavalli Cave Temples on the south side of Krishna River. While Uber works well in Vijayawada, beware that at the time of research only Rapido ride-hailing worked in Amaravathi. If you plan to visit Amaravathi by bus you might have to change in Gunter (an hour south of Vijayawada). If time is tight it can be easiest to hire a driver – Venkateswara Reddy *(WhatsApp 8919891479)* speaks English and knows the area very well. You could get to Kondapalli Fort by local train from Vijayawada. But by the time you've haggled with an auto driver for the return trip from the station – plus waiting time – you might realise that it would have been simplest and not much more expensive (especially if sharing) to take a chartered car all the way from the city.

Long-distance rail services connect Vijayawada to Warangal, Visakhapatnam, Hyderabad and Tirupati. For travel by road, comfortable private buses run from the old bus stand east of the train station, while government buses use Pandit Nehru Bus Station to the south. IndiGo flights buzz around the state from Vijayawada's expanding airport, 25km east of the centre.

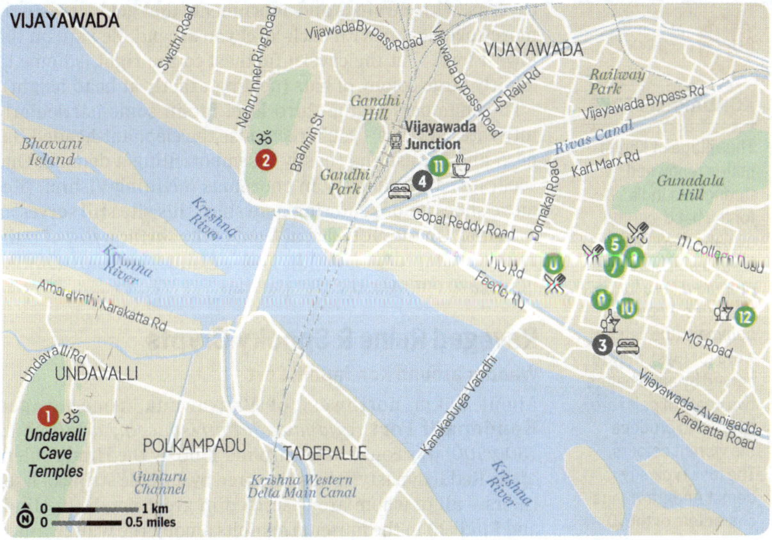

Colourful & Revered Temple

Join devotees at the Kanaka Durga Temple

Dating back to the 12th century, the important **Kanaka Durga Temple** *(kanakadurgamma.org)* has largely been swallowed whole by administration buildings and steel enclosures for channelling pilgrims. The temple's official name is Sri Durga Malleswara Swamy Varla Devasthanam (worth bearing in mind since Kanaka Durga places of worship are not uncommon; in fact there's one just 1.5km to the north). Once you get there the crowds will be enough to convince you that you're in the right place. During the Dussehra/Navarathri celebrations in September or October (dates change), the temple draws upwards of 100,000 Hindu faithful each day.

You can line up for free and face a long wait as you shuffle through a kilometre of wire cages, or pay ₹300 to be fast-tracked to the temple courtyard and into the sacred presence of the figure of the goddess Durga, in her domain high on on **Indrakeeladri Hill**, which also offers magnificent views across the mighty Krishna River.

HIGHLIGHTS
1 Undavalli Cave Temples

SIGHTS
2 Kanaka Durga Temple

SLEEPING
3 Grand Vijayawada
4 Hotel Sindhuri

EATING
5 Cross Roads
6 Eat Street
7 TFI
8 Under the Woods

DRINKING & NIGHTLIFE
9 10 Downing Street
10 Blue Fox
11 Hello Chai & Juice
12 Vault Brewery

Sculpted History

Clamber through the Undavalli Cave Temples

A 9km road trip southwest of Vijayawada, the impressive four-storey **Undavalli Cave Temples** *(vijayawadatourism.com; ₹300)* were carved into a rocky hillside by Buddhist monks in the 2nd century CE, but were converted to Hindu use in the 7th century.

As you enter the main gateway, turn left first to explore a shallower but less visited cave system before you venture to the main complex. Here you'll find four storeys of human-made

KONDAPALLI TOYS

The village of Kondapalli is renowned throughout India for the hand-carved miniature wooden figures that have been produced here for centuries. Known as *bommalu* (the Telugu word for toys), they're carved by hand before two coats of paint are applied to produce the vibrant colours. The toys typically depict Andhra village characters or the 10 principal incarnations of Vishnu. You'll see a large collection of such figurines in a display case in Kondapalli Fort museum, but some of the finest are among the vast collection of artefacts in Hyderabad's Salar Jung Museum (p850). If you want to see where they're created – or purchase some truly unique souvenirs – head for Killa Rd in Kondapalli village (known locally as the 'Bommalu Colony').

caverns, with carvings and adornments that get increasingly more spectacular with each level you ascend. Beware on the lowest level that the cavern furthest to the right is home to a fairly large colony of bats (nesting exactly at head height).

The chambers on the third level retain some particularly intricate carvings – you'll recognise the elephant-headed Ganesh and Narasimha (busily disembowelling a demon). One separate cavern houses an enormous reclining Vishnu. (Remove shoes before entering here since this site still serves as a shrine.) On the cliff edge in front of the shrine a row of rather over-restored, gnome-like *rishis* (saints) and cartoon-like lions gaze out over the rice paddies.

Ravaged Ruins & Spooky Crypts

Wander around Kondapalli Fort

About 25km northwest of Vijayawada, time-ravaged **Kondapalli Fort** *(vijayawadatourism.com; adult/child ₹300/200)* was constructed around 1360 by the Hindu rulers of the Reddi dynasty. It was captured by a whole string of later rulers – all of whom are described in great detail (in Hindi and English) in the museum exhibits among the whitewashed vaults of the restored Durbur Hall.

The kings of Vijayanagar, the Qutb Shahis of Golconda and the British all added to the fortifications and adapted them to their specific needs. Apart from the Durbar Hall (which also has a rooftop terrace offering fantastic views over distant Vijayawada) most other parts of the fort are open to the sky. Wandering the extensive grounds of Kondapalli is a magical experience; it could be a setting from *The Jungle Book*, complete with mischievous monkeys and venerable rock figs that seem to be doing their utmost to dismantle the great granite slabs.

It's easy to overlook the secluded passageway at the northeast edge of the fort, behind the Dhanyagara (granary), that leads to two evocative crypt-like buildings. As the jail and armoury, there were solid reasons for their sturdy construction and both (yet to be restored) have retained their roofs. The jail is still sealed by iron rails, but the armoury (last building at the northern edge of the complex) is particularly spooky, and some visitors shy away from stepping into the dark, pillared vaults that are home to a colony of bats.

It's possible catch a local train from Vijayawada but you'll need to haggle for a return trip by auto from the village up

DRINKING IN VIJAYAWADA: OUR PICKS

10 Downing Street: On the upper floor of PVP Square Mall is this English-style sports bar (with endless cricket on the TVs). *noon–11pm* ₹₹

Vault Brewery: Vijayawada's chicest bar, with a quirky design and tempting cocktails and bar snacks. *11am–11pm* ₹₹₹

Blue Fox: Licensed, mood-lit and refined, the restaurant at the Minerva Grand hotel serves the best cocktails in town. *11.30am–11pm* ₹₹₹

Hello Chai & Juice: The best fruit juices and milkshakes in town; also great for chai and coffee, especially ginger coffee. *7am (hot drinks 3.30am) –11.30pm* ₹

the very steep hill to the gates of the fort (30 minutes each way). Don't get a one-way trip since, even at the weekend, you're unlikely to find transport at the fort. In practice, it's most convenient to charter a taxi from the city (expect to pay around ₹2000 including an hour or so waiting time). Ask the driver to stop for a photo opportunity as you cross the sandy plain at the foot of the hill – it's particularly picturesque when the herds of water buffalo are being driven home through the towering pampas grass.

Supersized Religious History

Admire the giant stupa at Amaravathi

About 25km west of Vijayawada, ancient **Amaravathi** was a centre for Buddhist learning from the 2nd century BCE, and its **Mahachaitya Stupa** *(₹300)* was constructed in phases over the following five centuries. By the time it was completed it was 27m high by 49m wide and was the largest stupa in India. The site, near the banks of the mighty Krishna River, is a dramatic spot, with jet-black cormorants and snow-white egrets roosting by hundreds in the surrounding trees. Unfortunately, only the brick base of the once-statuesque stupa remains.

A distinct lack of information at the stupa site itself is made up for in the wonderfully curated little **Amaravathi Museum** *(₹5)*, which must be one of India's best bargains at the price. There are no guides in the museum but the artefacts are extremely well and thoughtfully explained in English both with signs and QR codes.

At the end of the main bazaar in Amaravathi, the **Sri Amareswara Swamy Vari Devasthanam Temple** enshrines a tall limestone lingam. It's said to be one of the five parts of the invincibility-granting Shiva lingam used by the demon-king Tarakasura to defeat the gods. It is of indeterminate age and you might be surprised to see that the limestone is being continuously eroded by holy water that is piped over it.

Walk 1km west through the predominantly Muslim riverside quarter and you'll soon see the looming **Dhyana Buddha Statue** *(adult/child ₹20/10)* rising 38m into the air.

ICONIC FORTS OF ANDHRA PRADESH

Kondaveedu Fort: Looming over the ridge 40km south of Amaravathi, this was one of the most important strategic points for the Reddi kings in the 14th and 15th centuries.

Gooty Fort: Looking almost like a natural extension of the granite cliffs, this fort served as a frontier garrison for the Chalukya dynasty from around 1050 CE.

Vijayanagaram Fort: A relative newcomer (from 1713). A garrison and administration centre for trade on the Bay of Bengal, it now houses a college.

Udayagiri Fort: Built by a local chieftain in the 14th century. Much of it is still standing strong today on a remote hilltop 140km north of Tirupati.

EATING IN VIJAYAWADA: OUR PICKS

Cross Roads: This family restaurant is ideal if you want to grab some quick sweet snacks (downstairs) or a great-value meal (upstairs). *11am-11pm* ₹₹

Under the Woods: Vijayawada's best upscale vegetarian restaurant with Indian, fusion and great international dishes, plus an irresistible dessert menu. *noon-11pm* ₹₹₹

Eat Street: Lively eating in the shopping district, with dozens of food stalls on Vemula Syamala Devi St by the stadium. *7am-10pm* ₹

TFL: 'The Food Lounge' is a hip, fun cafe with a covered terrace, a globe-trotting menu and great desserts. *10am-10pm* ₹₹

Visakhapatnam

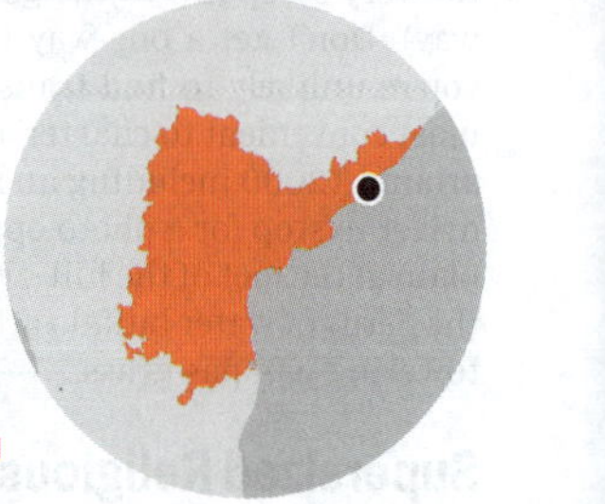

BEACHES | TEMPLES | FOOD

Visakhapatnam – known to locals as Vizag (vie-zag) – is Andhra Pradesh's largest city and a major hub for the steel industry, thanks to its busy port. It's also a popular seaside resort for domestic tourists, with a string of sandy beaches that the city authorities are taking increasingly good care of.

The city lacks a cohesive 'centre' – most sights of interest to travellers are strung out along Beach Rd, running northeast from Visakhapatnam port, while the main shopping hub is Town Kotha Rd. There are good hotels in the commercial part of town but most visitors will enjoy proximity to the Bay of Bengal breakers and the great selection of bars, restaurants and cafes along the coastline.

Beach Rd – the location of several fascinating museums – is the place to be after dawn, when citizens gather to stroll or jog, and around sunset, when strings of food-carts troop out.

GETTING AROUND

Vizag stretches almost 10km along the coast and the road system is convoluted, so getting around can take time. Autorickshaws are the least time-consuming option for accessing the northern beaches (best arranged through the Uber app), but taxis are recommended for longer journeys. From the RTC Complex bus stand (known locally simply as 'Complex'), public buses buzz around the city and to outlying communities.

The train station is 2km east of the bus stand but beware that some trains (eg to Vijayawada) leave from Duvvada train station (an hour's drive from the beach area). Visakhapatnam's international airport can be reached in half that time.

Ancient Carvings & Religious Devotion

Vizag's most famous temple

Set between forested hills north of Vizag, the **Varahalakshmi Narasimha Temple** is where the Hindu faithful pay their respects to Varaha (Vishnu in the form of a boar) and Narasimha, (Vishnu's demon-disembowelling man-lion avatar). Queuing for the free *darshan* (viewing) involves hours of slow shuffling, but a ₹300 ticket gets you processed rapidly through the claustrophobic metal cages.

A grand pavilion guards the inner courtyard and attendants hurry pilgrims through the main *mandapa* to the inner sanctum and the sacred statue of Varahalakshmi Narasimha. Before leaving the courtyard, pilgrims get a sip of holy water (said to have spectacular curative powers) and free *prasadam* (blessed food), which can be eaten in the courtyard or taken home.

Buses leave regularly from Vizag's RTC Complex bus stand or a taxi will cost about ₹600. Phones, cameras and bags must be left at the security desk.

HIGHLIGHTS
1 Kursura Submarine Museum
2 TU-142M Aircraft Museum

SIGHTS
3 Ramakrishna Beach
4 Sea Harrier Museum
5 UH-3H Helicopter Museum
6 Visakha Museum

SLEEPING
7 BacPac Monkey Co-Live
8 Daspalla Hotel
9 Dolphin Hotel
10 The Park

EATING
11 Cafooze Resto Cafe
12 Dharani
13 Dumont Creamery
14 Vintage Restaurant & Bar

THE LEGEND OF NARASIMHA

The story of Narasimha – the incarnation of Vishnu who disembowelled the demon Hiranyakashipu with his bare hands – is strongly associated with Andhra Pradesh. The man-lion deity, whose name comes from the Sanskrit words *nara* (man) and *simha* (lion), has been worshipped in this region since at least the 4th century CE, and pilgrims crowd the 32 Narasimha temples dotted around the state. In the highly revered Varahalakshmi Narasimha Temple (p864) 8km northwest of Visakhapatnam, are vivid depictions of Narasimha in the act of eviscerating Hiranyakashipu, on the threshold of his palace – thus overcoming the divine blessing, given by Brahma, that had supposedly guaranteed the demon's invulnerability.

ABIR ROY BARMAN/SHUTTERSTOCK

TU-142M Aircraft Museum

See the Military Museums

Dive into Indian naval history

Clustered together at the northern end of the city beach are four dramatic museums that shine a fascinating light on Visakhapatnam's background as a military and naval base.

It's hard to overlook the 91m-long whale-like structure of the Soviet-built, Indian Navy submarine, stranded high and dry right on the beach and now doing duty as **Kursura Submarine Museum** *(vmrda.gov.in/kursura.aspx)*. Inside it's impossible not to get a hint of the claustrophobia that submarine crews have to live with among the tiny sleeping quarters and cramped control rooms and engine rooms.

Directly across Beach Rd, the **TU-142M Aircraft Museum** offers a similar exploration of an enormous, Soviet-era Tupolev TU142M reconnaissance aircraft, used by the Indian Air Force to monitor its borders for nearly 29 years.

It doesn't end here: there's also a **Sea Harrier Museum** centred on a suspended British-built Harrier jump jet used by the Indian Navy's White Tigers squadron and a **UH-3H Helicopter Museum**, which opened in 2025, with one of the Indian Naval Air Squadron's last three operational UH-3H helicopters as its main exhibit.

The museums are open from 2pm to 8.30pm, and entry to each costs adult/child ₹70/40. An 'Integrated Ticket' (adult/child ₹200/120) covers admission for all four museums.

EATING IN VISAKHAPATNAM: OUR PICKS

Vintage Restaurant & Bar: Evocative archways make for an ideal (licensed) sundowner view along Ramakrishna Beach. *noon-3pm & 7-11pm* ₹₹

Dharani: Huge thalis are the stock in trade at the Daspalla Hotel's veg restaurant; for non-veg, try Dakshin in the next building. *6am-11pm* ₹₹

Cafooze Restro Cafe: A quirky cafe with original-flavoured shakes (try pina colada) and eclectic bar-style menu – masala fries to paneer enchiladas. *10.30am-10pm* ₹

Dumont Creamery: An eat-in ice-cream shop with some irresistible flavours – try 'South Indian Filter Coffee', 'Choco-orange' or 'Banana-caramel'. *10am-midnight* ₹₹₹

If you're still hankering for some extra military history, stroll 200m northeast to the small **Visakha Museum** *(₹50; 11am-7pm, closed Fri)* – which breaks with local tradition by opening in the morning. It features military models, bits of navy hardware, medieval arms and armour, and historic objects from the Andhra coast.

Hit the Beach

Stroll Andhra's best beaches

Ramakrishna Beach (Visakhapatnam's main beach) is at its best just after sunrise when hundreds of local people gather to walk and jog along in the cool hours. It might not be Waikiki but this wave-pounded arc of sand, with its sprinkling of palms here and there, is an unexpectedly pleasant (and surprisingly clean) urban beach by any standards. The promenade runs south for 4km, morphing into **Varun Beach** before it reaches the rocky breakwaters and the fishing harbour with its hundreds of boats.

Just 2.5km north you'll find coastline of a very different sort around the craggy **Tenneti Park Headland**. The headland is crowned – perhaps unusually anywhere other than India – by a monument to the 'Junior Cricketer'. But it's the dramatic rusting hulk of the 98m-long Bangladeshi cargo ship **MV Maa** that's the show-stealer here. It ran aground at this spot in 2020.

Pioneering Andhra's Unsurfed Waves

Surfing Rushikonda

With over 1000km of wave-pounded coastline, Andhra Pradesh might be one of the new frontiers in the sport of surfing. The coastline north of Visakhapatnam is particularly appealing (and clean), with a burgeoning surf scene at **Rushikonda Beach** (8km north of the city). The beach itself has a popular swimming area and sheltered right-hand wave that is ideal for longboards. In fact, you could be looking at Malibu as it might have been in the 1950s before the crowds paddled out.

OM Surf School *(@omsurfschool_vizag; from ₹1500 for 90min)* runs surf lessons here on a consistent and fun beach break. Kalyan and Chinnakonda Rayithi have been stoked on surfing since they first stole the wooden plank that served as a seat on their father's fishing boat, and the brothers have since competed (and frequently won) at national level. They run lessons each day at dawn but can also arrange multiday beginner courses exploring some of the best waves along the coastline north of Vizag.

Timeless Northern Beaches

Explore the waterfront at historic Bheemunipatnam

About 25km north of Vizag is the former Dutch settlement of **Bheemunipatnam**, the oldest municipality in mainland Andhra. It's worth the road trip out here along the coastline (about ₹400 by auto) for a breath of clean sea air and timeless

GREAT VIZAG SURF BREAKS

Kalyan Rayithi, co-founder of OM Surf School, won India's first surfing championship in 2011 and was shortlisted for the 2020 Tokyo Olympics. *@omsurfschool_vizag*

There are other great surf spots besides Rushikonda (few of which ever see a surfer).

Tenneti Park has a powerful right-hand point break that rumbles across the rocks near the MV *Maa* wreck.

Mangamaripeta Beach has spectacular rock formations and a wave that runs for 500m.

Bheemili Beach needs a big swell to work really well, but on a good day rides of several hundred metres are possible.

This is a land of right-handers, but Chintapalli Beach, at a historic fishing village of the same name, often has a great peak that breaks both right and left.

WELL-DRESSED ANDHRA PRADESH

Andhran men favour a shirt and trousers, but saris are the go-to outfit for women – the striking patterns of Andhran saris transform any gathering into a kaleidoscope of colour. The most sought-after sari patterns come from the townships of Mangalagiri (near Vijayawada) and Venkatagiri (northeast of Tirupati) and are typically woven from shimmering silk with a striking, multicoloured *pallu* – the decorative loose end of the sari.

The favoured way of wearing a sari in Andhra is known as *nivi*, with the *pallu* neatly pleated and draped over the left shoulder, and held in place with a pin. The style was invented in Andhra Pradesh but made popular across India by the early influencer and social reformer Jnanadanandini Devi Tagore, sister-in-law of the poet Rabindranath Tagore.

ABIR ROY BARMAN/SHUTTERSTOCK

Thotlakonda Ruins

scenes of timber fishing boats clustered in the sheltered inlets and fishing shacks roofed with palm leaves.

Bheemili Beach, as it's known, is decorated with gaudy sculptures. You walk through the concrete jaws of a huge fish to be faced with an oversized statue of a mermaid. The beach is clean and, with its peeling right-hand waves, has the makings of a surfers' paradise.

There's history here too in the form of an 1861 British lighthouse and the Flagstaff Cemetery – with gravestones, dating back to 1762, telling a harsh story of early European settlement on this fever-infested coast. Stroll to the colourful marketplace to check out the (very Dutch-looking) Clock Tower, which was built in 1948 to celebrate Indian independence.

Buddha's Resting Place

Pay homage at the site of Buddha's remains

About 12km north of Visakhapatnam you'll find the Buddhist ruins of **Bavikonda** *(₹50)*. They've been heavily restored, so you won't get a strong sense of history, but you can see substantial stupas from the 3rd century CE, and the views are spectacular. A reliquary was unearthed inside the *mahachaitya* (great stupa) at Bavikonda in 1993. It was believed to contain the ashes and a genuine bone fragment from the historical Buddha. It's now on display at the Telangana State Archaeology Museum (p851) in Hyderabad. You can take an auto to the main gates (it will cost about ₹250 from the city centre), but three-wheelers are not allowed inside, so you will need to walk about 300m up the hill.

The area was clearly an important Buddhist pilgrimage spot, and you can continue onward to the 2nd-century BCE **Thotlakonda Ruins** (where Roman coins were discovered), located 2km to the northwest.

Beyond Visakhapatnam

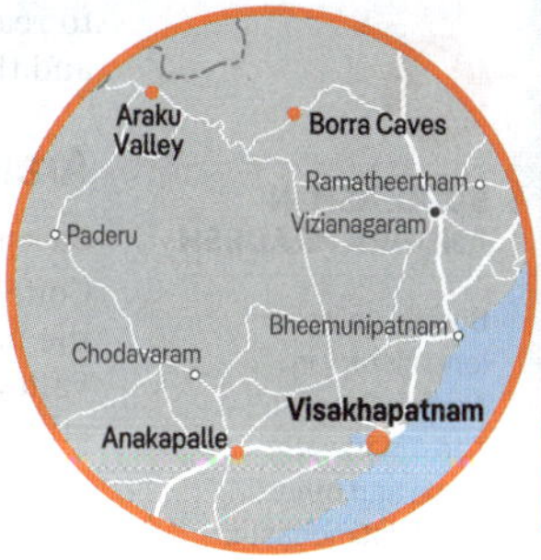

The notable highlight is the lush greenery of Araku Valley, famous with city-dwellers for the cool 'hill station' climate.

Well served by flights, trains and buses, Visakhapatnam is a handy hub for exploring the forested Eastern Ghats highlands of Andhra Pradesh, with their hills of coffee, pepper and cacao and their Adivasi communities. The scenic railway line that snakes up between soaring hills to the Araku Valley is reason enough to visit Andhra (be sure to book at least two months in advance). Nearby are the magnificent Borra Caves, one of India's most impressive cavern systems. A private car gives you more freedom to explore the sights beyond Araku town and turning a day trip into an overnight visit offers a chance to benefit more from the clean highland air and cool temperatures.

Places

Borra Caves

TIME FROM VISAKHAPATNAM: **2HR**

Clamber through a psychedelic cave experience

About 38km before Araku, on the winding approach road from Visakhapatnam, India's deepest cave system was hollowed out of the limestone hills by the Gosthani River, leaving behind a network of passages and dramatic stalactites and stalagmites. Adding to the drama, Andhra Pradesh Tourism has installed a psychedelic lighting display into **Borra Caves** (*vizagtourism.org.in/borra-caves-vizag; adult/child ₹60/60*), illuminating the vast chambers in vivid greens, reds, yellows and blues.

Slightly rickety metal steps wind through the interlinked caverns, with the tallest stairway providing access to a small sanctum containing a naturally formed Shiva lingam. The caves can get crowded at weekends, with visitors noisily testing the acoustics, to the chagrin of the bats roosting above.

The path to the caves is lined with stalls selling souvenirs, but the zip line by the cave entrance, offering out-and-back zooms for a very reasonable ₹500, was closed for maintenance at the time of writing. The train schedule for Borra Caves station doesn't allow for easy visits; it's better to come by chartered vehicle from Araku or Visakhapatnam.

Just a few hundred metres before arriving at the cave you'll see a dirt track heading off left. It runs for a very rocky and frequently extremely muddy 6km to **Katika Waterfalls**, a popular weekend spot despite its remoteness. The usual way

GETTING AROUND

Local buses go to the sights around Visakhapatnam but chartering a taxi saves a lot of time. Chukka Apparao *(WhatsApp 8143222535)* is a reliable, English-speaking, Visag-based driver. Book the train from Visakhapatnam to Araku at least two months in advance for a seat in the Vistadome air-con carriage. The 6.45am departure is perfect but the other (leaving at 9.20pm) gets you to Araku after midnight and, of course, you'll miss the views.

BUDDHISM IN ANDHRA PRADESH

Buddhism has a long history in Andhra Pradesh. The Amaravathi stupa and other Buddhist monastic sites were founded in the 2nd century CE, and the Chinese traveller Hiuen Tsang described a thriving religious community in the region in 630. Most of these ancient sites were abandoned in the medieval period. Andhra saw a massive upsurge in interest in Buddhism in the 1950s thanks to the speeches of social reformer BR Ambedkar, who helped draft India's constitution. He inspired hundreds of thousands of Dalit people to convert to Buddhism to escape the restrictions of the Hindu caste system. You'll see gigantic metal statues celebrating this inspirational politician in Hyderabad and Vijayawada.

to reach the falls is in a Mahindra 4WD *(₹200 per person)* and the spine-jarring journey is all part of the adventure.

Araku Valley

TIME FROM VISAKHAPATNAM: **4HR**

Sample Araku's heady mix of coffee and chocolate

Coffee has been a major commodity of Andhra Pradesh since the plant was introduced by the British in 1898. The Araku Valley, within the great ridge of the Eastern Ghats, is an evocative place to see it being grown and, of course, to sample some of the region's best.

The first big areas of cultivated coffee you'll see are the **Araku Anantagiri Coffee Plantations**, about 25km before you reach Araku town. This community co-operative was set up to give Adivasi people an income. You can have a direct positive impact if you stop here and buy a cup of fresh coffee from the string of stalls along the road; the water is boiled on little stoves formed from earth and the beans have been roasted in the village (about 3km walk back in the hills). You'll be welcome to take a closer look at the plants, which are shaded by soaring trees that also form a support for pepper vines (another marketable crop for the Indigenous communities here).

A few kilometres further up the highland road in Sunkarametta village a more accessible walkway into the plantation was opened by the Forest Development Corporation in early 2025. **Coffee Trail Sunkarametta** *(adult/child ₹50/20)* has some well-maintained trails and tree decks that serve as selfie spots. A 120m-long raised timber boardwalk gives a great opportunity to walk among and above the coffee plants and pepper vines.

In Araku town itself you'll find a small **Coffee Museum** *(₹20)* and – for those with a sweet tooth – the **Chocolate Factory** *(adult/child ₹50/40)*, a Willy Wonka–inspired house of fun that also does a good educational job of explaining how chocolate gets 'from bean to bar'.

Wander Araku's Tribal Museum

Araku's **Tribal Museum** *(adult/child ₹60/30)* introduces the region's many tribal communities, using colourful dioramas and artefacts. The museum is well laid-out with exhibits in a series of circular buildings representing tribal dwellings. Life-size dioramas bring to life everything from hunting and gathering to wedding ceremonies and housework in what is described on signboards as a 'museum of tribal habitate' (sic). Information boards (in Hindi and English) explain the rich

EATING BEYOND VISAKHAPATNAM: TOP PICKS

Araku Valley Coffee House: Araku's coffee co-op serves a vast menu of coffee-based treats plus tasty local chocolate and sweets. *8.30am-9pm* ₹

Mr Cram: A popular student hangout near Anakapalle bus stand, serving tasty biryanis at marble-topped tables. *10am-10pm* ₹₹

Royal Darbar: An inviting restaurant on Araku's main drag, serving quick meals downstairs and biryanis and curries in the air-con room above. *7am-11pm* ₹₹

Zad Restaurant: An unexpectedly upscale restaurant near Rushikonda Beach. Recommended for its tandooris and biryanis. *11.30am-4pm & 7-11pm* ₹₹₹

SATYA TEJA D/SHUTTERSTOCK

Araku Anantagiri Coffee Plantations

cultural diversity that exists among the ethnic groups known as Adivasis in India.

There are evening dance shows, and if the kids start to suffer from information overload there's a range of activities from zip lines, climbing walls and even a high-wire bicycle ride over a boating lake. You could easily spend half a day here and, if you're in need of refreshment, the museum cafe serves snacks and what it brands as 'Native Araku Coffee'.

Get to know highland flora in Padmapuram

North of Araku town, near the train station, the **Padmapuram Botanical Garden** *(adult/child ₹100/50)* is a peaceful sprawl of camphor, red sandalwood and cinnamon trees and ornamental topiary. Araku Valley is famous for its flowers and – especially in the months of December and January – is a riot of colour. The rose beds are a highlight but in general it's a lovely place to wander and relax in the shade. It's disappointing that there are no information boards providing an insight to the region's spectacular flora. Be sure to walk the raised timber walkway, overlooking paddy fields and weaving sinuously through a stand of giant bamboo (of the sort that serves as cooking pots even today in Adivasi villages).

Anakapalle

TIME FROM VISAKHAPATNAM: 1½HR

Andhra Pradesh's most spectacular Buddhist ruins

Ancient Buddhist sites are dotted around Visakhapatnam's coastline, but the most interesting remains are slightly inland at **Sankaram** (just outside the town of Anakapalle). **Bojjanakonda Buddhist Ruins** *(free)*, dating from the 3rd century BCE, are best accessed by chartered taxi since the busy road junction nearby doesn't make for pleasant walking.

BEST TIME TO BE IN ARAKU

Chukka Apparao is a reliable Visakhapatnam-based driver with good English and an in-depth knowledge of the whole region. *Tel/WhatsApp 8143222535*

If possible it's best to avoid weekends at Araku since the cool mountain temperatures frequently attract huge crowds and there can be queues to get into sights and museums. I'd say that December and January are the best months. The weather is perfect and the flowers are in full bloom so that the whole valley is a riot of colour. **Araku Utsav** (also known as Araku Chali Festival) is a cultural festival, celebrating tribal culture, and it's held for three days in January or February.

RESPECT & SAFETY AT TIRUMALA

Shanthi Kumar visits Sri Venkateshwara Temple at Tirumala at least once a month.

We appreciate it when foreign visitors come to experience our pilgrimage but there are a few things to bear in mind if you want to do it respectfully and safely. The walk to the top of the hill is 11km, but it is preferable that you complete it barefoot. For those who want to experience *darshan* (a glimpse inside the temple) the wait is often between eight and 16 hours, but a ticket costing ₹300 entitles you to a fast-track system (normally three to four hours). Some pilgrims prefer to go at night, but in this case you should never walk alone. There have been leopard attacks and recently a tiger was spotted near Alipiri steps.

Bojjanakonda Buddhist Ruins (p871), Sankaram

A well-maintained path leads from the security gate through tended gardens to the top of the hill, where dozens of small stupas surround a massive, damaged *mahachaitya* and the plinth of an enormous vanished temple, flanked on all sides by brick niches.

Two overgrown hills rising beside an irrigation canal are adorned with intriguing stone structures peeking through the vegetation. The eastern hill is known as **Bojjanakonda**, dominated by a split-level cave temple, sculpted inside and out with images of the Buddha and various bodhisattvas, and there are two levels of painstakingly excavated caves with supporting pillars (all apparently carved out of solid rock).

The western hill, known as **Lingalakonda**, is crowned by an incredible garden of stone *chaityas* (shrines) – carved at the same time as neighbouring Bojjanakonda. At the far end of the outcrop are two massive stupas, one flanking an unadorned cave temple. The views out across the palms and rice paddies are stunning and the rocky outcrop is also a spectacular vantage point for birdwatching, with flocks of egrets flying in V-formation across the paddies and vibrantly plumed India rollers hunting for insects among the ancient stones.

EATING IN ARAKU: OUR PICKS

Adivasi Bamboo Chicken: One of several roadside eateries that specialise in biryani prepared over coals in sections of bamboo. *9am-9pm* ₹

Vasundhara Restaurant: A firm favourite with weekend visitors from Vizag for its vast and varied menu and excellent value. *6am-10.15pm* ₹

MTR Restaurant: An eclectic menu – featuring everything from Old Delhi style to Mongolian – at this indoor/outdoor restaurant. *noon-10.30pm* ₹₹

Star Annapurna: Famous as the only upmarket eatery in Araku where you can sample the traditional Adivasi bamboo biryani. *7.30am-10pm* ₹₹₹

LALAM PHOTOGRAPHY/SHUTTERSTOCK

TOP EXPERIENCE

Sri Venkateshwara Temple

Reached by a steep 11km hike (or easy bus ride) from Tirupati town, the sacred hill of Tirumala, crowned by Sri Venkateshwara Temple, sees more than 50,000 pilgrims each day. The (barefoot) walk – almost all under cover – is a unique cultural experience. If you hope to enjoy *darshan* (a glimpse inside the temple), phones, bags and cameras must be left with the guards.

DON'T MISS

- Alipiri Metlu
- Religious bazaar
- Holding rooms
- Outer courtyard
- Inner courtyard
- Ladoo counters

Alipiri Metlu

Alipiri Metlu is the more popular and easier of the two pilgrim trails to Tirumala. Starting at Alipiri (accessible by shared auto for ₹50) it involves an 11km tramp up 3550 steps, under an all-weather canopy. The first stage climbs steeply from the enormous 16th-century **Raja Gopuram** at the base of the escarpment. At step 250, you'll pass under the **Mysore Gopuram**, then the tall **Gali Gopuram** at step 2083, where the path levels out and a cluster of food stands and shrines provides a perfect spot to break the climb. The remainder of

PRACTICALITIES

- Scan this QR code for prices and opening hours.

the ascent is much less steep, snaking up through peaceful forests dotted with statues and shrines. You'll pass under the **Mokalimitta Gali Gopuram** at step 2910, before following the access road to what is almost a sacred city around Sri Venkateshwara Temple.

Shortly after reaching the 3000th step (around 6km), you'll find yourself face-to-face with a gargantuan statue of Hanuman, the monkey king. It's a spectacular sight that, bizarrely, seems almost to lure wildlife – you'll see monkeys (of course), along with chital deer, majestic sambar stags and giant squirrels.

Religious Bazaar

Surrounding the Sri Venkateshwara Temple you'll find a veritable metropolis of subtemples, pilgrim rest houses and food stalls, centred on a frenetic religious market. Pilgrims stock up on everything from deity images to plastic toy guns to keep the kids happy. Near the temple's Supadham entrance, look out for vendors selling silver depictions of body parts, to be used as offerings by pilgrims seeking cures for ailments.

'Holding Rooms'

If you want a *darshan* with Lord Venkateshwara, you'll face hours of queuing inside cramped metal cages, but you'll get to break the trip in one of the special holding rooms, where attendants serve up a free meal of *prasadam* (blessed food) to the waiting crowds. Eventually, the gates open and pilgrims surge forwards with enthusiastic shouts of 'Govinda!' – an alternative name for the Tirumala deity.

Courtyards

The temple consists of two mighty granite courtyards entered via *gopuram*, constructed in the 15th century in the Vijayanagar era over 10th-century foundations. You'll first enter the outer courtyard, embellished with lavish carvings and dotted with sacred objects – including the metal crowbar with which the 11th-century yogi Ananthalwar accidentally thumped Lord Venkateshwara on the chin.

Passing the flower-adorned base of the temple's ceremonial flagstaff, you'll enter the inner courtyard and be ushered rapidly past the dark stone chamber containing the paste-daubed idol of Lord Venkateshwara, credited with the power to grant any wish. During the nine-day Srivari Brahmotsavam festival in September or October, the wait for a fleeting glimpse of this revered statue can exceed 24 hours.

Ladoo Counters

After leaving the temple, pilgrims head to the famous *ladoo* (sweet) counters, which dole out millions of free cakes made from chickpea flour, cardamom and dried fruits every day. *Darshan* entitles you to one free *ladoo* but most families buy extra to take home for neighbours.

DARSHAN EXPLAINED

For a *darshan* (sacred viewing) without the eight-plus hour wait, head to the Sarvadharshan Token Counters one block north of Tirupati's bus station (queues are quietest around 6pm). Join the 'Special ₹300 Darshan' queue and present your passport; on arrival you'll take the fast-track route to the inner sanctum, a process that can still take three to four hours for a five-second viewing.

TOP TIPS

- Sri Venkateshwara Temple is open 24 hours.
- The pilgrim trails are closed to children during the night because of wild animals.
- You need your passport to join the fast 'Special ₹300 Darshan' queue.
- The temple's valuables storage system is well organised, but for an easier *darshan*, leave your phone, camera and bag at your hotel.
- Food and drinks are widely available at the temple and along the pilgrim trail.
- While shorts are fine on the trail (you'll see many locals wearing them) you'll want smarter dress if you are heading for *darshan*.

Places We Love to Stay

₹ Budget ₹₹ Midrange ₹₹₹ Top End

Hyderabad

Map p846

Golden Glory Guesthouse ₹ A great budget option in posh Banjara Hills. Save on the room so you can splash out on great neighbourhood restaurants.

Hotel Urban Eminence ₹ Not in the most salubrious lane but handy for trendy Banjara Hills cafes and just a short stroll from Kasu Brahmananda Reddy National Park.

Taj Mahal Hotel ₹₹ A midrange Hyderabad favourite with a heritage wing, a smart modern annexe, a recommended restaurant and reliable service.

Royalton Hotel ₹₹ A solid all-rounder with well-appointed rooms and a good restaurant in a location that's convenient for the train station.

Hotel Raj Inn ₹₹ The rooms are less showy than the lobby, but Hotel Raj Inn scores points for cleanliness, comfort and being close to Secunderabad neighbourhood's restaurants.

The Park ₹₹₹ This stylish modern property offers beautifully appointed rooms near Hussain Sagar lake. The pool bar and generous buffet breakfasts are highlights.

Taj Falaknuma Palace ₹₹₹ Hyderabad's top hotel, filling a lavish palace that was owned by the sixth Nizam. Guests arrive by horsedrawn coach through peacock-filled grounds.

The Leela Hyderabad ₹₹₹ Offering all the comforts, facilities and seamless service that you'd expect from one of India's best hotels.

Warangal & Hanamkonda

Townhouse Oak Public Garden ₹ Within walking distance of the temples, you'll find spotless rooms and excellent service at Hanamkonda's newest and most appealing budget hotel.

Hotel Bhilva Inn ₹₹ If you don't mind traffic noise from the Kammam-Warangal Hwy, there are comfortable rooms in this Warangal property located close to Bhadrakali Temple.

Hotel Ashoka ₹₹ Set back from Hanamkonda's main road, with comfy air-con rooms and great meals at Kanishka (veg) and Kadambari (non-veg).

Vijayawada & Around

Map p861

Hotel Sindhuri ₹ Not the most welcoming staff but comfortable and clean rooms in a central location that's hard to beat.

Haritha Resorts ₹ Simple, clean rooms right by the Dhyana Buddha statue on the southern bank of the mighty Krishna River at Amaravathi.

Grand Vijayawada ₹₹₹ Great service and comfortable, spacious and beautifully appointed rooms at Vijayawada's plushest and most popular four-star hotel.

Visakhapatnam

Map p865

BacPac Monkey Co-Live ₹ The best of the absolute cheapies with comfortable air-con and fan rooms just a few blocks from Vizag's lively city beach.

Daspalla Hotel ₹₹ A home-from-home for many return guests at this perennial midrange favourite, with a restaurant that's famous for excellent veg thalis.

Dolphin Hotel ₹₹ Despite the name this stylish choice – with some of Vizag's most appealing rooms – is in the commercial district rather than beachside.

The Park ₹₹₹ Located at the northern end of Ramakrishna Beach, with extremely stylish rooms, three restaurants, two bars and an irresistible pool.

Araku Valley

Ushodaya Resorts ₹ Excellent value for spacious, clean rooms at this welcoming hotel that's just a short walk from the botanical gardens...and the chocolate factory!

Haritha Valley Resort ₹₹ An inviting government-run property, with a pool and spacious rooms around a garden on the edge of Araku.

Tirupati

Hotel Elite Fortune Inn ₹ A comfortable, clean, budget option right next to the bus station. Helpful staff can arrange your pilgrimage to Tirumala.

Minerva Grand ₹₹ Stylish midrange option within easy reach of buses and train station. The Minerva Coffee Shop (veg) and licensed Blue Fox (non-veg) are also recommended.

Marasa Sarovar Premiere ₹₹₹ Tirupati's best five-star resort is right at the foot of sacred Tirumala Hill. The restaurant is famous for its Sunday lunch buffet.

Researched by
Isabella Noble

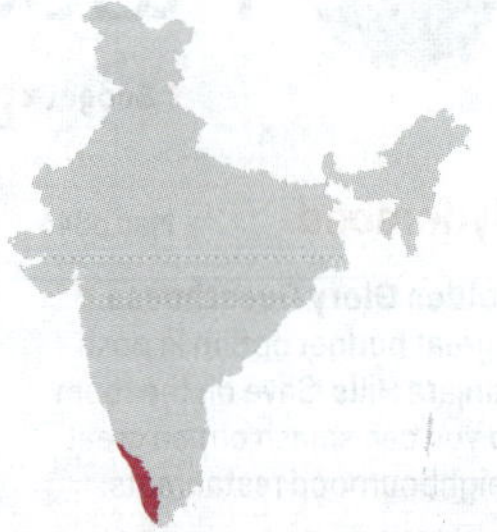

Kerala

BACKWATERS, BEACHES AND SOUTHERN CULTURE

From sultry palm-shaded backwaters and surf-pounded beaches to the wildlife-prowled mountains of the Western Ghats: welcome to one of India's most magical corners.

With a name born from the Malayalam words for 'land' and 'coconut', it's no surprise that Kerala's lush, palm-sprinkled landscapes have landed it a much-loved spot on India's tourism map. But all this immense natural beauty is just a taste of what makes India's southwesternmost state a joy to explore.

Defined both historically and culturally by its dramatic geography, Kerala has attracted traders for millennia with its fragrant spices. Butter-coloured beaches washed by tropical surf give way to sleepy backwaters reflecting endless palms, beyond which rise the misty peaks of the sparsely populated and wonderfully biodiverse Western Ghats, home to a string of fiercely protected wildlife reserves.

JIMMY KAMBALLUR/SHUTTERSTOCK

Go trekking, cycling, kayaking, surfing, boating and wildlife-spotting in nature, but don't miss the thrills of Kerala's dynamic cities – from Kochi's (Cochin's) dazzling contemporary-art scene to Thiruvananthapuram's (Trivandrum's) cultural wonders and Kannur's go-slow charm.

Before modern-day Kerala state was born in 1956, for centuries Arab, Portuguese, Dutch and British powers rivalled both each other and several powerful local dynasties here. Now, Kerala ranks among India's most progressive regions, with one of the highest literacy rates in the country and a history of democratically elected communist-led governments.

Many of Kerala's most memorable moments are still about quiet escapes, whether that means catching a peachy sunrise over the rippling backwaters, sharing a freshly cooked family meal at a homestay or soaking up the sounds of the forest on a trek through the ethereal Western Ghats.

THE MAIN AREAS

KOCHI (COCHIN)
Arty, culture-rich, historical hub. **p882**

ALAPPUZHA (ALLEPPEY)
Gateway to backwaters and houseboats. **p897**

MUNNAR
Tea capital, misty mountains and upland trekking. **p906**

PERIYAR TIGER RESERVE
Rich wildlife among spectacular mountain landscapes. **p911**

For places to stay in Kerala, see p938

DMITRY RUKHLENKO/SHUTTERSTOCK

Above: Tea plantations, Munnar (p906); Left: *Theyyam* performer (p928)

VARKALA
Beach time, surf scene and yoga centre. p915

KERALA'S NORTH COAST
Ancient arts, peaceful beaches and off-the-path backwaters. p927

WAYANAD
Into the hills: wildlife, trekking and homestays. p932

Find Your Way

Kerala's coastline stretches across almost 600km of southwest India, though this is still one the country's smaller states. Landscapes sweep from tropical shores to the mighty Western Ghats mountains, with road transport complementing efficient rail and air links across the state.

AIR

Kerala now has four international airports: Trivandrum, Kochi, Kozhikode (Calicut) and Kannur. An ever-growing number of airlines offers short hops. Karnataka's Mangaluru (Mangalore) airport is also convenient for northern Kerala. Kochi's airport was the world's first to power its electricity needs with solar energy.

CAR & BUS

The only way to reach Kerala's Western Ghats is by (winding) road, which means a bus (slow, budget-friendly) or hiring a car and driver (more expensive). State-run and private buses travel everywhere. Ongoing road upgrades, including the north–south NH66, should soon speed up travel.

TRAIN & BOAT

Trains are a fantastic way to explore much of Kerala, including new express services. Railways link most major lowland destinations, though it's best to allow a little flexibility for potential delays. Boat travel is usually most convenient (and fun!) for the backwaters.

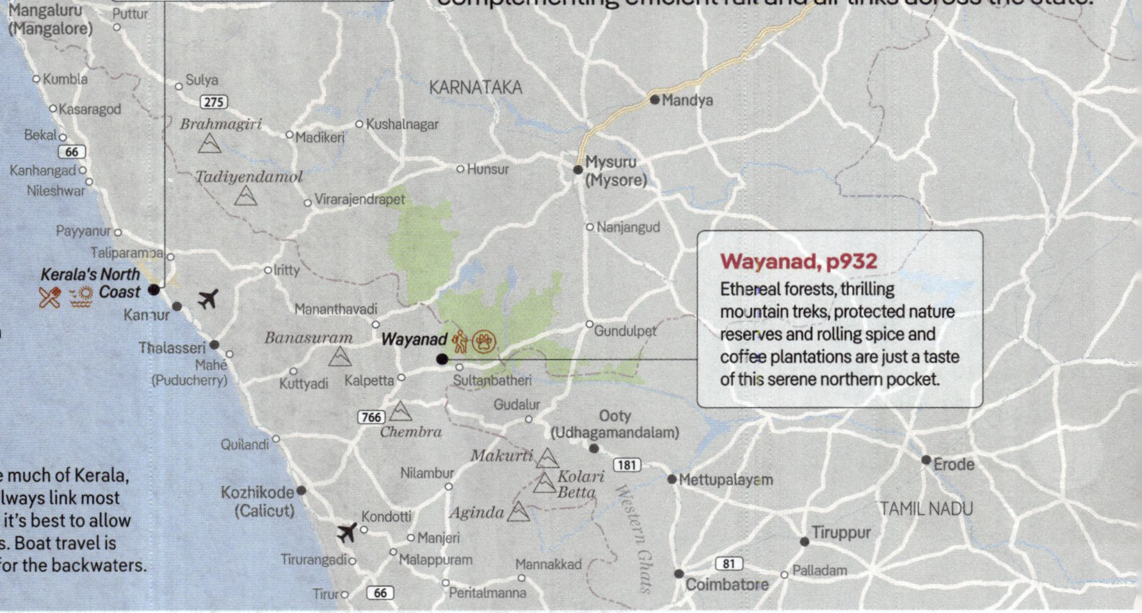

Kerala's North Coast, p927

Almost-empty beaches, vibrant *theyyam* (trance-induced rituals), peaceful backwaters, evocative accommodation and fabulous Malabar food await along Kerala's less-touristed northern shores.

Wayanad, p932

Ethereal forests, thrilling mountain treks, protected nature reserves and rolling spice and coffee plantations are just a taste of this serene northern pocket.

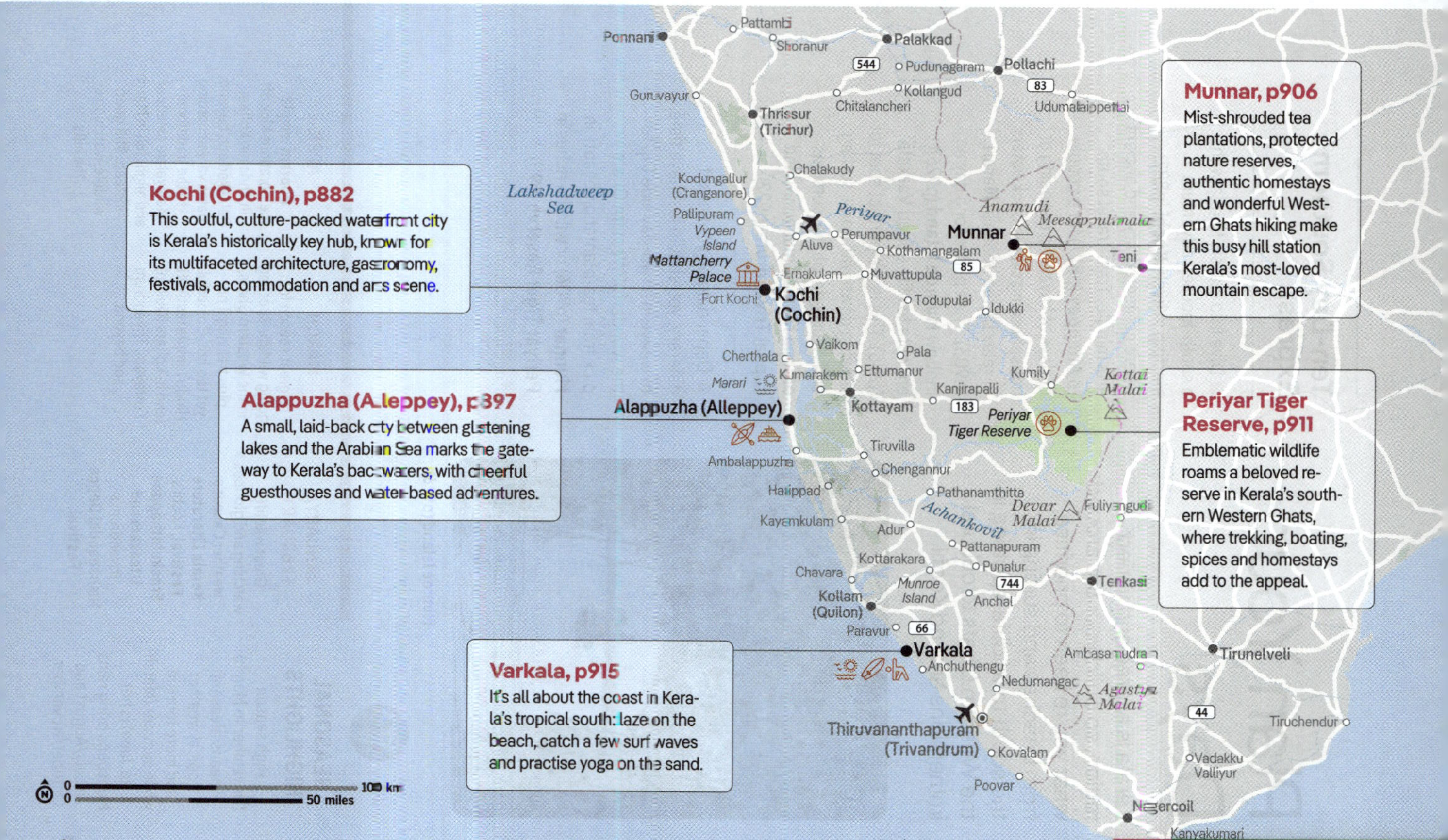
Ponnani
Pattambi
Shoranur
Palakkad
544
Pudunagaram
Pollachi
83
Kollangud
Udumalaippettai
Guruvayur
Thrissur
(Trichur)
Chitalancheri
Chalakudy
Kodungallur
(Cranganore)
Lakshadweep
Sea
Pallipuram
Vypeen
Island
Periyar
Aluva
Perumpavur
Anamudi
Meesapulimala
Munnar
Kothamangalam
Teni
85
Mattancherry
Palace
Ernakulam
Muvattupula
Fort Kochi
Kochi
(Cochin)
Todupulai
Idukki
Vaikom
Pala
Cherthala
Kumarakom
Ettumanur
Marari
Kumily
Kottai
Malai
Kanjirapalli
183
Alappuzha (Alleppey)
Kottayam
Periyar
Tiger Reserve
Tiruvilla
Ambalappuzha
Chengannur
Harippad
Pathanamthitta
Achankovil
Devar
Malai
Fuliyangudi
Kayamkulam
Adur
Pattanapuram
Kottarakara
Punalur
Chavara
Munroe
Island
744
Tenkasi
Anchal
Kollam
(Quilon)
Paravur
66
Varkala
Anchuthengu
Ambasamudram
Tirunelveli
Nedumangad
Agastya
Malai
44
Tiruchendur
Thiruvananthapuram
(Trivandrum)
Kovalam
Vadakku
Valliyur
Poovar
Nagercoil
Kanyakumari
0 100 km
0 50 miles
Munnar, p906
Mist-shrouded tea plantations, protected nature reserves, authentic homestays and wonderful Western Ghats hiking make this busy hill station Kerala's most-loved mountain escape.
Periyar Tiger Reserve, p911
Emblematic wildlife roams a beloved reserve in Kerala's southern Western Ghats, where trekking, boating, spices and homestays add to the appeal.
Alappuzha (Alleppey), p897
A small, laid-back city between glistening lakes and the Arabian Sea marks the gateway to Kerala's backwaters, with cheerful guesthouses and water-based adventures.
Varkala, p915
It's all about the coast in Kerala's tropical south: laze on the beach, catch a few surf waves and practise yoga on the sand.
Kochi (Cochin), p882
This soulful, culture-packed waterfront city is Kerala's historically key hub, known for its multifaceted architecture, gastronomy, festivals, accommodation and arts scene.

Plan Your Days

Kerala is a large and varied region, so build your trip around what you're keen to prioritise, from beaches and surfing in the south to wildlife-spotting in the Western Ghats to cultural immersions around Kochi.

KV NAUSHAD/SHUTTERSTOCK

Munroe Island (p926)

Ten-Day Southern Express

● Dive into classic Kerala with a south-focused adventure starting in lively **Kochi** (p882), where contemporary and ancient arts mingle. Train-travel south to **Alleppey** (p897) for a couple of days of kayaking, canoeing or houseboating on the backwaters, or relax by the beach in **Marari** (p903). Then pause for a day on mellow **Munroe Island** (p926) en route to cliff-edged **Varkala** (p915). This is the perfect spot for slowing down with yoga, surfing and Ayurveda, plus excursions around Kerala's museum-filled capital **Trivandrum** (p922).

● Depending on your exact itinerary, you should just have time to weave in a two-day side trip to the wonderful Western Ghats – pick from tea-plantation beauty in **Munnar** (p906) or wildlife riches in **Periyar Tiger Reserve** (p911).

SEASONAL HIGHLIGHTS

High season (November to March) means pleasant tropical weather and more tourism, while summer (March to June) is hot. Monsoons bring rains in July/August and October/November.

JANUARY/FEBRUARY

Great wildlife-watching and glorious weather.Calicut's **Kerala Literature Festival**, Kochi's **Ernakulathappan Utsavam** and Trivandrum's **Nishagandhi Dance Festival**.

MARCH

A great season for going wildlife-spotting in the Western Ghats, plus trekking if not yet too hot. Colourful Hindu temple festivals land in Kollam (Quilon), Kottayam, Trivandrum and beyond.

APRIL

Pooram temple celebrations kick off in Thrissur, Kollam, Palakkad and beyond; dates vary according to the traditional Malayalam calendar and might fall in March instead. Still good wildlife-watching in the hills.

A Taste of the North

- If you're keen to see Kerala's less touristed side, prioritise the quiet north over a two- to three-week trip. Spend a few days beach-lazing in **Bekal and Nileshwar** (p930) and boating around the **Valiyaparamba backwaters** (p929), before heading to **Kannur** (p927), known for its *theyyam* (a trance-induced ritual) and homestays along **Thottada Beach** (p927).

- Then it's inland to **Wayanad** (p932) for mountain treks, Western Ghats scenery and wildlife-spotting safaris. Head south via **Kozhikode** (p929) to **Kochi** (p882) for history walks, food tours, cosy cafes, art galleries and day trips to history-filled **Chennamangalam** (p894) or culture-packed **Thrissur** (p895). Alternatively, from Wayanad hop over into neighbouring Karnataka and well-connected **Mysuru** (Mysore; p804).

More Time

- Soak up Kerala's beauty on a south-to-north trip starting from surf-loving **Varkala** (p915). Spend time in the festival-loving capital **Trivandrum** (p922) or add on beachy **Kovalam** (p924), with spectacular **Padmanabhapuram Palace** (p925) nearby. Head north for backwaters scenery around **Munroe Island** (p926) and/or **Alleppey** (p897), both with canoeing and paddleboarding.

- Find more water adventures in **Kumarakom** (p903), fronting Vembanad Lake. Reaching the Western Ghats takes work, but it's worth it once you're trekking through **Periyar Tiger Reserve** (p911), from where roads lead to **Munnar** (p906) for tea plantations and homestays. Allow several days to soak up cultural **Kochi** (p882). Trains then zip you north; discover budget-friendly homestays in **Kannur** (p927) or luxury retreats in **Bekal** (p930), and don't miss beautiful **Wayanad** (p932).

JULY

Monsoon season is here, bringing along rains, rushing waterfalls and often good accommodation discounts (though some places close). This is also the traditional time for Ayurveda retreats (p920).

AUGUST/SEPTEMBER

Kerala's greatest cultural celebration–**Onam** (p918). Snake-boat races peak, including Alleppey's famous **Nehru Trophy Boat Race** (p902), which draws thousands of spectators in mid-August.

NOVEMBER

Catch the start of northern Kerala's ***theyyam*** season, as well as (usually) ideal trekking and surfing conditions (all until April). Good weather for beaches and exploring begins. Kollam hosts its prestigious **President's Trophy Boat Race**.

DECEMBER

Christmas festivities, Kochi's Carnival, **International Film Festival of Kerala** (p924) and the **Kochi-Muziris Biennale** (p883). Go surfing, swimming, trekking and wildlife-spotting, or head north to seek out *theyyam*.

Kochi (Cochin)

ARTS SCENE | FOOD CULTURE | KERALA HISTORY

TOP TIP
A rewarding way to explore Old Kochi is on two wheels; several operators offer tours and rentals. **Alphonso Stories** *(alphonsostories.com)* organises bike trips to off-the-beaten-track villages.

Set on a sweeping estuary that has drawn traders for centuries, Kochi is both a heritage-rich city with an evocative old quarter and a lively, dynamic hub known for its contemporary-art scene. This is the only place in India where three European powers took control one after the other – the Portuguese from 1500 onwards, the Dutch from the 1660s and the British from 1795 until Independence. Today, Kochi's spice-laden gastronomy, distinctive neighbourhoods and varied architecture spotlight countless different communities that have settled here.

Where vast Vembanad Lake opens into the Arabian Sea, laid-back Fort Kochi is the historical European part of the city. Murals adorn the streets, Chinese fishing nets dot the water, and heritage buildings have been reborn as stylish cafes, boutiques, art galleries and some of India's loveliest hotels. Around 3.5km southeast of Fort Kochi, Mattancherry is Kochi's old bazaar district and spice-trading hub. Together these two areas form Old Kochi.

Meanwhile, urban life rumbles on in busy mainland Ernakulam (especially around Broadway marketplace), which developed from the early 20th century and is now Kerala's business and transport epicentre.

GETTING AROUND

Fort Kochi and Mattancherry are walkable and increasingly wheelchair-accessible. It's a 2km (30-minute) walk or ₹80 autorickshaw between them. Use Uber and Ola to book taxis/autorickshaws. **Kochi Water Metro** *(watermetro.co.in)* links Fort Kochi with mainland Ernakulam (returning via Vypeen Island), and Mattancherry with Ernakulam (via Willingdon Island); check for expansion updates. Ferries *(swtd.kerala.gov.in)* also connect Fort Kochi with Ernakulam and Vypeen Island. Kochi's metro *(kochimetro.org)* runs across Ernakulam; at research time it ran from Aluva (northeast) to SN Junction (southeast). It will eventually reach the airport; until then, airport feeder buses go to/from Aluva metro. Airport taxis to/from Fort Kochi cost from ₹1600.

JOHNNYCHAOS/SHUTTERSTOCK

Chinese fishing nets, Kochi

An Ancient Art

Glimpse Kerala's Chinese fishing nets

Take a stroll along Fort Kochi's northwest waterfront (around Vasco da Gama Sq) and you'll instantly spot Kerala's unofficial backwaters emblem looming over the swooshing estuary – the cantilevered *cheenavala*, or **Chinese fishing nets**. Originally introduced to Kerala in around 1400 CE by Chinese traders from the court of Kublai Khan, the giant spider-evoking nets were then adapted and enlarged under Portuguese rule, using local bamboo, teak and other materials.

Today's large-scale fishing industry means many of these 10m tall contraptions have fallen into disuse, but a small handful are still in operation along Fort Kochi's harbourfront, and at the time of writing there were plans to restore others as heritage structures. The best time to see the *cheenavala* is at high tide, when five or six people work together to raise the catch in a delicate dance of balance and timing. Spotting the nets silhouetted against the sunset is mesmerising, too. Nearby Vypeen Island (p893) has more *cheenavala*, especially just inland from Cherai and Kuzhupilly Beaches, as does Kumbalangi island village just south of Old Kochi.

A special experience working to preserve Kochi's *cheenavala* is **Nilāvala** *(per person ₹3000-4600)* by conservation-driven **Blue Yonder** (p888). After a sunset punt-canoe journey near Ezhikkara village (20km north of Fort Kochi), you'll enjoy a home-cooked dinner served by local fishing communities on a repurposed lantern-lit Chinese fishing net.

BIENNALE & BEYOND

Edgar Pinto, owner of Kashi Art Cafe (p890) and Old Harbour Hotel (p938) in Fort Kochi. @ *iamedgarpinto*

Established in 2012 by artists, the Kochi-Muziris Biennale is also known as the People's Biennale, as it has made art much more accessible, putting it right on everyone's doorstep. The 2025–26 Biennale was its sixth edition, and we've had everything from street art to installations by Anish Kapoor. The Biennale involves local and international artists, a children's art programme and a students' platform, and has become South Asia's biggest platform for showcasing contemporary art, bringing creatives to our city. Many local artists have been picked up for shows overseas, international artists now do residencies in Kerala, and numerous galleries are opening here.

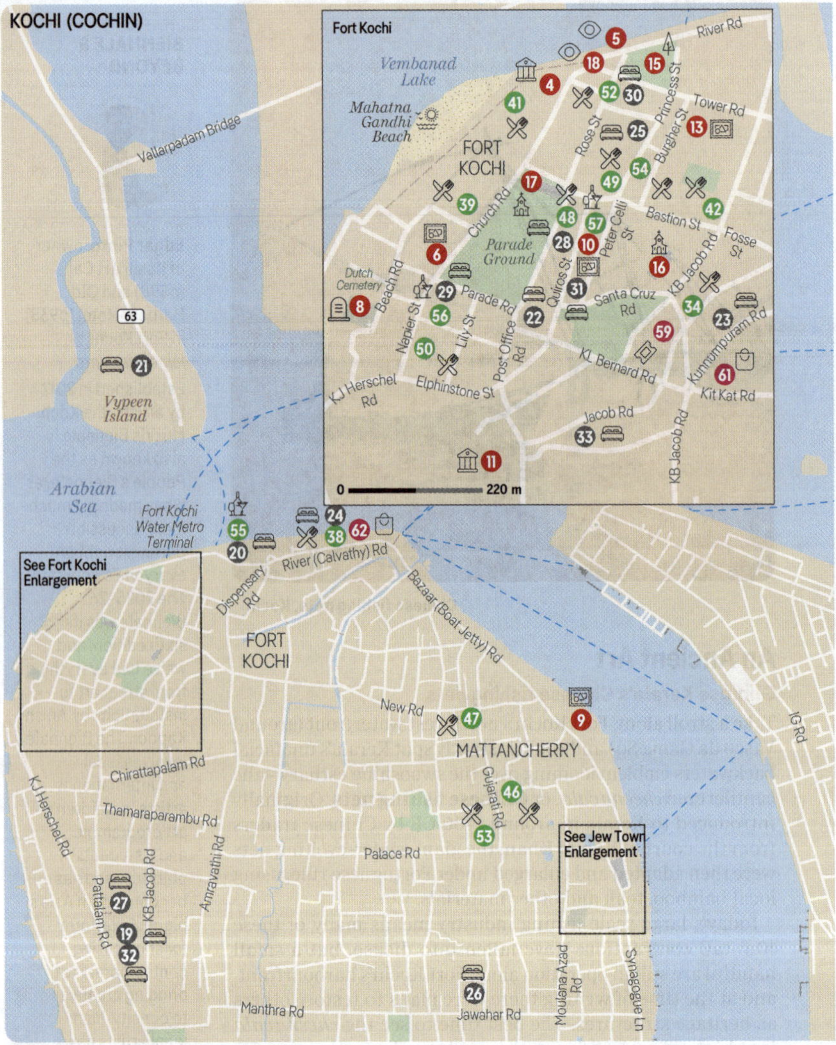

HIGHLIGHTS
1 Mattancherry Palace
2 Pardesi Synagogue

SIGHTS
3 Ambikapuram Church
4 Bastion Bungalow
5 Cheenavala (Chinese Fishing Nets)
6 David Hall
7 Durbar Hall Art Gallery
8 Dutch Cemetery
9 Gallery OED
10 Idha
11 Indo-Portuguese Museum
12 Jewish Cemetery
13 Kashi Art Gallery
14 Muziris Contemporary
15 Nehru Park
16 Santa Cruz Basilica
17 St Francis Church
18 Vasco da Gama Square

ACTIVITIES
see 21 Neema's Kitchen

SLEEPING
19 Beena Homestay
20 Brunton Boatyard
21 Bungalow Heritage Homestay
22 Delight Homestay
23 Fort Bungalow
24 Fort House Hotel
25 Forte Kochi
26 Govindamangalam Homestay
27 Green Woods Bethlehem
28 Kara
29 Malabar House
30 Old Harbour Hotel
31 Raintree Lodge
32 Reds Residency
33 Zostel

- **EATING**
- **34** Anantha Bhavan Inn
- **35** Cafficana
- **36** Chillies
- **37** Cocoa Tree
- **38** Fort House Restaurant
- **39** Fort Paragon
- **40** French Toast
- **41** French Toast
- **42** Fusion Bay
- **43** Ginger House
- **44** Gokul Oottupura
- **45** Grand Pavilion
- **46** Gujarat Road
- **see 20** History
- **see 13** Kashi Art Cafe
- **47** Kayees Rahmathulla Café
- **48** Lila Art Cafe
- **49** Loafers Corner Cafe
- **50** Loving Earth Cafe
- **see 29** Malabar Junction
- **51** Mocha Art Cafe
- **see 6** Pandhal Cafe & Deli
- **see 30** Restaurant 1788
- **52** Rose Street Food
- **53** Sri Krishna Cafe
- **54** Trouvaille

DRINKING & NIGHTLIFE
- **55** Armoury Restobar
- **56** DiVine
- **57** Francis
- **58** Velocity

ENTERTAINMENT
- **59** Kerala Kathakali Centre

SHOPPING
- **60** Ethnic Passage
- **61** One Zero Eight
- **62** Pepper House
- **63** Rouka
- **64** Sarah Cohen's Home

MATTANCHERRY CULTURES

Ajita Skaria is a local tour guide who grew up in Fort Kochi and runs **Kochi Stories** *(kochistories.com).*

In the courtyard of Mattancherry Palace, three temples are housed – the central one dedicated to Bhagavati, flanked by temples for Krishna and Shiva. Just beyond the palace are the Pardesi Synagogue (from 1568), and the Clock Tower, which was built in the 18th century and has numerals in Malayalam, Hebrew and Latin on its different sides. On the other side of the palace are a mosque and a Catholic church, all within a kilometre of each other. Here in Mattancherry we have 30 different communities speaking around 16 different languages, from Tamil to Gujarati.

Living Canvas

Dive into Kochi's contemporary-art scene

Much of Kochi's new-wave art scene revolves around evocative Fort Kochi, where artists showcase their work at cafes, museums, hotels and galleries. Wandering around, it often feels like every corner reveals a curious new mural. It all comes to a creative crescendo every two years for the four-month **Kochi–Muziris Biennale** *(kochimuzirisbiennale.org)*, which takes over the town with more than 90 international and Indian artists on the lineup.

Fort Kochi's galleries are mostly free to visit, with regularly changing shows, so spend a few hours exhibition-hopping. Pioneering **Kashi Art Gallery** *(instagram.com/kashiartcafe)* on Burgher St was founded in the 1990s by the late Anoop Scaria, a major force behind modern Kochi's art scene; it's still a favourite, with rotating exhibitions and the popular Kashi Art Cafe (p890) in a Dutch-era building. A few doors down, **Idha** *(instagram.com/idha.fortkochi)* is a charming gallery-studio where you can even stay overnight. Wander west towards the Parade Ground to dip into Kara (p938), a heritage-meets-boutique hotel hosting exhibitions, and Lila Art Cafe (p890) in a 400-year-old Dutch-built house *(instagram.com/lilaartcafe)*. Neighbouring **David Hall** *(instagram.com/davidhallartgallery_cghearth)* shows up-and-coming artists in a restored 17th-century Dutch-style bungalow.

Mattancherry's **Gallery OED** *(instagram.com/galleryoed)*, a converted pepper warehouse, also focuses on emerging creatives, while nearby, 2025-opened **Muziris Contemporary** *(muzirisconteporary.com)* is a Mumbai offshoot bringing top-tier art from India and beyond, in a 1947 warehouse with a speciality-coffee corner. Over in Ernakulam, check what's on at **Durbar Hall Art Gallery** *(lalithkala.org; closed Mon)*, a key Biennale venue in the restored 1850s former court of the Maharajas of Cochin.

Marvellous Royal Relic

Admire the Dutch Palace of Mattancherry

One of Kochi's most entrancing sights, the two-storey **Mattancherry Palace** *(keralatourism.org; adult/child ₹5/free; closed Fri)* was created by the Portuguese in the mid-16th century and gifted to the Raja of Kochi, Veera Kerala Varma (1537–65), before being rebuilt under Dutch rule in the 1660s (it's also known as the Dutch Palace). The building's graceful

DRINKING IN KOCHI: OUR PICKS

DiVine: Stylish rooftop wine lounge at Malabar House (p938) serving drops like Fratelli from Maharashtra and Grover Zampa from Karnataka, plus snacks. *11am-11pm*

Armoury Restobar: Harbour views, India-made wines and smart international cooking, on the waterfront terrace at Brunton Boatyard hotel (p938). *11am-10.30pm*

Francis: Laid-back bar in a three-century-old Fort Kochi house that gets busy for live music, cold Kingfishers, Indian wines and pub-style food. *11am-midnight*

Velocity: Top pick among Ernakulam's new wave of gastropubs, with a buzzy vibe, DJ beats, cocktails and Kerala-meets-international cooking. *11am-11pm*

A STROLL THROUGH FORT KOCHI'S HISTORY

With its pedestrian-friendly streets, a buzzing atmosphere and over 80 species of trees, Fort Kochi is a joy to explore on foot.

START	END	LENGTH
Bastion Bungalow	Santa Cruz Basilica	2km; 1hr

A distinctive Indo-European building turned excellent museum, ❶ **Bastion Bungalow** delves into the maritime and spice-trading history of Kochi and ancient Muziris (closed Monday). Pop around the corner to ❷ **Vasco da Gama Square** to see one of the few surviving sections of the 16th-century Portuguese Fort Immanuel. Coconut carts and street-food stalls congregate here next to banyan-dotted ❸ **Nehru Park**.

Wander 250m south along Rose St then turn west (right) to ❹ **St Francis Church**, the Portuguese-built church where Vasco da Gama was once buried. A wooden chapel was first established here in 1503 by Portuguese Franciscan friars, but the mid-16th-century church itself was remodelled after the Dutch took Kochi in the 1660s, then again under British rule in the 1800s. Opposite the Parade Ground, you'll spot ❺ **David Hall**, the only relic of three 17th-century Dutch-era houses, now a gallery-cafe.

A 200m meander along Parade Rd then Dutch Cemetery Rd brings you to the ❻ **Dutch Cemetery**, from 1724. Around 500m southeast, the ❼ **Indo-Portuguese Museum** has religious artefacts collected around Kochi (closed Monday); glimpse more Fort Immanuel remains in the basement. Head 500m northeast to the neoclassical ❽ **Santa Cruz Basilica**, built in 1902 on the site of a 16th-century Portuguese church demolished by the British; the beautiful frescoed interior is the work of Lombardy-born priest-and-artist Antonio Moscheni.

NCREATIVES/SHUTTERSTOCK

Pardesi Synagogue

mix of European and Kerala-style *nalukettu* architecture is a delight, but the highlights are the intricate Hindu murals depicting stories from the Ramayana, Mahabharata and Puranic legends. Dating from the 17th to 19th centuries, they were created using vibrant natural dyes – and many remain astonishingly well preserved, particularly in the royal bedchamber, which includes scenes of Hanuman, the monkey god, rescuing Sita from Lanka. Other standouts to look for are Vishnu's 10 avatars and his consort Lakshmi, and Tripura Sundari, one of the 10 *mahavidyas* (Hindu wisdom goddesses).

Visiting the palace with a guide who can unveil the murals' stories is highly recommended, though English-language panels outline key details so you can also explore independently for an hour or two. Braille signs and an outdoor staircase lift have increased accessibility in recent years.

A World in a Neighbourhood

Mattancherry's multicultural makeup

Old Kochi's trade centre, Mattancherry, revolves around the area known as **Jew Town**, once home to a thriving Jewish community who arrived here from the Kodungallur region (north of Kochi) from the 14th century onwards. A wide range of other communities has also coexisted here for centuries. Allow a few hours to soak up the neighbourhood's atmosphere, monuments and spice-scented streets.

Although Kochi's Jewish population has now almost disappeared (many people emigrated to Israel), the wonderfully preserved **Pardesi Synagogue** *(keralatourism.org; adult/child ₹100/free; closed Fri afternoon & Sat)* still welcomes visitors and has its own museum. The 1568 building was partly destroyed by the Portuguese in 1662, then restored under

TOUR COMPANIES

Blue Yonder: Conservation-focused tours across Kerala, including Kochi-region day trips showcasing arts, crafts and heritage. *(theblueyonder.com)*

Breakaway: Multiday itineraries and day trips with a focus on arts, textiles and crafts, by a women-founded operation. *(break-away.in)*

Kochi Heritage Project: Sharing Kochi's heritage through small-group storytelling walks, food tours and immersive experiences. *(kochiheritageproject.in)*

Pack Your Passport: Thoughtfully curated trips, mostly southern Kerala, including off-the-beaten-track destinations. *(pack-your-passport.in)*

Traveling Gecko: Outfitter specialising in Kerala, Puducherry and Tamil Nadu; Kochi highlights include meeting Kathakali performers. *(thetravelinggecko.com)*

Moksha Stories: Community-based experiences (dance, theatre, music) across Kerala, plus adventure activities. *(mokshastories.com)*

Tropiq Getaways: Birdwatching, kayaking and immersive tours with a reputable Kochi-based team. *(tropiqgetaways.com)*

Dutch rule two years later and renovated in 1762 by Ezekiel Rahabi, who added the landmark Clock Tower. It's impossible not to gasp in awe at the elaborate brass bimah surrounded by Belgian chandeliers, Murano-glass lamps and over 1000 hand-painted, willow-pattern tiles from Guangzhou (Canton) in China. Just outside, **Synagogue Lane** has old homes converted into shops including **Sarah Cohen's Home** (a historic Jewish embroidery shop) and **Ethnic Passage** (antiques, souvenirs, books). Ancient tombstones fill the nearby 16th-century **Jewish Cemetery**.

Just south of Jew Town is Kochi's old Muslim quarter, while northern Mattancherry has major Konkani and Gujarati communities. Along 1.6km Gujarati Road (p891), fruit stalls bustle beside generations-old restaurants. **Kochi Heritage Project** runs excellent storytelling walks *(₹2200 per person)* and bike tours exploring Mattancherry's multicultural identity.

Puttu, Parotta & Family Recipes

Get a taste of Kochi's kitchens

With its mix of cultures that have settled here over the centuries, Kochi is a culinary treat blending Kerala-style and other Indian flavours. Discover the secrets behind some of the city's favourite recipes at long-running **Neema's Kitchen** *(neemaskitchen.in; classes ₹4000-4500)*, a quick ferry ride over the water from Fort Kochi on southern Vypeen Island. Neema Veliyath runs hugely popular three-hour South Indian cook-a-thons in a 1930 home now converted into **Bungalow Heritage Homestay**; you'll get hands-on and tackle specialities like Kerala fish curry, vegetable *thoran* and spiced chutneys. Vegetarian, vegan and gluten-free diets can all be accommodated.

Or join **Kochi Heritage Project** for a lip-smacking evening food walk around Mattancherry *(₹3000 per person)*. From around 4pm, this spice-trading district springs to life with street-food stalls where people clamour around sizzling counters. Over three hours, taste flavours from all over India – Gujarati sweets, Konkani *goli bajji*, flaky Kerala *parotta* with juicy curry – and hear about lesser-known chapters from Kochi's culinary story, perhaps even stepping into a local spice mill en route.

CLASSIC KERALA DISHES

Maryann and Philip Dsouza, owners of Reds Residency (p938) and Reds Heritage homestays. *@redsresidency*

Kerala cuisine is a feast for the senses, and coconut is the key element. Start with gently spiced coconut-milk-based stew accompanied by soft *appam* (South Indian rice pancake). Next, artfully made *meen pollichatthu* (fish in banana leaf) is a treat. Another cult favourite is spice-enriched beef fry eaten with crisp *parotta* (watch how these are made, on any corner!). A wholesome *sadya* – a traditional banana-leaf vegetarian banquet – is an absolute must too. Don't miss *puttu kalada*, steamed rice flour and coconut accompanied by black-chickpea curry, or *avial*, a spiced vegetable delight flavoured with coconut yoghurt sauce and topped with coconut oil and fresh curry leaves (perfect with rice).

EATING IN KOCHI: ERNAKULAM SPOTS

Zera Noya: Stylish indoor-outdoor cafe in Kacheripady, popular for speciality coffee and freshly baked treats from a Dutch pastry chef. *10am-11pm* ₹₹

Gokul Oottupura: Arrive early to devour a Kerala-style banana-leaf lunch at this all-veg favourite in Panampilly Nagar. Great thalis and breakfasts, too. *7.30am-10pm* ₹

Grand Pavilion: The 1963-opened Grand Hotel's smart restaurant has Kerala classics and Indian wines on its global menu. *7-10am, noon-3.30pm & 7-10.30pm* ₹₹₹

Chillies: Kochi's best all-you-can-eat Andhra-style thalis and banana-leaf fare, plus a downstairs tandoori restaurant, near Durbar Hall. *hours vary* ₹₹

HOMESTAYS

Kerala has a rich and varied homestay scene, with local families providing some of South India's loveliest accommodation. Some have just a handful of simple rooms, while others are going increasingly upmarket with modern design and perks. Some of Kerala's best meals are served in these family homes; many also offer cooking classes. Kochi (particularly Fort Kochi) is a homestay hub with hundreds of options; others include Munnar, Kumily (for Periyar Tiger Reserve), Wayanad and Thottada Beach in Kannur (p927). Homestays are blossoming across Kerala's backwaters too, offering the chance to experience village life away from the crowds.

SAIKO3P/SHUTTERSTOCK

Kathakali performer

Out on the Water

Cruise Kochi's waterways and mangrove forests

There are plenty of ways to get out on the shimmering water around Kochi, with backwaters meandering north, south and inland. Active souls can paddle out with **Tropiq Getaways** (p888) on a three-hour sunrise kayak tour *(from ₹1500 per person)* through the mangroves in the Kadamakudy area, 14km north of Fort Kochi. **Blue Yonder** (p888) offers naturalist-led mangrove tours *(per person ₹2800-3600)* by punt canoe, including sapling collection.

Exploring by local ferry is a great, budget-friendly alternative; **State Water Transport Department** *(SWTD; swtd.kerala.gov.in)* ferries zip across the estuary between Fort Kochi, Ernakulam and Vypeen Island throughout the day. The 2023-launched **Kochi Water Metro** *(watermetro.co.in)*

EATING IN KOCHI: OLD KOCHI CAFES

Kashi Art Cafe: Kochi's original art cafe–gallery pairs a mellow indoor-outdoor setting with delicious coffee, fresh juices and organic-driven meals. *8.30am-10pm* ₹₹

French Toast: Mural-filled haven in Cochin Club. Cakes, strong coffee and sandwiches with sourdough. *9am-6pm Mon-Fri, to 8pm Sat & Sun* ₹₹

Loving Earth Cafe: Join a drop-in yoga class at this stylish studio, then grab a Buddha bowl or smoothie in its plant-based garden cafe. *noon-10pm* ₹₹

Trouvaille: Arty vibes, tip-top coffee and home-cooked breakfasts at this Fort Kochi favourite. Try the toffee-pudding cake. *9am-9pm Mon-Thu, 8.30am-10pm Fri-Sun* ₹₹

Pandhal Cafe & Deli: Beautiful garden cafe at David Hall (p886); Malabar coffee, homemade cakes and international bites including all-day breakfasts. *9am-9pm* ₹₹

Mocha Art Cafe: A 400-year-old spice warehouse opposite Mattancherry's synagogue, for iced coffees, cheese omelettes and spiced snacks. *10am-9pm* ₹₹

Loafers Corner Cafe: Long-running, super-central spot in a restored Dutch-Portuguese building, with window seating and French press coffee. *8.30am-10pm* ₹₹

Lila Art Cafe: Elegant heritage-building cafe opposite the Parade Ground with live music, art collections, chef pop-ups and a boutique. *9am-10pm* ₹₹

is opening up local water travel via electric-hybrid boats. At the time of writing, two Water Metro routes were operating (check for updates), with regular departures linking High Court (in Ernakulam) with Fort Kochi (via Vypeen Island) and Mattancherry (via Willingdon Island). One-way tickets cost from ₹40; factor in some flexibility time-wise as there can be long queues.

Be Entranced by Kerala's Arts

Dance, drama and martial arts

Kochi is a major centre for nurturing the traditional arts of Kathakali, a Kerala-born dance-drama from the 16th and 17th centuries, and *kalarippayat,* a fast-paced martial art inspired by animal movements, dating back to at least the 12th century.

During typical hours-long Kathakali performances, actors temporarily transform into gods, heroes and demons through intricate make-up, vibrant clothing, ornamental headpieces and meditation. Fort Kochi's long-running **Kerala Kathakali Centre** *(keralakathakali.com; shows ₹500-600)* hosts introductory two-hour performances. There are also *kalarippayat,* classical music and *bharatanatyam* (traditional classical Indian dance) shows, and workshops in which you'll learn classical dance steps or be immersed in the artistry of Kathakali make-up rituals. Keen to learn the *kalarippayat* ropes? Renowned **ENS Kalari** *(enskalari.org.in),* just southeast of Ernakulam, runs intensive training courses *(from ₹9000),* and also offers demonstrations *(₹8000 for up to 8 people)* by advance booking.

On any day, explore Kerala's traditional arts background at the family-owned **Kerala Folklore Museum** *(keralafolkloremuseum.org; ₹300),* built from ancient temples and homes; its impressive collections include performance costumes for *mohiniyattam* and *theyyam.*

Kochi Style

Explore a world of local design

Kochi's blossoming fashion-and-design scene is rooted in vibrant local textiles, independent boutiques and ancient handloom traditions. Dive in at Fort Kochi's **One Zero Eight** *(savetheloom.org),* a multibrand boutique founded by nonprofit Save the Loom in a restored Portuguese-era building. Around 1km northeast, **Pepper House** *(instagram.com/pepperhouseshop)* celebrates bold, artisanal fashion from

KERALA TEXTILES

Sreejith Jeevan, designer and founder at Rouka. @*roukabysreejithjeevan*

Kerala's handwoven cotton tradition is shaped by its warm, humid climate, resulting in a remarkable range of textiles – coarse cottons for the home, loosely woven *thorthu* towels, the exquisitely fine cotton Kerala *kaithari* (handloom) saris. Traditionally reserved for special occasions, these saris feature *zari* borders and are widely recognised as *kasavu* saris. Long rooted in local use and festive contexts, these crafts have, over the past decade, with designer interventions, embraced their inherent minimalism, to evolve into compelling contemporary expressions. Through my label, my focus has been on elevating the *kasavu* sari for a design-conscious audience. As a community we share pride in design processes that honour not just the product, but the craft traditions and communities they empower.

EATING IN KOCHI: MATTANCHERRY RESTAURANTS

Ginger House: Part of an antiques-filled warehouse, serving cashew-paneer curry, *pachakari* stew and Indian wines on a terrace. *8am-10pm* ₹₹₹

Kayees Rahmathulla Café: Locally famous 1940s-founded kitchen with a roaring lunchtime trade in mutton, chicken and seafood biryanis (arrive early!). *11am-4pm* ₹

Gujarati Road: Bustling hub of Mattancherry's thriving street-food scene; popular stops include Dudu's (veg snacks like *bonda*) and Puthu's Tea Shop. *hours vary* ₹

Sri Krishna Cafe: Classic fuss-free spot for masala dosa, thali lunches, *uttapam, idli* and other pure-veg South Indian favourites. *8am-9.30pm* ₹

TODDY SHOPS

Toddy – a fizzy white alcoholic drink sourced from palm trees around Kerala – has had a bit of a renaissance in recent years, with younger generations (and social media influencers) exploring toddy shops in scenic locations such as the backwaters. Known as *kallu* in Malayalam, Kerala toddy has a short shelf life (it ferments within three days in a bottle) and is typically enjoyed with famously spicy cuisine, often said to ease the alcoholic burn. Most toddy shops around Kerala are simple, rustic places, some more dimly lit than others, so seek out a local recommendation if you're keen to try one. More generally, Kerala's alcohol regulations include a dry day on the first day of every month and a legal drinking age of 23.

across India. Hop on the ferry or Water Metro to be immersed in colour at Ernakulam's **Rouka** *(shoprouka.com)*; this gorgeous boutique near Durbar Hall is the brainchild of Kochi-based designer Sreejith Jeevan. If you're heading to Edappally's **Lulu Mall** *(lulumall.in)*, don't miss **MANTRA** *(shalinijamesmantra.com)* for elegant womenswear by designer Shalini James, using handwoven textiles from Kerala and beyond. **Breakaway** (p888) offers a terrific full-day **Kochi Textile Trail** *(₹6500 per person, minimum 2 people)* that combines handloom heritage with meeting cutting-edge designers working in Kerala-made fabrics.

A Wander Around Panampilly Nagar

Enjoy neighbourhood vibes in Ernakulam

While most visitors focus on Old Kochi's historical riches, mainland Ernakulam showcases a flourishing, forward-looking South Indian city. Around 1.5km south of Ernakulam Junction train station, Panampilly Nagar counts among Kochi's smartest neighbourhoods. With leafy streets, peaceful parks, trendy cafes and celebrity residents, it's ideal for wandering, and was originally settled in the 1970s by communities from nearby Perumanoor (which was converted into Kochi's shipyard). Come for a couple of hours around lunchtime to savour the popular food scene. Step into **Ambikapuram Church**, a 1972 creation, before strolling along **Panampilly Nagar Avenue**. For a pause: industrial-vibe **Cafficana** *(cafficana.com)* serves espresso from Coorg-grown beans, Gokul Oottupura (p889) is a go-to for vegetarian cooking, or try sweet treats at stylish **French Toast** *(instagram.com/frenchtoastindia)* and **Cocoa Tree** *(instagram.com/_cocoatree)*.

EATING IN KOCHI: FORT KOCHI RESTAURANTS

Restaurant 1788: Lantern-lit garden setting as dazzling as the Indian-international menu, local wines and live music, at Old Harbour Hotel (p938). *7.30am-11.30pm* ₹₹₹

Fort Paragon: Busy branch of Calicut-born legend Paragon (with terrace), famous for chicken biryani, Kerala fish dishes and mango curry. *11.30am-11pm* ₹₹

Anantha Bhavan Inn: Devour perfect masala dosa, fresh *puttu* and fluffy *appam* with ginger tea under the trees at a low-key vegetarian terrace kitchen. *7.30am-11pm* ₹

Malabar Junction: Elegant culinary haven at Malabar House (p938), serving creative East-meets-West dishes and Indian wines; delicious Flavours of India platter. *12.30-11pm* ₹₹₹

Fort House Restaurant: Bougainvillea-filled waterside restaurant at Fort House Hotel (p938); highlights include signature seafood and *pachakari* stew with *appam*. *8am-10pm* ₹₹

Fusion Bay: Long-running, terracotta-adorned family restaurant known for its Kerala-Syrian delicacies, including fish or paneer in *pollichathu* style. *1-10.30pm* ₹₹

Rose Street Food Stalls: Opposite Nehru Park, a pair of well-established street-food stalls does fresh *vada*, filter coffee and other snacks at plastic tables. *5.30am-6.30pm* ₹

History: Brunton Boatyard's (p938) smart, wood-beamed dining room celebrates creative flavour fusions drawing on Kochi's multicultural backstory. *7.30am-10.30pm* ₹₹₹

Beyond Kochi

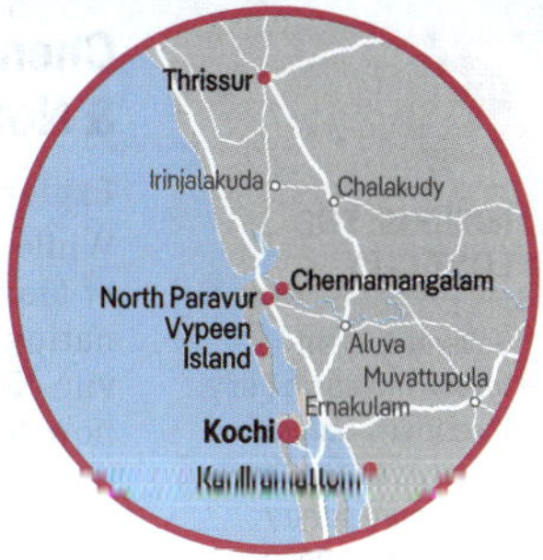

Ancient monuments, a mythical lost port, traditional handloom industries and an engaging temple-and-festival city mingle with backwater-fringed beaches.

Heading north along central Kerala's coastline reveals a slow-going world of expansive, sandy beaches backed by languid backwaters, particularly on 27km-long Vypeen Island. Roughly 30km north of Fort Kochi, fronting the Periyar River, the lush monument-rich area around Chennamangalam, North Paravur and Kodungallur is one of the most historically fascinating pockets of Kerala and an epicentre of the local handloom industry. Amid ongoing excavations, many historians believe the ancient pepper-trading port of Muziris once stood here.

Thrissur, 90km north of Kochi, is a buzzing city of 315,000 people and a major local-festival hub with a seemingly endless parade of celebrations, including Thrissur Pooram, while its surrounding region is renowned for its arts and crafts as well as a celebrated centuries-old temple at Guruvayur.

Places

GETTING AROUND

All these destinations are day-trippable from Kochi if you aren't staying closer. For Vypeen Island, take the vehicle ferry from Fort Kochi or the Kochi Water Metro from Ernakulam, then continue north by autorickshaw or bus (or bring a rental scooter/motorbike from Fort Kochi). The best way to explore the Chennamangalam/North Paravur area is by day tour with a Kochi-based operator (p888); buses from Ernakulam also serve this area. Thrissur has excellent train and bus links.

Vypeen Island

TIME FROM KOCHI: **15-20MIN**

Lazy beach days

Kochi isn't really a beach city, but you'll find delicious sands on mellow Vypeen Island. Hopping on the 15-minute roll-on roll-off vehicle ferry over from Fort Kochi sets the tone for a relaxed escape to 3km-long **Cherai Beach**. Around 25km north of Fort Kochi, this unhurried golden-hued strand is backed by miles of meandering backwaters that seem to almost touch the seafront, with spider-like *cheenavala* (Chinese fishing nets) dotted along their watery expanses. Plenty of Kochi residents head here for (usually) good swimming and easygoing beach restaurants (**Chilli Out** is a local favourite). Weekends can get busy, so for a quieter experience visit midweek. Nearby **Kuzhupilly** and **Munambam** beaches are worth seeking out too. On southern Vypeen (near the ferry and Water Metro jetties), check out the baroque-style **Church of Our Lady of Hope**, which dates from 1605 and has Portuguese roots.

MUZIRIS: THE LOST CITY

Several ancient texts – including Pliny the Elder's *Natural History* and the Tamil *Akananuru* poetry collection – mention a major port on the Malabar Coast that traded with Rome from the 1st century BCE. This was Muziris, a once-key trading hub for black pepper, spices, pearls and more. It is believed to have disappeared without a trace; many historians attribute this to a great 1341 flood, also thought to have created Kochi's harbour and Vypeen Island. Some experts believe Muziris was located in/near modern-day Kodungallur (35km north of Kochi), though the oldest relics excavated here so far date from the 13th century. More recent excavations revealed thousands of Roman amphorae (among other artefacts) at nearby Pattanam village, leading to a growing consensus that *this* was Muziris.

Chennamangalam & North Paravur

TIME FROM KOCHI: 1HR (car) OR (bus)

Explore sacred sites

While the exact location of the ancient pepper-trading city of Muziris is still being hotly debated, a collection of fascinating monuments in the Chennamangalam–North Paravur–Kodungallur area (25km to 35km north of Kochi) has now been restored under the **Muziris Heritage Project** *(muzirisheritage.in)*. The UNESCO-supported venture aims to revive the mythical lost port's forgotten story. Most monuments close on Monday.

If you only visit one place here, make it the beautifully rehabilitated **Chennamangalam Synagogue** *(keralatourism.org; ₹10)*; dating from 1420 (though rebuilt in 1614), this is one of Kerala's oldest synagogues, a testament to the fact that Kerala's Jewish communities first settled in this region before relocating to Kochi. In Paliam, 2km west of Chennamangalam, stroll the breezy corridors of **Paliam Kovilakam** *(keralatourism.org; adult/child ₹105/20)*, done in a mix of Dutch and Kerala styles; it was once the palace-home of the Paliath Achans, the wealthy chief ministers to the Maharajas of Cochin.

Around 5km west of Chennamangalam, in North Paravur, lies **Paravur Synagogue** *(keralatourism.org; adult/child ₹105/20)*, built around 1616 on the site of a 12th-century predecessor; the Kerala-style building now hosts a museum of Jewish history. Another 10km north from here, pause by the Periyar River at **Kottapuram village**, home to a prettily restored spice-trading market street and the scant remains of an early-16th-century Portuguese fort. Finally, Kodungallur's remodelled **Cheraman Juma Masjid** (3km north of Kottapuram) is said to be the oldest mosque in India, with roots dating from 629 CE (its current shape is more recent).

Home of the handloom

The Chennamangalam area is renowned for being home to one of Kerala's three traditional handloom-weaving communities granted Geographical Indication (GI) by the Indian government; the others are Balaramapuram near Trivandrum and Kuthampully northeast of Thrissur. Handloom-weaving in this region dates back to the 17th century, with today's industry employing around 500 weavers (most of them women over 40) crafting everything from saris to school uniforms. The white-and-gold Kerala *kasavu* cotton sari is a speciality. Regional tour companies, such as **Blue Yonder** (p888) and **Breakaway** (p888), organise behind-the-scenes visits to Chennamangalam's handful of weaving cooperatives. You'll hear the meditative click-clack of working looms echoing among the palm forests, get the chance to meet local weavers as they demonstrate their craft and (if lucky) glimpse yarns laid out for softening by the river in the morning.

Chennamangalam's handloom industry was devastated by Kerala's 2018 floods, which caused over 150 million rupees worth of damage. Happily, it is now slowly bouncing back,

AJP/SHUTTERSTOCK

Mask dancers during Onam (p918), Thrissur

partly in collaboration with contemporary Kochi-based designers showcasing local textiles.

Thrissur & Around

TIME FROM KOCHI: 2½HR (car) /1 1¼HR (train)

Meet a former royal capital

Festival-loving Thrissur played a key role as a second capital for the Cochin royal family in the 16th century when the Portuguese landed, then changed hands between Kozhikode's Zamorin rulers and Tipu Sultan before falling back under Kochi's control in the late 18th century. A day exploring the city's low-key monuments provides a taste of its backstory.

All visits should begin at the renowned **Vadakkunathan Temple** *(keralatourism.org)*, dedicated to Shiva, atop a small hill in Thrissur's heart. With roots in the 9th century (perhaps earlier), this is one of Kerala's oldest temples and a spiritual atmosphere pervades the surrounding tree-shaded grounds. Only Hindus are permitted to enter the temple's (main) inner complex. Non-Hindu visitors can admire the four elaborately carved Kerala-style *gopurams* (gateway towers; the southern gate hosts Thrissur's famous Pooram celebrations, while the pagoda-style eastern entrance is the main one); we recommend visiting with a guide who can evoke the building's stories.

Other Thrissur highlights include **Sakthan Thampuram Palace** *(keralatourism.org; adult/child ₹350/100; closed Mon)*, a restored 200-year-old Kerala-Dutch building with gorgeous Italian tilework, 800m north of Vadakkunathan Temple. Among its terrific archaeology collection, don't miss the Kerala bronze sculptures, distinctive for their Hoysala-influenced thick shapes. Around 1.5km east, **Thrissur District Heritage Museum** *(keralatourism.org; adult/child ₹200/50; closed Mon)* occupies Kollengode House, a 1904 Indo-European building housing fine hand-painted copies of famous Kerala

KERALA'S ELEPHANTS

Many of Kerala's most famous festivals (such as Thrissur Pooram and Kochi's Ernakulathappan Utsavam) traditionally involve processions of caparisoned elephants. In recent years animal-rights campaigns against this practice have been gaining momentum, amid growing concerns about the welfare of Kerala's estimated 500 captive temple elephants. After reportedly brutal, often-abusive training, many elephants are transported in trucks from one loud festival to another; there are many recent cases of elephants collapsing (and dying) during festivals or travel.

India banned buying and selling elephants in 2003, and there are growing calls for moving towards cruelty-free celebrations and creating sanctuaries for rehoming captive elephants. In 2023, the Irinjalakuda Sree Krishna Temple (near Thrissur) unveiled a life-size, 800kg robotic elephant called Irinjadapilly Raman to carry out rituals, donated by PETA.

NILA RIVER

Gopinath Parayil is the founder of conservation-focused tour company **Blue Yonder**. *@the.blue.yonder*

For an experience that combines both culture and nature, I recommend exploring the area around the Nila River (or Bharathappuzha) in the three districts of Thrissur, Palakkad and Malappuram. Vallachira is a village known for its Onam-related celebrations, while an arts-and-crafts trail along the Nila could include a unique Kathakali accessories workshop in Vellinezhi. The Vazhachal Forest Division is known for the mighty Athirappilly waterfalls and the biodiversity of the Chalakudy River, and there are some great rainforest treks here. And in Ponnani, where the River Nila joins the Arabian Sea, you can enjoy unique culinary experiences, such as dining with local families and learning regional recipes.

murals. Hungry? **Hotel Bharath** *(hotelbharathtcr.com)* is a 1960s-founded pure-veg institution serving delicious thalis and Kerala breakfasts, just south of the temple.

Savour arts old and new

The Thrissur region is a hub for Kerala's continually evolving art forms. **Blue Yonder** (p888) offers wonderful off-the-beaten-track arts-focused tours here, taking guests to meet local performers specialising in ancient arts such as *kalampattu* (sacred floor drawings), *thottampattu* (evocative ballads) and crafting Pooram ornaments and umbrellas.

At **Clayfingers** *(clayfingerspottery.com)*, 13km south of Thrissur, sculptor Haseena Suresh and photographer Suresh Subramanian have restored a century-old tile factory as their delightful indoor-outdoor home-and-studio. Book ahead for one-hour guided tours *(₹350)*, or join Haseena's hands-on pottery workshops, from beginner-friendly days *(₹3500)* to multi-week programmes. You can stay overnight in one of the six art-filled cottages.

The respected century-old training centre **Kerala Kalamandalam** *(kalamandalam.ac.in; closed Apr-May)*, 30km north of Thrissur in Cheruthuruthy, also welcomes visitors through its A Day With the Masters experience *(per person ₹2000)* by advance booking. Take in the intricately built temple-theatre and galleries of vibrant costumes, before learning how performance make-up is applied and catching demonstrations of Kathakali (Kerala dance-drama), *mohiniyattam* (dance of the enchantress), Kootiattam (Sanskrit drama), classical Carnatic music and more.

Flavours of Kerala

If a deep-dive into Kerala's delectable cuisine sounds tempting, join prize-winning food writer Nimi Surendran Kolatte – author of *Lip Smacking Dishes of Kerala* and *4 O'Clock Temptations of Kerala* – at **Nimi's Lip Smacking Classes** *(nimisrecipes.com; ₹3000 per person)*. Three- to four-hour sessions start with an introduction to Kerala's spices and feature daily changing, primarily vegetarian menus of seasonal ingredients. Get in touch ahead to confirm current location.

Kanjiramattom

TIME FROM KOCHI: 1HR

Discover reborn Kerala textiles

For a firsthand immersion into the revival of central Kerala's rural handloom industry, seek out **Kara Weaves** *(karaweaves.com)*, a mother-daughter-founded fair-trade textiles enterprise in Kanjiramattom, around 30km southeast of Fort Kochi. Co-owner Indu Menon and team have thrown open the doors of their charming studio wrapped in tropical greenery, where you can learn all about their creative home textiles, mostly inspired by the traditional Kerala *thorthu* (woven-cotton towel). Call ahead for studio drop-ins *(free)*, with the option of also visiting the weaving community Kara works with.

Alappuzha (Alleppey)

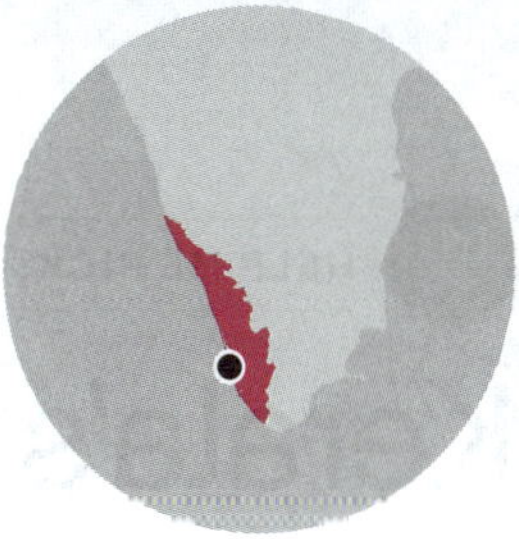

BACKWATERS ADVENTURES | HOUSEBOATS | VILLAGE LIFE

Surrounded by a sprawling network of waterways, 50km south of Kochi, Alappuzha (still mostly called Alleppey) is Kerala's vibrant backwaters hub and also a major coir producer.

The busy city centre revolves around a compact grid of canals set between a golden beach and Punnamada Lake, which spills into Kerala's largest lake, Vembanad. Beyond its traffic-heavy core, Alleppey morphs into a gorgeously green haven of meandering channels, palm-shaded villages, rustling paddy fields and thatched-roof *kettuvallam* (rice-barge houseboats). The region's waterways are the undisputed stars of any visit and jointly stretch all the way to Kochi (north), Kottayam (east) and Kollam (south).

Alleppey boomed as a spice-trading port for the Travancore rulers in the 18th century, when its custom-designed canals were created, and vestiges of this history can still be glimpsed around town. Houseboats first started carrying visitors across the waters in the 1990s, paving the way for today's (touristed) backwaters capital.

☑ TOP TIP

Alleppey's central canal grid has intriguing historical architecture, including ancient coir warehouses and other buildings restored under the Alappuzha Heritage Project; stroll along CCNB Rd (by the South Canal) or join a guided heritage tour. Alleppey Beach is one of Kerala's few with a wheelchair-friendly access point.

Paddling Out

Kayak and canoe the backwaters

Picture this: the sun blazes peach-and-pink as it sinks behind a forest of slender coconut palms fringing a shimmering lake, with just the leisurely sound of a paddle swooping

Continues on p900

GETTING AROUND

Alleppey is flat and walkable, but spread out and busy. The Mullackal bazaar area and bus stand are 3km and 3.5km inland (east) from Alleppey Beach respectively, and accommodation is all over the place (including along the beach and backwaters). Renting a scooter is popular, through guesthouses or agencies such as **Nanni Tours & Travels** *(nannibikerentals.com; per day ₹500)*. Autorickshaws charge ₹100 for quick hops. The well-connected train station is 4km southwest of the centre.

HELP ME PICK:

Kerala's Backwaters

Venturing out through Kerala's meandering network of backwaters counts among the region's most magical experiences, and there's an array of ways in which to get immersed in all this natural beauty. An overnight trip aboard a houseboat (meals included) is the classic adventure. Excellent kayaking, canoeing and paddleboarding tours also weave through the waterways, or hop on a local ferry to cruise between waterside towns and backwater villages.

Exploring the Backwaters If You Like...

Active Adventures

Kayaking, paddleboarding and punt-powered canoe trips with local guides are booming in popularity as a more sustainable way to roam around the backwaters than aboard a houseboat or other motorised boat. These rewarding, (generally) small-group tours open up areas that are trickier to reach by large boat and

LINKA A ODOM/GETTY IMAGES

offer a slow-travel experience on which you're likely to meet local villagers, learn about regional industries (from coir-making to fishing), catch the sunrise or sunset, and dine at small waterfront restaurants, rustic toddy shops or even family homes. Most places along Kerala's coast, lakes and backwaters offer kayaking, canoeing and paddleboarding trips. Munroe Island (p926) near Kollam is a scenic paddle hub; Alleppey, Varkala, Kochi, Kannur and Bekal have great tours available too.

Dipping into Local Life

Kerala's ever-expanding network of public ferries, run by the State Water Transport Department *(swtd.kerala.gov.in)*, provides a lifeline for local residents by linking backwater villages with hubs like Alleppey, Kollam, Kottayam and Kochi. SWTD ferry tickets typically cost just a few rupees and most schedules are available online (though it's still best to check locally for up-to-date details). Kochi's public ferries and still-growing Water Metro offer a great introduction (p890). The Alleppey–Kottayam ferry (around 2½ hours) is a popular trip (p900), and local ferries zip across Ashtamudi Lake from Kollam. Kerala's less-touristed northern backwaters, around Valiyaparamba Island between Kannur and Kasaragod, are also accessible by local ferry (p929).

Houseboat Escapes

With careful planning, spending a night aboard a houseboat designed like a *kettuvallam* (rice barge) can be a highlight of any India adventure. Feeling worlds away from everything, a typical houseboat trip looks something like this: fiery sunsets over the backwaters, freshly cooked Kerala-style meals, steaming chai sipped as the sun rises, glimpses of rare South Indian birds, seeing toddy-tapping and coir-making, hearing temple music echoing across the water. All that said, given the popularity of Kerala's houseboats (especially in the Alleppey area), it can be disappointing to find so many other boats plying the same waterways, so it's worth considering timing and location carefully. It's also important to know that there are growing environmental concerns involved (see p901).

NILADRILOVESPHOTOGRAPHY/SHUTTERSTOCK

Houseboat, Vembanad Lake (p904)

HOW TO

When to go If possible, skip the busy peak season and domestic holidays like Onam, when backwaters can get overwhelmed with houseboats (particularly around Alleppey).

Book ahead The most professional and responsible houseboats usually get booked up in advance, so it's worth reserving ahead. Kayaking and punt-canoeing trips are easily booked on location.

Budget Houseboat costs vary wildly, with prices also rising in high season. A one-night trip from Alleppey on a two-person boat typically costs from around ₹9000.

Finding a houseboat Ideally, choose your houseboat based on a strong local recommendation (a friend, local contact or reputable guesthouse); most bookings can be done online or by phone.

Houseboat Practicalities

The classic Kerala houseboat trip is an overnight cruise from Alleppey, but there are countless options and variations. A two-night trip, for example, will take you deeper into the rural backwaters. Houseboats (with drivers/captains) can be chartered through an almost overwhelming lineup of private operators in Kochi, Alleppey, Kollam, Kumarakom and, to a lesser extent, the Valiyaparamba backwaters area in northern Kerala.

The style and quality of boats varies hugely, from simple but well-maintained structures to palatial retreats, so it pays to do advance research by speaking with other travellers and local contacts. Reliable guesthouses and hotels are often a great starting point. Three meals a day cooked by an on-board chef are usually included in prices.

Alleppey has the biggest choice of houseboats in Kerala, with approximately 1000 floating around its waters. Concerns have grown in recent years about unlicensed houseboats operating in this region, however, so do check. With its social traveller atmosphere, Alleppey is also a great place for solo visitors to link up with others who might want to share houseboat costs and arrangements.

At the luxury end of the market, **Spice Coast Cruises** *(cghearth.com/spice-coast-cruises)* – by the sustainability-driven CGH Earth hotels chain – operates smart houseboats in the Vembanad Lake area near Alleppey. For northern Kerala's Valiyaparamba region, Lotus Houseboat (p930) and Bekal Ripples (p930) offer rewarding cruises.

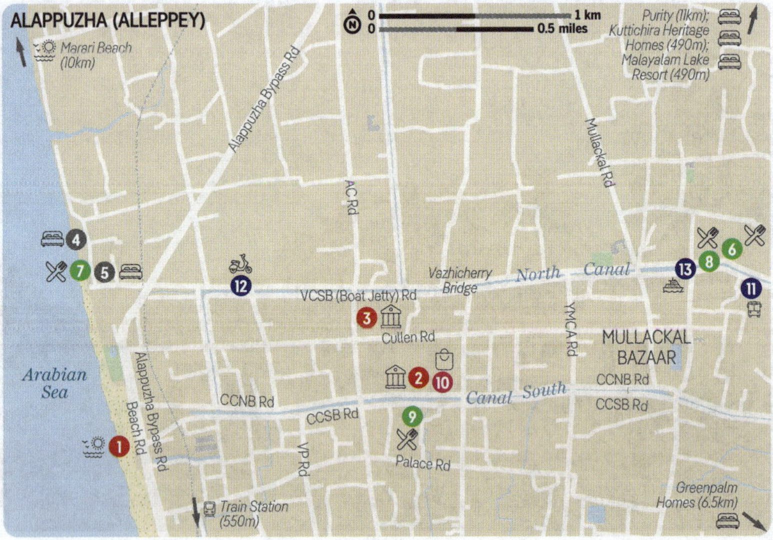

SIGHTS
1 Alleppey Beach
2 New Model Coir Society Building
3 RKK Memorial Museum

SLEEPING
4 Nanni Backpackers Hostel
5 Zostel

EATING
6 Borma
7 Cafe Catamaran
8 Cafe Paradiso
9 Halais

SHOPPING
10 Aspinwall & Co Warehouse

TRANSPORT
11 KSRTC Bus Stand
12 Nanni Tours & Travels
13 SWTD Boat Jetty

Continued from p897

through the water for company. Few Kerala moments rival catching a sunset or sunrise from a kayak, paddleboard or punt-powered canoe out in the midst of the backwaters. Visiting waterside villages, seeing coir-making and boat-building in action, learning about toddy-tapping, spotting a wide variety of birdlife and meeting local farmers and fishers are among many highlights en route.

Whether you prefer to paddle your own kayak or relax on a canoe led by a knowledgeable river guide, a slow-paced jaunt will immerse you in more off-the-beaten-track creeks and canals that larger boats are unable to navigate. Tours typically last anywhere between three hours and a full day (with a Kerala-style lunch included), and are easily booked through Alleppey-based operators. Reliable **Nanni Tours & Travels** *(nannibikerentals.com; tours per person from ₹1000)* offers private and small-group trips led by local guides or boat owners, mostly in the Kuttanad area just south of Alleppey; it also has a budget-friendly **guesthouse-and-hostel**. Similarly priced excursions by *shikara* (gondola-like boat) are also popular, and particularly convenient for travellers with young children in tow.

Catch a Local Ferry

All aboard for Kottayam

For the local-life experience of vast Vembanad Lake, take advantage of **State Water Transport Department** *(swtd.kerala.gov.in)* ferries departing from Alleppey's **SWTD boat jetty**, 3.5km east of the beach near Punnamada Lake. At a budget-friendly ₹29 per trip (buy tickets on board), boats ply the waters between Alleppey and Kottayam five times daily between 7.15am and 5.15pm. Trundling across **Vembanad Lake**, you'll catch the varied landscapes slipping by before arriving after 2½ hours in spice-trading **Kottayam**, from where there are handy onwards connections to Kerala's Western Ghats as well as Kochi, Kumarakom and beyond. Double-check the current Alleppey jetty location, amid ongoing construction works. A network of solar-powered public ferries is slowly being developed in the Alleppey area too; check locally for updates.

Boating Alleppey's Backwaters

The classic houseboat adventure

Chartering a houseboat for a night or two and floating past green paddy fields, lush palm forests, Chinese fishing nets and remote villages while feeling the tropical breeze on your face can be one of Kerala's (and indeed India's) most mesmerising experiences. Beautifully designed with wooden panels, thatched roofs and coconut-fibre rope, the *kettuvallam* has been used in this region since 3000 BCE to transport grain, spices and coconuts. It wasn't until the 1990s that tourism entered the picture, offering a new lease of life for these traditional boats, which had started to fade out as road links ramped up across the state.

Alleppey's houseboats offer diverse levels of comfort, style, budget and sustainability. Overtourism and houseboat pollution are increasingly serious concerns, so it's well worth researching (and booking) the most professional and responsible operators in advance (p899).

A Personal Collection

Take in the RKK Memorial Museum

Just south of central Alleppey's North Canal, **RKK Memorial Museum** (*rkkmuseum.com; ₹500; closed Mon*) houses the impressive private collection amassed by much-honoured local businessman Revi Karuna Karan. A grand building fronted by Greco-Roman columns, it was opened in memory of the late Alleppey-born personality by his wife Betty Karan. Wander through galleries bursting with extremely fine art and antiques from across India, as well as elsewhere in Asia and Europe – ceramics, porcelain and furniture. Don't miss the original antique Thanjavur paintings or the hundreds of beautiful Swarovski crystal animals and flowers. Afterwards, stroll 500m south to the South Canal for a taste of Alleppey's trading-port history; the restored **New Model Coir Society Building** (with a tiny free history museum) and **Aspinwall & Co Warehouse** are standout heritage buildings here.

Magical Backwaters Stays

Sink into only-in-Kerala accommodation

While you can certainly enjoy Alleppey's backwaters on a day tour, staying a night (or several) out among the waterways or along Vembanad Lake's shores fully immerses you in the region's slow beauty. Serene accommodation here ranges from charming little homestays to boutique-design

BACKWATERS: ENVIRONMENTAL ISSUES

With over 1000 houseboats (possibly even 2000) thought to be roaming Kerala's waterways (some unlicensed), the famous backwaters are facing increasing contamination from spilled fuel, plastic, food, noise and even human waste. This translates into water shortages, potential health hazards for local villagers, and declining bird and fish populations. Vembanad Lake also faces serious damage due to parts of it being reclaimed for agriculture from the 1880s onwards, and the creation of an enormous saltwater barrier in the 1970s. It isn't all bad news though: bio-toilets are now mandatory for houseboats, some owners are bringing in green initiatives like solar panels, and public solar-powered ferries are gaining traction. India's first solar-powered ferry has been cruising across Vembanad Lake from Vaikom to Thavanakkadav since 2017.

SNAKE-BOAT RACES

If you're anywhere near Alleppey in August, it's impossible to miss the sports-like fervour of the **Nehru Trophy Boat Race** *(nehrutrophy.nic.in)*, Kerala's most famous regatta. Beautifully carved *chundan vallam* (snake boats) propelled by up to 100 rowers battle it out on Punnamada Lake, drawing thousands of cheering spectators, many of them aboard houseboats. The race has been held almost every year since 1954 on the second Saturday in August. It is said to have evolved from water-based battles in the region over 400 years ago. Tickets are sold online and at on-site booths. Snake-boat races are big all over Kerala during monsoon season, with other highlights including Kollam's **President's Trophy Boat Race** (November) and **Aranmula Boat Race** (during Onam in the Kottayam region).

IMAGEBROKER.COM/ALAMY

Purity resort

retreats, all feeling galaxies away from the houseboat hubbub. Most places have immersive activities – village walks, sunrise kayaking, bike trips – on the doorstep. Long-running, community-driven **Greenpalm Homes** *(greenpalmhomes.com)* offers the chance to stay with local families in a collection of simple homestays on Chennamkary island, surrounded by backwaters and rice paddies 12km southeast of Alleppey. Luxury hotels cluster around Vembanad Lake, especially in nearby Kumarakom. Heritage-style **Purity** *(purityresort.com)*, 16km north of Alleppey, combines vibrant contemporary design with Indian antiques and Tamil Nadu-made tilework, creating a memorable setting for Kerala-style meals, Ayurvedic treatments, morning yoga and boat trips.

BACKWATERS PRACTICALITIES
For the lowdown on Kerala's backwaters scene – from booking tips to rewarding alternative regions beyond Alleppey – check out p898.

EATING IN ALLEPPEY: OUR PICKS

Cafe Catamaran: Breezy beachfront cafe under swaying lanterns, with live music, international dishes, fresh juices and evening tandoori. *8.30am-11pm* ₹₹

Halais: Step through a sweet shop to this locally renowned biryani spot famed for its chicken and mutton versions, plus Arabian and Yemeni dishes. *noon-10pm* ₹₹

Borma: Lovely garden cafe on the North Canal for international-style breakfasts, paneer wraps, strong coffee and freshly baked cakes. *9.30am-10pm Wed-Mon* ₹₹

Cafe Paradiso: Tiny coffee hangout doing espresso, lassis and simple breakfasts at canal-side tables, near the Mullackal bazaar and temple. *9am-8.30pm* ₹

Beyond Alappuzha

Gold-tinged beaches and palm-sprinkled lakes give way to nature reserves, islands reachable only by boat, ancient palaces and farming communities.

A string of powdery beaches and low-key fishing villages marks the evocative coast just north of Alleppey. Marari (or Mararikulam), 14km north of Alleppey, is growing into one of Kerala's most-loved beach escapes with both cheerful homestays and luxe hotels, but still retains its go-slow charm, making it a great alternative base for exploring this backwaters-laced region.

On the eastern shores of sprawling Vembanad Lake, a 30km drive northeast of Alleppey, Kumarakom hosts (mostly) high-end resorts from which to experience village life, water adventures and prime birdwatching. Heading inland unveils a green-clad agricultural region centred on Kottayam, a lively transport-hub city of 350,000 people and the heart of Kerala's rubber and spice trades, as well as its Christian community.

Places

GETTING AROUND

Marari is best explored on foot or by bike. Taxis between Alleppey and Marari cost ₹500; plenty of Cherthala-bound buses heading north from Alleppey stop in/near Marari, as do trains. Kottayam has excellent train and bus links to destinations across Kerala (including the Western Ghats), plus SWTD ferries to/from Alleppey (2½ hours; see p900). Kumarakom, easily reached by taxi or bus (30 minutes) from Kottayam, is ideal for kayaking and cycling.

Marari

TIME FROM ALAPPUZHA: **20MIN** (car) OR (train)

Slow down to beach mode

Wandering down tranquil sandy lanes to honey-gold, kilometres-long **Marari Beach** instantly soothes the soul, whether you're day-tripping from Alleppey or staying a few nights. Stalls selling fragrant chai and fresh coconuts congregate at the main beach entrance, though the sand is cleaner further south; people do swim, but take care as there's no lifeguard service and currents can be strong. Around sunset, locals and visitors converge along the sands fringed by palms and casuarinas. Or stroll the beach early in the morning to see colourful fishing boats out at work. Around 2km inland from central Marari Beach, the **Mahadeva Temple** is said to date back 700 years; an enormous, modern Shiva head marks the entrance.

For something even more low-key, head a few kilometres south to **Kattoor Beach**, which has a fishing-village feel and is known as Secret Beach for its often-empty golden sands. Yogis can join classes here at **Secret Beach Yoga Homestay**; *secretbeach.in*); owner Vimal also runs *kalarippayat* sessions.

Kumarakom & Vembanad Lake

TIME FROM ALAPPUZHA: **1HR** (car)

Cook, dine and stay on a farm

Hopping into a wooden boat across the water is the perfect introduction to **Philipkutty's Farm** *(philipkuttysfarm.com)*, a serene 14-hectare ancestral home and coconut farm

STATE BIRD

A thrill to see (and hear) in flight, the great Indian hornbill is known for its distinctive yellow bill and the astonishing whooshing sound made by its wing beats as it soars through the sky. It is celebrated as the state bird of both Kerala and Arunachal Pradesh. Female hornbills nest inside tree cavities for months, sealing the entrance except for a small slit through which they and any chicks are fed by their mate. Some of the best places to spot these graceful creatures in Kerala are Periyar Tiger Reserve, Nelliyampathy in Palakkad (northeast from Thrissur) and Thattekkad Bird Sanctuary near Kothamangalam (en route to Munnar).

on a human-made island just northwest of **Kumarakom**. Set where the Meenachil River meets Vembanad Lake, this biogas-powered property has been lovingly transformed into a luxury homestay with cottages and rooms inspired by Kerala architecture. Hosts Anu and Aniamma offer personalised cooking classes *(per person ₹2950)*, as well as wonderful home-cooked lunches and guided farm walks, all also open to outside guests by prior booking. Every meal is packed with family recipes and organic farm-to-table ingredients (taste the freshness in the rich coconut curries), and you'll learn all about the region's tradition of farming below lake level on reclaimed land.

Roam the lazy waterways

Getting lost in the endless blues of 2000-sq-km **Vembanad Lake** (Kerala's largest lake) and its wandering inlets is a key draw of the Kumarakom region. Most Kumarakom hotels (p938) can organise *kettuvalam* experiences, as well as paddleboarding, canoeing and kayaking tours.

Based in Maravantharathu village, 20km north of Kumarakom, **Kizhakku Kayaking** *(instagram.com/kizhakku_kayaking; tours per person ₹600-800)* runs guided excursions on the Muvattupuzha River and small uncrowded canals. Book ahead and catch the sun rising or sinking beyond the palms; traditional breakfasts of *puttu* and veg curry can be arranged for morning slots.

Spot protected birdlife

Around 150 species of feathered creatures are known to gather at forested **Kumarakom Bird Sanctuary** *(keralatourism.org)*. This 5-hectare nature reserve on a former rubber plantation on Vembanad Lake provides a refuge for local birds such as pond herons, egrets, little cormorants, kingfishers and Indian shags; as well as migratory species (October to February), including ospreys, garganey teals, marsh harriers, Siberian cranes and steppe eagles. First thing in the morning is usually best for bird-spotting. Bring binoculars, insect repellent and comfortable shoes. The sanctuary was undergoing renovations at research time, so it's best to check up-to-date visiting arrangements locally.

Kottayam

TIME FROM ALAPPUZHA: 2½HR /1¼HR

Step into ancient places of worship

Kottayam is the epicentre of Kerala's prominent Syrian Christian community, which according to legend traces its roots back to St Thomas bringing Christianity to India in 52 CE. Get a glimpse of this heritage by spending an hour or two exploring the fascinating Syrian Christian churches hidden near the Meenachil River, 2km northwest of central Kottayam (donations are welcome).

Also called Valiyapally, hilltop **St Mary's Syrian Knanaya Church** *(0481-2563324)* dates from 1588, though it was originally founded in 1550. The highlights are two granite-carved crosses inscribed with Pahalavi-language writing from the 7th century or earlier, brought from another church. Provided you don't arrive during the daily lunch break, staff offer

NEKOMURA/SHUTTERSTOCK

Kumarakom Bird Sanctuary

visiting leaflets, open the muralled main altar (otherwise behind a curtain) and point out details such as an original Kerala-influenced stone archway with carved elephants and peacocks. A five-minute walk away, **St Mary's Orthodox Church** *(kottayamcheriapally.com)* blends European-style baroque architecture with Kerala temple design, including elaborate wood carvings on its southern porch. Often called Kottayam Cheriapally, it was constructed by the Portuguese in 1579 and has vibrant vegetable-dye altar paintings. Ask the office for a highlights pamphlet.

More beautiful murals await at the renowned **Mahadeva Temple** *(ettumanoormahadevatemple.com)* in Ettumanur, 12km north of Kottayam. The oldest inscriptions go back to 1542, though this Hindu Shiva temple built in Dravidian style is thought to date in part from the 12th century.

Kayamkulam

TIME FROM ALAPPUZHA: **45MIN** /**1¼HR**

A jewel of royal architecture

Around 48km south of Alleppey, the restored **Krishnapuram Palace Museum** *(archaeology.kerala.gov.in; adult/child ₹350/100)* ranks among Kerala's most impressive royal buildings. While not *quite* as spectacular as Padmanabhapuram Palace (p925) in the south (now over the border in Tamil Nadu), it dates mostly from the mid-18th century and was once a home for the Travancore royal family. Wandering around its interconnected courtyards reveals a feast of gabled roofing, antique crafts, intricate woodwork and outward-curving balconies. But the undisputed highlight is a vibrantly painted 3m-tall mural of the Gajendra Moksha (the liberation of Gajendra, chief of the elephants), a legend from the Bhagavata Purana, painted in earthy blues, oranges and reds using natural dyes. Climb upstairs to weave through wooden galleries including the former dance room. Note that the palace is closed on Monday and from 1pm to 2pm on other days.

THE GOD OF SMALL THINGS

The small village of **Aymanam**, 5km northwest of Kottayam near the Meenachil River, is famously where Booker Prize–winning Indian author Arundhati Roy spent her childhood and set her internationally acclaimed 1997 debut novel *The God of Small Things*. The novel depicts mid-20th-century life (and its challenges) here through the story of a Syrian-Christian family, against a backdrop of India's caste system and the enduring effects of British colonialism. The area is now home to a blossoming rural-tourism scene and a few small charming places to stay, with birdwatching, temples, backwaters, paddy fields and heritage buildings on the doorstep.

Munnar

MOUNTAIN BEAUTY | TEA CULTURE | WILDLIFE RESERVES

Strategically located 1524m high at the meeting point of three rivers, 135km inland from Kochi, Munnar sits at the heart of the largest tea-producing region in South India. The cool, rugged mountain landscapes evoke everything that makes the UNESCO-listed Western Ghats magical, often cloaked in patches of swirling mist between which loom some of South India's tallest peaks.

Once positioned on an ancient trading route linking central Kerala with Madurai, this area was developed as a tea-growing hub from the 1880s onwards during the British colonial period, with Munnar itself established in 1901. Before all this, subsistent Adivasi communities lived in the region, which eventually became part of the princely state of Travancore.

Centred on a busy bazaar, modern-day Munnar is a working hill town and an immensely popular tourism destination drawing both domestic and international travellers. The mountainous surrounding area is known for its rich biodiversity, with wildlife corridors spilling over into neighbouring Tamil Nadu.

GETTING AROUND

Munnar's flat town centre is walkable, though traffic-heavy. Most accommodation and sights are scattered across the countryside. Autorickshaws, taxis, jeeps and buses get you there. Munnar's main KSRTC bus station (for services across Kerala and beyond) is at the town's south end; some buses stop in the bazaar instead. Full-day jeep or taxi tours of viewpoints and sights cost ₹2500 to ₹3500. **Gokulam Bike Hire** *(bikerentalmunnar.com)* rents scooters and motorbikes. The main NH85 Kochi–Munnar road was being redeveloped at the time of research; once complete, travel times should speed up.

MORE SOUTHERN TEA

Kerala's Periyar region (p911) is home to one of South India's oldest tea industries, while Wayanad (p932) and Tamil Nadu's Nilgiri Hills (p975) are also famous for tea.

All About Tea

Dive into Munnar's tea-producing history

Two ingredients – tea and cardamom – put Munnar on the modern-day world map. Tea-growing remains one of Munnar's key industries, with around 250 working plantations sprinkled around the hills, mostly owned by Harrisons Malayalam Ltd and the local

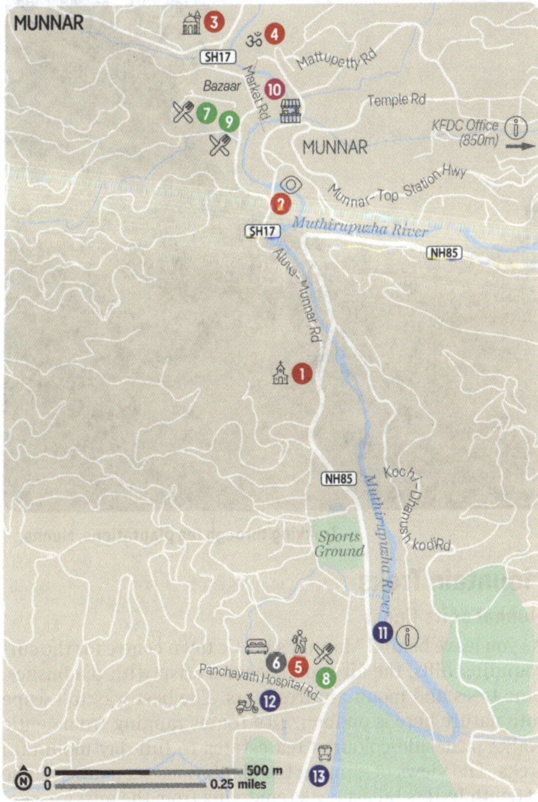

SIGHTS
1 CSI Christ Church
2 Kanan Devan Hills Plantation Company Building
3 Munnar Juma Masjid
4 Subramanya Swami Temple

ACTIVITIES
5 Munnar Trekking

SLEEPING
6 Green View Inn

EATING
see 10 Bazaar Food Stalls
7 Saravana Bhavan
8 Taste the Brews
9 Tea Tales

SHOPPING
10 Munnar Daily Vegetable Market

INFORMATION
11 DTPC Tourist Office

TRANSPORT
12 Gokulam Bike Hire
13 KSRTC Bus Station

cooperative Kanan Devan Hills Plantation Company (KDHP). Grown at altitudes of around 1400m to 2400m, tea here has a crisp, aromatic edge, thanks to the misty climate and elevated geography, with black, white and green teas all produced locally.

Around 10km southeast of Munnar along the NH85, 1879-founded **Lockhart Tea Factory** *(8921771287; adult/child ₹250/100)* is one of Kerala's oldest estates, now run by Harrisons Malayalam Ltd. With a spectacular view of Chokramudi peak, the current building dates from 1936. Half-hour guided tours unveil today's tea process, from picking to drying to export, and are professionally run (if a little cursory), ending with a multi-tea tasting in the on-site shop. A collaboration with eco-conscious hotel brand CGH Earth means you can now even stay overnight at **Lockhart Bungalow** *(cghearth.com)*, an original three-room bungalow among Lockhart's plantations. For a more in-depth experience, consider an immersive tea-themed tour with Blue Yonder or Breakaway (p888).

TOP TIP

Many visitors come to Munnar seeking mountain tranquillity, but this can be increasingly tricky to find amid growing overtourism. Avoid weekends and holidays, when the town, roads and viewpoints get packed.

A LOCAL'S MUNNAR GUIDE

Dileep Tomy runs Rosegardens Tours *(rosegardenstours.com)*.

Letchmi Hills: Go trekking just west of Munnar town to enjoy the mountain beauty and, if lucky, spot wild elephants. Treks can take from three hours to a whole day.

Top Station: On a 32km scenic drive to this viewpoint you'll cross two dams (Mattupetty and Kundaly), wonderful tea plantations and the spectacular Yellapatty vegetable plantation.

Marayoor: Around 40km from Munnar, this area is famous for its sandalwood forests and jaggery production. Another 15km on you reach the starting point for a guided 1½-hour trek to beautiful Thoovanam Waterfall in Chinnar Wildlife Sanctuary (p910).

Srishti Trust: A charitable TATA-founded project for children with disabilities, producing handmade papers and silk-dyed fabrics that make original gifts.

AZAD NECHIKKADE/SHUTTERSTOCK

Trekking through tea plantations, Munnar

Mountain Treks

Munnar at its finest

As you leave behind Munnar's hectic town centre for the surrounding hills, the air soon becomes crisp with tea bushes, pine trees and mountain freshness. The best way to escape into nature here is on foot, with routes ranging from gentle walks past jade-coloured tea estates to full-day mountain treks. The views of glinting tea plantations set against some of South India's tallest peaks emerging from the mist are genuinely mesmerising. Reputable **Munnar Trekking** *(munnartrekking.com)* offers expert-led treks including a 6km (return) early-morning route to catch the sunrise at 2000m high *(₹900 per person)*.

A popular official hike is the ascent of 2195m-high **Chokramudi** *(per person ₹800)*, a 6km (return) route often referred to as Bison Trail; it starts from Lockhart Gap (12km southeast of Munnar), with optional guides. Rewarding further-flung hiking areas include **Top Station**, 32km northeast of Munnar at 1880m and (when not cloaked in mist) with dramatic views from its **viewpoint** *(₹50)*; this was once the upper terminus of the Kottagudi Aerial Ropeway which, along with the Kundala Valley Railway, linked Munnar with Tamil Nadu for tea export. **Meesappulimala** (2650m), Kerala's second-highest peak on the remote Kerala–Tamil Nadu border, is another tempting challenge for trekkers; guided hikes of around 10km (return) must be prebooked and begin from an official Forest Department base camp, 20km west of Munnar.

At the time of writing, all three areas required Forest Department permits/tickets; check directly with your guesthouse or a local trekking company for updates. For Meesappulimala, there's also a mandatory return transfer charge from Munnar. You *may* be able to book some Forest Department routes online *(ecotourism.forest.kerala.gov.in)* or through Munnar's **KFDC Office** *(kfdcecotourism.com)*, though joining a local trekking company is often the easiest approach.

Munnar Town Stroll

Markets and monuments in the hill station's heart

Beyond all the tourism paraphernalia, Munnar is a bustling, working hill town. Soak up the local-life atmosphere with an hour or two of wandering its central streets, starting with the colourful bazaar area at the north end of town. On the east side of Market Rd, **Munnar Daily Vegetable Market** bursts with counters of aromatic spices and fresh produce laid out beneath dangling strings of bananas. Across the street, stalls sell everything from artisanal chocolates to flower garlands to deep-fried evening snacks. Munnar's **Juma Masjid** (main mosque) and Hindu **Subramanya Swami Temple** sit just north of the bazaar.

Head 500m south along the (usually busy) main road to the pale-yellow 20th-century **Kanan Devan Hills Plantation Company Building** *(kdhptea.com)*. Now housing KDHP offices and a shop, this was once Munnar's train station for the colonial-period Kundala Valley Railway, a 35km monorail turned narrow-gauge railway used to transport tea (and other products) up to Top Station for export through Tamil Nadu, until it was destroyed by a great flood in 1924. Around 600m further south, in what is known as Old Munnar, rises the neogothic **CSI Christ Church**, built in 1911, where many colonial-era planters were laid to rest.

Cook Up a Storm

Flavours of Munnar's kitchens

All those fragrant cardamom-coated hills and fresh-spice stalls around Munnar will have food lovers itching to get behind the stove. At lovely homestay **Rosegardens** (p938), 12km southwest of Munnar, botanist Tomy Joseph, his wife Raji and their close family host four-hour cooking experiences *(per person ₹2500)* that start with a tour of the property's organic gardens, cardamom plantations and spice crops. Depending on what's in season, you might be able to pick fresh ingredients yourself.

Rare Wildlife & Protected Hills

Explore Eravikulam National Park

The stocky Nilgiri tahr is one of the Western Ghats' signature species, but there are now thought to be only around 2660 of these endangered mountain goats remaining across Kerala and Tamil Nadu. The largest single population (around 840) inhabits the rolling expanses of the protected 97-sq-km **Eravikulam National Park** *(eravikulamnationalpark.in; ₹500; closed Feb & Mar)*, 11km north of Munnar. While trekking at

TREKKING PRACTICALITIES

Organising a trek in Munnar can feel complicated, but once you're out in the green hills, walking here is a joy. The Forest Department dictates which areas are officially open for trekking (you must usually purchase a ticket/permit) and a growing number of routes now require mandatory Forest Department guides. There are still walks to enjoy independently, though keep in mind that tea plantations are private property and traffic has increased along local roads. For updates on what's open, ask locally, ideally at your guesthouse or at Munnar's KFDC Office or **DTPC Tourist Office** *(dtpcidukki.com)*, or head out with a professional trekking company, such as Munnar Trekking or Green Valley Vista (p938). Factor in flexibility for unpredictable mountain weather.

Eravikulam wasn't permitted at the time of writing, park-operated buses travel 3km to an elevated drop-off point where you can walk a little further along a paved road, with a good chance of spotting Nilgiri tahrs as well as views of *shola* (virgin forest), grasslands and, on clear days, 2695m-tall Anamudi, South India's highest peak. Eravikulam is hugely popular, so prebook tickets and visit on weekdays (ideally early) to side-step the crowds; entry is from 8am to 2pm. The park is also a hotspot for *neelakurinji*, an endemic plant that bursts into purple-pink bloom once every 12 years (next due in 2030).

Eravikulam is an easy day trip from Munnar, often combined with Chinnar Wildlife Sanctuary. Buses heading along the SH17 road will get you there; taxis/jeeps from Munnar charge ₹3200 to ₹3500 for day trips.

Walk Through Protected Forests

Nature escapes in Chinnar Wildlife Sanctuary

Extending around the Pambar River, 50km northeast of Munnar on the Kerala–Tamil Nadu border, **Chinnar Wildlife Sanctuary** *(chinnar.in; treks per person ₹500-1500)* is a lushly forested 90-sq-km expanse favoured for its official hikes usually led by Adivasi guides from local communities. Among its grasslands, scrub jungle and *shola* roam deer, gaurs, langurs, giant grizzled squirrels, wild elephants and endangered Nilgiri tahrs, as well as much-harder-to-spot tigers and leopards. Go early to maximise chances of glimpsing wildlife, though it's often down to luck; November to March are the best months for wildlife.

Various guided treks were available at the time of writing, starting from official checkpoints on the SH17 road and lasting one, three or six hours. Options include threading through the forest to the rushing **Thoovanam Waterfalls**.

IDUKKI DISTRICT

Carved through by the Periyar and Pamba Rivers, spice-growing **Idukki** is Kerala's largest district, yet also one of its least densely populated areas. It stretches along the border with neighbouring Tamil Nadu, taking in the Munnar region, Kerala's highest peaks and a collection of interconnected wildlife reserves. The area has been inhabited since prehistoric times (as recovered cave art and dolmens show) and has a strong Adivasi population. In the 18th century it became part of the Kingdom of Travancore. Much of Kerala's power is sourced from Idukki's hydroelectric stations, often fuelled by enormous Idukki Dam, which is surrounded by the 77-sq-km Idukki Wildlife Sanctuary. **Vagamon** is another popular Idukki hill station, with a growing accommodation scene and similar mountain-adventure activities to Munnar.

EATING IN MUNNAR: OUR PICKS

Saravana Bhavan: Dosa, *vada*, *idli*, *uttapam*, filter coffee and other South Indian vegetarian classics, at a fuss-free restaurant next to the bazaar. *7am-9.30pm* ₹

Tea Tales: Modern 1st-floor cafe above Munnar's bazaar with a tiny terrace, serving local teas, espresso and international bites. *9.30am-8.30pm* ₹₹

Taste the Brews: Near the bus stand, this laid-back cafe does fresh juices and cakes, European-style breakfasts and Kerala tea and coffee. *8.30am-5pm* ₹

Bazaar Food Stalls: Simple stands serving deep-fried snacks like *pani puri* and chilli *bajji* burst into action every morning and evening in Munnar's bazaar area. *hours vary* ₹

Periyar Tiger Reserve

WILDLIFE | MOUNTAIN ADVENTURES | SPICES AND TEA

Hidden among the southern reaches of the UNESCO-listed, biodiverse Western Ghats, 925-sq-km Periyar Tiger Reserve is South India's most popular protected space and holds a special place in the hearts of many Keralites. Electric-green tea plantations sprawl across the surrounding hillsides, while lofty peaks rise above dense, untrammelled forest. Centred on a 26-sq-km artificial lake, this was Kerala's first tiger reserve, declared in 1978, though it had already been a protected sanctuary since 1934. Long before the late 19th century when British colonisers arrived, this area was home for Adivasi communities, many of whom still live here today.

Periyar now sits firmly on Kerala's travel map and is known for its pioneering, vehicle-free ecotourism programmes. Around 2000 elephants and 40 elusive tigers flit through the forests here, along with langurs, wild boars, giant squirrels, sambar, bison, otters and great Indian hornbills. Kumily, the park's lively access town, sits on the Kerala–Tamil Nadu border, with park facilities towards its south end, known as Thekkady.

GETTING AROUND

Compact Kumily is easily explored on foot. From Kumily bus stand and the bazaar, it's 600m to Bypass Rd where most accommodation gathers. The main Periyar Tiger Reserve entrance is 1.5km south of Kumily bus stand. Shuttle buses (₹30) run from the Bamboo Grove Ticket Office to Periyar Lake, 3km south of the park entrance; you *may* be able to walk this stretch (with a park ticket). Buses fan out across Kerala; there's a separate stop for Tamil Nadu buses, just north of town.

Wild Walks

Periyar Tiger Reserve on foot

Among the key factors that make the 925-sq-km **Periyar Tiger Reserve** *(periyartigerreserve.org; adult/child ₹500/180)* such an exciting natural space to explore are its pioneering trekking opportunities, through which you'll travel into the reserve on routes led by mostly Adivasi guides. Options range from two-hour wildlife-spotting hikes to adventurous overnight itineraries with forest camping, always in small groups and mostly accompanied by armed guards (for safety). Simply being out in the raw wild with birdcalls echoing through the forest canopy feels truly special. While wildlife sightings can

SLEEPING
1 Chrissie's Hotel
2 Green View
3 Spice Village

EATING
4 Bar-B-Que
see 1 Chrissie's Cafe
5 Friends Coffee Bar
see 3 Spice Village

INFORMATION
6 Bamboo Grove Ticket Office
7 Ecotourism Centre

TRANSPORT
8 Kumily Bus Stand
9 Park Shuttle Bus Stop
10 Tamil Nadu Bus Stand

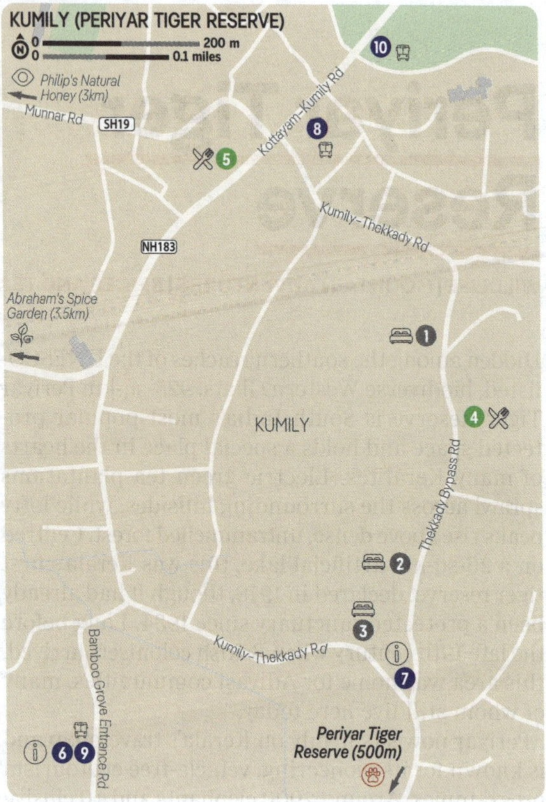

TOP TIP

The optimum season for wildlife is December to April, especially March/April when animals gather at water sources as the weather warms up. Early morning and late afternoon are often the best times of day.

never be guaranteed, you're highly likely to at least spot a rich variety of birds and deer, and very possibly Nilgiri langurs, giant squirrels or some tiger pugmarks.

The park's signature hike is the **Periyar Tiger Trail** *(per person ₹7200-10,000)* led by retrained former poachers now working as guides; with options for either one night/two days or two nights/three days, it's a challenging route covering 20km to 30km, with overnight accommodation at tented campsites. Also thrilling are the full-day **Border Hikes** *(per person ₹2000)*, which open up spectacular mountain views at between 900m and 1300m, with 16km of walking on the northern edges of the park. All these include meals.

But even the shorter **Green Walk** and **Nature Walk** routes *(per person ₹400)* are an adventure, immersing you in the dense forest over 4km to 5km (2½ hours). After-dark **Jungle Scout walks** *(per person ₹1500)* are popular too, offering visitors the chance to join 2½-hour nighttime patrols along the reserve's fringes.

ventures on the Water

oating, rafting and wildlife-watching

Glinting **Periyar Lake** – a 25-sq-km human-made expanse created in 1895 when the British built the Mullaperiyar Dam – dominates the northern core of Periyar Tiger Reserve. The 1½-hour **Periyar Lake boat cruises** *(periyartigerreserve.org; adult/child ₹255/85)* are the park's most popular, accessible and family-friendly activity. Snag the first or last boat of the day for the best chances of wildlife-sighting. Though the experience is really more of a scenic cruise than a wildlife-spotting expedition, guides do a good job of identifying and pointing out species along the way. Expect to spot birds flitting by or resting on tree trunks; bison, deer, otters or even elephants are sometimes spied on the lake's shores too. Book well ahead as tickets sell out (online reservations get the top seats), or try your luck on the day at the jetty counter 1½ hours before your ideal tour.

If you're keen to sidestep the crowds on a more in-depth experience, how about gliding across Periyar Lake on a punted bamboo raft? Half- and full-day guided **rafting expeditions** of up to 15 people start with a hike through the forest. Half-day options *(per person ₹2200)* involve an hour exploring by raft, while the full-day trip *(per person ₹2700)* means three hours on the water.

Periyar's Tea Story

From leaf to cup

The unique Western Ghats geography and warm, humid climate make for prime tea-growing land in the hills surrounding Periyar Tiger Reserve. This lush region is one of South India's earliest established tea regions, originally developed under British rule from the late 19th century, and still ranks among Kerala's key tea producers. Emerald-green plantations carpet the hillsides at between 750m and 1350m above sea level, particularly around **Vandiperiyar**, 14km southwest of Kumily.

At Vandiperiyar's well-established **Connemara Tea Factory** *(connemaratea.com; tours ₹250)*, going strong since 1945, excellent one hour guided tours offer a glimpse of the undulating plantations and an intriguing introduction to the intricate in-factory process of withering, rolling, oxidation and drying, before ending with a small tasting of the estate's brews. Connemara now employs around 80 tea-pickers (all women) and 30 other workers, producing black, green and white tea as well as coffee.

World of Spices

Learn at local spice farms

Kerala has been growing fragrant spices for thousands of years, attracting traders from across the globe. Many of these emerge from the Western Ghats, and the Periyar area is a major producer. **Abraham's Spice Garden** *(abrahamspice.com; tours*

PERIYAR PRACTICALITIES

Book Periyar activities well ahead, particularly for the peak November-to-March season. Bookings are theoretically available online *(periyartigerreserve.org)*, though foreign cards weren't working at time of writing. Periyar accommodation hosts can help with reservations. There may be slots available at shorter notice through the Forest Department's **Ecotourism Centre** *(6.30am-8.30pm)* in Thekkady, or at the lakeside jetty for boat cruises; cash, card and UPI payments were all accepted at research time. Many activities require at least two or four people; alternatively, join existing groups or pay the minimum fee. Most hikes are off-limits to kids under 12. Pack warm, waterproof layers and sensible footwear. All visitors must purchase a park entry ticket (in addition to booking activities), valid for one day.

SABARIMALA

Around 100km south from Kumily by road lies one of the world's busiest pilgrim destinations, the **Ayyappan Temple** at Sabarimala, drawing millions of Hindu devotees each year. Dedicated to the celibate god Ayyappan, Sabarimala has traditionally not permitted women of 'menstruating age' to enter the temple; widespread protests and violence erupted when India's Supreme Court overturned this ban in 2018, and the ruling remains controversial and politicised. On the way to Sabarimala, many Hindu pilgrims – who dress in black for the journey – also visit **Vavar Mosque** at Erumeli (50km from Sabarimala), a centuries-old place of worship dedicated to Vavar, a Muslim friend of Sabarimala's god Ayyappan. According to legend, Vavar helped Ayyappan defeat the demon Mahishi at Erumeli.

Bonnet Macaque, Periyar Tiger Reserve (p911)

₹300), 3km west of Kumily, is a long-running family-owned spice farm with 12 hectares of organic gardens, growing everything from cardamom to over 20 varieties of banana. On an informal one-hour tour, owner Justin Abraham and family will show you around some of their crops (the earliest planted in the 1950s), sharing stories about cardamom harvesting, the region's many orchids and countless local plants with medicinal uses. Also open for casual visits is **Philip's Natural Honey** *(instagram.com/philips_natural_honey)*, a small family-run bee farm that has been producing honey for over four decades, 3.5km northwest of Kumily.

EATING IN KUMILY: OUR PICKS

Chrissie's Cafe: Roof-terrace cafe for coffee, falafel wraps, biryani, fresh juices and water refills, plus breakfasts featuring home-baked bread. *8am-8.30pm* ₹₹

Spice Village: Swish resort with a cocktail bar, superb hyper-local cuisine at 50 Mile restaurant and delicious Kerala specialities at Tamarind. *hours vary* ₹₹₹

Friends Coffee Bar: Tiny no-fuss spot in Kumily's bazaar that does a roaring trade in *vada*, *bajjis* and other savoury snacks with steaming tea or coffee. *6.30am-8pm* ₹

Bar-B-Que: Get hands-on preparing spice-laden Kerala dishes, before enjoying a group dinner, at this long-running, family-owned cookery school. *hours vary* ₹₹

Varkala

SURF AND YOGA | BEAUTIFUL BEACHES | TEMPLE TOWN

Around 50km northwest of Kerala's capital Thiruvananthapuram (Trivandrum), Varkala has two identities. The first is the coastal town that ripples along a string of rust-coloured laterite cliffs towering 15m high above powdery gold-black beaches and some of South India's finest surf waves. But Varkala is also an important Hindu pilgrimage destination, home to the centuries-old Janardhana Temple, and Varkala Town (3km inland from the coast) has its own lively buzz.

The natural setting is spectacular, so it is no surprise that this laid-back beach town has morphed into one of Kerala's most-loved destinations, pulling in a mix of families, couples, groups of friends and solo travellers. Varkala was Kerala's original backpacker beach spot, and while it still retains its easygoing soul, in recent years things have smartened up with boutique guesthouses, vegan cafes, yoga centres and stylish sunset-view restaurants. The (main) North Cliff area can get busy, but it's easy to escape to quieter pockets of beachfront beauty.

GETTING AROUND

Varkala's beaches are 3km west of Varkala Town, where you'll find well-connected Varkala Sivagiri train station. Autorickshaws charge ₹150 between Varkala Town and the seafront, or hop on one of the regular local buses. Beachfront Varkala is generally walkable with paths threading along the cliffs, though watch your step at night. Autorickshaws gather at the North Cliff's helipad, by Papanasam Beach and outside the Janardhana Temple. Some travellers hire scooters to zip around locally, costing around ₹500 per day.

Beach Bliss

From quiet coves to pilgrimage spots

With earthy-red cliffs cascading down to meet broad stretches of gold-and-black sand washed by the often-bath-warm Arabian Sea, Varkala's naturally spectacular setting makes it a dreamy escape for beach lovers. It's all very laid-back, and most people simply pick a patch of sand and stretch our their towel before plunging in, though take care with large waves and potential riptides.

At the heart of it all lies cliff-edged **Papanasam Beach**, a powdery (often busy) strand. The middle of the beach (near the Beach Rd junction) is considered a holy spot by Hindus. For beach time, head further north or south; at the far southern end of Papanasam, there's a gorgeous slip of feathery sand just beneath the South Cliffs. Immediately north of the North Cliff, **Black Beach** (Thiruvambady Beach) is a pretty, sandy

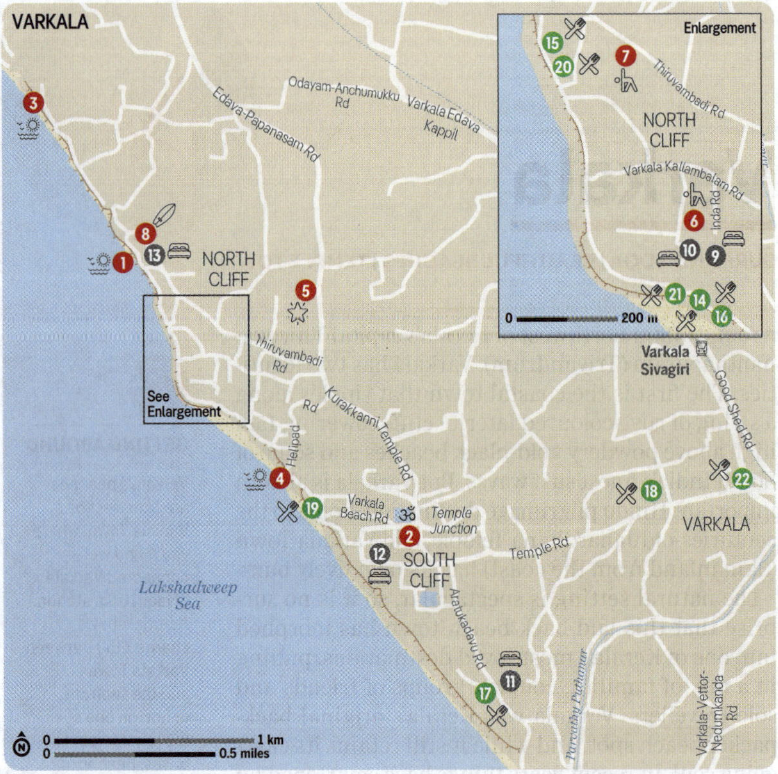

SIGHTS
1 Black Beach
2 Janardhana Temple
3 Odayam Beach
4 Papanasam Beach

ACTIVITIES
5 AyurSoul
6 Devvrat Yoga
7 Lumuma
8 Point Break

SLEEPING
9 InDa Hotel
10 Mad About Coco
11 Villa Akasa
12 Villa Jacaranda
13 Zostel

EATING
14 ABBA
15 Aum Cafe
16 Cafe del Mar
17 Cafe TripisLife
18 Chimney Family Restaurant
19 Cyra Cafe
see 9 InDa Cafe
20 Lumuma
21 Sun Francisco
22 Suprabhatham

TOP TIP

All beaches in this area can develop dangerous currents – take care when out in the water. Most clifftop restaurants offer wide-ranging Indian-international menus, but for more traditional South Indian meals head into Varkala Town.

stretch that draws surfers as well as beachgoers. Around 1km north of the North Cliff, honey-coloured **Odayam Beach** provides a refreshingly peaceful refuge, though it has suffered from erosion recently. From here, largely undeveloped sands (including **Kappil Beach**, which you can coastal-walk to) stretch north almost all the way to Kollam. Near Kappil Beach, the small **Edava Backwaters** extend inland, popular for paddleboarding and kayaking. Lucky beachgoers might spot dolphins skimming through the waters off Varkala's coast.

Surfers' Paradise

Catch the Varkala waves

Whether you're a complete beginner or a pro, surfing in Varkala is a tropical thrill thanks to the wave-whipped beaches north and south of town. The surf scene here has a strong community focus, tying in initiatives such as beach clean-ups and surf camps for local kids. Shops along the cliffs rent surfboards and boogie boards for experienced surfers, though take care with currents on Varkala's beaches.

To learn more about riding the waves here (and insider tips on the season's best spots), sign up for a multiday course with a reputable surf school. Classes typically kick off early in the morning when conditions are best, and the main surfing season runs roughly October to April. Non-Varkala-based surf centres often bring their own retreats to town too, including women-only trips. Long-running favourite **Soul & Surf** *(soulandsurf.com)* was due to close down at research time, but check social media for potential pop-ups or similar.

In a peaceful spot near Black Beach, **Point Break** *(pointbreakvarkala.in)* combines a small, beachy guesthouse with switched-on surf classes; sessions are sometimes available to outside guests on request. Popular **Surf Turf** *(surfturf.in; classes ₹1250-1900)*, founded in Tamil Nadu's top surf village Kovalam (p953), now has a Varkala branch near Edava Beach, offering regular beginner and group classes.

A Holy Hindu Town

Varkala's spiritual heart

Varkala might be a fun-loving beach and surf destination, but it is also a major Hindu pilgrimage town. Looming over Beach Rd just 500m inland from Papanasam Beach, the **Janardhana Temple** is devoted to Vishnu as Janardhana and draws pilgrims from across Kerala. It is believed to date in one shape or another from the 13th century. While only Hindus are permitted to enter the main shrine, the grounds are open to everyone from around 4am to noon and 5pm to 7pm. From the temple tank on Beach Rd, slip off footwear and climb the steep staircase to wander beneath an ancient banyan tree. A granite-built Tamil-style *mandapa* (pillared pavilion) leads to the central shrine and several smaller shrines devoted to other Hindu deities, including Hanuman and Shiva. It's particularly atmospheric in the evenings when lanterns are lit. On nearby Papanasam Beach (p915), priests perform *puja* for passed loves ones and pilgrims bathe in the sea, whose waters are believed to wash away sins.

Yoga by the Sea

Lean into a daily practice

Varkala has grown into one of Kerala's main yoga hubs, whether you fancy joining a casual drop-in class or a serious Yoga Teacher Training (YTT) course. Stretching, twisting and breathing into the day on an open-sided *shala* atop

SOUTHERN SURF

Aparna Sathianathan and **Nitisha Sethia**, surfers based in Varkala and founding members of Kerala Surf Association. *@that_crazy_brown_chick @nitishasethia*

The surf community in Varkala is the best part about surfing here. The joy of sharing your waves, of cheering each other on and being stoked about party waves! South Cliff gets good swell rarely, but when it works, it's the most magical place – a beautiful cliff full of greenery, crystal-clear blue waters and resident dolphins. Edava is great for catching barrels, while Cowies is good for longboarding. More women are in the water than ever before. Seeing international women surf with ease is surely an inspiration. At the same time, us women surfers in Kerala are developing our own relationship with the sea.

ONAM

Celebrated across Kerala during the Malayali month of Chingam (August/September), 10-day Onam is the state's greatest cultural festivity, honouring the mythical king Mahabali and marking the harvest season. Though traditionally a Hindu festival, it is also a celebration of arts, food, culture and family, in which Malayalis of all different religions get involved. Traditional *kasavu* saris are the dress of choice for many people, while the famous *onasadya* – an all-vegetarian banana-leaf feast of Kerala flavours – is another highlight. Traditional arts take over stages, from Kathakali to *mohiniyattam* (classical dance), and homes all over Kerala are beautifully decorated with floral *pookalam*. If you can't make it during Onam, Kerala Tourism's Local Cuisine programme helps you find restaurants and homes serving traditional *sadya* year-round *(keralatourism.org)*.

ASHTANGA YOGA

Anyone interested in serious yoga training in India will want to spend time in the world's capital of Ashtanga yoga, Mysuru (Mysore), in neighbouring Karnataka (p804).

the red-laterite cliffs here feels pretty special. There are excellent classes on offer with both locally based and visiting teachers; we always recommend doing your own research. Drop-in group classes are widely available all over town throughout the tourism season, though when it's quiet you might find it's mostly private classes.

Just back from the North Cliff, **Devvrat Yoga** *(devvratyoga.com)* runs well-regarded Yoga Alliance–certified 200-hour and 300-hour YTT programmes, plus daily hatha yoga and meditation classes *(₹500)* open to all. Popular boutique guesthouse Mad About Coco (p939) has regular drop-in classes *(₹500)*, plus breezy cafe **Sun Francisco** for post-yoga refuels. **Lumuma** *(lumuma.com)*, off the northern North Cliff, is a professionally run retreat centre in flower-filled grounds, with multiday wellness retreats, YTT courses, twice-daily drop-in classes *(₹600)* and a lovely plant-based **cafe**.

See Varkala from Sky & Water

Flying high or paddling out

On clear southern days, you'll often spot paragliders swooping around high above Varkala's beach, drinking in the panoramic views of this delicious stretch of cliff-edged coastline. Tempted to join in? Well-established **Can Fly Adventure** *(canfly adventure.com)* runs tandem flights of 10 to 20 minutes *(₹6000)*, led by a professional paragliding instructor. The paragliding season runs from around December to April, depending on conditions. The same team also organises four-hour kayaking and paddleboarding trips *(per person from ₹1200)* to catch sunrise or sunset on inland waterways near Varkala, from around October to May.

EATING IN VARKALA: OUR PICKS

ABBA: Long-running terrace halfway along North Cliff; great salads, breakfasts, sandwiches, curries, cakes and other treats. *8am-10.30pm* ₹₹

Cyra Cafe: Breezy little vegan spot by Papanasam's sands, with fresh juices, plant-based coffees and homemade bites like fruity smoothie bowls. *8am-8pm* ₹₹

Cafe del Mar: North Cliff long-timer serving reliably good favourites, from samosas and masala fries to international breakfasts. *7.30am-10.30pm* ₹₹

Aum Cafe: Laid-back hangout for sea breezes, plant-driven menus and some of Varkala's best espresso, on far North Cliff. *7am-10pm* ₹₹

EMILIO NAVARINO/SHUTTERSTOCK

Yoga by the sea (p917)

Explore an Isle of Gold

Hidden temple, ancient fort

Local legends tell how the Travancore royal family once hid riches on tiny, acacia-shaded **Ponnumthuruthu (Golden Island)**, flung out in the middle of a lake 10km south of Varkala. The islet centres on a Shiva/Parvati shrine thought to be at least a century old. The temple itself is closed to non-Hindus, but the chance to kayak or canoe across to Ponnumthuruthu is just as much of a draw. **Shiva Kayaking** *(varkalakayak.com; tours per person ₹650)* runs guided excursions, and most Varkala accommodation can organise rickshaw tours with waiting time. Go in the early morning before the heat picks up.

Just 6km southeast, **Anchuthengu Fort** *(free)* was built in 1695 by the British East India Company. Climbing to the top of the concrete-and-laterite walls opens up sprawling views across colourful Anchuthengu village. This was one of the earliest British trading posts established in India and it was here that the landmark 1721 Attingal Revolt happened.

LESSER-KNOWN NATURE RESERVES

Parambikulam Tiger Reserve: Gaurs, sambar, sloths, elephants and tigers roam this isolated park, with safaris and treks; access from Palakkad or Pollachi. *(parambikulam.org)*

Silent Valley National Park: Remote reserve in Palakkad district offering safaris, hikes, rare rainforests and biodiversity; bookings essential. *(silentvalley.gov.in)*

Thattekad Bird Sanctuary: Protects 300 bird species around the Periyar River between Kochi and Munnar; birdwatch by kayak, boat or expert-guided walk. *(ecotourism.forest.kerala.gov.in)*

Idukki Wildlife Sanctuary: Southeast of Munnar, this sanctuary centred on a reservoir is home to elephants, birds, deer and wild boars. *(forest.kerala.gov.in)*

Aralam Wildlife Sanctuary: Green 55-sq-km haven near Kannur, best known for butterflies and waterfalls, with guided trekking. *(keralatourism.org)*

Cafe TripisLife: Gorgeous South Cliffs restaurant, 1km south of the temple; bowl-style curries, lush gardens and fiery sunsets. *6.30am-9.30pm* ₹₹₹

Suprabhatham: Always-busy South Indian kitchen in Varkala Town serving masala dosa, thalis, *vadas*, *uttapam* and other pure-veg deliciousness. *8am-9.30pm* ₹

InDa Cafe: Stylish, relaxed place hidden back from North Cliff, with international menus (salad bowls, homemade pasta, fresh breakfasts). *8.30am-10pm* ₹₹

Chimney Family Restaurant: Popular, pavilion-style restaurant in Varkala Town, known for thalis, biryanis, tandoori and Kerala dishes. *11.30am-10.30pm* ₹₹

HELP ME PICK:

Ayurveda in Kerala

Believed to date back at least 2000 years (it was first documented in the Vedas), India's traditional medical system is intricately linked to Kerala's identity, climate and flora. It gets its name from the Sanskrit *'ayu'*, meaning life, and *'veda'*, which means knowledge or science. Ayurveda treatment centres are dotted all over the state, from small family-owned clinics with a well-established local reputation to five-star wellness havens where you can retreat for multiweek programmes in serious luxury.

Where to Experience Ayurveda

Kovalam, Varkala & Around

Somatheeram Ayurveda Village *(somatheeram.in)* One of southern Kerala's original Ayurvedic resorts, known for its prize-winning treatment plans, homemade oils and cottage-style accommodation overlooking Chowara Beach.

Niraamaya Retreats Surya Samudra *(niraamaya.com)* Luxe seafront escape in Pulinkudi (near Kovalam) with Kerala-architecture-inspired rooms, superb meals, infinity pool, yoga overlooking the waves and multi-night Ayurveda programmes.

Somatheeram Ayurvedic Health Resort *(somatheeram.org)* Respected centre on the hillside above Chowara Beach, with wide-ranging yoga, a pool and great food. Treatments open to outside guests with prior booking.

AyurSoul *(ayursoulindia.com)* Popular Ayurveda centre near Varkala's North Cliff, aimed at women and couples; drop-in treatments and extended programmes.

Bethsaida Hermitage *(bethsaidahermitage.com)* Long-running, professional retreat just outside Kovalam offering a wide range of accommodation and treatment plans, in pretty beachfront grounds.

Kalari Rasayana *(cghearthayurveda.com)* Top-end, NABH-accredited Ayurveda hospital on the backwaters between Varkala and Kollam, run by sustainability-focused CGH Earth hotels.

J Wellness Circle *(tajhotelhotels.com)* Luxe hotel-spa setting for Ayurveda-inspired treatments and yoga classes, at Taj Green Cove (p939) in Kovalam. Pool passes available, too.

Central Kerala

Ayurdara *(ayurdara.com)* Well-established Ayurveda centre on Vypeen Island, specialising in treatment plans of one or more weeks, with accommodation.

Niraamaya Retreats Backwaters & Beyond Kumarakom *(niraamaya.com)* Five-star Ayurvedic retreat on Lake Vembanad, for both short stays and in-depth programmes. Some rooms have private pools.

Sacred Lotus *(sacredlotusretreat.com)* Professional Fort Kochi centre among gardens, offering long-term plans, drop-in treatments and yoga classes.

Fort Ayurveda *(hotelforthouse.com)* Well-regarded Ayurvedic centre, with both day spa and longer packages, attached to the lovely Fort House Hotel (p938).

Carnoustie *(carnoustieresorts.com)* Refresh and rejuvenate in luxury at this beachside Ayurvedic resort in Marari, where programmes include *panchakarma* (cleansing).

Northern Kerala

Neeleshwar Hermitage (p939) A luxurious beachfront resort and reputable Ayurveda retreat with a sustainable ethos, yoga, meditation and wonderful cooking, near Bekal.

Thottada Beach (p927) Easygoing homestays along this beach just outside Kannur can arrange Ayurvedic therapies with small local treatment centres.

YADID LEVY/ALAMY

Ayurveda treatment, Kerala

HOW TO

When to go The traditional Ayurveda season is the monsoon, when the body is believed to be most receptive (with open pores etc). Most centres operate year-round.

Before you go It's important to understand the kinds of treatments involved in Ayurveda, some of which can be very intense (see below).

Choosing treatments In most cases an Ayurvedic doctor will recommend appropriate therapies, treatment plans and meal guidelines; prices vary widely.

Hotel spas Most serious centres only offer full programmes, but there are also spas offering Ayurveda-style treatments on a casual basis, often in high-end hotels.

Ayurveda: The Basics

Ayurveda was first recorded in the Vedas, but it is likely to be even older. Today practised by university-trained doctors, Ayurveda revolves around the idea that people have three *doshas* (humours), which together make up the *tridoshas* – *vata* (air/space), *pitta* (fire) and *kapha* (water/earth). The aim of Ayurveda is to restore the natural balance between them, as a lack or excess of a particular *dosha* can cause health problems. For most of us, there will be one (or maybe two) dominant *doshas*. Ayurveda focuses on maintaining balance and preventing illness, rather than curing external symptoms (though these often overlap).

There are two main treatment methods in Ayurveda – herbal massage (using oils made from herbs growing naturally across Kerala) and *panchakarma* (purification or cleansing), which is typically recommended for more serious medical issues and centres on five key types of detoxification therapies. Programmes are prescribed for individual requirements following a consultation with an Ayurvedic doctor, and typically also involve yoga, meditation and a tailored diet. Oil massages and herbal-steam baths help prepare the body for *panchakarma* cleansing.

Panchakarma therapies include *nasya* (eliminating toxins through the nose using oil), *vaman* (therapeutic vomiting), *virechan* (purgation), *vasti* (enemas) and *raktamoksha* (bloodletting). Ayurveda purification can be intense and it's important to read up on what to expect in advance, though the most extreme treatments are only used occasionally.

Beyond Varkala

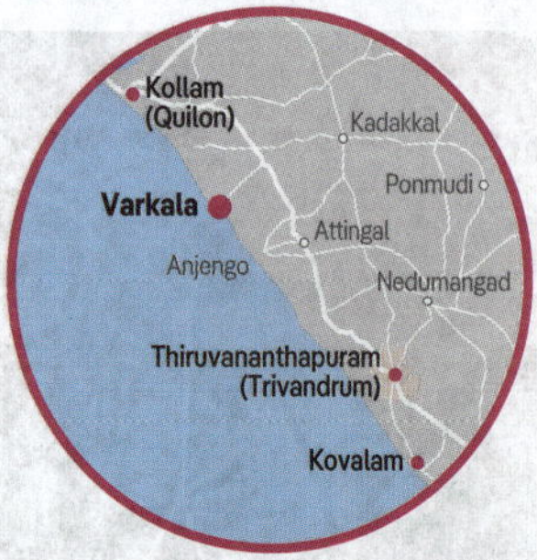

The far south: Kerala's culture-rich capital gives way to surf-pounded beaches, go-slow backwater islands, royal palaces and delicious tropical breezes.

Places

GETTING AROUND

Thiruvananthapuram International Airport is southern Kerala's air-transport hub; prepaid taxis cost ₹750 to Kovalam, ₹2500 to Varkala and ₹500 into Trivandrum centre. KSRTC Air-Rail buses link the airport with Trivandrum Central train station and the bus stand. For getting around Trivandrum, Ola and Uber taxi apps are best. Trivandrum and Kollam are well connected by train and bus; Kovalam is walkable and has good bus links, but no train station. Munroe Island is also accessible by train.

Kerala's sultry deep south unfolds in a swirl of sparkling-green palms, gold-and-black beaches and shimmering estuaries. The energetic state capital Thiruvananthapuram (Trivandrum), 50km southeast of Varkala, is home for around a million people. It also has superb museums, an increasingly exciting culinary scene and a revered Hindu temple. Just 15km southeast from Trivandrum, Kovalam rivals Varkala as Kerala's most-loved seaside playground. This now-developed beach town grew from a small fishing village from the 1930s onwards (there's still a village feel around the colourful backstreets) and is an important Ayurveda destination (p920).

North from Varkala, beach-lined shores stretch all the way to Kollam (Quilon), an ancient port town fringed by backwaters and several still-sleepy islands, including Munroe Island.

Thiruvananthapuram (Trivandrum)

TIME FROM VARKALA: **45MIN-1¾HR** (train)**/1¼HR** (car)

Fort stroll: Trivandrum's ancient core

The city's old heart is the lively **Fort area**, 1km southwest of Trivandrum Central station. A wander through this former royal neighbourhood is an essential piece of understanding the capital. **Storytrails** *(storytrails-walks.in; per group ₹8000)* offers Fort walking tours led by wonderfully engaging guides.

Framed by four elaborate gateways, the fort itself dates from the 14th century, but was substantially rebuilt in the mid-18th century under Marthanda Varma, the founding maharaja of the Kingdom of Travancore, who moved the capital here from Padmanabhapuram (p925). Spot some original wall remains near the West Gate. At the area's core lies the (mostly) 18th-century **Shri Padmanabhaswamy Temple** *(spst.in)*, a fusion of Kerala-style and Dravidian architecture devoted to the reclining Padmanabha (one of Vishnu's incarnations). Non-Hindus cannot enter the temple, but you can't miss the 30m-high Tamil Nadu–style *gopuram* (gateway tower) on the east side. The temple is also famous for the US$1 trillion of treasure that was discovered hidden in its vaults in 2011. Beside the temple tank, explore the sumptuous former home of the Travancore rulers at the **Puthe Maliga Palace**

Shri Padmanabhaswamy Temple, Thiruvananthapuram

Museum *(kuthiramaliga.in; ₹200)*, adorned with 122 teakwood-carved horses.

City of museums

Trivandrum's museum complex (all closed Monday) sits in lush parklands, 3km north of Fort. Begin a few hours' immersion at the superb **Keralam Museum** *(museumkeralam.org; adult/child ₹200/50)*, a restored 120-year-old Indo-European building now devoted to Kerala's history and culture. Highlights range from replicas of petroglyphs at Wayanad's Edakkal Caves (p936) to astonishing bronze figures. Just north across LMS Vellayambalam Rd, the dramatic **Napier Museum** *(museumandzoo.kerala.gov.in; adult/child ₹200/100)* unveils bronzes, woodcarvings and stone sculptures within an 1880 building mixing Kerala design with neogothic style, created by British architect Robert Chisholm. Behind, **Raja Ravi Varma Art Gallery** *(rajaravivarmaartgallery.kerala.gov.in; adult/child ₹50/20)* hosts works by celebrated 19th-century Keralite artist Ravi Varma, known for his fusion of Indian and European techniques. A fitting place to round off a culture-packed morning is **Baker's Arch** *(bakersarch.in)*, a gorgeous garden cafe set in a brick-clad 1980s building designed by British-Indian architect Laurie Baker, just 10 minutes' drive north.

CULTURAL TRIVANDRUM

Aditi Radhakrishnan is Operations Head and a Storyteller at Storytrails in Trivandrum. *@storytrails*

Thiruvananthapuram's bounty of beaches, hills, forests and rivers is easily accessible. But I recommend visitors to partake in its vibrant cultural scene, with programmes, celebrations and festivals year-round. The **Nishagandhi Dance and Music Festival** steals the spotlight in January, featuring classical talents from across India; Kathakali performances offer a captivating glimpse into traditional storytelling through dance. From January to March, temple festivals immerse devotees in a whirlwind of music and dance. As the year progresses from April to September, Thiruvananthapuram hosts myriad events, including flower shows, book fairs, and vibrant celebrations for Vishnu and Onam.

EATING IN TRIVANDRUM: OUR PICKS

Villa Maya: Trivandrum's top restaurant is housed in an 18th-century mansion as beautiful as its elevated Kerala-rooted menus and Indian wines. *11am-11pm* ₹₹₹

Ariya Nivaas: Well-established all-veg favourite near Trivandrum Central station, always packed for its fresh thalis, spicy *uttapam* and crispy dosas. *7am-10pm* ₹

Cafe Sarwaa: Easygoing garden cafe attached to a pretty crafts shop; enjoy fresh juices, French press and snacks like paneer-coriander sandwiches. *10am-9pm* ₹₹

Indian Coffee House: Busy branch serving up filter coffee, masala dosa and more in a spiralling Laurie Baker–designed building near the bus/train stations. *7am-10pm* ₹

INTERNATIONAL FILM FESTIVAL OF KERALA

Going strong since 1996 (when it was first held in Calicut), the International Film Festival of Kerala (IFFK) takes over Trivandrum every November/December in a cinematic celebration that ranks among India's finest cultural events. It is particularly renowned for its showcase of Malayali cinema, though many other Indian and international films debut during the festivities too, and there are also workshops and panel sessions, with events held at venues across town. Anyone keen to attend must register and pay for a pass in advance (online), then prebook screenings *(iffk.in)*; slots for the most popular films get filled up quickly, but not everything is bookable in advance.

Around 500m north of Fort's West Gate, the **Palm-Leaf Manuscripts Museum** *(keralatourism.org; adult/child ₹25/5; closed Mon)* charts Kerala's history through 160 intricately crafted manuscripts dating from the 13th century to the 1890s.

Market time

Heading south along Mahatma Gandhi (MG) Rd from Trivandrum's museum district, you'll pass the neogothic 1900 **State Central Library** and **St Joseph's Cathedral** (from 1873), before reaching the lively **Connemara Market**. First opened in 1857, it's best known for textiles, but wander through the red-and-white brick arch to be engulfed in everything from spices to pottery. Near the Padmanabhaswamy Temple (p922), sprawling **Chalai Market** traces its roots back to the 14th century and is made up of different streets with generations-old stalls devoted to particular products (vegetables, stationery, furniture).

Kovalam

TIME FROM VARKALA: 1½HR

Beautiful beaches and water adventures

Much of Kovalam life revolves around **Lighthouse Beach**, a broad strip of gold-and-black sand with good swimming, lifeguard services and surf waves. Well-established, community-focused **Kovalam Surf Club** *(kovalamsurfclub.com)* offers board rental *(half-day ₹800)* and classes *(group/private ₹1800/2500)*. Red-striped **Vizhinjam Lighthouse** *(lighthouse.nic.in; ₹50; closed Mon)* looms over the strand's south end; climb 144 steps or zip up by lift for sprawling panoramas.

Just north, busy **Hawa Beach** is framed by coconut-fringed cliffs and has snack stalls and sunbeds. **Samudra Beach**, Kovalam's northernmost strand, has a seafront mosque, rocky outcrops, chai stands and honey-coloured sand, drawing day trippers. The loveliest time out on the beaches is in the cool(er) early morning, when local fishers reel in nets, though a sunset stroll is a treat too. Take care with currents in the water.

Beneath the waves, this area takes in some of Kerala's top

EATING IN KOVALAM: OUR PICKS

Suprabhatham: Kerala-style breakfasts (dosas, *uttapam*) and fresh, tasty veg dishes like paneer-cashew curry, in a rustic courtyard near Lighthouse Beach. *8am-9pm* ₹

Bait: Gorgeous, driftwood-vibe spot at Taj Green Cove (p938); try Travancore curry or fish and paneer soaked in spices. *12.30-2.30pm & 7.30-10.30pm* ₹₹₹

Waves: Laid-back, breezy terrace on Lighthouse Beach; great for breakfast, French press coffee, Ayurvedic meals and world-roaming dinners. *7.30am-10pm* ₹₹

Leela: Elegant Thai-leaning cuisine at seaside Tides and Indian-international bites at all-day Terrace, or book the feast-like thali experience. *hours vary* ₹₹₹

Curry Leaf: Relaxed sea-view restaurant just above Samudra Beach; delicious pakora, masala-fried prawns, *pollichathu* fish and other fresh flavours. *8am-11pm* ₹₹

Fusion: Creative cooking and terrace vibes at south end of Lighthouse Beach – masala omelette with mint chutney, thalis, good coffee. *8am-10pm* ₹₹

Usthad Hotel: Long-running local haunt on Vizhinjam Harbour Rd, known for its fried fish with masala and other seafood plates. *9am-2am Sat-Thu* ₹

Varsha: Small, pure-veg South Indian kitchen down behind southern Lighthouse Beach (masala dosa, banana-leaf thalis, pumpkin curry). *hours vary* ₹

NESRU MARKMEDIA/SHUTTERSTOCK

Lighthouse Beach, Kovalam

dive sites, including several shipwrecks. Turtles, octopuses, stingrays, eels and all kinds of fish (from lionfish to red snapper) ply the waters. Reputable **Bond Safari & Cool Divers** *(bondsafarikovalam.com)* offers PADI courses, dive excursions and snorkelling trips.

Kerala's finest royal palace

The Kingdom of Travancore – one of the three major regions that became Kerala in 1956 – was once ruled from Padmanabhapuram village, 50km southeast of Kovalam in what is today the Kanyakumari district of neighbouring Tamil Nadu. Easily accessible from Kovalam, the exquisite **Padmanabhapuram Palace** *(padmanabhapurampalace.org; adult/child ₹500/100; closed Mon & lunchtime)* remains the greatest example of traditional Kerala architecture still standing, with its most ancient sections dating from 1550. Wandering through its labyrinth of walkways connecting 15 buildings, you'll spot beautifully carved rosewood ceilings, sloping gabled roofs, overhanging balconies and leafy courtyards. At the heart of the complex, the 16th-century timber-built Thai Kottaram is the oldest part of the palace, with a typical *nalukettu* (open courtyard) design. Kovalam-based taxis charge ₹3500 for Padmanabhapuram day trips.

Pick up Kerala-made crafts

Among peaceful 3.5-hectare grounds, 3km north of Kovalam, the government-run **Kerala Arts & Crafts Village** *(kacvkovalam.org; ₹200; closed Mon)* is devoted to preserving traditional regional handicrafts. Pop in to meet (and buy from) artisans crafting everything from dry flowers, handloom textiles and rosewood carvings to custom-designed ornaments for Pooram festivities. The centre also hosts events, including the fabulous **International Dance Festival** in October/November.

KERALA PRIDE

Kerala's LGBTIQ+ community continues to face discrimination, cyberbullying and other challenges. But there is also a growing LGBTIQ+ Pride movement spearheaded by organisations such as Queerala, Queerythm and Sahayathrika, which also provide safe spaces, support, representation and solidarity for the community. Kerala Queer Pride has been celebrated almost every year since 2010 in different cities across the state, with seminars, workshops and cultural events usually held alongside a Pride march or rally. Its 13th edition was hosted by Trivandrum in 2024. Queerythm has also organised several other Pride walks in Trivandrum. Cosmopolitan Kochi is another hub for the LGBTIQ+ community, including queer artists showing exhibitions at the Kochi-Muziris Biennale.

LAKSHADWEEP

Extending roughly 300km off Kerala's central and north coasts, the coral islands of Lakshadweep rank among India's finest dive spots, with salt-white beaches, pristine coral reefs and around 4200 sq km of warm lagoon-like waters. Lakshadweep's 36 islands – just 10 of which are inhabited (with a total population of around 70,000) – make up the smallest Union Territory in India. The Muslim communities here mostly speak Malayalam. To help preserve this fragile natural space, tourism is tightly controlled, though it is starting to grow. At the time of writing, only a few islands were open to visitors, with all access through tour packages offered by Lakshadweep's Society for Promotion of Nature Tourism and Sports (SPORTS), involving flights or ferry cruises from Kochi *(lakshadweeptourism.com)*.

Temples of the south coast

Around 1.5km east of Lighthouse Beach, the small banyan-shaded **Vizhinjam Rock-Cut Cave** *(keralatourism.org; free)* is believed to date from the 8th century – among the oldest of its kind in Kerala. Fine sculpturework shows Shiva as Dakshinamurthy, as well as Nataraja (with Parvati) and Tripurantaka, these last two unfinished. Head 5km southeast to discover the kaleidoscopic beachfront **Aazhimala Shiva Temple** *(keralatourism.org; caves ₹100)*, taking in a sculpture-studded *gopuram* and Kerala's tallest Shiva statue, a 17m-high, 2021 creation by a local artist. Then descend 24 steps into a series of cool caves adorned with strikingly contemporary sculptures, including a nude Shiva and Parvati. Though an Aazhimala shrine has existed for years, the caves are an immensely popular 2025 addition.

Munroe Island

TIME FROM VARKALA: **40MIN HR** (train)/**1¼HR** (car)

Cruise Munroe's quiet canals

Around 15km north of Kollam, lushly green Munroe Island was a pioneer of village tourism in Kerala and, despite its growing popularity, remains a rewarding place to retreat to. The highlight is the chance to explore meandering waterways known for their scenic narrow canals and low bridges – you'll find yourself ducking inside canoes or kayaks beneath bridges if the tide is high.

The best way to soak up the calm is by staying a night (or several), roaming around by bike, kayak or canoe. **Munroe Island Backwaters Homestay** *(instagram.com/munroeislandbackwatershomestay)* is a charmingly laid-back place run by Vijeesh Vimalan (a leader in Munroe tourism) and family. On their signature three-hour sunrise canoe tour *(per person ₹900)*, my entire small group was entranced into companionable silence while gliding across channels reflecting electric-green palms and lakes glowing under the day's first rays. Coir-making and toddy tapping are easily glimpsed along Munroe's backwaters, and you might even try your hand at canoe-steering.

Kollam (Quilon)

TIME FROM VARKALA: **20MIN** (train)/**50MIN** (car)

A taste of trading-port history

Hugging Ashtamudi Lake's shores, Kollam was once a major trading port for spices, cashews and other local products. It's still an important commercial hub today. At the northwest end of Kollam's harbour (3km west of the centre) lies **Thangassery**, a former Portuguese trading post that fell into Dutch hands from the 1650s, then to the British East India Company in the 1680s. The remains of the 1519 Portuguese-built **St Thomas Fort** are still visible here, along with a (climbable!) candy-striped 1902 **lighthouse** *(₹50)*. After strolling around Thangassery, head to **Meen by Chef Pillai** *(chefpillai.com)* for fine Kerala cuisine – mango curry, lunchtime thalis – in a lakeside setting.

Kerala's North Coast

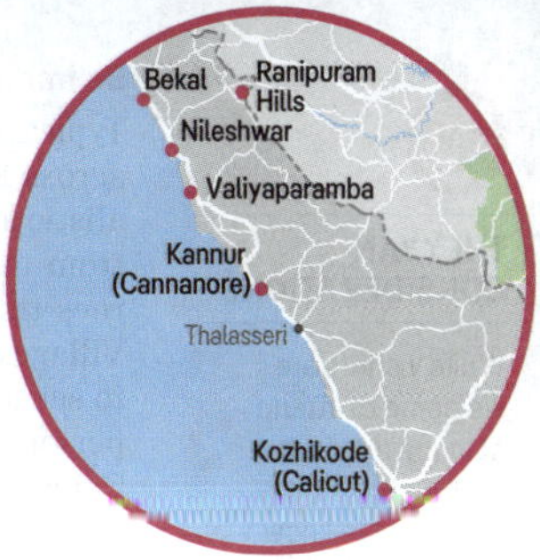

Stretching from Kozhikode (Calicut) to the border with neighbouring Karnataka, Kerala's northern Malabar Coast feels worlds away from the busier south. Quiet, undeveloped beaches stretch for miles along the palm-edged shores, where rust-coloured laterite cliffs tumble down to meet the Arabian Sea and lazy backwaters ripple inland. During the colonial period, the Portuguese, the Dutch and the British all vied for control of the region around the historically important spice-trading port of Kannur.

This is an area rich in ancient folk traditions that still hold strong, most famously the *theyyam* possession rituals held at local temples. It's also known for its market towns, centuries-old forts and delicious regional cuisine. Calicut is northern Kerala's largest city and transport hub, home to 430,000 residents, a raved-about food scene and the annual Kerala Literature Festival. Further north, near Kasaragod and Kanhangad, there's a peaceful beach scene around Bekal and Nileshwar, the latter of which has royal echoes as the former home of the Nileshwaram rajas.

Places

GETTING AROUND

The international airports at Kannur, Calicut and Mangaluru (in Karnataka) serve Kerala's northern coast. Kannur, Calicut and Kasaragod have good train links (including fast Vande Bharat trains); some trains also stop at Bekal Fort and Nileshwar stations. Kannur's sights are spread out; short autorickshaw hops cost ₹60. For Thottada Beach, buses run between central Kannur and Adikadalayi village (20 minutes), from where it's a 1km walk; rickshaws/taxis charge ₹300/800. For the Valiyaparamba backwaters, Payyanur is well-linked by train.

Kannur (Cannanore)

Chill on lesser-known beaches

Kannur's peaceful coast is all about slow explorations, so simply relax at one of the charming beachside homestays (p939) – some offer yoga, meditation and Ayurveda – and lean into it. Serene **Thottada Beach**, 8km southeast of central Kannur, is one of Kerala's loveliest strands, framed by rust-coloured laterite sea cliffs. A powder-soft sweep of honey-coloured sand and shingle backed by coconut palms, it makes a dreamy place for an early-morning swim; at sunset local kids play sports on the sand, and the water is usually calm. Be sure to take a stroll around the tidal lagoon just inland too, where you're likely to spot (and definitely hear) a rich variety of birds. Just north is secluded **Adikadalayi Beach**, while immediately south awaits palm-lined, little-explored **Ezhara Beach**. Take care with ocean currents, which can be strong.

Kannur's main urban strand, 4km-long **Payyambalam Beach** (just north of the city's historical cantonment area), has a local atmosphere, with people gathering for picnics, weekend strolls and sunset views.

THEYYAM CONSIDERATIONS

While visitors are welcome to attend at many *theyyam* performances, it is important to know that some *theyyam* still involve the ritual sacrifice of an animal (often, though not limited to, cockerels). Though these days many *theyyam* gatherings have moved away from this traditional element, we recommend consulting a local expert in each region to find a cruelty-free *theyyam*. It's also key to remember that this ancient ritual is about witnessing an intense spiritual experience of local importance, not watching a staged performance. Visitors should wear temple-appropriate clothing, ask before taking photographs or videos, and avoid disturbing performers and participants. Attending with a guide who can explain details throughout the *theyyam* is hugely rewarding.

Be immersed in ancient *theyyam*

Typically held in *kavus* (sacred groves), temples and homes across Kerala's Malabar region, *theyyam* is an ancient ritualistic art form in which respected male performers (usually from marginalised castes) seek to embody deities and heroes through dance, song, drumming and intricate dress. Villages in the Kannur region are the best places in Kerala to see a *theyyam* (the term refers both to the ritual and the performer); it can also be experienced around Kasaragod, Calicut and Wayanad.

This religious ritual is thought to predate Hinduism and have Adivasi roots, possibly emerging from early harvest festivities that involved folk dance. There are now around 450 different *theyyam* that can be portrayed, each with their own associations, significance and bright face make-up, skirts, jewellery and elaborate headdresses that can reach up to 7m tall. During a *theyyam*, the performer blesses devotees and offers the chance for the deity to manifest itself in human form.

The *theyyam* season runs from around November to April; during peak months (December to February) there is usually one happening most nights in the Kannur region. Local guesthouses can arrange visits and expert guides; **Kerala Tourism** *(keralatourism.org)* publishes a *theyyam* calendar. Dedicated *theyyam* tours (on which you might meet performers) are offered by culture-focused operators like **Moksha Stories** *(moskhastories.com)* and Blue Yonder (p888).

At any time of year, glimpse vibrant outfits used in *theyyam* and other traditional practices at the museum of **Kerala Folklore Academy** *(keralafolklore.org; adult/child ₹50/15)*, an arts-training centre 7km north of Kannur.

Step into Kannur's history

Today powered by cashew, fishing and handloom industries, Kannur was once a major spice-trading port. Dig into the city's tumultuous past with a morning's walk around its heritage monuments. Begin at the impressively preserved 1505 **Fort St Angelo** *(dtpckannur.com; adult/child ₹300/free)*, which overlooks Mappila Bay, 2km south of Kannur's flower-filled bazaar. Originally built by the Portuguese, the laterite complex has a distinctive blend of architectures and shady grounds for strolling. It passed from Portuguese to Dutch to British hands, but in between was bought by the powerful Arakkal family, Kerala's only Muslim royal family, whose roots date back to the 12th century.

EATING IN KANNUR: OUR PICKS

Hotel Odhen's: Lunch-only, queue-worthy classic near Kannur's bazaar, renowned for its banana-leaf thalis bursting with Malabar seafood flavours. *noon-4.30pm* ₹

Pulari Restaurant: Locally famous for fresh Malabar cuisine. Pick from changing whiteboard menus of fragrant biryani, lunchtime thalis, fish fry and other treats. *6am-11pm* ₹

Naura Bistro: Stylish little European-leaning spot with a loyal following for its delicious pizzas, pastas, steaks and creative specials. *12.30-3.30pm & 6-10.30pm Tue-Sun* ₹₹

MRA: Superb biryanis, tandoori platters, dosas and north-Kerala faves like *molee* fish and mango-laced curry, next to Kannur train station. *7.30am-11.30pm* ₹₹

Find out more about the Arakkal dynasty (who allied with Tipu Sultan against the British in the late 19th century) at their former palace nearby, now renovated as the **Arakkal Museum** *(dtpckannur.com; ₹50; closed Mon)*. Just across the road stands the **Moideen Palli**, a teal-coloured 18th-century mosque built by the Arakkal family, with Dutch-influenced architecture and lavish details like Malabar teakwood, French floor tiling and Austrian lanterns. Non-Muslims are welcome to visit respectfully outside worship hours (you might be able to climb the minaret), though it's best to drop by with a local expert. The team behind **City Heritage** *(cityheritage.in)* offer fascinating Kannur-heritage walks *(₹5000 for 2 people)* and other culture-focused experiences.

If you're passing Thalasseri en route to/from Kannur, consider a pitstop to check out British-built **Thalasseri Fort** *(dtpckannur.com; ₹10)*, which dates from 1708.

Kozhikode (Calicut)

TIME FROM KANNUR: 2½HR (car)/1¼-2HR (train)

Feast in a culinary capital

Ask any Keralite about Calicut and they're bound to gush about the fantastic food of northern Kerala's biggest city, which many international travellers simply breeze through en route to/from Wayanad or the north-coast beaches. Calicut is the epicentre of Kerala's famously delicious regional Mappila cuisine (p930) and the best way to get under the city's skin is through its kitchens. Malabar-region specialists **City Heritage** *(cityheritage.in)* offer a variety of immersive Calicut culinary tours on a personalised private basis, perhaps even including a meal in a local Mappila home. On a self-guided food trail, you can't miss 1939-founded **Paragon Restaurant**, which draws droves of diners each day and is best known for its perfectly spiced biryani.

Valiyaparamba

TIME FROM KANNUR: 1¼HR (car)/30-45MIN (train)

Glide across Kerala's northern backwaters

Halfway between Kannur and Kasaragod lies a completely entrancing stretch of coastline, where five rivers (including the Thejaswini) converge around Valiyaparamba and Kavvayi islands. Much less touristed than Kerala's southern waterways, the **Valiyaparamba Backwaters** offer blissful seclusion among a sea of bottle-green coconut palms. Whether on a kayaking adventure or a leisurely houseboat cruise, you're likely

KANNUR'S CHARM

Rosi and Nazir have welcomed guests at Kannur Beach House (p939) on Thottada Beach for two decades. *@kannurbeachhouse*

Born and raised in Kannur, we are well travelled, but still delight in sharing the quiet charm of Thottada Beach and the traditional hospitality of a Malabar coastal village. The sea in front of our homestay and the surrounding lagoon nourish mangroves and a lot of birds, and we all share a deep commitment to local, seasonal and community-based living. Stop to sip a tea or coconut water while taking a walk in the village, watch the local artisans at work and listen to the rhythms of the toddy tapper. Or see local weavers at their looms by wandering into our nearest cooperative **Kausalya Weavers**, at Thottada.

EATING IN CALICUT: OUR PICKS

Paragon Restaurant: Calicut's must-try kitchen, going strong since the 1930s; join the queue for the famous seafood plates, chicken biryani and coconut fish curry. *6am-11.30pm* ₹₹

Zains Hotel: Local family-owned favourite with three decades of history, specialising in fresh Mappila cooking, including delicate biryani and *meen pathiri* (rice-based pancake with fried fish). *12.30-11pm* ₹

Adaminde Chayakada: Retro tea-shop vibes and Malabar dishes near the beach; great Kerala-style breakfasts, lunchtime thalis and banana-leaf rice. *8am-11.30pm Mon-Fri, to 1am Sat & Sun* ₹₹

MAPPILA CUISINE

A particular speciality of the north-Kerala coast, Mappila (or Moppila) cuisine emerged over the centuries from a blend of Malabar Muslim cooking with Middle Eastern influences introduced by traders who arrived here from the 7th century CE onwards. Rich spices, roasted coconut, meaty recipes and fresh local seafood are all part of the menu. Classic dishes to look for include *kallumakai* (green Malabar Coast mussels), *kozhi ada* (deep-fried chicken dumplings), *pathiri* (rice-based pancake, often eaten with fried fish), *unnakkaya* (deep-fried banana stuffed with raisins, nuts and coconut), *erachi puttu* (made with meat masala) and a wide range of delectable *halwas* (soft sweets made with vegetables, cereals, lentils, nuts or fruit). For more on Calicut's Mappila cuisine, check out the written works of Ummi Abdulla, fondly known as 'the matriarch of Mappila food'.

to see coir-making, visit fishing villages, step into secluded temples, spot a rich variety of birds (such as kingfishers), and hear temple song echoing across the water in the evenings.

Locally based **Bekal Ripples** *(bekalripples.com)* offers houseboat cruises aboard elegant Alleppey-crafted *kettuvallam*. Make the most of the setting by booking a classic overnight trip *(₹14,000 for 2 people)* or hop on board for an evocative sunset journey *(₹7000 for 4 people)*. The beautiful **Lotus Houseboat** *(abchapriretreats.in; from ₹42,000 for 2 people)*, run by sustainability-driven resort Neeleshwar Hermitage (p939), is a luxurious way to experience Valiyaparamba's waterways.

Active souls can paddle out in the Kavvayi area on guided kayaking excursions travelling into the mangrove forests; these are easily organised through local accommodation or regional tour companies such as **City Heritage** *(cityheritage.in)* and **Muddy Boots** *(muddyboots.in)*. Alternatively, explore the waterways aboard **public ferries** operated by the SWTD *(swtd.kerala.gov.in)*; services travel several times most days between the jetties at Kotti (near Payyanur train station), Ayitti and Ori, but check schedules locally.

Bekal & Nileshwar

TIME FROM KANNUR: 1-1½HR (train)/1½-2HR (car)

Northern beach retreats

The tranquil, palm-bordered beaches stretching north and south from **Bekal** town are easily some of the most spectacular strands in Kerala (though take care with strong currents and shifting sandbars). With a crop of serene luxury resorts (p939) and a growing yet low-key homestay scene, it's the perfect recipe for a go-slow coastal escape in Kerala's northernmost corner, during which you can witness *pujas* at village temples, go birdwatching on the waterways, see *theyyam* in season or simply relax by the whooshing waves.

The long, golden beach surrounding Bekal Fort gets busy with a mixed crowd of locals and visitors, especially at weekends, while honey-sand **Kappil Beach** brings a taste of seclusion just 6km further north. Around 18km southeast of Bekal, **Nileshwar Beach** is a seemingly endless strand of cream-hued bliss, backed by quiet village streets and bright-green rice crops, all with the northern backwaters on the doorstep.

Roam Kerala's largest fort

Set on a rocky promontory looming over the sea (halfway between Kanhangad and Kasaragod), spectacular **Bekal Fort** *(dtpckasaragod.com; adult/child ₹300/free)* is Kerala's most expansive fortress and also its most historically intriguing. You can easily spend an hour or two wandering the irregular quadrangular complex, with its well-tended pathways, imposing laterite-brick walls and views of beaches disappearing into the tropical haze.

The fort was constructed between 1645 and 1660 by the Ikkeri Nayaks, a powerful dynasty that emerged from the

SRIDHAR.PRABHAKAR/SHUTTERSTOCK

Bekal Fort

Vijayanagar empire, and still retains its well-preserved moat and observation towers. It became part of the Kingdom of Mysore in the 1760s, before falling under British control in 1792. The main trail zigzags up past a small Hindu Hanuman temple, then crosses the sprawling grounds before dropping down to a laterite lookout protruding into the sea. A fun way to explore Bekal Fort and surrounds is on a half-day cycling tour with well-established adventure operator **Muddy Boots** *(muddyboots.in; per person ₹3540-4810)*.

Ranipuram Hills

TIME FROM BEKAL/NILESHWAR: **75-90MIN**

Hike through misty border forests

There's northern beauty beyond the beaches, too. Often called 'the Ooty of Kerala' for their dramatic mist-cloaked landscapes, the Ranipuram Hills sit on the Kerala–Karnataka border, around 55km inland from Bekal and Kasaragod. Soak up the scene on the 5km (return) **Ranipuram trek** *(ecotourism.forest.kerala.gov.in; permits ₹150)*, which tracks through cool *shola* and open grassland to 750m-high Ranipuram crag. Access times are 8am to 3pm. With luck, you might spot wild elephants, deer and birds.

WHY I LOVE KERALA'S NORTH COAST

Isabella Noble
Lonely Planet writer

There's a slow, quiet beauty to Kerala's far north coast, which feels markedly different to the busier scene in the south. It's possible to walk for miles along the gorgeous, undeveloped honey-toned beaches, where palms trickle along the edge of the soft sand, sparkling backwaters stretch inland and sunsets tinge the sky in irresistible peachy-pink shades. I love the chance to start the day with a yoga practice overlooking the sea or by cycling to a village temple, and some of the best meals I've ever enjoyed in India have been Malabar recipes with distinctive spices and historical influences. If you're planning just a day or two here, you'll almost certainly end up staying longer.

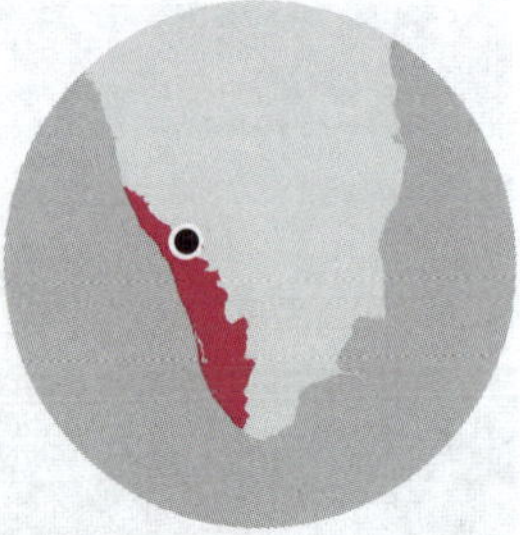

Wayanad

WILDLIFE ENCOUNTERS | MOUNTAIN ADVENTURE | HOMESTAYS

TOP TIP

Travelling back and forth around Wayanad can eat up valuable time, so it pays to carefully consider which area to base yourself in.

Dripping with moody mountainscapes and reached by spine-tingling hairpin-bend roads, the elevated Wayanad region is the only part of Kerala that borders both Karnataka and Tamil Nadu, with contiguous wildlife sanctuaries rippling between the three states. Here in the northernmost part of Kerala's Western Ghats, altitudes range from 700m to 2100m. Quiet forests emerge from the mist, rugged peaks loom beyond electric-green rice paddies, and coffee, pepper and cardamom plantations rest between spindly betel nut trees.

In recent years, Wayanad has grown into a hugely popular hill-country escape for wildlife-watching, trekking, cycling, rafting and natural tranquillity. At the same time, this region is also home for Kerala's largest Adivasi population (around 150,000 people including the Paniya, Adiya, Kurichiya and Kattunayakan communities) and many of these communities continue to face displacement.

Wayanad district has three main towns: Mananthavadi (northwest), Kalpetta (south) and Sultanbatheri (southeast). Just south, the Vythiri area is a weekend-escape destination with luxury resorts.

GETTING AROUND

Wayanad encompasses a large spread-out region and requires planning to explore, but it's easily reached from northern Kerala, as well as Tamil Nadu and Karnataka. Kannur and Calicut are the main, well-connected Kerala access towns for Wayanad, both with prepaid taxis from their airports. Local buses link Wayanad's three main towns and also run to/from the Tholpetty and Muthanga gates for Wayanad Wildlife Sanctuary. Taxis charge around ₹2500 for a full-day trip. Buses connect Wayanad with Kannur, Calicut, Ernakulam (Kochi) and even Trivandrum. There are also buses to/from Ooty (in Tamil Nadu), and Mysuru and Bengaluru (in Karnataka).

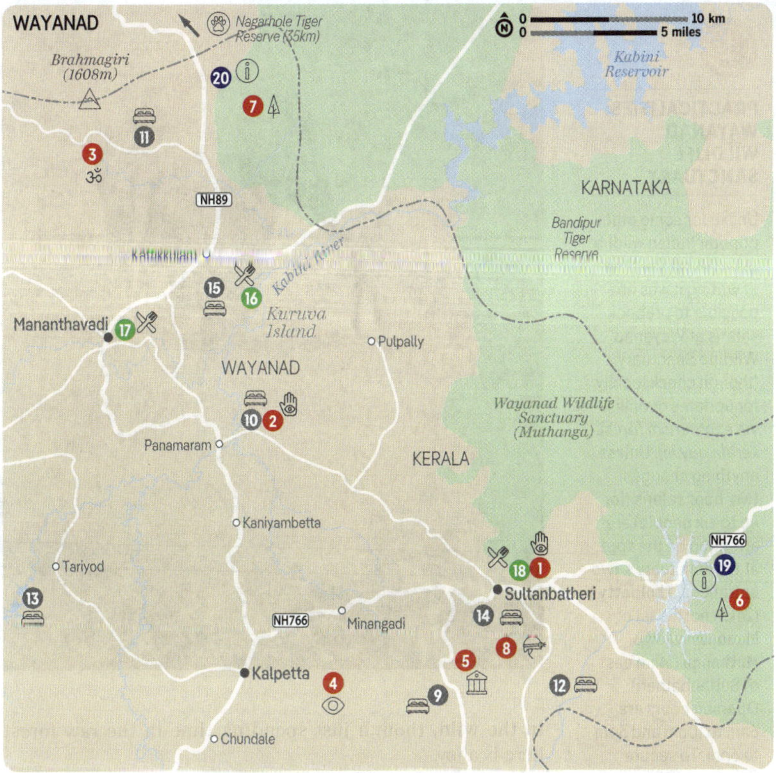

SIGHTS
1 Jain Temple
2 Panamaram Jain Temple
3 Thirunelly Temple
4 Uravu Bamboo Grove
5 Wayanad Heritage Museum
6 Wayanad Wildlife Sanctuary (Muthanga Range)
7 Wayanad Wildlife Sanctuary (Tholpetty Range)

ACTIVITIES
8 Edakkal Caves

SLEEPING
9 Amaryllis
10 Ente Veedu
11 Jungle Retreat Wayanad
12 Pepper Trail
13 Taj Wayanad
14 Tranquil
15 Varnam Homestay

EATING
16 Aswathi Bhavan
17 Indian Coffee House
see 13 Southern Spice
18 Wilton Restaurant

INFORMATION
19 Wayanad Wildlife Sanctuary (Muthanga Gate)
20 Wayanad Wildlife Sanctuary (Tholpetty Gate)

A Wild World

Wayanad Wildlife Sanctuary by safari

Thick with rosewood and other deciduous-forest trees, **Wayanad Wildlife Sanctuary** *(wayanadwildlifesanctuary.com)* is a serenely beautiful and biodiverse place where peacocks and langurs amble through a fiercely protected 345-sq-km expanse that's also home to wild elephants, sambars, turtles, chital deer, gaur and wild boars. While sightings can never be guaranteed, this pristine pocket of Western Ghats nature is one of the top places in Kerala to see elephants

PRACTICALITIES: WAYANAD WILDLIFE SANCTUARY

Unlike for some other popular Indian wildlife reserves, at the time of writing it was not possible to prebook safaris at Wayanad Wildlife Sanctuary (though check locally for updates or online via *ecotourism.forest.kerala.gov.in*). Unless anything changes, two-hour safaris (for up to six people) are arranged on the spot at the sanctuary's two entrances, **Tholpetty** (24km northeast of Mananthavadi) or **Muthanga** (14km east of Sultanbatheri). Opening hours are 6am to 10am and 3pm to 6pm. To secure tickets and a jeep, it's best to arrive at the gate an hour before opening time, especially during high season (November to March); you're likely to be asked for ID, so bring your passport. Only cashless payments (including international cards) are accepted.

PAUL HARDING 00/SHUTTERSTOCK

in the wild, though just spending time in the raw forest here is a joy.

Also part of the Nilgiri Biosphere Reserve, the sanctuary sits within a wider wildlife corridor linked up with several other nature reserves in Karnataka and Tamil Nadu, with the occasional tiger or leopard padding through too. It's rich in birdlife as well, providing a refuge for over 250 feathered species, including great hornbills, Bonelli's eagles and endangered vultures (whose numbers have been decimated across India in recent decades).

The sanctuary takes in four different ranges, two of which – Tholpetty (north) and Muthanga (southeast) – are open to visitors. The only way to drive in is by official two-hour jeep safari with a guide and a driver, which leave from the Tholpetty and Muthanga ticket offices *(up to 4/6 people ₹4200/4800)*. It's a bumpy, rattling ride in a semi-open jeep. Muthanga has also introduced safaris by larger bus vehicles. The top wildlife-spotting months are November to April, peaking in March/April when animals gather at dwindling water sources, though the sanctuary often closes from mid-March to mid-April due to fire risk. For the best chances of sighting wildlife, hop on the first or last trip of the day.

It's also possible to visit Karnataka's much-loved **Nagarhole Tiger Reserve** (p812) on a day trip from Wayanad, especially if you're staying in northern Wayanad.

Wild elephants, Wayanad Wildlife Sanctuary (p933)

Hike up to the Kerala–Karnataka Border

Brahmagiri peak and other trekking trails

Heading out on foot will get you to pockets of Wayanad that most visitors don't reach, and while trekking in Wayanad Wildlife Sanctuary itself is not permitted, rewarding routes weave through the surrounding hills.

There's no better way to savour Wayanad's natural beauty than from the wind-whipped summit of 1608m-tall **Brahmagiri**, which sits on the border of Kerala and Karnataka. This is arguably the region's most thrilling trek: a steep 10km return route (around four hours) through misty forests and sun-drenched slopes, starting 1km east of the revered Thirunelly Temple (p937). The reward is a spectacular view across the Wayanad plateau and Karnataka's Kodagu region, often from

EATING IN WAYANAD: OUR PICKS

Wilton Restaurant: Roadside hit on Sultanbatheri's western fringes, with multicuisine menus of richly spiced biryani, *sadya* spreads and tandoori dishes. *7am-10pm* ₹₹

Indian Coffee House: Fuss-free veg and nonveg bites at Mananthavadi's split-level ICH, which does all the usual filter coffee, fish curries and dosas. *6am-10pm* ₹

Southern Spice: Elegant deep-south cuisine paired with temple-inspired design at Taj Wayanad (p939). Reservations advised. *7.30-11.30pm Sun-Thu, 12.30-3pm & 7.30-11.30pm Fri & Sat* ₹₹₹

Aswathi Bhavan: Near the western raft jetty for Kuruva Island, this rustic north-Wayanad kitchen serves Kerala-style *sadya* on banana leaves; advance booking only. *11am-4pm* ₹

WAYANAD COFFEE

Kerala is one of India's four main coffee-growing states, producing around a quarter of the country's beans, and Wayanad counts among the state's most important coffee regions (alongside Idukki and Malappuram). Much like in Munnar, both coffee- and tea-growing were first introduced here during the British colonial period and today remain key industries. Grown at cool altitudes of around 600m to 900m, Wayanad beans are almost always strong Robusta, with around 50,000 to 60,000 tonnes produced each year. Harvesting is still mostly done by hand, and many coffee plantations use organic farming methods, such as growing banana plants for natural shade or intercropping coffee with spice plants such as pepper.

Edakkal Caves

above the clouds, and – if you're lucky – perhaps a glimpse of sambar deer, Nilgiri langurs or wild elephants.

At the time of research, two other main trekking areas were open. **Chembra**, the region's beloved highest peak, looms 2100m tall over southern Wayanad; trekking here is only permitted up to a heart-shaped lake at the halfway point (around 3km return). Or explore western Wayanad's **Banasura Hills**, home to peaceful *shola* and rushing waterfalls. All three areas open year-round (weather permitting) and require mandatory Forest Department guides and permits *(up to 5 people ₹7500-8000)*; starting times are usually 7am to 9.30am and payment is by card or UPI (no cash accepted). Online bookings *may* be doable via *ecotourism.forest.kerala.gov.in*. Bring layers, water and sun protection.

Reputable adventure operator **Muddy Boots** *(muddyboots.in)* runs expert-led treks across Wayanad, including half-day excursions along the Kabini River, crossing by raft at the end *(per person ₹2360-3540)*. The team also offers full-day trips to summit Brahmagiri and fun cycling tours of both south and north Wayanad.

Climb to Prehistoric Art

Wonders of the Edakkal Caves

Hidden at around 1200m high in southeastern Wayanad's Ambukuthi Hills, the set of natural rock shelters known as **Edakkal Caves** *(wayanad.gov.in; adult/child ₹50/30; closed Mon)* shines a light on South India's prehistory. Etched into the stone walls here is a series of vivid Neolithic petroglyphs thought to date from between 6000 BCE and 1000 BCE, depicting human figures, hunting scenes, various animals, abstract patterns and inscriptions in Sanskrit and Tamil-Brahmi. See if you can spot an elephant or a peacock. There is usually an official guide in the main cave sharing details about the petroglyphs and the history of this space, which is thought to have been lived in at several different times. The cave etchings were put on today's world map in the 1890s, when a British police officer stumbled across them (with the help of local Adivasi communities).

Reaching the caves involves a steep 1km, 15-minute walk up from a designated car park near Ambalavayal village (11km southwest of Sultanbatheri), then climbing 300 steps to enter the caves. Allow at least 45 minutes once you're past the ticket office; arrive early or last thing to beat the crowds, and skip busy weekends. While exploring this area, don't miss **Wayanad Heritage Museum** *(keralatourism.org; ₹30)* in Ambalavayal, which focuses on the region's Adivasi heritage and cultures.

Rural Crafts

Discover Uravu's bamboo world

Around 11km east from Kalpetta by road, nonprofit **Uravu Bamboo Grove** *(uravubamboogrove.com)* has been working with 200 local families specialising in bamboo-based crafts since the 1990s. Dig into Wayanad's bamboo artistry by visiting the artisans' studios on a two- to three-hour tour *(per person ₹750)*, joining a bamboo-crafting workshop *(per person ₹1200)* or popping into the small art gallery, where you can pick up handmade baskets, lampshades, bangles, decorative ornaments and other pieces. Sustainably built cottage accommodation is also available.

Sacred Places

Wayanad through its temples

Resting 900m high in the lower reaches of the Brahmagiri Hills, 25km north of Mananthavadi, **Thirunelly Temple** *(thirunellytemple.in)* is believed to be one of India's most ancient temples and plays an important part in Wayanad's identity. The complex honours Vishnu, drawing devotees from all over Kerala. While the main shrine is closed to non-Hindus, the mountain setting is as spectacular as the feast of elaborately carved granite pillars adorning the 15th-century Vilakkumadom building's exterior, and anyone can wander uphill to the sacred Papanasini stream.

Over in southeast Wayanad, **Sultanbatheri** gets its curious name from a fort built by Tipu Sultan in the 18th century, when the region was annexed by the Kingdom of Mysore. The fort itself disappeared long ago, but on the western edge of town you can still see a 13th-century granite-built **Jain Temple** in Vijayanaga style with intricately carved stone pillars showing elephants, snakes and lotus flowers. A relic from Wayanad's historically important Jain community, it was later used as an artillery base by the Mysore army. There's another beautifully carved, now-crumbling Jain temple on the roadside just northeast of **Panamaram**, 25km northwest of Sultanbatheri (or 13km southeast from Mananthavadi).

ACTIVE WAYANAD

Pradeep Murthy, Director at Muddy Boots Vacations *@muddybootsvacationsindia*

Wayanad has long been 'that wild place up in the hills', but now it's more accessible than ever. Soaring mountains, deep valleys, tiger reserves and stunning mountain passes encircle populated countryside in the middle, offering a great mix of nature, culture and adventure for pretty much everyone. In addition to hiking and cycling, bamboo rafting is a great way to get a very different perspective of the Kabini River. Pro tips: avoid the most popular tourist places and seek out hidden treasures with a local operator and budget enough time for local travel, as the twisty roads make for slow progress.

Places We Love to Stay

₹ Budget ₹₹ Midrange ₹₹₹ Top End

Kochi (Cochin)

Map p884

Zostel ₹ Well-equipped air-con dorms, private doubles, bright communal spaces and social vibes, in Fort Kochi.

Fort Bungalow ₹₹ Beautiful home where traditional-inspired clay-floor rooms surround a courtyard, near Santa Cruz Basilica.

Reds Residency ₹₹ Delightful Fort Kochi homestay with hotel-smart rooms, fresh breakfasts. There's also a sister property in Edakochi.

Beena Homestay ₹₹ Welcoming hosts, fresh rooms and delicious communal breakfasts, on a quiet Fort Kochi lane.

Delight Homestay ₹₹ Whitewashed heritage home turned charming six-room guesthouse, opposite the Parade Ground.

Raintree Lodge ₹₹ Restored, vine-covered 18th-century house; rooms mix contemporary style and heritage touches.

Green Woods Bethlehem ₹₹ Warm, long-running, lower-midrange guesthouse rambling amid palm gardens in Fort Kochi.

Kayal Island Retreat ₹₹₹ Serene, four-room, boat-access boutique hideaway on the backwaters, 20km south of Kochi.

Old Harbour Hotel ₹₹₹ A 300-year-old Dutch-Portuguese building turned elegant poolside escape; fabulous garden restaurant (p892).

Kara ₹₹₹ Boutique haven with eight design-led rooms and art exhibitions, in a gorgeous heritage building.

Malabar House ₹₹₹ Fort Kochi's original luxury-boutique retreat: an 18th-century building with pool and prize-winning restaurant (p892).

Brunton Boatyard ₹₹₹ This five-star heritage pick has Kerala-inspired style, a harbourfront pool and tip-top dining (p892).

Fort House Hotel ₹₹₹ Waterfront haven with a great restaurant (p892), tropical gardens and modern-Kerala design.

Govindamangalam Homestay ₹₹₹ Antique beds and traditional art adorn this smart four-room spot in a century-old Mattancherry home.

Forte Kochi ₹₹₹ Stylishly revamped, mango-yellow 19th-century house spread around a plant-filled pool courtyard.

Thrissur & Around

Chaayaa ₹₹ Sweeping verandahs, Kerala breakfasts and stylish bathrooms in a 70-year-old family home, south of Thrissur.

Alappuzha (Alleppey)

p900

Zostel ₹ Lively branch of the popular chain, near Alleppey's beach, with six-bed air-con dorms and private rooms.

Malayalam Lake Resort ₹₹ Orchid gardens, backwaters views and varnished-wood rooms with balconies, at a charming family-owned guesthouse.

Kuttichira Heritage Home ₹₹ Overlooking green fields north of town, with wood-built Kerala-style rooms and pretty gardens.

Marari

Peacock Marari ₹₹ Garden-terrace breakfasts, relaxed vibes and bright, contemporary rooms, just back from the beach.

Secret Beach Yoga Homestay ₹₹ See p903.

Marari Villas ₹₹₹ Gorgeous boutique-design serviced villas with private pools, Kerala-style meals and beachfront locations.

Marari Beach ₹₹₹ Serene, sustainability-driven resort: thatch-roof villas, saltwater pool and Ayurvedic spa amid 12-hectare gardens.

Kumarakom & Vembanad Lake

Philipkutty's Farm ₹₹₹ See p899.

Kumarakom Lake Resort ₹₹₹ Kerala-inspired architecture, tropical gardens and a lakefront setting make a palm-dotted beauty.

Munnar & Around

Map p907

Green View Inn ₹ Long-established, fresh, central guesthouse, by the switched-on team behind Munnar Trekking (p908).

Green Valley Vista ₹₹ Mountain-view balconies, modern rooms, home-cooked meals and community-based tours, in Anachal village.

Windermere Estate ₹₹₹ Century-old cardamom estate turned swish heritage hotel, with a pool overlooking tea plantations.

Rosegardens ₹₹₹ One of Kerala's loveliest homestays: a 100-year-old home with organic gardens, cosy rooms and biogas plant.

Mudhouse Marayoor ₹₹₹ Stylish, barefoot-vibe mud-built cottages, paired with home-style cooking, near Marayoor.

Kumily (Periyar Tiger Reserve)

Map p912

Green View ₹₹ Long-running, welcoming favourite featuring well-kept rooms with breezy terraces and solar-heated water.

Chrissie's Hotel ₹₹ Vibrant murals adorn this 15-room guesthouse; yoga, rooftop pool and popular cafe (p914).

Coffee & Pepper Plantation Homestay ₹₹ Stylish, contemporary-feel homestay surrounded by spice gardens, just outside Kumily.

Spice Village ₹₹₹ Elegant thatch-roof cottages, sparkling pool and local-sourced cooking at a gorgeous CGH Earth resort.

Varkala

Map p916

Zostel ₹ Near Black Beach, offers modern air-con dorms (including women only options) and private rooms.

Mad About Coco ₹₹ Boutique North Cliff guesthouse for boho-cool rooms, solar-heated water, sea-view cafe and yoga.

InDa Hotel ₹₹ This popular North Cliff bolthole has boutique flair, garden cottages and a peaceful cafe.

Villa Jacaranda ₹₹₹ Beautiful four-room house amid lush pool gardens, serving home-cooked breakfasts, near the South Cliffs.

Villa Akasa ₹₹₹ Bright floral fabrics, terracotta floors and lush gardens fill this boutique South Cliffs hideaway.

Thiruvananthapuram (Trivandrum)

Graceful Homestay ₹₹ Peaceful heritage homestay in leafy western Trivandrum; four fan-cooled rooms, lovely gardens, Kerala breakfasts.

Kovalam

Paradesh Inn ₹₹ Above Lighthouse Beach, this popular six-room guesthouse has Mediterranean design, rooftop views and great breakfasts.

Maharaju Palace ₹₹ Tranquil guesthouse just back from Lighthouse Beach, with charmingly styled rooms overlooking gardens.

Leela ₹₹₹ Elegant five-star luxury above Samudra Beach, from clifftop infinity pool to textile-clad rooms and royal thalis.

Taj Green Cove ₹₹₹ Luxe retreat amid palm-dotted gardens; thatched cottages, beautiful spa, wonderful dining.

Beach Hotel & Beach Hotel II ₹₹₹ Breezy sister properties with arty ochre-hued rooms and good restaurants, on Lighthouse Beach.

Munroe Island & Kollam (Quilon)

Munroe Island Backwaters Homestay ₹₹ See p922.

Ashtamudi Villas ₹₹ Charming, modern solar-powered cottages on Ashtamudi Lake, plus kayaks, home-cooked meals and swaying hammocks.

Kannur

Kannur Beach House ₹₹ Calming, long-established Thottada homestay, with rustic rooms, Kannur-made linens and Malabar-style cooking.

Costa Malabari ₹₹ Kannur's original guesthouse offers homestay-style rooms, home-cooked meals and *theyyam* expertise, just inland from Thottada's sands.

Blue Mermaid Homestay ₹₹ Contemporary-touch homestay set among tropical gardens by Thottada Beach, serving garden-fresh meals.

Ivory Coast'e ₹₹ Warmly run, modern-build home with spacious rooms, hidden amid greenery near Thottada Beach.

Bekal & Nileshwar

Neeleshwar Hermitage ₹₹₹ Fabulous, sustainability-focused resort inspired by Kerala Vastu architecture, with Ayurveda, yoga and dreamy pool.

Poothali ₹₹₹ Modern Kerala-style homestay overlooking Nileshwar's rice crops, delivering Malabar meals and culture-rich tours.

Aavi Beach Retreat ₹₹₹ Wake up to the waves at this ancestral Nileshwar home, stylishly revamped with beachy palettes.

Wayanad

Map p933

Varnam Homestay ₹₹ Standout homestay on an organic family-run spice plantation with homegrown meals, forest-view pool and cosy rooms.

Jungle Retreat Wayanad ₹₹ Rustic-vibe, 20-hectare resort bordering Wayanad Wildlife Sanctuary, with treehouses and cottages.

Ente Veedu ₹₹ A 150-year-old coffee estate hosts this charming homestay surrounded by crops and forest, near Mananthavadi.

Tranquil ₹₹₹ Century-old, family-owned coffee-and-spice estate, with custom-designed treehouses and farm-to-table meals; also runs serene Amaryllis.

Pepper Trail ₹₹₹ Immersed in cardamom plantations, this stylish property has pool villas, treehouses and a heritage house.

Taj Wayanad ₹₹₹ Earthy-toned rooms, soothing spa treatments and top-tier cuisine in a five-star setting overlooking Banasura Lake.

Researched by Meena Thiruvengadam

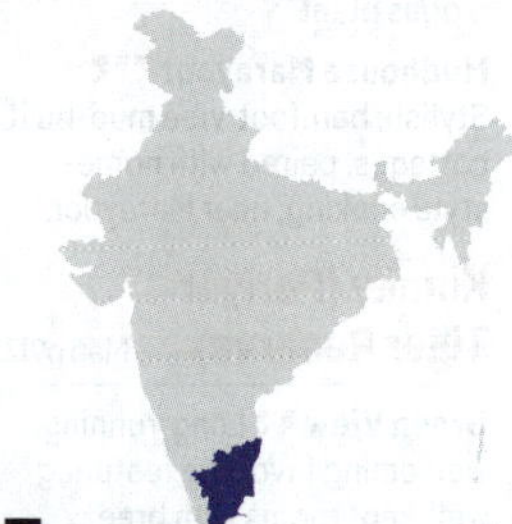

Tamil Nadu

ANCIENT HISTORY, GRAND TEMPLES AND NATURAL BEAUTY

This is where ancient history and modern India collide: discover magnificent temples, sandy beaches and mountain escapes in India's cradle of arts, culture and Tamil heritage.

The name Tamil Nadu means land of Tamils, an ethnic group native to India and Sri Lanka known for its contributions to arts, literature and language. This homeland of one of humanity's oldest living civilisations is rich with history and culture. Tamil Nadu stretches from the dense forests of the Western Ghats to the sandy beaches of the sun-drenched Coromandel Coast and the southern tip of the subcontinent. It is a land of incredible topological diversity, a place where bustling modern cities, vibrant historical villages and magical mountain towns coexist with nature and wildlife.

NDARU ANURADHA/SHUTTERSTOCK

Tamil Nadu is an economic powerhouse where there is always music in the air, be it a cacophony of horns, gentle carnatic melody or the rhythmic beats of *bharatanatyam*, a Tamil classical dance. Arts, culture and language have always flourished here. Experience fine examples of Dravidian architecture left behind by the Chola, Pallava and Maratha dynasties. Marvel at brightly colored Hindu temples in Madurai and Chennai (Madras) and ancient rock-cut temples on the beach in Mahabalipuram.

Often thought of as a vegetarian hotspot, Tamil Nadu has a long tradition of non-vegetarian cuisine reflecting a history influenced by Myanmar, France, the United Kingdom and centuries of dynastic rule. Indulge in fluffy croissants, artisanal chocolates and savoury delicacies like *kari dosa*, a hearty mutton-topped dosa (savoury crepe).

There's an unforgettable adventure waiting down the road in Tamil Nadu.

THE MAIN AREAS

CHENNAI
Arts, culture and big-city energy. **p946**

PUDUCHERRY (PONDICHERRY)
Seaside remnant of French colonial India. **p957**

For places to stay in Tamil Nadu, see p982

ILOSK50/SHUTTERSTOCK

Above: Meenakshi Amman Temple (p966), Madurai; Left: DakshinaChitra Heritage Museum (p950), Chennai

MADURAI
Ancient history and iconic street foods. **p966**

OOTY (UDHAGAMANDALAM)
Mountains, gardens and British colonial history. **p975**

Find Your Way

Tamil Nadu is India's 10th largest state and home to the southernmost city on the subcontinent. This is a place where distances can be deceiving.

Ooty (Udhagamandalam), p975

Known as the 'Queen of Hill Stations', this British colonial mountain retreat has sprawling botanical gardens, colonial-era bungalows and endless scenic views.

BUS & TRAIN

Tamil Nadu is served by extensive rail and bus networks. Trains link key destinations and are an economical way to travel long distances, but seats can sell out quickly. Buses offer connections to smaller towns and more remote areas.

AIR

Air travel is an efficient option for covering Tamil Nadu's vast distances quickly on a budget. Major cities, including Chennai, Madurai and Coimbatore, are served by rapidly developing airports that are useful gateways to harder-to-reach destinations.

CAR & DRIVER

India is home to some of the most chaotic roads in the world. Hire a car and driver for maximum flexibility with minimal stress. Chennai traffic and the hairpin bends of the Nilgiri Hills are not for the faint of heart.

Chennai, p946

The vibrant capital of Tamil Nadu offers lively arts and shopping scenes in a city where ancient temples and modern skyscrapers coexist.

Puducherry (Pondicherry), p957

This Franco-Tamil union territory is home to tranquil ashrams, several beaches, a scenic waterfront promenade and a burgeoning surf scene.

Madurai, p966

The soul of Tamil Nadu, this temple town is known for its spirited festivals, thriving cultural scene and as a gateway to the Nilgiri Hills.

Plan Your Time

Choose between beaches, mountains and cultural experiences if time is limited, or slow down to take in all Tamil Nadu has to offer.

VIKAS SHRIVASTAV/SHUTTERSTOCK

Old Lighthouse (p961), Puducherry

Pressed for Time

- Start in **Chennai** (p946) for South Indian art, history and culture. Visit colourful **Kapaleeshwarar Temple** (p952), gleaming white churches, and **Higginbothams** (p952), the oldest bookshop in India. Shop for handmade crafts and shimmering fabrics. Dine on crisp dosas or sip craft cocktails at a chic bar such as **La Cabana** (p952). Head to the sandy shores of **Mahabalipuram** (p954) to spend a day among rock-cut temples that captured the attention of Marco Polo. Make your way south to **Puducherry** (p957), a Franco-Tamil beach town filled with colourful villas, courtyard cafes and independent boutiques. Stroll the promenade to **Rock Beach** for sunset and you can learn to surf (p960) on the Bay of Bengal. Dine on Franco-Tamil dishes at **Coromandel Cafe** (p959), and carve out a few hours for a stop in **Auroville** (p964).

SEASONAL HIGHLIGHTS

December and January offer the most pleasant weather, and a robust festival calendar. Temperatures peak between March and May.

JANUARY

Celebrate **Pongal**, a Hindu harvest festival honouring the sun god Surya with colorful *kolams* and the cooking of *sakkarai pongal*, a sweet pudding made with fresh rice, jaggery and milk.

FEBRUARY

February is one of the best times to visit Tamil Nadu, after peak holiday and festival season has subsided and before the oppressive summer heat sets in.

APRIL/MAY

Witness the **Chithirai Festival** (967) at the Meenakshi Amman temple in Madurai. It marks the Tamil New Year and celebrates the union of the goddess Meenakshi (Parvati) and Lord Sundareshwar (Shiva).

Tamil Nadu in a Week

- After the above, dive into ancient history in **Madurai** (p966), one of India's oldest cities where you can marvel at the intricate **Meenakshi Amman Temple** (p966), explore the **Keeladi Heritage Museum** (p968) and excavation site and sample the local drink *jigarthanda*. Head to the hills of the Western Ghats at **Ooty** (p975), the cool resort town where the game of snooker was invented. Enjoy mountain breezes strolling through the **Botanical Garden** (p976) and the **Rose Garden** (p976). Sample handmade chocolates at **Moddy's** (p977) and ride the vintage **Nilgiri Mountain Railway** (p978), an hour-long scenic journey from Ooty to Coonoor passing mountain towns, tea terraces and Bollywood movie scenes.

Take It Slow

- With three weeks or more you can experience the best Tamil Nadu has to offer. In **Chennai** (p946) visit the **DakshinaChitra Heritage Museum** (p950) and **Government Museum** (p951), stroll **Marina Beach** (p947) and shop your way across lively **Thyagaraya Nagar** (p952). Travel to ancient monuments in **Mahabalipuram** (p954), community-led **Auroville** (p964) and Gallic seaside enclave **Puducherry** (p957). Detour to the temples and palaces of **Thanjavur** (p962) and the grand mansions of **Chettinadu** (p971), where you can watch artisans at work in open-air tile factories and try unique spice blends. Don't miss stops in **Madurai** (p966) and **Ooty** (p975) before ending with a road trip to the southernmost tip of India at **Kanyakumari** (p974), where the Bay of Bengal meets the Indian Ocean and Arabian Sea. Savour one of the best sunrises in the world at **Triveni Sangam** (p974).

MAY

Experience the **Ooty Summer Festival** during which Ooty shows off its abundance of flowers, fruits, vegetables, roses and spices. The event includes rowing and boat races on the lake.

OCTOBER

Navaratri is a nine-night festival honouring the goddess Durga and her nine divine forms. It happens seasonally, with the largest celebrations in autumn. In Tamil Nadu, it's known more for elaborate doll displays than the folk dances of the north.

OCTOBER/ NOVEMBER

Celebrate **Deepavali**, the Hindu festival of lights honouring good over evil, light over darkness and knowledge over ignorance. Tamils mark the day with oil baths, new clothes and evening firecrackers.

DECEMBER

Immerse yourself in Carnatic music and Bharatanatyam dance in Chennai during **Margazhi Mela**, a month-long celebration featuring a robust calendar of concerts and dance performances from mid-December to mid-January.

Chennai

BEACH STROLLS | HISTORY | ART, MUSIC & DANCE

TOP TIP
Chennai restaurants are often called hotels and are known for serving traditional cuisine at affordable prices.

Chennai is a vibrant capital city filled with art, architecture and ancient temples. This seaside city was called Madras from 1639 – when the British acquired the land for their first trading post in India – until 1996. Today Chennai is a modern city with a rich history spanning thousands of years. The area has an estimated population of around 12.5 million, making it smaller than Delhi and Mumbai but larger than London, Paris, New York and Hong Kong. Chennai is home to giant air-conditioned shopping malls, a sprawling national park and the second-largest urban beach in the world. A hub for medical tourism and the Indian auto industry, it's a place that drives innovation while celebrating South Indian heritage and the arts. One of the city's marquee events is a classical music and dance festival held each December.

Bastion of the Past

Discover the roots of British colonial India

Fort St George, historically known as White Town, was the first British fortress in India. Built by the British East India Company, it's now home to a collection of government buildings and barracks for military troops. Among them, you'll find **St Mary's Church**, India's oldest surviving British colonial building, constructed between 1678 and 1680 and used as a

GETTING AROUND

Chennai traffic is no joke, especially with a citywide metro system still under construction. Plan your sightseeing strategically and escape the traffic on the metro, whose elevated and underground stations connect the airport and certain key neighborhoods with fares between ₹10 and ₹50. The city has an extensive and affordable bus system, but they can get extremely crowded at peak travel times. Ridesharing is available in the city and at the airport through Ola and Uber. Taxis and autorickshaws are also available, but bike lanes are limited, as are walkable sidewalks.

JOOSTP/SHUTTERSTOCK

Marina Beach

barracks and granary during the Second Carnatic War and an invasion by the Mysore's Kingdom's King Hyder Ali in the 18th century. The small **Fort Museum** *(₹200; closed Fri)* contains thousands of items from British colonial India, including portraits, weapons and coins. It also houses the first flag flown over a newly independent India, hoisted at this site on 15 August, 1947. Admission must be made through a QR code (no cash). There's a parking lot across the street.

Vibrant Marina Beach

Escape to India's longest urban beach

The 3km stretch of **Marina Beach** is the longest natural urban beach in India, and visiting is a true cultural experience. It's about 300m wide on average and 437m at its widest point. Expect to walk through the sand for a while before you see the Bay of Bengal peek out over the horizon.

Strong riptides make swimming here dangerous, though people do sometimes cool off in the shallow water along the sand. Street-food stalls and restaurants dot this sandy landscape, where the biggest draw is the refreshing breeze blowing off the bay. Instead of sunbathers, you're more likely to run into kite flyers, fitness enthusiasts and families in search of affordable fun.

Continues on p952

TAMIL NADU TOUR OPERATORS

5 Senses Tours: Motorcycle tours of Tamil Nadu's Chola Temples, Chettinad mansion tours and walking tours in Chennai and Madurai. *5sensestours.com*

Madras Inherited: Cultural and heritage walking tours. *madrasinherited.in*

Chennai Photo Walk: Free walking tours led by local photographers. Check Instagram for upcoming dates and locations. *@the chennaiphotowalk*

Pondicherry Beach Escapes: Kayaking tours, surfing and scuba diving experiences, and exclusive visits to the typically off-limits parts of Auroville. *pondicherrybeach escapes.com*

Foodies Day Out: Madurai food tours sampling *idlis*, *dosas*, *parottas* and paratha. *foodiesdayout.com*

EATING IN CHENNAI: OUR PICKS

Wild Garden Cafe: Artsy garden cafe with a broad menu, cappuccinos and delicious baked goods. Also a clothing shop and flower shop. *10am-11.30pm* ₹₹

The Farm: A farm-to-table restaurant with wood-fired pizzas, fresh cheese and open-air dining at this farm. *11am-6pm Tue-Sun* ₹₹₹

Southern Spice: This award-winning restaurant feels like stepping into the heyday of the Chola, Pallava or Pandya dynasties. *12.30-2.45pm & 7-11pm* ₹₹₹

Chamiers: Adorable vegetarian- and vegan-friendly restaurant with a beautifully papered wall lined with historic photos. 8.30am-10.30pm ₹₹

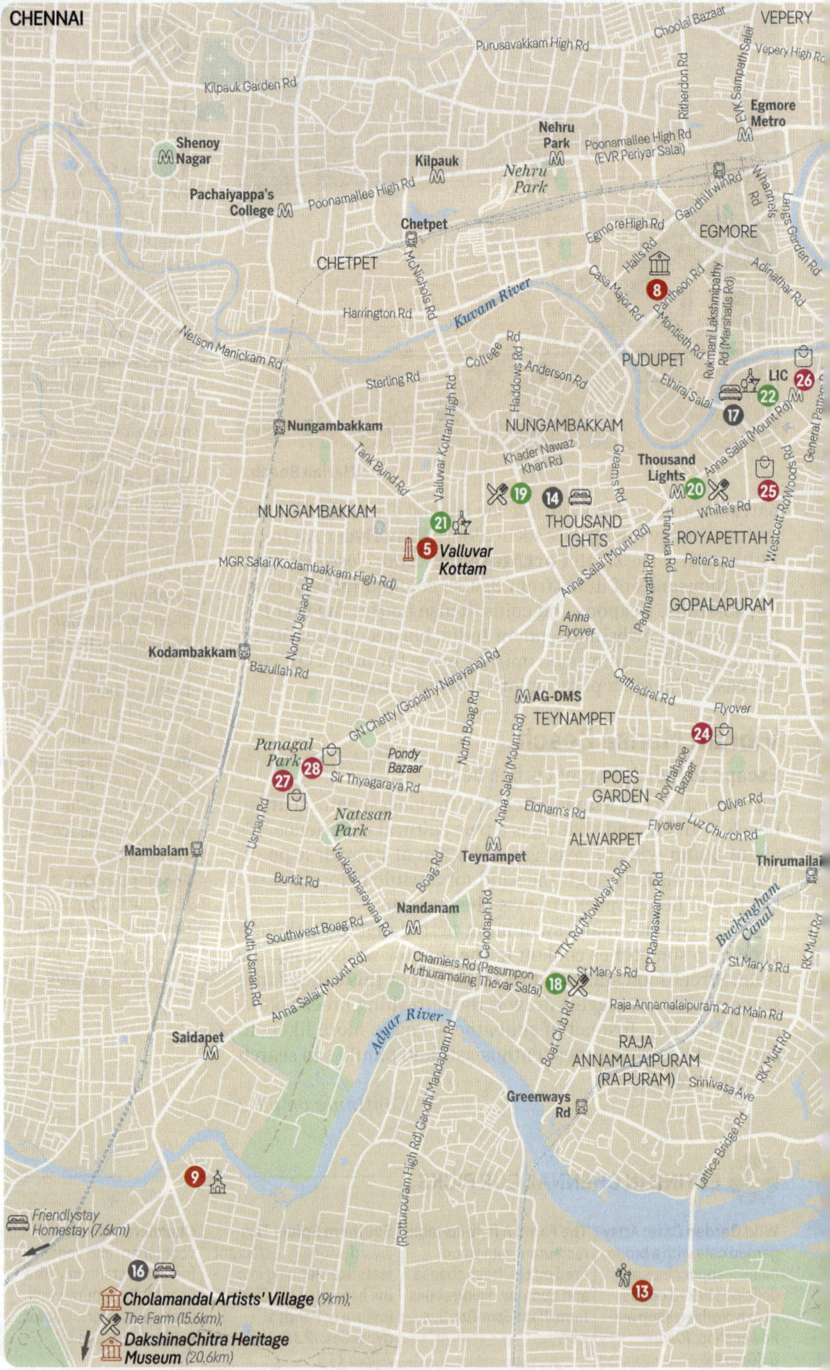
CHENNAI
VEPERY
Choolai Bazaar
Purusavakkam High Rd
Vepery High Rd
Kilpauk Garden Rd
Ritherdon Rd
EVK Sampath Salai
Egmore Metro
Shenoy Nagar
Nehru Park
Poonamallee High Rd (EVR Periyar Salai)
Kilpauk
Nehru Park
Pachaiyappa's College
Poonamallee High Rd
Gandhi Irwin Rd
Whannels Rd
Langs Garden Rd
Chetpet
Egmore High Rd
EGMORE
CHETPET
McNichols Rd
Halls Rd
Adinathar Rd
Casa Major Rd
Pantheon Rd
Rukmani Lakshmipathy Rd (Marshalls Rd)
Harrington Rd
Kuvam River
Montieth Rd
Nelson Manickam Rd
College Rd
Haddows Rd
Anderson Rd
PUDUPET
Sterling Rd
Ethiraj Salai
LIC
Valluvar Kottam High Rd
Nungambakkam
Tank Bund Rd
NUNGAMBAKKAM
Khader Nawaz Khan Rd
Greams Rd
Thousand Lights
Anna Salai (Mount Rd)
General Patters Rd
Woods Rd
Westcott Rd
White's Rd
NUNGAMBAKKAM
THOUSAND LIGHTS
Thiruvika Rd
ROYAPETTAH
Valluvar Kottam
MGR Salai (Kodambakkam High Rd)
Anna Salai (Mount Rd)
Peter's Rd
North Usman Rd
Padmavathi Rd
Anna Flyover
GOPALAPURAM
Kodambakkam
Bazullah Rd
GN Chetty (Gopathy Narayana) Rd
North Boag Rd
Cathedral Rd
AG-DMS
TEYNAMPET
Flyover
Panagal Park
Pondy Bazaar
Anna Salai (Mount Rd)
Sir Thyagaraya Rd
POES GARDEN
Royttahpe Bazaar
Oliver Rd
Eldham's Rd
Natesan Park
Flyover
Luz Church Rd
Usman Rd
ALWARPET
Mambalam
Teynampet
Thirumailai
Burkit Rd
Boag Rd
Venkatanarayana Rd
TTK Rd (Mowbray's Rd)
Nandanam
Cenotaph Rd
CP Ramaswamy Rd
Buckingham Canal
South Usman Rd
Southwest Boag Rd
Chamiers Rd (Pasumpon Muthuramaling Thevar Salai)
St Mary's Rd
St Mary's Rd
RK Mutt Rd
Anna Salai (Mount Rd)
Raja Annamalaipuram 2nd Main Rd
Adyar River
Boat Club Rd
Saidapet
RAJA ANNAMALAIPURAM (RA PURAM)
Srinivasa Ave
RK Mutt Rd
(Rotturpuram High Rd) Gandhi Mandapam Rd
Greenways Rd
Lattice Bridge Rd
Friendlystay Homestay (7.6km)
Cholamandal Artists' Village (9km);
The Farm (15.6km);
DakshinaChitra Heritage Museum (20.6km)
5 8 9 13 14 16 17 18 19 20 21 22 24 25 26 27 28

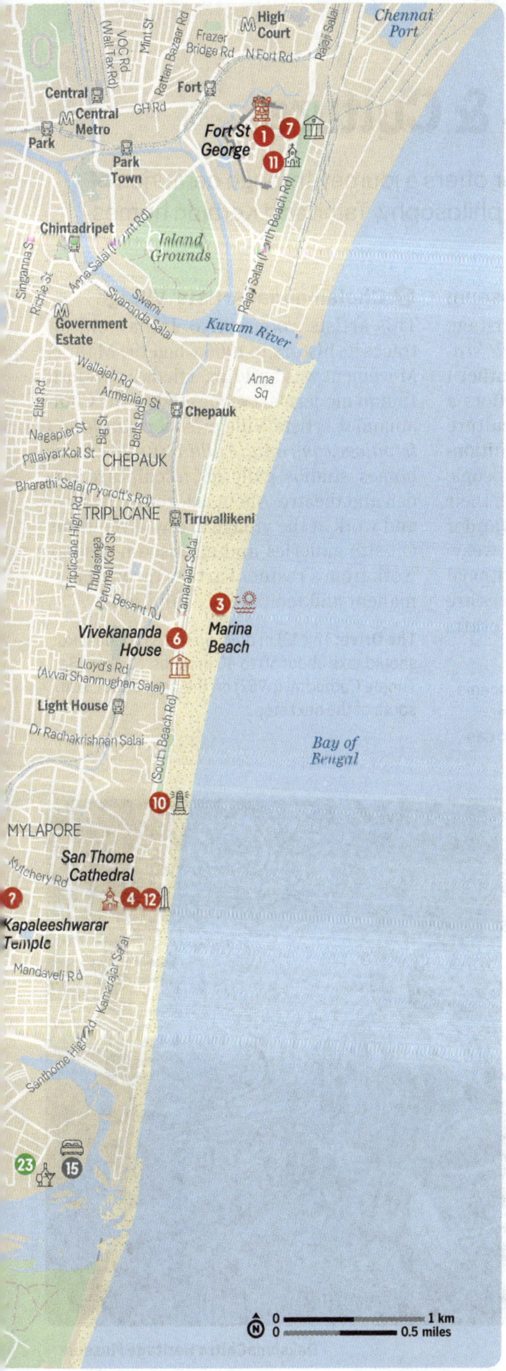

HIGHLIGHTS
1 Fort St George
2 Kapaleeshwarar Temple
3 Marina Beach
4 San Thome Cathedral
5 Valluvar Kottam
6 Vivekananda House

SIGHTS
7 Fort Museum
8 Government Museum
9 Little Mount Church
10 Madras Lighthouse
11 St Mary's Church
12 Tomb of St Thomas the Apostle

ACTIVITIES
13 Madras Inherited

SLEEPING
14 Hotel Ranjith
15 Leela Palace
16 Park Hyatt
17 Taj Connemara

EATING
18 Chamiers
19 Southern Spice
20 Wild Garden Cafe

DRINKING & NIGHTLIFE
see 16 Flying Elephant
21 La Cabana Rooftop Bar & Grill
22 Lady Connemara Bar
23 Radio Room

SHOPPING
24 Cottage Arts Emporium
25 Express Avenue Mall
26 Higginbothams
27 Nalli Silks
28 Thyagaraya Nagar

DRIVING TOUR

Chennai Arts & Culture

This scenic urban driving tour offers a journey through centuries of South Indian art, history and philosophy, Tamil and Keralan homes and modern art galleries.

1 DakshinaChitra Heritage Museum

Start at the DakshinaChitra Heritage Museum (*dakshinachitra.net; adult/student ₹250/70; closed Tue*) at the southern edge of Chennai. This museum offers a window into Tamil and Keralan culture through a collection of relocated traditional homes. See how merchants, craftspeople and others lived by walking through their meticulously recreated homes. Wander streetscapes, watch potters, basket weavers and bangle-makers at work. Traditional music and folk dancing performances are on show, and there's an arts and crafts market.

The Drive: An easy drive north along the scenic East Coast Rd to the next stop should take around 20 minutes, though Chennai traffic can be highly unpredictable.

2 Cholamandal Artists' Village

This artists' cooperative, India's oldest, traces its history to 1966 when the Madras Movement was building a fledgling South Indian modern art scene. Today, the Cholamandal Artists' Village (*cholamandalartistvillage.com; adult/child ₹50/10*) includes homes, studios, galleries, a sculpture garden and theatre. About a dozen artists live and work at the village at any given time. On-site galleries and a museum display work from a roster of artists through permanent and temporary exhibitions.

The Drive: This 18km drive up the East Coast Rd should take about 30 to 40 minutes. Look for San Thome Cathedral (p952) on the right about 3km south of the next stop.

RAJA MANNAR/SHUTTERSTOCK

DakshinaChitra Heritage Museum

3 Vivekananda House

The pastel-pink Vivekananda House *(vivekanandahouse.org; adult/child ₹50/40; closed Mon)*, a block back from Marina Beach, is where Swami Vivekanda stayed while visiting Madras in 1897. The Hindu monk, author and religious teacher is known for sparking the Western world's interest in yoga and Hindu philosophy with a speech at the 1893 Parliament of World Religions in Chicago. The museum offers a glimpse into his life and teachings through a number of multisensory exhibits. The round 19th-century building was originally built to store ice imported from the US.

The Drive: It's about 6km west into the city to Valluvar Kottam – as little as 15 minutes or as much as a half-hour depending on traffic and road closures.

4 Valluvar Kottam

Valluvar Kottam *(free; 10am-8pm)* is dedicated to the Tamil poet Valluvar, best known for writing *Kural*, a collection of 1330 couplets on ethics, virtue, wealth and love and built by the architect who created the Thiruvalluvar statue (p974) in Kanyakumari. The Chennai monument includes a 39m-high stone car made with 3000 blocks of granite. There's a life-size statue of Valluvar inside the chariot and inscriptions of *Kural*'s couplets at the site.

The Drive: Only about 3km northeast to the Government Museum, 10 to 20 minutes by car.

5 Government Museum

This treasure trove of history and art is India's second-oldest museum. Spread across several buildings, the Government Museum *(chennaimuseum.org; ₹250; closed Fri)* is home to bronze sculptures dating back to the 7th century when the Pallava dynasty ruled. It also has an extensive collection of stone sculptures, massive portraits of former British rulers and a selection of Tanjore paintings, as well as a children's museum featuring an expansive doll collection and a 3D show.

CHENNAI'S BEST SHOPPING

Nalli Silks: Family-owned boutique chain since 1928. The place to shop for traditional Indian clothing, fabrics and fine silk saris.

Thyagaraya Nagar: T Nagar is one of the busiest shopping districts in India. Shop for clothing, jewellery and household items.

Higginbothams: Opened in 1844, this is India's oldest bookshop with a wide selection of books in Tamil, English and Hindi from Indian and international authors.

Express Avenue Mall: Shop local and international brands at this air-conditioned mall with cinema.

Cottage Arts Emporium: One-stop shop for art from across South India. Shop for brass sculptures, Tanjore paintings, marble and high-end rugs.

Continued from p947

There's also a long promenade that runs parallel to the beach, making this one of the most walkable parts of Chennai. **Kamarajar Promenade** is lined with statues, monuments and memorials, including homages to Mahatma Gandhi and former local leaders MG Ramachandran and Jayaram Jayalalitha, beloved Tamil film stars who later went into politics. Several architectural icons are across the street, including the **Indo-Saracenic University of Madras**, an example of the hybrid Indian, Islamic, neogothic and neoclassical architectural style that was popular in British India.

The **Madras Lighthouse**, at the southern end of the beach, offers panoramic views of the city and the Coromandel Coast, with a lift to the top.

Divine Discoveries

Explore Chennai's religious landscape

Chennai is dotted with colourful Hindu temples and gleaming white Christian churches that can be explored on a self-guided tour. Start at the **Kapaleeshwarar Temple** in Mylapore. This masterpiece of Dravidian architecture is dedicated to Lord Shiva, and its colourful *gopuram* and pillared *mandapas* (pavilions) stand out in this residential area. It's here that the goddess Parvati, who Shiva turned into a peacock for failing to focus on his lessons, came to worship in an effort to regain her original form. The story is depicted on the western facade of the temple's inner courtyard.

It's a five-minute drive or 15-minute walk to **San Thome Cathedral**, built by the Portuguese in 1523 and rebuilt by the British in 1896. It houses the **Tomb of St Thomas the Apostle**, who is believed to have brought Christianity to India. The **Little Mount Church**, a 20-minute drive away, contains a cave where St Thomas is said to have lived or hid from persecutors. Look for what's believed to be his handprint on the rock near the window and check out the Bleeding Cross believed to have been made by the apostle.

DRINKING IN CHENNAI: OUR PICKS

Radio Room: A creative list of cocktails and mocktails served in a radio-themed bar at Somerset Greenways hotel. *noon-1am Mon-Thu, to 2am Fri & Sat*

Flying Elephant: Upscale bar and restaurant in the Park Hyatt Chennai with a creative list of craft cocktails and bar snacks. *5pm-1am*

La Cabana Rooftop Bar & Grill: Cocktails and mocktails on a rooftop with cabanas, an infinity pool and city views. *6-11.30pm*

Lady Connemara: Chennai's first licensed bar located inside the Taj Connemara hotel. Try an expertly crafted cocktail, like the signature Madras No 1. *3-10pm*

Beyond Chennai

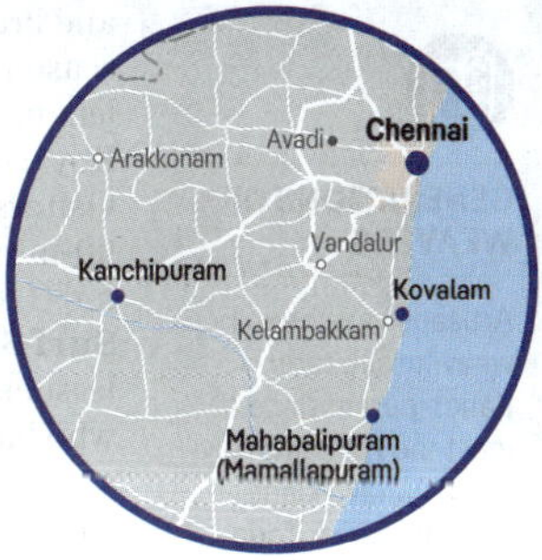

Surfing, fresh seafood and ancient temples are within a two-hour drive of Chennai.

Drive south along the scenic East Coast Rd long enough and Chennai's urban sprawl gives way to sandy beaches, fishing villages and magnificent stone-cut temples. Get to know Kovalam, a fishing village that's slowly transforming into a surf destination known for some of the best waves on the Coromandel Coast. Kovalam is also known for its fish curry made with red chillies, shallots and garlic. Keep driving south and you'll land in Mahabalipuram, a seaside town famous for its intricate bas-relief sculptures and rock-cut temples, some of which were hidden until the 2004 tsunami.

Two hours southwest of Chennai brings you to the ancient temples of Kanchipuram, the 'City of a Thousand Temples', where you can learn what makes Kanchipuram silk such a sought-after commodity.

Places

GETTING AROUND

Get to Kovalam, Mahabalipuram and Kanchipuram from Chennai by hired taxi, rideshare or bus. Expect to pay around ₹1000 each way to Mahabalipuram and Kovalam, and ₹1500 to Kanchipuram. Bus fares are significantly cheaper but schedules are limited. Locally you can hire a taxi or autorickshaw to get around town or consider renting a scooter.

Kovalam

TIME FROM CHENNAI: 1¼HR

Go surfing, kayaking or paddleboarding

Kovalam is a quaint fishing village that's grown into a surfing hotspot over the past decade, thanks to its warm waters, consistent sea breezes, a collection of independent surf schools

JAYBEE/GETTY IMAGES

Surfing, Kovalam

GENERATIONS OF WEAVERS

Artisans have been weaving silk saris in Kanchipuram since at least the 7th century, when Pallava kings ruled this area. Today, the saris, made from the silk of mulberry silkworms, are among the best in India, known for their thickness, intricate designs and use of silk threads dipped in liquid gold or silver, called *zari*. Kanchipuram saris are particularly popular wedding attire, for both brides and guests. Kanchipuram's army of skilled weavers uses a system of pedals and pulleys on giant looms to create their intricate designs. The silk is dyed with colours derived from plants, flowers and other natural sources to create vibrant hues.

and breaks that are suitable for surfers of all levels. Monsoon season can bring stronger swells that may be especially challenging for beginners but would suit more experienced surfers. Kovalam's certified surf guides can be invaluable for helping visitors navigate these waters. **Surf Turf** *(surfturf.in)* has 90-minute introductory lessons for ₹1900 or a group class for ₹1500. A three-day beginner course costs ₹5000. **Murthy Surf School** *(murthysurfschool.com)* also offers 90-minute lessons *(₹1500)* with local surfing legend Murthy Megavan, who has been surfing here for more than 20 years. Kayaking and paddleboarding classes are ₹1500 for 90 minutes. Hourly surfboard, kayak and paddleboard rentals are also available.

Kanchipuram

TIME FROM CHENNAI: **2HR**

Temple-hopping and silk shopping

Grand temples from the Pallava, Chola and Vijayanagar eras are the highlight in this former capital of the Pallava dynasty. The **Kailasanatha Temple** is one of the oldest surviving Hindu temples in the city, while the **Ekambareshwara Temple** is the largest Hindu temple in Kanchipuram. In between temple visits, head to Gandhi Rd to shop for Kanchipuram silk saris. These saris, made from the finest mulberry silk threads and handwoven by skilled artisans, are renowned for their high quality and intricate designs.

Mahabalipuram (Mamallapuram)

TIME FROM CHENNAI: **1½HR**

Lighthouse views of the coastline

Mahabalipuram is an ancient port city filled with treasure, some of which was unearthed by a 2004 tsunami. On the Coromandel Coast, the town also known as Mamallapuram is best known for its ancient temples, intricate stone sculptures and laid-back vibe. Head to the **Mahabalipuram Lighthouse** *(₹25)*, which has been guiding ships through the Bay of Bengal since 1900, for a bird's-eye view of this jewel of the Pallava dynasty. Climb to the top of its spiral staircase for 360-degree views of Mahabalipuram and the coast. Next door is the **Olakkannesvara Temple**, which is believed to have housed India's first lighthouse in the 7th century using an oil lamp that was relit every night to guide sailors to shore.

EATING IN MAHABALIPURAM: OUR PICKS

Joe's Cafe: A laid-back spot known for its Italian coffees, fresh fruit juices and lassis. Come here for crepes or a casual brunch. *9am-8pm* ₹

Arabian Garden: A multicuisine restaurant on East Raja St known for its seafood and biriyanis. *11am-11.45pm* ₹₹

L'attitude 49: Elegant restaurant with garden views, a broad selection of Indian and Southeast Asian dishes and the catch of the day. *7am-11pm* ₹₹₹

Wharf 2.0: International menu of dishes inspired by earth, water, wind, fire and air. Known for its grilled seafood, meats and pastas. *noon-3pm & 7-11pm* ₹₹₹

Shore Temple

TOP EXPERIENCE

Mahabalipuram Monuments

Mahabalipuram's collection of ancient temples and elaborate rock carvings has been recognised as a UNESCO World Heritage Site, one of four in Tamil Nadu. This set of 40 monuments includes one of the world's largest open-air rock reliefs, a soaring temple tower that guided ancient Greek and Roman traders to shore and several structures that re-emerged only after the 2004 tsunami.

DON'T MISS

- Shore Temple
- Krishna's Butterball
- Arjuna's Penance
- Tiger Cave
- Five Rathas
- Mahishasuramardini Cave
- Olakkanesvara Temple

Shore Temple

When this complex of temples and shrines was built together on a single platform in the early 8th-century CE, this area was a busy port overlooking the Bay of Bengal. The Shore Temple, dedicated to Lords Shiva, Vishnu and Ksatriyasimnesvara during the rule of Pallava King Narasimhavarman II (Rajasimha) around 675–728 CE, is one of the oldest structural stone temples in India. It drew visiting merchants from ancient Greece and Rome who likely used its pagodas as a navigational landmark. Greek and Roman coins have been found here.

Made of hard granite, the temple was built to survive tsunami waves like those that slammed this area in 2004. Look for the partially completed lion monolith with an opening in

PRACTICALITIES

● asi.nic.in/pages/WorldHeritageMahabalipuram ● ₹600 ● 6am-6pm
● book a slot and pay online at asi.payumoney.com/quick/mam

THE MARCO POLO CONNECTION

The famous Venetian merchant and explorer Marco Polo is believed to have been among the earliest European visitors to Mahabalipuram. He travelled through India on the way home from China, documenting the area's vast wealth and writing about its spices, textiles and customs. Polo marked Mahabalipuram on his *Catalan Map* of 1275, which he used to record his travels. The Mahabalipuram Shore Temple's pagoda is believed to be among the Seven Pagodas that Polo would have spotted off the coast India, later written about by European visitors.

TOP TIPS

- Visit between December and February for the most pleasant weather.
- Start your day before the tour buses begin arriving around 10am.
- Hire an Archaeological Survey of India guide at the monuments for a more in-depth experience.
- Hire a guide for a half-day tour for around ₹3000.

its torso, a sign it may have been a favourite creature, and the miniature Durga that's sculpted into the lion's back, the well-preserved water tank complex and the 16-sided miniature shrine.

Krishna's Butterball

This giant granite boulder defies gravity. Balanced on a short incline that's an easy climb, this natural wonder is believed to have influenced the development of Thanjavur's famous dancing dolls. Opt for shoes with a sturdy grip.

Descent of the Ganges (Arjuna's Penance)

This 29m by 13m open-air relief is carved into a pair of monolithic boulders. Facing the sea, it is one of the world's largest open-air rock reliefs and depicts the descent of the Ganges to earth from the heavens. Look for the snake carvings that symbolise fertility and water flowing down alongside gods, sages and animals. This scene was carved to celebrate King Narasimhavarman I's defeat of Chalukya Emperor Pulakesin II. It includes almost 150 intricate sculptures, including nearly life-sized carvings of elephants.

Five Rathas (Pancha Rathas)

This complex of five giant chariots was built during the reign of Pallava Kings Mahendravarman and his son Narasimhavarman. Each chariot is carved into a single piece of monolithic granite. Work on the chariots likely began in the 7th or 8th centuries and was never completed.

Tiger Cave

This 8th-century cave is named for the collection of tiger heads surrounding its mouth-like entrance, accessed by a handful of stairs. Stand back and the structure as a whole resembles a resting tiger. Tiger Cave is associated with King Narasimhavaram II,. Inscriptions found at this especially popular picnic spot in 2005 led to the discovery of a Sangam-era Murugan temple nearby.

Mahishasuramardini Cave

This hillside temple has three chambers and is dedicated to the goddess Mahishasuramardini, considered an incarnation of the Durga. Check out the carving of a battle between Durga and buffalo-headed demon Mahishaasura on the north wall of the cave.

Olakkanesvara Temple

This hilltop temple above the Mahishasuramardini Cave offers serene Bay of Bengal views. Built in honour of Lord Shiva during the Pallava dynasty in the 8th century, its roof served as a lighthouse directing early seafarers to shore. The temple can be accessed by a series of rock steps leading up from the cave.

Puducherry (Pondicherry)

FRANCO-INDIAN FLAIR | SURFING | ASHRAM LIFE

This union territory offers a taste of France on the eastern coast of India. Pondy, as it's known locally, was a French colony for 138 years until 1954. Known as the French Riviera of the East, this is the rare Indian city where Creole-style architecture accented with bougainvillaea-lined walkable boulevards is lit by 19th-century lamp posts.

The buildings in the French Quarter of this bohemian-chic beach town wear bright colours and look almost as if they fell from a box of crayons. Many of them have been converted into heritage hotels or modern restaurants with idyllic courtyards. Bakeries and boutiques are plentiful, French is still spoken, and the streets continue to tell the story of the city's Franco-Indian history.

Visitors come not only for Franco-Tamil culture but also for water sports like surfing and diving or to search for inner peace through yoga, meditation and a taste of ashram life.

GETTING AROUND

Hire a car and driver from Chennai (₹4000 one-way, three hours) with a stop at Auroville, or take a train from Egmore station (from ₹100, four hours). The French Quarter of Puducherry is walkable, but consider an autorickshaw (₹100 or more for a 1km journey) for longer distances. Scooter rentals start at ₹400 per day.

A Guide to Puducherry's Past

Learn Franco-Tamil history

Housed in a lateh18th-century villa, the **Puducherry Museum** *(art.py.gov.in/puducherry-museum; ₹50)* takes visitors on a journey through thousands of years of history. Learn about the ancient seaport of Arikamedu, a centuries-old Indo-Roman trading hub that once existed a few kilometres away. See

TOP TIP

Book walking tours, rickshaw tours and scuba-diving, surfing and kayaking excursions at the tour desk that shares a building with Le Cafe.

EATING IN PUDUCHERRY: BEST BAKERIES

Baker Street: Sandwiches, croissants and assorted pastries in a cute cafe across from the beach. Don't skip the macaroons. *7am-9.30pm* ₹

Le Petit Four: Fresh bread, ornate cakes, fancy coffees and fluffy croissants with indoor and outdoor seating. *7am-11pm* ₹

Auroville Bakery: Artisanal breads and organic treats at an eco-conscious bakery and cafe in Auroville. *7am-5.30pm Mon-Sat, to 1pm Sun* ₹

Bouche Sucree: A spacious cafe across from the beach that serves chocolate, almond and plain croissants and a range of rich desserts. *8am-10.30pm* ₹₹

HIGHLIGHTS
1 Cluny Embroidery Centre
2 Puducherry Museum
3 Sri Aurobindo Ashram

SIGHTS
4 French War Memorial
5 Notre Dame des Anges
6 Old Lighthouse
7 Rock Beach
8 Sri Manakula Vinayagar Temple

ACTIVITIES
9 École de Surf Pondy

SLEEPING
10 De Fleur Hotel
11 Gratitude Heritage
12 La Villa
13 Le Dupleix
14 Maison Perumal
15 Palais de Mahé
16 Villa Helena
17 Villa Shanti

EATING
18 Baker Street
19 Bouche Sucree
20 Cherrypond Garden Cafe and Bar
21 Chez Francis
22 Coromandel Cafe
23 Le Café
24 Le Petit Four
see 15 Les Alizes'
see 14 Maison Perumal
25 Surguru Spot
26 Wildfish Bistro

DRINKING & NIGHTLIFE
27 Catamaran Brewing Company
28 Flaming Dragons Lounge & Nightlife
29 Skol
30 The Storytellers Bar

SHOPPING
31 Anokhi
32 Aura Experience Store
33 Chintz Boutique
see 31 Hidesign & Le Pondichéry Boutique
34 Meraki

remnants of pottery, handmade beads and coins from the archaeological site, and browse bronze sculptures from the Chola, Vijayanagar and Nayak dynasties. The museum is also home to a Gutenberg printing press, a collection of weapons and an example of what the interior of a French Indian home may have looked like in the 17th century.

Yoga & Meditation Hub

Find calm amid chaos

Founded in 1926 by Sri Aurobindo and a French-born woman known as the Mother, the **Sri Aurobindo Ashram** *(sriaurobindoashram.org; tours ₹50 per person, 8.15am)* is a hub for integral yoga and meditation. Its goal is to help members 'manifest a higher consciousness' on Earth. The ashram welcomes visitors to join open meditation sessions *(free)*, attend yoga workshops *(from ₹12,000 for 3 days)* and to pay their respects at the flower-adorned funerary monument to Sri Aurobindo and the Mother inside the ashram. The ashram is open to visitors from 8am to 11am and 2pm to 6pm. Meditation sessions are held between 7.25pm and 7.50pm. Visitors must obtain a pass from Bureau Central, the administration centre of the ashram, to addend. Yoga classes are held between 6am and 7am and between 5.45pm and 7.15pm at the Matriniketan, a few blocks away. Two- and four-day residential yoga workshops are also available.

A Hub for Embroidery

Watch intricate scenes come to life

Since 1929, the Sisters of Cluny have run the **Cluny Embroidery Centre** *(free ; 8-11am & 2-5pm)* in this gigantic colonial bungalow with black-and-white chequered floors flanked by grand white pillars. Women, primarily widows, single mothers, divorcees and victims of domestic abuse, work in rows embroidering tablecloths, napkins and towels. Nuns here have been passing on their French embroidery skills, teaching other women how to create intricate pieces often inspired by nature. These pieces can take months to complete and are often sold

ASHRAM ETIQUETTE

The Mother described Sri Aurobindo Ashram as a place for yoga and quiet meditation. Members are expected to commit their lives to the divine and to contribute to the ashram in some way. Rudeness is not tolerated, and politeness and acceptance are paramount. Visitors are welcome and while there is no explicit dress code, the ashram expects visitors and members to dress modestly, often recommending clothing that covers the shoulders and knees. Members and visitors are expected to abstain from meat, smoking, alcohol, drugs and sexual relations while at the ashram. Some hotels near the ashram also prohibit alcohol and meat consumption.

EATING IN PUDUCHERRY: OUR PICKS

Le Cafe (p957): Come to this waterfront cafe for filter coffee, croissants, sandwiches and cooling breezes of the Bay of Bengal. *24hr* ₹	**Cherrypond Garden Cafe and Bar:** Bohemian cafe with a stylish bar and stunning murals. Come for breakfast or brunch, and cold coffees. *8am-11pm* ₹₹	**Coromandel Cafe:** Creative Franco-Tamil dishes at this elegant hotel in a charming historic building in White Town. *8.30am-11pm* ₹₹₹	**Wildfish Bistro:** Select your fish and your recipe at this upscale hotel restaurant with courtyard dining and Indian wines. *7-11pm* ₹₹
Surguru Spot: A casual eatery that serves up paper-thin dosas and filling thalis near the Sri Aurobindo Ashram. *7am-10.30pm* ₹	**Maison Perumal:** Hearty Creole dishes served in the courtyard of a restored mansion and heritage hotel. *noon-2.30pm & 7-10pm* ₹₹₹	**Les Alizes':** Indulge in fabulous Indo-Franco fusion cuisine at this rooftop restaurant within the luxurious Palais de Mahé hotel. *noon-3pm & 7-10.30pm* ₹₹₹	**Chez Francis:** Dine in luxury at this upscale courtyard restaurant, where French cuisine meets local charm. *noon-3pm & 7-10.30pm* ₹₹₹

PUDUCHERRY BOUTIQUES

Hidesign & Le Pondichéry Boutique: Expansive boutique selling clothing, accessories, jewellery and bags in a store that feels like a painting.

Anokhi: Founded in 1970, this handblock-printed clothing company prioritises craft conservation and doesn't have an online store.

Chintz Boutique: Shop for clothes from Indian designers, jewellery and home accessories at this stylish boutique.

Meraki: An expansive boutique selling unique jewellery, clothing and more, all sourced from designers across India.

Aura Experience Store: This seafront shop on Goubert Ave sells books and crafts from Auroville and the Sri Aurobindo Ashram.

HARI MAHIDHAR/SHUTTERSTOCK

Sri Aurobindo Ashram (p959)

before they're finished. The proceeds are used to pay workers a monthly salary. You can watch artisans at work during the centre's opening times.

A True Beach Town

Catch waves, kayak mangroves or go diving

Some of the best experiences in Puducherry are on the water. Like its neighbour Kovalam to the north, Puducherry offers ample opportunities to catch waves at reasonable prices. Take surfing lessons at the **Mother Ocean Surf School**, **Kallialay Surf School** or **École De Surf Pondy**. Pondicherry Beach Escapes (p947) runs scuba-diving excursions off the coast, beginner surf lessons at Serenity Beach and kayak tours through peaceful mangroves and backwaters. Kayak tours offer a look at changes to the city's landscape between low tide and high tide and provide ample opportunities for birdwatching. Keep an eye out for blue pipers, cormorants and kingfishers.

DRINKING IN PUDUCHERRY: OUR PICKS

Catamaran Brewing Company: Sip on a flight of craft beers and listen to live music at Puducherry's first microbrewery. *11am-midnight*

Flaming Dragons Lounge & Nightlife: Come here for a solid bar selection, Chinese food and a dance floor with great vibes. *11am-1am*

Skol Bar: A futuristic-looking cocktail bar that hosts party nights, has excellent mixologists and serves piña coladas in pineapples. *noon-midnight*

The Storytellers Bar: This cocktail bar is for book lovers. Located inside the Promenade Hotel. *7pm-midnight Wed-Mon*

A FRENCH QUARTER STROLL

Discover Puducherry's unique Franco-Tamil culture on a walking tour through the French Quarter.

START	END	LENGTH
Sri Manakula Vinayagar Temple	Cluny Embroidery Centre	1.2km; 30min

1 Sri Manakula Vinayagar Temple has stood in Puducherry for more than 500 years – more than a century before the French arrived. The temple walls show scenes from the Vedas and Upanishads, Hindu religious texts.

One block north is the **2 Sri Aurobindo Ashram** (p959), a 100-year-old spiritual community. Head east to the coastal promenade and **3 Rock Beach**, a popular local gathering spot and the city's best place to watch the sunrise.

Continue along Goubert Ave towards the **4 Old Lighthouse**, which guided ships along the Coromandel Coast between 1837 and 1979.

Stop at the **5 French War Memorial**, dedicated to the residents of French India killed in WWI. There's a statue of Gandhi on the other side of the street.

Walk a block inland and turn left on Dumas St to see **6 Notre Dame des Angels**. The oldest parts of the cathedral were built in the mid-1700s. Walk south for two more blocks, then go right on Bazaar St Laurent St and again on Rue Romain Rolland and look for the grand white bungalow that houses the **7 Cluny Embroidery Centre** (p959), where French nuns have been teaching local women embroidery for a century.

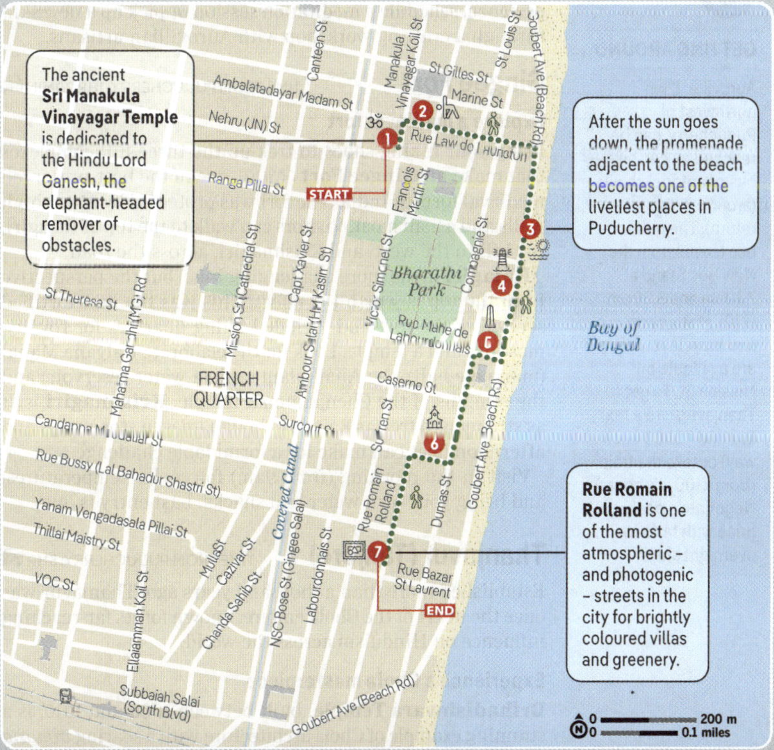

Beyond Puducherry

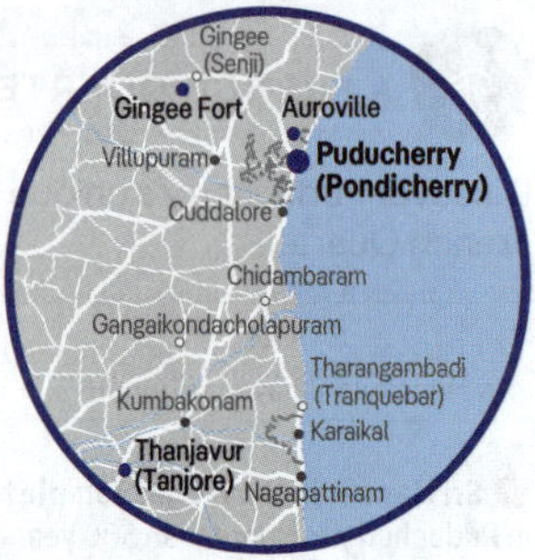

From sandy beaches to towering forts and sprawling temple complexes, the area surrounding Puducherry is rich with nature and history.

Places

Gingee Fort p962
Thanjavur (Tanjore) p962
Auroville p960

GETTING AROUND

Auroville, 12km northwest of Puducherry, can be reached by car, bike, bus or autorickshaw (around ₹700 return). The public bus leaves from the New Bus Stand at 7.30am and 3.30pm (₹10). Motorcycle and bicycle rentals are available on Mission St. To get to Thanjavur, hire a taxi (around ₹3500 each way) or take the train (from ₹100, 4½ hours). Negotiate a package price with taxis for overnight stays.

The area surrounding Puducherry is ripe for cultural experiences. Immerse yourself in art, history and music in Thanjavur, which became the capital of the powerful Chola Empire in the 9th century. Learn about the temple city's famous gold-foil paintings and handmade dancing dolls. See historic manuscripts at one of the oldest libraries in Asia, learn about the Dutch community that once made its home here or immerse yourself in Carnatic music. For an experience closer to town, explore Auroville, a self-sustaining commune at the edge of Puducherry where you can enjoy a farm-to-table dining experience, schedule a meditation session or pick up a new skill through a crafting workshop with Aurovillian artisans.

Gingee Fort

TIME FROM PUDUCHERRY: **1HR 20MIN**

Explore a medieval fort

Bring your hiking shoes to trek up the three hill complexes that make up **Gingee Fort** *(₹300)*, one of the best-preserved medieval forts in India. The fort was protected by 250m-high walls and a 25m moat. Visitors can walk to the top of Rajagiri, the hill to the west, and Krishnagiri, across the road.

Rajagiri is the more challenging hike, but the perspective from the top is worth the effort. This was the best-fortified section of the fort and included living quarters for royalty, mosques and a temple. Look for the elaborate Kalyana Mahal (marriage hall), the Anaikulam tank (a water reservoir) and the remains of the Chenjiamman temple. **Krishnagiri** isn't as strenuous a trek as Rajagiri, though uneven stone steps and afternoon heat can make for a formidable challenge.

Visit in the morning (from 9am) for cooler temperatures, and bring your own water and snacks. Last entry is 3pm.

Thanjavur (Tanjore)

TIME FROM PUDUCHERRY: **3HR**

Established more than a thousand years ago, Thanjavur was once the heart of the Chola empire, known for its far-reaching influence on Hinduism across the world.

Experience a Chola masterpiece

Brihadishwara Temple, built between 1003 and 1010, is a stunning example of Chola architecture with a soaring *vimana*

IKHWAN AMEER/SHUTTERSTOCK

Gingee Fort

(tower) that's among the tallest in South India. Stroll the meticulously maintained temple grounds and seek out the shrines that dot this complex, including a 6m Nandi, Shiva's sacred bull, cut from a single rock in the 16th century. Look for the colourful frescoes that were discovered underneath a layer of Nayak-era murals in 1931 and spend some time examining the temple's intricate granite facade, carved with a series of elaborate stucco sculptures.

Dive into art and literature

Thanjavur's **Royal Palace** *(₹200)* complex, built by the Nayak and Maratha dynasties, contains one of Asia's oldest libraries, the **Saraswathi Mahal Library**. The stacks are closed to visitors, but a small museum displays a collection of world atlases and ancient manuscripts. The **Maratha Palace** around the corner was originally built by the area's Nayak rulers, but became home to Maratha leaders after the fall of the Nayak kingdom and is now home to the **Royal Palace Museum**. Take some time to admire its Chola-era bronze sculptures before heading to the Durbar Hall to see the colourfully painted archways, intricate stucco sculptures and statue of Raja Serfoji, the last Maratha ruler of Thanjavur.

Shop for Thanjavur treasures

Thanjavur has long been a city of artists. Shop for some of its most famous treasures – gold-foil paintings, bronze sculptures and Thanjavur dancing dolls – at the **Government Handicrafts Sales Emporium** upstairs at the Sangeetha Mahal, a building known for its excellent natural acoustics.

THE ORIGINAL BOBBLEHEADS

Long before there were modern bobblehead dolls, there were the dancing dolls of Thanjavur. Known in Tamil as Thallayatti Bommai, these handmade dolls with bobbing heads, hands and bodies are designed to mimic the graceful movements of Indian classical dancers. Thallayatti is the Tamil word for head-shaking. The dolls have hollow bodies set on a heavier base. Touch them gently, and they'll dance. In the 17th century, these dolls were made for royalty and the wealthy using clay from the Kaveri River. Nowadays, they're easy to find and often made with papier-mâché.

EATING IN THANJAVUR: OUR PICKS

Nasar Idiyappa Paya Unavagam: This no-frills restaurant is known for goat curries, *kothu* parottas and steamed *idiyappams*. *11am-11pm* ₹

Thillana: Come here for generous lunchtime thalis. Masala dosas and fluffy *idlis* are also available for breakfast and dinner. *6.30am-11pm* ₹₹

Aswins Sweets and Snacks: Head to this bakery for sweet treats and savoury snacks. Try the *gulab jamun* if you have a sweet tooth. *24hr* ₹

Aaharam: An organic vegetarian restaurant serving traditional Tamil thalis in a stunning heritage hotel. *7am-11pm* ₹₹₹

VYAS ABHISHEK/SHUTTERSTOCK

The Matrimandir

TOP EXPERIENCE

Auroville: An Experimental Commune

Auroville is a self-sustaining community that's been around for almost 60 years. The cash-free society is home to more than 3000 residents representing 60 nationalities. Auroville prioritises self-reliance, sustainability and environmental stewardship, and residents participate in everything from organic farming to renewable energy projects, hospitality management and handicraft production.

DON'T MISS

- Visitor Centre
- Crafting Workshops
- Matrimandir Viewing Point
- Botanical Garden
- Solitude Farm
- Sustainable Handicrafts
- Fresh Smoothies

Start at the Visitor Centre

Auroville can be a lot to wrap your head around. Invest a half-hour learning about the community and its ethos at the Visitor Centre. Attendants at the front desk are happy to answer questions.

The section of Auroville that's open to visitors is easy to get around on foot, thanks to a network of roads and shady walkways. Bike rentals are available at the Visitor Centre. Auroville offers on-site accommodation *(guesthouses.auroville.org)*, and guests staying at Auroville can rent e-bikes *(kinisi.in/rental)*. There are restrooms, water fountains and cafes on the property.

PRACTICALITIES

● auroville.org ● free ● 8am inner chamber meditation, 9am-5pm (Matrimandir viewpoint), 9am-5.30pm (Visitor Centre)

Visitors wishing to join the community in Auroville can volunteer for a minimum term of three months *(atr@auroville.org.in)*.

Meditate in a Geodesic Dome

The **Matrimandir** – a marble-lined chamber with a crystal orb that diffuses sunlight – is the focal point of an Auroville visit. Visitors are not permitted on the grounds of the commune, but they are able to see its iconic gold dome from a designated viewpoint. Passes are required from the Visitor Centre, where you can learn more about the construction and structure of the dome. Morning meditation sessions are open to the public and held daily except Sunday and Tuesday. Advance booking is required.

Reconnect sith Nature

Auroville is home to a 20-hectare **botanical garden** with 1300 varieties of plants and more than 300 species of trees. Nature walks are open to visitors on Wednesday and Friday mornings from 9.30am to 11am (book via email at *avbgtours@gmail.com*). Auroville is also home to several banyan trees, which are considered sacred in India. The largest has a diameter of 50m and is estimated at 100 years old.

Learn Something New

Every resident of Auroville has a job that allows them to contribute to the community, and some artisans teach their skills to visitors through a series of workshops making baskets, bowls, coasters and more from recycled newspapers. Try your hand at turning coconut shells into artistic treasures, blend your own incense sticks or get your hands dirty during a pottery workshop.

Enjoy a Farm-to-Table Meal

Solitude Farm Cafe, Auroville's vegan farm-to-table restaurant, features produce grown in Auroville's gardens used in green smoothies, millet dosas and healthy bowls. Visit Auroville's farm on a free tour on Saturday mornings at 11.30am.

Shop for Crafts

As a self-sustaining commune, Aurovillians are asked to take on jobs to help support the community. Some Aurovillians make and sell jewellery, household goods, trinkets and accessories at on-site shops. Auroville also hosts art exhibits where works on display are offered for sale.

Guided Tours

Pondicherry Beach Escapes (p947) partners with Auroville residents on a four-hour tour that takes visitors behind the scenes of the commune. Tours *(₹2500)* start at 9.30am Monday to Saturday. A meal at Auroville's Solar Kitchen is included. See *pondicherrybeachescapes.com/package/special-auroville-experience* for more information and bookings.

ORIGINS OF AUROVILLE

Auroville is the brainchild of Mirra Alfassa, a French woman called 'The Mother', and Sri Aurobindo, an Indian yogi and philosopher. The pair envisioned Auroville as a self-sustaining utopian town existing beyond national boundaries and cultural lines. The international community was founded in 1968 as a cashless society without religion, politics or nationality. It's now home to thousands of residents from more than 60 countries.

TOP TIPS

- Start at the Visitor Centre to get a basic understanding.
- Book a slot to meditate inside the Matrimandir early as spaces fill up quickly. Sessions may be cancelled in wet weather.
- If travelling between Chennai and Puducherry by car, stop here on the way.
- The Visitor Centre closes for lunch between 1pm and 1.30pm Monday to Saturday.
- Bring a reusable water bottle and wear comfortable shoes.

Madurai

ANCIENT HISTORY | COLOURFUL TEMPLES | PIPING-HOT IDLIS

With more than 2500 years of history, Madurai is one of the oldest continuously inhabited cities in the world. It was once a trading hub, selling spices, fabrics and jewels to the Greek and Roman empires. Later, it became a key destination in the fight for Indian independence.

Often called the soul of Tamil Nadu, Madurai is a living museum of Tamil culture and history. It has been ruled by the Chola, Pandya, Vijayanagar, and Nayak empires – the last gave the city its signature lotus shape – as well as by Muslim sultans and the British Raj.

Legend suggests Madurai, a city surrounded by mountains and famous for its aromatic jasmine flowers, emerged from sacred drops of nectar that fell from Lord Shiva's hair. Shiva later married the goddess Meenakshi, whose namesake temple – one of the most famous Hindu temples in the world – continues to dictate the rhythms of the city.

GETTING AROUND

Madurai is well connected by air, train and bus. Madurai's local bus system covers the city's major sights and is the most affordable way to get around town. Expect to pay around ₹400 to hire an autorickshaw for a day or ₹2000 for a car and driver. Scooters and motorbikes are available for rent from ₹400 per day.

Centuries of Devotion

Visit Madurai's most sacred temple

In the heart of Madurai, the **Meenakshi Amman Temple** is one of the largest and oldest in India. It's also one of the few religious monuments in India devoted to a female deity.

Originally built in 600 CE, the temple was destroyed by Muslim conquerors and rebuilt between the 14th and 17th centuries. A colourful example of Dravidian architecture, it boasts 14 soaring *gopurams* decorated with thousands of sculptures of animals, gods and demons. Enter through the eastern *gopuram* for the shortest path to the 1000 Pillar Hall, where you'll find the **Temple Art Museum**. The museum contains a collection of bronzes, paintings and coins and offers the chance to see a replica of the goddess Meenakshi, whose original shrine is off-limits to non-Hindus. While you're in the hall, check out the pillars on its western side. When struck, each pillar produces a different musical note.

TOP TIP

Don't plan your Meenakshi Amman Temple visit for mid-afternoon. While the temple is open from 5am (for the first morning *puja*) to 10pm, it closes for a lengthy break between 12.30pm and 4pm.

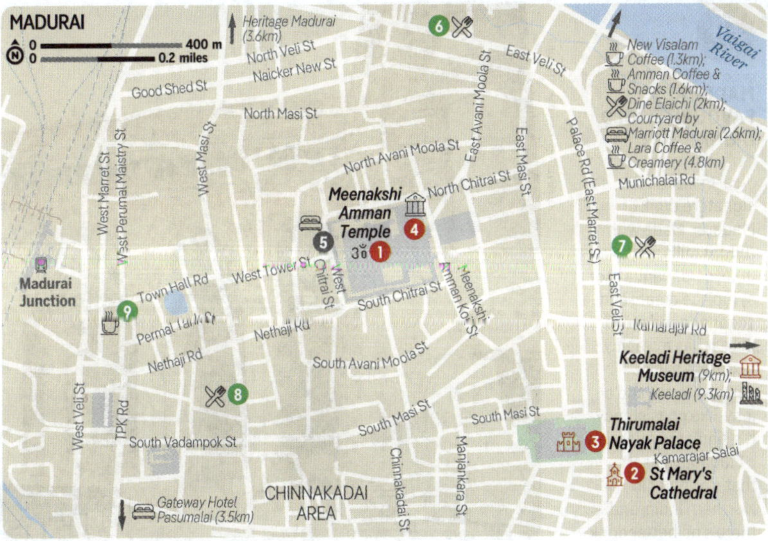

HIGHLIGHTS
1 Meenakshi Amman Temple
2 St Mary's Cathedral
3 Thirumalai Nayak Palace

SIGHTS
4 Temple Art Museum

SLEEPING
5 Gopuram Grand

EATING
6 Konar Kodai
7 Madurai Muniyandi Vilas
8 Murugan Idli Shop

DRINKING & NIGHTLIFE
9 Sree Sabarees

The temple opens at 5am but the best time to visit for minimal crowds is between 7am and 9am. Come at 9pm to watch a procession of priests carry the shrine of Shiva to Meenakshi for the evening. While it's not possible for non-Hindus to visit either shrine, a wander through the **Golden Lotus Tank** in the centre of the sprawling temple complex tells the story of their marriage through a collection of ceiling murals. Devotees often bathe in the tank, which holds a gold-gilded lotus, before visiting major shrines. Phones and bags are not allowed inside the temple.

In April and May the two-week Chithirai Festival (p944) is a celebration/reenactment of the marriage of Meenakshi to Sundareswarar (Shiva). The deities are wheeled around the Meenakshi Amman Temple in massive chariots forming part of long, colourful processions.

An Ancient Civilisation

See remnants of an egalitarian urban society

Archaeologists have spent more than a decade excavating the site of an ancient village that challenges widely held beliefs about urban traditions after the decline of the Harappan

EATING IN MADURAI: OUR PICKS

Murugan Idli Shop: Madurai's most famous *idli* shop. Known for its steaming hot *idlis*, chutneys and *jigarthanda*. *7am-11pm* ₹

Dine Elaichi: North Indian and Chinese dishes in an elegant setting. Try the chilli paneer, and start with a soup. *11.30am-3.30pm and 6.30-11pm* ₹₹

Madurai Muniyandi Vilas: Pop in for a *brotta*. This combination bun and *paratha* is a favourite local street food. *noon-midnight* ₹

Banyan Restaurant: Come for the lunchtime buffet of classic Tamil dishes. *7am-10.30pm Sun-Tue, from 7.30am Wed-Sat* ₹₹₹

MADURAI'S FAVOURITE COLD DRINK

Jigarthanda is the signature drink of Madurai. Made with full-fat milk, almond gum, sarsaparilla root syrup, ice cream and sugar or condensed milk, it has a creamy texture, a sweet, earthy flavour and a jelly-like consistency. It's similar to *falooda*, a Mughlai dessert that's popular in Northern India, and there's no better drink for cooling off on a sweaty summer day. *Jigarthanda* ('cold heart') is such an icon that two Tamil movies bear its name and the drink makes appearances in both. Try it at **Famous Jigarthanda** (multiple locations) or the Murugan Idli Shop (p967).

VIRTUALEXPLORING/SHUTTERSTOCK

civilisation in northern India. **Keeladi**, also known as Keezhadi, was an advanced urban civilisation near the Vaigai River that was on par with the early Greek and Roman empires around the 6th century BCE. Evidence shows that Keeladi was equipped with brick houses, ring wells and advanced drainage systems. It was a place where skilled craftspeople made household goods like pottery, etched with inscriptions that suggest widespread literacy.

The main way to get acquainted with this ancient civilization is through a visit to the **Keeladi Heritage Museum** *(₹100)*. The museum's 15,000-item collection is scattered among several Chettinad-style buildings set around a lush courtyard. The collection suggests the people of Keeladi were mariners who traded extensively with Europe and benefited from robust iron and ceramics industries. Dice, beads and toys show that play was as much a priority as work. Don't skip the introductory video, which includes interviews with archaeologists and historians. Keeladi is 12km southeast of Madurai (₹400 by taxi).

WHERE TO DRINK IN MADURAI: BEST FILTER COFFEE

New Visalam Coffee: It's standing room only at this local favourite. Look for the crowd to find this hole-in-the-wall spot. *5.15am-12.15pm & 3.15-7.45pm*

Amman Coffee and Snacks: Try a *vada* with your coffee at this standing-room only coffee bar. *6am-10.30pm*

Sree Sabarees: Eat vegetarian food off a banana leaf and finish your meal with a filter coffee. *6am-11.30pm, to midnight Sat*

Lara Coffee and Creamery: Come here for cute coffee shop vibes, filter coffee, cold coffee and cappuccinos. Also a great place for dessert. *11am-10.30pm*

Thirumalai Nayak Palace

The Nayaks' Palatial Pride

Walk through remnants of a grand dynasty

The grand **Thirumalai Nayak Palace** *(₹60)* was built by King Thirumalai Nayak in 1636. If it feels reminiscent of Italy, it's because the king is believed to have hired an Italian architect to help with its design. Only a quarter of the original palace remains, and it can be experienced in as little as half an hour. Despite peeling walls and stucco, the grandeur of this site continues to shine through. Stroll among the palace's massive pillars, arranged into perfectly straight lines. Pass a pair of massive stone-carved horses, and look up to admire the 25m-high dome inside the **Swarga Vilasam** (Celestial Pavilion). This was once a throne room, and a large red throne remains at its centre. Visit at 6.45pm to catch a 50-minute sound-and-light show *(₹50)* in English that aims to bring the Nayak dynasty to life.

A Cathedral among Temples

Step into the soft light of stained-glass windows

With its pointed arches, stained-glass windows and intricate blue and white facade, **St Mary's Cathedral** stands out in a city of Hindu temples. It was built by the British in 1840 to serve the growing Christian population and replaced by this neogothic cathedral in 1916. Step inside to experience its soaring pointed arches, bright-orange rib-vaulted ceiling and stained-glass windows depicting scenes from the Bible. Outside, take a moment to admire its crowning jewels – a pair of identical bell towers that soar 42m – and a collection of scenes depicting the Stations of the Cross, which recount the final hours of Jesus Christ's life on earth.

A DIFFERENT KIND OF DOSA

Madurai may feel like a vegetarian city, but one of its signature dishes is anything but. Madurai *kari dosa* looks more like a pizza than a light crispy dosa. Imagine a thick base of dosa batter topped with a crispy omelette and a generous layer of meat, typically minced mutton. The mutton is cooked with spices including cumin, coriander, turmeric and black pepper, aromatics including curry leaves and green chillies, and cold-pressed sesame oil until it becomes a thick brown mixture that can be spread over the dosa. This signature dish from Madurai's pastoral Konar community first emerged in 1959 at the **Konar Kodai** restaurant, which opened in 1943 and now has several Madurai locations. Madurai *kari dosa* can also be made with chicken.

Beyond Madurai

Beyond the ancient city of Madurai are some of southern Tamil Nadu's finest adventures, from the rolling hills of the Western Ghats to the mansions of the Chettiars and the southern tip of India.

Places

GETTING AROUND

The easiest way to travel outside of Madurai is to hire a car and driver from around ₹2500 a day. Buses connect Madurai with Kodaikanal (₹100 each way). The closest train station to Kodaikanal is a two-hour drive from key sites and hotels. Trains connect Virudunagar, 49km south of Madurai, with Karaikudi in Chettinadu. Express trains connect Madurai and Kanyakumari in just under four hours (from ₹125). Plan ahead and book tickets early.

Madurai is a gateway to the Western Ghats, where cooler weather, lush forests, luxurious hill station resorts and endless trekking opportunities await. Head two hours northeast, however, and you'll find yourself in the land of the Chettiars, a prosperous merchant community known for building grand mansions across the arid plains of Tamil Nadu. About 10,000 of these opulent estates remain standing. Some have been transformed into heritage hotels or tourist sites, but others remain private residences.

Four hours south of Madurai, Kanyakumari almost feels like the edge of India – at the southernmost tip of Tamil Nadu, it's here that the Bay of Bengal, Arabian Sea and Indian Ocean meet.

Samanar Hills

TIME FROM MADURAI: **30MINS**

Explore caves and Jain temples

Leave the chaos of Madurai behind and make the 10km journey to the Samanar Hills to discover stone beds and 10th-century Jain sculptures carved into the rocks. This collection of hills spread over 3km is known for its Jain and Hindu monuments. Start at the **Ayyanar Karuppanasamy Temple**, a peaceful spot where you'll find colourful *gopurams*, a lush lotus pond and a majestic banyan tree. Check out **Settipodavu**, a cave on the southwestern slope of the hill that was a favourite meditation spot of Jain monks for centuries. Look for inscriptions written in ancient scripts and the large seated sculpture of Lord Mahavira, the last saviour and supreme preacher, known as a *tirthankara*, of Jainism. Hike up the steep stairs towards the top of the hill to **Pechipallam**, where you'll find a collection of eight *thirthankara* sculptures from the 10th century and more inscriptions written in the Tamil-Brahmi script, believed to be about 2000 years old.

Kodaikanal

TIME FROM MADURAI: 3¼HR

Hike to ancient burial sites

Kodaikanal is dotted with megalithic stone structures believed to be ancient burial sites. These structures, called dolmens, pre-date the Iron Age and were built like boxes. A large stone slab rests on top of vertical stones to create a roof, slanted to allow for rainwater runoff. Because the slabs on top of these dolmen circles are about 1m from the ground, historians believe they were used for burials. Jesuit priests first wrote about these dolmens in 1928, warning that the historic structures were being destroyed to make way for roads. Only 60 of them remain today. As some access is on private land and trails are not well-marked, take a guided trek with naturalist Nithan Chandrasekaran of **Xacro Xperiences** *(xacro.in)*.

Go birdwatching

Kodaikanal is one of the best places for birdwatching in Tamil Nadu, home to more than 250 species of birds, some of which can only be found in India's Nilgiri Hills. Look for endemic birds like the Nilgiri wood oigeon, with its blue-grey head and hints of purple among its feathers, the tiny long-tailed Nilgiri flycatcher, or the Banasura laughingthrush, which looks almost like it's wearing a tiny black eye mask. Migratory birds, including brown fish owls and Eurasian wrynecks, also pass through this area. The Tamil Nadu Forest Department offers a four -hour birdwatching trek *(trektamilnadu.com; ₹999)* from the **Kodaikanal Solar Observatory** to the Gundar Zero Point.

Chettinadu

TIME FROM MADURAI: 2HR

Experience Chettinad hospitality

Feel like a Chettiar if only for a night when checking into one of the opulent mansions that have been transformed into some of the best heritage hotels in Tamil Nadu. At **Visalam** (p983; *cghearth.com)*, in **Kanadukathan**, the welcome ritual includes a lamp ceremony and small gifts of bracelets for women and shawls or dhotis for men. The hotel has just 15 rooms, each of them furnished with antiques, local textiles and traditional artwork. The on-site restaurant serves breakfast, lunch and dinner, sometimes overlooking the property's idyllic pool. Some hotels are just places to stay. This hotel offers a window into a lifestyle of yesteryear, a time when wealthy merchant families lived in sprawling mansions with extended

WHY I LOVE KODAIKANAL

Meena Thiruvengadam, Lonely Planet writer

Kodaikanal is as close as I expect to get to sipping tea while sitting on an actual cloud. Nestled high in the mountains, this scenic hill station is an escape from overwhelm. Getting here is an arduous journey that requires patience and the stomach for a winding drive through the Nilgiri Hills. Expect to lose cellular signals occasionally. It feels almost like nature's way of forcing disconnection to lay a foundation for a digital detox. It's easy to do nothing in this resort town, to settle into a hotel nestled into a granite cliff or sip on a flavourful Nilgiri tea while enjoying the view. I'm convinced this his has to be one of the world's greatest places to relax.

EATING IN KODAIKANAL: OUR PICKS

Sera's Cafe: Sip on lemongrass tea and dine on Maggi noodles while enjoying the views from this mountaintop outdoor cafe. *9am-9pm* ₹

Altaf's Cafe: Feel like you're dining in the clouds at this Middle Eastern restaurant with excellent hummus. *9am-9pm* ₹

Aromas of Kodai: Traditional Indian dishes in an elegant indoor setting that's especially suited for larger groups. *12.30-9pm* ₹₹

La Providence: Traditional Indian cuisine inside a beautiful former monastery. A vintage toy train winds through the restaurant. *7.30am-10pm* ₹₹₹

REVIVING THE TILE INDUSTRY

Local guide **Shivashankar Solamalai** has lived in the Chettinadu region of Tamil Nadu all his life and over the past few years has watched as social media and a construction boom in Bengaluru has revived this region's tile-making industry. 'Before the pandemic, there were only a handful of handmade tile workshops in Chettinadu. Now, there are more than 100. Some people took up tile making as a pandemic hobby. Others got to work preserving Chettiar mansions – many of which used decorative tiles from Japan, the Netherlands and beyond. People continue to use the grand estates as backdrops for YouTube videos and Instagram Reels, helping to drive Chettinadu's tilemaking renaissance.

To see how these tiles are made without firing or electricity, visit Ganapathy Tiles or Athangudi Palace Tiles factories.

family on beautifully manicured estates. Relax on a verandah that doubles as an entertainment room, the only place on the property where you'll find a TV. Learn how to make spicy fish curry during a complimentary Chettinad cooking class or how to create a colourful *kolam*. Or relax with a bicycle ride, spa treatment or walk through the hotel's vegetable garden.

Watch artisans at work

Head to the village of Athangudi, about a 30-minute drive north of Karaikudi, to watch master tile makers at work. Artisans here have been making tiles by hand for centuries. At the **Athangudi Palace Tiles** *(athangudipalacetile.com)* workshop you can watch artisans transform a mix of cement, river sand and natural pigments into works of art like those found in this region's grand mansions. Artisans here began making tiles as a cheaper alternative to repairing imported tiles from Japan, the Netherlands and other far-flung locales. They started by making replicas of those foreign tiles and have since become known for creating their own distinct geometric and floral patterns.

Mahalakshmi Handloom Weaving Centre in Kanadukathan is one of the oldest in the region, where Chettinadu's famous cotton towels and saris are made. Make a quick trip to **Chettinad Sweets** in Kottaiyar to see how some of this region's favourite savoury snacks are made by hand.

Visit Chettiar mansions

You don't have to stay in one of this region's Chettinad mansions to experience their grandeur. Just head to **Athangudi Palace** *(₹120)* or the **VVR House** *(₹100)* in Kanadukathan. These Chettiar mansions have been converted into tourist sites and offer a peek at all the features Nattukottai Chettiars aspired to incorporate into their homes, including egg-plaster walls – which kept interiors cool before air-conditioning – patterned tile floors, intricate Burmese teak carvings, and family photographs. Be sure to look up when you're inside the palace, which is known for its grandeur and floral tiled ceilings.

The Nattukottai Chettiars were a community of well-travelled merchants and traders who built these homes to showcase their wealth and worldliness. Living spaces were built around an open courtyard, and extended families often lived together. VVR House is so large that its back door and front door open to different streets.

EATING IN KARAIKUDI: OUR PICKS

The Bangala: Hotel restaurant with dishes like tamarind crab curry and black-pepper chicken. *12.30-2.30pm & 7.30-9.30pm* ₹₹₹

Annalakshmi Restaurant: A bright restaurant serving up filling thalis and crispy dosas with fresh chutneys on banana leaves. *7.30am-10pm* ₹

Sri Priya Mess: Authentic Chettinad cuisine and efficient service make for the perfect lunch, especially if you're tight on time. *noon-4.30pm* ₹

Karaikudi Garden Biriyani: Come here to eat mutton and chicken biriyanis off banana leaves in a tropical garden. *11am-11pm* ₹

MANIVANNAN T/SHUTTERSTOCK

Athangudi Palace, Chettinadu

Shop for antiques

As trade declined and local fortunes dried up in the aftermath of WWII, many Chettinad mansions were abandoned. Some of the treasures from those homes landed in antique shops in Karaikudi. Head to **Mangalam Arts**, **South Indian Crafts Centre** and **MC Crafters** on Kovil St to shop for furniture, paintings, wood carvings, kitchenware, phonographs and more.

Experience ancient temples

This region is a Hindu temple-hopper's delight. If time is tight, prioritise the **Solai Andavar** and **Sri Vairavar Temples**. The Solai Andavar Temple – known for its collection of terracotta horses – is dedicated to Ayannar, the deity believed to protect rural communities from misfortune. The Sri Vairavar Temple is both an architectural gem and a mystery. Dedicated to Lord Shiva, it's known for its intricate stone sculptures, musical pillars and the water that collects on the floor during rainy seasons. No architect or engineer has been able to find the source of the leak.

A CULINARY LEGACY

While you will find Tamil staples like dosas, *idli* and curd rice here, you'll quickly notice Chettinad cuisine isn't quite the same as in Madurai or Chennai. This fiery twist on Tamil cuisine is known for unique spice blends featuring star anise, cardamom, cinnamon, cloves and dried red chillies. It has been heavily influenced by Burmese food, a reflection of trading ties between the Chettiar community and Myanmar. Chettinad menus offer a mix of vegetarian and non-vegetarian options, often incorporating shallots, garlic, ginger and tomatoes. Some of the most popular dishes are Chettinad chicken, *kuzhi paniyaram* – a fluffy ball made of rice and lentils – and *eral kuzhambu*, a prawn curry.

EATING IN KANADUKATHAN: OUR PICKS

Vaadhyar's House: Authentic Chettinad dishes cooked in wood-fired stoves and served in a charming setting across from The Lotus Hotel. *noon-9pm* ₹₹

Sri Narayana Coffee House: Don't let its name fool you. This full-service restaurant serves veg and non-veg cuisine, including generous thalis. *8am-8pm* ₹

Visalam (p983): Spicy Chettinad dishes served on an expansive verandah. Don't skip the *paniyaram* with mutton curry or *adhirasam*. *7.30am-9.30pm* ₹₹₹

Chettinadu Mansion: Choose from an elaborate multicourse meal or a lighter à la carte lunch at this palatial mansion built in 1902. *11am-3pm & 5-9.30pm* ₹₹

WHERE THE WATERS MEET

Kanyakumari is filled with unforgettable views. Here at **Triveni Sangam**, the greenish tint of the Arabian Sea meets the blueish hues of the Bay of Bengal and the dark water of the Indian Ocean , creating a blueish-green mix that looks like a watercolour painting. At sunrise, it looks as if the sun is rising directly from the water. The landscape becomes even more colorful as hints of pink, orange and gold reflect off the water, creating one of the most interesting photo spots in Tamil Nadu.

VIEW360INDIA/SHUTTERSTOCK

Vivekananda Rock Memorial , Kanyakumari

Kanyakumari

TIME FROM MADURAI: **4HR**

Pay homage to Swami Vivekananda

Hinduism and Vedanta yoga began their spread to the West from an island a short ferry ride away from the coast. A few days of meditation here in December 1892 drove Swami Vivekananda to begin preaching about Hinduism and Vedanta yoga in the United States. The **Vivekananda Rock Memorial** *(₹20)*, a short ferry ride from Kanyakumari *(₹50 return, ₹200 to skip the line)*, recounts the story and honours Vivekananda's efforts. Spend some time in the meditation hall before strolling across the glass bridge connecting to a neighbouring island that's home to a 40m-high statue honouring the Tamil poet **Thiruvalluvar**.

Honour a virgin goddess

The **Kumari Amman Temple** is the southernmost Hindu temple in India. It has stood here for more than 3000 years and is considered one of the holiest places on Earth. The temple is the home of the virgin goddess Devi Kanya Kumari, also known as Bhagavathi Amman. Visit during the **Vaisakhi festival** in May to watch elaborate processions featuring the idol of goddess Kumari.

EATING IN KANYAKUMARI: OUR PICKS

Taj Hotel: Straightforward Tamil restaurant in a casual eatery unrelated to the luxury hotel brand. Ideal for a quick meal. *7am-10pm* ₹

Ocean Restaurant: Upscale hotel restaurant with a broad international menu and a Bay of Bengal view. *6am-11pm* ₹₹

Zam Zam Restaurant: Soups, salads and sizzlers with a particularly extensive non-veg menu. Try the creamy *malai* chicken sizzler. *11am-11pm* ₹₹

The Curry: Elegant hotel restaurant with a stylish buffet and à la carte dining inside the Gopinivas Grand hotel. *7am-10pm* ₹₹

Ooty (Udhagamandalam)

BOTANICAL GARDENS | STUNNING VIEWS | INDIGENOUS COMMUNITIES

Long before it became a summer outpost for the British, Ooty was – and still is – home to Indigenous tribes, including the Toda people, who were among the earliest inhabitants of this mountainous region. This community of farmers and herders has been in the Nilgiri Hills for an estimated 2000 years and continues to live in small villages outside of the town nicknamed the 'Queen of Hill Stations'. The nearest Toda village is about 15km from the town centre.

The East India Company arrived in Ooty in the 18th century, building bungalows to help officials escape the oppressive summer heat in Madras. Like other hill stations developed by the British, Ooty is built around an idyllic, albeit human-made, lake where boating, scenic walks and horseback riding are popular activities. Ooty, the birthplace of the table game snooker, is known for its horticultural prowess, and its vast gardens are among its most frequented sights.

GETTING AROUND

A taxi or hired car (from ₹1500) is the best way to get around Ooty. Autorickshaws are a convenient option for short rides around the town centre. Check the board at the auto stands for rates to key destinations. The Nilgiri Mountain Railway (p978) is the most nostalgic way to arrive in Ooty, but tickets are limited. Public buses are plentiful and are the most affordable option for travel in this area.

Origins of Ooty

Discover Ooty's Indigenous history

While Toda villages typically aren't open to independent tourists, visitors can get an introduction to the culture of the Toda people at the **Government Museum** *(free; closed Fri)* in Ooty, with artefacts from the dozen or so tribes that have called this area home. Delve into Nilgiri tribal culture through exhibits on clothing styles, traditional homes, jewellery and farming tools. Ceremonial items and buffalo skulls are among the items on display. Take a minute to examine its exterior facade – this is Stone House, the first bungalow built in Ooty in 1822.

A **Tribal Research Centre** *(nilgiris.nic.in/tourist-place/tribal-museum; ₹100)*, home to a collection of tribal artefacts from the Todas, Paniyas, Kurumbas and others, is located about 10km from Ooty. The only way to visit a Toda village is by hiring a local Toda guide, typically from Pykara falls.

TOP TIP

Dress in layers when travelling to Ooty. Even in summer, temperatures can fall as low as 12°C in the evenings. Daytime temperatures rise as high as 25°C during summer. A light jacket is required year-round. There are several roadside stands along the way to Ooty selling sweatshirts, jackets, hats and gloves.

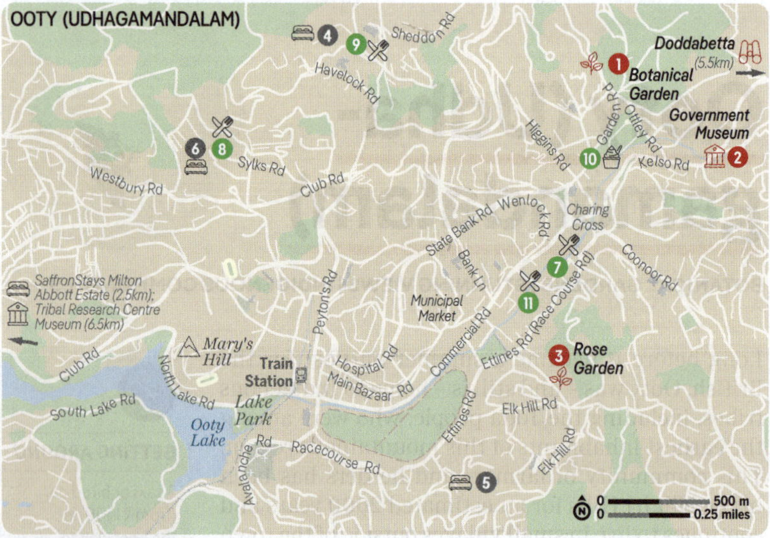

HIGHLIGHTS
1 Botanical Garden
2 Government Museum
3 Rose Garden

SLEEPING
4 King's Cliff
5 Marli Hill Bungalow Ooty
6 Savoy

EATING
7 Adyar Ananda Bhavan
8 Dining Room
9 Earl's Secret
10 Moddy's
11 Willy's Coffee Pub

TAMIL TEA

India is one of the largest tea producers – and tea drinkers – in the world. Only China produces more tea than India. Over 70% of the tea grown in India is consumed in India. The British East India Company began large-scale tea production in Assam in the 1820s. By the 1840s, it had brought Chinese tea seeds to the Nilgiri Hills of South India where abundant rainfall allowed for year-round tea harvesting. These hills are the heart of Tamil Nadu's tea sector and anchored by large tea plantations. The tea grown here is known for its delicate floral notes, bright aromas and distinctive flavours, a reflection of the region's climate and high altitude.

A Floral Paradise

Explore Ooty's botanical diversity

Ooty's top sight is its sprawling **Botanical Garden** *(₹100)*, established in 1948. These carefully manicured grounds are home to over 300 species of plants from around the world, including towering maple trees, delicate ferns and bonsai plants. There's a fossilised tree trunk in the centre of the garden that's estimated to be 20 million years old. Look for the map of the Indian Union that's made of plants and the Italian Garden, which was created by Italian prisoners of war during WWI. The garden's flowers are especially popular, and a summer flower show draws an estimated 150,000 visitors each year.

Ooty's tropical mountain climate makes it ideal for growing roses, and the city's **Rose Garden** *(₹100)* is among the largest in India. It's home to more than 20,000 varieties of roses, including miniature roses, hybrid tea roses and exceptionally rare black and green roses. Visit during the **Ooty Summer Festival** in May when the city's flower and produce crops are at their most abundant.

ALBIN RAJ/SHUTTERSTOCK

Botanical Garden

Top of the Nilgiris

Take in Ooty's best view

Head 7km from Ooty to ascend **Doddabetta**, the highest peak in the Nilgiri Hills. This is one of the best places to take in the views on a clear day. Visit early in the morning to beat the crowds and enjoy panoramic views without the mist that often blankets this area. Hire a taxi from Charing Cross (₹1000 round trip) or take a bus, which will drop you at Doddabetta Junction. From there, it's a steep 3km hike to the top or take a jeep for about ₹200.

CHOCOLATE TOWN

Ooty's subtropical highland climate isn't just great for roses. It's great for chocolate. The cool, temperate environment in this part of the Nilgiri Hills is ideal for growing cocoa. Local chocolatiers have been combining cocoa with spices, nuts and fruits for decades, satisfying sweet tooths all over southern India. The British are believed to have begun this region's love affair with chocolate. Cadbury, the British chocolatemaker, stoked it with investments in cocoa farms so much that some South Indians call cocoa trees Cadbury trees. Ooty's chocolatiers tend to use 40% cocoa solids, creating a richer, more intense flavour than American milk chocolates. Try Ooty's handmade preservative-free chocolate at **Moddy's**, which has been making chocolates in Ooty since 1951.

EATING IN OOTY: OUR PICKS

Willy's Coffee Pub: Quiet cafe with a lending library and extensive menu of coffee, tea, toasties, pizzas and pastries. *10am-9.30pm* ₹

Adyar Ananda Bhavan: Head to this South Indian chain to satisfy your *idli* and dosa cravings without queues. *7.30am-3.30pm & 6-10.30pm* ₹₹

Dining Room: Contemporary Indian, pan-Asian and European cuisine at the Savoy, one of Ooty's oldest hotels. *7.30-10.30am, 12.30-3pm & 7.30-10.30pm* ₹₹₹

Earl's Secret: Perched above Ooty in a 19th-century British manor, this is as much about the views as for its North Indian food. *8-10am, noon-3pm & 7-10pm* ₹₹₹

DETHAN PUNALUR/GETTY IMAGES

TOP EXPERIENCE

Nilgiri Mountain Railway

Before this railway opened in 1899, it took two weeks to travel the 45.8km between Mettapalayam and Ooty. Now, the nostalgic journey takes around five hours. Pulled by a steam engine, classic rail cars – some 80 years old – wind through a scenic stretch of the Western Ghats on Tamil Nadu's most beloved train ride.

DON'T MISS

- Terraced tea plantations
- Eucalyptus forests
- Wellington Bridge
- Ooty train station
- Coonoor train station
- Lovedale train station

The Route

The Nilgiri Mountain Railway weaves through the mountains between Ooty and Mettapalayam, though you can choose to ride a portion of the route, either between Ooty and Coonoor or Coonoor and Mettapalayam – the most scenic stretch. This is where it's easiest to understand what makes this engineering innovation so special.

PRACTICALITIES

● irctctourism.com/gallery/nilgiri.html ● Ooty to Coonoor ₹80-290, Ooty to Mettapalayam ₹175 ● depart Ooty at 9.15am, 12.15pm, 2pm & 5.30pm, depart Mettapalayam at 7.10am

Built by the British, the Nilgiri Mountain Railway is Asia's steepest and India's only cog railway. It uses the Abt rack-and-pinion system, developed by Swiss engineer Carl Roman Abt, to climb a 2203m – too steep for conventional railroad construction methods. The complete journey takes riders across 250 bridges and takes almost five hours uphill and four hours downhill.

A Beloved Toy Train

Boarding the Nilgiri Mountain Railway feels like travelling back in time. Steam engines pull a handful of blue-and-yellow vintage train coaches in and out of grand colonial-era train stations as the sounds of chugs and whistles fill the air. The train has a maximum speed of 30km but is capped at 13km per hour during the ascent from Kallar to Coonoor.

The Nilgiri Mountain Railway is nicknamed the 'Ooty Toy Train' because of its size – the miniature steam engines and carriages look like toys barrelling down the narrow-gauge railroad track. Tickets for these adorable trains can sell out months in advance.

A handful of trains run between Ooty and Coonoor each day, but on most days there's only one departure a day between Ooty to Mettapalayam. A second train runs from Ooty to Mettapalayam on Friday and from Mettapalayam to Ooty on Sunday.

This UNESCO World Heritage–listed experience is more than just a train ride. It has been a lifeline connecting remote hill stations to facilitate trade and tourism. In the process, it's driven the development of these small mountain communities.

Tickets for Spontaneous Travellers

It's not impossible to get a ticket for last-minute travel on the Nilgiri Mountain Railway, but it will take effort. There are around 50 seats per train available for travellers booking same-day travel between Ooty and Coonoor or Coonoor and Ooty, and 15 seats for last-minute travel each way between Ooty to Mettapalayam. You can buy up to four tickets per person between Ooty and Coonoor and two per person between Ooty and Mettapalayam.

Travellers need to wait in line in person at their departure station to claim these seats. Sales open about an hour before departure, but getting in line at least an hour before sales open offers the best chances at securing a seat.

A POP CULTURE ICON

The Nilgiri Mountain Railway is no stranger to the big screen. See the Shah Rukh Khan dance on the top of the iconic train in the 1998 Bollywood movie *Dil Se*. The Nilgiri Mountain Railway also makes an appearance in *Barfi!*, a 2012 movie starring Priyanka Chopra and Ranbir Kapoor. The train's locomotive is also the inspiration for Ashima in the British animated series *Thomas & Friends*.

TOP TIPS

- Purchase tickets online *(irctc.co.in)* a few months in advance, especially if you plan to experience the entire route.
- Choose a seat on the right side of the train when travelling from Mettapalayam to Ooty and on the left side of the train when travelling in the reverse direction.
- Travel light as space for luggage can be tight.

Beyond Ooty

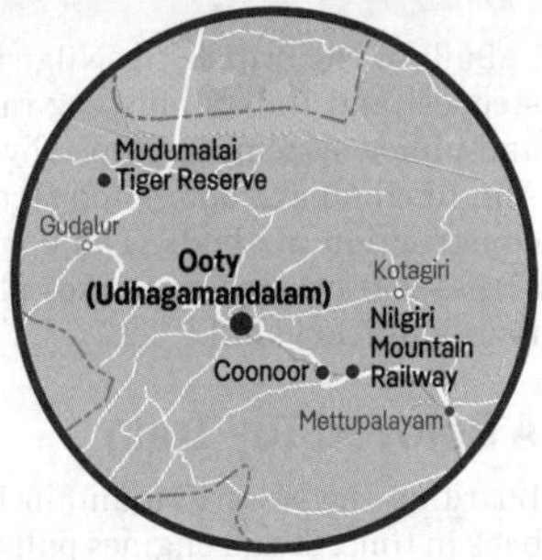

The Nilgiris' serene scene: rolling tea plantations, colonial-era bungalows and the impeccable beauty of Tamil Nadu's Western Ghats.

GETTING AROUND

Drive from Coonoor to Ooty in about an hour or take the scenic Nilgiri Mountain Railway (p978). Train fares start at ₹80, but availability is extremely limited. It's an hour's drive between Ooty and Kotagiri. Buses run from Ooty to Coonoor and from Ooty to Kotagiri but can be crowded. Expect to pay around ₹2000 for a long-distance taxi in this area. The Kerala border is around two hours' drive from Ooty and Mysuru (Mysore) is 3½ hours away.

Nestled into the Western Ghats, Ooty is surrounded by lush greenery, rich history, ample lakes and seemingly endless tea estates. There's a Toda village 3km north and a tiger reserve a few hours' drive away. A tea destination on par with Darjeeling, Coonoor is about an hour southwest of Ooty. Take the Nilgiri Mountain Railway for the most scenic journey. The railway cuts through colourful mountain towns, stopping at elegant colonial-era train stations and passing countless tea plantations. For a true nature escape, make the one-hour drive to Kotagiri for waterfalls, views and *shola* forests. Whatever you do, don't let the distance fool you. With sharp, hairpin turns, single-lane roadways and traffic jams, journeys are almost always longer than expected.

Coonoor

TIME FROM OOTY: **50MIN** (car) **/70MIN** (train)

Enjoy Coonoor's best views

Like Ooty, Kodaikanal and Kotagiri, Coonoor is a town filled with breathtaking views. Take in views of sprawling tea and coffee plantations over a picnic at **Lamb's Rock**, a viewpoint 6km east of town. Marvel at **Catherine Falls** from **Dolphin's Nose**, a viewpoint 10km west of Coonoor that's named for its unique shape. If you're on the lookout for birds, bring a pair of binoculars.

Ultimate nature walk

Established in 1874, **Sim's Park** *(₹30; 7.30am-6.30pm)*, named after British colonial official JD Sim, is a living museum that showcases a century of plant cultivation in the Nilgiris. Due to a steady distribution of rainfall throughout the year and steady temperatures, the region has an exceptionally long flowering season. Meandering paths wind through fields of flowers, rows of *shola* trees and a glass greenhouse. This 12-hectare garden is home to more than 1000 species of plants and trees from around the world, including rarities like the Rudraksh bead tree, whose seeds are revered in Hinduism. Called the tears of Shiva, these beads are used for chanting and meditation. A fruit and vegetable show is held in May.

TOP EXPERIENCE

Mudumalai Tiger Reserve

There's more to Mudumalai Tiger Reserve than tigers. One of India's earliest wildlife preservation efforts, this park is also home to elephants, bison, deer and birds. Book a safari through the Forest Department – tiger sightings are not guaranteed but they do happen. Take a taxi from Ooty (₹2500) to enjoy the spectacular scenery and 36 hairpin bends along the Sighur Ghat road.

Indian elephant

An Unforgettable Safari Experience

Begin your journey into the wilds of Mudumalai at the visitor centre where you board minibuses, open-top Gypsy vehicles and SUVs for an hour-long off-road drive through this sprawling park in the eastern hills of the Western Ghats. The reserve is home to just over 100 Bengal tigers.

Sightings of tigers are rare but elephants and sambar deer are virtually guaranteed. An estimated 500 to 1000 elephants live in this area, including 28 who make their home at the nearby **Theppakadu Elephant Camp**, also operated by the Forest Department. Theppakadu has been caring for elephants here since 1910. Guests can visit the camp *(₹300)* from 8.30am to 9am and 5.30pm to 6pm to watch caretakers feed their giant charges.

Wild elephants meander through the park, which is part of a major elephant corridor, in herds as large as 22. Leopards – including the rare black leopard – also live in the area.

The best time to visit is between October and February. Tours are also available through private tour operators, though their off-road access is restricted.

TOP TIPS

- Book an early-morning safari to increase your chances of spotting animals.
- Sit near the river across the street from the safari meeting point to watch elephants bathe from 7.30am to 8.30am and 3.30pm to 4.30pm.
- Wear earth-toned clothing to minimise disturbances to wildlife, and bring a reusable water bottle.

PRACTICALITIES

- mudumalaitigerreserve.com
- ₹2500 for a shared bus safari through the Forest Department, from ₹4600 for a private vehicle
- safaris 6.30-10am & 2-5pm

Places We Love to Stay

₹ Budget ₹₹ Midrange ₹₹₹ Top End

Chennai

Map p948

Friendlystay Homestay ₹ A welcoming homestay with simple, straightforward rooms in a quiet neighbourhood near the airport.

Hotel Ranjith ₹₹ Modern decor and quality food in a contemporary hotel in Nungambakkam near shopping and nightlife.

Taj Connemara ₹₹₹ Chennai's oldest hotel blends old-world charm with modern luxury near shopping and the Government Museum.

Leela Palace ₹₹₹ Staying at this historic hotel near the coast is a cultural experience complete with live music, expansive buffets and local art.

Park Hyatt ₹₹₹ This Western-style luxury hotel blends top-notch service and premium amenities to create one of the most comfortable stays in the city.

Kovalam

Surf Turf (p954) **₹** Affordable beachside property with comfortable rooms and a relaxed vibe.

Taj – Fisherman's Cove ₹₹₹ A luxurious resort at the edge of the Bay of Bengal, featuring well-appointed rooms, a private beach and seaside dining with a menu filled with fresh seafood.

Mahabalipuram

Grande Bay Resort ₹₹ A colourful resort with stylish rooms, a private beach and a pool with a lifeguard.

Welcomhotel By ITC Hotels, Kences Palm Beach ₹₹ Spacious accommodation and an outdoor pool overlooking the Bay of Bengal at this family-friendly resort.

Intercontinental Resort ₹₹₹ Stylish beachfront resort offering plush rooms with sunken tubs, a luxurious Ayurvedic spa, a beach bar and multiple dining options.

Radisson Blu Resort ₹₹₹ A waterfront luxury resort with panoramic sea views and one of India's longest swimming pools (220m).

Puducherry (Pondicherry)

Map p958

De Fleur Hotel ₹₹ A mid-price hotel in White Town with clean, comfortable rooms, an all-day restaurant and rooftop bar.

La Villa ₹₹ A stunning six-room boutique hotel with contemporary rooms and curved wooden beds. Don't miss the rooftop pool or the outdoor restaurant.

Gratitude Heritage ₹₹ An adults-only bed and breakfast with a shaded courtyard in a carefully restored 19th-century home.

Le Dupleix ₹₹ Beautiful hotel blending traditional architecture and modern comfort inside a converted 18th-century townhouse that was once home to the Mayor of Pondicherry.

Maison Perumal ₹₹₹ A heritage hotel from CGH Earth set in a beautifully restored 130-year-old Tamil mansion with exquisite architecture. Dine at the on-site Franco-Tamil restaurant.

Villa Shanti ₹₹₹ Housed in a centuries-old building and revamped by two French architects, this hotel expertly blends contemporary design with traditional Tamil elements. The courtyard restaurant is also popular.

Villa Helena ₹₹₹ A gracefully restored property with elegantly furnished rooms and a charming courtyard cafe.

Palais de Mahé ₹₹₹ A boutique heritage hotel by the eco-friendly proprietor CGH Earth. Rooms are spacious and there's a courtyard pool and rooftop restaurant.

Thanjavur (Tanjore)

Sangam Hotel ₹₹ Straightforward hotel near the city's main sights ,with efficient rooms, a pool and a South Indian restaurant.

Svatma ₹₹₹ A stylish heritage hotel blending traditional Tamil architecture, vintage Indian furniture and modern comfort in a 150-year-old building with a pool.

Chettinadu

Chidambara Vilas ₹₹ Intricately carved woodwork, stained-glass windows and custom tile work combine to form a luxurious heritage hotel that's also an architectural delight. The on-site restaurant is known for its Chettiar-style lunches served on banana leaves.

The Bangala (p972) **₹₹₹** Chettinadu's first heritage hotel in Karaikkudi, known for its sumptuous banana-leaf feasts, refreshing pool and charming verandahs.

Visalam ₹₹₹ This ecofriendly luxury hotel in Kanadukathan has a large swimming pool and spacious rooms filled with vintage furniture. Don't miss the coffee cart.

Chettinadu Mansion (p973) ₹₹₹ Experience grandeur at this heritage hotel located inside a centuries-old 126-room mansion in Kanadukathan. The family of the home's original owner still runs the hotel and lives on the property.

Madurai

Map p967

Gopuram Grand ₹₹ A glamorous new hotel with plush rooms and a vegetarian restaurant walking distance from the Meenakshi Amman Temple.

Heritage Madurai ₹₹₹ Luxury hotel designed by renowned architect Geoffrey Bawa. Some rooms are styled as 'villas' with private plunge pools.

Gateway Hotel Pasumalai ₹₹₹ This hilltop Taj hotel is a peaceful retreat with resident peacocks and panoramic views.

Courtyard by Marriott Madurai ₹₹₹ A reliable chain with modern rooms and a pool.

Kodaikanal

Tomorrowland Farms & Suites ₹₹ A collection of cabins and glamping domes located high in the mountains a 15-minute drive from town. There's a restaurant serving vegetarian and non-vegetarian cuisine on-site.

The Tamara Kodai ₹₹₹ A luxurious hilltop escape with outdoor dining, a swimming pool and a restaurant located inside a former monastery.

Kanyakumari

Hotel Sivamurugan ₹ A clean, well-located hotel with fixed prices year-round. Upgraded rooms offer air-conditioning and sea views.

Sparsa Resort ₹₹ A stylish resort across from the beach. Offers sea views, a restaurant, a huge pool, a spa and a gym.

Ooty (Udhagamandalam)

Map p976

SaffronStays Milton Abbott Estate ₹₹ Surrounded by forest, this serene four-bedroom bungalow features airy rooms and access to hiking trails. The outdoor lawn fireplace is perfect for chilly nights.

King's Cliff ₹₹ Perched atop the hills, this historic mansion-turned-charming heritage hotel boasts enviable views of the misty Ooty hillside. Don't miss a cosy fireside dinner of North Indian specialties at Earl's Secret.

Marli Hill Bungalow Ooty ₹₹₹ Quaint six-bedroom heritage B&B that blends luxury with history, offering personalised service and an intimate experience in the heart of Ooty's charming landscape.

Savoy, IHCL SeleQtions ₹₹₹ Ooty's oldest heritage hotel dates back to 1829. Choose from chic cottages facing the well-manicured gardens. The on-site restaurant serves delicious local Badaga dishes.

Maison Meraki ₹₹ A stylish boutique hotel with modern, elegant rooms located next door to the Savoy.

Coonoor & Around

YWCA Wyoming Guesthouse ₹ A budget-friendly guesthouse in a centuries-old building offering simple, clean rooms with nice views.

Ibex Stays and Trails ₹₹ This 113-year-old bungalow offers cosy rooms with breathtaking mountain views, and is especially popular among trekkers. There's another Ibex property on the road to Kotagiri.

Gateway ₹₹₹ A Luxurious Taj-group heritage hotel with evening bonfires in a former monastery set amid lush greenery.

La Maison ₹₹₹ A homestay in a renovated 19th-century Scottish bungalow near Kotagiri. Don't skip a soak in the mountain-facing hot tub.

Rose garden (p976), Ooty

Researched by
Mark Eveleigh

Andaman Islands

IDYLLIC, TROPICAL ADVENTURE

The Andamans (1200km from the mainland) are India's remotest islands, but even if it weren't for the affordable, convenient flights, they'd be well worth the journey.

With the Nicobar Islands officially out of bounds, it's the Andamans that lure visitors with their promise of tropical island adventure. The turquoise reefs and shimmering white beaches are famous, but the densely forested interiors offer an extra jolt of excitement to heighten the sense of adventure. Diving, snorkelling and 'sunset watching' are the main crowd pullers here, but allow extra time for walking and jungle-trekking.

For thousands of years, Indigenous people have lived on the islands, but it's against the law to interact with any of these groups. Travellers can, however, spend time exploring the capital, and are often charmed to find a surprisingly cosmopolitan self-proclaimed 'settler' community. Despite rapid growth, Port Blair (officially renamed as Sri Vijaya Puram in 2024) has managed to retain a delightfully welcoming small-town atmosphere. The murky past of British colonial oppression is still very visible, however, especially on Netaji Subhash Chandra Bose Island (previously Ross Island) and around the Cellular Jail, which was used as a penal colony for 'political' prisoners.

EUGENE GA/SHUTTERSTOCK

These days most visitors hurry though Sri Vijaya Puram (Port Blair) on their way to Swaraj Island (Havelock) and Shaheed Island (Neil). Take time to explore southwards, both on South Andaman and further south still to the remote surf spots on Little Andaman, and you're sure to sink into the sort of chilled island lifestyle where you lose track of the days.

THE MAIN AREAS

SRI VIJAYA PURAM (PORT BLAIR)
Bustling historical capital of the Andamans. p988

SWARAJ ISLAND (HAVELOCK)
Beach-lined, densely forested island paradise. p995

SHAHEED ISLAND (NEIL)
Charming, pint-sized and pleasantly laid-back. p1000

For places to stay in the Andaman Islands, see p1003

PREM SS/SHUTTERSTOCK

Above: Lakshmanpur Beach (p1002), Shaheed Island (Neil);
Left: Kingfisher, Swaraj Island (Havelock; p997)

Find Your Way

Anyone who plans to explore beyond the tourist centres should bear in mind that most of the Andamans' 325 islands (and all the Nicobars) are off-limits to give peace and space to the Indigenous communities who call them home.

AIR

Flying to Veer Savarkar International Airport from one of India's mainland cities is the easiest way to reach the islands. Routes link to Chennai, Delhi, Kolkata (Calcutta), Hyderabad and Mumbai (Bombay) daily.

FERRY

There are three main ferry companies: Nautika *(gonautika.com)* and Makruzz *(makruzz.com)* are best for the 1½-hour voyages to Swaraj and Shaheed Islands, but the more unpredictable eight-hour government ferries are the only way to get to Little Andaman. (Get up-to-date local advice.)

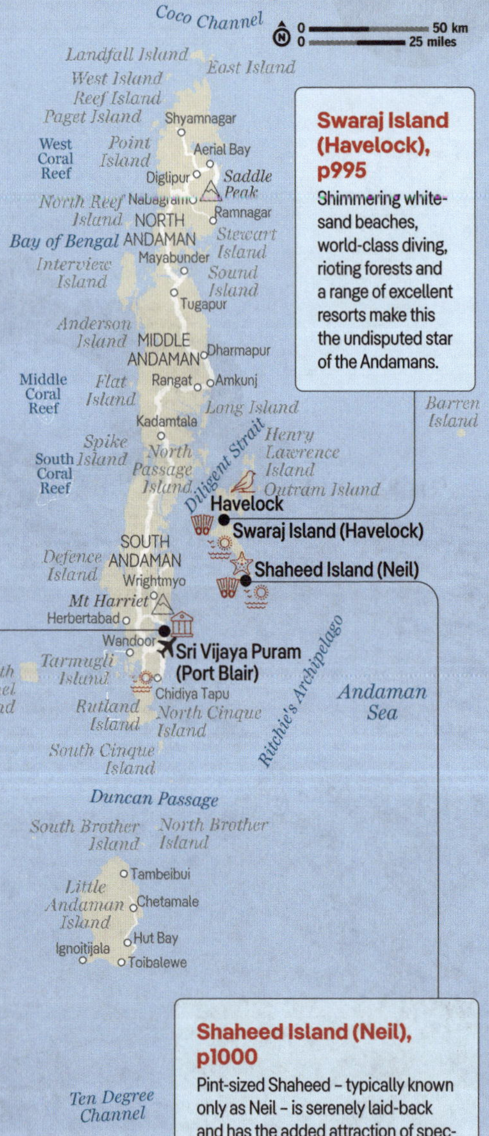

Swaraj Island (Havelock), **p995**

Shimmering white-sand beaches, world-class diving, rioting forests and a range of excellent resorts make this the undisputed star of the Andamans.

Sri Vijaya Puram (Port Blair), **p988**

A vibrant little capital with a rich history to explore, plus excitingly wild waterways and pristine beaches.

Shaheed Island (Neil), **p1000**

Pint-sized Shaheed – typically known only as Neil – is serenely laid-back and has the added attraction of spectacular reefs, frequented by dugong.

DOCTORS PHOTOGRAPHY/SHUTTERSTOCK

Chidiya Tapu (p993)

Plan Your Time

Whether you're in the Andamans for island-hopping, diving or 'surfaris', it is not a place to rush around. Ferries are weather dependent, so go with the flow and try to enjoy a slower pace.

A Long Weekend

- Land in Port Blair in time for the last (2pm) boat trip to **Netaji Subhash Chandra Bose (Ross) Island** (p989). That evening head off on a guided kayaking excursion amid the fairy-light bioluminescence on **Flat Bay** (p991). Next morning hop on a ferry to **Swaraj Island** (p955). Spend two days snorkelling with turtles and exploring the rock pools before sailing back to Port Blair.

Three Weeks

- If adventure is on your mind, spend a few days exploring the coastline south of Port Blair around **Chidiya Tapu** (p993). Spend a few days on **Swaraj Island** (p955) then fully immerse yourself into island life on **Shaheed Island** (p1000). You might find it hard ever to leave, but **Little Andaman** (p994) may entice you with further thoughts of adventure and uncrowded surf spots.

SEASONAL HIGHLIGHTS

SPRING
Ideal temperatures and smaller crowds make this the perfect time to go, particularly for surfers, who head to Little Andaman for the swells.

SUMMER
Around June the monsoon starts in earnest; unreliable ferry connections but uncrowded beaches and cheaper accommodation.

AUTUMN
As monsoon ends (around September) visitors flock back. With jungle trails drying you can start to look forward to long treks.

WINTER
With peak season in full swing, December is a great time to search out post-dive parties, particularly on lively Swaraj Island.

Sri Vijaya Puram (Port Blair)

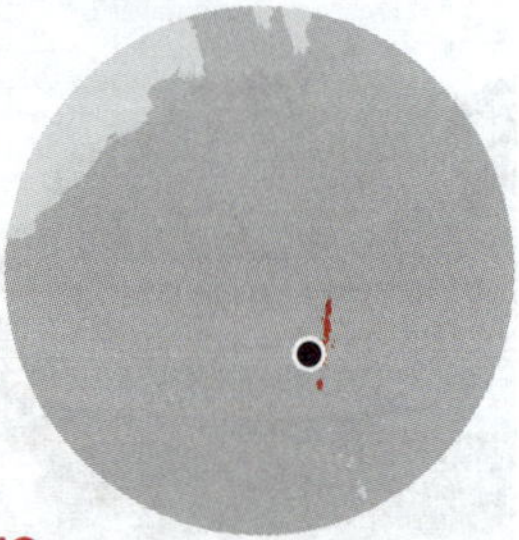

MOVING HISTORY | TRANSPORT HUB | TOP KAYAKING

GETTING AROUND

Autorickshaws are the easiest way to whip around town. Ride-hailing apps don't yet function here so you'll have to haggle – a ride anywhere around the centre shouldn't cost more than ₹200. Taxis from the airport or ferry terminal to the centre will set you back closer to ₹300. **Saro Tours & Travel** *(03192-242027)* is highly recommended for scooter hire (₹500 per day). When heading out to the islands of Swaraj and Shaheed, it's easiest to book ferry tickets with **Nautika** *(gonautika.com)* or **Makruzz** *(makruzz.com)*.

Renamed in 2024 as Sri Vijaya Puram, the Andamans' financial, industrial and transport centre is still holding on to its colonial-era Port Blair moniker. This little state capital of 165,000 inhabitants is so compact that it almost feels wrong to call it a city. As it has the only airport on the islands, most international visitors land here and, all too often, bustle onwards to the ferry terminal for departures to Swaraj Island and Shaheed Island (more commonly known as Havelock Island and Neil Island, respectively).

Most of Port Blair's inhabitants denominate themselves as 'settlers', having arrived here from all over India in the 1970s and 1980s to create what's become a vibrant cosmopolitan community. Visitors who take time to soak up traditional life beyond the bustling little bazaar discover unexpectedly rich history and the spectacular nature of South Andaman. It's surprising how many overlooked gems you can discover almost on the city's doorstep.

The Cellular Jail's Imperial Shadows

India's fight for independence remembered

A national monument and a powerful icon of India's long struggle for independence from the British empire, Port Blair's **Cellular Jail** *(₹100)* draws large numbers of visitors from across the country. A moving place to visit, it should be on the list of every visitor who wants to get under the skin of these islands on India's remotest eastern fringe.

It was cleverly designed as a wheel-shaped complex of cells – not 'dorms', hence apparently the 'cellular' – with a tall watchtower at the centre of seven long, three-storey spokes. Three of these wings remain, with the longest stretching 130m. When it was opened in 1906 this 'Indian Bastille' had 693 cells (or 663, or 698, depending which of the museum's information boards you choose to believe).

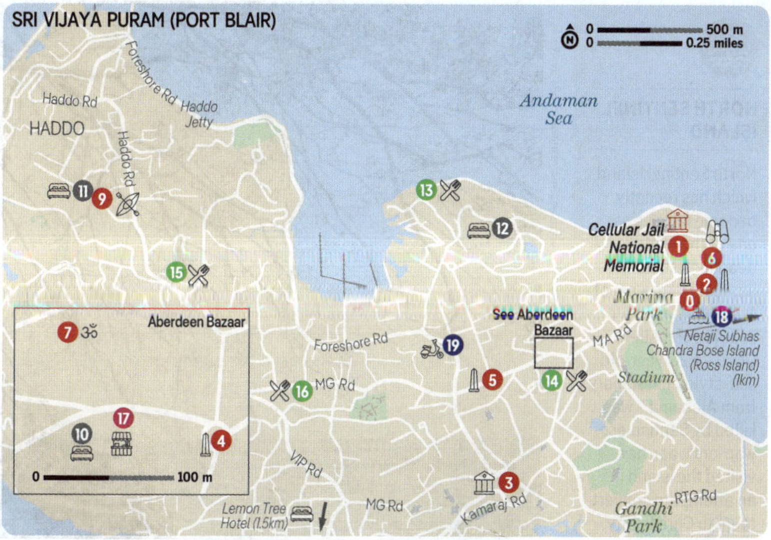

HIGHLIGHTS
1 Cellular Jail National Memorial

SIGHTS
2 Aberdeen Memorial
3 Anthropological Museum
4 Clock Tower
5 Gandhi Statue
6 Marina Viewpoint
7 Shri Ganesha Temple
8 Tsunami Memorial

ACTIVITIES
9 Port Blair Kayaking

SLEEPING
10 Amina Lodge
11 Andaman Homestay
12 SeaShell Port Blair

EATING
13 Amaya
14 Anju Coco Resto
15 Driftwood
16 Mavi Rooftop Lounge

SHOPPING
17 Aberdeen Bazaar

TRANSPORT
18 Aberdeen Jetty
19 Saro Tours & Travels

Notwithstanding the conflicting information, the museum is a fascinating place to learn what life was like for the criminals and political prisoners (freedom fighters). Signs in the well-tended gardens exhort visitors to 'maintain silence as a mark of respect to freedom fighters', but it's such a powerfully evocative place that it can only really be contemplated in silent wandering. There are guides available, however, and (for an added fee) they will explain the intricacies of daily life and the diabolical design of the flogging pillory and the gallows that were rigged to hang three men at a time.

The silence is broken each evening at 6.50pm when the popular **Cellular Jail Sound & Light Show** brings the stories to life in the prison courtyard.

TOP TIP

Only a few of Andaman's Indigenous inhabitants are assimilated into city life. The majority live in the centre of the island along the ATR (Andaman Trunk Road). As it's illegal to visit or communicate with them, relatively few travellers make the arduous and expensive 10-hour journey to the island's northern tip.

A Haunting British Village

Visit the ruins on Ross Island

A 10-minute boat ride (₹470 return) from Aberdeen Jetty, **Netaji Subhash Chandra Bose Island** is as picturesque as it is eerie. Known as Chong-Ekee-Bood in Andaman dialect, it became Ross Island under the British (and most islanders still refer to it as such). The British officers and staff in charge of the Cellular Jail and all the horrors that went on there lived

NORTH SENTINEL ISLAND

North Sentinel Island, which has recently become famous as one of the world's deadliest islands, lies just 50km west of Port Blair city centre. In 2018 John Allen Chau – a 26-year-old self-styled missionary from Alabama – was killed by Sentinelese warriors when he visited the island in an attempt to convert them to Christianity.

As with other traditional communities in the islands, it is illegal (not to mention incredibly foolhardy) to visit here. A major risk lies in the transmission of contagious germs that could easily wipe out an entire tribe. The population of North Sentinel remains unknown, but the right of the islanders to retain their traditional ways is supported by Indian law – to the extent that it proved impossible even to retrieve Chau's body for Christian burial.

SAIKAT_PHOTOGRAPHER/SHUTTERSTOCK

on this island in a beautifully constructed and laid-out community that became known to its 500 or so privileged inhabitants as the Paris of the East.

There were churches, barracks, stores, a printing press, hospital, bakery, library, water-purification plant and three palatial separate clubs (all built, of course, with prisoner labour), one of which was fitted with a sprung teak dance floor. During WWII the clubs, tennis courts and swimming pools became the domain of the Japanese forces and the British themselves had a taste of prison life on the main island.

These days the jungle is reclaiming the site with giant fig trees patiently doing their best to dismantle the sturdy walls. It's an eerie spot to wander but, since the return boat trip only allows for an hour on the island, consider paying for a golf cart driven by knowledgeable guides *(₹450)* to shuttle you to **Ross Island Lighthouse** on the island's northern tip. From there you can easily stroll back in half an hour.

Apart from the rioting vegetation, the wild peacocks and hundreds of resident deer (imported by the hunt-loving British) have become a natural phenomenon of the island and one of its many photogenic aspects.

EATING IN PORT BLAIR: BEST RESTAURANTS

Anju Coco Resto: The service might not be the quickest (or friendliest) but this restaurant has the most extensive menu in Aberdeen Bazaar. *8am-10.30pm* ₹

Driftwood: A lively bar with a terrace serving cold beer and the world's spiciest and tastiest jalapeno pizza. *11am-midnight* ₹₹

Mavi Rooftop Lounge: A cosy terrace vibe for a full meal or what the quirky and eclectic menu describes as 'between the buns' snacks. *4-11.45pm* ₹₹

Amaya: The rooftop restaurant at SeaShell hotel boasts sea views as good as its tiger tandoori prawns – pair with a cocktail. *11am-11pm* ₹₹₹

Netaji Subhash Chandra Bose Island (p989)

Perhaps the World's Best Kayaking Experience

A nocturnal star-trip through blazing bioluminescence

Port Blair is home to one of the world's most exciting kayaking excursions. Professionally and responsibly run by record-breaking local expedition kayaker Tanaz Noble *(@kayakwalla)* and her brother Shiraz, the double-seater kayak excursions at **Port Blair Kayaking** *(andamanhomestay.com; ₹3500)* are open to adults, and children from five years old.

You leave Port Blair around sunset and, after a safety and strategy briefing, paddle out onto the normally serene mangrove-lined inlet known as **Flat Bay**. The real highlight (figuratively and literally) of this experience is a chance to see the magical bioluminescent plankton that's typical of these nutrient-rich waters. The Noble family own a stilted house on Flat Bay and, while the shimmering blue is spectacular even in the moonlit channel, it's an unforgettable once-in-a-lifetime experience to paddle into the almost impenetrable darkness under the house. While you play with what appears to be glittering neon-confetti, Tanaz explains the scientific phenomenon along with some fun anecdotes about this hypnotically beautiful water-bound fairy dust.

No real kayaking experience is necessary on what is less a boating excursion than a stargazing tour that takes in the constellations above you as well as below. As you rock gently on the star-studded water in the open channel, you'll enjoy an in-depth introduction to the stars, learning how they change with the tropical seasons, along with the fascinating nuances of traditional navigation in the northern hemisphere and southern hemisphere.

ANDAMAN TRUNK ROAD TRAVEL RESTRICTIONS

The Andaman Trunk Road (ATR) runs 298km from Port Blair to Diglipur, the main town in North Andaman. International travellers are only permitted to make the journey (of 10 hours or more, depending on rainfall and fluctuating potholes) in a private vehicle and as part of a convoy. There are interesting geological and natural sights in the far north, but the real fascination lies in the Adivasi (tribal) community land that the ATR passes through.

However, it is strictly forbidden for travellers to stop in communities or to have any interaction with the inhabitants of the area. While some (mostly domestic) tourists make the journey, there are worries that it is turning into something akin to a 'human safari', with cameras pointed at the island's traditional inhabitants through car windows. For a more meaningful insight into the islands' traditional communities visit Port Blair's Zonal **Anthropological Museum** *(andaman tourism.org.in; ₹150)*.

PORT BLAIR ON FOOT

Wander among the historic buildings and iconic monuments of the old quarters of Port Blair.

START	END	LENGTH
Aberdeen Clock Tower	Mahatma Gandhi Statue	3km; 1hr

Start at 1 **Aberdeen Clock Tower**, built in 1922 to commemorate British and Indian troops who died in WWI. Head northeast on Rina Rd towards Atlanta Point until you reach 2 **Cellular Jail** (p988). This poignant memorial to the evils of colonial oppression is worth exploring in depth. Walk around the back road to pass the central watchtower and you'll eventually emerge at 3 **Marina Viewpoint** where you'll have your first uninterrupted view of the historic Netaji Subhash Chandra Bose (Ross) Island, where prison staff once lived in sumptuous comfort.

Continue down to the shoreline to reach the 4 **Aberdeen Memorial**, which commemorates the Andamanese inhabitants who died resisting the British in May 1859. The nearby 5 **Tsunami Memorial** is a reminder of the 2004 tsunami that caused so much destruction throughout the region (although Port Blair was largely spared since Ross Island took the brunt of the force). You can take a short detour up 6 **Aberdeen Jetty**, from where boats depart for Ross Island. Then continue up the hill to 7 **Aberdeen Bazaar**, the town centre, with its vibrant storefronts and the colourful 8 **Shri Ganesha Temple**, surrounded by flower stalls stocked with the marigolds that are reputedly the elephant-headed god's favourite. End your walk at the 9 **Mahatma Gandhi Statue**, celebrating the man who did so much to break the yoke of British imperialism.

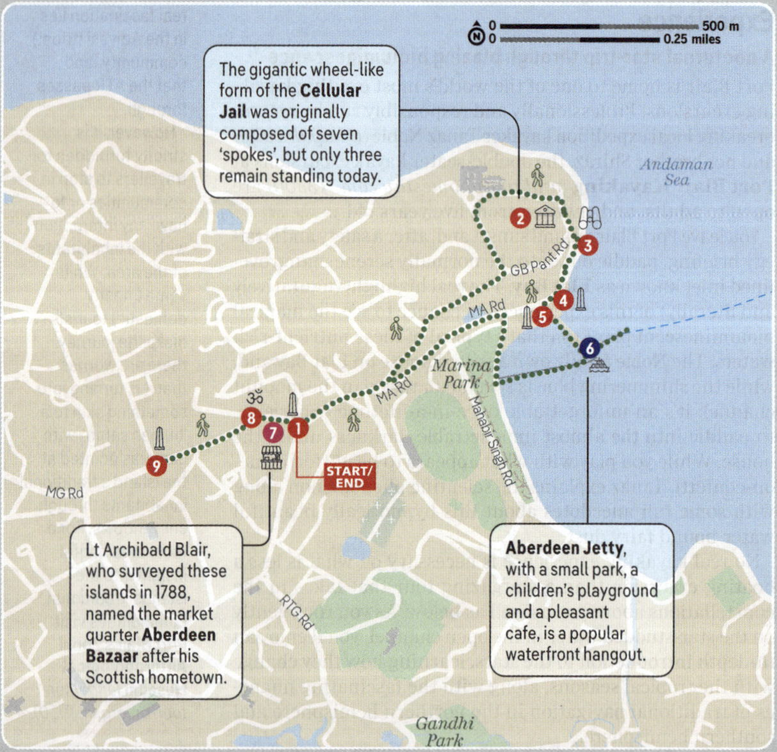

Beyond Port Blair

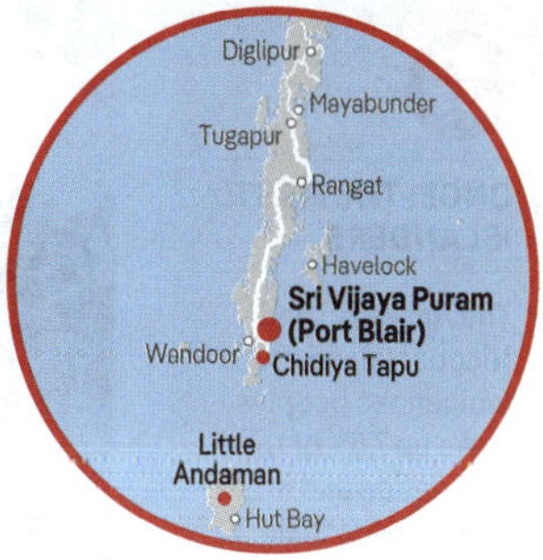

Historic city highlights aside, the rural corners of the Andamans are where the real magic lies.

Most tourists make a beeline for Swaraj Island and/or Shaheed Island, but if time is short, the little coastal community of Chidiya Tapu makes for an idyllic escape in its own right, seemingly overlooked even by the city's inhabitants.

Some visitors head to Diglipur (10 hours drive to the north) to see the turtle nesting grounds on Kalipur Beach or the uninhabited Ross and Smith Islands, but in truth there is more to lure visitors in the south. Eight hours south from Port Blair by ferry, Little Andaman is a sleepy outpost...unless you're here to conquer the Indian Ocean surf. Arranging the ferry ride to Little Andaman is easy enough through the government ferry offices, but departures can be erratic.

Places

Chidiya Tapu p993
Little Andaman p994

Chidiya Tapu

TIME FROM PORT BLAIR: **40MIN**

Peaceful vibes on South Andaman's southern shore

Near the southern tip of South Andaman the tiny hamlet of Chidiya Tapu pulls in the weekend Port Blair crowd for the simple reason that it's one of the region's most idyllic corners. Chidiya Tapu (meaning Bird Hill) is particularly popular with birdwatchers and those searching out vibrant sunsets. It's also renowned among experienced divers who are keen to tackle celebrated dive spots like **Corruption Rock** and a WWII British minesweeper wreck. Unfortunately for them, in recent years the area has become equally famous for its large and active saltwater crocodile population.

You can get to Chidiya Tapu by bus (about an hour from Port Blair) or hire an auto for the return trip (about ₹1600), but a scooter affords ideal flexibility. Our suggestion would be to overnight at Wild Grass Resort (p1003) to enjoy the real charm of this birding area or at least stop for lunch on the resort's lovely terrace.

The potholed coastal lane finally dwindles to a halt at **Munda Pahar Beach**, 2km south of Chidiya Tapu. You'll have to sign in at the ranger office here and will be warned to be vigilant since big crocs are frequently spotted. At the end of the beach a well-maintained track leads through the jungle to the remote lighthouse that stands at the southern end of Andaman's biggest island.

GETTING AROUND

Government ferries can be booked by anyone with a login so your hotel or homestay staff should be able to help you book. No private tour companies as yet serve this route. Local buses run to Chidiya Tapu several times a day, but for more flexibility an autorickshaw driver will charge around ₹1600 (for the return journey and waiting time). For more flexibility still, rent a scooter (about ₹500/day).

If you want to visit northern Andaman you'll need to hire a driver to take you along the ATR and will have to check timing as it is compulsory to travel in convoy.

ONGE: THE FIRST ISLANDERS

The Andaman and Nicobar Islands' Indigenous peoples make up 7.5% of the population and in recent years their numbers have been increasing. The Onge, Sentinelese, Andamanese and Jarawa have a strong resemblance to people from Africa, but anthropologists are at a loss as to how and when they arrived. Tragically, numerous groups have become extinct. Part of Little Andaman Island was taken over by the Forest Department and 'settled' in 1977. The 140 or so remaining members of the Onge people – traditionally hunters – are now dependent on government handouts and some anthropologists report that the reserve (around Dugong Creek and South Bay) has been overrun by poachers. As with all Indigenous communities of the Andaman Islands, it's illegal to visit or communicate with the Onge.

JOHN SEATON CALLAHAN/GETTY IMAGES

Surfing, Little Andaman

Little Andaman

TIME FROM PORT BLAIR: **8HR**

Surf Little Andaman

Little Andaman has a very small tourism scene, which is not surprising given that it's quite a commitment to get there. So if you're after an idyllic, quiet haven to relax in a hammock uninterrupted, this is your place. It does, however, have an under-the-radar, nascent surfing culture for a few months of the year. The surf season tends to run from February to late April when the monsoon rains roll in. Ferry access can be erratic at times (and more so during the October–December cyclone season).

Little Andaman offers the best swell exposure in the archipelago, as it isn't blocked by the Nicobar Islands. While the waves can sometimes be challenging, there are also sheltered bays and beaches that are suited to learners. Ferries dock in **Hut Bay**, which is dotted with small homestays, most of which have surfboards (long, short and bodyboards) to rent.

Kumari Point in the far southwest is renowned as a 'wave magnet' but can be hard to access, while **Jackson Creek** (predominantly a left-hand reef break) and **Tochangeou** (lefts and rights) get consistent swell. It's a very low-key surf scene for a couple of very good reasons – surfers want to keep it that way and the local government does too, probably due to the ever-lingering possibility of crocodiles appearing. There's a large and growing population of crocs on the island (see p1001). For once the words 'here be dragons' hold more than a hint of truth.

If you're up for braving it though, a Little Andaman surfari is an adventure into one of the lesser-known frontiers of the surfing atlas.

Swaraj Island (Havelock)

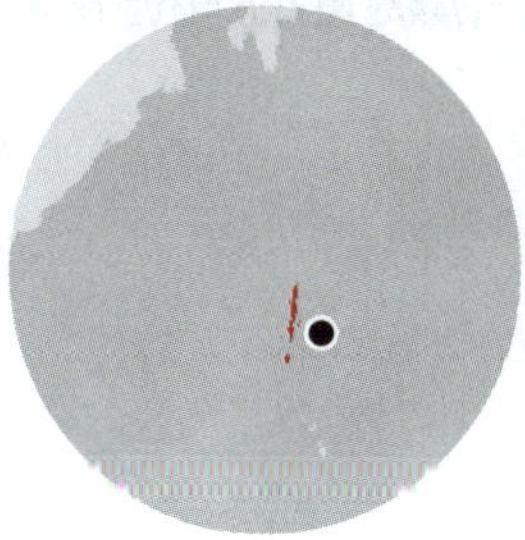

PALM-LINED BEACHES | SEA LIFE | RELAXATION

Swaraj Island (named for a Hindi word meaning 'independence') is indisputably the Andamans' headline destination. With sweeping white-sand beaches, thick tropical forests, rare flora and fauna, and appealing resorts, the island that was known as Havelock until 2018 lives up to its paradise-island reputation.

Even as the number of tourists (especially domestic) increases, the island still maintains an undeveloped and laid-back vibe. It's easy to avoid the tour-group crowds and find your own quiet patch of paradise. Swaraj is the sort of place you might settle into for a long weekend and still find yourself chilling there two weeks later.

Swaraj is primarily famous for its spectacular marine life thanks to Jacques Cousteau, and a handful of reputable dive centres have been operating here for decades, along with a few newer arrivals. Nature thrives on land too, and guided rock-pooling walks, birdwatching and nature walks are major drawcards.

GETTING AROUND

From the ferry terminal either arrange transport through your accommodation or expect to pay around ₹300/200 for a taxi/auto. Local buses leave from the ferry jetty every 40 minutes, charging ₹30 for a ride anywhere. There's really only one main road on Swaraj and with very little traffic most visitors opt for the flexibility that comes with a rented scooter (from ₹500 a day). It's easiest to arrange this through your homestay/resort.

Underwater Adventures

Diving-central at any skill level

Since the godfather of scuba diving Jacques Cousteau focused on the wonders of the Andaman deeps in a TV program called *Invisible Islands* in 1989, Swaraj Island has been a bucket-list destination for international divers. While here, Cousteau discovered dive sites populated by pelagic fish like tuna, barracuda and marbled stingray and (now world-famous) **Minerva Ledge**. The ledge is too large to take in on one dive, so knowledgeable guides will usually suggest one of several locations, depending on your preference for coral gardens, steep walls or dramatic gorges. The currents at this site allow for drift diving, if you're an advanced diver.

There are now around 50 dive centres on the island. It's important you select a top-quality dive centre that is a PADI or SSI member so that they follow responsible diving protocol and work effectively to protect marine ecology. Many of these

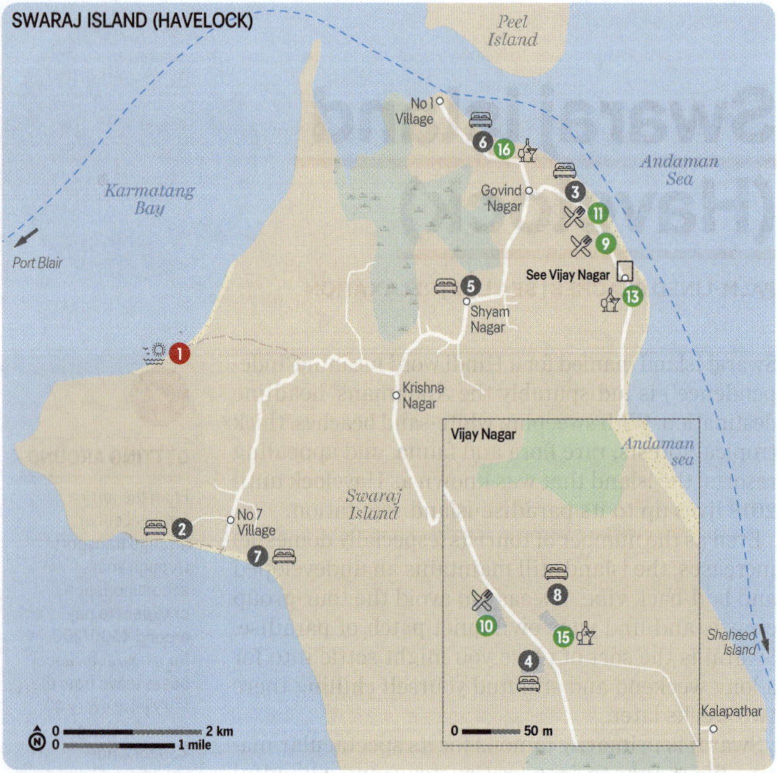

SIGHTS
1 Elephant Beach

SLEEPING
2 Barefoot at Havelock
3 Barefoot Scuba
4 Havelock Farms Resort
5 Matsya Island Retreat
6 SeaShell Havelock
7 Taj Exotica
8 Wild Orchid

EATING
9 Anju Coco Resto
10 Famous Seafood Restaurant
11 Full Moon Cafe
see 2 The Swimming Elephant

DRINKING & NIGHTLIFE
13 5th Bistro Cafe and Bar
see 6 High Tide
15 Narra
16 Something Different

TOP TIP

Saltwater crocodiles live along the Swaraj waterfront, especially near river-mouths. While you're unlikely to see one (it's been over a decade since the last fatal incident), do ask locals before swimming or kayaking, and heed their advice.

centres offer everything from introductory dives for absolute novices to lengthier courses in specialisations like night diving and dive-master.

Whatever your level, an important thing to consider is your sunscreen: buy environmentally sound, biodegradable sunscreen before your trip – it's hard to come by here and as diving becomes increasingly popular this toxic substance is wreaking havoc on the reefs.

Rare Birds Galore

Best birdwatching ever? Probably

Whether you're an experienced birdwatcher looking to tick once-in-a-lifetime sightings or a novice who appreciates a colourful flutter, Swaraj Island is a great spot to embrace your inner twitcher. Almost 300 species live on the island, including 19 that are endemic. As it's such a peaceful and relatively undeveloped region, you'll see colourful plumage whizzing by wherever you turn. To learn more about these winged wonders, join one of the excellent birdwatching tours run by a handful of resorts (see p1003): Barefoot at Havelock, Matsya and Taj Exotica.

Barefoot at Havelock is set in 10 hectares of forest abutting the unspoiled **Radhanagar Beach**, and since more than half the resort's land has been replanted and preserved with indigenous forest three decades ago, the area offers ideal forest and shoreline habitat for most of the island's avian species. Whether you join the sunrise or sunset birding tours you have a great chance of seeing white-throated and collared kingfishers, chestnut-headed bee-eaters and white-bellied sea eagles. There are five species of noisy parakeets here, along with the bizarre hanging parrot. Andaman serpent eagles, green imperial pigeons, Andaman wood pigeons and shy Andaman crakes are harder to spot.

Nor is it only about birds; a knowledgeable and enthusiastic guide will also be sure to point out other wildlife, such as the territorial Andaman Bay lizards that seem to defend every trunk, and flora, including some of the eight endemic orchid species. Nocturnal bird-watching tours can reveal Andaman scops owls, oriental scops owls, Andaman boobooks and Hume's boobooks, to name just a few of the iconic nocturnal species.

Get Your Feet Wet in Swaraj's Rock Pools

Guided intertidal walks with a difference

Rock pools are ever changing habitats, but naturalist and wildlife photographer Prathamesh B Khedwan has explored one section of the Blue Flag Radhanagar Beach so tirelessly and minutely that he knows it better than his own backyard. Departures from the Barefoot at Havelock resort for his rock-pool tours *(barefoot-andaman.com; ₹2000)* are dictated by the tides. Dawn is a gorgeous time to be in what naturalists refer to as the 'intertidal zone', but evening rock-pool walks

DIVING WITH DUGONGS

Tanya Deborah Abraham is a marine biologist and certified AOW scuba diver. *@tany_deborah*

Swaraj Dweep and Shaheed Dweep (Havelock and Neil Islands) stand out as rare places on our planet where the dugong can still be observed in the wild. A gentle and slow-moving marine mammal, it's also known as the sea cow and is sometimes confused with the manatee (a distinct species found in Africa and the Americas).

Recognised for its ecological importance, the dugong holds the distinction of being the state animal of the Andaman and Nicobar Islands, serving as a living emblem of the region's exceptional marine biodiversity and of the state's continuing efforts towards marine protection.

EATING ON SWARAJ ISLAND: BEST DINING

Famous Seafood Restaurant: Easily overlooked (but for the crowds) this roadside eatery serves the best-value prawn curries and lobster. *7am-11pm* ₹

Full Moon Cafe: Laid-back beachside vibe and an extensive library so you can grab a book after lunch. A wide variety of local and international dishes. *9am-10.30pm* ₹₹

Anju Coco Resto: Great meals all day, from breakfast to Indian and Western dinners; famous for grilled seafood. *8am-10.30pm* ₹₹

The Swimming Elephant: Better for lunch than dinner (since the rough access road is best avoided in the dark), but there's an idyllic jungle vibe. *6.30am-10.30pm* ₹₹₹

ENDEMIC SPECIES

Prathamesh B Khedwan abandoned a career as a software engineer to follow his passion as a naturalist on Swaraj Island. He works as naturalist and guide at Barefoot at Havelock. *@sea__dweller*

The Andaman Islands are a biodiversity hothouse that's incredibly rich in endemic species. Swaraj Island, known for its lush forests and diverse marine habitats, is a great place to spot rare birds such as the Andaman woodpecker, Andaman serpent eagle, Andaman hawk owl, Andaman drongo, Andaman teal and Andaman cuckoo-dove.

Among the endemic mammals that you might spot on Swaraj are Andaman wild pig (a distinct subspecies), Andaman masked palm civet and the bizarre Andaman spiny shrew. Avid sunset watchers frequently catch sight of the haunting silhouette of our Andaman flying fox.

NEIL BOWMAN/SHUTTERSTOCK

Imperial pigeon and Alexandrine parakeets

are particularly 'illuminating', coinciding as they do with the emergence of nocturnal creatures such as octopi and lionfish.

Prathamesh advises his guests to wear sunhats and waterproof sports sandals and to keep any skin that's been treated with sunblock out of the water. His enthusiasm is matched by his knowledge of marine species and by his incredible familiarity with the area of watery wilderness that he's explored so thoroughly. He can show you the spots where several of the Andamans' 13 species of clown fish (that elusive 'Nemo') defend their anemones so fearlessly and lead you to a spectacular coral formation decorated with more than 400 christmas tree worms in every colour imaginable. In general the experience is a far more vibrantly colourful one than most people would expect, and it's fascinating also, both for adults and kids (minimum age three), to learn about the habits of the bizarre 'solar-powered sea slug' or to understand the symbiosis between the goby fish and the pistol shrimp that at first glance would seem to be unlikely flat-mates in their shared submarine burrows.

DRINKING ON SWARAJ: TOP SPOTS FOR COCKTAILS

Narra: This elegant restobar has a tasting menu and perhaps the island's best cocktails. It's a great party spot with occasional live music. *7.30am-10.30pm*

Something Different: A busy restaurant and Swaraj's most popular cocktail spot for sundowners or nightcaps. *11.30am-10pm*

5th Bistro Cafe and Bar: Air-con and friendly service make this an unbeatable spot for morning cappuccinos or Havelock Sour nightcaps. *11am-10pm*

High Tide: Set in a coconut grove in the grounds of the SeaShell hotel, this semi-outdoor bar has great cocktails and live entertainment. *11am-10.30pm*

Seeing the Island from Two Wheels

Getting under Swaraj's skin by pedal-power

Havelock might be known for its gorgeous beaches, but pedaling along its lanes on a bicycle is a fantastic way to get to know the island beyond the postcard images – and there's a lot to hold your interest. **SeaShell Havelock** offers an easygoing 4km bicycle tour *(seashellhotels.net/havelockisland; ₹1770)* guided by the resort's resident naturalist, who will not only point out various plants, trees and birds along the route, but also explain some of the island's geological history and agricultural industries, including tropical fruits, coconuts and the ever-present betel-nut palms. You might even glean intriguing insights about the Indigenous islanders, including those who still live (almost entirely uncontacted) on outlying islands.

At the time of writing, the bicycles were in need of maintenance but the cycling route is flat and easy and could, if you chose, easily be walked in any case. You'll pass through quiet villages and, despite being close to town, even visit a beach that's so far overlooked by tourists that it doesn't yet have a name. More than a physical outing, this cycle tour is a fantastic way to get your bearings and gather some sort of understanding of Swaraj from a cultural and natural history perspective.

A Taste of Swaraj Island's Jungle Habitat

A jungle hike to Elephant Beach

From the so-called 'tourist shed' on the main road that marks the trailhead it's just 1.7km to **Elephant Beach**. During the height of the dry season it's a negligible stroll (a bit sweaty at most), but at most other times it can be extremely muddy. Don't be surprised to find yourself stumbling through knee-high mud and slithering along what seem to be greased trails.

While it's only a relatively small stretch of jungle, it's worth bearing in mind that every year tourists get lost on the labyrinth of trails. The official guides at the tourist shed *(₹500 each way)* are adamant that the only way to approach the trail is barefoot – any footwear is invariably engulfed and then retained by the mud. Apart from showing you the easiest routes, the experienced guides have a wealth of fascinating anecdotes about the snakes, crocodiles and wild pigs that inhabit these forests – and about Swaraj's last wild elephant.

The remote Elephant Beach is the only place where jet skis, banana boats, parasailing and other water sports are allowed. It's with a sense of culture shock that you emerge from the jungle to find refreshment stalls, hundreds of holidaymakers (up to 2000 at the height of the season) and fleets of lurid banana boats. Needless to say, these people didn't all walk here: it's possible to access Elephant Beach by boat from town *(₹1000 return)*. It's safe to say, however, that the most fascinating and fulfilling experience that Elephant Beach has to offer is the guided jungle walk to get there.

SWARAJ'S LAST ELEPHANT

Swaraj resident **Monojit Monday** has been a jungle guide working around Elephant Beach for 12 years.

When I was a kid there were several elephants roaming the forests of Swaraj Island. Now 30-year-old Laxmi is the last elephant standing. Unlike the others who came here as logging elephants and were habituated to humans, she was born semi-wild. Perhaps that has made her unpredictable and we rarely know how she's going to react when we come across her on the trail: half the time we watch; half the time we run!

She roams wild but forest rangers are always up to date with her whereabouts. She's a regular visitor at Elephant Beach, but when she turns up there the authorities close the beach to humans. Effectively it's Laxmi's private beach.

Shaheed Island (Neil)

INCREDIBLE REEFS | BEST DIVING | TOTAL SERENITY

GETTING AROUND

The government bus goes from the Neil Kendra bazaar to Sitapur Beach (at the island's eastern extreme) once an hour, but you're unlikely to need it. The roads are flat and distances short (the island's longest road is 7km), so hiring a bicycle or scooter (per hour/day ₹150/500) through your homestay or resort is your best bet. Autorickshaws charge ₹200 from the jetty to almost anywhere on the island.

An hour by boat from Swaraj, charming Shaheed Island (renamed from Neil in 2018, but it's still not catching on locally) is the more laid-back of the two islands. At first glance it's prettier than the bigger islands, and with its relaxed village vibe, it's popular with long-stay travellers. The island takes 15 minutes to drive end-to-end along a sweeping road that breezes you effortlessly past rice paddies and through betel-nut groves.

Before divers came to the island in the 1990s, the small local population worked in farming or fishing, but now tourism is a big part of the economy. Shaheed Island still has a village feel; everyone is friendly and welcoming. For such a small island there's a wealth of white-sand beaches (many of which put those on Swaraj Island's developed north coast to shame) and you'll find the most spectacular natural rock and coral formations anywhere in the archipelago.

ROSTASEDLACEK/SHUTTERSTOCK

Shaheed Island (Neil)

TOP TIP

There's no pharmacy or doctor's surgery on Shaheed and the grocery shops are small. Bring any medical supplies you're likely to need with you. If you plan to dive or snorkel, simple first-aid supplies for coral cuts and grazes can come in handy.

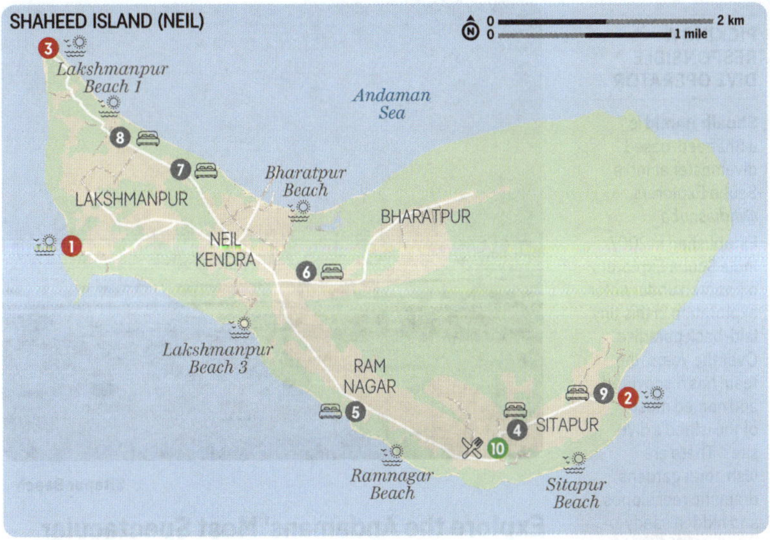

SIGHTS
1 Lakshmanpur Beach
2 Sitapur Beach
3 Sunset Point

ACTIVITIES
see 8 India Scuba Explorers

SLEEPING
4 Blue Lagoon
5 Break Water Beach Resort
6 Save Green Resort
7 SeaShell Neil
8 SeaShell Samssara
9 TSG Aura Resort

EATING
see 7 Dugong
10 Garden View Restaurant
see 8 Kamari
see 9 Vibes & Dives

Dugongs & How to Find Them

Diving among 'mermaids'

One of the rarest mammals in the ocean, dugongs are said to be the creatures that gave rise to the myth of the mermaid. There are less than 30 left in these islands, with a large population being found among the seagrass pastures around Shaheed Island.

Your best chance of seeing a dugong is to join a company such as **India Scuba Explorers** *(indiascubaexplorers.com; ₹2500)* for a high-tide snorkelling excursion off Shaheed's northern shores. You usually depart by boat from the Fisheries Jetty (next to Shaheed's big passenger jetty), but the area of reef and seagrass meadow you're likely to search is within a few minutes puttering, to the east and west of the jetty.

Even when visibility is good the huge mammals (weighing as much as 900kg) are surprisingly hard to spot, and while there's never a guarantee, dive guides claim that once they are spotted in a given area they remain there for some time. Should you encounter one, relax your movements to the same pace as theirs and savour the moment. Some divers say you can feel your heart beat in time with the peaceful dugongs.

CROCODILE ROCK

Crocodiles are found in most parts of the Andamans. They're common at river-mouths on Swaraj Island and often seen at Corbyn's Cove and Wandoor near Port Blair, as well as North Andaman. Little Andaman has large populations.

While deaths are relatively uncommon, a tourist was killed at Wandoor Beach in 2017 and another was eaten by a big saltwater crocodile on Swaraj Island (near Neil's Cove) in 2010. A high level of vigilance is advised – locals will tell you it's foolhardy to swim in spots that do not have lifeguards on watch. Keep informed, listen to warnings by authorities and avoid murky water, especially around dawn or dusk.

PICKING A RESPONSIBLE DIVE OPERATOR

Shoaib Hamid is a Shaheed-based divemaster at India Scuba Explorers. *@indiascuba*

Established in 2007, India Scuba Explorers pioneered underwater exploration in this tiny, laid-back paradise. Over the years, the team has discovered and named most of the island's dive sites. There are lush coral gardens, dramatic reef slopes and hidden sandy lagoons, all teeming with life. As the diving industry increases, marine conservation has become crucial. Check that the operator you want to book with is actively involved in beach and reef clean-ups and/or works closely with the community to spread awareness about waste management and sustainability. Shaheed is a place where life revolves around the rhythm of the tides. We must all play a part in keeping it that way.

SWAPAN KUMAR SAHANA/SHUTTERSTOCK

Sitapur Beach

Explore the Andamans' Most Spectacular Coastline

Shaheed's best beaches

The number of visitors on Shaheed's beaches tends to fluctuate wildly depending upon the tides. If low tide coincides with sunset you're likely to find the vast majority of the island's visitors at **Lakshmanpur Beach**, where two spectacular natural coral bridges arch out into the breaking waves, providing some of the Andamans' best photo opportunities.

That location is impossible to reach at high tide, however, so at that time those same crowds gather at the northernmost tip of the island, the spot known appropriately to locals as **Sunset Point**. The hour around sunset is what amounts to 'rush hour' on Shaheed.

The most spectacular beauty spot is certainly the more isolated **Sitapur Beach** – a patch of tropical beauty that very much lives up to the paradise epithet. The southern end of the beach is famous as Shaheed's 'sunrise viewing spot', but walk just 1km north and you'll find yourself in a series of blissfully deserted coves and reefs. There's a hidden cave here and even the picturesque wreck of a Burmese fishing vessel, just to make the scene look even more Crusoe-esque. Be aware that it's easy to get trapped by the rising tide here.

EATING ON SHAHEED: SEAFOOD & MORE

Garden View Restaurant: A welcoming eatery with excellent seafood curries. The sort of place you'll want to visit regularly. *10am-9pm* ₹

Vibes & Dives: Cafe by day, vibrant restaurant by night, with great vibes, from the music to the fish menu. Don't miss the butter garlic squid. *hours vary* ₹₹

Kamari: The quintessential dive-hangout for hearty après-dive feasts (especially barbecued seafood) and 'buccaneer stories'. *11am–10.30pm* ₹₹

Dugong: This luxurious hotel restaurant serves excellent grilled fish, lobster, tiger prawns and more. *7.30am-10.30pm* ₹₹₹

Places We Love to Stay

₹ Budget ₹₹ Midrange ₹₹₹ Top End

Sri Vijaya Puram (Port Blair)

Map p989

Amina Lodge ₹ The simple rooms are made homely by kind Raksha and Bobby, who've been running this centrally located little guesthouse for decades.

Andaman Homestay ₹ The helpful and welcoming Noble family offer well-equipped fan and air-con rooms, along with the Andamans' best kayaking experiences.

Lemon Tree Hotel ₹₹₹ Five-star service at Port Blair's best-known four-star hotel. Ideally located just across the road from the airport.

SeaShell Port Blair ₹₹₹ This branch of the Andamans' local chain, on quiet Marine Hill, has a rooftop restaurant with the best views in town.

Chidiya Tapu

Wild Grass Resort ₹₹ There's an idyllic rural wilderness vibe at this timber-cabin 'resort' on a forested hillside. The restaurant has some of the best meals on the big island.

Big Tree Cottages ₹₹₹ Expect far more than just humble 'cottages' at this sumptuous retreat set between an organic farm and a forest reserve.

Little Andaman

Ieshika Resort ₹₹ Everything you need in these concrete and bamboo cottages, with friendly service, home-cooked meals and surfboards for hire (on a learner-friendly beach).

Hawa Beach Resort ₹₹ This laid-back family-run resort has a handful of simple concrete cottages and surfboard rental. Mimi cooks Little Andaman's most delicious meals.

Swaraj Island (Havelock)

Map p996

Havelock Farms Resort ₹₹ Ideal budget option, with great service, lush gardens and immaculate chalets. A small fleet of electric scooters for rent.

Wild Orchid ₹₹ Impeccable rooms, excellent service and instant access to some of Swaraj's best cocktails and meals at the resort's Narra restaurant.

Barefoot Scuba ₹₹ This veteran dive centre has bijou two-storey sea-facing huts, as well as handy basic hut options for long stayers on a budget.

Barefoot at Havelock ₹₹₹ Set in a private jungle reserve, this resort is Swaraj's most sumptuous nature retreat. The unforgettable rock-pooling experience is open to non-guests.

Matsya Island Retreat ₹₹₹ A boutique guesthouse and oasis of calm, with elegantly designed interiors with natural fabrics to enhance the rustic vibes.

SeaShell Havelock (p999) ₹₹₹ Lavish beach huts and villas set among palm trees. Unwind at the best spa on the island or join the in-house divemasters for scuba/snorkelling.

Taj Exotica ₹₹₹ As luxurious as it gets, with decadent villas, outstanding restaurants and the infinity pool, which stretches parallel to the popular Radhanagar Beach.

Shaheed Island (Neil)

Map p1001

Blue Lagoon ₹₹ The best-value family-run resort on Shaheed Island with comfortable, well-equipped rooms and delicious Indian breakfasts. Five-star service at budget prices.

TSG Aura Resort ₹₹ At the more expensive end of the midrange bracket, this resort is ideally located on Sitapur Beach and right next door to Vibes & Dives Cafe.

Break Water Beach Resort ₹₹ Easygoing ambience, with thatched huts, whitewashed concrete bungalows and a good restaurant with direct access to a great snorkelling beach.

Save Green Resort ₹₹ A reliable midrange bet, close to the ferry jetty and just a short stroll from the town centre and the bustling fishing beach.

SeaShell Neil ₹₹₹ Lovely suites and the excellent Dugong restaurant combine with a fabulous pool and access through coconut palms directly to the beach.

SeaShell Samssara ₹₹₹ A notch above anything else in the area, this sleek yet welcoming resort is Neil's finest, with iconic tropical design and perfect pampering.

SmartBike
PROMOTE YOUR BRAND THROUGH SmartBik
For more info, Contact: + 91 40 48211777
20390
SmartBike
20085

Bike-share station, Delhi (p52)

HISTORICALPITARA7/SHUTTERSTOCK

TOOLKIT

The chapters in this section cover the most important topics you'll need to know about in India. They're full of nuts-and-bolts information and valuable insights to help you understand and navigate India and get the most out of your trip.

Arriving

Almost everyone arrives in India by air, though India shares land border crossings with Pakistan, Bangladesh, Nepal, Tibet and Myanmar. The key ports of arrival are Delhi, Mumbai, Kolkata, Chennai, Bengaluru and Hyderabad. Note that international airport terminals are often separate to domestic terminals – be sure to go to the right terminal as transport between terminals can be limited.

Visas

Most nationalities can apply for a tourist E-Visa valid for anything from 30 days to five years. Apply at least four days in advance at *indianvisaonline.gov.in*. Carry a printout of your ETA, E-Visa confirmation and E-arrival card.

ATMs

ATMs are everywhere in India. Most dispense ₹500 bills with a ₹10,000 cap per transaction. Try to break big bills down to smaller change; shops and autorickshaw drivers may not have change.

Mobile Phones

Local three-month tourist SIM cards are fairly easy to obtain through official phone company desks – Reliance, Jio and Airtel are the biggest operators. City-centre offices are the best places to get reliably set up on a local network.

Prepaid Transport

Most airports and many train stations have prepaid taxi and autorickshaw stands, where you can pay a fair fixed price to reach your hotel, or you can book a ride via Uber or Ola.

Transport from Airport to City Centre

	Delhi	Mumbai	Bengaluru
METRO	₹54 25min	₹70 45min	n/a
AIRPORT BUS	₹50-70 1½hr	₹125-175 1-2hr	₹210-410 1hr
TAXI	₹550-600 1½hr	₹800-1000 1-2hr	₹900-1500 1hr

WIDESPREAD SECURITY

On arrival in India, you'll quickly get a sense that India is very concerned about security. To enter or leave airports, you'll need to pass all your bags (including suitcases and shoulder bags) through X-ray machines. The same applies at Metro and train stations and when entering many top-end hotels and some tourist sites. Note that Indian airlines are quite strict about what can go into your luggage – power banks and any kind of batteries can only be carried in carry-on bags, spices must go in the hold, e-cigarettes may be barred, and dried coconut is banned from luggage completely!

FROM LEFT: FUSE/GETTY IMAGES, GOGLIK83/GETTY IMAGES

Getting Around

India has excellent bus and rail networks and plentiful domestic flights. Because of local driving conditions, road travel can be risky at night; travel by day where possible.

TRAVEL COSTS

Car & driver
₹3000–5500 per day

Petrol
Approx ₹100/ litre

Delhi–Agra AC class train ticket
from ₹600

Mumbai–Goa bus
₹800–1000

Best Ways to Get Around

Trains should be your first choice – they're faster and more comfortable than buses, and stations are often (though not always) centrally located. Buses are cheap and go everywhere, ranging in comfort from basic local services to deluxe sleeper coaches. Consider domestic flights to avoid long overland trips. Hiring a car and driver is a good option for day trips (or when a train or bus is cancelled).

INDIA TRAIN TIPS

Many cities have multiple train stations, so check which station your train arrives in and departs from via the 'Reserved trains between stations' link at *indianrail.gov.in*. Arrive at the station an hour early – some are huge, with multiple platforms. Trains can have dozens of carriages; check your carriage in advance and use platform signs to position yourself in the right place on the platform. Find out more about Indian train travel at *seat61.com/India*.

Bargaining for Transport

While autorickshaws and taxis may have meters, they're rarely used. To guarantee a fair fare, look for prepaid taxi and autorickshaw booths at bus and train stations and airports, or book a ride through Uber or Ola. Elsewhere, you'll need to agree a fare with the driver, which can involve some bargaining. Ask at your hotel to get a sense of what a ride should cost.

Hiring a Vehicle

Self-drive car hire is rare in India, but many travellers rent scooters and motorcycles. By law you should have a national driving licence covering motorcycles, plus an International Driving Permit (IDP). Chartering a car (or taxi) and driver – ideally an experienced driver – can be very cost-effective if shared between several people; ask hotels to help, or negotiate a fare directly with drivers.

To Fly or Not to Fly

Domestic flights in India can save days of uncomfortable overland travel, and some routes offer amazing views, but there's an environmental impact. Delays are common, particularly in North India during the foggy winter, and many airlines charge extra for more than 15kg of check-in luggage. IndiGo, Air India and Spicejet are the biggest domestic carriers. Domestic airport terminals may be in a different location to the international terminal.

Buses

Buses operated by state bus companies go everywhere for pocket-friendly prices, but luggage space is limited and buses get crowded. Ask around at stations to find the right stand and ticket booking desk. For longer trips, there are hundreds of private companies, offering comfy air-con buses with reclining seats or sleeping berths; book online via apps such as Redbus, MakeMyTrip and Abhibus. Always check the departure point – it may be outside the centre.

DRIVING ESSENTIALS

Drive on the left

70
Speed limits range from 70km/h (cities) to 120km/h (expressways)

.03
Blood alcohol limit is 0.03%

DINESH HUKMANI/SHUTTERSTOCK

HOW TO... Book Train Tickets

Train travel is one of India's great joys, but booking tickets for this behemoth rail network is an initiation in the complex ways of the subcontinent.

Booking Tickets Online

The Indian Railway Catering and Tourism Corporation *(IRCTC; irctc.co.in)* offers online train bookings via its website. You'll also need an IRCTC account to book trains via sites such as MakeMyTrip.

To register on the IRCTC website, you'll need to provide a mobile phone number (which can be an international number) and an email address (and verify via both), and also pay a small registration fee with a credit card when you log in for the first time. For subsequent bookings, you may need to search about for the international payment option.

If you'll only be using trains for major routes, international payments are straightforward through 12GoAsia *(12go.asia)*.

Other Methods

Booking in person at the 'reserved' booking desk at train stations is another option, but you'll need to know the correct station names (each has a unique code) and train number. Find out these details on the Indian Railways website *(indianrail.gov.in)*, via the 'Reserved trains between stations' link. Book at least a few days ahead; local and international travel agencies can do the hard work on your behalf.

PNRs, Wait Lists & Quotas

Your train seat number isn't 100% confirmed until a few hours before travel, when the 'chart is prepared'. Use the 10-digit 'PNR' number from your booking to confirm your seat via the PNR link at *indianrail.gov.in*.

Tickets may be available as Wait List. If a seat comes free (assuming there aren't too many people ahead of you) your ticket will be 'confirmed'; if not, you get a refund. Again, check against your PNR for updates.

Indian Railways also has a special Foreign Tourist Quota for rides between major stations; reserve at special station desks, with your passport, using cash.

Types of Train

Express and mail trains form the bulk of services. Shatabdi Express trains are same-day seating-only services. Rajdhani Express trains are long-distance overnight services between Delhi and state capitals. Duronto Express trains and gleaming new Vande Bharat trains (pictured; seating only) link major cities at high speed.

TRAIN CLASSES

Air-Conditioned 1st Class (1AC) The most costly option; two- or four-berth compartments with locking doors and meals included.

Air-Conditioned 2-Tier (2AC) Two-tier berths with bed sheets in an open-plan carriage; ticket may include meals.

Air-Conditioned 3-Tier (3AC) Three-tier berths arranged in groups of six in an open-plan carriage.

AC Executive Chair (ECC) & AC Chair (CC) Comfortable, reclining chairs and air-con; usually on Shatabdi and Vande Bharat services.

Sleeper Class (sl) Open-plan carriages with three-tier bunks and no AC; inexpensive and reasonably comfortable.

Unreserved/reserved 2nd Class (II/SS or 2S) Aka 'general' class – shared bench seats, cheap, often crowded, but no reservation required.

Nuts & Bolts

OPENING HOURS

The following are guidelines; hours may vary;

Banks (nationalised) 10am–4pm Monday to Friday, to noon, 1pm or 4pm Saturday; closed second and fourth Saturday of the month

Bars and clubs Noon–11.30am or midnight, clubs with entry fees may open later

Islamic sites May be closed Friday for prayers

Markets 10am–7pm in major cities, with one closed day; rural markets once weekly, early morning to lunchtime

Museums/sights Often closed Monday

Post offices 9.30am–5pm Monday to Saturday

Restaurants 8am–10pm, or lunch (noon–3pm) and dinner (7pm–10pm). Tourist restaurants often close at 11pm

Shops 10am–7pm or 8pm, some close Sunday

Weights & Measures

India uses the metric system, including for road distances. Fruit and vegetables are usually sold by weight, though large items like coconuts are sold individually and bananas are often sold in bunches. Local units you're likely to come across are lakh (100,000) and crore (10 million).

Tap Water

Don't drink tap water. Stick to purified water; where possible, refill from hotel communal supplies.

Toilets

Public toilets charge and usually have squat toilets. Find sit-down toilets at tourist sites, upmarket restaurants and hotels.

GOOD TO KNOW

Time zone
India Standard Time (GMT+5.30)

Country code
+91

Emergency number
100 or 112

Population
1.45 billion

Electricity

Type C and D, 220V/50Hz

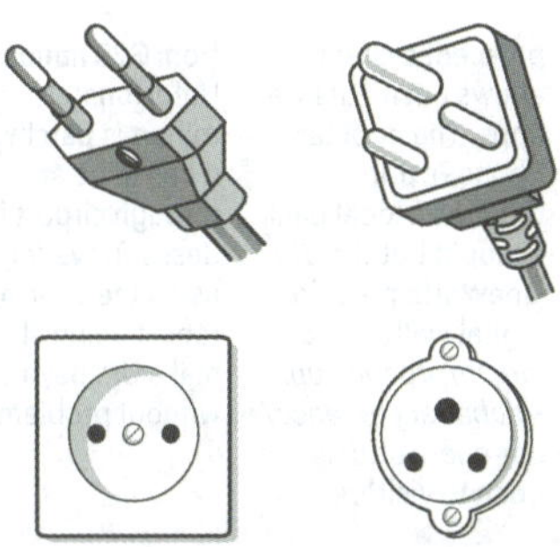

PUBLIC HOLIDAYS

On gazetted holidays (see *india.gov.in/calendar* for dates) most businesses, offices, banks and tourist sites close, but transport is usually unaffected. Most states also have local holidays.

Republic Day 26 January

Holi February/March

Mahavir Jayanti March/April

Ram Navami March/April

Buddha Purnima April/May

Good Friday April

Eid al-Fitr March

Eid al-Adha (Id ul-Zuha) May/June

Muharram June/July

Independence Day 15 August

Janmastami August/September

Eid-Milad-un-Nabi August/September

Gandhi Jayanti 2 October

Dussehra September/October

Diwali October/November

Guru Nanak Jayanti November

Christmas Day 25 December

Money

CURRENCY: INDIAN RUPEE (₹)

Cash

Cash is still king in much of India, though paying by phone is growing in popularity. Bills come in denominations of ₹500, ₹200, ₹100, ₹50, ₹20 and ₹10, plus rarely seen ₹2000 bills. Pay with big bills at restaurants, shops and hotels so you have change for autorickshaws and street vendors.

Foreign Exchange

Larger banks such as State Bank of India (SBI) and private money changers can exchange cash (and travellers cheques) in major currencies such as US$, UK£ and euros. Ask for smaller Indian bills when you exchange money. To avoid being scammed, don't change money on the street and count your currency before leaving forex offices.

ATMs

ATMs are found everywhere, but they don't all accept foreign cards, and some charge high transaction fees. State Bank of India (SBI) ATMs are a safe bet.

Debit & Credit Cards

Visa and Mastercard are accepted by many upmarket hotels, restaurants and shops. You may need to tap, enter your PIN or provide a signature.

HOW MUCH FOR...

Museum entry
₹25–600

Short autorickshaw ride
₹100–150

Metro ticket
₹10–70

4WD tiger safari
from ₹3500

HOW TO... Tip

There are two tiers of tipping in India: tipping for service, which may be included in the bill (on top of GST) at posher establishments; and *baksheesh*, which covers everything from alms for beggars and tips for someone who was particularly helpful to 'unofficial' payments to officials to expedite slow procedures. When tipping drivers and guides or for meals, 10% is a good starting point.

LOCAL TIP

Booking rooms via Booking.com or Agoda.com can bring lots of discounts, but you may need to pay a deposit electronically. Always confirm with the hotel to make sure they're expecting you.

PAYING BY PHONE

You'll see QR codes for payments by phone displayed everywhere in India, from museum ticket desks to tea stands. Apple Pay doesn't cover India, and Google Pay requires an Indian bank account, but the local UPI payment system allows payments via apps. The popular PhonePe app requires a local bank account but the UPI OneWorld prepaid digital wallet (*npci.org.in/product/upi-global-acceptance/upi-one-world*) is open to visitors from G20 nations. Unfortunately, rollout is patchy, and it has to be arranged through airport forex desks. Travellers using the Wise app report being able to make UPI payments without problems.

Accommodation

Hostels

Hostel chains such as Hosteller, Zostel and Moustache are sweeping across India, significantly improving the hostel experience. Most offer clean dorms with shared bathrooms and lockers (usually with single sex dorms for women), plus a cafe and/or kitchen and sometimes even a pool, plus fun activities such as games and tours. Some budget hotels also offer simple dorms without the extras.

Homestays

Homestays are common, both in cities and in rural areas such as the Himalayan foothills. You'll usually get a simple room, tasty home-cooked food, and sometimes extras like guided walks. Some places are very comfortable, but for more basic properties, bring a mosquito net. Find listings on sites such as *homestaysofindia.com* and *homestay.com/india*, as well as Booking.com and Agoda.com.

Guesthouses

Filling the gap between hostels and hotels, India's guesthouses offer simple but comfortable accommodation, sometimes with perks such as home-cooked meals or cooking classes. Many are located in city suburbs, offering a window onto life away from the tourist hustle. Sometimes there'll be green space to relax in. In rural areas, guesthouses can feel more like homestays.

Hotels

Hotels in India range from basic bus-stand flophouses to former royal palaces. In cheaper hotels, look at several rooms before deciding, as some may be worn or musty. Many hotels are listed on sites such as Booking.com, Agoda.com and MakeMyTrip.com, but always check your booking with the venue, as online bookings don't always filter through to the check-in desk.

HOW MUCH FOR A NIGHT IN A...

Hostel dorm bed
₹500–1000

Midrange hotel room
₹1000–5000

Top-end hotel room
₹5000–60,000

Ashrams & Pilgrim Rest Houses

Many religious sites offer free accommodation to devotees, pilgrims and travellers, though a donation is appropriate. There are usually rules banning alcohol and smoking, but a stay at a major shrine such as Amritsar's Golden Temple (pictured) can be an amazing experience. In remote areas, you'll also find so-called rest houses, dak bungalows and circuit houses, offering simple rooms aimed at travelling officials.

REGAL SLEEPS

India's very best hotels are housed in the former palaces of maharajas, and there are dozens to choose from. Sometimes the royal family is resident in an adjacent wing, and rooms often overflow with antiques, chandeliers, royal portraits and hunting trophies. Properties such as Jaipur's Rambagh and Hyderabad's Falaknuma Palace offer a taste of princely life at a princely price, with fabulous fine dining as part of the package. If you can't afford a room, book in for dinner or a drink at the bar for an excuse to wander the grounds.

Family Travel

India can be an amazing place to travel with kids, but there are challenges, including traffic, hygiene, mosquitoes and feral animals. Unfamiliar food, climate and crowds can also be wearing for kids. A shawl can provide privacy while breastfeeding, or use breastfeeding rooms at stations and malls. Nappies, wipes and formula are available from pharmacies.

Plan Realistically

Bustle and noise that is thrilling for adults can be exhausting for children, particularly when it's hot. Don't be too ambitious when sightseeing, and build in rest stops in air-conditioned spaces. Minimise long journeys and plan days out around kid-friendly food stops, parks and uncrowded spaces. For a first-time trip, try Goa or Kerala, with the beach as a fallback when kids tire of the sights.

Food for Small Diners

Indian food can be a challenge for young palates, but not everything is spicy, and international food – often branded as 'continental' – is widely available. Indian Chinese food is often lightly spiced, and dosas (rice and lentil-flour crepes) and Indian breads are fun finger food. Fruit goes down well, but wash or peel before eating to avoid germs.

Kids' Essentials

Most hotels have family rooms or can provide extra beds; cots are harder to find. Consider bringing a travel cot with a zip-up mosquito net; a child carrier is more practical than a pushchair (stroller). Upmarket restaurants have highchairs; bring a car seat from home.

Hygiene & Health

Arrange recommended vaccinations and pack the family travel trinity – sunscreen, mosquito spray and anti-bacterial hand gel. Bites can get infected so use antiseptic and always clean hands before eating. Be careful of the heat – listlessness and headaches can be a sign of heatstroke.

BEST FAMILY EXPERIENCES

The beaches

Goa (p739) and Kerala (p876) are beach playgrounds. In the Andamans (p984, add in dugong and bioluminescence encounters.

The wildlife

Monkeys are everywhere; spot dolphins in Goa (p739), elephants at Bandipur (p810) or Periyar (p911) and tigers at Ranthambore (p127) or Kanha (p619).

The forts

Kids love castles, and Rajasthan (p104) has forts to spare – start with Amber (p112) near Jaipur.

Easy adventures

Himachal Pradesh (p257) offers plentiful family adventures, from zip lines to rafting and short hikes.

SMALL CELEBRITIES

Family life is hugely important in Indian culture and children are adored, so kids will get a lot of attention, most of it well intended. However, being touched by strangers and regularly asked to pose with locals for selfies can be stressful for small travellers. Wearing sunglasses and using a music player with headphones can give kids some privacy. Crowds can be tiring for smaller kids, so plan days around stops in quieter, less-crowded spaces, even if that means sacrificing sightseeing for time by the hotel pool and chill-out breaks in local parks and mall play areas.

Health & Safe Travel

STAYING HEALTHY

There are many tropical diseases in India, so visit your doctor a month before travel to discuss vaccinations and anti-malarial tablets. Take steps to avoid mosquito bites to avoid infections such as dengue fever, and be careful of street dogs, cats and monkeys – they can carry rabies. Take hygiene seriously – before eating anything, clean your hands with soap or antibacterial hand gel.

Environmental Hazards

The sun can be intense, so use sunscreen and cover up, and be alert to the signs of heatstroke. A face-mask can help with pollution and prevent respiratory illnesses. Other risks include road accidents, train derailments, earthquakes, severe storms, and flooding and landslides during the monsoon. Avoid road travel at night and take steps to avoid acute mountain sickness (AMS) above 2500m.

Local Healthcare

Doctors surgeries are easy to find, but try to use well-funded private hospitals in large cities over government hospitals or rural healthcare facilities. Always take out travel insurance with repatriation cover for serious emergencies, and check if you need to pay first and claim back later or if the insurer will settle costs directly with the hospital.

TRANSPORT SAFETY

Politely decline offers of food or drink from strangers on public transport – travellers have been drugged and robbed.

DANGERS TO BE AWARE OF

Weather Look out for warnings of heatwaves or flooding.

Water safety Watch for riptides on India's beaches.

Animals Be wary of feral dogs, aggressive monkeys, tigers, leopards and elephants.

Traffic Be very careful crossing the road – it's probably the biggest danger in India.

Crime & Violence

Violent crime is rare but opportunistic theft is a risk, so be cautious with your valuables and lock your hotel room at night. Monitor the media and government travel advisories for warnings of terrorism, communal violence, political unrest and natural disasters, and avoid angry crowds. Be cautious about terrorist threats around high-risk sites, such as important temples and areas close to the Pakistan border.

ESSENTIAL VACCINATIONS

Most medics recommend vaccination against diphtheria, hepatitis A, tetanus and typhoid. For longer stays in rural areas, consider vaccinations against hepatitis B and rabies – your doctor can advise. If you get bitten by an animal, commence anti-rabies treatment immediately. Talk to your doctor about anti-malarial tablets – they're not required for all regions, and may not be needed in the dry, cool winter months.

CLOCKWISE FROM TOP RIGHT: GENGWIT WATTAKAWIGRAN/SHUTTERSTOCK, AKM CREATIVES/SHUTTERSTOCK

Food, Drink & Nightlife

When to Eat

Breakfast: (6am to 10am) A light meal with chai – dosas, kachori, *idli*, *parathas* and *poha* (flattened rice) are popular.

Lunch: (noon to 3pm) Often a thali (plate meal) with sauces, rice, chapatis and sides.

Tiffin: (3pm to 6pm) A snack, at mid-afternoon or anytime.

Dinner: (6pm to 10.30pm) Usually the big, sit-down meal of the day.

Where to Eat

Bhojnalayas Local restaurants, serving simple meals from the local regional cuisine.

Restaurants Ranging from hole-in-the-wall tandoori joints to lavish eateries in palace hotels.

Misthan bhandars Serving *mithai* (sweets), *namkeen* (savoury crisp snacks) and vegetarian food, found India-wide.

Dhabas: Punjabi-style roadhouses, serving quick meals to drivers, truckers and bus passengers.

South Indian cafes Found everywhere, serving dosas, *idlis*, *vada* and *appam* from breakfast till late evening.

Street food: Stalls are concentrated in business districts, at markets and close to transport hubs.

MENU DECODER

Achar pickle

Appam rice pancake (*uttapam* if topped)

Bhajia & pakora vegetable fritters

Biryani steamed rice with meat or vegetables

Chaat salad-like snacks

Chai sweet milky tea

Channa chickpeas

Dhal lentils

Dosa lentil and rice-flour crepes

Idli spongy rice cake

Kulfi Indian ice cream

Lassi yoghurt drink

Mithai & ladoo: Indian sweets

Momo savoury Tibetan dumpling

Naan, chapati & roti Indian flatbreads

Namkeen savoury nibbles

Paan areca nut and betel leaf parcels

Paneer unfermented cheese

Pappadam:crispy savoury wafer

Paratha/parantha flaky flatbread

Pilau rice cooked in spiced stock

Puri fried bread puffs

Raita spiced yoghurt

Sabzi:vegetables

Sambar spicy lentil dip

Samosa filled pastry triangles

Tandoori cooked in a clay oven

Thali all-you-can-eat meal

Tiffin snack

Tikka grilled chunks of meat, paneer or fish

Vada doughnut-shaped lentil fritter

HOW TO... Eat Without Cutlery

Traditionally, most people in India eat with their right hand, while the left hand is reserved for ablutions. You can use your left hand for holding drinks and serving from a communal bowl, but don't use it to bring food to your mouth.

When we say eating with the right hand, we mean it literally – locals often eschew cutlery, instead mopping up sauces with Indian breads, or scooping mixed rice and sauces into their mouths with their fingers. In the south, your food may be served on a banana leaf instead of a plate.

The finger-scoop technique is easy to master. Wash your hands, mix your rice and sauce together, then use your fingers like a shovel and your thumb to push food into your mouth. When eating rice, *sabzi* (vegetables) and dhal (stewed lentils), often just the lentils and rice are mixed. You can always ask for a spoon if you're struggling.

HOW MUCH FOR A...

Cup of chai
₹10–30

Samosa
₹15–30

Stuffed masala dosa
₹50–250

Thali plate meal
₹150–500

Tandoori chicken (half)
₹350–600

Posh restaurant dinner (per person)
From ₹1500

660ml bottle of Kingfisher beer
₹400–600

HOW TO... Order an Indian Meal

For those unfamiliar with Indian food, or used to Indian menus outside India, the first trip to a local restaurant can be confusing. Where's the chicken *korma* and lamb *dhansak*? The first thing to realise is that restaurants often specialise in the local cuisine, so menus will be dominated by food from that region. Dishes are often named for their ingredients (eg *aloo ghobi* – spiced potato and cauliflower) or cooking style (eg chicken *karahi*, cooked in a *karahi* wok). If you see a dish described as masala, it means 'in a spiced sauce'.

Curry

The word 'curry' comes from the Tamil word *kari*, meaning a spiced sauce, but in India, dishes tend to be named for their ingredients, the style of cooking, or the region they come from.

To sample the restaurant's specialities, order a thali – a selection of sauces, rice or chapatis, and often some curd, pickles and a dessert. Sometimes called a 'meal' in the south, it's often the best thing on the menu, but sometimes only served at lunchtime. Alternatively, order a few sauces and bread or a rice dish. A bowl of *dahi* (curd) is a useful side-order as a chilli douser. Note that dishes such as *pilau* rice or fried rice are often stand-alone main courses rather than sides.

Meats and kebabs grilled in the tandoor (clay oven) make a great meal with naan, but waiters may encourage you to order a sauce so your meal isn't 'dry'. A bowl of dhal (say, the ubiquitous 'dhal fry') goes down well with any meal. Ordering starters then mains tends to be reserved for posher restaurants.

EATING SAFELY IN INDIA

With restaurants, cafes and ood stalls on every corner, dining options are almost limitless. But how do you know if a restaurant will be culinary perfection or a recipe for disaster?

The main risk is stomach upsets, which visitors tend to be more vulnerable to than locals. The golden rule is to eat at busy establishments; if there's a queue of locals waiting outside, chances are the food is excellent and the kitchen is clean.

Also think about what you are eating. Food that has been cooked and left to sit at room temperature is potentially risky; food freshly cooked to order will usually be fine. Fried and tandoor-cooked food gets an ultra-high blast of heat to kill off nasties before it is served.

Anything uncooked is a gamble; this includes salad and fresh vegetables, which may have been washed in dirty water. If you buy fruit, wash or peel it before eating. Avoid ice and cups of water offered at restaurants for the same reason.

Dairy (including ice cream) is a common source of bugs, but paneer and curd are fermented (and curd will help populate your gut with healthy bacteria). Undercooked meat and fish are a higher risk than vegetables.

Some travellers choose to go vegetarian as a precaution but it's easy to have a trouble-free non-veg trip if you're careful. Remember, always wash your hands before you eat – germs on your fingers are the most likely source of infection.

Responsible Travel

Climate Change & Travel

It's impossible to ignore the impact we have when travelling; Lonely Planet urges all travellers to engage with their travel carbon footprint, which will mainly come from air travel. While there often isn't an alternative, travellers can look to minimise the number of flights they take, opt for newer aircrafts and use cleaner ground transport, such as trains. One proposed solution – purchasing carbon offsets – unfortunately does not cancel out the impact of individual flights. While most destinations will depend on air travel for the foreseeable future, for now, pursuing ground-based travel where possible is the best course of action.

The **UN Carbon Offset Calculator** shows how flying impacts a household's emissions:

The **ICAO's carbon emissions calculator** allows visitors to analyse the CO2 generated by point-to-point journeys:

Support National Parks & Reserves

Just 5.3% of India is officially protected and the expanding population is a growing threat. Visiting national parks with local guides channels money from tourism to local communities, providing a direct incentive for conservation.

Avoid Plastic Bottles

Avoid disposable plastic bottles; bring a bottle and purify your own water (or use hotel communal supplies), or drink fresh coconut water or chai, preferably in a glass or clay *kulhad* (pictured above) rather than a plastic or paper cup.

Seek out hotels that use solar power, recycle wastewater and use natural materials and homegrown produce, such as **Pench Tree Lodge** in Madhya Pradesh, **Neeleshwar Hermitage** in Kerala and **Barefoot at Havelock** in the Andaman Islands.

If you go trekking, carry out your rubbish (and any rubbish you can pick up and carry) for disposal in the nearest town. **India Hikes** *(indiahikes.com)* is a pioneer of waste-free trekking.

PEDAL OR WALK

Cut the carbon by exploring on foot or by bicycle; rental bikes are available in many tourist hotspots. Set out early in the morning before the traffic builds up; you'll breathe easier and be safer too.

GIVE RESPONSIBLY

Rather than handing out cash to beggars, you can make a more lasting difference by donating to local nongovernment organisations (see *ngodarpan.gov.in* for a directory) or buying crafts from government or community-run cooperatives (*handicrafts.nic.in* has listings).

Bring a Tote Bag

In many regions, particularly in the mountains, plastic bags are banned, along with plastic bottles, to protect watercourses and wildlife. Bring a fabric tote bag and use this instead of accepting plastic bags from shops.

Watch Your Water Use

To avoid contributing to water shortages, minimise water use by showering rather than taking a bath, and wash clothes less frequently. Only put out your hotel towels to be laundered at the end of your stay.

Turn Off the Power

Turn off the master electricity switch to your hotel room (normally by the door) whenever you go out. That way, the air-con, fan, lights and water heater won't consume unnecessary energy while you're out.

Don't Buy Animal Souvenirs

Avoid souvenirs made from animal parts, including seashells, teeth, skin, claws and fur. Crafts made from endangered animals are sold widely – including shawls made from endangered shahtoosh wool – so shop carefully and seek out sustainable mementos instead.

Don't Contribute to the Human Zoo

When visiting Adivasi (Indigenous community) villages, go with a local guide and stay in local homestays, to avoid contributing to the exploitation of tribal people. Responsible operators such as Odisha's **Desia Koraput** (*desiakoraput.com*) directly support local people.

Riding elephants can cause them physical harm – avoid rides in national parks and at tourist sites.

Giving pens or sweets to children does little to help their situation – consider donating to local schools or community organisations instead.

Pollution

Particle pollution in cities such as Delhi can reach 30 times the WHO-recommended safe limit – monitor air-quality levels at *aqi.in/dashboard/india*. Use battery-powered electric autorickshaws rather than petrol-powered vehicles to help reduce emissions.

RESOURCES

responsibletourismindia.com
A useful resource for ethical and sustainable tours and activities.

rtsoi.org
Certifies responsible tourism projects in India.

wti.org.in
Raising awareness of conservation issues.

CLOCKWISE FROM TOP LEFT: VEK_SAN/SHUTTERSTOCK, INNA DODOR/SHUTTERSTOCK, PRADEEPGAURS/SHUTTERSTOCK, DHAN PAL SINGH/SHUTTERSTOCK

LGBTIQ+ Travellers

While urban areas are more open, much of India is still socially conservative. Larger cities and tourist hubs such as Goa are more welcoming of queer people, but it's still best to be discreet. You are unlikely to face overt discrimination on the street or in hotels. The local queer scene is largely underground, though some major cities host pride marches, film festivals and events.

Travel Advice

When booking rooms, you are likely to be given twin beds (unless you request otherwise) – staff often assume same-sex couples are friends sharing a room to save costs. Big hotel chains usually welcome queer guests even if they don't advertise it. Generally, discretion is key for trouble-free LGBTIQ+ travel. Avoid public displays of affection (the same applies for heterosexual travellers), especially in rural areas. Indian men and women often hold hands with members of the same sex, regardless of sexual orientation, so this won't raise eyebrows. If questioned about your relationship, 'just friends' usually works.

QUEER RIGHTS IN INDIA

In 2018, the Supreme Court decriminalised homosexuality in India, removing laws put in place in colonial times. However, the same court, while recognising the rights of gay couples, declined to legalise same-sex marriages in 2023. In 2026, India rolled back trans people's once-constitutional right to self-identify and placed restrictions on who can receive gender-affirming surgery.

QUEER TOURISM

Reach out to LGBTIQ+-friendly tour operators like **Gay Tours India** *(gaytoursindia.com)*, **Indja Pink** *(indjapink.co.in)*, **Out & About** *(instagram.com/out_and_about____)*, **Pink Vibgyor** *(pinkvibgyor.com)* and **Gay Trip India** *(gaytripindia.com)*. International operators such as Intrepid welcome LGBTIQ+ travellers. **Delhi Queer Heritage Walks** *(instagram.com/delhiqueerheritagewalks)* runs walking tours exploring the city's queer history.

WHERE TO GO

Mumbai has the LaLit hotel's inclusive club **Kitty Su Mumbai**; **Salvation Star** *(facebook.com/SalvationStar)* organises queer events. Delhi has queer-friendly cafe **Jugmug Thela** (p61), music spot **Depot 48** (p61), and **Kitty Su** (p61) at Connaught Place.

In Goa, find queer parties at **BudXLoft** *(instagram.com/budxloft)*, **Five 44** *(five44.bar)* and **Hopping Frog** *(hoppingfrog.in)*. Follow **Queer Kinara Goa** *(instagram.com/queer_kinara_goa)* for upcoming events.

Bengaluru queer-friendly spaces include **Urban Solace**, **Kitty Ko** and rooftop bar **Toit** (p801). In Kolkata, visit **Tavern** (p420) and **Marbella's**.

Queer Festivals

Mumbai hosts the **Kashish Mumbai International Queer Film Festival** *(mumbaiqueerfest.com)*, with Indian and foreign LGBTIQ+ films. Delhi has the **Rainbow Lit Fest** *(rainbowliteraturefestival.com)*. Bengaluru has the **Bangalore Queer Film Festival** *(bqff.in)*, while Kolkata has LGBTIQ+ film festival **Dialogues** *(instagram.com/dialoguesfilmfest.in)*.

Accessible Travel

With its uneven streets, heavy traffic and crowds, India can be a tricky destination for travellers with mobility issues, particularly wheelchair users. Many travellers overcome the obstacles and have an amazing trip, but it's easiest with the support of an able-bodied companion.

Travel by Air & Rail

India's rail and airline staff are experienced in assisting passengers with mobility issues, and larger stations have elevators. Travel 1st class on trains or use Vande Bharat services for maximum space to manoeuvre.

Airport

Major airports such as Delhi, Mumbai, Bengaluru, Hyderabad, Kolkata and Chennai meet international accessibility standards. Allow extra time for check-in and speak to airlines (particularly domestic carriers) in advance about your needs.

Accommodation

Midrange and top-end accommodation is more likely to be accessible. However, steps are common and lifts are often small (or stop at mezzanines between floors). Fully accessible bathrooms are uncommon; suite rooms usually have roomier facilities.

CAR & DRIVER

Chartering a taxi is the most stress-free way to explore if you have mobility issues. Drivers can help you access the vehicle, and taxis have air-con and can usually fit a small folding wheelchair.

Dangerous Drains

Pavements in India are often formed by placing concrete slabs over open drains. These slabs can be uneven and often break, creating hazardous terrain for the mobility impaired – navigate slowly and cautiously.

Be Careful on the Streets

Be careful crossing the road; vehicles routinely ignore pedestrian crossings, and pavements are crowded and full of trip hazards. Taking taxis or autorickshaws from point to point can minimise the need for road crossings.

HISTORIC SIGHTS

Many sights in India were constructed centuries before accessibility laws were passed. Major attractions such as Jaipur's City Palace and the Taj Mahal have ramps, but access to some areas is still limited by steps and narrow passageways.

RESOURCES

Association of People with Disability *(apd-india.org)* Represents the needs of people with disabilities in India.

Disabled Holidays *(disabledholidays.com)* Offers accessible holidays to many destinations in India.

Responsible Travel *(responsibletravel.com)* Specialises in responsible holidays, including wheelchair-accessible India trips.

Enable Holidays *(enableholidays.com/india)* Specialist agent offering supported and wheelchair accessible trips.

Intrepid *(intrepidtravel.com)* Reputable tour agency that welcomes travellers with disabilities.

Most Indian Metro networks and many major train stations have lifts from street level, and step-free access to platforms, with space on board for wheelchairs. India's new Vande Bharat trains also have accessible carriages with ramps and accessible toilets.

Women Travellers

Women travelling to India have extra considerations to keep in mind – from harassment and safety in crowds to finding menstrual products. While most women travel to India without problems, it pays to be cautious in some situations. As anywhere, following the lead of local women is the best way to stay safe.

Unwanted Attention & Harassment

Unwanted attention from men is a common problem. Local women often use phones, dark glasses, headphones and wedding rings (or pretend ones) to avert this kind of attention. While India's anti-rape laws were tightened following some high-profile gang-rape and murder cases, incidents of rape and sexual assault continue to be common (and often under-reported).

Negative attitudes towards darker-skinned people from South India have existed in India since Mughal and colonial times, and some Black travellers have reported facing particular harassment and racism.

Buses & Trains

Harassment on public transport can be an issue, but urban trains often have special sections or carriages for women travellers. Conductors on buses will often make space for women to sit with local women (who travel for free in some areas).

Booking higher-class berths on trains will ensure curtains for privacy. Some women prefer travelling in 2AC class with several other passengers around, rather than travelling with just one stranger in a two-berth 1st-class compartment.

Local Transport

Touristy destinations (such as Goa) and large cosmopolitan cities tend to be less conservative in terms of dress than more rural areas. The locally popular *salwar kameez* (loose trousers with a long tunic) is practical, and suitable for visits to sites where 'modesty' is expected. The accompanying dupatta (long scarf) is handy for covering your head in places of worship.

Many women in India wear long shorts and a T-shirt when swimming in public; having a sarong handy for covering up when appropriate at the beach or pool is recommended. If in doubt, follow the example of local women.

Women's Health

Seek medical advice from women doctors if you become ill, and bring sufficient supplies of your chosen contraception, menstrual products and treatment for UTIs. Sanitary pads are readily available, but tampons and menstrual cups are harder to find.

OTHER TIPS

- Use women-only dorms, and choose better-quality hotels in safer neighbourhoods.
- Look out for all-women group tours led by female guides.
- Try to avoid arriving in an unfamiliar destination after dark, and be cautious of walking alone, particularly in empty areas or at night.

Scams

Regrettably, scams are a common pitfall in India, so be cautious, without being paranoid. You can normally tell quite quickly if you are being pressured into doing something you weren't planning on doing – if something doesn't feel right, politely decline whatever is being offered.

Touts

If someone starts an unsolicited conversation and tries to steer you towards – or away from – a specific business, they may be seeking a commission. If you agree to be led somewhere you weren't planning to visit, you might find yourself at a souvenir shop, hotel or travel agency where you'll pay a mark-up.

When taking autorickshaws or taxis, decline any detours on the way to your destination, and be sceptical of claims that your chosen hotel is shut, closed down or full – ask to be dropped nearby, and check for yourself, unaccompanied.

Rickshaw and taxi prices are often hiked at transport hubs and tourist sites; use prepaid counters where available or summon a ride via Uber or Ola.

Bargaining

Haggling is a feature of life in India, but it's a game, not a battle, and shouldn't be an angry process. Unless prices are fixed, vendors will typically suggest a price that is a little high, so offer 30% to 40% less and see how they respond. After a little back and forth, you should reach a mutually acceptable price. If not, politely decline and try elsewhere.

Shopping Scams

Expect a bit of a mark-up from souvenir sellers – be prepared to bargain. Be wary of vendors promising you can sell things for a profit back home, particularly gems and carpets. Unless you're an experienced dealer, buy things because you like them, not in the hope of making a profit. Jewellery hubs such as Jaipur have dedicated testing labs that can confirm your gems are genuine.

Druggings

Politely decline offers of food and drink from strangers – travellers have been given spiked food or drinks by thieves, particularly on public transport. As anywhere, be cautious of accepting drinks from strangers in bars and clubs because of the risk from date-rape drugs.

Money Scams

Credit cards are vulnerable to cloning or theft so be careful at ATMs and keep your PIN hidden. Always make sure credit card transactions are carried out in front of you. Never change money in the street, and always count your money before you leave forex counters.

TOURIST OFFICE OR TRAVEL AGENT?

Some travel agencies masquerade as 'tourist offices' but actually exist to sell (often overpriced) tours and transport tickets. If someone offers to lead you to the 'tourist office', you may end up at an agency, paying a 1st-class price for a 3rd-class seat. If asked if this is your first time in India, say you've made many visits, to be less of a target.

FROM LEFT: DON MAMMOSER/SHUTTERSTOCK, DON MAMMOSER/SHUTTERSTOCK

Religious Etiquette

Religion plays an massive role in Indian society, despite this being the largest secular democracy in the world. For the most part, India's varied faiths coexist harmoniously, but communal tensions surface periodically. It is important to be respectful when entering religious sites or participating in religious festivals. Images and likenesses of gods and goddesses demand a similar reverence, as do people at prayer.

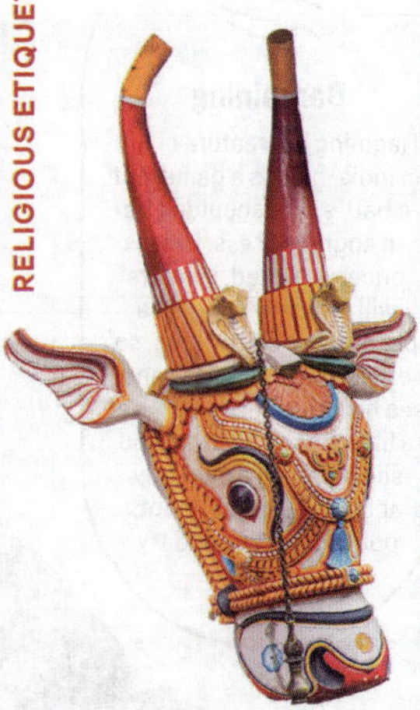

Holy Cow

Cows are deeply venerated in Hindu culture, both as a source of dairy products and manure for fuel and fertiliser and as a symbol of the divine – Shiva's *vahana* (divine vehicle) is the bull Nandi, and Krishna spent his childhood as a cowherd.

Cows are treated with respect (within limits – market traders are not averse to shooing away cows trying to steal their produce). In particular, killing cows and eating beef is considered sinful, and it is banned in some states. In recent years, Hindu nationalist 'cow vigilantes' have targeted minorities perceived to be harming cattle.

Dress Appropriately

Dress modestly when visiting temples. Avoid tight or revealing clothes, shorts, short dresses and sleeveless outfits. In many mosques, women are not allowed to enter the area used by men, and may also need to cover their heads – also a requirement in *gurdwaras* (Sikh temples). Some mosques and Jain and Hindu temples (particularly in the south) are closed to non-believers. In some South Indian Hindu temples, men may be asked to remove their shirts and women must cover their legs.

Go Barefoot

Remove your shoes before entering religious sites, from temples to monasteries and mosques. Going barefoot is a sign of respect and humility, and shoe racks (sometimes charging a nominal fee) are usually provided near the entrance. Stricter temples may ask you to remove socks as well.

No Photos

Many religious sites have a 'no photography' policy, especially in the inner sanctum. This includes some Tibetan Buddhist monasteries, and waterside ghats (ceremonial steps) at Hindu shrines. Respect this rule – there will usually be signs; check with the priest if in doubt. At some shrines, phones and cameras must be left with guards or in lockers at the entrance. Even if cameras are permitted, be respectful and avoid taking photos of people praying.

Pluralism

Religious pluralism is a core value in India. Nearly 80% of Indians practise Hinduism, with Muslims (14%) being the largest minority. Other important faiths include Christianity (2.3%), Sikhism (1.7%), Buddhism (0.7%) and Jainism (0.4%), with smaller numbers of animists and Zoroastrian Parsis.

OTHER RELIGIOUS PROSCRIPTIONS

Menstruating women are prohibited from entering many Hindu temples and almost all Jain temples, a practice that dates back to Vedic times, linked to outdated attitudes to menstrual blood being 'unclean'. While attitudes are slowly changing, respect signs asking menstruating women not to enter. Many Jain temples also ban leather items, food and drink.

FROM LEFT: MIFFIN THOMAS/SHUTTERSTOCK, AKELLA SRINIVAS RAMALINGASWAMI/SHUTTERSTOCK

Festivals

India's festival calendar is packed with spectacular celebrations, from secular art and crafts fairs and celebrations of dance and music to vast religious festivals that draw millions of devotees.

Hindu Festivals

Hindu festivals are often linked to the birth dates of deities, changes in the season and legendary events – from Shiva's cosmic dance to historical battles from the Ramayana. Festivals relating to Shiva, Krishna, Rama and Ganesh feature particularly vibrant celebrations.

The most famous Hindu festivals are Holi, which sees coloured powder thrown about enthusiastically in February/March, and Diwali in October/November, marked by fireworks and butter lamps. Held in September/October, Dussehra sees huge parades of temple deities (pictured), while clay deity idols are immersed to mark the victory of good over evil for Navratri and Durga Puja in autumn.

Pilgrimages

Hindu pilgrimages such as Tirumala Brahmotsavam at Tirumala in Andhra Pradesh can draw millions of pilgrims – visit cautiously as there's a risk of stampedes. The biggest festival of all is the Kumbh Mela, which takes place every 12 years at Haridwar, Prayagraj (Allahabad), Ujain or Nashik (with smaller festivals held in the same locations every three years). Prayagraj's 2025 festival attracted an estimated 660 million devotees!

Buddhist, Jain & Sikh Celebrations

Many Jain and Buddhist festivals are linked to major events in the lives of the Buddha and the Jain *tirthankars* (great teachers). The Tibetan Buddhist new year, Losar, sees masked dancers in Himalayan regions, while Buddha Purnima in April/May marks the birth, enlightenment and liberation of the Buddha. For Sikhs, the birthday of Guru Nanak in November and Vaisakhi in April, marking the arrival of spring and the birth of the Sikh religion, see huge celebrations in Punjab.

Islamic Festivals

Muslim festivals follow the Islamic lunar calendar, which moves forward around 11 days every year compared to the Gregorian calendar. During Ramadan (Ramazan), the month of fasting, many Muslims avoid eating or drinking from dawn until sunset, breaking the fast with a feast at Eid al-Fitr. There are more celebrations for Eid al-Adha, commemorating Ibrahim's willingness to sacrifice his son, and the Shia festival of Muharram, commemorating Hussein Ibn Ali. Sufi sites hold Urs festivals to mark the death anniversaries of Sufi saints.

Festival Practicalities

Festivals can impact transport schedules and hotel availability – always book well ahead for festival travel. Extra public transport is laid on for major celebrations, along with special pilgrim accommodation and food, but the crowds can be phenomenal and many years see deadly crushes – take extra care when travelling.

LUNAR CALENDARS

Most religious festivals in India are tied to ancient lunar calendars, with dates that change every year compared to the Gregorian calendar. The government site *india.gov.in/calendar* features dates of major celebrations. Muslim festivals may be dependent on sightings of the moon – always check dates before you travel.

Language

India is a vastly multilingual nation. Of the 121 languages spoken here, 22 are recognised as official by the Indian Constitution. Possibly because of this linguistic diversity, English is still widely used as the lingua franca. Efforts to promote Hindi, the predominant language in the North, as the national language have been ongoing. However, few people speak Hindi in the South as it bears no resemblance to longstanding Dravidian languages like Tamil.

Hindi Basics

Hello./Goodbye. नमस्ते na·ma·ste

Yes. जी हाँ jee haang

No. जी नही jee na·heeng

Excuse me. सुनिए su·ni·ye

Sorry. माफ़ कीजिये
maaf kee·ji·ye

Please ... कृपया ... kri·pa·yaa ...

Thank you. थैंक यू thayn·kyoo

What's your name?
आपका नाम क्या है
aap kaa naam kyaa hay

My name is ... मेरा नाम है
me·raa naam ... hay

Do you speak English?
क्या आपको अंग्रेजी आती है
kyaa aap ko an·gre·zee aa·tee hay

I don't understand.
मैं नहीं समझा / समझी
mayng na·heeng sam·jaa/sam·jee (m/f)

Where's ...? कहाँ है
ka·haang hay

What's the address?
पता क्या है pa·taa kyaa hay

Can you show me (on the map)?
नक्शे पर दिखा सकते हैं
(nak·she par) di·kaa sak·te hayng

Help! मदद कीजिए
ma·dad kee·ji·ye

Where is the toilet?
टॉयलेट कहां है
taa·i·let ka·haang hay

Tamil Basics

Hello. வணக்கம். va·nak·kam

Goodbye. போய் வருகிறேன்.
po·i va·ru·ki·reyn

Yes./No. ஆமாம்./இல்லை.
aa·maam/il·lai

Excuse me. தயவு செய்து.
ta·ya·vu sei·du

Sorry. மன்னிக்கவும.
man·nik·ka·vum

Please. தயவு செய்து.
ta·ya·vu chey·tu

Thank you. நன்றி. nan·dri

What's your name?
உங்கள் பெயர் என்ன?
ung·kal pe·yar en·na

My name is ... என் பெயர்...
en pe·yar ...

Do you speak English?
நீங்கள் ஆங்கிலம பேசுவீர்களா?
neeng·kal aang·ki·lam pey·chu·veer·ka·la

I don't understand.
எனக்கு விளங்கவில்லை.
e·nak·ku vi·lang·ka·vil·lai

Where's ...?
... எங்கே இருக்கிறது?
... eng·key i·ruk·ki·ra·tu

What's the address?
விலாசம் என்ன? vi·laa·cham en·na

Can you show me (on the map)?
எனக்கு (வரைபடத்தில்) காட்ட முடியுமா?
e·nak·ku (va·rai·pa·tat·til) kaat·ta mu·ti·yu·maa

Help! உதவி! u·ta·vi

Where is the toilet?
கழிவறைகள் எங்கே?
ka·zi·va·rai·kal eng·key

HINDI NUMBERS

1	ek
2	do
3	teen
4	chaar
5	paanch
6	chhe
7	saat
8	aath
9	nau
10	dus

DONATIONS TO ENGLISH FROM HINDI

Numerous – including chutney, jungle, thug, bandana, bungalow, loot, shampoo and guru.

Hindi to English

English borrows generously from Hindi. The first known inclusion, according to the Oxford English Dictionary, was *qila* (fort) in 1761 and countless others have followed since.

Street Talk

Yaar Friend
Arre! Hey!
Bas That's it/ Enough
Theek Hai OK
Bindaas Cool

CARRYING CURRENCY

If you look closely at an Indian banknote, you'll find 15 languages listed in a narrow panel on the reverse. These appear in English alphabetical order: Assamese, Bengali, Gujarati, Kannada, Kashmiri, Konkani, Malayalam, Marathi, Nepali, Oriya, Punjabi, Sanskrit, Tamil, Telugu and Urdu.

Polyglot India

India's linguistic vibrancy means it is almost natural for Indians to speak more than one language. As per the 2011 census, over 26% Indians are bilingual while 7.10% are trilingual. Most educated Indians speak English, which makes it easy to get around the country, but it always helps to know a little of the local language.

Language Groups

All Indian languages fall into one of four groups: Indo-Aryan, Dravidian, Sino-Tibetan and Afro-Asiatic. Although writing came much later to India, all Indian scripts originate from the same Brahmi script. This explains why both Sanskrit and Tamil have strong oral traditions.

WHO SPEAKS HINDI?

Hindi and English are the official languages of India, and Hindi is the official language of nine states. In addition, versions of Hindi are spoken by the Indian diaspora around the globe. It's the third most spoken language in the world.

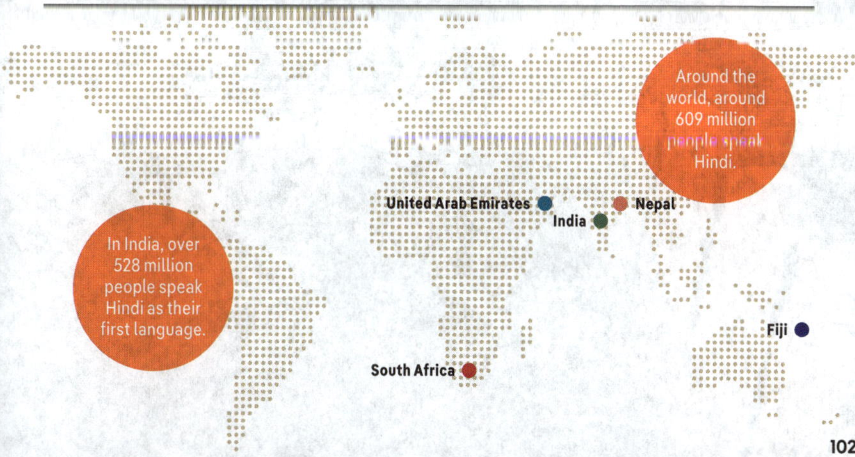

THE INDIA

STORYBOOK

Our writers delve deep into different aspects of Indian life.

Nahargarh fort (p121)
TRAVELPHOTOBLOGGERS/SHUTTERSTOCK

A HISTORY OF INDIA IN 15 PLACES

With its ruins of forgotten cities, vanished and vanquished empires and a history that scrolls back to the Stone Age, Indian history is best described as kaleidoscopic. Combined with waves of multicultural immigration as the birthplace of three major religions, this peninsular nation's past makes it anything but boring.

By Dr Ruchika Sharma

INDIA'S HISTORY STRETCHES back to the Palaeolithic period, with two-million-year-old sites such as the Soan Valley. However, it was the Neolithic site of Mehrgarh that kickstarted India's rich history of civilisations. This 7000 BCE site became the launchpad for the Indus Valley civilisation (which extended into present-day Pakistan), known for its meticulous urban planning and standardisation. Although the decline of the Indus Valley civilisation remains a mystery, what followed it was waves of steppe pastoralist migrants who composed and later wrote the Vedas (Hindu scriptures). City states came up in the 3rd century BCE when Buddhism flourished and the Mauryan king Ashoka's inscriptions were put on pillars and rocks. More criss-crossing of people followed and brought Arabian traders into contact with 8th-century India via the Arabian Sea.

At the heels of these traders came the Turkic sultans in the 12th century, who established sultanates in Delhi, Bengal, Malwa (present-day Madhya Pradesh and Rajasthan) and the Deccan. This cultural melting pot then bubbled to greater heights under the Mughal empire, which, at its peak in the 16th century, contributed 25% of the world's GDP. It was eventually reduced to a meagre 3% in the 20th century due to heavy European colonial exploitation. Regardless, India's battle with colonialism was nothing short of heroic and inspired many nations and leaders alike. Colonialism did leave an indelible impact on India in terms of poverty and communalism fuelled by the horrors of partition, which continue to be considerable challenges to the country in modern times.

1. Bhimbetka, Madhya Pradesh

ONE OF INDIA'S EARLIEST SETTLEMENTS

India's antiquity is beautifully illustrated on the rock shelters of Bhimbetka, where red pigment paintings, engravings and carvings depict fierce battles, intense hunts and totemic animals as well as mythical creatures. With some rock shelters dated to a million years ago, the caves also bear other markers of habitation such as ostrich eggshell beads and quartzite cleavers and hand axes. While human settlement in these caves was continuous from the Stone Age to the Mesolithic period, rock art featured intermittently even till the medieval period, making Bhimbetka a valuable record of Indian history.

For more on Bhimbetka, see p608.

2. Dholavira, Gujarat

5000-YEAR-OLD CITY

In the heart of the harsh Kachchh (Kutch) desert, Dholavira is a 5000-year-old story of human resilience. The city was built largely out of stone, starting in 3000 BCE with a fortress that was destroyed by an earthquake in 2600 BCE. But that only matured it, and between 2500 and 2000 BCE, Dholavira's dwellers built a well-planned citadel and lower town with extra care given to the drainage system. Huge reservoirs built for rainwater harvesting can still be seen. Ceremonies and markets were held at an open area dubbed today as the 'stadium'. For the weary desert traveller, signboards were installed; one still stands at the northern entrance of the citadel, with 10 symbols of the Indus script. As part of the Indus Valley civilisation, this city was contemporaneous with the Mesopotamian and Egyptian civilisations.

For more on Dholavira, see p656.

3. Bodhgaya, Bihar

CRADLE OF BUDDHISM

Siddhartha Gautama, the prince of Kosala, earned his famous epithet, 'Buddha' (the Enlightened One), at Bodhgaya. The Mahabodhi temple here is said to mark the exact spot where the Buddha, after years of wandering and asceticism, took a seat under a tree and passed eight stages of wisdom (Bodhi) to attain enlightenment. The Mahabodhi temple has a fascinating history of lying forgotten for centuries and then being partially reconstructed in the 19th century. Bodhgaya also features temples and monasteries built by people from Sri Lanka, Korea, Japan, China and other countries with a considerable Buddhist population. Each temple has its unique architecture and history.

For more on Bodhgaya, see p480.

Mahabodhi Temple (p482), Bihar

PACCEKA/SHUTTERSTOCK

4. Ajanta & Ellora Caves, Maharashtra

HISTORY THROUGH ART

The rock-cut caves of Ajanta and Ellora in the Western Ghats have a history of at least 1200 years, most of which is depicted on their walls as paintings or in stone as sculptures. While the Ajanta Caves, starting from the 2nd century BCE, were exclusively Buddhist caves made as monasteries and worship halls for the monks, the Ellora Caves, starting from the 7th century CE, are multireligious with Hindu, Buddhist and Jain caves. The walls of Ajanta are adorned with a stunning array of paintings depicting scenes from the life of the Buddha, while Ellora's walls sport lifelike rock-cut sculptures of deities along with the Kailasanatha Temple, hewn from a single rock.

For more on the Ajanta & Ellora Caves, see p720.

5. Nalanda, Bihar

WORLD'S FIRST RESIDENTIAL UNIVERSITY

While the antiquity of Nalanda goes back to the 5th century BCE as an important trade centre, its prominence began in the 5th century CE with the establishment of the Nalanda university. Predating the University of Oxford by almost 500 years, this Buddhist university was visited by Chinese pilgrims Hieun Tsang and I-Tsing, who wrote interesting accounts of the university's rules for admission and registration. The university offered courses on grammar, philology, medicine and logic. Overshadowed by other universities in the vicinity, Nalanda university faded into oblivion for lack of proper patronage in the 13th century, leaving behind its haunting ruins.

For more on Nalanda, see p488.

6. Mehrauli Archaeological Park, Delhi

TALLEST BRICK MINARET IN THE WORLD

Delhi's story of being India's seat of power starts from the 12th century with Mehrauli. Capital of the Delhi sultans, Mehrauli boasts many 800-year-old structures along with its crowning glory, the 72.5m-high minaret, the Qutb Minar. Built in three stages and over a period of 200 years, this sandstone and marble marvel is a palimpsest built next to Delhi's oldest mosque, the Qutb Mosque. The Minar was built in honour of Delhi's patron saint, Qutbuddin

Bakhtiyar Kaki, whose hospice is not far from it. An ornate gateway, the Alai Darwaza, featuring the first true dome in India, stands next to the Minar, as do many other tombs and palaces dated variously from the 12th to 19th centuries.

For more on Mehrauli Archaeological Park, see p97

7. Mandu, Madhya Pradesh

FIRST EXTANT HOSPITAL IN INDIA

A 14th-century poet described the fort of Mandu as 'high as the sky', and with its height of 61m, it does indeed give that impression. Capital of the 14th-century Malwa sultanate, Mandu also has a Dar-us-Shifa (hospital) that currently bears the misnomer of 'Gada Shah's shop'. A Persian text describes the hospital as two storeys with a separate section reserved for treatment of mental health. Besides this, Mandu's water scarcity led its patrons to build numerous water management structures, many of which still sustain its population.

For more on Mandu, see p614.

8. Hampi, Karnataka

THE DESERTED CITY

Capital of the Vijayanagar kingdom, the city of Hampi flourished for two centuries before being abruptly deserted in the 16th century. The city continues to be eerily deserted but boasts a set of impressive monuments, such as the Hazararama Temple, where the walls have elaborate sculptures depicting scenes from the Hindu epic Ramayana. The fortress of Hampi itself was a formidable one as reported by the 16th-century Portuguese traveller Domingo Paes. Signs of the city's sacking are still imprinted in the Vitthala Temple as well as the damaged Lakshmi Narasimha statue.

For more on Hampi, see p823.

9. Kumbhalgarh, Rajasthan

INDIA'S GREAT WALL

A 14th-century wonder, the fort of Kumbhalgarh with its encircling wall was constructed over a period of 15 years. Named after its patron Maharana Kumbha, the fort serves as an excellent representative of medieval Indian military genius. The Kumbhalgarh wall is also famous as India's Great Wall, a 36km-long serpentine construction 1100m above sea level. The battlements and the high walls ensured that this became an impregnable fortress that the Udaipur Maharana could take refuge in when under attack. Interspersed with palaces, guard rooms and temples, the wall is quite a hiking experience.

For more on Kumbhalgarh, see p157.

10. Old Goa, Goa

THE PORTUGUESE INTERREGNUM

Established by the Bijapur sultanate and wrested by the Portuguese, Old Goa preserves India's maritime history. The 16th-century Portuguese thalassocracy left behind a series of mostly mannerist-style churches before ending abruptly in the 17th century due to a malaria epidemic. The largest church is the Sé Cathedral, which took 60 years to construct. The murals on the walls of the Church of St Francis of Assisi have an unmistakable Indic influence in the way the angels and saints are depicted. Stone used for some of these churches, such as the Basilica de Bom Jesus, was quarried at Bassein, another Portuguese stronghold adjacent to Goa.

For more on Old Goa, see p751.

11. Vijayapura (Bijapur), Karnataka

SECOND-LARGEST DOME IN THE WORLD

The seat of the Bijapur sultanate contains architecture that is beautifully syncretic, a perfect synthesis of Timurid domes and Indic carvings. The epitome of this is the Gol Gumbaz, the 17th-century mausoleum of its patron Sultan Mohammad Adil Shah, who lies buried under its huge dome measuring 44m in diameter. Its 'whispering gallery' has brilliant acoustics, a penchant for which was shared by Sultan Mohammad's father, Ibrahim II, who built a new city, Nauraspur, adjacent to Vijayapura and dedicated to his practice of Hindustani classical music. Sultan Ibrahim lies buried in an ornate mausoleum decorated with the finest arabesques in India.

For more on Vijayapura, see p833.

12. Agra, Uttar Pradesh

THE TAJ OF INDIA

While Agra is famous for the Taj Mahal, its blueprint lies not far from it, in the tomb of Itimad-ud-Daulah. Made from white marble

Red Fort (p64), Old Delhi

and pietra dura mosaics, this mausoleum is an ode to a father from a daughter. The tomb was commissioned by Mughal queen Nur Jahan, who minted coins in her name in the city. Fatehpur Sikri at Agra was the seat of the Mughals for a considerable period and features the serene white marble tomb of saint Shaikh Salim Chishti and the lofty Buland Darwaza. The likeness of the Darwaza can be found in Mughal emperor Akbar's red sandstone tomb that lies a few kilometres away in Sikandra.

For more on Agra, see p310.

13. Old Delhi, Delhi

SEAT OF THE MUGHALS

The city of Shahjahanabad, now known as Purani Dilli (Old Delhi), is one of nine historical cities of Delhi. Located on what were once the banks of the Yamuna River, this city was the seat of the Mughal empire for most of 17th to the middle of the 19th century. The city was envisioned as a macrocosm of the Mughal court, where the throne of the Mughal emperor, the Red Fort, was the axis mundi, with the rest of the double-walled city in front of it. The Chandni Chowk market commissioned by Mughal emperor Shahjahan's daughter, Jahanara, still bears signs of colonial destruction in the wake of the 1857 revolt.

For more on Old Delhi, see p60.

14. Fort, Mumbai (Bombay)

GOTHIC GALORE

Dubbed by the British as the 'Urbs Prima in Indis' (most important city in India), Bombay, as it was then known, was made by artificially joining seven different islands in the Arabian Sea. The heart of British occupation in Bombay was the Fort (previously Fort George, built over the site of the Maratha Dongri Fort). Today, the area is littered with the remains of India's colonial past (which started in the 18th century). Most prominently, the Elphinstone Circle, later renamed the Horniman Circle in honour of an English editor who supported Indian independence, is built in a neoclassical style with its covered arcade and lofty pillars. The dominant style is neogothic as the Secretariat, the University of Mumbai, the David Sassoon Library and Reading Room, the Rajabai clock tower and Chhatrapati Shivaji Terminus (formerly Victoria Terminus) are all made with pointed arches and high ceilings.

For more on Fort, see p679.

15. Jhansi, Uttar Pradesh

A QUEEN'S FIGHT AGAINST COLONIALISM

Part of the kingdom of Orchha, the Jhansi fort was built in the early 17th century by a high-ranking Mughal officer, Bir Singh Bundela. The tall granite walls would later be bravely defended by the queen of Jhansi, Rani Lakshmibai, during the Indian rebellion of 1857 against the British. Using the Kadak Bijli cannon (which is proudly featured in the fort today), Lakshmibai fought British commander Hugh Rose and his forces, albeit unsuccessfully. Lakshmibai died heroically on the battlefield. Scenes of this epic battle still adorn the walls of the adjacent Lakshminarayan Temple, which was also built first in the 17th century.

MEET THE INDIANS

Friendly, feisty and frequently late. With over a billion people, stereotypes about Indians are as true as they are untrue. Dr Ravikant Kisana introduces his people.

FEW COUNTRIES POSSESS the name-recall that India does. It conjures up vivid images of bustling streets, colourful festivals, historical monuments and natural beauty. Yet, the people who make up this land are understood in flattening stereotypes: we like food, Bollywood and cricket.

While most people's understanding of Indian food comes from restaurant menus (notably butter chicken, naan and biryani), there exists a vast diversity of cuisines. From the complexity of Odia and Bengali fish and chutneys to the bamboo and fiery chilli pork from the Northeast, the food variety is so vast that even Indians themselves keep 'discovering' different kinds of Indian foods.

Our Bollywood obsession is all-consuming, but in truth, Bollywood is just one of the many film industries in India, such as the larger-than-life melodrama of Tollywood and the homespun mass appeal of Bhojpuri films. Fans of each are convinced that their cinema and stars are the best – and debates are heated.

Beyond cinema, only sport gets Indians as animated. Exhilaration and heartbreak flow in a collective delirium for those who see cricketers as gods and rockstars rolled into one. Football fires up similar emotions, bringing traffic to a standstill as teenagers in Messi and Ronaldo jerseys dribble down the lanes in Kolkata (Calcutta), Shillong, Goa and beyond. Elsewhere kabaddi, chess, wrestling and badminton draw huge crowds, attesting that Indians love a good contest and are not a one-sport people.

We love a spectacle! And none is bigger than the 'great Indian wedding'. From the loud, alcohol-soaked, nocturnal Punjabi weddings to the muted elegance of Tamil weddings to the community pride and dignity of Scheduled Caste Buddhist marriages, every community and region has its rituals and carousing traditions. It remains the ultimate honour – and often the most fun experience – to be invited to one.

But beyond the bright lights, India can also be a dark place. Inequity and social discrimination along religious and caste lines run deep even as most live distressed lives, with over 90% of rural Indian households living on less than US$110 per month. Air pollution and climate change, exacerbated by indifferent planning priorities, have heightened these challenges. With law and order stretched, crimes against women have grabbed headlines. While most Indians will go out of their way to help visitors, overcommercialisation of popular tourist sites, crowding and scams have soured some experiences.

Nonetheless, Indians remain positive and welcoming. We are a young nation, with over 65% below the age of 35. From social media creators to entrepreneurs, vibrant people are trying to give wings to their aspirations even in difficult circumstances. That is, in a nutshell, the vibe of Indians. Persevering and retaining the capacity to smile, 'Jeena Isi Ka Naam Hai' (This Is What Is Called Life) goes an old Bollywood song by Mukesh. We nod and agree.

Same but Different

Indians are divided across hundreds of languages and castes, each with its own unique culture. Large sections of the poorest come from marginalised castes, while most urban, English-speaking elites are minority dominant castes. The cultural balance of India hangs between these two.

CLOCKWISE FROM TOP LEFT: OSCAR ESPINOSA/SHUTTERSTOCK, ASH DANIEL/SHUTTERSTOCK, ELENA_ALEX_FERNS/SHUTTERSTOCK, DIETMAR TEMPS/SHUTTERSTOCK

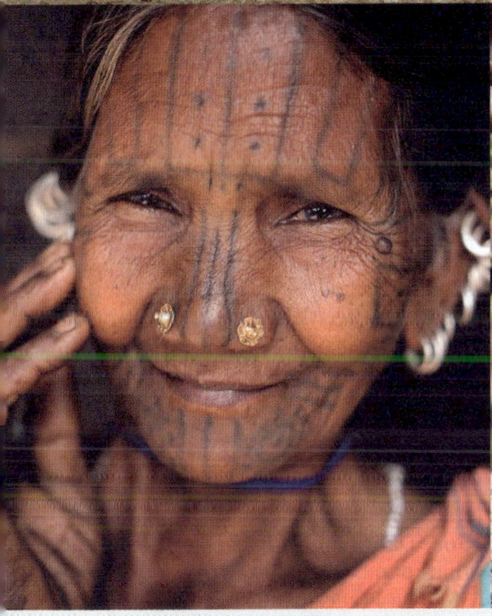

FROM THE 'OTHER' KOLKATA

I grew up in Kolkata, a city believed to be a bastion of progressive thought, intellectual discourse and art. But in India, caste shapes which stories get primacy and which are sidelined. As a child of 'lower'-caste Punjabi immigrants, I walked the streets of the rougher neighbourhoods of Topsia and Tangra, where I found freedom, joy and some life lessons too. My father, a Gujjar (semi-nomadic animal-rearing caste), instilled in me the hardy ethos of always being ready to move. My mother, a Dalit Sikh woman, kept me close to her faith and cultivated in me her love of sharing stories. Through them I saw stories of marginalised-caste, working-class poor and migrant workers, a heaving mass of humanity seeking a better, dignified life in the packed metropolis, beyond the popular elite narratives. The Kolkata my parents showed me forever shaped my gaze, which now looks for what has been overlooked.

Bonda woman, Odisha

DIETMAR TEMPS/SHUTTERSTOCK

INDIGENOUS INDIANS

Despite being pushed to the margins, India's tribes and Indigenous peoples continue to flourish, explains Adivasi writer Ruby Hembrom

IT IS NOT uncommon to hear 'I didn't know India has Indigenous peoples' from both foreigners and Indians alike, but Indigenous Indians account for 104 million of India's 1.43 billion people. That's nearly 9% – slotted across 705 ethnic groups recognised by the government. Dotting the entire country, their distribution is spread across terrains, from dense forests and lush valleys to arid deserts.

During British rule, these communities were identified and enumerated as 'tribes', distinct from the non-tribal majority. Later, after Indian independence, they were reclassified as 'Scheduled Tribes' (ST) when the Constitution was adopted in 1950, and subsequently gained administrative and political provisions and safeguards. The ST status transformed tribes from a vague social and cultural category to a political and administrative one, fully recognised as citizens of India (albeit marginalised ones). But the manner in which this was done continues to be a point of contention, with tribal groups being miscategorised across states and census listings, which have missed groups altogether at times. The result? Estimates of the ST numbers in India are ever-fluctuating, if not wholly inaccurate.

The People

Despite being such a small minority, STs make for an expansive diversity of groups. Between groups, not only do they vary linguistically and in their numerous belief systems (which exist outside Hinduism and the caste system), but there is diversity in physicality, individual population sizes, means of livelihood, degrees of development, social stratification and assimilation too.

India's central and eastern, and western regions, in particular – spanning from the states of Rajasthan, Gujarat, Maharashtra, Goa, Dadra and Nagar Haveli to Bihar, Jharkhand, West Bengal, Odisha (Orissa), Madhya Pradesh and Chhattisgarh – are home to over 55% of India's tribal groups. These include tribes like the Gonds, Bhils, Santals, Mundas, Oraons and Minas (Meenas), with populations that range from one million (Ho, Kharia) to a little over seven million people (Gonds, Bhils, Santals). Conversely, tribes like the Andamanese Islanders (island region), and the Birjia, Asur, Birhor (middle and eastern regions) have a population of less than 200 people.

Strikingly, Indigenous peoples make India's linguistic terrain kaleidoscopic. Although three-quarters of India speaks Indo-European languages, only a little over

1% of the tribal population speaks them as a native language (namely the Bhil and Halbi tribes). Meanwhile, tribes such as the Gond, Khond, Koya, Oraon and Toda speak Dravidian languages, while tribes of the Himalaya and Northeast India speak Sino-Tibetan languages, and tribes such as the Santal (Santhal), Munda, Kharia and Ho speak Austro-Asiatic ones.

Their Story

People from these tribal groups don't often have access to education, and those who do undertake it in the dominant mainstream languages (the official modes of instruction). And although constitutional provisions exist, STs remain among the poorest and most marginalised of Indian society. For 8.6% of the population, they are disproportionately overrepresented in those living below the poverty line. What's more, they have low literacy rates, poor physical health, and low life expectancies and incomes.

Most STs depend on agriculture, either as subsistence farmers or agricultural labourers, as a means of income. They are also collectors of forest produce, hunter-gatherers, pastoralists, nomadic herders and artisans. Traditional occupations of tribal groups range from honey collection to hunting small animals to engaging in metalwork and rope-making. Sadly, none of these roles is financially viable, leading to an increasing number of STs moving away from their traditional means of livelihood, and working as labourers on plantations or in mines and factories. Worse still, displacement due to financially motivated land grabs and changes in government policies has led to an increasing number of STs working as contract labourers in the construction industry and as domestic workers (such as household staff) in major cities, entering the unregulated informal labour market.

'Indigenous', 'Tribal' or 'Adivasi'?

Although the terms 'Adivasi', 'tribal', 'Scheduled Tribe' and 'Indigenous' each have their own histories, the use of 'Indigenous' is not officially recognised. And neither is Adivasi – so 'tribal' or 'ST' becomes a functional catch-all term to refer to India's Indigenous population.

The relationship the tribes and subtribes of India's Northeastern States have with both the colonial and Indian State is different from that of the central Indian tribes, and this difference plays out in how the tribes address themselves. The central Indian tribes call themselves Adivasi (*adi* meaning first and *vasis* meaning inhabitants). According to Adivasi sociologist Virginius Xaxa, the use of the term 'Adivasi' as being 'Indigenous' emerged more as a political self-reference than an anthropological definition. The term encapsulates the demand for recognition of identity, and rights over ancestral lands, forests and customary practices among other things. The Northeast has not adopted this nomenclature.

In a series of Constituent Assembly Debates about tribal groups between 1946 and 1949, the general opinion became an estimation of Adivasi backwardness, that their 'general level had to be raised'. The underlying conclusion was that tribal people being 'still in such a subhuman state of existence is something, for which [non-tribal Indians] should be ashamed'; that the existence of the STs was a 'stigma on our nation' and that they needed to 'come up to the level of the rest of the population' and be 'developed so quickly that they may become indistinguishable from the rest of the Indian population'.

The 'backwardness, upliftment, and development paradigm' currently operating within the middle ground of 'integration', as opposed to the extremes of assimilation or isolation, continues to determine national and legal frameworks for Adivasis.

Being 'Adivasi'

The term 'Adivasi' conveys a sense of empowerment, augmented by self-identification and solidarity with indigenous peoples' movements across the world. However, being Adivasi is not about suffering, but about the resilience emerging from it, and a celebration of ancestral approaches to life.

Faced with market-oriented forays into their regions, land dispossession and the undermining of their sovereignty, Adivasi history has also been marked by protests and rebellions against the British empire and the Indian zamindars (landowners) in the late 18th, 19th and early 20th centuries, like the Chuar rebellion in Bengal (1795–1809), the Bhil rebellion (1822–57), the Santhal Hul of 1855–56, the Birsa Ulgulan of 1895–1900, and the Bastar Bhumkal of 1910. The commemoration of these rebellions, and the ones who led them like Komaram Bheem, Birsa Munda, and the Santal siblings Sido, Kanhu, Phulo and Jhanu Murmu, is an important cultural marker for Adivasis.

Indigenous Renaissance

Adivasi identities are tied to their ancestral ways, rooted in land. They live in forested areas that comprise 15% of the country's land mass, which holds 80% of the biodiversity, making them stewards of biodiversity. It's no wonder India, like the rest of the world, is turning to Indigenous knowledge and practices to find solutions to the many crises humanity faces – the climate crisis and beyond. In India, where the male-to-female ratio is often skewed, Indigenous groups average 990 females for every 1000 males in comparison to the overall ratio of 943 to 1000, according to the most recent census in 2011, making them more equitable.

The emphasis on community, cultural heritage, performing arts, social practices, rituals, festive events, food, knowledge and practices concerning nature and the universe, medicinal knowledge and skills in traditional arts and crafts make these rich, dynamic living cultures that need to flourish; promoting preservation and parity, in the face of modernity and dispossession.

Indigenous knowledge systems have stood the test of time. They can be seen in the 100 identified living root bridges (Jingkieng Jri) across 72 villages in the East Khasi Hills and West Jaintia Hills of the northeastern state of Meghalaya, where the Khasis wove, and still weave, the roots of the Indian rubber tree along hollowed-out trunks of the areca palm and bamboo; these turn into sturdy foot bridges in about 15 to 30 years, spanning from 4.5m to 76m in length, and enduring for over 500 years. It's in the popularisation of Adivasi cuisine like Aruna Tirkey's eatery and cooking school Ajam Emba ('delectable' in Kurukh/Oraon) in Ranchi, Jharkhand, reviving and upholding the culinary heritage of central Indian tribes. Adivasi food of mainly the Oraon, Munda, Santal and Ho tribes – rice tea, *jil pitha* (rice dough with meat barbecued on sal leaves), *marh jhor* (boiled rice water curried broth, with native leafy vegetables and whole spices), *marwa roti* (finger millet flat bread) – are served here, ensuring ancient recipes and staples diets remain in circulation. Traditional art forms like Sohrai (harvest festival) wall paintings by Santal women on their mud homes, across Jharkhand, Bihar, Odisha and West Bengal, turn their villages into arresting compositions of flora, fauna, and geometrical designed canvasses, crafted from natural pigments. They lament that concrete housing alternatives and aspirations threaten this ancient ritualistic and ornamental art form, which is replicable on cement and mortar but only ever comes alive on mud.

Adivasi activist Dr Ram Dayal Munda once called upon Adivasis to *'naachi se baanchi'* – dance to survive. Adivasis, he believed, would survive if they remained intentionally connected to their practices. Dancing was an expression of their indigeneity, an act of defiance – a move towards cultural preservation and endurance.

THE TERM 'ADIVASI' ENCAPSULATES THE DEMAND FOR RECOGNITION OF IDENTITY, AND RIGHTS OVER ANCESTRAL LANDS, FORESTS AND CUSTOMARY PRACTICES

Living bridge (p562), Meghalaya

EHUNRISA SUMER/SHUTTERSTOCK

LAND BEFORE TIME

India is a hotbed of fossils, including those of blue-green algae, plants, and marine and land vertebrates, waiting to be fully explored. By Khursheed Dinshaw

THE VILLAGE OF Raiyoli in Gujarat, India, may not ring a bell for many, but for a palaeontologist, it holds a very special place. In 1997, based on the findings of almost 50 palaeontologists from around the world, this village was considered one of the largest dinosaur egg sites (hatcheries) in the world, with over 1000 eggs found at the site. *Rajasaurus narmadensis,* a carnivorous dinosaur found only in India, lived here. The village is also unique because it is the only place in India which has a dinosaur museum attached to the actual dinosaur site. Princess Aaliya Sultana Babi, fondly known as the 'Dinosaur Princess', has been instrumental in creating awareness about the site and museum.

India's unique geological history continues to be narrated through its diverse fossils. Spanning eras, the fossils, be they plants or marine or land vertebrates, preserve links of the past for future generations. It's not just dinosaurs – the evolution of whales from the land ancestor *Indohyus* in the Himalayas is also significant. Few know that the country also has well-preserved spiders, mosquitoes and termites in amber. Even though recent discoveries have put India on the world map, the country's fossil potential is still waiting to be discovered.

Clockwise from top left: *Carnotaurus* skeleton, Raiyoli; *Rajasaurus* statue at the Indroda Dinosaur and Fossil Park (p639), Gujarat; Stegosaurus statue, Hyderabad; Stromatolites, Sonbhadra Fossils Park, Uttar Pradesh

CLOCKWISE FROM TOP LEFT: HAPPY HONEY/SHUTTERSTOCK, DYNAMOLAND/SHUTTERSTOCK, ARUN SAMBHU MISHRA/SHUTTERSTOCK, KHURSHEED DINSHAW

New Discoveries with Far-Reaching Global Implications

Fresh discoveries in India include the finding of *Vasuki indicus,* one of the largest prehistoric snakes in the world. Found in a lignite mine in Kachchh (Kutch) in Gujarat, the 47-million-year-old snake is almost 15m in length. Palaeontologists have also found fossils of 55-million-year old *Cambaytherium,* the most primitive ancestor of the modern horse, in a lignite mine in Gujarat. In Telangana, a carnivorous dinosaur dating back 220 million years has been discovered.

The general lack of awareness about India's fossils, the absence of a world-class museum where the country's rich fossil wealth can be displayed, inadequate funding and only a handful of palaeontologists are some of the challenges of palaeontology in India. In addition, fossil sites are being destroyed by mining or vandalism. 'I am optimistic that our fossil heritage will thrive once we attract younger talent, financially invest and enforce stronger laws to protect our sites,' says Sunil Bajpai, a Professor of Vertebrate Paleontology at IIT Roorkee. Bajpai, with Post-Doctoral Fellow Debajit Datta, led the group that discovered *Vasuki indicus* and *Cambaytherium.*

India's Rich Fossil Parks

Prominent fossil parks include Sonbhadra Fossils Park (also known as Salkhan Fossil Park), Akal Wood Fossil Park, Siwalik Fossil Park, Ghughua Fossil National Park, Dinosaur Fossil National Park Bagh, Kutch Fossil Park, and Indroda Dinosaur and Fossil Park.

At Sonbhadra Fossils Park in Uttar Pradesh, 1.4-billion-year-old rare stromatolites (layered rocks) formed by blue-green algae, which are living fossils, can be viewed. Some of the big coniform formations are 1m in height. Smaller columns measuring a couple of centimetres are also present. The fossil park has been included in UNESCO's Tentative List for World Heritage Sites.

Akal Wood Fossil Park in Rajasthan is a National Geological Monument. It contains both fossilised tree trunks and invertebrates linked to the Jurassic period. The 180-million-year-old well-preserved plant and animal fossils are spread over 21 hectares.

Siwalik Fossil Park in Himachal Pradesh houses a museum displaying fossils of animals that existed in the area one to 2.5 million years ago. Fossils of turtles, hippopotamuses and fish are exhibited alongside skulls, teeth and bones of prehistoric extinct elephants, sabre-toothed tigers and ancestors of the modern giraffe.

Stegodon ganesa is an extinct elephant species with a heavy trunk and a long pair of tusks. While giraffes may not roam in India, their ancestors ambled in the Siwaliks. One such ancestor was 4m tall, had four horns and a small neck in contrast to present-day giraffes. The fauna faced extinction with the coming of the Ice Age.

Ghughua Fossil National Park in Madhya Pradesh is a significant site for 65-million-year-old plant fossils. The park is home to fossils of palm, mango, coconut and eucalyptus trees alongside leaf and seed fossils. Dinosaur Fossil National Park Bagh in Madhya Pradesh has fossilised eggs of dinosaurs as well as marine life that thrived in what was then a sea.

The Kutch Fossil Park in Gujarat exhibits marine and plant fossils. It was founded by Mohan Singh Sodha, who discovered a new sea-cow fossil that was named after him.

At Indroda Dinosaur and Fossil Park in Gujarat, marine fossils are displayed. The park is famous for fossilised eggs and bones of dinosaurs that have been sourced from Raiyoli.

'The general perception is that palaeontology has no real value in nation building. Slowly and gradually, it is giving way to applied geology. Many universities have stopped teaching it. Also the employment scene is not very good. But there is hope. Palaeontology will bounce back because youngsters and their parents are enthused about becoming palaeontologists,' says Dr Ashok Sahni, Professor Emeritus, Panjab University, Chandigarh.

With the media and movies enamouring audiences, and with the latest fossil findings becoming dinner-table conversations, palaeontology in India has much to look forward to, one brush at a time.

BEYOND BOLLYWOOD

Alternative spaces for film exhibitions in Mumbai (Bombay) offer breathing room for critical and creative conversations, writes filmmaker Jyoti Nisha.

WHEN TRAVELLERS COME to India, many things strike them about our beautiful country – the colours, the architecture, the people, local attire, our food and warmth – the list is long! Yet the most inescapable thing about India is its cinema. As the hub of Bollywood, Mumbai has a long history of film – one almost as old as cinema itself. The first film premiered here in 1896 by the Lumière Brothers, just six months after they exhibited in Paris for the first time.

Single Screens & Documentaries

Of course the city offers big multiplex experiences with every Friday release, but it's the single-screen theatres that still make the average Mumbaikar nostalgic. In 2021, there were 259 multiplexes versus 65 single-screen ones – to name a few: Regal Cinema in Colaba, Gaiety, Galaxy, Gem at Bandra and Maratha Mandir at Mumbai Central (which, for nearly 30 years, has screened Shahrukh Khan and Kajol's *Dilwale Dulhania Le Jayenge*).

Away from commercial films, Mumbai's film clubs offer a peek into Indian cinema beyond Bollywood. These spaces nurture the spirit of the artist or filmmaker (artistic and critical conversations are a standard part of the deal) and the films screened here are curated in favour of independent filmmaking.

'Independent filmmaking in India is a thankless job with no structural or institutional support,' explains Paloma Joseph, curator at Soho House Mumbai, Juhu, adding, 'Unfortunately, barring the festival circuit it's very hard to find independent films online or offline.' Even with Soho House's 'something for everyone' approach (it screens about 30 films each month), it makes room for independent Indian films that push the envelope. Its screening of *Land of the Breasted Woman* by Natasha Mendonca and Suman Sridhar was well received and reignited conversations about Nangeli, an early-19th-century peasant whose death remains a subject of debate – did Nangeli mutilate herself in protest of the British-imposed 'breast tax', which forced oppressed-caste women to pay a fee to cover their breasts in public, or was she killed for her bold resistance?

'Any film that has something important to convey about the human condition and is done with passion and integrity

 Left: Regal Cinema (p669), Colaba; Right: Maratha Mandir, Mumbai (p664)

is worth showing,' says Anand Patwardhan, a documentary filmmaker and curator for Vikalp@Prithvi, which exclusively screens documentaries and short films. Located in the heart of Juhu, Vikalp@Prithvi defines itself as a 'platform to defend freedom of expression and resist censorship'. Screenings are typically followed by lively discussions with the filmmaker. Since Prithvi Theatre charges Vikalp no money, exhibiting filmmakers charge no money and screenings at Vikalp are free – 'in that sense Vikalp@Prithvi is a valuable democratic space'. For over 20 years, it has screened brilliant documentaries, from *Manufacturing Consent,* on Noam Chomsky by Peter Wintonick and Mark Achbar, to *The Golden Harvest* by Alia Younis, and Bedabrata Pain's *Déjà Vu*: Pain's documentary is 'the amazing story of how American farmers were destroyed over the last 40 years by huge agro-business corporations in league with the government,' says Patwardhan. 'The exact story of what's happening to Indian farmers!'

In nearby Versova, Harkat Studios (which also has a branch in Berlin) actively engages with Indian and global politics. 'We try to be very responsive to the world – in a political sense,' says curator Karan Suri Talwar. 'We make our point through what we choose to programme [...] sometimes we want to excavate narratives from the past, pair new things together and just play around to evoke new conversations.'

Independent Spaces

In recent times, India has seen a spike in censorship in cinema. For independent filmmakers, spaces like these are a boon.

Further south of Juhu, tucked away in Pali Village, these spaces are blossoming. 'Art needs a space for its expression and for it to be experienced the way a maker has intended it to,' says Shubhika Sharma, a film editor and co-creator of Chhat Chitra Talkies, one of two prominent spaces in the neighbourhood. 'We curate films by independent filmmakers and help build an audience for them – that also helps us stay away from the legalities involved in screening films commercially.' In an independent setup, Shubhika and co-creator Harshita Sabnis, a producer, get in touch with film directors and producers, seeking permission to screen their films. As an entirely bootstrapped venture, they charge a minimal fee (₹350). The result is something of a rarity in today's Marvel-DC-stream-on-demand world. 'Directors come and interact with the audience within the intimate walls of our mini cinema,' Shubhika says, adding, 'The boundaries between the art and artist tend to blur as we question, interact and hang out together.'

Similarly, the second Pali Village space, Art and Charlie, achieves that same level of boundary-blurring in its quaint rust-coloured bungalow-turned-art-gallery. It has become a hotspot of critical and artistic conversations replete with the undercurrents that are not part of popular culture (it's also housed above Mumbai's tiniest cafe, Subko Mini).

I screened my documentary *Dr. B.R. Ambedkar: Now and Then* (about the titular Indian social reformer) here because I appreciate the effort that the founder, Ayesha Parikh, brings to platform people from the margins. It's non-exclusive and caters to a mixed audience. An artist's agency requires a space to have critical, artistic conversations, and as an Ambedkarite filmmaker, Art and Charlie did just that for me.

Parikh says she likes 'platforming independent filmmakers and contemporary artists from India whose practices raise anthropological questions relevant to our times'. When curating, she tends to gravitate towards artists whose practices 'add value to contemporary society by holding up a mirror or through subversion'.

'Once I believe in the artist, my focus shifts to helping them platform their work in the right way as well as creating space for new experiments that allow the artist to grow – their growth and the growth of our space is symbiotic and inextricably linked, shared,' Parikh says.

Mumbai is full of film clubs that lift the curtain to expose the depth of Indian cinema. Here are a few more to add to your list: Enlighten Film Society, The Bimal Roy Memorial & Film Society, FD Zone (a film club by Film Division) and Alliance Française, and G5A, a space for experimental and independent arts.

FROM LEFT: RAMESH R NAIR/SHUTTERSTOCK; DINOCIA PHOTO/GETTY IMAGES

INDEX

A

B

Map Pages **000**

INDEX B-D

Map Pages **000**

Map Pages **000**

Map Pages **000**

Q

R

S

A statement of royal power executed in stone, the mighty walls of the Mehrangarh loom over Jodhpur's Old City, seeming to emerge organically from the rocky cliffs.

Few Kerala moments rival catching a sunset or sunrise from a kayak, paddleboard or punt-powered canoe out in the midst of the backwaters.

FROM LEFT: FOTONIUM/SHUTTERSTOCK, WAJ/SHUTTERSTOCK

Mapping data sources:
© Lonely Planet
© OpenStreetMap http://openstreetmap.org/copyright

THIS BOOK

The 21st edition of Lonely Planet's *India* guidebook was written and researched by Isabella Noble, Margot Bigg, Joe Bindloss, Mark Eveleigh, Prachi Joshi, Puneetinder Kaur Sidhu, Christabel Lobo, Joanna Lobo, Pooja Naik, Paul Stafford, Meena Thiruvengadam, Shikha Tripathi and Dr Jenny Walker. The previous edition was written by Monique Choy, Mark Elliot, Lucie Grace, John Noble and Kevin Raub. This guidebook was produced by the following:

Destination Editor
Akanksha Singh

Coordinating Editor
Andrea Dobbin

Production Editor
Kate James

Image Editor
Dermot Hegarty

Cartographer
Valentina Kremenchutskaya

Assisting Editors
Holly Alexander, Bridget Blair, Kate Chapman, Katie Connolly, Nigel Chin, Melanie Dankel, Paul Harding, Anna Kaminski, Anne Mulvaney, Karyn Noble, Kathryn Rowan, Clifton Wilkinson

Cover Researcher
Beatriz Atunes

MIX
Paper | Supporting responsible forestry
FSC™ C021741
www.fsc.org

Paper in this book is certified against the Forest Stewardship Council™ standards. FSC™ promotes environmentally responsible, socially beneficial and economically viable management of the world's forests.

Published by Lonely Planet Global Limited
CRN 554153
21st edition - Oct 2026
ISBN 978 1 83869 801 0

10 9 8 7 6 5 4 3 2 1
Printed in Malaysia